Stanley Gibbons
Stamp Catalogue

Germany

(also covering German States, Occupation Issues and German Colonies)

12th Edition 2018

STANLEY GIBBONS LTD
London and Ringwood

By Appointment to
Her Majesty The Queen
Philatelists
Stanley Gibbons Ltd,
London

1st Edition in this form – 1979
2nd Edition – 1982
3rd Edition – 1987
4th Edition – 1992
5th Edition – 1996
6th Edition – 2002
7th Edition – 2005
8th Edition – 2007
9th Edition – 2011
10th Edition – 2012
11th Edition – 2014
12th edition – 2018

Published by Stanley Gibbons Ltd
Editorial, Publications Sales Offices
7 Parkside, Christchurch Road, Ringwood,
Hants BH24 3SH

© Stanley Gibbons Ltd 2018

Copyright Notice

The contents of this Catalogue, including the numbering system and illustrations, are fully protected by copyright. No part of this publication may be reproduced, stored in a retrieval system, or transmitted in any form or by any means, electronic, mechanical, photocopying, recording or otherwise, without the prior permission of Stanley Gibbons Limited. Requests for such permission should be addressed to the Catalogue Editor. This Catalogue is sold on condition that it is not, by way of trade or otherwise, lent, re-sold, hired out, circulated or otherwise disposed of other than in its complete, original and unaltered form and without a similar condition including this condition being imposed on the subsequent purchaser.

British Library Cataloguing in Publication Data.
A catalogue record for this book is available from the British Library.

Errors and omissions excepted. The colour reproduction of stamps is only as accurate as the printing process will allow.

ISBN-13: 978-1-911304-22-7

Item No. R 2836-18

Printed by
Latimer Trend, Plymouth

Stanley Gibbons Foreign Catalogue

ABOUT THIS EDITION

It is over 35 years since the present split into 'Parts 2 to 22' was announced, dividing up what had up to then been an alphabetical listing of European and Overseas countries over seven large volumes into handy-sized catalogues, bringing together countries or groups of countries, generally united by geography or political affiliations.

Back in 1979 the new 'Parts' catalogues proved to be very popular with collectors, but over time these volumes have grown in size, with the ever increasing numbers of new issues.

In 2015 Stanley Gibbons celebrated 150 years of catalogue production and it seemed the right time to take a look at the structure and break down of our Foreign catalogue range.

The Stanley Gibbons Germany catalogue contains all the stamps of Germany from the early states, through the two World Wars, the reunification in 1990 up to modern-day Germany, as well as covering the German Colonies.

- Specimen stamps have been included for the first time.
- The Germany design index has been updated.
- New varieties have been listed, many of which are priced.
- Pricing has been revised throughout the catalogue.

Germany new issue listings have been updated to February 2018:

The first supplement to this catalogue appeared in *Gibbons Stamp Monthly* for November 2018.

Addresses for specialist societies for this area are on page iv.

We would like to thank James Bendon for all his advice with the listing of specimen stamps in this catalogue.

Hugh Jefferies, Editor
Clare de la Feuillade, Deputy Editor
Sue Price, New Issues Listings
Barbara Hawkins, Pricing Assistant
Emma Fletcher, Designer and page layout

STAMPS ADDED

BAVARIA
123a
154a
155a
203Aa
207Aa

EAST GERMANY
E632a

LITHUANIAN OCCUPATION OF MEMEL
7a

SAAR
53c
55c
55ca/55cb
56b
57b, 57c, 57ca/57cb
58b
61b
70c, 70ca, 70cb
71b
72b
73c
76c

NUMBERS DELETED

GERMANY
3323, 3323a
3324

NUMBERS ALTERED

GERMANY

OLD	NEW
34bc	34ba

Germany 2005-2018 Flowers Definitive Series –
3306/3334 now Y3306/Y3374

SAAR

OLD	NEW
53b	53c
55b	55c
55ba	55ca
57b	57c
57ba	57ca
70b	70c

SPECIALIST SOCIETIES

Germany and Colonies Philatelic Society
Website: www.germanphilately.org /index.html

Germany Philatelic Society Inc
Secretary: Michael Peter
PO Box 6547
Chesterfield
MO 63006-65647
USA
Website: www.germanyphilaticsocietyusa.org/wordpress/

Contents

Stanley Gibbons Holdings Plc vii
General Philatelic Information and
 Guidelines to the Scope of Stanley
 Gibbons Foreign Catalogues viii
Abbreviations xv
International Philatelic Glossary .. xvi
Guide to Entries xx

I. German States 1
Baden 1
Bavaria 1
  Stamp Booklets 7
Bergedorf 7
Bremen 7
Brunswick 8
Hamburg 8
Hanover 9
Lübeck 10
Mecklenburg-Schwerin 10
Mecklenburg-Strelitz 11
Oldenburg 11
Prussia 12
Saxony 12
Schleswig-Holstein 13
Thurn and Taxis 14
Württemberg 15

Heligoland 19

North German Confederation 21

Alsace and Lorraine 22

Inscriptions on German
 Stamp Issues 22

II. Germany (1871–1945) 23
Empire 23
The Weimar Republic 27
Third Reich 36
  Stamp Booklets 49
  Design Index 51

III. Allied Occupation 52
A. Allied Military Post 52
B. American, British and Soviet
   Russian Zones, 1946–1948 52
   Stamp Booklets 53
C. British and American Zones,
   1948–1949 54
D. French Zone 56
E. Russian Zone 59

IV. German Federal Republic 63
A. West Germany 63
B. Germany Reunified 114
   Machine Labels 204
   Stamp Booklets 204
   Design Index 207

V. Berlin (Western Sectors) 216
Machine Labels 239
Stamp Booklets 239

VI. German Democratic Republic
 (East Germany) 239
Stamp Booklets 331

Belgian Occupation, 1919-1921 332
I. For Belgian Forces in the
   Rhineland 332
II. For the Districts of Eupen
    and Malmedy 332

German Occupation Issues,
 1914-1918 333
A. Belgium 333
B. Eastern Military Command Area .. 334
C. Estonia 334
D. Poland 334
E. Romania 334
F. Western Military Command Area .. 335

Allenstein 335

Danzig 336
Free City 336
Stamp Booklets 342
Polish Post in Danzig 342

Marienwerder 343

Memel 344
Lithuanian Occupation 346

Saar 349
I. League of Nations Commission
   (1920–1935) 349
II. Return to Germany 352
III. French Occupation 352
IV. Return to Germany 357
   Stamp Booklets 358

Schleswig (Slesvig) 359

Upper Silesia 359
Inter-allied Commission 360

German Occupation Issues,
 1939–45 361
A. Albania 361
B. Bohemia and Moravia 361
C. Estonia 364
D. France 365
E. Ionian islands 365
F. Latvia 365
G. Lithuania 366

H. Luxembourg 366
I. Poland 367
J. Russia 370
K. Serbia 370
L. Yugoslavia 372
M. Channel Islands 376
   Guernsey 376
   Jersey 376

Cameroun 378
Stamp Booklets 379
British Occupation 379

Caroline Islands 380

German East Africa 381
Lamu 381
Zanzibar 381
Other Post Offices in East Africa 382
   Stamp Booklets 382
Mafia Island 383

German New Guinea 384
New Guinea 384

German Post Offices in China 387

German Post Offices in Morocco 389

German Post Offices in
 Turkish Empire 390

German South-West Africa 391
Otyimbingue 391
Other Post Offices in German
   South-West Africa 391
   Stamp Booklets 392

Kiaochow 393

Mariana Islands 394

Marshall Islands 394

Samoa 395
New Zealand Occupation 396

Togo 397
Anglo-French Occupation 397
   French Issues 397
   British Issues 398

Index 400

Beautiful stamps from the island of Jersey

The island of Jersey is rich in history and culture and, over the years, Jersey Post has produced stamps on a wide range of topics and a number of innovative world firsts.

A constant mix of heritage, innovation and creatively packaged special issues keeps Jersey Post at the forefront of the philatelic world and helps to make Jersey stamps such sought-after and fascinating collections.

Jersey Icons
Lillie Langtry – 100 years since leaving the stage

Flora and Fauna
Links with China - Butterflies

Striking Illustrations
100 Years of the RAF

Fascinating Themes
Frankenstein – 200 years

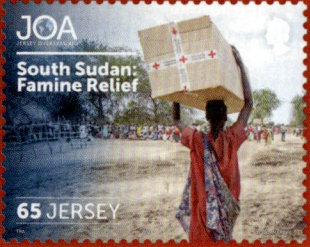

Events & Anniversaries
50 years of Jersey Overseas Aid

Stunning Photography
Jersey Seasons - Spring

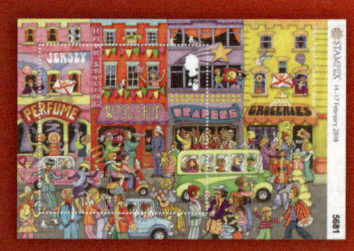

Limited Editions
Popular Culture – The 1960s
Miniature Sheet Stampex Overprint

Nostalgia
A Traditional Christmas

Royal Family
HM Queen Elizabeth II and HRH Prince Philip's Platinum Wedding Anniversary

Innovative techniques
Including printing on wood and silk, honey-scented stamps, 3D lenticular imagery and metallic finishes
Durrell & Darwin
25 years of the Darwin Initiative

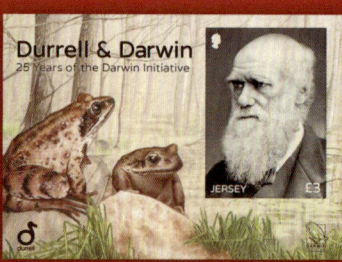

All our issues are available on First Day Covers and in Presentation Packs. Visit the website to see our full range and to order online

www.jerseystamps.com

Email: stamps@jerseypost.com   Tel: +44(0) 1534 516320

www.facebook.com/jerseystamps   @JerseyStamps

Free postage and packing for Subscription Customers!
Open your account today

Jersey Post

Stanley Gibbons Holdings Plc

Stanley Gibbons Limited,
Stanley Gibbons Auctions
399 Strand, London WC2R 0LX
Tel: +44 (0)207 836 8444
Fax: +44 (0)207 836 7342
E-mail: help@stanleygibbons.com
Website: www.stanleygibbons.com
for all departments, Auction and
Specialist Stamp Departments.
Open Monday–Friday 9.30 a.m. to 5 p.m.
Shop. Open Monday–Friday 9 a.m. to
5.30 p.m. and Saturday 9.30 a.m.
to 5.30 p.m.

Stanley Gibbons Publications,
Gibbons Stamp Monthly and
Philatelic Exporter
7 Parkside, Christchurch Road,
Ringwood, Hampshire BH24 3SH.
Tel: +44 (0)1425 472363
Fax: +44 (0)1425 470247
E-mail: help@stanleygibbons.com
Publications Mail Order.
FREEPHONE 0800 611622
Monday–Friday 8.30 a.m. to 5 p.m.

Stanley Gibbons (Jersey) Limited
18 Hill Street, St Helier, Jersey,
Channel Islands JE2 4UA.
Tel: +44 (0)1534 766711
Fax: +44 (0)1534 766177
E-mail: investment@stanleygibbons.com

Stanley Gibbons (Asia) Limited
12/F, 100 Queen's Road Central
Central Hong Kong
Tel: +852 3180 9370
E-mail: elee@stanleygibbons.com

Stanley Gibbons Publications Overseas Representation
Stanley Gibbons Publications are represented overseas by the following

Australia
Renniks Publications PTY LTD
Unit 3 37-39 Green Street,
Banksmeadow, NSW 2019, Australia
Tel: +612 9695 7055
Website: www.renniks.com

Canada
Unitrade Associates
99 Floral Parkway, Toronto,
Ontario M6L 2C4, Canada
Tel: +1 416 242 5900
Website: www.unitradeassoc.com

Germany
Schaubek Verlag Leipzig
Am Glaeschen 23, D-04420
Markranstaedt, Germany
Tel: +49 34 205 67823
Website: www.schaubek.de

Italy
Ernesto Marini S.R.L.
V. Struppa, 300, Genova, 16165, Italy
Tel: +3901 0247-3530
Website: www.ernestomarini.it

Japan
Japan Philatelic
PO Box 2, Suginami-Minami,
Tokyo 168-8081, Japan
Tel: +81 3330 41641
Website: www.yushu.co.jp

Netherlands (also covers Belgium
Denmark, Finland & France)
Uitgeverij Davo BV
PO Box 411, Ak Deventer, 7400
Netherlands
Tel: +315 7050 2700
Website: www.davo.nl

New Zealand
House of Stamps
PO Box 12, Paraparaumu,
New Zealand
Tel: +61 6364 8270
Website: www.houseofstamps.co.nz

Philatelic Distributors
PO Box 863
15 Mount Edgecumbe Street
New Plymouth 4615, New Zealand
Tel: +6 46 758 65 68
Website: www.stampcollecta.com

Norway
SKANFIL A/S
SPANAV. 52 / BOKS 2030
N-5504 HAUGESUND, Norway
Tel: +47-52703940
E-mail: magne@skanfil.no

Singapore
C S Philatelic Agency
Peninsula Shopping Centre #04-29
3 Coleman Street, 179804, Singapore
Tel: +65 6337-1859
Website: www.cs.com.sg

South Africa
Peter Bale Philatelics
P.O. Box 3719
Honeydew 2040
Gauteng
South Africa
Tel: +27 11 462 2463
E-mail: balep@iafrica.com

Sweden
Chr Winther Sorensen AB
Box 43, S-310 20 Knaered, Sweden
Tel: +46 43050743
Website: www.collectia.se

General Philatelic Information and Guidelines to the Scope of Stanley Gibbons Foreign Catalogues

These notes reflect current practice in compiling the Foreign Catalogue.

The *Stanley Gibbons Stamp Catalogue* has a very long history and the vast quantity of information it contains has been carefully built up by successive generations through the work of countless individuals. Philately itself is never static and the Catalogue has evolved and developed during this long time-span. These notes apply to current policy – some of the older listings were prepared using slightly different criteria – and we hope you find them useful in using the catalogue.

THE CATALOGUE IN GENERAL

Contents. The Catalogue is confined to adhesive postage stamps, including miniature sheets. For particular categories the rules are:
(a) Revenue (fiscal) stamps or telegraph stamps are listed only where they have been expressly authorised for postal duty.
(b) Stamps issued only precancelled are included, but normally issued stamps available additionally with precancel have no separate precancel listing unless the face value is changed.
(c) Stamps prepared for use but not issued, hitherto accorded full listing, are nowadays footnoted with a price (where possible).
(d) Bisects (trisects, etc.) are only listed where such usage was officially authorised.
(e) Stamps issued only on first day covers and not available separately are not listed but priced (on the cover) in a footnote.
(f) New printings, as such, are not listed, though stamps from them may qualify under another category, e.g. when a prominent new shade results.
(g) Official and unofficial reprints are dealt with by footnote.
(h) Stamps from imperforate printings of modern issues which also occur perforated are covered by footnotes or general notes, but are listed where widely available for postal use.

Exclusions. The following are excluded:
(a) non-postal revenue or fiscal stamps;
(b) postage stamps used fiscally;
(c) local carriage labels and private local issues;
(d) telegraph stamps;
(e) bogus or phantom stamps;
(f) railway or airline letter fee stamps, bus or road transport company labels;
(g) cut-outs;
(h) all types of non-postal labels;
(i) documentary labels for the postal service, e.g. registration, recorded delivery, airmail etiquettes, etc.;
(j) privately applied embellishments to official issues and privately commissioned items generally;
(k) stamps for training postal officers;
(l) specimen stamps.

Full listing. 'Full listing' confers our recognition and implies allotting a catalogue number and (wherever possible) a price quotation.

In judging status for inclusion in the catalogue broad considerations are applied to stamps. They must be issued by a legitimate postal authority, recognised by the government concerned, and must be adhesives valid for proper postal use in the class of service for which they are inscribed. Stamps, with the exception of such categories as postage dues and officials, must be available to the general public, at face value, in reasonable quantities without any artificial restrictions being imposed on their distribution.

We record as abbreviated Appendix entries, without catalogue numbers or prices, stamps from countries which either persist in having far more issues than can be justified by postal need or have failed to maintain control over their distribution so that they have not been available to the public in reasonable quantities at face value. Miniature sheets and imperforate stamps are not mentioned in these entries.

The publishers of this catalogue have observed, with concern, the proliferation of 'artificial' stamp-issuing territories. On several occasions this has resulted in separately inscribed issues for various component parts of otherwise united states or territories.

Stanley Gibbons Publications have decided that where such circumstances occur, they will not, in the future, list these items in the SG catalogue without first satisfying themselves that the stamps represent a genuine political, historical or postal division within the country concerned. Any such issues which do not fulfil this stipulation will be recorded in the Catalogue Appendix only.

For errors and varieties the criterion is legitimate (albeit inadvertent) sale over a post office counter in the normal course of business. Details of provenance are always important; printers' waste and fraudulently manufactured material is excluded.

Certificates. In assessing unlisted items due weight is given to Certificates from recognised Expert Committees and, where appropriate, we will usually ask to see them.

New issues. New issues are listed regularly in the Catalogue Supplement in *Gibbons Stamp Monthly*, then consolidated into the next available edition of the Catalogue.

Date of issue. Where local issue dates differ from dates of release by agencies, 'date of issue' is the local date. Fortuitous stray usage before the officially intended date is disregarded in listing.

Catalogue numbers. Stamps of each country are catalogued chronologically by date of issue. Subsidiary classes (e.g. postage due stamps) are integrated into one list with postage and commemorative stamps and distinguished by a letter prefix to the catalogue number.

The catalogue number appears in the extreme left column. The boldface type numbers in the next column are merely cross-references to illustrations. Catalogue

Information and Guidelines

numbers in the *Gibbons Stamp Monthly* Supplement are provisional only and may need to be altered when the lists are consolidated. Miniature sheets only purchasable intact at a post office have a single MS number; sheetlets – individual stamps available – number each stamp separately. The catalogue no longer gives full listing to designs originally issued in normal sheets, which subsequently appear in sheetlets showing changes of colour, perforation, printing process or face value. Such stamps will be covered by footnotes.

Once published in the Catalogue, numbers are changed as little as possible; really serious renumbering is reserved for the occasions when a complete country or an entire issue is being rewritten. The edition first affected includes cross-reference tables of old and new numbers.

Our catalogue numbers are universally recognised in specifying stamps and as a hallmark of status.

Illustrations. Stamps are illustrated at three-quarters linear size. Stamps not illustrated are the same size and format as the value shown unless otherwise indicated. Stamps issued only as miniature sheets have the stamp alone illustrated but sheet size is also quoted. Overprints, surcharges, watermarks and postmarks are normally actual size. Illustrations of varieties are often enlarged to show the detail.

CONTACTING THE CATALOGUE EDITOR

The editor is always interested in hearing from people who have new information which will improve or correct the Catalogue. As a general rule he must see and examine the actual stamps before they can be considered for listing; photographs or photocopies are insufficient evidence. Neither he nor his staff give opinions as to the genuineness of stamps.

Submissions should be made in writing to the Catalogue Editor, Stanley Gibbons Publications, 7 Parkside, Christchurch Road, Ringwood, Hants BH24 3SH. The cost of return postage for items submitted is appreciated, and this should include the registration fee if required.

Where information is solicited purely for the benefit of the enquirer, the editor cannot undertake to reply if the answer is already contained in these published notes or if return postage is omitted. Written communications are greatly preferred to enquiries by telephone or e-mail and the editor regrets that he or his staff cannot see personal callers without a prior appointment being made.

The editor welcomes close contact with study circles and is interested, too, in finding local correspondents who will verify and supplement official information in overseas countries where this is deficient.

We regret we do not give opinions as to the genuineness of stamps, nor do we identify stamps or number them by our Catalogue.

TECHNICAL MATTERS

The meanings of the technical terms used in the Catalogue will be found in *Philatelic Terms Illustrated*, published by Stanley Gibbons (Price £14.95 plus postage).

1. Printing

Printing errors. Errors in printing are of major interest to the Catalogue. Authenticated items meriting consideration would include background, centre or frame inverted or omitted; centre or subject transposed; error of colour; error or omission of value; double prints and impressions; printed both sides; and so on. Designs *tête-bêche*, whether intentionally or by accident, are listable. *Se-tenant* arrangements of stamps are recognised in the listings or footnotes. Gutter pairs (a pair of stamps separated by blank margin) are excluded unless they have some philatelic importance. Colours only partially omitted are not listed, neither are stamps printed on the gummed side.

Printing varieties. Listing is accorded to major changes in the printing base which lead to completely new types. In recess-printing this could be a design re-engraved, in photogravure or photolithography a screen altered in whole or in part. It can also encompass flat-bed and rotary printing if the results are readily distinguishable.

To be considered at all, varieties must be constant. Early stamps, produced by primitive methods, were prone to numerous imperfections; the lists reflect this, recognising re-entries, retouches, broken frames, misshapen letters, and so on. Printing technology has, however, radically improved over the years, during which time photogravure and lithography have become predominant. Varieties nowadays are more in the nature of flaws and these, being too specialised for a general catalogue, are almost always outside the scope. We therefore do not list such items as dry prints, kiss prints, doctor-blade flaws, blanket set-offs, doubling through blanket stretch, plate cracks and scratches, registration flaws (leading to colour shifts), lithographic ring flaws, and so on. Neither do we recognise fortuitous happenings like paper creases or confetti flaws.

Overprints (and surcharges). Overprints of different types qualify for separate listing. These include overprints in different colours; overprints from different printing processes such as litho and typo; overprints in totally different typefaces, etc.

Overprint errors and varieties. Major errors in machine-printed overprints are important and listable. They include overprint inverted or omitted; overprint double (treble, etc.); overprint diagonal; overprint double, one inverted; pairs with one overprint omitted, e.g. from a radical shift to an adjoining stamp; error of colour; error of type fount; letters inverted or omitted, etc. If the overprint is handstamped, few of these would qualify and a distinction is drawn.

Varieties occurring in overprints will often take the form of broken letters, slight differences in spacing,

ix

Information and Guidelines

rising spacers, etc. Only the most important would be considered for footnote mention.

Sheet positions. If space permits we quote sheet positions of listed varieties and authenticated data is solicited for this purpose.

2. Paper

All stamps listed are deemed to be on 'ordinary' paper of the wove type and white in colour; only departures from this are mentioned.

Types. Where classification so requires we distinguish such other types of paper as, for example, vertically and horizontally laid; wove and laid bâtonné; card(board); carton; cartridge, enamelled; glazed; GC (Grande Consommation); granite; native; pelure; porous; quadrillé; ribbed; rice; and silk thread.

The 'traditional' method of indentifying chalk-surfaced papers has been that, when touched with a silver wire, a black mark is left on the paper, and the listings in this catalogue are based on that test. However, the test itself is now largely discredited, for, although the mark can be removed by a soft rubber, some damage to the stamp will result from its use.

The difference between chalk-surfaced and pre-war ordinary papers is fairly clear: chalk-surfaced papers being smoother to the touch and showing a characteristic sheen when light is reflected off their surface. Under good magnification tiny bubbles or pock marks can be seen on the surface of the stamp and at the tips of the perforations the surfacing appears 'broken'. Traces of paper fibres are evident on the surface of ordinary paper and the ink shows a degree of absorption into it.

The various makeshifts for normal paper are listed as appropriate. They include printing on: unfinished banknotes, war maps, ruled paper, Post Office forms, and the unprinted side of glossy magazines. The varieties of double paper and joined paper are recognised.

Descriptive terms. The fact that a paper is hand-made (and thus probably of uneven thickness) is mentioned where necessary. Such descriptive terms as 'hard' and 'soft'; 'smooth' and 'rough'; 'thick', 'medium' and 'thin' are applied where there is philatelic merit in classifying papers.

Coloured, very white and toned papers. A coloured paper is one that is coloured right through (front and back of the stamp). In the Catalogue the colour of the paper is given in italics, thus

black/*rose* = black design on rose paper.

Papers have been made specially white in recent years by, for example, a very heavy coating of chalk. We do not classify shades of whiteness of paper as distinct varieties. There does exist, however, a type of paper from early days called toned. This is off-white, often brownish or buffish, but it cannot be assigned a definite colour. A toning effect brought on by climate, incorrect storage or gum staining is disregarded here, as this was not the state of the paper when issued.

Safety devices. The Catalogue takes account of such safety devices as varnish lines, grills, burelage or imprinted patterns on the front or moiré on the back of stamps.

Modern developments. Two modern developments also affect the listings, printing on self-adhesive paper and the tendency, philatelic in origin, for conventional paper to be reinforced or replaced by different materials. Some examples are the use of foils in gold, silver, aluminium, palladium and steel; application of an imitation wood veneer; printing on plastic moulded in relief; and use of a plastic laminate to give a three-dimensional effect. Examples also occur of stamps impregnated with scent; printed on silk; and incorporating miniature gramophone records.

3. Perforation and Rouletting

Perforation gauge. The gauge of a perforation is the number of holes in a length of 2 cm. For correct classification the size of the holes (large or small) may need to be distinguished; in a few cases the actual number of holes on each edge of the stamp needs to be quoted.

Measurement. The Gibbons Instanta gauge is the standard for measuring perforations. The stamp is viewed against a dark background with the transparent gauge put on top of it. Though the gauge measures to decimal accuracy, perforations read from it are generally quoted in the Catalogue to the nearest half. For example:

Just over perf.
12¾ to just under perf. 13¼   = perf. 13
Perf. 13¼ exactly, rounded up   = perf. 13½
Just over perf.
13¼ to just under perf. 13¾   = perf. 13½
Perf. 13¾ exactly, rounded up   = perf. 14

However, where classification depends on it, actual quarter-perforations are quoted.

Notation. Where no perforation is quoted for an issue it is imperforate. Perforations are usually abbreviated (and spoken) as follows, though sometimes they may be spelled out for clarity. This notation for rectangular stamps (the majority) applies to diamond shapes if 'top' is read as the edge to the top right.

P 14: perforated alike on all sides (read: 'perf. 14').

P 14×15: the first figure refers to top and bottom, the second to left and right sides (read: 'perf. 14 by 15'). This is a compound perforation. For an upright triangular stamp the first figure refers to the two sloping sides and the second to the base. In inverted triangulars the base is first and the second figure refers to the sloping sides.

P 14-15: perforation measuring anything between 14 and 15: the holes are irregularly spaced, thus the gauge may vary along a single line or even along a single edge of the stamp (read: 'perf. 14 to 15').

P 14 irregular. perforated 14 from a worn perforator, giving badly aligned holes irregular spaced (read 'irregular perf. 14').

Information and Guidelines

P *comp(ound)* 14×15: two gauges in use but not necessarily on opposite sides of the stamp. It could be one side in one gauge and three in the other, or two adjacent sides with the same gauge (Read: 'perf. compound of 14 and 15'). For three gauges or more, abbreviated as 'P 14, 14½, 15 or compound' for example.

P 14, 14½: perforated approximately 14¼ (read: 'perf. 14 or 14½'). It does not mean two stamps, one perf. 14 and the other perf. 14½. This obsolescent notation is gradually being replaced in the Catalogue.

Imperf: imperforate (not perforated).

Imperf × P 14: imperforate at top and bottom and perf 14 at sides.

P 14 × *imperf* = perf 14 at top and bottom and imperforate at sides.

Such headings as 'P 13 × 14 (vert) and P 14 × 13 (horiz)' indicate which perforations apply to which stamp format – vertical or horizontal.

Some stamps are additionally perforated so that a label or tab is detachable; others have been perforated suitably for use as two halves. Listings are normally for whole stamps, unless stated otherwise.

Other terms. Perforation almost always gives circular holes; where other shapes have been used they are specified, e.g. square holes; lozenge perf. Interrupted perfs are brought about by the omission of pins at regular intervals. Perforations have occasionally been simulated by being printed as part of the design. With few exceptions, privately applied perforations are not listed.

Perforation errors and varieties. Authenticated errors, where a stamp normally perforated is accidentally issued imperforate, are listed provided no traces of perforation (blind holes or indentations) remain. They must be provided as pairs, both stamps wholly imperforate, and are only priced in that form.

Stamps merely imperforate between stamp and margin (fantails) are not listed.

Imperforate-between varieties are recognised, where one row of perfs has been missed. They are listed and priced in pairs:

Imperf between (horiz pair): a horizontal pair of stamps with perfs all around the edges but none between the stamps.

Imperf between (vert pair): a vertical pair of stamps with perfs all around the edges but none between the stamps.

Where several of the rows have escaped perforation the resulting varieties are listable. Thus:

Imperf vert (horiz pair): a horizontal pair of stamps perforated top and bottom; all three vertical directions are imperf – the two outer edges and between the stamps.

Imperf horiz (vert pair): a vertical pair perforated at left and right edges; all three horizontal directions are imperf – the top, bottom and between the stamps.

Straight edges. Large sheets cut up before issue to post offices can cause stamps with straight edges, i.e. imperf on one side or on two sides at right angles. They are not usually listable in this condition and are worth less than corresponding stamps properly perforated all round. This does not, however, apply to certain stamps, mainly from coils and booklets, where straight edges on various sides are the manufacturing norm affecting every stamp. The listings and notes make clear which sides are correctly imperf.

Malfunction. Varieties of double, misplaced or partial perforation caused by error or machine malfunction are not listable, neither are freaks, such as perforations placed diagonally from paper folds. Likewise disregarded are missing holes caused by broken pins, and perforations 'fading out' down a sheet, the machinery progressively disengaging to leave blind perfs and indentations to the paper.

Centering. Well-centred stamps have designs surrounded by equal opposite margins. Where this condition affects the price the fact is stated.

Type of perforating. Where necessary for classification, perforation types are distinguished. These include:

Line perforation from one line of pins punching single rows of holes at a time.

Comb perforation from pins disposed across the sheet in comb formation, punching out holes at three sides of the stamp a row at a time.

Harrow perforation applied to a whole pane or sheet at one stroke.

Rotary perforation from the toothed wheels operating across a sheet, then crosswise.

Sewing-machine perforation. The resultant condition, clean-cut or rough, is distinguished where required.

Pin-perforation is the commonly applied term for pin-roulette in which, instead of being punched out, round holes are pricked by sharp-pointed pins and no paper is removed.

Punctured stamps. Perforation holes can be punched into the face of the stamp. Patterns of small holes, often in the shape of initial letters, are privately applied devices against pilferage. These 'perfins' are outside the scope. Identification devices, when officially inspired, are listed or noted; they can be shapes, or letters or words formed from holes, sometimes converting one class of stamp into another.

Rouletting. In rouletting the paper is cut, for ease of separation, but none is removed. The gauge is measured, when needed, as for perforations. Traditional French terms descriptive of the type of cut are often used and types include:

Arc roulette (percé en arc). Cuts are minute, spaced arcs, each roughly a semicircle.

Cross roulette (percé en croix). Cuts are tiny diagonal crosses.

Line roulette (parcé en ligne or en ligne droite). Short straight cuts parallel to the frame of the stamp. The commonest basic roulette. Where not further described, 'roulette' means this type.

Rouletted in colour or coloured roulette (percé en lignes colorees or en lignes de coleur). Cuts with

xi

coloured edges, arising from notched rule inked simultaneously with the printing plate.

Saw-tooth roulette (percé en scie). Cuts applied zigzag fashion to resemble the teeth of a saw.

Serpentine roulette (percé en serpentin). Cuts as sharply wavy lines.

Zigzag roulettes (percé en zigzags). Short straight cuts at angles in alternate directions, producing sharp points on separation. US usage favours 'serrate(d) roulette' for this type.

Pin-roulette (originally *percé en points* and now *perforés trous d'epingle*) is commonly called pin-perforation in English.

4. Gum

All stamps listed are assumed to have gum of some kind; if they were issued without gum this is stated. Original gum (o.g.) means that which was present on the stamp as issued to the public. Deleterious climates and the presence of certain chemicals can cause gum to crack and, with early stamps, even make the paper deteriorate. Unscrupulous fakers are adept in removing it and regumming the stamp to meet the unreasoning demand often made for 'full o.g.' in cases where such a thing is virtually impossible.

Until recent times the gum used for stamps has been gum arabic, but various synthetic adhesives – tinted or invisible-looking – have been in use since the 1960s. Stamps existing with more than one type of gum are not normally listed separately, though the fact is noted where it is of philatelic significance, e.g. in distinguishing reprints or new printings.

The distinct variety of grilled gum is, however, recognised. In this the paper is passed through a gum breaker prior to printing to prevent subsequent curling. As the patterned rollers were sufficient to impress a grill into the paper beneath the gum we can quote prices for both unused and used examples.

Self-adhesive stamps are issued on backing paper from which they are peeled before affixing to mail. Unused examples are priced as for backing paper intact. Used examples are best kept on cover or on piece.

5. Watermarks

Stamps are on unwatermarked paper except where the heading to the set says otherwise.

Detection. Watermarks are detected for Catalogue description by one of four methods:

(1) holding stamps to the light;
(2) laying stamps face down on a dark background;
(3) adding a few drops of petroleum ether 40/60 to the stamp laid face down in a watermark tray; or
(4) by use of the Stanley Gibbons Detectamark, or other equipment, which works by revealing the thinning of the paper at the watermark. (Note that petroleum ether is highly inflammable in use and can damage photogravure stamps.)

Listable types. Stamps occurring on both watermarked and unwatermarked papers are different types and both receive full listing.

Single watermarks (devices occurring once on every stamp) can be modified in size and shape as between different issues; the types are noted but not usually separately listed. Fortuitous absence of watermark from a single stamp or its gross displacement would not be listable.

To overcome registration difficulties the device may be repeated at close intervals (a **multiple watermark**), single stamps thus showing parts of several devices. Similarly a large **sheet watermark** (or all-over watermark) covering numerous stamps can be used. We give informative notes and illustrations for them. The designs may be such that numbers of stamps in the sheet automatically lack watermark; this is not a listable variety. Multiple and all-over watermarks sometimes undergo modifications, but if the various types are difficult to distinguish from single stamps notes are given but not separate listings.

Papermakers' watermarks are noted where known but not listed separately, since most stamps in the sheet will lack them. Sheet watermarks which are nothing more than officially adopted papermakers' watermarks are, however, given normal listing.

Marginal watermarks, falling outside the pane of stamps, are ignored except where misplacement causes the adjoining row to be affected, in which case they may be footnoted.

Watermark errors and varieties. Watermark errors are recognised as of major importance. They comprise stamps intended to be on unwatermarked paper but issued watermarked by mistake, or stamps printed on paper with the wrong watermark. Watermark varieties, on the other hand, such as broken or deformed bits on the dandy roll, are not listable.

Watermark positions. Paper has a side intended for printing and watermarks are usually impressed so that they read normally when looked through from that printed side.

Illustrations in the Catalogue are of watermarks in normal positions (from the front of the stamps) and are actual size where possible.

Differences in watermark position are collectable as distinct varieties. In this Catalogue, however, only normal sideways watermarks are listed (and 'sideways inverted' is treated as 'sideways'). Inverted and reversed watermarks have always been outside its scope: in the early days of flat-bed printing, sheets of watermarked paper were fed indiscriminately through the press and the resulting watermark positions had no particular philatelic significance. Similarly, the special make-up of sheets for booklets can in some cases give equal quantities of normal and inverted watermarks.

6. Colours

Stamps in two or three colours have these named in order of appearance, from the centre moving outwards.

Four colours or more are usually listed as multicoloured.

In compound colour names the second is the predominant one, thus:
orange-red = a red tending towards orange;
red-orange = an orange containing more red than usual.

Standard colours used. The 200 colours most used for stamp identification are given in the Stanley Gibbons Colour Key. The Catalogue has used the Key as a standard for describing new issues for some years. The names are also introduced as lists are rewritten, though exceptions are made for those early issues where traditional names have become universally established.

Determining colours. When comparing actual stamps with colour samples in the Key, view in a good north daylight (or its best substitute: fluorescent 'colour-matching' light). Sunshine is not recommended. Choose a solid portion of the stamp design; if available, marginal markings such as solid bars of colour or colour check dots are helpful. Shading lines in the design can be misleading as they appear lighter than solid colour. Postmarked portions of a stamp appear darker than normal. If more than one colour is present, mask off the extraneous ones as the eye tends to mix them.

Errors of colour. Major colour errors in stamps or overprints which qualify for listing are: wrong colours; one colour inverted in relation to the rest; albinos (colourless impressions), where these have Expert Committee certificates; colours completely omitted, but only on unused stamps (if found on used stamps the information is footnoted).

Colours only partially omitted are not recognised.

Colour shifts, however spectacular, are not listed.

Shades. Shades in philately refer to variations in the intensity of a colour or the presence of differing amounts of other colours. They are particularly significant when they can be linked to specific printings. In general, shades need to be quite marked to fall within the scope of this Catalogue; it does not favour nowadays listing the often numerous shades of a stamp, but chooses a single applicable colour name which will indicate particular groups of outstanding shades. Furthermore, the listings refer to colours as issued: they may deteriorate into something different through the passage of time.

Modern colour printing by lithography is prone to marked differences of shade, even within a single run, and variations can occur within the same sheet. Such shades are not listed.

Aniline colours. An aniline colour meant originally one derived from coal-tar; it now refers more widely to colour of a particular brightness suffused on the surface of a stamp and showing through clearly on the back.

Colours of overprints and surcharges. All overprints and surcharges are in black unless otherwise in the heading or after the description of the stamp.

7. Luminescence

Machines which sort mail electronically have been introduced in recent years. In consequence some countries have issued stamps on fluorescent or phosphorescent papers, while others have marked their stamps with phosphor bands.

The various papers can only be distinguished by ultraviolet lamps emitting particular wavelengths. They are separately listed only when the stamps have some other means of distinguishing them, visible without the use of these lamps. Where this is not so, the papers are recorded in footnotes or headings. (Collectors using the lamps should exercise great care in their use as exposure to their light is extremely dangerous to the eyes).

Phosphor bands are listable, since they are visible to the naked eye (by holding stamps at an angle to the light and looking along them, the bands appear dark). Stamps existing with and without phosphor bands or with differing numbers of bands are given separate listings. Varieties such as double bands, misplaced or omitted bands, bands printed on the wrong side, are not listed.

8. Coil Stamps

Stamps issued only in coil form are given full listing. If stamps are issued in both sheets and coils the coil stamps are listed separately only where there is some feature (e.g. perforation) by which singles can be distinguished. Coil strips containing different stamps *se-tenant* are also listed.

Coil join pairs are too random and too easily faked to permit of listing; similarly ignored are coil stamps which have accidentally suffered an extra row of perforations from the claw mechanism in a malfunctioning vending machine.

9. Booklet Stamps

Single stamps from booklets are listed if they are distinguishable in some way (such as watermark or perforation) from similar sheet stamps. Booklet panes, provided they are distinguishable from blocks of sheet stamps, are listed for most countries; booklet panes containing more than one value *se-tenant* are listed under the lowest of the values concerned.

Lists of stamp booklets are given for certain countries and it is intended to extend this generally.

10. Forgeries and Fakes

Forgeries. Where space permits, notes are considered if they can give a concise description that will permit unequivocal detection of a forgery. Generalised warnings, lacking detail, are not nowadays inserted since their value to the collector is problematic.

Fakes. Unwitting fakes are numerous, particularly 'new shades' which are colour changelings brought about by exposure to sunlight, soaking in water contaminated with dyes from adherent paper, contact with oil and dirt from a pocketbook, and so on. Fraudulent operators, in addition, can offer to arrange: removal of hinge marks; repairs of thins on white or coloured

Information and Guidelines

papers; replacement of missing margins or perforations; reperforating in true or false gauges; removal of fiscal cancellations; rejoining of severed pairs, strips and blocks; and (a major hazard) regumming. Collectors can only be urged to purchase from reputable sources and to insist upon Expert Committee certification where there is any doubt.

The Catalogue can consider footnotes about fakes where these are specific enough to assist in detection.

PRICES

Prices quoted in this Catalogue are the selling prices of Stanley Gibbons Ltd at the time when the book went to press. They are for stamps in fine condition for the issue concerned; in issues where condition varies they may ask more for the superb and less for the sub-standard.

All prices are subject to change without prior notice and Stanley Gibbons Ltd may from time to time offer stamps at other than catalogue prices in consequence of special purchases or particular promotions.

No guarantee is given to supply all stamps priced, since it is not possible to keep every catalogued item in stock. Commemorative issues may, at times, only be available in complete sets and not as individual values.

Quotations of prices. The prices in the left-hand column are for unused stamps and those in the right-hand column are for used.

Prices are expressed in pounds and pence sterling. One pound comprises 100 pence (£1 = 100p).

The method of notation is as follows: pence in numerals (e.g. 10 denotes ten pence); pounds and pence up to £100, in numerals (e.g. 4·25 denotes four pounds and twenty-five pence); prices above £100 expressed in whole pounds with the '£' sign shown.

Unused stamps. Prices for stamps issued up to the end of the Second World War (1945) are for lightly hinged examples and more may be asked if they are in unmounted mint condition. Prices for all later unused stamps are for unmounted mint. Where not available in this condition, lightly hinged stamps are often available at a lower price.

Used stamps. The used prices are normally for stamps postally used but may be for stamps cancelled-to-order where this practice exists.

A pen-cancellation on early issues can sometimes correctly denote postal use. Instances are individually noted in the Catalogue in explanation of the used price given.

Prices quoted for bisects on cover or on large piece are for those dated during the period officially authorised.

Stamps not sold unused to the public but affixed by postal officials before use (e.g. some parcel post stamps) are priced used only.

Minimum price. The minimum catalogue price quoted is 10p. For individual stamps prices between 10p and 95p are provided as a guide for catalogue users. The lowest price charged for individual stamps purchased from Stanley Gibbons Ltd. is £1.

Set prices. Set prices are generally for one of each value, excluding shades and varieties, but including major colour changes. Where there are alternative shades, etc, the cheapest is usually included. The number of stamps in the set is always stated for clarity.

Where prices are given for *se-tenant* blocks or strips any mint price quoted is for the complete *se-tenant* strip or block. Mint and used set prices are always for a set of single stamps.

Repricing. Collectors will be aware that the market factors of supply and demand directly influence the prices quoted in this Catalogue. Whatever the scarcity of a particular stamp, if there is no one in the market who wishes to buy it it cannot be expected to achieve a high price. Conversely, the same item actively sought by numerous potential buyers may cause the price to rise.

All the prices in this Catalogue are examined during the preparation of each new edition by expert staff of Stanley Gibbons and repriced as necessary. They take many factors into account, including supply and demand, and are in close touch with the international stamp market and the auction world.

GUARANTEE

All stamps are guaranteed genuine originals in the following terms:

If not as described, and returned by the purchaser, we undertake to refund the price paid to us in the original transaction. If any stamp is certified as genuine by the Expert Committee of the Royal Philatelic Society, London, or by B.P.A. Expertising Ltd, the purchaser shall not be entitled to make claim against us for any error, omission or mistake in such certificate. Consumers' statutory rights are not affected by this guarantee.

The establishment Expert Committees in this country are those of the Royal Philatelic Society, 41 Devonshire Place, London W19 6JY, and B.P.A. Expertising Ltd, P.O. Box 1141, Guildford, Surrey GU5 0WR. They do not undertake valuations under any circumstances and fees are payable for their services.

Abbreviations

Printers
A.B.N. Co.	American Bank Note Co, New York.
B.A.B.N.	British American Bank Note Co. Ottawa
B.D.T.	B.D.T. International Security Printing Ltd, Dublin, Ireland
B.W.	Bradbury Wilkinson & Co, Ltd.
Cartor	Cartor S.A., La Loupe, France
C.B.N.	Canadian Bank Note Co, Ottawa.
Continental	Continental Bank Note Co. B.N. Co.
Courvoisier	Imprimerie Courvoisier S.A., La-Chaux-de-Fonds, Switzerland.
D.L.R.	De La Rue & Co, Ltd, London.
Enschedé	Joh. Enschedé en Zonen, Haarlem, Netherlands.
Format	Format International Security Printers Ltd., London
Harrison	Harrison & Sons, Ltd. London
J.W.	John Waddington Security Print Ltd., Leeds
P.B.	Perkins Bacon Ltd, London.
Questa	Questa Colour Security Printers Ltd, London
Walsall	Walsall Security Printers Ltd
Waterlow	Waterlow & Sons, Ltd, London.

General Abbreviations
Alph	Alphabet
Anniv	Anniversary
Comp	Compound (perforation)
Des	Designer; designed
Diag	Diagonal; diagonally
Eng	Engraver; engraved
F.C.	Fiscal Cancellation
H/S	Handstamped
Horiz	Horizontal; horizontally
Imp, Imperf	Imperforate
Inscr	Inscribed
L	Left
Litho	Lithographed
mm	Millimetres
MS	Miniature sheet
N.Y.	New York
Opt(d)	Overprint(ed)
P or P-c	Pen-cancelled
P, Pf or Perf	Perforated
Photo	Photogravure
Pl	Plate
Pr	Pair
Ptd	Printed
Ptg	Printing
R	Right
R.	Row
Recess	Recess-printed
Roto	Rotogravure
Roul	Rouletted
S	Specimen (overprint)
Surch	Surcharge(d)
T.C.	Telegraph Cancellation
T	Type
Typo	Typographed
Un	Unused
Us	Used
Vert	Vertical; vertically
W or wmk	Watermark
Wmk s	Watermark sideways

(†) = Does not exist
(–) (or blank price column) = Exists, or may exist, but no market price is known.
/ between colours means 'on' and the colour following is that of the paper on which the stamp is printed.

Colours of Stamps
Bl (blue); blk (black); brn (brown); car, carm (carmine); choc (chocolate); clar (claret); emer (emerald); grn (green); ind (indigo); mag (magenta); mar (maroon); mult (multicoloured) mve (mauve); ol (olive); orge (orange); pk (pink); pur (purple); scar (scarlet); sep (sepia); turq (turquoise); ultram (ultramarine); verm (vermilion); vio (violet); yell (yellow).

Colour of Overprints and Surcharges
(B.) = blue, (Blk.) = black, (Br.) = brown, (C.) = carmine, (G.) = green, (Mag.) = magenta, (Mve.) = mauve, (Ol.) = olive, (O.) = orange, (P.) = purple, (Pk.) = pink, (R.) = red, (Sil.) = silver, (V.) = violet, (Vm.) or (Verm.) = vermilion, (W.) = white, (Y.) = yellow.

Arabic Numerals
As in the case of European figures, the details of the Arabic numerals vary in different stamp designs, but they should be readily recognised with the aid of this illustration.

٠ ١ ٢ ٣ ٤ ٥ ٦ ٧ ٨ ٩
0 1 2 3 4 5 6 7 8 9

International Philatelic Glossary

English	French	German	Spanish	Italian
Agate	Agate	Achat	Agata	Agata
Air stamp	Timbre de la poste aérienne	Flugpostmarke	Sello de correo aéreo	Francobollo per posta aerea
Apple Green	Vert-pomme	Apfelgrün	Verde manzana	Verde mela
Barred	Annulé par barres	Balkenentwertung	Anulado con barras	Sbarrato
Bisected	Timbre coupé	Halbiert	Partido en dos	Frazionato
Bistre	Bistre	Bister	Bistre	Bistro
Bistre-brown	Brun-bistre	Bisterbraun	Castaño bistre	Bruno-bistro
Black	Noir	Schwarz	Negro	Nero
Blackish Brown	Brun-noir	Schwärzlichbraun	Castaño negruzco	Bruno nerastro
Blackish Green	Vert foncé	Schwärzlichgrün	Verde negruzco	Verde nerastro
Blackish Olive	Olive foncé	Schwärzlicholiv	Oliva negruzco	Oliva nerastro
Block of four	Bloc de quatre	Viererblock	Bloque de cuatro	Bloco di quattro
Blue	Bleu	Blau	Azul	Azzurro
Blue-green	Vert-bleu	Blaugrün	Verde azul	Verde azzuro
Bluish Violet	Violet bleuâtre	Bläulichviolett	Violeta azulado	VioItto azzurrastro
Booklet	Carnet	Heft	Cuadernillo	Libretto
Bright Blue	Bleu vif	Lebhaftblau	Azul vivo	Azzurro vivo
Bright Green	Vert vif	Lebhaftgrün	Verde vivo	Verde vivo
Bright Purple	Mauve vif	Lebhaftpurpur	Púrpura vivo	Porpora vivo
Bronze Green	Vert-bronze	Bronzegrün	Verde bronce	Verde bronzo
Brown	Brun	Braun	Castaño	Bruno
Brown-lake	Carmin-brun	Braunlack	Laca castaño	Lacca bruno
Brown-purple	Pourpre-brun	Braunpurpur	Púrpura castaño	Porpora bruno
Brown-red	Rouge-brun	Braunrot	Rojo castaño	Rosso bruno
Buff	Chamois	Sämisch	Anteado	Camoscio
Cancellation	Oblitération	Entwertung	Cancelación	Annullamento
Cancelled	Annulé	Gestempelt	Cancelado	Annullato
Carmine	Carmin	Karmin	Carmín	Carminio
Carmine-red	Rouge-carmin	Karminrot	Rojo carmín	Rosso carminio
Centred	Centré	Zentriert	Centrado	Centrato
Cerise	Rouge-cerise	Kirschrot	Color de ceresa	Color Ciliegia
Chalk-surfaced paper	Papier couché	Kreidepapier	Papel estucado	Carta gessata
Chalky Blue	Bleu terne	Kreideblau	Azul turbio	Azzurro smorto
Charity stamp	Timbre de bienfaisance	Wohltätigkeitsmarke	Sello de beneficenza	Francobollo di beneficenza
Chestnut	Marron	Kastanienbraun	Castaño rojo	Marrone
Chocolate	Chocolat	Schokolade	Chocolate	Cioccolato
Cinnamon	Cannelle	Zimtbraun	Canela	Cannella
Claret	Grenat	Weinrot	Rojo vinoso	Vinaccia
Cobalt	Cobalt	Kobalt	Cobalto	Cobalto
Colour	Couleur	Farbe	Color	Colore
Comb-perforation	Dentelure en peigne	Kammzähnung, Reihenzähnung	Dentado de peine	Dentellatura e pettine
Commemorative stamp	Timbre commémoratif	Gedenkmarke	Sello conmemorativo	Francobollo commemorativo
Crimson	Cramoisi	Karmesin	Carmesí	Cremisi
Deep Blue	Blue foncé	Dunkelblau	Azul oscuro	Azzurro scuro
Deep bluish Green	Vert-bleu foncé	Dunkelbläulichgrün	Verde azulado oscuro	Verde azzurro scuro
Design	Dessin	Markenbild	Diseño	Disegno

International Philatelic Glossary

English	French	German	Spanish	Italian
Die	Matrice	Urstempel. Type, Platte	Cuño	Conio, Matrice
Double	Double	Doppelt	Doble	Doppio
Drab	Olive terne	Trüboliv	Oliva turbio	Oliva smorto
Dull Green	Vert terne	Trübgrün	Verde turbio	Verde smorto
Dull purple	Mauve terne	Trübpurpur	Púrpura turbio	Porpora smorto
Embossing	Impression en relief	Prägedruck	Impresión en relieve	Impressione a relievo
Emerald	Vert-eméraude	Smaragdgrün	Esmeralda	Smeraldo
Engraved	Gravé	Graviert	Grabado	Inciso
Error	Erreur	Fehler, Fehldruck	Error	Errore
Essay	Essai	Probedruck	Ensayo	Saggio
Express letter stamp	Timbre pour lettres par exprès	Eilmarke	Sello de urgencia	Francobollo per espresso
Fiscal stamp	Timbre fiscal	Stempelmarke	Sello fiscal	Francobollo fiscale
Flesh	Chair	Fleischfarben	Carne	Carnicino
Forgery	Faux, Falsification	Fälschung	Falsificación	Falso, Falsificazione
Frame	Cadre	Rahmen	Marco	Cornice
Granite paper	Papier avec fragments de fils de soie	Faserpapier	Papel con filamentos	Carto con fili di seta
Green	Vert	Grün	Verde	Verde
Greenish Blue	Bleu verdâtre	Grünlichblau	Azul verdoso	Azzurro verdastro
Greenish Yellow	Jaune-vert	Grünlichgelb	Amarillo verdoso	Giallo verdastro
Grey	Gris	Grau	Gris	Grigio
Grey-blue	Bleu-gris	Graublau	Azul gris	Azzurro grigio
Grey-green	Vert gris	Graugrün	Verde gris	Verde grigio
Gum	Gomme	Gummi	Goma	Gomma
Gutter	Interpanneau	Zwischensteg	Espacio blanco entre dos grupos	Ponte
Imperforate	Non-dentelé	Geschnitten	Sin dentar	Non dentellato
Indigo	Indigo	Indigo	Azul indigo	Indaco
Inscription	Inscription	Inschrift	Inscripción	Dicitura
Inverted	Renversé	Kopfstehend	Invertido	Capovolto
Issue	Émission	Ausgabe	Emisión	Emissione
Laid	Vergé	Gestreift	Listado	Vergato
Lake	Lie de vin	Lackfarbe	Laca	Lacca
Lake-brown	Brun-carmin	Lackbraun	Castaño laca	Bruno lacca
Lavender	Bleu-lavende	Lavendel	Color de alhucema	Lavanda
Lemon	Jaune-citron	Zitrongelb	Limón	Limone
Light Blue	Bleu clair	Hellblau	Azul claro	Azzurro chiaro
Lilac	Lilas	Lila	Lila	Lilla
Line perforation	Dentelure en lignes	Linienzähnung	Dentado en linea	Dentellatura lineare
Lithography	Lithographie	Steindruck	Litografía	Litografia
Local	Timbre de poste locale	Lokalpostmarke	Emisión local	Emissione locale
Lozenge roulette	Percé en losanges	Rautenförmiger Durchstich	Picadura en rombos	Perforazione a losanghe
Magenta	Magenta	Magentarot	Magenta	Magenta
Margin	Marge	Rand	Borde	Margine
Maroon	Marron pourpré	Dunkelrotpurpur	Púrpura rojo oscuro	Marrone rossastro
Mauve	Mauve	Malvenfarbe	Malva	Malva
Multicoloured	Polychrome	Mehrfarbig	Multicolores	Policromo
Myrtle Green	Vert myrte	Myrtengrün	Verde mirto	Verde mirto
New Blue	Bleu ciel vif	Neublau	Azul nuevo	Azzurro nuovo
Newspaper stamp	Timbre pour journaux	Zeitungsmarke	Sello para periódicos	Francobollo per giornali
Obliteration	Oblitération	Abstempelung	Matasello	Annullamento
Obsolete	Hors (de) cours	Ausser Kurs	Fuera de curso	Fuori corso

xvii

GERT MÜLLER AUCTIONS
Your competent partners

CARSTEN BERNHARD
Head of philately

HOLGER THULL
CEO & auctioneer

VERA SEEBACHER
Administration

- Rare Stamps and Covers from Europe, especially Germany
- More than 3000 collections, lots and worldwide estates each auction

CONSIGNMENTS WELCOME!

Please order the <u>free catalogues</u> now!
Phone: 0049 7243 561740

CONSIGNMENTS WELCOME — FOUR INTERNATIONAL AUCTIONS A YEAR

GERT MÜLLER
Auctions since 1951

Gert Müller GmbH & Co. KG • International stamp and coin auctions
Carl-Zeiss-Str. 2 • 76275 Ettlingen/Germany • P: 0049 7243 561740 • F: 0049 7243 5617429
E-Mail: info@gert-mueller-auktion.de • Internet: www.gert-mueller-auktion.de

STANLEY GIBBONS
LONDON 1856

LUXURY HINGELESS COUNTRY ALBUMS
Germany and German States

Germany (Deutsches Reich)	Vol I	1872-1945	R5313LX	£191
GERMANY (West) Zones	27 pages		R5212LXSL	£89
GERMANY (East) Zones	20 pages		R5213LXSL	£67
BRD (West)	Vol I	1949-1969	R5314LX	£141
BINDER/SLIPCASE			R5314L/RB	£64
BRD (West)	Vol II	1970-1990	R5315LX	£219
BINDER/SLIPCASE			R5315L/RB	£64
BERLIN	Vol I	1948-1990	R5316LX	£198
BINDER/SLIPCASE			R5316L/RB	£64
Complete set BRD/Berlin	Vol I,II,I	1948-1990	R5314LX(SO)	£288
BINDER/SLIPCASE			R5646L/RB	£64
DDR (East)	Vol I	1949-1965	R5317LX	£191
BINDER/SLIPCASE			R5317L/RB	£64
DDR East	Vol II	1966-1974	R5318LX	£198
BINDER/SLIPCASE			R5317L/RB	£64
DDR East	Vol III	1975-1979	R5319LX	£156
BINDER/SLIPCASE			R5319L/RB	£64
DDR East	Vol IV	1980-1985	R5432LX	£174
BINDER/SLIPCASE			R5432L/RB	£64
DDR East	Vol V	1986-1990	R5551LX	£141
BINDER/SLIPCASE			R5551L/RB	£64
Complete set	Vol I-V	1949-1990	R5317LX(SO)	£688
GERMANY (unified)	Vol I	1990-1999	R5528LX	£198
BINDER/SLIPCASE			R5528L/RB	£64
GERMANY (unified)	Vol II	2000-2009	R5572LX	£208
GERMANY (unified)	Vol III	20010-2017	R5623LX	£156
Complete set		1990-2017	R5528LX(SO)	£446

With a space for each stamp and with crystal clear protective mounts already affixed for immediate insertion of your stamps, this luxury stamp album really is the stamp album for the collector who wants to give his collection a touch of class.

The leaves, which are of finest quality paper, have been expertly arranged and include selected illustrations and descriptions for your guidance.

Visit **stanleygibbons.com/davo05** to view the full range.

Also available in Standard (without mounts) - check the website for the full range or contact Customer Services for a Davo brochure.

399 Strand, WC2R 0LX, London | Phone: **+44 1425 472 363** | Email: **support@stanleygibbons.com**
www.stanleygibbons.com

www.jennes-und-kluettermann.de

Three times a year - first Saturday in April + August + December - we offer collectors and researchers auctions of numerous single lots from all philatelic areas of stamps, covers and postal history as well as large collections. The main focus is on the German area. Our auctions are a treasure trove for specialists with rarities from A (Altdeutschland) to Z (Zonen). We also provide favourable terms for sale of your philatelic holdings. We are always ready to answer your queries and strive to give you the very best personal service.

J&K

Wolfgang Jennes & Peter Klüttermann
Briefmarkenauktionen - Clarenbach Straße 182 - 50931 Köln
FON +49 221 - 940 53 20 FAX +49 221 - 940 53 26
e-mail info@jennes-und-kluettermann.de

GERMANY & COLONIES PHILATELIC SOCIETY

JOIN ONE OF THE LEADING
PHILATELIC SOCIETIES IN THE UK
LEARN MORE ABOUT THE WIDE
RANGE OF GERMAN PHILATELY

WWW.GERMANPHILATELY.ORG

Full-colour 72-page quarterly magazine, exchange packet, three postal auctions annually of 700 to 800 lots, postal lending library for UK members. Catalogues and collecting accessories at discount prices. Regional Group meetings in Central London, Eastleigh, Brighton, Taunton, Frodsham, Solihull, Durham and Linlithgow. Study Groups researching specific areas. Comprehensive website with message boards for queries. and free youth membership.

Germany

I. German States

CONDITION. The condition of all early issues of the German States is an important factor in establishing catalogue value. The prices for imperf stamps are for stamps in good condition with four margins, but naturally stamps in very fine condition with large margins all round are worth very much more, whilst medium and close-cut copies are supplied at lower prices.

BADEN

60 Kreuzer = 1 Gulden

Grand Duke Leopold I
30 March 1830–24 April 1852

(Eng C. Naumann, Frankfurt-am-Main. Typo W. Hasper, Karlsruhe)

1851 (1 May)–**52**. Black impression, on coloured paper. Imperf.

1	1	1k. on *buff*	£5500	£1300
1a		1k. on *brown* (15.9.1851)	£800	£425
2		3k. on *orange*	£2500	60·00
3		3k. on *yellow* (19.8.1852)	£400	26·00
4		6k. on *blue-green*	£6000	£140
5		6k. on *yellow-green* (15.3.1852)	£1300	80·00
6		9k. on *rose*	£7000	£250
6a		9k. on *dull rose* (21.10.1851)	£325	46·00
		b. Error. On *green*		

The date on the stamps is that of the treaty establishing a German-Austrian postal union.

Only three examples of No. 6*ab* are known, one on piece (*Price £1,300,000*) and two on cover (*Price £2,300,000*), one of the latter being in the German Post Office Museum. Examples cancelled '164', 'WERTHRIM' or 'ALTHAUSEN 28 SEP 56' are forgeries.

Friedrich Prince Regent
24 April 1852–5 September 1856

Later Grand Duke
5 September 1856–28 September 1907

1853 (20 Aug)–**58**. Black impression. Imperf.

8	1	1k. on *white* (18.10)	£600	46·00
9		3k. on *green* (1.12.58)	£425	13·00
10		3k. on *blue* (8.58)	£1900	50·00
11		6k. on *orange* (1.1.54)	£700	46·00

Reprints of all the above stamps except the 9kr. were made in 1867 in different shades. The paper used is thicker for all values except the 6k. on *orange*, and the gum is white and smooth.

(Des C. A. Weber. Eng L. Kurz, Frankfurt-am-Main. Typo Hasper, Karlsruhe)

1860 (June)–**62**. P 13½.

13	2	1k. black	£140	39·00
14		3k. Prussian blue	£500	£120
15		3k. deep blue	£650	£325
16		3k. ultramarine (1861)	£160	39·00
17		6k. orange (1861)	£170	£130
18		6k. orange-yellow (1862)	£325	£160
19		9k. rose (1861)	£425	£275

1862. P 10.

20	2	1k. silver-grey	£12000	£12000
21		1k. black (*shades*)	£100	£160
22		6k. blue	£250	£170
23		6k. deep blue	£200	£130
24		9k. brown	£600	£450
25		9k. bistre	£170	£200
25a		9k. yellow-brown	£200	£425

(Eng L. Kurz. Typo W. Hasper, Karlsruhe)

1862 (26 Mar). P 13½.

26	3	3k. rose	£3750	£475

1862–05. P 10.

27	3	1k. black (1864)	80·00	20·00
28		3k. pale rose	£100	5·75
		a. Imperf	£65000	£65000
29		3k. deep rose	£100	5·75
30		6k. ultramarine (1864)	20·00	42·00
30a		6k. light blue	80·00	£100
31		6k. Prussian blue (1865)	£1000	£110
32		9k. yellow-brown	£650	£140
		a. Printed both sides		£10000
33		9k. pale brown	26·00	50·00
34		9k. brown	£325	80·00
35		9k. deep brown	£900	£800
36		18k. green	£650	£900
37		18k. deep green	£2250	£2500
38		30k. orange	50·00	£4250

Only one unused example of No. 28a is known, plus several used examples.

1862 (1 Oct). RURAL POSTAGE DUE. Thin paper. P 10.

D39	D 4	1k. black/*yellow*	7·75	£500
		b. Thicker, deeper yellow paper	£225	£1000
D40		3k. black/*yellow*	4·50	£200
		b. Thicker, deeper yellow paper	£200	£650
D41		12k. black/*yellow*	60·00	£28000
		a. Bisected (*on cover*)	†	£33000

In the 12k. 'LAND-POST' is in a straight line.

(Eng Mayer. Typo W. Hasper, Karlsruhe)

1868 (1 Oct). P 10.

39	4	1k. pale green	7·25	14·50
40		1k. green	7·25	14·50
41		3k. rose	4·50	9·00
42		3k. deep rose	4·50	9·00
43		7k. sky blue	70·00	£170
44		7k. blue (*to deep*)	33·00	50·00

Separate issues for Baden ceased in 1871, when the Baden postal administration was incorporated in that of the German Empire.

BAVARIA

1849. 60 Kreuter = 1 Gulden
1874. 100 Pfennig = 1 Mark

King Maximilian II
21 March 1848 – 10 March 1864

(Des P. Haseney. Eng F. X. Seitz. Plates by Gustav Lorenz. Typo J. G. Weiss, Munich)

1849 (1 Nov). Imperf.

1	1	1k. black	£1700	£3750
		a. With silk thread in paper	£6500	
2		1k. grey-black	£4500	£4500
		a. Tête-bêche (pair)	£130000	

No. 1a is probably a proof.

Only three examples of No. 2a are known, all unused and part of a larger block.

GERMANY/ German States - Bavaria

1849–62. Labels at top, bottom and sides cut the circle. Paper with silk thread. Imperf.

2b	2	3k. bright Prussian blue (plate 1)	£4000	£120
2c		3k. blue-black	£6500	£200
3		3k. grey-blue (plate 2) (9.1850–54)	£400	6·50
4		3k. greenish blue (plate 3) (12.1854–58)	£200	6·50
5		3k. deep blue (plate 4) (5.1856–62)	£250	7·75
6		3k. blue (plate 5) (8.1858–62)	£100	6·50
7		6k. brown (*shades*)	£12000	£400

Most so-called unused copies of No. 7 offered for sale are pen-cancelled stamps that have been washed. The same remark applies to No. 15.

1850–58. Paper with silk thread. Imperf.

8	2a	1k. rose	£300	£300
8a		1k. pink	£600	£600
9		6k. cinnamon	£225	£225
10		6k. bistre-brown	£160	£160
11		6k. brown	80·00	80·00
12		6k. bright brown	80·00	80·00
13		6k. chestnut	80·00	80·00
14		6k. deep brown	80·00	80·00
15		9k. pale blue-green	£6500	£6500
16		9k. pale yellow-green	£325	£325
17		9k. deep yellow-green	£120	£120
18		12k. red (1.7.58)	£225	£225
19		18k. orange-yellow (19.7.54)	£225	£225

Examples of the 18k. without silk thread are forgeries.

1862 (1 Oct)–**63**. Colours changed. Paper with silk thread. Imperf.

20	2a	1k. yellow	£130	39·00
21		1k. orange-yellow	£130	39·00
21a		1k. greenish yellow (1863)		
22	2	3k. rose	£225	13·00
23		3k. carmine	85·00	13·00
24		3k. crimson	85·00	13·00
25	2a	6k. blue	£100	65·00
26		6k. deep blue	£250	20·00
27		6k. ultramarine	£4000	£13000
28		9k. pale bistre	£200	26·00
29		9k. bistre-brown	£200	26·00
30		12k. yellow-green	£160	£130
31		12k. green	£160	£130
32		12k. brick-red	£225	£800
33		18k. bright red	£1600	£250

Examples of the 18k. without silk thread are forgeries. No. 27 is a proof.

(Type-set. J. G. Weiss, Munich)

1862 (1 Oct). POSTAGE DUE. Silk thread. Imperf.

D34	3	3k. black	£200	£500
		a. 'Empfänge' ('r' omitted)	£650	£1700
		b. 'Bom' instead of 'Vom' (pos. 18 and 60)	£400	£1000

No. D34a occurs on Row 2, stamp 4 in the sheet of 90 (9×10). Examples of No. D34 without silk thread are forgeries.

King Ludwig II
10 March 1864 – 10 June 1886

3

(Eng P. Riess. Embossed and typo Mint, Munich)

1867 (1 Jan)–**69**. With silk thread. Imperf.

34	3	1k. yellow-green	£100	20·00
35		1k. green	£300	46·00
36		1k. blue-green	£500	85·00
37		3k. rose	£110	13·00
38		3k. rose-carmine		
39		6k. pale blue	80·00	33·00
40		6k. blue		
41		6k. pale bistre (1.10.68)	£130	80·00
42		6k. deep bistre (1869)		
43		7k. blue (1.10.68)	£650	26·00
44		7k. deep blue (1869)		£850
45		7k. Prussian blue (1869)	£3750	£1300
46		9k. pale bistre	80·00	70·00
47		9k. yellow-bistre		
48		12k. mauve	£600	£160
49		12k. dull mauve		
50		18k. brick-red	£225	£275

See also Nos. 51/64 and 67/74.

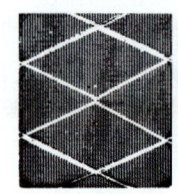

4    **5**    D **6**

1870 (1 July)–**73**. P 11½.

A. W **4** (*width of mesh 17 mm*)

51A	3	1k. pale green	20·00	2·50
52A		1k. deep green	50·00	7·75
53A		3k. rose	39·00	2·50
54A		3k. rose-carmine		
55A		6k. bistre	50·00	50·00
56A		7k. pale blue	6·50	7·75
57A		7k. blue	33·00	23·00
58A		7k. ultramarine	£1000	£275
59A		9k. brown (1.1.73)	9·00	6·50
60A		10k. ochre (1.1.73)	10·50	26·00
61A		12k. dull mauve	£2000	£8000
63A		18k. pale red	26·00	26·00
64A		18k. red	£200	£120

B. W **5** (*width of mesh 14 mm*)

51B	3	1k. pale green	£170	16·00
52B		1k. deep green	£250	60·00
53B		3k. rose	£160	4·00
54B		3k. rose-carmine		
55B		6k. bistre	£275	£120
56B		7k. pale blue	£225	60·00
57B		7k. blue	£275	80·00
59B		9k. brown (1.1.73)	£475	£800
60B		10k. ochre (1.1.73)	£400	£600
61B		12k. dull mauve	£600	£1800
63B		18k. pale red	£500	£400
64B		18k. red	£650	£300

(Typo J. G. Weiss, Munich)

1870 (1 July). POSTAGE DUE. P 11½.

A. W **4**

D65A	D **6**	1k. black	90·00	£2750
D66A		3k. black	90·00	£2000

B. W **5**

D65B	D **6**	1k. black	23·00	£1300
D66B		3k. black	23·00	£800

6 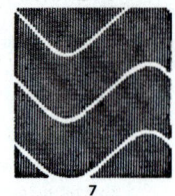   **7**

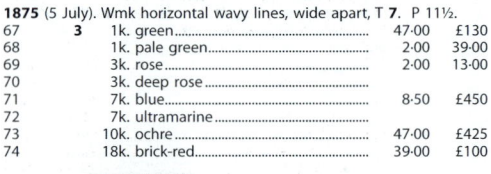

(Eng P. Riess. Embossed and typo Mint, Munich)

1874 (5 Aug). W **4**. Imperf.

65	**6**	1m. mauve	£1100	£140

See also Nos. 66, 88/89, 99/101*a*, 131/132*b* and 134/137.

1875 (June). W **4**. P 11½.

66	**6**	1m. mauve	£350	90·00
		a. Dark violet	£800	£225

1875 (5 July). Wmk horizontal wavy lines, wide apart, T **7**. P 11½.

67	3	1k. green	47·00	£130
68		1k. pale green	2·00	39·00
69		3k. rose	2·00	13·00
70		3k. deep rose		
71		7k. blue	8·50	£450
72		7k. ultramarine		
73		10k. ochre	47·00	£425
74		18k. brick-red	39·00	£100

8

(D **9**) ('Payable by the Recipient')

GERMANY / German States - Bavaria

(Eng P. Riess. Embossed and typo Mint, Munich)

1876 (1 Jan)–**80**. New currency. W **7**. P 11½.

75	8	3pf. yellow-green	£130	39·00
76		3pf. pale green	60·00	2·50
77		5pf. pale green	£140	26·00
78		5pf. deep blue-green	£500	34·00
79		5pf. sage-green	£2250	£1200
80		5pf. mauve (9.78)	£275	39·00
81		10pf. rose	£1300	£180
82		10pf. carmine	£300	2·50
83		20pf. Prussian blue	£1400	£325
84		20pf. blue	£300	5·25
85		25pf. brown	£275	10·50
85a		25pf. pale brown		
86		50pf. vermilion	90·00	11·50
87		50pf. orange-brown (9.78)	£1400	50·00
88	6	1m. pale mauve (5.79)	£3250	£140
89		2m. orange (1880)	46·00	21·00

See also Nos. 90/98, 102/129 and 133.

1876 (1 Jan). POSTAGE DUE. Optd with Type D **9**, in red. W **7**. P 11½.

D90	8	3pf. grey	26·00	65·00
D91		5pf. grey	20·00	26·00
D92		10pf. grey	6·50	2·50

See also Nos. D102/D104 and D130/D133.

9 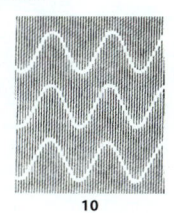   10

(Embossed and typo J. G. Weiss; from Jan 1883, Mint, Munich)

1881 (15 Nov)–**1903**. Wmk close vertical wavy lines. Type **9**. P 11½.

90	8	3pf. yellow-green	20·00	1·60
91		5pf. mauve	29·00	2·10
92		5pf. pale mauve		
93		10pf. carmine	21·00	1·30
94		10pf. aniline red	39·00	7·75
95		20pf. ultramarine	23·00	1·30
96		25pf. bistre-brown	£200	5·75
97		50pf. orange-brown	£225	5·25
98		50pf. brown		
99	6	1m. red-mauve/*rose*	£120	9·00
100		1m. mauve/(toned)	10·50	7·75
101		2m. orange-yellow/*rose* (1.12.90)	£140	23·00
101a		2m. orange-yellow/*white* (1903)	8·50	16·00

1883 (10 June)–**87**. POSTAGE DUE. Optd with Type D **9**, in red. W **9**. P 11½.

D102	8	3pf. grey	£140	£170
D103		5pf. grey	90·00	£120
D104		10pf. grey (1887)	4·00	2·50

Prince-Regent Luitpold
10 June 1886 – 12 December 1912

1888 (1 Jan)–**1900**. Wmk close horizontal wavy lines. Type **10**. P 14×14½.

(a) Toned paper

102	8	2pf. grey (1900)	20·00	8·50
103		3pf. yellow-green	17·00	3·25
104		3pf. brown (10.2.90)	13·00	1·00
105		3pf. grey-brown (10.2.90)	46·00	11·00
106		5pf. mauve	39·00	13·00
107		5pf. pale mauve	34·00	16·00
108		5pf. deep green (10.2.90)	17·00	1·00
109		5pf. deep blue-green (10.2.90)		
110		10pf. rose	11·00	1·30
111		10pf. carmine	39·00	17·00
		a. Imperf (pair)	£250	£650
112		20pf. blue	17·00	2·10
113		20pf. ultramarine	23·00	6·50
114		25pf. bistre-brown	50·00	22·00
115		25pf. orange (10.2.90)	29·00	4·50
		a. Orange-yellow	29·00	4·50
116		50pf. grey-brown		
117		50pf. deep grey-brown	£100	22·00
118		50pf. maroon	80·00	5·25
119		50pf. deep maroon (10.2.90)	80·00	5·25
119a		80pf. mauve (1900)	50·00	20·00

(b) White paper (1900)

120	8	2pf. grey	3·50	1·30
121		3pf. deep brown	50	1·00
122		5pf. deep green	50	1·00
123		10pf. carmine	65	1·30
		a. Imperf (pair)	£130	
124		20pf. bright ultramarine	65	1·30
125		25pf. orange	1·00	2·00
126		30pf. olive-green	1·30	2·00
127		40pf. yellow-ochre	1·30	2·10
128		50pf. maroon	1·30	2·75
129		80pf. mauve	4·50	7·75
120/129		Set of 10	14·00	20·00

1888 (5 Mar)–**1903**. POSTAGE DUE. Optd with Type D **9**, in red. W **10**. Rose-tinted paper. P 14×14½.

D130	8	2pf. grey (1895)	3·25	7·75
		a. White paper (1903)	1·30	4·00
D131		3pf. grey	4·50	5·00
		a. White paper (1903)	1·30	7·25
D132		5pf. grey	4·50	5·00
		a. White paper (1903)	1·80	6·50
D133		10pf. grey	4·50	2·50
		a. White paper (1903)	1·30	4·00
D130/D133		Set of 4	15·00	18·00
D130a/D133a		Set of 4	5·25	20·00

1895 (4 Sept)–**1903**. POSTAGE DUE. No. D131A surch '2' in each corner.

D134	8	2 on 3pf. grey/*rose* (R.)	†	£80000

D134 was never issued, only six copies, all used, exist.

1900 (1 Apr)–**06**. W **9**. P 11½.

(a) Toned paper

131	6	3m. olive-brown	39·00	50·00
132		5m. pale green	39·00	50·00

(b) White paper (1906)

132a	6	3m. olive-brown	£275	£800
132b		5m. pale green	£250	£600

E
(R **11**)

1908 (1 Jan). RAILWAY OFFICIAL. Nos. 121/4 and 128 optd with T R **11**.

R133	8	3pf. deep brown (R.)	1·30	7·25
R134		5pf. deep green (R.)	40	65
R135		10pf. carmine (G.)	40	65
R136		20pf. ultramarine (R.)	80	1·30
R137		50pf. maroon (G.)	7·75	13·00
R133/R137		Set of 5	9·50	21·00

The so-called Return Letter stamps formerly catalogued are not postage stamps in any sense, but simply labels applied by the Post Office officials for their own convenience.

1911 (23 Jan). W **9**. P 14×14½.

133	8	5pf. green	1·00	22·00

1911 (Jan). Thick white paper. W **10**. P 11½.

134	6	1m. mauve	13·00	23·00
135		2m. orange-yellow	14·50	37·00
136		3m. olive-brown	14·50	55·00
137		5m. pale green	14·50	60·00
134/137		Set of 4	50·00	£160

11    12    13

Prince Luitpold

I.

II.

Pfennig values

I. 'E' of 'MAERZ' has short centre bar; 'R' of 'MAERZ' with small head and long tail.
II. 'E' with long centre bar; 'R' with large head.

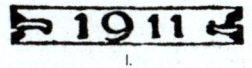

I.

GERMANY/ German States - Bavaria

1911
II.

Mark values

I. Thin figures in '1911'; bottom serifs of figures '1' very short.
II. Figures thicker; serifs thick.

(Des F. A. v. Kaulbach. Photo-litho by Oskar Consee, Munich, but early supplies of the 30, 40, 50 and 80pf. by Topographical Institute of the Ministry of War).

1911 (10 Mar)–**13**. 90th Birthday of Prince-Regent Luitpold. W **9** (30pf. to 20m.) or W **10** (others). P 14 ×14½ (3pf. to 25pf.) or 11½ (others).

No.	Type	Description	Un	Used
138	11	3pf. brown/*drab*	2·75	1·30
		a. Deep brown/*drab*	3·50	2·50
		b. '911' for '1911'	£500	£500
		c. Date as Type II (10.11)	50	1·30
139		5pf. green/*green* (I)	1·80	1·30
		a. Tête-bêche (pair)	6·50	10·50
		b. Booklet pane. No. 139×4 plus two labels	£200	
		c. Date as Type II (10.11)	50	1·30
		ca. Tête-bêche (pair)	6·50	10·50
		cb. Booklet pane No. 139c×4 plus two labels	£200	
		cc. Booklet pane No. 139c×5 plus advertising label (1912)	£300	
		cd. As cc. but St. Andrew's Cross on label (1.13)	£160	
140	11	10pf. carmine/*buff* (I)	1·80	1·30
		a. '911' for '1911'	26·00	36·00
		b. Tête-bêche (pair)	65·00	£100
		c. Booklet pane. No. 140×5 plus advertising label	£150	
		d. Date as Type II (10.11)	50	1·30
		db. Tête-bêche (pair)	65·00	£100
		dc. Booklet pane. No. 140d×5 plus advertising label	£150	
		dd. As dc. but St. Andrew's Cross on label (1.13)	£160	
141		20pf. blue/*blue* (I)	17·00	4·50
		a. Bright ultramarine/*blue*	17·00	13·00
		b. Date as Type II (10.11)	3·25	2·10
142		25pf. purple-brown/*buff* (I)	31·00	5·25
		a. Date as Type II (10.11)	5·25	4·00
143	12	30pf. orange/*buff* (I)	18·00	6·50
		a. Date as Type II (10.11)	4·00	4·00
144		40pf. olive-green/*buff* (I)	29·00	6·50
		a. Date as Type II (10.11)	6·50	4·00
145		50pf. claret/*drab* (I)	31·00	17·00
		a. Date as Type II (10.11)	5·25	5·25
146		60pf. blue-green/*buff* (Type II) (1.10.11)	5·25	5·25
147		80pf. violet/*drab* (I)	70·00	39·00
		a. Date as Type II (10.11)	16·00	18·00
148	13	1m. brown/*drab* (I)	90·00	25·00
		a. Date as Type II (10.11)	5·25	10·50
149		2m. green/*green* (I)	£225	£100
		a. Date as Type II (10.11)	7·75	20·00
150		3m. carmine/*buff* (I)	31·00	70·00
		a. Date as Type II (as 149a) (10.11)	21·00	£100
151		5m. grey-blue/*buff* (I)	42·00	80·00
		a. Date as Type II (10.11)	21·00	£275
152		10m. orange/*yellow* (I)	70·00	£110
		a. Date as Type II (10.11)	46·00	£500
153		20m. chocolate/*yellow* (I)	42·00	50·00
		a. Date as Type II (10.11)	39·00	£600

There are shades in most values of the above series, but we only list those which vary in value.

The Tête-bêche pairs are from sheets made up to be bound into booklets.

The 5pf. and 10pf. from booklets listed under Type I differ from those from sheets in that they contain the 'E' of Type I and the 'R' of Type II.

No. 138b occurs on position 83 and No. 140a on position 30 of part of the printing.

14

(Des F. A. v. Kaulbach. Litho Oskar Consee)

1911 (10 June). 25th Anniv of Regency of Prince Luitpold. Background in black. No wmk. P 11½.

154	14	5pf. yellow, green and black	1·30	2·30
		a. Imperf (vert pair)	£225	£400
155		10pf. yellow, carmine and black	2·00	4·00
		a. Imperf (vert pair)	£225	£400

1912 (1 July). RAILWAY OFFICIAL. Nos. 138II/42II and 145II punctured 'E'.

R156	11	3pf. brown/*drab*	4·00	5·25
R157		5pf. green/*green*	65	65
R158		10pf. carmine/*buff*	50	65
R159		20pf. blue/*blue*	90	65
R160		25pf. purple-brown/*buff*	9·00	13·00
R161	12	50pf. claret/*drab*	10·50	20·00
R156/R161	Set of 6		23·00	36·00

Ludwig Prince Regent
12 Dec 1912 – 5 Nov 1913

Later King Ludwig III
5 Nov 1913 – 8 Nov 1918

15 **16** **17**

King Ludwig III

(Des Schirnböck. Photo F. A. Bruckmann, Munich)

1914 (31 Mar)–**20**. W **10** (2pf. to 80pf. and 5m. to 20m.) or W **9** (others).

A. P 14×14½ (2pf. to 80pf.) or 11½ (others)

171A	15	2pf. slate	40	4·25
172A		'2½' on 2pf. slate	40	4·25
173A		3pf. brown	40	4·25
174A		5pf. deep green	2·50	4·25
		a. Tête-bêche (pair)	13·00	33·00
		b. Tête-bêche (imperf pair)	£100	
		c. Booklet pane. No. 174A×5 plus label (4.14)	65·00	
175A		5pf. yellow-green	40	4·25
176A		7½pf. green	40	4·25
		a. Tête-bêche (pair)	7·75	11·50
177A		10pf. scarlet	2·50	4·25
		a. Tête-bêche (pair)	11·50	20·00
		b. Tête-bêche (imperf pair)	£100	
		c. Booklet pane. No. 177A×5 plus label (4.14)	65·00	
178A		10pf. crimson	40	4·25
179A		15pf. scarlet	40	4·25
		a. Tête-bêche (pair)	7·75	11·50
		b. Booklet pane. No. 179A×5 plus label (2.17)	29·00	
180A		15pf. carmine	2·75	60·00
181A		20pf. blue	40	4·25
182A		20pf. greenish blue	40	4·25
183A		25pf. grey	40	4·25
184A		30pf. orange	2·00	4·25
185A		40pf. olive	40	4·50
186A		50pf. chocolate	40	4·25
187A		60pf. blue-green	2·00	4·25
188A		80pf. violet	40	4·25
189A	16	1m. grey-brown	40	4·25
190A		2m. deep violet	50	4·50
191A		3m. scarlet	65	9·00
192A	17	5m. Prussian blue	90	33·00
193A		10m. green	2·75	90·00
194A		20m. deep brown	5·25	£130

B. Imperf (1920)

171B	15	2pf. slate	40	22·00
173B		3pf. brown	40	23·00
175B		5pf. yellow-green	40	22·00
176B		7½pf. green	40	22·00
		a. Tête-bêche (pair)	13·00	
178B		10pf. crimson	40	22·00
179B		15pf. scarlet	40	22·00
		a. Tête-bêche (pair)	13·00	
181B		20pf. blue	40	23·00
182B		20pf. greenish blue	40	23·00
183B		25pf. grey	40	23·00
184B		30pf. orange	40	23·00
185B		40pf. olive	40	23·00
186B		50pf. chocolate	40	23·00

GERMANY/ German States - Bavaria

187B		60pf. blue-green	40	26·00
188B		80pf. violet	40	26·00
189B	16	1m. grey-brown	50	26·00
190B		2m. deep violet	65	33·00
191B		3m. scarlet	80	44·00
192B	17	5m. Prussian blue	1·60	70·00
193B		10m. green	2·50	£110
194B		20m. deep brown	3·75	£180

The *tête-bêche* pairs are from sheets made up to be bound into booklets.

There are two printings of Nos. 171/94, except the 2, 2½, 7½ and 15pf., the early (1914) printings showing clear impression, bright colours, and smooth creamy paper, while the later war-time printings show coarse impression, poor colours and rough white paper. Prices quoted are for the latter, the 1914 printings being worth considerably more.

The colours of these stamps run badly in water.

1914–16. RAILWAY OFFICIAL. Nos. 173, 175, 178 and 181 punctured 'E'.

R195	15	3pf. brown (1916)	39·00	£180
R196		5pf. yellow-green	1·60	2·30
R197		10pf. crimson	1·60	1·60
R198		20pf. blue	4·00	8·50
R195/R198 *Set of* 4			42·00	£170

The 25 and 50pf. values were also puncutred but not issued (*Price:* £39 *each*).

O 18

(Des Otto Hupp. Typo Mint, Munich)

1916–20. OFFICIAL. W **10**. P 11½.

O195	O **18**	3pf. brown	40	1·30
O196		5pf. yellow-green	40	1·30
O197		7½pf. green/*green*	65	80
O198		7½pf. green	40	2·50
O199		10pf. crimson	40	2·50
O200		15pf. red/*buff*	1·00	1·70
O201		15pf. red	40	2·50
O202		20pf. indigo/*blue*	3·25	3·75
O203		20pf. blue	40	2·50
O204		25pf. grey	40	1·00
O205		30pf. orange	40	1·00
O206		60pf. myrtle-green	40	2·00
O207		1m. deep purple/*buff*	1·60	5·25
O208		1m. purple (1920)	4·50	£800
O195/O208 *Set of* 14			13·00	£750

Republic, 8 Nov, 1918

The republic declared in November 1918 was first known as People's State (Volksstaat); after the adoption of a constitution in 1919 the title was changed to Free State (Freistaat).

Volksstaat Bayern (**19**)   **Freistaat Bayern** (**20**)

1919 (1 Mar)–**20**. People's State issue. Optd with T **19** or larger (Nos. 212/214).

A. Perf

195A	15	3pf. brown	40	4·25
196A		5pf. yellow-green	40	4·25
197A		7½pf. green	40	4·25
198A		10pf. crimson	40	4·25
199A		15pf. scarlet	40	4·25
200A		20pf. greenish blue	40	4·25
201A		25pf. grey	40	4·25
202A		30pf. orange	40	4·25
203A		35pf. orange	40	5·25
		a. Opt omitted	£200	
204A		40pf. olive	40	4·25
205A		50pf. chocolate	40	4·25
206A		60pf. grey-green	40	4·25
207A		75pf. chocolate	40	4·25
		a. Opt omitted	46·00	£450
208A		80pf. dull violet	40	4·25
209A	16	1m. grey-brown	40	4·25
210A	16	2m. deep violet	50	4·25
211A		3m. scarlet	80	7·75
212A	17	5m. Prussian blue	1·60	20·00
213A		10m. green	2·30	80·00
214A		20m. deep brown	4·00	85·00

B. Imperf (4.3.20)

195B	15	3pf. brown	40	31·00
196B		5pf. yellow-green	40	31·00
197B		7½pf. green	40	31·00
198B		10pf. crimson	40	31·00
199B		15pf. scarlet	40	31·00
200B		20pf. greenish blue	40	31·00
201B		25pf. grey	40	31·00
202B		30pf. orange	40	31·00
203B		35pf. orange	40	33·00
		a. Opt omitted	26·00	
204B		40pf. olive	40	31·00
205B		50pf. chocolate	40	31·00
206B		60pf. grey-brown	40	31·00
207B		75pf. chocolate	40	33·00
		a. Opt omitted	£400	
208B		80pf. dull violet	40	33·00
209B	16	1m. grey-brown	40	39·00
210B		2m. deep violet	80	46·00
211B		3m. scarlet	1·20	31·00
212B	17	5m. Prussian blue	1·60	90·00
213B		10m. green	2·30	£130
214B		20m. deep brown	4·50	£130

IMPERF STAMPS. This issue and Nos. 231/249 and 253/255 were issued imperf to collectors but are known postally used.

1919 (1 Mar)–**20**. OFFICIAL. Optd with T **19**.

O215	O **18**	3pf. brown (1.9.19)	65	22·00
O216		5pf. yellow-green	65	4·25
O217		7½pf. green (1.9.19)	65	21·00
O218		10pf. crimson	65	4·25
O219		15pf. red	65	4·25
O220		20pf. blue (1.9.19)	65	4·25
O221		25pf. grey	65	4·25
O222		30pf. orange (1.9.19)	65	4·25
O223		35pf. orange (7.7.19)	65	4·25
O224		50pf. olive (1.8.19)	65	4·25
O225		60pf. myrtle-green (1.9.19)	65	22·00
O226		75pf. brown (1.8.19)	65	6·50
O227		1m. deep purple/*buff* (1.9.19)	2·50	23·00
O228		1m. purple (1.3.20)	7·75	£600
O215/O228 *Set of* 14			16·00	£650

1919 (17 May–30 Sept). First Free State issue. Nos. 83/104 of Germany optd with T **20**.

215	24	2½pf. grey	40	4·25
216	17	3pf. brown	40	4·25
217		5pf. green	40	4·25
218	24	7½pf. orange	40	4·25
219	17	10pf. carmine	40	4·25
220	24	15pf. slate-violet	40	4·25
221	17	20pf. ultramarine	40	4·25
222		25pf. black and red/*yellow*	40	4·25
223	24	35pf. chocolate	40	4·25
224	17	40pf. black and carmine	65	4·25
225		75pf. black and myrtle-green	90	5·25
226		80pf. black and carmine/*rose*	90	5·25
227	18	1m. carmine	2·10	7·75
228	20	2m. blue	2·50	18·00
229	21	3m. violet-black	2·50	21·00
230	22	5m. lake and black	2·50	21·00
		a. Opt inverted	£7000	
215/230 *Set of* 16			14·00	£110

Nos. 215 and 217/219 were first issued on 17 May in the Rhine Palatinate to meet a shortage of stamps; the whole series was issued throughout Bavaria on 30 September.

Freistaat Bayern (**21**)   **Freistaat Bayern** (**22**)

1919 (6 Aug)–**20**. Second Free State issue. Optd with T **21** or **22** (Nos. 247/249).

A. Perf (1919–20)

231A	15	3pf. brown	40	4·25
232A		5pf. yellow-green	40	4·25
233A		7½pf. green	40	26·00
234A		10pf. crimson	40	4·25
235A		15pf. scarlet	40	4·25
236A		20pf. greenish blue	40	4·25
237A		25pf. grey	40	4·25
238A		30pf. orange	40	4·25
239A		40pf. olive	40	23·00
240A		50pf. chocolate	40	4·25
241A		60pf. grey-green	40	23·00
242A		75pf. bistre	65	23·00
243A		80pf. dull violet	40	5·75
244A	16	1m. grey-brown	40	5·25
245A		2m. deep violet	40	9·00

5

GERMANY/ German States - Bavaria

246A		3m. scarlet	1·00	11·50
247A	17	5m. Prussian blue	1·80	29·00
248A		10m. green	3·25	60·00
249A		20m. deep brown	4·00	£100
231A/249A		Set of 19	14·50	£325

B. Imperf (4.3.20)

231B	15	3pf. brown	40	20·00
232B		5pf. yellow-green	40	20·00
233B		7½pf. green	40	36·00
234B		10pf. crimson	40	20·00
235B		15pf. scarlet	40	20·00
236B		20pf. greenish blue	40	20·00
237B		25pf. grey	40	20·00
238B		30pf. orange	40	22·00
239B		40pf. olive	40	23·00
240B		50pf. chocolate	40	23·00
241B		60pf. grey-green	40	23·00
242B		75pf. bistre	40	60·00
		a. Opt omitted	10·50	
243B		80pf. dull violet	40	23·00
244B	16	1m. grey-brown	40	36·00
245B		2m. deep violet	40	36·00
246B		3m. scarlet	1·00	46·00
247B	17	5m. Prussian blue	1·80	65·00
248B		10m. green	3·25	£120
249B		20m. deep brown	4·00	£180
231B/249B		Set of 19	14·50	£750

(23)

1919 (25 Aug). War Wounded Fund. Surch with T **23**. P 14×14½.

250	15	10pf. +5pf. crimson	65	4·25
		a. Opt inverted	£140	£300
251		15pf. +5pf. scarlet	65	4·25
		a. Opt inverted	£140	£300
252		20pf. +5pf. greenish blue	65	4·25
		a. Opt inverted	£140	£300
250/252		Set of 3	1·80	11·50

(24)  **(25)**

1919 (17 Dec)–**20**. T **16**, in various colours, optd with T **21** and surch as T **24**.

A. Perf

253A	16	1,25 M on 1m. yellow-green	40	4·25
254A		1,50 M on 1m. yellow-orange (5.1.20)	40	5·25
255A		2,50 M on 1m. slate (17.1.20)	80	10·50
253A/255A		Set of 3	1·40	18·00

B. Imperf (4.3.20)

253B	16	1,25 M on 1m. yellow-green	50	60·00
254B		1,50 M on 1m. yellow-orange	50	60·00
		a. Opt omitted	20·00	
255B		2,50 M on 1m. slate	1·00	60·00
		a. Opt omitted	20·00	
253B/255B		Set of 3	1·80	£160

1920 (28 Jan). No. 105 surch with T **25**.

256	8	20 on 3pf. grey-brown (B.)	40	4·25
		a. Surch inverted	16·00	50·00

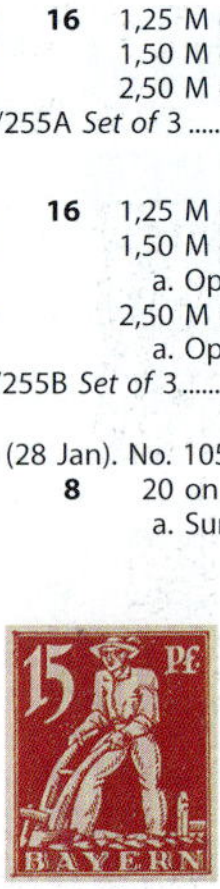

26  **27**  **28**

29  **30**

I.  II.

Two types of the 20pf. I. Foot of '2' turned downwards. II. Foot of '2' turned upwards.

(Des V. Zietara (**26**), F. P. Glass (**27** and **28**), S. von Weech (**29**), F. A. v. Kaulbach (**30**). Nos. 257/69 typo von Hamböck; No. 269a litho Oskar Consée; Nos. 270/3 recess F. A. Bruckmann, Munich)

1920.

(a) W 10. P 14×14½

257	26	5pf. yellow-green	40	4·25
		a. Imperf (pair)	£100	£750
		b. '5' omitted	80·00	£300
258		10pf. yellow-orange	40	4·25
259		15pf. carmine	40	4·25
260	27	20pf. violet (I)	40	4·25
		a. 'BAYEFN' for 'BAYERN' (pos. 4, 9, 54, 59)	2·00	10·50
260b		20pf. violet (II)	16·00	£2500
261		30pf. deep blue	40	5·25
262		40pf. bistre-brown	40	4·25
263	28	50pf. scarlet	40	4·25
264		60pf. blue-green	40	4·25
265		75pf. claret	40	4·25
257/269		Set of 10 (cheapest)	4·75	95·00

(b) W 9. P 11½

266	29	1m. crimson and grey	50	4·25
		a. Imperf (pair)	13·00	50·00
267		1¼m. blue and bistre	40	4·25
		a. Imperf (pair)	13·00	50·00
		b. 'LAVARIAE' for 'BAVARIE' (pos. 32)	6·50	33·00
		c. Diagonal stroke of '¼' in '1¼' missing (pos. 4)	10·50	39·00
268		1½m. green and grey	40	5·25
		a. Imperf (pair)	13·00	50·00
269		2½m. black and grey (typo)	40	50·00
		a. Lithographed	80	£100
266/269		Set of 4	4·75	95·00

(c) W 10. P 11½

270	30	3m. pale blue	1·00	23·00
		a. Imperf (pair)	26·00	£130
271		5m. yellow-orange	1·00	23·00
		a. Imperf (pair)	26·00	£130
272		10m. deep green	1·60	39·00
		a. Imperf (pair)	26·00	£160
273		20m. black	2·30	55·00
		a. Imperf (pair)	26·00	£200
270/273		Set of 4	5·25	£130

Types I and II of the 20pf. occur in the same sheet, Type II occupying the upper right-hand block of 25 (positions 6-10, 16-20, 26-30, 36-40 and 46-50). The variety is found only in early printings as it was soon corrected, later printings consisting of Type I only.

In the typographed 2½m. the edges of the black impression are sharp and firm, while in the lithographed stamps they are irregular and rough.

There are numerous minor varieties of design and lettering in this issue.

O **31**  O **32**  O **33**

(Des. S. von Weech (O **31**/2), J. Nitsche (O **33**). Typo Mint, Munich)

1920 (24 Mar). OFFICIAL.

(a) W 10. P 14×14½

O274	O **31**	5pf. green	40	10·50
O275		10pf. orange	40	10·50
O276		15pf. carmine-red	40	10·50
O277		20pf. violet	40	10·50

GERMANY/ German States – Bavaria / Bergedorf / Bremen

O278	30pf. Prussian blue	40	11·50
O279	40pf. bistre-brown	40	11·50

(b) W 9. P 14½×14

O280	O **32**	50pf. scarlet	40	36·00
O281		60pf. blue-green	40	16·00
O282		70pf. lilac	40	47·00
O283		75pf. claret	40	60·00
O284		80pf. dull blue	40	60·00
O285		90pf. olive	40	90·00
O286	O **33**	1m. chocolate	40	80·00
O287		1¼m. green	40	£100
O288		1½m. scarlet	40	£100
O289		2½m. dull blue	40	£120
O290		3m. lake	80	£170
		a. Imperf (pair)	39·00	
O291		5m. olive-black	3·25	£200
O274/O291	Set of 18		9·50	£1000

The Bavarian Post Office was incorporated in that of Germany on 29 April 1920; German stamps were in use from 1 April and Bavarian stamps ceased to be valid on 30 June 1920 Remainders of Nos. 257/73 were overprinted 'Deutsches Reich' for use throughout Germany (see Germany Nos. 117/36).

STAMP BOOKLETS

The following checklist covers, in simplified form, booklets issued by Bavaria. It is intended that it should be used in conjunction with the main listings and details of stamps and panes listed there are not repeated.

Prices are for complete booklets

Booklet No.	Date	Contents and cover price	Price
SB1	21.12.11–12	Luitpold (T **11**) 5 panes, No. 139bl; 2 panes, No 140cl (2m.)	£6500
		(a) Black on blue-green cover with text each side of Arms	£7000
		(b) As a. but containing No. 140cll (2.12)	£3500
		(c) Nos. 139bll and 140cll. Blue on red cover with text below Arms (6.12)	£2500
		(ca) As c. but black on green cover (10.12)	£6000
SB2	10.12–13	Luitpold (T **11**) 1 pane, No. 139bll; 2 panes, No. 139c; 1 pane, No. 139ll×6; 2 panes, No. 140cll (2m.)	£3250
		(a) Black on green cover	£8000
		(b) Black on blue cover (5.13)	£6000
SB3	1.13	Luitpold (T **11**) 4 panes, No. 139ca; 2 panes, No 140ca (2m.)	
		(a) Black on blue cover	£1600
		(b) Black on orange cover (3.13)	£3250
SB4	3.13	Luitpold (T **11**) 4 panes, No. 139c; 2 panes, No. 140cll (2m.)	
		(a) Black on blue cover	£2000
		(b) Black on red cover (10.13)	£6500
SB5	4.14	Ludwig (T **15**) 4 panes, No. 174b; 2 panes, No 177b (2m.)	£3250
		(a) Blue cover	£1000
		(b) Grey cover	£1300
		(c) Black on red cover	£1800
SB6	2.17	Ludwig (T **15**) 2 panes, No. 176×6; 2 panes, No 179b (2m.40)	£500

BERGEDORF

Bergedorf is a small town S.E. of Hamburg which belonged jointly to the Free Cities of Hamburg and Lübeck from 1420 to 1867.

16 Schilling = 1 Mark

'LHPA' = Lübeck, Hamburg Post Anstalt (Post Office)

(Litho K. Fuchs, Hamburg)

1861 (1 Nov)–**67**. T **1** and **2** (and varying intermediate sizes). Imperf.
1		½s. black/*pale lilac*		£700
2		½s. black/*pale blue*	70·00	£1300
3		½s. black/*deep blue* (1867)	£200	£8500
4		1s. black/*white*	70·00	£650
		a. Tête-bêche (pair)		£850
5		1½s. black/*yellow*	33·00	£2500
		a. Tête-bêche (pair)		£400
6		3s. black/*rose*		£1100
7		3s. blue/*rose*	39·00	£3250
8		4s. black/*brown*	39·00	£3750

The 1s. (£1300 *un*) and 1½s. (£650 *un*) on thick paper, and the 4s. black on pale brown (£2500 *un*) are from the unissued trial printing of June 1861. Nos. 1 and 6 are also part of this trial printing but these were put on sale, although no used copies are known.

These stamps have been several times reprinted. The 1½ SCHILLINGE, with final 'E', is believed to be an essay. The ½s. black/*lilac*, and the 3s. black/*rose*, were reprinted in 1867. The impression of the first is less sharp, and the 'H' of 'SCHILLING' has either no crossbar or it is hardly visible. The tint of the paper is also slightly different. The reprint of the 3s. is on thin instead of thick paper, and there are two dots on the centre of the letter 'S' of 'POSTMARKE'. The other stamps were reprinted in 1872 and 1887; the 4s. also in 1874, and the 1s. and 3s. again in 1888. All the reprints of the 1½s. have 'SCHILLINGE' with final 'E'. The impressions of all the values are less sharp, and the shades of the papers differ from those of the original stamps.

Modern forgeries of the ½ and 1½s. can be identified by the fraction touching the containing square; which does not occur on genuine stamps. Similar forgeries of the 3s. show the dash above the second 'E' of 'BERGEDORF' omitted and the right leg of 'M' in 'Marke' is straight instead of rough. On forgeries of the 4s. the two dots in 'B' of 'BERGEDORF' are missing.

On 8 August 1867 Hamburg purchased Lübeck's share of Bergedorf. From that date the stamps of Hamburg were used.

BREMEN

Bremen joined the Hanseatic League in 1276 and became an Imperial Free City in 1646.

72 Grote = 1 Thaler (internal)
22 Grote = 10 Silbergröschen (overseas mail)

PRINTERS. All the stamps of Bremen were lithographed by G. Hunckel Lithographic Co.

There are three types of the 3 grote (all issues), shown above in the variations of the central ornament at the foot of the stamp below the 'EM' of 'BREMEN'; these types exist in horizontal *se-tenant* strips (same price all types). Types I and II can also be found with an additional broken line between 'STADT POST AMT' and the crown, from positions 29 (Type II), 40, 41 and 43 in the sheet of 120 (12×10).

1855 (10 Apr). Laid paper:—(a) Horizontal. (b) Vertical. Imperf.
1	**1**	3gr. black/*blue* (a)	£350	£450
2		3gr. black/*blue* (b)	£800	£1000

No. 1 exists from the first printing on paper with a lily watermark covering four stamps (*Price for single stamp*: £1200 *un*., £1700 *us*.). Strips and blocks are also known with watermark 'H A S' extending over several stamps.

Modern forgeries are without vertical lines through the lower central loop.

Two types of the 5gr. varying in the arrangement of the background lines. These occur in the same sheet.

7

1856–63. Wove paper. Imperf.

3	2	5gr. black/*rose* (A) (4.4.56)	£250	£500
3*a*		5gr. black/*rose* (B)	£250	£500
4		7gr. black/*yellow* (10.7.60)	£400	£1200
5	3	5sgr. deep green (22.8.59)	£250	£500
6		5sgr. moss green (4.6.63)	£900	£500
		On thick chalky paper		
7	3	5sgr. bright green (20.10.59)	95·00	£3250

The 5gr. black/*rose* exists with the value spelt 'Marken' but it was never issued. (*Price* £23).

4

5

1861–64. Laid paper (3gr., 5gr. (a: horizontal; b: vertical)) or wove paper (others). Percés én scie 16.

8	4	2gr. orange (1863)	£600	£3250
9		2gr. orange-red	£3250	£6000
		a. Chalky paper (*either shade*) .... *from*	£650	£5000
10	1	3gr. black/*blue* (a) (1864)	£5000	£5000
11		3gr. black/*blue* (b) (1864)	£1000	£1200
12	2	5gr. black/*rose* (a) (1862)	£600	£400
12*a*		5gr. black/*rose* (b)	£600	£400
13	5	10gr. black (11.61)	£1300	£1600
14		10gr. grey-black	£1300	£1600
15	3	5sgr. pale yellow-green (1863)	£2000	£325
15*a*		5sgr. green (*chalky paper*) (14.9.63)	£850	£800
16		5sgr. bright green (1864)	£2000	£400

1866–67. Horiz laid paper (3gr., 5gr.) or wove paper (others). P 13.

17	4	2gr. orange (14.12.66)	£200	£600
18		2gr. red orange (14.12.66)	£900	£1300
19	1	3gr. black/*blue* (4.9.66)	£160	£600
20	2	5gr. black/*pale rose* (a) (1866)	£200	£500
20*a*		5gr. black/*pale rose* (b)	£200	£500
21		7gr. black/*yellow* (9.67)	£250	£7000
22	5	10gr. black (4.5.67)	£325	£1800
23		10gr. grey-black	£325	£1800
24	3	5sgr. yellow-green (1866)	£900	£325
25		5sgr. blue-green	£225	£6500
26		5sgr. green (*chalky paper*)	£1600	£500

Nos. 13 and 14 always have an outer single-line frame but in Nos. 22 and 23 this outer line is often absent or very weak.

Forged examples of the 2gr. show more than the genuine 12 vertical lines in the oval containing the key.

Having joined the North German Confederation, Bremen ceased to have a separate issue of stamps after 31 December 1867.

BRUNSWICK

30 Silbergröschen = 1 Thaler

PRINTERS. All the stamps of Brunswick were typographed by J. H. Meyer, Brunswick.

Duke Wilhelm I

28 April 1831 – 18 Oct 1884

1

2

(Eng C. Petersen)

1852 (1 Jan). No wmk. Imperf.

1	1	1sgr. rose	£3750	£500
2		2sgr. blue	£2500	£450
3		3sgr. vermilion	£2500	£450

These stamps are often met with washed, but are *very rare* in *fine mint* condition.

Nos. 1/3, although printed in sheets of 120 (12×10), were sold in horizontal strips of ten. Vertical pairs and strips are extremely rare.

1853 (1 Mar)–**56**. Black impression. W **2**. Imperf.

4	1	¼ggr. on *brown* (1.3.56)	£1300	£425
5		⅓ggr. on *white* (1.3.56)	£225	£600
6		1sgr. on *brown-buff*	£650	90·00
7		1sgr. on *buff*	£650	£100
8		2sgr. on *blue*	£500	£100
9		2sgr. on *pale blue*		£275
10		3sgr. on *pale rose*	£800	£130
11		3sgr. on *rose*	£900	£275

3

4

1857 (1 Mar). W **2**. Imperf.

12	3	4/4ggr. black/*brown*	65·00	£160
		a. On *pale brown*	£130	£325
		b. Quarter stamp (*on cover*)		£225
		c. Half stamp (*on cover*)		£180
		d. Three-quarter stamp (*on cover*)		£225

A similar stamp in brown on white paper was prepared, but not used for postal purposes (*Price* £22).

No. 12 was for use on internal mail. It was intended that the four quarters would be used separately to provide frankings of ¼ggr., ½ggr. or ¾ggr.

1861–64. W **2**.

		(a) Imperf		
15	1	½sgr. black/*blue-green* (1.1.63)	65·00	£600
16		½sgr. black/*yellow-green* (1.1.63)	65·00	£600
17		1sgr. black/*yellow* (1.1.61)	£700	90·00
18		3sgr. rose (1862)	£1000	£375
19		3sgr. deep rose (1862)		£450
		(b) Rouletted 12 (1864)		
19*a*	1	½sgr. black/*yellow-green*		
20		1sgr. yellow	£1000	£500
20*a*		1sgr. black/*yellow*		£20000
21		3sgr. rose		£6500
		(c) Percés en arc 16½ to 17½ (1864)		
22	1	⅓ggr. black/*white*	£800	£3750
23		½sgr. black/*yellow-green*	£325	£5000
24		1sgr. black/*yellow*	£5000	£2500
25		1sgr. yellow/*white*	£650	£225
26		2sgr. black/*blue*	£650	£550
27		3sgr. rose/*white*	£1300	£850

1865 (1 Oct). Embossed. No wmk. Percés en arc 16½ to 17½.

28	4	⅓gr. black	46·00	£600
		a. Imperf (pair)	£200	
29		1gr. red	6·50	90·00
		a. Imperf (pair)	£100	
30		1gr. rose-red	6·50	90·00
31		1gr. rose	6·50	90·00
32		2gr. blue	16·00	£200
		a. Imperf (pair)	£130	
33		2gr. ultramarine	16·00	£200
34		3gr. bistre	13·00	£250
		a. Imperf (pair)	£180	
35		3gr. bistre-brown	13·00	£250
		a. On thick paper	65·00	

Having joined the North German Confederation, Brunswick ceased to have a separate issue of stamps after 31 December 1867.

HAMBURG

Hamburg allied with Lübeck in 1241 to form the nucleus of the Hanseatic League; it became a Free City in 1510.

16 Schilling = 1 Mark

GUM. The large remainders of these stamps are all without gum. Our unused prices are for the stamps as issued with the old *brown* gum; stamps without gum are worth considerably less.

1

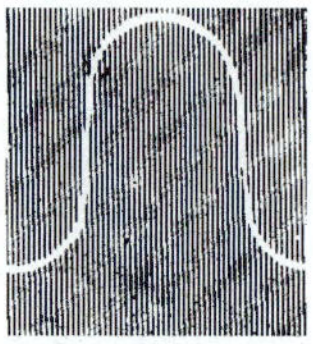

2

(Des C. G. Hencke. Eng J. F. R. Ziesenist. Typo. Th. G. Meissner, Hamburg)

1859 (1 Jan). Wmk wavy lines, Type **2**. Imperf.

1	1	½s. black	£170	£1000

GERMANY/ German States - Hamburg / Hanover

2	1s. brown		£170	£160
3	2s. red		£170	£170
4	3s. Prussian blue		£170	£200
5	4s. yellow-green		£130	£2000
6	4s. green		£250	
7	7s. orange		£170	90·00
8	7s. orange-yellow		£170	90·00
9	9s. yellow		£325	£3250
10	9s. pale yellow		£325	£3250

3   **4**

(Litho C. Adler, Hamburg)

1864 (29 Feb–Apr). W **2**. Imperf.

11	**3**	1¼s. deep lilac	£250	£160
12		1¼s. mauve	£1000	£1600
13		1¼s. dull lilac	£225	£130
14		1¼s. bluish grey	£225	£140
15		1¼s. grey	£140	£130
16		1¼s. greenish grey	£200	£170
17		1¼s. blue	£1000	£1900
18	**4**	2½s. blue-green	£225	£225

(Type **1** typo Th. G. Meissner; Type **3/4** litho C. Adler. Perforated by C. Adler.)

1864–65. W **2**. P 13½.

19	**1**	½s. black	14·50	21·00
20		1s. brown	21·00	29·00
21	**3**	1¼s. mauve	£170	20·00
22		1¼s. deep lilac	£170	20·00
23		1¼s. dull lilac	£170	21·00
24		1¼s. grey-lilac	£170	21·00
25	**1**	2s. red	26·00	35·00
26	**4**	2½s. green	£250	65·00
27		2½s. yellow-green	£200	60·00
28		2½s. pale green	£250	65·00
29	**1**	3s. Prussian blue	£225	£180
30		3s. ultramarine	70·00	60·00
		a. Imperf	£130	
31		3s. deep ultramarine	65·00	65·00
32		4s. bright green	23·00	65·00
33		4s. dull green	£375	90·00
34		7s. orange	£250	£200
35		7s. orange-yellow	£250	£200
36		7s. dull mauve (9.2.65)	20·00	26·00
37		7s. mauve (9.2.65)	20·00	26·00
		a. Imperf	£225	
38		9s. yellow	50·00	£3500
39		9s. pale yellow	50·00	£3500

Nos. 30a and 37a were probably not issued.

The 1¼s. and 2½s. were privately reprinted about 1872 and later, on white wove *unwatermarked* paper and also on the surplus of the old *watermarked* paper, both imperf and perf roughly 13½, and also clean-cut 11½. The 1¼s. is found in *reddish lilac* (imperf only), *lilac, brownish lilac, greyish lilac* and *reddish brown* (perf only); the 2½s. in *deep green, yellow-green* and *pale yellow-green*.

5   **6**

(Embossed and typo Prussian State Printing Office)

1866 (4 Apr–June). No wmk. Rouletted 10.

43	**5**	1¼s. mauve	£130	£120
44		1¼s. dull lilac	65·00	60·00
45	**6**	1½s. rose (4.4)	21·00	£200

Reprints of both values were made about 1872 and in later years, on white wove unwatermarked paper, and are found rouletted 8½ or 10. The reprint of the 1¼s. is from a retouched die, and has the circles in the centres of the four 'stars' filled in with colour, and no line in the upper part of 'g' of 'Schilling'.

The 1½s. was reprinted from the envelope die, and has a longer line in the upper part of the 'g' of 'Schilling'. The paper is thicker, and the impression does not show through as it does in the originals. The reprints are often found with forged postmarks.

(Typo Th. G. Meissner, Hamburg)

1867 (5 May). W **2**. P 13½.

46	**1**	2½s. dull green	21·00	£130
		a. Imperf	£200	
47		2½s. deep green	£100	£160
		a. Imperf	£200	

Having joined the North German Confederation, Hamburg ceased to have a separate issue of stamps after 31 December 1867.

HANOVER

1850. 12 Pfennig = 1 Gutengröschen
24 Gutengröschen = 1 Thaler
1858. 10 (new) Pfennig = 1 (new) Gröschen
30 (new) Gröschen = 1 Thaler

King Ernst

August, 24 June 1837 – 18 Nov 1851

1

(Des A. Jürgens, eng J. F. Fickenscher. Typo Senator Culemann, Hanover)

1850 (1 Dec). Wmk a Rectangle. Imperf.

1	**1**	1ggr. black/*grey-blue*	£5500	90·00

This stamp was reprinted on unwatermarked paper in 1864, without gum. The colour of the paper is grey.

King George V

18 Nov 1851– 20 Sept 1866

2   **3**

(T **2** eng J. F. Fickenscher. Typo Senator Culemann, Hanover)

1851–55. Black impression. W **3**. Imperf.

2	**1**	1ggr. on *grey-green* (21.7.51)	£130	20·00
2a		1ggr. on *sea-green* (1855)	£1600	50·00
3	**2**	1/30th. on *salmon* (21.7.51)	£160	85·00
4		1/30th. on *crimson* (15.2.55)	£160	85·00
5		1/15th. on *blue* (21.7.51)	£250	£130
6		1/10th. on *carmine* (21.7.51)	£300	£100
7		1/10th. on *orange-yellow*	£300	£100

The 1/10th. was reprinted on unwatermarked paper in 1889, with white gum, and this reprint is found tête-bêche.

4   **5** King George V

(Eng Fickenscher. Typo Senator Culemann, Hanover)

1853 (15 Apr). Inscr 'EIN DRITTEL SILBERGROSCHEN'. White paper. W **3**. Imperf.

8	**4**	3pf. pale rose	£600	£500
8a		3pf. deep rose	£3250	£1600

1855. Fine coloured network in second colour. No wmk. Imperf.

9	**2**	1/10th. black and yellow	£700	£450
10		1/10th. black and orange	£300	£250

The other values found with the fine network are essays.

1856. Coloured network of larger meshes in second colour. No wmk. Imperf.

11	**4**	3pf. pale rose and grey	£650	£600
12		3pf. pale rose and black	£450	£450
14	**1**	1ggr. black and green	£100	20·00
15	**2**	1/30th. black and rose	£200	50·00
16		1/15th. black and blue	£160	£130
17		1/10th. black and orange	£1000	90·00

9

GERMANY/ German States - Hanover / Lübeck / Mecklenburg-Schwerin

All five values were reprinted in 1864 on white wove unwatermarked paper, with yellowish white gum. The network on the reprints only extends over blocks of four stamps, whereas on the originals it extends over the entire sheet. The ⅒th. was again reprinted in 1889, on similar paper, and with white gum. In this reprint the network was applied stamp by stamp. These reprints are found *tête-bêche*. The original stamps have rose gum.

(Des and eng Brehmer. Typo Senator Culemann, Hanover)
1859 (15 Feb)–**61**. New currency. Rose gum. No wmk. Imperf.

18	**4**	3pf. dull rose	£225	£250
19		3pf. bright rose	£130	£140
20		3pf. deep rose	£225	£250
21	**5**	1gr. deep claret	£200	£140
22		1gr. carmine	46·00	39·00
23		1gr. rose	7·75	9·00
24		1gr. pale rose	13·00	14·50
25		2gr. Prussian blue	34·00	65·00
25a		2gr. deep blue	26·00	70·00
26		2gr. ultramarine	26·00	70·00
27		3gr. orange-yellow	£425	£110
28		3gr. yellow	£250	£160
29		3gr. brown (11.61)	46·00	90·00
30		3gr. deep brown (11.61)	£650	£650
31		10gr. olive-green (1.3.61)	£475	£1600

The 3pf. was reprinted in 1889 on yellowish white wove unwatermarked paper, with brownish gum applied in stripes. In the reprint, the ends of the scroll at the right and left sides of the stamp point downwards, whereas on the originals they bend slightly towards the side borders of the stamp. The 3gr. was reprinted in yellow and in brown in 1891, with white gum.

6

7

(Typo Senator Culemann, Hanover)
1860 (1 Apr)–**62**. No wmk. Rose gum. Imperf.

32	**6**	½gr. Black	£650	£500
		a. White gum (1862)	£225	£325

The ½gr. was reprinted in 1883 on toned wove paper, with yellowish gum, and is found *tête-bêche*.

1863 (Nov). Inscr 'DREI ZEHNTEL SILBERGROSCHEN'. No wmk. Rose gum. Imperf.

34	**7**	3pf. yellow-green	£650	£1600

Modern forgeries show only three, instead of five, lines of vertical shading left of 'DREI'.

1864 (Mar)–**65**. No wmk. Yellow or white gum (2gr.) or rose gum (others). Percés en arc 16.

35	**7**	3pf. green	£130	£140
		a. Yellow or white gum	50·00	£110
36	**6**	½gr. black	£800	£700
		a. Yellow or white gum	£400	£450
37	**5**	1gr. rose	65·00	39·00
		a. Yellow or white gum	20·00	20·00
38	**5**	2gr. ultramarine	£180	£100
39		3gr. brown	£2000	£2000
		a. Yellow or white gum	£100	£120

The 3gr. was reprinted in 1891 with white gum, and *percés en arc* 13½.

Hanover was annexed by Prussia on 20 September 1866 after the Austro-Prussian War, in which it fought on the side of Austria; Prussian stamps were on sale on 1 October 1866, but Hanoverian stamps could be used until 31 October; mixed frankings may be found.

LÜBECK

Lübeck, a Free City since 1226, allied with Hamburg in 1241 to form the nucleus of the Hanseatic League.

16 Schilling = 1 Mark

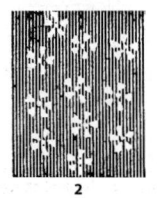

1

2

(Litho H. G. Rahtgens, Lübeck)
1859 (1 Jan). Wmk. Myosotis flowers, T **2**. Imperf.

1	**1**	½s. slate-lilac	£3750	£3250
2		1s. orange	£4000	£3250
3		2s. brown	£180	£400
		a. Error. 'ZWEI EIN HALB'	£1600	£12000
4		2½s. rose-red	£350	£1400
5		2½s. rose	£350	£1400
6		4s. deep green	£140	£1000

A 4s. yellow-green was prepared but not issued (*price* £50). No. 3a occurs on positions 96 and 97 in the sheet of 100. Modern forgeries of all values show the ornament at the top of the design as a short horizontal line instead of two dots separated by a horizontal line.

1862 (5 Apr). No wmk. Imperf.

9	**1**	½s. dull lilac	70·00	£2500
10		1s. orange-yellow	£140	£2500

All five values were reprinted in 1871 on thin, white wove unwatermarked paper, with smooth white gum, and in shades different from those of the originals.

3

4

(Eng H. G. Schilling. Embossed and typo Prussian State Ptg Wks, Berlin)
1863 (1 July)–**67**. No wmk. Rouletted 11½.

11	**3**	½s. green	70·00	£120
12		½s. yellow-green	70·00	£120
13		1s. orange-vermilion	£200	£300
		a. Rouletted 10 (1867)	£325	£800
14		2s. rose-red	46·00	£110
15		2s. rose	46·00	£110
16		2½s. ultramarine	£200	£650
17		4s. bistre	90·00	£170

All five values were reprinted in 1871. The reprints show no embossing, and are imperforate.

(Litho H. G. Rahtgens, Lübeck)
1864 (1 Apr). No wmk. Imperf.

18	**4**	1¼s. chestnut	50·00	£200
19		1¼s. pale brown	50·00	£200
20		1¼s. deep brown	80·00	90·00

5

(Eng H. G. Schilling. Embossed and typo Prussian State Ptg Wks, Berlin)
1865 (1 Dec). No wmk. Rouletted 11½.

21	**5**	1½s. mauve	50·00	£140

This stamp was reprinted in 1871, but the reprint shows no embossing, and is imperforate.

Having joined the North German Confederation, Lübeck ceased to have a separate issue of stamps after 31 December 1867.

MECKLENBURG-SCHWERIN

48 Schilling = 1 Thaler

Grand Duke Friedrich Franz II

8 March 1842 – 15 April 1883

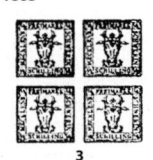

1   **2**   **3**

Type **1** has a *dotted* ground and Type **3** a *plain* ground. Prices are for complete stamp (four quarters) as illustrated. It was intended that the four quarters would be used separately to provide frankings of ¼s. ½s. or ¾s.

(Des Otto in Güstrow. Die eng H. G. Schilling. Typo Prussian State Ptg Wks, Berlin)

1856 (1 July). Imperf.

1	1	4/4s. red	£250	£200
		a. Quarter stamp (*on cover*)	†	£225
		b. Half stamp (*on cover*)	†	£325
		c. Three quarter stamp (*on cover*)	†	£450
2	2	3s. yellow	£160	£100
3		3s. orange-yellow	£130	£100
4		5s. blue	£375	£475

1864 (1 July). Rouletted 11½.

5	1	4/4s. red	£4500	£3000
		a. Quarter stamp (*on cover*)	†	£4000
		b. Half stamp (*on cover*)	†	£5000

1864. Rouletted 11½.

6	3	4/4s. red (9.64)	£650	£130
		a. Quarter stamp (*on cover*)	†	£225
		b. Half stamp (*on cover*)	†	£275
7	2	5s. bistre (9.64)	£250	£400
		a. Thick paper	£400	£550

1865–67. Rouletted 11½. Distance of roulette from frame of stamp varies: (a) Stamp 23 mm square; (b) Stamp 24 mm. square.

9	2	3s. orange-yellow (a) (9.65)	£250	£200
10		3s. orange-yellow (b) (6.67)	80·00	£500

1866–67. Rouletted 11½.

11	2	2s. purple (1.10.66)	£400	£400
12		2s. grey-lilac (7.9.67)	£225	£2500
13		2s. bluish lilac (1867)	£225	£2500

Having joined the North German Confederation, Mecklenburg-Schwerin ceased to have a separate issue of stamps after 31 December 1867.

MECKLENBURG-STRELITZ

30 Silbergröschen = 1 Thaler

Grand Duke Friedrich Wilhelm

6 Sept 1860 – 29 May 1904

1

2

(Die eng Otto in Güstrow. Embossed and typo Prussian State Ptg Wks, Berlin)

1864 (Oct). Rouletted 11½.

1	1	¼sgr. orange-yellow	£600	£6500
2		¼sgr. orange-red	£275	£4000
3		⅓sgr. pale green	£140	£2250
4		⅓sgr. deep green	£225	£4000
6		1sch. deep mauve	£475	£5000
7	2	1sgr. rose	£225	£300
8		1sgr. rose-carmine	£225	£300
9		2sgr. pale ultramarine	80·00	£1300
10		2sgr. bright ultramarine	80·00	£1300
11		3sgr. bistre	65·00	£2000

Having joined the North German Confederation, Mecklenburg-Strelitz ceased to have a separate issue of stamps after 31 December 1867.

OLDENBURG

72 Grote = 1 Thaler

Grand Duke Peter II

27 Feb 1853 –13 June 1900

1

A.

B.

C.

Three types of 1/30 thaler:
A. Ornament in lower part of shield joins left stroke of 'H'.
B. Ornament is 1 mm. below 'H'.
C. Ornament under 'H' is rounded and further away.

Three types of 1/15 thaler:
(a) 'H' of 'THALER' almost touches indentation of shield.
(b) 'H' is well above indentation of shield.
(c) Similar to (b), but mantle is fully shaded beneath the arms.

(Litho Gerhard Stalling, Oldenburg)

1852 (5 Jan)–**59**. Black impression. Imperf.

1	1	⅓sgr. on *green* (30.1.55)	£2000	£1700
2		1/30th. on *blue* (A)	£600	46·00
3		1/30th. on *blue* (B)	£1000	£160
4		1/30th. on *blue* (C) (1854)	£650	46·00
5		1/15th. on *rose* (a)	£1300	£130
6		1/15th. on *rose* (b)	£2000	£350
7		1/15th. on *rose* (c) (1859)	£2250	£425
8		1/10th. on *yellow*	£1300	£160
9		1/10th. on *lemon*	£1600	£200

2

3

(Litho Gerhard Stalling, Oldenburg)

1859 (10 July). Black impressions. Imperf.

10	2	⅓g. on *green*	£4250	£4750
11		1g. on *blue*	£1000	80·00
12		1g. on *grey-blue*	£1000	80·00
13		1g. on *bright blue*	£1000	80·00
14		1g. on *indigo*	£12000	£11000
15		2g. on *rose*	£1700	£1000
16		3g. on *yellow*	£1700	£1000
		a. Error 'OLBENBURG'	£2500	£2000

1861 (1 Jan). Imperf.

17	2	¼g. orange-yellow	£500	£6500
18		⅓g. green	£800	£1300
19		⅓g. pale bluish green	£800	£1300
		a. Printed both sides		£12000
		b. Error. 'Dritto'	£1400	£2250
		c. Error. 'Drittd'	£1400	£2250
		d. Error. 'OLDEIBURG'	£1400	£2250
20		⅓g. moss-green	£2500	£4250
21		½g. chestnut	£700	£850
22		½g. brown	£700	£850
23		1g. bright blue	£800	£425
24		1g. pale blue	£400	£275
		a. Printed both sides	—	£9000
25		1g. dull blue	£2000	£6500
26		2g. red	£700	£700
27		2g. rose-red	£700	£700
28		3g. pale yellow	£700	£700
29		3g. deep yellow	£700	£700
		a. Printed both sides	—	£12000
		b. Error 'OLDENDURG'	£1300	£1400
		c. Error. '8' for '3'	£1300	£1400
		d. Error 'Croshen'	£1300	£1400
		e. Error 'OLDENDURG'	£1300	£1400

Several other varieties of lettering and in the frame are found in the ⅓g. and 3g., whilst the 1g. is known with pointed figure '1' at right.

(Eng E. Schilling. Embossed and typo Prussian State Ptg Wks, Berlin)

1862–67.

(a) Rouletted 11½ (1862)

30	3	⅓g. pale green	£325	£300
31		⅓g. green	£325	£300
32		½g. orange	£325	£180
33		½g. orange-red	£400	£250
34		1g. rose-red	£180	29·00
35		1g. rose-carmine	£180	29·00
36		2g. Prussian blue	£325	80·00
37		2g. ultramarine	£325	80·00
38		3g. bistre	£350	85·00
39		3g. bistre-brown	£350	85·00

(b) Rouletted 10 (1867)

40	3	⅓g. pale green	50·00	£1200
41		½g. pale orange	50·00	£600
42		1g. rose-carmine	33·00	90·00
43		2g. ultramarine	33·00	£800
44		3g. bistre	65·00	£650

Having joined the North German Confederation, Oldenburg ceased to have a separate issue of stamps after 31 December 1867.

GERMANY/ German States - Prussia / Saxony

PRUSSIA

1850. 12 Pfennig = 1 Silbergröschen
30 Silbergröschen = 1 Thaler
1867. 60 Kreuzer = 1 Gulden

PRINTERS. All stamps of Prussia were printed by the Prussian State Printing Works, Berlin.

King Friedrich Wilhelm IV
7 June 1840 – 2 Jan 1861

1 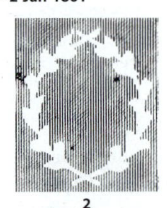   **2**

(Des F. E. Eichens; eng on steel H. G. Schilling. Recess)

1850 (15 Nov)–**56**. Background of crossed lines. Wmk Laurel Wreath, Type **2**. Imperf.

1	1	4pf. yellow-green (1856)	£180	£120
2		4pf. deep yellow-green (1856)	£250	£200
3		6pf. orange	£160	90·00
4		6pf. vermilion	£160	90·00
5		1sgr. black/rose	£130	26·00
5a		1sgr. black/carmine	£33000	£800
6		2sgr. black/blue	£180	26·00
7		3sgr. black/orange	£500	50·00
8		3sgr. black/yellow	£180	26·00

The shape of the watermark varies considerably in different specimens. All five values were reprinted in 1864 on unwatermarked paper, and a second time in 1873 on paper with a similar watermark to that of the originals. The reprints in both sets vary in shade from the originals.

(Eng on wood H. G. Schilling. Typo)

1857 (1 Apr). Smaller head. Solid background. No wmk. Imperf.

9	1	1sgr. rose	£500	46·00
10		2sgr. pale blue	£2000	£140
11		2sgr. deep blue	£2750	£200
12		3sgr. yellow	£2500	£160
13		3sgr. orange	£250	65·00

The so-called reprints of this issue are nothing better than official imitations. Two printings were made in 1864 and in 1873. The letters of 'FREIMARKE', and of the words of value, and the numerals differ in type from the originals, and there is only one period in place of two after the word 'SILBERGR'.

1858 (15 Sept). Smaller head, but background of crossed lines. No wmk. Imperf.

14	1	4pf. yellow-green	£120	60·00
15		4pf. green	£130	£130
16		1sgr. pale rose	50·00	6·50
17		1sgr. carmine-rose	£200	13·00
18		2sgr. pale blue	£180	29·00
19		2sgr. indigo	£250	65·00
20		3sgr. pale orange-yellow	£225	33·00
21		3sgr. deep orange-yellow	£160	26·00

(Eng on steel H. G. Schilling. Recess)

1860 (Nov). No wmk. Imperf.

22	1	½sgr. (=6pf.) pale vermilion	£325	£250
23		½sgr. (=6pf.) deep vermilion	£450	£375

King Wilhelm I
2 Jan 1861–9 March 1888

3    **4**

(Eng H. G. Schilling. Typo)

1861 (1 Oct)–**67**. Arms embossed. Rouletted 11½.

24	3	3pf. dull lilac (1.4.65)	46·00	70·00
25		3pf. mauve (1867)	£500	£450
26		4pf. green	20·00	18·00
27		4pf. pale green	65·00	90·00
28		6pf. orange	20·00	22·00
29		6pf. orange-red	£200	£100
30	4	1sgr. rose	5·75	2·50
31		1sgr. dull rose	5·75	2·50
32		1sgr. carmine	20·00	26·00
33		2sgr. Prussian blue	£650	47·00
34		2sgr. pale ultramarine	20·00	2·50
35		2sgr. deep ultramarine	20·00	2·50
36		3sgr. bistre-yellow	14·50	3·25
37		3sgr. bistre-brown (1865)		47·00

All six values are found *imperf*, but in this state must be looked upon as proofs, although postmarked specimens are known. The stamps with an inscription at the back are essays.

5    **6**    **7**

1866 (15 Dec). Printed in reverse on back of specially treated transparent paper. Rouletted 10.

38	5	10sgr. rose	£130	£170
39	6	30sgr. blue	£160	£375

These two stamps were not sold to the public, but were affixed in the Post Office to heavy packets requiring them.

(Eng H. G. Schilling. Typo)

1867 (1 July). New currency. Embossed. Rouletted 16.

40	7	1k. green	50·00	70·00
41		1k. yellow-green	50·00	70·00
42		2k. orange	80·00	£160
43		3k. rose	39·00	43·00
44		3k. carmine-rose	39·00	43·00
45		6k. ultramarine	39·00	70·00
46		9k. bistre	46·00	80·00

This set of stamps was issued for use in the States served by the Thurn and Taxis office, Prussia having taken over the management of those Post Offices from July 1st 1867. The remarks appended to Nos. 24/37 apply equally to Nos. 40/46.

Many envelope stamps of Prussia were cut out and used as adhesives; the value of these varies.

Having joined the North German Confederation, Prussia ceased to have a separate issue of stamps after 31 December 1867.

SAXONY

10 Pfennig = 1 Neugröschen
30 Neugröschen = 1 Thaler

King Friedrich August II,
6 June 1836–9 Aug 1854

1    **2**    **3** Friedrich August II

(Des and typo J. B. Hirschfeld, Leipzig)

1850 (29 June). Imperf.

1	1	3pf. pale red to brick-red	£13000	£12000
2		3pf. cherry-red	£20000	£21000
3		3pf. brownish red	£20000	£17000

(Des Holzschnitt. Typo J. B. Hirschfeld)

1851 (29 July). Imperf.

(a) 1st printing. Thin hard white paper. Fine impression

4	2	3pf. green	£1300	£450
5		3pf. light green	£1600	£700
6		3pf. yellow-green	£2750	£1300

(b) Later printings. Thick yellow paper

7	2	3pf. green	£200	£160
8		3pf. light green	£250	£200
9		3pf. yellow-green	£400	£400

The first printing was in sheets of ten (two rows of five stamps) and vertical pairs with large margins exist. Later printings were in sheets of 120 (10×12) and afterwards in sheets of 100.

Nos. 1/9 were intended for the payment of postage on newspapers.

(Des Ulbricht. Eng and recess C. C. Meinhold & Sons, Dresden)
1851 (1 Aug). Imperf.
10	3	½ngr. black/grey	£120	20·00
11		½ngr. black/greenish to blue-grey	£425	60·00
		a. Error. On *pale blue*	£32000	
12		1ngr. black/rose (*shades*)	£160	20·00
13		2ngr. black/pale blue (*shades*)	£425	£120
14		3ngr. black/yellow (*shades*)	£250	60·00

1852 (Nov). Colour changed. Imperf.
15	3	2ngr. black/*deep blue*	£1200	90·00

King Johann
9 August 1854–29 October 1873

4 King Johann I **5** **6**

(Des Ulbricht. Recess C. C. Meinhold & Sons, Dresden)
1855 (1 June)–**63**. Imperf.
16	4	½ngr. black/grey to blue-grey	65·00	12·00
		a. '½' double		
17		½ngr. black/grey to blue/grey (1859)	26·00	12·00
18		1ngr. black/rose (*shades*)	26·00	12·00
19		1ngr. black/*deep red*	£325	£160
20		2ngr. black/*deep blue*	39·00	33·00
21		2ngr. black/*dull greenish blue*	39·00	33·00
22		2ngr. black/*bright blue*	£120	80·00
23		3ngr. black/*yellow*	39·00	26·00
24		5ngr. brick-red (*shades*) (24.4.56)	£130	£100
25		5ngr. orange-red (1860)	£500	£500
26		5ngr. carmine-red	£450	£200
27		5ngr. rose-brown (2.63)	£650	£1000
28		10ngr. milky blue (24.4.56)	£400	£400
29		10ngr. deep blue (1859)	£500	£500
30		10ngr. blue (1861)	£350	£550

(Typo Giesecke & Devrient, Leipzig)
1863 (1 July)–**67**. Arms embossed. P 13.
31	5	3pf. green to blue-green	6·50	65·00
32		3pf. yellow-green	£160	£200
33		3pf. emerald-green	£1200	£1200
34		½ngr. reddish orange	39·00	9·75
35		½ngr. red	80·00	£160
36		½ngr. pale dull orange (1866)	4·00	4·50
37		½ngr. orange (11.67)	10·50	60·00
38		½ngr. lemon-yellow to ochre-yellow (1867)	£2500	£6500
39	6	1ngr. rose (*shades*)	2·50	4·50
		a. Imperf between (horiz pair)	£650	
40		2ngr. blue, pale blue	4·50	13·00
41		2ngr. deep blue	20·00	50·00
42		3ngr. reddish brown	7·75	20·00
43		3ngr. brown	39·00	16·00
44		3ngr. chocolate-brown	£1000	£1000
45		5ngr. grey-blue to greenish blue	33·00	80·00
46		5ngr. purple (1866)	50·00	80·00
47		5ngr. deep grey (1867)	39·00	£450
48		5ngr. brownish lilac (1867)	26·00	£1000
49		5ngr. brownish grey	33·00	£1300
50		5ngr. pure grey	£190	£1800

Having joined the North German Confederation, Saxony ceased to have a separate issue of stamps after 31 December 1867.

SCHLESWIG-HOLSTEIN
I. Provisional Government

The King of Denmark was Duke of the Duchies of Schleswig and Holstein. Attempts to integrate Schleswig with Denmark led to a revolt, the establishment of a Schleswig Provisional Government on 24 March 1848, and war between Prussia and Denmark.

96 Skilling = 1 Rigsbankdaler (Danish)

1

(Des and eng M. Claudius. Typo H. W. Köbner & Lemkuhl, Altona)
1850 (15 Nov). Arms in centre embossed. Imperf.
1	1	1s. Prussian blue	£1600	
2		1s. deep blue	£1200	£13000
2a		1s. pale blue	£500	£8500
4		2s. pale rose	£900	£12000
5		2s. deep rose	£1200	£16000

Nos. 1 and 5 were not issued.
Nos. 2/4 were only available in Holstein and were withdrawn at the end of March 1851.

After peace was signed in 1850, Danish stamps were in use from 1 May 1851 to 31 March 1864 in Schleswig and from 1 July 1853 to 29 February 1864 in Holstein.

A renewed attempt by Denmark in 1863 to annex Schleswig led to invasion of the Duchies by Prussia and Austria on 1 February 1864. By the Convention of Gastein, 14 August 1865, Holstein was placed under Austrian control with Prussia administering Schleswig and Lauenburg, which had previously been part of Holstein.

JOINT ADMINISTRATION BY AUSTRIA AND PRUSSIA
16 Schilling = 1 Mark

2 **3**

(Typo Prussian State Printing Works)
1865. White parts embossed. Rouletted 11½.
6	2	½s. rose (15.2)	65·00	70·00
7		1¼s. green (18.4)	33·00	33·00
8	3	1⅓s. lilac-mauve (14.8)	80·00	£200
9	2	2s. ultramarine (14.8)	80·00	£400
10	3	4s. bistre (8.9)	£100	£2000

The 1⅓s. is found *imperf*, and was apparently issued in this condition, as pairs are known used.

Nos. 6/10 replaced the individual issues for Schleswig and Holstein from February 1865 until replaced by Nos. 24/9 and 61/5. The Joint issue was re-introduced from 6 November 1866 and remained in use until replaced by North German Confederation issues.

II. Schleswig
JOINT ADMINISTRATION BY AUSTRIA AND PRUSSIA
96 Skilling = 1 Rigsbankdaler

4 **5**

(Type **4** and **5**. Typo Prussian State Printing Works)
1864. Rouletted 11½.
21	4	1¼s. green (1.4)	70·00	33·00
22		4s. rose (10.3)	£160	£800
23		4s. carmine	£160	£800

Nos. 21/23 were replaced by the joint issue for both Duchies, Nos. 6/10.

PRUSSIAN ADMINISTRATION
16 Schilling = 1 Mark

1865 (1 Nov). Rouletted 11½.
24	4	½s. yellow-green	50·00	90·00
25		1¼s. dull mauve	90·00	39·00
26		1¼s. grey-lilac	90·00	39·00
27	5	1⅓s. rose	47·00	£100
28	4	2s. ultramarine	47·00	90·00
29		4s. bistre	50·00	£130

1867 (June). Rouletted 10.
30	4	1¼s. dull mauve	£250	£100
31		1¼s. lilac	50·00	£225
32		1¼s. grey	£650	£180

Nos. 24/32 were replaced by the re-issued Nos. 6/10.

III. Holstein

GERMAN FEDERAL COMMISSION ADMINISTRATION

On 7 December 1863 the states of the German Confederation agreed, under a Federal Execution, to undertake administration of Holstein. This lasted until administration was handed over to Austria under the Convention of Gastein.

96 Skilling = 1 Rigsbankdaler

6

7

8

(Ptd by H. W. Köbner & Lemkuhl, Altona)

1864 (1 Mar). Imperf.

(a) Litho. Small lettering in frame, 'SCHILLING' large

51	**6**	1¼s. pale blue	90·00	£100
52		1¼s. blue	90·00	£100
		a. Rouletted 9½ (privately)		

(b) Litho. Larger lettering in frame, 'SCHILLING' small, wavy lines in spandrels wider apart

54	**7**	1¼s. blue	£1300	£4500

(c) Typo. Still larger and thicker lettering, 'SCHILLING' small no dots over the two letters 'I'

55	**8**	1¼s. blue	80·00	£100
		a. Rouletted 9½ (privately)		
56		1¼s. pale blue	80·00	£100

9

(Typo H. W. Köbner & Lemkuhl)

1864 (15 May). Rouletted 8.

59	**9**	1¼s. pale blue	65·00	39·00
		a. Bisected (½s.) (*on cover*) (23.6.64)		£3250
60		1¼s. deep blue	65·00	39·00

Type **6**, **7** and **8** are printed on white paper with a *grey* network, while Type **9** is on paper with a *rose* network.

Nos. 51/60 were replaced by the joint issue for both duchies, Nos. 6/10.

AUSTRIAN ADMINISTRATION

16 Schilling = 1 Mark

10

11

12

(Eng M. Claudius. Typo Köbner, Altona)

1865 (1 Nov). Rouletted 8.

61	**10**	½s. pale green	£100	£160
62		1¼s. pale mauve	80·00	39·00
63	**11**	1⅓s. carmine-rose	£100	70·00
64	**10**	2s. pale blue	85·00	85·00
65	**11**	4s. bistre	£100	£130

(Typo Köbner, Altona)

1866. Rouletted 8.

66	**12**	1¼s. purple (2.66)	£100	39·00
67		2s. pale blue (7.66)	£225	£250

Nos. 61/67 were replaced by the re-issued Nos. 6/10 from 6 November 1866.

The Duchies were annexed by Prussia on 24 January 1867 after the Austro-Prussian War of 1866. Nos. 6 to 10 were superseded by the stamps of the North German Confederation on 1 January 1868.

THURN AND TAXIS

The postal monopoly possessed and managed by the Counts of Thurn and Taxis – a princely house of Austria – extended throughout those States and parts of Germany, afterwards forming part of the German Empire, which did not possess a postal administration of their own, or separate issues of stamps.

NORTHERN DISTRICT

The Northern District comprised Bremen (until 1855), Camburg, Gotha, Hamburg (until 1859), Hesse-Kassel, Lippe-Detmold, Lübeck (until 1859), Reuss, Saxe-Weimar-Eisenach, Schaumburg-Lippe and Schwarzburg-Sondershausen.

30 Silbergröschen = 1 Thaler

1

2

(Typo C. Naumann, Frankfurt-am-Main)

1852 (29 Jan)–**58**. Black impression. Imperf.

1	**1**	¼sgr. on *red-brown* (1.1.54)	£275	46·00
2		⅓sgr. on *flesh* (1.7.58)	£120	£200
3		½sgr. on *pale green*	£900	26·00
4		½sgr. on *pale bluish green*	£800	39·00
5		1sgr. on *deep blue*	£1300	£120
6		1sgr. on *blue* (5.6.53)	£1000	23·00
7		1sgr. on *grey-blue* (1858)	£850	23·00
8		2sgr. on *rose*	£850	26·00
9		2sgr. on *pale rose*	£850	26·00
10		3sgr. on *yellow*	£1000	26·00
11		3sgr. on *yellow-buff*	£1000	65·00

In 1910 all values were reprinted in a very limited number. The colours are too bright, the paper rather smooth and glossy and every stamp has on the back 'N.D.' in large letters.

(Type **2** des and eng F. M. Kepler. Typo)

1859 (14 Sept)–**61**. Coloured impression. Imperf.

12	**1**	¼sgr. pale red (1861)	85·00	60·00
13		½sgr. blue-green (1.60)	£350	85·00
14		1sgr. pale blue (1.60)	£350	39·00
15		2sgr. rose (1861)	£180	65·00
16		2sgr. pale rose (1861)	£180	65·00
17		3sgr. brown-red (1861)	£180	£100
18	**2**	5sgr. mauve	5·25	£400
19		10sgr. orange	5·25	£800

The last two values are known *rouletted*, and also *perforated*, but both these additions are of a purely private nature.

All values up to 3sgr. were reprinted in 1910 on very white thickish wove paper, and each stamp has on the back 'N.D.' in large type. The 10sgr. was also reprinted in *black* on *blue paper*.

1862–64. Imperf.

20	**1**	¼sgr. black (12.1.63)	33·00	65·00
21		⅓sgr. yellow-green (13.1.63)	46·00	£225
22		⅓sgr. blue-green (13.1.63)	46·00	£225
23		½sgr. orange	£100	39·00
24		½sgr. orange-yellow (1863)	£100	39·00
25		1sgr. pale rose (9.1 63)	85·00	20·00
26		1sgr. deep rose (9.1.63)	85·00	20·00
27		2sgr. pale blue (1863)	60·00	85·00
28		2sgr. deep blue (1864)	60·00	85·00
29		3sgr. bistre (1863)	33·00	46·00
30		3sgr. yellow-brown (1863)	33·00	46·00

All values were reprinted in 1910 on the same paper as the last set, and with the letters 'N.D' at back. The colour of the reprinted 3sgr. is a *purple-brown*.

1865 (July). Rouletted 16.

31	**1**	¼sgr. black	13·00	£650
32		⅓sgr. green	20·00	£400
33		½sgr. orange-yellow	39·00	60·00
34		1sgr. rose	42·00	26·00
35		2sgr. blue	2·50	90·00
36		3sgr. bistre	4·50	39·00
37		3sgr. bistre-brown	4·50	39·00

The ½sgr. and 1sgr. were reprinted in 1910 on the same paper and lettered 'N.D' as described above.

1866 (31 Aug)–**67**. Rouletted 16, in colour.

38	**1**	¼sgr. black (1867)	4·00	£1700

GERMANY/ German States - Thurn and Taxis / Württemberg

39	½sgr. pale green (1867)	4·00	£1000
40	½sgr. green (1867)	4·00	£1000
41	½sgr. orange-yellow	4·00	£200
42	1sgr. rose	3·25	90·00
	a. Not rouletted between, vert (pair)	£300	£2250
43	2sgr. blue (1867)	3·25	£900
44	3sgr. yellow-brown	3·25	£250

SOUTHERN DISTRICT

The Southern District comprised Coburg, Frankfurt-am-Main, Hesse-Darmstadt, Hesse-Homburg, Hohenzollern-Hechingen, Hohenzollern-Sigmaringen, Nassau, Saxe-Meiningen and Schwarzburg-Rudolstadt.

60 Kreuzer = 1 Gulden

3   4

(Typo C. Naumann, Frankfurt-am-Main)

1852 (29 Jan)–**58**. Black impression. Imperf.

51	3	1k. on *pale green*	£225	16·00
52		1k. on *pale bluish green*	£500	39·00
53		3k. on *deep blue*	£1000	46·00
54		3k. on *blue* (5.6.53)	£1000	23·00
55		3k. on *grey-blue* (1858)	£850	23·00
56		6k. on *rose*	£800	16·00
57		6k. on *pale rose*	£1200	13·00
58		9k. on *yellow*	£850	20·00
59		9k. on *yellow-buff*	£850	43·00

This set was reprinted in 1910. (See note after No. 11).

(Type **4** des and eng F. M. Kepler. Typo)

1859 (2 Oct)–**60**. Coloured impression. Imperf.

60	3	1k. blue-green (1.60)	26·00	13·00
61		1k. green (1.60)	26·00	13·00
62		3k. pale blue (1.60)	£600	20·00
62a		3k. deep blue (1.60)	£600	20·00
63		6k. rose (1.60)	£600	60·00
64		9k. orange-yellow (1.60)	£800	£120
65		9k. yellow (1.60)	£550	80·00
66	4	15k. purple	5·25	£160
67		30k. orange	5·25	£425

The same remarks apply to Nos. 66 and 67 as are appended to Nos. 18 and 19.
The 3k. *yellow-green*, formerly catalogued as an 'error' is now looked upon as a proof.
These stamps were reprinted in 1910, the 1k. to 9k. being on thick white wove paper, with the letters 'N.D' at back, and the 15k. and 30k. in *black on thin blue paper*.

1862–63. Imperf.

68	3	3k. pale rose (24.3.62)	13·00	23·00
69		3k. deep rose (24.3.62)	13·00	23·00
70		6k. pale blue (26.6.62)	33·00	39·00
71		6k. deep blue (26.6.62)	13·00	29·00
72		9k. bistre (1863)	13·00	29·00
73		9k. brown (1863)	16·00	31·00

These stamps were reprinted in 1910 similarly to the last issue.

1865 (July). Rouletted 16, uncoloured.

74	3	1k. pale green	22·00	20·00
75		3k. rose	33·00	14·50
76		6k. blue	3·25	33·00
77		9k. bistre	5·00	46·00
78		9k. bistre-brown	4·50	33·00

The 1k. was reprinted in 1910 on the same paper, and lettered 'N.D' as described above.

1866 (31 Aug). Rouletted 16, in colour.

79	3	1k. green	4·00	33·00
80		1k. pale green	4·00	33·00
81		3k. rose	4·00	26·00
82		6k. blue	4·00	50·00
83		9k. yellow-bistre	5·25	70·00
84		9k. yellow-ochre	4·00	46·00

Variety, rouletted plain, and also in colour

| 85 | 3 | 3k. bright rose (pair) | | |

The Thurn and Taxis postal service ceased on 1 July 1867 when the network was sold to Prussia for 3 million thalers. At that time Prussia had only an issue in silbergröschen; the 1867 issue of Prussia was therefore created for use in the Southern District, formerly served by the Thurn and Taxis administration.

WÜRTTEMBERG

1851. 60 Kreuzer = 1 Gulden
1875.100 Pfennig = 1 Mark

King Wilhelm I
30 June 1816–25 June 1864

1   2

(Centre eng J. Schuster. Typo J. B. Mezler)

1851 (15 Oct)–**52**. Black impression. Imperf.

1	1	1k. on *buff*	£1800	£170
3		3k. on *yellow*	£450	17·00
4		3k. on *orange-yellow*	£2750	95·00
5		6k. on *yellow-green*	£2250	50·00
6		6k. on *blue-green*	£4500	81·00
7		9k. on *pale rose*	£8000	65·00
8		9k. on *rose*	£15000	£170
9		18k. on *slate-lilac* (1852)	£3000	£1200

The date on the stamps is that of the treaty establishing a German-Austrian postal union.
The word 'Württemberg' varies in length, measuring 18, 18½ or 19 mm. The so-called reprints of this issue are nothing better than official imitations. They were made in 1864, and they have the letter 'W' of 'Wurttemberg' 1½ mm from the left side-line of the label, instead of 1 mm as in the originals.
No. 2 is vacant.

(Des P. Reusch. Embossed and typo Railway Commission Ticket-printing Office)

1857 (22 Sept). With orange silk thread. Imperf.

10	2	1k. pale brown	£1300	£130
11		1k. deep brown	£2500	£600
12		3k. orange	£700	46·00
13		3k. orange-yellow	£650	22·00
14		6k. pale yellow-green	£1300	£100
15		6k. green	£1300	£100
16		6k. deep green	£1300	£100
17		9k. rose	£3000	£120
18		9k. carmine	£3000	£120
19		18k. blue	£6500	£2750
20		18k. pale blue	£5000	£2000

All five values were reprinted in 1864 with a *red* silk thread, and the 6k. also with a *yellow* silk thread. On the sheets of reprints the stamps are 1¾ mm. apart, instead of ¾ mm. as in the originals.

1859–62. Without silk thread.

(a) Imperf

21	2	1k. brown	£1000	£170
22		1k. deep brown	£3250	£1100
23		3k. orange	£450	23·00
24		3k. orange-yellow	£650	39·00
25		6k. pale green	£16000	£180
26		6k. deep green	£16000	£180
27		9k. rose	£2000	£130
28		9k. carmine	£2000	£130
29		18k. blue	£5000	£2250
30		18k. deep blue	£5000	£2250

(b) P 13½. Thick paper. (1860)

31	2	1k. brown	£1800	£200
32		3k. orange	£500	16·00
33		3k. orange-yellow	£650	26·00
34		6k. green	£5000	£170
35		6k. deep green	£6000	£375
36		9k. carmine	£2000	£200

(c) P 13½. Thin paper. (1861)

37	2	1k. brown	£1600	£450
38		1k. deep brown	£1600	£450
39		1k. black-brown	£1700	£425
40		3k. orange-yellow	£325	£100
41		6k. green	£650	£180
42		9k. carmine	£2000	£425
43		9k. purple	£2500	£600
44		18k. blue	£5000	£3750

(d) P 10. Thin paper. (1862)

45	2	1k. black-brown	£1000	£700
46		3k. orange-yellow	£1300	85·00
47		6k. green	£850	£250
48		9k. purple	£6500	£1200

This issue, like the last, was reprinted in 1864 *imperf* but the reprints have a space of 2 mm. between the stamps, whereas the originals have only 1.5 mm.

15

GERMANY/ German States - Württemberg

King Karl
25 June 1864–6 October 1891

1863 (Jan)–**64**. Colours changed. P 10.

49	**2**	1k. yellow-green	70·00	22·00
50		1k. green	70·00	22·00
51		1k. blue-green	£650	£160
52		3k. carmine	£500	9·00
53		3k. deep rose	£650	33·00
54		6k. blue (1864)	£250	90·00
55		6k. deep blue (1864)	£800	£275
56		9k. yellow-brown	£1300	£275
57		9k. chestnut	£425	90·00
58		9k. black-brown	£1600	£275
59		18k. orange (1864)	£2000	£650

1865 (Nov)–**68**. Rouletted 10.

60	**2**	1k. yellow-green	80·00	20·00
61		1k. pale green	£1000	£450
62		3k. pale rose	80·00	6·50
63		3k. rose	£130	17·00
64		6k. blue	£475	85·00
65		6k. deep blue	£1300	£400
66		7k. slate-blue (2.4.68)	£1600	£200
67		7k. indigo (1868)	£2000	£275
68		9k. brown (1867)	£2000	£130
69		9k. chestnut	£2000	£130
70		9k. bistre (1867)	£2500	£200
71		18k. orange (1867)	£3000	£1400

(Des Kast. Embossed and typo Traffic Institute)

1869 (1 Jan)–**73**. Rouletted 10.

72	**3**	1k. blue-green	£425	£180
73		1k. yellow-green	50·00	4·00
74		2k. orange (1872)	£275	£225
75		2k. deep orange (1872)	£500	£400
76		3k. pale rose	26·00	3·25
77		3k. deep rose	26·00	3·25
78		7k. blue	£110	29·00
79		7k. deep blue	£250	£100
80		9k. bistre (1873)	£130	65·00
81		14k. dull yellow (1872)	£2500	£2500
82		14k. orange-yellow (1872)	£140	80·00
83		14k. orange (1872)	£400	£200

The 14k. is found *imperf*, but is not known used. (*Price unused*, £31).
The 1k. is also known *imperf*.

(Embossed and typo Traffic Institute)

1873 (1 Jan). Imperf.

84	**2**	70k. purple	£5000	£9000
85		70k. red-violet	£3000	£6500

(Typo J. B. Mezler)

1874 (5 Nov). P 11½×11.

86	**3**	1k. yellow-green	£180	65·00
87		1k. green	£180	65·00

Other values of this type are sometimes seen perforated, but these are fraudulent productions.

(Typo Eisenlohr and Weigle, Stuttgart)

1875 (1 Jan)–**79**. New currency. P 11½×11.

88	**4**	3pf. pale blue-green	£500	£130
89		3pf. green	34·00	2·50
90		5pf. bright mauve	16·00	1·30
91		5pf. mauve	16·00	1·30
92		10pf. pale rose	£140	2·00
		a. Imperf (pair)	£130	
93		10pf. carmine	2·50	1·30
94		20pf. Prussian blue	£450	27·00
94a		20pf. dull blue	3·50	2·50
95		20pf. ultramarine	2·50	2·50
96		20pf. pale ultramarine	2·50	2·50
97		25pf. pale brown	£200	20·00
98		25pf. chestnut	£425	36·00
99		50pf. grey	£1200	65·00
100		50pf. grey-green (1878)	£100	9·75
101		50pf. sage-green (1878)	£100	9·75
102		2m. orange-yellow	£1200	£425
103		2m. vermilion/*orange* (1879)	£4250	£200

See also Nos. 123/132.

1875 (1 July). MUNICIPAL SERVICE. Typo. No wmk. P 11½×11.

M104	M **5**	5pf. mauve	£1000	50·00
M105		5pf. pale mauve	80·00	4·00
		a. Imperf (pair)	—	£3250
M106		10pf. rose	70·00	10·50
		a. Imperf (pair)	£120	
M107		10pf. carmine	16·00	4·00

See also Nos. M144/M150, M153/M157, M168/M180, M222/31, M261/M269 and M270/M299.

1881 (1 Apr). OFFICIAL. Typo. No wmk. P 11½×11.

O108	O **5**	3pf. pale yellow-green	39·00	7·75
O109		3pf. pale blue-green	39·00	7·75
O110		5pf. pale mauve	13·00	4·25
O111		5pf. mauve	13·00	4·25
O112		5pf. deep mauve	13·00	4·25
O113		10pf. pale rose	33·00	4·50
O114		10pf. rose	5·25	3·50
		a. Imperf (pair)	90·00	
O115		20pf. ultramarine	1·70	3·50
O116		20pf. pale ultramarine	£100	11·50
		a. Imperf (pair)	£140	
O117		25pf. chestnut	60·00	10·50
O118		25pf. brown	£170	£160
O119		50pf. grey-green	10·50	17·00
O120		1m. yellow (1882)	£120	£275
O108/O120 Set of 7 (cheapest)			£225	£300

See also Nos. O133/O143, O181/O198 and O200/O201.

1881 (1 Nov)–**83**. Typo. P 11½×11.

121	**5**	2m. black and orange	13·00	20·00
		a. Black and yellow (1883)	£700	£120
		b. Imperf (pair)	£250	
122		5m. black and pale blue	70·00	£250

See also Nos. 151/152.

1890 (5 Feb)–**94**. Colours changed and new value. No wmk. P 11½×11.

123	**4**	2pf. slate-grey (1894)	3·75	1·70
124		3pf. brown	1·30	90
125		3pf. deep brown	1·30	90
		a. Imperf (pair)	£250	
126		5pf. yellow-green	2·50	90
127		5pf. green	2·50	90
		a. Imperf (pair)	£275	
128		5pf. blue-green	£500	39·00
129		25pf. orange-yellow	£550	£250
130		25pf. deep orange	4·50	2·50
		a. Imperf (pair)	£275	
131		50pf. pale red-brown	£900	£110
132		50pf. purple-brown (1891)	5·25	1·60
		a. Imperf (pair)	£275	

The imperf stamps in genuinely used condition are very scarce.

1890–1902. OFFICIAL. Colours changed and new values. No wmk. P 11½×11.

O133	O **5**	2pf. grey (1896)	2·50	3·75
		a. Imperf (pair)	90·00	
O134		3pf. brown	2·50	4·25
		a. Imperf (pair)	65·00	
O135		5pf. green	4·00	4·25
		a. Imperf (pair)	65·00	
O136		5pf. deep green	4·00	4·25
O137		25pf. orange	8·50	4·25
		a. Imperf (pair)	85·00	
O138		25pf. deep orange	8·50	4·25
O139		30pf. black and orange (1902)	3·25	5·50
		a. Imperf (pair)	90·00	
O140		40pf. black and carmine (1902)	3·25	5·50
		a. Imperf (pair)	90·00	
O141		50pf. red-brown	£400	£2750
O142		50pf. deep maroon (1891)	47·00	6·50
		a. Imperf (pair)	90·00	
O143		1m. violet	9·00	26·00
		a. Imperf (pair)	65·00	

1890. MUNICIPAL SERVICE. Colour changed. No wmk. P 11½×11.

M144	M **5**	5pf. yellow-green	3·00	4·25
M145		5pf. green	3·00	4·25
		a. Imperf (pair)	90·00	
M146		5pf. deep blue-green	£300	36·00

GERMANY/ German States - Württemberg

King Wilhelm II
6 Oct 1891–30 November 1918

1896–1900. MUNICIPAL SERVICE. New values. No wmk. P 11½×11.
M147	M 5	2pf. grey	6·50	4·50
		a. Imperf (pair)	90·00	
M148		2pf. slate-grey	6·50	4·50
M149		3pf. brown (1896)	5·25	4·50
		a. Imperf (pair)	90·00	
M150		25pf. orange	39·00	13·50
		a. Imperf (pair)	90·00	
		s. Optd 'Specimen'	£100	

1900. Numeral in black. Typo. P 11½×11.
151	5	30pf. grey	6·50	9·00
152		40pf. carmine	6·50	10·50

Dies and electrotypes for all the stamps of the above issues and for the Municipal and Official stamps (except the water-marked series) were made by the Mint, Stuttgart.

USED PRICES. Used prices quoted for Nos. M153/M299 are for cancelled-to-order examples. Prices for postally used vary, with some values being very scarce.

1806 – 1906
(M 6)   M 7

1906 (Feb). MUNICIPAL SERVICE. Centenary of Establishment of Kingdom. Optd with Type M 6. P 11½×11.
M153	M 5	2pf. grey	70·00	26·00
M154		3pf. brown	26·00	16·00
M155		5pf. green	10·50	6·00
M156		10pf. rose	10·50	6·00
M157		25pf. orange	80·00	22·00
M153/M157 Set of 5			£180	70·00

Nos. M153/M157 exist imperf (Price £375 un. in pairs).

1906 (Feb). OFFICIAL. Centenary of Establishment of Kingdom. Optd with Type M 6. P 11½×11.
O158	O 5	2pf. grey	46·00	33·00
O159		3pf. brown	9·00	90
O160		5pf. green	7·75	90
O161		10pf. rose	7·25	90
O162		20pf. ultramarine	7·75	90
O163		25pf. orange	18·00	13·00
O164		30pf. black and orange	16·00	11·50
O165		40pf. black and carmine	60·00	33·00
O166		50pf. deep maroon	50·00	33·00
O167		1m. violet	£100	36·00
O158/O167 Set of 10			£300	£150

Nos. O158/O167 exist imperf (Price £180 set un. in pairs).

(Typo German Imperial Printing Office, Berlin)

1906–19. MUNICIPAL SERVICE. Wmk Type M 7. P 11½×11.
M168	M 5	2pf. grey	6·50	90
M169		2½pf. grey (1916)	1·30	50
M170		3pf. brown	1·60	65
M171		5pf. green	1·30	65
M172		7½pf. orange (1916)	1·30	50
M173		10pf. rose	1·30	65
M174		15pf. yellow-brown (1916)	3·50	60
M175		15pf. violet (1917)	2·00	50
M176		20pf. deep blue	2·50	65
M177		25pf. orange	1·60	65
M178		25pf. black and brown (1917)	2·00	50
M179		35pf. red-brown (1919)	2·50	1·60
M180		50pf. deep maroon	23·00	65
M168/M180 Set of 13			45·00	8·00

(Typo, German Imperial Printing Office, Berlin)

1906–19. OFFICIAL. Wmk Type M 7. P 11½×11.
O181	O 5	2pf. grey	80	65
O182		2½pf. grey (1916)	90	90
O183		3pf. brown	80	80
O184		5pf. green	80	80
O185		7½pf. orange (1916)	90	90
O186		10pf. rose	80	80
O187		15pf. yellow-brown (1916)	1·00	90
O188		15pf. purple (1.11.17)	2·00	65
O189		20pf. ultramarine	1·00	80
O190		20pf. bright blue (1.11.17)	20·00	1·30
O191		25pf. orange	1·30	80
O192		25pf. black and brown (1917)	80	65
O193		30pf. black and orange	80	80
O194		35pf. red-brown (1.2.19)	2·50	4·25
O195		40pf. black and carmine	80	80
O196		50pf. deep maroon	1·00	80
O197		1m. violet	4·00	80
O198		1m. black and grey (1.11.17)	4·00	1·30
O181/O198 Set of 18			40·00	17·00

25 Pf.
(M 8)   M 9   O 10 King Wilhelm II

1916 (10 Sept). MUNICIPAL SERVICE. No. M177 surch with Type M 8.
M199	M 5	25pf. on 25pf. orange	6·25	1·50
		a. No watermark	65·00	

1916–19. OFFICIAL. Surch.
O200	O 5	25pf. on 25pf. orange (20.9.16)	5·25	1·30
		a. No watermark	60·00	
O201		50pf. on 50pf. deep maroon (1.2.19)	2·50	1·80

1916 (6 Oct). MUNICIPAL SERVICE. Jubilee of King Wilhelm II. P 14½×14.
M202	M 9	2½pf. blue-grey	2·50	2·50
M203		7½pf. orange-red	2·50	2·50
M204		10pf. carmine	2·50	2·50
M205		15pf. bistre	2·50	2·50
M206		20pf. blue	2·50	2·50
M207		25pf. grey	6·50	4·00
M208		50pf. red-brown	13·00	5·25
M202/M208 Set of 7			29·00	20·00

1916 (6 Oct). OFFICIAL. Jubilee of King Wilhelm II. Typo. P 14.
O209	O 10	2½pf. blue-grey	1·60	1·30
O210		7½pf. orange-red	1·60	1·00
O211		10pf. carmine	1·60	1·00
O212		15pf. bistre	1·60	1·00
O213		20pf. blue	1·60	1·00
O214		25pf. grey	2·50	1·30
O215		30pf. black and orange	2·50	2·20
O216		40pf. claret	4·50	2·50
O217		50pf. red-brown	5·75	4·00
O218		1m. mauve	5·75	5·25
O209/O218 Set of 10			26·00	18·00

Provisional Government
30 November 1918–26 April 1919

Republic, 26 April 1919

Volksstaat

2 75 Württemberg
(M 11)   (O 12)   (M 13)

1919. MUNICIPAL SERVICE. No. M169 surch with T M 11.
M219	M 5	2 on 2½pf. grey (B.)	1·30	80

1919. OFFICIAL. Nos. O182 surch with T M 11.
O220		2 on 2½pf. grey (B.)	2·50	2·50

1919. MUNICIPAL SERVICE. Stamps of 1906–19 optd with T M 13.
M222	M 5	2½pf. grey	65	80
M223		3pf. brown	19·00	2·00
M224		5pf. green	50	80
M225		7½pf. orange	1·70	80
M226		10pf. rose	50	80
M227		15pf. purple	50	80
M228		20pf. deep blue	65	80
M229		25pf. black and brown	65	1·30
M230		35pf. red-brown	6·25	1·60
M231		50pf. deep maroon	9·00	1·60
M222/M231 Set of 10			35·00	10·00

1919. OFFICIAL. Stamps of 1906–19, optd with T M 13.
O232	O 5	2½pf. grey	90	65

17

GERMANY/ German States - Württemberg

O233	3pf. brown	11·50	1·30
	a. No watermark	85·00	
O234	5pf. green	65	65
O235	7½pf. orange	65	65
O236	10pf. rose	65	65
O237	15pf. purple	65	65
O238	20pf. ultramarine	65	65
O239	25pf. black and brown	80	65
	a. Opt inverted	£160	
O240	30pf. black and orange	1·30	65
	a. Opt inverted	£800	
O241	35pf. red-brown	90	65
O242	40pf. black and carmine	90	65
O243	50pf. deep maroon	1·30	1·00
O244	1m. black and grey-green	1·30	1·30
O232/O244 Set of 13		20·00	9·00

1919. OFFICIAL. No. O233 additionally surch with T O **12**.

O245	75 on 3pf. brown (R)	2·00	2·00
	a. No watermark	£130	33·00

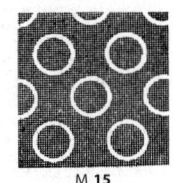

(Des and eng M. Körner. Typo)

1920 (29 Mar). MUNICIPAL SERVICE. Wmk T M **15**. P 14½.

M245	M **14**	10pf. claret	2·30	2·50
M246		15pf. brown	2·30	2·30
M247		20pf. deep blue	2·30	2·10
M248		30pf. blue-green	2·30	2·30
M249		50pf. yellow	5·25	4·00
M250		75pf. olive-bistre	5·75	5·25
M245/M250 Set of 6			18·00	17·00

O **16** Ulm

(Des Kissling and Raible. Litho K. Ebner, Stuttgart)

1920 (29 Mar). OFFICIAL. T O **16** and similar views. Wmk T M **15**. P 14½.

O251	10pf. claret (Stuttgart)	90	1·90
O252	15pf. brown (Ulm)	90	1·90
O253	20pf. indigo (Tübingen)	90	1·90
O254	30pf. blue-green (Ellwangen)	90	1·90
O255	50pf. yellow (Stuttgart)	90	2·00
O256	75pf. olive-bistre (Ulm)	90	2·00
O257	1m. vermilion (Tübingen)	1·30	2·00
O258	1m.25 violet (Ellwangen)	1·30	2·00
O259	2m.50 ultramarine (Stuttgart)	4·00	2·50
O260	3m. green (Stuttgart)	4·00	2·50
O251/O260 Set of 10		14·50	19·00

Prices are for cancelled to order.

1921 (1 Jan)–**22**. MUNICIPAL SERVICE. Wmk Type M **7**. P 11½×11.

M261	M **5**	10pf. orange	50	65
M262		15pf. reddish violet	50	65
M263		20pf. green	50	65
M264		40pf. carmine	50	65
M265		50pf. claret	50	90
M266		60pf. olive-green (1921)	80	1·20
M267		1.25m. light green	50	90
M268		2m. greenish slate (9.22)	50	90
M269		3m. chestnut (9.22)	80	90
M261/M269 Set of 9			4·50	6·75

5 Mark (M **17**)   **60** Mark (M **18**)

1922 (Dec)–**23**. MUNICIPAL SERVICE. Surch as T M **17** (to 50m.) or T M **18** (others).

M270	M **5**	5m. on 10pf. orange	40	80
M271		10m. on 15pf. reddish violet	40	80
M272		12m. on 40pf. carmine (12.22)	40	80
M273		20m. on 10pf. orange	1·20	1·30
M274		25m. on 20pf. green	40	80
M275		40m. on 20pf. green	40	80
M276		50m. on 20pf. olive-green	40	80
M277		60m. on 1.25m. light green (12.22)	40	80
M278		100m. on 40pf. carmine	40	80
M279		200m. on 2m. greenish slate (R.)	40	80
M280		300m. on 50pf. claret (B.)	40	80
M281		400m. on 3m. chestnut (B.)	40	80
M282		1000m. on 60pf. olive-green	65	80
M283		2000m. on 1.25m. light green	50	80
M270/M283 Set of 14			6·00	10·50

5 Tausend (M **19**)   **3** (M **20**)

1923 (10 Aug). MUNICIPAL SERVICE. Surch as T M **19**. T = Tausend (thousand). M = Million. Md = Milliard.

M284	M **5**	5T. on 10pf. orange	50	80
M285		20T. on 40pf. carmine	50	80
M286		50T. on 15pf. reddish violet	2·00	80
M287		75T. on 2m. greenish slate	2·50	80
M288		100T. on 20pf. green	40	80
M289		250T. on 3m. chestnut	40	80
M290		1M. on 60pf. olive-green	2·50	80
M291		2M. on 50pf. claret	40	80
M292		5M. on 1.25m. light green	65	80
M293		4Md. on 50pf. claret	8·50	80
M294		10Md. on 3m. chestnut	6·50	80
M284/M294 Set of 11			22·00	8·00

1923 (Dec). MUNICIPAL SERVICE. No. M177 surch as T M **20**, in gold pfennige.

M295	M **5**	3pf. on 25pf. orange	90	65
M296		5pf. on 25pf. orange	80	65
M297		10pf. on 25pf. orange	80	65
M298		20pf. on 25pf. orange	90	65
M299		50pf. on 25pf. orange	80	65
M295/M299 Set of 5			3·75	3·00

The Kingdom of Württemberg ceased to have separate postage stamps on 1 April 1902, the stamps of the German Empire superseding them. Official stamps continued to be issued until 1 April, 1920, and Municipal Service stamps until 1924, from which date only German stamps were used.

Heligoland

Stamps of HAMBURG were used in Heligoland until 16 April 1867. The Free City of Hamburg ran the Heligoland postal service between 1796 and 1 June 1866. Its stamps continued in use on the island until replaced by Heligoland issues.

PRICES FOR STAMPS ON COVER
Nos. 1/19 — *from* × 3

PRINTERS. All the stamps of Heligoland were typographed at the Imperial Printing Works, Berlin.

REPRINTS. Many of the stamps of Heligoland were subsequently reprinted at Berlin (between 1875 and 1885), Leipzig (1888) and Hamburg (1892 and 1895). Of these only the Berlin productions are difficult to distinguish from the originals so separate notes are provided for the individual values. Leipzig reprints can be identified by their highly surfaced paper and those from Hamburg by their 14 perforation. All of these reprints are worth much less than the original stamps priced below.

There was, in addition, a small reprinting of Nos. 13/19, made by the German government in 1890 for exchange purposes, but examples of this printing are far scarcer than the original stamps.

Forgeries, printed by lithography instead of typography, also exist for Nos. 1/4, 6 and 8 perforated 12½ or 13. Forged cancellations can also be found on originals and, on occasion, genuine postmarks on reprints.

1

(Currency. 16 schillings = 1 mark)

Three Dies of Embossed Head for Types **1** and **2**:

Die I

Die II

Die III

Die I. Blob instead of curl beneath the chignon. Outline of two jewels at top of diadem.
Die II. Curl under chignon. One jewel at top of diadem.
Die III. Shorter curl under chignon. Two jewels at top of diadem.

(Des Wedding. Die eng E. Schilling)

1867 (21 Mar)–**68**. Head Die I embossed in colourless relief. Roul.

1	1	½sch. blue-green and rose	£350	£850
		a. Head Die II (7.68)	£800	£1200
2		1sch. rose and blue-green	£180	£200
3		2sch. rose and grass-green	20·00	65·00
4		6sch. green and rose	21·00	£275

For Nos. 1/4 the second colour given is that of the spandrels on the ½ and 1sch., and of the spandrels and central background for the 2 and 6sch.

All four values exist from the Berlin, Leipzig and Hamburg reprintings. The following points are helpful in identifying originals from Berlin reprints; for Leipzig and Hamburg reprints see general note above:

½sch. – Reprints are all in yellowish green and show Head Die II
1sch. – All reprints are Head Die III
2sch. – Berlin reprints are in dull rose with a deeper blue-green
6sch. – Originals show white specks in green. Berlin reprints have a more solid bluish green

1869 (Apr)–**73**. Head embossed in colourless relief. P 13½×14½.

5	1	¼sch. rose and green (background) (I) (*quadrillé paper*) (8.73)	35·00	£1600
		a. Error. Green and rose (background) (9.73)	£190	£3250
		b. Deep rose and pale green (background) (11.73)	95·00	£1600
6		½sch. blue-green and rose (II)	£225	£250
		a. Yellow green and rose (7.71)	£160	£225
		b. Quadrillé paper (6.73)	£110	£170
7		¾sch. green and rose (I) (*quadrillé paper*) (12.73)	50·00	£1200
8		1sch. rose and yellow-green (III) (11.71)	£160	£200
		a. Quadrillé paper. *Rose and pale blue-green* (6.73)	£140	£200
9		1½sch. green and rose (I) (*quadrillé paper*) (9.73)	95·00	£275

For Nos. 5/9 the second colour given is that of the spandrels on the ½ and 1sch., of the central background on the ¼ and 1½sch., and of the central background, side labels and side marginal lines of the ¾sch.

No. 5a was a printing of the ¼sch. made in the colour combination of the 1½sch. by mistake.

A further printing of the ½sch. (Head die I) in deep rose-red and yellowish green (background), on non-*quadrillé* paper, was made in December 1874, but not issued (*Price* £15, *unused*).

All five values exist from the Berlin, Leipzig and Hamburg reprintings. The following points are helpful in identifying originals from Berlin reprints; for Leipzig and Hamburg reprints see general note above:

¼sch. – All Berlin and some Hamburg reprints are Head Die II
½sch. – Berlin reprints on thinner paper with solid colour in the spandrels
¾sch. – Berlin reprints on thinner, non-quadrillé paper
1sch. – Berlin reprints are on thinner paper or show many breaks in the rose line beneath 'SCHILLING' at the top of the design or in the line above it at the foot
1½sch.– All Berlin and some Hamburg reprints are Head Die II

Berlin, Leipzig and Hamburg reprints also exist of the 2 and 6sch., but these values do not come as perforated originals.

(New Currency. 100 pfennig = 1 mark)

2

3

4

5

(Des H. Gätke. Die eng E. Schilling (Type **2**), A. Schiffner (others))

1875 (Feb)–**90**. Head Die II on Type **2** embossed in colourless relief. P 13½×14½.

10	2	1pf. (¼d.) deep green and rose	20·00	£550
11		2pf. (½d.) deep rose and deep green	20·00	£650
12	3	3pf. (⅜d.) pale green, red and yellow (6.76)	£250	£1200
		a. Green, red and orange (6.77)	£170	£900
13	2	5pf. (¾d.) deep yellow-green and rose	23·00	20·00
		a. Deep green and rose (6.90)	27·00	55·00
14		10pf. (1½d.) deep rose and deep green.	42·00	23·00
		a. Scarlet and pale blue-green (5.87)	17·00	24·00
15	3	20pf. (2½d.) rose, green and yellow (6.76)	£275	£120
		a. Rose-carmine, deep green and orange (4.80)	£180	55·00
		b. Dull red, pale green and lemon (7.88)	26·00	30·00

GERMANY / Heligoland

		c. Aniline vermilion, bright green and lemon (6.90)..............................	16·00	55·00
16	2	25pf. (3d.) deep green and rose	24·00	29·00
17		50pf. (6d.) rose and green	26·00	42·00
18	4	1m. (1s.) deep green, scarlet and black (8.79)..	£170	£200
		a. Perf 11½	£1400	
		b. Deep green, aniline rose and black (5.89)	£170	£200
19	5	5m. (5s.) deep green, aniline rose, black and yellow (8.79)	£225	£950
		a. Perf 11½	£1400	
		ab. Imperf between (horiz pair).............	£6000	

For stamps as Type **2** the first colour is that of the central background and the second that of the frame. On the 3pf. the first colour is of the frame and the top band of the shield, the second is the centre band and the third the shield border. The 20pf. is similar, but has the centre band in the same colour as the frame and the upper band on the shield in the second colour.

The 1, 2 and 3pf. exist from the Berlin, Leipzig and Hamburg reprintings. There were no such reprints for the other values. The following points are helpful in identifying originals from Berlin reprints; for Leipzig and Hamburg reprints see general note above:

1pf. – Berlin printings show a peculiar shade of pink
2pf. – All reprints are much lighter in shade than the deep rose and deep green of the originals
3pf. – Berlin reprints either show the band around the shield in brownish orange, or have this feature in deep yellow with the other two colours lighter

Heligoland was ceded to Germany on 9 August 1890.

GERMANY/ North German Confederation

North German Confederation

Northern District. 30 Gröschen = 1 Thaler

Southern District. 60 Kreuzer = 1 Gulden

The North German Confederation was set up on 1 Jan 1868. Its postal services replaced those of Bremen, Brunswick, Hamburg, Lübeck, Mecklenburg (both), Oldenburg, Prussia and Saxony.

1 **2**

(Type **1/4** des C. Schwatlo; eng H. G. Schilling. Typo Prussian State Printing Works, Berlin)

1868 (1 Jan). Rouletted 8½ to 10, and 11 to 12½.

(a) Northern District

1	1	¼g. deep purple	26·00	26·00
2		¼g. purple	46·00	23·00
3		⅓g. green	50·00	7·75
4		⅓g. pale green	50·00	7·75
		a. Unroletted (pair)	£300	
5		½g. orange	50·00	5·75
6		1g. rose	33·00	4·50
		a. Unroletted (pair)	£250	
7		1g. carmine-rose	33·00	4·50
8		2g. blue	£130	7·75
9		2g. ultramarine	£130	7·75
10		5g. bistre	£130	17·00
		a. Unroletted (pair)	£900	

(b) Southern District

11	2	1k. pale green	60·00	13·00
12		1k. deep green	60·00	13·00
		a. Imperf (pair)	£225	£400
13		2k. orange	90·00	90·00
		a. Unroletted (pair)	£650	£300
14		3k. rose	60·00	5·25
		a. Unroletted (pair)	£250	£350
15		3k. carmine-rose	60·00	5·25
16		7k. deep blue	£250	20·00
17		7k. ultramarine	£250	20·00
18		18k. bistre	60·00	£100

1869 (17 Feb)–**70**. P 14×14½.

(a) Northern District

19	1	¼g. pale mauve	23·00	26·00
20		¼g. purple	39·00	31·00
21		⅓g. green	8·50	5·25
22		⅓g. yellow-green	8·50	5·25
23		½g. orange	8·50	6·50
24		½g. orange-vermilion	8·50	6·50
25		1g. rose	6·50	2·75
26		1g. rose-carmine	6·50	2·75
27		2g. ultramarine	11·50	4·00
28		2g. pale ultramarine	11·50	4·00
29		5g. bistre	14·50	18·00

(b) Southern District

30	2	1k. green	21·00	17·00
31		1k. yellow-green	21·00	17·00
32		2k. orange	65·00	£180
33		3k. rose	11·50	7·75
34		3k. rose-carmine	11·50	7·75
35		7k. ultramarine	18·00	20·00
36		7k. pale ultramarine	18·00	20·00
37		18k. bistre (1870)	£250	£2750

3 **4**

1869 (1 Mar). P 14½×14.

38	3	10g. grey	£500	£100
39	4	30g. pale blue	£425	£225

These two stamps were not sold to the public, but were affixed in the Post Office to packets requiring them, and cancelled with pen and ink. Used prices are for stamps thus cancelled.

O **5**

(Typo. Prussian State Printing Works, Berlin)

1870 (1 Jan). OFFICIAL. P 14½×14.

(a) Northern District

O40	O **5**	¼g. black and pale red-brown	46·00	70·00
O41		⅓g. black and pale red-brown	16·00	33·00
O42		½g. black and pale red-brown	5·25	7·75
O43		1g. black and pale red-brown	4·50	4·00
O44		2g. black and pale red-brown	11·50	7·75

(b) Southern District

O45	O **5**	1k. black and grey	50·00	£425
O46		2k. black and grey	£130	£1300
O47		3k. black and grey	46·00	80·00
O48		7k. black and grey	70·00	£450

The background consists of a repetition of the words. 'NORDD. POSTBEZIRK'.

Local issue for Hamburg

H **1**

(Des C. Schwertler; eng J. G. Schilling. Typo Prussian State Printing Works, Berlin)

1868 (1 Jan). Rouletted 8½ to 10 and 11 to 12½.

H1	H **1**	(½s.) purple-brown	£200	90·00

1869. P 14×14 ½.

H2	H **1**	(½s.) purple-brown	7·75	14·50
H3		(½s.) purple	17·00	39·00

The postal services of the North German Confederation were merged in a German Reichspost on 4 May 1871 and the stamps of Germany were brought into use on 1 January 1872.

21

GERMANY/ Alsace and Lorraine / Inscriptions on German Stamp Issues

Alsace and Lorraine

German Army of Occupation 1870–71

These stamps were used in those parts of France occupied by the German Army in the war of 1870–71, and afterwards provisionally in the annexed provinces of Alsace and Lorraine, until superseded by the issues for the German Empire.

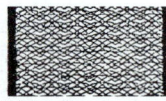

| 1 | I Points upwards | II Points downwards |

The word 'POSTES' varies in length resulting in many variations in the relative positions of the different parts of the inscription. The following are the more prominent types:—

Three types of 4c.

| CENTIMES | CENTIMES | CENTIMES |
| A | B | C |

A. Foot of '4' over 'IM' of 'CENTIMES'.
B. Foot of '4' further left, over 'TIM'.
C. Foot of '4' still further left, over 'TI'.

Two types of 10c.

| CENT | CENT |
| D | E |

D. Foot of '1' over 'N' of 'CENTIMES'.
E. Foot of '1' further left, over 'EN'.

(Typo Prussian State Ptg Wks, Berlin)
1870 (10 Sept). P 13½×14½.

I. With points of the net upwards

1	1	1c. olive-green	90·00	£160
2		1c. sage-green	£200	£200
3		2c. chestnut	£120	£225
4		2c. deep brown	£350	£400
5		4c. grey (A)	£120	£120
6		4c. grey (B)	£180	£180
7		4c. grey (C)		
8		5c. pale yellow-green	80·00	16·00
9		5c. deep yellow-green	£160	23·00
10		10c. pale brown (D)	£100	22·00
11		10c. pale brown (E)	90·00	22·00
12		10c. bistre (E)	£100	22·00
13		10c. bistre-brown (E)	£100	22·00
14		20c. pale ultramarine	£100	18·00
15		20c. deep ultramarine	£100	18·00
16		25c. deep brown	£170	£120

II. With points of the net downwards

17	1	1c. olive-green	£450	£1300
18		1c. sage-green	£450	£1300
19		2c. chestnut	£160	£1200
20		4c. grey (B)	£160	£160
21		4c. grey (C)	£200	£200
22		5c. pale yellow-green	£4000	£800
23		10c. pale brown (D)	70·00	20·00
24		10c. pale brown (E)	70·00	20·00
25		10c. bistre-brown (E)	£100	26·00
26		20c. ultramarine	£170	£160
27		25c. brown	£350	£350

An official imitation of all the values was made in 1885. In the imitations the 'P' of 'POSTES' is only 2½ mm. from the left border, whereas in the originals the distance is 3 to 3½ mm. Almost all the imitations have the points of the network downwards.

Inscriptions on German Stamp Issues

A number of different forms of inscription have been used on the stamps of Germany. They are useful in identifying the period from which the issue comes. A chronological list is given below, together with the catalogue numbers on which they occur.

DEUTSCHE REICHSPOST	First issues of the German Empire, Nos. 1 to 44
REICHSPOST	Empire issues from 1889, Nos. 45 to 66
DEUTSCHES REICH	The most extensively used of the pre-1945 inscriptions, lasting from Empire issues of 1902 up to Nazi stamps issued in 1944, between Nos. 67 and 851, also 876/881
DEUTSCHE NATIONAL VERSAMMLUNG	'German National Assembly' (Weimar Republic), Nos. 107/10
DEUTSCHE FLUGPOST	Airmail issues 1919 to 1923, between Nos. 111 and 273
DEUTSCHE LUFTPOST	Airmail issues 1926 to 1938, between Nos. 392 and 658
GROSSDEUTSCHES REICH	Style adopted by the Nazi State from 1943, between Nos. 850 and 898
DEUTSCHE FELDPOST	Military Field Post issues of 1942 and 1944, Nos. M805. M895/M896
DIENSTMARKE	Official Stamps from 1920, No. O117 onwards

NOTE Stamps inscribed 'DEUTSCHES (or GROSSDEUTSCHES) REICH GENERALGOUVERNEMENT', and with face values in gröschen and zloty, are issues of the German Occupation of Poland, and are listed with that country.

DEUTSCHE POST	Used for many issues during the immediate post-war period; the joint issues of the American, British and Russian Zones 1946 to 1948, Nos. 899 to 956; Civil Government issues for the British and American Zones 1948/1949, Nos. A36 to A111. Russian Zone issues for Saxony North-West and South-East 1945/1946, and General issues to 1949, Nos. RD1/RD36, RE24/RE25, R31/R61; stamps for West Berlin until 1954 and West Germany until 1949, Nos. B35 to B124 and 1033/1042; the first three and last six issues of East Germany, Nos. E1/E4 and E3040/E3061
A.M. POST DEUTSCHLAND	Military Government issue, British and American Zones 1945, Nos. A1/A35
ZONE FRANCAISE	French Zone, General issues 1945/1946, Nos. F1/F13
BADEN, RHEINLANDPFALZ, WÜRTTEMBERG	Territories of the French Zone 1947/1949, Nos. FB1 to FW52
STADT BERLIN, MECKLENBURG VORPOMMERN PROVINZ SACHSEN, THURINGEN	Districts of the Russian Zone, 1945/1946, between Nos. RA1 and RF13
POST ПУТА	Saxony (South-Eastern) district, Russian Zone 1945, No. RE1
POST	Saxony (South-Eastern) district, Russian Zone, 1945/1946, Nos. RE2/RE23
DEUTSCHE BUNDESPOST	The German Federal Republic 1950-95, Nos. 1043/2626 and 2628/2630

Stamps additionally inscribed 'BERLIN' are for use in West Berlin.

DEUTSCHE DEMOKRATISCHE REPUBLIK	The German Democratic Republic or DDR (East Germany)
DEUTSCHLAND	The German Federal Republic from April 1995, Nos. 2627 and 2631 onwards

II. Germany (1871–1945)

1872. Northern areas including Alsace and Lorraine:
30 Gröschen = 1 Thaler
Southern areas: 90 Kreuzer = 1 Gulden
1875. Throughout Germany: 100 Pfennig = 1 Mark
1923. 100 Renten-pfennig = 1 Rentenmark (gold currency)
1928. 100 Pfennig = 1 Reichsmark

EMPIRE

Emperor Wilhelm I
18 January 1871–9 March 1888

> **PRINTERS.** The stamps of Germany were printed until May, 1879, by the Prussian State Printing Office, which from that date was known as the Reichsdruckerei (Imperial Printing Office), and was responsible for the printing of all subsequent issues, *unless otherwise stated.*

1 **A**

(Eng H. G. Schilling. Background and inscriptions typo.
Arms embossed in colourless relief)

1872 (1 Jan–Apr). Eagle with small shield (Type A). P 13½×14½.

(a) Issue for districts with 'thaler' currency

1	1	¼g. violet	£375	£150
2		⅓g. yellow-green	£800	65·00
		a. Imperf	—	†
3		½g. orange-vermilion	£1800	70·00
4		½g. orange-yellow (4.72)	£1900	80·00
5		1g. rose-carmine	£500	12·50
		a. Bisected (on cover)	—	£88000
		b. Imperf	—	
6		2g. blue	£2750	25·00
		a. Imperf	—	£15000
7		5g. bistre	£1500	£150
		a. Imperf		£18000

(b) Issue for districts with 'gulden' currency

8	1	1k. yellow-green	£1100	90·00
9		2k. orange-vermilion	£1000	£500
10		2k. orange-yellow (4.72)	65·00	£325
11		3k. rose-carmine	£3000	25·00
12		7k. blue	£4000	£150
13		18k. bistre	£800	£650

Stamps with embossed eagle inverted are forgeries.

> **PRICES.** — The prices quoted for the early embossed issues of Germany are for stamps with average embossing and centring. Stamps perfectly centred and with very sharp embossing are worth more.

2 **3**

(Eng H. G. Schilling. Typo)

A. Unused.
B. Handwritten cancellation.
C. Postmarked.

Stamps with handwritten cancellation and complete postmark are worth about one-third the prices quoted under *C*.

1872 (15 Jan). P 14½×13½.

			A	B	C
14	2	10g. grey	95·00	£300	£2250
15	3	30g. blue	£180	£950	£4250

B **4**

1872 (July–Dec). As Type **1**, but eagle with large shield (Type B). P 13½×14½.

(a) issue for districts with 'thaler' currency

16	1	¼g. purple (9.72)	£140	£160
17		⅓g. yellow-green (8.72)	55·00	25·00
		a. Pale blue-green	£225	£190
18		½g. orange (8.72)	65·00	15·00
19		1g. rose-carmine (7.72)	£130	10·00
		a. Bisected (on cover)	—	£100000
20		2g. blue (10.72)	38·00	11·50
21		2½g. chestnut (1.11.72)	£3250	£130
		a. Deep brown	£9000	£1000
22		5g. bistre (12.72)	50·00	50·00
		a. Imperf	—	£14000

(b) Issue for districts with 'gulden' currency

23	1	1k. yellow-green (10.72)	60·00	55·00
		a. Pale blue-green	£500	£900
24		2k. orange (12.72)	£800	£4000
25		3k. rose-carmine (9.72)	38·00	11·50
26		7k. blue (3.72)	55·00	£110
27		9k. chestnut (1.11.72)	£750	£700
		a. Deep brown	£2500	£800
28		18k. bistre (7.72)	65·00	£3500

Stamps with embossed eagle inverted are forgeries.

1874. Nos. 21 and 27 with large figures over central eagle in colour of stamps as Type **4**.

29	4	2½g. on 2½g. chestnut (8.1.74)	70·00	75·00
		a. '1' in fraction to left of '2'	£900	£900
30		9k. on 9k. chestnut (3.74)	£140	£750

No. 29a occurs on Row 12, stamp 4 and Row 15, stamp 1 in the sheet of 150 (10×15).
Dates quoted for Nos. 29 and 30 are those of earliest known use.

5 **6** **7**

(Typo, eagle in Type **6** embossed)

1875 (1 Jan)–79. 'PFENNIGE' with final 'E'. P 13½×14½.

31	5	3pf. blue-green	£100	8·75
		a. Yellow-green	£160	15·00
32		5pf. mauve	£160	6·25
33	6	10pf. carmine	70·00	3·25
		a. Bisected (on cover)	†	—
		b. Deep carmine-red	£160	5·75
34		20pf. blue	£900	50·00
		a. Ultramarine	£750	3·25
35		25pf. red-brown	£800	30·00
		a. Yellow-brown (1877)	£1500	£130
		b. Deep brown (1879)	£5000	£375
36		50pf. grey-black	£6500	£550
		a. Grey (1876)	£2750	19·00
37		50pf. grey green (1877)	£3250	23·00
		a. Deep olive-green	£6500	£250

A. Unused.
B. Pen-cancellation.
C. Postmarked.

1875–99. P 14½ ×13½.

			A	B	C
38	7	2m. dull violet (1875)	£3250	65·00	£550
		a. Purple (1880)	£5000	65·00	£650
		b. Dull rose (1884)	£2000	£650	21·00
		c. Mauve (1889)	£2500	£550	£100
		d. Deep claret (1890)	£130	—	10·00
		e. Red-lilac (1899)	£180	—	65·00

A. Early printings. Dull colours. Matt ink. Thick paper.
Yellowish crackled gum.

B. Later printings (from 1885). Brighter colours. Shiny, fugitive ink.
Thinner, white, smooth paper. Smooth, white gum.

1880–87. 'PFENNIG' without final 'E'. P 13½×14½.

39	5	3pf. dull green (A.) (2.80)	50·00	2·50
		a. Bright yellow-green (B.)	5·00	2·50
		b. Imperf (pair)		
40		5pf. purple (A.) (2.80)	21·00	2·50
		a. Bright mauve (B.)	3·75	2·50
41	6	10pf. rose (A.) (1.80)	40·00	2·50
		a. Imperf (pair)	£1100	
		b. Carmine (B.)	15·00	2·50
		ba. Imperf (pair)	£900	

www.robstine-stamps.com

A fantastic array of fine used stamps is now available!

- Fine used stamps of most areas of Germany
- Full stock list on the web site which is regularly updated
- More material on my second website www.robstineextra.com
- Many more countries available with lists on the site
- Orders processed fast

www.robstine-stamps.com
EXCELLENT QUALITY ✦ PROMPT SERVICE

---

50 years of experience, covering 100 years of the stamps of

GERMANY & AUSTRIA

Comprehensive stock of regular stamps 1850 to 1950, definitives offered singly, commemoratives in sets, all priced (cheaply!) for u/m, mint light hinge, fine used - we're THE philatelic source for English readers. Fill your gaps now!

Specialist material (lots!) with varieties, proofs, se tenants and booklets, postmarks, postal history, locals and stadtpost, revenues, inflation, Zeppelins and airmail, Sudetenland, concentration camp mail, feldpost, 1945 Soviet locals, 1948 currency reform, Austrian Empire, Austrian Levant cancels etc.

Essential reading!

John BAREFOOT

203 Clifford House (GG)
7-9 Clifford Street
YORK YO1 9RA
Tel 01904 426879

email : JBarefootL@AOL.com
websites :
www.stampsofgermany.com
www.stampsofaustria.com

GERMAN STATES
Baden to Wurttemberg, plus Stadtpost.

GERMANY 1872-1918
Definitives, Colonies, WWI Occupations.

GERMANY 1919-1932
Weimar period plus Plebiscites.

GERMANY III REICH
Defins, commemoratives, WWII Occupations.

GERMAN POSTWAR
Zones, West Germany, Berlin, DDR.

AUSTRIA EMPIRE
Classics to Franz Joseph, WWI, Levant.

AUSTRIA REPUBLIC
Interwar period plus postwar to 1956.

Which lists would you like to receive?

42		20pf. pale blue (A.) (1.80)	£150	5·75
		a. Bright blue (B.)	10·00	2·50
43		25pf. yellow-brown (A.) (9.80)	£450	44·00
		a. Bright red-brown (A.) (1883)	£1000	44·00
		b. Deep chestnut (B.)	30·00	8·50
44		50pf. pale grey-olive (A.) (7.80)	£350	2·50
		a. Dull olive-green (B.) (1886)	24·00	2·40
		b. Blackish olive (B.) (1887)	£200	23·00
		c. Bronze-green (B.)	£400	40·00
		d. Central projection of right frame-line missing	£160	55·00

No. 44d occurs in part of the printing on Row 1, stamp 2 of the upper pane of 50 in the sheet of 100.

Forgeries of the 10pf. and 50pf. were made to deceive the postal authorities.

Emperor Friedrich III
9 March – 15 June 1888

Emperor Wilhelm II
15 June 1888 – 9 November 1918

8  **9**

1889–1900. Typographed. P 13½ ×14½.

45	8	2pf. slate (29.3.00)	1·50	1·50
		a. 'REIGHSPOST'	95·00	£225
46		3pf. grey-brown (11.89)	5·00	2·30
		a. Imperf (pair)	£450	
		b. Deep brown	£1000	£110
		ba. Imperf (pair)	£2000	
		c. Orange-brown	25·00	8·75
		d. Bistre-brown	12·00	5·50
47		5pf. yellow-green (2.90)	£190	6·25
		a. Blue-green	4·50	2·30
		b. Cedilla on 'C' of 'REICHSPOST'	12·50	65·00
48	9	10pf. rose-carmine (10.89)	£400	5·75
		a. Imperf (pair)	£700	
		b. Carmine (1890)	6·25	2·50
		c. Stroke through 'T' of 'REICHSPOST'	£130	70·00
49		20pf. violet-blue (11.89)	12·50	2·30
		a. Dull blue	95·00	2·75
50		25pf. orange-yellow (3.90)	£300	12·50
		a. Imperf (pair)	£900	
		b. Orange	50·00	3·50
51		50pf. lake-brown (11.89)	£1900	£100
		a. Imperf (pair)	£1500	
		b. Chocolate (9.90)	50·00	2·30
45/51		Set of 7 (cheapest)	£120	15·00

There were several settings of No. 45 in which the incidence and position of No. 45a vary. It exists on positions 21, 26, 71 or 76, occurring once or twice in the same sheet although sheets also exist without the error.

The imperforate stamps listed above are from unfinished sheets sent to the Berlin Postal Museum or from trial sheets which found their way on to the market. There are, in addition, imperf specimens of the 3pf. in red-brown, the 25pf. in orange-yellow and the 50pf. in chocolate which are reprints made specially for the Berlin Postal Museum (*Prices for un. singles:* 3pf. £250; 25pf. £375; 50pf. £375).

Postal forgeries of the 10pf. exist.

10 'Germania'    **11** 'Germania'

12 General Post Office, Berlin    **13** Allegory of Union of North and South Germany (after Anton von Werner)

14 Unveiling of memorial to Wilhelm I in Berlin (after W. Pape)

15 25th Anniversary of German Empire Address by Wilhelm II (after W. Pape)

Two types of Type **11**:

(A)    (B)

A. 'REICHSPOST'. 12 mm. long, just over 1½ mm. high, *thick lettering* (1st printing).
B. 'REICHSPOST', 11½ mm. long, just over 1¼ mm. high, *thinner lettering*.

Two types of Type **14**:

3m. I    3m. II

3 MARKS. There are two types of this stamp, all the stamps in the second and third horizontal rows being Type II. In Type I the front of the Kaiser's cuirass is curved, making it appear that he is leaning back in the saddle, and traces of the right hand and reins can be seen between his body and the horse's mane. In Type II the cuirass slopes sharply back from its most forward point, giving the Kaiser a more erect appearance and the space between the cuirass and the horse's mane is empty.

Two types of Type **15**:

5M. I    5M. II

5 MARKS. Typo I. Figures '5' thick. Serifs of letters 'M' small and pointed.
Type II. Figures '5' thinner. Letters 'M' with pronounced serifs.
There is another type found only in the trial printing, perf 11½, in which the flags of the figures '5' are not cut into by the margins of the value tablets. There are 58 lines of shading instead of 64 between the value tablet and the Arms in the left border, and 55 instead of 63 at right. Numerous other minor differences.

(T **10/11** des Paul Waldraff, from portrait of the actress Anna Führing, typo. T **13/15** eng Prof. W. Roese, recess).

1899–1900. Inscr 'REICHSPOST'. P 14 (2pf. to 80pf.) or 14½ (1m. to 5m.).

52	10	2pf. grey (7.00)	1·40	1·00
		a. Imperf (pair)	£900	
53		3pf. brown (10.4.00)	1·40	1·80
		a. Imperf (pair)	£900	
54		5pf. green (4.1900)	2·50	1·50
55		10pf. carmine (1.1.00)	3·75	1·30
		a. Imperf (pair)	£150	
		b. Imperf double impression	£900	
56		20pf. blue (8.1.1900)	18·00	1·50
57	11	25pf. black and red/*yellow* (A.) (30.3.00)	£3250	£12000
		a. Type B	25·00	7·00
58		30pf. black and orange/*rose* (A.) (12.99).	£3250	£7500
		a. Type B	38·00	1·50
59		40pf. black and carmine (A.) (12.99)	£3250	£7500
		a. Type B	44·00	2·50
60		50pf. black and purple/*rose* (A.) (2.00)	£3250	£7500
		a. Type B	44·00	1·90
61		80pf. black and carmine/*carmine* (A.) (12.99)	£3250	£7500
		a. Type B	65·00	3·75
62	12	1m. carmine-red (1.1.00)	£180	5·00
		a. Dull lake	£500	
		b. Perf 11½	£3500	

GERMANY/ Germany (1871-1945)

63	13	2m. blue (1.6.00)	£180	12·50
		a. Perf 11½	£3500	
64	14	3m. violet-black (I) (1.8.00)	£190	75·00
		a. Perf 11½	£5500	
		b. Type II	£225	£100
65	15	5m. crimson and black (I) (15.12.00)	£2250	£3500
		a. Type II	£600	£650
		ab. Perf 11½	£3750	
		b. Hand-painted borders (I)	£600	£650
		c. As b. Type II	£1000	£1000
62s/65s Optd 'Specimen' Set of 4			£600	

Hand-painted borders. Stamps in which the central design did not 'register' accurately with the frame were touched up by hand in red and white (Types I and II) or in white only (Type I) and then issued.

3PF
(16)

1901 (13 Apr). No. 54 bisected vertically and each half handstamped with T **16**.

66	10	3pf. on half of 5pf. green (V.)	£17000	£13000

This provisional was issued on the German cruiser *Vineta* during a temporary shortage of 3pf. stamps.
One example with inverted surcharge is known.

17 **18**
19 **20**
21 **22**

Three types of 2m.

Type I: inscription in gothic lettering, sun-rays formed by straight lines.
Type II: inscriptions in Roman lettering, sun-rays formed by shading.
Type III: (prepared for use but not issued), inscriptions as Type II, sun-rays as Type I.

1902 (1 Apr–May). Inscr 'DEUTSCHES REICH'.

(a) Typo. No wmk. P 14

67	17	2pf. grey	2·50	1·00
68		3pf. brown	1·30	1·60
		a. Yellow-brown	£375	70·00
		b. 'DFUTSCHES' for 'DEUTSCHES'	16·00	70·00
69		5pf. green	6·25	1·60
		a. Dull blue-green	£450	15·00
70		10pf. carmine	15·00	1·60
71		20pf. blue	50·00	1·60
72		25pf. black and red/*yellow*	75·00	3·50
73		30pf. black and orange/*rose*	£100	1·00
74		40pf. black and carmine	£150	1·80
75		50pf. black and purple/*rose*	£110	1·90
76		80pf. black and carmine/*carmine*	£325	4·75

(b) Recess. No wmk

A. P 14½ or 14½×14 (26×17 perforation holes)

77A	18	1m. carmine-red	£450	4·50
78A	19	2m. blue (I)	£150	£160
79A	20	2m. blue (II) (5.02)	£200	8·25
		a. Typo III	£14000	
80A	21	3m. violet-black	£375	31·00
81A	22	5m. crimson and black	£450	31·00

B. P 13¾×(25×16 perforation holes)

77B	18	1m. carmine-red	£1000	44·00
79B	20	2m. blue (II) (5.02)	£1600	50·00
80B	21	3m. violet-black	£1100	44·00
81B	22	5m. crimson and black	£41000	£7500
67s/78As, 80As/81As Optd 'Specimen' Set of 14			£2000	

No. 68b occurs on positions 35 or 90 on some sheets.
All values from the 2pf. to the 5m. (except the 2m. Type I) exist imperforate from sheets handed over to the Berlin Postal Museum for exchange purposes (*Prices un. (pairs)* 2 to 80pf. (*set*) £325; 1m. £1500; 2m. (Type II); £1500; 3m. £1500; 5m. £1500).
Postal forgeries of the 10pf. exist.
The above series was the first issue for the whole of Germany except Bavaria.
See also Nos. 82/96, 97/104. 113/116, 140/152 and 196/7.

23 **24**

Kingdom of Prussia

1903 (1 Jan). OFFICIAL. Typo. P 14.

O82	O **23**	2pf. grey	1·90	7·50
O83		3pf. brown	1·90	7·50
O84		5pf. green	40	90
O85		10pf. carmine	40	90
O86		20pf. ultramarine	40	90
O87		25pf. black and red/*yellow*	1·30	2·75
O88		40pf. black and carmine	1·30	3·25
O89		50pf. black and purple/*rose*	1·50	3·25
O82/O89 Set of 8			8·25	24·00

Grand-Duchy of Baden

1905 (1 Jan). OFFICIAL. Typo. P 14.

O90	O **24**	2pf. grey	90·00	£130
O91		3pf. brown	10·00	18·00
O92		5pf. green	7·00	15·00
O93		10pf. carmine	1·30	3·50
O94		20pf. ultramarine	2·50	5·00
O95		25pf. black and red/*yellow*	50·00	90·00
O90/O95 Set of 6			£140	£225

There were 30 different States and Administrations which possessed the privilege of having their official correspondence franked. Hitherto this had been carried out without stamps. The above two sets were issued, each to be used for 12 months, in order to ascertain the amount to be credited to the revenue of the Post Office for the conveyance of official correspondence in the States named.

BOOKLET PANES. Those panes which have two or more values *se-tenant*, or include *se-tenant* labels, are listed under the lowest value stamp included in each pane. In the listings which include printed advertisements prices quoted are for the cheapest version of that particular pane. A checklist of booklets is given at the end of section II.
Most booklet panes were also available to collectors as uncut sheets. Many combinations not occurring in the normal panes can be found from such sheets but, with the exception of *tête-bêche* pairs of the same value, these are not listed.

23

1905–21. W **23** (Lozenges).

(a) Typo. P 14

82	17	2pf. grey (20.11.05)	2·75	4·50
83		3pf. brown (29.10.05)	3·75	2·50
		a. Dark brown (1915)	1·00	2·50
84		5pf. green (30.10.05)	2·75	2·50
		a. Deep green (1915)	1·00	2·50
		b. Double impression	£450	£3250
		c. Booklet pane. No. 84×4 plus two labels (St. Andrew's Cross) (1.11.10)		£1900
		ca. As c. but with advertising labels (2.11)		£2250
		d. Booklet pane. No. 84×5 plus label (1911)		£300
		e. Booklet pane. No. 84×2 plus four labels (7.12)		£1900
		f. Booklet pane. No. 84×2 (at top) and 85×4 (5.13)		£425
		fa. As f. but No. 84 at bottom (5.20)		50·00
		g. Booklet pane. Nos. 84×4 and 101×2 (2.18)		£600

GERMANY/Germany (1871–1945)

	h. Booklet pane. Nos. 84 and 85×5 (2.18)	£650		
	i. Booklet pane. Nos. 84×2 (on right) and 99×4 (11.18)	£550		
	ia. As i. but No. 84 on left (6.19)	£150		
	j. Booklet pane. Nos. 84×4 and 85×2 (12.19)	75·00		
85	10pf. rose-carmine (25.11.05)	18·00	2·50	
	a. *Bright carmine* (1911)	5·00	2·50	
	b. *Double impression*	£450	£3750	
	c. Booklet pane. No. 85×5 plus label (1911)	£1200		
	d. Booklet pane. No. 85×4 plus two labels (7.12)	£1800		
	e. Booklet pane. Nos. 85×2 (on right) and 101×4 (11.18)	£550		
	ea. As e. but No. 85 on left (6.19)	£100		
86	20pf. cobolt blue (1.06)	19·00	2·50	
	a. *Bisected* (*on cover*)	—	£4500	
	b. *Deep blue* (1907)	£325	8·75	
	c. *Prussian blue* (4.18)	19·00	5·75	
	d. *Violet-blue* (15.5.15)	1·90	2·50	
	da. *Imperf* (*pair*)	£13000	£7500	
87	25pf. black and red/*yellow* (1.06)	65·00	4·50	
88	30pf. black and orange/*buff* (23.12.05)	55·00	2·75	
	a. *Black and orange/cream* (1915)	1·30	2·50	
89	40pf. jet black and deep carmine (1.06)	65·00	3·50	
	a. *Black and carmine* (1915)	2·20	2·50	
90	50pf. black and purple/*buff* (1.06)	£100	3·50	
	a. *Black and purple/cream* (1915)	1·30	2·50	
91	60pf. rose-purple (1.10.11)	£325	23·00	
	a. *Deep purple* (1915)	3·25	2·50	
92	80pf. black and lake/*carmine* (1.06)	31·00	5·00	
	a. *Black and bright carmine/carmine* (1915)	1·90	3·25	

Forgeries of the 5pf. and 10pf. were made to deceive the postal authorities. The 10pf. (and the 15pf., No. 101) were also forged in England during the 1914–18 war for use by British intelligence agents in Germany.

(b) Recess
A. P 14½×14 (26×17 perforation holes)

93A	18	1m. carmine-red (9.12.05)	£110	3·75
		a. *Bright rose-red*	£110	3·75
94A	20	2m. deep blue (II) (25.2.06)	£110	5·00
95A	21	3m. violet-black (21.3.11)	90·00	44·00
96A	22	5m. carmine and black (24.1.06)	75·00	35·00

B. P 14½×14 (25×17 perforation holes) (1916–17)

93B	18	1m. carmine-red	4·50	3·75
		a. *Bright rose-red*	4·50	3·75
94B	20	2m. deep blue (II)	8·75	8·25
		a. *Bright blue*	90·00	50·00
95B	21	3m. violet-black	5·00	7·50
		a. *Wmk Circles* (1921)	£3250	£6500
		b. *Slate-purple*	19·00	44·00
96B	22	5m. carmine and black	5·00	8·25
		a. *Frame inverted*	£75000	£110000

No. 95Ba was printed in error on paper used for insurance stamps.

Pre-war printings have clear impressions and smooth white gum. Printings from 1915 onwards are less clear, on paper with indistinct watermark and often with yellowish or brownish gum.

24 Unshaded background

1916 (1 Aug)–**20**. Typo. W **23** (Lozenges). P 14.

97	24	2pf. yellowish grey (1.10.18)	50	6·25
98		2½pf. grey	40	3·25
		a. *Coil pair. Nos. 98 and 99*	20·00	35·00
		b. *Coil pair. Nos. 98 and 99a*	7·50	15·00
99		7½pf. orange-yellow	5·75	3·75
		a. *Orange* (1918)	90	3·75
		b. Booklet pane. Nos. 99×2 and 100×4 (12.16)	£750	
		c. Booklet pane. Nos. 99×2 and 101×4 (13.6.17)	£800	
		d. Booklet pane. Nos. 99×4 and 101×2 (2.18)	£600	
100		15pf. yellow-brown	5·00	3·75
101		15pf. slate-violet (5.17)	65	3·75
102		15pf. brown-purple (1.20)	40	3·25
		a. *Imperf* (*pair*)	£110	
		b. Booklet pane. Nos. 102×2 and 86×4 (5.20)	38·00	
103		35pf. red-brown (6.2.19)	50	3·75
104	**17**	75pf. black and blue-green (20.2.19)	50	3·75
97/104		Set of 8 (*cheapest*)	8·00	28·00

Nos. 97/98 exist in war-time and peace-time printings, the latter distinguishable by its smooth white gum.

Forgeries of No. 101 exist (see note after No. 92a).

THE WEIMAR REPUBLIC
9 November 1918–30 January 1933

USED STAMPS. From No. 105 to No. 351 faked postmarks are found on genuine stamps. It is recommended that higher-priced used examples should be expertised and our prices from £5 are for such items: unexpertised examples are generally worth the same as unused.

25 5 Pf. für Kriegs=beschädigte

1919 (1 May). War Wounded Fund. Surch with T **25**.

105	**17**	10 +5pf. carmine (No. 85)	1·00	7·25
106	**24**	15 +5pf. slate-violet (No. 101)	1·00	7·75

26 **27** **28**

(Designs symbolic of the new order. T **26** by H. Frank, T **27** by E. Böhm, T **28** by G. A. Mathey. Typo)

1919 (1 July)–**20**. National Assembly at Weimar. P 13×13½.

107	**26**	10pf. carmine	40	2·50
		a. *Bisected* (*on cover*)		2·50
108	**27**	15pf. blue and chocolate	40	2·50
109	**28**	25pf. scarlet and green	40	2·50
		a. '1019' for '1919'	£170	£500
110		30pf. scarlet and purple (2.20)	40	4·00
		a. '1019' for '1919'	80·00	£250
107/110		Set of 4	1·40	10·50

No. 109a occurs on positions 7, 23, 5, 8 and 73 and No. 110a on positions 99 and 100, both in part of the printing only.

29   **30** LVG Schneider Biplane

(T **29** des G. A. Mathey. Typo)

1919 (Oct). AIR. P 14½×14.

111	**29**	10pf. orange	40	4·50
112	**30**	40pf. green	40	5·25
		a. *Imperf* (*ungummed pair*)	£6500	

1920. T **18** and **20** re-drawn. Offset printing. W **23** (Lozenges). P 14½×14.

113	**18**	1m. carmine-red (5.20)	5·75	4·00
		a. *Double impression*	£200	£1000
		b. *Bright rose-carmine*	60·00	44·00
114		1m.25 green (3.20)	5·75	3·00
		a. *Double impression*	£1600	
		b. *Deep green*	5·75	3·00
115		1m.50 yellow-brown (3.20)	80	3·00
		a. *Double impression*	£170	£1200
		b. *Brown*	26·00	33·00
116	**20**	2m.50 lilac-rose (3.20)	17·00	16·00
		a. *Double impression*	£170	£1200
		b. *Claret*	80	4·00
		c. *Purple*	2·50	22·00

There are numerous differences in the designs of the re-drawn types. In the 1m., the only value which might be confused with previous issues, there is one pedestrian behind the carriage in the right foreground instead of three in front of the carriage.

GERMANY/ Germany (1871-1945)

Deutsches Reich

O 31   O 32   (O 33)

1920 (1 Apr). OFFICIAL. T O **31**, O **32** and similar types. differing for each value. With figures '21' for use in all areas outside Prussia. Typo. W **23** (Lozenges). P 14.

O117	5pf. green	40	5·25
O118	10pf. carmine	1·30	2·50
O119	15pf. chocolate	25	4·00
	a. Imperf (pair)		£1200
O120	20pf. violet-blue	25	3·25
	a. Prussian blue		£1200
O121	30pf. orange/rose	25	2·50
O122	50pf. violet/rose	50	2·50
O123	1m. red/rose	14·50	6·50
O117/O123 Set of 7		16·00	24·00

1920 (1 Apr)–**22**. OFFICIAL. T O **31**, O **32** and similar types but without figures '21'. Typo. W **23** (Lozenges). P 14.

O124	5pf. green	1·60	23·00
O125	10pf. carmine	25	2·75
O126	10pf. orange (3.21)	1·00	£800
O127	15pf. brown-purple	25	4·00
	a. Imperf (pair)	£2500	£2500
O128	20pf. violet-blue	25	3·25
O129	30pf. orange/rose	25	3·25
O130	40pf. carmine (10.20)	25	3·25
O131	50pf. violet/rose	25	3·25
O132	60pf. purple-brown (5.21)	50	2·50
O133	1m. red/rose	25	3·25
O134	1m.25 indigo/yellow (9.20)	25	6·50
O135	2m. slate-blue (9.20)	7·25	5·25
	a. Wmk Mesh (2.22)	25	2·50
	ab. Ditto. Imperf (pair)	£350	
O136	5m. brown/yellow (9.20)	25	5·25
	a. Red-brown/yellow	2·00	5·25
O124/O136 Set of 12 (*Exc.* O126) (*cheapest*)		4·25	55·00

This issue was originally for Prussian areas only but from 1 July 1920 it was available for all areas.

No. O126 exists punctured 'FM' (=Finanz Ministerium) (*Price:* £6.50 un, £1200 used).

1920 (1 Apr). OFFICIAL. For use in Bavaria only Official stamps of Bavaria optd as T O **33** (opt spaced 8 *mm.* on mark values).

O137	O **31**	5pf. yellow-green	25	5·25
		a. Imperf (pair)	£160	
O138		10pf. orange	25	3·00
O139		15pf. carmine-red	25	3·25
O140		20pf. purple	25	2·50
		a. Pair, one with opt omitted	33·00	
O141		30pf. Prussian blue	25	2·50
		a. Opt double	50·00	£650
O142		40pf. bistre-brown	25	2·50
O143	O **32**	50pf. scarlet	25	3·25
		a. Opt inverted	£1400	£4500
		b. Imperf (pair)	£160	
O144		60pf. blue-green	25	2·50
O145		70pf. dull violet	3·25	4·50
		a. Opt double	£2000	
O146		75pf. carmine	50	2·30
		a. Opt double		
O147		80pf. dull blue	25	2·30
O148		90pf. olive-green	2·50	5·75
O149	O **33**	1m. deep brown	25	3·25
		a. Imperf (pair)	£160	
O150		1¼m. green	25	3·25
O151		1½m. vermilion	25	3·25
O152		2½m. dull blue	25	3·25
		a. Opt inverted	£200	£2000
		b. Imperf (pair)	£180	£3000
O153		3m. lake	25	3·25
O154		5m. olive-black	14·50	46·00
O137/O154 Set of 18			22·00	90·00

1920 (1 Apr). OFFICIAL. For use in Württemberg only. Municipal Service stamps of Württemberg, 1906–19. optd with T O**33**.

O155	M **5**	5pf. green	6·50	17·00
O156		10pf. rose	4·00	7·75
O157		15pf. violet	4·00	8·50
O158		20pf. blue	6·50	14·50
		a. Wmk Circles	7·75	14·50
O159		50pf. maroon	10·50	33·00
O155/O159 Set of 5			28·00	75·00

All values excluding O158a exist imperforate *Price* £120.
O158a imperforate *Price* £130.

1920 (1 Apr). OFFICIAL. For use in Württemberg only. Official Stamps of Württemberg, 1906–19, optd with T O **33**.

O160	O **5**	5pf. green	4·00	6·50
O161		10pf. rose	2·50	5·25
O162		15pf. purple	2·50	5·25
O163		20pf. ultramarine	2·50	2·50
		a. Wmk Circles	£200	£500
O164		30pf. black and orange	2·50	6·50
O165		40pf. black and carmine	2·50	5·25
O166		50pf. deep maroon	2·50	6·50
O167		1m. black and grey-green	4·00	13·00
O160/O167 Set of 8			21·00	46·00

All values excluding O163a exist imperforate *Price* £90.
O163a imperforate *Price* £250.

Issues for all Germany, including Bavaria and Württemberg

Deutsches Reich (31)   Deutsches Reich (32)

Deutsches Reich (33)

1920 (6 Apr)–**21**. T **26** to **30** of Bavaria optd in Munich.

117	**31**	5pf. bright green	25	2·50
		a. Figure '5' omitted	£450	£2000
		b. Opt double	26·00	£2000
		c. Imperf (pair)	90·00	£1200
		d. Opt inverted	50·00	
		e. Pair, one with opt omitted	90·00	£325
118		10pf. orange	25	2·50
		a. Opt inverted	50·00	£1000
		b. Opt double	26·00	
		c. Imperf (pair)	90·00	£1200
		d. Pair, one with opt omitted	90·00	£325
119		15pf. carmine	25	2·50
		a. Opt inverted	50·00	
		b. Opt double	26·00	£850
		c. Pair, one with opt omitted	90·00	£325
120		20pf. purple (No. 260)	25	2·50
		a. 'BAYEFN' for 'BAYERN'	2·50	16·00
		b. Opt inverted	50·00	£1300
		c. Opt double	26·00	
		d. Opt treble		
		e. Imperf (pair)	£100	
		f. Pair, one with opt omitted	65·00	£250
121		30pf. deep blue	25	2·50
		a. Opt inverted	£100	£1200
		b. Opt inverted	50·00	
		c. Pair, one with opt omitted	65·00	£250
122		40pf. bistre-brown	25	2·50
		a. Opt inverted	50·00	£1300
		b. Imperf (pair)	£100	
123		50pf. vermilion	25	4·00
		a. Pair, one with opt omitted	£130	£400
124		60pf. blue-green	25	2·30
125		75pf. claret	80	8·50
		a. Opt inverted	50·00	
126		80pf. deep blue (6.20)	65	4·50
		a. Imperf (pair)	£100	
127	**32**	1m. carmine and grey	80	4·50
		a. Opt inverted	90·00	
		b. Imperf (pair)	£120	£3000
128		1¼m. blue and bistre	80	4·50
		a. 'LAVARIAE' for 'BAVARIAE'	13·00	65·00
		b. Diagonal stroke of '¼' in '1¼' missing	33·00	£180
		c. Imperf (pair)	£120	
129		1½m. blue-green and grey	80	5·75
		a. Imperf (pair)	£120	
130		2m. violet and bistre (6.20)	1·30	6·50
		a. Imperf (pair)	£120	
		b. Opt omitted		
131		2½m. black and grey (Typo) (R.) (20.4.20)	25	5·25
		a. Grey background omitted	£250	£2250
		b. Imperf (pair)	£120	
131c		2½m. black and grey (Litho) (R.) (4.21)*	1·60	£160
		ca. Imperf (pair)	£120	
132	**33**	3m. pale blue	5·25	16·00
		a. Straight top to 'R' in 'Reich'	47·00	£130
		b. Five flowers on spray in woman's hand	65·00	£225
133		4m. dull red (6.20)	5·25	17·00
		a. Five flowers on spray in woman's hand	80·00	£250
		b. Straight top to 'R' in 'Reich'	70·00	£350
		c. Imperf (pair)	£200	

GERMANY / Germany (1871-1945)

	d. Opt omitted			£650
134	5m. orange-yellow		5·25	16·00
	a. Straight top to 'R' in 'Reich'		50·00	£160
	b. Imperf (pair)			£200
135	10m. green (5.20)		8·50	26·00
	a. Straight top to 'R' in 'Reich'		£180	£1200
	b. Imperf (pair)			£200
	ba. Opt double			
136	20m. black (5.20)		9·75	21·00
	a. Straight top to 'R' in 'Reich'		70·00	£250

*The 2½m. was printed both by typography and by lithography. In the latter, the fine lines in the shield below the Madonna are not so clear as in the former.

On the 20m. the word 'BAYERN' was partially erased from the plate before the stamps were overprinted.

The straight top to 'R' variety occurs on position 3 for the 3, 4, 10m., positions 3 and 15 for the 5m. and position 15 for the 20m. No. 117a occurs on position 4 and No. 133a on position 7.

Printings were made both from the original plates and from new plates; in the latter some of the listed plate errors were corrected.

On the original plates No. 120a occurs on positions 4, 9, 54 and 59, but later printings show either position 4 or 4, 9 and 54 corrected.

✱ 1,25 m. ✱
(34)

1920 (June). T **18** and **20** recess-printed in new colours and surch as T **34**. W **23** (Lozenges). P 14½×14.

137	**18**	1,25m. on 1m. green	65	10·50
138		1,50m. on 1m. brown	65	11·50
139	**20**	2,50m. on 2m. rosy purple	14·50	£325
		a. Brown-purple	16·00	£325
137/139	Set of 3		14·00	£300

PLATE I of the values indicated below was the old double plate, printing the centre and inscriptions at one operation and the frame at another. Stamps thus printed can be distinguished by the fact that the centre and inscriptions are rarely exactly centred in relation to the frame, and the cross on the crown of Germania is almost invisible. This plate was used for coil stamps only.

PLATE II is the new single plate, printing the whole stamp at one operation, so that the centre and inscription are always accurately placed. The cross on the crown is clearer.

1920 (Sept)–**21**. New colours and values and changes of type. W **23** (Lozenges). P 14.

140	**17**	5pf. brown	40	3·25
		a. Red-brown	1·80	4·50
		b. Deep brown	2·50	10·50
141		10pf. orange	25	2·50
		a. Orange-yellow	25	2·50
		b. Tête-bêche (pair)	3·00	11·50
		c. Bisected (on cover)		
		d. Booklet pane. Nos. 141×4 and 143×2 (11.20)	14·50	
142		20pf. green	40	4·00
		a. Bright green	2·00	5·25
		b. Imperf (pair)	—	£2000
143		30pf. dull blue (Pl. I)	4·50	50·00
		a. Plate II	25	2·50
		aa. Plate II, imperf (pair)	£800	£2500
		b. Tête-bêche (pair) (Pl. II)	6·25	21·00
		c. Booklet pane. Nos. 143a×2 and 144×4 (11.20)	14·50	
144		40pf. carmine (Pl. I)	7·25	50·00
		a. Plate II	25	3·25
		aa. Plate II, imperf (pair)	£500	£2000
		b. Tête-bêche (pair) (Pl. II)	3·25	11·50
		c. Booklet pane. Nos. 144a×2 and 146×4 (1921)	20·00	
145		50pf. purple (Pl. I) (12.20)	5·25	50·00
		a. Plate II	1·00	4·00
146		60pf. olive-green	25	2·50
		a. Tête-bêche (pair)	4·75	33·00
147		75pf. purple (Pl. I) (12.20) (shades)	4·00	70·00
		a. Purple (Pl. II) (shades)	1·00	3·25
		b. Claret (Pl. II) (1921)	£200	£170
148		80pf. ultramarine (Pl. 11) (10.20)	2·00	90·00
		a. Plate II	40	4·00
		b. Plate II, imperf (pair)	£600	
149		1m. green and violet (12.20)	25	4·00
		a. Imperf (pair)	£225	
150		1¼m. purple and vermilion (12.20)	25	3·25
		a. Fiscal paper. W **46**	£800	£1700
151		2m. blue and lake (12.20)	1·00	3·50
		a. Fiscal paper. W **46**	—	£60000
152		4m. carmine and black (12.20)	25	4·00
140/152	Set of 13 (cheapest)		5·25	39·00

The 60pf. without watermark and perf 13 is a postal forgery.

35	**36** Blacksmiths	**37** Miners
38 Reapers	**39** Posthorn	
40	**41** Ploughman	

(Des W. Geiger (T **35**), P. Neu (T **36**/8), W. Szeztokat (T **39**), H. Haas (T **40**) or Scharff (T **41**). Typo (T **35**/9), recess (T **41**) or recess; background litho (T **39**))

1921 (May–Dec). W **23** (Lozenges). P 14.

153	**35**	5pf. claret	25	3·25
154		10pf. olive-green	25	3·25
		a. Imperf (pair)		
		b. Tête-bêche (pair)	8·75	60·00
		c. Booklet pane. Nos. 154×5 and 157	20·00	
155		15pf. turquoise-blue (8.21)	25	2·50
156		25pf. brown (8.21)	25	2·50
157		30pf. blue-green	25	2·50
		a. Tête-bêche (pair)	8·50	60·00
		b. Booklet pane. Nos. 157×4 and 144a×2	20·00	
158		40pf. orange-vermilion (8.21)	25	2·50
159		50pf. purple (8.21)	50	2·50
160	**36**	60pf. claret	25	2·50
161		80pf. carmine	25	9·00
162	**37**	100pf. green	50	3·25
163		120pf. ultramarine	25	2·50
164	**38**	150pf. orange	40	3·25
165		160pf. myrtle-green	25	14·50
166	**39**	2m. violet and rose (12.21)	65	5·75
167		3m. scarlet and yellow (29.12)	65	26·00
168		4m. green and yellow-green (12.21)	40	5·75
169	**40**	5m. orange-red (9.21)	65	4·00
170		10m. carmine (9.21)	80	5·25
171	**41**	20m. indigo and green (9.21)	4·00	4·50
		a. Printed on both sides		
		b. Green background inverted	£325	£1700
153/171	Set of 19		10·00	95·00

See also Nos. 176/195, 204/217, 230/246 and 249/256.

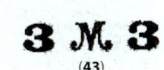

✱ ✱
1,60 M   3 M 3
(42)   (43)

1921 (Aug). T **17** surch.

172	**42**	1m.60 on 5pf. brown	25	4·00
		a. Deep brown	£110	£700
173	**43**	3m. on 1¼m. purple and vermilion	25	4·50
174	**42**	5m. on 75pf. purple (G.)	40	4·00
175	**43**	10m. on 75pf. purple	65	4·00
172/175	Set of 4		1·40	15·00

These surcharges may be found in dull or shiny ink.

45 (Vertical)    **46**

29

GERMANY/ Germany (1871-1945)

1921 (Dec)–**22**. W **45** (Mesh). P 14.

176	35	5pf. claret (5.22)	1·30	£350
177		10pf. olive-green (2.22)	11·50	£300
178		15pf. turquoise-blue (5.22)	80	£375
179		25pf. brown (3.22)	25	5·25
180		30pf. blue-green (5.22)	1·30	£550
181		40pf. orange (1.22)	25	6·50
182		50pf. purple (1.22)	40	2·50
183	36	60pf. claret (1.22)	25	34·00
184	35	75pf. violet-blue (8.22)	25	4·75
185	36	80pf. carmine (3.22)	65	£100
186	37	100pf. green (1.22)	25	2·50
		a. Imperf (pair)	£200	£5000
187		120pf. violet-blue (5.22)	1·20	£180
188	38	150pf. orange (3.22)	25	2·50
		a. Imperf (pair)	£130	
189		160pf. myrtle green (5.22)	1·20	£275
190	39	2m. violet and rose (1.22)	25	2·50
191		3m. scarlet and yellow (29.12.21)	25	2·50
		a. Imperf (pair)	£130	£1300
192		4m. green and yellow-green (1.22)	25	2·50
193	40	5m. orange-red (2.22)	50	3·25
		a. Imperf (pair)	£350	£8000
194		10m. carmine (3.22)	50	4·00
195	41	20m. indigo and green (5.22)	25	5·25
		a. Green background inverted	50·00	£1200
		b. Imperf (pair)	£350	£7500
176/195 Set of 20			20·00	£2000

1922 (Mar). W **45** (Mesh). P 14.

196	17	75pf. claret	65	4·50
197		1¼m. purple and vermilion	40	3·00

47 Arms of Munich

(Des Prof. Ehmcke. Typo)

1922 (2 Apr). Munich Exhibition. P 13×13½.

(a) Wmk Mesh, T **45**

198	47	1¼m. lake	50	3·25
199		2m. violet	40	3·25
200		3m. vermilion	40	3·25
201		4m. ultramarine	40	3·25

(b) Wmk Lozenges, T **23** *(horiz)*

202	47	10m. brown/*flesh*	1·00	4·50
203		20m. carmine/*rose* (ribbed gum)	6·50	21·00
		a. Smooth gum	21·00	90·00
198/203 Set of 6			8·25	35·00

The colours of stamps of this issue run very quickly in water.

I (Flat) II (Rotary) I (Flat) II (Rotary)

1922–23. New colours and values. Wmk Mesh, T **45**. P 14.

204	39	2m. purple (5.22)	40	2·50
		a. Imperf (pair)	£250	
205		3m. vermilion (5.22)	40	2·50
206		4m. deep green (5.22)	40	2·50
		a. Imperf (pair)	£180	
207		5m. orange and yellow (3.6.22)	40	3·75
		a. Imperf (pair)	£500	
208		5m. orange (10.22)	40	2·50
		a. Imperf (pair)	£200	
209		6m. blue (I) (10.22)	40	2·50
		a. Rotary printing (II)	65	3·25
		b. Imperf (pair)	£200	
210		8m. olive-green (I) (11.22)	40	2·50
		a. Rotary printing (II)	65	47·00
211		10m. carmine and rose (6.22)	40	2·50
		a. Background omitted	80·00	£1700
212		20m. violet and red (10.22)	65	2·50
213		20m. violet (1.23)	40	2·50
214		30m. brown and yellow (10.22)	25	2·50
215		30m. chocolate (2.23)	40	13·00
216		40m. apple-green (1.23)	40	4·00
217		50m. myrtle-green and purple (12.22)	40	3·00
		a. W **46** (3.3.23)	4·00	£1400
204/217 Set of 14			5·25	44·00

The following were printed from flat and rotary plates: 5m. (No. 208). 6m., 8m., 20m. (No. 212), 30m. (No. 214), 40m. and 50m. The printings can be distinguished by small differences in the shape of the figures. As only the 6 and 8m. are easily distinguishable, we only list those values separately.

48   49

1922 (July)–**23**. AIR.

(a) Wmk Mesh, T **45** *(vert). P 14*

218	48	25pf. brown	80	31·00
219		40pf. orange	65	42·00
220		50pf. purple	40	14·50
221		60pf. carmine	90	34·00
222		80pf. pale emerald	65	34·00

(b) Background in second colour. W **45** *(horiz). P 13×13½*

223	49	1m. deep green and pale green	25	6·50
224		2m. lake and grey	25	6·50
225		3m. violet-blue and grey	40	7·75
		a. Background omitted	£250	£1000
226		5m. red-orange and violet	25	6·50
227		10m. purple and rose (2.23)	25	16·00
228		25m. brown and yellow (2.23)	25	14·50
229		100m. olive-green and rose (4.23)	25	11·50
218/229 Set of 12			4·75	£200

See also Nos. 269/273 and 358/364.

1922–23. Offset printing. P 14½×14.

(a) Wmk Lozenges, T **23**

230	40	100m. purple/*buff* (10.22)	40	2·30
231		200m. carmine/*buff* (11.22)	25	2·30
232		300m. green/*buff* (11.22)	25	2·30
233		400m. yellow-brown/*buff* (12.22)	90	4·00
234		500m. orange/*buff* (12.22)	25	2·30
230/234 Set of 5			1·80	12·00

(b) Wmk Mesh, T **45**

235	40	50m. slate-black (10.22)	40	2·50
		a. 'c' for 'e' in 'Reich'	4·00	16·00
236		100m. purple/*buff* (2.23)	25	2·30
237		200m. carmine/*buff* (2.23)	40	3·25
238		300m. green/*buff* (2.23)	25	2·30
239		400m. yellow-brown/*buff* (1.23)	25	2·30
240		500m. orange/*buff* (3.22)	25	2·30
241		1,000m. grey (*shades*) (1.23)	25	2·30
242		2,000m. blue (*shades*) (1.23)	50	3·25
		a. Imperf (pair)		
243		3,000m. brown (*shades*) (2.23)	40	2·50
244		4,000m. violet (7.23)	25	2·50
		a. Imperf (pair)	£130	£650
245		5,000m. grey-green (8.23)	50	2·50
		a. Imperf (pair)	£180	£800
246		100,000m. scarlet (9.23)	25	2·30
		a. Imperf (pair)	£180	£800
235/246 Set of 12			3·50	27·00

No. 235a occurs on position 2 of some sheets.

O 48   O 49   O 50

1922 (Nov)–**23**. OFFICIAL. Typo. P 14.

(a) Wmk Lozenges, T **23**

O247	O **49**	3m. brown/*carmine*	25	2·50
O248	O **50**	10m. green/*carmine*	25	2·50

(b) Wmk Mesh, T **45**

O249	O **48**	75pf. blue	40	13·00
O250	O **50**	10m. green/*carmine* (2.23)	40	16·00
O251		20m. blue/*carmine* (1.23)	25	2·50
O252		50m. violet/*carmine* (1.23)	25	2·50
		a. Imperf (pair)	£350	
O253		100m. carmine/*carmine* (3.23)	25	2·50
		a. Imperf (pair)	£400	£2500
O247/O253 Set of 7			1·80	37·00

30

GERMANY/Germany (1871-1945)

50 Allegory of Charity

51 Miners

(Des J. V. Cissarz. Litho)

1922 (11 Dec). Fund for the Old and for Children. Premium in second colour. W **45** (Mesh). P 14.
247	50	6m. +4m. blue and bistre	25	39·00
248		12m. +8m. red and lilac	25	39·00

1922–23. Typo. W **45** (Mesh). P 14.
249	51	5m. orange (24.2.23)	25	21·00
250	38	10m. bright blue (12.22)	25	2·50
251		12m. scarlet (12.22)	25	2·50
252	51	4m. claret (4.23)	25	2·50
		a. Wmk horizontal	1·30	£100
253	38	25m. olive-bistre (1.23)	25	2·50
254	51	30m. olive-green (6.23)	25	4·00
		a. Olive-black	1·30	65·00
255	38	40m. blue-green (3.23)	40	2·50
		a. Yellow-green	80	4·50
256	51	50m. turquoise-blue (3.23)	65	£200
249/256 Set of 8			2·30	£225

No. 256 was only issued in coils. Blocks and horizontal pairs therefore do not exist.

(52) (53)

1923 (19 Feb). Relief Fund for Sufferers in the Rhine and Ruhr Occupation Districts. Surch as T **52** or with T **53** (No. 259).
257	51	5 +100m. orange	25	16·00
		a. No hyphens after 'Ruhr' (pos. 51)	46·00	£600
258	38	25 +500m. olive-bistre	40	39·00
		a. Surch inverted	£130	
259	41	20 +1000m. indigo and green (No. 195)	3·50	£140
		a. Green background inverted	£650	£2750
		b. Surch inverted	£1700	£6500
257/259 Set of 3			3·75	£180

54

55 Wartburg Castle

56 Cologne Cathedral

1923. Typo. W **45** (Mesh). P 14.
260	54	100m. deep reddish purple (3.23)	40	2·50
261		100m. purple (5.23)	40	2·50
262		200m. carmine (3.23)	25	2·50
263		300m. green (4.23)	25	2·50
264		400m. brown (4.23)	25	9·75
265		500m. orange-red (4.23)	25	10·50
266		1000m. grey (8.23)	25	2·50
260/266 Set of 7			1·80	29·00

No. 261 is a definitely ordered colour change, not a shade.

1923. Recess. W **45** (Mesh). P 14.
267	55	5,000m. indigo (5.23)	50	5·25
		a. Imperf (pair)	£1000	£4000
268	56	10,000m. grey-olive (7.23)	50	6·50

1923 (May–June). AIR. W **45** (Mesh). P 13×13½.
269	49	5m. orange-red	25	70·00
270		10m. purple	25	17·00
271		25m. deep brown	25	17·50
272		100m. olive-green	25	20·00
273		200m. violet-blue (6.23)	25	60·00
		a. Imperf (pair)		£200
269/273 Set of 5			1·10	£170

(O **57**)

1923 (May). OFFICIAL. Contemporary postage stamps optd with Type O **57**.
O274	51	20m. claret	50	13·00
		a. Wmk horizontal	65	£250
O275		30m. olive-green	25	60·00
O276	38	40m. green	50	5·25
O277	54	200m. carmine	25	2·50
O278		300m. green	25	2·50
O279		400m. brown	25	2·50
O280		500m. orange-red	25	2·50
O274/O280 Set of 7			2·00	80·00

Inflation Provisionals

The rapid fall in the value of the mark during the second half of 1923 necessitated such frequent changes of postal rates that it was found impossible to keep pace with them by issuing stamps in definitive designs. The authorities therefore had recourse to surcharging, not only in Berlin but also at other places. These local printings can be distinguished in complete sheets by variations in the marginal inscriptions, etc., and in single specimens, in some cases, by minor variations in the surcharge, but their differentiation is outside the scope of a general catalogue.

(57) (58)

(59) (60)

1923 (24 Aug–Oct). Previous types in old or new colours and values surch as T **57** to **60** (T **35** surch as T **57**; T **38** as T **58**; T **54**, Nos. 279, 282–5 and 288 as T **59**, remainder as T **60**; T **61** as T **60**). Wmk Mesh, T **45**.

T =Tausend (thousand). M=Million(en)

(a) P 14
274	35	5T. on 40pf. orange (3.9)	15	2·75
275		8T. on 30pf. blue-green (3.9)	39·00	£11000
		a. Wmk lozenges	15	2·50
		aa. Wmk lozenges. '8' inverted	36·00	£600
276	38	15T. on 40m. green (3.9)	40	3·25
277		20T. on 12m. scarlet (25.8)	15	2·50
278		20T. on 25m. olive-bistre	15	4·00
279	54	20T. on 200m. carmine	40	4·00
		a. Surch 17 instead of 16 mm high	65	4·50
		b. Surch inverted	£100	£1300
280	38	25T. on 25m. olive-bistre (15.9)	15	23·00
281		30T. on 10m. bright blue (3.9)	15	2·50
		a. Surch inverted	£120	
282	54	30T. on 200m. pale blue (B.) (7.9)	15	2·50
		b. Surch omitted	£200	
283		75T. on 300m. yellow-green (17.9)	15	23·00
		a. Imperf (pair)	£160	
284		75T. on 400m. yellow-green (1.9)	40	2·50
285		75T. on 1000m. yellow-green (1.9)	40	3·25
		a. Surch 16½ instead of 15½ mm high	40	4·50
		b. Surch omitted	£200	
286	54	100T. on 100m. purple (20.9)	40	4·00
		a. Surch inverted	30·00	£1000
		b. Surch double	65·00	£800
		c. Deep purple	50	£180
		ca. Surch double	£275	£3250

31

GERMANY / Germany (1871-1945)

287		100T. on 400m. blue-green (G.) (20.9)	15	2·50
		a. Imperf (pair)	£140	£2500
		b. Surch double	£130	
		c. Surch omitted	£200	
288		125T. on 1000m. rose-pink (20.9)	25	3·25
		a. Salmon	1·30	90·00
289		250T. on 200m. carmine (22.9)	15	9·00
		a. Surch inverted	60·00	
		b. Surch double	90·00	
290		250T. on 300m. green (20.9)	15	29·00
		a. Surch inverted	60·00	
291		250T. on 400m. brown (22.9)	15	33·00
		a. Surch inverted	46·00	
292		250T. on 500m. pink (20.9)	15	2·50
		a. Imperf (pair)	£180	£3000
293		250T. on 500m. orange-red (20.9)	15	33·00
		a. Surch inverted	65·00	
		b. Surch double	50·00	£1700
294	35	800T. on 5pf. apple-green (G.) (1.10)	25	7·25
		a. Imperf (pair)	90·00	£400
295		800T. on 10pf. apple-green (G.) (1.10)	25	8·50
296	54	800T. on 200m. carmine 11.10)	25	£130
		a. Surch inverted	65·00	
		b. Surch double	£130	£1700
297		800T. on 300m. yellow-green (G.) (1.10)	25	8·50
298		800T. on 400m. yellow-green (G.) (1.10)	25	6·50
299		800T. on 400m. deep brown (1.10)	25	21·00
		a. Surch inverted	70·00	
		b. Surch double	£130	
300		800T. on 500m. yellow-green (G.) (1.10)	25	£2500
301		800T. on 1000m. yellow-green (G.) (11.10)	40	2·50
302		2M. on 200m. rose-pink (1.10)	25	3·75
		a. Rose-red	40	2·50
		b. Wmk horizontal	5·25	£600
303		2M. on 300m. green (1.10)	25	3·75
		a. Surch inverted	70·00	
		b. Surch double	£130	
304		2M. on 500m. dull rose (9.10)	25	10·50
305	61	2M. on 5T. rose (4.10)	50	2·50
		a. Imperf (pair)	£130	£500
		b. Rose-red	2·00	23·00

(b) Zigzag roulette

306	35	400T. on 15pf. bistre (Br.) (1.10)	25	7·75
		a. Imperf (pair)	£180	£900
307		400T. on 25pf. bistre (Br.) (1.10)	25	7·75
308		400T. on 30pf. bistre (Br.) (1.10)	25	7·75
		a. Imperf (pair)	£160	
		b. Surch double	£160	
309		400T. on 40pf. bistre (Br.) (1.10)	25	7·75
		a. Imperf (pair)	£160	
		b. Surch double	£160	
310	54	2M. on 200m. bright rose (16.10)	25	£250
		a. Rose-red	26·00	£21000
311	61	2M. on 5T. rose (4.10)	25	16·00
		a. Rose-red	2·00	23·00

Several different overprinting formes were used. No. 275aa is found on position 44 or 96 of two formes.

The following were prepared for use, but not officially issued: 800T. on 300m green (£50 *un*), 800T. on 500m. orange-red (£50 *un*).

The 800T. on 500m. rose, with green overprint, imperforate, is a trial printing (*Price £650 un*).

1923 (Aug–Oct). OFFICIAL. Official stamps, 1920–23 (earlier types without figures '21'). Surch as T **57**.

(a) Wmk Lozenges

O312		5T. on 5m. brown/*yellow*	15	5·25
		a. Surch inverted	85·00	£4000
O313		20T. on 30pf. orange/*rose*	15	5·25
		a. Surch inverted	90·00	
		b. Imperf (pair)	£200	
O314		100T. on 15pf. brown-purple	15	5·25
		a. Imperf (pair)	£200	
O315		250T. on 10pf. carmine	15	5·25
		a. Surch inverted	85·00	
		b. Surch double	65·00	
		c. Pair, one with surch omitted	£100	£450
O316		800T. on 30pf. orange/*rose*	80	£500

(b) Wmk Mesh

O317		75T. on 50M. violet/*carmine*	15	5·25
		a. Surch inverted	85·00	
		b. Pair, one with surch omitted	90·00	
O318		400T. on 15pf. brown-purple	15	47·00
O319		800T. on 30pf. orange/*rose*	50	7·75
O320		1M. on 75pf. blue	15	65·00
O321		2M. on 10pf. carmine	50	6·50
		a. Wmk horizontal	13·00	£5000
		b. Imperf (pair)	£300	
O322		5M. on 100m. carmine/*carmine*	15	9·75

Nos. O318, O319 and O321 were not previously issued with Mesh wmk.

61   62   (63)

1923 (15–20 Sept). Typo. W **45** (Mesh). P 14.

312	61	5T. greenish blue	25	29·00
		a. Imperf (pair)	£300	
313		50T. yellow-bistre (20.9)	25	2·50
		a. Imperf (pair)	80·00	£11000
		b. Olive-brown	2·00	11·50
		ba. Imperf (pair)	£100	
314		75T. purple	25	18·00

1923 (Oct–Nov). Value (in first colour) inserted at second printing. Slanting figures as in T **63** on the milliard values. Typo. W **45** (Mesh).

T = Thousand. M = Million. Md = Milliard.

(a) P 14

315	62	500T. brown	25	4·50
316		1M. greenish blue	25	2·75
		a. Imperf (pair)	£180	£2000
317		2M. grey	25	34·00
318		4M. yellow-green	25	2·50
		a. Imperf (pair)	£140	
319		5M. carmine	25	2·50
320		10M. scarlet	25	2·50
		a. Value double	80·00	£6500
321		20M. blue	25	3·25
322		30M. maroon	25	16·00
323		50M. grey-green	40	3·25
		a. Imperf (pair)	£180	£1200
		b. Value inverted	80·00	
324		100M. grey	25	2·50
		a. Imperf (pair)	£225	£1300
		b. Value double	80·00	
325		200M. yellow-brown	25	2·50
		a. Imperf (pair)	£140	
326		500M. sage green	25	2·50
327		1Md. chocolate	50	3·25
		a. Imperf (pair)	£225	
328		2Md. green and flesh	25	3·25
329		5Md. brown and yellow	25	2·50
330		10Md. green and apple green	25	2·50
		a. Imperf (pair)	£160	£900
331		20Md. brown and emerald	25	3·25
332		50Md. light blue	40	60·00

(b) Zigzag roulette

333	62	10M. scarlet	90	80·00
334		20M. blue	90	£500
335		50M. grey-green	90	10·50
336		200M. yellow-brown	90	20·00
337		1Md. chocolate	90	13·00
338		2Md. green and flesh	90	5·75
339		5Md. brown and yellow	1·30	4·00
340		20Md. brown and emerald	1·30	20·00
341		50Md. light blue	3·25	£1200

Nos. 315/316, 318/321, 324/327, 329 and 331/332 exist with value omitted (*Price: from £90 each un*.).

1923 (Oct). OFFICIAL. Optd with T O **57**.

O342	62	100M. grey	25	£250
O343		200M. yellow-brown	50	£250
O344		2Md. green and flesh	25	£200
O345		5Md. brown and yellow	25	£140
O346		10Md. green and apple green	6·50	£225
O347		20Md. brown and emerald	6·50	£250
O348		50Md. light blue	3·25	£350

1923 (7 Nov). Surch with T **63**.

342	54	1Md. on 100M. purple	40	49·00
		a. Surch inverted	£200	
		b. Deep reddish purple	£100	£6000

The above stamp was issued in Bavaria only, and is known as the Hitler provisional as it was issued on the day before his *Putsch*. Many forgeries of the surcharge on No. 342b exist.

1923 (Nov). Surch in 'milliarden' as T **60**.

(a) P 14

343	62	5Md. on 2M. purple	40	£225
		a. Surch inverted	33·00	
		b. Surch double	80·00	
344		5Md. on 4M. yellow-green	25	39·00
		a. Surch inverted	65·00	£2000
		b. Surch double	65·00	
345		5Md. on 10M. scarlet	25	4·50
		a. Surch inverted	33·00	£2000
		b. Surch double	65·00	

GERMANY / Germany (1871-1945)

346		10Md. on 20M. blue	40	7·75
		a. Surch inverted	46·00	
		b. Surch double	80·00	
		c. Surch triple		£900
347		10Md. on 50M. grey-green	25	7·75
		a. Surch inverted	33·00	£1600
		b. Surch double	80·00	
348		10Md. on 100M. grey	25	13·00
		a. Surch inverted	46·00	£2500

(b) Zigzag roulette

349	62	5Md. on 10M. scarlet	3·25	£300
		a. Surch inverted	46·00	£2000
		b. Surch double	80·00	
350		10Md. on 20M. blue	6·50	£180
351		10Md. on 50M. grey-green	3·25	65·00
		a. Surch inverted	46·00	£2000

The following so-called 'errors' are recorded in some catalogues: 10Md. on 2M. purple, perf (ungummed) (£160 *un*); 5Md. and 10Md. surcharges together on 2M. purple, perf (£800 *un*); 10Md. on 10m. scarlet (£500 *un*).

Gold Currency

64  **65**  **66**

1923 (1 Dec). Values in 'renten-pfennige' (gold currency). Typo. W **45** (Mesh). P 14.

352	64	3pf. brown	65	40
		a. Value omitted	£300	£500
		b. Imperf (pair)	£375	£900
353		5pf. green	65	40
		a. Value omitted	£250	£500
		b. Imperf (pair)	£350	
354		10pf. carmine	65	40
		a. Value omitted	£250	£500
355		20pf. violet-blue	2·00	65
		a. Imperf (pair)	£475	£900
356		50pf. orange	4·50	1·70
		a. Imperf (pair)	£2500	
357		100pf. purple	14·50	2·00
		a. Value omitted	£250	
352/357		Set of 6	21·00	5·00

1923 (1 Dec). OFFICIAL. Optd with T O **57**.

O358	64	3pf. brown	40	1·30
		a. Value omitted	£200	£500
O359		5pf. green	40	1·30
		a. Value omitted	£200	£500
		b. Opt inverted	£200	£500
O360		10pf. carmine	40	1·30
		a. Value omitted	£200	£1300
		b. Opt inverted	£200	£500
O361		20pf. violet-blue	1·00	2·00
O362		50pf. orange	1·00	2·50
		a. Value omitted	£650	£6500
O363		100pf. purple	6·50	13·00
		a. Opt inverted	£200	£500
O358/O363		Set of 6	8·75	19·00

1924 (11 Jan). AIR. W **45** (Mesh). P 14.

358	48	5pf. yellow-green	2·20	4·00
		a. Wmk horizontal	£160	£225
359		10pf. carmine	2·20	4·00
360		20pf. violet blue	11·50	9·00
		a. Wmk horizontal	£400	£400
361		50pf. orange	20·00	46·00
362		100pf. purple	50·00	£100
363		200pf. greenish blue	£100	£130
		a. Wmk horizontal		
364		300pf. grey	£170	£180
358/364		Set of 7	£325	£425

(Des E. Böhm after paintings by Moritz von Schwind. Illustrating the life of St. Elizabeth. Typo)

1924 (25 Feb). Welfare Fund. T **65** (and similar designs). W **45** (Mesh). P 14½.

365	65	5pf. +15pf. blue-green	3·00	5·75
366	–	10pf. +30pf. scarlet	3·00	5·75
367	–	20pf. +60pf. blue	10·50	14·50
368	–	50pf. +1.50m. red-brown	39·00	£110

365/368	Set of 4	50·00	£120

Designs: St. Elizabeth—5pf., feeding the hungry; 10pf. giving drink to the thirsty; 20pf. clothing the naked; 50pf. caring for the sick. See also Nos. 522/525.

(Des S. von Weech. Typo)

1924. W **45** (Mesh). P 14.

369	66	3pf. bistre (3.24)	50	65
		a. Wmk horizontal	£160	65·00
		b. Imperf (pair)	£400	£1300
370		5pf. green (3.24)	50	65
		a. Imperf (pair)	£500	£1300
371		10pf. scarlet (3.24)	65	65
		a. Wmk horizontal	33·00	20·00
		b. Imperf (pair)	£650	
372		20pf. blue (6.24)	3·25	65
		a. Imperf (pair)	£450	
373		30pf. claret (3.24)	3·25	80
		a. Imperf (pair)	£450	
374		40pf. olive-green (5.24)	22·00	1·20
		a. Imperf (pair)	£500	
375		50pf. orange (11.24)	26·00	2·00
369/375	Set of 7		50·00	6·00

The values from 10pf. upwards have 'pf.' in right top corner instead of figures of value.

Unwatermarked forgeries of the 10pf. exist made to deceive the postal authorities.

1924 (Mar). OFFICIAL. Optd with T O **57**.

O376	66	3pf. bistre	1·00	4·00
		a. Imperf (pair)	£250	
		b. Surch inverted	£100	
O377		5pf. green	80	1·30
		a. Imperf (pair)	£250	
		b. Surch inverted	£180	
O378		10pf. scarlet	60	1·30
O379		20pf. blue	65	1·30
O380		30pf. claret	2·10	1·30
O381		40pf. olive-green	2·10	1·30
O382		50pf. orange	11·00	6·50
O376/O382	Set of 7		16·00	15·00

67 Rheinstein  **68** Cologne

69 Marienburg  **70** Speyer Cathedral

1924–27. Recess. W **45** (Mesh). P 14.

376	67	1m. green (11.24)	20·00	5·75
		a. Wmk horizontal (1927)	50·00	21·00
377	68	2m. blue (11.5.24)	29·00	5·75
378	69	3m. brown-lake (6.24)	36·00	10·50
379	70	5m. grey-green (1.9.25)	60·00	26·00
376/379	Set of 4		£130	43·00

See also No. 458.

71 Dr. von Stephan  **72** Dr. von Stephan

1924–28. 50th Anniv of Universal Postal Union. Typo. W **45** (Mesh). P 14.

380	71	10pf. deep green (9.10.24)	1·00	50
381		20pf. deep blue (9.10.24)	2·50	1·30
382	72	60pf. Venetian red (5.24)	6·50	1·30
		a. Chalky paper (1928)	39·00	23·00
383		80pf. slate (5.24)	17·00	2·50
380/383	Set of 4		24·00	5·00

1924 (June). OFFICIAL. Optd as T O **57**, but horizontal and smaller.

O384	72	60pf. Venetian red	4·00	6·50
O385		80pf. slate	11·50	60·00

GERMANY / Germany (1871-1945)

73 German Eagle and Rhine
74 

(Des Otto Firie. Typo)

1925. Rhineland Millenary. W **45** (Mesh). P 14.
384	73	5pf. green (30.5.25)	80	65
385		10pf. scarlet (7.25)	1·40	65
386		20pf. blue (7.25)	9·00	1·80
384/386	Set of 3		10·00	2·75

(Des S. von Weech. Typo)

1925 (30 May). Munich Exhibition. W **45** (Mesh). P 13½×13.
387	74	5pf. green	5·50	9·00
		a. Wmk horizontal	5·50	9·00
388		10pf. scarlet	6·50	17·00
		a. Wmk horizontal	8·25	26·00

75  **76**  **78**

(Des S. von Weech. Typo)

1925 (15 Dec). Welfare Fund. Various Arms. dated 1925. W **45** (Mesh). P 14.
389	75	5pf. +5pf. yellow, black and green	1·00	3·25
390		10pf. +10pf. buff, pale blue and red	3·00	3·25
391		20pf. +20pf. buff, green, black and blue	13·50	23·00
		a. Booklet pane. No. 391×2 plus two labels	£600	
389/391	Set of 3		16·00	27·00

Arms are of Prussia, Bavaria and Saxony respectively.

(Des O. H. W. Hadank. Typo)

1926 (1 Apr)–**31**. AIR. W **45** (Mesh). P 14.
392	76	5pf. green	2·00	2·00
393		10pf. carmine	3·25	2·00
		a. Tête-bêche (pair)	£275	£450
		b. Booklet pane. Nos. 393×6 and 394×4 (14.7.31)	£400	
394		15pf. purple (15.6.27)	3·25	3·25
395		20pf. dull blue	3·25	3·25
		a. Tête-bêche (pair)	£275	£450
		b. Booklet pane. No. 395×5 plus five labels (18.12.30)	£800	
		c. Booklet pane. No 395×4 plus six labels (14.7.31)	£400	
396		50pf. orange	31·00	9·00
397		1m. rose and black	31·00	10·50
398		2m. pale blue and black	31·00	39·00
399		3m. olive-green and black	90·00	£160
392/399	Set of 8		£180	£200

1926 (1 Oct)–**27**. T **78** and similar portraits. Typo. W **45** (Mesh). P 14.
400		3pf. dark brown	2·00	65
		a. Imperf (pair)	£500	
401		3pf. yellow-brown (8.27)	2·00	65
		a. Imperf (pair)	£500	
402		5pf. dark green	2·00	65
		a. Booklet pane. No. 402×10	£950	
		b. Imperf (pair)	£500	
403		5pf. light green (8.27)	2·50	65
		a. Imperf (pair)	£500	
404		8pf. deep green (8.27)	2·50	65
		a. Booklet pane. No. 404×10	£2000	
		b. Imperf (pair)	£500	
405		10pf. carmine	2·50	65
		a. Booklet pane. No. 405×10	£1800	
406		15pf. scarlet	4·00	65
		a. Booklet pane. No. 406×8 plus two labels (10.27)	£2000	
		b. Imperf (pair)	£500	
407		20pf. greenish slate	18·00	2·00
		a. Wmk horizontal	£4000	£650
408		25pf. blue	5·75	1·60
409		30pf. olive-green	11·00	1·60
410		40pf. violet	20·00	1·60
411		50pf. brown	25·00	13·00
412		80pf. chocolate	50·00	8·50
400/412	Set of 13		£130	28·00

Portraits:—3pf., 25pf. Goethe; 5pf. Schiller; 8pf., 20pf. Beethoven; 10pf. Frederick the Great; 15pf. Kant; 30pf. Lessing; 40pf. Leibniz; 50pf. Bach; 80pf. Dürer.

1926 (1 Dec). Welfare Fund. Various Arms as T **75** dated 1926. W **45** (Mesh – vert on 25pf.) P 14.
413		5pf. +5pf. buff, red. black and green	2·00	4·00
		a. Wmk vertical	£700	£1200
414		10pf. +10pf. red, gold and carmine	3·00	5·25
		a. Wmk vertical	£650	£1600
		b. Booklet pane. No. 414×6 plus two labels	£400	
		ba. As b. but containing No. 414a		
415		25pf. +25pf. yellow, red and blue	17·00	33·00
416		50pf. +50pf. yellow, blue, red and chocolate	£160	£5500
		a. Wmk vertical	70·00	£170
413/416a	Set of 4 (cheapest)		85·00	£190

Arms of Württemberg, Baden, Thuringia and Hesse respectively.

I.A.A.

79 President von Hindenburg
(80) 'Internationales Arbeits Amt'
O **81** 

10.–15. 10. 1927

(Des E. Smith. Photo)

1927 (26 Sept–Nov). Welfare Fund. 80th Birthday of President. W **45** (Mesh). P 14.
417	79	8pf. +7pf. deep green	1·30	2·50
		a. Booklet pane. Nos. 417×4, 418×3 plus label (11.24)	£200	
418		15pf. +15pf. scarlet	2·00	4·00
419		25pf. +25pf. blue	14·50	36·00
420		50pf. +50pf. bistre-brown	20·00	42·00
417/420	Set of 4		34·00	75·00

1927 (10 Oct). Session of International Labour Office at Berlin. Nos. 404, 406 and 408 optd with T **80**.
421		8pf. deep green	29·00	£110
422		15pf. scarlet	29·00	£110
423		25pf. blue	29·00	£110
421/423	Set of 3		80·00	£300

1927–33. OFFICIAL. Typo. W **45** (Mesh). P 14.
O424	O **81**	3pf. ochre	50	1·30
O425		4pf. greenish blue (1931)	65	1·60
O426		4pf. deep grey-blue (12.33)	21·00	23·00
O427		5pf. green	25	1·30
O428		6pf. yellow-olive (1932)	1·20	1·60
O429		8pf. deep grey-green	50	1·30
O430		10pf. carmine	11·50	10·50
O431		10pf. vermilion (1929)	29·00	44·00
		a. Wmk horizontal	26·00	33·00
O432		10pf. bright purple (1930)	65	1·60
		a. Imperf (pair)	£500	
O433		10pf. reddish brown (12.33)	9·00	16·00
O434		12pf. orange (1932)	65	1·60
O435		15pf. orange-red	2·50	1·60
O436		15pf. carmine (1929)	65	1·60
O437		20pf. deep turquoise	11·50	5·25
		a. Wmk horizontal	35·00	£130
O438		20pf. brownish grey (1930)	3·25	2·00
		a. Wmk horizontal	£1700	£800
O439		30pf. bronze green	1·50	1·60
O440		40pf. purple	1·60	1·60
		a. Wmk horizontal	14·00	50·00
O441		60pf. lake-brown (1928)	2·10	3·25
O424/O441	Set of 18 (cheapest)		85·00	£100

81 Pres. Ebert
82 Pres. von Hindenburg 

(Des E. Smith. Typo)

1928 (1 Sept)–**32**. W **45** (Mesh). P 14.
424	81	3pf. bistre-brown	40	1·00
425	82	4pf. light blue (25.2.31)	1·70	2·10
		a. Tête-bêche (pair)	39·00	65·00

GERMANY / Germany (1871-1945)

		c. Booklet pane. No. 425×9 plus label (15.4.32)	£170		
426		5pf. green	65	1·00	
		a. Imperf (pair)	£375		
		b. Tête-bêche (pair)	31·00	50·00	
		c. Booklet pane. No. 426×6 plus four labels	£140		
		d. Booklet pane. Nos. 426×4 and 427×6 (15.4.32)	£170		
427	81	6pf. sage-green (25.1.32)	1·60	1·20	
		a. Booklet pane. Nos. 427×2 and 431×8 (15.4.32)	£170		
428		8pf. deep green	40	1·00	
		a. Tête-bêche (pair)	31·00	50·00	
		b. Wmk horizontal	£100	£225	
429		10pf. scarlet	3·25	4·00	
430		10pf. bright magenta (8.2.30)	2·00	1·30	
431	82	12pf. orange (21.1.32)	2·30	1·20	
		a. Tête-bêche (pair)	39·00	65·00	
432		15pf. carmine	1·00	1·00	
		a. Tête-bêche (pair)	31·00	50·00	
		b. Booklet pane. No. 432×6 plus four labels	£140		
433	81	20pf. deep blue-green	11·00	6·50	
434		20pf. pearl-grey (8.2.30)	11·00	1·30	
435	82	25pf. blue	13·00	1·60	
436	81	30pf. olive-green	9·00	1·60	
437	82	40pf. purple	26·00	1·60	
438	81	45pf. orange	16·00	5·25	
439	82	50pf. brown	17·00	4·50	
440	81	60pf. Venetian red	20·00	5·25	
441	82	80pf. chocolate	39·00	11·50	
442		80pf. ochre (9.30)	15·00	4·00	
424/442		Set of 19	£170	50·00	

The 3pf. and 4pf. exist on thick white gummed card and are perforated 11½. These originated as printed impressions on postcards ordered by a private firm in connection with the Mophila exhibition in 1932. For some reason the cards were not used, but the Stuttgart Oberpostdirektion allowed the firm to cut the printed impressions from the cards, gum them and perforate them.

No. 428 also exists with greenish gum.

83 Airship LZ-127 *Graf Zeppelin*

84 Cologne

1928–31. AIR- Photo. W **45** (Mesh). P 14.

443	83	1m. carmine (8.5.31)	42·00	60·00	
444		2m. bright blue (20.9.28)	70·00	85·00	
445		4m. sepia (20.9.28)	46·00	60·00	
443/445		Set of 3	£140	£180	

1928 (15 Nov). Welfare Fund. Various Arms as T **75**, dated 1928. W **45** (Mesh) horizontal. P 14.

446		5pf. +5pf. orange, red and green	1·20	6·50	
		a. Wmk vertical	£3000	£5000	
447		8pf. +7pf. yellow, black, red and deep green	90	6·50	
		a. Wmk vertical	23·00	£850	
		b. Booklet pane. Nos. 447×4, 448×3 plus label (St. Andrew's Cross)	£400		
		ba. As b. but with advertising label	£400		
448		15pf. +15pf. yellow, blue and carmine	1·40	6·50	
		a. Wmk vertical	39·00	£850	
449		25pf. +25pf. yellow, red and indigo	23·00	85·00	
		a. Wmk vertical	39·00	£850	
450		50pf. +50pf. yellow, black, red and chocolate..	80·00	£160	
446/450		Set of 5	95·00	£250	

The Arms are those of Hamburg, Mecklenburg-Schwerin, Oldenburg, Brunswick and Anhalt respectively.

1929 (1 Nov–Dec). Welfare Fund. Various Arms as T **75**, dated 1929. W **45** (Mesh). P 14.

451		5pf. +2pf. yellow, red and green	1·10	3·25	
		a. Booklet pane. No. 451×6 plus two labels (1.12)	£160		
452		8pf. +4pf. yellow, red and deep green	1·30	3·25	
		a. Booklet pane. Nos 452×4. 453×3 plus label (1.12)	£200		
453		15pf. +5pf. yellow, black and carmine	1·70	2·50	
454		25pf. +10pf. yellow, black, red and indigo	22·00	85·00	
455		50pf. +40pf. yellow, red and chocolate	65·00	£160	
		a. 'PE' for 'PF'	£250	£650	
451/455		Set of 5	80·00	£225	

The Arms are those of Bremen, Lippe, Lübeck, Mecklenburg-Strelitz and Schaumburg-Lippe respectively.

1930 (26 Apr). AIR. First South American Flight of *Graf Zeppelin*. As Nos. 444/445 but additionally inscr 'I. SUDAMERIKA FAHRT'. Photo. W **45** (Mesh) horizontal. P 14.

456	83	2m. bright blue	£500	£650	
		a. Wmk vertical	£425	£500	
457		4m. sepia	£500	£650	
		a. Wmk vertical	£425	£500	

1930 (May). Inscr 'Reichsmark'. Recess. W **45** (Mesh). P 14.

458	84	2m. blue	46·00	25·00	

The 1m. green as T **67** but inscribed 'Reichsmark' instead of 'Mark' was not officially issued.

85 30. JUNI 1930

1930 (30 June). Evacuation of Rhineland by Allied Forces. Optd with T **85**.

459	81	8pf. deep green	3·50	1·60	
460	82	15pf. carmine	3·50	1·60	

86 Aachen

87 Berlin

88 Marienwerder

89 Wurzburg

90

1930 (12 Sept). International Philatelic Exhibition, Berlin. Recess. W **90** with 'IPOSTA' at top and '1930' below in sheet margins in double-lined capitals and figures. P 14.

461	86	8pf. +4pf. green	50·00	£180	
462	87	15pf. +5pf. carmine	50·00	£180	
463	88	25pf. +10pf. blue	50·00	£180	
464	89	50pf. +40pf. brown	50·00	£180	
MS464a		195×148 mm. Nos. 461/464 (sold at 2m.70 in the Exhibition)	£700	£2500	

1930 (1 Nov). Welfare Fund. W **45** (Mesh). P 14.

465	86	8pf. +4pf. green	1·20	2·30	
		a. Booklet pane. No. 465×7 plus label	£140		
		b. Booklet pane. Nos. 465×3, 466×4 plus label	£180		
466	87	15pf. +15pf. carmine	1·60	3·25	
467	88	25pf. +10pf. blue	12·50	39·00	
468	89	50pf. +40pf. brown	36·00	£140	
465/468		Set of 4	46·00	£170	

1931 (22 July). AIR. Polar Flight of *Graf Zeppelin*. Optd 'POLAR-FAHRT 1931' in upper left-hand corner. W **45** (Mesh). P 14.

469	83	1m. carmine (Br.)	£200	£180	
		a. Opt without hyphen	£800	£2000	
470		2m. bright blue (Br.)	£275	£350	
		a. Opt without hyphen	£900	£2000	
471		4m. sepia (Br.)	£700	£1200	
469/471		Set of 3	£1100	£1600	

Nos. 469a and 470a occur on position 41 of part of the printing.

91 Town Hall. Breslau

92 Heidelberg Castle

1931 (1 Nov). Welfare Fund. T **91/2** and similar designs. Recess. W **45** (Mesh). P 14.

472	–	8pf. +4pf. green	90	3·00	
		a. Booklet pane. No. 472×7 plus label	£160		

ROBERT UDEN
PHILATELY

Your specialist for Germany and its territories from 1872 - 2000

In addition to our extensive range of general issue stamps, we also stock postal stationery, covers, booklets and propaganda cards etc. Our other related speciality is Zeppelin flown mail, and we pride ourselves in being probably the number one dealer in the UK in this fascinating subject.

If you collect Germany, then look no further. We can send free price lists upon request, whether it is Third Reich stamps, the attractive issues from the German Colonies or mail flown on the giant Zeppelins.

Exclusive

'Exclusive' is our exciting 32 page colour publication. A retail list that touches on most philatelic collecting areas, that showcases new and unusual stock items. Request your free copy today.

Customer satisfaction is very important to us, so every item we send can be returned for a full refund within 30 days. Our aim is to develop a long term relationship with you. Together with our supportive advice and guidance when requested, we hope to help build and enhance your collection. We look forward to hearing from you.

PO Box 183, Hythe, Kent CT21 4GP   Telephone: 01303 238807

Email: robertuden@btopenworld.com

GERMANY/ Germany (1871-1945)

		b. Booklet pane. Nos. 472×3, 473×4 plus label............	£170		
473	91	15pf. +5pf. carmine		90	3·00
474	92	25pf. +10pf. blue		16·00	50·00
475	–	50pf. +40pf. brown		49·00	£130
472/475 Set of 4............				60·00	£170

Designs: Vert—8pf. The Zwinger, Dresden; 50pf. The Holstentor, Lübeck.
See also Nos. 485/489.

(93)

94 Pres von Hindenburg

1932 (2 Feb). Welfare Fund. Nos. 472/473 surch as T **93**.
| 476 | – | 6 +4pf. on 8pf.+4pf. green............ | 6·75 | 17·00 |
| 477 | 91 | 12 +3pf. on 15pf.+5pf. carmine............ | 8·50 | 20·00 |

(Des from a bronze plaquette by K. Goetz. Typo)

1932 (1 Oct)–**33**. 85th Birthday of Pres. von Hindenburg. W **45** (Mesh). P 14.
478	**94**	4pf. light blue............	85	1·00
479		5pf. emerald-green............	1·30	1·00
		a. Booklet pane Nos. 479×4 and 500A×4 (5.8.33)............	£140	
480		12pf. orange-red............	8·25	1·00
481		15pf. carmine............	5·00	17·00
482		25pf. ultramarine............	3·50	1·30
483		40pf. violet............	31·00	2·50
484		50pf. chocolate............	8·50	18·00
478/484 Set of 7............			55·00	38·00

See also Nos. 493/509 and for stamps with black borders see Nos. 545/550.

1932 (1 Nov). Welfare Fund. Designs as T **92**. Recess. W **45** (Mesh). P 14.
485		4pf. +2pf. pale blue............	1·30	3·00
		a. Booklet pane. Nos 485×5 and 486×5....	80·00	
486		6pf. +4pf. olive-green............	1·70	3·00
487		12pf. +3pf. vermilion............	1·30	3·00
		a. Tête-bêche (pair)............	20·00	33·00
		b. Booklet pane. No. 487×8 plus two labels............	80·00	
488		25pf. +10pf. blue............	14·50	31·00
489		40pf. +40pf. slate-purple............	47·00	£110
485/489 Set of 5............			60·00	£130

Designs:—4pf. Wartburg Castle; 6pf. Stolzenfels Castle; 12pf. Nüremberg Castle; 25pf. Lichtenstein Castle; 40pf. Marburg Castle.

THIRD REICH
30 January 1933–8 May 1945

PRICES. For Nos. 490/898 prices are given in three columns: for unmounted mint (full own gum), for lightly hinged unused, and for used.

96 Frederick the Great (after A. von Menzel)

97

1933 (12 Apr–May). Opening of the Reichstag in Potsdam (21.3.33). Photo. W **45** (Mesh). P 14.

			Unmtd Mint	Mtd Mint	Used
490	**96**	6pf. myrtle green............	7·50	1·10	1·50
		a. Tête-bêche (pair)............	50·00	30·00	50·00
491		12pf. rosine............	11·50	1·60	1·50
		a. Tête-bêche (pair)............	50·00	30·00	50·00
		b. Booklet pane. No. 491×5 plus label (5.33)............	£100	65·00	
492		25pf. ultramarine............	£400	65·00	35·00
490/492 Set of 3............			£375	60·00	34·00

1933–41. New values and colours changed. Typo. P 14×14½.

A. W **45** (Mesh)
494A	**94**	3pf. yellow-brown (4.33)............	£150	28·00	1·30
495A		4pf. dull blue (5.33)............	28·00	6·25	1·30
497A		6pf. deep dull green (4.33)............	12·50	3·25	1·30
498A		8pf. orange-red (4.33)............	25·00	10·00	1·30
		a. Booklet pane. Nos. 498A×3 and 500A×5 (5.8.33)............	£300	£180	
499A		10pf. reddish brown (5.33)............	38·00	6·25	1·30
500A		12pf. rosine (4.33)............	25·00	3·75	1·30
501A		15pf. deep reddish purple (8.33)	35·00	8·75	44·00
502A		20pf. new blue (5.33)............	90·00	11·50	2·50
504A		30pf. olive-green (5.33)............	30·00	11·50	2·30
505A		40pf. bright purple (8.33)............	£375	50·00	4·50
506A		50pf. black and green (7.33)............	£180	25·00	3·75
507A		60pf. black and deep claret (5.33)............	£325	50·00	1·60
508A		80pf. black and blue (7.33)............	38·00	15·00	1·90
509A		100pf. black and yellow-orange (7.33)............	£225	44·00	21·00
494A/509A Set of 14............			£1400	£250	80·00

No. 494A exists with yellowish gum (*Price* Unmtd Mint £130, Mtd Mint £650).
For 496A and 503A with mash wmk see Nos. 479 and 482.

B. W **97** (Swastikas)
493B	**94**	1pf. black (12.33)............	65	25	65
		a. Tête-bêche (pair) (1939)	3·75	2·30	4·50
		b. Booklet pane. Nos. 493B×3, 494B×3 and 496B×2 (6.34)............	£110	70·00	
		c. Booklet pane. Nos. 493B×2, 498B×5 plus label (8.36)............	65·00	38·00	
		d. Booklet pane. Nos. 493B×4 and 500B×4 (10.37)............	55·00	35·00	
		e. Booklet pane. Nos. 493B×4, 495B×3 plus label (10.39)............	44·00	25·00	
		f. Coil strip. Nos. 493B×2, 494B, 496B plus label (arr. 1, 5, label, 3, 1pf.) (10.39)............	6·75	3·00	
		fa. Coil strip. As f. but arranged 5.1, label, 1, 3pf. (2.41)............	7·00	3·50	
494B	**94**	3pf. yellow-brown (1.34)............	65	25	65
		a. Tête-bêche (pair) (1940)............	1·30	75	1·30
		b. Booklet pane. Nos. 494B×4 and 496B×4 (8.36)............	65·00	38·00	
		c. Booklet pane. Nos. 494B×4 and 497B×4 (10.37)............	55·00	35·00	
		d. Booklet pane. Nos. 494B×6, 500B plus label (10.39)............	31·00	19·00	
495B		4pf. slate-blue (2.34)............	65	25	65
		a. Booklet pane. Nos. 495B×3 500B×4 plus label (10.37)............	55·00	35·00	
		b. Coil pair. Nos. 495B and 497B (1939)............	5·00	3·75	
496B		5pf. emerald (2.34)............	65	25	65
		a. Booklet pane. Nos. 496B×4 and 498B×4 (6.34)............	£110	70·00	
		b. Booklet pane. Nos. 496B×2, 497B×3 and 498B×3 (10.37)............	55·00	35·00	
		c. Booklet pane. Nos. 496B×2 (on right), 497B×5 plus label (10.39)............	44·00	25·00	
		ca. As c. but No. 496B in middle (4.40)............	44·00	25·00	
497B		6pf. deep dull green (2.34)............	65	25	65
		a. Booklet pane. Nos. 497B, 500B×6 plus label (6.34)....	£190	£110	
		b. Booklet pane. No. 497B×7 plus label (8.36)............	65·00	38·00	
498B		8pf. orange-red (2.34)............	65	25	65
		a. Booklet pane. Nos. 498B×3 (at bottom), 500B×4 plus label (10.37)............	55·00	25·00	
		ab. As a. but No. 498B at top (4.40)............	55·00	25·00	
499B		10pf. reddish brown (2.34)............	1·30	25	65
500B		12pf. rosine (2.34)............	65	25	65
		a. Booklet pane. No. 500B×7 plus label (8.36)............	65·00	38·00	
501B		15pf. deep reddish purple (4.34)	2·50	50	65
502B		20pf. light blue (4.34)............	5·75	75	65
503B		25pf. ultramarine (4.34)............	5·75	75	65
504B		30pf. olive-green (2.34)............	11·50	1·30	65
505B		40pf. bright purple (2.34)............	16·00	2·50	65
506B		50pf. black and green (9.34)............	24·00	5·00	65
507B		60pf. black and deep claret (5.34)............	10·00	1·30	65

37

GERMANY/ Germany (1871-1945)

508B		80pf. black and blue (2.36)	10·50	3·75	2·00
509B		100pf. black and yellow-orange (9.34)	14·00	5·00	1·90
493B/509B Set of 17			95·00	21·00	12·50

(98)  99 Tannhäuser  O 100

1933 (25 Sept). AIR. Chicago World Exhibition Flight of *Graf Zeppelin*. Optd with T **98**. W **45** (Mesh). P 14.

510	83	1m. carmine	£4250	£1200	£650
511		2m. bright blue	£375	£110	£325
512		4m. sepia	£375	£110	£325
510/512 Set of 3			£4500	£1300	£1200

(Des Alois Kolb. Recess)

1933 (1 Nov). Welfare Fund. T **99** and similar designs showing scenes from Wagners' Operas. W **97**. P 14×13.

513		3pf. +2pf. brown	38·00	4·50	9·50
514		4pf. +2pf. deep blue	25·00	2·50	3·75
		a. Perf 14	25·00	2·50	5·00
		ab. Booklet pane. Nos. 514a×5 and 516a×5	£375	£225	
515		5pf. +3pf. light green	65·00	6·25	11·50
516		6pf. +4pf. myrtle green	25·00	2·50	3·75
		a. Perf 14	25·00	2·50	8·25
517		8pf. +4pf. orange-red	38·00	3·75	6·25
		a. Perf 14	31·00	3·50	7·00
		ab. Booklet pane. Nos. 517a×5, 518a×4 plus label	£375	£225	
518		12pf. +3pf. carmine-red	38·00	3·50	4·50
		a. Perf 14	31·00	3·75	10·50
519		20pf. +10pf. greenish blue	£1900	£325	£325
		a. Perf 14	£1200	£200	£160
520		25pf. +15pf. ultramarine	£450	50·00	65·00
521		40pf. +35pf. magenta	£1200	£200	£220
513/521 Set of 9 (*cheapest*)			£2750	£450	£450

Designs:—3pf. T **99**; 4pf. *The Flying Dutchman*; 5pf. *Rhinegold*; 6pf. *The Mastersingers*; 8pf. *The Valkyries*; 12pf. *Siegfried*; 20pf. *Tristan and Isolde*; 25pf. *Lohengrin*; 40pf. *Parsifal*.

1933 (29 Nov). Welfare Fund. As Nos. 365/8, each optd '1923–1933' and printed together horizontally, in miniature sheet. Hand-made paper of varying thickness. W **97**. P 14½.

522	65	5 +15pf. blue-green	£375	£150	£650
523	–	10 +30pf. scarlet	£375	£150	£650
524	–	20 +60pf. blue	£375	£150	£650
525	–	50pf. +1.50m. red-brown	£375	£150	£650
MS525*a* 210×148 mm. Nos. 522/5			£8500	£2250	£1600

1934 (18 Jan). OFFICIAL. Typo. W **97** (Swastikas). P 14.

O526	O **100**	3pf. bistre-brown	5·00	1·30	1·90
O527		4pf. slate-blue	1·50	45	1·50
O528		5pf. emerald green	1·00	25	1·90
O529		6pf. deep green	1·00	25	1·50
		a. Imperf (pair)	£400	£130	£800
O530		8pf. vermilion	11·50	3·00	1·50
O531		10pf. chocolate	2·30	60	12·50
O532		12pf. carmine	19·00	4·00	2·50
O533		15pf. claret	7·50	2·00	15·00
O534		20pf. light blue	2·75	70	2·50
O535		30pf. bronze-green	4·50	1·20	2·50
O536		40pf. magenta	4·50	1·20	2·50
O537		50pf. yellow	7·50	2·00	6·25
O526/O537 Set of 12			60·00	15·00	47·00

For this issue without watermark, see Nos. O809/O820.

100 Golden Eagle, Globe and Swastika

101 Count Zeppelin and Airship LZ-127 *Graf Zeppelin*

RIBBED GUM. On many issues from No. 526 a gum-breaker was used, giving a ribbed effect. This ribbing is listed where a stamp was issued with both horizontally and vertically ribbed gum. As the pressure exerted often left an impression in the actual paper, prices are in some cases given for used examples; where this impression is unclear the cheapest price should be taken.

(Des H. Bastanier. Typo)

1934 (21 Jan). AIR. W **97**. Vertically ribbed gum.
(*a*) P 14

526	**100**	5pf. emerald	8·75	1·90	1·50
		a. Horizontally ribbed gum	19·00	2·50	15·00
527		10pf. scarlet	8·75	1·90	1·50
		a. Horizontally ribbed gum	16·00	2·50	15·00
528		15pf. dull ultramarine	10·00	3·00	2·00
		a. Horizontally ribbed gum	50·00	7·50	15·00
529		20pf. steel blue	20·00	5·75	2·75
		a. Horizontally ribbed gum	48·00	7·50	15·00
530		25pf. yellow-brown	65·00	7·50	3·25
		a. Horizontally ribbed gum	65·00	7·50	15·00
531		40pf. magenta	£100	11·50	1·90
		a. Horizontally ribbed gum	£110	15·00	33·00
532		50pf. deep grey-green	£160	20·00	1·50
		a. Horizontally ribbed gum	£180	25·00	33·00
533		80pf. yellow-orange	80·00	6·25	6·25
		a. Horizontally ribbed gum	95·00	12·50	21·00
534		100pf. black	£100	12·50	4·50
		a. Horizontally ribbed gum	£150	25·00	31·00

(*b*) T **101** and another inscr 'Otto Lilienthal'. P 13½×13

535	–	2m. black and green	£180	28·00	31·00
		a. Horizontally ribbed gum	£5500	£1300	£5500
536	**101**	3m. black and blue	£250	50·00	70·00
		a. Horizontally ribbed gum	£500	£130	£750
526/536 Set of 11			£900	£130	£110
526a/536a Set of 11			£6000	£1400	£6000

Design:—2m. Otto Lilienthal and Lilienthal biplane glider.

103 Franz A. E. Lüderitz    **104** 'Saar Ownership'    **105** Nüremberg Castle

1934 (30 June). German Colonisers' Jubilee. T **103** and similar designs. Typo. W **97**. Ribbed gum, vertically (6pf.) or horizontally (others). P 13×13½.

537		3pf. deep red-brown and chocolate	40·00	4·25	10·00
538		6pf. deep red-brown and myrtle green	15·00	1·80	2·50
539		12pf. deep red-brown and carmine	44·00	4·50	2·50
		a. Vertically ribbed gum	55·00	5·75	6·25
540		25pf. deep red-brown and greenish blue	£150	16·00	33·00
537/540 Set of 4 (*cheapest*)			£225	24·00	43·00

Portraits:—3pf. T **103**; 6pf. Gustav Nachtigal; 12pf. Karl Peters; 25pf. Hermann von Wissmann.

(Des K. Schulpig and W. Brand, resp. Typo)

1934 (26 Aug). Saar Plebiscite. T **104** and similar type. W **97** (Swastikas). P 14.

541		6pf. deep green	50·00	5·00	1·00
542		12pf. scarlet	65·00	6·75	1·00

Designs:— 3pf. T **104**; 12pf. Eagle inscr 'Saar' in rays from a swastika eclipsed sun.

(Des Mjölnir-Schweitzer. (Photo))

1934 (29 Aug). Nüremberg Congress. W **97**. P 14.

543	**105**	6pf. dull blue-green	44·00	4·50	1·00
		a. Imperf (pair)	—	—	
544		12pf. rose-red	65·00	6·75	1·00
		a. Imperf (pair)	£2500	£950	—

1934 (4 Sept). Hindenburg Memorial. Black borders. Typo. W **97** (Swastikas). P 14.

545	**94**	3pf. bistre-brown	6·25	1·10	75
546		5pf. emerald-green	6·25	1·10	90
547		6pf. deep green	13·00	2·00	75
548		8pf. orange-red	31·00	4·00	75
549		12pf. carmine	38·00	4·50	75
550		25pf. ultramarine	95·00	12·00	14·00
545/550 Set of 6			£170	22·00	16·00

106 Blacksmith    **107** Friedrich von Schiller    **108** The 'Saar comes home'

38

GERMANY / Germany (1871-1945)

(Des F. Spiegel. Recess)

1934 (2–5 Nov). Welfare Fund. T **106** and similar vert designs. W **97**. P 13×13½.

551	3pf. +2pf. brown	12·00	1·80	2·50
552	4pf. +2pf. black	7·50	1·30	2·50
	a. Booklet pane. Nos. 552×5 and 554×5 (2.11)	£150	90·00	
553	5pf. +2pf. green	55·00	9·50	12·50
554	6pf. +4pf. myrtle green	7·00	1·30	1·00
555	8pf. +4pf. Indian red	12·00	1·80	3·25
	a. Booklet pane. Nos. 555×5, 556×4 plus label (2.11)	£225	£140	
556	12pf. +3pf. brown-red	5·75	95	1·00
557	20pf. +10pf. deep bluish green	£150	26·00	35·00
558	25pf. +15pf. dull ultramarine	£160	26·00	35·00
559	40pf. +35pf. brown-lilac	£350	70·00	£110
551/559	Set of 9	£700	£120	£180

Designs:—3pf. Merchant; 4pf. Mason; 5pf. Mason; 6pf. Miner; 8pf. Architect; 12pf. Farmer; 20pf. Scientist; 25pf. Sculptor; 40pf. Judge.

(Des K. Bauer. Typo)

1934 (5 Nov). 175th Anniv of Schillers' Birth (10 Nov). W **97** (Swastikas). P 14.

560	**107**	6pf. green	41·00	4·00	1·00
561		12pf. carmine	90·00	8·00	1·00

(Des Emmy Glintzer. Photo)

1935 (16 Jan). Saar Restoration. W **97** (Swastikas). P 14.

562	**108**	3pf. brown	5·00	1·00	1·90
563		6pf. green	5·00	1·00	1·30
564		12pf. lake	31·00	3·50	1·30
565		25pf. blue	£110	12·50	14·00
562/565	Set of 4		£140	16·00	17·00

109 'Steel Helmet'  **110** 'Victors' Crown'  **111** Heinrich Schutz

(Des Mjölnir-Schweitzer. Photo)

1935 (15 Mar). War Heroes' Day. W **97**. Horizontally ribbed gum. P 14.

566	**109**	6pf. bottle green	12·50	2·20	2·50
		a. Vertically ribbed gum	55·00	11·50	18·00
567		12pf. brown-lake	14·00	2·50	2·50
		a. Vertically ribbed gum	55·00	11·50	18·00

(Des K. Diebitsch. Photo)

1935 (26 Apr). Apprentices Vocational Contest. W **97**. Vertically ribbed gum. P 14.

568	**110**	6pf. bottle green	12·50	1·80	2·30
569		12pf. bright scarlet	19·00	2·75	2·30
		a. Horizontally ribbed gum	£200	34·00	95·00

(Des Ferdinand Spiegel. Recess)

1935 (21 June). Musicians' Anniversaries. T **111** and similar portraits. Other types inscr '1685–1935'. W **97** (Swastikas). P 14.

570	**111**	6pf. deep green	10·00	1·30	1·30
571	–	12pf. brown-lake (Bach)	12·50	1·80	1·30
572	–	25pf. blue (Handel)	19·00	2·75	1·50
		a. Inscr '1585-1935' in error	90·00	13·00	95·00
570/572	Set of 3		37·00	5·25	3·75

112 Allenstein Castle. (Background, E. Prussia)  **113** Stephenson Locomotive *Adler*

(Des Franz Marten. Recess)

1935 (23 June). International Philatelic Exhibition, Königsberg. T **112** and similar horiz designs printed together in miniature sheets of four stamps. Wmk Cross of the Teutonic Order of Knighthood on stamps, with 'OSTROPA' at top and '1935' below in sheet margins. P 13½×14.

		Un	Used
573	3pf. brown	55·00	60·00
574	6pf. deep blue-green	55·00	60·00
575	12pf. deep scarlet	55·00	60·00
576	25pf. Blue	55·00	60·00

MS576*a* 148×105 mm. Nos. 573/6 .... £1500 £1400

Designs:—3pf. T **112**; 6pf. Tannenberg Memorial; 12pf. Königsberg Castle; 25pf. Heilsberg Castle. Backgrounds – Eagle, Shield and Oak Leaf. The gum used for this issue contained an acid which slowly dissolved the paper and the gum has therefore been removed in most cases. Prices are for stamps or sheet without gum.

(Des Karl Diebitsch. Recess)

1935 (10 July). German Railway Centenary. T **113** and similar vert designs. W **97**. P 14×13½.

			Unmtd Mint	Mtd Mint	Used
577		6pf. green	10·00	1·60	1·30
		a. Imperf (pair)	£4750	£1400	
578		12pf. brown-red	10·00	1·60	1·30
		a. Imperf (pair)	£4750	£1400	
579		25pf. blue	55·00	8·75	3·00
		a. Imperf (pair)	£5000	£1500	
		b. Double impression	£450	£100	£450
580		40pf. bright purple	95·00	14·50	3·00
		a. Imperf (pair)	£5000	£1500	
577/580	Set of 4		£150	24·00	7·75

Designs:—6pf. T **113**; 12pf. Class 03 steam train, 1930s; 25pf. Diesel train 'Flying Hamburger'; 40pf. Class 05 streamlined steam locomotive No. 001, 1935.

114 Trumpeter  **115** Nüremberg

(Des Karl Diebitsch. Photo)

1935 (25 July). World Jamboree of Hitler Youth. W **97**. Vertically ribbed gum. P 14.

581	**114**	6pf. green	12·00	1·90	3·75
		a. Horizontally ribbed gum	25·00	2·50	9·50
582		15pf. deep claret	25·00	3·00	5·00
		a. Horizontally ribbed gum	38·00	7·50	10·00

(Des Karl Diebitsch. Recess)

1935 (7 Sept). Nüremberg Congress. W **97**. Vertically ribbed gum. P 14×13½.

583	**115**	6pf. deep green	10·00	2·00	90
		a. Horizontally ribbed gum	£1500	£475	£1500
584		12pf. brown-red	18·00	3·50	90

116 East Prussia  **117** SA Man and Feldherrnhalle, Munich

(Des Karl Diebitsch. Recess)

1935 (4 Oct–15 Nov). Welfare Fund. T **116** and similar vert designs. W **97**. P 14×13½.

585	3pf. +2pf. brown	2·50	55	65
	a. Booklet pane. Nos. 585×4, 590×5 plus label (15.11)	£110	70·00	
586	4pf. +3pf. grey-blue	9·50	2·00	2·50
587	5pf. +3pf. emerald	2·50	55	1·60
	a. Booklet pane. Nos. 587×5 and 588×5 (15.11)	75·00	45·00	
588	6pf. +4pf. myrtle green	1·30	30	65
589	8pf. +4pf. orange-brown	14·50	3·00	2·50
590	12pf. +6pf. scarlet	1·90	45	65
591	15pf. +10pf. purple-brown	34·00	7·00	9·50
592	25pf. +15pf. dull ultramarine	60·00	12·50	10·00
593	30pf. +20pf. drab	70·00	17·00	33·00
594	40pf. +35pf. deep magenta	65·00	14·00	24·00
585/594	Set of 10	£225	50·00	75·00

Designs: Women in provincial costumes—3pf. T **116**; 4pf. Silesia; 5pf. Rhineland; 6pf. Lower Saxony; 8pf. Kurmark; 12pf. Black Forest; 15pf. Hesse; 25pf. Upper Bavaria; 30pf. Friesland; 40pf. Franconia.

(Des Heinz Raebiger. Photo)

1935 (5 Nov). 12th Anniv of First Hitler Putsch (9.11.23). W **97**. Vertically ribbed gum. P 14×13½.

595	**117**	3pf. brown	5·00	50	1·10
		a. Horizontally ribbed gum	25·00	5·00	50·00
596		12pf. scarlet	15·00	1·30	1·10
		a. Imperf (pair)	£1800	£650	£1500

39

GERMANY/ Germany (1871-1945)

118 Skating

119 Heinkel He 70 Blitz

(Des Max Eschle. Recess)

1935 (25 Nov). Winter Olympic Games, Garmisch-Partenkirchen. T **118** and similar types. W **97** (Swastikas). P 13½×14.

597	6pf. +4pf. green	7·50	1·50	2·30
598	12pf. +6pf. carmine	15·00	3·00	2·00
599	25pf. +15pf. ultramarine	65·00	12·50	12·50
597/599	Set of 3	80·00	15·00	15·00

Designs:—6pf. T **118**; 12pf. Ski jumping; 25pf. Bobsleighing.

(Des Karl Diebitsch. Photo)

1936 (6 Jan). Tenth Anniv of Lufthansa Airways. W **97** (Swastikas). P 14×13½.

| 600 | **119** | 40pf. bright blue | 75·00 | 10·00 | 5·00 |

120 Gottlieb Daimler

121 Airship LZ-129 *Hindenburg*

1936 (15 Feb). Berlin Motor Show and 50th Anniv of Invention of First Motor Car. T **120** and similar portrait. Photo. W **97** (Swastikas). P 14.

601	6pf. green	9·50	1·10	1·60
602	12pf. lake (Carl Benz)	12·00	1·40	1·60

(Des Karl Diebitsch. Recess)

1936 (16 Mar). AIR. W **97**. P 14.

			Un	Used
603	**121**	50pf. deep blue	30·00	1·30
604		75pf. deep green	33·00	1·80

Unused prices are for stamps without gum (see note below No. **MS**576a).

122 Otto von Guericke

123 Gymnastics

(Des Richard Klein. Photo)

1936 (4 May). 250th Death Anniv of Otto von Guericke (scientist). W **97**. P 14.

			Unmtd Mint	Mtd Mint	Used
605	**122**	6pf. deep green	2·00	50	90

(Des Max Eschle. Recess)

1936 (9 May–1 Aug). Summer Olympic Games, Berlin. T **123** and similar horiz designs. Nos. W **97** (Swastikas). P 13½×14.

606		3pf. +2pf. brown	3·25	55	75
		a. Booklet pane. Nos. 606×5 and 610×5 (15.6)	75·00	45·00	
607		4pf. +3pf. slate-blue	2·50	50	1·30
		a. Booklet pane. Nos. 607×5 and 608×5 (15.6)	75·00	45·00	
608		6pf. +4pf. green	2·50	50	75
609		8pf. +4pf. vermilion	31·00	5·00	2·10
610		12pf. +6pf. carmine-red	3·75	65	75
611		15pf. +10pf. deep claret	55·00	9·00	5·00
612		25pf. +15pf. dull ultramarine	30·00	5·00	6·25
613		40pf. +35pf. reddish violet	55·00	9·00	12·50
606/613	Set of 8	£160	27·00	26·00

MS613a Two sheets, each 148×105 mm. (a) Nos. 606/8 and 613; (b) Nos. 609/12 (1.8.36) £350 £130 £225

Designs:—3pf. T **123**; 4pf. Diver; 6pf. Footballer; 8pf. Javelin thrower; 12pf. Olympic torchbearer; 15pf. Fencer; 25pf. Double scullers; 40pf. Show jumper.

In the miniature sheets Wmk **97** occurs only on the stamps; the sheet margins have the watermark 'XI. OLYMPISCHE SPIELE BERLIN 1936'. The sheets exist in two thicknesses of paper *(Prices £750, £250, £700)*.

124 Symbolical of Local Government

125 Brown Ribbon Race

(Des Richard Klein. Photo)

1936 (3 June). Sixth International Local Govt Congress. W **97** (Swastikas). P 14.

614	**124**	3pf. deep brown	3·25	75	50
615		5pf. green	4·50	90	50
616		12pf. lake	5·75	1·40	1·00
617		25pf. deep blue	12·00	2·75	1·80
614/617	Set of 4	23·00	5·25	3·50

(Des Richard Klein. Recess)

1936 (22 June). Brown Ribbon of Germany. CHARITY. Single stamp in miniature sheet (148×105 *mm*). W **97** (Swastikas). Marginal wmk 'MUNCHEN RIEM' above and '1936' below design. P 14.

MS618 **125** 42pf. (+108pf.) deep brown 40·00 20·00 23·00

Sold at 1.50 Reichsmarks at the Munich-Riem Race Course and selected post offices.
See also No. **MS**637a, 659, 687, 735, 768, 805, 842 and 887.

126 Leisure Time

127 Saluting the Swastika

(Des Sepp Semar. Photo)

1936 (30 June). International Recreational Congress, Hamburg. W **97** (Swastikas). P 14.

619	**126**	6pf. green	7·50	1·00	90
620		15pf. claret	15·00	1·90	1·60

1936 (3 Sept). Nüremberg Congress. Photo. W **97** (Swastikas). P 14.

621	**127**	6pf. green	7·00	95	1·00
622		12pf. scarlet	10·50	1·50	1·00

128 Luitpoldhain Heroes Memorial, Nüremberg

129 'R(eichs) L(uftschutz) B(und)' (Civil Defence Union)

(Eng G. Fritz. Recess)

1936 (21 Sept–Nov). Winter Relief Fund. T **128** and similar horiz designs. no wmk. P 13½×14.

623		3pf. +2pf. sepia	1·50	35	65
		a. Booklet pane. Nos. 623×4, 628×5 plus label (2.11)	75·00	45·00	
624		4pf. +3pf. black (26.10)	1·90	40	75
625		5pf. +3pf. emerald (26.10)	1·50	35	65
		a. Booklet pane. Nos. 625×5 and 626×5 (2.11)	38·00	23·00	
626		6pf. +4pf. bottle green	1·50	35	65
627		8pf. +4pf. red-brown (26.10)	8·75	1·50	2·10
628		12pf. +6pf. brown-red	1·50	35	65
629		15pf. +10pf. chocolate (26.10)	31·00	4·75	5·75
630		25pf. +15pf. deep blue (horizontal ribbed gum)	21·00	3·75	6·25
		a. Vertically ribbed gum	£300	£160	£1100
631		40pf. +35pf. deep magenta (26.10)	35·00	5·75	10·50
623/631	Set of 9	95·00	16·00	25·00

Designs—3pf. Munich Frontier road; 4pf. Air Ministry, Berlin; 5pf. T **128**; 6pf. Bridge over River Saale; 8pf. Deutschlandhalle, Berlin; 12pf. Alpine road; 15pf. Führerhaus, Munich; 25pf. Bridge over River Mangfall; 40pf. German Art Museum, Munich.

40

GERMANY / Germany (1871-1945)

(Des L. Hohlwein. Recess)
1937 (3 Mar). Fourth Anniv of Civil Defence Union. No wmk. P 14.
632	**129**	3pf. brown	3·75	75	65
633		6pf. green	5·00	1·00	65
634		12pf. bright rose	10·00	2·00	1·30
632/634	Set of 3		17·00	3·25	2·30

130 Adolf Hitler    **131** Fishing Smacks

(Des R. Klein (frame and marginal inscription). Photo)
1937. Hitler's Culture Fund and 48th birthday. Four stamps in miniature sheet (148×105 mm). W **97** (Swastikas). Marginal inscr 'WER EIN VOLK RETTEN WILL KANN NUR HEROISCH DENKEN'.

(a) P 14. (5.4.37)
MS635	**130**	6+19pf. blue-green	90·00	30·00	20·00

(b) Imperf (16.4.37)
MS636	**130**	6+19pf. blue-green	£275	65·00	38·00

(c) No. **MS**635, but with margins rouletted, continuing the lines of perforation, except at foot, and inscr '25 Rpf einschliesslich Kulturspende' opposite each stamp. (10.6.37)
MS637	**130**	6+19pf. blue-green	£400	£110	£110

Used singles of No. **MS**637 cannot be distinguished from No. **MS**635.
No. **MS**636 was sold at the Berlin Philatelic Exhibition for 1 Rm.+50 Rpf. entrance fee.

1937 (1 Aug). Brown Ribbon of Germany. No. **MS**618 optd with German eagle and ornamental border surrounding, '1. AUGUST 1937 MUNCHEN-RIEM' in red.
MS637a	**125**	42pf.(+108pf.) deep brown	£225	95·00	£160

1937 (3 Sept). Nüremberg Congress. Four stamps in miniature sheet, as No. **MS**637, but optd 'REICHSPARTEITAG NÜRNBERG 1937' in panels of stamps.
MS638	**130**	6+19pf. blue-green	£400	£120	75·00

(Eng Axster-Heudtlass. Recess)
1937 (4 Nov). Winter Relief Fund. T **131** and similar horiz designs. No wmk. P 13½×14.
639		3pf. +2pf. bistre-brown	65	30	65
	a. Booklet pane. Nos. 639×4 and 644×5 plus label		75·00	45·00	
640		4pf. +3pf. blue-black	12·00	1·80	1·90
641		5pf. +3pf. emerald	65	30	65
	a. Booklet pane. Nos. 641×5 and 642×5		38·00	23·00	
642		6pf. +4pf. deep grey-green	65	30	65
643		8pf. +4pf. Indian red	7·50	1·10	1·90
644		12pf. +6pf. brown-red	1·30	35	65
645		15pf. +10pf. chocolate	16·00	2·50	6·25
646		25pf. +15pf. dull ultramarine	36·00	5·00	6·25
647		40pf. +35pf. purple (*horizontal ribbed gum*)	60·00	9·00	12·50
	a. Vertically ribbed gum		£800	£120	£800
639/647	Set of 9		£120	19·00	28·00

Designs:—3pf. *Bremen* (lifeboat), 1931; 4pf. *Burgemeister Oswald* (lightship); 5pf. T **131**; 6pf. *Wilhelm Gustloff* (liner); 8pf. *Padua* (barque); 12pf. *Tannenberg* (liner); 15pf. *Schwerin* (train ferry); 25pf. *Hamburg* (liner); 40pf. *Europa* (liner).

P **132** Party Badge    **132** Hitler Youth    **133** Unity

NSDAP = National Socialist German Workers Party

(Des R. Klein. Typo)
1938 (26 Jan). PARTY OFFICIAL. For use of Officials of National Socialist German Workers Party. W **97** (Swastikas). P 14.
O648	P **132**	1pf. black	9·50	1·40	5·00
O649		3pf. bistre-brown	9·50	1·40	3·25
O650		4pf. slate-blue	11·50	1·60	2·50
O651		5pf. emerald-green	4·25	1·20	2·50
O652		6pf. deep green	4·25	1·20	2·50
O653		8pf. vermilion	38·00	5·00	2·50
O654		12pf. carmine	70·00	8·50	2·50
O655		16pf. grey	8·25	1·70	15·00
O656		24pf. sage-green	18·00	2·75	8·25
O657		30pf. bronze-green	14·00	2·00	12·50
O658		40pf. magenta	16·00	2·20	19·00
O648/O658	Set of 11		£180	26·00	70·00

For stamps without watermark in Type P **132**, see Nos. O798/O808.

(Des A. Kolb. Photo)
1938 (28 Jan). Hitler Culture Fund. Fifth Anniv of Hitler's Leadership. W **97** (Swastikas). P 14×13½.
648	**132**	6pf. +4pf. green	12·50	1·90	3·25
649		12pf. +8pf. carmine	12·50	1·90	3·25

(Des E. Puchinger. Photo)
1938 (8 Apr). Austrian Plebiscite.

*(a) Berlin printing (23×28 mm). W **97** (Swastikas). P 14×13½*
650	**133**	6pf. green	3·00	1·30	1·00

(b) Vienna printing (21×26 mm). No wmk. P 12½
651	**133**	6pf. green	3·00	1·30	2·10

134 Adolf Hitler    **135** Breslau Cathedral

(Eng R. Klein. Recess)
1938 (13 Apr). Hitler's Culture Fund and 49th Birthday. No wmk. P 14.
652	**134**	12pf. +38pf. carmine-red	16·00	3·25	4·50

See also No. 660.

(Des G. Fritz. Recess)
1938 (21 June). 16th German Sports Tournament, Breslau. As T **135** (inscr 'Breslau 1938 Deutsches Turn-u. Sportfest'). No wmk. P 14.
653		3pf. brown	1·90	55	90
654		6pf. green	1·90	55	90
655		12pf. rose-red	5·00	1·30	90
656		15pf. brown-lake	11·50	2·75	1·30
653/656	Set of 4		18·00	4·75	3·50

Designs:—3pf. T **135**; 6pf. Hermann Goring Stadium; 12pf. Breslau Town Hall; 15pf. Centenary Hall.

136 Airship gondola and Airship CZ-127 *Graf Zeppelin*    **137** Horsewoman

(Eng. Axster-Heudtlass. Recess)
1938 (5 July). AIR. Birth Centenary of Count Zeppelin. T **136** and similar design. No wmk. P 13½×14.
657		25pf. blue	28·00	4·50	2·50
658		50pf. green	43·00	7·00	2·50

Designs:—25pf. Count Zeppelin in primitive airship gondola and airship LZ-5; 50pf. T **136**.

(Des. R. Klein. Recess)
1938 (22 July). Brown Ribbon of Germany. No wmk. Horizontally ribbed gum. P 14.
659	**137**	42pf. +108pf. brown	£190	35·00	75·00
	a. Vertically ribbed gum		£350	£100	£450

1938 (1 Sept). Nüremburg Congress and Hitler's Culture Fund. As No. 652, but inscr 'Reichsparteitag 1938' below portrait. Vertically ribbed gum. P 14.
660	**134**	6pf. +19pf. green	30·00	3·75	7·00
	a. Horizontally ribbed gum		£250	55·00	£250

41

GERMANY/ Germany (1871-1945)

138 Saarpfalz Gautheater, Saarbrücken
139 Forchtenstein Castle, Burgenland 
144 Horticultural Exhibition Entrance and Arms Stuttgart
145 Adolf Hitler Speaking

(Des G. Fritz. Photo)

1938 (9 Oct). Opening of Gautheater and Hitler's Culture Fund. W **97** (Swastikas). P 14.

661	**138**	6pf. +4pf. blue-green	15·00	2·30	3·25
662		12pf. +8pf. carmine	19·00	3·00	4·50

(Eng Axster-Heudtlass. Recess)

1938 (18 Nov–Dec). Winter Relief Fund. T **139** and similar vert designs. No wmk. P 13½×14.

663	3pf. +2pf. bistre-brown	1·00	35	70
	a. Booklet pane. Nos. 663×4, 668×5 plus label (12.38)	75·00	45·00	
664	4pf. +3pf. slate-blue	14·00	2·75	1·90
665	5pf. +3pf. yellowish green	75	35	75
	a. Booklet pane. Nos. 665×5 and 666×5 (12.38)	38·00	23·00	
666	6pf. +4pf. deep green	75	35	75
667	8pf. +4pf. red	14·00	2·75	1·90
668	12pf. +6pf. brown-red	90	40	75
669	15pf. +10pf. maroon	25·00	5·00	7·50
670	25pf. +15pf. deep blue	21·00	4·50	7·50
671	40pf. +35pf. deep magenta	50·00	10·00	12·50
663/671	Set of 9	£110	24·00	31·00

Designs:—3pf. T **139**; 4pf. Flexenstrasse; 5pf. Zell am See; 6pf. Grossglockner; 8pf. Wachau (Augstein Castle); 12pf. Wien (Prince Eugene statue, Vienna); 15pf. Erzberg, Steiermark; 25pf. Hall i. Tirol; 40pf. Braunau.

140 Sudeten Miner and Wife
141 Racing Cars 

(Des Axster-Heudtlass. Photo)

1938 (2 Dec). Acquisition of Sudetenland and Hitler's Culture Fund. W **97**. Horizontally ribbed gum. P 14.

672	**140**	6pf. +4pf. deep blue-green	21·00	2·50	5·00
		a. Vertically ribbed gum	50·00	12·50	80·00
673		12pf. +8pf. deep rose-red	30·00	3·75	5·00

(Des E. Meerwald. Photo)

1939 (17 Feb). International Motor Show, Berlin and Hitler's Culture Fund. T **141** and similar designs. W **97** (Swastikas). P 14×13½.

674	6pf. +4pf. blue-green	38·00	5·75	5·75
675	12pf. +8pf. carmine	38·00	5·75	5·75
676	25pf. +10pf. blue	65·00	11·00	10·00
674/676	Set of 3	£130	19·00	19·00

Designs:—6pf. Early Benz and Daimler cars; 12pf. T **141**; 25pf. Volkswagen car.

142 Eagle and Laurel Wreath
143 Adolf Hitler in Braunau 

(Des E. Meerwald. Photo)

1939 (4 Apr). Apprentices' Vocational Contest. W **97** (Swastikas). P 14.

677	**142**	6pf. blue-green	14·00	3·00	6·25
678		12pf. carmine	18·00	3·75	6·25

(Eng R. Klein. Recess)

1939 (13 Apr). Hitler's 50th Birthday and Culture Fund. No wmk. P 13½×14.

679	**143**	12pf. +38pf. carmine	14·00	2·75	7·50

(Des H. L. Schmitt. Photo. State Printing Works, Vienna)

1939 (22 Apr). Stuttgart Horticultural Exhibition and Hitler's Culture Fund. No wmk. P 12½.

680	**144**	6pf. +4pf. green	10·00	2·00	5·00
681		15pf. +5pf. claret	15·00	3·00	6·25

1939 (28 Apr). National Labour Day and Hitler's Culture Fund. Photo. W **97** (Swastikas). P 14×13½.

682	**145**	6pf. +19pf. sepia	20·00	6·25	8·25

See also No. 689.

(146) 
147 'Investment' and Jockey

1939 (18 May). Nürburgring Races and Hitler's Culture Fund. Nos. 674/6 optd with T **146**.

683	6pf. +4pf. blue-green	£120	31·00	44·00
684	12pf. +8pf. carmine	£120	31·00	44·00
685	25pf. +10pf. blue	£120	31·00	44·00
683/685	Set of 3	£325	85·00	£120

(Des Hadank. Recess)

1939 (18 June). 70th Anniv of German Derby. P 14×13½.

686	**147**	25pf. +50pf. ultramarine	£100	25·00	25·00

148 Training Thoroughbred Horses
149 Young Venetian Woman after A. Dürer 

(Des R. Klein. Recess)

1939 (3 July). Brown Ribbon of Germany. P 14×13½.

687	**148**	42pf. +108pf. deep brown	£100	25·00	40·00

1939 (12 July). German Art Day. Photo. W **97**. P 13½×14.

688	**149**	6pf. +19pf. green	44·00	8·75	16·00

1939 (25 Aug). Nüremberg Congress. As No. 682 but inscr 'REICHS/PARTEITAG/1939'.

689	6pf. +19pf. sepia	30·00	7·00	15·00

150 Mechanics at Work and Play
151 St. Mary's Church, Danzig 

(Des Axster-Heudtlass. Photo State Ptg Works, Vienna)

1939 (15 Sept). Postal Employees' and Hitler's Culture Funds. As T **150** (inscr 'Kameradschaftsblock der Deutschen Reichspost'). P 13½×14.

690	3pf. +2pf. brown	20·00	3·75	8·75
691	4pf. +3pf. grey-blue	18·00	3·25	8·75

692	5pf. +3pf. emerald-green	5·00	1·00	2·50	
693	6pf. +4pf. blue-green	6·25	1·20	2·50	
694	8pf. +4pf. orange	6·25	1·20	2·50	
695	10pf. +5pf. chocolate	6·25	1·20	3·25	
696	12pf. +6pf. red	7·50	1·40	3·25	
697	15pf. +10pf. claret	6·25	1·20	3·75	
698	16pf. +10pf. slate-green	6·25	1·20	3·75	
699	20pf. +10pf. ultramarine	6·25	1·20	3·75	
700	24pf. +10pf. olive-green	16·00	3·25	6·25	
701	25pf. +15pf. indigo	16·00	3·25	5·00	
690/701	*Set of 12*	£110	21·00	49·00	

Designs:—3pf. Postal Employees' Rally; 4pf. Review in Vienna; 5pf. T **150**; 6pf. Youths on parade; 8pf. Flag bearers; 10pf. Distributing prizes; 12pf. Motor race; 15pf. Women athletes; 16pf. Postal police; 20pf. Glider workshop; 24pf. Mail coach; 25pf. Sanatorium, Königstein. See also. Nos. 761/6 and 876/81.

1939 (18 Sept). Occupation of Danzig. T **151** and similar design inscr 'DANZIG IST DEUTSCH'. Photo. W **97** (Swastikas). P 14.

702	6pf. green	2·50	70	1·30	
703	12pf. red (Crane Gate)	3·75	1·10	1·40	

Rpf   4 Rpf 4
Deutsches   Deutsches
Reich   Reich

Rpf   4 Rpf 4
(152)   (153)

1 Reichsmark

Deutsches Reich
(154)

1939 (1 Oct). Stamps of Danzig, T **39** (Arms) and T **42** (Views), optd as T **152** or surch as T **153** and **154**.

704	**39**	Rpf. on 3pf. brown	3·50	1·00	3·50
705		4Rpf. on 35pf. bright blue	3·25	1·00	3·75
706		Rpf. on 5pf. orange	3·25	1·00	4·50
707		Rpf. on 8pf. yellow-green	5·75	1·60	6·25
708		Rpf. on 10pf. green	10·00	3·25	6·25
709		12Rpf. on 7pf. yellow-green	7·50	2·30	3·50
710		Rpf. on 15pf. scarlet	30·00	9·50	18·00
711		Rpf. on 20pf. grey	15·00	4·50	12·50
712		Rpf. on 25pf. carmine	23·00	7·00	16·00
713		Rpf. on 30pf. purple	10·00	3·25	7·00
714		Rpf. on 40pf. indigo	12·00	3·75	8·75
715		Rpf. on 50pf. scarlet and blue	19·00	5·75	10·50
716	**42**	1Rm. on 1g. black and orange	70·00	21·00	90·00
717	–	2Rm. on 2g. black and carmine	90·00	28·00	95·00
		a. 'Deutsches Reich' omitted	£13000		
		b. '2 Reichsmark' omitted	£6500		
704/717	*Set of 14*		£275	85·00	£250

The Danzig stamps used for the above issue have the Swastika watermark, except for the 7, 20 and 35pf. (Small Honeycomb) and the 2g. (Lozenges). The 30pf., wmk Swastikas, does not exist without the overprint.

Nos. 716/717 were issued with yellow or white gum.

Nos. 704/717 are often found with commemorative postmarks dated 1 or 28 September. These cancellations were used without change of date for about three months.

155 Elbogen Castle

N **156** Newspaper Messenger and Globe

(Des H. Trier. Recess)

1939 (27 Oct–Dec). Winter Relief Fund. T **155** and similar horiz designs. P 14.

718	3pf. +2pf. deep brown	1·50	30	75	
	a. Booklet pane. Nos. 718×4, 723×5 plus label (12.39)	75·00	45·00		
719	4pf. +3pf. slate-black	11·50	2·50	3·25	

GERMANY/ Germany (1871-1945)

720	5pf. +3pf. emerald	2·50	50	90	
	a. Booklet pane Nos. 720×5 and 721×5 (12.39)	38·00	23·00		
721	6pf. +4pf. bronze green	1·50	30	65	
722	8pf. +4pf. orange-red	11·50	2·50	2·75	
723	12pf. +6pf. deep rose-red	5·00	90	2·50	
724	15pf. +10pf. chocolate	18·00	3·75	7·50	
725	25pf. +15pf. dull ultramarine	14·00	3·25	7·50	
726	40pf. +35pf. deep claret	19·00	4·25	10·00	
718/726	*Set of 9*	75·00	16·00	32·00	

Designs:—3pf. T **155**; 4pf. Drachenfels; 5pf. Goslar Castle; 6pf. Clocktower, Graz; 8pf. The Römer, Frankfurt; 12pf. City Hall, Klagenfurt; 15pf. Ruins of Schreckenstein Castle; 25pf. Salzburg Fortress; 40pf. Hohentwiel Castle.

1939 (1 Nov). NEWSPAPER. Photo. W **97** (Swastikas). P 14.

N727	N **156**	5pf. green	3·75	95	8·75
N728		10pf. brown	3·75	95	8·75

156 Leipzig Library and Gutenberg

157 Courtyard of Chancellery, Berlin

(Des R. Engelhardt (25pf.), Axster-Heudtlass (others). Photo State Ptg Wks, Vienna)

1940 (3 Mar). Leipzig Fair. As T **156** (inscr 'Leipziger Messe'). P 10½.

727	3pf. brown	2·50	75	75
728	6pf. grey-green	2·50	75	75
729	12pf. carmine	2·50	75	75
730	25pf. ultramarine	4·75	1·50	1·90
727/730	*Set of 4*	11·00	3·50	3·75

Designs (Leipzig views):—3pf. T **156**; 6pf. Augustusplatz; 12pf. Old Town Hall; 25pf. View of the Fair.

(Des G. Fritz. Recess)

1940 (28 Mar). Second Berlin Philatelic Exhibition. P 14.
731 **157** 24pf. +76pf. green .... 45·00 10·00 28·00

158 Hitler and Child    **159** Wehrmacht Symbol

(Des R. Klein. Photo)

1940 (10 Apr). Hitler's 51st Birthday. W **97** (Swastikas). P 14×13½.
732 **158** 12pf. +38pf. brown-red .... 20·00 5·00 10·00

(Des A. Grögerchen. Photo State Ptg Wks, Vienna)

1940 (30 Apr). National Fête Day and Hitler's Culture Fund. P 14.
733 **159** 6pf. +4pf. green .... 2·30 50 2·10

160 Horseman    **161** Chariot

(Des E. Stahl. Photo)

1940 (22 June). Hamburg Derby and Hitler's Culture Fund. W **97** (Swastikas). P 14×13½.
734 **160** 25pf. +100pf. ultramarine .... 33·00 7·00 19·00

(Des R. Klein. Eng F. Lorber. Recess State Ptg Wks, Vienna)

1940 (20 July). Brown Ribbon Race and Hitler's Culture Fund. P 14.
735 **161** 42pf. +108pf. brown .... £150 38·00 44·00

GERMANY/ Germany (1871-1945)

162 Malmedy    **163** Heligoland

(Des Vogenauer. Photo)

1940 (25 July). Re-incorporation of Eupen and Malmedy and Hitler's Culture Fund. T **162** and similar type inscr 'Eupen-Malmedy/wieder deutsch'. W **97** (Swastikas). P 14×13½.
736		6pf. +4pf. green	8·25	1·90	4·75
737		12pf. +8pf. brown-red	8·25	1·90	4·75

Designs:—6pf. T **162**; 12pf. View of Eupen.

(Des Meerwald. Photo State Ptg Wks, Vienna)

1940 (9 Aug). 50th Anniv of Cession of Heligoland to Germany and Hitler's Culture Fund. P 14×13½.
738	**163**	6pf. +94pf. red and green	38·00	9·50	19·00

164 Artushof, Danzig    **165** Emil von Behring (bacteriologist)    **166** Postilion and Globe

(Des L. Wüst. Recess)

1940 (5 Nov–Dec). Winter Relief Fund. T **164** and similar vert designs. P 14.
739		3pf. +2pf. deep brown	1·50	45	75
		a. Booklet pane. Nos. 739×4, 744×5 plus label (12.40)	75·00	45·00	
740		4pf. +3pf. indigo	5·00	1·40	1·30
741		5pf. +3pf. yellowish green	1·50	45	75
		a. Booklet pane. Nos. 741× 5 and 742×5 (12.40)	38·00	23·00	
742		6pf. +4pf. bottle green	1·80	55	75
743		8pf. +4pf. red-orange	7·50	2·10	1·40
744		12pf. +6pf. scarlet	1·90	55	75
745		15pf. +10pf. purple-brown	8·25	2·40	4·50
746		25pf. +15pf. blue	10·50	3·25	4·50
747		40pf. +35pf. deep claret	20·00	5·25	10·00
739/747 Set of 9			50·00	14·50	22·00

Designs:—3pf. T **164**; 4pf. Town Hall, Thorn; 5pf. Kaub Castle; 6pf. City Theatre, Posen; 8pf. Heidelberg Castle; 12pf. Porta Nigra, Trier; 15pf. New Theatre, Prague; 25pf. Town Hall, Bremen; 40pf. Town Hall, Münster.

(Photo State Ptg Wks, Vienna)

1940 (26 Nov). 50th Anniv of Development of Diphtheria Antitoxin. P 14.
748	**165**	6pf. +4pf. green	7·50	1·60	3·50
749		25pf. +10pf. ultramarine	11·50	2·75	3·75

(Des Meerwald. Photo State Ptg Wks, Vienna)

1941 (12 Jan). Stamp Day. P 14.
750	**166**	6pf. +24pf. green	8·25	1·90	5·00

167 Mussolini and Hitler    **168** House of Nations, Leipzig

(Des R. Klein. Photo)

1941 (30 Jan). Hitler's Culture Fund. W **97** (Swastikas). P 13½×14.
751	**167**	12pf. +38pf. carmine	10·50	1·90	7·00

(Des E. Stahl. Photo State Ptg Wks, Vienna)

1941 (1 Mar). Leipzig Fair. As T **168** (buildings, inscr 'REICHSMESSE LEIPZIG 1941'). P 14×13½.
752		3pf. brown	3·25	50	1·60
753		6pf. green	3·25	50	1·60
754		12pf. rose-red	3·25	50	1·90
755		25pf. blue	7·50	1·20	2·50
752/755 Set of 4			16·00	2·40	6·75

Designs:—3pf. T **168**; 6pf. Cloth Hall; 12pf. Exhibition Building; 25pf. Railway station.

169 Dancer    **170** Adolf Hitler

(Des W. Dachauer. Photo State Ptg Wks, Vienna)

1941 (8 Mar). Vienna Fair. T **169** and similar designs. P 13½×14.
756		3pf. brown	3·25	70	90
757		6pf. green	3·25	70	90
758		12pf. scarlet	3·25	70	1·00
759		25pf. blue	9·50	2·00	2·50
756/759 Set of 4			17·00	3·75	4·75

Designs:—3pf. T **169**; 6pf. Arms and Exhibition Building; 12pf. Allegory and Municipal Theatre; 25pf. Prince Eugene's Equestrian Monument.

(Des. E. Vogenauer. Photo)

1941 (17 Apr). Hitler's 52nd Birthday and Culture Fund. W **97**. Vertically ribbed gum. P 14×13½.
760	**170**	12pf. +38pf. red	12·50	1·90	5·00
		a. Horizontally ribbed gum	25·00	5·75	28·00

1941 (16 May). Postal Employees' and Hitler's Culture Fund. Inscr 'Kameradschaftsblock der Deutschen Reichspost' as Nos. 693/4, 696 and 698/700, but premium values and colours changed.
761		6pf. +9pf. yellow-green	6·25	1·10	3·75
762		8pf. +12pf. brown-red	9·50	1·80	2·50
763		12pf. +18pf. lake	9·50	1·80	3·25
764		16pf. +24pf. black	9·50	1·80	6·25
765		20pf. +30pf. ultramarine	12·50	2·30	6·25
766		24pf. +46pf. violet	31·00	6·75	19·00
761/766 Set of 6			70·00	14·00	37·00

171 Racehorse    **172** Two Amazons

(Des E. Meerwald. Recess State Ptg Wks, Vienna)

1941 (20 June). 72nd Anniv of the Hamburg Derby. P 14.
767	**171**	25pf. +100pf. blue	21·00	5·00	12·50

(Des R. Klein. Recess State Ptg Wks, Vienna)

1941 (20 July). Brown Ribbon of Germany. P 14.
768	**172**	42pf. +108pf. brown	15·00	3·25	8·25

173 Adolf Hitler    **174** Brandenburg Gate, Berlin

(Des R. Klein)

1941 (1 Aug)–**42**. P 14.

(a) Typo. Size 18½×22½ mm
769	**173**	1pf. deep grey	50	25	50
		a. Booklet pane. Nos. 769×4 and 772×4 (12.41)	19·00	11·50	
770		3pf. yellow-brown	50	25	50
		a. Booklet pane. Nos. 770×6 and 773×2 (12.41)	19·00	11·50	
771		4pf. slate-blue	50	25	50
		a. Booklet pane. Nos. 771×4, 774×2 plus two labels (12.41)	19·00	11·50	
		b. Coil pair. Nos. 771 and 773 (1942)	3·75	2·30	6·25

GERMANY/Germany (1871-1945)

772		5pf. dull yellowish green	50	25	50
773		6pf. reddish violet	50	25	50
		a. Booklet pane. No. 773×7 plus label (12.41)	38·00	23·00	
774		8pf. bright orange-red	50	25	50
775		10pf. brown (12.42)	65	35	75
		a. Imperf (pair)	£350	£130	£500
776	173	12pf. scarlet-vermilion (12.42)	65	35	75
		a. Imperf (pair)	£350	£150	£650

(b) Recess. Size 18½×22½ mm

777	173	10pf. brown	1·50	65	65
778		12pf. carmine-red	1·50	65	65
		a. Booklet pane. No. 778×6 plus two labels (12.41)	12·50	7·50	
779		15pf. lake	65	25	2·50
780		16pf. deep bluish green	50	25	2·50
781		20pf. blue	50	25	65
782		24pf. orange-brown	50	25	2·50

(c) Recess. Size 21½×26 mm

783	173	25pf. ultramarine	50	25	75
784		30pf. olive-green	50	25	75
785		40pf. deep magenta	50	25	75
786		50pf. bottle green	50	25	75
787		60pf. purple-brown	50	25	75
788		80pf. deep blue	50	25	75
769/788	*Set of 20*		11·00	5·75	17·00

There is a range of shades for Nos. 769/788.
6pf. violet stamps in a similar design but portraying Himmler are propaganda forgeries made by British Intelligence.
For 42pf. inscribed 'GROSSDEUTSCHESREICH', see No. 894.

(Des E. Meerwald. Recess)

1941 (9 Sept). Berlin Grand Prix and Hitler's Culture Fund. P 14.

789	174	25pf. +50pf. ultramarine	18·00	4·50	11·50

175 Belvedere Palace, Vienna
176 Belvedere Gardens, Vienna 

(Des E. Puchinger (12pf.), F. Zerritsch (15pf.). Recess State Ptg Wks, Vienna)

1941 (16 Sept). Vienna Fair and Hitler's Culture Fund. P 14.

790	175	12pf. +8pf. rose-red	7·50	2·00	6·25
791	176	15pf. +10pf. violet	8·75	2·30	6·25

177 Marburg
178 Veldes 

(Des E. Meerwald. Photo State Ptg Wks, Vienna)

1941 (29 Sept). Annexation of Northern Slovenia, and Hitler's Culture Fund. As T **177/8** (views). P 14.

792	177	3pf. +7pf. brown	5·75	1·30	3·75
793	178	6pf. +9pf. violet	5·75	1·30	3·75
794	—	12pf. +13pf. lake (Pettau)	5·75	1·30	4·50
795	—	25pf. +15pf. blue (Triglav)	11·50	2·50	4·50
792/795	*Set of 4*		29·00	5·75	15·00

179 Mozart
180 Philatelist 

(Des and eng H. Ranzoni. Recess State Ptg Wks, Vienna)

1941 (28 Nov). 150th Anniv of Mozart and Hitler's Culture Fund. P 14.

796	179	6pf. +4pf. purple	1·30	40	1·50

(Des E. Stahl. Photo State Ptg Wks, Vienna)

1942 (11 Jan). Stamp Day and Hitler's Culture Fund. P 14.

797	180	6pf. +24pf. violet	5·00	90	4·75

1942 (2 Mar). PARTY OFFICIAL. For use of Officials of National Socialist German Workers Party. No wmk. P 14.

O798	P 132	1pf. grey	6·25	1·50	50·00
O799		3pf. brown	1·50	45	1·90
O800		4pf. slate-blue	6·25	1·50	5·00
O801		5pf. olive-green	1·50	45	38·00
O802		6pf. deep violet	1·50	45	3·75
O803		8pf. vermilion	2·00	50	3·75
O804		12pf. carmine	2·00	50	1·90
O805		16pf. greenish blue	31·00	6·25	£130
O806		24pf. yellow-brown	3·75	90	50·00
O807		30pf. bronze-green	5·00	1·20	38·00
O808		40pf. magenta	5·00	1·20	75·00
O798/O808	*Set of 11*		60·00	13·50	£350

181 Symbolical of Heroism
182 Adolf Hitler 

(Des R. Klein. Photo)

1942 (10 Mar). Heroes' Remembrance Day and Hitler's Culture Fund. P 14.

798	181	12pf. +38pf. slate	3·00	75	2·75

(Des W. Dachauer. Eng F. Lorber. Recess State Ptg Wks, Vienna)

1942 (20 Mar)–**44**. P 12½.

799	182	1rm. bottle green	6·25	2·50	10·00
		a. Perf 14 (1944)	1·90	75	8·75
800		2rm. blackish purple	5·00	2·00	10·00
		a. Perf 14 (1944)	6·25	2·50	12·50
801		3rm. brown-red	6·25	2·50	25·00
		a. Perf 14 (1944)	38·00	15·00	44·00
802		5rm. deep blue	11·50	5·00	80·00
		a. Perf 14 (1944)	19·00	7·50	65·00
799/802	*Set of 4*		26·00	11·00	£110
799a/802a	*Set of 4*		60·00	23·00	£120

Nos. 800a/802a (perf 14) are extremely rare genuinely used, our prices are for cancelled to order.

183 Adolf Hitler
M **184** Junkers Ju 52/3m 

(Des E. Vogenauer. Photo)

1942 (13 Apr). Hitler's 53rd Birthday and Culture Fund. Horizontally ribbed gum. P 14.

803	183	12pf. +38pf. claret	19·00	2·50	10·00
		a. Vertically ribbed gum	31·00	4·25	35·00

(Des E. Meerwald. Typo)

1942 (18 Apr)–**43**. MILITARY FIELD POST FOR AIR MAIL. P 13½.

M804	M **184**	(—) ultramarine	1·10	55	75
		a. Rouletted (1943)	75	45	7·30

Stamps perf 12, in litho or typo, are forgeries, some of which were produced during the war by British Intelligence.

184 Jockey and Three-year-old Horse
M **185** 

45

GERMANY / Germany (1871-1945)

(Des L. Hohlwein. Recess State Ptg Wks, Vienna)

1942 (16 June). Hamburg Derby and Hitler's Culture Fund. P 14.
804	**184**	25pf. +100pf. blue	28·00	7·50	19·00

(Des Marggraff. Typo)

1942 (10 July). MILITARY FIELD POST for PARCELS. Size 28×23 mm. P 13½.
M805	M **185**	(–) lake-brown	1·10	50	19·00
		a. Rouletted	75	40	£150

See No. M895.

Nos. M804/M805 also exist overprinted 'INSELPOST' in various types for use in Crete and the Aegean Islands and there are various other local fieldpost issues.

185 Equine Trio   **186** Cream Jug and Loving Cup

(Des R. Klein. Recess State Ptg Wks, Vienna)

1942 (14 July). Brown Ribbon of Germany and Hitler's Culture Fund. P 14.
805	**185**	42pf. +108pf. brown	12·50	2·50	8·75

No. 805 was issued with yellow or white gum.

1942 (28 July). OFFICIAL. No wmk. P 14.
O809	O **100**	3pf. brown	1·00	40	1·90
O810		4pf. slate-blue	90	30	5·00
O811		5pf. green	1·50	40	25·00
O812		6pf. deep violet	1·00	40	1·90
O813		8pf. vermilion	1·00	40	1·90
O814		10pf. deep brown	2·50	65	19·00
O815		12pf. carmine	1·90	50	7·50
O816		15pf. claret	19·00	4·75	90·00
O817		20pf. blue	1·50	50	12·50
O818		30pf. bronze-green	1·50	50	12·50
O819		40pf. magenta	3·25	1·00	31·00
O820		50pf. deep green	25·00	5·75	£500
O809/O820	Set of 12		55·00	14·00	£650

(Des G. Tischer. Photo State Ptg Wks, Vienna)

1942 (8 Aug). Tenth Anniv of National Goldsmiths' Institution. P 14.
806	**186**	6pf. +4pf. brown-lake	2·20	50	2·50
807		12pf. +88pf. green	3·25	85	3·75

187 Badge of Armed SA   **188** Peter Henlein

(Des Axster-Heudtlass. Photo State Ptg Wks, Vienna)

1942 (12 Aug). Armed Sports Day of Sturm Abteilung (Nazi Militia). P 14.
808	**187**	6pf. violet	1·30	40	1·30

(Des Manz. Photo State Ptg Wks, Vienna)

1942 (29 Aug). 400th Death Anniv of Henlein (inventor of the watch). P 14.
809	**188**	6pf. +24pf. violet	2·75	75	2·50

189 Mounted Postilion   (**190**)

(Des E. Meerwald. No. 810 photo State Ptg Wks, Vienna. No. 811 eng Schuricht, recess State Ptg Wks, Vienna. No. 812 eng Zenziger, recess, Berlin)

1942 (12 Oct). European Postal Congress, Vienna. T **189** and similar designs. P 14.
810		3pf. +7pf. blue	1·30	45	2·50
811		6pf. +14pf. brown and blue	1·90	65	2·50
812		12pf. +38pf. brown and carmine	3·25	95	4·50
810/812	Set of 3		5·75	1·50	8·50

Designs: Horiz—3pf. Postilion and map of Europe; 12pf. T **189**. Vert—6pf. mounted postilion and globe.

1942 (19 Oct). Signing of European Postal Union Agreement. Nos. 810/812 optd with T **190**.
813		3pf. +7pf. blue	3·75	1·10	4·50
814		6pf. +14pf. brown and blue	3·75	1·10	4·50
815		12pf. +38pf. brown and carmine	5·00	1·70	7·50
813/815	Set of 3		11·00	3·50	15·00

191 Mail Coach   **192** Brandenburg Gate and Torchlight Parade

(Des Erich Meerwald. Centre recess, frame litho)

1943 (10 Jan). Stamp Day and Hitler's Culture Fund. P 13½×14.
816	**191**	6pf. +24pf. brown, yellow and grey-black	1·30	40	1·50

(Des G. Klein. Photo State Ptg Wks, Vienna)

1943 (26 Jan). Tenth Anniv of Third Reich. P 14.
817	**192**	54pf. +96pf. brown-lake	4·50	75	3·75

193   **194** Machine Gunners

(Des G. Marggraff. Photo State Ptg Wks, Vienna)

1943 (26 Jan). P 14.
818	**193**	3pf. +2pf. olive-bistre	1·10	40	1·50

The use of this stamp secured special philatelic cancellations.

(Des E. Meerwald. Eng W. Hertz (3pf.), F. Lorber (4, 5pf.) J. Piwczyk (6, 25pf.), L. Schnell (8, 12pf.), R. Zenziger (15, 50pf.), A. Schuricht (20pf.), W. Goritz (30pf.) and B. Chabada (40pf.). Recess Govt Printing Works, Berlin or (Nos. 820/821 825/826 and 830) State Ptg Wks, Vienna)

1943 (21 Mar). Armed Forces' and Heroes' Day. T **194** and similar horiz designs. P 14.
819		3pf. +2pf. sepia	2·50	80	2·00
820		4pf. +3pf. brown	2·50	80	2·00
821		5pf. +4pf. green	1·90	60	2·00
		a. Imperf (pair)	£650	£250	
822		6pf. +9pf. violet	1·90	60	2·00
823		8pf. +7pf. Indian red	2·00	65	2·00
824		12pf. +8pf. carmine-red	3·25	1·00	2·00
825		15pf. +10pf. brown-purple	3·25	1·00	2·00
		a. Imperf (pair)	£650	£250	
826		20pf. +14pf. indigo	3·25	1·00	2·00
827		25pf. +15pf. deep blue	3·75	1·20	2·00
828		30pf. +20pf. green	3·25	1·00	3·25
829		40pf. +40pf. deep claret	3·25	1·00	3·25
830		50pf. +50pf. blackish green	3·25	1·00	5·00
819/830	Set of 12		31·00	9·50	27·00

Designs:—3pf. U-boat Type V11A (submarine); 4pf. T **194**; 5pf. Armed motorcyclists; 6pf. Wireless operators; 8pf. Engineers making pontoon; 12pf. Grenade thrower; 15pf. Heavy artillery; 20pf. Anti-aircraft gunners; 25pf. Junkers Ju 87B Stuka dive bombers; 30pf. Parachutists; 40pf. Tank; 50pf. S-22 (motor torpedo-boat).

195 Hitler Youth   **196** Adolf Hitler

(Des E. Meerwald. Photo State Ptg Wks, Vienna)

1943 (26 Mar). Youth Dedication Day. P 14.
831	**195**	6pf. +4pf. green	1·80	40	2·10

GERMANY/ Germany (1871-1945)

(Des G. Klein. Photo State Ptg Wks, Vienna)
1943 (13 Apr). Hitler's 54th Birthday and Culture Fund. P 14.

832	196	3pf. +7pf. black	3·25	1·00	2·50
		a. Imperf (pair)	£650	£250	
833		6pf. +14pf. deep dull green	1·90	70	2·50
834		8pf. +22pf. deep blue	1·90	70	2·50
835		12pf. +38pf. brown-red	1·90	70	2·50
836		24pf. +76pf. maroon	4·50	1·40	5·75
837		40pf. +160pf. blackish olive	4·50	1·40	5·75
832/837	Set of 6		16·00	5·25	19·00

197 Attestation  **198** Huntsman

(Des K. Müller-Rabe. Eng R. Zenziger (3pf.), A. Schuricht (5 and 6pf.) and F. Lorber (12pf.). Recess State Ptg Wks, Vienna)
1943 (26 June). Labour Corps. T **197** and similar vert designs. P 14.

838		3pf. +7pf. brown	1·30	30	1·30
		a. Imperf (pair)	£375	£110	
839		5pf. +10pf. deep yellow-green	1·30	30	1·30
		a. Imperf (pair)	£375	£110	
840		6pf. +14pf. blue	1·20	25	1·30
841		12pf. +18pf. red	1·90	55	2·30
		a. Imperf (pair)	£500	£140	
838/841	Set of 4		5·25	1·30	5·50

Designs:—3pf. T **197**; 5pf. Harvester sharpening scythe; 6pf. Labourer wielding sledge-hammer; 12pf. 'Pick and shovel fatigue'.

(Des R. Klein. Eng R. Zenziger. Recess State Ptg Wks, Vienna)
1943 (27 July). Brown Ribbon of Germany. P 14.

842	198	42pf. +108pf. deep brown	1·50	40	2·00
		a. Imperf (pair)	£1300	£500	

199 Birthplace of Peter Rosegger  **200** Peter Rosegger

(Des Brunlechner (6pf.), Fuchs (12pf.). Photo State Ptg Wks, Vienna)
1943 (27 July). Birth Centenary of Peter Rosegger (poet). P 14.

843	199	6pf. +4pf. green	1·30	25	1·50
		a. Imperf (pair)	£1800	£800	
844	200	12pf. +8pf. deep rose-red	1·30	25	1·50
		a. Imperf (pair)	£1800	£800	

201 Racehorse  **202** Mother and Children  **203** St. George and the Dragon

(Des H. Ranzoni. Recess State Ptg Wks, Vienna)
1943 (14 Aug). Grand Prix, Vienna. P 14.

845	201	6pf. +4pf. carmine	1·40	35	2·00
846		12pf. +88pf. brown-lake	1·40	35	2·00

(Des Axster-Heudtlass. Eng F. Lorber. Recess State Ptg Wks, Vienna)
1943 (1 Sept). Tenth Anniv of Winter Relief Fund. P 14.

847	202	12pf. +38pf. brown-lake	1·40	40	2·00

(Des E. R. Vogenauer. Eng J. Piwczyk. Recess)
1943 (1 Oct). 11th Anniv of National Goldsmiths' Institution. P 14.

848	203	6pf. +9pf. green	90	30	1·30
849		12pf. +88pf. purple	1·00	35	1·90

204 Lübeck  **205**

(Des A. Mahlau. Photo State Ptg Wks, Vienna)
1943 (24 Oct). 800th Anniv of Lübeck. P 14.

850	204	12pf. +8pf. deep rose-red	1·10	30	1·90
		a. Imperf (pair)	£1000	£425	

(Des F. Roubal. Photo State Ptg Wks, Vienna)
1943 (5 Nov). 20th Anniv of Munich Rising. P 14.

851	205	24pf. +26pf. brown-red	1·90	30	2·50
		a. Imperf (pair)	£900		

206 Dr. Robert Koch  **207** Adolf Hitler

(Des E. R. Vogenauer. Eng J. Piwczyk. Recess State Ptg Wks, Vienna)
1944 (25 Jan). Birth Centenary of Dr. Robert Koch (bacteriologist). P 14.

852	206	12pf. +38pf. sepia	1·30	30	1·90

(Des G. Klein. Photo State Ptg Wks, Vienna)
1944 (29 Jan). 11th Anniv of the Third Reich. P 14.

853	207	54pf. +96pf. brown	2·50	40	3·75

208 Focke Wulf Fw 200 Condor over Tempelhof Airport  **209** Dornier Do-26 Flying Boat

(Des E. Meerwald (6pf.), E. R. Vogenauer (others). Photo State Ptg Wks, Vienna)
1944 (11 Feb). 25th Anniv of Airmail Services. T **208/209** (and similar type). P 14.

854	208	6pf. +4pf. green	90	35	1·90
855	209	12pf. +8pf. claret	90	35	1·90
856	—	42pf. +108pf. blue	2·10	50	3·75
854/856	Set of 3		3·50	1·10	6·75

Design: Vert—42pf. Junkers Ju 90B aeroplane.

210 Day Nursery  **211** Mothers' Help

(Des Axster-Heudtlass. Photo State Ptg Wks, Vienna)
1944 (2 Mar). Tenth Anniv of 'Mother and Child' Organisation. T **210/211** and similar vert designs. P 14.

857	210	3pf. +2pf. reddish brown	65	20	1·30
858	211	6pf. +4pf. bottle green	65	20	1·30
		a. Imperf (pair)	£1100		
859	—	12pf. +8pf. carmine	65	20	1·30
860	—	15pf. +10pf. brown-purple	65	20	1·30
857/860	Set of 4		2·30	70	4·75

Designs:—12pf. Child auscultation; 15pf. Mothers at convalescent home.

GERMANY / Germany (1871-1945)

212 Landing Craft

213 Fulda monument

(Des O. Anton. Photo)
1944 (11 Mar). Armed Forces and Heroes' Day. T **212** and similar horiz designs. Horizontally ribbed gum. P 14.

861	3pf. +2pf. light brown	1·90	50	1·90
	a. Vertically ribbed gum	£350	90·00	£375
862	4pf. +3pf. Prussian blue	1·90	50	1·90
863	5pf. +3pf. dull yellowish green	1·10	25	90
	a. Vertically ribbed gum	25·00	8·50	38·00
864	6pf. +4pf. violet	1·10	25	90
865	8pf. +4pf. bright scarlet	25·00	7·50	80·00
	a. Vertically ribbed gum	1·10	20	1·00
866	10pf. +5pf. deep brown	1·10	25	90
867	12pf. +6pf. carmine	1·10	25	90
	a. Vertically ribbed gum	75·00	20·00	90·00
868	15pf. +10pf. claret	1·10	25	1·30
	a. Vertically ribbed gum	95·00	25·00	£100
869	16pf. +10pf. deep bluish green	1·60	45	2·00
870	20pf. +10pf. blue	2·50	55	3·25
871	24pf. +10pf. chestnut	2·50	55	3·25
872	25pf. +15pf. ultramarine	5·00	1·20	6·25
873	30pf. +20pf. deep olive	5·00	1·20	6·25
861/873	Set of 13 (cheapest)	24·00	5·75	28·00

Designs:—3pf. T **212**; 4pf. Caterpillar tricar; 5pf. Parachutists; 6pf. Submarine officer; 8pf. Mortar-firing party; 10pf. Searchlight unit; 12pf. Machine gunners; 15pf. Tank; 16pf. *S-128* (motor torpedo-boat); 20pf. Arado Ar 196A seaplane; 24pf. Railway gun; 25pf. Rocket projectiles; 30pf. Alpine trooper.

No. 865 was issued with yellowish or white gum.

(Des F. Woltt. Photo State Ptg Wks, Vienna)
1944 (11 Mar). 1200th Anniv of Fulda. P 14.

874	**213**	12pf. +38pf. brown	1·00	25	1·50

214 Hitler

215 Postwoman

(Des G. Klein. Eng J. Piwczyk. Recess)
1944 (14 Apr). Hitler's 55th Birthday. P 14.

875	**214**	54pf. +96pf. carmine	3·00	50	5·00

(Des Axster-Heudtlass. Photo State Ptg Wks, Vienna)
1944 (3 May). Postal Employees and Hitler's Culture Funds. As T **150**, but reduced to 30×24½ mm and T **215** (various designs) inscr 'Kameradschaftsblock der Deutschen Reichspost'. P 14.

876	6pf. +9pf. deep ultramarine	90	30	1·30
877	8pf. +12pf. deep greenish slate	90	30	1·30
878	12pf. +18pf. deep claret	90	30	1·30
879	16pf. +24pf. myrtle green	90	30	1·30
880	20pf. +30pf. blue	90	30	2·30
881	24pf. +36pf. deep lilac	1·10	55	2·30
876/881	Set of 6	5·00	1·80	8·75

Designs:—6pf. T **215**. As T **150**—8pf. Mail coach; 16pf. Motor car race; 20pf. Postal police march; 24pf. Glider workshop. As T **215**—12pf. The Field Post on the Eastern Front.

216 Girl Worker

217 Labourer

(Des R. Ahrlé. Eng L. Schnell (6pf) and J. Piwczyk (12pf). Recess)
1944 (June). Labour Corps. P 14.

882	**216**	6pf. +4pf. green	65	25	1·10
883	**217**	12pf. +8pf. scarlet	75	30	1·10

218 Rifleman

219 Duke Albrecht

(Des L. Alton. Photo State Ptg Wks, Vienna)
1944 (2 July). Seventh Innsbruck Shooting Competition. P 14.

884	**218**	6pf. +4pf. green	65	25	1·40
885		12pf. +8pf. lake	75	30	1·40

(Des Prof Marten. Photo State Ptg Wks, Vienna)
1944 (7 July). Fourth Centenary of Foundation of Albert University Königsberg. P 14.

886	**219**	6pf. +4pf. green	1·30	40	2·00

220 Racehorse and Foal

221 Racehorse and Laurel Wreath

(Des R. Klein. Eng A. Schuricht. Recess)
1944 (23 July). Brown Ribbon of Germany. P 14.

887	**220**	42pf. +108pf. brown	1·80	40	3·50

(Des H. Frank. Photo State Ptg Wks, Vienna)
1944 (Aug). Vienna Grand Prix. P 14.

888	**221**	6pf. +4pf. deep bluish green	90	25	1·80
889		12pf. +88pf. carmine-red	90	25	1·80

222 Chambered Nautilus Beaker

223 Posthorn

(Des. E. R. Vogenauer. Photo State Ptg Wks, Vienna)
1944 (11 Sept). National Goldsmiths Institution. T **222** and similar vert design. P 14.

890	**222**	6pf. +4pf. deep green	90	25	1·80
891		12pf. +88pf. brown lake	90	25	1·80
		a. Imperf (pair)	£375	£150	

(Des E. Meerwald. Photo State Ptg Wks, Vienna)
1944 (2 Oct). Stamp Day. P 14.

892	**223**	6pf. +24pf. green	1·10	25	2·00

224 Eagle and Dragon

225 Adolf Hitler

(Des K. Diebitsch. Photo)
1944 (9 Nov). 21st Anniversary of Munich Rising. P 14.

893	**224**	12pf. +8pf. scarlet	1·30	25	2·00

(Des R. Klein. Recess)
1944. P 14.
894   225   42pf. emerald green...................   50   25   3·25

(M **226**)   **226** Count Anton Günther

1944 (20 Oct). MILITARY FIELD POST for CHRISTMAS PARCELS. Size 22½×18 mm. P 14.
M895   M **185**   – bright green...................   2·10   1·00   4·50

Used prices for Nos. M895 and M896 are for cancelled-to-order; postally used examples are rare.

1944 (24 Nov). MILITARY FIELD POST for 2 KILO PARCELS. No. 785 optd with Type M **226**.
M896   **173**   – on 40pf. magenta............   1·90   95   5·50

See note below No. M895.

(Des E. R. Vogenauer. Litho)
1945 (6 Jan). 600th Anniversary of Oldenburg. P 14.
895   226   6pf. +14pf. brown-purple.........   1·30   25   2·00

227 Home Guard   **228** SS Troopers

(Des E. Meerwald. Photo State Ptg Wks, Vienna)
1945 (6 Feb). Mobilisation of Home Guard. P 14.
896   227   12pf. +8pf. carmine...............   2·30   50   4·50

(Des E. Meerwald (897), R. Ahrlé (898). Photo State Ptg Wks,Vienna)
1945 (21 Apr). 12th Anniv of Third Reich. T **228** and similar type. P 14.
897   **228**   12pf. +38pf. scarlet...............   65·00   16·00   90·00
898   –   12pf. +38pf. scarlet................   44·00   12·50   90·00

Design:—No. 898, SA man with flaming torch.

These stamps were on sale only in Berlin for a short period before street-fighting made further postal activity impossible. Used prices are for cancelled-to-order; postally used examples are rare.

Imperforate examples were not issued.

Two 12pf.+38pf. stamps in carmine, one a vertical design showing three servicemen and the other a horizontal design showing a glider with a cloud behind it, were prepared but not issued.

STAMP BOOKLETS

The following checklist covers, in simplified form, booklets issued by Germany from 1910 to 1941. It is intended that it should be used in conjunction with the main listings and details of stamps and panes listed there are not repeated.

Prior to the issue of No. SB1, three experimental booklets were prepared, containing 2, 4 or 8 panes, each No. 55×6. These were not issued.

Prices are for complete booklets

Booklet No.	Date	Contents and cover price	Price
SB1	1.11.10	Germania (T **17**) 2 panes, No. 84×6; 1 pane. No. 84c; 2 panes, No. 85×6. Rose or Green cover (2m.)	£12000
SB2	2.11	Germania (T **17**) As No. SB1 but with No. 84ca	£13000
SB3	1911	Germania (T **17**) 4 panes, No. 84d; 2 panes, No. 85c (2m.)	£13000
SB4	7.12	Germania (T **17**) 3 panes, No. 84×6; 1 pane No. 84e; 1 pane, No. 85×6; 1 pane No. 85d (2m.)	£14000
SB5	5.13	Germania (T **17**) 3 panes, No. 84×6; 1 pane, No. 84f; 1 pane, No. 85×6 (2m.)	£9500
SB6	9.16	Germania (T **24**) 5 panes, No. 98×6 (75pf.)	£2250
SB7	9.16	Germania (T **24**) 3 panes, No. 99×6; 1 pane, No. 99b; 1 pane, No. 100×6 (3m.)	£7500
SB8	9.17	Germania (T **24**) 3 panes, No. 99×6; 1 pane, No. 99c; 1 pane, No. 101×6 (3m.)	£8000
SB9	2.18	Germania (T **17** and **24**) 1 pane, No. 84g; 1 pane, No. 84h; 1 pane, No. 99×6; 1 pane, No. 99d; 1 pane, No. 101×6 (3m.)	£5000
SB10	11.18	Germania (T **17** and **24**) 1 pane, No. 84×6; 1 pane, No. 84i; 1 pane, No. 85×6; 1 pane, No. 85e; 1 pane, No. 101×6 (3m.)	£5000
SB11	6.19	Germania (T **17** and **24**) 1 pane, No. 84×6; 1 pane. No. 84ia; 1 pane, No. 85×6; 1 pane, No. 85ea; 1 pane, No. 101×6 (3m.)	£1100
SB12	12.19	Germania (T **17** and **24**) 1 pane, No. 84×6; 1 pane, No. 84j; 1 pane, No. 85×6; 1 pane, No. 85ea; 1 pane, No. 101×6 (3m.)	£600
SB13	5.20	Germania (T **17** and **24**) 1 pane, No. 84×6; 1 pane, No. 84fa; 1 pane, No. 102×6; 1 pane, No. 102b; 1 pane, No. 86d×6 (4m.)	£375
SB14	11.20	Germania (T **17**) 1 pane, No. 141×6; 1 pane, No. 141d; 1 pane, No. 143a×6; 1 pane, No. 143c; 1 pane, No. 144a×6 (8m.)	£300
SB15	1921	Germania (T **17**) and Numeral (T **35**) 1 pane, No. 154c; 1 pane, No. 157b, 1 pane, No. 144a×6; 1 pane, No. 144c; 1 pane, No. 146×6 (12m.)	£1100
SB16	10.25	Eagle (T **66**) 2 panes, No. 370×10; 1 pane, No. 371×10 (2m.)	£10000
SB17	12.10.25	Rhineland Millenary (T **73**) 2 panes, No. 384×10; 1 pane, No. 385×10 (2m.)	£8000
SB18	15.12.25	Welfare Fund (as T **75**) 1 pane, No. 389×4; 1 pane, No. 390×4; 1 pane, No. 391a (2m.)	£2250
		a. As above but third pane contains No. 391×2 (no labels)	£3000
SB19	11.26	Schiller and Frederick the Great (as T **78**) 2 panes, No. 402a; 1 pane. No. 405a (2m.)	£7500
SB20	1.12.26	Welfare Fund (as T **75**) 1 pane, No. 413×8; 1 pane, No 414b (2m.)	£1400
		a. As above but No. 414ba	
SB21	10.27	Beethoven and Kant (as T **78**) 1 pane, No. 404a; 1 pane, No 406a (2m.)	£7500
SB22	11.27	Welfare Fund. Hindenburg (T **79**) 1 pane, No. 417a (1m.50)	£425
SB23	9.28	Hindenburg (T **82**) and Ebert (T **81**) 1 pane, No. 426c; 1 pane, No. 428×10; 1 pane. No. 432b	£3750
		a. As above but No. 428b	£9000
SB24	15.11.28	Welfare Fund (as T **75**) 1 pane, No. 447b (1m.50)	£750
		a. No. 447ba	£900
SB25	1.12.29	Welfare Fund (as T **75**) 1 pane, No. 451a; 1 pane, No. 452a (1m.50)	£700
SB26	1.11.30	Welfare Fund (T **86, 88**) 1 pane, No. 465a; 1 pane, No. 465b	£600
SB27	18.12.30	AIR (T **76**) 1 pane, No. 393×10; 1 pane, No 395b (2m.)	£3000
SB28	14.7.31	AIR (T **76**) 1 pane, No. 393c; 1 pane, No. 395d (2m.)	£1400
SB29	1.11.31	Welfare Fund (as T **91**) 1 pane, No. 472a; 1 pane, No. 472b (2m.)	£600
SB30	15.4.32	Hindenburg (T **82**) and Ebert (T **81**) 1 pane, No. 425c; 1 pane, No. 426d; 1 pane, No. 427a (2m.)	£1400
SB31	1.11.32	Welfare Fund (as T **92**) 1 pane, No. 485a; 1 pane, No. 487b (2m.)	£425
SB32	5.33	Frederick the Great (T **96**) 1 pane, No. 490×6; 1 pane, No. 491b (96pf.)	£225
SB33	5.8.33	Hindenburg (T **94**). Wmk Mesh 1 pane, No. 479a; 1 pane, No. 497A×6; 1 pane, No: 498Aa (2m.)	£1100

49

GERMANY/ Germany (1871-1945)

No.	Date	Description	Price
SB34	11.33	Welfare Fund. Wagner's Operas (as T **99**) 1 pane, No. 514ab; 1 pane, No. 517ab	£1200
SB35	6.34	Hindenburg (T **94**). Wmk Swastikas 1 pane, No. 493Bb; 1 pane, No. 496Ba; 1 pane, No. 497B×6; 1pane, No. 497Ba (2m.)	£1100
SB36	2.11.34	Welfare Fund (as T **106**) 1 pane, No. 552a; 1 pane, No. 555a (2m.)	£600
SB37	15.11.35	Welfare Fund (as T **116**) 1 pane, No. 585a; 1 pane, No. 587a (2m.)	£250
SB38	15.6.36	Olympic Games (as T **123**) 1 pane, No. 606a; 1 pane, No. 607a (2m.)	£250
SB39	8.36	Hindenburg (T **94**) 1 pane, No. 493Bc; 1 pane, No. 494Bb; 1 pane, No. 497Bb; 1 pane, No. 500Ba (2m.)	£600
SB40	2.11.36	Winter Relief Fund (as T **128**) 1 pane, No. 623a; 1 pane, No. 625a (2m.)	£180
SB41	10.37	Hindenburg (T **94**) 1 pane, No. 493Bd; 1 pane, No 494Bc; 1 pane, No. 495Ba; 1 pane, No. 496Bb (2m.)	£450
SB42	11.37	Winter Relief Fund (as T **131**) 1 pane, No. 639a; 1 pane, No. 641a (2m.)	£180
SB43	12.38	Winter Relief Fund (as T **139**) 1 pane, No. 663a; 1 pane, No. 665a (2m.)	£180
SB44	10.39	Hindenburg (T **94**) 1 pane, No. 493Be; 1 pane, No. 494Bd; 1 pane, No. 496Bc; 1 pane, No. 497Bb; 1 pane, No. 498Ba (2m.)	£325
SB45	12.39	Winter Relief Fund (as T **155**) 1 pane. No. 718a; 1 pane, No. 720a (2m.)	£180
SB46	4.40	Hindenburg (T **94**) 1 pane, No. 493Be; 1 pane, No. 494Bd; 1 pane, No. 496Bca; 1 pane, No. 497Bb; 1 pane, No. 498Bab (2m.)	£325
SB47	12.40	Winter Relief Fund (as T **164**) 1 pane, No. 739a; 1 pane, No. 741a (2m.)	£180
SB48	12.41	Hitler (T **173**) 1 pane, No. 769a; 1 pane, No. 770a; 1 pane, No. 771a; 1 pane, No. 773a; 1 pane, No. 778a (2m.)	£170

No. SB49 is listed below No. 956 of Section III: Allied Occupation and SB50 onwards at the end of Section IV: German Federal Republic.

DESIGN INDEX

I. Issues to 1945

This is divided into three sections: A. Definitive, B. Airmail and C. Charity, Commemorative and Pictorial issues. Only the first stamp in a set sharing the same design is given. Portraits are listed under surnames and buildings, etc. under the town or city in which they are situated.
Part II of this index, covering the post-war Occupation Zones, West Berlin and West Germany will be found at the end of West Berlin.

A. DEFINITIVE ISSUES

These designs are listed with their Type numbers as well as the catalogue numbers on which they occur. Surcharged stamps are included, but only the first stamp on which a design appears in a set is listed.

Design	*Type No.*	*Catalogue Nos.*
'Anniv of Empire Address'	**15, 22**	65, 81, 96
Blacksmiths	**36**	160, 183
Cologne	**68, 84**	377, 458
Cologne Cathedral	**56**	268
Eagle	**66**	369
Eagle, globe and Swastika	**100**	526
Eagle (embossed) (1872)	**1, 4**	1, 8, 16, 23, 29
Eagle ('Flugpost')	**48, 49**	218, 358
Eagle ('Luftpost')	**76**	392
Ebert	**81**	424, 459
GPO Berlin	**12, 18**	62, 77, 93, 113, 137
'Germania'	**10, 11, 17, 24**	52, 57, 66, 67, 82, 97, 105, 140, 172, 196
Hindenburg (medallion)	**94**	478, 493, 545
Hindenburg (portrait)	**82**	425, 460
Hitler types	**173, 182, 225**	769, 799, 894
Marienburg	**69**	378
'Memorial to William 1'	**14, 21**	64, 80, 95
Miners	**37, 51**	162, 186, 249, 257
Numeral (in square)	**35**	153, 176, 274
Numeral (inflation types)	**54, 61/3, 64**	260, 279, 312, 315, 342, 343; 352
Numeral (oblong type)	**40**	169, 193, 230
Numeral (1872 'gröschen')	**2, 3, 7**	14, 38
Numeral & eagle types (1875)	**5, 6**	31, 39
Numeral & eagle types (1889)	**8, 9**	45
Ploughman	**41**	171, 195
Posthorn	**39**	166, 190, 204
Reapers	**38**	164, 188, 250, 258, 276
Rheinstein	**67**	376
Speyer Cathedral	**70**	379
'Union of North and South' (allegory)	**13, 19, 20**	63, 78, 94, 116, 139
Wartburg	**55**	267

B. AIRMAIL ISSUES

The following is a checklist of all issues to 1945 which were inscribed 'FLUGPOST' or 'LUFTPOST'; 111/12, 218/29, 269/73, 358/64, 392/9, 443/5, 456/7, 469/71, 510/12, 526/36, 603/4, 657/8.
No. M804 is a military field post issue for use as an airmail stamp.

C. CHARITY, COMMEMORATIVE AND PICTORIAL ISSUES

A
Aachen ... 461, 465
Air Defence League ... 632
Air Post Offices ... 854
Albrecht (Duke) ... 886
Allenstein ... 573
Alpine road ... 628
Anhalt ... 450
Armed Forces ... 556, 733, 798, 819, 838, 861, 882, 884, 896, 897
Arms ... 198, 389, 413, 446, 451
Austria ... 650

B
Bach ... 411, 571
Baden ... 414
Bavaria ... 390
Beethoven ... 404
Behring ... 748
Benz ... 602, 674, 683
Berlin ... 462, 466, 624, 731, 789, 817
Braunau ... 671, 679
Bremen ... 451, 746
Breslau ... 473, 477, 653
Brown Ribbon (horse race) ... **MS**618, **MS**637*a*, 659, 687, 735, 768, 805, 842, 887
Brunswick ... 449

C
Carinthia ... 792
Children's Charity ... 247
Cologne ... 268, 377, 458
Costumes ... 585

D
Daimler ... 601, 674, 683
Danzig ... 702, 704, 739
Drachenfels ... 719
Dresden ... 472, 476
Dürer ... 412, 688

E
Eagle and Dragon ... 893
Eagle and Wreath ... 677, 818
Ebert ... 424, 459
Elbogen ... 718
Empire, 25th Anniv Address ... 65, 81, 96
Erzberg ... 669
Eupen ... 737

F
Flexenstrasse ... 664
Flying Dutchman ... 514
Forchenstein ... 663
Frankfurt ... 722
Frederick the Great ... 405, 490
Fulda ... 874

G
German Derby (horse race) ... 686
Goethe ... 400
Goldsmiths' Institution ... 806, 848, 890
Goslar ... 720
Graf Zeppelin (airship) ... 443, 456, 469, 510, 536, 657
GPO, Berlin ... 62, 77, 93
Grand Prix Vienna (horse race) ... 845, 888
Graz ... 721
Grossglockner ... 666
Guericke ... 605
Gunther (Count) ... 895

H
Hall i. Tirol ... 670
Hamburg ... 446
Hamburg Derby (horse race) ... 734, 767, 804
Handel ... 572
Heidelberg ... 474, 743
Heligoland ... 738
Helisberg ... 576
Henlein ... 809
Hesse ... 416
Hindenburg ... 417, 425, 460, 478, 493, 545
Hindenburg (airship) ... 603
Hitler ... **MS**635, **MS**638, 652, 660, 679, 682, 689, 732, 751, 760, 769, 799, 803, 832, 853, 875, 894
Hitler Youth ... 581, 648, 831
Hohentwiel ... 726

I
IAA ... 421
Innsbruck ... 884
International Labour Office ... 421

K
Kant ... 406
Kaub ... 741
Klagenfurt ... 723
Koch ... 852
Königsberg ... 575, 886
Köningstein ... 701

L
Leibniz ... 410
Leipzig ... 727, 752
Lessing ... 409
Lichtenstein ... 488
Lifeboat ... 639
Lightship ... 640
Lilienthal ... 535
Lippe ... 452
Local Government ... 614
Lohengrin ... 520
Lübeck ... 453, 475, 850
Luderitz ... 537
Lufthansa (airline) ... 600

M
Malmedy ... 736
Mangfall (river) ... 630
Marburg ... 489, 792
Marienburg ... 378
Marienwerder ... 463, 467
Mastersingers ... 516
Mecklenburg-Schwerin ... 447
Mecklenburg-Strelitz ... 454
Mother and Children ... 847, 857
Motor Show ... 674, 683
Mozart ... 796
Munich ... 198, 387, 595, 623, 851, 893
Münster ... 747
Mussolini ... 751

N
Nachtigal ... 538
National Assembly ... 107
Nazi Party ... 595
Nürburgring (motor) races ... 683
Nüremberg ... 487, 543, 583, 621, 625, **MS**638, 660, 689

O
Oldenburg ... 448, 895
Olympic Games ... 597, 606
OSTROPA ... 573

P
Parsifal ... 521
Peters ... 539
Pettau ... 794
Posen ... 742
Postal Congress ... 810, 813
Postal Employees Fund (inscr 'Kameradschaftsblock der Deutschen Reichspost') ... 690, 761, 876
Prague ... 745
Prussia ... 389

R
RAD (Labour Corps) ... 882
Railway ... 577
Recreation ... 619
Reichstag ... 490
Rheinstein ... 376
Rhinegold ... 515
Rhineland ... 384, 459
Rosegger ... 843

S
SA and SS ... 808, 851, 897
Saale (river) ... 626
Saar ... 541, 562
Saarbrücken ... 661
Sailing ship ... 643
Salzburg ... 725
Saxony ... 391
Schaumburg-Lippe ... 455
Schiller ... 402, 560
Schreckenstein ... 724
Schütz ... 570
Ships ... 639
Siegfried ... 518
Speyer ... 379
St. Elizabeth ... 365, 522
St. George ... 848
Stamp Day ... 750, 797, 816, 892
Stephan ... 380
Stolzenfels ... 486
Stuttgart ... 680
Styria ... 792
Sudetenland ... 672
Swastika ... 568, 621, 650, 808, 851

T
Tannenberg ... 574
Tannhäuser ... 513
Thorn ... 740
Thuringia ... 415
Trades ... 551
Trier ... 744
Triglav ... 795
Tristan and Isolde ... 519

U
'Union' (allegory) ... 63, 78, 94
UPU ... 380

N
Valkyries ... 517
Veldes ... 793
Vienna (Wien) ... 668, 691, 756, 790, 810, 813, 845, 888
Volkswagen ... 676, 685

W
Wachau ... 667
Wagner ... 513
Wartburg ... 267, 485
Wien (Vienna) ... 813, 845, 888
William 1 Memorial Berlin ... 64, 80, 95
Winter Relief Fund ('Winterhilfswerk') ... 623, 639, 663, 718, 739, 847
Wissmann ... 540
Workers ... 551
Württemberg ... 413
Würzburg ... 464, 468

Z
Zell am See ... 665
Zeppelin (Count) (see also *Graf Zeppelin*) ... 536, 657

GERMANY / Allied Occupation

III. Allied Occupation

At the Yalta Conference in February 1945 J. V. Stalin, President Roosevelt and Winston Churchill decided that Germany, after surrender, should be divided into four Zones of Occupation (British, American, French and Soviet Russian). Berlin was to be under joint allied control and to be divided into four sectors.

Germany surrendered on 7 May 1945, and Allied Military Post stamps, which had first been issued in Aachen on 19 March, came into use throughout the British and American Zones. The French issued special stamps in their Zone and in the Soviet Russian Zone the first issues were made by local postal administrations.

100 Pfennig = 1 Reichsmark
From 21.6.48. 100 Pfennig = 1 Deutsche Mark (West)
From 24.6.48. 100 Pfennig = 1 Deutsche Mark (East)

A. ALLIED MILITARY POST
(BRITISH AND AMERICAN ZONES)

Two types of Spandrels:—
In Type A the space between the scroll and the rectangular frame lines is filled with colour. The scrolls are well drawn and the corner-bud is broad and projects closely into the angle.

In Type B the space has white patches, the scrolls are roughly drawn and the bud is thin and farther away from the angle.

Two types of the 6pf.:— In Type D the '6' is larger than in Type C and the top is shorter.

(Des W. A. Roach. Die eng E. H. Helmuth)

1945–46.

I. Typo by Bureau of Engraving and Printing, Washington (19 Mar –1 July, 1945). Thick paper. Spandrels as A. P 11

			Unmtd Mint	Used
A1	A 1	3pf. violet (1.7.45)	40	3·25
A2		4pf. grey (1.7.45)	40	2·50
A3		5pf. emerald-green	40	65
A4		6pf. yellow (C.)	40	65
A5		8pf. orange	40	65
A6		10pf. chocolate (1.7.45)	40	65
A7		12pf. purple	1·30	65
A8		15pf. carmine (1.7.45)	40	2·50
A9		25pf. blue (1.7.45)	40	2·50
A1/A9	Set of 9.		4·00	12·50

Nos. A3/A5 and A7 were first issued at Aachen, which had been captured by American troops on 21 October 1944. The Allied Military Post System was not operative until June 1945.
Nos. A10/A15 were only on sale in the British Zone.

II. Photo by Harrison & Sons Ltd, London (28 Aug-19 Sept 1945). P 14

A10	A 1	3pf. violet (19.9.45)	40	1·00
		a. Perf 14 ×14½	80·00	£450
		b. Perf 14½×14	2·50	33·00
		c. Perf 14½	16·00	£130
A11		4pf. grey (14.9.45)	40	1·00
		a. Perf 14 ×14½	50	7·75
A12		5pf. emerald-green (4.9.45)	2·20	21·00
		a. Perf 14 ×14½	2·50	50·00
		b. Perf 14½×14	1·00	21·00
		c. Perf 14½	9·00	80·00
A13		6pf. yellow (D.)	40	1·00
		a. Perf 14 ×14½	1·80	7·25
		b. Perf 14½×14	10·50	20·00
		c. Perf 14½	£325	£400
A14		8pf. orange (14.9.45)	2·20	10·50
		a. Perf 14 ×14½	1·00	5·25
		b. Perf 14½ ×14	1·30	8·50
		c. Perf 14½	9·75	46·00
A15		12pf. purple	60	1·00
		a. Perf 14 ×14½	3·25	7·75
		b. Perf 14½×14	10·50	10·50
		c. Perf 14½	39·00	65·00
A10/A15	Set of 6 (cheapest)	3·50	27·00

III. Litho by G. Westerman, Brunswick (Aug 1945–Jan 1946). Medium paper. Spandrels as B. P 11

(a) 19×22 mm

A16	A 1	1pf. grey-black (3.10.45)	65	6·50
		a. Perf 11×11½	65	6·50
		b. Perf 11½×11	5·00	20·00
		c. Perf 11½	9·00	46·00
A17		3pf. violet (11.10.45)	65	1·60
		a. Perf 11×11½	65	2·50
		b. Perf 11½×11	2·50	9·00
		c. Perf 11½	2·20	16·00
A18		4pf. grey (31.10.45)	65	2·00
		a. Perf 11×11½	4·50	80·00
		b. Perf 11½×11	2·00	17·00
		c. Perf 11½	2·00	20·00
A19		5pf. emerald-green (3.9.45)	1·60	33·00
		a. Perf 11×11½	65	6·50
		c. Perf 11½	9·00	£100
A20		6pf. yellow (D.) (18.8.45)	65	1·60
		a. Perf 11×11½	1·30	4·75
		b. Perf 11½×11	13·00	39·00
		c. Perf 11½	1·30	6·50
A21		8pf. orange (9.10.45)	10·50	50·00
		b. Perf 11½×11	£160	£1200
		c. Perf 11½	10·50	50·00
A22		10pf. chocolate (29.8.45)	65	4·00
		a. Perf 11×11½	65	7·00
		c. Perf 11½	£600	£5000
A23		12pf. purple (25.8.45)	65	1·30
		a. Perf 11×11½	1·30	2·00
		b. Perf 11½×11	£120	£160
		c. Perf 11½	7·75	11·50
A24		15pf. carmine (28.8.45)	65	5·25
		a. Perf 11×11½	65	8·25
		b. Perf 11½×11	10·50	90·00
A25		16pf. blue-green (10.10.45)	65	20·00
		a. Perf 11×11½	80	26·00
A26		20pf. light blue (23.10.45)	65	6·50
		a. Perf 11×11½	4·00	65·00
		b. Perf 11½×11	1·30	26·00
		c. Perf 11½	16·00	£100
A27		24pf. purple-brown (19.10.45)	1·20	39·00
		a. Perf 11×11½	65	18·00
		b. Perf 11½×11	7·75	£110
A28		25pf. blue (29.8.45)	65	20·00
		a. Perf 11×11½	1·20	39·00
		b. Perf 11½×11	30·00	£650

(b) Size 22×25 mm

A29	A 1	30pf. olive (11.9.45)	65	2·75
		a. Perf 11×11½	2·00	6·50
		b. Perf 11½ × 11	9·00	50·00
A30		40pf. magenta (11.9.45)	90	6·00
		a. Perf 11×11½	65	7·75
		b. Perf 11½ × 11	7·75	60·00
A31		42pf. green (17.9.45)	65	3·25
		a. Perf 11×11½	1·30	13·00
		b. Perf 11½ × 11	1·00	9·00
		c. Perf 11½	33·00	£200
A32		50pf. slate (19.9.45)	65	23·00
		a. Perf 11×11½	65	25·00
		b. Perf 11½ × 11	£250	£2000
A33		60pf. plum (20.9.45)	1·30	26·00
		a. Perf 11×11½	14·50	90·00
		b. Perf 11½ × 11	2·50	39·00
		c. Perf 11½	£200	£1300
A34		80pf. indigo (20.9.45)	60·00	£650
		a. Perf 11×11½	£250	£3250
		b. Perf 11½ × 11	50·00	£425
		c. Perf 11½	60·00	£650

(c) Size 25×29½ mm

| A35 | A 1 | 1m. myrtle-green (P11×11½) (17.1.46) | 10·50 | £700 |
| A16/A35 | Set of 20 (cheapest) | 75·00 | £1200 |

Stamps overprinted 'German', 'ZONE FRANCAISE'. '6' or '8' are bogus. The 8 and 12pf. values overprinted 'Military Permit Office Stamps' were used as travel permit stamps.

Nos. A1/A35 were replaced by Nos. 899/925 from January 1946 onwards.
Lots of shades are known, prices are for the cheapest.

B. AMERICAN, BRITISH AND SOVIET RUSSIAN ZONES 1946–1948

From February 1946 to June 1948 the following general issues were provided for all of occupied Germany, except the French Zone.

GERMANY / Allied Occupation

After the early occupation issues for the American, British, French and Russian Zones in 1945–46 (Nos. A1/A35, F1/F13 and RA1/**MS**RF17), it was intended that general issues should be made for all four Zones. The French continued, however, to issue stamps for each of the three *Länder* in their Zone (Nos. FB1/FW52), so that Nos. 899/956 listed below, were issued in the American, British and Russian Zones.

When the Western Powers effected a Currency Reform in their Zones in June 1948, the Russians again made separate issues in their Zone.

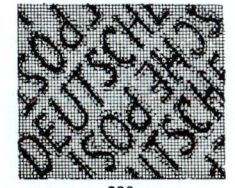

229 Numeral   **230**

(Typo State Ptg Works, Berlin)

1946 (Feb)–**47** (May). W **230**. P 14.

(a) Size 18×22½ mm

899	**229**	1pf black	35	5·25
900		2pf black	35	40
901		3pf yellow-brown	35	6·50
902		4pf slate-blue	35	7·75
903		5pf emerald-green	35	1·00
904		6pf violet	35	35
905		8pf vermilion	35	40
906		10pf brown	35	70
907		12pf scarlet	35	40
908		12pf blue-grey	35	40
		a. Booklet pane. Nos. 908a×5 and 911×3 (5.47)	35·00	
909		15pf claret	35	12·50
910		15pf yellow-green	35	50
911		16pf bluish green	35	50
912		20pf pale blue	35	50
913		24pf chestnut	35	40
914		25pf ultramarine	35	12·50
915		25pf yellow-orange	35	2·00
916		30pf olive-green	35	40
917		40pf bright purple	35	50
918		42pf green	4·00	50·00
919		45pf scarlet	35	65
920		50pf myrtle-green	35	40
921		60pf red	35	60
922		75pf ultramarine	35	40
923		80pf violet-blue	35	60
924		84pf green	35	40

(b) Size 24×30 mm

925	**229**	1m olive-green	35	60
899/925		Set of 27	12·00	95·00
MS925a		107×51 mm. Nos. 912/913 and 917 (sold for 5m.) (8.12.46). Perf.	80·00	£250
		ab. Imperf	90·00	£325

231 1160: Leipzig obtains Charter   **232**

(Des E. Gruner. Eng K. Wolf. Recess Giesecke & Devrient. Leipzig)

1947 (5 Mar). Leipzig Spring Fair. T **231** and similar design inscr 'LEIPZIGER MESSE 1947'. W **232**. P 13½×13.

926	**231**	24pf. +26pf. lake-brown	2·00	8·50
927		– 60pf. +40pf. ultramarine	2·00	8·50

Design:—60+40pf. 1268: Foreign merchants at Fair.

These stamps were reprinted in 1948, perf 13, by the State Printing Works, Berlin.

233 Gardener   **234** Sower   **235** Labourer

236 Bricklayer and Reaper   **237** 'Dove of peace'

(Des L. Brand (T **233**), H. Luckenbach (T **234**). J. Rogmann (T **235**), G. Barach (T **236**), Typo. T **237** des H. W. Hoepner, recess State Ptg Wks, Berlin)

1947 (7 Mar)–**48**. W **230**. P 14.

928	**233**	2pf. brown-black	40	65
929		6pf. violet	40	40
930	**234**	8pf. vermilion	40	65
931		10pf. yellow-green (1.2.48)	40	1·00
932	**235**	12pf. grey	40	40
933	**233**	15pf. chocolate (1.2.48)	90	9·00
934	**236**	16pf. blue-green	40	65
935	**234**	20pf. light blue	40	2·50
936	**236**	24pf. brown	40	65
937	**233**	25pf. yellow-orange	40	2·50
938	**235**	30pf. red (1.2.48)	90	5·25
939	**234**	40pf. magenta	50	1·00
940	**236**	50pf. ultramarine (1.2.48)	90	3·25
941	**235**	60pf. red	40	65
942		60pf. red-brown (1.3.48)	40	1·30
943		80pf. grey-blue	40	2·50
944	**236**	84pf. emerald-green	65	4·00
945	**237**	1m. olive-green (1.5.47)	50	65
946		2m. violet (27.5.47)	50	2·50
947		3m. brown-lake (27.5.47)	65	33·00
948		5m. indigo (1.2.48)	4·50	£120
928/948		Set of 21	13·50	£170

238 Dr. von Stephan   **239** Weighing Goods

(Litho State Ptg Wks, Berlin)

1947 (15 May). 50th Death Anniv of Dr. von Stephan (founder of Universal Postal Union & former P.M.G.) W **230**. P 14.

949	**238**	24pf. brown-orange	65	2·50
950		75pf. blue	65	2·50

(Des E. Gruner. Litho State Ptg Wks, Berlin)

1947 (2 Sept). Leipzig Autumn Fair. As T **231** inscr 'LEIPZIGER MESSE 1947'. W **230**. P 13½×13.

951		12pf. carmine red	80	4·50
952		75pf. ultramarine	80	4·50

Designs:—12pf. 1497: Maximilian I granting Charter; 75pf. 1365: Assessment and Collection of Ground Rents.

(Des E. Gruner. Eng L. Schnell. Recess State Ptg Wks, Berlin)

1948 (2 Mar). Leipzig Spring Fair. As T **231** inscr 'LEIPZIGER MESSE 1948'. W **230**. P 13½×13.

953		50pf. blue	80	2·50
954		84pf. green	80	4·00

Designs:—50pf. 1388: At the Customs Barrier; 84pf. 1433: Bringing merchandise.

For similar types, dated '1948', '1949' or '1950', but with premium values, see Russian Zone Nos. R31/R32, R51/R52, R60/R61 and E7/E8 of East Germany.

(Des H. W. Hoepner. Litho State Ptg Wks, Berlin)

1948 (22 May). Hanover Trade Fair. W **230**. P 14.

955	**239**	24pf. carmine	65	2·50
956		50pf. ultramarine	65	4·00

Nos. 955/6 were issued both in separate sheets and together in sheets containing *se-tenant* pairs (*Price for se-tenant pair*: £13 un, £33 used).

STAMP BOOKLET

1947 (May). Black on light brown cover inscr. 'Deutsche Post'.

SB49	3m. booklet containing pane No. 908a and No. 913×8	80·00

GERMANY / Allied Occupation

C. BRITISH AND AMERICAN ZONES 1948–1949

On 18 June 1948 the British, American and French governments announced the introduction of a reformed currency, the Deutsche Mark, in their Zones. The Soviet government reacted by introducing their own currency reform in the Russian Zone, and from 24 June 1948 separate issues of stamps were produced for use there.

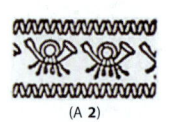

(A **2**) 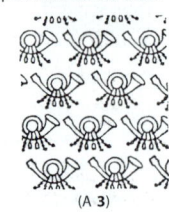 (A **3**)

1948. Currency Reform.

(a) On Nos. 928 to 944 (21.6.48)
(i) Optd with Type A **2**

A36	2pf. brown-black	80	1·00
A37	6pf. violet	80	80
A38	8pf. vermilion	80	80
A39	10pf. yellow-green	80	80
A40	12pf. grey	80	80
A41	15pf. chocolate	14·50	26·00
A42	16pf. blue-green	3·25	5·25
A43	20pf. light blue	1·00	2·00
A44	24pf. brown	80	80
A45	25pf. yellow-orange	80	80
A46	30pf. red	4·50	7·75
A47	40pf. magenta	2·00	4·00
A48	50pf. ultramarine	2·00	3·25
A49	60pf. red-brown	1·60	1·60
A50	60pf. red	£140	£400
A51	80pf. grey-blue	2·10	4·00
A52	84pf. emerald-green	7·75	10·50
A36/A52	Set of 17	£170	£425

(ii) Optd with Type A **3**

A53	2pf. brown-black	2·00	4·00
A54	6pf. violet	1·60	2·50
A55	8pf. vermilion	2·00	3·25
A56	10pf. yellow-green	1·30	1·30
A57	12pf. grey	2·50	3·25
A58	15pf. chocolate	1·30	2·00
A59	16pf. blue-green	2·50	4·50
A60	20pf. light blue	1·30	1·30
A61	24pf. brown	1·30	2·50
A62	25pf. yellow-orange	13·00	26·00
A63	30pf. red	1·30	2·30
A64	40pf. magenta	1·30	1·30
A65	50pf. ultramarine	1·30	1·30
A66	60pf. red-brown	1·30	2·00
A67	60pf. red	4·50	6·50
A68	80pf. grey-blue	1·30	2·00
A69	84pf. emerald-green	2·50	2·50
A53/A69	Set of 17	38·00	60·00

(b) On Nos. 900 to 924 (July–Aug 1948)
(i) Optd with Type A **2**

A70	2pf. black	10·50	55·00
A71	8pf. vermilion	20·00	£110
A72	10pf. brown	1·60	8·50
A73	12pf. scarlet	14·50	90·00
A74	12pf. blue-grey	£225	£1000
A75	15pf. claret	14·50	90·00
A76	15pf. yellow-green	4·50	29·00
A77	16pf. blue-green	50·00	£350
A77a	20pf. light blue	£100	£425
A78	24pf. chestnut	£130	£475
A79	25pf. ultramarine	26·00	£110
A80	25pf. yellow-orange	2·30	18·00
A81	30pf. olive-green	4·00	18·00
A82	40pf. bright purple	£100	£375
A83	45pf. scarlet	5·25	18·00
A84	50pf. myrtle-green	3·25	13·00
A85	75pf. ultramarine	9·00	42·00
A86	84pf. green	10·50	42·00
A70/A86	Set of 18	£650	£2750

(ii) Optd with Type A **3**

A87	2pf. black	39·00	£120
A88	8pf. vermilion	65·00	£300
A89	10pf. brown	65·00	£325
A90	12pf. scarlet	21·00	£120
A91	12pf. blue-grey	£500	£1800
A92	15pf. claret	21·00	90·00
A93	15pf. yellow-green	2·50	14·50
A94	16pf. blue-green	70·00	£275
A94a	20pf. light blue	£140	£400
A95	24pf. chestnut	80·00	£375
A96	25pf. ultramarine	21·00	£110
A97	25pf. yellow-orange	70·00	£350
A98	30pf. olive-green	3·25	11·50
A99	40pf. bright purple	£100	£425
A100	45pf. scarlet	6·50	21·00
A101	50pf. myrtle-green	6·50	21·00
A102	75pf. ultramarine	4·50	21·00
A103	84pf. green	5·00	22·00
A87/A103	Set of 18	£1100	£4250

All values, Nos. A36/A103, exist with overprint inverted or double. Nos. A36/A69 were also in use in the Western Sectors of Berlin.

A **4** Crowned Head 
A **5** The Three Wise Men 
A **6** Cologne Cathedral

A **7** Cologne Cathedral
A **8** 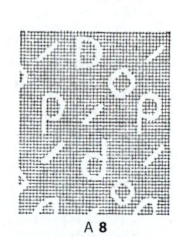

(Des Anton Wolff (6pf), Prof Hausmann (12 and 24pf.) and Alfred Will (50pf.). Litho G. Westermann, Brunswick)

1948 (12 Aug). 700th Anniv of Cologne Cathedral and Restoration Fund. Wmk Type A **8**. P 11.

A104	A **4**	6pf. +4pf. yellow-brown	1·30	1·30
A105	A **5**	12pf. +8pf. greenish blue	2·50	3·25
A106	A **6**	24pf. +16pf. carmine	7·25	6·50
A107	A **7**	50pf. +50pf. blue	10·50	16·00
A104/A107		Set of 4	19·00	24·00

A **9** The Römer, Frankfurt-am-Main 
A **10** Frauenkirche, Munich 
A **11** Cologne Cathedral

A **12** Brandenburg Gate
A **13** Holstentor, Lübeck 

Type A **11**. Three types

I Narrow divisions of shading on transept roof
II and III Wide divisions of shading on transept roof 

54

GERMANY / Allied Occupation

I and II No threshold to middle door at right

III Threshold to middle door at right

Type A **13**. Two types

IV Roadway under arch with four white lines

V Roadway extended to seven white lines

Perforations. A number of perforating machines were used. Our perf 11 includes both comb and line perfs gauging between 10¾ and 11½ including compounds. We only distinguish the perf 14 and compounds of 14 and 11.

Watermark. The wmk is found upright, sideways and reversed.

(Des M. Bittrof. Litho A. Bagel, München-Gladbach or G. Westermann, Brunswick)

1948 (1 Sept)–**50**. Wmk Type A **8**. P 11.

A108	A **9**	2pf. black	65	80
		a. Perf 14	4·50	8·50
A109	A **10**	4pf. brown (shades)	65	80
		a. Perf 14	2·30	80
A110	A **11**	5pf. blue (shades) (I)	2·75	2·00
		a. Type III	1·00	80
		ab. Perf 14	2·75	90
A111	A **10**	6pf. orange-brown	65	1·60
A112		6pf. orange	80	80
		a. Perf 14	22·00	7·75
A113	A **9**	8pf. orange-yellow	80	85
A114	A **10**	8pf. slate	65	80
A115	A **11**	10pf. yellow-green (I)	3·25	1·30
		a. Type III	80	80
		ab. Perf 14	2·50	80
A116	A **10**	15pf. orange	3·25	7·75
A117	A **9**	15pf. deep violet	1·80	80
		a. Perf 14	17·00	80
		b. Bright violet (P 14)	33·00	1·30
A118		16pf. bluish green	1·00	1·00
A119		20pf. light blue	1·60	5·25
A120	A **12**	20pf. carmine	1·30	80
		a. Perf 14	6·50	80
A121		24pf. carmine	80	80
A122	A **11**	25pf. vermilion (II)	2·30	80
		a. Perf 14	£200	£2250
		b. Type III	1·80	80
		ba. Perf 14	£100	£275
		bb. Comp Perf	29·00	50·00
A123	A **12**	30pf. blue	2·00	80
		a. Perf 14	34·00	80
A124	A **10**	30pf. scarlet	4·50	9·00
A125	A **11**	40pf. bright mauve (I)	2·50	80
		a. Type II	16·00	1·00
		ab. Perf 14	£650	£500
		b. Type III	5·75	80
		ba. Perf 14	36·00	9·75
		bb. Comp Perf	39·00	9·75
A126	A **12**	50pf. blue	2·00	4·00
A127	A **10**	50pf. bluish green	2·50	80
		a. Perf 14	£225	80
A128	A **11**	60pf. brown-purple (I)	£130	80
		a. Perf 14	4·00	80
		b. Type II	£160	80
		c. Type III	£160	80
		ca. Perf 14	39·00	7·75
A129	A **12**	80pf. magenta	4·50	80
		a. Perf 14	£160	80
A130	A **10**	84pf. bright purple	2·75	10·50
A131	A **11**	90pf. bright mauve (I)	16·00	80
		a. Type II	50·00	80
		b. Type III	7·75	80
		ba. Perf 14	£225	90
A132	A **13**	1Dm. yellow-green (IV)	50·00	1·00
		a. Type V (1949)	65·00	1·30
		ab. Perf 14 (10.50)	£200	80
A133		2Dm. violet (IV)	46·00	1·30
		a. Type V (1949)	80·00	80
A134		3Dm. magenta (IV)	50·00	4·50
		a. Type V (1949)	£225	1·80
A135		5Dm. blue (IV)	80·00	36·00
		a. Type V (1949)	£275	5·75
A108/A135	Set of 28 (cheapest)		£250	55·00

AT **14**

A **15** Brandenburg Gate, Berlin

(Typo A. Wegener, Ahlfeld, or G. Westermann, Brunswick)

1948 (1 Dec)–**49**. OBLIGATORY TAX. Aid for Berlin.

(a) Wmk Type A **8**

AT136	AT **14**	2pf. blue (imperf)	1·30	40
AT137		2pf. blue (P11½×11)	4·50	40
		a. Compound perf 12 and 14–14½*	2·50	65
		b. Perf 11	£160	10·50
		c. Perf 11½	13·00	2·00
		d. Perf 12	£225	£100
		e. Compound perf 11½ and 12*	—	£650
		f. Perf 9 -10	£225	£100

(b) W **258a**

AT138	AT **14**	2pf. blue (imperf)	80·00	2·50
AT139		2pf. blue (P 11½.11)	3·25	40
		a. Compound perf 12 and 14–14½*	4·50	65
		b. Perf 11	50·00	5·25
		c. Perf 11½	£1000	£650
		d. Perf 12 (1949)	£375	7·75
		e. Perf 12×11 (1949)	47·00	80
		f. Perf 12×12½ (1949)	43·00	60
		g. Perf 12×13½	£800	33·00

*The compound perforation 12 and 14–14½ has three sides gauging 14–14½ and one side 12. The compound perforation 11½ and 12 exists with three sides 11½ and one side 12 and also as a regular 12×11½.

No. AT137f covers various perforations between 9 and 10 made by local postmasters and put on sale thus. Stamps also exist privately rouletted, and with one, two or three sides imperforate.

There is a wide variety of shades in this issue, ranging from pale blue to blue-black, and differences in thickness of lettering can also be found.

For litho printings, perf 14, see Nos. T1043 and T1103 of the Federal Republic.

Following a blockade of the Western sectors of Berlin by the USSR, the allied forces mounted an airlift to the city. To help defray the cost of this and the expenses of maintaining the city a tax was imposed on all internal mail posted in the Western zones (except in and to Berlin itself). At first it was compulsory only in the British and American zones but it was subsequently enforced in the French zone at varying dates (but not in the Saar). After the formation of the Federal Republic the tax stamp remained in use until the end of March 1956, although its use on various classes of mail was gradually relaxed and firms were allowed to include the 2pf. tax in a single franking.

(Des M. Bittrof. Litho Bagel, München-Gladbach)

1948 (9 Dec). Aid to Berlin. Wmk Type A **8**. P 11.

A140	A **15**	10pf. +5pf. green	10·50	11·50
		a. Perf 11×11½	10·50	11·50
A141		20pf. +10pf. carmine	10·50	11·50
		a. Perf 11×11½	10·50	11·50

A **16** Herman Hillebrant Wedigh (after Holbein)

A **17** Racing Cyclists

(Des Axster-Heudtlass. Recess State Ptg Wks, Berlin)

1949 (22 Apr). Hanover Trade Fair. Wmk Type M **7** of Württemberg (Mult Crosses and Circles). P 14.

A142	A **16**	10pf. green	5·25	4·50
A143		20pf. carmine	5·25	4·00
A144		30pf. blue	7·75	5·75
A142/A144	Set of 3		16·00	13·00
MSA145	110×65 mm. Nos. A142/A144 (sold at 1Dm.).		£140	£450

55

GERMANY / Allied Occupation

(Recess State Ptg Wks, Berlin)
1949 (15 May). Trans-German Cycle Race. Wmk Type M **7** of Württemberg. P 14.
A146	A **17**	10pf. +5pf. green	7·75	10·50
A147		20pf. +10pf. chestnut	18·00	26·00

A **18** Goethe in Italy    A **19** Goethe

(Recess State Ptg Wks, Berlin)
1949 (15 Aug). Bicentenary of Birth of Johann Wolfgang von Goethe (poet). T A **18/19** and similar portrait. Wmk Type M **7** of Württemberg. P 14.
A148	A **18**	10pf. +5pf. green	6·50	7·25
A149	A **19**	20pf. +10pf. scarlet	9·00	13·00
A150	–	30pf. +115pf. blue	39·00	39·00
A148/A150	Set of 3		49·00	55·00

Design:—30pf. Profile portrait of Goethe.

The British and American Zones, together with the French Zone, became the Federal German Republic (West Germany) on 21 Sept 1949 (see section IV).

D. FRENCH ZONE

(a) GENERAL ISSUE, 1945–1946

F **1** Arms of the Palatinate    F **2** Goethe

(Des and eng A. Ouvré (1 to 5m.). Des R. Louis; die eng H. Cortot 5, 8, 20, 30pf.), J. Piel (others). Ptd French Govt Ptg Works, Paris)

1945 (17 Dec)–**46**.
(a) Arms. Vert designs as Type F **1**. Typo. P 14×13½
F1	1pf. emerald, black and pale yellow (11.1.46)	40	40
F2	3pf. yellow, black and red (11.1.46)	40	40
F3	5pf. black, orange-yellow and light brown (11.1.46)	40	40
F4	8pf. red, orange-yellow and light brown (11.1.46)	40	40
F5	10pf. emerald, light brown and pale yellow	19·00	95·00
F6	12pf. orange-yellow, black and red	40	40
F7	15pf. dull ultramarine, black and red (11.1.46)	40	40
F8	20pf. black, orange-yellow and black	40	40
F9	24pf. ultramarine, black and red (11.1.46)	40	40
F10	30pf. orange-yellow and black	40	40

Arms:—1, 10pf. Type F **1**; 3, 12pf. Rhineland; 5, 20pf. Württemberg; 8, 30pf. Baden; 15, 24pf. Saar.

(b) Poets. Vert designs as Type F **2**. Recess. P 13
F11	1m. chocolate	5·75	30·00
F12	2m. deep blue (1.4.46) (Schiller)	5·75	90·00
F13	5m. brown-lake (1.4.46) (Heine)	6·25	£110
F1/F13	Set of 13	36·00	£300

From 1947 to 1949 the French made separate issues for each of the Länder within the Zone.

(b) BADEN, 1947–1949

PRINTERS. All stamps of Baden were printed by F. Burda, Offenburg.

FB **1** J. P. Hebel    FB **2** Rastatt

FB **3** Höllental, Black Forest    FB **4** Freiburg Cathedral

(Des V. K. Jonynas. Photo)
1947–48. Types FB **1/4** and similar designs inscr 'BADEN'. P 14.
FB1	FB **1**	2pf. grey (1.12.47)	40	65
FB2	–	3pf. brown (1.12.47)	40	65
FB3	–	10pf. grey-blue (8.12.47)	40	65
FB4	FB **1**	12pf. blue-green (12.5.47)	40	65
FB5	–	15pf. violet (12.12.47)	40	65
FB6	FB **2**	16pf. olive-green (15.12.47)	40	2·50
FB7	–	20pf. blue (16.1.48)	40	65
FB8	FB **2**	24pf. carmine (1.5.47)	40	65
FB9	–	45pf. magenta (18.7.47)	40	1·50
FB10	FB **1**	60pf. brown-orange (12.1.48)	40	65
FB11	–	75pf. blue (23.6.47)	40	3·25
FB12	FB **3**	84pf. green (22.8.47)	40	3·25
FB13	FB **4**	1m. brown (18.8.47)	40	5·30
FB1/FB13	Set of 3		4·75	15·00

Designs: As Type FB **1**–3, 15, 45pf. Badensian girl and yachts; 10, 20, 75pf. Hans Baldung Grien (artist).

1948 (21 June)–**49** (9 July). Currency Reform. As last but colours changed, new values and designs. P 14.
(a) Values in 'PF.'
FB14	FB **1**	2pf. orange	40	50
FB15	–	6pf. chocolate	40	50
FB16	–	10pf. olive-brown (9.7)	65	50
FB17	FB **1**	12pf. scarlet	65	50
FB18	–	15pf. light blue	75	1·00
FB19	FB **2**	20pf. blue-green	90	50
FB20	–	30pf. magenta (9.7)	1·80	1·90
FB21	–	50pf. blue	1·80	50

(b) Values in 'DPF' or 'DM' 'Deutschpfennig' or 'Deutschmark'
FB22	–	8dpf. blue-green	90	1·90
FB23	FB **2**	16dpf. violet	1·90	3·25
FB24	–	20dpf. brown	6·25	1·60
FB25	FB **1**	60dpf. grey	8·75	1·00
FB26	FB **3**	84dpf. brown-lake	11·50	7·50
FB27	FB **4**	1m. blue	10·00	7·50
FB14/FB27	Set of 14		42·00	26·00

Designs: As Types FB **1/2**–6, 15pf. Badensian girl and yachts; 10pf, 20dpf. Hans Baldung Grien; 8dpf., 16dpf. Black Forest girl in festive headdress; 50pf. Grand-Duchess Stephanie of Baden. Nos. FB14/FB21 were sold on the new currency basis though not inscribed 'DPF'.

1948 (Nov)–**49**. As before but 'PF' omitted. Colours changed, new values and designs. P 14.
FB28	FB **1**	2pf. brown-orange	1·90	90
FB29	–	4pf. violet	1·30	75
FB30	–	5pf. light blue	1·50	1·00
FB31	–	6pf. blackish brown (1949)	40·00	23·00
FB32	–	8pf. red-brown	1·90	1·80
FB33	–	10pf. blue-green	5·00	90
FB34	–	20pf. magenta (1949)	2·30	65
FB35	–	40pf. olive-brown (1949)	95·00	£130
FB36	FB **1**	80pf. scarlet	15·00	10·00
FB37	FB **3**	90pf. brown-purple (1949)	95·00	£130
FB28/FB37	Set of 10 (cheapest)		£225	£275

Designs: As Types FB **1/2**–4, 40pf. Rastatt; 5, 6pf. Badensian girl and yachts; 8pf. Black Forest girl in festive headdress; 10, 20pf. Hans Baldung Grien.

FB **5** Cornhouse, Freiburg    FB **6** Arms of Baden

(Des Dietrich. Photo)
1949 (24 Feb). Freiburg Rebuilding Fund. Type FB **5** and similar types. P 14.
FB38	4pf. +16pf. deep violet	23·00	65·00

GERMANY/ Allied Occupation

FB39	10pf. +20pf. green		23·00	65·00
FB40	20pf. +30pf. scarlet		23·00	65·00
FB41	30pf. +50pf. light blue		25·00	75·00
FB38/FB41 Set of 4			85·00	£250
MSFB41a 65×78 mm. Nos. FB38/41			95·00	£350
MSFB41b Ditto but imperf			95·00	£350

Designs:—4pf. Type FB **5**; 10pf. Freiburg Cathedral; 20pf. Trumpeting Angel, Freiburg; 30pf. 'Fischbrunnen'. Freiburg.

(Des E. Bargatzky. Photo)

1949 (25 Feb). Red Cross. Cross in red. P 14.

FB42	**6**	10pf. +20pf. green	31·00	£130
FB43		20pf. +40pf. lilac	31·00	£130
FB44		30pf. +60pf. blue	31·00	£130
FB45		40pf. +80pf. grey	31·00	£130
FB42/FB45 Set of 4			£110	£475
MSFB45a 90×100 mm. Nos. FB42/FB45 imperf without gum			£140	£1900

Forgeries of the miniature sheet exist in different shades.

FB **7** Seehof Hotel, Constance

(Des P. Hund. Photo)

1949 (22 June). Engineers' Congress, Constance. P 14.

FB46	FB **7**	30pf. blue	33·00	£110
		a. Second printing	£800	£2500

In the first printing the frame lines and inscription are thick and the upper loop of the 'B' partly filled in. In the second printing the lines and inscription are fine, the shading lighter and the 'B' is clear.

FB **8** Goethe (relief, Johann Peter Melchior)

FB **9** Carl Schurz and Revolutionary Scene

FB **10** Conradin Kreutzer

1949 (12 Aug). Birth Bicentenary of Goethe (poet). Type FB **8** and similar portraits inscr '1749 GOETHE 1949'. Photo. P 14.

FB47	10pf. +5pf. green	12·50	31·00
FB48	20pf. +10pf. magenta	15·00	31·00
FB49	30pf. +15pf. blue	20·00	75·00
FB47/FB49 Set of 3		43·00	£120

Portraits:—10pf. Type FB **8**; 20pf. Drawing by Johann Lips; 30pf. Profile relief by Angelica Facius.

(Des V. K. Jonynas. Photo)

1949 (23 Aug). Centenary of Rastatt Insurrection. P 14.

FB50	FB **9**	10pf. +5pf. green	15·00	48·00
FB51		20pf. +10pf. magenta	15·00	48·00
FB52		30pf. +15pf. blue	18·00	48·00
FB50/FB52 Set of 3			43·00	£130

(Des H. Thorweger. Photo)

1949 (27 Aug). Death Centenary of Conradin Kreutzer (composer). P 14.

FB53	FB **10**	10pf. green	5·75	19·00

FB **11** Mail Coach in 1849

FB **12** Posthorn and Globe

(Des Meyer (10pf.) and Pixa (20pf.). Photo)

1949 (17 Sept). German Stamp Centenary. T FB **11** and similar type. P 14.

FB54	10pf. green	8·25	18·00
FB55	20pf. brown	8·25	18·00

Designs:—10pf. T FB **11**; 20pf. Postal motor-coach with trailer and Douglas DC-4 airliner.

(Des Meyer and Pixa. Photo)

1949 (4 Oct). 75th Anniv of Universal Postal Union. P 14.

FB56	FB **12**	20pf. brown-lake	8·75	18·00
FB57		30pf. blue	8·75	15·00

(c) RHINELAND-PALATINATE, 1947–1949

FR **1** Porta Nigra, Trier

FR **2** Karl Marx

FR **3** Gutenfels Castle and River Rhine

FR **4** Statue of Charlemagne

A.

B.

Two types of 15pf. Type B ('K' without hook) occurs in the third and eighth vertical rows of the sheet of 100 (10×10), the other rows being Type A.

(Des V. K. Jonynas. Photo F. Burda, Offenburg)

1947. Types FR **1**/**4** and similar designs inscr 'RHEINLAND-PFALZ'. P 14.

FR1	2pf. grey	40	50
FR2	3pf. brown	40	50
FR3	10pf. grey-blue (8.9.47)	40	50
FR4	12pf. blue-green	40	50
FR5	15pf. dull violet (A)	40	50
	a. 'K' without hook (B)	2·50	3·25
FR6	16pf. yellow-green	40	1·80
FR7	20pf. blue	40	50
FR8	24pf. carmine (7.4.47)	40	50
FR9	30pf. magenta	40	3·75
FR10	45pf. magenta	40	1·00
FR11	50pf. blue	40	3·75
FR12	60pf. brown-orange	40	50
FR13	75pf. blue	40	1·00
FR14	84pf. dark green	50	2·30
FR15	1m. brown	50	1·30
FR1/FR15 Set of 15		5·50	17·00

Designs: 18×23 mm.—2pf., 60pf. Beethoven's death mask; 3pf. Baron von Ketteler, Bishop of Mainz; 10pf. Girl vintager; 12pf. Type FR **1**; 15pf. Type FR **2**; 16pf. Rocks at Arnweiler; 20pf. Palatinate village house; 24pf. Worms Cathedral; 30pf., 75pf. Gutenberg (printer); 45pf., 50pf. Mainz Cathedral.

1948 (21 June). Currency Reform. As last but colours changed and new values. P 14.

(a) Values in 'PF.'

FR16	2pf. brown-orange	40	50
FR17	6pf. chocolate	40	50
FR18	10pf. olive-brown	65	50
FR19	12pf. scarlet	65	50
FR20	15pf. light blue (A)	1·90	1·00
	a. 'K' without hook (B)	6·25	5·00
FR21	24pf. blue-green	65	50
FR22	30pf. magenta	1·90	65
FR23	50pf. magenta	2·50	65

(b) Values in 'DPF' or 'DM' 'Deutschpfennig' or 'Deutschmark'

FR24	8dpf. blue-green	65	1·90
FR25	16dpf. violet	1·00	2·30

57

GERMANY / Allied Occupation

FR26	20dpf. brown		5·00	1·00
FR27	60dpf. grey		12·50	65
FR28	84dpf. brown-lake		8·25	9·50
FR29	1dm. blue		8·75	9·50
FR16/FR29 Set of 14			41·00	27·00

Designs: 18×22 mm.—2pf., 60dpf. Beethoven's death mask; 6pf. Baron von Ketteler, Bishop of Mainz; 10pf. Girl vintager; 12pf., 8dpf. as Type FR **1**; 15pf. Type FR **2**; 24pf. Worms Cathedral; 30pf. Mainz Cathedral; 50pf. Gutenberg (printer); 16dpf. Rocks at Arnweiler; 20dpf. Palatinate village house. 40×23 mm.—84dpf. Type FR **3**. 23×40 mm.—dm. Type FR **4**.

Nos. FR16/FR23 were sold on the new currency basis though not inscribed 'DPF'.

FR **5** St. Martin

(Des Speyer. Photo)

1948 (Oct). Ludwigshafen Explosion Relief Fund. Type FR **5** and similar design. P 14.

FR30	20pf. +30pf. magenta	3·25	95·00
FR31	30pf. +50pf. bright blue	3·25	95·00

Designs:—20pf. Type FR **5**; 30pf. St Christopher.

1948 (Nov)–**49**. As before but 'PF' omitted. Colours changed, new values and designs. P 14.

FR32	—	2pf. brown-orange	1·20	60
FR33	—	4pf. violet (1949)	1·20	60
FR34	FR **2**	5pf. light blue (A.) (1949)	1·20	95
		a. 'K' without hook (B.)	7·75	8·50
FR35	—	6pf. sepia	42·00	24·00
FR36	FR **1**	8pf. brown-lake (1949)	£110	£600
FR37	—	10pf. blue-green	1·60	60
FR38	—	20pf. magenta	1·60	60
FR39	—	40pf. olive-brown (1949)	6·00	6·00
FR40	FR **1**	80pf. scarlet (1949)	7·25	7·75
FR41	FR **3**	90pf. brown-purple (1949)	12·00	24·00
FR32/FR41 Set of 10			£170	£600

Designs: 18×23 mm.—2pf. Beethoven's death mask; 4pf. Rocks at Arnweiler; 6pf. Baron von Ketteler, Bishop of Mainz; 10pf. Girl vintager; 20pf. Palatinate village house; 40pf. Worms Cathedral.

1949 (25 Feb). Red Cross. As Type FB **6** of Baden but Arms of Rhine, and and inscr 'RHEINLAND/PFALZ'. Cross in red. P 14.

FR42	10pf. +20pf. green	26·00	£130
FR43	20pf. +40pf. lilac	26·00	£130
FR44	30pf. +60pf. blue	26·00	£130
FR45	40pf. +80pf. grey	26·00	£130
FR42/FR45 Set of 4		95·00	£475

MSFR45a 90×100 mm. Nos. FR42/FR45 imperf without gum | £140 | £1800

Forgeries of the miniature sheet exist in different shades.

1949 (12 Aug). Birth Bicentenary of Goethe (poet). As Nos. FB47/FB49 of Baden, but inscr 'RHEINLAND PFALZ'. Photo. P 14.

FR46	10pf. +5pf. green	9·50	29·00
FR47	20pf. +10pf. magenta	9·50	29·00
FR48	30pf. +15pf. blue	17·00	65·00
FR46/FR48 Set of 3		32·00	£110

1949 (17 Sept). Centenary of First German Stamp. As Nos. FB54/FB55 of Baden, but inscr 'RHEINLAND PFALZ'. Photo. P 14.

FR49	10pf. green	13·00	30·00
FR50	20pf. brown	13·00	30·00

1949 (4 Oct). 75th Anniv of UPU. As Nos. FB56/FB57 of Baden but inscr 'RHEINLAND-PFALZ'. Photo. P 14.

FR51	20pf. brown-lake	9·50	18·00
FR52	30pf. blue	9·50	16·00

(d) SAAR, 1945–1947

The Saar District, from 1945 to 1947 part of the French Zone, also had its own stamps, but as it was in a different political category. we list its stamps for convenience of reference all together; see under Saar in this catalogue.

(e) WÜRTTEMBERG, 1947–1949

For use in South Württemberg, Hohenzollern and the Bavarian district of Kreis Lindau.

FW **1** Fr. von Schiller

FW **2** Bebenhausen Monastery

FW **3** Lichtenstein Castle

(Des V. K. Jonynas. Photo F. Burda)

1947 (15 May)–**48**. Types FW **1**/**3** and similar designs inscr 'WÜRTTEMBERG'. P 14.

FW1	2pf. grey (13.1.48)	35	95
FW2	3pf. brown (16.1.48)	35	50
FW3	10pf. grey-blue (22.1.48)	35	60
FW4	12pf. blue-green (19.6.47)	35	50
FW5	15pf. violet (2.2.48)	35	70
FW6	16pf. olive-green (4.2.48)	35	1·90
FW7	20pf. blue (7.2.48)	35	1·90
FW8	24pf. carmine (15.6.47)	35	50
FW9	45pf. magenta	35	1·90
FW10	60pf. brown-orange (10.2.48)	35	1·20
FW11	75pf. blue	60	2·20
FW12	84pf. green (27.8.47)	60	2·20
FW13	1m. brown (2.9.47)	60	2·20
FW1/FW13 Set of 13		4·75	16·00

Designs: 18×23 mm.—2pf., 12pf., 60pf. Type FW **1**; 3pf., 15pf., 45pf. Portrait of Hölderlin (poet); 10pf., 20pf., 75pf. Wangen Gate; 16pf. Type FW **2**. 22×40 mm.–1m. Zwiefalten Monastery Church.

1948 (21 June). Currency Reform. As last but colours changed, new values and designs. P 14.

(a) Values in 'PF'

FW14	2pf. brown-orange	35	60
FW15	6pf. chocolate	35	50
FW16	10pf. olive-brown	35	60
FW17	12pf. scarlet	35	50
FW18	15pf. light blue	1·20	60
FW19	24pf. blue-green	1·80	95
FW20	30pf. magenta	1·80	95
FW21	50pf. blue	3·50	95

(b) Values in 'DPF' or 'DM' 'Deutschpfennig' or 'Deutschmark'

FW22	8dpf. green	1·80	3·50
FW23	16dpf. violet	1·40	2·40
FW24	20dpf. brown	3·00	1·80
FW25	60dpf. grey	18·00	95
FW26	84dpf. brown-lake	4·75	7·25
FW27	1dm. light blue	4·75	7·25
FW14/FW27 Set of 14		39·00	26·00

Designs: 18×22 mm.—2pf., 12pf., 60dpf. Type FW **1**; 6pf., 15pf. Fr. Hölderlin (poet); 10pf., 20dpf. Wangen Gate; 16dpf., 24pf. Type FW **2**; 8 dpf., 30pf. Waldsee Castle; 50pf. Ludwig Uhland (poet). 22×40 mm.—1dm. Zwiefalten Monastery Church.

Nos. FW14/FW21 were sold on the new currency basis though not inscr 'DPF'.

1948 (Nov)–**49**. As before but 'PF' omitted. Colours changed, new values and designs. P 14.

FW28	FW **1**	2pf. brown-orange	1·60	95
FW29	FW **2**	4pf. violet	3·50	60
FW30	—	5pf. light blue (1949)	9·00	3·50
FW31	—	6pf. sepia (1949)	12·00	9·00
FW32	—	8pf. brown-lake (1949)	12·00	3·50
FW33	—	10pf. blue-green (1949)	11·00	60
FW34	—	20pf. magenta (1949)	12·00	60
FW35	FW **2**	40pf. olive-brown (1949)	30·00	60·00
FW36	FW **1**	80pf. scarlet (1949)	60·00	60·00
FW37	FW **3**	90pf. brown-purple (1949)	90·00	£160
FW28/FW37 Set of 10			£225	£275

Designs: 18×23 mm.—5pf. and 6pf. Portrait of Hölderlin (poet); 8pf. Waldsee Castle; 10pf. and 20pf. Wangen Gate.

FW **4** Isny and Coat of Arms

FW **5** Gustav Werner (founder)

GERMANY / Allied Occupation

(Des J. Dorner. Litho State Ptg Works, Berlin)

1949 (11 Feb). Ski Championships (Northern Combination) at Isny/Allgau. Type FW **4** and similar type. Wmk Type M **7** of Württemberg (Mult Crosses and Circles). P 14.

| FW38 | 10pf. +4pf. blue-green | 12·00 | 36·00 |
| FW39 | 20pf. +6pf. brown-lake | 12·00 | 36·00 |

Designs:—10pf. Type FW **4**; 20pf. Skier and view of Isny.

1949 (25 Feb). Red Cross. As Type FB **6** of Baden, but Arms of Württemberg and inscr 'WÜRTTEMBERG'. Cross in red. P 14.

FW40	10pf. +20pf. green	48·00	£140
FW41	20pf. +40pf. lilac	48·00	£140
FW42	30pf. +60pf. blue	48·00	£140
FW43	40pf. +80pf. grey	48·00	£140
FW40/FW43	Set of 4	£170	£500
MSFW43a	90×100 mm. Nos. FW40/FW43 imperf without gum	£180	£2250

Forgeries of the miniature sheet exist in different shades.

1949 (12 Aug). Birth Bicentenary of Goethe (poet). As Nos. FB47/FB49 of Baden, but inscr 'WÜRTTEMBERG'.

FW44	10pf. +5pf. green	11·00	30·00
FW45	20pf. +10pf. magenta	16·00	42·00
FW46	30pf. +15pf. blue	16·00	60·00
FW44/FW46	Set of 3	39·00	£120

(Photo F. Burda, Offenburg)

1949 (4 Sept). Centenary of the Christian Institution 'Zum Bruderhaus'. P 14.

| FW47 | FW **5** | 10pf. +5pf. blue-green | 7·75 | 20·00 |
| FW48 | | 20pf. +10pf. purple | 7·75 | 20·00 |

1949 (17 Sept). German Stamp Centenary. As Nos. FB54/FB55 of Baden, but inscr 'WÜRTTEMBERG'.

| FW49 | 10pf. green | 9·50 | 19·00 |
| FW50 | 20pf. brown | 9·50 | 19·00 |

1949 (4 Oct). 75th Anniv of UPU. As Nos. FB56/FB57 of Baden, but inscr 'WÜRTTEMBERG'.

| FW51 | 20pf. brown-lake | 7·75 | 16·00 |
| FW52 | 30pf. blue | 7·75 | 14·50 |

The French Zone became part of the German Federal Republic (West Germany) on 21 Sept 1949. French Zone stamps in use and issued after that date could be used throughout the Federal Republic until 31 December 1949 (commemorative stamps until 31 March 1950).

E. RUSSIAN ZONE

I. PROVINCIAL ADMINISTRATIONS

Of the many issues of the Russian Zone, we restrict our listing to those issues made under the various Provincial Administrations which were in general use. We do not list the many 'town' issues.

Until the issue of Nos. 899/956 for general use in the British, American and Soviet Russian Zones the Soviet authorities decided to organise the posts within their Zone on the basis of the Higher Postal Directorates, *Oberpostdirektionen* (OPD), of the principal cities.

(a) BERLIN—BRANDENBURG (OPD. Berlin)

RA **1** Arms of Berlin

(Des H. Goldammer (5, 8, 30pf.) and H. Schwab. Litho State Ptg Works, Berlin)

1945 (9 June–6 Dec). Type RA **1** and similar designs inscr 'Stadt Berlin'. P 14.

RA1	5pf. yellow-green (9.6.45)	50	85
RA2	6pf. violet (18.7.45)	50	60
RA3	8pf. red-orange (9.6.45)	50	60
RA4	10pf. brown (18.7.45)	50	85
RA5	12pf. carmine (5.7.45)	50	60
RA6	20pf. blue (18.7.45)	50	80
RA7	30pf. olive-green (18.7.45)	50	1·20
RA1/RA7	Set of 7	3·25	5·00

B. Zigzag Roulette (6 Dec)

RA8	5pf. yellow-green	13·00	£190
RA9	6pf. violet	25·00	£140
RA10	8pf. red-orange	13·00	£140
RA11	10pf. brown	25·00	£140
RA12	12pf. carmine	31·00	£190
RA13	20pf. blue	25·00	£160
RA14	30pf. olive-green	38·00	£200
RA8/RA14	Set of 7	£150	£1000

Designs:—5pf. Type RA **1**; 6pf. Bear with spade; 8pf. Bear on shield; 10pf. Bear holding brick; 12pf. Bear carrying plank; 20pf. Bear on small shield; 30pf. Oak sapling amid ruins.

All values were issued rouletted in December, 1945, but in this condition seem to be speculative and not intended for postal use. The 5pf. in this issue can only be distinguished from an earlier printing, issued normally, by the gum.

Stamps overprinted 'Berlin im Aufbau', etc., were privately produced to defraud collectors.

(b) MECKLENBURG-VORPOMMERN (OPD Schwerin)

RB **1**    RB **2**    RB **3**

(Des G. Otto. Typo W. Sandmeyer, Schwerin)

1945 (28 Aug)**–46**. P 10½.

RB1	RB **1**	6pf. black/*green* (31.8.45)	60	3·50
RB2		6pf. violet (16.11.45)	4·75	7·75
RB3		6pf. violet/*green* (11.1.46)	4·75	6·00
RB4	RB **2**	8pf. red/*red* (6.10.45)	95	3·50
RB5		8pf. black/*red* (19.10.45)	7·25	16·00
RB6		8pf. lilac/*green* (3.11.45)	1·80	7·25
RB7		8pf. black/*green* (2.1.46)	16·00	23·00
RB8		8pf. brown (7.1.46)	1·40	7·25
RB9	RB **3**	12pf. black/*red* (28.8.45)	85	3·25
RB10		12pf. brownish lilac (9.11.45)	1·10	3·50
RB11		12pf. red (20.12.45)	8·50	19·00
RB12		12pf. lilac (30.1.46)	1·20	3·75
RB1/RB12	Set of 12		44·00	95·00

There are many shades of the above stamps. With overprint '20.12.45' they are bogus.

RB **4** Rudolf Breitscheid    RB **5** Sower

(Des H. Bartholomäus. Typo P. Niemann, Ludwigslust)

1945 (21 Oct). Victims of Fascism. Type RB **4** and similar vert portraits. P 10½.

RB13	6pf. +14pf. emerald	42·00	95·00
RB14	8pf. +22pf. reddish violet	42·00	95·00
RB15	12pf. +28pf. red	42·00	95·00
RB13/RB15	Set of 3	£110	£250

Portraits:—6pf. Type RB **4**; 8pf. Dr. Klausener; 12pf. Ernst Thälmann.

(Des H. Bartholomäus. Typo P. Niemann, Ludwigslust)

1945 (8–31 Dec). CHARITY. Land Reform. Type RB **5** and similar vert designs inscr 'JUNKERLAND IN BAUERNHAND'. P 10½.

RB16	6pf. +14pf. blue-green	11·00	65·00
	a. Bright green (31.12)	11·00	65·00
RB17	8pf. +22pf. brown	11·00	65·00
	a. Chestnut (31.12)	11·00	65·00
RB18	12pf. +28pf. rose-red	11·00	65·00
	a. Red-orange (31.12)	11·00	65·00
RB16/RB18	Set of 3	30·00	£180

Designs:—6pf. Horse-ploughing; 8pf. Typr RB **5**; 12pf. Reaper.

RB **6** Child in Hand    RB **7** Village Street

(Des H. Bartholomäus. Typo P. Niemann, Ludwigslust)

1945 (31 Dec). Child Welfare. Type RB **6** and similar vert designs. P 10½.

RB19	6pf. +14pf. orange-red	9·00	70·00
RB20	8pf. +22pf. blue	4·75	70·00
RB21	12pf. +28pf. rose-red	4·75	70·00

59

GERMANY / Allied Occupation

RB19/RB21 Set of 3		17·00	£190

Designs:—6pf. Type RB **6**; 8pf. Schoolgirl in Winter; 12pf. Boy.

(Des E. Wriedt. Die eng H. Bartholomäus. Typo P. Niemann, Ludwigslust, later W. Sandmeyer, Schwerin)

1946 (17 Jan–25 Feb). As Type RB **7** (inscr 'MECKLENBURG VORPOMMERN' at base).

I. Imperf

RB22	3pf. brown	4·75	70·00
RB23	4pf. blue	55·00	95·00
RB24	4pf. claret	4·75	70·00
RB25	5pf. green (shades)	4·75	65·00
RB26	8pf. vermilion	4·25	65·00
RB27	10pf. chocolate	4·25	65·00
RB22/RB27 Set of 6		70·00	£375

II. P 10½

RB28	6pf. blue	20·00	48·00
	a. Violet	2·40	11·00
RB29	12pf. rose-red	2·40	5·50
RB30	15pf. brown	2·40	12·00
RB31	20pf. blue	3·50	16·00
RB32	30pf. turquoise-green	3·00	18·00
RB33	40pf. bright purple	3·00	18·00
RB28/RB33 Set of 6 (cheapest)		15·00	70·00

Designs:—3pf. Type RB **7**; 4pf. Deer; 5pf. Fishing Boats; 6pf. Harvesting; 8pf. Windmill; 10pf. Two-horse Plough; 12pf. Scaffolding; 15pf. Ploughing by Tractor; 20pf. Ship and Warehouse; 30pf. Factory; 40pf. Woman spinning.

(c) SAXONY (OPD Halle)

RC **1** Coat of Arms    RC **2** Ploughing    RC **3** Rehousing

(Des E. Manz. Typo Giesecke and Devrient, Leipzig)

1945–46. W **232**.

(a) Imperf (10.10.45, except 10pf, Jan 1946)

RC1	**1** 1pf. slate	95	7·25
RC2	3pf. yellow-brown	95	4·75
RC3	5pf. green	2·40	18·00
RC4	6pf. violet	1·70	3·50
RC5	8pf. orange	95	4·75
RC6	10pf. brown	16·00	£225
RC7	12pf. carmine	95	3·50
RC1/RC7 Set of 7		22·00	£250

The 10pf. imperf was issued in Naumburg.

(b) P 13×12½ (Dec 1945)

RC8	**1** 1pf. slate	35	3·50
RC9	3pf. yellow-brown	35	3·50
RC10	5pf. green	35	3·50
RC11	6pf. violet	2·40	4·50
RC12	8pf. orange	35	4·25
RC13	10pf. brown	2·40	4·25
RC14	12pf. carmine	35	4·25
RC15	15pf. claret	£300	£850
RC16	20pf. blue	50	5·75
RC17	24pf. red-brown	50	5·75
RC18	30pf. olive-green	50	5·75
RC19	40pf. purple	2·40	11·50
RC8/RC19 Set of 11 (excl. RC15)		9·75	80·00

(Des Gebauer. Typo)

1945–46. Land Reform.

A. Ptd by Ebelt, Halle-on-Saale on unwatermarked white paper (17.12.45).

(a) Imperf

RC20	**2** 6pf. green	50	3·50
RC21	12pf. carmine	50	3·50

(b) P 11

RC22	**2** 6pf. green	8·50	36·00
RC23	12pf. carmine	8·50	36·00

B. Redrawn and ptd by Giesecke and Devrient on thin, transparent, wmkd paper P 13×13½ (21.2.46).

RC24	**2** 6pf. green	50	10·00
RC25	12pf. red	50	10·00

(Des Gebauer. Typo Giesecke and Devrient)

1946. Reconstruction Fund. Type RC **3** and similar types inscr 'WIEDERAUFBAU'.

(a) P 13 (19 Jan)

RC26	6pf. +4pf. green	50	3·50

RC27	12pf. +8pf. rose	50	3·50
RC28	42pf. +28pf. violet	50	3·50
RC26/RC28 Set of 3		1·40	9·50

(b) Imperf (21 Feb)

RC29	6pf. +4pf. green	70	30·00
RC30	12pf. +8pf. rose	70	30·00
RC31	42pf. +28pf. violet	85	30·00
RC29/RC31 Set of 3		2·00	80·00

Designs:—6pf. Type RC **3**; 12pf. Bridge-building; 42pf. Locomotives.

(d) WEST SAXONY (OPD Leipzig)

PRINTERS. All issues were typographed by Giesecke and Devrient, Leipzig.

RD **1**    RD **2**    RD **3**

1945. W **232**.

(a) Imperf (28 Sept)

RD1	**1** 5pf. green	35	3·50
RD2	6pf. violet	35	3·50
RD3	8pf. orange	35	3·50
RD4	12pf. carmine	35	3·50
RD1/RD4 Set of 4		1·30	12·50

(b) P 13×12½ (9–15 Nov)

RD5	**1** 3pf. brown	35	3·50
RD6	4pf. blue-grey	60	5·50
RD7	5pf. green	35	3·50
RD8	6pf. violet	35	3·50
RD9	8pf. orange	35	7·25
RD10	10pf. grey	35	6·50
RD11	12pf. carmine	35	3·50
RD12	15pf. claret	1·20	6·50
RD13	20pf. blue	1·20	6·00
RD14	30pf. olive-green	1·20	3·50
RD15	40pf. magenta	2·40	7·25
RD16	60pf. purple-brown	5·50	30·00
RD5/RD16 Set of 12		13·00	80·00

The 5, 6, 8 and 12pf. values also exist rouletted locally at Rosswein and other places and with an experimental perf 11.

1945 (18 Oct). Leipzig Fair. W **232**. P 13½.

RD17	**2** 6pf. green	1·40	4·50
RD18	12pf. carmine	1·40	4·50

(Des Otto Horn)

1946 (7 Jan). Relief Fund. W **232**. P 13×12½.

RD19	**3** 3pf. +2pf. brown	85	4·75
RD20	4pf. +3pf. slate	85	4·75
RD21	5pf. +3pf. yellow-green	85	4·75
RD22	6pf. +4pf. lilac	85	4·75
RD23	8pf. +4pf. orange	85	4·75
RD24	10pf. +5pf. grey	85	4·75
RD25	12pf. +6pf. carmine	85	4·75
RD26	15pf. +10pf. red-brown	85	4·75
RD27	20pf. +10pf. blue	85	4·75
RD28	30pf. +20pf. olive-green	85	5·75
RD29	40pf. +30pf. magenta	85	4·75
RD30	60pf. +40pf. claret	85	7·00
	a. Error 'DFUTSCHE POST'	48·00	£140
RD19/RD30 Set of 12		9·25	55·00

No. RD30a occurs on positions 87 and 100 of part of the printing.

RD **4** Leipzig Arms    RD **5** Leipzig Town Hall    RD **6** Market and Old Town Hall

1946 (12 Feb–15 Mar). Types RD **4/5** and similar type. P 13×12½.

*(a) W **232***

RD31	3pf. brown	60	9·50
RD32	4pf. slate	60	9·50
RD33	5pf. green	60	9·50
RD34	6pf. violet	60	9·50
RD35	8pf. orange	60	9·50

GERMANY/ Allied Occupation

RD36	12pf. scarlet		60	9·50
RD31/RD36	Set of 6		3·25	50·00

(b) No wmk (15 Mar)

RD37	3pf. brown		70	14·50
RD38	4pf. slate		70	14·50
RD39	5pf. green		70	14·50
RD40	6pf. violet		70	14·50
RD41	8pf. orange		70	14·50
RD42	12pf. scarlet		70	14·50
RD37/RD42	Set of 6		3·75	80·00

Designs:—3pf., 4pf. Type RD **4**; 5pf., 6pf. St. Nicholas Church, Leipzig; 8pf., 12pf. Type RD **5**.

1946. Leipzig Fair. W **232**.

(a) P 13½×13 (8 May)

RD43	RD **6**	6pf. +14pf. violet		35	4·25
		a. No wmk		1·40	5·50
RD44		12pf. +18pf. slate-blue		1·20	7·25
		a. No wmk		1·40	9·50
RD45		24pf. +26pf. yellow-brown		60	4·25
		a. No wmk		1·40	3·50
RD46		84pf. +66pf. green		60	11·00
RD43/RD46	Set of 4			2·50	23·00

(b) Imperf (20 May)

RD47	RD **6**	6pf. +14pf. violet		1·60	18·00
RD48		12pf. +18pf. slate-blue		1·60	20·00
RD49		24pf. +26pf. yellow-brown		1·60	20·00
RD50		84pf. +66pf. green		1·60	32·00
RD47/RD50	Set of 4			5·75	95·00
MSRD51	105×105 mm. Nos. RD47/RD50			£275	£425

(e) EAST SAXONY (OPD Dresden)

RE **1**

RE **2** Zwinger, Dresden

(Des P. Chemnitz)

1945 (23 June). Type RE **1** but inscr 'ПОЧАТ' below value. Photo Welzel, Dresden or Hoesch Bros, Hutten. White chalky paper. Imperf.

RE1	12pf. red		£800	£1000

14,500 copies of a printing of 1,030,000 of this stamp were put on sale in Dresden before it was ordered to be withdrawn on the day of issue, because the Russian inscription was contrary to Allied agreements. The withdrawn stamps were officially destroyed.

Used price for No. RE1 was for cancelled to order.

Forgeries printed by typography exist.

1945–46. Type RE **1**.

(a) Photo Welzel. Dresden or Hoesch Bros, Hutten. White chalky paper. Imperf (1945)

RE2	5pf. brown (6.7)		1·20	3·00
RE3	6pf. green to yellow-green (30.6)		12·00	14·50
	aa. Grey-green (26.7)		36·00	42·00
	a. Blackish green (26.7)		£1800	£4000
	b. Rouletted (shades) (3.7)		12·00	16·00
	c. Perf 11 (26.7)		£180	£275
RE4	8pf. violet (3.7)		1·60	3·00
RE5	10pf. deep brown (3.7)		1·80	6·50
RE6	12pf. rose-carmine (28.6)		1·80	3·00
RE7	15pf. olive-yellow (10.7)		1·40	4·25
RE8	20pf. grey-blue (26.7)		1·90	4·25
RE9	25pf. blue (5.7)		1·40	4·25
RE10	40pf. magenta (7.7)		1·40	4·25
RE2/RE10	Set of 9		22·00	42·00

(b) Litho J. R. Ulbricht, Limbach. Grey paper. Imperf (1945)

RE11	3pf. sepia (5.12)		1·20	4·25
	a. Rectangular right end to top of '3'		4·75	38·00
RE12	10pf. grey (3.11)		1·20	4·25
	a. Error. Black		£600	£1100

(c) Photo Sächsische Volkszeitung, Dresden. Imperf (1945)

RE13	4pf. blue-green (5.11)		60	3·00
RE14	20pf. blue (3.11)		50	3·00
RE15	30pf. yellow (5.11)		50	3·00
RE13/RE15	Set of 3		1·40	8·00

(d) Typo Giesecke and Devrient, Leipzig. Grey paper. P 13×12½. (1945)

RE16	3pf. brown (21.12)		60	3·00
RE17	5pf. green (3.11)		60	3·00
RE18	6pf. violet (3.11)		60	3·00
RE19	8pf. orange (3.11)		60	3·00
RE20	12pf. red (3.11)		60	3·00
RE16/RE20	Set of 5		2·75	13·50

(e) Photo Sächsische Volkszeitung, Dresden. Chalky paper (4pf and 6pf). Ordinary greyish paper (12pf). Imperf (1946)

RE21	4pf. dark greenish-grey (15.1)		50	1·80
RE22	6pf. violet (22.1)		50	1·80
	a. Grey-violet		6·00	19·00
RE23	12pf. red (1.2)		50	1·80
RE21/RE23	Set of 3		1·40	4·75

Shades of all the above exist.

Several post offices perforated or rouletted stamps for convenience. Ten sheets of 100 of No. RE3*a* were issued.

No. RE11a occurs on positions 11, 31, 51, 71 and 91 in the sheet of 100 (10×10).

Imperforate remainders of Nos. RE16/RE20 were put on sale in limited quantities on 23.4.1946.

Nos. RE21 and RE23 can be distinguished from Nos. RE13 and RE6 respectively by the differences in the paper.

(Des H. Walter. Photo Sächsische Volkszeitung, Dresden)

1946 (6 Feb). Reconstruction Fund. Type RE **2** (and similar type). P 11.

RE24	6pf. +44pf. green		1·60	10·00
RE25	12pf. +88pf. red		1·60	10·00

Designs:—6pf.+44pf. Type RE **2**; 12pf.+88pf. Town Hall, Dresden.

(f) THURINGIA (OPD Erfurt)

RF **1** Posthorn

RF **2** Schiller

(Des E. Schoner. Typo Ohlenroth, Erfurt)

1945–46. Types RF **1/2** and similar designs. P 11.

RF1	–	3pf. brown (1.1.46)	60	4·75
RF2	–	4pf. grey-black (1.1.46)	60	4·75
RF3	–	5pf. yellow-green (15.10.45)	60	6·00
RF4	RF **1**	6pf. blue-green (1.10.45)	60	3·50
RF5	–	8pf. orange (24.10.45)	60	4·25
RF6	RF **2**	12pf. red (15.10.45)	60	3·50
RF7	–	20pf. blue (19.11.45)	60	3·50
		a. Imperf	60	5·50
RF8	–	30pf. grey (22.12.45)	2·40	5·50
		a. Imperf	14·50	46·00
RF1/RF8	Set of 8		6·00	32·00
MSRF9	78×38 mm. Nos. RF1/RF3 (18.12.45). Imperf		£450	£1300
MSRF10	120×120 mm. Nos. RF2, RF4 and RF6/RF7 (18.12.45). Roul		£2250	£4000

Designs:—3pf. to 5pf. Fir trees; 20pf, 30pf. Goethe.

Numerous shades and various types of paper exist.

Unused prices are for stamps with smooth gum. All values were also issued with 'economy' gum in which a regular pattern of ungummed circles appear. (*Price for Set of 8 with economy gum*: £30 *un*.)

Modern forgeries of No. **MS**RF9 exist, printed in photogravure instead of typography.

RF **3** Schiller

RF **4** Saalburg Bridge

1946 (27 Mar). Rebuilding of German National Theatre, Wiemar. Sheets 105×105 mm, containing Type RF **3** and similar designs.

(a) W **232**. *White gummed paper. Imperf*
MSRF11 6(pf.) grey-brown; 10(pf.) grey-green; 12(pf.) grey-violet; 16(pf.) red-brown; 40(pf.) ultramarine
(29×22 *mm*) (*sold at 7.50Rm*) .... 24·00 95·00

(b) No watermark. Brownish paper with gum. Roul
MSRF12 Designs as **MS**RF11 (*sold at 7.50Rm*) .... 85·00 £275

Designs:—6(pf.) Type RF **3**; 10(pf.) Goethe; 12(pf.) Liszt; 16(pf.) Wieland; 40(pf.) National Theatre.

(Des E. Schoner. Typo Ohlenroth, Erfurt)

1946 (30 Mar). Bridge Reconstruction Fund Type RF **4** and similar bridge designs. Imperf.

RF13	10pf. +60pf. chocolate		1·20	14·50
RF14	12pf. +68pf. vermilion		1·20	14·50
RF15	16pf. +74pf. deep bluish green		1·20	14·50
RF16	24pf. +76pf. orange-brown		1·20	14·50
RF13/RF16	Set of 4		4·25	50·00
MSRF17	119×119 mm. Nos. RF13/16		£500	£2000

Designs:—10pf. Type RF **4**; 12pf. Camsdorf Bridge, Jena; 15pf. Göschwitz Bridge; 24pf. Ilm Bridge, Mellingen.

GERMANY / Allied Occupation

II. GENERAL ISSUES

From February 1946 until June 1948 the Soviet Russian Zone used Nos. 899/956.

The Soviet authorities introduced their currency reform in a hurry, and as an emergency control measure Nos. 928/44 were handstamped with Postal District names and OPD numbers and placed on sale from 24 June 1948. There are over 1900 different handstamps, originating in about 1100 postal districts. These handstamps are outside the scope of this catalogue.

(R 1) R 2

1948. Optd with Type R **1**.

(a) On Pictorial issue of 1947–48, Nos. 928/44 (3 July)

R1	2pf. brown-black	60	60
R2	6pf. violet	60	60
R3	8pf. vermilion	60	60
R4	10pf. yellow-green	60	70
R5	12pf. grey	60	60
R6	15pf. chocolate	70	70
R7	16pf. blue-green	60	95
R8	20pf. light blue	60	70
R9	24pf. brown	60	50
R10	25pf. yellow-orange	60	50
R11	30pf. red	3·00	70
R12	40pf. magenta	60	70
R13	50pf. ultramarine	85	2·40
R14	60pf. red-brown (No. 942)	1·80	2·40
R15	60pf. red (No. 941)	85·00	£225
R16	80pf. grey-blue	3·50	4·75
R17	84pf. emerald green	4·25	4·75
R1/R17	Set of 17	95·00	£225

(b) On Numeral issue of 1946, Nos. 899, etc. (Sept)

R18	5pf. emerald-green	1·20	2·40
R19	30pf. olive-green	1·90	4·75
R20	45pf. scarlet	95	1·80
R21	75pf. ultramarine	95	1·80
R22	84pf. green	2·20	4·75
R18/R22	Set of 5	6·50	14·00

(c) On Berlin Russian Zone issue, Nos. RA1/RA7 (Sept)

R23	5pf. yellow-green	60	2·75
R24	5pf. yellow-green (No. RA8) (roul)	60	2·40
R25	6pf. violet	60	2·40
R26	8pf. red-orange	60	3·00
R27	10pf. brown	60	3·00
R28	12pf. carmine	85	24·00
R29	20pf. blue	60	1·40
R30	30pf. olive-green	60	10·00
R23/R30	Set of 8	4·50	44·00

(Des E. Gruner. Litho Giesecke & Devrient, Leipzig)

1948 (29 Aug). Leipzig Autumn Fair. As T **231** of Allied Occupation, but inscr '1948'. Wmk Type R **2**. P 13½.

R31	16pf. +9pf. brown-purple	1·10	95
R32	50pf. +25pf. ultramarine	1·10	95

Designs:—16pf. 1459: The first Spring Fair; 50pf. 1469: Foreign merchants displaying cloth.

R **3** Käthe Kollwitz

R **4**

(Des H. Ilgenfritz. Typo Giesecke & Devrient, Leipzig)

1948 (from Oct). Portraits of politicians, artists and scientists as Type R **3**. Wmk Type R **2**. P 13×12½.

R33	2pf. slate-grey	2·40	2·40
R34	6pf. violet	2·40	2·40
R35	8pf. brown-red	2·40	2·40
R36	10pf. bluish green	2·40	1·80
R37	12pf. light blue	5·50	1·20
R38	15pf. brown	1·80	3·50
R39	16pf. greenish blue	7·75	3·50
R40	20pf. brown-purple	2·40	2·40
R41	24pf. carmine	6·00	2·40
R42	25pf. olive-green	2·40	3·00
R43	30pf. vermilion	6·00	3·50
R44	40pf. bright purple	24·00	4·25
R45	50pf. blue	2·40	3·00
R46	60pf. dark green	12·00	4·25
R47	80pf. blackish blue	2·40	2·40
R48	84pf. red-brown	3·75	7·25
R33/R48	Set of 16	75·00	45·00

Portraits:—2pf., 20pf. Käthe Kollwitz; 6pf., 40pf. Gerhart Hauptmann; 8pf., 50pf. Karl Marx; 10pf., 84pf. August Bebel; 12pf., 30pf. Friedrich Engels; 15pf., 60pf. G. F. W. Hegel; 16pf., 25pf. Rudolf Virchow; 24pf., 80pf. Ernst Thälmann.

For similar stamps but wmkd E **30**, see Nos. E82/E96 of East Germany.

(Des E. Müller. Litho Giesecke and Devrient)

1948 (23 Oct). Stamp Day. Wmk Type R **2**. P 13×13½.

R49	R **4**	12pf. +3pf. vermilion	1·20	1·60

PRINTERS. Nos. R50/R61 were printed by the German Bank Note Ptg Co., Leipzig (formerly Giesecke & Devrient).

R **5** Karl Liebknecht and Rosa Luxemburg

R **6** Dove

(Des E. Müller. Litho.)

1949 (15 Jan). 30th Death Anniv of K. Liebknecht and R. Luxemburg (revolutionaries). Wmk Type R **2**. P 13½×13.

R50	R **5**	24pf. pale red	1·20	1·60

(Des E. Gruner. Eng K. Wolf. Litho)

1949 (6 Mar). Leipzig Spring Fair. As T **231** of Allied Occupation but inscr 'LEIPZIGER MESSE 1949'. Wmk Type R **2**. P 13½.

R51	30pf. +15pf. vermilion	5·25	6·50
R52	50pf. +25pf. deep ultramarine	6·00	7·25

Designs:—30pf. First Neubau Town Hall bazaar, 1556; 50pf. Italian merchants at Leipzig, 1536.

(Des F. Gravenhorst. Litho.)

1949 (13 May). Third German People's Congress. Wmk Type R **2**. P 13.

R53	R **6**	24pf. rose	2·40	3·00

3. Deutscher Volkskongreß

29.- 30 Mai 1949

(R **7**)

1949 (29 May). Third German People's Congress. No. R53 optd with Type R **7**.

R54	R **6**	24pf. rose	3·00	4·50

R **8** Goethe (after Schmoll)

R **9** Goethe (after Ludwig Sebbers)

(Des E. Schoner. Litho.)

1949 (20 July). Birth Bicentenary of Goethe (poet). Type R **8** and similar portraits inscr '1749 1949 GOETHE'. Wmk Type R **2**. P 13½×13.

R55	6pf. +4pf. violet	3·50	4·25

R56	12pf. +8pf. brown	3·50	4·25
R57	24pf. +16pf. brown-lake	3·00	3·50
R58	50pf. +25pf. blue	3·00	3·50
R59	84pf. +36pf. greenish grey	4·75	7·25
R55/R59	Set of 5	16·00	20·00

Portraits:—12pf. *Goethe in the Campagna* (Johann Tischbein the elder); 24pf. After Johann Lips; 50pf. After Josef Stieler; 84pf. After Schwerdtgeburth.

(Des F. Gravenhorst. Recess)

1949 (22 Aug). Goethe Festival Week, Weimar. Sheet 106×104 mm. Wmk Type R **2**. P 14.

| MSR59a | R **9** | 50pf.(+Dm.4.50) ultramarine | £275 | £700 |

(Des E. Gruner. Litho)

1949. Leipzig Autumn Fair. As T **231** of Allied Occupation (inscr 'LEIPZIGER MESSE 1949'). Wmk Type R **2**. P 13½.

| R60 | 12pf. +8pf. slate (30.8.49) | 7·25 | 12·00 |
| R61 | 24pf. +16pf. red-brown (28.8.49) | 8·50 | 14·50 |

Designs:—12pf. 1650: Russian merchants; 24pf. 1765: Goethe at Fair. The Russian Zone became the German Democratic Republic (East Germany) on 7 October 1949 (see Section VI).

IV. German Federal Republic

100 Pfennig = 1 Deutsche Mark (West)

PRINTERS. All the issues of the German Federal Republic were printed at the State Printing Works, Berlin, *unless otherwise stated.*

A. WEST GERMANY

The German Federal Republic as instituted by the Basic Law of 23 May 1949 consisted of the territory which had formed the British, American and French zones of occupation; it formally came into existence on 21 September 1949. West Berlin was constituted a Land of the Federal Republic on 1 September 1950 but until 1990 had special stamp issues (q.v.).

257 Constructing Parliament Building

258 Reproduction of T **1** of Bavaria

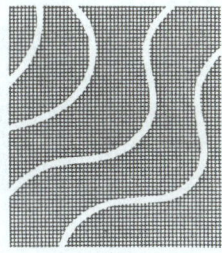

258a

(Des M. Bittrof. Litho A. Bagel, München-Gladbach)

1949 (7 Sept). Opening of West German Parliament, Bonn. Wmk Type A **8**. P 14.

| 1033 | **257** | 10pf. blue-green | 70·00 | 27·00 |
| 1034 | | 20pf. carmine-red | 75·00 | 34·00 |

Modern imperforate forgeries exist on unwatermarked paper.

(Litho F. Bruckmann, Munich)

1949 (30 Sept). Centenary of First German Stamps. T **258** and similar vert designs. W **258a**. P 14.

1035	10pf. +2pf. black and green	23·00	41·00
	a. Without wmk	£2750	
1036	20pf. grey-blue and vermilion	55·00	60·00
1037	30pf. brown and blue	70·00	95·00
1035/1037	Set of 3	£130	£180

Designs: Reproductions of Bavarian stamps—10pf. T **258**; 20pf. (Type **2**); 30pf. (No. 7).
Modern imperforate forgeries exist on unwatermarked paper.

259 Heinrich von Stephan, Old GPO Berlin and Ständehaus, Berne

260 St. Elisabeth of Thuringia

(Des M. Bittrof. Photo F. Burda, Offenburg)

1949 (9 Oct). 75th Anniv of Universal Postal Union. Wmk Type A **8**. P 14.

| 1038 | **259** | 30pf. ultramarine | 90·00 | 60·00 |

(Des after portraits. Recess)

1949 (14 Dec). Refugees' Relief Fund. T **260** and similar types inscr 'HELFT DER FREIEN WOHLFAHRTSPFLEGE...'. Wmk Type A **8**. P 14.

1039	8pf. +2pf. purple	25·00	34·00
1040	10pf. +5pf. yellow-green	19·00	19·00
1041	20pf. +10pf. scarlet	19·00	19·00
1042	30pf. +15pf. blue	£110	£160
1039/1042	Set of 4	£160	£200

Portraits:—8pf. T **260**; 10pf. Paracelsus von Hohenheim; 20pf. F. W. A. Froebel; 30pf. J. H. Wichern.

(Litho A. Wegener, Ahlfeld)

1950 (Mar). OBLIGATORY TAX. Aid for Berlin. W **258a**. P 14.

| T1043 | AT **14** | 2pf. blue | 1·40 | 40 |

See also No. T1103.

261 J. S. Bach's Seal

262 Numeral and Posthorn

263

264 Figures

(Des after Trump. Recess)

1950 (28 July). Death Bicentenary of Bach (composer). Wmk Type A **8**. P 14.

| 1043 | **261** | 10pf. +2pf. myrtle-green | 80·00 | 70·00 |
| 1044 | | 20pf. +3pf. claret | 90·00 | 75·00 |

(Des Mathey)

1951–52. W **263**. P 14.

(a) Size 18½×22½ mm. Typo

1045	**262**	2pf. apple green (1.8.51)	8·00	1·80
1046		4pf. yellow-brown (20.6.51)	8·00	55
		a. Booklet pane. Nos. 1046×3, 1048×3 and 1052×4 (30.10.51)	£500	
		b. Imperf (pair)	£1600	£2000
1047		5pf. bright purple (1.8.51)	22·00	55
1048		6pf. orange (20.9.51)	30·00	5·50
		a. Imperf (pair)	£800	£950
1049		8pf. grey (20.9.51)	30·00	11·00
1050		10pf. green (20.6.51)	16·00	55
		a. Booklet pane. Nos. 1050×4, 1052×5 plus one label (30.10.51)	£500	
		b. Imperf (pair)	£2000	£2000
1051		15pf. violet (20.9.51)	60·00	1·80
1052		20pf. carmine (20.6.51)	13·50	55
1053		25pf. plum (20.9.51)	£140	9·50

(b) Size 20×24½ mm. Recess

1054	**262**	30pf. blue (1.8.51)	80·00	1·10
1055		40pf. purple (20.12.51)	£190	1·10
1056		50pf. blue-grey (11.3.52)	£275	1·10
		a. Imperf (pair)	£800	£950

63

GERMANY/German Federal Republic

1057	60pf. red-brown (20.12.51)	£200	1·10
1058	70pf. yellow (11.3.52)	£700	26·00
1059	80pf. rose-red (16.4.52)	£700	4·00
1060	90pf. yellow-green (16.4.52)	£750	4·75
1045/1060 Set of 16		£3000	65·00

The 4, 10 and 20pf. were also issued in coils.

(Des M. Bittrof. Litho G. Westermann)

1951 (30 Aug). CHARITY. 700th Anniv of St. Mary's Church, Lübeck. Wmk Type A **8**. P. 14.

1065	264	10pf. +5pf. black and green	£150	£110
		a. Imperf (pair)	£4750	
1066		20pf. +5pf. black and claret	£150	£110
		a. Imperf (pair)	£4750	

Modern imperforate forgeries exist on unwatermarked paper.

265 Stamps under Magnifier
266 St. Vincent de Paul 

(Des Prof. Schardt. Litho)

1951 (14 Sept). National Philatelic Exhibition, Wuppertal. W **263** (sideways). P. 14.

| 1067 | 265 | 10pf. +2pf. yellow, black and green | 60·00 | 70·00 |
| 1068 | | 20pf. +3pf. yellow, black and claret | 70·00 | 75·00 |

Modern imperforate forgeries exist on unwatermarked paper.

(Des Zapf. Eng L. Schnell and J. Piwczyk. Recess)

1951 (23 Oct). Humanitarian Relief Fund. T **266** and similar vert portraits. W **263**. P. 14.

1069	4pf. +2pf. brown	13·50	13·50
1070	10pf. +3pf. green	18·00	11·00
1071	20pf. +5pf. scarlet	18·00	11·00
1072	30pf. +10pf. blue	£150	£160
1069/1072 Set of 4		£180	£180

Portraits:—4pf. T **266**; 10pf. F. Von Bodelschwingh; 20pf. Elsa Brandström; 30pf. J. H. Pestalozzi.

267 W. C. Röntgen (physicist)
268 Mona Lisa 

(Des Prof. Barth. Eng J. Piwczyk. Recess)

1951 (10 Dec). 50th Anniv of Award to Röntgen of First Nobel Prize for Physics. W **263**. P. 14.

| 1073 | 267 | 30pf. blue | £110 | 27·00 |

(Des Zapf. Litho A. Bagel, Düsseldorf)

1952 (15 Apr). Fifth Birth Centenary of Leonardo da Vinci. Multicoloured centre. W **258a**. P. 13½.

| 1074 | 268 | 5pf. red-brown | 2·20 | 4·00 |

269 Martin Luther
270 A. N. Otto and Diagram 

(Des H. Zapf. Eng J. Piwczyk. Recess)

1952 (25 July). Lutheran World Federation Assembly, Hanover. W **263**. P. 14.

| 1075 | 269 | 10pf. green | 20·00 | 8·00 |

(Des and eng L. Schnell. Recess)

1952 (25 July). 75th Anniv of Otto Gas Engine. W **263**. P. 14.

| 1076 | 270 | 30pf. deep blue | 43·00 | 22·00 |

271 Nüremberg Madonna
272 Senator Schaffer (trawler) off Heligoland 
273 Carl Schurz 

(Des A. Goldammer. Eng L. Schnell. Recess)

1952 (9 Aug). Centenary of German National Museum, Nüremberg. W **263** (sideways). P. 14.

| 1077 | 271 | 10pf. +5pf. green | 23·00 | 27·00 |

(Des A. Goldammer. Eng L. Schnell. Recess)

1952 (7 Sept). Rehabilitation of Heligoland. W **263**. P. 14.

| 1078 | 272 | 20pf. scarlet | 20·00 | 9·50 |

(Des and litho A. Bagel, Düsseldorf)

1952 (17 Sept). Centenary of Arrival of Carl Schurz in America. W **258a**. P. 13½.

| 1079 | 273 | 20pf. salmon, black and pale blue | 27·00 | 13·50 |

274 Boy Hikers
275 Elizabeth Fry 

(Des M. Bittrof. Eng J. Piwczyk. Recess)

1952 (17 Sept). Youth Hostels' Fund. T **274** and similar vert design inscr 'JUGENDMARKE 1952'. W **263**. P. 14.

| 1080 | 10pf. +2pf. green | 30·00 | 31·00 |
| 1081 | 20pf. +3pf. scarlet (Girl hikers) | 30·00 | 31·00 |

(Des and eng J. Piwczyk (20pf.), L. Schnell (others). Recess)

1952 (1 Oct). Humanitarian Relief Fund. T **275** and similar vert portraits. W **263** (sideways). P. 14.

1082	4pf. +2pf. orange-brown	15·00	11·00
1083	10pf. +5pf. green	15·00	11·00
1084	20pf. +10pf. lake	30·00	23·00
1085	30pf. +10pf. black-blue	£120	£110
1082/1085 Set of 4		£160	£140

Portraits:—4pf. T **275**; 10pf. Dr. C. Sonnenschein; 20pf. T. Fliedner; 30pf. H. Dunant.

276 Postman, 1852
277 P. Reis 

(Litho A. Bagel, Düsseldorf)

1952 (25 Oct). Thurn and Taxis Stamp Centenary. W **258a**. P. 13½.
| 1086 | 276 | 10pf. multicoloured | 11·00 | 4·75 |

(Des H. Zapf. Litho F. Bruckmann, Munich)

1952 (27 Oct). 75th Anniv of German Telephone Service. W **258a**. P. 14.
| 1087 | 277 | 30pf. blue | 75·00 | 24·00 |

278 Road Accident Victim
279 
280 Red Cross and Compass

GERMANY / German Federal Republic

(Des K. Weinert. Litho A. Bagel, Düsseldorf)
1953 (30 Mar). Road Safety Campaign. W **258a**. P 13½.
| 1088 | **278** | 20pf. multicoloured | 24·00 | 8·00 |

(Des E. Cordier. Eng G. Schulz. Recess)
1953 (7 May). 50th Anniv of Science Museum, Munich. W **263** (sideways). P 14.
| 1089 | **279** | 10pf. +5pf. green | 41·00 | 43·00 |

(Des W. Baum. Litho A. Bagel, Düsseldorf)
1953 (8 May). 125th Birth Anniv of Henri Dunant (founder of Red Cross). W **258a**. P 13½.
| 1090 | **280** | 10pf. red and bronze-green | 30·00 | 10·00 |

281 Prisoner of War
282 J. von Liebig 
283 Rail Transport (train, semaphore and hand signal) 

(Des K. H. Walter. Centre embossed; background typo)
1953 (9 May). Commemorating Prisoners of War. No wmk. P 14.
| 1091 | **281** | 10pf. black and grey | 9·50 | 70 |

(Des L. Schnell after Trautschold. Recess)
1953 (12 May). 150th Birth Anniv of Liebig (chemist). W **263**. P 14.
| 1092 | **282** | 30pf. deep blue | 60·00 | 34·00 |

(Des M. Bittrof. Eng J. Piwczyk (4pf.), G. Schulz (others). Recess)
1953 (20 June). Transport Exhibition, Munich. T **283** and similar vert designs. W **263**. P 14.
1093		4pf. brown	10·00	6·75
1094		10pf. green	20·00	11·00
1095		20pf. red	23·00	13·50
1096		30pf. deep blue	70·00	27·00
1093/1096	Set of 4		£110	50·00

Designs:—4pf. T **283**; 10pf. Air (dove and aeroplanes); 20pf. Road (traffic lights and cars); 30pf. Sea (buoy and ships).

284 Gateway, Thurn and Taxis Palace
285 A. H. Francke 
286 President Heuss 

(Des W. Brudi. Litho A. Bagel, Düsseldorf)
1953 (29 July). International Philatelic Exhibition, Frankfurt-am-Main. T **284** and similar design inscr 'IFRABA 1953'. W **258a**. P 13½.
| 1097 | | 10pf. +2pf. chestnut, black and green | 34·00 | 38·00 |
| 1098 | | 20pf. +3pf. grey, indigo and brown-red | 34·00 | 38·00 |

Designs: Vert—10pf. T **284**; 20pf. Telecommunications Buildings, Frankfurt-am-Main.

(Des and eng L. Schnell. Recess)
1953 (2 Nov). Humanitarian Relief Fund. T **285** and similar vert portraits. W **263** (sideways). P 14.
1099		4pf. +2pf. brown	8·00	13·50
1100		10pf. +5pf. myrtle green	13·50	13·50
1101		20pf. +10pf. red	20·00	13·50
1102		30pf. +10pf. deep blue	80·00	£100
1099/1102	Set of 4		£110	£130

Portraits:—4pf. T **285**; 10pf. Sebastian Kneipp; 20pf. Johann Senckenberg; 30pf. Fridtjof Nansen.

(Litho A. Wegener, Ahlfeld)
1954 (Jan). OBLIGATORY TAX. Aid for Berlin. W **263**. P 14.
| T1103 | AT **14** | 2pf. blue | 95 | 40 |

(Des M. Bittrof)
1954–60. Ordinary paper (white). P 14.

*(a) Size 18½×22½ mm. Typo. W **263***
1103	**286**	2pf. light olive-green (15.6.54)	40	40
		a. Booklet pane. Nos. 1103×5, 1105×4, plus label (15.1.55)	80·00	
		b. Booklet pane. Nos. 1103×3,1105×6, plus label (3.56)	20·00	
		c. Booklet pane. Nos. 1103×3, 1108, 1109×5, plus label (3.56)	30·00	
1104		4pf. orange-brown (31.1.54)	40	40
1105		5pf. mauve (1.4.54)	40	40
		a. Booklet pane. Nos. 1105×2,1109×7 plus label (15.1.55)	80·00	
		b. Fluorescent paper (cream)	15·00	60·00
		c. Wmk sideways (2.60)	1·20	1·40
1106		6pf. brown (1.4.54)	1·00	1·40
1107		7pf. turquoise-green (28.7.54)	40	55
		a. Fluorescent paper (cream)	1·10	6·75
1108		8pf. grey (1.4.54)	40	1·10
		a. Wmk sideways (2.60)	80·00	£190
1109		10pf. emerald (31.1.54)	40	40
		a. Booklet pane. Nos. 1109×4, 1111×5 plus label (15.1.55)	80·00	
		b. Fluorescent paper (cream)	1·40	1·60
		c. Wmk sideways (2.60)	1·20	1·40
1110		15pf. chalky blue (1.4.54)	1·10	80
		a. Fluorescent paper (cream)	12·00	60·00
1111		20pf. carmine (31.1.54)	40	40
		a. Fluorescent paper (cream)	3·75	5·75
		b. Wmk sideways (2.60)	1·20	1·40
1112		25pf. brown-purple (15.6.54)	1·30	1·10
		a. Fluorescent paper (cream)	23·00	£180

*(b) Size 20×24 mm. Recess. W **263**.*
1113	**286**	30pf. pale blue (31.1.54)	20·00	8·00
1114		40pf. reddish blue (1.4.54)	8·00	55
1115		50pf. slate-black (15.6.54)	£275	80
1116		60pf. lake-brown (15.6.54)	60·00	1·10
1117		70pf. yellow-olive (15.6.54)	24·00	3·50
1118		80pf. deep rose-red (15.6.54)	4·00	8·00
1119		90pf. green (15.6.54)	20·00	4·00

*(c) Size 25×30 mm. Recess. W **263** (sideways).*
1120	**286**	1Dm. olive-green (1.4.54)	2·30	55
1121		2Dm. lavender (15.6.54)	4·00	2·00
1122		3Dm. crimson (15.6.54)	11·00	4·00
1103/1122	Set of 20		£400	36·00

*(d) Size 18×22 mm. Recess. W **294**.*
1122a	**286**	30pf. grey-green (5.57)	70	1·10
		b. Fluorescent paper (cream)	41·00	£250
1122c		40pf. blue (11.56)	2·75	55
		d. Fluorescent paper (cream)	4·50	27·00
1122e		50pf. deep yellow-olive (2.57)	1·80	55
1122f		60pf. brown (9.57)	5·25	80
1122g		70pf. violet (2.57)	15·00	80
1122h		80pf. orange-red (6.57)	9·50	3·50
1122i		90pf. bluish green (6.57)	24·00	1·80
1122a/1122i	Set of 7		55·00	8·25

The stamps on fluorescent paper were all issued in August 1960. Nos. 1105, 1107, 1109, 1109b, 1110/a, 1111/a, 1112/a, 1122c/d and 1122g were also issued in coils with every fifth stamp numbered on the back.
Nos. 1105c, 1108a, 1109c and 1111b were issued in booklets only (see booklet pane No. 1152bca).
Nos. 1122a/1122i exist with both ribbed gum (as Nos. 1103/1122) and flat shiny gum. Our prices are for the latter, which were issued in 1958. Stamps with ribbed gum are scarcer.

287 P. Ehrlich and E. Behring
288 Gutenberg and Printing-press 

(Des J. Boehland. Litho A. Bagel, Düsseldorf)
1954 (13 Mar). Centenaries of Births of Ehrlich and Von Behring (bacteriologists). W **258a**. P 13½.
| 1123 | **287** | 10pf. green | 16·00 | 6·00 |

(Des W. Brudi. Typo)
1954 (5 May). 500th Anniv of *Gutenberg Bible*. W **263**. P 14.
| 1124 | **288** | 4pf. deep brown | 2·40 | 1·10 |

65

GERMANY/ German Federal Republic

289 Sword-pierced Mitre
290 Käthe Kollwitz 
291 C. F. Gauss 

(Des E Göhlert. Eng G Schulz. Recess; centre embossed)
1954 (5 June). 1200th Anniv of Martyrdom of St. Boniface. No wmk. P 14.
1125   289   20pf. red and grey-brown.................... 12·00   6·75

(Des K. H. Walter. Eng G. Schulz (7pf., 10pf.), L. Schnell (others). Recess)
1954 (28 Dec). Humanitarian Relief Fund. T **290** and similar vert portraits. W **263** (sideways). P 14.
1126   7pf. +3pf. red-brown .... 5·50   5·50
1127   10pf. +5pf. green .... 2·75   2·75
1128   20pf. +10pf. red .... 15·00   8·00
1129   40pf. +10pf. blue .... 49·00   60·00
1126/1129 Set of 4 .... 65·00   70·00
Portraits:—7pf. T **290**; 10pf. L. Werthmann, 20pf. J. F. Oberlin, 40pf. Bertha Pappenheim.

(Des H. Eidenbenz. Eng L. Schnell. Recess)
1955 (23 Feb). Death Centenary of Gauss (mathematician). W **263** (sideways). P 14.
1130   291   10pf. green.. 7·75   1·10

292 Flight 
293 Oskar von Miller

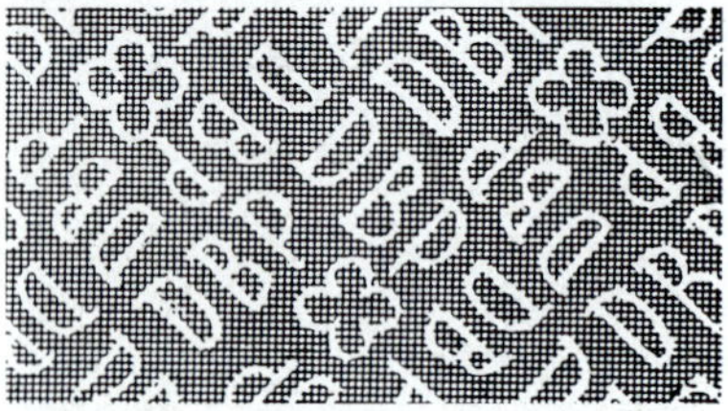

294

(Des Müller and Blase. Litho A. Bagel, Düsseldorf)
1955 (31 Mar). Re-establishment of Lufthansa Airways. W **263**. P 13½×13.
1131   292   5pf. magenta and black...................... 1·80   1·40
1132   10pf. blue-green and black.................. 2·20   2·00
1133   15pf. blue and black........................... 11·00   9·50
1134   20pf. scarlet and black....................... 30·00   11·00
1131/1134 Set of 4 .... 41·00   22·00

(Des M. Cordier. Litho)
1955 (7 May). Birth Centenary of Oskar von Miller (electrical engineer). W **263**. P 14.
1135   293   10pf. pale emerald............................. 8·00   2·40

295 Schiller
296 Motor Coach, 1906 

(Des K. H. Walter. Eng G. Schulz. Recess; centre embossed)
1955 (9 May). 150th Death Anniv of Schiller (poet). No wmk. P 14.
1136   295   40pf. blue.. 24·00   8·75

(Des Müller and Blase. Typo)
1955 (1 June). 50th Anniv of Postal Motor Transport. W **294**. P 14.
1137   296   20pf. black and scarlet..................... 16·00   7·50

297 Arms of Baden-Württemberg
298 Earth and Atom 

(Des H. Bentele. Litho A. Bagel, Düsseldorf)
1955 (15 June). Baden-Württemberg Agricultural Exhibition, Stuttgart. W **263** (sideways). P 13×13½.
1138   297   7pf. black, red-brown and olive-bistre ..... 7·50   5·50
1139   10pf. black, green and olive-bistre .... 8·75   4·00

(Des K. Kranz and F. Bruckmann. Photo)
1955 (24 June). Cosmic Research. W **263** (sideways). P 14.
1140   298   20pf. lake .... 16·00   1·80

299 Refugees
300 Orb, Arrows and Waves 

(Des Hahn. Eng E. Falz. Recess)
1955 (2 Aug). Tenth Anniv of Expulsion of Germans from beyond the Oder-Neisse Line. W **294**. P 14.
1141   299   20pf. brown-lake............................... 5·75   95
See also No. 1400.

(Des E. Göhlert. Litho; centre embossed)
1955 (10 Aug). Millenary of Battle of Lechfeld. No wmk. P 14.
1142   300   20pf. reddish purple......................... 13·50   5·50

301 Magnifying Glass and Carrier Pigeon
302 Railway Signal 

(Des H. Bentele. Eng E. Falz (10pf.), H.-J. Fuchs (20pf.). Recess)
1955 (14 Sept). West European Postage Stamps Exhibition. T **301** and similar vert design inscr 'WESTROPA 1955'. W **294**. P 14.
1143   10pf. +2pf. bluish green............................ 7·00   9·50
1144   20pf. +3pf. Red..................................... 16·00   18·00
Designs:—10pf. T **301**; 20pf. Tweezers and posthorn.

(Des A. Stankowski. Litho)
1955 (5 Oct). Railway Timetable Conference. W **294**. P 14.
1145   302   20pf. black and vermilion................... 13·50   4·00

303 Stifter Monument
304 United Nations Emblem 

(Des A. Stankowski. Eng H.-J. Fuchs. Recess)
1955 (22 Oct). 150th Birth Anniv of Stifter (Austrian poet). W **294**. P 14.
1146   303   10pf. green.. 6·00   4·00

GERMANY / German Federal Republic

(Des K. H. Walter. Litho; centre embossed)

1955 (24 Oct). United Nations Day. No wmk. P 14.
| 1147 | 304 | 10pf. dull yellow-green and red-brown.. | 5·75 | 6·75 |

305 Amalie Sieveking

(Des H. Berke. Recess)

1955 (15 Nov). Humanitarian Relief Fund. T **305** and similar vert portraits. Litho burelage background of vert lines in colour of stamps. W **294**. P 14.
1148		7pf. +3pf. olive-brown	5·50	5·50
1149		10pf. +5pf. deep dull green	4·00	2·75
1150		20pf. +10pf. orange-red	4·00	2·75
1151		40pf. +10pf. light blue	41·00	55·00
1148/1151	*Set of 4*...	49·00	60·00

Portraits:—7pf. T **305**; 10pf. A. Kolping; 20pf. Dr. S. Hahnemann; 40pf. Florence Nightingale.

306

307 Von Stephan's Signature

(Des A. Schraml. Typo)

1955 (1 Dec)–**63**. Ordinary paper (white). P 14.
| 1152 | 306 | 1pf. grey.. | 40 | 70 |
| | | a. Fluorescent paper (cream) (1963).. | 40 | 95 |

(b) Booklet stamps. W **263** *(26.3.58–60)*
1152b	306	1pf. grey...	16·00	34·00
		ba. Booklet pane. Nos. 1152b×2 1105×2, 1108, 1109×2 and 1111×3	41·00	
		c. Wmk sideways (2.60)..	27·00	60·00
		ca. Booklet pane. As No. 1152bba but wmk sideways (2.60)...................................	£150	

(Des A. Schraml. Eng H.-J. Fuchs. Recess)

1956 (7 Jan). 125th Birth Anniv of Heinrich von Stephan. W **294**. P 14.
| 1153 | 307 | 20pf. brown-red .... | 11·00 | 4·00 |

308 Spinet and Opening Bars of Minuet

309 Heinrich Heine

(Des Michel and Kieser. Litho)

1956 (27 Jan). Birth Bicentenary of Mozart (composer). No wmk. P 14.
| 1154 | 308 | 10pf. slate-violet and black........................ | 1·60 | 70 |

(Des Müller and Blase. Litho A. Bagel)

1956 (17 Feb). Death Centenary of Heine (poet). W **263**. P 13½×13.
| 1155 | 309 | 10pf. light bronze-green and black............ | 4·75 | 5·50 |

310 Old Houses and Crane

311

(Des A. Mahlau. Eng H.-J. Fuchs. Recess)

1956 (2 May). Millenary of Lüneburg. W **294**. P 14.
| 1156 | 310 | 20pf. red.. | 11·00 | 13·50 |

(Des H. Bentele. Eng E. Falz. Recess)

1956 (9 June). Olympic Year. W **294**. P 14.
| 1157 | 311 | 10pf. dull green.. | 1·40 | 1·10 |

312 Boy and Dove

313 Schumann

(Des Michel and Kieser. Litho)

1956 (21 July). Youth Hostels' Fund T **312** and similar horiz design inscr 'JUGEND'. No wmk. P 14.
| 1158 | | 7pf. +3pf. grey, black and chestnut .... | 3·50 | 5·50 |
| 1159 | | 10pf. +5pf. grey, black and yellow-green......... | 9·75 | 13·50 |

Designs:—7pf. T **312**; 10pf. Girl playing flute and flowers.

(Des Michel and Kieser. Litho)

1956 (28 July). Death Centenary of Schumann (composer). No wmk. P 14.
| 1160 | 313 | 10pf. black, red and bistre.............................. | 1·40 | 80 |

314

315 Thomas Mann (author)

(Des H. Stelzer. Litho A. Bagel)

1956 (8 Aug). Evangelical Church Convention, Frankfurt-am-Main. W **294**. P 13×13½.
| 1161 | 314 | 10pf. dull green.. | 5·50 | 6·00 |
| 1162 | | 20pf. brown-lake... | 6·75 | 8·00 |

(Des K. H. Walter. Eng E. Falz. Recess)

1956 (11 Aug). Thomas Mann Commemoration. W **294**. P 14.
| 1163 | 315 | 20pf. claret.. | 4·75 | 3·75 |

316

317 Ground Plan of Cologne Cathedral and Hand

(Des E. Göhlert. Litho A. Bagel)

1956 (24 Aug). 800th Anniv of Maria Laach Abbey. W **294**. P 13×13½.
| 1164 | 316 | 20pf. grey and brown-lake............................ | 3·75 | 3·50 |

(Des J. Fassbender. Litho)

1956 (29 Aug). 77th Meeting of German Catholics, Cologne. W **294**. P 13×13½.
| 1165 | 317 | 10pf. dull green and chocolate.................. | 4·75 | 4·50 |

318

319

67

GERMANY / German Federal Republic

(Des Michel and Kieser. Litho A. Bagel)
1956 (1 Sept). International Police Exhibition, Essen. W **294**. P 13½×13.
1166 **318** 20pf. bright green, red-orange and black............... 4·75 4·75

(Des Gonzague. Eng Schulz. Recess)
1956 (15 Sept). Europa. W **294**. P 14.
1167 **319** 10pf. deep green................... 1·50 40
1168   40pf. blue............................. 12·00 1·80

320 Midwife and Baby    **321** Carrier Pigeon

(Des B. Jäger. Litho)
1956 (1 Oct). Humanitarian Relief Fund. T **320** and similar horiz designs. Centres in black. No wmk. P 14.
1169 7pf. +3pf. orange-brown............ 2·75 4·00
1170 10pf. +5pf. green..................... 2·00 1·40
1171 20pf. +10pf. vermilion............... 2·00 1·40
1172 40pf. +10pf. light blue............... 23·00 22·00
1169/1172 Set of 4......................... 27·00 26·00
Designs:—7pf. T **320**; 10pf. I. P. Semmelweis and cot; 20pf. Mother and baby in cradle; 40pf. Nursemaid and children.

(Des U. Huber. Recess)
1956 (27 Oct). Stamp Day. W **294**. P 14.
1173 **321** 10pf. green......................... 2·75 1·20

322 'Military Graves'    **323** Arms

(Des H. Klein. Eng E. Falz. Recess)
1956 (17 Nov). War Graves Commission. W **294**. P 13½×14.
1174 **322** 10pf. blackish green............ 2·75 1·20

(Des H. Kern. Litho A. Bagel)
1957 (2 Jan). Return of the Saar to West Germany. W **294**. P 13½×13½.
1175 **323** 10pf. brown and light grey-green............ 95 80

324 Children with Luggage    **325** Heinrich Hertz

(Des E. Krauss-Guyer. Litho A. Bagel, Düsseldorf)
1957 (1 Feb). Berlin Children's Holiday Fund. T **324** and similar horiz design. No wmk. P 13½×13.
1176 10pf. +5pf. red-orange and dull green............ 2·00 3·50
1177 20pf. +10pf. pale blue and red-orange........... 4·75 6·75
Designs:—10pf. T **324**; 20pf. Girl returning from holiday.

(Des Müller and Blase. Litho)
1957 (22 Feb). Birth Centenary of Hertz (physicist). W **294**. P 13½×14.
1178 **325** 10pf. black and pale bronze-green......... 2·30 1·10

326 Paul Gerhardt    **327** 'Flora and Philately'

(Des and eng L. Schnell. Recess)
1957 (18 May). 350th Birth Anniv of Paul Gerhardt (hymn-writer). W **294**. P 14.
1179 **326** 20pf. carmine-lake................. 1·10 95

(Des E. Göhlert. Eng E. Falz. Recess)
1957 (8 June). Exhibition and Eighth Congress of the International Federation of 'Constructive Philately'. W **294**. P 14.
1180 **327** 20pf. red-orange................... 1·10 95

328 Emblem of Aschaffenburg    **329** University Class

(Des H. Noeth. Litho A. Bagel, Düsseldorf)
1957 (15 June). Millenary of Aschaffenburg. W **294**. P 13×13½.
1181 **328** 20pf. light red and black......... 1·10 95

(Des B. Jäger. Litho A. Bagel, Düsseldorf)
1957 (24 June). Fifth Centenary of Freiburg University. W **294**. P 13½×13.
1182 **329** 10pf. black, orange-red and blue-green........... 80 70

330 *Bayernstein* (freighter)

(Des Müller and Blase. Litho)
1957 (25 June). German Merchant Shipping Day. W **294**. P 14.
1183 **330** 15pf. black, red and blue......... 1·90 1·90

331 Justus Liebig University    **332** Albert Ballin

(Des H. Lortz. Eng E. Falz. Recess)
1957 (3 July). 350th Anniv of Justus Liebig University, Giessen. W **294**. P 14.
1184 **331** 10pf. deep green.................. 80 80

(Des A. Goldammer. Litho)
1957 (15 Aug). Birth Centenary of Albert Ballin (director of Hamburg—America Shipping Line). W **294**. P 14.
1185 **332** 20pf. black and pale lake......... 2·30 80

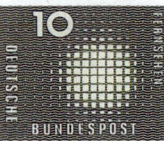

333 Television Screen    **334** 'Europa' Tree

GERMANY/ German Federal Republic

(Des Michel and Kieser. Recess)
1957 (23 Aug). Publicising West German Television Service. W **294**. P 14.
1186   **333**   10pf. green and deep blue 80   80

(Des R. Blank. Litho; centre embossed)
1957 (16 Sept)–**58**. Europa. P 14.
1187   **334**   10pf. green and pale turquoise............... 70   35
     a. Imperf (pair) £1000   £950
     b. Wmk **294** (8.58) .... 11·00   19·00
1188   40pf. deep bright blue and pale turquoise .... 7·75   70

335 Young Miner
336 Water Lily 

(Des B. Jäger. Litho)
1957 (1 Oct). Humanitarian Relief Fund. T **335** and similar horiz designs. W **294**. P 14×13½.
1189   7pf. +3pf. black and yellow-brown................. 2·00   2·75
1190   10pf. +5pf. black and yellow-green................. 1·40   1·40
1191   20pf. +10pf. black and red........................... 2·00   1·40
1192   40pf. +10pf. black and blue........................ 24·00   30·00
1189/1192 *Set of* 4... 26·00   32·00
Designs:—7pf. T **335**; 10pf. Miner drilling coal-face; 20pf. Miner with coal-cutting machine; 40pf. Operator at mine lift-shaft.

(Des R. Gerhardt (10pf); A. Goldammer (20pf.). Litho)
1957 (4 Oct). Nature Protection Day. T **336** and similar design. W **294**. P 14 ×13½ (10pf.) or 13½ ×14 (20pf.).
1193   10pf. orange, yellow and green.................. 90   75
1194   20pf. blue, black, brown-red and yellow-bistre 95   80
     a. Error. Face value and 'DEUTSCHE BUNDESPOST' missing £2000
Designs: Horiz—10pf. T **336**. Vert—20pf. European robin.

337 Carrier Pigeons
338 Baron vom Stein 

(Des W. Neufeld. Litho)
1957 (5 Oct). International Correspondence Week. W **294**. P 14×13½.
1195   **337**   20pf. black and carmine................... 1·50   95

(Des P. Dietrich. Eng H.-J. Fuchs. Recess)
1957 (26 Oct). Birth Bicentenary of Baron vom Stein (statesman). W **294**. P 14.
1196   **338**   20pf. red.. 2·40   1·10

339 Dr. Leo Baeck
340 Württemberg Parliament House 
341 Stage Coach 

(Des P. Dietrich. Eng E. Falz. Recess)
1957 (2 Nov). First Death Anniv of Dr. Leo Baeck (philosopher). W **294**. P 14.
1197   **339**   20pf. brown-red .... 2·40   1·10

(Des W. Brudi. Litho A. Bagel, Düsseldorf)
1957 (16 Nov). 500th Anniv of First Württemberg Parliament. W **294**. P 13×13½.
1198   **340**   10pf. sage-green and deep grey-green.. 1·50   95

(Des H. Willberg. Eng E. Falz. Recess)
1957 (26 Nov). Death Centenary of Joseph von Eichendorff (novelist). W **294**. P 14.
1199   **341**   10pf. green .... 1·40   95

342 Max and Moritz (cartoon characters)
343 'Prevent Forest Fires!' 

(Litho A. Bagel, Düsseldorf)
1958 (9 Jan). 50th Death Anniv of Wilhelm Busch (writer and illustrator). T **342** and similar horiz design. W **294**. P 13½×13.
1200   10pf. yellow-olive and black.................. 40   40
1201   20pf. light red and black........................ 1·40   1·10
Designs:—10pf. T **342**; 20pf. Wilhelm Busch.

(Des H. Kern. Litho)
1958 (5 Mar). Forest Fires Prevention Campaign. W **294**. P 14.
1202   **343**   20pf. black and vermilion................. 1·20   95

344 Rudolf Diesel and First Oil Engine
345 The Fox who stole the Goose 

(Des H. Schardt. Eng E. Falz. Recess)
1958 (18 Mar). Centenary of Birth of Rudolf Diesel (engineer). W **294**. P 14.
1203   **344**   10pf. deep bluish green..................... 70   70

(Des E. Göhlert. Litho)
1958 (1 Apr). Berlin Students' Fund. T **345** and similar vert design inscr 'Für die Jugend'. W **294**. P 14.
1204   10pf. +5pf. brown-red, black and dull green.. 2·75   3·50
1205   20pf. +10pf. olive-brown, dull green and red   4·75   6·00
Designs:—10pf. T **345**; 20pf. *A hunter from the Palatinate* (horseman).

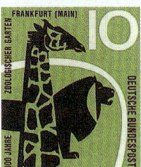

346 Giraffe and Lion
347 Old Munich 

(Des A. Haller. Litho A. Bagel, Düsseldorf)
1958 (7 May). Centenary of Frankfurt-am-Main Zoo. W **294**. P 13×13½.
1206   **346**   10pf. black and green 95   70

(Des E. Ege. Eng E. Falz. Recess)
1958 (22 May). 800th Anniv of Munich. W **294**. P 14.
1207   **347**   20pf. carmine-red............................. 95   70

348 Trier and Market Cross
349 Deutsche Mark (coin) 

(Des H. Stelzer. Eng E. Falz. Recess)
1958 (3 June). Millenary of Trier Market. W **294**. P 14.
1208   **348**   20pf. brown-red and black................. 95   70

(Des G. Kühlborn. Litho A. Bagel, Düsseldorf)
1958 (20 June). Tenth Anniv of Currency Reform. W **294**. P 14.
1209   **349**   20pf. black and red-orange................. 1·20   1·60

GERMANY / German Federal Republic

350 Emblem of Gymnastics

351 H. Schulze-Delitzsch

(Des E. Göhlert. Litho)
1958 (21 July). 150th Anniv of German Gymnastics. W **294**. P 14.
1210   350   10pf. black, green and pale grey............ 70   80

(Des H. Eidenbenz. Eng L. Schnell. Recess)
1958 (29 Aug). 150th Anniv of Birth of Schulze-Delitzsch (pioneer of German co-operative movement). W **294**. P 14.
1211   351   10pf. green.. 80   70

351a 'Europa'

(Des A. van der Vossen. Litho)
1958 (13 Sept). Europa. W **294**. P 14.
1212   351a   10pf. blue and green............................ 70   40
1213   40pf. red and blue................................ 5·50   70

352 Friedrich Raiffeisen (philanthropist)

353 Dairymaid

(Des E. Meerwald. Litho)
1958 (1 Oct). Humanitarian Relief and Welfare Funds. T **352** and other vert designs as T **353**. W **294**. P 14.
1214   7pf. +3pf. brown, yellow-brown and chestnut.. 80   80
1215   10pf. +5pf. red, yellow and green............ 80   80
1216   20pf. +10pf. new blue, bright yellow-green and red.. 80   80
1217   40pf. +10pf. yellow, reddish orange and blue.. 11·00   13·00
1214/1217   Set of 4.. 12·00   14·00
Designs:—7pf. T **352**; 10pf. T **353**; 20pf. Vine-dresser; 40pf. Farm labourer.

354 Cardinal Nicholas of Cues (founder)

354a President Heuss

(Des H. Kern. Litho)
1958 (3 Dec). 500th Anniv of Hospice of St. Nicholas. W **294**. P 14.
1218   354   20pf. black and deep magenta................ 80   70
               a. Imperf (pair)............................ £1100   £1100

1959 (31 Jan–22 May). W **294**. P 14.
               (a) Typo
1219   354a   7pf. blue-green (10.4)............................ 40   40
1220   10pf. green... 70   40
1221   20pf. carmine... 70   40
               (b) Recess
1222   354a   40pf. blue (22.5).................................... 19·00   1·60
1223   70pf. violet (22.5).................................... 6·75   1·40
1219/1223   Set of 5.. 25·00   3·75

Nos. 1219/1221 were also issued in coils with every fifth stamp numbered on the back.

355 Jakob Fugger

356 Adam Riese

(Des after woodcut by H. Burgckmair. Litho A. Bagel, Düsseldorf)
1959 (6 Mar). 500th Anniv of Birth of Fugger (merchant prince). W **294**. P 13×13½.
1224   355   20pf. grey-black and brown-red................ 70   80

(Litho A. Bagel)
1959 (28 Mar). 400th Anniv of Death of Adam Riese (mathematician). W **294**. P 13½×13.
1225   356   10pf. black and yellow-green.................. 70   80

357 A. von Humboldt

358 First Hamburg Stamp of 1859

(Des H. Kern. Eng E. Falz. Recess)
1959 (6 May). Death Centenary of Alexander von Humboldt (naturalist). W **294**. P 14.
1226   357   40pf. Prussian blue.................................... 3·00   2·30

(Des A. Schraml. Recess)
1959 (22 May–22 Aug). International Stamp Exhibition, Hamburg, and Centenary of First Postage Stamps of Hamburg and Lübeck. T **358** and a similar vert design inscr 'INTERPOSTA'. W **294**. P 14.
1227   358   10pf. +5pf. deep brown and blue-green   1·40   3·75
1228   10pf. +5pf. brown and green (22.8.59)...   40   1·40
1229   20pf. +10pf. brown and carmine-red........ 2·00   3·75
1230   20pf. +10pf. brown and orange–red (22.8.59).. 40   1·40
1227/1230   Set of 4.. 3·75   9·25
Designs:—10pf. T **358**; 20pf. (2) First Lübeck stamp of 1859.

359 Buxtehude

360 Holy Tunic of Trier

(Des O. Rohse. Litho)
1959 (20 June). Millenary of Buxtehude. W **294**. P 14.
1231   359   20pf. red, black and light blue.................. 75   75

(Des E. Göhlert. Litho; centre embossed)
1959 (18 July). Holy Tunic of Trier Exhibition. W **294**. P 14.
1232   360   20pf. black, buff and claret........................ 70   70

361 Congress Emblem

361a Beethoven

(Des H. Bentele. Litho)
1959 (12 Aug). German Evangelical Church Day and Congress, Munich. W **294**. P 14.
1233   361   10pf. reddish violet, yellow-green and black.. 60   60

GERMANY/ German Federal Republic

(Des H. Kern. Eng H.-J. Fuchs (10pf., 25pf.), E. Falz (15pf.), G. Schulz (20pf.), H. Braband (40pf.). Recess)

1959 (8 Sept). Inauguration of Beethoven Hall, Bonn. T **361a** and similar horiz designs in sheet 148×104 mm with extract from Beethoven's music notebooks. W **294**. P 14.
MS1233a 10pf. myrtle-green (Handel); 15pf. blue (Spohr); 20pf. red (T **361a**); 25pf. bistrebrown (Haydn); 40pf. deep blue (Mendelssohn)...... 34·00   70·00

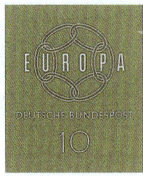

361b 'Europa'

362 Feeding the Poor

(Des W. Brudi. Litho)

1959 (19 Sept). Europa. W **294**. P 14.
1234 **361b** 10pf. olive-green 55 40
              a. Imperf (pair) £650
1235   40pf. grey-blue .... 2·20 70

(Des B. Jäger (40pf.), E. Sporer (others). Litho)

1959 (1 Oct). Humanitarian Relief and Welfare Funds. T **362** and similar horiz designs. W **294**. P 14.
1236   7pf. +3pf. sepia and yellow 40 70
1237   10pf. +5pf. deep green and yellow 40 70
1238   20pf. +10pf. brown-red and yellow 55 70
1239   40pf. +10pf. black, ochre, green and blue ... 5·50 8·00
1236/1239 Set of 4 .... 6·25 9·00

Designs:—7pf. T **362**; 10pf. Clothing the Naked; 20pf. Bounty from Heaven (scenes from the Brothers Grimm story *The Star Thaler*); 40pf. The Brothers Grimm.

363 'Uprooted Tree'

364 P. Melanchthon

(Des H. Rastorfer. Litho A. Bagel)

1960 (7 Apr). World Refugee Year. W **294**. P 13½×13.
1240 **363** 10pf. black, purple and green 40 40
1241   40pf. black, red and blue .... 3·75 3·75

(Des Michel and Kieser. Litho)

1960 (19 Apr). 400th Anniv of Death of Melanchthon (Protestant reformer). W **294**. P 14.
1242 **364** 20pf. black and crimson .... 2·00 2·00

365 Cross and Symbols of the Crucifixion

366

(Des H. Kern. Litho)

1960 (17 May). Oberammergau Passion Play. W **294**. P 14.
1243 **365** 10pf. grey, ochre and deep greenish blue 55 55

(Des E. Ege. Recess)

1960 (30 July). 37th World Eucharistic Congress of Roman Catholics, Munich. W **294**. P 14.
1244 **366** 10pf. deep grey-green 95 70
1245   20pf. deep claret .... 1·40 1·40

367 Wrestling

368 St. Michael's Church Hildesheim

(Des R. Heinsdorff. Eng G. Schulz. Recess)

1960 (8 Aug). Olympics Year. As T **367** inscr 'OLYMPISCHES JAHR 1960'. W **294**. P 14.
1246   7pf. red-brown 40 35
1247   10pf. bronze-green 55 40
1248   20pf. red 55 40
1249   40pf. deep blue .... 2·00 2·00
1246/1249 Set of 4 .... 3·25 2·75

Designs:—7pf. T **367**; 10pf. Running; 20pf. Throwing the javelin and discus; 40pf. Chariot-racing.

(Des E. Ege. Eng G. Braband. Recess)

1960 (6 Sept). 1,000th Anniv of Birth of St. Bernward and St. Godehard. W **294**. P 14.
1250 **368** 20pf. brown-purple .... 1·40 80

368a Conference Emblem

369 Red Riding Hood meeting Wolf

(Eng H. Braband. Recess)

1960 (19 Sept). Europa. W **294**. P 14.
1251 **368a** 10pf. green and olive-green 40 40
1252   20pf. vermilion and red .... 1·40 40
1253   40pf. light blue and blue .... 2·00 1·80
1251/1253 Set of 3 .... 3·50 2·30

(Des Michel and Kieser. Litho)

1960 (1 Oct). Humanitarian Relief Funds. T **369** and similar designs. W **294**. P 14.
1254   7pf. +3pf. black, red and bistre 80 80
1255   10pf. +5pf. black, red and green 80 70
1256   20pf. +10pf. black, emerald and brown-red 80 70
1257   40pf. +20pf. black, red and blue .... 3·50 6·75
1254/1257 Set of 4 .... 5·25 8·00

Designs:—7pf. T **369**; 10pf. Red Riding Hood, and wolf disguised as grandmother; 20pf. Woodcutter and dead wolf; 40pf. Red Riding Hood with grandmother.

370 Gen. George Marshall

371 Stephenson Locomotive *Adler*, 1835

(Des Michel and Kieser. Litho A. Bagel)

1960 (15 Oct). First Anniv of Death of General Marshall. W **294**. P 13×13½.
1258 **370** 40pf. black and blue .... 4·50 3·75

(Des H. Bentele. Litho)

1960 (7 Dec). 125th Anniv of German Railways. W **294**. P 14.
1259 **371** 10pf. black and bistre 55 70

372 St. George and the Dragon

372a Albertus Magnus

71

GERMANY / German Federal Republic

(Des E. Ege. Eng H. Braband. Recess)

1961 (22 Apr). 50th Anniv of Pathfinders (German Boy Scouts). W **294**. P 14.

| 1260 | **372** | 10pf. green | 40 | 55 |

(Des Michel and Kieser)

1961–64. Famous Germans. T **372a** and similar portraits. W **294**. P 14.

(a) Typo. Ordinary paper (white)

1261	5pf. olive (18.9.61)	40	40
	a. Fluorescent paper (cream)	40	40
	ab. Tête-bêche (pair)	1·10	1·90
1262	7pf. yellow-brown (3.8.61)	40	40
	a. Fluorescent paper (cream)	40	40
1263	8pf. reddish violet (3.8.61)	40	70
	a. Fluorescent paper (cream)	40	40
1264	10pf. yellow-green (15.6.61)	40	40
	a. Fluorescent paper (cream)	40	40
	ab. Tête-bêche (pair)	1·10	2·75
1265	15pf. pale blue (18.9.61)	70	1·40
	a. Fluorescent paper (cream)	40	40
	ab. Tête-bêche (pair)	1·60	3·75
1266	20pf. carmine-red (28.6.61)	70	55
	a. Fluorescent paper (cream)	40	40
	ab. Tête-bêche (pair)	1·10	3·50
1267	25pf. orange-brown (fluorescent paper cream) (7.10.61)	40	40

(b) Recess. Fluorescent paper (cream)

1268	30pf. black-brown (7.10.61)	40	40
1269	40pf. blue (28.6.61)	40	40
	a. Ordinary paper (white)	80	1·20
1270	50pf. brown (1.12.61)	55	40
1271	60pf. claret (12.4.62)	55	40
1272	70pf. dark green (1.12.61)	40	40
	a. Deep grey-green (11.62)	1·10	40
1273	80pf. yellow-brown (1.12.61)	70	70
1274	90pf. bistre (3.8.64)	55	40
1275	1Dm. bluish violet (18.9.61)	95	40
1276	2Dm. green (12.4.62)	4·75	95

Portraits:—5pf. T **372a**; 7pf. St. Elisabeth of Thuringia; 8pf. Johannes Gutenberg (inventor of printing); 10pf. Albrecht Dürer (artist); 15pf. Martin Luther (Protestant reformer); 20pf. Johann Sebastian Bach (composer); 25pf. Balthasar Neumann (architect); 30pf. Immanuel Kant (philosopher); 40pf. Gotthold Lessing (writer); 50pf. Johann Wolfgang von Goethe (writer); 60pf. Friedrich von Schiller (writer); 70pf. Ludwig van Beethoven (composer); 80pf. Heinrich von Kleist (writer); 90pf. Franz Oppenheimer (political economist); 1Dm. Annette von Droste-Hülshoff (writer); 2Dm. Gerhart Hauptmann (writer).

The 5, 7, 10, 15, 20, 40pf. on both ordinary and fluorescent papers and the 25, 60 and 70pf. (both shades) were also issued in coils with every fifth stamp numbered on the back.

373 Early Daimler Motor Car

374 Nüremberg Messenger of 1700

(Des H. Siegmund. Litho)

1961 (3 July). 75th Anniv of Daimler-Benz Patent. T **373** and similar horiz design. W **294**. P 14.

1277	10pf. blue-green and black	40	40
	a. Black 'G. Daimler' omitted	£1000	£1000
1278	20pf. red and black	55	55

Designs:—10pf. T **373**; 20pf. Early Benz Motor Car.

(Des R. Heinsdorff. Recess; background litho)

1961 (31 Aug). The Letter during Five Centuries Exhibition, Nüremberg. W **294**. P 14.

| 1279 | **374** | 7pf. black and Venetian red | 55 | 55 |

375 Speyer Cathedral

376 Doves

(Des E. Ege. Eng H.-J. Fuchs. Recess)

1961 (2 Sept). 900th Anniv of Speyer Cathedral. W **294**. P 14.

| 1280 | **375** | 20pf. red | 55 | 80 |

(Des T. Kurpershoek. Litho A. Bagel (1281a) or State Ptg Works, Berlin (others))

1961 (18 Sept)–**62**. Europa. W **294**. P 14.

1281	**376**	10pf. bronze-green	40	40
		a. Fluorescent paper (15.2.62)	55	80
1282		40pf. dull ultramarine	70	95

377 Hansel and Gretel in the Wood

378 Telephone Apparatus

(Des B. Jäger. Litho)

1961 (2 Oct). Humanitarian Relief Funds. T **377** and similar designs. W **294**. P 14.

1283	7pf. +3pf. black, red, green and yellow-olive	40	55
1284	10pf. +5pf. black, red, blue and green	40	55
1285	20pf. +10pf. black, blue, green and red	40	55
1286	40pf. +20pf. black, red, olive and greenish blue	1·60	3·25
1283/1286	Set of 4	2·50	4·50

Designs:—7pf. T **377**; 10pf. Hansel, Gretel and the Witch; 20pf. Hansel in the Witch's cage; 40pf. Hansel and Gretel reunited with their father.

(Des K. Blase. Eng H. Braband. Recess)

1961 (26 Oct). Centenary of Philipp Reis's Telephone. W **294**. P 14.

| 1287 | **378** | 10pf. deep green | 55 | 70 |

A 20pf. black and a red stamp showing a hungry child was prepared for a 'Bread for the World' (Freedom from Hunger campaign) issue but was not put on sale. It only exists overprinted 'Muster' (Specimen).

379 Baron W. E. von Ketteler

380 Drusus Stone

(Des G. and E. Aretz. Litho)

1961 (22 Dec). 150th Anniv of Birth of Baron von Ketteler (Catholic leader). W **294**. P 14.

| 1288 | **379** | 10pf. black and olive-green | 55 | 70 |

FLUORESCENT PAPER was used for all issues from No. 1289 onwards *unless otherwise stated.*

(Des E. Ege. Eng H. Braband. Recess)

1962 (10 May). Bimillenary of Mainz. W **294**. P 14.

| 1289 | **380** | 20pf. maroon | 55 | 70 |

381 *Parnassius apollo*

382 Part of *In Dulci Jubilo* from *Musae Sioniae* (M. Praetorius)

(Des K. Blase. Litho)

1962 (25 May). Child Welfare. T **381** and similar horiz designs. Multicoloured. W **294**. P 14.

1290	7pf. +3pf. Type **381**	70	1·10
1291	10pf. +5pf. *Nymphalis antiopa*	70	1·10
	a. Without wmk	£1400	£1800
1292	20pf. +10pf. *Aglais urticae*	1·40	2·00
	a. Without wmk	£1400	£1800
1293	40pf. +20pf. *Iphiclides podalirius*	2·00	3·50
	a. Without wmk	£1400	£1800
1290/1293	Set of 4	4·25	7·00

GERMANY / German Federal Republic

(Des W. Brecker. Litho)
1962 (12 July). Song and Choir (Summer Music Festivals). W **294**. P 14.
1294   382   20pf. red and black 55   80

383 'Belief, Thanksgiving and Service'
384 Open Bible 

(Des E. Ege. Eng E. Falz. Recess)
1962 (22 Aug). Catholics' Day. W **294**. P 14.
1295   383   20pf. magenta 55   80

(Des O. Rohse. Litho)
1962 (11 Sept). 150th Anniv of Württembergische Bibelanstalt (Bible publishers). W **294**. P 14.
1296   384   20pf. black and red 55   80

385 Europa 'Tree'
386 Snow White and Seven Dwarfs 

(Des Lex Weyer. Eng H.-J. Fuchs. Recess)
1962 (17 Sept). Europa. W **294**. P 14.
1297   385   10pf. green 40   40
1298   40pf. ultramarine 80   95

(Des H. Börnsen. Litho)
1962 (10 Oct). Humanitarian Relief and Welfare Funds. T **386** and similar designs. W **294**. P 14.
1299   7pf. +3pf. multicoloured 40   40
1300   10pf. +5pf. multicoloured 40   40
1301   20pf. +10pf. multicoloured 40   40
1302   40pf. +20pf. multicoloured .... 1·40   2·20
1299/1302 Set of 4 .... 2·30   3·00
Designs:—7pf. The Magic Mirror; 10pf. T **386**; 20pf. The Poisoned Apple; 40pf. Snow White and Prince Charming. All from *Snow White and the Seven Dwarfs* (Brothers Grimm).

387 'Bread for the World'
388 Relief Distribution 

(Des H. Kern. Litho; centre embossed)
1962 (23 Nov). Freedom from Hunger. W **294**. P 14.
1303   387   20pf. brown-red and black 55   80

(Des E. Ege. Eng E. Falz. Recess)
1963 (9 Feb). CRALOG and CARE Relief Organisations. W **294**. P 14.
1304   388   20pf. lake 55   70

389 Ears of Wheat, Cross and Globe
390 Snake's Head Lily 

(Des B. Jäger. Recess and litho)
1963 (27 Feb). Freedom from Hunger. W **294**. P 14.
1305   389   20pf. black, red and grey 55   70

(Des O. Rohse. Litho)
1963 (26 Apr). Flora and Philately Exhibition, Hamburg. T **390** and similar vert designs. Multicoloured. W **294**. P 14.
1306   10pf. Type **390** 40   40
1307   15pf. Lady's Slipper Orchid 40   40
          a. Imperf (pair) £7000
1308   20pf. Columbine 40   40
1309   40pf. Sea Holly 45   60
1306/1309 Set of 4 .... 1·50   1·60

391 'Heidelberger Catechismus'
392 Cross, Sun and Moon 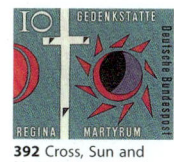

(Des N. Müller. Recess and litho)
1963 (2 May). 400th Anniv of Heidelberg Catechism. W **294**. P 14.
1310   391   20pf. black, brown-red and red-orange.. 55   70

(Des O. Rohse. Litho)
1963 (4 May). Consecration of Regina Martyrum Church, Berlin. W **294**. P 14.
1311   392   10pf. black, violet, carmine and bluish green 40   55

393 Emblems of Conference Participating Countries
394 'Bird-flight' Railway Map and Flags 

(Des E. Ege. Eng H.-J. Fuchs. Recess)
1963 (7 May). Centenary of Paris Postal Conference. W **294**. P 14.
1312   393   40pf. ultramarine 70   95

(Des K. Blase. Litho)
1963 (14 May). Opening of Denmark-Germany Railway (Vogelfluglinie). No wmk. P 14.
1313   394   20pf. red, olive-green, black and yellow   55   55
No. 1313 was a joint issue with Denmark.

395 Red Cross Emblem
396 Hoopoe 

(Des H. Bentele. Litho; outline of cross and frame embossed)
1963 (24 May). Centenary of Red Cross. No wmk. P 14.
1314   395   20pf. red, purple and olive-yellow 55   55

(Des H. Schillinger. Litho)
1963 (12 June). Child Welfare. T **396** and similar vert bird designs inscr 'FUR DIE JUGEND 1963'. Multicoloured. W **294**. P 14.
1315   10pf. +5pf. T **396** 80   1·10
1316   15pf. +5pf. Golden Oriole 70   1·10
1317   20pf. +10pf. Bullfinch 70   1·10
1318   40pf. +20pf. Common Kingfisher .... 3·00   4·25
1315/1318 Set of 4 .... 4·75   6·75

397 Congress Emblem
398 'Co-operation'

GERMANY / German Federal Republic

(Des H.-J. Rau. Litho A. Bagel)

1963 (24 July). German Evangelical Church Day and Congress, Dortmund. W **294**. P 13½×13.
1319 **397** 20pf. black and orange-brown 55 70

(Des A. Holm. Eng P. Nowraty. Recess)

1963 (14 Sept). Europa. W **294**. P 14.
1320 **398** 15pf. green 40 55
1321   20pf. scarlet 40 40

399 Mother Goat warning Kids
400 Atlantic Herring 

(Des H. Börnsen. Litho)

1963 (23 Sept). Humanitarian Relief and Welfare Funds. T **399** and similar horiz designs. W **294**. P 14.
1322   10pf. +5pf. black, red, green and yellow-bistre 40 40
1323   15pf. +5pf. black, red, yellow and green 40 40
1324   20pf. +10pf. black, yellow, green and red 40 40
1325   40pf. +20pf. black, red, olive-yellow and blue . 95 2·00
1322/1325 Set of 4 .... 1·90 3·00
Designs:—10pf. T **399**; 15pf. Wolf entering house; 20pf. Wolf in house, threatening kids; 40pf. Mother Goat and kids dancing round wolf in well.
From Grimm's *Wolf and the Seven Kids*.

(Des R. Heinsdorff. Litho)

1964 (10 Apr). Child Welfare. T **400** and similar horiz fish designs inscr 'Für die Jugend 1964'. Fish in natural colours. No wmk. P 14.
1326   10pf. +5pf. orange-brown (T **400**) 40 55
1327   15pf. +5pf. green (Greater Red-fish) 40 55
1328   20pf. +10pf. red (Mirror Carp) 55 80
1329   40pf. +20pf. blue (Atlantic Cod) .... 1·60 3·50
1326/1329 Set of 4 .... 2·75 4·75

401 Old Town Hall, Hanover
402 Ottobeuren Abbey 

(Des H. and H. Schillinger. Litho)

1964–65. Capitals of the Federal Lands. T **401** and similar horiz designs. Multicoloured. W **294**. P 14.
1330   20pf. Type **401** (29.4.64) 40 55
1331   20pf. *Lichtenfels* (liner) and St. Michael's Church, Hamburg (775th anniv) (6.5.64) 40 55
1332   20pf. *Kronprinz Harald* (ferry), Kiel (6.5.64) 40 55
1333   20pf. National Theatre, Munich (6.5.64) 40 55
1334   20pf. Kurhaus, Wiesbaden (6.5.64) 40 55
1335   20pf. Reichstag, Berlin (19.9.64) 40 55
1336   20pf. Gutenberg Museum, Mainz (25.9.64) 40 55
1337   20pf. Jan Wellem's Monument and Town Hall, Düsseldorf (24.10.64) 40 55
1338   20pf. Town Hall, Bonn (17.5.65) 40 55
1339   20pf. Market Hall, Bremen (17.5.65) 40 55
1340   20pf. View of Stuttgart (17.5.65) 40 55
1340a   20pf. Ludwig's Church, Saarbrücken (23.10.65) 40 55
1330/1340a Set of 12 .... 4·25 6·00

(Des E. Ege. Recess and litho)

1964 (29 May). 1,200th Anniv of Benedictine Abbey, Ottobeuren. No wmk. P 14.
1341   **402** 20pf. black, red and pink 40 55

402a Pres. Lübke
402b Sophie Scholl 

1964 (1 July). Re-election of President Lübke. No wmk. P 14.
1342   **402a** 20pf. carmine-red 40 40
1343   40pf. blue 40 55
See also Nos. 1447/1448.

(Des G. and E. Aretz. Recess and litho)

1964 (20 July). 20th Anniv of Attempt on Hitler's Life. Sheet 148×105 mm. containing eight 20pf. stamps depicting anti-Hitlerite Martyrs. Printed in black and bluish grey. P 14.
1343a   20pf. Type **402b** .... 1·10 2·00
1343b   20pf. Ludwig Beck .... 1·10 2·00
1343c   20pf. Dietrich Bonhoeffer .... 1·10 2·00
1343d   20pf. Alfred Delp .... 1·10 2·00
1343e   20pf. Karl Friedrich Goerdeler .... 1·10 2·00
1343f   20pf. Wilhelm Leuschner .... 1·10 2·00
1343g   20pf. Helmuth James (Von Moltke) .... 1·10 2·00
1343h   20pf. Claus Schenk (Von Stauffenberg) .... 1·10 2·00
1343a/1343h Set of 8 .... 8·00 14·50
MS1343i The sheet .... 11·00 20·00
The individual stamps from this sheet were valid for postage but the sheet itself had no postal validity, although some are known used in Brunswick. Such use was also tolerated on first day covers.

403 Calvin
404 Diagram of Benzene Formula 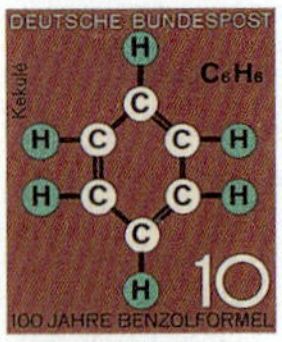

(Des K. O. Blase. Litho)

1964 (3 Aug). World Council of Reformed Churches. No wmk. P 14.
1344   **403** 20pf. black and vermilion 40 55

(Des K. O. Blase. Litho)

1964 (14 Aug). Scientific Anniversaries (1st series). T **404** and similar vert designs. No wmk. P 14.
1345   10pf. green, black and chocolate 40 40
1346   15pf. light blue, blue, black and green 40 40
1347   20pf. green, black and red 40 40
1345/1347 Set of 3 .... 1·10 1·10
Designs:—10pf. T **404** (centenary of publication of Kekulé's benzene formula); 15pf. Diagram of nuclear reaction (25th anniv of publication of Hahn-Strassman treatise on splitting the nucleus of the atom); 20pf. Gas engine (centenary of Otto-Langen internal-combustion engine).
A used copy of No. 1346 has been seen with black omitted.
See also Nos. 1426/1427 and 1451/1453.

405 F. Lassalle
406 'The Sun' 

(Des H. A. Rischka. Litho)

1964 (31 Aug). Death Centenary of Ferdinand Lassalle (Socialist founder and leader). No wmk. P 14.
1348   **405** 20pf. black and light blue 40 55

(Des W. Neufeld. Eng E. Falz. Recess)

1964 (2 Sept). 80th Catholics' Day. No wmk. P 14.
1349   **406** 20pf. carmine-red and grey-blue 40 55

407 Europa 'Flower'
408 The Sleeping Beauty 

(Des G. Bétemps. Litho)

1964 (14 Sept). Europa. No wmk. P 14.
1350   **407** 15pf. reddish violet and yellow-green 40 40
1351   20pf. reddish violet and rose-red 40 40
              a. Imperf (pair) £1200 £1600

74

GERMANY / German Federal Republic

(Des H. Börnsen. Litho)
1964 (6 Oct). Humanitarian Relief and Welfare Funds. T **408** and similar horiz designs. No wmk. P 14.

1352	10pf. +5pf. multicoloured	40	40
1353	15pf. +5pf. multicoloured	40	40
1354	20pf. +10pf. multicoloured	40	40
1355	40pf. +20pf. multicoloured	60	1·60
1352/1355	Set of 4	1·60	2·50

Designs:—10pf. T **408**; 15pf., 20pf., 40pf. Various scenes from Grimm's *The Sleeping Beauty*.

409 Judo

410 Prussian Eagle

(Des H. and H. Schillinger. Litho)
1964 (10 Oct). Olympic Year. No wmk. P 14.
1356 **409** 20pf. multicoloured 40 55

(Des H. Kern. Litho; centre embossed)
1964 (30 Oct). 250th Anniv of German Court of Accounts. No wmk. P 14.
1357 **410** 20pf. orange-red and black 40 55

411 Pres. Kennedy

412 Castle Gateway, Ellwangen (Jagst)

(Des R. Gerhardt. Eng E. Falz. Recess)
1964 (21 Nov). President Kennedy Commemoration. W **294**. P 14.
1358 **411** 40pf. ultramarine 55 55

(Des O. Rohse. Eng P. Nowraty (5pf., 40pf. (1362), 50pf. (1363), 60pf. (1364), 80pf. (1366)); H. Fuchs (10pf. (1368), 20pf. (1369), 40pf. (1372), 70pf. (1375), 80pf. (1376), 1Dm.30); E. Falz (30pf., 50pf. (1373), 60pf. (1374), 1Dm., 1Dm.10, 2Dm.); H. Kummer (90pf.). Typo (1359/61), recess (others))

1964 (15 Dec)–**69**. 12 Centuries of German Architecture. T **412** and similar vert designs. No wmk. P 14.

(a) Size 18½×22 mm on slightly greyish paper. Plain backgrounds

1359	10pf. brown (12.3.65)	55	40
1360	15pf. deep green (12.3.65)	55	40
	a. Tête-bêche (pair) (8.65)	2·00	3·00
1361	20pf. brown-red (12.3.65)	60	40
	a. Tête-bêche (pair) (2.66)	2·00	2·75
1362	40pf. ultramarine (12.3.65)	60	40
1363	50pf. bistre-brown	1·10	40
1364	60pf. scarlet	1·90	70
1365	70pf. bronze-green (29.5.65)	2·00	70
1366	80pf. chocolate	2·00	70
1359/1366	Set of 8	8·25	3·75

(b) Size 19½×24 mm on cream paper. Coloured backgrounds

1367	5pf. bistre-brown (15.6.66)	40	35
1368	10pf. deep purple-brown (21.6.67)	40	35
1369	20pf. emerald-green (17.11.67)	40	35
1370	30pf. olive-brown (7.1.66)	40	35
1371	30pf. rose-red (17.2.67)	40	40
1372	40pf. bistre (4.8.67)	55	40
1373	50pf. deep blue (4.8.67)	70	25
1374	60pf. orange-red (14.4.67)	5·25	2·75
1375	70pf. bronze-green (14.4.67)	2·20	40
1376	80pf. red-brown (21.6.67)	4·00	2·75
1377	90pf. black (15.6.66)	1·50	55
1378	1Dm. Prussian blue (7.11.66)	1·50	40
1379	1Dm.10 chestnut (13.12.66)	1·50	70
1380	1Dm.30 yellow-green (26.3.69)	4·00	2·40
1381	2Dm. purple (13.12.66)	4·00	1·10
1367/1381	Set of 15	24·00	12·00

Buildings:—5pf. Berlin Gate, Stettin; 10pf. Zwinger Pavilion, Dresden; 15pf. Tegel Castle, Berlin; 20pf. Monastery Gate, Lorsch; 30pf. North Gate, Flensburg; 40pf. Trifels Castle (Palatinate); 50pf. T **412**; 60pf. Treptow Portal, Neubrandenburg; 70pf. Osthofen Gate, Soest; 80pf. Ellingen Portal, Weissenburg (Bavaria); 90pf. Zschokk's Convent, Königsberg; 1Dm. Melanchthon House, Wittenberg; 1Dm.10, Trinity Hospital, Hildesheim; 1Dm.30, Tegel Castle, Berlin (*different*); 2Dm. Burghers' Hall, Lowenberg Town Hall (Silesia).

Nos. 1359/1362 and 1364/1366 were also issued in coils with every fifth stamp numbered on the back.

413 Owl, Hat, Walking-stick and Satchel

414 Woodcock

(Des R. Heinsdorff. Eng H.-J. Fuchs. Recess)
1965 (21 Jan). 150th Death Anniv of Matthias Claudius (poet). No wmk. P 14.
1383 **413** 20pf. black and red/*pale grey* 40 55
        a. Imperf (pair) £750

(Des P. Froitzheim. Litho)
1965 (1 Apr). Child Welfare. T **414** and similar horiz bird designs inscr 'FUR DIE JUGEND 1965'. Multicoloured. No wmk. P 14.

1384	10pf. +5pf. Type **414**	40	55
1385	15pf. +5pf. Ring-necked Pheasant	40	55
1386	20pf. +10pf. Black Grouse	40	55
1387	40pf. +20pf. Capercaillie	45	1·60
1384/1387	Set of 4	1·50	3·00

415 Bismarck

416 Boeing 727-100 Jetliner and Space Capsule

(Des R. Gerhardt. Litho)
1965 (1 Apr). 150th Birth Anniv of Otto von Bismarck (statesman). No wmk. P 14.
1388 **415** 20pf. black and brown-red 40 55
        a. Imperf (pair) £2250

(Des G. Magnus. Photo)
1965 (1 Apr–25 June). International Transport Exhibition, Munich. T **416** and similar horiz designs. Multicoloured. No wmk. P 14.

1389	5pf. Road signs and railway crossing sign	40	55
	a. Imperf (pair)	£800	
1390	10pf. *Syncom* satellite and tracking station	40	55
1391	15pf. Old and modern postal buses	40	55
1392	20pf. Old semaphore station and modern signal tower	40	55
1393	40pf. Stephenson locomotive *Adler* (1835) and Class E10.12 electric locomotive (1960s)	40	55
1394	60pf. Type **416**	40	55
1395	70pf. *Bremen* (liner) and *Hammonia* (19th-century steamship)	55	55
1389/1395	Set of 7	2·75	3·50

Dates of issues:—60pf. 1 April (to mark tenth anniv of Lufthansa's renewed air services); others, June.

417 Bouquet

418 ITU Emblem

(Des K. O. Blase. Litho)
1965 (30 Apr). 75th Anniv of May 1st (Labour Day). No wmk. P 14.
1396 **417** 15pf. multicoloured 40 40

(Des F. Lichtwitz. Litho)
1965 (17 May). Centenary of International Telecommunications Union. No wmk. P 14.
1397 **418** 40pf. black and deep dull blue 55 70

75

GERMANY/German Federal Republic

419 A. Kolping

420 *Theodor Heuss* (rescue vessel)

(Des H. Kern. Eng E. Falz. Recess)

1965 (26 May). Death Centenary of Adolf Kolping (miners' padre). No wmk. P 14.
1398   **419**   20pf. black, red and grey 40   55

(Des K. Blase. Litho and recess)

1965 (29 May). Centenary of German Sea-Rescue Service. No wmk. P 14.
1399   **420**   20pf. deep violet, black and red 40   55

1965 (28 July). 20th Anniv of Influx of East German Refugees. As T **299** but inscr 'ZWANZIG JAHRE VERTREIBUNG 1945 1965'. W **294**. P 14.
1400   20pf. slate-purple 40   55

421 Evangelical Church Emblem

422 Radio Tower

(Des H.-J. Rau. Litho and recess)

1965 (28 July). German Evangelical Church Day and Synod, Cologne. No wmk. P 14.
1401   **421**   20pf. black, turquoise-blue and blue 40   55

(Des H. and H. Schillinger. Litho A. Bagel, Düsseldorf)

1965 (28 July). Radio Exhibition, Stuttgart. No wmk. P 14.
1402   **422**   20pf. black, new blue and magenta 40   55

423 Thurn and Taxis 1, 2, and 5sgr. Stamps of 1852

424 Europa 'Sprig'

(Des E. Poell. Litho)

1965 (28 Aug). 125th Anniv of First Postage Stamp. No wmk. P 14.
1403   **423**   20pf. multicoloured 40   55
           a. Imperf (pair) £2250

(Des H. Karlsson. Eng H.-J. Fuchs. Recess)

1965 (27 Sept). Europa. W **294**. P 14.
1404   **424**   15pf. green 40   40
1405   20pf. carmine-red 40   40

425 Cinderella with Birds

426 Nathan Söderblom

(Des G. Stefula. Litho)

1965 (6 Oct). Humanitarian Relief Funds. T **425** and similar horiz designs. Multicoloured. No wmk. P 14.
1406   10pf. +5pf. Type **425** 40   40
1407   15pf. +5pf. Cinderella and birds with dress 40   40
1408   20pf. +10pf. Prince offering slipper to Cinderella 40   40
1409   40pf. +20pf. Cinderella and Prince on horse .. 70   1·20
1406/1409   Set of 4 .... 1·70   2·20

(Des H. Michel. Litho A. Bagel)

1966 (15 Jan). Birth Centenary of Nathan Söderblom, Archbishop of Uppsala. No wmk. P 14.
1410   **426**   20pf. black and lilac 40   55

427 Cardinal von Galen

428 Brandenburg Gate, Berlin

429 Roe Deer

(Des K. Blase. Litho)

1966 (22 Mar). 20th Death Anniv of Cardinal Clemens von Galen. No wmk. P 14.
1411   **427**   20pf. light red, magenta and black 40   55

1966–68. Typo. P 14.
1412   **428**   10pf. chocolate (24.10.66) 55   40
         a. Tête-bêche (pair) (1966) .... 1·40   1·40
         b. Booklet pane. Nos. 1412×4, 1413×2 and 1413×4 (17.2.67) ...... 8·00
         c. Booklet pane. Nos. 1412×2 and 1413×4 (8.3.68) .... 4·75
1413   20pf. myrtle-green (24.10.66) 55   40
         a. Tête-bêche (pair) (1968) .... 1·60   1·80
         b. Booklet pane. Nos. 1413×2 and 1414×2 (8.3.68) .... 3·50
1414   30pf. carmine-red (1.4.66) 55   40
         a. Tête-bêche (pair) (1968) .... 1·80   2·40
1415   50pf. deep blue (24.10.66) .... 2·20   70
1415*a*   100pf. Prussian blue (14.4.67) .... 18·00   1·10
1412/1415*a* Set of 5 .... 20·00   2·75

Nos. 1412/1415*a* were issued both in sheets and in coils, the latter having every fifth stamp numbered on the back.

(Des P. Froitzheim. Photo)

1966 (22 Apr). Child Welfare. T **429** and similar horiz designs. Multicoloured. P 14.
1416   10pf. +5pf. Type **429** 40   55
1417   20pf. +10pf. Chamois 40   55
1418   30pf. +15pf. Fallow Deer 40   55
1419   50pf. +25pf. Red Deer .... 1·10   1·60
1416/1419 Set of 4 .... 2·10   3·00

430 Christ and Fishermen (*Miracle of the Fish*)

431 19th-century Postman

432 G. W. Leibniz

(Des J. Oberberger. Litho)

1966 (13 July). Catholics' Day. P 14.
1420   **430**   30pf. black and salmon-red 40   55

(Des H. and H. Schillinger. Litho)

1966 (13 July–24 Sept). International Philatelic Federation Meeting, Munich. T **431** and similar vert design. Multicoloured. P 14.
1421   30pf. +15pf. Bavarian mail coach (24.9) 70   1·20
1422   50pf. +25pf. Type **431** (13.7) 95   1·20

(Des K. O. Blase. Recess and litho)

1966 (24 Aug). 250th Death Anniv of Gottfried Leibniz (scientist). P 14.
1423   **432**   30pf. black and magenta 40   55

433 Europa 'Ship'

434 Diagram of AC Transmission

GERMANY / German Federal Republic

(Des G. and J. Bender. Photo)

1966 (24 Sept). Europa. P 14.
1424	**433**	20pf. mauve, green, black and light green	40	55
1425		30pf. light blue, crimson, black and pink	40	40

(Des K. O. Blase. Litho)

1966 (28 Sept). Scientific Anniversaries (2nd Series). T **434** and similar vert design. P 14.
1426		20pf. black, purple, yellow, green and blue	40	40
1427		30pf. black, green, blue and red	40	40

Designs:—20pf. T **434** (75th Anniv of alternating current transmission); 30pf. Diagram of electric dynamo (centenary).

435 Princess and Frog
436 UNICEF Emblem 

(Des G. Stefula. Litho)

1966 (5 Oct). Humanitarian Relief Funds. T **435** and similar horiz designs. Multicoloured. P 14.
1428		10pf. +5pf. Type **435**	40	40
1429		20pf. +10pf. Frog dining with Princess	40	40
1430		30pf. +15pf. Prince and Princess	40	40
1431		50pf. +25pf. In coach	60	1·60
1428/1431	Set of 4		1·60	2·50

Designs from Grimm's *The Frog Prince*.

(Des N. Müller. Litho)

1966 (24 Oct). Award of Nobel Peace Prize to United Nations Children's Fund. P 14.
| 1432 | **436** | 30pf. sepia, black and scarlet-vermilion | 40 | 55 |

437 Werner von Siemens
438 Common Rabbit 

(Des H. Kern. Eng E. Falz. Recess)

1966 (13 Dec). 150th Birth Anniv of Werner von Siemens (electrical engineer). P 14.
| 1433 | **437** | 30pf. brown-lake | 40 | 55 |

(Des P. Froitzheim and S. Tonis. Litho)

1967 (4 Apr). Child Welfare. T **438** and similar horiz designs. Multicoloured. P 14.
1434		10pf. +5pf. Type **438**	40	70
1435		20pf. +10pf. Stoat	40	70
1436		30pf. +15pf. Common Hamster	80	1·40
1437		50pf. +25pf. Red Fox	1·80	2·75
1434/1437	Set of 4		3·00	5·00

See also Nos. 1454/1457.

439 Cogwheels
440 Francis of Taxis 
441 Evangelical Symbols 

(Des O. Bonnevalle. Photo)

1967 (2 May). Europa. P 14.
1438	**439**	20pf. multicoloured	55	55
1439		30pf. multicoloured	40	40

(Des K. O. Blase. Eng H.-J. Fuchs. Recess and litho)

1967 (3 June). 450th Death Anniv of Francis of Taxis. P 14.
| 1440 | **440** | 30pf. black and red-orange | 40 | 55 |

(Des E. Ege. Eng H-J. Fuchs. Recess and litho)

1967 (21 June). 13th German Evangelical Churches Day. P 14.
| 1441 | **441** | 30pf. black and light magenta | 40 | 55 |

442 Friedrich von Bodelschwingh (Head of Hospital, 1910–46)
443 Frau Holle at Spinning-wheel 

(Des H. Michel. Litho A. Bagel)

1967 (1 July). Centenary of Bethel Hospital, Bielefeld. P 13½×13.
| 1442 | **442** | 30pf. black and red-brown | 40 | 55 |

(Des G. Stefula. Litho)

1967 (3 Oct). Humanitarian Relief Funds. T **443** and similar horiz designs. P 14.
1443		10pf. +5pf. multicoloured	40	40
1444		20pf. +10pf. multicoloured	40	40
1445		30pf. +15pf. multicoloured	40	40
1446		50pf. +25pf. multicoloured	80	2·00
1443/1446	Set of 4		1·80	3·00

Designs:—10pf. T **443**; 20pf. In the clouds; 30pf. With shopping-basket and cockerel; 50pf. Covered with soot. From Grimm's *Frau Holle* (Mother Carey).

1967 (14 Oct). Re-election of President Lübke. P 14.
1447	**402a**	30pf. carmine-red	40	55
1448		50pf. blue	70	70

444 Wartburg Castle, Eisenach
445 Cross on South American Map 

(Des E. Ege. Eng H.-J. Fuchs. Recess)

1967 (31 Oct). 450th Anniv of Luther's *Theses* and the Reformation. P 14.
| 1449 | **444** | 30pf. red | 55 | 70 |

(Des H. Klein. Photo)

1967 (17 Nov). Adveniat (Aid for Catholic Church in Latin America). P 14.
| 1450 | **445** | 30pf. multicoloured | 40 | 55 |

446 Koenig's Printing Machine
447 Trade Symbols 

(Des K. O. Blase. Litho)

1968 (12 Jan). Scientific Anniversaries (3rd series). T **446** and similar vert designs. Multicoloured. P 14.
1451		10pf. Type **446**	35	35
1452		20pf. Ore Crystals	35	35
1453		30pf. Lens Refraction	40	40
1451/1453	Set of 3		1·00	1·00

Anniversaries:—10pf. 150th Anniversary of invention; 20pf. Millenary of ore mining in Harz Mountains; 30pf. Centenary of the Abbé-Zeiss Scientific Microscope.

(Des P. Froitzheim. Photo)

1968 (2 Feb). Child Welfare. Horiz designs as T **438**, but inscr '1968'. Multicoloured. P 14.
1454		10pf. +5pf. Wild Cat	40	80
1455		20pf. +10pf. European Otter	70	1·40
1456		30pf. +15pf. Eurasian Badger	95	1·90
1457		50pf. +25pf. Eurasian Beaver	3·00	5·50
1454/1457	Set of 4		4·50	8·75

(Des K. O. Blase. Litho A. Bagel)

1968 (8 Mar). German Crafts and Trades. P 14.
| 1458 | **447** | 30pf. multicoloured | 55 | 70 |

77

GERMANY / German Federal Republic

448 Dr. Adenauer
449 Europa 'Key' 

1968 (19 Apr). Adenauer Commemoration (1st issue). T **448** and similar horiz designs in sheet 149×106 mm. P 14.
MS1459 10pf. red-brown and black; 20pf. bluish green and black; 30pf. brown-red and black; 50pf. new blue and black .... 4·00 4·00
Designs:—10pf. Sir Winston Churchill; 20pf. Alcide de Gasperi; 30pf. Robert Schuman; 50pf. T **448**. See also No. 1469.

(Des H. Schwarzenbach. Photo)
1968 (29 Apr). Europa. P 14.
1460 **449** 20pf. yellow, yellow-brown and emerald 40 55
1461 30pf. yellow, yellow-brown and carmine-red 40 40

450 Karl Marx
451 F. von Langen (horseman) 

(Des H. Kern. Eng E. Falz. Recess and litho)
1968 (29 Apr). 150th Birth Anniv of Karl Marx. P 14.
1462 **450** 30pf. bright red, black and grey 40 55

(Des K. O. Blase. Eng E. Falz (No. 1465) or H.-J. Fuchs (others). Recess and litho)
1968 (6 June). Olympic Games (1972) Promotion Fund (1st series). T **451** and similar vert portrait designs. P 14.
1463 10pf. +5pf. black and light olive-green 80 55
1464 20pf. +10pf. black and bright green 95 60
1465 30pf. black and light reddish lilac .... 1·10 70
1466 30pf. +15pf. black and light rose-red .... 1·60 1·40
1467 50pf. +25pf. black and light new blue .... 2·00 1·90
1463/1467 Set of 5 .... 5·75 4·75
Portraits:—10pf. T **451**; 20pf. R. Harbig (runner); T **451** (No 1465); Pierre de Coubertin (founder of modern Olympics); 30pf. (No. 1466); Helene Mayer (fencer); 50pf. Carl Diem (sports organiser).
See also Nos. 1493/1496, 1524/1527, 1589/1593, 1621/1624, **MS**1625 and 1629/**MS**1633.

452 Opening Bars of *The Mastersingers*
453 Dr. Adenauer 

(Des H. Kern. Eng E. Falz. Recess and litho)
1968 (21 June). Centenary of First Performance of Richard Wagner's Opera, *The Mastersingers*. P 14.
1468 **452** 30pf. black, brown-red, grey and pale brown 40 55

(Des H. and H. Schillinger. Litho)
1968 (19 July). Adenauer Commemoration (2nd issue). P 14.
1469 **453** 30pf. black and red-orange 55 55
A similar stamp in black and scarlet was prepared, but not issued. Copies exist overprinted 'Muster' (Specimen).

454 Cross, Dove and 'The Universe'
455 Northern District 1g. and Southern District 7k. Stamps of 1868 

(Des H. Stelzer. Eng H.-J. Fuchs. Recess and litho)
1968 (19 July). Catholics' Day. P 14.
1470 **454** 20pf. violet, greenish yellow and light myrtle-green 55 55

(Des H. Stelzer. Eng H.-J. Fuchs. Recess)
1968 (5 Sept). Centenary of North German Postal Confederation and First Stamps. P 14.
1471 **455** 30pf. brown-red, dull ultramarine and black 40 55

456 Arrows
457 Doll of 1878 

(Des 'Acon'. Photo)
1968 (26 Sept). Centenary of German Trade Unions. P 14.
1472 **456** 30pf. multicoloured 40 55

(Des H. and H. Schillinger. Litho)
1968 (3 Oct). Humanitarian Relief Funds. T **457** and similar vert designs showing standing dolls. Multicoloured. P 14.
1473 10pf. +5pf. Type **457** 40 40
1474 20pf. +10pf. Doll of 1850 .... 40 40
1475 30pf. +15pf. Doll of 1870 .... 40 40
1476 50pf. +25pf. Doll of 1885 .... 95 1·60
1473/1476 Set of 4 .... 1·90 2·50

458 Human Rights Emblem
459 Pony 

1968 (10 Dec). Human Rights Year. Photo. P 14.
1477 **458** 30pf. multicoloured 40 55

(Des D. von Andrian. Photo)
1969 (6 Feb). Child Welfare. T **459** and similar horiz designs. P 14.
1478 10pf. +5pf. brown, black and olive-yellow 55 80
1479 20pf. +10pf. chestnut, black and buff 55 80
1480 30pf. +15pf. blackish brown, black and red ... 95 1·40
1481 50pf. +25pf. grey, yellow, black and blue .... 3·00 2·75
1478/1481 Set of 4 .... 4·50 5·25
Designs:—10pf. T **459**; 20pf. Draught-horse; 30pf. Saddle-horse; 50pf. Thoroughbred.

460 Junkers Ju 52/3m D-2201 *Boelke*
461 Colonnade

GERMANY / German Federal Republic

(Des K. Blase. Litho)
1969 (6 Feb). 50th Anniv of German Airmail Services. T **460** and similar horiz design. Multicoloured. P 14.
| 1482 | 20pf. Type **460** | 70 | 40 |
| 1483 | 30pf. Boeing 707 airliner | 1·10 | 40 |

(Des L. Gasbarra and G. Belli. Photo)
1969 (28 Apr). Europa. P 14.
| 1484 | **461** | 20pf. greenish yellow, yellow-green and blue | 70 | 40 |
| 1485 | | 30pf. yellow, brown-red and slate-violet | 70 | 40 |

462 'The Five Continents'
463 Eagle Emblems of Weimar and Federal Republics 

(Des B. K. Wiese. Litho A. Bagel)
1969 (28 Apr). 50th Anniv of International Labour Organisation. P 13½×13.
| 1486 | **462** | 30pf. multicoloured | 80 | 55 |

(Des H. Stelzer. Photo)
1969 (23 May). 20th Anniv of German Federal Republic. P 14 ×13½.
| 1487 | **463** | 30pf. black, gold and red | 2·00 | 80 |

464 'War Graves'
465 Lakeside Landscape 

(Des E. J. Sauer. Eng M. Spiegel. Recess and litho)
1969 (4 June). 50th Anniv of German War Graves Commission. P 14.
| 1488 | **464** | 30pf. deep blue and pale yellow | 80 | 55 |

(Des O. Rohse. Eng E. Falz (10pf., 30pf.), M. Spiegel (20pf., 50pf.). Recess and litho)
1969 (4 June). Nature Protection. T **465** and similar horiz designs. Multicoloured. P 14.
1489	10pf. Type **465**	40	40
1490	20pf. Highland landscape	1·10	70
1491	30pf. Alpine landscape	40	40
1492	50pf. River landscape	1·40	95
1489/1492	Set of 4	3·00	2·20

466 Running Track
467 'Longing for Justice' 

(Des W. H. Schmidt. Photo)
1969 (4 June). Olympic Games (1972) Promotion Fund (2nd series). T **466** and similar vert designs. Multicoloured. P 14.
1493	10pf. +5pf. Type **466**	70	55
1494	20pf. +10pf. Hockey	95	80
1495	30pf. +15pf. Shooting target	1·40	1·10
1496	50pf. +25pf. Sailing	2·40	2·00
1493/1496	Set of 4	5·00	4·00

(Des H.-J. Rau. Litho)
1969 (7 July). 14th German Protestant Congress, Stuttgart. P 14.
| 1497 | **467** | 30pf. multicoloured | 80 | 55 |

468 Electro-Magnetic Field
469 Marie Juchacz 

(Des G. H. Magnus. Litho)
1969 (11 Aug). German Radio Exhibition, Stuttgart. P 14.
| 1498 | **468** | 30pf. multicoloured | 80 | 55 |

(Des K. H. Walter. Eng H.-J. Fuchs (30pf.), E. Falz (others). Recess.)
1969 (11 Aug). Fifty Years of German Women's Suffrage. Sheet 102× 61 mm containing T **469** and similar vert portraits of women politicians. P 14.
MS1499 10pf. olive; 20pf. myrtle green; 30pf. claret ..... 2·40 1·60
Designs:—10pf. T **469**; 20pf. Marie-Elizabeth Luders; 30pf. Helene Weber.

470 Maltese Cross Symbol
471 Bavaria 3k. Stamp of 1867 

(Des D. Peters. Litho A. Bagel)
1969 (11 Aug). Malteser Hilfsdienst (welfare organisation) Commemoration. P 13½×13½.
| 1500 | **470** | 30pf. red and black | 80 | 55 |

(Des E. Poell. Embossed and litho)
1969 (4 Sept). German Philatelic Federation Congress and Exhibition, Garmisch-Partenkirchen. P 14.
| 1501 | **471** | 30pf. rose and slate | 80 | 55 |

472 Map of Pipeline
473 Rothenburg ob der Tauber 

(Des K. O. Blase. Litho A. Bagel)
1969 (4 Sept). 350th Anniv of Bad Reichenhall-Traunstein Brine Pipeline. P 13½×13.
| 1502 | **472** | 20pf. multicoloured | 80 | 55 |

(Des H. and H. Schillinger. Eng M. Spiegel. Recess and litho)
1969 (4 Sept). Tourism. P 14.
| 1503 | **473** | 30pf. black and carmine-red | 80 | 55 |
See also Nos. 1523, 1558, 1564, 1587, 1606, 1641/1642, 1655/1656 and 1680/1682.

474 Mahatma Gandhi
475 Pope John XXIII
476 Stephenson Locomotive *Adler*, 1835 

(Des K. O. Blase. Litho)
1969 (2 Oct). Birth Centenary of Mahatma Gandhi. P 14.
| 1504 | **474** | 20pf. black and yellow-green | 55 | 55 |
| | | a. Imperf (pair) | | |

GERMANY / German Federal Republic

(Des H. and H. Schillinger. Eng E. Falz. Recess)
1969 (2 Oct). Sixth Death Anniv of Pope John XXIII. P 14.
1505   475   30pf. brown-red 70   55

(Des H. and H. Schillinger. Litho)
1969 (20 Oct–13 Nov). Humanitarian Relief Funds. Pewter Models. T **476** and similar vert designs. Multicoloured. P 14.
(a) Inscr 'WOHLFAHRTSMARKE' (2 Oct)
1506   10pf. +5pf. Type **476** 35   35
1507   20pf. +10pf. Gardener watering flowers (1780) 40   40
1508   30pf. +15pf. Bird salesman (1850) 55   55
1509   50pf. +25pf. Mounted dignitary (1840) ..... 1·50   2·00
1506/1509 Set of 4 .... 2·50   3·00

(b) Christmas. Inscr 'WEIHNACHTSMARKE' (13 Nov)
1510   10pf. +5pf. Child Jesus in crib 70   55

477 E. M. Arndt   **478** Heinrich von Rugge

(Des H. and H. Schillinger. Eng M. Spiegel. Recess and litho)
1969 (13 Nov). Birth Bicentenary of Ernst Arndt (writer). P 14.
1511   477   30pf. lake and pale bistre 70   55

(Des P. Froitzheim. Photo)
1970 (5 Feb). Child Welfare. Miniatures of Minnesingers. T **478** and similar vert designs. Multicoloured. P 14.
1512   10pf. +5pf. Type **478** 70   55
1513   20pf. +10pf. Wolfram von Eschenbach .... 1·10   70
1514   30pf. +15pf. Walther von Metz .... 1·40   1·10
1515   50pf. +25pf. Walther von der Vogelweide ...... 3·00   2·75
1512/1515 Set of 4 .... 5·50   4·50

479 Beethoven   **480** Saar 1m. Stamp of 1947

(Des H. and H. Schillinger. Recess and litho)
1970 (20 Mar). Birth Bicentenaries. T **479** and similar vert portraits. P 14.
1516   10pf. black and pale violet-blue .... 1·40   40
1517   20pf. black and yellow-olive 80   40
1518   30pf. black and pink 80   40
1516/1518 Set of 3 .... 2·75   1·10
Designs:—10pf. T **479**; 20pf. G. W. Hegel (philosopher); 30pf. F. Hölderlin (poet).
A 20pf. 'stamp' commemorating the birth centenary of Lenin is bogus.

(Des E. Poell. Photo)
1970 (29 Apr). SABRIA 70 Stamp Exhibition, Saarbrücken. P 14.
1519   480   30pf. dull green, black and vermilion 70   55

481 'Flaming Sun'   **482** Von Münchhausen on Severed Horse

(Des L. le Brocquy. Eng E. Falz. Recess)
1970 (4 May). Europa. P 14.
1520   481   20pf. green 55   40
1521   30pf. red 60   40

(Des G. Stefula. Litho A. Bagel)
1970 (11 May). 250th Birth Anniv of Baron H. von Münchhausen (writer). P 13½×13.
1522   482   20pf. multicoloured 70   55

(Des H. and H. Schillinger. Eng E. Falz. Recess and litho)
1970 (11 May). Tourism. Horiz design similar to T **473**, but with view of Oberammergau. P 14.
1523   30pf. black and red-orange 70   55

483 Royal Palace   **484** Kungsholm IV (liner) in Kiel Canal and Road-tunnel

(Des H. Kern. Eng E. Falz (5, 15pf.), H.-J. Fuchs (10, 25pf.). Recess)
1970 (5 June). Olympic Games (1972) Promotion Fund (3rd series). T **483** and similar horiz designs. P 14.
1524   10pf. +5pf. bistre-brown 70   55
1525   20pf. +10pf. turquoise 95   70
1526   30pf. +15pf. carmine-red .... 1·40   1·40
1527   50pf. +25pf. new blue .... 2·00   2·00
1524/1527 Set of 4 .... 4·50   4·25
Designs: Munich Buildings—10pf. T **483**; 20pf. Propylaea; 30pf. Glyptothek; 50pf. Bavaria (statue and colonnade).

(Des K. O. Blase. Litho)
1970 (18 June). 75th Anniv of Kiel Canal. P 14.
1528   484   20pf. multicoloured 70   55

485 Nurse with Invalid   **486** President Heinemann   **487** Illuminated Cross

(Des H. Förtsch and S. von Baumgarten. Photo)
1970 (18 June–21 Sept). Voluntary Relief Services. T **485** and similar vert designs. Multicoloured. P 14.
1529   5pf. Oxygen-lance operator (21.9) 40   40
1530   10pf. Mountain rescue (21.9) 40   40
1531   20pf. Type **485** (18.6) 55   40
1532   30pf. Fireman with hose (18.6) .... 1·40   40
1533   50pf. Road-accident casualty (21.9) .... 1·40   70
1534   70pf. Rescue from drowning (21.9) .... 1·60   1·40
1529/1534 Set of 6 .... 5·25   3·25

(Des K. Walter. Eng H.-J. Fuchs. Recess)
1970–73. P 14.
1535   486   5pf. black (23.7.70) 55   40
1536   10pf. brown (23.10.70) 55   40
1537   20pf. deep green (23.10.70) 55   40
1538   25pf. deep yellow-green (27.8.71) 80   40
1539   30pf. lake-brown (6.1.71) 70   40
1540   40pf. brown-orange (8.4.71) 70   40
1541   50pf. steel-blue (8.4.71) .... 2·75   40
1542   60pf. deep ultramarine (25.6.71) .... 1·50   40
1543   70pf. agate (8.4.71) .... 1·40   55
1544   80pf. slate-green (8.4.71) .... 1·40   55
1545   90pf. deep claret (6.1.71) .... 2·75   2·00
1546   1Dm. yellow-olive (23.7.70) .... 2·00   55
1547   110pf. olive-grey (16.1.73) .... 2·40   1·40
1548   120pf. yellow-brown (8.3.72) .... 3·00   1·40
1549   130pf. ochre (20.6.72) .... 3·00   1·40
1550   140pf. deep bluish green (16.1.73) .... 3·00   1·60
1551   150pf. brown-lake (5.7.72) .... 3·00   1·40
1552   160pf. orange (8.3.72) .... 4·25   1·90
1553   170pf. orange (11.9.72) .... 3·75   1·40
1554   190pf. brown-purple (16.1.73) .... 4·75   1·40
1555   2Dm. bluish violet (6.1.71) .... 4·75   65
1535/1555 Set of 21 .... 43·00   17·00

(Des L. Staedler. Litho)
1970 (25 Aug). Catholic Church World Mission. P 14.
1556   487   20pf. greenish yellow and green 55   40

GERMANY / German Federal Republic

488 Stylised Cross
489 Jester 

(Des P. Froitzheim. Litho A. Bagel)

1970 (4 Sept). Catholics Day and 83rd German Catholic Congress, Trier. P 13×13½.
| 1557 | **488** | 20pf. multicoloured | 55 | 40 |

(Des H. and H. Schillinger. Eng M. Spiegel. Recess and litho)

1970 (21 Sept). Tourism. Horiz design similar to T **473**, but with view of Cochem. P 14.
| 1558 | | 20pf. black and apple-green | 80 | 55 |

(Des E. de Vries. Litho)

1970 (6 Oct–12 Nov). Humanitarian Relief Funds. Puppets. T **489** and similar vert designs. Multicoloured. P 14.

(a). Relief Funds (6 Oct)
1559		10pf. +5pf. Type **489**	40	40
1560		20pf. +10pf. Buffoon	40	55
1561		30pf. +15pf. Clown	70	70
1562		50pf. +25pf. Harlequin	1·80	1·80
1559/1562	*Set of 4*		3·00	3·00

(b) Christmas (12 Nov)
| 1563 | | 10pf. +5pf. Angel | 70 | 55 |

(Des H. and H. Schillinger. Eng H.-J. Fuchs. Recess and litho)

1970 (4 Nov). Tourism. Horiz design similar to T **473**, but with view of Freiburg im Breisgau. P 14.
| 1564 | | 20pf. sepia and bronze-green | 80 | 55 |

490 Comenius
491 F. Engels as Young Man 

(Des H. and H. Schillinger. Eng H.-J. Fuchs. Recess and litho)

1970 (12 Nov). 300th Death Anniv of Amos Comenius (Jan Komensky, scholar), and International Education Year. P 14.
| 1565 | **490** | 30pf. red and black | 80 | 55 |

(Des H. Kern. Litho)

1970 (27 Nov). 150th Birth Anniv of Friedrich Engels. P 14.
| 1566 | **491** | 50pf. royal blue and bright red | 2·40 | 1·40 |

492 German Eagle
493 'Ebert' Stamp of 1928 and inscr 'To the German people' 

(Des O. J. Stanik. Recess and litho)

1971 (18 Jan). Centenary of German Unification. P 14.
| 1567 | **492** | 30pf. black, vermilion and orange | 2·40 | 55 |

(Des H. Kern. Litho A. Bagel)

1971 (18 Jan). Birth Centenary of Friedrich Ebert (Chancellor 1918 and President 1919–25). P 13½×13½.
| 1568 | **493** | 30pf. olive-green, black and brown-lake | 2·40 | 55 |

494 King of Blackamoors
495 Molecular Chain 

(Des from Children's drawings. Litho)

1971 (5 Feb). Child Welfare. Drawings. T **494** and similar vert designs. Multicoloured. P 14.
1569		10pf. +5pf. Type **494**	55	55
1570		20pf. +10pf. Flea	70	70
1571		30pf. +15pf. Puss-in-Boots	1·10	1·10
1572		50pf. +25pf. Serpent	1·90	1·90
1569/1572	*Set of 4*		3·75	3·75

(Des K. O. Blase. Litho A. Bagel)

1971 (18 Feb). 125 Years of Chemical Fibre Research. P 13½×13.
| 1573 | **495** | 20pf. black, red and blue-green | 55 | 40 |

496 Road-crossing Patrol
497 Luther before Charles V 

(Des H. Wöhrle. Photo)

1971 (18 Feb). New Road Traffic Regulations (1st series). T **496** and similar vert designs. P 14.
1574		10pf. black, blue and red	40	35
1575		20pf. black, red and green	55	40
1576		30pf. orange-red, black and pale grey	80	40
1577		50pf. black, blue and red	1·40	80
1574/1577	*Set of 4*		2·75	1·80

Road signs:—10pf. T **496**; 20pf. Right-of-way across junction; 30pf. STOP; 50pf. Pedestrian Crossing.
See also Nos. 1579/1582.

(Des B. Jäger. Litho)

1971 (18 Mar). 450th Anniv of *Diet of Worms*. P 14.
| 1578 | **497** | 30pf. black and red | 1·10 | 55 |

(Des B. Siegel. Photo)

1971 (16 Apr). New Road Traffic Regulations (2nd series). Designs similar to T **496**, but all horiz. P 14.
1579		5pf. red, black and blue	45	40
1580		10pf. red, deep olive-green, yellow and black	55	40
1581		20pf. scarlet, black and bright emerald	70	40
1582		30pf. yellow, black and bright rose-red	1·20	40
1579/1582	*Set of 4*		2·50	1·40

New Highway Code regulations:—5pf. Overtaking; 10pf. Warning of obstruction; 20pf. Lane discipline; 30pf. Pedestrian Crossing.

498 Europa Chain
499 Thomas à Kempis writing *The Imitation of Christ* 

(Des H. Haflidason. Photo)

1971 (3 May). Europa. P 14.
| 1583 | **498** | 20pf. gold, green and black | 55 | 40 |
| 1584 | | 30pf. gold, magenta and black | 55 | 40 |

(Des M. Mahlstedt. Eng H.-J. Fuchs. Recess)

1971 (3 May). 500th Death Anniv of Thomas à Kempis (devotional writer). P 14.
| 1585 | **499** | 30pf. black and red | 95 | 55 |

81

GERMANY / German Federal Republic

500 Dürer's Monogram    **501** Meeting Emblem

(Des E. J. Sauer. Eng H.-J. Fuchs. Recess)

1971 (21 May). 500th Birth Anniv of Albrecht Dürer (artist). P 14.
1586 500 30pf. sepia and brown-red .... 2·20 55

(Des H. and H. Schillinger. Eng E. Falz. Recess and litho)

1971 (21 May). Tourism. Horiz design similar to T **473**, but with view of Nüremberg. P 14.
1587   30pf. black and orange-red 80 55

(Des A. H. Marschler. Litho A. Bagel)

1971 (28 May). Whitsun Ecumenical Meeting, Augsburg. P 13½×13.
1588 501 30pf. black, orange and vermilion 80 55

502 Ski Jumping    **503** Astronomical Calculus

(Des K. Sugiura. Litho)

1971 (4 June). Olympic Games (1972) Promotion Fund (4th series). Winter Games, Sapporo, Japan. Vert designs as T **502**. P 14.
1589   10pf. +5pf. black and yellow-brown 55 45
1590   20pf. +10pf. black and emerald .... 1·10 80
1591   30pf. +15pf. black and carmine .... 1·60 1·40
1592   50pf. +25pf. black and new blue .... 2·75 2·40
1589/1592 Set of 4 .... 5·50 4·50
MS1593 112×66 mm. Nos. 1589/1592 .... 5·75 5·00
Designs:—10pf. T **502**; 20pf. Ice dancing; 30pf. Skiing start; 50pf. Ice hockey.
Stamps from No. **MS**1593 do not have '1971' at foot.

(Des H. Kern. Photo)

1971 (25 June). 400th Birth Anniv of Johannes Kepler (astronomer). P 14.
1594 503 30pf. gold, magenta and black 95 55

504 Dante    **505** Alcohol and Front of Car (Don't Drink and Drive)

(Des K. Walter. Eng E. Falz. Recess)

1971 (3 Sept). 650th Death Anniv of Dante Alighieri. P 14.
1595 504 10pf. black 40 40

(Des H. Förtsch and S. von Baumgarten. Typo)

1971 (10 Sept)–**74**. Accident Prevention. T **505** and similar vert designs. P 14.
1596   5pf. orange-red (29.10.71) 55 35
    a. Booklet pane. Nos. 1596×2, 1599×2, 1600×2 and 1601×2 (8.73) .... 9·50
1597   10pf. reddish brown (8.3.72) 55 35
    a. Booklet pane. Nos. 1597×4 and 1600×2 (3.72) .... 5·50
    b. Booklet pane. Nos. 1597×2, 1598×2, 1600×2 and 1601×2 (perf all edges) (11.72) .... 12·00
    c. Perf 3 sides. Booklets (1974) .... 2·75 2·75
    ca. Booklet pane. Nos. 1597c×2, 1598a×2, 1600b×2 and 1601b×2 (imperf top and bottom) (1974) .... 24·00
1598   20pf. violet (5.7.72) 70 40
    a. Perf 3 sides. Booklets (1974) .... 3·50 3·50
1599   25pf. myrtle green (10.9.71) 80 40
    a. Tête-bêche (pair) (11.71) .... 4·00 5·50
1600   30pf. carmine-red (8.3.72) 80 40
    a. Tête-bêche (pair) (3.72) .... 8·00 8·00
    b. Perf 3 sides. Booklets (1974) .... 3·50 3·50
1601   40pf. magenta (20.6.72) 80 40
    a. Tête-bêche (pair) (11.72) .... 2·20 2·30
    b. Perf 3 sides. Booklets (1974) .... 2·75 2·75
1602   50pf. turquoise-blue (16.1.73) .... 3·50 40
1603   60pf. ultramarine (10.9.71) .... 2·00 80
1603a   70pf. ultramarine and emerald (5.6.73) ..... 2·00 55
1604   100pf. olive (5.7.72) .... 3·50 40
1605   150pf. chestnut (11.9.72) .... 8·75 2·00
1596/1605 Set of 11 (*cheapest*) .... 22·00 5·75
Designs:—5pf. Man within flame and spent match (Fire Prevention); 10pf. Fall from ladder; 20pf. Unguarded machine (Factory Safety); 25pf. T **505**; 30pf. Falling brick and protective helmet; 40pf. Faulty electric plug; 50pf. Protruding nail in plank; 60, 70pf. Ball in front of car (Child Road Safety); 100pf. Crate on hoist; 150pf. Open manhole.
Nos. 1596/1605 were issued both in sheets and in coils, the latter having every fifth stamp numbered on the back.
In booklet panes Nos. 1597b and 1597ca the stamps are arranged in different orders.

(Des H. and H. Schillinger. Eng H.-J. Fuchs. Recess and litho)

1971 (15 Sept). Tourism. Horiz design similar to T **473**, but with view of Goslar. P 14.
1606   20pf. black and emerald 80 70

506 Women churning Butter    **507** Deaconess and Nurse

(Des H. and H. Schillinger. Litho)

1971 (5 Oct–11 Nov). Humanitarian Relief Funds. Wooden Toys. T **506** and similar vert designs. Multicoloured. P 14.

(a) Inscr 'WOHLFAHRTSMARKE' (5 Oct)
1607   20pf. +10pf. Type **506** 40 40
1608   25pf. +10pf. Horseman on wheels 40 40
1609   30pf. +15pf. Nutcracker man 80 80
1610   60pf. +30pf. Dovecote .... 2·20 2·20
1607/1610 Set of 4 .... 3·50 3·50

(b) Christmas. Inscr 'WEIHNACHTSMARKE' (11 Nov)
1611   20pf. +10pf. Angel with three candles .... 1·10 70

1972 (20 Jan). Death Centenary of Johann Wilhelm Löhe (founder of Deaconesses Mission, Neuendettelsau). P 13×13½.
1612 507 25pf. slate, black and bright green 80 55

508 Ducks crossing Road    **509** Senefelder's Press

(Des E. Kößlinger. Litho A. Bagel)

1972 (4 Feb). Youth Welfare. Protection of Animals. T **508** and similar horiz designs. Multicoloured. P 14.
1613   20pf. +10pf. Type **508** 95 80
1614   25pf. +10pf. Hunter scaring deer 95 80
1615   30pf. +15pf. Child protecting bird from cat ... 1·40 1·40
1616   60pf. +30pf. Boy annoying mute swans .... 2·40 2·40
1613/1616 Set of 4 .... 5·25 4·75

(Des K. O. Blase. Litho A. Bagel)

1972 (14 Apr). 175 Years of Offset Lithography. P 13½×13.
1617 509 25pf. multicoloured 80 55

GERMANY/ German Federal Republic

510 'Communications'
511 *Lucas Cranach* (Dürer) 

(Des P. Houvinen. Photo)
1972 (2 May). Europa. P 14.
1618 510 25pf. multicoloured .... 1·10 40
1619   30pf. multicoloured .... 1·10 40

(Des E. Sauer. Eng H. Fuchs. Recess and litho)
1972 (18 May). 500th Birth Anniv of Lucas Cranach the Elder (painter). P 14.
1620 511 25pf. black, stone and deep green............ 95 55

512 Wrestling
513 Gymnastics Stadium 

(Des G. Haller. Photo)
1972 (5 June). Olympic Games, Munich (5th series). T **512** and similar vert designs. Multicoloured. P 14.
1621   20pf. +10pf. Type **512** .... 1·40 1·10
1622   25pf. +10pf. Sailing .... 1·40 1·10
1623   30pf. +15pf. Gymnastics .... 1·40 1·10
1624   60pf. +30pf. Swimming .... 3·50 3·25
1621/1624 Set of 4 .... 7·00 6·00
For similar designs, see Nos. 1629/**MS**1633.

(Des H. Steltzer. Litho)
1972 (5 July). Olympic Games, Munich (6th series). Sheet 148×105 mm containing T **513** and similar multicoloured designs. P 14.
MS1625 25pf.+10pf. Type **513**; 30pf.+15pf. Athletics stadium; 40pf.+20pf. Tented area; 70pf.+35pf. TV tower .... 8·75 8·75

514 Invalid Archer
515 Posthorn and Decree 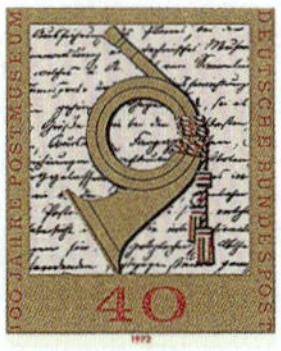

(Des K. Schwartz. Litho)
1972 (18 July). 21st International Games for the Paralysed, Heidelberg. P 14.
1626 514 40pf. brown-red, black and yellow .... 1·10 55

(Des K. H. Walter. Photo)
1972 (18 Aug). Centenary of German Postal Museum. P 14.
1627 515 40pf. multicoloured .... 1·40 55

516 K. Schumacher
517 Open Book 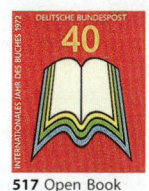

(Des K. O. Blase. Eng E. Falz. Recess and photo)
1972 (18 Aug). 20th Death Anniv of K. Schumacher (politician). P 14.
1628 516 40pf. black and red .... 1·90 55

(Des G. Haller. Photo)
1972 (18 Aug). Olympic Games, Munich (7th series). Vertical designs as T **512**. Multicoloured. P 14.
1629   25pf. +5pf. Long jumping..................... 80 80
    a. Booklet pane. Nos. 1629/32 .... 12·00
1630   30pf. +10pf. Basketball .... 2·20 2·20
1631   40pf. +10pf. Throwing the discus.......... 3·00 3·00
1632   70pf. +10pf. Canoeing .... 1·50 1·50
1629/1632 Set of 4 .... 6·75 6·75
MS1633 111×66 mm. Nos. 1629/1632 .... 8·00 8·00
    a. Green (background of 30pf.) omitted.... £4000
Nos. 1629/1632 only come from booklets.

(Des B. Knoblauch. Litho A. Bagel)
1972 (22 Sept). International Book Year. P 13×13½.
1634 517 40pf. multicoloured .... 1·10 55

518 Music and Signature
519 Knight 

(Des P. Konig. Litho)
1972 (29 Sept). 300th Death Anniv of Heinrich Schütz (composer). P 14.
1635 518 40pf. multicoloured .... 1·40 55

(Des H. and H.-J. Schillinger. Litho)
1972 (5 Oct–10 Nov). Humanitarian Relief Funds. Multicoloured. P 14.
    (a) 19th-century Faience Chessmen. T **519** and similar vert designs inscr 'WOHLFAHRTSMARKE' (5 Oct)
1636   25pf. +10pf. Type **519** 55 55
1637   30pf. +15pf. Rook 55 40
1638   40pf. +20pf. Queen 95 40
1639   70pf. +35pf. King .... 3·50 3·25
1636/1639 Set of 4 .... 5·00 4·25
    (b) Christmas. Horiz design inscr 'WEIHNACHTSMARKE' (10 Nov)
1640   30pf. +15pf. The Three Wise Men.......... 1·60 95

(Des H. and H. Schillinger. Eng M. Spiegel and E. Falz. Recess and litho)
1972 (20 Oct). Tourism. Horiz designs similar to T **473**. P 14.
1641   30pf. black and blue-green................... 80 40
1642   40pf. black and orange........................ 95 40
Views:—30pf. *Wappen von Hamburg* (liner), Heligoland; 40pf. Heidelberg.

520 Revellers

(Des E. de Vries. Litho)
1972 (10 Nov). 150th Anniv of Cologne Carnival. P 14.
1643 520 40pf. multicoloured .... 1·60 55

521 Heinrich Heine

(Des K. O. Blase. Litho)
1972 (13 Dec). 175th Birth Anniv of Heinrich Heine (poet). P 14.
1644 521 40pf. black, red and pink..................... 1·60 55

GERMANY / German Federal Republic

522 'Brot für die Welt'

523 Würzburg Cathedral (from ancient seal)

1972 (13 Dec). Freedom from Hunger Campaign. Photo. P 14.
1645   522   30pf. red and green 80   80

(Des C. Ackermann. Litho)

1972 (13 Dec). Catholic Synod '72. P 14.
1646   523   40pf. black, bright purple and carmine.. 95   55

524 National Colours of France and Germany

(Des H. and H. Schillinger. Litho)

1973 (22 Jan). Tenth Anniv of Franco-German Treaty. P 14.
1647   524   40pf. multicoloured .... 1·90   70
A stamp of a similar design was issued by France.

525 Osprey

526 Copernicus

(Des G. H. Magnus. Photo)

1973 (6 Feb). Youth Welfare. Birds of Prey. T **525** and similar vert designs. Multicoloured. P 14.
1648   25pf. +10pf. Type **525** .... 1·40   1·40
1649   30pf. +15pf. Common Buzzard .... 1·60   1·60
1650   40pf. +20pf. Red Kite .... 2·40   2·40
1651   70pf. +35pf. Montagu's Harrier .... 6·00   6·00
1648/1651 Set of 4 .... 10·50   10·50

(Des H. Kern. Litho)

1973 (19 Feb). 500th Birth Anniv of Copernicus (astronomer). P 14.
1652   526   40pf. black and vermilion .... 1·90   55

527 Radio Mast and Transmission

528 Weather Chart

(Des K. O. Blase. Litho A. Bagel)

1973 (19 Feb). 50th Anniv of International Criminal Police Organisation (Interpol). P 13½×13.
1653   527   40pf. black, red and grey 80   55

(Des K. O. Blase. Litho)

1973 (19 Feb). Centenary of World Meteorological Organisation. P 14.
1654   528   30pf. multicoloured 80   55

(Des H. and H. Schillinger. Eng H. Fuchs and E. Falz. Recess and litho)

1973 (15 Mar). Tourism. Horiz designs similar to T **473**. P 14.
1655   40pf. black and red .... 1·40   40
1656   40pf. black and red-orange .... 1·40   40
Views:—No. 1655, Container ship, Hamburg; 1656, *Loreley* (Rhine steamer), Rudesheim.

529 Gymnast (poster)

530 Kassel (Hesse) Sign

(Des S. and H. Lämmle. Photo)

1973 (15 Mar). Gymnastics Festival, Stuttgart. P 14.
1657   529   40pf. multicoloured 80   55

(Des H. and H. Schillinger. Litho)

1973 (5 Apr). IBRA 73 International Stamp Exhibition and International Philatelic Federation Congress, Munich. Posthouse Signs. T **530** and similar vert designs. Multicoloured. P 14.
1658   40pf. +20pf. Type **530** .... 1·20   1·20
1659   70pf. +35pf. Prussia .... 2·20   2·20
MS1660 74×105 mm. 40pf.+20pf. Württemberg; 70pf.+35pf. Kurpfalz (Bavaria) (*sold at 220Dm.*) .... 6·00   6·00

531 Europa Posthorn

532 'R' Motif

(Des L. F. Anisdahl. Photo)

1973 (30 Apr). Europa. P 14.
1661   531   30pf. yellow, myrtle-green and turquoise-green 70   40
1662   40pf. yellow, lake and rose 95   40

(Des R. Lederbogen. Litho)

1973 (25 May). 1000th Death Anniv of Roswitha von Gandersheim (poetess). P 14.
1663   532   40pf. yellow, black and red 95   55

533 Maximilian Kolbe

534 'Profile' (from poster)

(Des B. Knoblauch. Litho)

1973 (25 May). Father Maximilian Kolbe (concentration camp victim) Commemoration. P 14.
1664   533   40pf. red, brown and black 95   55

(Des C. Piatti. Photo)

1973 (25 May). 15th German Protestant Church Conference. P 14.
1665   534   30pf. multicoloured 70   55

535 Environmental Conference Emblem and 'Waste'

536 Schickard's Calculating Machine

(Des H. and H. Schillinger. Litho)

1973 (5 June). Protection of the Environment. T **535** and similar horiz designs. Multicoloured. P 14.
1666   25pf. Type **535** 70   40
1667   30pf. Emblem and 'Water' 70   40
1668   40pf. Emblem and 'Noise' .... 1·60   40

GERMANY / German Federal Republic

1669	70pf. Emblem and 'Air'	2·40	1·20
1666/1669	Set of 4	4·75	2·20

(Des K. O. Blase. Litho)

1973 (12 June). 350th Anniv of Schickard's Calculating Machine. P 14.
| 1670 | 536 | 40pf. black, red and yellow-orange | 1·10 | 70 |

537 Otto Wels

538 Lübeck Cathedral

(Des K. O. Blase. Litho)

1973 (14 Sept). Birth Centenary of Otto Wels (Social Democratic Party leader). P 14.
| 1671 | 537 | 40pf. brown-purple and lilac | 1·20 | 55 |

(Des H. Kern. Eng M. Spiegel. Recess and litho)

1973 (14 Sept). 800th Anniv of Lübeck Cathedral. P 14.
| 1672 | 538 | 40pf. multicoloured | 1·60 | 55 |

539 UN and German Eagle Emblems

540 French Horn

(Des K. O. Blase. Litho)

1973 (21 Sept). Admission of German Federal Republic to United Nations Organisation. P 14.
| 1673 | 539 | 40pf. multicoloured | 2·00 | 55 |

(Des I. Monson-Baumgart. Recess and litho (30pf.) or litho (others))

1973 (5 Oct–9 Nov). Humanitarian Relief Funds. Musical Instruments. T **540** and similar vert designs. Muiticoloured. P 14.

(a) Inscr 'WOHLFAHRTSMARKE' (5 Oct)
1674	25pf. +10pf. Type **540**	95	70
1675	30pf. +15pf. Grand piano	1·10	70
1676	40pf. +20pf. Violin	1·40	80
1677	70pf. +35pf. Harp	3·00	2·75
1674/1677	Set of 4	5·75	4·50

(b) Christmas. Inscr 'WEIHNACHTSMARKE' (9 Nov)
| 1678 | 30pf. +15pf. Christmas Star | 1·60 | 95 |

541 Radio Set of 1923

542 Louise Otto-Peters

(Des P. Froitzheim. Photo)

1973 (19 Oct). 50 Years of German Broadcasting. P 14.
| 1679 | 541 | 30pf. multicoloured | 70 | 40 |

(Des H. and H. Schillinger. Eng E. Falz (Nos. 1680/1) and L. Lück (No. 1682). Recess and litho)

1973 (19 Oct). Tourism. Horiz designs similar to T **473**. P 14.
1680	30pf. black and apple-green	95	40
1681	40pf. black and brown-red	95	40
1682	40pf. black and scarlet	95	40
1680/1682	Set of 3	2·50	1·10

Views:—No. 1680, Barge, Saarbrücken; 1681, Aachen; 1682, Freighters, Bremen.

(Des H. Förtsch and S. von Baumgarten. Recess and litho)

1974 (15 Jan). Women in German Politics. T **542** and similar horiz designs. Each black and orange. P 14.
1683	40pf. Type **542**	1·10	80
1684	40pf. Helene Lange	1·10	80
1685	40pf. Rosa Luxemburg	1·10	80
1686	40pf. Gertrud Bäumer	1·10	80
1683/1686	Set of 4	4·00	3·00

543 Drop of Blood and Emergency Light

(Des H. Langer. Photo)

1974 (15 Feb). Blood Donor and Accident/Rescue Services. P 14.
| 1687 | 543 | 40pf. red and ultramarine | 1·40 | 55 |

544 Deer in Red (Franz Marc)

545 St. Thomas teaching Pupils

1974 (15 Feb–29 Oct). German Expressionist Paintings. T **544** and similar multicoloured designs. Photo. P 14.
1688	30pf. Type **544**	80	40
1689	30pf. Girls under Trees (A. Macke) (16.8)	1·40	40
1690	40pf. Portrait in Blue (A. von Jawlensky) (vert)	95	40
1691	50pf. Pechstein Asleep (E. Heckel) (vert) (16.8)	1·40	55
1692	70pf. Still Life with Telescope (M. Beckmann) (29.10)	1·60	1·40
1693	120pf. Old Peasant (L. Kirchner) (vert) (29.10)	3·25	2·75
1688/1693	Set of 6	8·50	5·25

(Des L. Stadler. Litho)

1974 (15 Feb). 700th Death Anniv of St. Thomas Aquinas. P 14.
| 1694 | 545 | 40pf. black and red | 95 | 55 |

546 Disabled Persons in Outline

547 Construction (Bricklayer)

(Des H. Langer. Litho)

1974 (15 Feb). Rehabilitation of the Disabled. P 14.
| 1695 | 546 | 40pf. red and black | 1·40 | 55 |

(Des P. Lorenz. Photo)

1974 (17 Apr). Youth Welfare. Youth Activities. T **547** and similar vert designs. Multicoloured. P 14.
1696	25pf. +10pf. Type **547**	95	80
1697	30pf. +15pf. Folk dancing	1·60	1·40
1698	40pf. +20pf. Study	2·75	2·40
1699	70pf. +35pf. Research	4·75	4·75
1696/1699	Set of 4	9·00	8·50

548 Ascending Youth (W. Lehmbruck)

549 Immanuel Kant

(Des B. Wiese. Litho)

1974 (17 Apr). Europa. T **548** and similar vert design, showing another sculpture by Lehmbruck. P 14.
| 1700 | 30pf. black, emerald and silver | 95 | 40 |
| 1701 | 40pf. black, carmine and pale reddish lilac | 95 | 40 |

Designs:—30pf. T **548**; 40pf. Kneeling Woman.

85

GERMANY/German Federal Republic

(Des K. Walter. Eng H.-J. Fuchs. Recess)

1974 (17 Apr). 250th Birth Anniv of Immanuel Kant (philosopher). P 14.
1702   549   90pf. crimson .... 3·50   80

550 Federal Arms and National Colours   **551** Country Road

(Des H. Langer. Litho (Arms embossed))

1974 (15 May). 25th Anniv of Formation of Federal Republic. Sheet 94×64 mm. P 14.
MS1703   550   40pf. multicoloured .... 2·30   3·50

(Des R. Lederbogen. Litho A. Bagel)

1974 (15 May). Rambling, and Birth Centenaries of Richard Schirrman and Wilhelm Münker (founders of Youth Hostelling Association). P 14.
1704   551   30pf. multicoloured 70   55

552 Friedrich Klopstock   **553** 'Crowned Cross' Symbol

(Des E. Sauer. Eng E. Falz. Recess and litho)

1974 (15 May). 250th Birth Anniv of Friedrich Gottlieb Klopstock (poet). P 14.
1705   552   40pf. black and scarlet 95   55

(Des R. Lederbogen. Litho)

1974 (15 May). 125th Anniv of German Protestant Church Diaconal Association (charitable organisation). P 14.
1706   553   40pf. multicoloured 95   55

554 Goalkeeper saving Goal   **555** Hans Holbein (self-portrait)

(Des E. Poell. Litho)

1974 (15 May). World Cup Football Championship. T **554** and similar horiz design. Multicoloured. P 14.
1707   30pf. Type **554** .... 1·60   40
1708   40pf. Mid-field mêlée .... 3·25   40

(Des P. Froitzheim. Eng E. Falz. Recess and litho)

1974 (16 July). 450th Death Anniv of Hans Holbein the Elder (painter). P 14.
1709   555   50pf. black and bright crimson .... 1·40   55

556 Broken Bars of Prison Window

(Des J. Gassner. Litho)

1974 (16 July). Commemoration of Amnesty International (Organisation which gives help to Political Prisoners). P 14.
1710   556   70pf. black and dull ultramarine .... 1·80   80

557 Man and Woman looking at the Moon   **558** Campion

(Des B. Knoblauch. Photo)

1974 (16 Aug). Birth Bicentenary of Caspar David Friedrich (artist). P 14.
1711   557   50pf. multicoloured .... 1·80   55

(Des Hella and Heinz Schillinger. Litho)

1974 (15 Oct–29 Oct). Humanitarian Relief Funds. Flowers. T **558** and similar vert designs. Multicoloured. P 14.

(a) Inscribed '25 Jahre Wohlfahrtsmarken' (25 Years Welfare Stamps). (15 Oct)

1712   30pf. +15pf. Type **558** 55   55
1713   40pf. +20pf. Foxglove 70   55
1714   50pf. +25pf. Mallow 80   70
1715   70pf. +35pf. Campanula .... 2·30   2·30
1712/1715 Set of 4 .... 4·00   3·75

(b) Christmas. Inscribed 'Weihnachtsmarke 1974'. (29 Oct)

1716   40pf. +20pf. Poinsettia .... 1·60   95

559 Early German Post-boxes   **560** Annette Kolb

(Des G. Kühlborn. Litho)

1974 (29 Oct). Centenary of Universal Postal Union. P 14.
1717   559   50pf. multicoloured .... 1·90   70

(Des G. Aretz. Litho)

1975 (15 Jan). International Women's Year. Women Writers. T **560** and similar horiz designs. Multicoloured. P 14.
1718   30pf. Type **560** .... 1·10   55
1719   40pf. Ricarda Huch 95   55
1720   50pf. Else Lasker-Schüler 95   55
1721   70pf. Gertrud Freiin von le Fort .... 1·60   1·60
1718/1721 Set of 4 .... 4·25   3·00

561 Hans Böckler (Trade Union leader)   **562** Mother with Child and Emblem

(Des F. Busse. Eng H.-J. Fuchs. Recess)

1975 (15 Jan–14 Aug). Birth Centenaries of Famous Germans. T **561** and similar horiz designs. P 14.
1722   40pf. black and deep yellowish green (14.2) . 1·40   55
1723   50pf. black and scarlet (14.8) .... 1·10   55
1724   70pf. black and deep dull blue .... 3·00   1·40
1722/1724 Set of 3 .... 5·00   2·30
   Designs:—40pf. T **561**; 50pf. Matthias Erzberger (statesman); 70pf. Albert Schweitzer (medical missionary).

(Des H. Holzing. Litho A. Bagel)

1975 (15 Jan). 25th Anniv of Organisation for the Rest and Recuperation of Mothers. P 13×13½.
1725   562   50pf. multicoloured .... 1·40   55

GERMANY/ German Federal Republic

563 Detail of Ceiling Painting, Sistine Chapel

564 Plan of St. Peter's Cathedral, Rome, within a Cross

(Des F. Fischer. Photo)
1975 (14 Feb). 500th Birth Anniv of Michelangelo. P 14.
1726 563 70pf. black and dull ultramarine .... 2·75 2·40

(Des H. Börnsen. Photo)
1975 (14 Feb). Holy Year (Year of Reconciliation). P 14.
1727 564 50pf. multicoloured .... 1·40 55

565 Ice Hockey

566 Class 218 Diesel Locomotive

(Des E. Poell. Litho)
1975 (14 Feb). World Ice Hockey Championship, Munich and Düsseldorf. P 14.
1728 565 50pf. multicoloured .... 1·80 55

(Des Heinz and Hella Schillinger. Litho)
1975 (15 Apr). Youth Welfare. Railway Locomotives. T 566 and similar horiz designs. Multicoloured. P 14.
1729   30pf. +15pf. Type 566 .... 80 70
1730   40pf. +20pf. Class 103 electric locomotive ...... 1·20 1·10
1731   50pf. +25pf. Class 403 electric railcar .... 1·80 1·60
1732   70pf. +35pf. Transrapid Magler train (model) .. 3·00 2·75
1729/1732 Set of 4 .... 6·00 5·50

567 Concentric Group

568 Mörike's Silhouette and Signature

(Des B. K. Wiese. Eng State Ptg Wks, Berlin. Recess and litho)
1975 (15 Apr). Europa. Paintings by Oskar Schlemmer. T 567 and similar vert design. Multicoloured. P 14.
1733   40pf. Type 567 .... 80 40
1734   50pf. *Bauhaus* staircase .... 1·20 40

(Des G. Jacki. Eng E. Falz. Recess and litho)
1975 (15 May). Death Centenary of Eduard Mörike (writer). P 14.
1735 568 40pf. multicoloured 70 55

569 Nuis (wood-carving)

570 Jousting

(Des C. Keidel. Eng State Ptg Wks, Berlin. Recess and litho)
1975 (15 May). 500th Anniv of Siege of Neuss. P 14.
1736 569 50pf. multicoloured .... 1·10 55

(Des B. Knoblauch. Photo)
1975 (15 May). 500th Anniv of 'Landshut Wedding' (festival). P 14.
1737 570 50pf. multicoloured .... 1·60 55

571 Mainz Cathedral

572 Telecommunications Satellite

(Des O. Rohse. Eng L. Lück. Recess and litho)
1975 (15 May). Millenary of Mainz Cathedral. P 14.
1738 571 40pf. multicoloured .... 1·60 55

(Des R. Gerstetter (110pf.), H.-J. Fuchs (130pf.), E. Falz (300pf.), B. Knoblauch (others). Eng H.-J. Fuchs (5, 10, 130, 140, 160, 180, 230, 250pf.), L. Lück (20, 120, 500pf.), M. Spiegel (30, 40, 50, 70, 100, 150, 190pf.), E. Falz (80, 110, 200, 300pf.). Recess)
1975 (15 May)–**82**. Industry and Technology. T 572 and similar vert designs. P 14.
1739   5pf. bronze-green (14.11.75) 35 25
1740   10pf. deep magenta (14.8.75) 35 25
1741   20pf. orange-vermilion (17.2.76) 35 25
1742   30pf. slate-lilac (14.8.75) 40 35
1743   40pf. blue-green 55 40
1744   50pf. bright magenta 70 40
1745   60pf. rose-red (16.11.78) .... 1·40 40
1746   70pf. blue (14.8.75) .... 1·10 40
1747   80pf. deep bluish green (1510.75) .... 1·10 40
1748   100pf. deep brown .... 1·20 40
1748a 110pf. plum (16.6.82) .... 2·75 1·10
1749   120pf. deep blue (1510.75) .... 1·60 55
1749a 130pf. deep claret (16.6.82) .... 3·25 1·10
1750   140pf. carmine-red (14.11.75) .... 1·80 70
1751   150pf. brown-red (12.7.79) .... 4·00 1·40
1752   160pf. deep yellowish green (15.10.75) .... 2·40 1·10
1753   180pf. sepia (12.7.79) .... 3·75 1·40
1753a 190pf. orange-brown (15.7.82) .... 4·00 1·10
1754   200pf. deep rose-lilac (14.11.75) .... 2·75 55
1754a 230pf. purple (17.5.79) .... 5·50 1·60
1754b 250pf. green (15.7.82) .... 6·00 2·50
1754c 300pf. brown-olive (16.6.82) .... 6·75 2·50
1755   500pf. blue-black (17.2.76) .... 7·25 2·00
1739/1755 Set of 23 .... 55·00 19·00

Designs:—5pf. T 572; 10pf. Electric train; 20pf. Modern lighthouse; 30pf. MBB-Bolkow Bo 105P rescue helicopter; 40pf. Space laboratory; 50pf. Dish aerial; 60pf. X-ray apparatus; 70pf. Tanker under construction; 80pf. Farm tractor; 100pf. Lignite excavator; 110pf. Colour television camera; 120pf. Chemical plant; 130pf. Brewery plant; 140pf. Power station; 150, 190pf. Mechanical shovel; 160pf. Tipper wagons at blast furnace; 180pf. Wheel loader; 200pf. Marine drilling platform; 230, 250pf. Frankfurt Airport; 300pf. Electromagnetic monorail; 500pf. Radio telescope.

573 Town Hall and Market, Alsfeld

574 Effects of Drug-taking

(Des O. Rohse. Eng M. Spiegel (Nos. 1756, 1758), E. Falz (1757), L. Lück (1759). Recess and litho)
1975 (15 July). European Architectural Heritage Year. German Buildings. T 573 and similar horiz designs. Multicoloured. P 14.
1756   50pf. Type 573 .... 1·40 95
1757   50pf. Plönlein corner, Siebers tower and Kobolzeller gate, Rothenburgon-Tauber .... 1·40 95
1758   50pf. Town Hall ('The Steipe'), Trier .... 1·40 95
1759   50pf. View of Xanten .... 1·40 95
1756/1759 Set of 4 .... 5·00 3·50

(Des K.-P. Spreen. Photo)
1975 (14 Aug). Campaign to Fight the Abuse of Drugs and Intoxicants. P 14.
1760 574 40pf. multicoloured 70 55

87

GERMANY / German Federal Republic

575 Posthouse Sign, Royal Prussian Establishment for Mail Transport, 1776

576 Edelweiss

581 Junkers F-13 D-183 *Herta*

582 Emblem and Commemorative Inscription

(Des Hella and Heinz Schillinger. Litho A. Bagel)

1975 (14 Aug). Stamp Day. P 14.
1761 575 10pf. multicoloured 70 40

(Des Hella and Heinz Schillinger. Litho)

1975 (15 Oct–14 Nov). Humanitarian Relief Funds. Alpine Flowers. T **576** and similar vert designs. Multicoloured. P 14.

(a) Inscribed 'Wohlfahrtsmarke 1975' (15 Oct)
1762 30pf. +15pf. Type **576** 70 55
1763 40pf. +20pf. Trollflower 70 55
1764 50pf. +25pf. Alpine Rose .... 1·10 80
1765 70pf. +35pf. Pasqueflower .... 2·40 2·40
1762/1765 Set of 4 .... 4·50 3·75

(b) Christmas. Inscribed 'Weihnachtsmarke 1975' (14 Nov)
1766 40pf. +20pf. Christmas Rose .... 2·30 1·60

See also Nos. 1796/1799, 1839/1842 and 1873/1876.

1976 (5 Jan). 50th Anniv of Lufthansa (German civil airline). P 14.
1771 581 50pf. multicoloured .... 1·60 55

(Des Hella and Heinz Schillinger. Photo)

1976 (17 Feb). 25th Anniv of the Federal Constitutional Court. P 14.
1772 582 50pf. multicoloured .... 1·40 55

583 Letters 'E G' representing Steel Girders

584 Monorail Train

(Des H. Kroehl. Photo)

1976 (6 Apr). 25th Anniv of European Coal and Steel Community. P 14.
1773 583 40pf. multicoloured .... 1·40 55

(Des A. Ade. Litho)

1976 (6 Apr). 75th Anniv of Wuppertal Monorail. P 14.
1774 584 50pf. multicoloured .... 1·40 55

577 Gustav Stresemann (statesman)

578 Stylised Ski-runner

(Des K. Kutemeier and B. K. Wiese. Eng E. Falz. Recess)

1975 (14 Nov). German Nobel Peace Prize Winners. Sheet 100×70 mm containing T **577** and similar vert designs in black. P 14.
MS1767 50pf. Type **577**; 50pf. Ludwig Quidde (Reichstag deputy); 50pf. Carl von Ossietzky (journalist) .... 4·00 3·50

(Des A. Zelger. Eng State Ptg Wks, Berlin. Recess and litho)

1976 (5 Jan). Winter Olympic Games, Innsbruck. P 14.
1768 578 50pf. multicoloured .... 2·00 95

585 Basketball

(Des Hella and Heinz Schillinger. Litho)

1976 (6 Apr). Youth Welfare. Training for Olympic Games. T **585** and similar vert designs. Multicoloured. P 14.
1775 30pf. +15pf. Type **585** 80 55
1776 40pf. +20pf. Rowing .... 1·50 1·10
1777 50pf. +25pf. Gymnastics .... 1·90 1·60
1778 70pf. +35pf. Volleyball .... 2·50 2·30
1775/1778 Set of 4 .... 6·00 5·00

579 Konrad Adenauer

580 Cover Pages from Hans Sachs' Books

(Des K. H. Walter. Eng E. Falz. Recess)

1976 (5 Jan). Birth Centenary of Konrad Adenauer (Chancellor 1949–63). P 14.
1769 579 50pf. bottle green .... 3·75 55

(Des Hella and Heinz Schillinger. Litho)

1976 (5 Jan). 400th Death Anniv of Hans Sachs (poet and composer). P 14.
1770 580 40pf. multicoloured .... 1·10 55

586 Swimming

(Des K.-P. Spreen. Photo)

1976 (6 Apr). Olympic Games, Montreal T **586** and similar horiz designs. P 14.
1779 40pf. +20pf. black, bright blue-green and pale yellowish green .... 1·80 1·10
1780 50pf. +25pf. black, bright magenta and pale rose-pink .... 2·40 1·90
MS1781 110×70 mm. 30pf.+15pf. black, orange-red and pale yellow; 70pf.+35pf. black, new blue and pale blue .... 3·75 3·25

Designs:—30pf. Hockey; 40pf. T **586**; 50pf. High jumping; 70pf. Rowing four.

GERMANY/ German Federal Republic

587 Girl selling Trinkets and Copperplate Prints

588 Carl Sonnenschein

(Des B. K. Wiese. Photo)
1976 (13 May). Europa. Ludwigsburg China Figures. T **587** and similar vert design. Multicoloured. P 14.
| 1782 | 40pf. Type **587** | 95 | 40 |
| 1783 | 50pf. Boy selling copperplate prints | 95 | 40 |

(Des B. Knoblauch. Litho)
1976 (13 May). Birth Centenary of Dr. Carl Sonnenschein (clergyman). P 14.
| 1784 | **588** | 50pf. multicoloured | 1·10 | 55 |

589 Opening lines of Hymn *Entrust Yourself to God*

590 Carl Maria von Weber conducting

(Des H. Börnsen. Eng State Ptg Wks, Berlin. Recess and litho)
1976 (13 May). 300th Death Anniv of Paul Gerhardt (composer). P 14.
| 1785 | **589** | 40pf. multicoloured | 80 | 55 |

(Des H. Hölzing. Litho)
1976 (13 May). 150th Death Anniv of Carl Maria von Weber (composer). P 14.
| 1786 | **590** | 50pf. black and brown-red | 1·40 | 55 |

591 Carl Schurz (United States politician and reformer)

592 Wagnerian Stage

(Des B. Knoblauch. Litho)
1976 (13 May). Bicentenary of American Revolution. P 14.
| 1787 | **591** | 70pf. multicoloured | 1·80 | 70 |

(Des E. Poell. Litho)
1976 (14 July). Centenary of Bayreuth Festival. P 14.
| 1788 | **592** | 50pf. multicoloured | 2·20 | 55 |

593 Bronze Ritual Chariot

594 Golden Plover

(Des Hella and Heinz Schillinger. Litho)
1976 (14 July). Archaeological Heritage. T **593** and similar horiz designs. Multicoloured. P 14.
1789	30pf. Type **593**	70	55
1790	40pf. Gold-ornamented bowl	95	55
1791	50pf. Silver necklet	1·40	80
1792	120pf. Roman gold goblet	3·00	3·00
1789/1792	Set of 4	5·50	4·50

(Des P. Froitzheim. Litho)
1976 (17 Aug). Protection of Birds. P 14.
| 1793 | **594** | 50pf. multicoloured | 1·90 | 55 |

595 Mythical Creature

596 18th-century Posthouse Sign, Höchst am Main

1976 (17 Aug). 300th Death Anniv of Johann Jacob Christoph von Grimmelshausen (writer). P 14.
| 1794 | **595** | 40pf. multicoloured | 1·90 | 55 |

(Des Hella and Heinz Schillinger. Litho A. Bagel)
1976 (14 Oct). Stamp Day. P 14.
| 1795 | **596** | 10pf. multicoloured | 55 | 40 |

(Des Hella and Heinz Schillinger. Litho)
1976 (14 Oct). Humanitarian Relief Funds. Garden Flowers. Horiz designs similar to T **576**. Multicoloured. P 14.
1796	30pf. +15pf. Phlox	80	70
1797	40pf. +20pf. Marigolds	1·10	95
1798	50pf. +25pf. Dahlias	1·20	1·10
1799	70pf. +35pf. Pansies	2·00	2·00
1796/1799	Set of 4	4·50	4·25

597 Sophie Schröder ('Sappho')

598 *Madonna and Child* ('Marienfenster' window, Frauenkirche, Esslingen)

599 Eltz Castle

(Des D. Fischer-Nosbisch. Photo)
1976 (16 Nov). Famous German Actresses. T **597** and similar vert designs. Multicoloured. P 14.
1800	30pf. Caroline Neuber ('Medea')	1·10	40
1801	40pf. Type **597**	1·10	40
1802	50pf. Louise Dumont ('Hedda Gabler')	1·20	55
1803	70pf. Hermine Körner ('Macbeth')	2·20	1·60
1800/1803	Set of 4	5·00	2·75

(Des D. von Andrian. Eng State Ptg Wks, Berlin. Recess and litho)
1976 (16 Nov). Christmas. Sheet 71×101 mm. P 14.
| MS1804 | **598** | 50pf.+25pf. multicoloured | 1·60 | 1·50 |

(Des Hella and Heinz Schillinger. Typo)
1977 (13 Jan)–**90**. German Castles. T **599** and similar vert designs. P 14.
1805	10pf. deep blue (14.4.77)	35	25
	a. Perf 3 sides. Booklets (1.6.77)	35	25
	ab. Booklet pane. Nos. 1805a×4, 1806a×2 and 1808ba×2 (1.6.77)	7·50	
	ac. Booklet pane. Nos. 1805a×4, 1806a×2 and 1808bba×2 (4.80)	5·50	
	ad. Booklet pane. Nos. 1805a×2, 1806a×2, 1808bba×2 and 1809aab×2 (10.80)	16·00	
	ae. Booklet pane. Nos. 1805a×4, 1808bba×2 and 1810aab×2 (6.82)	10·00	
	b. Litho* (15.6.87)	40	1·40
	ba. Perf 3 sides. Booklets (4.90)	40	1·40
	bb. Booklet pane. Nos. 1805ba×4, 1806ba×2 and 1808bca×2 (4.90)	7·50	

89

GERMANY/ German Federal Republic

1805c	20pf. red-orange (14.2.79)	40	35
1805d	25pf. scarlet (11.1.79)	70	40
1806	30pf. bistre (14.4.77)	55	35
	a. Perf 3 sides. Booklets (1.6.77)	70	70
	b. Litho* (17.8.87)	1·10	3·25
	ba. Perf 3 sides. Booklets (4.90)	70	1·40
1806c	35pf. brown-red (16.6.82)	95	70
1807	40pf. blue-green (16.2.77)	80	35
1807a	40pf. deep brown (14.2.80)	1·10	40
1808	50pf. rose-carmine (17.5.77)	95	40
	a. Perf 3 sides. Booklets (1.6.77)	2·20	2·20
1808b	50pf. yellowish green (14.2.80)	1·20	40
	ba. Perf 3 sides. Booklets (4.80)	1·20	95
	c. Litho* (15.6.87)	2·20	2·20
	ca. Perf 3 sides. Booklets (4.90)	2·00	3·50
1809	60pf. bistre-brown	1·40	40
1809a	60pf. carmine (14.11.79)	1·20	55
	ab. Perf 3 sides. Booklets (10.80)	6·00	8·00
	b. Litho* (1.4.87)	2·75	2·00
1810	70pf. new blue (17.5.77)	1·40	40
1810a	80pf. yellow-olive (16.6.82)	1·80	55
	ab. Perf 3 sides. Booklets (6.82)	3·00	4·00
	b. Litho* (1.4.87)	3·50	3·25
1810c	90pf. ultramarine (11.1.79)	2·00	70
1810d	120pf. reddish violet (15.7.82)	2·75	95
1811	190pf. Venetian red (16.2.77)	3·50	1·40
1812	200pf. bronze green	4·00	1·40
1812a	210pf. red-brown (14.2.79)	5·50	2·00
1812b	230pf. deep bluish green (16.11.78)	5·50	2·00
1812c	280pf. greenish blue (15.7.82)	5·75	1·50
1812d	300pf. red-orange (16.6.82)	6·50	1·20
	e. Litho* (1.4.87)	13·50	32·00
1805/1812d Set of 21 (cheapest)		43·00	16·00

Designs:—10pf. Glücksburg; 20, 190pf. Pfaueninsel, Berlin; 25pf. Gemen; 30pf. Ludwigstein, Werratal; 35pf. Lichtenstein; 40pf. (1807) Type **599**; 40pf. (1807a) Wolfsburg; 50pf. Neuschwanstein; 50pf. (1808b) Inzlingen; 60pf. (1809) Marksburg; 60pf. (1809a) Rheydt; 70pf. Mespelbrunn; 80pf. Wilhelmsthal; 90pf. Vischering; 120pf. Charlottenburg, Berlin; 200pf. Bürresheim; 210pf. Schwanenburg; 230pf. Lichtenstein; 280pf. Ahrensburg; 300pf. Herrenhausen, Hanover.

Nos. 1805/1812d (typo) were issued both in sheets and in coils, the latter having every fifth stamp numbered on the back.

The booklet panes are imperforate top and bottom, giving stamps with one side imperf.

*For the 'litho' printed stamps (more correctly termed letterset or dry-offset printed) the original typo plates were used in a litho process with a blanket offsetting the ink from the plates to the paper. They can be distinguished by the smoother, more even appearance of the ink. They were issued in coils only, with three values also in booklets.

Nos. 1809, 1810c, 1812 and 1812b printed by lithography and perf 11 are postal forgeries.

600 Palais de l'Europe

(Des E. Poell. Eng H.-J. Fuchs. Recess)

1977 (13 Jan). Inauguration of Palais de l'Europe (Council of Europe building), Strasbourg. P 14.
| 1813 | **600** | 140pf. deep green and black | 3·00 | 95 |

601 Book Illustrations

602 Floral Ornament

(Des H. Börnsen. Litho)

1977 (13 Jan). *Till Eulenspiegel* (popular fable). P 14.
| 1814 | **601** | 50pf. multicoloured | 95 | 55 |

(Des P. Steiner. Litho)

1977 (16 Feb). German Art Nouveau. Sheet 116×86 mm containing T **602** and similar vert designs. Multicoloured. P 14.
MS1815 30pf. Type **602**; 70pf. Woman's head; 90pf. Chair .... 4·25 2·75

603 Jean Monnet

(Des M. Langer-Rosa and H. Langer. Litho)

1977 (16 Feb). Award of Citizen of Europe honour to Jean Monnet (French statesman). P 14.
| 1816 | **603** | 50pf. black, greenish grey and bistre-yellow | 1·10 | 55 |

604 'Flower'

605 Plane of Complex Numbers

(Des O. Rieger. Litho)

1977 (14 Apr). 25th Anniv of Federal Horticultural Show. P 14.
| 1817 | **604** | 50pf. multicoloured | 1·40 | 55 |

(Des B. K. Wiese. Litho)

1977 (14 Apr). Birth Bicentenary of Carl Friedrich Gauss (mathematician). P 14.
| 1818 | **605** | 40pf. multicoloured | 2·20 | 55 |

606 Wappen von Hamburg, 1731

607 Head of Barbarossa

(Des Hella and Heinz Schillinger. Litho)

1977 (14 Apr). Youth Welfare. Ships. T **606** and similar horiz designs. Multicoloured. P 14.
1819	30pf. +15pf. Type **606**	95	95
1820	40pf. +20pf. *Preussen* (full-rigged sailing ship), 1902	1·20	1·10
1821	50pf. +25pf. *Bremen* (liner), 1929	1·60	1·50
1822	70pf. +35pf. *Sturmfels* (container ship), 1972	2·30	2·30
1819/1822 Set of 4	5·50	5·25

(Des H. Lohrer. Litho)

1977 (14 Apr). Staufer Year, Baden-Württemberg. P 14.
| 1823 | **607** | 40pf. multicoloured | 2·00 | 55 |

608 Rhön Autobahn

609 Self Portrait (Rubens)

(Des Hella and Heinz Schillinger. Recess and litho)

1977 (17 May). Europa. T **608** and similar horiz design. P 14.
| 1824 | 40pf. black and emerald | 1·10 | 40 |
| 1825 | 50pf. black and scarlet | 1·10 | 40 |

Designs:—40pf. T **608**; 50pf. Rhine landscape.

GERMANY/ German Federal Republic

(Des H. Stelzer. Eng E. Falz. Recess)
1977 (17 May). 400th Birth Anniv of Peter Paul Rubens. P 14.
1826   609   30pf. black .... 1·40   55

610 Ulm Cathedral

611 Rector's Seal, Mainz University (500th Anniv)

(Des H. Kern. Eng E. Falz. Recess and litho)
1977 (17 May). 600th Anniv of Ulm Cathedral. P 14.
1827   610   40pf. deep brown, green and new blue   1·10   55

1977 (17 May–16 Aug). University Anniversaries. T **611** and similar vert designs. P 14.
1828   50pf. black and orange-red .... 1·40   55
1829   50pf. black and orange-red .... 1·40   55
1830   50pf. black and orange-red (16.8) .... 1·60   55
1828/1830 Set of 3 .... 4·00   1·50
Designs:—No. 1828, T **611**; No. 1829, Great Seal, Marburg University (450th Anniv); No. 1830, Great Seal, Tübingen University (500th Anniv).

612 *Morning*

(Des A. Mavignier. Litho)
1977 (13 July). Birth Bicentenary of Philipp Otto Runge (artist). P 14.
1831   612   60pf. multicoloured .... 2·00   70

613 Ketteler's Coat of Arms

614 Fritz von Bodelschwingh

(Des P. Steiner. Litho)
1977 (13 July). Death Centenary of Bishop Wilhelm Emmanuel von Ketteler. P 14.
1832   613   50pf. multicoloured .... 1·10   55

(Des G. Aretz. Recess and litho)
1977 (13 July). Birth Centenary of Pastor Fritz von Bodelschwingh (pioneer of welfare work for the disabled). P 14.
1833   614   50pf. multicoloured .... 1·40   55

615 Golden Hat

616 Operator and Switchboard

(Des Hella and Heinz Schillinger. Litho)
1977 (16 Aug). Archaeological Heritage. T **615** and similar vert designs. Multicoloured. P 14.
1834   30pf. Type **615** 70   55
1835   120pf. Gilt helmet .... 2·75   2·00
1836   200pf. Bronze centaur head .... 3·50   3·00
1834/1836 Set of 3 .... 6·25   5·00

(Des Elisabeth von Janota-Bzowski. Litho)
1977 (13 Oct). Centenary of Telephone in Germany. P 14.
1837   616   50pf. multicoloured .... 1·90   55

617 19th-century Posthouse Sign, Hamburg

618 Travelling Surgeon

(Des Hella and Heinz Schillinger. Litho A. Bagel)
1977 (13 Oct). Stamp Day. P 14.
1838   617   10pf. multicoloured 70   55

(Des Hella and Heinz Schillinger. Litho)
1977 (13 Oct). Humanitarian Relief Funds. Meadow Flowers. Vert designs similar to T **576**. Multicoloured. P 14.
1839   30pf. +15pf. Caraway 95   55
1840   40pf. +20pf. Dandelion .... 1·10   70
1841   50pf. +25pf. Red Clover .... 1·20   80
1842   70pf. +35pf. Meadow Sage .... 2·40   2·00
1839/1842 Set of 4 .... 5·00   3·75

(Des H. Börnsen. Litho)
1977 (10 Nov). 250th Death Anniv of Dr. Johann Andreas Eisenbarth. P 14.
1843   618   50pf. multicoloured .... 1·40   55

619 Wilhelm Hauff

620 King presenting Gift (stained glass window, Basilica of St. Gereon, Cologne)

(Des Elisabeth von Janota-Bzowski. Photo)
1977 (10 Nov). 150th Death Anniv of Wilhelm Hauff (poet and novelist). P 14.
1844   619   40pf. multicoloured 80   55

(Des C. Hansmann. Litho)
1977 (10 Nov). Christmas. Sheet 70×105 mm. P 14.
MS1845   620   50pf.+25pf. multicoloured .... 1·60   1·50

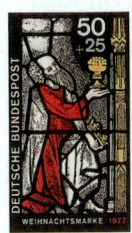

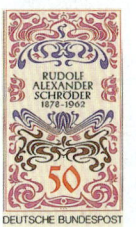

621 Book Cover Designs

622 Refugees

91

GERMANY / German Federal Republic

(Des G. Jacki. Litho)
1978 (12 Jan). Birth Centenary of Rudolf Alexander Schröder (writer). P 14.
1846 **621** 50pf. multicoloured .... 1·10 55

(Des A. Ade. Photo)
1978 (12 Jan). 20th Anniv of Friedland Aid Society. P 14.
1847 **622** 50pf. multicoloured .... 1·10 55

623 Skiing

(Des P. Lorenz. Litho)
1978 (12 Jan–13 Apr). Sport Promotion Fund. T **623** and similar horiz design. Multicoloured. P 14.
1848   50pf. +25pf. Type **623** .... 2·40 2·00
1849   70pf. +35pf. Show jumping (13.4) .... 5·50 4·75

624 Gerhart Hauptmann    **625** Martin Buber

(Des G. Aretz. Litho)
1978 (16 Feb). German Winners of Nobel Prize for Literature. T **624** and similar horiz designs. Multicoloured. P 14.
1850   30pf. Type **624** .... 1·10 45
1851   50pf. Hermann Hesse .... 1·20 55
1852   70pf. Thomas Mann .... 1·40 95
1850/1852 Set of 3 .... 3·25 1·80
MS1853 120×70 mm. Nos. 1850/1852 .... 4·25 2·40

(Des G. Aretz. Litho)
1978 (16 Feb). Birth Centenary of Martin Buber (religious philosopher). P 14.
1854 **625** 50pf. multicoloured .... 1·20 55

626 Museum Tower and Cupola    **627** Wilhelmine Reichart's Balloon, Munich October Festival, 1820

(Des Hella and Heinz Schillinger. Litho)
1978 (13 Apr). 75th Anniv of German Scientific and Technical Museum, Munich. P 14.
1855 **626** 50pf. black, yellow and red .... 1·20 55

(Des F. Haase. Litho)
1978 (13 Apr). Youth Welfare. Aviation History (1st series). T **627** and similar horiz designs. Multicoloured. P 14.
1856   30pf. +15pf. Type **627** .... 1·00 80
1857   40pf. +20pf. Airship LZ-1, 1900 .... 1·20 1·10
1858   50pf. +25pf. Blériot XI monoplane, 1909 .... 1·60 1·50
1859   70pf. +35pf. Hans Grade's monoplane, 1909.. 2·00 2·00
1856/1859 Set of 4 .... 5·25 4·75
See also Nos. 1886/1889 and 1918/1921.

628 Old Town Hall, Bamberg

(Des O. Rohse. Eng O. Lück (40pf.), M. Spiegel (others). Recess and litho)
1978 (22 May). Europa. T **628** and similar horiz designs. Multicoloured. P 14.
1860   40pf. Type **628** .... 1·10 45
1861   50pf. Old Town Hall, Regensburg .... 1·60 55
1862   70pf. Old Town Hall, Esslingen am Neckar...... 2·00 1·10
1860/1862 Set of 3 .... 4·25 1·90

629 Piper and Children 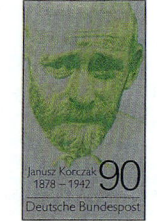   **630** Janusz Korczak

(Des G. Jacki. Litho)
1978 (22 May). Pied Piper of Hamelin. P 14.
1863 **629** 50pf. multicoloured .... 1·40 55

(Des G. H. Magnus. Litho)
1978 (13 July). Birth Centenary of Dr. Janusz Korczak (educational reformer). P 14.
1864 **630** 90pf. multicoloured .... 1·90 95

631 Fossil Bat    **632** Parliament Building, Bonn

(Des P. Froitzheim. Litho)
1978 (13 July). Archaeological Heritage. Fossils. T **631** and similar horiz design. Multicoloured. P 14.
1865   80pf. Type **631** .... 2·75 2·40
1866   200pf. Horse (*eohippus*) skeleton .... 3·00 2·75

(Des E. Poell. Litho)
1978 (17 Aug). 65th Interparliamentary Union Conference, Bonn. P 14.
1867 **632** 70pf. multicoloured .... 1·90 70

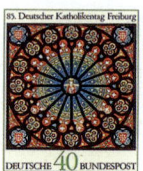

633 Rose window Freiburg Minster    **634** Silhouette

(Des P. Froitzheim. Litho)
1978 (17 Aug). 85th Congress of German Catholics, Freiburg. P 14.
1868 **633** 40pf. multicoloured 80 55

(Des Elisabeth von Janota-Bzowski. Litho)
1978 (17 Aug). Birth Bicentenary of Clemens Brentano (poet). P 14.
1869 **634** 30pf. multicoloured 80 55

GERMANY/ German Federal Republic

635 Text **636** Baden Posthouse Sign

(Des P. Steiner. Litho)

1978 (17 Aug). 25th Anniv of European Convention for the Protection of Human Rights. P 14.
1870   **635**   50pf. multicoloured .... 1·40   55

(Des H. Stelzer. Litho A. Bagel)

1978 (12 Oct). Stamp Day and World Philatelic Movement. T **636** and similar vert design. Multicoloured. P 14.
1871   40pf. Type **636** 80   40
   a. Horiz pair. Nos. 1871/1872 .... 1·70   85
1872   50pf. 1850 3pf. stamp of Saxony 80   40
Nos. 1871/1872 were issued together in horizontal *se-tenant* pairs within the sheet.

(Des Hella and Heinz Schillinger. Litho)

1978 (12 Oct). Humanitarian Relief Funds. Woodland Flowers. Vert designs similar to T **576**. Multicoloured. P 14.
1873   30pf. +15pf. Arum 70   55
1874   40pf. +20pf. Weasel-snout 95   80
1875   50pf. +25pf. Turk's-cap Lily .... 1·40   1·20
1876   70pf. +35pf. Liverwort .... 1·80   1·80
1873/1876 Set of 4 .... 4·25   4·00

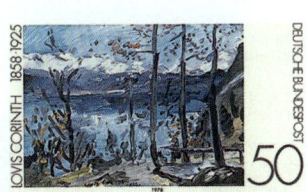

637 Easter at the *Walchensee* (Lovis Corinth)

(Des H. P. Schall. Photo)

1978 (16 Nov). Impressionist Paintings. T **637** and similar vert designs. Multicoloured. P 14.
1877   50pf. Type **637** .... 1·40   80
1878   70pf. *Horseman on the Shore turning Left* (Max Liebermann) .... 2·00   1·10
1879   120pf. *Lady with a Cat* (Max Slevogt) .... 2·75   2·40
1877/1879 Set of 3 .... 5·50   3·75

638 Christ Child (stained glass window, Frauenkirche, Munich)   **639** Child

(Des W. Fleckhaus. Litho)

1978 (16 Nov). Christmas. Sheet 65×93 mm. P 14.
MS1880   **638**   50pf.+25pf. multicoloured .... 1·90   1·40

(Des K. O. Blase. Photo)

1979 (11 Jan). International Year of the Child. P 14.
1881   **639**   60pf. multicoloured .... 1·60   55

640 Agnes Miegel   **641** Seating Plan

(Des Elisabeth von Janota-Bzowski. Photo)

1979 (14 Feb). Birth Centenary of Agnes Miegel (poet). P 14.
1882   **640**   60pf. multicoloured .... 1·10   55

(Des E. Poell. Litho)

1979 (14 Feb). First Direct Elections to European Parliament. P 14.
1883   **641**   50pf. multicoloured .... 1·60   55

642 Film   **643** Rescue Services Emblems

(Des D. Urban. Litho)

1979 (14 Feb). 25th West German Short Film Festival. P 13½×14.
1884   **642**   50pf. black and blue-green .... 1·40   55

(Des H. Klein. Litho)

1979 (14 Feb). Rescue Services on the Road. P 14.
1885   **643**   50pf. multicoloured .... 1·40   55

(Des F. Haase. Litho)

1979 (5 Apr). Youth Welfare. Aviation History (2nd series). Horiz designs as T **627**. Multicoloured. P 14.
1886   40pf. +20pf. Dornier Do-J Wal flying boat, 1922 95   95
1887   50pf. +25pf. Heinkel He Blitz, 1932 .... 1·40   1·40
1888   60pf. +30pf. Junkers W.33 D-1167 *Bremen*, 1928 .... 1·60   1·60
1889   90pf. +45pf. Focke Achgelis Fa 61 helicopter, 1936 .... 2·20   2·20
1886/1889 Set of 4 .... 5·50   5·50

644 Handball   **645** Telegraph Office, 1863

(Des H. P. Hoch. Litho)

1979 (5 Apr). Sport Promotion Fund. T **644** and similar horiz design. Multicoloured. P 14.
1890   60pf. +30pf. Type **644** .... 1·60   1·50
1891   90pf. +45pf. Canoeing .... 2·40   2·20

(Des Elisabeth von Janota-Bzowski. Litho)

1979 (17 May). Europa. T **645** and similar horiz design. Multicoloured. P 14.
1892   50pf. Type **645** .... 1·10   40
1893   60pf. Post office counter, 1854 .... 1·40   40

646 Anne Frank   **647** Werner von Siemens Electric Railway, 1879

93

GERMANY/ German Federal Republic

(Des Elisabeth von Janota-Bzowski. Photo)
1979 (17 May). 50th Birth Anniv of Anne Frank (concentration camp victim and diary writer). P 14.
1894   **646**   60pf. black, brownish grey and rose-red   1·60   55

(Des Hella and Heinz Schillinger. Litho)
1979 (17 May). International Transport Exhibition, Hamburg. P 14.
1895   **647**   60pf. multicoloured .... 1·60   55

648 Hand operating Radio Dial

649 Moses receiving the Tablets of the Law (woodcut, Cranach the elder)

(Des W. P. Seiter. Litho)
1979 (12 July). World Administrative Radio Conference, Geneva. P 14.
1896   **648**   60pf. multicoloured .... 1·60   55

(Des W. Neufeld. Eng H.-J. Fuchs. Recess and litho)
1979 (12 July). 450th Anniv of Publication of Martin Luther's *Catechisms*. P 14.
1897   **649**   50pf. black and myrtle green .... 1·60   55

650 Cross and Orb

651 Hildegard von Bingen

(Des K. H. Walter. Embossed and litho)
1979 (12 July). Pilgrimage to Aachen. P 14.
1898   **650**   50pf. multicoloured .... 1·10   55

(Des P. Steiner. Litho)
1979 (9 Aug). 800th Death Anniv of Hildegard von Bingen (writer and mystic). P 14.
1899   **651**   110pf. multicoloured .... 1·90   95

652 Photo-electric Effect

653 Pilot and Helmsman

(Des Brigitte von der Linde. Photo)
1979 (9 Aug). Birth Centenaries of Nobel Prize Winners. T **652** and similar horiz designs. Multicoloured. P 14.
1900   60pf. Type **652** (Albert Einstein, Physics, 1921) .... 1·40   70
1901   60pf. Splitting of uranium nucleus (Otto Hahn, Chemistry, 1944) .... 2·75   70
1902   60pf. Diffraction pattern of X-rays passed through crystal (Max von Laue, Physics, 1914) .... 1·40   70
1900/1902 *Set of 3* .... 5·00   1·90

(Des A. Löffelhardt. Eng E. Falz. Recess and litho)
1979 (11 Oct). 300th Anniv of First Pilotage Regulations. P 14.
1903   **653**   60pf. deep brown and brown lilac .... 1·10   55

654 Posthouse Sign, Altheim, Saar, 1754 (German side)

655 Red Beech

(Des Hella and Heinz Schillinger. Litho)
1979 (11 Oct). Stamp Day. P 13½.
1904   **654**   60pf. +30pf. multicoloured .... 1·90   1·90

(Des Hella and Heinz Schillinger. Litho)
1979 (11 Oct). Humanitarian Relief Funds. Woodland Flowers and Fruits. T **655** and similar horiz designs. Multicoloured. P 14.
1905   40pf. +20pf. Type **655** .... 1·10   80
1906   50pf. +25pf. English Oak .... 1·20   1·10
1907   60pf. +30pf. Hawthorn .... 1·40   1·20
1908   90pf. +45pf. Mountain Pine .... 2·00   2·00
1905/1908 *Set of 4* .... 5·25   4·50

656 Bird Garden

(Des H. P. Schall. Photo)
1979 (14 Nov). Birth Centenary of Paul Klee (artist). P 14.
1909   **656**   90pf. multicoloured .... 1·80   95

657 Faust and Mephistopheles

658 Lightbulb

(Des H. Burkert. Litho)
1979 (14 Nov). Doctor Johannes Faust. P 14.
1910   **657**   60pf. multicoloured .... 2·00   55

(Des C. von Mannstein. Litho A. Bagel, Düsseldorf)
1979 (14 Nov). Save Energy. P 13×13½.
1911   **658**   40pf. multicoloured .... 1·10   55

659 Nativity (Altenberg medieval manuscript)

660 Iphigenia

(Des P. Steiner. Litho)
1979 (14 Nov). Christmas. P 13½.
1912   **659**   60pf. +30pf. multicoloured .... 1·60   1·60

(Des H. P. Schall. Litho)
1980 (10 Jan). Death Centenary of Anselm Feuerbach (artist). P 14.
1913   **660**   50pf. multicoloured .... 1·90   55

GERMANY/ German Federal Republic

661 Flags of NATO Members

662 Town Hall, St. Mary's Church and St. Peter's Cathedral

(Des H. Börnsen. Litho)
1980 (10 Jan). 25th Anniv of North Atlantic Treaty Organisation Membership. P 14.
1914   **661**   100pf. multicoloured .... 2·75   1·40

(Des O. Rohse. Eng E. Falz. Recess and litho)
1980 (10 Jan). 1200th Anniv of Osnabrück Town and Bishopric. P 14.
1915   **662**   60pf. multicoloured .... 1·40   55

663 Götz von Berlichingen (glass picture)

664 Texts from 1880 and 1980 Duden Dictionaries

(Des G. Jacki. Litho)
1980 (10 Jan). 500th Birth Anniv of Götz von Berlichingen (Frankish knight). P 14.
1916   **663**   60pf. multicoloured .... 1·40   55

(Des P. Froitzheim. Litho)
1980 (14 Feb). Centenary of Konrad Duden's First Dictionary. P 14.
1917   **664**   60pf. multicoloured .... 1·40   55

(Des F. Haase. Litho)
1980 (10 Apr). Youth Welfare. Aviation History (3rd series). Horiz designs as T **627**. Multicoloured. P 14.
1918   40pf. +20pf. Phoenix FS 24 glider, 1957 70   70
1919   50pf. +25pf. Lockheed L1049G Super Constellation D-ALID (wrongly dated '1950') .... 1·10   1·10
1920   60pf. +30pf. Airbus Industrie A300B2 F-OCAZ of Air France, 1972 .... 1·50   1·50
1921   90pf. +45pf. Boeing 747-100 jetliner, 1969 ...... 2·20   2·20
1918/1921 Set of 4 .... 5·00   5·00

665 Emblems of Association Members

666 Frederick I with his Sons (Welt Chronicle)

(Des K. O. Blase. Litho)
1980 (10 Apr). Centenary of German Association of Welfare Societies. P 14.
1922   **665**   60pf. blue, dull vermilion and black .... 1·40   55

(Des K. H. Walter. Litho)
1980 (10 Apr). 800th Anniv of Imperial Diet of Gelnhausen. P 14.
1923   **666**   60pf. multicoloured .... 1·80   55

667 Football

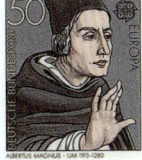

668 Albertus Magnus (scholar)

(Des H. P. Hoch. Photo)
1980 (8 May). Sport Promotion Fund. T **667** and similar horiz designs. Multicoloured. P 14.
1924   +25pf. +25pf. Type **667** 95   80
1925   60pf. +30pf. Dressage .... 1·40   1·10
1926   90pf. +45pf. Skiing .... 2·40   2·40
1924/1926 Set of 3 .... 4·25   3·75

(Des Elisabeth von Janota-Bzowski. Litho)
1980 (8 May). Europa. T **668** and similar vert design. Multicoloured. P 14.
1927   50pf. Type **668** .... 1·40   40
1928   60pf. Gottfried Wilhelm Leibniz (philosopher) .... 1·50   40

669 Reading Augsburg Confession (engraving, G. Kohler)

670 Nature Reserve

(Des Hella and Heinz Schillinger. Litho)
1980 (8 May). 450th Anniv of Augsburg Confession (creed of Lutheran Church). P 14.
1929   **669**   50pf. black, pale stone and blue-green.. 1·20   55

(Des Hella and Heinz Schillinger. Photo)
1980 (8 May). Nature Conservation. P 14.
1930   **670**   40pf. multicoloured .... 1·80   55

671 Ear and Oscillogram Pulses

(Des E. Poell. Embossed and litho)
1980 (10 July). International Congress for the Training and Education of the Hard of Hearing, Hamburg. P 14.
1931   **671**   90pf. multicoloured .... 2·00   70

672 First Book of Daily Bible Readings, 1731

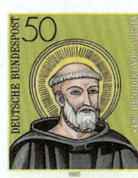

673 St. Benedict

(Des P. Steiner. Litho)
1980 (10 July). 250th Edition of Moravian Brethren's Book of Daily Bible Readings. P 14.
1932   **672**   50pf. multicoloured .... 1·20   55

(Des Elisabeth von Janota-Bzowski. Litho A. Bagel, Düsseldorf)
1980 (10 July). 1500th Birth Anniv of St. Benedict of Nursia (founder of Benedictine Order). P 13×13½.
1933   **673**   50pf. multicoloured .... 1·10   55

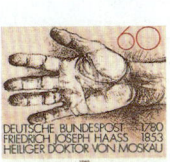

674 Helping Hand

675 Marie von Ebner-Eschenbach

95

GERMANY/ German Federal Republic

(Des G. Aretz. Recess and litho)

1980 (14 Aug). Birth Bicentenary of Friedrich Joseph Haass (physician and prison welfare pioneer). P. 14.
1934   **674**   60pf. multicoloured .... 1·40   55

(Des B. K. Wiese. Photo)

1980 (14 Aug). 150th Birth Anniv of Marie von Ebner-Eschenbach (novelist). P. 14.
1935   **675**   60pf. pale grey brown, blackish brown and orange .... 1·40   55

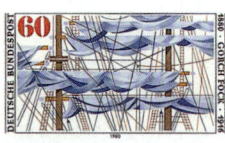

676 Rigging

677 Positioning Keystone of South Tower Finial (engraving)

(Des G. Jacki. Litho)

1980 (14 Aug). Birth Centenary of Johann Kinau ('Gorch Fock') (poet). P. 14.
1936   **676**   60pf. multicoloured .... 2·75   55

> A 60pf.+30pf. stamp depicting the Olympic rings was prepared for the Moscow Olympic Games but not issued due to the international boycott. Most of the printed stamps were destroyed, but one sheet in the possession of the then Federal Minister of Posts K. Gscheidle was missed and examples from it were inadvertently used for postage some time later. A single mint example is known, some used and several on cards or covers. (Price £48000 used).
> Facsimiles of the unissued stamp were produced for a stamp exhibition in 1983, but these have their status indicated by a statement on the reverse.

(Des P. Steiner. Litho)

1980 (9 Oct). Centenary of Completion of Cologne Cathedral. P. 14.
1937   **677**   60pf. multicoloured .... 2·75   55

678 *Ceratocephalus falcatus*

679 Wine-making (woodcuts)

(Des Hella and Heinz Schillinger. Litho)

1980 (9 Oct). Humanitarian Relief Funds. Endangered Wild Flowers. T **678** and similar square designs. Multicoloured. P. 14.
1938   40pf. +20pf. Type **678**   95   80
1939   50pf. +25pf. Yellow Vetchling .... 1·20   1·10
1940   60pf. +30pf. Corn Cockle .... 1·40   1·40
1941   90pf. +45pf. Tassel Hyacinth .... 2·20   2·20
1938/1941 Set of 4 .... 5·25   5·00
See also Nos. 1972/1975.

(Des E. Poell. Litho)

1980 (9 Oct). Bimillenary of Vine Growing in Central Europe. P. 14.
1942   **679**   50pf. multicoloured .... 1·40   55

680 Posthouse Sign, Altheim, Saar, 1754 (French side)

681 *Nativity* (Altomünster manuscript)

(Des Hella and Heinz Schillinger. Litho)

1980 (13 Nov). 49th International Philatelic Federation Congress, Essen. P 13½.
1943   **680**   60pf. +30pf. multicoloured .... 1·40   1·20
Issued in sheets of ten.

(Des H. Stelzer. Litho)

1980 (13 Nov). Christmas. P 13½.
1944   **681**   60pf. +30pf. multicoloured .... 1·80   1·60

682 *Landscape with Two Fir Trees* (etching)

(Des P. Steiner. Eng H.-J. Fuchs. Recess and litho)

1980 (13 Nov). 500th Birth Anniv of Albrecht Altdorfer (painter, engraver and architect). P. 14.
1945   **682**   40pf. pale grey-brown, black and reddish brown .... 1·10   55

683 Elly Heuss-Knapp

684 Society accepting the Disabled

(Des Elisabeth von Janota-Bzowski. Photo)

1981 (15 Jan). Birth Centenary of Elly Heuss-Knapp (social reformer). P. 14.
1946   **683**   60pf. multicoloured .... 1·40   55

(Des A. Löffelhardt. Litho)

1981 (15 Jan). International Year of Disabled Persons. P. 14.
1947   **684**   60pf. multicoloured .... 1·40   55

685 Old Town Houses

686 Telemann and Title Page of *Singet dem Herrn*

(Des O. Rohse. Eng E. Falz. Recess and litho)

1981 (15 Jan). European Campaign for Urban Renaissance. P. 14.
1948   **685**   60pf. multicoloured .... 1·50   55

(Des Elisabeth von Janota-Bzowski. Photo)

1981 (12 Feb). 300th Birth Anniv of Georg Philipp Telemann (composer). P. 14.
1949   **686**   60pf. multicoloured .... 1·40   55

687 Visiting a Foreign Family

688 Polluted Butterfly, Stylised Cyprinid Fish and Plant

(Des A. Ade. Litho)

1981 (12 Feb). Integration of Guest Worker Families. P. 14.
1950   **687**   50pf. multicoloured .... 1·40   55

(Des Hella and Heinz Schillinger. Litho)

1981 (12 Feb). Preservation of the Environment. P 13½.
1951   **688**   60pf. multicoloured .... 2·20   55

GERMANY/German Federal Republic

689 Patent Office Emblem and Scientific Signs

690 Scintigram showing Distribution of Radioactive Isotope

(Des E. Poell. Litho)
1981 (12 Feb). Establishment of European Patent Office, Munich. P 14.
1952   **689**   60pf. grey, orange-vermilion and black..   1·40   55

(Des W. Götzinger. Litho A. Bagel, Düsseldorf)
1981 (12 Feb). Cancer Prevention through Medical Check-ups. P 13×13½.
1953   **690**   40pf. multicoloured ....   1·10   55

691 Borda Circle, 1800

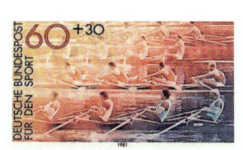

692 Rowing

(Des Hella and Heinz Schillinger. Litho)
1981 (10 Apr). Youth Welfare. Optical Instruments. T **691** and similar square designs. Multicoloured. P 13½.
1954   40pf. +20pf. Type **691**   95   70
1955   50pf. +25pf. Reflecting telescope, 1770..........   1·60   1·40
1956   60pf. +30pf. Binocular microscope, 1860........   1·60   1·40
1957   90pf. +45pf. Octant, 1775................................   2·30   2·30
1954/1957 Set of 4..   5·75   5·25

(Des G. Artez. Litho)
1981 (10 Apr). Sport Promotion Fund. T **692** and similar horiz design. Multicoloured. P 14.
1958   60pf. +30pf. Type **692** ....   1·50   1·40
1959   90pf. +45pf. Gliding..   2·30   2·20

693 South German Dancers

694 Convention Cross

(Des Elisabeth von Janota-Bzowski. Litho)
1981 (7 May). Europa. T **693** and similar vert design. Multicoloured. P 14.
1960   50pf. Type **693** ....   1·10   40
1961   60pf. North German dancers............................   1·40   40

(Des G. Jacki. Photo)
1981 (7 May). 19th German Protestant Convention, Hamburg. P 14.
1962   **694**   50pf. multicoloured...............................   1·40   55

695 Group from Crucifixion Altar

696 Georg von Neumayer German Antarctic Research Station

(Des B. K. Wiese. Litho)
1981 (7 May). 450th Death Anniv of Tilman Riemenschneider (woodcarver). P 14.
1963   **695**   60pf. multicoloured................................   1·40   55

(Des R. Blumenstein. Litho)
1981 (16 July). Polar Research. P 13½×14.
1964   **696**   110pf. multicoloured.............................   3·00   80

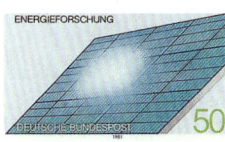

697 Solar Generator

698 Hand holding Common Coot (chick)

(Des E. Jünger. Litho)
1981 (16 July). Energy Research. P 14.
1965   **697**   50pf. multicoloured................................   1·80   55

(Des Erna de Vries. Litho)
1981 (16 July). Protection of Animals. P 14×13½.
1966   **698**   60pf. multicoloured................................   1·90   55

699 Arms of different Races forming Square

700 Wilhelm Raabe

(Des A. Ade. Litho)
1981 (16 July). Co-operation with Developing Countries. P 14.
1967   **699**   90pf. multicoloured................................   2·20   80

(Des B. K. Wiese. Recess and litho)
1981 (13 Aug). 150th Birth Anniv of Wilhelm Raabe (poet). P 14.
1968   **700**   50pf. green and bottle green..................   1·40   55

701 Constitutional Freedom

702 Posthouse Scene, c. 1855

(Des G. Jacki. Litho)
1981 (13 Aug). Fundamental Concepts of Democracy. T **701** and similar horiz designs quoting text of Article 20 of the Basic Law. Multicoloured. P 14.
1969   40pf. Type **701** ....   1·50   40
1970   50pf. Separation of Powers............................   1·50   40
1971   60pf. Sovereignty of the People......................   1·90   40
1969/1971 Set of 3...   4·50   1·10

(Des Hella and Heinz Schillinger. Litho)
1981 (8 Oct). Humanitarian Relief Funds. Endangered Wild Flowers. Square designs as T **678**. Multicoloured. P 14.
1972   40pf. +20pf. Water Nut....................................   80   70
1973   50pf. +25pf. Floating Heart..............................   1·10   95
1974   60pf. +30pf. Water Gillyflower.........................   1·40   1·40
1975   90pf. +45pf. Water Lobelia..............................   2·40   2·40
1972/1975 Set of 4...   5·25   5·00

(Des Elisabeth von Janota-Bzowski. Litho)
1981 (8 Oct). Stamp Day. P 14×13½.
1976   **702**   60pf. multicoloured................................   1·90   55

97

GERMANY/German Federal Republic

703 Nativity (glass painting)

704 St. Elisabeth

(Des P. Froitzheim. Litho)
1981 (12 Nov). Christmas. P 14.
1977   **703**   60pf. +30pf. multicoloured .... 1·80   1·50

(Des R. Lederbogen. Photo)
1981 (12 Nov). 750th Death Anniv of St. Elisabeth of Thüringia. P 14.
1978   **704**   50pf. multicoloured .... 1·80   55

705 Carl von Clausewitz (after W. Wach)

706 People forming Figure '100'

(Des Elisabeth von Janota-Bzowski. Photo)
1981 (12 Nov). 150th Death Anniv of General Carl von Clausewitz (military writer). P 14.
1979   **705**   60pf. multicoloured .... 1·80   55

(Des C. von Mannstein. Photo)
1981 (12 Nov). Centenary of Social Insurance. P 14.
1980   **706**   60pf. multicoloured .... 1·40   55

707 Map of Antarctica

708 Pot with Lid

1981 (12 Nov). 20th Anniv of Antarctic Treaty. P 14.
1981   **707**   100pf. deep ultramarine, azure and black   2·40   80

(Des G. Jacki. Litho)
1982 (13 Jan). 300th Birth Anniv of Johann Friedrich Böttger (founder of Meissen China Works). P 14.
1982   **708**   60pf. multicoloured .... 1·40   55

709 Insulated Wall

710 Silhouette (Dora Brandenburg-Polster)

(Des E. Jünger. Litho)
1982 (13 Jan). Energy Conservation. P 14.
1983   **709**   60pf. multicoloured .... 1·40   55

(Des Elisabeth von Janota-Bzowski. Litho)
1982 (13 Jan). The Town Band of Bremen (German fairy tale). P 14.
1984   **710**   40pf. black and scarlet .... 1·10   55

711 Goethe (after Georg Melchior Kraus)

712 Robert Koch

(Des Elisabeth von Janota-Bzowski. Photo)
1982 (18 Feb). 150th Death Anniv of Johann Wolfgang von Goethe (writer). P 14.
1985   **711**   60pf. multicoloured .... 3·75   55

(Des Marina Langer-Rosa and H. Langer. Photo)
1982 (18 Feb). Centenary of Discovery of Tubercule Bacillus. P 14.
1986   **712**   50pf. multicoloured .... 4·25   55

713 Benz Patent Motorwagen, 1886

(Des Hella and Heinz Schillinger. Litho)
1982 (15 Apr). Youth Welfare. Motor Cars. T **713** and similar horiz designs. Multicoloured. P 14.
1987   40pf. +20pf. Type **713**   95   80
1988   50pf. +25pf. Mercedes Tourenwagen, 1913 .....   1·20   1·10
1989   60pf. +30pf. Hanomag Kommissbrot, 1925......   1·60   1·40
1990   90pf. +45pf. Opel Olympia, 1937....................   3·00   3·00
1987/1990 Set of 4...   6·00   5·75

714 Jogging

(Des H. Buschfeld. Litho)
1982 (15 Apr). Sport Promotion Fund. T **714** and similar horiz designs. Multicoloured. P 14.
1991   60pf. +30pf. Type **714** ....   1·50   1·50
1992   90pf. +45pf. Disabled archers ....   2·30   2·30

715 'Good Helene'

716 Procession to Hambach Castle, 1832 (wood engraving)

(Des P. Froitzheim. Litho)
1982 (15 Apr). 150th Birth Anniv of Wilhelm Busch (writer and illustrator). P 14.
1993   **715**   50pf. black, bright apple green and greenish yellow .... 1·80   55

(Des K. O. Blase. Litho)
1982 (5 May). Europa. T **716** and similar horiz design. P 14.
1994   50pf. black, lemon and rosine ....   1·80   40
       a. Black double...
1995   60pf. multicoloured ....   2·30   40
Designs:—50pf. T **716**; 60pf. Excerpt from *Treaty of Rome* (instituting European Economic Community), 1957, and flags.

717 Racing Yachts

98

GERMANY / German Federal Republic

(Des H. Börnsen. Litho A. Bagel, Düsseldorf)
1982 (5 May). Centenary of Kiel Regatta Week. P 14.
1996 **717** 60pf. multicoloured .... 1·80 55

718 Young Couple

(Des P. Steiner. Litho)
1982 (5 May). Centenary of Young Men's Christian Association in Germany. P 14.
1997 **718** 50pf. multicoloured .... 1·40 55

719 Polluted Sea

(Des E. Göttner. Litho)
1982 (15 July). Prevent Pollution of the Sea. P 14.
1998 **719** 120pf. multicoloured .... 4·50 80

720 Battered Licence Plate
721 Doctor Examining Leper 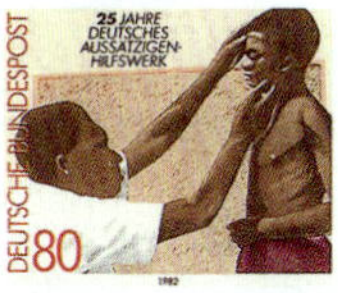

(Des G. Gamroth. Photo)
1982 (15 July). Don't Drink and Drive. P 14.
1999 **720** 80pf. multicoloured .... 1·80 55

1982 (15 July). 25th Anniv of German Lepers' Welfare Organisation. P 14.
2000 **721** 80pf. multicoloured .... 1·80 55

722 James Franck and Max Born
723 Atomic Model of Urea 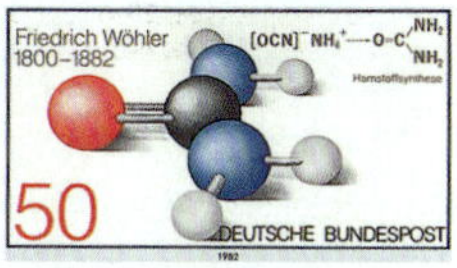

(Des K.-H. Walter. Recess and litho)
1982 (12 Aug). Birth Centenaries of James Franck and Max Born (physicists and Nobel Prize winners). P 14.
2001 **722** 80pf. grey, slate-black and scarlet............ 2·20 55

(Des E. Jünger. Photo)
1982 (12 Aug). Death Centenary of Friedrich Wöhler (chemist). P 14.
2002 **723** 50pf. multicoloured .... 1·60 55

724 St. Francis preaching to the Birds (after fresco by Giotto)
725 Hybrid Tea Rose 

(Des P. Steiner. Litho)
1982 (12 Aug). 87th German Catholics' Congress, Düsseldorf, and 800th Birth Anniv of St. Francis of Assisi. P 14.
2003 **724** 60pf. multicoloured .... 1·60 55

(Des Hella and Heinz Schillinger. Litho)
1982 (14 Oct). Humanitarian Relief Funds. Roses. T **725** and similar vert designs. Multicoloured. P 14.
2004 50pf. +20pf. Type **725** 95   80
2005 60pf. +30pf. Floribunda .... 1·20 1·10
2006 80pf. +40pf. Bourbon .... 1·90 1·80
2007 120pf. +60pf. Polyantha hybrid .... 2·75 2·40
2004/2007 Set of 4 .... 6·00 5·50

726 Letters on Desk
727 Gregorian Calendar by Johannes Basch. 1586 

(Des G. Aretz. Photo)
1982 (14 Oct). Stamp Day. P 14.
2008 **726** 80pf. multicoloured .... 2·40 55

(Des Elisabeth von Janota-Bzowski. Litho)
1982 (14 Oct). 400th Anniv of Gregorian Calendar. P 14.
2009 **727** 60pf. multicoloured .... 1·60 55

728 Theodor Huess
729 Nativity (detail from St. Peter altar by Master Bertram) 

(Des G. Aretz. Litho)
1982 (10 Nov). Presidents of the Federal Republic. Sheet 130×100 mm containing T **728** and similar horiz designs. Multicoloured. P 14.
MS2010 80pf. Type **728**; 80pf. Heinrich Lübke; 80pf. Gustav Heinemann; 80pf. Walter Scheel; 80pf. Karl Carstens.. 8·50 8·00

(Des B. K. Wiese. Litho)
1982 (10 Nov). Christmas. P 14.
2011 **729** 80pf. +40pf. multicoloured............... 2·75 1·90

730 Edith Stein
731 White Rose and Barbed Wire 

(Des F. Lüdtke. Litho)
1983 (13 Jan). 40th Death Anniv (1982) of Edith Stein (philosopher). P 14.
2012 **730** 80pf. olive-grey, deep brownish grey and black... 2·75 80

(Des H. Kern. Litho A. Bagel, Düsseldorf)
1983 (13 Jan). Persecution and Resistance 1933–1945. P 14.
2013 **731** 80pf. multicoloured .... 3·00 85

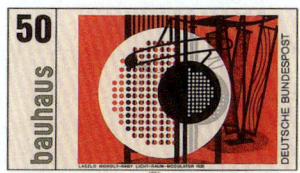

732 Light Space Modulator (Laszlo Moholy-Nagy)

GERMANY / German Federal Republic

(Des E. Nitsche. Litho)

1983 (8 Feb). Birth Centenary of Walter Gropius (founder of Bauhaus School of Art, Weimar). Bauhaus Art. T **732** and similar horiz designs. Multicoloured. P 14.

2014	50pf. Type **732**	1·50	60
2015	60pf. *Sanctuary* (lithograph by Josef Albers)	1·70	60
2016	80pf. *Skylights of Bauhaus Archives, Berlin* (Walter Gropius)	2·00	60
2014/2016	Set of 3	4·75	1·60

733 Federahannes (Rottweil carnival figure)

734 Daimler-Maybach, 1885

(Des P. Steiner. Litho)

1983 (8 Feb). Carnival. P 14.

2017	**733** 60pf. multicoloured	1·90	60

(Des H. Schillinger. Litho)

1983 (12 Apr). Youth Welfare. Motorcycles. T **734** and similar horiz designs. Multicoloured. P 14.

2018	50pf. +20pf. Type **734**	1·00	85
2019	60pf. +30pf. NSU, 1901	1·30	1·20
2020	80pf. +40pf. Megola Sport, 1922	2·30	2·20
2021	120pf. +60pf. BMW world record holder, 1936	3·50	3·25
2018/2021	Set of 4	7·25	6·75

735 Gymnastics (German Festival, Frankfurt-am-Main)

736 Stylised Flower

(Des F.-D. Rothacker. Photo)

1983 (12 Apr). Sport Promotion Fund. T **735** and similar horiz design. Multicoloured. P 14.

2022	80pf. +40pf. Type **735**	2·20	1·90
2023	120pf. +60pf. Modern pentathlon (world championships, Warendorf)	3·50	3·25

(Des Antonia Graschberger. Litho)

1983 (12 Apr). Fourth International Horticultural Show, Munich. P 14.

2024	**736** 90pf. multicoloured	1·90	60

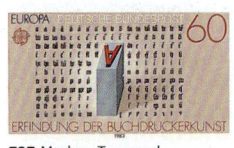

737 Modern Type and Gutenberg Letters

738 Johannes Brahms

(Des E. Jünger. Litho)

1983 (5 May). Europa. T **737** and similar horiz design. Multicoloured. P 14.

2025	60pf. Type **737**	3·75	75
2026	80pf. Resonant circuit and electric flux lines	2·20	75

(Des Elisabeth von Janota-Bzowski. Photo)

1983 (5 May). 150th Birth Anniv of Johannes Brahms (composer). P 14.

2027	**738** 80pf. multicoloured	3·00	85

739 Kafka's Signature and Teyn Church, Prague

740 Brewing (frontispiece of 1677 treatise)

(Des H.-G. Schmitz. Photo)

1983 (5 May). Birth Centenary of Franz Kafka (writer). P 14.

2028	**739** 80pf. multicoloured	3·00	85

(Des E. Poell. Litho)

1983 (5 May). 450th Anniv of Beer Purity Law. P 14.

2029	**740** 80pf. multicoloured	3·00	85

741 Concord

742 Children crossing Road

(Des R. Schlecht. Eng H.-J. Fuchs. Recess and litho)

1983 (5 May). 300th Anniv of First German Settlers in America. P 14.

2030	**741** 80pf. multicoloured	3·00	85

(Des L. Fromm. Litho)

1983 (14 July). Children and Road Traffic. P 14.

2031	**742** 80pf. multicoloured	3·00	85

743 Flags forming Car

744 Otto Warburg (after Oberland)

(Des E. Nitsche. Litho)

1983 (14 July). 50th International Motor Show, Frankfurt-am-Main. P 14.

2032	**743** 60pf. multicoloured	1·50	60

(Des Elisabeth von Janota-Bzowski. Photo)

1983 (11 Aug). Birth Centenary of Otto Warburg (physiologist and chemist). P 14.

2033	**744** 50pf. multicoloured	1·70	85

745 Wieland (after G. B. Bosio)

746 Rosette in National Colours

(Des Elisabeth von Janota-Bzowski. Litho)

1983 (11 Aug). 250th Birth Anniv of Cristoph Martin Wieland (writer). P 14.

2034	**745** 80pf. multicoloured	2·30	85

(Des J. Spohn. Photo)

1983 (11 Aug). Tenth Anniv of United Nations Membership. P 14.

2035	**746** 80pf. multicoloured	3·25	85

747 Das Rauhe Haus and Children

748 Surveying Maps

1983 (11 Aug). 150th Anniv of Das Rauhe Haus (children's home, Hamburg). P 14.

2036	**747** 80pf. multicoloured	2·50	85

(Des E. Jünger. Litho)

1983 (11 Aug). International Geodesy and Geophysics Union General Assembly, Hamburg. P 14.

2037	**748** 120pf. multicoloured	3·00	1·00

GERMANY/German Federal Republic

749 Swiss Androsace
750 Horseman with Posthorn 
757 Mendel and Genetic Diagram
758 Town Hall

(Des Karin Blume. Litho)
1983 (13 Oct). Humanitarian Relief Funds. Endangered Alpine Flowers. T **749** and similar vert designs. Multicoloured. P 14.
2038	50pf. +20pf. Type **749**	85	85
2039	60pf. +30pf. Krain Groundsel	1·20	1·20
2040	80pf. +40pf. Fleischer's Willow Herb	2·20	2·20
2041	120pf. +60pf. Alpine Sow-thistle	3·25	3·25
2038/2041	Set of 4	6·75	6·75

(Des P. Steiner. Litho)
1983 (13 Oct). Stamp Day. P 14.
2042	**750**	80pf. multicoloured	2·50	85

751 Luther (engraving by G. König after Cranach)
752 Interwoven National Colours 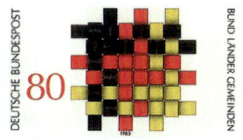

(Des Elisabeth von Janota-Bzowski. Litho)
1983 (13 Oct). 500th Birth Anniv of Martin Luther (Protestant reformer). P 14.
2043	**751**	80pf. multicoloured	4·25	85

(Des K. Ganzenmüller. Litho)
1983 (10 Nov). Federation, Länder and Communities Co-operation. P 14.
2044	**752**	80pf. multicoloured	2·75	80

753 Customs Stamps
754 Epiphany Carol Singers 

(Des U. Hoffmann. Litho)
1983 (10 Nov). 150th Anniv of German Customs Union. P 14.
2045	**753**	60pf. multicoloured	2·75	55

(Des P. Steiner. Litho)
1983 (10 Nov). Christmas. P 14.
2046	**754**	80pf. +40pf. multicoloured	2·75	2·20

755 Black Gate, Trier
756 Reis and Telephone Apparatus 

(Des O. Rohse. Recess and litho)
1984 (12 Jan). 2000th Anniv of Trier. P 14.
2047	**755**	80pf. multicoloured	3·00	80

(Des Elisabeth von Janota-Bzowski. Litho)
1984 (12 Jan). 150th Birth Anniv of Philipp Reis (telephone pioneer). P 14.
2048	**756**	80pf. multicoloured	3·00	80

(Des Elisabeth von Janota-Bzowski. Litho)
1984 (12 Jan). Death Centenary of Gregor Mendel (geneticist). P 14.
2049	**757**	50pf. multicoloured	1·80	55

(Des H. Burkert. Litho)
1984 (16 Feb). 500th Anniv of Michelstadt Town Hall. P 14.
2050	**758**	60pf. multicoloured	1·80	55

759 Cloth draped on Cross
760 Trichodes apiarus 

(Des G. Jacki, Photo)
1984 (16 Feb). 350th Anniv of Oberammergau Passion Play. P 14.
2051	**759**	60pf. multicoloured	1·80	55

(Des E. Nitsche. Litho)
1984 (12 Apr). Youth Welfare. Pollinating Insects. T **760** and similar vert designs. Multicoloured. P 14.
2052	50pf. +20pf. Type **760**	95	95
2053	60pf. +30pf. *Vanessa atalanta*	1·80	1·80
2054	80pf. +40pf. *Apis mellifera*	2·30	2·30
2055	120pf. +60pf. *Chrysotoxum festivium*	3·75	3·75
2052/2055	Set of 4	8·00	8·00

761 Throwing the Discus
762 Parliament Emblem 

(Des F. Kefer and P. Münch. Litho)
1984 (12 Apr). Sport Promotion Fund. T **761** and similar horiz designs. Multicoloured. P 14.
2056	60pf. +30pf. Type **761**	2·40	1·80
2057	80pf. +40pf. Rhythmic gymnastics	3·00	2·75
2058	120pf. +60pf. Windsurfing	5·50	4·75
2056/2058	Set of 3	9·75	8·25

(Des E. Poell. Litho)
1984 (12 Apr). Second Direct Elections to European Parliament. P 14.
2059	**762**	80pf. greenish yellow, dull ultramarine and cobalt	3·75	95

763 Bridge
764 St. Norbert (sculpture) 

(Des J. Larrivière. Photo)
1984 (8 May). Europa. 25th Anniv of European Post and Telecommunications Conference. P 14.
2060	**763**	60pf. ultramarine, violet-blue and black	2·30	70
2061		80pf. deep reddish purple, dull rose and black	2·30	70

GERMANY/ German Federal Republic

(Des B. K. Wiese. Photo)
1984 (8 May). 850th Death Anniv of St. Norbert von Xanten. P 14.
2062 764 80pf. yellowish green and deep green ... 2·30 85

765 Nursery Rhyme Illustration
766 Cross and Shadow 

(Des Marina Langer-Rosa and H. Langer. Recess)
1984 (8 May). Death Centenary of Ludwig Richter (illustrator). P 14.
2063 765 60pf. black and reddish brown .... 1·50 55

(Des H. G. Schmitz. Litho)
1984 (8 May). 50th Anniv of Protestant Churches' Barmen Theological Declaration. P 14.
2064 766 80pf. multicoloured .... 2·30 85

767 Letter sorting, 1800s
768 Groom leading Horse (detail from tomb of Oclatius) 

(Des E. Nitsche and H.-P. Hoch. Litho)
1984 (19 June). 19th Universal Postal Union Congress, Hamburg. Sheet 138×104 mm containing T **767** and similar square designs. P 14.
MS2065 60pf. light brown and black; 80pf. multicoloured; 120pf. yellow-olive, black and grey... 6·50 5·25
Designs:—60pf. T **767**; 80pf. Modern automatic letter sorting machine scanning device; 120pf. Heinrich von Stephan (founder of UPU).

(Des R. Lederbogen. Eng E. Falz. Recess and litho)
1984 (19 June). 2000th Anniv of Neuss. P 14.
2066 768 80pf. multicoloured .... 2·30 85

769 Bessel
770 Eugenio Pacelli (Pope Pius XII) 

(Des H. Schwahn. Eng H.-J. Fuchs. Recess and litho)
1984 (19 June). Birth Bicentenary of Friedrich Wilhelm Bessel (astronomer and mathematician). P 14.
2067 769 80pf. brownish grey, black and scarlet ... 2·30 85

(Des G. Aretz. Photo)
1984 (19 June). 88th German Catholics' Congress, Munich. P 14.
2068 770 60pf. multicoloured .... 1·90 55

771 Town Hall
772 Medieval Document and Visual Display Unit 

(Des Isolde Monson-Baumgart. Litho)
1984 (21 Aug). 750th Anniv of Duderstadt Town Hall. P 14.
2069 771 60pf. multicoloured .... 1·70 55

(Des Elisabeth von Janota-Bzowski. Litho)
1984 (21 Aug). Tenth International Archive Congress, Bonn. P 14.
2070 772 70pf. multicoloured .... 2·20 85

773 Merchant Ship, Knoop Lock
774 Research Centre and Storage Rings 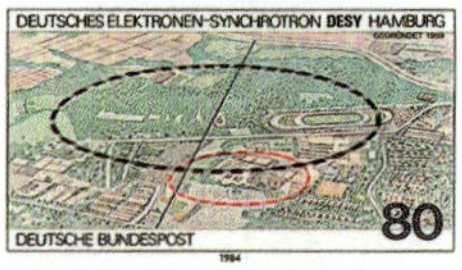

(Des W. P. Seiter. Litho)
1984 (21 Aug). Bicentenary of Schleswig-Holstein Canal. P 14.
2071 773 80pf. multicoloured .... 2·50 85

(Des E. Nitsche. Photo)
1984 (21 Aug). 25th Anniv of German Electron Synchrotron (physics research centre), Hamburg-Bahrenfeld. P 14.
2072 774 80pf. multicoloured .... 3·00 85

775 Aceras anthropophorum
776 Taxis Posthouse, Augsburg 

(Des G. Jacki. Litho)
1984 (18 Oct). Humanitarian Relief Funds. Orchids. T **775** and similar horiz designs. Multicoloured. P 14.
2073 50pf. +20pf. Type **775** .... 1·30 1·30
2074 60pf. +30pf. *Orchis ustulata* .... 1·30 1·30
2075 80pf. +40pf. *Limodorum abortivum* .... 2·00 2·00
2076 120pf. +60pf. *Dactylorhiza sambucina* .... 4·25 4·25
2073/2076 Set of 4 .... 8·00 8·00

(Des Dorothea Fischer Nosbisch. Litho)
1984 (8 Nov). Stamp Day. P 14.
2077 776 80pf. multicoloured .... 3·00 85

777 Burning Match
778 Male and Female Symbols 

(Des N. Vogel. Litho A. Bagel, Düsseldorf)
1984 (8 Nov). Anti-smoking Campaign. P 14.
2078 777 60pf. multicoloured .... 2·00 55

(Des H. Tröger. Photo)
1984 (8 Nov). Equal Rights for Men and Women. P 14.
2079 778 80pf. black, magenta and light blue ...... 2·50 85

779 Ballot Slip
780 St. Martin giving Cloak to Beggar 

(Des Corinna Ludwig. Litho)
1984 (8 Nov). For Peace and Understanding. P 14.
2080 779 80pf. pale olive-grey, black and deep blue .... 2·00 85

(Des P. Steiner. Litho)
1984 (8 Nov). Christmas. P 14.
2081 780 80pf. +40pf. multicoloured .... 2·30 2·20

GERMANY / German Federal Republic

781 Emperor Augustus (bust), Buildings and Arms

782 Spener (engraving by Batholome Kilian after J. G. Wagner)

789 Hebel and the Margravine

790 Draisienne Bicycle, 1817

(Des H. J. Volbracht. Litho A. Bagel, Düsseldorf)

1985 (10 Jan). 2000th Anniv of Augsburg. P 14.
2082 **781** 80pf. multicoloured .... 2·50 70

(Des G. Jacki. Litho)

1985 (10 Jan). 350th Birth Anniv of Philipp Jakob Spener (church reformer). P 14.
2083 **782** 80pf. black and blue-green .... 2·30 85

783 Grimm Brothers (engraving by Lazarus Sichling)

784 Romano Guardini

(Des Elisabeth von Janota-Bzowski. Litho)

1985 (10 Jan). Birth Bicentenaries of Grimm Brothers (folklorists) and Seventh International Union for German Linguistics and Literature Congress, Göttingen. P 14.
2084 **783** 80pf. black, deep bluish grey and scarlet .... 3·00 85

(Des G. Aretz. Litho)

1985 (10 Jan). Birth Centenary of Romano Guardini (theologian). P 14.
2085 **784** 80pf. multicoloured .... 2·30 85

785 Verden

786 Flags and German–Danish Border

(Des P. Steiner. Litho)

1985 (21 Feb). Millenary of Market and Coinage Rights in Verden. P 14.
2086 **785** 60pf. multicoloured .... 3·25 55

(Des E. Jünger. Litho)

1985 (21 Feb). 30th Anniv of Bonn-Copenhagen Declarations. P 14.
2087 **786** 80pf. multicoloured .... 3·50 1·10

787 Bowling

788 Kisch

(Des. F.-D. Rothacker. Photo)

1985 (21 Feb). Sport Promotion Fund. T **787** and similar horiz design. Multicoloured. P 14.
2088   80pf. +40pf. Type **787** (centenary of German Nine-pin Bowling Association) .... 2·30 2·00
2089   120pf. +60pf. Kayak (world rapid-river and slalom canoeing championships) .... 3·75 3·25

(Des A. Ade. Litho)

1985 (16 Apr). Birth Centenary of Egon Erwin Kisch (journalist). P 14.
2090 **788** 60pf. multicoloured .... 1·90 55

(Des Elisabeth von Janota-Bzowski. Litho)

1985 (16 Apr). 225th Birth Anniv of Johann Peter Hebel (poet). P 14.
2091 **789** 80pf. multicoloured .... 2·00 85

(Des H. Schillinger. Litho)

1985 (16 Apr). Youth Welfare. International Youth Year. Cycles. T **790** and similar horiz designs. Multicoloured. P 14.
2092   50pf. +20pf. Type **790** .... 1·50 1·40
2093   60pf. +30pf. NSU Germania ordinary, 1866 .... 1·70 1·70
2094   80pf. +40pf. Cross-frame low bicycle 1887 .... 2·30 2·20
2095   120pf. +60pf. Adler tricycle, 1888 .... 4·75 4·50
2092/2095 Set of 4 .... 9·25 8·75

791 Handel

792 Saint George's Cathedral

(Des K.-H. Walter. Photo)

1985 (7 May). Europa. Composers' 300th Birth Anniversaries. T **791** and similar vert design. Multicoloured. P 14.
2096   60pf. Type **791** .... 3·25 70
2097   80pf. Bach .... 3·25 70

(Des H. Schillinger. Litho)

1985 (7 May). 750th Anniv of Limburg Cathedral. P 14.
2098 **792** 60pf. multicoloured .... 1·70 85

793 Capital (presbytery, Wies Church)

794 Josef Kentenich

(Des E. Nitsche. Photo)

1985 (7 May). 300th Birth Anniv of Dominikus Zimmermann (architect). P 14.
2099 **793** 70pf. multicoloured .... 2·00 85

(Des F. Lüdtke. Litho)

1985 (7 May). Birth Centenary of Father Josef Kentenich (founder of International Schönstatt (Catholic laymen's) Movement). P 14.
2100 **794** 80pf. multicoloured .... 2·00 85

795 Clock and Forest

796 Tug of War and Scouting Emblem

(Des K. Ganzenmüller. Litho)

1985 (16 July). Save the Forests. P 14.
2101 **795** 80pf. multicoloured .... 3·25 85

(Des F. Lüdtke. Litho)

1985 (16 July). 30th World Scouts Conference, Munich. P 14.
2102 **796** 60pf. multicoloured .... 2·00 85

GERMANY/ German Federal Republic

797 *Sunday Walk*

798 *Horses and Postilion*

(Des F. Lüdtke. Litho)
1985 (13 Aug). Death Centenary of Carl Spitzweg (artist). P 14.
2103   797   60pf. multicoloured .... 3·00   85

(Des H. Schillinger. Litho)
1985 (13 Aug). Mophila 1985 Stamp Exhibition, Hamburg. T **798** and similar horiz design. Multicoloured. P 14.
2104   60pf. +20pf. Type **798** .... 4·25   3·50
   a. Horiz pair. Nos. 2104/2105 .... 8·75   7·25
2105   80pf. +20pf. Mail coach .... 4·25   3·50
Nos. 2104/2105 were issued together in horizontal *se-tenant* pairs within the sheet, each pair forming a composite design.

799 *Stock Exchange*

800 *Flowers and Butterfly*

(Des F. Kefer and L. Münch. Litho)
1985 (13 Aug). 400th Anniv of Frankfurt Stock Exchange. P 14.
2106   799   80pf. black, orange-red and greenish slate .... 2·50   85

(Des H. Börnsen. Litho)
1985 (15 Oct). Humanitarian Relief Funds. T **800** and similar horiz designs depicting motifs from borders of medieval prayer book. Multicoloured. P 14.
2107   50pf. +20pf. Type **800** .... 1·60   1·10
2108   60pf. +30pf. Flowers, bird and butterfly .... 1·70   1·40
2109   80pf. +40pf. Flowers, berries and snail .... 2·00   1·80
2110   120pf. +60pf. Flowers, snail and butterfly .... 3·50   3·25
2107/2110 Set of 4 .... 8·00   6·75

801 *Fritz Reuter*

802 *Inauguration of First German Railway* (Heim)

(Des P. Steiner. Litho)
1985 (15 Oct). 175th Birth Anniv of Fritz Reuter (writer). P 14.
2111   801   80pf. black, brownish grey and royal blue .... 3·50   85

(Des H. Schillinger. Litho)
1985 (12 Nov). 150th Anniv of German Railways and Birth Bicentenary of Johannes Scharrer (joint founder). P 14.
2112   802   80pf. multicoloured .... 3·50   85

803 *Carpentry Jointing National Colours*

804 *Iron Cross and National Colours*

(Des K. Przewieslik. Litho)
1985 (12 Nov). 40th Anniv of Integration of Refugees. P 14.
2113   803   80pf. multicoloured .... 3·25   85

(Des B. K. Wiese. Litho)
1985 (12 Nov). 30th Anniv of Federal Armed Forces. P 14.
2114   804   80pf. bright rose-red, black and lemon .. 5·00   85

805 *Nativity* (detail, High Altar, Freiburg)

806 *Early and Modern Cars*

(Des F. Lüdtke. Litho)
1985 (12 Nov). Christmas. 500th Birth Anniv of Hans Baldung Grien (artist). P 14.
2115   805   80pf. +40pf. multicoloured .... 2·75   2·75

(Des H. Schillinger. Litho)
1986 (16 Jan). Centenary of Motor Car. P 14.
2116   806   80pf. multicoloured .... 3·50   85

807 *Town Buildings*

808 *Self-portrait*

(Des F. Lüdtke. Litho A. Bagel, Düsseldorf)
1986 (13 Feb). 1250th Anniv of Bad Hersfeld. P 14.
2117   807   60pf. multicoloured .... 2·00   85

(Des B. K. Wiese. Litho)
1986 (13 Feb). Birth Centenary of Oskar Kokoschka (artist and writer). P 14.
2118   808   80pf. black, pale grey and scarlet .... 2·00   85

809 *Comet and* Giotto *Space Probe*

810 *Running*

(Des E. Jünger. Photo)
1986 (13 Feb). Appearance of Halley's Comet. P 14.
2119   809   80pf. multicoloured .... 3·50   1·00

(Des H. P. Hoch. Litho)
1986 (13 Feb). Sport Promotion Fund. T **810** and similar horiz design. Multicoloured. P 14.
2120   80pf. +40pf. Type **810** (European Athletics Championships, Stuttgart .... 3·00   2·75
2121   120pf. +55pf. Bobsleigh (World Championships, Königsee) .... 4·25   4·25

811 *Optician*

812 *Walsrode Monastery*

(Des H. Schillinger. Litho)
1986 (10 Apr). Youth Welfare. Trades (1st series). T **811** and similar horiz designs. Multicoloured. P 14.
2122   50pf. +25pf. Type **811** .... 1·90   1·80
2123   60pf. +30pf. Bricklayer .... 2·20   2·10
2124   70pf. +35pf. Hairdresser .... 2·50   2·40
2125   80pf. +40pf. Baker .... 3·25   3·00
2122/2125 Set of 4 .... 8·75   8·25
See also Nos. 2179/2182.

(Des O. Rohse. Eng W. Maurer. Recess and litho)
1986 (5 May). Millenary of Walsrode. P 14.
2126   812   60pf. multicoloured .... 2·30   85

104

GERMANY/ German Federal Republic

813 Ludwig and Neuschwanstein Castle
814 Mouth 

(Des Antonia Graschberger. Litho)
1986 (5 May). Death Centenary of King Ludwig II of Bavaria. P 14.
2127   813   60pf. multicoloured .... 4·00   85

(Des H. G. Schmitz. Photo)
1986 (5 May). Europa. T **814** and similar horiz design showing details of *David* (sculpture) by Michelangelo. Multicoloured. P 14.
2128   60pf. Type **814** .... 2·20   70
2129   80pf. Nose .... 2·20   70

815 Karl Barth
816 Ribbons 

(Des H. Schwahn. Recess)
1986 (5 May). Birth Centenary of Karl Barth (theologian). P 14.
2130   815   80pf. black, scarlet and bright purple ..... 2·50   85

(Des W. Rogger. Litho)
1986 (5 May). Union of German Catholic Students' Societies 100th Assembly, Frankfurt-am-Main. P 14.
2131   816   80pf. multicoloured .... 2·50   85

817 Weber and Score of *Gloria*
818 TV-Sat and Earth 

(Des G. Gamroth. Litho)
1986 (20 June). Birth Bicentenary of Carl Maria von Weber (composer). P 14.
2132   817   80pf. chestnut, black and rosine .... 3·50   85

(Des Sibylle and F. Haase. Litho)
1986 (20 June). Launch of German *TV-Sat* and French *TDF-1* Broadcasting Satellites. P 14.
2133   818   80pf. multicoloured .... 3·75   1·00

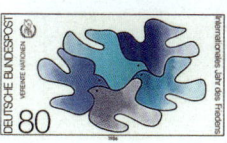

819 Doves
820 Liszt 

(Des J. Lenica. Litho)
1986 (20 June). International Peace Year. P 14.
2134   819   80pf. multicoloured .... 3·25   85

(Des F.-D. Rothacker. Litho)
1986 (20 June). Death Centenary of Franz Liszt (composer). P 14.
2135   820   80pf. deep violet-blue and orange-red ..... 3·25   85

821 Reichstag, Berlin

(Des N. Vogel. Litho)
1986 (20 June). Important Buildings in West German History. Sheet 100×130 mm containing T **821** and similar horiz designs. Multicoloured. P 14.
MS2136 80pf. Type **821**; 80pf. Koenig Museum, Bonn (venue of 1948-49 Parliamentary Council); 80pf. Bundeshaus, Bonn (parliamentary building) .... 7·25   6·75

822 Pollution Damage of Stained Glass Window

(Des F. Lüdtke. Litho)
1986 (14 Aug). Protection of Monuments. P 14.
2137   822   80pf. multicoloured .... 3·75   85

823 Frederick the Great (after Anton Graff)
824 Congress Card 

(Des Elisabeth von Janota-Bzowski. Litho)
1986 (14 Aug). Death Bicentenary of Frederick the Great. P 14.
2138   823   80pf. multicoloured .... 5·00   85

(Des Erna de Vries. Litho)
1986 (14 Aug). Centenary of First German Skat Congress and 24th Congress, Cologne. P 14.
2139   824   80pf. multicoloured .... 3·50   85

825 Opposing Arrows
826 Old University 

(Des Michaela Graml. Embossed and litho)
1986 (14 Aug). 25th Anniv of Organisation for Economic Co-operation and Development. P 14.
2140   825   80pf. multicoloured .... 2·50   85

(Des O. Rohse. Eng W. Mauer. Recess and litho)
1986 (16 Oct). 600th Anniv of Heidelberg University. P 14.
2141   826   80pf. multicoloured .... 3·00   85

827 Fan of Stamps behind Stagecoach
828 Ornamental Flask, 300 AD 

(Des Antonia Graschberger. Litho)
1986 (16 Oct). 50th Anniv of Stamp Day. P 14.
2142   827   80pf. multicoloured .... 3·00   85

(Des P. Steiner. Litho)
1986 (16 Oct). Humanitarian Relief Funds. Glassware. T **828** and similar vert designs. Multicoloured. P 14.
2143   50pf. +25pf. Type **828** .... 1·30   1·10

105

GERMANY/ German Federal Republic

2144	60pf. +30pf. Goblet with decorated stem, 1650	1·70	1·50
2145	70pf. +35pf. Imperial Eagle tankard, 1662......	2·00	1·70
2146	80pf. +40pf. Engraved goblet, 1720...........	2·30	2·10
2143/2146	Set of 4...................................	6·50	5·75

829 Dance in Silence from Autumnal Dances

830 Cross over Map

(Des Karin Blume-Zander. Litho)

1986 (13 Nov). Birth Centenary of Mary Wigman (dancer). P 14.
| 2147 | 829 | 70pf. multicoloured.............................. | 1·90 | 85 |

(Des F. Lüdtke. Photo)

1986 (13 Nov). 25th Anniv of Adveniat (Advent collection for Latin America). P 14.
| 2148 | 830 | 80pf. bright green, blue and black............ | 1·90 | 85 |

831 Adoration of the Infant Jesus (Ortenberg altarpiece)

832 Christine Teusch (politician)

(Des F. Lüdtke. Litho)

1986 (13 Nov). Christmas. P 14.
| 2149 | 831 | 80pf. +40pf. multicoloured.................... | 2·50 | 2·40 |

(Des G. Aretz. Eng W. Mauer (5, 10, 20, 70, 140, 150, 170, 240, 250pf.), H.-J. Fuchs (30, 130, 200, 350pf.), J. Kanior (40, 60, 80 (2156a), 100 (2157), 180pf.), J. Kanior and W. Mauer (50pf.), E. Falz and H.-J. Fuchs (80pf. (2156)), Petra Schlumbohm (100pf. (2157a)), E. Falz (120pf.), L. Lück (300, 500pf.). Recess)

1986 (13 Nov)–**94**. Famous German Women. T **832** and similar vert designs. P 14.

2150	5pf. orange-brown and slate (9.2.89)	60	50
2151	10pf. yellow-brown and violet (14.4.88)	85	65
2152	20pf. deep turquoise-blue and carmine-lake (5.5.88)	1·50	70
2152a	30pf. bistre and maroon (8.1.91)	75	55
2153	40pf. crimson and deep ultramarine (17.9.87)	1·50	40
2154	50pf. deep bluish green and olive-brown	1·50	40
2155	60pf. slate-lilac and bronze green (17.9.87)....	1·70	40
2155a	70pf. olive-green and brown-lake (8.1.91).....	2·20	1·10
2156	80pf. red-brown and bottle green	1·70	40
2156a	80pf. brown and deep turquoise-blue (13.10.94).............................	1·60	85
2157	100pf. olive-grey and brown-red (10.11.88) ...	2·20	70
2157a	100pf. olive-bistre and blackish lilac (13.10.94).............................	1·60	85
2158	120pf. brown-olive and chocolate (6.11.87).....	3·00	1·70
2159	130pf. deep violet and Prussian blue (5.5.88) ..	4·25	1·40
2160	140pf. brown-ochre and deep violet-blue (10.8.89)	5·00	2·50
2161	150pf. royal blue and brown-lake (14.2.91).....	5·00	2·50
2162	170pf. deep dull purple and deep olive (10.11.88).............................	3·75	2·10
2163	180pf. maroon and new blue (13.7.89)	4·25	2·10
2164	200pf. brown-red and purple-brown (14.2.91)..	3·75	1·40
2165	240pf. light brown and slate-green (10.11.88)..	5·00	3·50
2166	250pf. royal blue and bright magenta (13.7.89)	7·25	3·50
2167	300pf. deep green and plum (10.8.89)..........	4·25	2·10
2168	350pf. lake-brown and greenish black (10.11.88).............................	8·00	4·25
2168a	400pf. black and lake (9.1.92)................	8·75	6·25
2168b	450pf. deep ultramarine and greenish blue (11.6.92)	9·50	7·00
2169	500pf. brown-red and brown-olive (12.1.89) ...	9·50	5·50
2150/2169	Set of 26	90·00	48·00

Designs:—5pf. Emma Ihrer (politician and trade unionist); 10pf. Paula Modersohn-Becker (painter); 20pf. Cilly Aussem (tennis player); 30pf. Käthe Kollwitz (artist); 40pf. Maria Sibylla Merian (artist and naturalist); 50pf. T **832**; 60pf. Dorothea Erxleben (first German woman Doctor of Medicine); 70pf. Elisabet Boehm (founder of Agricultural Association of Housewives); 80pf. (2156) Clara Schumann (pianist and composer); 80pf. (2156a) Rahel Varnhagen von Ense (humanist) (after Wilhelm Hensel); 100pf. (2157) Therese Giehse (actress); 100pf. (2157a) *Luisa Henriette of Orange* (mother of King Friedrich I of Prussia) (after Gerhard von Honthorst); 120pf. Elisabeth Selbert (politician); 130pf. Lise Meitner (physicist); 140pf. Cécile Vogt (medical researcher); 150pf. Sophie Scholl (resistance member); 170pf. Hannah Arendt (sociologist); 180pf. Lotte Lehmann (opera singer); 200pf. Bertha von Suttner (novelist and pacifist); 240pf. Mathilde Franziska Anneke (women's rights activist); 250pf. Queen Louise of Prussia; 300pf. *Fanny Hensel* (composer) (after Eduard Magnus); 350pf. Hedwig Dransfeld (politician); 400pf. Charlotte von Stein (friend of Goethe); 450pf. Hedwig Courths-Mahler (novelist); 500pf. Alice Salomon (women's rights activist).

Postal forgeries of the 100pf. (No. 2157a) exist. These can be identified by irregular corners and a patchy blue reaction under UV light.

See also Nos. 2785/2789.

For similar designs, but in Euros, see Nos. 3017/3020 and 3190/3193.

833 Berlin Landmarks

(Des P. Steiner. Litho)

1987 (15 Jan). 750th Anniv of Berlin. P 14.
| 2170 | 833 | 80pf. multicoloured........................... | 3·50 | 1·10 |

834 Staircase, Residenz Palace, Würzburg

835 Ludwig Erhard

(Des H. Schwahn. Photo)

1987 (15 Jan). 30th Birth Anniv of Balthasar Neumann (architect). P 14.
| 2171 | 834 | 80pf. light grey, brownish black and vermillion .... | 3·00 | 85 |

(Des G. Aretz. Photo)

1987 (15 Jan). 90th Birth Anniv of Ludwig Erhard (former Chancellor). P 14.
| 2172 | 835 | 80pf. multicoloured........................... | 3·50 | 70 |

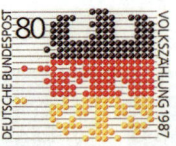

836 Abacus Beads forming Eagle

837 Clemenswerth Castle

(Des B. K. Wiese. Litho)

1987 (15 Jan). Census. P 14.
| 2173 | 836 | 80pf. multicoloured........................... | 3·25 | 85 |

(Des Sibylle and F. Haase. Litho)

1987 (12 Feb). 250th Anniv of Clemenswerth Castle. P 14.
| 2174 | 837 | 60pf. multicoloured........................... | 2·50 | 85 |

838 Chief Winnetou (from book cover)

839 Solar Spectrum

106

GERMANY / German Federal Republic

(Des Helga Regenstein. Photo)
1987 (12 Feb). 75th Death Anniv of Karl May (writer). P 14.
2175   838   80pf. multicoloured .... 2·75   85

(Des E. Kößlinger. Recess and litho)
1987 (12 Feb). Birth Bicentenary of Joseph von Fraunhofor (optician and physicist). P 14.
2176   839   80pf. multicoloured .... 2·50   85

840 Racing Yachts, World Sailing Championships, Kiel
841 Clefs, Notes and Leaves 

(Des H. P. Hoch. Litho)
1987 (12 Feb). Sport Promotion Fund. T **840** and similar horiz design. Multicoloured. P 14.
2177   80pf. +40pf. Type **840** .... 2·50   2·40
2178   120pf. +55pf. Skiers, World Nordic Skiing Championships, Oberstdorf .... 4·00   4·00

(Des H. Schillinger. Litho)
1987 (9 Apr). Youth Welfare. Trades (2nd series). Horiz designs as T **811**. Multicoloured. P 14.
2179   50pf. +25pf. Plumber .... 2·20   2·00
2180   60pf. +30pf. Dental technician .... 2·50   2·40
2181   70pf. +35pf. Butcher .... 3·00   2·50
2182   80pf. +40pf. Bookbinder .... 4·00   3·75
2179/2182 Set of 4 .... 10·50   9·50

(Des P. Steiner. Litho)
1987 (9 Apr). 125th Anniv of German Choir Association. P 14.
2183   841   80pf. multicoloured .... 2·50   85

842 Pope's Arms, Madonna and Child, and Kevelaer

(Des Antonia Graschberger. Litho)
1987 (9 Apr). Visit of Pope John Paul II to Kevelaer (venue for 17th Marian and tenth Mariological Congresses). P 14.
2184   842   80pf. multicoloured .... 3·25   85

843 Dülmen's Wild Horses
844 German Pavilion, International Exhibition, Barcelona, 1929 (Ludwig Mies van der Rohe) 

(Des R. Lüdtke. Photo)
1987 (5 May). European Environment Year. P 14.
2185   843   60pf. multicoloured .... 3·25   85

(Des B. K. Wiese. Litho State Ptg Wks, Berlin (60pf.), Schwann-Bagel, Düsseldorf (80pf.))
1987 (5 May). Europa. Architecture. T **844** and similar horiz design. Multicoloured. P 14.
2186   60pf. Type **844** .... 2·30   70
2187   80pf. Köhlbrand Bridge, Hamburg (Thyssen Engineering) .... 3·00   70

845 Emblem and Globe
846 Without Title (with an Early Portrait) 

(Des H. Stelzer. Litho)
1987 (5 May). Rotary International Convention, Munich. P 14.
2188   845   70pf. ultramarine, greenish yellow and new blue .... 2·30   85

(Des Karin Blume-Zander. Litho)
1987 (5 May). Birth Centenary of Kurt Schwitters (artist and writer). P 14.
2189   846   80pf. multicoloured .... 2·30   85

847 Organ Pipes and Signature
848 Bengel 

(Des G. Jacki. Litho)
1987 (5 May). 350th Birth Anniv of Dietrich Buxtehude (composer). P 14.
2190   847   80pf. brownish black, stone and bright scarlet .... 1·90   85

(Des H. Schall. Photo)
1987 (5 May). 300th Birth Anniv of Johann Albrecht Bengel (theologian). P 14.
2191   848   80pf. lake-brown, yellow-ochre and black .... 2·20   85

849 Kaisen
850 Charlemagne, Bishop Willehad, Bremen Cathedral and City Arms (after mural) 

(Des G. Aretz. Litho)
1987 (5 May). Birth Centenary of Wilhelm Kaisen (Senate president and Mayor of Bremen). P 14.
2192   849   80pf. multicoloured .... 2·30   85

(Des F.-D. Rothacker. Litho)
1987 (16 July). 1200th Anniv of Bremen Bishopric. P 14.
2193   850   80pf. multicoloured .... 2·20   85

851 Target, Crossed Rifles and Wreath
852 4th-century Roman Bracelet 

(Des P. Steiner. Litho)
1987 (20 Aug). Seventh European Riflemen's Festival, Lippstadt. P 14.
2194   851   80pf. multicoloured .... 2·20   85

(Des F. Lüdtke. Litho)
1987 (15 Oct). Humanitarian Relief Funds. Precious Metal Work. T **852** and similar horiz designs. Multicoloured. P 14.
2195   50pf. +25pf. Type **852** .... 2·20   2·10
2196   60pf. +30pf. 6th-century East Gothic buckle.. 2·20   2·10
2197   70pf. +35pf. 7th-century Merovingian disc fibula .... 2·20   2·10

GERMANY/German Federal Republic

2198	80pf. +40pf. 8th-century reliquary	3·00	2·75
2195/2198	Set of 4	8·75	8·25

853 Loading and Unloading Mail Train, 1887

854 Corner Tower, Celle Castle

(Des Elisabeth von Janota-Bzowski. Litho)

1987 (15 Oct). Stamp Day. P 14.

2199	853	80pf. multicoloured	2·20	1·50

(Des Sibylle and F. Haase. Litho)

1987 (6 Nov)–**96**. Tourist Sights. T **854** and similar vert designs. Inscr 'DEUTSCHE BUNDESPOST'. P 14.

2200	5pf. turquoise-blue and grey (15.2.90)	60	50
2201	10pf. cobalt and indigo (14.1.88)	85	35
	a. Perf 3 sides. Booklets (6.89)	75	50
	ab. Booklet pane. Nos. 2201a×4 (at left), 2208a×2 (in middle) and 2211a×2 (6.89)	9·75	
	ac. Booklet pane. Nos. 2201a×2, 2209a×2, 2211a×2 and 2213a×2 (6.89)	17·00	
	ad. Booklet pane. As ab. but Nos. 2201a (in middle) and 2208a (at left) (11.93)	9·75	
	ae. Booklet pane. Nos. 2201a×4, 2208a×2, 2211a×2, 2213a×2 (14.8.96)	18·00	
2202	20pf. flesh and Prussian blue (12.1.89)	80	50
	a. Perf 3 sides. Booklets (24.3.93)	3·50	3·50
	ab. Booklet pane. Nos. 2202a×2 and 2211a×2 (24.3.93)	11·00	
	ac. Booklet pane. Nos. 2202a×2, 2208a×2, 2211a×2 and 2213a×2 (9.11.94)	22·00	
2203	30pf. chestnut and greenish-green	1·30	40
2204	33pf. turquoise-green and Venetian red (12.1.89)	85	55
2205	38pf. drab and greenish blue (12.1.89)	1·50	85
2206	40pf. chocolate, dull scarlet and ultramarine (11.8.88)	1·10	85
2206a	41pf. drab and lemon (12.8.93)	1·30	70
2207	45pf. flesh and turquoise-blue (21.6.90)	85	70
2208	50pf. ochre and ultramarine	1·30	40
	a. Perf 3 sides. Booklets (6.89)	1·50	1·10
2209	60pf. dull blue-green and greenish black	1·50	40
	a. Perf 3 sides. Booklets (6.89)	1·50	1·40
2210	70pf. flesh and Prussian blue (14.7.88)	1·60	40
2210a	70pf. chestnut and dull violet-blue (21.6.90)	85	55
2211	80pf. brownish grey and deep bluish green	1·50	40
	a. Perf 3 sides. Booklets (6.89)	1·70	1·70
2212	90pf. olive-bistre and bistre-yellow (11.8.88)	3·25	3·50
2213	100pf. blue-green and dull orange (9.2.89)	4·25	55
	a. Perf 3 sides. Booklets (6.89)	4·00	2·75
	ab. Booklet pane. No. 2213a×10 (5.5.95)	41·00	
2214	120pf. turquoise-green and Venetian red (14.7.88)	3·00	1·30
2215	140pf. olive-bistre and bistre-yellow (12.1.89)	3·50	1·10
2216	170pf. drab and lemon (4.6.91)	3·50	1·40
2216a	200pf. blue and ochre (15.4.93)	4·00	1·30
2217	280pf. drab and greenish blue (11.8.88)	7·25	6·00
2218	300pf. flesh and red-brown (14.1.88)	5·00	85
2219	350pf. drab and deep ultramarine (9.2.89)	5·75	1·10
2220	400pf. carmine-lake and cinnamon (10.10.91)	6·50	1·10
2220a	450pf. chalky blue and chestnut (13.8.92)	7·25	2·10
2220b	500pf. stone and brown-purple (17.6.93)	8·00	2·50
2220c	550pf. chestnut and dull violet-blue (11.8.94)	9·25	4·25
2220d	700pf. grey-olive and greenish yellow (16.9.93)	11·50	4·25
2200/2220d	Set of 28 (cheapest)	90·00	36·00

Designs:—5pf. Brunswick Lion; 10pf. Frankfurt airport; 20, 70pf. (2210) Head of Nefertiti, Berlin Museum; 30pf. T **854**; 33, 120pf. Schleswig Cathedral; 38, 280pf. Statue of Roland, Bremen; 40pf. Chile House, Hamburg; 41, 170pf. Russian Church, Wiesbaden; 45pf. Rastatt Castle; 50pf. Freiburg Cathedral; 60pf. *Bavaria* (bronze statue), Munich; 70pf. (2210a) Heligoland; 80pf. Zollern II Dortmund Mine Industrial Museum, Westphalia; 90, 140pf. Bronze flagon, Reinheim; 100pf. Pilgrimage Chapel, Altötting; 200pf. Magdeburg Cathedral; 300pf. Hamback Castle; 350pf. Externsteine (rock formation), Horn-Bad Meinberg; 400pf. Dresden Opera House; 450pf. New Gate, Neubrandenburg; 500pf. Cottbus State Theatre; 550pf. Suhl-Heinrichs Town Hall, Thuringia; 700pf. National Theatre, Berlin.

Nos. 2200/20d were each issued both in sheets and in coils, the latter having every fifth stamp numbered on the back.

No. 2202ab must have margin attached at one side to distinguish it from a block removed from No. 2202ac.

Postal forgeries exist for several values; the gum and paper are more yellow and the printing less sharp than the genuine, and the reaction under a UV lamp is greenish white rather than yellow. Forged examples of the 100pf. show the 'R' of 'WALLFAHRTSKAPELLE' with straight, instead of diagonal, right leg.

For 10, 60, 80 and 100pf. self-adhesive and die cut, see Nos. 2377/2380.

For similar design inscribed 'DEUTSCHLAND', see Nos. 2654/66.

855 Gluck and Score of *Armide*

856 Poster by Emil Orlik for *The Weavers*

(Des H. Schwahn. Eng J. Kanior. Recess and litho)

1987 (6 Nov). Death Bicentenary of Christoph Willibald Gluck (composer). P 14.

2221	855	60pf. black, brownish grey and brown-lake	1·70	70

(Des R. Schwarz. Litho)

1987 (6 Nov). 125th Birth Anniv of Gerhart Hauptmann (playwright). P 14.

2222	856	80pf. dull scarlet, black and bright scarlet	2·50	85

857 Paddy Field

858 Birth of Christ (13th-century Book of Psalms)

(Des U. Amann. Photo)

1987 (6 Nov). 25th Anniv of German Famine Aid. P 14.

2223	857	80pf. multicoloured	2·50	85

(Des F. Lüdtke. Litho)

1987 (6 Nov). Christmas. P 14.

2224	858	80pf. +40pf. multicoloured	2·50	2·50

859 Jester

860 Jakob Kaiser

(Des G. Jacki. Litho)

1988 (14 Jan). 150th Anniv of Mainz Carnival. P 14.

2225	859	60pf. multicoloured	2·00	85

(Des G. Aretz. Eng W. Mauer. Recess and litho)

1988 (14 Jan). Birth Centenary of Jakob Kaiser (trade unionist and politician). P 14.

2226	860	80pf. black and pale bluish grey	1·90	85

861 Stein and Mayer

(Des Margret Fackelmann. Photo)

1988 (14 Jan). Beatification of Edith Stein and Father Rupert Mayer. P 14.

2227	861	80pf. multicoloured	2·00	85

GERMANY/ German Federal Republic

862 Dr. Konrad Adenauer (West German Chancellor) and Charles de Gaulle (French President)

(Des J.P. Véret-Lemarinier. Eng E. Falz. Recess)
1988 (14 Jan). 25th Anniv of Franco-German Co-operation Treaty. P 14.
2228   862   80pf. deep dull purple and grey-black ......   3·00   1·10

863 Solitude of the Green Woods (woodcut of poem, Ludwig Richter)

864 Raiffeisen and Ploughed Field

(Des Isolde Monson-Baumgart. Litho)
1988 (18 Feb). Birth Bicentenary of Joseph von Eichendorff (writer). P 14.
2229   863   60pf. multicoloured ....   2·00   85

(Des S. Förtsch-von Baumgarten and H. Förtsch. Litho)
1988 (18 Feb). Death Centenary of Friedrich Wilhelm Raiffeisen (philanthropist and agricultural co-operative founder). P 14.
2230   864   80pf. bright green and black ....   3·00   85

865 A. Schopenhauer

866 Football (European Championship)

(Des Elisabeth von Janota-Bzowski. Photo)
1988 (18 Feb). Birth Bicentenary of Arthur Schopenhauer (philosopher). P 14.
2231   865   80pf. red-brown and black ....   2·50   85

(Des H. G. Schmitz. Litho)
1988 (18 Feb). Sport Promotion Fund. T **866** and similar horiz designs. Multicoloured. P 14.
2232   60pf. +30pf. Type 866 ....   3·00   2·40
2233   80pf. +40pf. Tennis (Olympic Games) ......   4·25   3·50
2234   120pf. +55pf. Diving (Olympic Games) ....   5·00   4·25
2232/2234   Set of 3...   11·00   9·25

867 Buddy Holly

868 Hutten (wood engraving from Conquestiones)

(Des Antonia Graschberger. Litho)
1988 (14 Apr). Youth Welfare. Pop Music. T **867** and similar horiz designs. Multicoloured. P 14.
2235   50pf. +25pf. Type 867 ....   2·20   2·50
2236   60pf. +30pf. Elvis Presley ....   5·00   4·25
2237   70pf. +35pf. Jim Morrison ....   2·50   2·75
2238   80pf. +40pf. John Lennon ....   4·75   4·00
2235/2238   Set of 4...   13·00   12·00

(Des H. Stelzer. Eng J. Kanior. Recess and litho)
1988 (14 Apr). 500th Birth Anniv of Ulrich von Hutten (writer). P 14.
2239   868   80pf. multicoloured ....   2·00   1·00

869 City Buildings and Jan Wellem Monument

(Des Karin Blume-Zander. Litho Schwann-Bagel, Düsseldorf)
1988 (5 May). 700th Anniv of Düsseldorf. P 14.
2240   869   60pf. multicoloured ....   2·30   85

870 Airbus Industrie A320 and Manufacturing Nations' Flags

871 University Buildings and City Landmarks

(Des E. Jönger. Litho)
1988 (5 May). Europa. Transport and Communications. T **870** and similar horiz design. Multicoloured. P 14.
2241   60pf. Type 870 ....   2·00   85
2242   80pf. Diagram of Integrated Services Digital Network ....   2·00   85

(Des O. Rohse. Litho)
1988 (5 May). 600th Anniv of Cologne University. P 14.
2243   871   80pf. multicoloured ....   2·00   85

872 Jean Monnet

873 Theodor Storm

(Des G. Aretz. Litho)
1988 (5 May). Birth Centenary of Jean Monnet (statesman). P 14.
2244   872   80pf. multicoloured ....   2·00   85

(Des G. Jacki. Litho)
1988 (5 May). Death Centenary of Theodor Storm (writer). P 14.
2245   873   80pf. multicoloured ....   2·00   85

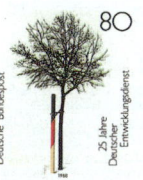

874 Tree supported by Stake in National Colours

875 Meersburg

(Des B. K. Wiese. Litho)
1988 (5 May). 25th Anniv of German Volunteer Service. P 14.
2246   874   80pf. multicoloured ....   2·00   85

(Des Isolde Monson-Baumgart. Litho Schwann-Bagel, Düsseldorf)
1988 (14 July). Millenary of Meersburg. P 14.
2247   875   60pf. multicoloured ....   1·70   85

109

GERMANY/ German Federal Republic

876 Leopold Gmelin

877 Vernier Caliper Bulb in National Colours

(Des H. Schwahn. Eng E. Faiz. Recess and litho)
1988 (14 July). Birth Bicentenary of Leopold Gmelin (chemist). P 14.
2248   876   80pf. multicoloured .... 1·90   85

(Des E. Jünger. Litho)
1988 (14 July). Made in Germany. P 14.
2249   877   140pf. multicoloured .... 3·50   1·70

878 August Bebel

879 Carrier Pigeon

(Des H. G. Schmitz. Photo)
1988 (11 Aug). 75th Death Anniv of August Bebel (Social Democratic Labour Party co-founder). P 14.
2250   878   80pf. magenta, dull ultramarine and silver .... 2·50   85

(Des P. Steiner. Litho)
1988 (13 Oct). Stamp Day. P 14.
2251   879   20pf. multicoloured .... 1·20   70

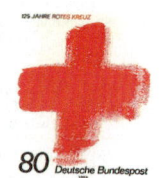

880 13th-century Rock Crystal Reliquary

881 Red Cross

(Des F. Lüdtke. Litho)
1988 (13 Oct). Humanitarian Relief Funds. Precious Metal Work. T **880** and similar square designs. Multicoloured. P 14.
2252   50pf. +25pf. Type **880** .... 1·20   1·10
2253   60pf. +30pf. 14th-century bust of Charlemagne .... 1·70   1·70
2254   70pf. +35pf. 10th-century crown of Otto III ... 1·70   1·70
2255   80pf. +40pf. 17th-century jewelled flowers .... 2·50   2·50
2252/2255 Set of 4 .... 6·50   6·25

(Des J. Wilke. Eng W. Mauer. Recess and litho)
1988 (13 Oct). 125th Anniv of Red Cross. P 14.
2256   881   80pf. bright scarlet and black .... 2·50   85

882 Burning Synagogue, Baden-Baden

883 Cancelled Postage Stamps

(Des F. Lüdtke. Photo)
1988 (13 Oct). 50th Anniv of Kristallnacht (Nazi pogrom). P 14.
2257   882   80pf. slate-purple and black .... 1·90   85

(Des E. Poell. Litho Schwann-Bagel, Düsseldorf)
1988 (10 Nov). Centenary of Collection of Used Stamps for the Bethel Charity. P 14.
2258   883   60pf. multicoloured .... 2·00   85

884 Linked Arms

885 *Adoration of the Magi* (illustration from *Henry the Lion's Gospel Book*)

(Des Corinna Rogger. Litho Schwann-Bagel, Düsseldorf)
1988 (10 Nov). Centenary of Samaritan Workers' (first aid) Association. P 14.
2259   884   80pf. multicoloured .... 2·00   85

(Des Silvia Runge. Litho)
1988 (10 Nov). Christmas. P 14.
2260   885   80pf. +40pf. multicoloured .... 2·50   2·20

886 *Bluxao I*

(Des H. Burkert. Litho)
1989 (12 Jan). Birth Centenary of Willi Baumeister (painter). P 14.
2261   886   60pf. multicoloured .... 1·90   85

887 Bonn

(Des P. Steiner. Litho)
1989 (12 Jan). 2000th Anniv of Bonn. P 14.
2262   887   80pf. multicoloured .... 3·00   1·30

888 Grass growing from Dry, Cracked Earth

889 *Cats in the Attic* (woodcut)

(Des W. Rogger. Photo)
1989 (12 Jan). 30th Anniversaries of Misereor and Bread for the World (Third World relief organisations). P 14.
2263   888   80pf. multicoloured .... 2·20   85

(Des G. Jacki. Litho)
1989 (9 Feb). Birth Centenary of Gerhard Marcks (artist). P 14.
2264   889   60pf. black, stone and bright scarlet .... 1·90   85

890 Table Tennis (World Championships)

891 Elephants

(Des H. P. Hoch. Litho)
1989 (9 Feb). Sport Promotion Fund. T **890** and similar horiz designs. Multicoloured. P 14.
2265   100pf. +50pf. Type **890** .... 3·25   3·00
2266   140pf. +60pf. Gymnastics (World Championships) .... 5·00   4·75

110

GERMANY / German Federal Republic

(Des E. Kößlinger. Litho)
1989 (20 Apr). Youth Welfare. Circus. T **891** and similar horiz designs. Multicoloured. P 14.
2267	60pf. +30pf. Type **891**	3·00	2·75
2268	70pf. +30pf. Acrobat on horseback	3·75	3·50
2269	80pf. +35pf. Clown	5·00	4·25
2270	100pf. +50pf. Caravans and Big Top	7·25	5·00
2267/2270 Set of 4		17·00	14·00

892 Posthorn and Book of Stamps

893 European and Members' Flags

(Des Antonia Graschberger. Litho)
1989 (20 Apr). IPHLA '89 International Philatelic Literature Exhibition, Frankfurt. P 14.
| 2271 | **892** 100pf. +50pf. multicoloured | 5·00 | 4·50 |

The premium was for the benefit of the Foundation for Promotion of Philately and Postal History.

(Des B. K. Wiese. Litho Schwann-Bagel, Düsseldorf)
1989 (20 Apr). Third Direct Elections to European Parliament. P 14.
| 2272 | **893** 100pf. multicoloured | 3·75 | 1·70 |

894 *Tsurumi Maru* (tanker), Tug, Fireboat and *Rickmer Rickmers* (full-rigged ship)

895 Asam (detail of fresco, Weltenburg Abbey)

(Des W. P. Seiter. Litho)
1989 (5 May). 800th Anniv of Hamburg Harbour. P 14.
| 2273 | **894** 60pf. multicoloured | 2·50 | 85 |

(Des E. Kößlinger. Litho)
1989 (5 May). 250th Death Anniv of Cosmas Damian Asam (painter and architect). P 14.
| 2274 | **895** 60pf. multicoloured | 1·50 | 85 |

896 Kites

(Des Erna de Vries. Litho)
1989 (5 May). Europa. Children's Toys. T **896** and similar horiz design. Multicoloured. P 14.
| 2275 | 60pf. Type **896** | 2·20 | 65 |
| 2276 | 100pf. Puppet show | 3·00 | 70 |

897 Emblem, National Colours and Presidents' Signatures

(Des E. Jünger. Photo)
1989 (5 May). 40th Anniv of German Federal Republic. P 14.
| 2277 | **897** 100pf. multicoloured | 3·50 | 1·30 |

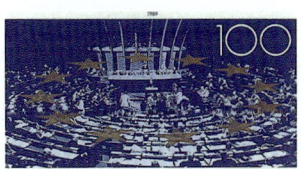

898 Council Assembly and Stars

(Des Margit Zauner. Photo)
1989 (5 May). 40th Anniv of Council of Europe. P 14.
| 2278 | **898** 100pf. dull ultramarine and gold | 3·25 | 1·40 |

899 Gabelsberger and Shorthand

900 Score of *Lorelei* and Silhouette of Silcher

(Des B. K. Wiese. Litho)
1989 (5 May). Birth Bicentenary of Franz Xaver Gabelsberger (shorthand pioneer). P 14.
| 2279 | **899** 100pf. multicoloured | 3·25 | 1·00 |

(Des R. Meyn. Litho)
1989 (15 June). Birth Bicentenary of Friedrich Silcher (composer). P 14.
| 2280 | **900** 80pf. multicoloured | 1·90 | 85 |

901 Saints Kilian, Totnan and Colman (from 12th-century German manuscript)

(Des P. Effert. Litho)
1989 (15 June). 1300th Death Anniversaries of Saints Kilian, Colman and Totnan (Irish missionaries to Franconia). P 14.
| 2281 | **901** 100pf. multicoloured | 3·00 | 1·20 |

A stamp of a similar design was issued by Ireland.

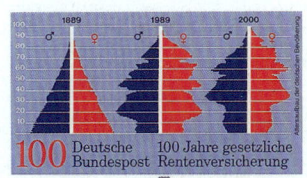

902 Age Graphs of Men and Women

(Des E. Poell. Litho)
1989 (15 June). Centenary of National Insurance. P 14.
| 2282 | **902** 100pf. bright new blue, bright scarlet and cobalt | 2·75 | 1·10 |

903 *Summer Evening* (Heinrich Vogler)

(Des Sybille and F. Haase. Litho)
1989 (13 July). Centenary of Worpswede Artists' Village. P 14.
| 2283 | **903** 60pf. multicoloured | 1·70 | 90 |

GERMANY / German Federal Republic

904 Paul Schneider

905 List (after Kriehuber) and 19th-century Train

(Des G. Jacki. Photo)
1989 (13 July). 50th Death Anniv of Reverend Paul Schneider (concentration camp victim). P 14.
2284   904   100pf. black, grey and olive-grey .... 2·30   1·10

(Des D. von Andrian. Eng J. Kanior. Recess)
1989 (13 July). Birth Bicentenary of Friedrich List (economist). P 14.
2285   905   170pf. black and scarlet .... 4·75   1·80

906 Cathedral

907 Children building House

(Des E. Kößlinger. Litho)
1989 (10 Aug). 750th Anniv of Frankfurt Cathedral. P 14.
2286   906   60pf. multicoloured .... 2·20   90

(Des L. Fromm. Litho)
1989 (10 Aug). Don't Forget the Children. P 14.
2287   907   100pf. multicoloured .... 2·75   1·10

908 Ammonite and Union Emblem

909 18th-century Mounted Courier, Thurn and Taxis

(Des E. Poell. Litho Schwann-Bagel, Düsseldorf)
1989 (10 Aug). Centenary of Mining and Power Industries Trade Union. P 14.
2288   908   100pf. multicoloured .... 2·20   1·10

(Des P. Steiner. Litho)
1989 (12 Oct). Humanitarian Relief Funds. Postal Deliveries. T **909** and similar square designs. Multicoloured. P 14.
2289   60pf. +30pf. Type 909 .... 2·30   2·10
2290   80pf. +35pf. Postal messenger, Hamburg, 1808 .... 4·00   3·00
2291   100pf. +50pf. Bavarian mail coach, 1900 .... 5·50   4·75
2289/2291 Set of 3 .... 10·50   8·75

910 Maier

911 Organ Pipes

(Des G. Aretz. Litho)
1989 (12 Oct). Birth Centenary of Reinhold Maier (politician). P 14.
2292   910   100pf. multicoloured .... 2·75   1·10

(Des P. Steiner. Litho Schwann-Bagel, Düsseldorf)
1989 (16 Nov). 300th Anniv of Arp Schnitger Organ, St. James's Church, Hamburg. P 14.
2293   911   60pf. multicoloured .... 2·20   90

912 Angel

913 Speyer

(Des H. Stelzer. Litho)
1989 (16 Nov). Christmas. 16th-century Carvings by Veit Stoss, St. Lawrence's Church, Nüremberg. T **912** and similar square design. Multicoloured. P 14.
2294   60pf. +30pf. Type 912 .... 2·50   2·10
2295   100pf. +50pf. Nativity .... 3·00   2·75

(Des P. Steiner. Litho)
1990 (12 Jan). 2000th Anniv of Speyer. P 14.
2296   913   60pf. multicoloured .... 2·20   90

914 Courier Albrecht Dürer

915 Vine forming Initial 'R'

(Eng J. Kanior. Recess and litho)
1990 (12 Jan). 500th Anniv of Regular European Postal Services. P 14.
2297   914   100pf. chocolate, pale cinnamon and grey-brown .... 4·00   1·20

(Des E. Kößlinger. Litho)
1990 (12 Jan). 500 Years of Riesling Grape Cultivation. P 14.
2298   915   100pf. multicoloured .... 2·20   1·20

916 Old Lübeck

917 15th-century Seal and Grand Master's Arms

(Des O. Rohse. Eng W. Mauer. Recess and litho)
1990 (12 Jan). UNESCO. World Heritage Site. Old Lübeck. P 14.
2299   916   100pf. multicoloured .... 2·75   1·20

(Des F. Lüdtke. Litho)
1990 (15 Feb). 800th Anniv of Teutonic Order. P 14×13½.
2300   917   100pf. multicoloured .... 3·00   1·20

918 Frederick II's Seal and Fair Entrance Hall

919 Maze

(Des H. G. Schmitz. Litho Schwann-Bagel, Düsseldorf)
1990 (15 Feb). 750th Anniv of Granting of Fair Privileges to Frankfurt. P 14.
2301   918   100pf. multicoloured .... 3·00   1·20

(Des F. Lüdtke. Litho)
1990 (15 Feb). 25th Anniv of Youth Research Science Competition. P 14.
2302   919   100pf. multicoloured .... 3·00   1·20

GERMANY/ German Federal Republic

920 Wildlife

(Des K. Przewieslik. Litho)
1990 (15 Feb). North Sea Protection. P 14.
2303   920   100pf. multicoloured .... 3·75   1·20

921 Handball   **922** Widow Bolte

(Des G. Aretz. Litho)
1990 (15 Feb). Sport Promotion Fund. T **921** and similar horiz design. Multicoloured. P 14.
2304   100pf. +50pf. Type **921** .... 5·00   3·00
2305   140pf. +60pf. Keep-fit .... 6·00   4·50

(Des H. Schillinger. Litho)
1990 (19 Apr). Youth Welfare. 125th Anniv of Max and Moritz (characters from books by Wilhelm Busch). T **922** and similar horiz designs. Multicoloured. P 14.
2306   60pf. +30pf. Type **922** .... 1·70   1·70
2307   70pf. +30pf. Max asleep .... 2·50   2·40
2308   80pf. +35pf. Moritz watching Max sawing through bridge .... 3·50   3·00
2309   100pf. +50pf. Max and Moritz .... 4·00   3·75
2306/2309 Set of 4 .... 10·50   9·75

923 '1.MAI' and Factory Silhouette   **924** Woman's Face

(Des H. P. Hoch. Photo)
1990 (19 Apr). Centenary of Labour Day. P 14.
2310   923   100pf. vermilion and black .... 2·50   1·20

(Des E. Poell. Litho)
1990 (19 Apr). 75th Anniv of German Association of Housewives. P 14.
2311   924   100pf. multicoloured .... 2·50   1·20

925 Collection Box   **926** Thurn and Taxis Palace, Frankfurt

(Des Sibylle and F. Haase. Litho)
1990 (3 May). 125th Anniv of German Lifeboat Institution. P 14.
2312   925   60pf. multicoloured .... 2·20   1·10

(Des K. Przewieslik. Litho)
1990 (3 May). Europa. Post Office Buildings. T **926** and similar horiz design. Multicoloured. P 14.
2313   60pf. Type **926** .... 2·50   85
2314   100pf. Postal Giro Office, Frankfurt .... 2·75   90

927 St. Philip's Church, Protestant Church Flag and Candle Flames   **928** Wilhelm Leuschner

(Des W. P. Seiter. Litho Schwann-Bagel, Düsseldorf)
1990 (3 May). Centenary of Rummelsberg Diaconal Institution. P 14.
2315   927   100pf. multicoloured .... 2·20   1·20

(Des G. Aretz. Recess and litho)
1990 (3 May). Birth Centenary of Wilhelm Leuschner (trade unionist and member of anti-Hitler Resistance). P 14.
2316   928   100pf. black and grey-lilac .... 3·00   1·20

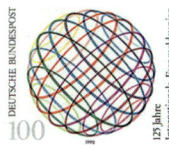

929 Globe   **930** National Colours and Students

(Des Marina Langer-Rosa and H. Langer. Litho)
1990 (3 May). 125th Anniv of International Telecommunications Union. P 14.
2317   929   100pf. multicoloured .... 2·50   1·20

(Des P. Effert. Recess and litho)
1990 (3 May). 175th Anniv of German Students' Fraternity and of their Colours (now National Colours). P 14.
2318   930   100pf. multicoloured .... 3·00   1·20

931 Hands exchanging Money and Goods

(Des P. Effert. Litho)
1990 (21 June). 30th World Congress of International Chamber of Commerce, Hamburg. P 14.
2319   931   80pf. multicoloured .... 2·20   1·50

932 Closing Sentence of Charter

(Des F. Lüdtke. Photo)
1990 (21 June). 40th Anniv of Expelled Germans Charter. P 14.
2320   932   100pf. multicoloured .... 2·75   1·10

933 Children of Different Races

(Des H. Ullmann. Litho)
1990 (21 June). Tenth International Youth Philatelic Exhibition, Düsseldorf. Sheet 165×101 mm. P 14.
MS2321   933   100pf.+50pf.×6 multicoloured .... 34·00   38·00
The premium was for the benefit of the Foundation for the Promotion of Philately and Postal History.

934 Matthias Claudius   **935** Mail Motor Wagon, 1900

113

GERMANY/ German Federal Republic

(Des F. Lüdtke. Litho)
1990 (9 Aug). 250th Birth Anniv of Matthias Claudius (writer). P 14.
2322 934 100pf. Prussian blue, black and bright crimson .... 2·75 90

(Des P. Steiner. Litho)
1990 (27 Sept). Humanitarian Relief Funds. Posts and Telecommunications. T **935** and similar square designs. Multicoloured. P 14.
2323 60pf. +30pf. Type **935** .... 1·70 1·70
2324 80pf. +35pf. Telephone exchange, 1890.......... 2·75 2·75
2325 100pf. +50pf. Parcel sorting office, 1900 .... 4·00 4·00
2323/2325 Set of 3.................. 7·50 7·50

B. GERMANY REUNIFIED

On 3 October 1990 the former territory of the Democratic Republic (East Germany) was absorbed into the Federal Republic. From this date separate issues for West Berlin and East Germany ceased.

936 'German Unity' and National Colours
937 H. Schliemann and Lion Gate, Mycenae 

(Des P. Effert. Litho Schwann-Bagel, Düsseldorf (50pf.), State Ptg Wks, Berlin (100pf.))
1990 (3 Oct). Reunification of Germany. P 14.
2326 **936** 50pf. black, orange-vermilion and lemon 2·30 75
2327 100pf. black, orange-vermilion and lemon 3·00 1·10

(Des E. Jünger. Litho)
1990 (11 Oct). Death Centenary of Heinrich Schliemann (archaeologist). P 14.
2328 **937** 60pf. multicoloured .... 2·50 90

938 Penny Black, Bavaria 1k. and West Germany 1989 100pf. Stamps
939 National Colours spanning Breach in Wall 

(Des Silvia Runge. Litho Schwann-Bagel, Düsseldorf)
1990 (11 Oct). Stamp Day. 150th Anniv of the Penny Black. P 14.
2329 **938** 100pf. multicoloured .... 2·75 90

(Des M. Gottschall. Litho (MS2332), photo (others) German Bank Note Ptg Co, Leipzig)
1990 (6 Nov). First Anniv of Opening of Berlin Wall. T **939** and similar vert design. P 14.
2330 50pf. Type **939** .... 2·30 1·40
2331 100pf. Brandenburg Gate and crowd .... 3·75 1·40
MS2332 146×100 mm. As Nos. 2330/2331 .... 7·00 6·25

940 Angel with Candles
941 Käthe Dorsch in *Mrs. Warren's Profession* 

(Des H. Schillinger. Litho)
1990 (6 Nov). Christmas. T **940** and similar square designs. Multicoloured. P 14.
2333 50pf. +20pf. Type **940** .... 1·60 1·50
2334 60pf. +30pf. Figure of man smoking .... 1·90 1·80
2335 70pf. +30pf. 'Soldier' nutcrackers .... 2·50 2·40
2336 100pf. +50pf. Tinsel Angel .... 4·00 3·75
2333/2336 Set of 4 .... 9·00 8·50

(Des Ursula Kahrl. Photo)
1990 (6 Nov). Birth Centenary of Käthe Dorsch (actress). P 14.
2337 **941** 100pf. bluish violet and rosine .... 2·75 1·20

942 View of City
943 Three Golden Circles with a Full Circle in Blue (relief in wood) 

(Des P. Steiner. Litho)
1991 (8 Jan). 750th Anniv of Hanover. P 14.
2338 **942** 60pf. multicoloured .... 2·20 90

(Des S. Denkhaus. Photo)
1991 (8 Jan). Birth Centenary of Erich Buchholz (artist). P 14.
2339 **943** 60pf. multicoloured .... 1·90 90

944 Miniature from 13th-century French Code
945 Brandenburg Gate (from Old Engravings of Berlin) 

(Des B. K. Wiese. Litho)
1991 (8 Jan). 750th Anniv of Promulgation of Pharmaceutical Ethics in Germany. P 14.
2340 **944** 100pf. multicoloured .... 3·00 1·20

(Des Antonia Graschberger. Eng H–J. Fuchs. Recess and litho)
1991 (8 Jan). Bicentenary of Brandenburg Gate. P 14.
2341 **945** 100pf. blue-black, brown-lake and brownish grey .... 3·50 90

946 Walter Eucken
947 Globe and '25' (poster) 

(Des H. G. Schmitz. Litho)
1991 (8 Jan). Birth Centenary of Walter Eucken (economist). P 14.
2342 **946** 100pf. multicoloured .... 2·75 1·20

(Des B. Görs. Litho)
1991 (8 Jan). 25th International Tourism Fair, Berlin. P 14.
2343 **947** 100pf. multicoloured .... 2·75 90

948 Two-man Bobsleigh
949 Weightlifting (World Championships) 

(Des L. Grünewald. Litho German Bank Note Ptg Co, Leipzig)
1991 (8 Jan). World Bobsleigh Championships, Altenberg. Sheet 55×80 mm. P 12½×13.
MS2344 **948** 100pf. multicoloured .... 3·75 4·50

114

(Des Karin Blume-Zander. Litho)
1991 (14 Feb). Sport Promotion Fund. T **949** and similar square designs. Multicoloured. P 14.
2345	70pf. +30pf. Type **949**	3·00	3·00
2346	100pf. +50pf. Cycling (world championships) ..	3·00	3·00
2347	140pf. +60pf. Basketball (centenary)	4·75	4·50
2348	170pf. +80pf. Wrestling (European championships)	4·75	4·50
2345/2348	*Set of* 4...	14·00	13·50

950 Title Page of *Cautio Criminalis* (tract against witch trials), Langenfeld and Score of *Trutz-Nachtigall*

951 Androsace

(Des Antonia Graschberger. Litho Schwann-Bagel, Düsseldorf)
1991 (14 Feb). 400th Birth Anniv of Friedrich Spee von Lagenfeld (poet and human rights pioneer). P 14.
2349   **950**   100pf. multicoloured .... 2·75   90

(Des Hannelore Heise. Litho German Bank Note Ptg Co, Leipzig)
1991 (12 Mar). Plants in Rennsteiggarten (botanical garden), Oberhof. T **951** and similar square designs. Multicoloured. P 13.
2350	30pf. Type **951**	80	75
2351	50pf. Primula..	1·10	1·10
2352	80pf. Gentian	1·90	75
2353	100pf. Cranberry	2·75	90
2354	350pf. Edelweiss	7·75	6·00
2350/2354	*Set of* 5	13·00	8·50

952 Werth (attr. Wenzel Hollar)

953 Ludwig Windthorst

(Des Elisabeth von Janota-Bzowski. Litho)
1991 (12 Mar). 400th Birth Anniv of Jan von Werth (military commander). P 14.
2355   **952**   60pf. multicoloured .... 1·90   90

(Des G. Aretz. Litho)
1991 (12 Mar). Death Centenary of Ludwig Windthorst (politician). P 14.
2356   **953**   100pf. multicoloured .... 2·75   90

954 Junkers F-13, 1930

955 *Colias phicomone*

(Des J. Bertholdt. Photo German Bank Note Ptg Co, Leipzig)
1991 (9 Apr). Historic Mail Aircraft. T **954** and similar horiz designs. Multicoloured. P 14.
2357	30pf. Type **954**	80	75
2358	50pf. Hans Grade's monoplane, 1909	1·10	75
2359	100pf. Fokker F.111, 1922...............................	3·00	75
2360	165pf. Airship LZ-127 *Graf Zeppelin*	4·75	4·25
2357/2360	*Set of* 4	8·75	5·75

(Des H. Schillinger. Litho)
1991 (9 Apr). Youth Welfare. Endangered Butterflies. T **955** and similar square designs. Multicoloured. P 14.
2361	30pf. +15pf. Type **955**	80	75
2362	50pf. +25pf. *Limenitis populi*	95	90
2363	60pf. +30pf. *Apatura iris*	1·90	1·80
2364	70pf. +30pf. *Lycaena helle*	2·00	2·00
2365	80pf. +35pf. *Papilio machaon*	2·50	2·40
2366	90pf. +45pf. *Parnassius phoebus*	3·00	3·00
2367	100pf. +50pf. *Colias palaeno*	4·00	3·75
2368	140pf. +60pf. *Lycaena dispar*	4·75	5·25
2361/2368	*Set of* 8..	18·00	18·00

See also Nos. 2449/2453.

956 Academy Building, 1830

957 Typesetting School, 1875

(Des F.-D. Rothacker. Recess and litho)
1991 (9 Apr). Bicentenary of Choral Academy, Berlin. P 14.
2369   **956**   100pf. multicoloured .... 2·75   1·20

(Des B. Görs. Photo)
1991 (9 Apr). 125th Anniv of Lette Foundation (institute for professional training of women). P 14.
2370   **957**   100pf. multicoloured .... 2·75   1·00

958 Battle (detail of miniature, *Schlackenwerth Codex*, 1350)

959 Arms

(Des F. Lüdtke. Recess and litho)
1991 (9 Apr). 750th Anniv of Battle of Legnica. P 14.
2371   **958**   100pf. multicoloured .... 3·00   1·80
A stamp of a similar design was issued by Poland.

(Des B. K. Wiese. Litho)
1991 (2 May). 700th Anniv of Granting of Charters to Six Towns of Trier. P 14.
2372   **959**   60pf. multicoloured .... 1·90   90

960 Speeding Train

961 *ERS-1* European Remote Sensing Satellite

(Des Sibylle and F. Haase. Litho)
1991 (2 May). Inauguration of Inter-City Express (ICE) Railway Service. P 14.
2373   **960**   60pf. multicoloured .... 1·90   90

(Des F. Lüdtke. Litho)
1991 (2 May). Europa. Europe in Space. T **961** and similar square design. Multicoloured. P 14.
2374	60pf. Type **961**	2·30	75
2375	100pf. *Kopernikus* telecommunications satellite	4·00	75

962 Max Reger and Organ Pipes

963 Ruffs

(Des E. Jünger. Litho Schwann-Bagel, Düsseldorf)
1991 (2 May). 75th Death Anniv of Max Reger (composer). P 14.
2376   **962**   100pf. multicoloured .... 3·00   90

GERMANY

(Des Sibylle and F. Haase. Litho)

1991 (4 June). Tourist Sights. Booklet stamps. As Nos. 2201, 2209, 2211 and 2213 but self-adhesive. Die-cut.

2377	10pf. dull blue and indigo	4·00	3·75
2378	60pf. dull blue-green and slate-green	4·00	3·75
2379	80pf. brownish grey and blue-green	4·00	3·75
2380	100pf. blue-green and orange-yellow	4·00	3·75
2377/2380	Set of 4	14·50	13·50

The individual stamps are peeled directly from the booklet cover and it is not therefore possible to collect these as booklet panes.

Nos. 2381/9 are vacant.

(Des J. Riess. Litho)

1991 (4 June). Seabirds. T **963** and similar vert designs. Multicoloured. P 14.

2390	60pf. Type **963**	1·60	90
2391	80pf. Little Terns	2·30	1·50
2392	100pf. Brent Geese	2·30	1·50
2393	140pf. White-tailed Sea Eagles	4·25	3·75
2390/2393	Set of 4	9·50	7·00

964 Wilhelm August Lampadius (gas pioneer)

(Des D. Glinski. Litho German Bank Note Ptg Co, Leipzig)

1991 (4 June). 18th World Gas Congress, Berlin. T **964** and similar horiz design, each black and light turquoise-blue. P 13×12½.

2394	60pf. Type **964**	2·00	90
	a. Horiz strip. Nos. 2394/2395 plus label	4·50	1·90
2395	100pf. Gas street lamp, Berlin	2·00	90

Nos. 2394/5 were issued together se-tenant with an intervening half stamp-size label bearing the Congress emblem.

965 Paul Wallot (after Franz Würbel) and Reichstag Building, Berlin

966 *Libellula depressa*

(Des B. Görs. Recess and litho)

1991 (4 June). 150th Birth Anniv of Paul Wallot (architect). P 14.

2396	**965** 100pf. multicoloured	3·00	90

(Des L. Grünewald. Photo German Bank Note Ptg Co, Leipzig)

1991 (9 July). Dragonflies. T **966** and similar horiz designs. Multicoloured. P 14.

2397	50pf. Type **966**	1·20	60
2398	60pf. Type **966**	2·30	1·20
	a. Block of 4. Nos. 2398/2401	9·50	
2399	60pf. *Sympetrum sanguineum*	2·30	1·20
2400	60pf. *Cordulegaster boltonii*	2·30	1·20
2401	60pf. *Aeshna viridis*	2·30	1·20
2402	70pf. As No. 2399	1·90	1·50
2403	80pf. As No. 2400	2·00	1·50
2404	100pf. As No. 2401	2·20	1·50
2397/2404	Set of 8	15·00	9·00

Nos. 2398/2401 were issued together in se-tenant blocks of four within the sheet.

967 Hand clutching Cloak

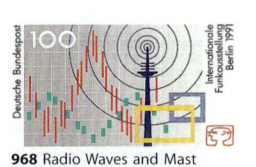

968 Radio Waves and Mast

(Des H. G. Schmitz. Litho)

1991 (9 July). 40th Anniv of Geneva Convention on Refugees. P 14.

2405	**967** 100pf. grey-lilac and grey-black	2·75	90

(Des Antonia Graschberger. Litho)

1991 (9 July). International Radio Exhibition, Berlin. P 14.

2406	**968** 100pf. multicoloured	3·00	90

969 Pedestrians and Traffic

970 Otto Lilienthal

(Des E. Kößlinger. Litho Schwann-Bagel, Düsseldorf)

1991 (9 July). Road Safety Campaign. P 14.

2407	**969** 100pf. multicoloured	3·00	1·20

(Des H. Detlefsen. Litho German Bank Note Ptg Co, Leipzig)

1991 (9 July). Centenary of First Heavier-than-Air Manned Flight by Otto Lilienthal and Lilienthal '91 European Airmail Exhibition, Dresden. Sheet 57×82 mm. P 14.

MS2408	**970** 100pf.+50pf. blackish brown, greenish blue and vermilion	7·00	6·00

971 August Heinrich Hoffmann von Fallersleben (lyricist) and Third Verse

972 Reinold von Thadden-Trieglaff

(Des Antonia Graschberger. Litho)

1991 (8 Aug). 150th Anniv of *Song of the Germans* (National Anthem). P 14.

2409	**971** 100pf. bright crimson, blue-black and brown-olive	2·75	90

(Des G. Aretz. Litho)

1991 (8 Aug). Birth Centenary of Reinold von Thadden-Trieglaff (founder of German Protestant Convention). P 14.

2410	**972** 100pf. multicoloured	2·75	90

973 Transmission Test between Lauffen-am-Neckar and Frankfurt-am-Main

974 Quill Pen and Sword

(Des P. Effert. Litho)

1991 (8 Aug). Centenary of Three-phase Energy Transmission. P 14.

2411	**973** 170pf. multicoloured	4·75	2·30

(Des R.-J. Lehmann. Litho German Bank Note Ptg Co, Leipzig)

1991 (12 Sept). Birth Bicentenary of Theodor Körner (poet). Sheet 55×80 mm containing T **974** and similar vert design. Multicoloured. P 13×12½.

MS2412	60pf. Type **974**; 100pf. Körner	4·75	6·00

975 Hans Albers in *The Winner*

976 Harbour

(Des Ursula Kahrl. Photo)

1991 (12 Sept). Birth Centenary of Hans Albers (actor). P 14.

2413	**975** 100pf. multicoloured	3·75	90

(Des H. Ullmann. Litho)

1991 (12 Sept). 275th Anniv of Rhine-Ruhr Port, Duisburg. P 14.

2414	**976** 100pf. multicoloured	2·75	90

GERMANY

977 Bethel Post Office
978 Postal Delivery in Spreewald Region 

(Des Karin Blume-Zander. Litho)

1991 (10 Oct). Humanitarian Relief Funds. Postal Buildings. T **977** and similar square designs. Multicoloured. P 14.
2415	30pf. +15pf. Type **977**	1·20	1·20
2416	60pf. +30pf. Büdingen post station	1·90	1·80
2417	70pf. +30pf. Stralsund post office	2·30	2·30
2418	80pf. +35pf. Lauscha post office	2·75	2·75
2419	100pf. +50pf. Bonn post office	4·00	3·50
2420	140pf. +60pf. Weilburg post office	5·00	4·50
2415/2420	Set of 6	15·00	14·50

(Des Dorothea Fischer-Nosbisch. Litho)

1991 (10 Oct). Stamp Day. P 14.
2421	**978** 100pf. multicoloured	2·75	90

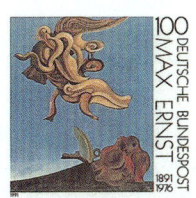

979 Bird Monument (detail)
980 Portrait of the Dancer Anita Berber 

(Des J.-P. Véret-Lemarinier. Litho)

1991 (10 Oct). Birth Centenary of Max Ernst (painter). P 14.
2422	**979** 100pf. multicoloured	2·75	90

A stamp of a similar design was issued by France.

(Des L. Lüders. Photo German Bank Note Ptg Co, Leipzig)

1991 (5 Nov). Birth Centenary of Otto Dix (painter). T **980** and similar vert design. Multicoloured. P 14.
2423	60pf. Type **980**	1·60	90
2424	100pf. *Self-portrait in Right Profile*	3·00	90

981 The Violinist and the Water Sprite
982 Angel (detail of *The Annunciation*) 

(Des Ursula Abramowski-Lautenschläger. Litho German Bank Note Ptg Co, Leipzig)

1991 (5 Nov). Sorbian Legends. T **981** and similar square design. Multicoloured. P 13.
2425	60pf. Type **981**	1·90	90
2426	100pf. *The Midday Woman and the Woman from Nochten*	2·75	90

(Des H. Stelzer. Litho)

1991 (5 Nov). Christmas. T **982** and similar square designs showing works by Martin Schongauer. Multicoloured. P 14.
2427	60pf. +30pf. Type **982**	2·00	1·80
2428	70pf. +30pf. Virgin Mary (detail of *The Annunciation*)	2·50	2·30
2429	80pf. +35pf. Angel (detail of *Madonna in a Rose Garden*)	5·00	4·25
2430	100pf. +50pf. *Nativity*	6·25	5·25
2427/2430	Set of 4	14·00	12·00

983 Julius Leber
984 Nelly Sachs 

(Des Antonia Graschberger. Litho Schwann-Bagel, Düsseldorf)

1991 (5 Nov). Birth Centenary of Julius Leber (politician). P 14.
2431	**983** 100pf. multicoloured	2·75	90

(Des G. Jacki. Litho)

1991 (5 Nov). Birth Centenary of Nelly Sachs (writer). P 14.
2432	**984** 100pf. deep violet and slate-violet	2·75	1·10

985 Mozart
986 Base of William I Monument and City Silhouette 

(Des J. Riess. Litho German Bank Note Ptg Co, Leipzig)

1991 (5 Nov). Death Bicentenary of Wolfgang Amadeus Mozart (composer). Sheet 82×56 mm. P 14.
MS2433	**985** 100pf. slate-lilac and grey-brown	4·75	5·25

(Des J. Bertholdt. Litho German Bank Note Ptg Co, Leipzig)

1992 (9 Jan). 2000th Anniv of Koblenz. P 13×12½.
2434	**986** 60pf. multicoloured	3·50	1·10

No. 2434 was issued on both fluorescent and ordinary paper. (*Price for ordinary paper £55 unused*).

987 Martin Niemöller
988 Child's Eyes 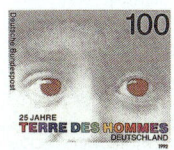

(Des G. Aretz. Litho)

1992 (9 Jan). Birth Centenary of Martin Niemöller (theologian). P 14.
2435	**987** 100pf. multicoloured	2·20	90

(Des Erna de Vries. Litho)

1992 (9 Jan). 25th Anniv of Terre des Hommes (child welfare organisation) in Germany. P 14.
2436	**988** 100pf. multicoloured	3·00	1·20

989 Arms of Baden-Württemberg
990 Fencing 

(Des E. Jünger. Litho)

1992 (9 Jan). Länder of the Federal Republic. P 14.
2437	**989** 100pf. multicoloured	3·00	1·40

For further designs in this series see under entry Arms of Länder in Design Index.

(Des G. Aretz. Litho)

1992 (6 Feb). Sport Promotion Fund. Olympic Games, Albertville and Barcelona. T **990** and similar square designs. Multicoloured. P 14.
2438	60pf. +30pf. Type **990**	2·20	2·10
2439	80pf. +40pf. Rowing eight	2·75	2·50
2440	100pf. +50pf. Dressage	5·50	5·25
2441	170pf. +80pf. Skiing (slalom)	7·75	7·50
2438/2441	Set of 4	16·00	16·00

117

GERMANY

991 Arthur Honegger and Score of Ballet *Semiramis*

992 Zeppelin and LZ-127 *Graf Zeppelin*

(Des F. Lüdtke. Photo German Bank Note Ptg Co, Leipzig)
1992 (6 Feb). Birth Centenary of Arthur Honegger (composer). P 14.
2442 991 100pf. black and grey-brown.................. 3·00 1·40

(Des E. Jünger. Litho).
1992 (6 Feb). 75th Death Anniv of Ferdinand von Zeppelin (airship manufacturer). P 14.
2443 992 165pf. multicoloured............................ 4·75 2·40

993 *Gorch Fock* (cadet barque) and Tug, Kiel City and Harbour

994 Andreas Marggraf, Beet, Franz Achard and Carl Scheibler

(Des P. Korn. Litho Schwann-Bagel, Düsseldorf)
1992 (12 Mar). 750th Anniv of Kiel. P 14.
2444 993 60pf. multicoloured............................ 2·20 1·10

(Des E. Jünger. Litho German Bank Note Ptg Co, Leipzig)
1992 (12 Mar). 125th Anniv of Berlin Sugar Institute. P 13×12½.
2445 994 100pf. multicoloured.......................... 3·00 1·40
The stamp depicts the discoverer of beet sugar, the founder of the beet sugar industry and the founder of the Institute respectively.

995 Horses and Renz

996 Adenauer

(Des Erna de Vries. Photo)
1992 (12 Mar). Death Centenary of Ernst Jakob Renz (circus director). P 14.
2446 995 100pf. multicoloured.......................... 3·00 1·10

(Des H. G. Schmitz. Litho)
1992 (12 Mar). 25th Death Anniv of Konrad Adenauer (Chancellor, 1949–63). P 14×13½.
2447 996 100pf. agate and cinnamon................ 3·75 1·10

(Des E. Jünger. Litho)
1992 (12 Mar). Länder of the Federal Republic. Square design as T **989**. Multicoloured. P 14.
2448   100pf. Bavaria.. 3·00 1·40

(Des H. Schillinger. Litho)
1992 (9 Apr). Youth Welfare. Endangered Moths. Square designs as T **955**. Multicoloured. P 14.
2449   60pf. +30pf. Purple Tiger Moth .... 2·75 2·75
2450   70pf. +30pf. Hawk Moth .... 3·00 3·00
2451   80pf. +40pf. *Noctuidae* sp .... 4·00 4·00
2452   100pf. +50pf. Tiger Moth .... 4·25 4·25
2453   170pf. +80pf. *Arichanna melanaria*..... 5·00 4·75
2449/2453 Set of 5... 17·00 17·00

997 Adam Schall

998 Cathedral and St. Severus's Church

(Des H. Zill. Litho German Bank Note Ptg Co, Leipzig)
1992 (9 Apr). 400th Birth Anniv of Adam Schall (missionary astronomer). P 13×12½.
2454 997 140pf. black, yellow and new blue .... 4·00 2·00

(Des P. Steiner. Litho)
1992 (7 May). 1250th Anniv of Erfurt. P 14.
2455 998 60pf. multicoloured............................ 2·20 1·10

999 Woodcut from 1493 Edition of *Columbus's Letters*

1000 'Consecration of St. Ludgerus' (from *Vita Liudgeri* by Altfridus)

(Des Erna de Vries. Litho)
1992 (7 May). Europa. 500th Anniv of Discovery of America by Columbus. T **999** and similar vert design. Multicoloured. P 14.
2456   60pf. Type **999** .... 2·30 75
2457   100pf. René de Laudonnière and Chief Athore (Jacques le Moyne de Morgues, 1564).. 3·00 85

(Des H. Börnsen. Litho)
1992 (7 May). 1250th Birth Anniv of St. Ludgerus (first Bishop of Münster). P 14.
2458 1000 100pf. multicoloured.......................... 2·75 1·20

1001 Arithmetric Sum

1002 Order of Merit

(Des H. Scheuner. Litho Schwann-Bagel, Düsseldorf)
1992 (7 May). 500th Birth Anniv of Adam Riese (mathematician). P 14.
2459 1001 100pf. multicoloured.......................... 3·00 1·10

(Des P. Effert. Litho German Bank Note Ptg Co, Leipzig)
1992 (7 May). 150th Anniv of Civil Class of Order of Merit (for scientific or artistic achievement). P 13.
2460 1002 100pf. multicoloured.......................... 2·75 1·10

1003 *Landscape with Horse* (Franz Marc)

1004 Lichtenberg

(Des E. Jünger. Litho)
1992 (11 June). 20th-century German Paintings (1st series). T **1003** and similar horiz designs. Multicoloured. P 14.
2461   60pf. Type 1003.................................... 1·60 1·20
2462   100pf. *Fashion Shop* (August Macke)...... 2·30 1·20
2463   170pf. *Murnau with Rainbow* (Wassily Kandinsky) .... 4·00 3·25
2461/2463 Set of 3... 7·00 5·00
See also Nos. 2507/2509, 2590/2592, 2615/2617 and 2704/2706.

(Des G. Aretz. Litho)
1992 (11 June). 250th Birth Anniv of Georg Christoph Lichtenberg (physicist and essayist). P 14.
2464 1004 100pf. multicoloured.......................... 2·75 1·20

(Des E. Jünger. Litho)
1992 (11 June). Länder of the Federal Republic. Square design as T **989**. Multicoloured. P 14.
2465   100pf. Berlin.. 3·00 1·40

GERMANY

1005 Rainforest    **1006** Garden

(Des Sabine Wilhelm. Litho German Bank Note Ptg Co, Leipzig)

1992 (11 June). Save the Tropical Rain Forest. P 13.
2466   **1005** 100pf. +50pf. multicoloured.......................... 3·75   4·00
The premium was for the benefit of environmental projects.

(Des W. Seiter. Litho German Bank Note Ptg Co. Leipzig)

1992 (16 July). Leipzig Botanical Garden. P 13×12½.
2467   **1006** 60pf. multicoloured... 1·90   1·10

1007 Stylised House and Globe    **1008** Family

(Des P. Effert. Photo)

1992 (16 July). 17th International Home Economics Congress, Hanover. P 14.
2468   **1007** 100pf. multicoloured.. 2·75   1·20

(Des J. Riess. Litho)

1992 (16 July). Family Life. P 14.
2469   **1008** 100pf. multicoloured.. 3·00   1·10

(Des E. Jünger. Litho)

1992 (16 July). Länder of the Federal Republic. Multicoloured. Square design as T **989**. P 14.
2470   100pf. Brandenburg .... 3·00   1·40

1009 Assumption of the Virgin Mary (Rohr Monastery Church)   **1010** Opera House (Georg von Knobelsdorff)

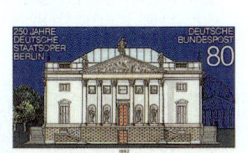

(Des H. Detlefsen. Litho German Bank Note Ptg Co, Leipzig)

1992 (13 Aug). 300th Birth Anniv of Egid Quirin Asam (sculptor). P 14.
2471   **1009** 60pf. multicoloured... 2·30   1·10

(Des E. Jünger. Litho Schwann-Bagel, Düsseldorf)

1992 (13 Aug). 250th Anniv of German State Opera House, Berlin. P 14.
2472   **1010** 80pf. multicoloured... 2·75   1·10

1011 Masked Actors    **1012** Globe

(Des P. Steiner. Litho)

1992 (13 Aug). Centenary of German Amateur Theatres Federation. P 14.
2473   **1011** 100pf. multicoloured.. 2·75   1·10

(Des E. Jünger. Litho)

1992 (13 Aug). Länder of the Federal Republic. Multicoloured. Square design as T **989**. P 14.
2474   100pf. Bremen .... 3·00   1·40

(Des H. Schillinger. Litho)

1992 (10 Sept). 500th Anniv of Martin Behaim's Terrestrial Globe. P 14.
2475   **1012** 60pf. multicoloured... 2·20   1·10

1013 1890 Pendant and 1990 Clock    **1014** Bergengruen (after Hanni Fries)

(Des Annegret Ehmke. Litho)

1992 (10 Sept). 225th Anniv of Jewellery and Watchmaking in Pforzheim. P 14.
2476   **1013** 100pf. multicoloured.. 2·50   1·10

(Des Elisabeth von Janota-Bzowski. Litho German Bank Note Ptg Co, Leipzig)

1992 (10 Sept). Birth Centenary of Werner Bergengruen (writer). P 14.
2477   **1014** 100pf. grey, ultramarine and black .... 2·50   1·10

1015 Neue Holzbrücke Bridge, nr. Essing    **1016** Turret Clock, 1400

(Des H. Schillinger. Litho)

1992 (10 Sept). Inauguration of Main–Donau Canal. P 14.
2478   **1015** 100pf. multicoloured.. 2·50   1·10

(Des E. Jünger. Litho)

1992 (10 Sept). Länder of the Federal Republic. Multicoloured. Square design as T **989**. P 14.
2479   100pf. Hamburg .... 3·00   1·40

(Des H. Schillinger. Litho)

1992 (15 Oct). Humanitarian Relief Funds. Clocks. T **1016** and similar square designs. Multicoloured. P 14.
2480   60pf. +30pf. Type **1016** .... 2·20   2·10
2481   70pf. +30pf. Astronomical mantel clock,1738   2·75   2·75
2482   80pf. +40pf. Flute clock, 1790 .... 2·75   2·75
2483   100pf. +50pf. Figurine clock, 1580 .... 3·50   3·25
2484   170pf. +80pf. Table clock, 1550 .... 4·75   4·50
2480/2484 Set of 5.. 14·50   14·00

1017 Distler and Score of *We Praise Our Lord Jesus Christ*   **1018** Balloon Post

(Des Ursula Kahrl. Litho German Bank Note Ptg Co, Leipzig)

1992 (15 Oct). 50th Death Anniv of Hugo Distler (composer). P 14.
2485   **1017** 100pf. black and violet..................................... 2·75   1·10

(Des E. Kößlinger. Litho)

1992 (15 Oct). Stamp Day. P 14.
2486   **1018** 100pf. multicoloured.. 2·75   1·20

119

GERMANY

1019 Otto Engine, 1892, Cogwheel and Laser Beam
1020 Adoration of the Magi 
1027 Route Map and Compass Rose
1028 Emblem and Safety Stripes

(Des F. Lüdtke. Eng H.-J. Fuchs. Recess and litho)
1992 (15 Oct). Centenary of German Plant and Machine Builders Association. P 14.
2487 **1019** 170pf. multicoloured .... 3·75   2·10

(Des Annegret Ehmke. Litho)
1992 (5 Nov). Christmas. Carvings by Franz Maidburg, St. Anne's Church, Annaberg-Buchholz. T **1020** and similar square design. Multicoloured. P 14.
2488   60pf. +30pf. Type **1020** .... 2·20   2·10
2489   100pf. +50pf. *Birth of Christ* .... 2·75   2·75

(Des Marina Langer-Rosa. Litho German Bank Note Ptg Co, Leipzig)
1993 (14 Jan). 125th Anniv of North German Naval Observatory, Hamburg. P 14.
2496 **1027** 100pf. multicoloured .... 2·20   1·10

(Des H. and Linde Detlefsen. Photo)
1993 (14 Jan). European Year of Health, Hygiene and Safety in the Workplace. P 14.
2497 **1028** 100pf. deep bright blue, bright lemon and black .... 2·30   1·10

1021 Blücher (after Simon Meister)
1022 Werner von Siemens
1029 Wires and Wall Socket forming House
1030 Ski-jumping Hill, Garmisch-Partenkirchen 

(Des Elisabeth von Janota-Bzowski. Litho German Bank Note Ptg Co, Leipzig)
1992 (5 Nov). 250th Birth Anniv of Field Marshal Gebhard Leberecht von Blücher. P 14.
2490 **1021** 100pf. multicoloured .... 2·75   1·10

(Des Margit Zauner. Photo)
1992 (5 Nov). Death Centenary of Werner von Siemens (electrical engineer). P 14.
2491 **1022** 100pf. bistre-brown and blackish brown .... 2·75   1·10

(Des G. Gamroth. Photo)
1993 (14 Jan). Centenary of German Association of Electrical Engineers. P 14.
2498 **1029** 170pf. multicoloured .... 3·75   2·10

(Des J. Riess. Litho)
1993 (11 Feb). Sport Promotion Fund. German Olympic Venues. T **1030** and similar square designs. Multicoloured. P 14.
2499   60pf. +30pf. Type **1030** .... 4·00   3·50
2500   80pf. +40pf. Olympiapark, Munich .... 4·75   3·75
2501   100pf. +50pf. Olympic Stadium, Berlin .... 5·75   5·25
2502   170pf. +80pf. Olympic Harbour, Kiel .... 6·75   6·50
2499/2502 Set of 4 .... 19·00 17·00

1023 Jochen Klepper
1024 Star in German Colours
1031 Stylised Sound Vibration
1032 Statue of St. John and Charles Bridge, Prague 

(Des G. Aretz. Eng J. Kanior. Recess and litho)
1992 (5 Nov). 50th Death Anniv of Jochen Klepper (writer). P 14.
2492 **1023** 100pf. multicoloured .... 2·75   1·10

(Des H. G. Schmitz. Litho Schwann-Bagel, Düsseldorf)
1992 (5 Nov). European Single Market. P 14.
2493 **1024** 100pf. multicoloured .... 3·75   1·20

(Des Sonja Wunderlich. Litho German Bank Note Ptg Co, Leipzig)
1993 (11 Feb). 250th Anniv of Leipzig Gewandhaus Orchestra. P 13×12½.
2503 **1031** 100pf. gold and black .... 2·20   1·10

(Des J. Riess. Litho German Bank Note Ptg Co, Leipzig)
1993 (11 Mar). 600th Death Anniv of St. John of Nepomuk. P 13×12½.
2504 **1032** 100pf. multicoloured .... 2·50   1·10

1025 Cathedral and Überwasser Church
1026 Newton, Sketch of Refraction of Light and Formula
1033 Diagram explaining New Postcodes
1034 Abbeys 

(Des Isolde Monson-Baumgart. Litho)
1993 (14 Jan). 1200th Anniv of Münster. P 14.
2494 **1025** 60pf. multicoloured .... 1·90   ...

(Des H. Zill. Eng H.-J. Fuchs. Recess and litho)
1993 (14 Jan). 350th Birth Anniv of Sir Isaac Newton (scientist). P 14.
2495 **1026** 100pf. multicoloured .... 2·75   1·10

(Des E. Jünger. Litho Schwann-Bagel, Düsseldorf)
1993 (11 Mar). Introduction of Five-digit Postcode System. P 14.
2505 **1033** 100pf. multicoloured .... 3·00   1·10

GERMANY

(Des E. Jünger. Litho)

1993 (11 Mar). Länder of the Federal Republic. Square design as T **989**. Multicoloured. P 14.
2506   100pf. Hesse .... 2·50   1·40

1993 (11 Mar). 20th-century German Paintings (2nd series). Horiz designs as T **1003**. P 14.
2507   100pf. multicoloured .... 2·75   1·50
2508   100pf. black, brownish grey and deep mauve...... 2·75   1·50
2509   100pf. multicoloured .... 2·75   1·50
2507/2509 Set of 3 .... 7·50   4·00
Designs:—No. 2507, *Café* (George Grosz); 2508, *Sea and Sun* (Otto Pankok); 2509, *Audience* (Andreas Paul Weber).

(Des O. Rohse. Eng Petra Schlumbohm. Recess and litho)

1993 (15 Apr). 900th Anniversaries of Maria Laach and Bursfelde Benedictine Abbeys. P 14.
2510   **1034**   80pf. multicoloured .... 2·75   1·10

1035 Alpine Longhorn Beetle

1036 Plants

(Des Annegret Ehmke. Litho)

1993 (15 Apr). Youth Welfare. Endangered Beetles. T **1035** and similar square designs. Multicoloured. P 14.
2511   80pf. +40pf. Type **1035** .... 3·00   3·00
2512   80pf. +40pf. Rose Chafer .... 3·00   3·00
2513   100pf. +50pf. Stag Beetle .... 3·75   3·50
2514   100pf. +50pf. Tiger Beetle .... 3·75   3·50
2515   200pf. +50pf. Cockchafer .... 6·00   5·75
2511/2515 Set of 5 .... 18·00   17·00

(Des Silvia Runge. Litho German Bank Note Ptg Co, Leipzig)

1993 (15 Apr). Fifth International Horticultural Show, Stuttgart. P 13×12½.
2516   **1036**   100pf. multicoloured .... 2·20   1·10

1037 Horse Race

(Des D. Glinski. Litho)

1993 (5 May). 125th Anniv of Hoppegarten Racecourse. P 14.
2517   **1037**   80pf. multicoloured .... 2·20   1·20

1038 Storage Place (Joseph Beuys)

(Des E. Jünger. Litho)

1993 (5 May). Europa. Contemporary Art. T **1038** and similar horiz design. Multicoloured. P 14.
2518   80pf. Type **1038** .... 2·30   1·40
2519   100pf. *Homage to the Square* (Josef Albers) ...... 2·30   1·40

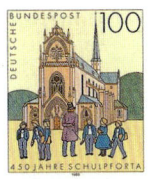

1039 Church and Pupils

1040 Students, Flag, City Hall and Castle

(Des A. Zander and Karin Blume-Zander. Litho German Bank Note Ptg Co, Leipzig)

1993 (5 May). 450th Anniv of Pforta School. P 14.
2520   **1039**   100pf. multicoloured .... 2·20   1·10

(Des P. Effert. Eng Petra Schlumbohm. Recess and litho)

1993 (5 May). 125th Anniv of Coburg Association of University Student Unions. P 14.
2521   **1040**   100pf. black, emerald and bright scarlet .... 2·20   1·10

1041 *Hohentwiel* (lake steamer) and Flags

1042 Old Market—View of St. Nicholas's Church (detail, Ferdinand von Arnim)

(Des A. Wittmer. Photo)

1993 (5 May). Lake Constance European Region. P 14.
2522   **1041**   100pf. multicoloured .... 2·75   1·10
Stamps of a similar design were issued by Austria and Switzerland.

(Des L. Lüders. Litho German Bank Note Ptg Co, Leipzig)

1993 (17 June). Millenary of Potsdam. P 13×12½.
2523   **1042**   80pf. multicoloured .... 2·75   1·10

1043 Hölderlin (after Franz Hiemer)

1044 'If People can fly to the Moon, why can't they do anything about so many Children dying?'

(Des Elisabeth von Janota-Bzowski. Photo)

1993 (17 June). 150th Death Anniv of Friedrich Hölderlin (poet). P 14.
2524   **1043**   100pf. multicoloured .... 2·75   1·10

(Des Vera Braesecke-Kaul. Litho Schwann-Bagel, Düsseldorf)

1993 (17 June). 40th Anniv of German United Nations Children's Fund Committee. P 14.
2525   **1044**   100pf. multicoloured .... 2·20   1·10

(Des E. Jünger. Litho)

1993 (17 June). Länder of the Federal Republic. Square design as T **989**. Multicoloured. P 14.
2526   100pf. Mecklenburg-Vorpommern .... 2·50   1·40

(Des E. Jünger. Litho)

1993 (15 July). Länder of the Federal Republic. Square design as T **989**. Multicoloured. P 14.
2527   100pf. Lower Saxony .... 2·50   1·40

1045 Fallada (after E. O. Plauen)

1046 Harz Mountain Range

121

GERMANY

(Des P. Nitzsche. Litho German Bank Note Ptg Co, Leipzig)

1993 (15 July). Birth Centenary of Hans Fallada (writer). P 14.
2528   1045   100pf. light brown-olive, brown and scarlet .... 2·75   1·10

(Des H. Schillinger. Litho)

1993 (15 July). Landscapes (1st series). T **1046** and similar horiz designs. Multicoloured. P 14.
2529   100pf. Type **1046** .... 2·75   1·40
2530   100pf. Rügen Island .... 2·75   1·40
2531   100pf. Hohe Rhön .... 2·75   1·40
2529/2531 *Set of 3* .... 7·50   3·75

See also Nos. 2585/2588, 2646/2649, 2709/2712 and 2806/2808.

1047 Stages of Manufacture

1048 George as Götz von Berlichingen in Goethe's *Urgötz*

(Des H. Scheuner. Litho German Bank Note Ptg Co, Leipzig)

1993 (12 Aug). 250th Death Anniv of Mathias Klotz (violin maker). P 13×12½.
2532   **1047**   80pf. multicoloured .... 2·20   90

(Des G. Aretz. Litho)

1993 (12 Aug). Birth Centenary of Heinrich George (actor). P 14.
2533   **1048**   100pf. multicoloured .... 2·20   1·10

(Des E. Jünger. Litho)

1993 (12 Aug). Länder of the Federal Republic. Square design as T **989**. Multicoloured. P 14.
2534   100pf. Nordrhein–Westfalen .... 2·50   1·40

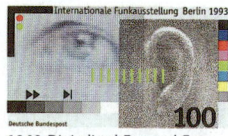

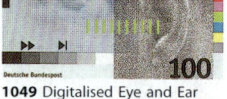

1049 Digitalised Eye and Ear

1050 Swedish Flag, Heart and Cross

(Des H. G. Schmitz. Litho)

1993 (12 Aug). International Radio Exhibition, Berlin. P 14.
2535   **1049**   100pf. multicoloured .... 2·50   1·10

(Des H. Zill. Litho)

1993 (16 Sept). Birth Centenary of Birger Forell (founder of Espelkamp (town for war refugees)). P 14.
2536   **1050**   100pf. greenish yellow, deep ultramarine and bright new blue   3·00   1·10

1051 *Tuledu Bridge* (engraving)

1052 Singing Clown

(Des H. G. Schmitz. Litho German Bank Note Ptg Co, Leipzig)

1993 (16 Sept). Birth Centenary of Hans Leip (writer and artist). P 13.
2537   **1051**   100pf. black, rosine and ultramarine......   3·00   1·10

(Des T. Müller. Litho)

1993 (16 Sept). For Us Children. Sheet 49×83 mm. P 14.
MS2538   **1052**   100pf. multicoloured ....   3·50   3·25

(Des E. Jünger. Litho)

1993 (16 Sept). Länder of the Federal Republic. Square design as T **989**. Multicoloured. P 14.
2539   100pf. Rheinland-Pfalz .... 2·50   1·40

1053 Postman delivering Letter

1054 Swan Lake

(Des R. Peter. Litho Schwann-Bagel, Düsseldorf)

1993 (16 Sept). Stamp Day. P 13½.
2540   **1053**   100pf. +50pf. multicoloured ....   3·00   3·25

(Des J. Riess. Litho Schwann-Bagel, Düsseldorf)

1993 (14 Oct). Death Centenary of Pyotr Tchaikovsky (composer). P 14.
2541   **1054**   80pf. multicoloured ....   2·75   1·10

1055 Föhr, Schleswig-Holstein

1056 St. Jadwiga (miniature, *Schlackenwerther Codex*)

(Des Hannelore Heise. Litho)

1993 (14 Oct). Humanitarian Relief Funds. Traditional Costumes (1st series). T **1055** and similar square designs. Multicoloured. P 14.
2542   80pf. +40pf. Type **1055** .... 2·75   2·75
2543   80pf. +40pf. Rügen, Mecklenburg Vorpommern .... 2·75   2·75
2544   100pf. +50pf. Oberndorf, Bavaria......... 3·00   3·00
2545   100pf. +50pf. Schwalm, Hesse............. 3·00   3·00
2546   200pf. +40pf. Ernstroda, Thuringia ..... 4·00   3·75
2542/2546 *Set of 5* .... 14·00   13·50

See also Nos. 2598/2602.

(Des A. Heidrich. Litho)

1993 (14 Oct). 750th Death Anniv of St. Jadwiga of Silesia. P 14.
2547   **1056**   100pf. multicoloured ....   3·00   1·10

Stamps of a similar design were issued by Poland.

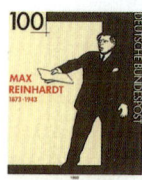

1057 Reinhardt on Stage

1058 Willy Brandt

(Des Sibylle and F. Haase. Litho German Bank Note Ptg Co, Leipzig)

1993 (14 Oct). 50th Death Anniv of Max Reinhardt (theatrical producer). P 14.
2548   **1057**   100pf. black, yellow-ochre and bright scarlet ....   2·75   1·10

(Des Ursula Kahrl. Litho)

1993 (10 Nov). 80th Birth Anniv of Willy Brandt (statesman). P 14.
2549   **1058**   100pf. multicoloured ....   4·00   1·80

1059 Claudio Monteverdi

1060 Paracelsus (after Augustin Hirschvogel)

122

GERMANY

(Des Antonia Graschberger. Litho German Bank Note Ptg Co, Leipzig)

1993 (10 Nov). 350th Death Anniv of Claudio Monteverdi (composer). P 13×12½.
2550   1059   100pf. multicoloured .... 2·75   1·10

(Des H. Zill. Recess and litho)

1993 (10 Nov). 500th Birth Anniv of Paracelsus (physician and philosopher). P 14.
2551   1060   100pf. yellow-ochre, deep brown and emerald .... 2·75   1·10

1061 Adoration of the Magi
1062 Quayside Buildings, Town Hall and St. Cosmas's Church

(Des Antonia Graschberger. Litho)

1993 (10 Nov). Christmas. Carvings from Altar Triptych, Blaubeuren Minster. T **1061** and similar square design. Multicoloured. P 14.
2552   80pf. +40pf. Type **1061** .... 1·90   1·80
2553   100pf. +50pf. Birth of Christ .... 3·50   3·00

(Des O. Rohse. Recess and litho)

1994 (13 Jan). Millenary of Stade. P 14.
2554   **1062**   80pf. lake, chestnut and deep ultramarine .... 2·20   1·10

1063 'FAMILIE'
1064 Heinrich Hertz and Electromagnetic Waves

(Des N. Höchtlen. Litho Schwann-Bagel, Düsseldorf)

1994 (13 Jan). International Year of the Family. P 14.
2555   **1063**   100pf. multicoloured .... 2·75   1·40

(Des E. Jünger. Litho)

1994 (13 Jan). Länder of the Federal Republic. Square designs as T **989**. Multicoloured. P 14.
2556   100pf. Saarland .... 2·75   1·40

(Des P. Steiner. Litho German Bank Note Ptg Co, Leipzig)

1994 (13 Jan). Death Centenary of Heinrich Hertz (physicist). P 13×12½.
2557   **1064**   200pt. black, scarlet and drab .... 5·00   2·10

1065 Frankfurt-am-Main
1066 Ice Skating

(Des E. Kößlinger. Litho German Bank Note Ptg Co, Leipzig)

1994 (10 Feb). 1200th Anniv of Frankfurt-am-Main. P 13×12½.
2558   **1065**   80pf. multicoloured .... 2·20   1·10

(Des F. Lüdtke. Litho)

1994 (10 Feb). Sport Promotion Fund. Sporting Events and Anniversaries. T **1066** and similar square designs. Multicoloured. P 14.
2559   80pf.. +40pf. Type **1066** (Winter Olympic Games, Lillehammer, Norway).................... 4·00   2·75
2560   100pf. +50pf. Football and trophy (World Cup Football Championship, USA)................... 4·25   3·00
2561   100pf. +50pf. Flame (centenary of International Olympic Committee).......... 4·25   3·00
2562   200pf. +80pf. Skier (Winter Paralympic Games, Lillehammer)............................ 6·25   6·00
2559/2562 Set of 4... 17·00   13·50

1067 Cathedral, St. Michael's Church and Castle
1068 Council Emblem

(Des D. Glinski. Litho)

1994 (10 Mar). 1250th Anniv of Fulda. P 14.
2563   **1067**   80pf. multicoloured .... 2·50   1·10

(Des Corinna Rogger. Litho German Bank Note Ptg Co, Leipzig)

1994 (10 Mar). Centenary of Federation of German Women's Associations – German Women's Council. P 13×12½.
2564   **1068**   100pf. black, bright scarlet and bright lemon... 2·75   1·20

1069 Members' Flags as Stars
1070 People holding Banner

(Des B. K. Wiese. Litho Schwann-Bagel, Düsseldorf)

1994 (10 Mar). Fourth Direct Elections to European Parliament. P 14.
2565   **1069**   100pf. multicoloured .... 3·00   1·40

(Des Sibylle and F. Haase. Litho)

1994 (10 Mar). 'Living Together' (integration of foreign workers in Germany). P 14.
2566   **1070**   100pf. multicoloured .... 2·50   1·40

(Des E. Jünger. Litho)

1994 (10 Mar). Länder of the Federal Republic. Square design as T **989**. Multicoloured. P 14.
2567   100pf. Saxony .... 2·75   1·40

1071 Johnny Head-in-the-Air
1072 Frauenkirche

(Des Annegret Ehmke. Litho)

1994 (14 Apr). Youth Welfare. Death Centenary of Heinrich Hoffmann (writer). T **1071** and similar square designs illustrating characters from *Slovenly Peter*. Multicoloured. P 13½.
2568   80pf. +40pf. Type **1071** .... 4·00   3·25
2569   80pf. +40pf. Little Pauline........................ 4·00   3·25
2570   100pf. +50pf. Naughty Friederich .... 4·25   3·75
2571   100pf. +50pf. Slovenly Peter .... 4·25   3·75
2572   200pf. +80pf. Fidget-Philipp....................... 5·50   4·75
2568/2572 Set of 5.. 20·00   17·00

(Des E. Kößlinger. Litho)

1994 (14 Apr). 500th Anniv of Frauenkirche, Munich. P 14.
2573   **1072**   100pf. multicoloured .... 3·75   1·50

1073 Resistor and Formula
1074 Pfitzner (after Emil Orlik)

(Des Margit Zauner. Photo)

1994 (5 May). Europa. Discoveries. T **1073** and similar horiz design. Multicoloured. P 14.
2574   80pf. Type **1073** (Ohm's Law) .... 1·90   90

123

GERMANY

2575	100pf. Radiation from black body and formula (Max Planck's Quantum Theory)		2·00	90

(Des P. Nitzsche. Litho German Bank Note Ptg Co, Leipzig)

1994 (5 May). 125th Birth Anniv of Hans Pfitzner (composer). P 14.

2576	**1074**	100pf. royal blue, new blue and vermilion	2·75	1·20

1075 Hagenbeck and Animals
1076 Spandau Castle

(Des J. Riess. Litho)

1994 (5 May). 150th Anniversaries. Sheet 77×108 mm containing T **1075** and similar horiz design. Multicoloured. P 14.

MS2577	100pf. birth anniv of Carl Hagenbeck (circus owner and founder of first zoo without bars)); 200pf. Animals and entrance to Berlin Zoo	7·25	8·25

(Des E. Kößlinger. Litho Schwann-Bagel, Düsseldorf)

1994 (16 June). 400th Anniv of Spandau Castle. P 14.

2578	**1076**	80pf. multicoloured	2·30	1·10

1077 Village Sign showing Society Emblem
1078 Heart inside Square

(Des K. Przewieslik. Litho German Bank Note Ptg Co, Leipzig)

1994 (16 June). Centenary of Herzogsägmühle (Society for the Domestic Missions welfare village). P 13×12½.

2579	**1077**	100pf. multicoloured	2·30	1·20

(Des E. Jünger. Litho)

1994 (16 June). Länder of the Federal Republic. Square design as T **989**. Multicoloured. P 14.

2580	100pf. Saxony-Anhalt	2·75	1·40

(Des Heike Schmidt. Litho German Bank Note Ptg Co, Leipzig)

1994 (16 June). Environmental Protection. P 13.

2581	**1078**	100pf. +50pf. bright yellowish green and black	3·00	3·00

1079 Friedrich II (13th-century miniature, *Book of Falcons*)
1080 '20 JULY 1944' behind Bars

(Des H. Scheuner. Litho German Bank Note Ptg Co, Leipzig)

1994 (16 June). 800th Birth Anniv of Emperor Friedrich II. P 14.

2582	**1079**	400pf. multicoloured	8·50	7·50

(Des H. P. Hoch. Litho)

1994 (14 July). 50th Anniv of Attempt to Assassinate Hitler. Sheet 105×70 mm. P 14.

MS2583	**1080**	100pf. black, orange-yellow and bright scarlet	4·00	5·00

(Des E. Jünger. Litho)

1994 (14 July). Länder of the Federal Republic. Square designs as T **989**. Multicoloured. P 14.

2584	100pf. Schleswig-Holstein	2·75	1·40

(Des H. Schillinger. Litho)

1994 (14 July). Landscapes (2nd series). Horiz designs as T **1046**. Multicoloured. P 14.

2585	100pf. The Alps	2·20	1·50
2586	100pf. Erzgebirge	2·20	1·50
2587	100pf. Main valley	2·20	1·50
2588	100pf. Mecklenburg lakes	2·20	1·50
2585/2588	Set of 4	8·00	5·50

1081 J. Herder (after Anton Graff)
1082 Early 20th-century Makonde Mask (Tanzania)

(Des Ursula Kahrl. Photo)

1994 (11 Aug). 250th Birth Anniv of Johann Gottfried Herder (philosopher). P 14.

2589	**1081**	80pf. multicoloured	1·90	1·10

(Des E. Jünger. Litho)

1994 (11 Aug). 20th-century German Paintings (3rd series). Horiz designs as T **1003**. Multicoloured. P 14.

2590	100pf. *Maika* (Christian Schad)	1·90	1·20
2591	200pf. *Dresden Landscape* (Erich Heckel)	3·50	3·00
2592	300pf. *Aleksei Javlensky and Marianne Werefkin* (Gabriele Münter)	5·00	4·75
2590/2592	Set of 3	9·25	8·00

(Des Silvia Runge. Litho German Bank Note Ptg Co, Leipzig)

1994 (8 Sept). 125th Anniv of Leipzig Ethnology Museum. P 13.

2593	**1082**	80pf. multicoloured	2·30	1·10

1083 Helmholtz, Eye and Colour Triangle
1084 W. Richter

(Des Margit Zauner. Eng J. Kanior. Recess and litho)

1994 (8 Sept). Death Centenary of Hermann von Helmholtz (physicist). P 14.

2594	**1083**	100pf. multicoloured	2·75	1·10

(Des R. Grüttner. Litho German Bank Note Ptg Co, Leipzig)

1994 (8 Sept). Birth Centenary of Willi Richter (President of Confederation of German Trade Unions). P 14.

2595	**1084**	100pf. deep brown, dull purple and black	2·30	1·10

1085 Flying on Dragon
1086 St. Wolfgang with Church Model (woodcut)

(Des L. Romboy. Litho)

1994 (8 Sept). For Us Children. Sheet 106×61 mm. P 14.

MS2596	**1085**	100pf. multicoloured	4·00	3·75

(Des E. Jünger. Litho)

1994 (8 Sept). Länder of the Federal Republic. Square design as T **989**. Multicoloured. P 14.

2597	100pf. Thuringia	2·75	1·40

(Des Hannelore Heise. Litho)

1994 (13 Oct). Humanitarian Relief Funds. Traditional Costumes (2nd series). Square designs as T **1055**. Multicoloured. P 14.

2598	80pf. +40pf. Bückeburg	2·30	2·30
2599	80pf. +40pf. Halle an der Saale	2·30	2·30

GERMANY

2600	100pf. +50pf. Minden....................	3·00	3·00
2601	100pf. +50pf. Hoyerswerda..............	3·00	3·00
2602	200pf. +70pf. Betzingen................	5·00	4·75
2598/2602	Set of 5...............................	14·00	14·00

(Des P. Steiner. Litho German Bank Note Pty Co, Leipzig)

1994 (13 Oct). Death Millenary of St. Wolfgang, Bishop of Regensburg. P 14.
2603   **1086** 100pf. gold, cream and black............ 2·30   1·20

1087 Hans Sachs

1088 Spreewald Postman, 1900

(Des P. Nitzsche. Eng W. Mauer. Recess)

1994 (13 Oct). 500th Birth Anniv of Hans Sachs (mastersinger and poet). P 14.
2604   **1087** 100pf. maroon and olive-green/*greyish*.   2·30   1·20

(Des E. Kößlinger. Litho Schwann-Bagel, Düsseldorf)

1994 (13 Oct). Stamp Day. P 14.
2605   **1088** 100pf. multicoloured .... 2·30   1·20

1089 Quedlinburg

1090 *Adoration of the Magi*

(Des E. Kößlinger. Eng Petra Schlumbohm. Recess and litho)

1994 (9 Nov). Millenary of Quedlinburg. P 14.
2606   **1089** 80pf. multicoloured .... 1·90   1·10

(Des P. Steiner. Litho)

1994 (9 Nov). Christmas. 500th Death Anniv of Hans Memling (painter). T **1090** and similar square design showing details of his triptych in St. John's Hospice, Bruges. Multicoloured. P 14.
2607   80pf. +40pf. Type **1090**........................ 2·50   2·75
2608   100pf. +50pf. *Nativity*............................ 3·00   3·00

1091 Steuben and *Surrender of Cornwallis at Yorktown* (detail, John Trumbull)

1092 Cemetery

(Des L. Grünewald. Litho)

1994 (9 Nov). Death Bicentenary of General. Friedrich Wilhelm von Steuben (Inspector General of Washington's Army). P 14.
2609   **1091** 100pf. multicoloured .... 2·30   1·20

(Des Margit Zauner. Litho)

1994 (9 Nov). 75th Anniv of National Association for the Preservation of German Graves Abroad. P 14.
2610   **1092** 100pf. black and vermilion................. 2·30   1·20

1093 Obersuhl Checkpoint, 11 November 1989

1094 T. Fontane (after Max Liebermann) and Lines from Prussian Song

(Des G. Lienemeyer. Litho German Bank Note Ptg Co, Leipzig)

1994 (9 Nov). Fifth Anniv of Opening of Borders between East and West Germany. P 13½×12½.
2611   **1093** 100pf. multicoloured .... 2·30   1·20

(Des P. Nitzsche. Litho)

1994 (9 Nov). 175th Birth Anniv of Theodor Fontane (writer). P 14.
2612   **1094** 100pf. bright green, black and magenta.. 2·30   1·20

1095 Simson Fountain, Town Hall and St. Mary's and St. Salvator's Churches

1096 Emperor Friedrich III, First Page of *Libellus* and *Zur Münze* (venue)

(Des D. Glinski. Litho Schwann-Bagel, Düsseldorf)

1995 (12 Jan). Millenary of Gera. P 13½×13.
2613   **1095** 80pf. multicoloured .... 2·30   1·10

1995 (12 Jan). 500th Anniv of Diet of Worms. P 13×12½.
2614   **1096** 100pf. black and bright scarlet............. 2·30   1·20

(Des E. Jünger. Litho)

1995 (12 Jan). 20th-century German Paintings (4th series). Horiz designs as T **1003**. Multicoloured. P 14.
2615   100pf. *The Water Tower, Bremen* (Franz Radziwill) .... 2·30   1·10
2616   200pf. *Still Life with Cat* (Georg Schrimpf)......... 3·75   3·00
2617   300pf. *Estate in Dangast* (Karl Schmidt Rottluff) .... 5·50   4·50
2615/2617 Set of 3.. 10·50   7·75

1097 Canoeing

1098 Friedrich Wilhelm (after A. Romandon)

(Des G. Aretz. Photo)

1995 (9 Feb). Sport Promotion Fund. T **1097** and similar square designs. Multicoloured. P 14.
2618   80pf. +40pf. Type **1097** (27th World Canoeing Championships, Duisburg)..... 2·30   2·75
2619   100pf. +50pf. Hoop exercises (tenth International Gymnastics Festival, Berlin)... 2·30   2·75
2620   100pf. +50pf. Boxing (eighth World Amateur Boxing Championships, Berlin) .... 2·30   2·75
2621   200pf. +80pf. Volleyball (centenary) .... 4·75   5·25
2618/2621 Set of 4... 10·50   12·00

(Des H. Schall. Litho German Bank Note Ptg Co, Leipzig)

1995 (9 Feb). 375th Birth Anniv of Friedrich Wilhelm of Brandenburg, The Great Elector. P 14.
2622   **1098** 300pf. multicoloured .... 6·25   4·75

125

GERMANY

1099 Deed of Donation (995) and Arms of Mecklenburg-Vorpommern

(Des Annegret Ehmke. Litho)

1995 (9 Mar). Millenary of Mecklenburg. P 14.
2623   1099   100pf. multicoloured .... 1·90   1·20

1100 Computer Image of Terminal and Lion

(Des Karen Scholz. Litho Schwann-Bagel. Düsseldorf)

1995 (9 Mar). 250th Anniv of Carolo-Wilhelmina Technical University, Braunschweig. P 14.
2624   1100   100pf. multicoloured .... 2·00   1·20

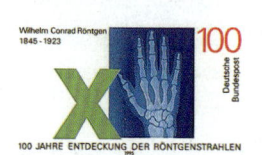

1101 X-ray of Hand
1102 Globe and Rainbow 

(Des Margit Zauner. Litho)

1995 (9 Mar). 150th Birth Anniv of Wilhelm Röntgen and Centenary of his Discovery of X-rays. P 14.
2625   1101   100pf. multicoloured .... 1·90   1·20

(Des R.-J. Lehmann. Litho German Bank Note Ptg Co, Leipzig)

1995 (9 Mar). First Conference of Signatories to General Convention on Climate, Berlin. P 14.
2626   1102   100pf. multicoloured .... 1·90   1·20

1103 Old Town Hall Reliefs

(Des E. Kößlinger. Litho)

1995 (6 Apr). 750th Anniv of Regensburg. P 14.
2627   1103   80pf. multicoloured .... 1·70   1·10

1104 Dietrich Bonhoeffer
1105 Symbols of Speech, Writing and Pictures 

(Des Antonia Graschberger. Photo)

1995 (6 Apr). 50th Death Anniv of Dietrich Bonhoeffer (theologian). P 14.
2628   1104   100pf. black, blue and lavender-grey...... 1·90   1·20

(Des P. Effert. Photo)

1995 (6 Apr). Freedom of Expression. P 14.
2629   1105   100pf. multicoloured .... 1·90   1·20

1106 St. Clement's Church, Münster
1107 Friedrich Schiller, Signature and Schiller Museum, Marbach 

(Des H. Scheuner. Litho German Bank Note Ptg Co, Leipzig)

1995 (6 Apr). 300th Birth Anniv of Johann Conrad Schlaun (architect). P 13.
2630   1106   200pf. multicoloured .... 4·00   3·25

(Des Antonia Graschberger. Photo)

1995 (5 May). Centenary of German Schiller Society. P 14.
2631   1107   100pf. multicoloured .... 1·90   1·20

1108 St. Vincent de Paul
1109 Number on Cloth and Barbed Wire  

(Des F. Lüdtke. Litho German Bank Note Ptg Co, Leipzig)

1995 (5 May). 150th Anniv of Vincent Conferences (charitable organisation) in Germany. P 14.
2632   1108   100pf. multicoloured .... 1·90   1·40

(Des E. Jünger. Litho)

1995 (5 May). 50th Anniv of Liberation of Concentration Camps. Sheet 105×70 mm. P 14.
MS2633   1109   100pf. grey, dull violet-blue and black .... 3·00   3·75

1110 City Ruins
1111 Returning Soldiers ('End of War') 

(Des E. Jünger. Litho)

1995 (5 May). 50th Anniv of End of Second World War. Sheet 104×70 mm containing T **1110** and similar square design. Multicoloured. P 14.
MS2634   100pf. Type **1110**; 100pf. Refugees .... 5·50   6·00

(Des E. Jünger. Litho)

1995 (5 May). Europa. Peace and Freedom. T **1111** and similar square design. P 14.
2635   100pf. black and vermilion .... 2·30   1·50
2636   200pf. bright blue, lemon and black .... 3·50   3·00
Designs:—100pf. T **111**; 200pf. Emblem of European Community ('Moving towards Europe').

1112 Shipping Routes before and after 1895
1113 Guglielmo Marconi and Wireless Equipment 

126

(Des Annegret Ehmke. Litho German Bank Note Ptg Co, Leipzig)
1995 (8 June). Centenary of Kiel Canal. P 14.
2637   **1112**   80pf. multicoloured .... 2·30   1·10

(Des E. Jünger. Litho)
1995 (8 June). Centenary of First Radio Transmission. P 14.
2638   **1113**   100pf. multicoloured .... 2·50   1·70
A stamp of a similar design was also issued by Ireland, Italy, San Marino and the Vatican City.

1114 UN Emblem   **1115** Münsterländer

(Des P. Effert. Litho)
1995 (8 June). 50th Anniv of United Nations Organisation. P 14.
2639   **1114**   100pf. lavender, gold and brownish grey..................................... 1·90   1·20

(Des J. Riess. Litho)
1995 (8 June). Youth Welfare. Dogs (1st series). T **1115** and similar square designs. Multicoloured. P 14.
2640   80pf. +40pf. Type **1115** .... 2·00   2·30
2641   80pf. +40pf. Giant schnauzer .... 2·00   2·30
2642   100pf. +50pf. Wire-haired Dachshund .. 2·30   2·50
2643   100pf. +50pf. German Shepherd .... 2·30   2·50
2644   200pf. +80pf. Keeshond .... 4·75   5·25
2640/2644 Set of 5................................... 12·00   13·50
See also Nos. 2696/2700.

1116 Opening Bars of *Carmina Burana* and Characters   **1117** Lion (from 12th-century coin)

(Des E. Kößlinger. Litho Schwann-Bagel, Düsseldorf)
1995 (6 July). Birth Centenary of Carl Orff (composer). P 13×13½.
2645   **1116**   100pf. multicoloured .... 1·90   1·20

(Des H. Schillinger. Litho)
1995 (6 July). Landscapes (3rd series). Horiz designs as T **1046**. Multicoloured. P 14.
2646   100pf. Franconian Switzerland .... 1·70   1·50
2647   100pf. River Havel, Berlin........................ 1·70   1·50
2648   100pf. Oberlausitz.................................... 1·70   1·50
2649   100pf. Sauerland..................................... 1·70   1·50
2646/2649 Set of 4... 6·00   5·50
Used examples of No. 2646 are known showing the bright yellow-green and yellow-olive omitted.

(Des A. von Bodecker. Litho German Bank Note Ptg Co, Leipzig)
1995 (6 July). 800th Death Anniv of Henry the Lion, Duke of Saxony and Bavaria. P 14.
2650   **1117**   400pf. multicoloured .... 6·25   6·00

1118 Kaiser Wilhelm Memorial Church   **1119** F. Werfel and Signature

(Des P. Steiner. Photo)
1995 (10 Aug). Centenary of Kaiser Wilhelm Memorial Church, Berlin. P 14.
2651   **1118**   100pf. multicoloured .... 2·20   1·20

(Des G. Aretz. Litho Schwann-Bagel, Düsseldorf)
1995 (10 Aug). 50th Death Anniv of Franz Werfel (writer). P 14.
2652   **1119**   100pf. deep magenta, blue and black.... 1·90   1·20

(Des Sibylle and F. Haase. Litho)
1995 (10 Aug)–**98**. Tourist Sights. Vert designs as T **854**, but inscr 'DEUTSCHLAND'. P 14.
2654   47pf. light green and greenish black (17.7.97)... 1·00   90
2656   100pf. grey-blue and black (28.8.97)......... 1·60   1·50
   a. Perf 3 sides. Booklets (22.1.98) .... 1·60   1·50
   ab. Booklet pane. No. 2656a×10................ 17·00
2657   110pf. cinnamon and blackish brown (14.8.97).. 1·70   75
   a. Perf 3 sides. Booklets............................ 1·70   1·50
   ab. Booklet pane. No. 2657a×10................ 18·00
2658   110pf. bright orange and greenish blue (10.9.98).. 2·00   1·20
   a. Perf 3 sides. Booklets (10.6.99) .... 2·00   1·50
   ab. Booklet pane. No. 2658a×10................ 21·00
2659   220pf. dull blue green and brownish black (14.8.97).. 3·00   1·50
2661   440pf. dull orange and light blue (14.8.97)....... 7·75   6·75
2663   510pf. Venetian red and deep blue (28.8.97) ... 7·75   7·50
2665   640pf. dull violet-blue and red-brown............. 11·50   6·75
2666   690pf. black and dull blue-green (13.6.96)...... 11·00   6·25
2654/2666 Set of 9... 43·00   35·00
Designs:—47pf. Berus Monument, Überherrn; 100pf. Goethe-Schiller Monument, Weimar; 110pf. (No. 2657) Bellevue Castle, Berlin; 110pf. (No. 2658) Emblem of EXPO 2000 World's Fair, Hanover; 220pf. Brühl's Terrace, Dresden; 440pf. Town Hall, Bremen; 510pf. Holsten Gate, Lübeck; 640pf. Speyer Cathedral; 690pf. St. Michael's Church, Hamburg.
Nos. 2654/2666 were each issued both in sheets and in coils, the latter having every fifth stamp numbered on the back.
For similar designs with face values in German currency and euros see Nos. 2988/3003.

Nos. 2667/2674 are vacant.

1120 F. J. Strauss   **1121** Postwoman

(Des G. Aretz. Photo)
1995 (6 Sept). 80th Birth Anniv of Franz Josef Strauss (politician). P 14.
2675   **1120**   100pf. multicoloured .... 2·30   1·50

(Des E. Kösslinger. Litho German Bank Note Ptg Co, Leipzig)
1995 (6 Sept). Stamp Day. P 13.
2676   **1121**   200pf. +100pf. multicoloured .... 5·00   5·25

1122 *Metropolis* (dir. Fritz Lang)   **1123** Eifel

(Des E. Jünger. Photo)
1995 (6 Sept). Centenary of Motion Pictures. Sheet 100×130 mm containing T **1122** and similar horiz designs showing frames from films. Multicoloured. P 14.
MS2677   80pf. Type **1122**; 100pf. *Little Superman* (dir Wolfgang Staudte); 200pf. *The Sky over Berlin* (dir. Wim Wenders) .... 9·25   12·00

(Des D. Glinski. Litho)
1995 (12 Oct). Humanitarian Relief Funds. Farmhouses (1st series). T **1123** and similar horiz designs. Multicoloured. P 14.
2678   80pf. +40pf. Type **1123** .... 2·00   2·00
2679   80pf. +40pf. Saxony................................ 2·00   2·00
2680   100pf. +50pf. Lower Germany .... 2·30   2·30
2681   100pf. +50pf. Upper Bavaria .... 2·30   2·30
2682   200pf. +70pf. Mecklenburg .... 4·00   3·75
2678/2682 Set of 5.. 11·50   11·00
See also Nos. 2742/2746.

127

GERMANY

1124 K. Schumacher

(Des Angelika Winkhaus. Litho German Bank Note Ptg Co, Leipzig)
1995 (12 Oct). Birth Centenary of Kurt Schumacher (politician). P 13.
2683   1124   100pf. multicoloured .... 1·90   1·20

1125 Animals gathered on Hill

(Des Christiane Hemmerich. Litho)
1995 (12 Oct). For Us Children. Sheet 110×60 mm. P 14.
MS2684   1125   100pf. multicoloured .... 5·50   6·00

1126 L. Ranke    **1127** P. Hindemith

(Des Elisabeth von Janota-Bzowski. Litho)
1995 (9 Nov). Birth Bicentenary of Leopold von Ranke (historian). P 14.
2685   1126   80pf. multicoloured .... 1·60   1·10

(Des I. Wulff. Litho German Bank Note Ptg Co, Leipzig)
1995 (9 Nov). Birth Centenary of Paul Hindemith (composer). P 14.
2686   1127   100pf. multicoloured .... 1·90   1·20

1128 Alfred Nobel and Will    **1129** 'CARE' in American Colours

(Des S. Ehrén. Eng C. Slania. Recess and litho)
1995 (9 Nov). Centenary of Nobel Prize Trust Fund. P 14.
2687   1128   100pf. multicoloured .... 2·50   1·80

(Des J. Bertholdt. Litho German Bank Note Ptg Co, Leipzig)
1995 (9 Nov). 50th Anniv of CARE (Co-operative for Assistance and Remittances Overseas). P 13×12½.
2688   1129   100pf. multicoloured .... 1·90   1·20

1130 Berlin Wall    **1131** The Annunciation

(Des Corinna Rogger. Litho)
1995 (19 Nov). Commemorating Victims of Political Oppression, 1945–89. P 14.
2689   1130   100pf. multicoloured .... 2·00   1·20

(Des E. Kößlinger. Litho)
1995 (9 Nov). Christmas. Stained Glass Windows in Augsburg Cathedral. T **1131** and similar square design. Multicoloured. P 14.
2690   80pf. +40pf. Type **1131** .... 2·30   2·30
2691   100pf. +50pf. *Nativity* .... 3·00   3·00

1132 Dribbling

(Des Margit Zauner. Photo)
1995 (6 Dec). Borussia Dortmund, German Football Champions. P 14.
2692   1132   100pf. multicoloured .... 2·75   1·50

1133 Auguste von Sartorius (founder)    **1134** Bodelschwingh

(Des E. Jünger. Litho Schwann-Bagel, Düsseldorf)
1996 (11 Jan). 150th Anniv of German Institute for Children's Missionary Work. P 14.
2693   1133   100pf. multicoloured .... 1·90   1·40

(Des H. Schwahn. Litho)
1996 (11 Jan). 50th Death Anniv of Friedrich von Bodelschwingh (theologian). P 14.
2694   1134   100pf. black and deep rose-red .... 1·90   1·40

1135 Luther (after Lucas Cranach)    **1136** P. Siebold

(Des D. Heidenreich. Litho)
1996 (8 Feb). 450th Death Anniv of Martin Luther (Protestant reformer). P 14.
2695   1135   100pf. multicoloured .... 2·00   1·70

1996 (8 Feb). Youth Welfare. Dogs (2nd series). Square designs as T **1115**. Multicoloured. P 14.
2696   80pf. +40pf. Borzoi .... 2·50   2·75
2697   80pf. +40pf. Chow Chow .... 2·50   2·75
2698   100pf. +50pf. St. Bernard .... 3·00   3·00
2699   100pf. +50pf. Rough Collie .... 3·00   3·00
2700   200pf. +80pf. Briard .... 4·75   4·50
2696/2700   Set of 5 .... 14·00   14·50

(Des G. Jacki. Litho German Bank Note Ptg Co, Leipzig)
1996 (17 Feb). Birth Bicentenary of Philipp Franz von Siebold (physician and Japanologist). P 13×12½.
2701   1136   100pf. multicoloured .... 2·00   1·70
A stamp of a similar design was issued by Japan.

1137 Cathedral Square    **1138** Galen

GERMANY

(Des J. Bertholdt. Litho German Bank Note Ptg Co, Leipzig)

1996 (7 Mar). Millenary of Cathedral Square, Halberstadt. P 13.
2702 **1137** 80pf. multicoloured .... 1·60 90

(Des Antonia Graschberger. Litho)

1996 (7 Mar). 50th Death Anniv of Cardinal Count Clemens von Galen, Bishop of Münster. P 14.
2703 **1138** 100pf. brownish grey, royal blue and gold .... 1·90 1·20

(Des E. Jünger. Litho)

1996 (7 Mar). 20th-century German Paintings (5th series). Horiz designs as T **1003**. Multicoloured. P 14.
2704 100pf. *Seated Female Nude* (Max Pechstein)...... 1·90 1·50
2705 200pf. *For Wilhelm Runge* (Georg Muche) .... 3·75 3·00
2706 300pf. *Still Life with Guitar, Book and Vase* (Helmut Kolle) .... 4·75 4·50
2704/2706 Set of 3 .... 9·25 8·00

1139 Detail of Ceiling Fresco, Prince-bishop's Residence, Würzburg

1140 Post Runner

(Des F. Lüdtke. Litho German Bank Note Ptg Co, Leipzig)

1996 (7 Mar). 300th Birth Anniv of Giovanni Battista Tiepolo (artist). P 13×12½.
2707 **1139** 200pf. multicoloured .... 3·50 2·75

(Des Erna de Vries. Litho)

1996 (11 Apr). For Us Children. Sheet 83×67 mm. P 14.
MS2708 **1140** 100pf. multicoloured .... 3·50 3·50

(Des H. Schillinger. Litho)

1996 (11 Apr). Landscapes (4th series). Horiz designs as T **1046**. Multicoloured. P 14.
2709 100pf. Eifel .... 1·90 1·50
2710 100pf. Holstein Switzerland .... 1·90 1·50
2711 100pf. Saale .... 1·90 1·50
2712 100pf. Spreewald .... 1·90 1·50
2709/2712 Set of 4 .... 6·75 5·50

1141 Paula Modersohn-Becker (self-portrait)

1142 Opening Lines of Document and Town (1642 engraving, Matthaeus Merian)

(Des M. Gottschall. Litho)

1996 (3 May). Europa. Famous Women. T **1141** and similar horiz design. P 14.
2713 80pf. multicoloured .... 1·90 75
2714 100pf. black, pale brownish-grey and magenta .... 2·00 1·50
Designs:—80pf. T **1141**; 100pf. *Käthe Kollwitz* (self-portrait).

(Des Karin Blume-Zander and A. Zander. Litho Schwann-Bagel, Düsseldorf)

1996 (3 May). Millenary of Freising's Right to hold Markets. P 14.
2715 **1142** 100pf. multicoloured .... 1·60 1·40

1143 Wolfgang Borchert

1144 Emblem

(Des G. and O. Aretz. Litho German Bank Note Ptg Co, Leipzig)

1996 (3 May). 75th Birth Anniv of Wolfgang Borchert (writer). P 13.
2716 **1143** 100pf. multicoloured .... 1·60 1·40

(Des Angelika Winkhaus. Litho German Bank Note Ptg Co, Leipzig)

1996 (13 May). 50th Anniv of Ruhr Festival, Recklinghausen. P 13.
2717 **1144** 100pf. multicoloured .... 1·60 1·40

1145 Ticket and Stage Curtain

1146 Gottfried Leibniz and Mathematical Diagram

(Des E. Jünger. Photo)

1996 (3 May). 150th Anniv of German Theatre Association. P 14.
2718 **1145** 200pf. multicoloured .... 3·00 2·30

(Des Elisabeth von Janota-Bzowski. Litho)

1996 (13 June). 350th Birth Anniv of Gottfried Leibniz (mathematician). P 14.
2719 **1146** 100pf. brown-red and black .... 1·60 1·40

1147 Kneeling Figure and Motto forming 'A'

1148 Carl Schuhmann (wrestling, equestrian sports and gymnastics, 1896)

(Des P. Steiner. Litho German Bank Note Ptg Co, Leipzig)

1996 (13 June). 300th Anniv of Berlin Academy of Arts. P 13.
2720 **1147** 100pf. multicoloured .... 1·60 1·40

(Des Margit Zauner. Photo)

1996 (13 June). Sport Promotion Fund. Centenary of Modern Olympic Games. T **1148** and similar square designs showing German Olympic Champions. Multicoloured. P 14.
2721 80pf. +40pf. Type **1148** .... 4·25 3·00
2722 100pf. +50pf. Josef Neckermann (dressage, 1964 and 1968)... 5·25 4·25
2723 100pf. +50pf. Annie Hübler-Horn (ice skating, 1908) .... 5·25 4·25
2724 200pf. +80pf. Alfred and Gustav Flatow (gymnastics, 1896).. 7·25 5·75
2721/2724 Set of 4 .... 20·00 16·00

1149 Townscape

1150 Children's Handprints

(Des D. Glinsky. Litho)

1996 (18 July). 800th Anniv of Heidelberg. P 14.
2725 **1149** 100pf. multicoloured .... 1·60 1·40
 a. Booklet pane. No. 2725×10, with margins all round .... 17·00

(Des L. Romboy. Litho Schwann-Bagel, Düsseldorf)

1996 (18 July). 50th Anniv of United Nations Children's Fund. P 14.
2726 **1150** 100pf. multicoloured .... 1·60 1·40

129

GERMANY

1151 *Wedding* (illustration by Bruno Paul)
1152 Beach 

(Des H. Zill. Litho German Bank Note Ptg Co, Leipzig)

1996 (18 July). 75th Death Anniv of Ludwig Thoma (satirist). P 13.
2727   1151   100pf. multicoloured ....   1·60   1·40

(Des Silvia Runge. Litho)

1996 (18 July). Western Pomerania National Park. Sheet 166×111 mm containing T **1152** and similar horiz designs showing Park landscapes. Multicoloured. P 14.
MS2728 100pf. Type **1152**; 200pf. Mudflat; 300pf. Sea inlet.................   12·50   12·00

1153 Map and Tropical Wildlife

(Des E. Jünger. Photo)

1996 (18 July). Environmental Protection. Preservation of Tropical Habitats. P 14.
2729   1153   100pf. +50pf. multicoloured........................   3·00   3·00

1154 Völklingen Blast Furnace
1155 Paul Lincke 

(Des R. Lederbogen. Litho)

1996 (14 Aug). UNESCO World Heritage Sites. P 13½.
2730   1154   100pf. multicoloured ....   1·60   1·40

(Des P. Nitzsche. Litho German Bank Note Ptg Co, Leipzig)

1996 (14 Aug). 50th Death Anniv of Paul Lincke (composer and conductor). P 13.
2731   1155   100pf. multicoloured ....   1·60   1·40

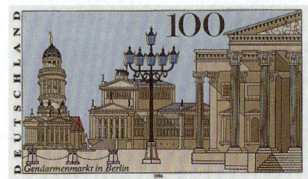

1156 Gendarmenmarkt, Berlin

(Des H. Schillinger. Litho)

1996 (14 Aug). Images of Germany. P 14.
2732   1156   100pf. multicoloured ....   1·60   1·40

1157 '50' comprising Stamp under Magnifying Glass
1158 Book 

(Des M. Bollwage. Photo)

1996 (14 Aug). Stamp Day. 50th Anniv of Association of German Philatelists. P 14.
2733   1157   100pf. multicoloured ....   1·60   1·40

(Des B. Wiese. Litho)

1996 (14 Aug). Centenary of German Civil Code. P 13½.
2734   1158   300pf. multicoloured ....   5·00   4·50

1159 Players
1160 Bamburg Old Town 

(Des H. G. Schmitz. Litho Schwann-Bagel, Düsseldorf)

1996 (27 Aug). Borussia Dortmund's Victory in German Football Championship. P 14.
2735   1159   100pf. multicoloured ....   2·00   1·40

(Des Isolde Monson-Baumgart. Litho)

1996 (12 Sept). UNESCO World Heritage Sites. P 14.
2736   1160   100pf. multicoloured ....   1·70   1·40

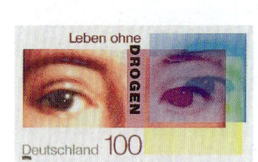

1161 Eyes
1162 'Like will Cure Like' and Samuel Hahnemann (developer of principle) 

(Des G. Gamroth. Photo)

1996 (12 Sept). Life without Drugs. P 14.
2737   1161   100pf. multicoloured ....   1·70   1·40

(Des H. Scheuner. Litho German Bank Note Ptg Co, Leipzig)

1996 (12 Sept). Bicentenary of Homeopathy. P 14.
2738   1162   400pf. multicoloured ....   6·25   6·25

1163 Bruckner and *Symphony No. III*
1164 Mueller, Map and Plants 

(Des Antonia Graschberger. Litho German Bank Note Ptg Co, Leipzig)

1996 (9 Oct). Death Centenary of Anton Bruckner (composer). P 13.
2739   1163   100pf. dull purple, lake-brown and black................   1·70   1·40

130

GERMANY

(Des J. Sellito and D. Blyth. Litho)

1996 (9 Oct). Death Centenary of Ferdinand von Mueller (botanist). P 14.

| 2740 | **1164** | 100pf. multicoloured | 1·70 | 1·40 |

A stamp of a similar design was issued by Australia.

1165 Score by John Cage

1166 Titles of Plays and Zuchmayer

(Des Margit Zauner. Litho Schwann-Bagel, Düsseldorf)

1996 (9 Oct). 75th Anniv of Donaueschingen Music Festival. P 13.

| 2741 | **1165** | 100pf. blue, black and magenta | 1·70 | 1·40 |

(Des D. Glinski. Litho)

1996 (9 Oct). Humanitarian Relief Funds. Farmhouses (2nd series). Horiz designs as T **1123**. Multicoloured. P 14.

2742	80pf. +40pf. Spree Forest	1·90	1·50
2743	80pf. +40pf. Thuringia	1·90	1·50
2744	100pf. +50pf. Black Forest	2·30	1·80
2745	100pf. +50pf. Westphalia	2·30	1·80
2746	200pf. +70pf. Schleswig-Holstein	4·00	4·00
2742/2746	Set of 5	11·00	9·50

(Des P. Steiner. Litho German Bank Note Ptg Co, Leipzig)

1996 (14 Nov). Birth Centenary of Carl Zuckmayer (dramatist). P 13.

| 2747 | **1166** | 100pf. multicoloured | 1·70 | 1·40 |

1167 Adoration of the Magi

1168 Carlo Schmid

(Des P. Steiner. Litho)

1996 (14 Nov). Christmas. Illustrations from Henry II's *Book of Pericopes* (illuminated manuscript of readings from the Gospels). T **1167** and similar square design. Multicoloured. P 14.

| 2748 | 80pf. +40pf. Type **1167** | 2·20 | 2·40 |
| 2749 | 100pl. +50pf. *Nativity* | 2·50 | 3·00 |

(Des G. and O. Aretz. Photo)

1996 (3 Dec). Birth Centenary of Carlo Schmid (politician and writer). P 14.

| 2750 | **1168** | 100pf. multicoloured | 1·60 | 1·40 |

1169 Friends of Schubert in Afzenbrugg (detail, L. Kupelwieser)

1170 Pitch, Player and Herberger

(Des P. Nitzsche. Litho)

1997 (16 Jan). Birth Bicentenary of Franz Schubert (composer). P 14.

| 2751 | **1169** | 100pf. multicoloured | 1·70 | 1·40 |

(Des Irmgard Hesse. Litho)

1997 (16 Jan). Birth Centenary of Sepp Herberger (National Football Team coach, 1936–64). P 14.

| 2752 | **1170** | 100pf. light green, orange-red and black | 1·90 | 1·40 |

1171 Motor Cars

1172 Melanchthon (after Lucas Cranach the younger)

(Des B. Bexte. Litho Schwann-Bagel, Düsseldorf)

1997 (16 Jan–9 Oct). More Safety for Children (road safety campaign). P 14.

| 2752a | **1171** | 10pf. multicoloured (9.10) | 60 | 45 |
| 2753 | | 100pf. multicoloured | 1·70 | 1·40 |

(Des P. Steiner. Litho)

1997 (4 Feb). 500th Birth Anniv of Philipp Melanchthon (religious reformer). P 14.

| 2754 | **1172** | 100pf. multicoloured | 1·70 | 1·40 |

1173 Revellers 'Wiggling'

1174 Ludwig Erhard

(Des H. Scheuner. Litho German Bank Note Ptg Co, Leipzig)

1997 (4 Feb). 175th Anniv of Cologne Carnival. P 14.

| 2755 | **1173** | 100pf. multicoloured | 1·70 | 1·40 |

(Des E. Jünger. Photo)

1997 (4 Feb). Birth Centenary of Ludwig Erhard (Chancellor, 1963–66). P 14.

| 2756 | **1174** | 100pf. black and vermilion | 1·90 | 1·40 |

1175 Aerobics

1176 New Pavilion

(Des Renate Riek-Bauer. Litho)

1997 (4 Feb). Sport Promotion Fund. Fun Sports. T **1175** and similar square designs. Multicoloured. P 14.

2757	80pf. +40pf. Type **1175**	2·20	3·00
2758	100pf. +50pf. Inline skating	2·75	3·25
2759	100pf. +50pf. Streetball	2·75	3·25
2760	200pf. +80pf. Free climbing	4·75	6·00
2757/2760	Set of 4	11·00	14·00

(Des Sibylle and F. Haase. Litho German Bank Note Ptg Co, Leipzig)

1997 (6 Mar). 500th Anniv of Granting of Imperial Fair Rights to Leipzig. P 13×12½.

| 2761 | **1176** | 100pf. silver, bright scarlet and ultramarine | 1·70 | 1·40 |

1177 Philharmonic, Berlin (Hans Scharoun)

1178 Straubing

131

GERMANY

(Des Karen Scholz. Litho)

1997 (6 Mar). Post-1945 German Architecture. Sheet 137×101 mm containing T **1177** and similar square designs. Multicoloured. P 14.

MS2762 100pf. Type **1177**; 100pf. National Gallery, Berlin (Ludwig Mies van der Rohe); 100pf. St. Mary, Queen of Peace Pilgrimage Church, Neviges (Gottfried Böhm); 100pf. German Pavilion, 1967 World's Fair, Montreal (Frei Otto)................. 9·25 10·50

(Des Vera Braesecke-Kaul and H. Kaul. Litho German Bank Note Ptg Co, Leipzig)

1997 (6 Mar). 1100th Anniv of Straubing. P 13×12½.
2763 **1178** 100pf. multicoloured...................... 1·90 1·40

1179 Stephan, Telephone and Postcards

(Des E. Jünger. Litho German Bank Note Ptg Co, Liepzig)

1997 (8 Apr). Death Centenary of Heinrich von Stephan (founder of Universal Postal Union). P 14.
2764 **1179** 100pf. multicoloured...................... 2·00 1·40

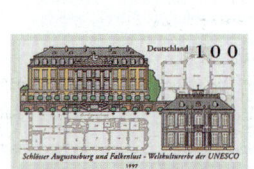

1180 Augustusburg and Falkenlust Castles **1181** Diamonds

(Des Vera Braesecke-Kaul and H. Kaul. Litho)

1997 (8 Apr). UNESCO World Heritage Sites. P 14.
2765 **1180** 100pf. multicoloured...................... 1·70 1·40

(Des Annegret Ehmke. Litho Schwann-Bagel, Düsseldorf)

1997 (8 Apr). 500th Anniv of Idar-Oberstein Region Gem Industry. P 14.
2766 **1181** 300pf. multicoloured...................... 5·25 5·00

1182 St. Adalbert **1183** *The Fisherman and His Wife* (Brothers Grimm)

(Des V. Suchánek. Recess)

1997 (23 Apr). Death Millenary of St. Adalbert (Bishop of Prague). P 14.
2767 **1182** 100pf. blackish lilac...................... 1·70 1·40
   No. 2767 was a joint issue with Poland, Czech Republic, Hungary and Vatican City.

(Des E. Kößlinger. Litho)

1997 (5 May). Europa. Tales and Legends. T **1183** and similar square design. Multicoloured. P 14.
2768   80pf. Type **1183**.............................. 1·90 1·20
2769   100pf. *Rübezahl*.............................. 2·20 1·50

1184 Knotted Ribbons **1185** Deciduous Trees

(Des H. Hoch. Litho Schwann-Bagel, Düsseldorf)

1997 (5 May). 50th Anniv of Town Twinning Movement. P 14.
2770 **1184** 100pf. multicoloured...................... 1·90 1·40

(Des J. Riess. Litho)

1997 (5 May). 50th Anniv of Society for the Protection of the German Forest. Sheet 105×70 mm containing T **1185** and similar square design. Multicoloured. P 14.

MS2771 100pf. Type **1185**; 200pf. Evergreen trees........ 6·50 7·25
   The stamps in No. **MS**2771 form a composite design.

1186 Kneipp **1187** United States Flag, George Marshall and Bomb Site

(Des G. Jacki. Litho German Bank Note Ptg Co, Leipzig)

1997 (9 June). Death Centenary of Father Sebastian Kneipp (developer of naturopathic treatments). P 13.
2772 **1186** 100pf. multicoloured...................... 2·00 1·40

(Des Corinna Rogger. Litho German Bank Note Ptg Co, Leipzig)

1997 (9 June). 50th Anniv of Marshall Plan (European Recovery Programme). P 13×13½.
2773 **1187** 100pf. multicoloured...................... 1·90 1·40

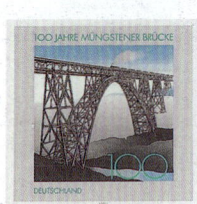

1188 Rheno-German Heavy Horse **1189** Train on Bridge

(Des Hannelore Heise. Litho)

1997 (9 June). Youth Welfare. Horses. T **1188** and similar square designs. P 14.
2774   80pf. +40pf. Type **1188**........................ 3·00 2·75
2775   80pf. +40pf. Shetland ponies................... 3·00 2·75
2776   100pf. +50pf. Frisian.......................... 3·50 3·00
2777   100pf. +50pf. Haflinger........................ 3·50 3·00
2778   200pf. +80pf. Hanoverian with foal............. 7·00 6·00
2774/2778 Set of 5..................................... 18·00 16·00

(Des L. Grünewald. Litho Schwann-Bagel, Düsseldorf)

1997 (20 June). Centenary of Müngsten Railway Bridge. P 14.
2779 **1189** 100pf. multicoloured...................... 1·70 1·40

1190 *Composition* (Fritz Winter)

GERMANY

(Des Sibylle and F. Haase. Litho)
1997 (20 June). Tenth Documenta Modern Art Exhibition, Kassel. Sheet 137×97 mm containing T **1190** and similar horiz designs. Multicoloured. P 14.
MS2780 100pf. Type **1190**; 100pf. *Mouth No. 15* (Tom Wesselmann); 100pf. *Quathlamba* (Frank Stella); 100pf. *Beuys/Bois* (Nam June Paik) .... 9·25 10·00

1191 Children holding Envelopes

1192 Arms of Brandenburg

(Des L. Fromm. Photo)
1997 (17 July). For Us Children. Sheet 70×105 mm. P 14.
MS2781 **1191** 100pf. multicoloured................... 3·50 3·75

(Des G. Aretz. Eng E. Falz (110pf.), J. Kanior (100, 220 pf.), W. Mauer (300, 440pf.). Recess)
1997 (14 Aug)–**98**. Famous Women. Vert designs as T **832** but inscr 'Deutschland'. P 14.
2782   100pf. orange-brown and deep bluish green
             (16.10.97)..................................... 2·00 1·40
2783   110pf. drab and deep violet....................... 2·00 1·40
2784   220pf. deep ultramarine and deep turquoise-
             blue (28.8.97)................................ 4·00 3·50
2785   300pf. yellow-brown and deep violet-blue
             (16.10.97).................................... 4·75 3·75
2786   440pf. lake-brown and deep violet (8.10.98).... 8·50 8·25
2782/2786 *Set of 5*..................................... 19·00 16·00
Designs:—100pf. Elisabeth Schwarzhaupt (politician); 110pf. Marlene Dietrich (actress); 220pf. Marie-Elisabeth Lüders (politician); 300pf. Maria Probst (social reformer and politician); 440pf. Gret Palucca (dancer).
Postal forgeries of the 110pf. exist. These can be identified by irregular corners and a patchy blue reaction to UV light.

Nos. 2787/2804 are vacant.

(Des E. Jünger. Litho)
1997 (19 Aug). Flood Relief Funds. P 14.
2805   **1192** 110pf. +90pf. multicoloured.............. 3·75 4·75

(Des H. Schillinger. Litho)
1997 (28 Aug). Landscapes (5th series). Horiz designs as T **1046**. Multicoloured. P 14.
2806   110pf. Bavarian Forest .... 2·00 1·50
2807   110pf. North German Moors......................... 2·00 1·50
2808   110pf. Lüneburg Heath .... 2·00 1·50
2806/2808 *Set of 3*..................................... 5·50 4·00

1193 Rudolf Diesel (engineer) and First Oil Engine

1194 Potato Plant and Cultivation

(Des P. Effert. Litho German Bank Note Ptg Co, Leipzig)
1997 (28 Aug). Centenary of Diesel Engine. P 13.
2809   **1193** 300pf. black, grey and new blue .... 5·50 4·50

(Des P. Steiner. Litho German Bank Note Ptg Co, Leipzig)
1997 (17 Sept). 350th Anniv of Introduction of the Potato to Germany. P 13×13½.
2810   **1194** 300pf. multicoloured...................... 4·75 4·50

1195 Biplane and Motorised Tricycle

1196 Mendelssohn-Bartholdy and Music Score

(Des J. Riess. Litho)
1997 (17 Sept). Stamp Day. Sheet 70×105 mm. P 14.
MS2811 **1195** 440pf.+220pf. multicoloured.............. 11·00 12·00
The premium was for the benefit of the Foundation for the Promotion of Philately and Postal History.

No. 2812 is vacant.

(Des Annegret Ehmke. Litho German Bank Note Ptg Co, Leipzig)
1997 (9 Oct). 150th Death Anniv of Felix Mendelssohn-Bartholdy (composer). P 13×13½.
2813   **1196** 110pf. deep olive, brown-olive and
             yellow .... 1·90 1·50

1197 Watermill, Black Forest

1198 Emblem

(Des O. Rohse. Litho)
1997 (9 Oct). Humanitarian Relief Funds. Mills. T **1197** and similar square designs. Multicoloured. P 14.
2814   100pf. +50pf. Type **1197** .... 3·75 3·50
2815   110pf. +50pf. Watermill, Hesse.................... 4·00 4·00
2816   110pf. +50pf. Post mill, Lower Rhine.............. 4·00 4·00
2817   110pf. +50pf. Scoop windmill, Schleswig
             Holstein..................................... 4·00 4·00
2818   220pf. +80pf. Dutch windmill...................... 5·75 6·00
2814/2818 *Set of 5*..................................... 19·00 19·00

(Des C. Broutin. Litho)
1997 (16 Oct). Saar-Lor-Lux European Region. P 14.
2819   **1198** 110pf. multicoloured..................... 2·00 1·50
A stamp of a similar design was issued by France and Luxembourg.

1199 Team celebrating

(Des Sabine Bucher. Photo)
1997 (16 Oct). Bayern München's Victory in German Football Championship. P 14.
2820   **1199** 110pf. multicoloured..................... 2·00 1·50

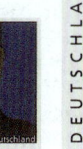

1200 Thomas Dehler

1201 Heine (after Wilhelm Hensel)

(Des G. and O. Aretz. Litho Schwann-Bagel, Düsseldorf)
1997 (6 Nov). Birth Centenary of Thomas Dehler (politician). P 14.
2821   **1200** 110pf. multicoloured..................... 1·90 1·50

GERMANY

(Des G. Lienemeyer. Litho German Bank Note Ptg Co, Leipzig)

1997 (6 Nov). Birth Bicentenary of Heinrich Heine (journalist and poet). P 13.

| 2822 | **1201** | 110pf. multicoloured | 1·90 | 1·50 |

The original printing of No. 2822 was withdrawn due to the appearance of runic symbols on the sheet margin which had previous Nazi connotations. Subsequent supplies omitted the runes from the sheet margins.

1202 Tree and Title of Hymn

1203 Emblem

(Des Antonia Graschberger. Litho)

1997 (6 Nov). 300th Birth Anniv of Gerhard Tersteegen (religious reformer). P 14.

| 2823 | **1202** | 110pf. lake-brown, bluish grey and black | 1·90 | 1·50 |

(Des Sibylle and F. Haase. Photo)

1997 (6 Nov). Centenary of Deutscher Caritas Verband (Catholic charitable association). P 14.

| 2824 | **1203** | 110pf. multicoloured | 1·90 | 1·50 |

1204 Three Kings

1205 Monastery Plan and Church

(Des J. Lenica. Litho)

1997 (6 Nov). Christmas. T **1204** and similar square design. Multicoloured. P 14.

| 2825 | 100pf. +50pf. Type **1204** | 2·50 | 2·40 |
| 2826 | 110pf. +50pf. Nativity | 3·00 | 2·75 |

The premium was for the benefit of the Federal Association of Free Welfare Work, Bonn.

(Des R. Lederbogen. Litho)

1998 (22 Jan). UNESCO World Heritage Site, Maulbronn Monastery. P 14.

| 2827 | **1205** | 100pf. multicoloured | 1·90 | 1·50 |

1206 Walled City

1207 Glienicke Bridge, Potsdam–Berlin

(Des H. Schillinger. Litho)

1998 (22 Jan). 1100th Anniv of Nördlingen. P 14.

| 2828 | **1206** | 110pf. multicoloured | 1·90 | 1·50 |

(Des R. Blumenstein. Litho German Bank Note Ptg Co, Leipzig)

1998 (22 Jan). Bridges (1st series). P 14.

| 2829 | **1207** | 110pf. multicoloured | 1·90 | 1·50 |

See also Nos. 2931, 2956 and 3046.

1208 Football

1209 Characters in Brecht's Head

(Des Irmgard Hesse. Photo)

1998 (5 Feb). Sport Promotion Fund. International designs. Championships. T **1208** and similar horiz Multicoloured. P 14.

2830	100pf. +50pf. Type **1208** (World Cup Football Championship, France)	4·00	3·50
2831	110pf. +50pf. Ski jumping (Winter Olympic Games, Japan) Nagano	4·25	3·75
2832	110pf. +50pf. Rowing (World Rowing Championships, Cologne)	4·25	3·75
2833	300pf. +100pf. Disabled skier (Winter Paralympic Games Nagano)	9·25	9·00
2830/2833	Set of 4	20·00	18·00

(Des J. Lenica. Litho Schwann-Bagel, Düsseldorf)

1998 (5 Feb). Birth Centenary of Bertolt Brecht (dramatist). P 14.

| 2834 | **1209** | 110pf. multicoloured | 1·90 | 1·50 |

1210 X-ray Photographs of Moon, Ionic Lattice Structure and Nerve of Goldfish and Founding Assembly

(Des Sibylle and F. Haase. Litho German Bank Note Ptg Co, Leipzig)

1998 (5 Feb). 50th Anniv of Max Planck Society for the Advancement of Science. P 14.

| 2835 | **1210** | 110pf. multicoloured | 1·90 | 1·50 |

1211 Bad Frankenhausen

(Des D. Glinski. Litho German Bank Note Ptg Co, Leipzig)

1998 (12 Mar). Millenary of First Documentary Reference to Bad Frankenhausen. P 13½×13.

| 2836 | **1211** | 110pf. multicoloured | 1·90 | 1·50 |

1212 Signatories

(Des M. Gottschall. Litho)

1998 (12 Mar). 350th Anniv of Peace of Westphalia ending Thirty Years' Wars. P 14.

| 2837 | **1212** | 110pf. black, bluish grey and bright magenta | 1·90 | 1·50 |

1213 Baden-Württemberg (Kurt Viertel)

(Des G. and O. Aretz. Litho)

1998 (12 Mar). Federal State Parliament Buildings (1st series). T **1213** and similar horiz designs. Multicoloured. P 14.
2838	110pf. Type **1213**	2·00	1·50
2839	110pf. Bavaria (Friedrich Bürklein)	2·00	1·50
2840	110pf. Chamber of Deputies, Berlin (Friedrich Schulze)	2·00	1·50
2841	110pf. Brandenburg (Franz Schwecten)	2·00	1·50
2838/2841	Set of 4	7·25	5·50

See also Nos. 2885, 2893/2894, 2897, 2953, 2957, 2978, 3025, 3043, 3052, 3064 and 3072.

1214 Hildegard's Vision of Life Cycle

(Des P. Nitzsche. Litho)

1998 (16 Apr). 900th Birth Anniv of Hildegard von Bingen (writer and mystic). P 14.
| 2842 | **1214** 100pf. multicoloured | 1·90 | 1·50 |

1215 Marine Life

(Des Verena Schmidmaier. Litho)

1998 (16 Apr). For Us Children. Sheet 110×66 mm. P 14.
| MS2843 | **1215** 110pf. multicoloured | 3·50 | 3·75 |

1216 St. Marienstern Abbey

(Des H. Zill. Litho German Bank Note Ptg Co, Leipzig)

1998 (16 Apr). 750th Anniv of St. Marienstern Abbey, Panschwitz-Kuckau. P 13×12½.
| 2844 | **1216** 110pf. multicoloured | 1·90 | 1·50 |

1217 Auditorium

(Des H. Schillinger. Litho)

1998 (16 Apr). 250th Anniv of Bayreuth Opera House. P 13½.
| 2845 | **1217** 300pf. multicoloured | 5·00 | 4·75 |

1218 Ernst Jünger    **1219** Doves and Tree (German Unification Day)

(Des Antonia Graschberger. Litho Schwann-Bagel, Düsseldorf)

1998 (22 Apr). Ernst Jünger (writer) Commemoration. P 14.
| 2846 | **1218** 110pf. multicoloured | 1·90 | 1·50 |

(Des J. Lenica. Litho)

1998 (7 May). Europa. National Festivals. P 14.
| 2847 | **1219** 110pf. multicoloured | 2·30 | 1·50 |

1220 Association Manifesto    **1221** Opening Session of Parliamentary Council, 1948

(Des Irmgard Hesse. Litho German Bank Note Ptg Co, Leipzig)

1998 (7 May). 50th Anniv of German Rural Women's Association. P 13.
| 2848 | **1220** 110pf. apple green, emerald and black | 1·90 | 1·50 |

(Des I. Wulff. Litho)

1998 (7 May). Parliamentary Anniversaries. Sheet 105×70 mm containing T **1221** and similar square design. Multicoloured. P 14.
| MS2849 | 110pf. Type **1221**; 220pf. First German National Assembly, St. Paul's Church, Frankfurt, 1848 | 7·00 | 8·25 |

1222 Coast and Ocean

(Des M. Gottschall. Litho)

1998 (7 May). Environmental Protection. P 14.
| 2850 | **1222** 110pf. +50pf. multicoloured | 4·00 | 5·00 |

See also No. 3864.

1223 The Mouse    **1224** Crowds of People and Cross

(Des Erna de Vries. Litho)

1998 (10 June). Youth Welfare. Children's Cartoons. T **1223** and similar square designs. Multicoloured. P 14.
2851	100pf. +50pf. Type **1223**	2·75	2·75
2852	100pf. +50pf. *The Sandman*	2·75	2·75
2853	110pf. +50pf. *Maja the Bee*	3·00	3·00
2854	110pf. +50pf. *Captain Bluebear*	3·00	3·00
2855	220pf. +80pf. *Pumuckl*	5·00	4·75
2851/2855	Set of 5	15·00	14·50

GERMANY

(Des L. Romboy. Litho Schwann-Bagel, Düsseldorf)
1998 (10 June). 150th Anniv of First Congress of German Catholics. P 13×13½.
2856   **1224**   110pf. multicoloured .... 1·90   1·40

1225 One Deutschmark Coin
1226 Harvesting Hops 

(Des E. Jünger. Litho German Bank Note Ptg Co, Leipzig)
1998 (19 June). 50th Anniv of the Deutschmark. P 13.
2857   **1225**   110pf. multicoloured .... 3·00   1·80

(Des P. Steiner. Litho German Bank Note Ptg Co, Leipzig)
1998 (16 July). 1100 Years of Hop Cultivation in Germany. P 13.
2858   **1226**   110pf. multicoloured .... 1·90   1·50

1227 Euro Banknotes forming 'EZB'

(Des P. Effert. Litho)
1998 (16 July). Inauguration of European Central Bank, Frankfurt-am-Main. P 14.
2859   **1227**   110pf. multicoloured .... 2·50   1·80

1228 Rock Face, Elbe Sandstone Mountains
1229 Crocodile Skeleton 

(Des D. Glinski. Litho)
1998 (16 July). Saxon Switzerland National Park. Sheet 105×70 mm containing T **1228** and similar square design. Multicoloured. P 14.
MS2860 110pf. Type **1228**; 220pf. Elbe Sandstone Mountains .... 7·00   8·00
The stamps in No. **MS**2860 form a composite design.

(Des Isolde Monson-Baumgart. Litho German Bank Note Ptg Co, Leipzig)
1998 (20 Aug). UNESCO World Heritage Sites. Grube Messel Fossil Deposits. P 13×12½.
2861   **1229**   100pf. multicoloured .... 1·90   1·40

1230 Coloured Squares and Ludolphian Number
1231 Würzburg Palace 

(Des N. Höchtlen. Photo)
1998 (20 Aug). 23rd International Congress of Mathematicians, Berlin. P 14.
2862   **1230**   110pf. multicoloured .... 1·90   1·50

(Des Xiao Yutian. Litho)
1998 (20 Aug). UNESCO World Heritage Sites. T **1231** and similar vert design. Multicoloured. P 14.
2863   110pf. Type **1231** .... 2·30   1·40
2864   110pf. Puning Temple, Chengde, China .... 2·30   1·40

1232 Glasses (Peter Behrens)

(Des I. Wulff. Litho)
1998 (20 Aug). Contemporary Design (1st series). Sheet 138×97 mm containing T **1232** and similar horiz designs. Multicoloured. P 14.
MS2865 110pf. Type **1232**; 110pf. Teapot (Marianne Brandt); 110pf. Table lamp (Wilhelm Wagenfeld); 110pf. 'Wassily' Chair (Marcel Breuer) .... 11·00   12·50
See also No. **MS**2922.

1233 Players, Ball and Pitch
1234 Main Building 

(Des L. Menze. Litho Schwann-Bagel, Düsseldorf)
1998 (10 Sept). 1.FC Kaiserslautern's Victory in German Football Championship. P 14.
2866   **1233**   110pf. multicoloured .... 2·20   1·50

(Des Barbara Dimanski. Litho German Bank Note Ptg Co, Leipzig)
1998 (10 Sept). 300th Anniv of Francke Charitable Institutions, Halle. P 13.
2867   **1234**   110pf. multicoloured .... 1·90   1·50

1235 Hausmann and Book Cover
1236 Hands on T-shirt 

(Des P. Nitzsche. Litho)
1998 (10 Sept). Birth Centenary of Manfred Hausmann (writer). P 14.
2868   **1235**   110pf. multicoloured .... 1·90   1·50

(Des T. Ottenfelt. Litho German Bank Note Ptg Co, Leipzig)
1998 (10 Sept). Child Protection. P 14.
2869   **1236**   110pf. scarlet, olive-grey and black .... 1·90   1·50

1237 Hen Harriers and Chicks
1238 Ear

GERMANY

(Des J. Riess. Litho)

1998 (8 Oct). Humanitarian Relief Funds. Birds. T **1237** and similar square designs. Multicoloured. P 14×13½.
2870	100pf. +50pf. Type **1237**	2·75	2·75
2871	110pf. +50pf. Great Bustards	3·00	3·00
2872	110pf. +50pf. White-eyed Ducks	3·00	3·00
2873	110pf. +50pf. Sedge Warblers on reeds	3·00	3·00
2874	220pf. +80pf. Woodchat Shrike	4·75	5·25
2870/2874	*Set of 5*	15·00	15·00

(Des Susanne Oesterlee. Litho German Bank Note Ptg Co, Leipzig)

1998 (8 Oct). Telephone Help Lines. P 13.
2875	**1238** 110pf. black and red-orange	1·90	1·50

1239 Hiorten (sailing packet), 1692

1240 Günther Ramin

(Des H. Zill. Litho)

1998 (8 Oct). Stamp Day. P 13.
2876	**1239** 110pf. multicoloured	1·90	1·50

(Des G. Lienemeyer. Photo)

1998 (8 Oct). Birth Centenary of Günther Ramin (choirmaster and organist). P 14.
2877	**1240** 300pf. multicoloured	5·00	4·50

1241 Shepherds following Star

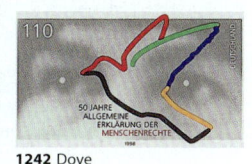

1242 Dove

(Des J. Lenica. Photo)

1998 (12 Nov). Christmas. T **1241** and similar square design. Multicoloured. P 14.
2878	100pf. +50pf. Type **1241**	2·30	2·30
2879	110pf. +50pf. Baby Jesus	2·50	2·40

(Des E. Jünger. Litho German Bank Note Ptg Co, Leipzig)

1998 (12 Nov). 50th Anniv of Declaration of Human Rights. P 13×12½.
2880	**1242** 110pf. multicoloured	1·90	1·50

For charity stamp for Kosovo Relief Fund in similar design see No. 2899.

1243 Conductor's Hands and Baton

1244 National Theatre, Schiller, Goethe, Wieland and Herder

(Des M. Gottschall. Litho Schwann-Bagel, Düsseldorf)

1998 (12 Nov). 450th Anniv of Saxon State Orchestra, Dresden. P 14.
2881	**1243** 300pf. multicoloured	5·50	4·50

(Des Vera Braesecke-Kaul and H. Kaul. Litho)

1999 (14 Jan). 1100th Anniv of Weimar, European City of Culture. P 14.
2882	**1244** 100pf. multicoloured	1·90	1·70

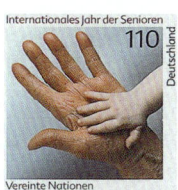

1245 Hands of Elderly Person and Child

1246 Katharina von Bora

(Des L. Menze. Litho German Bank Note Ptg Co, Leipzig)

1999 (14 Jan). International Year of the Elderly. P 13.
2883	**1245** 110pf. multicoloured	2·00	1·70

(Des H. Schall. Litho Schwann-Bagel, Düsseldorf)

1999 (14 Jan). 500th Birth Anniv of Katharina von Bora (wife of Martin Luther). P 14.
2884	**1246** 110pf. multicoloured	2·00	1·70

(Des G. and O. Aretz. Litho)

1999 (14 Jan). Federal State Parliament Buildings (2nd series). Horiz design as T **1213**. P 14.
2885	110pf. Hesse (Richard Goerz) (former palace of Dukes of Hesse)	2·00	1·70

1247 Cycle Racing

(Des F.-D. Rothacker. Photo)

1999 (18 Feb). Sport Promotion Fund. T **1247** and similar horiz designs. Multicoloured. P 14.
2886	100pf. +50pf. Type **1247**	2·75	3·00
2887	110pf. +50pf. Horse racing	3·00	3·25
2888	110pf. +50pf. Motor racing	3·00	3·25
2889	300pf. +100pf. Motorcycle racing	6·25	6·50
2886/2889	*Set of 4*	13·50	14·50

1248 Cover Illustration (by Walter Trier) of *Emil and the Detectives* (children's novel)

1249 Coloured Diodes

(Des G. Lienemeyer. Litho German Bank Note Ptg Co, Leipzig)

1999 (18 Feb). Birth Centenary of Erich Kästner (writer). P 13.
2890	**1248** 300pf. multicoloured	5·00	4·75

(Des P. Krüll. Litho German Bank Note Ptg Co, Leipzig)

1999 (11 Mar). 50th Anniv of Fraunhofer Society (for applied research). P 13.
2891	**1249** 110pf. multicoloured	2·00	1·70

1250 Emblem and Initials

1251 Maybach Cabriolet of 1936 and Club Emblem

(Des P. Effert. Photo)

1999 (11 Mar). 50th Anniv of North Atlantic Treaty Organisation. P 13½.
2892	**1250** 110pf. multicoloured	2·00	1·70

GERMANY

(Des G. and O. Aretz. Litho)
1999 (11 Mar). Federal State Parliament Buildings (3rd series). Horiz designs as T **1213**. Multicoloured. P 14.
2893 110pf. City Parliament of Hamburg .... 2·00 1·70
2894 110pf. Mecklenburg-Western Pomerania (Schwerin Castle, rebuilt by Georg Demmler and Friedrich Stüler)................... 2·00 1·70

(Des Heike Ullmann. Photo)
1999 (27 Apr). Centenary of German Automobile Club. P 14.
2895 **1251** 110pf. multicoloured .... 2·00 1·70

1252 Emblem

1253 Man, Nature, Technology

(Des Lorli and E. Jünger. Litho German Bank Note Ptg Co, Leipzig)
1999 (27 Apr). 25th Anniv of German Cancer Relief. P 13.
2896 **1252** 110pf. multicoloured .... 2·00 1·70

(Des G. and O. Aretz. Litho)
1999 (27 Apr). Federal State Parliament Buildings (4th series). Horiz design as T **1213**. P 14.
2897 110pf. Bremen (Wassili Luckhardt)....................... 2·00 1·70

(Des J. Riess. Litho Schwann-Bagel, Düsseldorf)
1999 (27 Apr). EXPO 2000 World's Fair, Hanover (1st series). P 14.
2898 **1253** 110pf. multicoloured .... 2·00 1·70
See also Nos. 2936, 2959, 2966/2971 and 2979.

(Des E. Jünger. Litho German Bank Note Ptg Co, Leipzig)
1999 (27 Apr). Kosovo Relief Fund. As T **1242** but with inscription changed to 'KOSOVO—HILFE 1999'. P 14.
2899 110pf. +100pf. multicoloured .... 3·75 3·50

1254 Bavaria 1849 1k. and Saxony 1850 3pf. Stamps

(Des P. Nitzsche. Litho)
1999 (27 Apr). IBRA'99 International Stamp Exhibition, Nüremberg. Sheet 140×100 mm. P 13½.
MS2900 **1254** 300pf.+110pf. black, rose-red and gold/*cream*.. 9·25 10·50

1255 Berchtesgaden National Park

(Des Silvia Runge. Litho)
1999 (4 May). Europa. Parks and Gardens. Sheet 110×66 mm. P 14.
MS2901 **1255** 110pf. multicoloured................................ 4·75 5·25

1256 Cross of St. John

1257 Flags and Children

(Des L. Romboy. Litho German Bank Note Ptg Co, Leipzig)
1999 (4 May). 900th Anniv of Orders of Knights of St. John of Jerusalem. P 13½×13.
2902 **1256** 110pf. multicoloured .... 2·00 1·70

(Des Angela Kühn. Photo)
1999 (4 May). 50th Anniv of Berlin Airlift of 1948–49. P 14.
2903 **1257** 110pf. multicoloured .... 2·00 1·70

1258 Emblem

(Des M. Gottschall. Litho German Bank Note Ptg Co, Leipzig)
1999 (4 May). 50th Anniv of Council of Europe. P 13.
2904 **1258** 110pf. multicoloured .... 2·30 1·70

1259 State Arms and Article 1

(Des Lorli and E. Jünger. Litho)
1999 (21 May). 50th Anniv of German Basic Law. Sheet 110×66 mm. P 14.
MS2905 **1259** 110pf. multicoloured............................... 3·00 5·25

1260 Politicians and New Parliament Chamber, Berlin

(Des Antonia Graschberger. Litho)
1999 (21 May). 50th Anniv of Federal Republic of Germany. Sheet 138×97 mm containing T **1260** and similar horiz designs. Multicoloured. P 14.
MS2906 110pf. Type **1260**; 110pf. Child playing in rubble and child among flowers; 110pf. Berlin Wall and its fall; 110pf. Soldiers confronting civilians and debating chamber............................... 10·00 12·00

1261 *Lars*, the Little Polar Bear

1262 Cross Clasp, Altar, Cathedral Spire and Time-line

(Des P. Steiner. Litho)

1999 (10 June). Youth Welfare. Cartoon Characters. T **1261** and similar square designs. Multicoloured. P 14.

2907	100pf. +50pf. Type **1261**	2·75	3·00
2908	100pf. +50pf. *Rudi* the Crow	2·75	3·00
2909	110pf. +50pf. *Twipsy* (mascot of EXPO 2000 World's Fair, Hanover)	3·00	3·50
2910	110pf. +50pf. *Mecki* (hedgehog)	3·00	3·50
2911	220pf. +80pf. *Tabaluga* (dragon)	4·75	5·25
2907/2911	Set of 5	14·50	16·00

(Des P. Steiner. Litho German Bank Note Ptg Co, Leipzig)

1999 (10 June). 1200th Anniv of Paderborn Diocese. P 14.

| 2912 | **1262** 110pf. multicoloured | 2·00 | 1·50 |

1263 House (child's painting)

1264 *Ball at the Viennese Hofburg* and Score

(Des Marie-Helen Geisselbrecht. Litho German Bank Note Ptg Co, Leipzig)

1999 (10 June). 50th Anniv of SOS Children's Villages. P 14.

| 2913 | **1263** 110pf. multicoloured | 2·00 | 1·50 |

(Des Ursula Kahrl. Litho)

1999 (10 June). Death Centenary of Johann Strauss the younger (composer). P 14.

| 2914 | **1264** 300pf. multicoloured | 5·25 | 4·50 |

1265 Children at Desks (tapestry)

1266 Gustav Heinemann

(Des Barbara Dimanski. Litho)

1999 (15 July). 115th Anniv of Dominikus-Ringeisen Institute for Disabled People, Ursberg. P 14.

| 2915 | **1265** 110pf. multicoloured | 2·00 | 1·50 |

(Des Antonia Graschberger. Litho Schwann-Bagel, Düsseldorf)

1999 (15 July). Birth Centenary of Gustav Heinemann (President 1969–74). P 14.

| 2916 | **1266** 110pf. olive-grey and bright scarlet | 2·00 | 1·50 |

1267 *Old Woman laughing* (Ernst Barlach)

1268 Participating Countries and Dove

(Des F. Lüdtke. Litho)

1999 (15 July). Cultural Foundation of the Federal States (1st series). Sculptures. T **1267** and similar horiz design. Multicoloured. P 14.

| 2917 | 110pf. Type **1267** | 2·00 | 1·50 |
| 2918 | 220pf. *Bust of a Thinker* (Wilhelm Lehmbruck) | 3·50 | 3·00 |

See also Nos. 2960/1.

(Des G. and O. Aretz. Litho German Bank Note Ptg Co, Leipzig)

1999 (15 July). Centenary of First Peace Conference, The Hague. P 13.

| 2919 | **1268** 300pf. violet-grey, rosine and new blue | 5·25 | 4·25 |

1269 Goethe (after J. K. Stieler)

1270 Mouse carrying Letter

(Des Ursula Kahrl. Litho)

1999 (12 Aug). 250th Birth Anniv of Johann Wolfgang von Goethe (poet and playwright). P 14.

| 2920 | **1269** 110pf. multicoloured | 2·00 | 1·70 |

A stamp of a similar design was issued by South Korea.

(Des Barbara Dimanski. Litho German Bank Note Ptg Co, Leipzig)

1999 (12 Aug). For Us Children. Sheet 105×71 mm. P 13.

| MS2921 | **1270** 110pf. multicoloured | 3·00 | 4·50 |

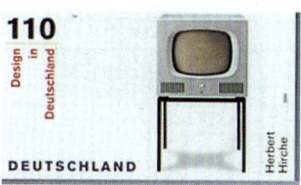

1271 HF1 Television Set (Herbert Hirche)

(Des I. Wulff. Litho)

1999 (12 Aug). Contemporary Design (2nd series). Sheet 138×97 mm containing T **1271** and similar horiz designs. Multicoloured. P 14.

| MS2922 | 110pf. Type **1271**; 110pf. 'Mono-a' cutlery (Peter Raacke); 110pf. Pearl bottles (Gunter Kupetz); 110pf. Transrapid Maglev train (Alexander Neumeister) | 10·00 | 11·50 |

1272 Player

1273 Book and Bookmark

(Des L. Menze. Litho Schwann-Bagel, Mönchengladbach)

1999 (16 Sept). FC Bayern Münich's Victory in German Football Championship. P 14.

| 2923 | **1272** 110pf. multicoloured | 2·00 | 1·70 |

(Des G. and O. Aretz. Photo)

1999 (16 Sept). 50th Anniv of Federal Association of German Book Traders' Peace Prize. P 14.

| 2924 | **1273** 110pf. multicoloured | 1·90 | 1·70 |

1274 Srauss and Poster from *Salome* (opera)

(Des P. Nitzsche. Litho German Bank Note Ptg Co, Leipzig)

1999 (16 Sept). 50th Death Anniv of Richard Strauss (composer). P 13.

| 2925 | **1274** 300pf. multicoloured | 5·25 | 4·75 |

GERMANY

1275 Andromeda Galaxy

(Des B. Blase. Litho and holography (Nos. 2929/30) or litho (others))

1999 (14 Oct). Humanitarian Relief Funds. Outer Space. T **1275** and similar horiz designs. Multicoloured. P 14.
2926	100pf. +50pf. Type **1275**	2·50	2·40
2927	100pf. +50pf. Swan constellation	2·50	2·40
2928	110pf. +50pf. X-ray image of exploding star	2·75	2·75
2929	110pf. +50pf. Comet colliding with Jupiter	2·75	2·75
2930	300pf. +100pf. Gamma ray image of sky	6·50	6·25
2926/2930	Set of 5	15·00	15·00

1276 Göltzsch Valley Railway Bridge

(Des W. Schmidt. Litho German Bank Note Ptg Co, Leipzig)

1999 (14 Oct). Bridges (2nd series). P 14.
2931	**1276** 110pf. multicoloured	1·90	1·70

1277 'DGB'

1278 Greater Horseshoe Bats

(Des H. G. Schmitz. Litho Schwann-Bagel, Mönchengladbach)

1999 (14 Oct). 50th Anniv of German Federation of Trade Unions. P 14.
2932	**1277** 110pf. black and bright scarlet-vermilion	1·90	1·70

(Des H. Zill. Litho Schwann-Bagel, Mönchengladbach)

1999 (4 Nov). Endangered Species. P 14.
2933	**1278** 110pf. multicoloured	1·90	1·70

1279 The Annunciation

1280 Emblem and Eye

(Des P. Steiner. Litho)

1999 (4 Nov). Christmas. T **1279** and similar square design. Multicoloured. P 14.
2934	100pf. +50pf. Type **1279**	2·50	2·50
2935	110pf. +50pf. Nativity	2·75	2·75

(Des H. G. Schmitz. Litho)

2000 (13 Jan). EXPO 2000 World's Fair, Hanover (2nd issue). P 14.
2936	**1280** 100pf. multicoloured	1·90	1·70

1281 Emblem

1282 Charlemagne and Plan of Palace Chapel

(Des G. and O. Aretz. Litho)

2000 (13 Jan). Holy Year 2000. P 14.
2937	**1281** 110pf. multicoloured	2·00	1·70

(Des P. Nitzsche. Litho)

2000 (13 Jan). 1200th Anniv of Aachen Cathedral. P 14.
2938	**1282** 110pf. multicoloured	2·00	1·70

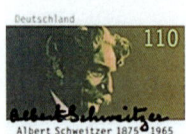

1283 Schweitzer and Signature

1284 Football

(Des H. G. Schmitz. Litho German Bank Note Ptg Co, Leipzig)

2000 (13 Jan). 125th Birth Anniv of Albert Schweitzer (missionary doctor). P 14.
2939	**1283** 110pf. multicoloured	2·00	1·70

(Des H. G. Schmitz. Photo)

2000 (13 Jan). Centenary of German Football Association. P 13½.
2940	**1284** 110pf. multicoloured	2·50	1·70

No. 2940 is perforated as a circle contained within an outer perforated square.

1285 Herbert Wehner

1286 Woman

(Des G. and O. Aretz. Photo)

2000 (13 Jan). Tenth Death Anniv of Herbert Wehner (politician). P 14.
2941	**1285** 110pf. multicoloured	2·00	1·70

(Des Irmgard Hesse. Litho Schwann-Bagel, Mönchengladbach)

2000 (13 Jan). Prevention of Violence Against Women. P 14.
2942	**1286** 110pf. scarlet-vermilion, grey and black	2·00	1·70

1287 '2000' in Moving Film Sequence

(Des H. G. Schmitz, Litho German Bank Note Ptg Co, Leipzig)

2000 (17 Feb). 50th Berlin International Film Festival. P 14.
2943	**1287** 100pf. multicoloured	1·90	1·70

1288 Boxing

GERMANY

(Des L. Menze. Litho)

2000 (17 Feb). Sport Promotion Fund. T **1288** and similar horiz designs. Multicoloured. P 14.
2944	100pf. +50pf. Type **1288** (fair play)	3·50	3·00
2945	110pf. +50pf. Rhythmic gymnastics (beauty)	3·75	3·25
2946	110pf. +50pf. Running (competition)	3·75	3·25
2947	300pf. +100pf. Raised hands (culture of interaction)	6·75	6·00
2944/2947	Set of 4	16·00	14·00

1289 Gutenberg (after engraving by A. Thevet) and Letters from *Gutenberg Bible*

1290 Jester

(Des Regina and P. Steiner. Litho)

2000 (17 Feb). 600th Birth Anniv of Johannes Gutenberg (inventor of printing press). P 14.
| 2948 | **1289** 110pf. black and orange-red | 2·00 | 1·70 |

(Des E. Kößlinger. Litho Schwann-Bagel, Mönchengladbach)

2000 (17 Feb). 175th Anniv of First Düsseldorf Carnival. P 13×13½.
| 2949 | **1290** 110pf. multicoloured | 2·20 | 1·70 |

1291 Friedrich Ebert

1292 Weill at Rehearsal of *One Touch of Venus* (musical), 1943

(Des H. G. Schmitz. Photo)

2000 (17 Feb). 75th Death Anniv of Friedrich Ebert (President, 1919–25). P 13½.
| 2950 | **1291** 110pf. multicoloured | 2·00 | 1·70 |

(Des Sibylle and F. Haase. Litho)

2000 (17 Feb). Birth Centenary of Kurt Weill (composer). P 14.
| 2951 | **1292** 300pf. multicoloured | 5·25 | 4·75 |

1293 Passau

(Des H. Schillinger. Litho)

2000 (16 Mar). Images of Germany. P 14.
| 2952 | **1293** 110pf. multicoloured | 2·00 | 1·70 |

(Des G. and O. Aretz. Litho)

2000 (16 Mar). Federal State Parliament Buildings (5th series). Horiz design as T **1213**. Multicoloured. P 14.
| 2953 | 110pf. Leine Palace, Lower Saxony | 2·00 | 1·70 |

1294 Trees

1295 Toy Windmill and 'Post!'

(Des J. Riess. Litho German Bank Note Ptg Co, Leipzig)

2000 (16 Mar). Hainich National Park. Sheet 105×70 mm. P 13.
| MS2954 | **1294** 110pf. multicoloured | 3·00 | 4·25 |

(Des Regina and P. Steiner. Litho)

2000 (16 Mar). P 14.
| 2955 | **1295** 110pf. multicoloured | 2·50 | 2·40 |

1296 'Blue Wonder' Bridge, Dresden

1297 City Buildings

(Des H. Zill. Litho German Bank Note Ptg Co, Leipzig)

2000 (13 Apr). Bridges (3rd series). P 13.
| 2956 | **1296** 100pf. multicoloured | 1·90 | 1·50 |

(Des G. and O. Aretz. Litho)

2000 (13 Apr). Federal State Parliament Buildings (6th series). Horiz design as T **1213**. Multicoloured. P 14.
| 2957 | 110pf. North-Rhine/Westphalia (Fritz Eller) | 2·20 | 1·70 |

(Des Regina and P. Steiner. Recess and litho)

2000 (13 Apr). 750th Anniv of Greifswald. P 14.
| 2958 | **1297** 110pf. multicoloured | 2·00 | 1·70 |

(Des J. Riess. Litho Schwann-Bagel, Mönchengladbach)

2000 (13 Apr). EXPO 2000 World's Fair, Hanover (3rd issue) As No. 2898 but self-adhesive. Die-cut perf 11.
| 2959 | **1253** 110pf. multicoloured | 9·75 | 7·50 |

No. 2959 is peeled directly from the cover of the booklet. It is not therefore possible to collect these as booklet panes.

1298 *Expulsion from Paradise* (Leonhard Kern)

1299 'Building Europe'

(Des F. Lüdtke. Litho)

2000 (13 Apr). Cultural Foundation of the Federal States (2nd series). Sculptures. T **1298** and similar horiz design. Multicoloured. P 14.
| 2960 | 110pf. Type **1298** | 2·30 | 2·10 |
| 2961 | 220pf. Silver table fountain (Melchior Gelb) | 3·50 | 3·25 |

(Des J.-P. Cousin. Litho Schwann-Bagel, Mönchengladbach)

2000 (12 May). Europa.

(a) Sheet stamp. P 13½
| 2962 | **1299** 110pf. multicoloured | 2·75 | 1·80 |

(b) Booklet stamp. Self-adhesive. Die-cut perf 11
| 2963 | **1299** 110pf. multicoloured | 4·00 | 2·40 |

No. 2963 is peeled directly from the cover of the booklet. It is not therefore possible to collect these as booklet panes.

Nos. 2962/2963 are denominated both in German currency and in euros. See note after No. 3027.

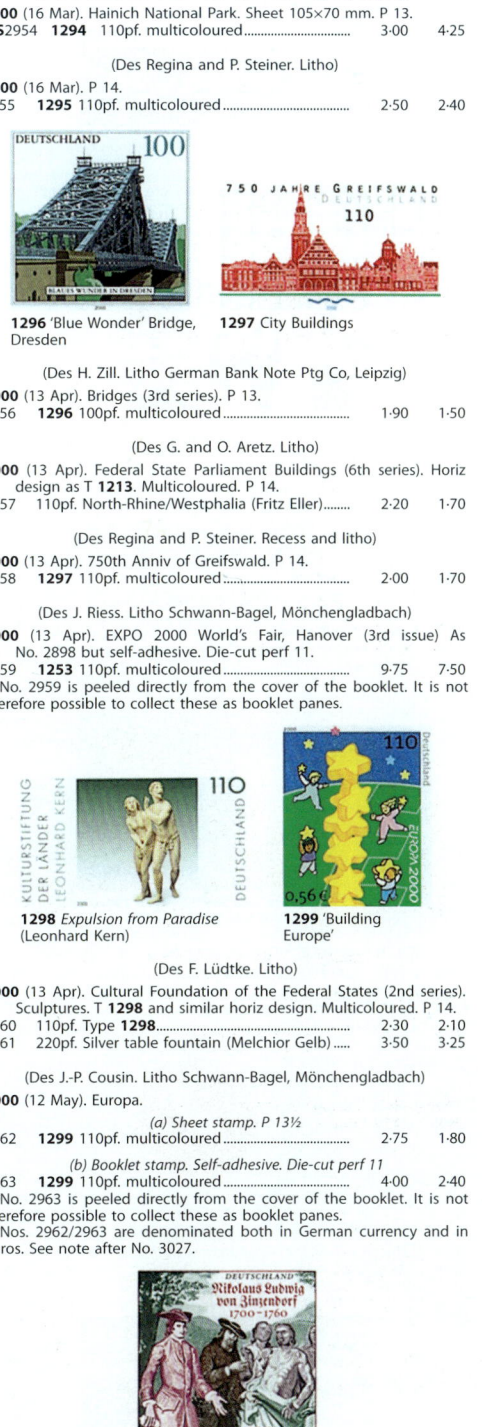

1300 Von Zinzendorf and Red Indians

(Des P. Nitzsche. Litho)

2000 (12 May). 300th Birth Anniv of Nikolaus Ludwig von Zinzendorf (leader of Moravian Brethren). P 13½.
| 2964 | **1300** 110pf. multicoloured | 2·00 | 1·50 |

141

GERMANY

1301 Countryside

(Des P. Steiner. Litho German Bank Note Ptg Co, Leipzig)
2000 (12 May). Environmental Protection. P 14.
2965 **1301** 110pf. +50pf. multicoloured .... 4·00 4·25

1302 Crowd at Music Festival

(Des A. Choiniere, Julia Henning, M. Koopmann, Wang Yanhui LiuNan, Wu Wenyue and Katrin Storm. Litho)
2000 (8 June). Youth Welfare. EXPO 2000 World's Fair, Hanover (4th issue). T **1302** and similar horiz designs. Multicoloured. P 14.
2966 100pf. +50pf. Type **1302** .... 2·75 2·75
2967 100pf. +50pf. Back-packers .... 2·75 2·75
2968 110pf. +50pf. Map of Africa and text .... 3·00 3·00
2969 110pf. +50pf. Eye of Buddha .... 3·00 3·00
2970 110pf. +50pf. Chinese calligraphy .... 3·00 3·00
2971 300pf. +100pf. Psychedelic swirl .... 5·00 5·00
2966/2971 Set of 6 .... 18·00 18·00

1303 Front Page of Issue 17, 1650, and Modern Pages of Newspaper

(Des F. Lüdtke. Litho German Bank Note Ptg Co, Leipzig)
2000 (8 June). 350th Anniv of *Einkommende Zeitungen* (first German daily newspaper). P 14.
2972 **1303** 110pf. multicoloured .... 2·20 1·70

1304 Emblem

(Des P. Effert. Litho Schwann-Bagel, Mönchengladbach)
2000 (8 June). Centenary of Chambers of Handicrafts. P 14.
2973 **1304** 300pf. bright orange and black .... 5·25 4·75

1305 Meteorological Station

(Des E. Kößlinger. Litho)
2000 (13 July). Centenary of Zugspitze Meteorological Station. P 14.
2974 **1305** 100pf. multicoloured .... 2·30 1·70

1306 Road Sign and Flashing Light  **1307** Bach

(Des Corinna Rogger. Litho)
2000 (13 July). 50th Anniv of Technisches Hilfwerk (Federal disaster relief organisation). P 14.
2975 **1306** 110pf. multicoloured .... 2·30 1·70

(Des Irmgard Hesse. Litho German Bank Note Ptg Co, Leipzig)
2000 (13 July). 250th Death Anniv of Johann Sebastian Bach (composer). P 13.
2976 **1307** 110pf. multicoloured .... 2·30 1·70

1308 Airship LZ-1  **1309** Emblem, Globe and Fingerprint

(Des Angela Kühn. Litho German Bank Note Ptg Co, Leipzig)
2000 (13 July). Centenary of Inaugural Flight of LZ-1 (Zeppelin airship). P 13.
2977 **1308** 110pf. multicoloured .... 2·30 1·70

(Des G. and O. Aretz. Litho)
2000 (14 Aug). Federal State Parliament Buildings (7th series). Horiz designs as T **1213**. Multicoloured. P 14.
2978 110pf. Rhineland-Palatinate, Mainz .... 2·20 1·80

(Des H. G. Schmitz. Litho)
2000 (14 Aug). EXPO 2000 World's Fair, Hanover (5th issue). P 14.
2979 **1309** 110pf. multicoloured .... 2·30 1·70

1310 Wiechert  **1311** Nietzsche (Edvard Munch)

(Des P. Nitzsche. Photo)
2000 (14 Aug). 50th Death Anniv of Ernst Wiechert (writer). P 14.
2980 **1310** 110pf. multicoloured .... 2·50 1·70

(Des Elisabeth von Janota-Bzowski. Litho German Bank Note Ptg Co, Leipzig)
2000 (14 Aug). Death Centenary of Friedrich Nietzsche (philosopher). P 13.
2981 **1311** 110pf. multicoloured .... 2·30 1·70

1312 'For You'

(Des E. Jung and F. Pfeffer. Litho Schwann-Bagel, Mönchengladbach)
2000 (14 Sept). Greetings Stamp. P 13×13½.
2982 **1312** 100pf. multicoloured .... 1·90 1·70

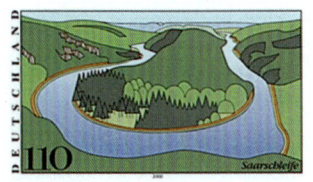

1313 Saar River, Mettlach

(Des H. Schillinger. Litho)

2000 (14 Sept). Images of Germany. P 14.
2983   **1313**   110pf. multicoloured .... 2·00   1·70

1314 Adolph Kopling    **1315** Building

(Des E. Jung and F. Pfeffer. Litho German
Bank Note Ptg Co, Leipzig)

2000 (14 Sept). 150th Anniv of Kopling Society (voluntary organisation). P 13.
2984   **1314**   110pf. multicoloured .... 2·00   1·70

(Des Regina and P. Steiner. Recess and litho)

2000 (14 Sept). 50th Anniv of Federal Court of Justice. P 14.
2985   **1315**   110pf. multicoloured .... 1·90   1·70

1316 Clown's Face    **1317** Nocht (founder), World Map and Microscope Images of Pathogens

(Des Jennifer Rothkopf. Litho German
Bank Note Ptg Co, Leipzig)

2000 (14 Sept). For Us Children. Sheet 55×82 mm. P 14.
MS2986 **1316** 110pf. multicoloured .... 3·00   4·50

(Des Corinna Rogger. Litho German Bank
Note Ptg Co, Leipzig)

2000 (14 Sept). Centenary of Bernard Nocht Institute for Tropical Medicine. P 14.
2987   **1317**   300pf. multicoloured .... 5·50   5·25

1318 Town Hall, Wernigerode    **1319** National Colours

(Des Sibylle and F. Hasse. Litho)

2000 (28 Sept)–**01**. Tourist Sights. T **1318** and similar vert designs showing face values in German currency and euros.
(a) Ordinary gum. P 14
2988	10pf. olive-grey, salmon and greenish slate ...	95	60
2989	20pf. salmon and black (8.11.01)	1·10	90
2990	47pf. dull mauve and deep grey-green (5.4.01)	95	90
2991	50pf. dull ochre and maroon (5.9.01)	1·60	1·40
2992	80pf. turquoise-green and reddish brown	1·40	1·20
2993	100pf. steel-blue and yellow-ochre (11.1.01)	2·30	2·30
2994	110pf. dull purple, chocolate and red-orange .	2·20	1·50
	a. Perf 3 sides. Booklets	2·30	2·30
	ab. Booklet pane. No. 2994a×10	24·00	

2995	220pf. steel-blue and brown (11.1.01)	4·00	3·75
2996	300pf. chestnut and indigo	4·75	4·50
2997	400pf. dull ochre and maroon (5.9.01)	6·25	6·00
2998	440pf. black and brownish grey (9.8.01)	7·00	6·75
2999	510pf. flesh and brown-lake (8.11.01)	8·50	8·25
3000	720pf. slate-purple and dull mauve (2.7.01) ...	11·50	11·50
2988/3000 Set of 13		47·00	45·00

(b) Self-adhesive booklet stamps. Die-cut perf 10½×11 (3 sides)
3001	10pf. olive-grey, salmon and greenish slate (25.5.01)	5·50	5·00
3002	100pf. steel-blue and yellow-ochre (25.5.01)	5·50	5·25
3003	110pf. dull purple, reddish brown and red-orange (25.5.01)	4·25	3·75
3001/3003 Set of 3		13·50	12·50

Designs:—10pf. (2988, 3001) T **1318**; 20pf. Böttcherstrasse, Bremen; 47pf. Wilhelmshöhe Park, Kassel; 50pf. Ceiling decoration, Kirchein Castle; 80pf. St. Reinoldi Church, Dortmund; 100pf. (2993, 3002) Schwerin Castle, Mecklenburg; 110pf. (2994, 3003) Stone bridge, Regensburg; 220pf. St. Nikolai Cathedral, Greifswald; 300pf. Town Hall, Grimma; 400pf. Wartburg Castle, Eisenach; 440pf. Cologne Cathedral; 510pf. Heidelberg Castle; 720pf. Town Hall, Hildesheim.

Nos. 2988/2993 and 2995/3000 were each issued both in sheets and in coils, the latter having every fifth stamp numbered on the reverse. No. 2994 was issued both in coils and booklets.

Nos. 3001/3003 are peeled directly from the cover of the booklet. It is not therefore possible to collect these as booklet panes.

See also Nos. 3150/3166.

Nos. 3004/3009 are vacant.

(Des Angela Kühn. Litho German Bank Note Ptg Co, Leipzig)

2000 (28 Sept). Tenth Anniv of Reunification of Germany. P 13.
3010   **1319**   110pf. black, vermilion and yellow .... 2·00   1·70

1320 Curd Jürgens

(Des Antonia Graschberger. Litho)

2000 (12 Oct). Humanitarian Relief Funds. Actors. T **1320** and similar horiz designs. Multicoloured. P 14.
3011	100pf. +50pf. Type **1320**	2·75	2·75
3012	100pf. +50pf. Lilli Palmer	2·75	2·75
3013	110pf. +50pf. Heinz Rühmann	3·00	3·00
3014	110pf. +50pf. Romy Schneider	3·00	3·00
3015	300pf. +100pf. Gert Fröbe	6·25	6·00
3011/3015 Set of 5		16·00	16·00

1321 Pens, Envelope and 1999 110pf. Stamp    **1322** Grethe Weiser (actress and singer)

(Des G. Fiedler. Litho German Bank
Note Ptg Co, Leipzig)

2000 (12 Oct). Stamp Day. P 13.
3016   **1321**   110pf. multicoloured .... 1·90   1·70

(Des G. and O. Aretz. Recess)

2000 (9 Nov)–**01**. Famous German Women. T **1322** and similar vert designs showing face values in German currency and euros. P 14.
3017	100pf. deep bluish green and light brown	1·70	1·50
3018	110pf. brown-red and brown-olive	1·90	1·50
3019	220pf. red-brown and blackish green (11.1.01)	3·00	3·00
3020	300pf. deep reddish purple and chocolate (11.1.01)	4·75	4·50
3017/3020 Set of 4		10·00	9·50

Designs:—100pf. T **1322**; 110pf. Käte Strobel (politician); 220pf. Marieluise Fleisser (writer); 300pf. Nelly Sachs (writer).

Nos. 3021/3024 are vacant.

(Des G. and O. Aretz. Litho)

2000 (9 Nov). Federal State Parliament Buildings (8th series). Horiz design as T **1213**. Multicoloured. P 14.
3025   110pf. Saarland .... 1·90   1·70

GERMANY

1323 Book Cover
1324 Bode 

(Des Elisabeth von Janota-Bzowski. Litho Schwann-Bagel, Mönchengladbach)

2000 (9 Nov). 125th Birth Anniv of Rainer Maria Rilke (poet). P 13×13½.
3026 **1323** 110pf. multicoloured .... 1·90 1·70

(Des C. Wolff. Litho German Bank Note Ptg Co, Leipzig)

2000 (19 Nov). Birth Centenary of Arnold Bode (artist). P 13.
3027 **1324** 110pf. black and vermilion .... 1·90 2·20

DENOMINATION. From No. 3028 stamps are denominated both in German currency and in euros. No cash for the latter was in circulation until 1 January 2002 so face values before that date are shown in pfennig.

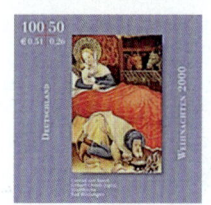

1325 Birth of Christ (Conrad von Soest)
1326 Indian Pepper (illustration from *New Book of Herbs*) 

(Des Lorli and E. Jünger (No. 3028), Christiane Hemmerich (3029). Litho)

2000 (9 Nov). Christmas. T **1325** and similar square design. Multicoloured. P 14.
3028 100pf. +50pf. Type **1325** .... 2·30 2·20
3029 110pf. +50pf. *Nativity* .... 2·50 2·30

(Des P. Nitzsche. Litho)

2001 (11 Jan). 500th Birth Anniv of Leonhart Fuchs (physician and botanist). P 13½.
3030 **1326** 100pf. multicoloured .... 1·70 1·50

1327 'VdK'

(Des Corinna Flogger. Photo)

2001 (11 Jan). 50th Anniv (2000) of Disabled War Veterans' Association. P 14.
3031 **1327** 110pf. multicoloured .... 1·70 1·50

1328 Prussian Eagle
1329 Lortzing and Music Score 

(Des G. and O. Aretz. Litho)

2001 (11 Jan). 300th Anniv of the Kingdom of Prussia. P 14.
3032 **1328** 110pf. multicoloured .... 1·70 1·50

(Des H. G. Schmitz. Litho)

2001 (11 Jan). Birth Bicentenary of Albert Lortzing (composer). P 14.
3033 **1329** 110pf. multicoloured .... 1·70 1·50

1330 Telephone Handset and Number

(Des Andrea Acker. Litho German Bank Note Ptg Co, Leipzig)

2001 (11 Jan). National Federation of Child and Youth Telephone Helplines. P 14.
3034 **1330** 110pf. orange-yellow, orange-vermilion
              and black... 1·70 1·50

1331 Martin Bucer

(Des Regina and P. Steiner. Litho Schwann-Bagel, Mönchengladbach)

2001 (8 Feb). 450th Death Anniv of Martin Bucer (teacher and Protestant reformer). P 14.
3035 **1331** 110pf. multicoloured .... 1·70 1·50

1332 Children running

(Des F.-D. Rothacker. Litho)

2001 (8 Feb). Sport Promotion Fund. T **1332** and similar horiz designs. Multicoloured. P 14.
3036 100pf. +50pf. Type **1332** .... 2·50 2·30
3037 110pf. +50pf. Disabled and able-bodied
              athletes... 2·75 2·50
3038 110pf. +50pf. Adult and children skating............ 2·75 2·50
3039 300pf. +100pf. Men playing basketball.............. 6·50 6·25
3036/3039 Set of 4... 13·00 12·00

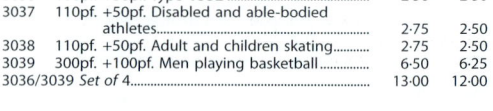

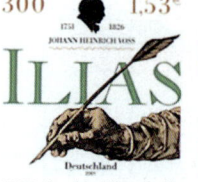

1333 Hand holding Quill
1334 Erich Ollenhauer 

(Des H. Zill. Litho German Bank Note Ptg Co, Leipzig)

2001 (8 Feb)–**02**. 250th Birth Anniv of Johann Heinrich Voss (writer and translator).
  (a) Sheet stamp. Ordinary gum. P 14
3040 **1333** 300pf. multicoloured .... 5·25 5·00
  (b) Coil stamp. Self-adhesive gum. Die-cut perf 10½ (4.4.02)
3040a **1333** €1.53 multicoloured .... 7·25 6·50
No. 3040a was only issued in boxes containing coils of 100 stamps. Strips of five stamps were available from philatelic outlets.

(Des E. Jung and F. Pfeffer. Litho)

2001 (8 Mar). Birth Centenary of Erich Ollenhauer (politician). P 14.
3041 **1334** 110pf. vermilion, black and silver............ 1·70 1·50

GERMANY

1335 Karl Arnold  **1336** Badge

(Des Ursula Kahrl. Litho German Bank Note Ptg Co, Leipzig)
2001 (8 Mar). Birth Centenary of Karl Arnold (politician). P 13.
3042 **1335** 110pf. black, yellowish green and
                    vermilion... 1·70 1·50

(Des G. and O. Aretz. Litho)
2001 (8 Mar). Federal State Parliament Buildings (9th series). Horiz designs as T **1213**. Multicoloured. P 14.
3043   110pf. Saxony.. 1·70 1·50

(Des Corinna Rogger. Photo)
2001 (8 Mar). 50th Anniv of Federal Border Police. P 14.
3044 **1336** 110pf. multicoloured................................ 1·70 1·50

1337 Suspension Railway

(Des H. G. Schmitz. Litho)
2001 (8 Mar). Centenary of Suspension Railway, Wuppertal. P 14.
3045 **1337** 110pf. +50pf. multicoloured........................ 3·50 3·00

1338 Rendsberg Railway Viaduct

(Des J. Bertholdt. Litho German Bank Note Ptg Co, Leipzig)
2001 (5 Apr). Bridges (4th series). P 14.
3046 **1338** 100pf. multicoloured................................ 2·00 1·50

1339 'Post!'

(Des G. Gamroth. Photo)
2001 (5 Apr). P 14.
3047 **1339** 110pf. multicoloured................................ 1·70 1·50

1340 Accordion

(Des Lorli and E. Jünger. Litho Schwann-Bagel, Mönchengladbach)
2001 (5 Apr). Folk Music. P 13×13½.
3048 **1340** 110pf. multicoloured................................ 1·70 1·50

1341 World Map  **1342** Glass of Water

(Des Irmgard Hesse. Litho)
2001 (5 Apr). 50th Anniv of Goethe Institute. P 14.
3049 **1341** 300pf. multicoloured................................ 4·75 4·25

(Des H. G. Schmitz. Litho)
2001 (10 May). Europa. Water Resources. P 14.
3050 **1342** 110pf. multicoloured................................ 2·30 2·00

1343 Werner Egk

(Des Sibylle and F. Haase. Litho German Bank Note Ptg Co, Leipzig)
2001 (10 May). Birth Centenary of Werner Egk (composer and conductor). P 14.
3051 **1343** 110pf. multicoloured................................ 2·00 1·50

(Des G. and O. Aretz. Litho)
2001 (10 May). Federal State Parliament Buildings (10th series). Horiz designs as T **1213**. Multicoloured. P 14.
3052   110pf. Saxony-Anhalt............................... 1·70 1·50

1344 Mountain Gorilla with Young  **1345** Pinocchio

(Des G. Jacki. Litho)
2001 (10 May–12 July). Endangered Species. T **1344** and similar horiz design. Multicoloured.
   (a) Sheet stamps. Ordinary gum. P 14
3053   110pf. Type **1344**................................... 1·90 1·80
3054   110pf. Indian rhinoceros with young.......... 1·90 1·80
   (b) Self-adhesive booklet stamps. Die-cut perf 11 (12 July)
3055   110pf. Type **1344**................................... 2·75 2·50
3056   110pf. Indian rhinoceros with young.......... 2·75 2·50
   Nos. 3055/3056 are peeled directly from the cover of the booklet. It is not therefore possible to collect these as booklet panes.

(Des G. and O. Aretz. Litho)
2001 (13 June). Youth Welfare. Characters from Children's Stories. T **1345** and similar square designs. Multicoloured. P 14.
3057   100pf. +50pf. Type **1345**........................ 2·75 2·75
3058   100pf. +50pf. Pippi Longstocking.............. 2·75 2·75
3059   110pf. +50pf. Heidi and Peter.................... 3·00 3·00
3060   110pf. +50pf. Jim Knopf............................. 3·00 3·00
3061   300pf. +100pf. Tom Sawyer and Huckleberry
                    Finn... 7·00 6·75
3057/3061 Set of 5.. 17·00 16·00

1346 St. Catherine's Monastery and Oceanographic Chart

145

GERMANY

(Des W. Schmidt. Litho Schwann-Bagel, Mönchengladbach)
2001 (13 June). 750th Anniv of St. Catherine's Monastery and 50th Anniv of German Oceanographic Museum, Stralsund. P 13×13½.
3062   **1346**   110pf. multicoloured ....   1·70   1·50

1347 Church Exterior and Plan
1348 Church Bell Tower, Canzow 

(Des W. Schmidt. Litho German Bank Note Ptg Co, Leipzig)
2001 (13 June). 250th Anniv of Catholic Court Church, Dresden. P 13.
3063   **1347**   110pf. multicoloured ....   1·70   1·50

(Des G. and O. Aretz. Litho)
2001 (12 July). Federal State Parliament Buildings (11th series). Horiz design as T **1213**. Multicoloured. P 14.
3064   110pf. Schleswig-Holstein ....   1·70   1·50

(Des Marie-Helen Geisselbrecht. Litho)
2001 (12 July). P. 14.
3065   **1348**   110pf. black, new blue and magenta .....   1·70   1·50

1349 Hand (circulatory disease)

(Des H. G. Schmitz. Litho Schwann-Bagel, Mönchengladbach)
2001 (12 July). Health Awareness Campaign. Sheet 138×110 mm containing T **1349** and similar horiz designs. Multicoloured. P 13×13.
MS3066   110pf. Type **1349**; 110pf. Torso (cancer); 110pf. Lower body (infectious diseases); 110pf. Man holding head (depression) ....   10·00   9·75

1350 Emblem

(Des D. Glinski. Litho German Bank Note Ptg Co, Leipzig)
2001 (9 Aug). Dragon Lancing Festival, Furth im Wald. P 13.
3067   **1350**   100pf. multicoloured ....   1·60   1·40

1351 Lime Tree, Himmelsberg

(Des F. Lüdtke. Litho)
2001 (9 Aug–13 Sept). Natural Heritage.
     (a) Sheet stamp. Ordinary gum. P 14
3068   **1351**   110pf. multicoloured ....   1·70   1·50
     (b) Self adhesive booklet stamp. Die cut perf 10×10½ (13 Sept)
3069   **1351**   110pf. multicoloured ....   4·25   3·50
No. 3069 is peeled directly from the cover of the booklet. It is not therefore possible to collect these as booklet panes.

1352 Schoolmaster Lämpel (Wilhelm Busch) and Text

(Des Sibylle and F. Haase. Litho)
2001 (9 Aug). Lifelong Learning. P. 14.
3070   **1352**   110pf. multicoloured ....   1·70   1·50

1353 Felix standing on Cat

(Des Regina and P. Steiner. Litho German Bank Note Ptg Co, Leipzig)
2001 (5 Sept). For Us Children. Sheet 110×66 mm. P 14.
MS3071   **1353**   110pf. multicoloured ....   2·50   2·75

(Des G. and O. Aretz. Litho)
2001 (5 Sept). Federal State Parliament Buildings (12th series). Horiz design as T **1213**. Multicoloured. P 14.
3072   110pf. Thüringia ....   1·70   1·50

1354 Justice (sculpture)

(Des F. Lüdtke. Litho)
2001 (5 Sept). 50th Anniv of Federal Constitutional Court. P 14.
3073   **1354**   110pf. multicoloured ....   1·70   1·50

1355 Members' Flags

(Des L. Menze. Litho Schwann-Bagel, Mönchengladbach)
2001 (5 Sept). First Union Network International World Congress, Berlin. P 13×13½.
3074   **1355**   110pf. multicoloured ....   1·70   1·50

1356 Museum Floor Plan    **1357** Marilyn Monroe

(Des H. G. Schmitz. Photo)
2001 (5 Sept). Jewish Museum, Berlin. P 14.
3075   **1356**   110pf. multicoloured ....   1·70   1·50

(Des Antonia Graschberger. Litho)
2001 (11 Oct). Humanitarian Relief Funds. Film Industry. T **1357** and similar horiz designs. Multicoloured. P 14.
3076   100pf. +50pf. Type **1357** ....   2·75   2·75

146

GERMANY

3077	100pf. +50pf. Charlie Chaplin	2·75	2·75
3078	110pf. +50pf. Greta Garbo	3·00	3·00
3079	110pf. +50pf. Film reel	3·00	3·00
3080	300pf. +100pf. Jean Gabin	7·00	6·75
3076/3080	Set of 5	17·00	16·00

MS3080*a* 205×156 mm. As No. 3076 (P 13, 13, 13½, 13); 3077 (P 13½×13); 3078 (P 13½,13, 13, 13); 3079 (P 13½×13); 3080 (P 13) .... 25·00 24·00

The stamps in No. **MS**3080*a* as Nos. 3076 and 3078 are perforated 13 on three sides and 13½ on the fourth side.

No. **MS**3080*a* was issued, attached at left, in a card cover.

A 110pf.+50pf. stamp depicting Audrey Hepburn was prepared as part of the Humanitarian Relief Funds (Film Industry) set, but was not issued. A number are known used.

1358 Ribbon and 'für Dich'

(Des E. Jung and F. Pfeffer. Litho Schwann-Bagel, Mönchengladbach)

2001 (11 Oct). Greetings Stamp. P 13×13½.
3081 **1358** 110pf. bright carmine and black............. 1·70 1·50

1359 *Virgin and Child*
(Alfredo Roldán)

(Des J. Villalba. Photo)

2001 (8 Nov). Christmas. Religious Paintings. T **1359** and similar square design. Multicoloured. P 13½.
| 3082 | 100pf. +50pf. Type **1359** | 2·30 | 2·30 |
| 3083 | 110pf. +50pf. *The Shepherd's Adoration* (Jusepe de Ribera) | 2·50 | 2·40 |

MS3083*a* 106×133 mm. Nos. 3082/3083 together with Nos. 3788/3789 of Spain .... 8·50 8·25

Stamps of a similar design were also issued by Spain.

1360 *Gauss* (survey barquentine)

(Des E. Kößlinger. Litho German Bank Note Ptg Co, Leipzig)

2001 (8 Nov). Centenary of German Antarctic Research. Sheet 135×105 mm, containing T **1360** and similar horiz design. Multicoloured. P 14.
MS3084 110pf. Type **1360**; 220pf. *Polarstern* (exploration ship) .... 6·50 6·75

1361 Werner Heisenberg

(Des I. Wulff. Litho Schwann-Bagel, Mönchengladbach)

2001 (8 Nov). Birth Centenary of Werner Heisenberg (physicist). P 14.
3085 **1361** 300pf. black and bright blue .... 5·50 4·75

New Currency
100 cents = 1 euro

1362 Bautzen   **1363** Hans von Dohnanyi

(Des Regina and P. Steiner. Litho Schwann-Bagel, Mönchengladbach)

2002 (10 Jan–7 Mar). Millenary of Bautzen. P 14.
(a) Sheet stamps. Ordinary gum
3086 **1362** 56c. multicoloured .... 1·70 1·50
(b) Self-adhesive booklet stamp. Die-cut perf 11 (7 Mar)
3086*a* **1362** 56c. multicoloured .... 7·00 6·00

No. 3086*a* is peeled directly from the cover of the booklet. It is not therefore possible to collect these as booklet panes.

(Des C. Gassner. Photo)

2002 (10 Jan). Birth Centenary of Hans von Dohnanyi (German resistance co-ordinator). P 14.
3087 **1363** 56c. multicoloured .... 1·70 1·50

1364 Graffiti

(Des Regina and P. Steiner. Litho German Bank Note Ptg Co, Leipzig)

2002 (10 Jan). Tolerance. P 14.
3088 **1364** 56c. multicoloured .... 1·70 1·50

1365 '€'   **1366** Mountains

(Des Lorli and E. Jünger. Litho)

2002 (10 Jan). New Currency. P 14.
(a) Sheet stamp. Ordinary gum
3089 **1365** 56c. greenish yellow and bright blue... 2·75 2·50
(b) Coil stamp. Self-adhesive gum. Die-cut perf 10½
3090 **1365** 56c. greenish yellow and bright blue... 6·25 5·25

No. 3089 was only issued in boxes containing coils of 100 stamps, with every fifth stamp in the coil numbered on the back.

(Des G. Gamroth. Litho)

2002 (10 Jan). International Year of Mountains. P 14.
3091 **1366** 56c. +26c. multicoloured......................... 2·75 2·40

No. 3091 was sold with a premium towards environmental protection.

1367 Cross-country Skier (biathlon)

(Des L. Menze)

2002 (7 Feb). Winter Olympic Games, Salt Lake City, USA. T **1367** and similar horiz designs. Multicoloured. P 14.
(a) Litho State Ptg Wks, Berlin
3092 51c. +26c. Type **1367**....................................... 2·50 2·40

147

GERMANY

3093	56c. +26c. Ice skater (speed skating)...............	2·75	2·50
3094	56c. +26c. Skier (ski jumping)........................	2·75	2·50
3095	153c. +51c. Man in helmet (luge)....................	6·25	6·00

(b) Litho Schwann-Bagel, Mönchengladbach

3092/3095 Set of 4 .... 13·00 12·00
MS3096 142×98 mm. As Nos. 3092/3095 .... 17·00 17·00

No. **MS**3096 was issued, attached at top, in a card cover.

Nos. 3092/**MS**3096 were sold with a premium towards Foundation for the Promotion of Sport in Germany.

1368 Adolf Freiherr Knigge and Books

1369 Front of Train Carriage

(Des P. Nitzsche. Litho)

2002 (7 Feb). 250th Birth Anniv of Adolf Freiherr Knigge (author of *Über den Umgang mit Menschen* (book on etiquette)). P 14.
3097   1368   56c. multicoloured ....   1·90   1·70

(Des I. Wulff. Litho German Bank Note Ptg Co, Leipzig)

2002 (7 Feb). Centenary of Berlin Subway. P 13.
3098   1369   56c. multicoloured ....   2·00   1·70

1370 Deggendorf

(Des W. Schmidt. Litho Schwann-Bagel, Mönchengladbach)

2002 (7 Mar). Millenary of Deggendorf. P 14.
3099   1370   56c. multicoloured ....   1·70   1·50

1371 Mechanical Calculator (Johann Christoph Schuster)

1372 Ecksberg Pilgrimage Church

(Des F. Lüdtke. Litho Schwann-Bagel, Mönchengladbach)

2002 (7 Mar). Cultural Foundation of the Federal States. P 14.
3100   1371   56c. multicoloured ....   1·90   1·70

(Des L. Menze. Recess and litho)

2002 (4 Apr). 150th Anniv of Ecksberg Foundation (for people with disabilities). P 14.
3101   1372   56c. multicoloured ....   1·70   1·50

1373 Exhibits and Building

1374 Armorial Lions

(Des P. Effert. Litho)

2002 (4 Apr). Centenary of Freemason's Museum, Bayreuth. P 14.
3102   1373   56c. multicoloured ....   1·90   1·70

(Des Angela Kühn. Litho German Bank Note Ptg Co, Leipzig)

2002 (4 Apr). 50th Anniv of Baden-Württemberg State. P 13.
3103   1374   56c. black, gold and orange-yellow ....   1·90   1·70

1375 'post'

(Des G. Fiedler. Litho Schwann-Bagel, Mönchengladbach)

2002 (4 Apr). P 13×13½.
3104   1375   56c. multicoloured ....   1·70   1·50

1376 Emblem

(Des F. Lüdtke. Litho)

2002 (4 Apr). 50th Anniv of Federal Employment Services. P 14.
3105   1376   €1.53 bright scarlet and black................   5·00   4·50

1377 Modern Student and Elector Friedrich the Wise (founder of Wittenberg University)

1378 'KINDERGOTTESDIENST!'

(Des L. Menze. Litho)

2002 (2 May). 500th Anniv of Martin Luther University, Halle-Wittenberg. P 14.
3106   1377   56c. greenish grey, ultramarine and bright magenta.................   1·70   1·50

(Des Angela Kühn. Litho German Bank Note Ptg Co, Leipzig)

2002 (2 May). 150th Anniv of Children's Church Services. P 13.
3107   1378   56c. multicoloured ....   1·90   1·70

1379 'Documenta11'

(Des Regina and P. Steiner. Litho German Bank Note Ptg Co, Leipzig)

2002 (2 May). 11th Documenta Modern Art Exhibition, Kassel. Sheet 100×70 mm. P 14.
3108   1379   56c. dull ultramarine, reddish lilac and dull violet-blue ....   3·00   3·00

1380 Flags of Championship Winners and Football

1381 Clown

148

GERMANY

(Des Andrea Acker. Litho Schwann-Bagel, Mönchengladbach)

2002 (2 May). 20th-century World Cup Football Champions. T **1380** and similar multicoloured design. P 13½×14.
3109		56c. Type **1380**	1·90	1·80
		a. Horiz pair. Nos. 3109/3110	4·00	3·75
3110		56c. German footballer	1·90	1·80

Nos. 3109/3110 were issued together in horizontal *se-tenant* pairs within sheets of ten stamps. No. 3110 is perforated in a circle contained within an outer perforated square.

Stamps of a similar design were also issued by Argentina, Brazil, France, Italy and Uruguay.

(Des D. Glinski. Litho German Bank Note Ptg Co, Leipzig)

2002 (2 May–4 July). Europa. Circus.

(a) Sheet stamp. Ordinary gum P 13.
3111	**1381**	56c. black, orange-vermilion and green	1·70	1·50

(b) Coil stamp. Self-adhesive gum. Die-cut perf 10½ (4 July)
3112	**1381**	56c. black, orange-vermilion and green	4·25	4·25

No. 3112 was only issued in boxes containing coils of 100 stamps, with every fifth stamp in the coil numbered on the back. Strips of five stamps were available from philatelic outlets.

1382 Dessau-Wörlitz

(Des Hannelore Heise. Litho)

2002 (2 May–8 Aug). UNESCO World Heritage Site. Dessau-Wörlitz Gardens.

(a) Ordinary gum P 14.
3113	**1382**	56c. multicoloured	1·90	1·70

(b) Self-adhesive booklet stamps. Die-cut perf 11 (8 Aug)
3114	**1382**	56c. multicoloured	3·00	2·50

No. 3114 is peeled directly from the cover of the booklet. It is not therefore possible to collect these as booklet panes.

1383 Albrecht Daniel Thaer

(Des G. Lienemeyer. Litho Schwann-Bagel, Mönchengladbach)

2002 (2 May). 250th Birth Anniv of Albrecht Daniel Thaer (agronomist). P 13×13½.
3115	**1383**	€2.25 multicoloured	7·75	7·50

1384 Desmoulin's Whorl Snail  **1385** Chess Pieces

(Des G. Jacki. Litho German Bank Note Ptg Co, Leipzig)

2002 (6 June). Endangered Species. Molluscs. T **1384** and similar horiz design. Multicoloured. P 14.
3116		51c. Type **1384**	1·60	1·50
3117		56c. Freshwater pearl mussel	1·90	1·70

Stamps of a similar design were also issued by Czech Republic.

(Des H. Scheuner. Litho Schwann-Bagel, Mönchengladbach)

2002 (6 June). Youth Welfare. Toys. T **1385** and similar square designs. Multicoloured. P 14.
3118		51c. +26c. Type **1385**	2·50	2·40
3119		51c. +26c. Wooden crane	2·50	2·40
3120		56c. +26c. Doll	2·75	2·75
3121		56c. +26c. Teddy bear	2·75	2·75
3122		153c. +51c. Electric train	6·25	6·00
3118/3122		*Set of 5*	15·00	15·00

1386 Yellow Feather in Red

(Des Lorli and E. Jünger. Litho)

2002 (6 June). Birth Centenary of Ernst Wilhelm Nay (artist). P 14.
3123	**1386**	56c. multicoloured	1·70	1·50

1387 Leaves and Silhouettes

(Des Regina and P. Steiner. Litho)

2002 (4 July). 40th Anniv of Deutsche Welthungerhilfe (humanitarian aid organisation). P 14.
3124	**1387**	51c. multicoloured	1·60	1·50

1388 Way of Human Rights (sculpture, Danni Karavan)

(Des Regina Winkler and O. Jäger. Litho German Bank Note Ptg Co, Leipzig)

2002 (4 July). 150th Anniv of National Museum of German Art and Culture, Nüremberg. P 14.
3125	**1388**	56c. multicoloured	1·70	1·50

1389 Hermann Hesse

(Des Corinna Rogger. Litho)

2002 (4 July). 125th Birth Anniv of Hermann Hesse (writer). P 14.
3126	**1389**	56c. greenish blue and olive-yellow	1·90	1·70

1390 Trees and Rocks

(Des D. Glinski. Litho German Bank Note Ptg Co, Leipzig)

2002 (4 July). Hochharz National Park. Sheet 110×66 mm. P 14.
MS3127	**1390**	56c. multicoloured	2·75	2·50

149

GERMANY

1391 Josef Felder
1392 Museum Buildings 

(Des G. and O. Aretz. Litho German Bank Note Ptg Co, Leipzig)

2002 (8 Aug). Second Death Anniv of Josef Felder (politician and journalist). P 13.
| 3128 | **1391** | 56c. multicoloured | 2·10 | 1·80 |

(Des H. Schillinger. Recess and litho)

2002 (8 Aug). UNESCO World Heritage Site. Museum Island, Berlin. P 14.
| 3129 | **1392** | 56c. black and deep bluish green | 2·10 | 1·80 |

1393 Firemen fighting Fire

(Des P. Effert. Litho)

2002 (8 Aug). Voluntary Fire Brigades. P 14.
| 3130 | **1393** | 56c. multicoloured | 2·10 | 1·80 |

1394 Building Façade

(Des Corinna Rogger. Litho Schwann-Bagel, Mönchengladbach)

2002 (8 Aug). 130th Anniv of Communications Museum, Berlin. P 14.
| 3131 | **1394** | 153c. multicoloured | 5·25 | 5·00 |

(Des M. Gottscall. Litho Schwann-Bagel, Mönchengladbach)

2002 (30 Aug). Flood Relief. Design as T **1222** but with 'HOCHWASSERHILFE 2002' inscribed at left and new face value. P 13×13½.
| 3132 | | 56c. +44c. multicoloured | 4·50 | 3·75 |
| | a. | Perf 13×14 | 17·00 | 16·00 |

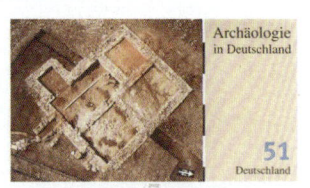

1395 Walls of Roman Bathhouse, Wurmlingen (illustration from *Die Alammannen* by Konrad Theiss)

(Des Jünger and Michel. Litho German Bank Note Ptg Co, Leipzig)

2002 (5 Sept). Archaeology. P 14.
| 3133 | **1395** | 51c. multicoloured | 1·80 | 1·70 |

1396 Face painted on Child's Toe

(Des Birgit Hogrefe. Litho Schwann-Bagel, Mönchengladbach)

2002 (5 Sept). For Us Children. Sheet 110×66 mm. P 13×13½.
| 3134 | **1396** | 56c. multicoloured | 2·50 | 2·40 |

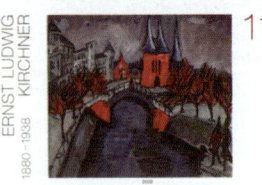

1397 *Rotes Elisabeth-Ufer* (painting, Ernst Ludwig Kirchner)

(Des Lorli and E. Jünger. Litho German Bank Note Ptg Co, Leipzig)

2002 (5 Sept). P 14.
| 3135 | **1397** | 112c. multicoloured | 3·75 | 3·25 |

1398 Heinrich von Kleist (miniature, Peter Friedel)
1399 Eugen Jochum rehearsing 

(Des I. Wulff. Litho German Bank Note Ptg Co, Leipzig)

2002 (10 Oct). 225th Birth Anniv of Heinrich von Kleist (writer). P 13.
| 3136 | **1398** | 56c. multicoloured | 1·90 | 1·70 |

(Des G. Lienemeyer. Photo)

2002 (10 Oct). Birth Centenary of Eugen Jochum (conductor). P 14.
| 3137 | **1399** | 56c. multicoloured | 1·90 | 1·70 |

1400 Diagram of Planets (Copernicus), Horsemen and Sphere
1401 Angel (detail, *The Annunciation*) 

(Des C. Gassner. Photo)

2002 (10 Oct). 400th Birth Anniv of Otto von Guericke (engineer and physicist). P 14.
| 3138 | **1400** | 153c. multicoloured | 6·25 | 5·25 |

(Des D. Glinski. Litho Schwann-Bagel, Mönchengladbach)

2002 (7 Nov). Christmas. Paintings by Rogier van der Weyden. T **1401** and similar square design. Multicoloured. P 14.
| 3139 | | 51c. +26c. Type **1401** | 2·75 | 2·30 |
| 3140 | | 56c. +26c. The Holy Family (detail, Miraflores alterpiece) | 2·75 | 2·50 |

1402 Arrows
1403 Clock and Eye 

(Angela Kühn. Litho German Bank Note Ptg Co, Leipzig)

2002 (7 Nov). 50th Anniv of Federal Agency for Civic Education. P 13.
| 3141 | **1402** | 56c. black, vermilion and orange yellow | 1·90 | 1·70 |

(Des Andrea Acker. Photo)

2002 (7 Nov). 50th Anniv of German Television. P 14.
| 3142 | **1403** | 56c. multicoloured | 2·10 | 1·70 |

No. 3143 is vacant.

1404 BMW Isetta 300 (1960)

(Des Lorli and E. Jünger. Litho)

2002 (5 Dec). Cars (1st series). T **1404** and similar horiz designs. Multicoloured. P 14.

3144	45c. +20c. Type **1404**	2·75	2·75
3145	55c. +25c. Volkswagen Beetle (1949)	3·00	2·75
3146	55c. +25c. Mercedes Benz 300 SL (1954)	3·00	2·75
3147	55c. +25c. VEB Sachsenring Trabant P50 (1961)	3·00	2·75
3148	144c. +56c. Borgward Isabella Coupé (1957)	8·00	7·50
3144/3148	Set of 5	18·00	17·00

See also Nos. 3238/3242.

1405 Halle Market Church (Lyonel Feininger)

(Des Lorli and E. Jünger. Litho German Bank Note Ptg Co. Leipzig)

2002 (5 Dec). P 14.
3149	**1405**	55c. multicoloured	1·90	1·70

(Des Sybille and F. Haase. Litho)

2002 (27 Dec)–**04**. Tourist Sights. Vert designs as T **1318** but with face value in new currency.

(a) Sheet stamps P 14.
3150	5c. olive-brown and turquoise-green (5.2.04)	45	40
3151	25c. deep olive and violet (8.1.04)	90	85
3152	40c. multicoloured (8.1.04)	1·40	1·30
3153	44c. orange-yellow and grey-black	1·80	1·50
3154	45c. rose-pink and grey-black	1·80	1·70
3155	55c. orange-yellow and grey-black	1·90	1·80
3156	€1 bluish grey and grey-black	3·50	3·00
3157	€1.44 pink and myrtle-green (16.1.03)	5·75	5·25
3158	€1.60 bluish grey, grey-black and bright reddish orange	5·25	5·00
3159	€1.80 myrtle-green and chestnut (13.2.03)	7·00	5·75
3160	€2 carmine-lake and blackish olive (13.2.03)	7·00	6·50
3161	€2.20 light blue and grey-black (16.1.03)	8·75	8·25
3162	€2.60 deep blue and orange-vermilion (6.3.03)	10·50	9·00
3163	€4.10 bright purple and deep turquoise-blue (6.3.03)	15·00	13·00

(b) Coil stamps. Self-adhesive. Die-cut perf 10×11
3164	55c. orange-yellow and grey-black	2·10	2·00

(c) Self-adhesive booklet stamps. Die-cut perf 10×11 (3 sides)
3165	45c. rose-pink and grey-black	4·50	4·25
3166	55c. orange-yellow and grey-black	2·75	2·50
3150/3166	Set of 17	70·00	65·00

Designs:—5c. Erfster Cathedral; 25c. J. S. Bach (statue), Leipzig; 40c. Schloss, Arolsen; 44c. Philharmonic Hall, Berlin; 45c. Canal warehouse, Tonning; 55c. Old Opera House, Frankfurt; €1 Porta Niga (black gate), Trier; €1.44 Beethoven's birthplace, Bonn; €1.60 Bauhaus, Dessau; €1.80 Staatsgalerie, Stuttgart; €2 *Bamberger Reister* (statue); €2.20 Theodor Fontane monument, Neuruppin; €2.60 *Seute Dern* (four-mast barque), Maritime Museum, Bremerhaven; €4.10 Houses, Wismar.

The outer edges of the booklet panes are imperforate, giving stamps with either top or bottom edge imperforate.

Nos. 3165/3166 are peeled directly from the corner of the booklet. It is not therefore possible to collect these as booklet panes.

Nos. 3167/3189 are vacant.

(Des G. and O. Aretz. Recess)

2002 (27 Dec)–**03**. Famous German Women. Vert designs as T **1322** but with face value in new currency. P 14.

3190	45c. brown-olive and deep turquoise blue	1·60	1·50
3191	55c. scarlet-vermilion and grey-black	1·80	1·70
3192	€1 deep reddish purple and steel blue (16.1.03)	3·50	3·00
3193	€1.44 orange-brown and indigo	4·50	4·25
3190/3193	*Set of 4*	10·50	9·50

Designs:—45c. Annette von Droste-Hülshoff (writer); 55c. Hildegard Knef (actress); €1 Marie Juchacz (politician); €1.44 Esther von Kirchbach (writer).

1406 Town Buildings

(Des E. Kößlinger. Litho Schwann-Bagel, Mönchengladbach)

2003 (16 Jan). Millenary of Kronach. P 14.
3194	**1406**	45c. multicoloured	1·80	1·50

1407 Georg Elser  **1408** Bridge joined by Heart

(Des Lorli and E. Jünger. Litho Schwann-Bagel, Mönchengladbach)

2003 (16 Jan). Birth Centenary of Georg Elser (attempted assassination of Adolf Hitler). P 13.
3195	**1407**	55c. multicoloured	2·10	1·80

(Des T. Ungerer and Jünger & Michel. Litho Schwann-Bagel, Mönchengladbach)

2003 (16 Jan). 40th Anniv of German—French Co-operation Treaty. P 13½.
3196	**1408**	55c. multicoloured	2·10	1·80

1409 Hand and Page

(Des Marie-Helen Geißelbrecht. Litho)

2003 (16 Jan). Year of the Bible. P 14.
3197	**1409**	55c. multicoloured	2·10	1·80

1410 Proun 30t (El Lissitzky)

(Des F. Lüdtke. Litho)

2003 (16 Jan). Cultural Foundation of the Federal States. P 14.
3198	**1410**	€1.44 multicoloured	5·25	4·25

1411 St. Thomas Church Choir, Leipzig

(Des Barbara Dimanski. Litho Schwann-Bagel, Mönchengladbach)

2003 (13 Feb). Boys' Choirs. Sheet 172×77 mm containing T **1411** and similar horiz designs. Multicoloured. P 14.
MS3199 45c. Type **1411**; 55c. Dresden Church choir; 100c. St. Peter's Cathedral choir, Regensburg ... 8·00 8·25

GERMANY

151

GERMANY

1412 Rose

(Des Antonia Graschberger. Litho)

2003 (13 Feb). Greetings Stamp.
(a) Sheet stamp. Ordinary gum. P 14
3200 1412 55c. multicoloured .... 1·90 1·70
(b) Self-adhesive booklet stamp. Die-cut perf 10
3201 1412 55c. multicoloured .... 2·50 1·80

No. 3201 is peeled directly from the cover of the booklet. It is not therefore possible to collect these as booklet panes.

1413 *Junger Argentier* (Max Beckman)

(Des Lorli and E. Jünger. Litho German Bank Note Ptg Co, Leipzig)

2003 (13 Feb). Artists' Anniversaries. T **1413** and similar horiz design. Multicoloured. P 14.
3202   55c. Type **1413** (53rd death anniv) .... 2·10 1·70
3203   €1 *Komposition* (Adolf Hölzel) (150th birth anniv) .... 3·25 3·00

1414 Football Player

(Des L. Metz. Litho Schwann-Bagel, Mönchengladbach)

2003 (6 Mar). Sports Promotion Fund. World Cup Football Championship (2006), Germany. T **1414** and similar horiz designs. Multicoloured. P 13½.
3204   45c. +20c. Type **1414** .... 3·00 2·75
3205   55c. +25c. Boys playing football .... 3·25 3·00
3206   55c. +25c. Fan with arms raised .... 3·25 3·00
3207   55c. +25c. Young player heading ball .... 3·25 3·00
3208   €1.44 +56c. Boy kicking ball to older man .. 7·00 6·50
3204/3208 Set of 5 .... 18·00 16·00

1415 Building Façade   **1416** Flower

(Des J. Reiss. Litho German Bank Note Ptg Co, Leipzig)

2003 (6 Mar). UNESCO World Heritage Sites. Cologne Cathedral.
(a) Sheet stamp. Ordinary gum P 13.
3209 1415 55c. lavender-grey, carmine-lake and grey-black .... 2·10 1·80
(b) Coil stamp. Self-adhesive gum. Die-cut perf 10½
3210 1415 55c. lavender-grey, carmine-lake and grey-black .... 2·50 2·00

No. 3210 was issued in coils of 100, the stamps spaced along the coil with every fifth stamp in the coil numbered on the back.

(Des Karin Blume-Zander and A. Zander. Litho German Bank Note Ptg Co, Leipzig)

2003 (10 Apr). International Horticultural Exhibition, Rostock. P 13.
3211 1416 45c. multicoloured .... 1·90 1·70

1417 Oskar von Miller (founder) and Technological Symbols   **1418** Cut-out Figures

(Des Lorli and E. Jünger. Photo)

2003 (10 Apr). Centenary of Deutsches Museum, Munich. P 14.
3212 1417 55c. multicoloured .... 2·10 1·80

(Des Angela Kühn. Litho German Bank Note Ptg Co, Leipzig)

2003 (10 Apr). 50th Anniv of Deutscher Kinderschutzbund (children's organisation). P 13.
3213 1418 55c. multicoloured .... 2·10 1·80

1419 Map and Representation of Radio Waves   **1420** Aviators and Junkers W 33 *Bremen*

(Des Andrea Akker. Litho)

2003 (10 Apr). 50th Anniv of Deutsche Welle (radio station). P 14.
3214 1419 55c. multicoloured .... 2·10 1·80

(Des Corinna Rogger. Litho Schwann-Bagel, Mönchengladbach)

2003 (10 Apr). 75th Anniv East—West North Atlantic Flight. P 13½.
3215 1420 144c. +56c. multicoloured .... 8·00 7·00

1421 1960s Posters

(Des C. Gassner. Litho Schwann-Bagel, Mönchengladbach)

2003 (8 May). Europa. Poster Art. P 13×13½.
3216 1421 55c. multicoloured .... 2·10 1·80

1422 Justus von Liebig   **1423** Reinhold Schneider and Text

(Des G. Lienemeyer. Litho German Bank Note Ptg Co, Leipzig)

2003 (8 May). Birth Bicentenary of Justus von Liebig (chemist). P 14.
3217 1422 55c. multicoloured .... 2·10 1·80

(Des Ursula Kahrl. Litho German Bank Note Ptg Co, Leipzig)

2003 (8 May). Birth Centenary of Reinhold Schneider (writer). P 13½.
3218 1423 55c. multicoloured .... 1·90 1·80

1424 Helicopter and Patrol Vehicle

(Des C. Wolff. Litho Schwann-Bagel, Mönchengladbach)

2003 (8 May). Centenary of ADAC (automobile association). P 13×13½.
3219 **1424** 55c. multicoloured .... 2·10 1·80

1425 Rainbow

(Des Angela Kühn. Litho)

2003 (8 May). Ecumenical Church Conference, Berlin. P 14.
3220 **1425** 55c. multicoloured .... 2·10 1·80

1426 Hands and Text

(Des L. Menze. Litho)

2003 (8 May). Centenary of Hans Jonas (philosopher). P 14.
3221 **1426** 220c. multicoloured .... 8·00 7·00

1427 Hand with Face and Feet

(Des E. Jung and F. Pfeffer. Litho)

2003 (12 June). Tenth Anniv of Postal Codes. P 14.
3222 **1427** 55c. multicoloured .... 2·10 1·80

1428 Bridge over Salzach River

(Des H. Margreiter. Litho)

2003 (12 June). Centenary of Oberndorf—Laufen Bridge. P 14.
(a) Sheet stamp. Ordinary gum
3223 **1428** 55c. multicoloured .... 2·10 1·80
(b) Self-adhesive booklet stamp. Die-cut perf 14
3224 **1428** 55c. multicoloured .... 3·25 2·50
No. 3224 is peeled directly from the cover of the booklet. It is not therefore possible to collect these as booklet panes.
A stamp of the same design was issued by Austria.

1429 Lake, Trees and Islands

(Des D. Glinski. Litho Schwann-Bagel, Mönchengladbach)

2003 (12 June). Unteres Odertal National Park. Sheet 111×66 mm. P 13×13½.
MS3225 **1429** 55c. multicoloured .... 2·30 2·50

1430 Protesters and Tanks   **1431** Musical Notations

(Des Lorli and E. Jünger. Photo)

2003 (12 June). 50th Anniv of Uprising in East Berlin. P 14.
3226 **1430** 55c. +25c. multicoloured.......................... 3·25 3·00

(Regina and P. Steiner. Litho)

2003 (12 June)–04. 50th Anniv of Deutscher Musikrat (music association). P 14.
(a) Sheet stamp. Ordinary gum
3227 **1431** €1.44 silver and dull ultramarine............. 5·25 4·50
(b) Self-adhesive booklet stamp. Die-cut perf 11 (8.1.04)
3227a **1431** €1.44 silver and dull ultramarine
           (8.1.04) .... 5·25 4·50
No. 3227a is peeled directly from the cover of the booklet. It is not therefore possible to collect these as booklet panes.

1432 Father chasing Son

(Regina and P. Steiner. Litho)

2003 (10 July). For Us Children. Father and Son (cartoon by E. O. Plauen (Erich Ohser)). Sheet 111×191 mm containing T **1432** and similar horiz designs. Multicoloured. Litho. P 13×13½.
MS3228 45c.+20c. Type **1432**; 55c.+25c. Father and son falling; 55c.+25c. Father looking over shoulder at son running away; 55c.+25c. Father chasing son in a circle; €1.44+56c. Father and son sliding .... 19·00 18·00

1433 Winding Gear and Trees

(Des H. Schillinger. Litho Schwann-Bagel, Mönchengladbach)

2003 (10 July). Ruhr District Industrial Landscape. P 13×13½.
3229 **1433** 55c. multicoloured .... 2·10 1·80

1434 Andres Hermes

GERMANY

(Des C. Wolff. Litho)
2003 (10 July). 125th Birth Anniv of Andreas Hermes (politician). P 14.
3230 **1434** 55c. multicoloured .... 1·90 1·70

1435 Market Stalls, Munich

1436 Petrified Forest, Chemnitz

(Des G. Fiedler. Litho German Bank Note Ptg Co, Leipzig)
2003 (7 Aug)–04. German Cities. T **1435** and similar multicoloured designs. P 14.

(a) Sheet stamps. Ordinary gum
3231 45c. Type **1435** .... 1·80 1·50
3232 55c. Building façades, Altstadt Gorlitz
       (51×30 *mm*) .... 1·90 1·70

(b) Self-adhesive booklet stamp. Die-cut perf 11 (8.1.04)
3233 45c. As No. 3231 .... 2·30 1·70
No. 3233 is peeled directly from the cover of the booklet. It is not therefore possible to collect these as booklet panes.

(Des J. Reis. Litho German Bank Note Ptg Co, Leipzig)
2003 (7 Aug). P 13.
3234 **1436** 144c. multicoloured .... 5·25 5·00

1437 Viaduct and Enz River

(Des G. Fiedler. Litho Schwann-Bagel, Mönchengladbach)
2003 (11 Sept). 150th Anniv of Enztal Viaduct (railway). P 13×13½.
3235 **1437** 55c. multicoloured .... 2·10 1·80

1438 Theodor Adorno and Manuscript

(Des G. Lienemeyer. Litho)
2003 (11 Sept). Birth Centenary of Theodor Adorno (philosopher and sociologist). P 14.
3236 **1438** 55c. multicoloured .... 1·90 1·70

1439 Elephant and Bird

(Des Nina Clausing. Litho German Bank Note Ptg Co, Leipzig)
2003 (11 Sept). For Us Children. Sheet 111×65 mm. P 14.
MS3237 **1439** 55c. multicoloured .... 2·50 2·50

(Des Lorli and E. Jünger. Litho)
2003 (9 Oct). Cars (2nd series). Horiz designs as T **1404**. Multicoloured. P 14.
3238 45c. +20c. Wartburg 311 Coupé (1962) .... 2·75 2·50
3239 55c. +25c. Ford Taunus 17 M P3 (1960)......... 3·00 2·75
3240 55c. +25c. Porsche 356 B Coupé (1959) .... 3·00 2·75
3241 55c. +25c. Opel Olympia Rekord P1 (1957) .. 3·00 2·75
3242 144c. +56c. Auto Union 1000 S (1959)............ 8·00 7·50
3238/3242 Set of 5 .... 18·00 16·00

1440 Posting Letter

1441 Lifeguards

(Des Emma de Vries. Litho German Bank Note Ptg Co, Leipzig)
2003 (9 Oct). Post. P 13.
3243 **1440** 55c. multicoloured .... 2·10 1·80

(Des Corinna Rogger. Litho)
2003 (9 Oct). 90th Anniv of DLRG (safety organisation). P 14.
3244 **1441** 144c. multicoloured .... 5·25 4·50

1442 Nativity Figures (19th-century)

(Des G. Lienemeyer. Litho)
2003 (13 Nov). Christmas. T **1442** and similar square design. Multicoloured. P 14.
3245 45c. +20c. Type **1442** .... 2·50 2·30
3246 55c. +25c. Holy Family .... 2·75 2·50

1443 Dresden Opera House

(Des P. Effert. Litho Schwann-Bagel, Mönchengladbach)
2003 (13 Nov). Birth Bicentenary of Gottfried Semper (architect). P 13×13½.
3247 **1443** 55c. multicoloured .... 2·20 1·90

1444 Hands and Women

(Des L. Menze. Litho)
2003 (13 Nov). Centenary of German Catholic Women's Federation. P 14.
3248 **1444** 55c. multicoloured .... 2·20 1·90

1445 Stars

(Des Andrea Acker. Litho)
2003 (13 Nov). Tenth Anniv of Maastricht Treaty. P 14.
3249 **1445** 55c. ultramarine and greenish yellow 2·40 2·00

1446 St. Martin's Church

(Des F. Lüdtke. Litho)
2004 (8 Jan). 800th Anniv of Landshut. P 14.
3250 1446 45c. multicoloured............ 1·80 1·70

1447 Cathedral and Images of Schleswig

1448 Clouds, Sun and Trees

(Des E. Kößlinger. Litho German Bank Note Ptg Co, Leipzig)
2004 (8 Jan). 1200th Anniv of Schleswig. P 13.
3251 1447 55c. multicoloured............ 2·20 1·90

(Des Klein und Neumann. Litho Schwann-Bagel, Mönchengladbach)
2004 (8 Jan). Environmental Protection and Renewable Energy. P 14.
3252 1448 55c. +25c. multicoloured......... 3·50 3·25

1449 Football Players

(Des Andrea Acker. Litho Schwann-Bagel, Mönchengladbach)
2004 (5 Feb). Sport Promotion Fund. T **1449** and similar horiz designs. Multicoloured. P 13.
3253 45c. +20c. Type **1449** (European Football Championship)............ 3·25 3·00
3254 55c. +25c. Wheelchair athlete (Paralympics)....... 3·50 3·25
3255 55c. +25c. Runner (Olympic Games, Athens).......... 3·50 3·25
3256 55c. +25c. Footballer (50th anniv of Germany winning World Cup)....... 3·50 3·25
3257 144c. +56c. Hands holding trophy (Centenary of FIFA)............ 9·00 8·25
3253/3257 Set of 5 .... 20·00 19·00

1450 Paper Aeroplanes

(Des R. Lederbogen. Litho)
2004 (5 Feb). Post. P 14.
3258 1450 55c. multicoloured............ 2·40 2·00

1451 Buildings

1452 Shadow of Boy, Apple and Arrow

GERMANY

(Des W. Schmidt. Litho German Bank Note Ptg Co, Leipzig)
2004 (5 Feb). 1300th Anniv of Arnstadt. P 13.
3259 1451 55c. multicoloured............ 2·40 2·00

(Des Barbara Dimanski. Litho Schwann-Bagel, Mönchengladbach)
2004 (11 Mar). Classic Theatre. Sheet 102×73 mm containing T **1452** and similar square design. Multicoloured. P 14.
MS3260 45c. Type **1452** (William Tell (Friedrich von Schiller) (200th anniv)); 100c. Faust and the Devil (Faust II (Johann Wolfgang von Goethe) (150th anniv))............ 6·50 6·50

1453 Joseph Schmidt

(Des Jennifer Rothkopf. Litho)
2004 (11 Mar). Birth Centenary of Joseph Schmidt (singer). P 14.
3261 1453 55c. Light brown............ 2·40 2·00

1454 Paul Ehrlich (chemistry) and Emil von Behring (medicine)

(Des Ursula Maria Kahrl. Litho German Bank Note Ptg Co, Leipzig)
2004 (11 Mar). 150th Birth Anniv of Nobel Prize Winners. P 14.
3262 1454 144c. multicoloured............ 6·00 5·25

1455 White Stork in Flight

(Des Regina and P. Steiner. Litho)
2004 (7 Apr). Endangered Species. White Stork (Circona circona). P 14.
3263 1455 55c. black, new blue and orange-vermilion............ 2·40 2·00

1456 Master House, Dessau

(Des Sibylle and F. Haase. Litho)
2004 (7 Apr). Bauhaus (design group). P 14.
3264 1456 55c. multicoloured............ 2·40 2·00

1457 Kurt Kiesinger

1458 Early and Modern Light Bulbs

155

GERMANY

(Des G. and O. Aretz. Litho Schwann-Bagel, Mönchengladbach)
2004 (7 Apr). Birth Centenary of Kurt Georg Kiesinger (politician). P 14.
| 3265 | **1457** | 55c. multicoloured | 2·30 | 1·90 |

(Des S. Klein and O. Neumann. Litho Schwann-Bagel, Mönchengladbach)
2004 (7 Apr). 150th Anniv of Electric Light Bulb. P 14.
| 3266 | **1458** | 220c. multicoloured | 9·50 | 8·25 |

1459 Sunflower and Holiday Symbols

1460 New Members' Flags as Cones

(Des Christiane Hemmerich. Litho German Bank Note Ptg Co, Leipzig)
2004 (6 May). Europa. Holidays. P 13.
| 3267 | **1459** | 45c. multicoloured | 2·10 | 1·70 |

(Des P. Effert. Litho German Bank Note Ptg Co, Leipzig)
2004 (6 May). Enlargement of European Union. P 13.
| 3268 | **1460** | 55c. multicoloured | 2·30 | 1·90 |

1461 Reinhard Schwarz-Schilling

1462 St. Boniface under Attack

(Des Birgit Hogrefe. Litho)
2004 (6 May). Birth Centenary of Reinhard Schwarz-Schilling (composer). P 14.
| 3269 | **1461** | 55c. sepia | 2·30 | 1·90 |

(Des L. Menze. Litho Schwann-Bagel, Mönchengladbach)
2004 (6 May). 350th Anniv of Martyrdom of St. Boniface (papal envoy to Germany). P 14.
| 3270 | **1462** | 55c. multicoloured | 2·30 | 1·90 |

1463 Schloss Ludwigsburg

(Des Vera and H. Kaul. Litho)
2004 (6 May). 300th Anniv of Schloss Ludwigsburg. P 14.
| 3271 | **1463** | 144c. multicoloured | 6·25 | 5·25 |

1464 Two Kittens playing with String

(Des Annegret Ehmke. Litho)
2004 (3 June). For Us Children. Cats. T **1464** and similar horiz designs. Multicoloured. P 14.
3272	45c. +20c. Type **1464**	3·25	3·00
3273	55c. +25c. Three kittens playing with ball	3·50	3·25
3274	55c. +25c. Mother and kitten	3·50	3·25
3275	55c. +25c. Cat washing paw	3·50	3·25
3276	144c. +56c. Two kittens asleep	9·50	8·25
3272/3276	Set of 5	21·00	19·00

1465 Sea and Sand

1466 National Flags as Heart-shaped Kite

(Des Barbara Dimanski. Litho German Bank Note Ptg Co, Leipzig)
2004 (3 June). Wattenmeer National Park. P 14.
| 3277 | **1465** | 55c. multicoloured | 2·30 | 1·90 |

(Des A. Osolin. Litho Schwann-Bagel, Mönchengladbach)
2004 (3 June). 21st-century German—Russian Youth Forum. P 14.
| 3278 | **1466** | 55c. multicoloured | 2·30 | 1·90 |
A stamp of a similar design was issued by Russia.

1467 Greifswalder Oie, Baltic Sea

1468 *Bremen* (passenger ship) and New York Harbour

(Des J. Count. Litho Schwann-Bagel, Mönchengladbach)
2004 (8 July). Lighthouses. T **1467** and similar square design. Multicoloured.
   (a) Sheet stamps. Ordinary gum. P 14.
| 3279 | 45c. Type **1467** | 2·30 | 1·90 |
| 3280 | 55c. Roter Sands | 2·30 | 1·90 |
   (b) Coil stamp. Self-adhesive gum. Die-cut perf 10½
| 3281 | 55c. As No. 3280 (32×35 *mm*) | 2·30 | 1·90 |
| 3279/3281 | Set of 3 | 6·25 | 5·25 |
No. 3281 was only issued in boxes containing coils of 100 stamps, with every fifth stamp in the coil numbered on the back.
See also Nos. 3365/3367 and 3486/3487.

(Des Sybille and F. Haase. Litho German Bank Note Ptg Co, Leipzig)
2004 (8 July–12 Aug). *Bremen*—1929 Winner of Blue Ribbon (Europe to America speed record).
   (a) Sheet stamp. Ordinary gum. P 14.
| 3282 | **1468** | 55c. multicoloured | 2·30 | 1·90 |
   (b) Self-adhesive booklet stamp. Die-cut perf 14 (12 Aug)
| 3283 | **1468** | 55c. multicoloured | 2·30 | 1·90 |

1469 Ludwig Fuerbach

1470 Camellia

(Des P. Effert. Litho)
2004 (8 July). Birth Bicentenary of Ludwig Fuerbach (philosopher). P 14.
| 3284 | **1469** | 144c. rosine and black | 6·25 | 5·25 |

(Des Antonia Graschberger. Litho)
2004 (12 Aug). Greetings Stamp.
   (a) Sheet stamp. Ordinary gum. P 14.
| 3285 | **1470** | 55c. multicoloured | 2·30 | 1·90 |
   (b) Self-adhesive booklet stamp. Die-cut perf 10
| 3286 | **1470** | 55c. multicoloured | 3·00 | 2·20 |
No. 3286 was issued in self-adhesive booklets with No. 3201.

1471 Church Façade

1472 Scene from *Hansel and Gretel* (opera) and Engelbert Humperdinck

(Des W. Schmidt. Litho Schwann-Bagel, Mönchengladbach)

2004 (12 Aug). Centenary of Protestant Regional Church, Speyer. P 14.
3287 1471 55c. multicoloured .... 2·50 2·00

(Des Lorli and E. Jünger. Litho German Bank Note Ptg Co, Leipzig)

2004 (9 Sept). 150th Birth Anniv of Engelbert Humperdinck (composer). P 14.
3288 1472 45c. multicoloured .... 2·10 1·70

1473 Ink Pot, Quill Pen, Manuscript and Glasses

1474 Feet and Hand Prints forming Face

(Des F. Lüdtke. Litho German Bank Note Ptg Co, Leipzig)

2004 (9 Sept). Birth Bicentenary of Eduard Mörike (writer). P 14.
3289 1473 55c. multicoloured .... 2·30 1·90

(Des R. Terpitz. Litho Schwann-Bagel, Mönchengladbach)

2004 (9 Sept). For Us Children. P 14.
3290 1474 55c. multicoloured .... 2·30 1·90

1475 Kaiser Wilhelm Cathedral Church, Berlin and Egon Eiermann

1476 Court Seal

(Des C. Wolff. Litho)

2004 (9 Sept). Birth Centenary of Egon Eiermann (architect). P 14.
3291 1475 100c. multicoloured .... 4·25 3·25

(Des W. Schmidt. Litho and embossed Schwann-Bagel, Mönchengladbach)

2004 (9 Sept). 50th Anniv of Federal Social Court. P 14.
3292 1476 144c. multicoloured .... 6·25 5·25

1477 Iceberg, Greenland

(Des C. Gassner. Litho)

2004 (7 Oct). Climate Zones. T **1477** and similar horiz designs. Multicoloured. P 14.
3293 45c. +20c. Type **1477** (arctic) .... 3·25 3·00
3294 55c. +25c. Mountains, Tibet (alpine) .... 3·50 3·25

GERMANY

3295 55c. +25c. River and grazing animals, Mecklenburg-Vorpommern (temperate) .... 3·50 3·25
3296 55c. +25c. Dunes, Sahara (desert) .... 3·50 3·25
3297 144c. +56c. Rainforest, Galapagos Islands (tropics) .... 9·50 8·25
3293/3297 Set of 5 .... 21·00 19·00

1478 Flying Boat Do X (1930)

1479 Flight into Egypt

(Des Klein and Neumann. Litho German Bank Note Ptg Co, Leipzig)

2004 (7 Oct). Stamp Day. P 14.
3298 1478 55c. deep ultramarine and vermilion . 2·50 2·10

(Des Lorli and E. Jünger. Litho Schwann-Bagel, Mönchengladbach)

2004 (4 Nov). Christmas. T **1479** and similar square design showing paintings by Peter Paul Rubens. Multicoloured. P 14.
3299 45c. +20c. Type **1479** .... 3·25 2·75
3300 55c. +25c. *Adoration of the Magi* .... 3·75 3·25
Stamps of the same design were issued by Belgium.

1480 Snow-covered Avenue

(Des J. Graf. Litho German Bank Note Ptg Co, Leipzig)

2004 (4 Nov). Post. P 14.
3301 1480 55c. multicoloured .... 2·50 2·10

1481 *Das Geheimnis*

(Des Lorli and E. Jünger. Litho German Bank Ptg Note Co, Leipzig)

2004 (4 Nov). Birth Centenary of Felix Nussbaum (artist). P 14.
3302 1481 55c. multicoloured .... 2·50 2·10

1482 International Space Station

1483 City Hall

(Des I. Wulff. Litho)

2004 (4 Nov). P 14.
3303 1482 55c. multicoloured .... 2·50 2·10

(Des G. Fiedler. Litho German Bank Note Ptg Co, Leipzig)

2005 (3 Jan). 1200th Anniv of Forchheim. P 13.
3304 1483 45c. multicoloured .... 2·10 1·70

157

GERMANY

1484 Three Kings (board painting, Cologne (c. 1350))

1485 Sunflower

(Des W. Schmidt. Litho German Bank Note Ptg Co, Leipzig)

2005 (3 Jan). Art. P 13.
| 3305 | 1484 | 55c. multicoloured | 2·50 | 2·10 |

See also No. 3566.

(Des W. Schmidt. Litho Giesecke & Devrient GmbH, Security Ptg, Leipzig)

2005 (3 Jan)–**18**. Flowers. T **1485** and similar vert designs. Multicoloured.

(a) Ordinary gum. P 14

Y3306	5c. Crocus tommasinianus (11.8.05)	45	40
Y3307	5c. Phlox (13.4.17)	45	40
Y3308	10c. Tulipa (8.9.05)	60	55
Y3309	10c. Eranthis hyemalis (8.6.17)	60	55
Y3310	20c. Tagetes erecta (7.7.05)	90	85
Y3311	20c. Hyacinthoides non-scripta (8.6.17)	90	85
Y3312	25c. Dianthus (9.10.08)	1·40	1·10
Y3313	25c. Lavatera trimestris (2.6.05)	1·40	1·10
Y3314	28c. Centaurium erythraea (3.7.14)	1·50	1·20
Y3315	35c. Dahlia variabilis (2.1.06)	1·60	1·50
Y3316	40c. Hepatica (8.9.05)	1·80	1·70
Y3317	45c. Chrysanthemum (7.4.05)	2·10	1·70
Y3318	45c. Convallaria majalis (6.5.10)	2·10	1·70
Y3319	45c. Nymphaea alba (11.5.17)	2·10	1·70
Y3320	50c. Aster novae (2.6.05)	2·30	1·90
Y3321	55c. Papaver rhoeas (7.7.05)	2·75	2·10
Y3322	55c. Rosa (12.6.08)	2·50	2·10
Y3323	58c. Pulsatilla vulgaris (6.12.12)	2·75	2·50
Y3324	60c. Fritillaria imperialis (5.12.13)	2·75	2·50
Y3325	62c. Paeonia (4.12.14)	3·00	2·75
Y3326	65c. Rudbeckia fulgida (2.3.06)	3·25	2·75
Y3327	70c. Dianthus carthusianorum (13.4.06)	3·50	2·75
Y3328	70c. Cosmos atrosanguineus (3.12.15)	3·50	2·75
Y3329	75c. Platycodon grandifloras (3.1.11)	3·25	3·00
Y3330	80c. Primula denticulate (4.12.14)	3·50	3·25
Y3331	85c. Dianthus plumarius (4.12.14)	3·75	3·25
Y3332	90c. Narcissus (2.1.06)	4·00	3·50
Y3333	90c. Hypericum hircinum (11.5.17)	4·00	3·50
Y3334	95c. Type **1485**	5·75	4·25
Y3335	100c. Dicentra spectabilis (13.7.06)	4·50	3·75
Y3336	145c. Nigella damascena (2.1.18)	6·00	5·50
Y3337	145c. Iris xiphium (2.1.16)	6·00	5·50
Y3338	180c. Aquilegia caerulea (5.6.14)	8·25	7·50
Y3339	200c. Eschscholzia californica (9.11.06)	9·25	7·50
Y3340	220c. Leontopodium alpinum (13.4.06)	10·50	8·75
Y3341	240c. Gaura lindheimeri (6.12.12)	11·00	10·00
Y3342	250c. Carduus defloratus (2.1.16)	11·50	10·50
Y3343	260c. Lilium candidum (11.12.16)	12·00	11·00
Y3344	345c. Myosotis (10.8.17)	17·00	16·00
Y3345	390c. Lilium bulbiferum (4.5.06)	18·00	17·00
Y3346	395c. Heuchera (4.12.14)	18·00	17·00
Y3347	400c. Fuschia (3.12.15)	19·00	17·00
Y3348	410c. Cypripedium (2.1.10)	18·00	16·00
Y3349	430c. Consolida regalis (2.1.09)	25·00	23·00
Y3350	440c. Lilium mortagon (4.12.14)	20·00	18·00
Y3351	450c. Ophrys apifera (3.12.15)	20·00	18·00
Y3352	500c. Gentiana acaulis (7.7.11)	21·00	19·00

(b) Self-adhesive. Die-cut perf 10½

Y3360	25c. Dianthus (2.1.06)	1·40	1·10
Y3361	25c. Lavatera trimestris (9.10.08)	1·20	1·10
Y3362	28c. Centaurium erythraea (3.7.14)	1·40	1·30
Y3363	35c. Dahlia variabilis (2.1.06)	1·60	1·50
Y3364	45c. Convallaria majalis	2·10	1·90
Y3365	55c. Papaver rhoeas (7.7.05)	2·75	2·10
Y3366	55c. Rosa (12.6.08)	2·50	2·10
Y3367	58c. Pulsatilla vulgaris (6.12.12)	2·75	2·50
Y3368	60c. Fritillaria imperialis (5.12.13)	2·75	2·50
Y3369	62c. Paeonia (4.12.14)	3·00	2·75
Y3370	65c. Rudbeckia fulgida (2.1.09)	3·25	3·00
Y3371	70c. Dianthus carthusianorum (2.1.09)	3·50	3·25
Y3372	70c. Cosmos atrosanguineus (3.12.15)	3·50	3·25
Y3373	90c. Narcissus (2.1.06)	4·25	3·75
Y3374	100c. Dicentra spectabilis (10.10.13)	4·50	4·25

No. Y3312 is reported issued in small sheets of ten stamps.
No. Y3322 is reported issued both in small sheets of ten stamps and in coils.

Nos. Y3364 and Y3368 were printed both in booklets with the surplus paper around the stamp retained and in coils with the surplus paper removed.
No. Y3366 in coils of 100 stamps with the paper removed.
Nos. Y3370 and Y3371 were issued in single sided booklets of five stamps and five labels inscribed 'LUFTPOST', with the surplus paper around each stamp removed.
Nos. Y3373/Y3374 were both issued in booklets of ten with the surplus paper around each stamp retained.

1486 Celtic Statue, Glauberg

(Des W. Schmidt. Litho Schwann-Bagel, Mönchengladbach)

2005 (3 Jan). Archaeology. P 13.
| 3335 | 1486 | 144c. multicoloured | 7·00 | 6·00 |

1487 Championship Mascot
(½-size illustration)

(Des E. Jünger. Litho)

2005 (10 Feb). Sport Promotion Fund. T **1487** and similar horiz designs. Multicoloured. P 14.

3336	45c. +20c. Type **1487** (World Cup Football Championship, Germany 2006)	3·75	3·25
3337	55c. +25c. Footballers (World Cup Football Championship, Germany 2006)	4·00	3·50
3338	55c. +25c. Skier (Nordic World Ski Championships, Oberstdorf)	4·00	3·50
3339	55c. +25c. Gymnasts (International German Gymnastics Festival, Berlin)	4·00	3·50
3340	144c. +56c. Fencers (Fencing World Championships, Leipzig)	10·50	9·50
3336/3340	Set of 5	24·00	21·00

1488 Pillar

(Des E. Kößlinger. Litho Schwann-Bagel, Mönchengladbach)

2005 (10 Feb). 150th Anniv of Advertisement Pillars. P 14.
| 3341 | 1488 | 55c. multicoloured | 2·50 | 2·10 |

1489 Cathedral Façade

(Des Barbara Dimanski. Litho German Bank Note Ptg Co, Leipzig)

2005 (10 Feb). Centenary of Berlin Cathedral. P 13.

(a) Sheet stamps. Ordinary gum
| 3342 | 1489 | 95c. multicoloured | 4·25 | 3·50 |

(b) Self-adhesive booklet stamp. Die-cut perf 11
| 3343 | 1489 | 95c. multicoloured | 5·00 | 3·75 |

No. 3343 is peeled directly from the cover of the booklet. It is not therefore possible to collect these as booklet panes.

GERMANY

1490 Postman walking in Mountains

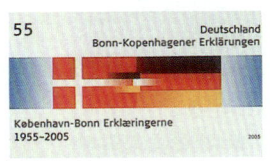

1491 Danish and German Flags

(Des D. Ziegenfeuter. Litho Schwann-Bagel, Mönchengladbach)
2005 (3 Mar). Postal Service (1st issue). T **1490** and similar square design. Multicoloured. P 13.
3344		95c. Type **1490**	2·75	2·10
3345		55c. Postman cycling	2·75	2·10

See also Nos. 3370/3371.

(Des Angela Kühn. Litho)
2005 (3 Mar). 50th Anniv of Germany—Denmark Relations. P 14.
| 3346 | **1491** | 55c. multicoloured | 2·50 | 2·10 |

A stamp of the same design was issued by Denmark.

1492 Lockhead L-1049 Super Constellation

(Des Angela Kühn. Litho)
2005 (3 Mar). 50th Anniv of Resumption of German Air traffic. P 14.
| 3347 | **1492** | 155c. multicoloured | 7·00 | 6·00 |

1493 Aquaduct

(Des J. Berholdt. Litho)
2005 (7 Apr). Centenary of Mittelland Canal. P 14.
| 3348 | **1493** | 45c. multicoloured | 2·30 | 2·10 |

1494 Rock, Ferns and Tree

1495 Silhouettes of Characters

(Des J. Graf. Litho)
2005 (7 Apr). National Parks. Bavarian Forest. P 14.
| 3349 | **1494** | 55c. multicoloured | 2·50 | 2·10 |

(Des Karin Blume-Zander. Litho)
2005 (7 Apr). Birth Bicentenary of Hans Christian Andersen (writer).
(a) Ordinary gum. P 10½.
| 3350 | **1495** | 144c. pale orange, orange and black | 7·00 | 6·25 |
(b) Coil Stamp. Self-adhesive gum. Die-cut perf 14
| 3351 | **1495** | 144c. pale orange, orange and black | 8·00 | 7·25 |

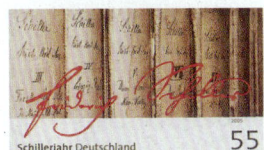

1496 Book Bindings and Signature

(Litho German Bank Ptg Co, Leipzig)
2005 (12 May). Birth Bicentenary of Friedrich Schiller (poet). Schiller Year. P 14.
| 3352 | **1496** | 55c. multicoloured | 2·50 | 2·10 |

1497 Signatories

1498 *Sitzende Fränzi* (woodcut) (Erich Heikel)

(Des C. Gassner. Litho Schwann-Bagel, Mönchengladbach)
2005 (12 May). 50th Anniv of Paris Contracts (establishing Federal Democratic Republic of Germany in Western European Union (WEU) and North Atlantic Treaty Organisation (NATO). P 14.
| 3353 | **1497** | 55c. black and vermilion | 2·50 | 2·10 |

(Litho Schwann-Bagel, Mönchengladbach)
2005 (12 May). Centenary of Die Brücke (The Bridge) (group of Expressionist artists). P 14.
| 3354 | **1498** | 55c. black, vermilion and pale stone | 2·50 | 2·10 |

1499 Wine Glass, Wine Bottle, Candle and Cup

(Des Nina Clausing. Litho German Bank Ptg Co, Leipzig)
2005 (12 May). Europa. Gastronomy. P 14.
| 3355 | **1499** | 55c. chocolate, pale yellow-orange and bright rose | 2·50 | 2·10 |

1500 Pope John Paul II

(Des W. Schmidt. Litho Schwann-Bagel, Mönchengladbach)
2005 (12 May). Pope John Paul II Commemoration. P 14.
| 3356 | **1500** | 55c. multicoloured | 2·50 | 2·10 |

1501 Kraftpost Omnibus

(Des Gerda and H. Neumann. Litho)
2005 (12 May). Stamp Day. Centenary of Post Bus. P 14.
| 3357 | **1501** | 55c. +25c. multicoloured | 4·00 | 3·50 |

1502 *Greif* ('Reach') (training ship) (⅔-*size illustration*)

159

GERMANY

(Des Klein and Neumann. Litho)

2005 (2 June). Youth Welfare. Ships. T **1502** and similar horiz designs. Multicoloured. P 14.

3358	45c. +20c. Type **1502**	3·75	3·25
3359	55c. +25c. *Passat* ('Trade Wind') (four-mast bark)	4·00	3·50
3360	55c. +25c. *Rickmer Rickmers* (cargo ship)	4·00	3·50
3361	55c. +25c. *Grand Duchess Elizabeth* (schooner)	4·00	3·50
3362	144c. +56c. *Deutschland* (training ship)	10·50	9·50
3358/3362	Set of 5	24·00	21·00

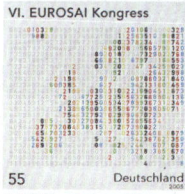

1503 Numbers as Map of Europe

1504 Cross and Globe

(Des Angela Kühn. Litho)

2005 (2 June). EUROSAI (European Organisation of Supreme Audit Institutions) Conference, Bonn. P 14.

| 3363 | **1503** | 55c. multicoloured | 2·50 | 2·10 |

(Des Andrea Voß-Acker. Litho)

2005 (2 June). World Youth Day. P 14.

| 3364 | **1504** | 55c. multicoloured | 2·50 | 2·10 |

A stamp of the same design was issued by Vatican City.

1505 Brunsbüttel Lighthouse

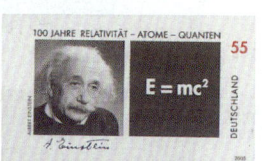

1506 Albert Einstein and 'E=mc²'

(Des J. Graf. Litho Bagel Security-Print, Mönchengladbach)

2005 (7 July). Lighthouses. T **1505** and similar square design. Multicoloured.

(a) Ordinary gum. P 14

| 3365 | 45c. Type **1505** | 2·10 | 1·70 |
| 3366 | 55c. Westerheversand | 2·50 | 2·10 |

(b) Self-adhesive booklet stamps. Die-cut perf 11

3366a	45c. As No. 3365	2·30	1·70
3367	45c. As Type **1467**	2·30	1·70
3365/3367	Set of 2	8·25	6·50

See also Nos. 3429/3430.

(Des G. Lienemeyer. Litho German Bank Ptg Co, Leipzig)

2005 (7 July). Centenary of *Special Theory of Relativity* by Albert Einstein (physicist). P 14.

| 3368 | **1506** | 55c. black and scarlet | 2·50 | 2·10 |

1507 New Palace, Sanssouci Park, Potsdam

(Des J. Graf. Litho Bagel Security-Print, Mönchengladbach)

2005 (7 July). Prussian Schlosses (1st issue). Sheet 98×70 mm. P 14.

| MS3369 | **1507** | 220c. multicoloured | 10·00 | 9·50 |

See also No. 3386.

(Des D. Ziegenfeuter. Litho Schwann-Bagel, Mönchengladbach)

2005 (11 Aug). Postal Service (2nd issue). Square designs as T **1490**. Multicoloured. P 14.

| 3370 | 55c. Postman with trolley | 2·50 | 2·10 |
| 3371 | 55c. Postman in boat | 2·50 | 2·10 |

1508 Tree and Figure

1509 Chickens

(Des Karin Blume-Zander and A. Zander. Litho German Bank Ptg Co. Leipzig)

2005 (11 Aug). Centenary of NaturFreunde Deutschlands (conservation organisation). P 13½.

| 3372 | **1508** | 144c. deep blue-green and pale rose | 7·00 | 6·00 |

(Des Kathrin Armbrust. Litho)

2005 (8 Sept). For us Children. P 14.

| 3373 | **1509** | 55c. multicoloured | 2·50 | 2·10 |

1510 City from River (15th-century woodcut)

1511 Angel

(Des H. Schillinger. Litho German Bank Ptg Co, Leipzig)

2005 (8 Sept). 1200th Anniv of Magdeburg. P 14.

| 3374 | **1510** | 55c. multicoloured | 2·50 | 2·10 |

(Des P. Effert. Litho Bagel Security-Print, Mönchengladbach)

2005 (8 Sept). 450th Anniv of Religious Freedom. P 14.

| 3375 | **1511** | 55c. multicoloured | 2·50 | 2·10 |

See also No. 3567.

1512 Max Schmeling

(Des Irmgard Hesse. Litho German Bank Ptg Co, Leipzig)

2005 (8 Sept). Birth Centenary of Max Schmeling (boxer). P 14.

| 3376 | **1512** | 100c. black and scarlet vermilion | 2·50 | 2·10 |

1513 Church

(Des Andrea Voß-Acker. Litho German Bank Ptg Co, Leipzig)

2005 (13 Oct). Completion of Reconstruction of Frauenkirche (Church of our Lady) Dresden (2004). P 14.

| 3377 | **1513** | 55c. multicoloured | 2·50 | 2·10 |

1514 Script and Pen Nib

160

(Des Regina and P. Steiner. Litho Bagel Security-Print, Mönchengladbach)

2005 (13 Oct). Birth Bicentenary of Adalbert Stifter (writer). P 14.
3378 **1514** 95c. multicoloured .... 4·50 4·25

1515 Horse-drawn Procession

1516 Adoration of the Child Jesus

(Des M. Gottscall. Litho German Bank Ptg Co, Leipzig)

2005 (3 Nov). 150th Anniv of Bad Tölz Leonhardifahrt (festival). P 14.
3379 **1515** 45c. multicoloured .... 2·10 1·70

(Litho Bagel Security-Print, Mönchengladbach)

2005 (3 Nov). Christmas. T **1516** and similar square design showing paintings by Stefan Lochner. Multicoloured. P 14.
3380 **1516** 45c. +20c. Type **1516** .... 3·25 2·75
3381 55c. +25c. *Madonna of the Rose Bush* .... 4·00 3·25

1517 Israeli and German Flags

1518 Bertha von Suttner and *Die Waffen nieder*

(Des S. Klein and O. Neumann. Litho)

2005 (3 Nov). 40th Anniv of Diplomatic Relations with Israel. P 14.
3382 **1517** 55c. multicoloured .... 2·50 2·10
A stamp of a similar design was issued by Israel.

(Des Sibylle and F. Haase. Litho)

2005 (3 Nov). Centenary of Bertha von Suttner's Nobel Peace Prize. P 14.
3383 **1518** 55c. multicoloured .... 2·50 2·10

1519 '50 JAHRE BUNDES WEHR'

1520 Robert Koch and Microscope

(Des Nina Clausing. Litho)

2005 (3 Nov). 50th Anniv of German Federal Armed Forces. P 14.
3384 **1519** 55c. multicoloured .... 2·50 2·10

(Des Sibylle and F. Haase. Litho)

2005 (3 Nov). Centenary of Robert Koch's Nobel Prize for Physiology and Medicine. P 14.
3385 **1520** 144c. multicoloured .... 7·00 6·00

(Des J. Graf. Litho Bagel Security-Print, Mönchengladbach)

2005 (3 Nov). Self-adhesive Booklet Stamp. Prussian Schlosses. New Palace, Sanssouci Park, Potsdam (2nd issue). Die-cut perf 11.
3386 **1507** 220c. multicoloured .... 10·50 9·50

1521 *Gonepteryx rhamni*

2005 (1 Dec). Butterflies and Moths. T **1521** and similar horiz designs. Multicoloured.

(a) Sheet stamps. P 14
3387 45c. +20c. Type **1521** .... 3·25 3·00
3388 55c. +25c. *Panaxia quadripunctaria* .... 3·50 3·25
3389 55c. +25c. *Inachis io* .... 3·50 3·25
3390 145c. +55c. *Brintesia circe* .... 9·75 9·00

(b) Self-adhesive. Die-cut perf 14
3391 55c. +25c. As No. 3389 .... 4·25 3·25
3387/3391 Set of 5 .... 22·00 20·00

No. 3391 was available in coils, with the surplus paper around the stamp removed and in booklets with the paper retained.

1522 Sights of Halle

1523 Wolfgang Mozart

(Des I. Wulff. Litho German Bank Ptg Co, Leipzig)

2006 (2 Jan). 1200th Anniv of Halle. P 14.
3392 **1522** 45c. multicoloured .... 2·10 1·70

(Des I. Hess. Litho German Bank Ptg Co, Leipzig)

2006 (2 Jan). 250th Birth Anniv of Wolfgang Amadeus Mozart (composer). P 13½.
3393 **1523** 55c. multicoloured .... 2·50 2·10

1524 Snow-covered Tree

(Des J. Graf. Litho German Bank Ptg Co, Leipzig)

2006 (2 Jan). Winter. P 14.
3394 **1524** 55c. multicoloured .... 2·50 2·10
See also No. 3452.

1525 Clouds over Earth

(Des J. Graf. Litho Bagel Security-Print, Mönchengladbach)

2006 (2 Jan). Climate Protection Awareness. P 14.
3395 **1525** 55c. +25c. multicoloured .... 4·25 3·50

1526 Bull (detail) and Charles IV's Seal

GERMANY

(Des Antonia Graschberger. Litho Bagel Security-Print, Mönchengladbach)

2006 (2 Jan). 650th Anniv of Charles IV's Golden Bull (document creating constitutional structure).

(a) Ordinary gum. P 14
| 3396 | 1526 | 145c. multicoloured | 7·00 | 6·25 |

(b) Self-adhesive Booklet Stamp. Die-cut perf 10½
| 3397 | 1526 | 145c. multicoloured | 8·00 | 6·25 |

1527 German Flags *(Illustration further reduced. Actual size 55×33 mm)*

(Des Andrea Acker. Litho Bagel Security-Print, Mönchengladbach)

2006 (9 Feb). Sport Promotion Fund. World Cup Football Championship, Germany. T **1527** and similar horiz designs. Multicoloured. P 14.

3398	45c. +20c. Type **1527**	3·25	3·00
3399	55c. +25c. Horse and rider (World Equestrian Games, Aachen 2006)	3·50	3·25
3400	55c. +25c. Stadium lights (opening game)	3·50	3·25
3401	55c. +25c. Pitch (final)	3·50	3·25
3402	145c. +56c. Fireworks and emblem	9·25	8·50
3398/3402	Set of 5	21·00	19·00

See also No. **MS**3412.

1528 Rooftops

(Litho German Bank Ptg Co, Leipzig)

2006 (9 Feb). 850th Anniv of Michaelskirche, Schwäbisch Hall. P 14.
| 3403 | 1528 | 55c. multicoloured | 2·50 | 2·10 |

1529 'Fräiske Räid'

(Des C. Gassner. Litho)

2006 (9 Feb). 50th Anniv of Friesenrat (Frisian council). P 14.
| 3404 | 1529 | 90c. multicoloured | 4·25 | 3·50 |

1530 Braille *(Illustration further reduced. Actual size 55×32 mm)*

(Des C. Gassner. Litho and embossed Bagel Security-Print, Mönchengladbach)

2006 (2 Mar). Bicentenary of Blind School, Berlin. 150th Anniv of Nikolauspflege (charitable organisation). P 14.
| 3405 | 1530 | 55c. black and pale brown-grey | 2·50 | 2·10 |

1531 Early Town and Map  **1532** Altes Museum, Lustgarten

(Des H. Scheuner. Litho)
2006 (2 Mar). 1200th Anniv of Ingolstadt. P 14.
| 3406 | 1531 | 55c. multicoloured | 2·50 | 2·10 |

(Des G. Lienemeyer. Litho)
2006 (2 Mar–13 July). 225th Birth Anniv of Karl Friedrich Schinkel (architect).

(a) Ordinary gum. P 14
| 3407 | 1532 | 55c. multicoloured | 2·50 | 2·10 |

(b) Self-adhesive gum. Die-cut perf 11
| 3407a | 1532 | 55c. multicoloured (13.7) | 3·50 | 2·75 |

1533 Johannes Rau  **1534** Emblem

(Des G. Aretz and O. Aretz. Litho German Bank Ptg Co, Leipzig)
2006 (2 Mar). Johannes Rau (president 1999–2004) Commemoration. P 14.
| 3408 | 1533 | 55c. multicoloured | 2·50 | 2·10 |

(Des Sibylle and F. Haase. Litho and embossed Bagel Security-Print, Mönchengladbach)
2006 (13 Apr). 500th Anniv of European University Viadrina Frankfurt (Oder). P 14.
| 3409 | 1534 | 55c. light blue and brownish black | 2·50 | 2·10 |

1535 Blossom-covered Trees  **1536** Self-Portrait (Albrecht Dürer)

(Des J. Graf. Litho German Bank Ptg Co, Leipzig)
2006 (13 Apr). Spring. P 14.
| 3410 | 1535 | 55c. multicoloured | 2·50 | 2·10 |

See also No. 3449.

(Des W. Schmidt. Litho)
2006 (13 Apr). Art. P 14.
| 3411 | 1536 | 145c. light blue and brownish black | 6·50 | 5·50 |

(Des Andrea Acker. Litho Bagel Security-Print, Mönchengladbach)
2006 (4 May). World Cup Football Championship, Germany. Sheet 130×180 mm containing T **1527** and similar horiz designs. Multicoloured. P 14.
MS3412 130×180 mm. Nos. 3398, 3400/3402 ... 20·00 18·00

1537 'Integration' on Jacket  **1538** Rhine Valley

GERMANY

(Des Irmgard Hesse. Litho German Bank Ptg Co, Leipzig)

2006 (4 May). Europa. Integration. P 14.
3413 1537 55c. multicoloured .... 2·50 2·10

(Des D. Ziegenfeuter. Litho Bagel Security-Print, Mönchengladbach)

2006 (4 May). Upper Central Rhine Valley (Oberes Mittelrheintal). World Heritage Site.

(a) Ordinary gum. P 14
3414 1538 55c. multicoloured .... 2·50 2·10

(b) Self-adhesive Booklet Stamp. Die-cut perf 11
3415 1538 55c. multicoloured .... 2·75 2·50

1539 Gerd Bucerius

(Des Birgit Hogrefe. Litho)

2006 (4 May). Birth Centenary of Gerd Bucerius (politician). P 14.
3416 1539 85c. multicoloured .... 4·25 3·25

1540 Pine Marten

(Des C. Lienemeyer. Litho German Bank Ptg Co, Leipzig)

2006 (8 June). Youth Welfare. Animals. T **1540** and similar horiz designs. Multicoloured. P 14.
3417 45c. +20c. Type 1540 .... 3·00 2·75
3418 55c. +25c. Hares .... 3·75 3·25
3419 55c. +25c. Red Squirrel .... 3·75 3·25
3420 55c. +25c. Roe Deer and fawn .... 3·75 3·25
3421 145c. +55c. Wild Boar and young .... 9·25 8·50
3417/3421 Set of 5 .... 21·00 19·00

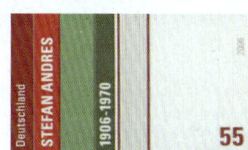

1541 Stripes

(Des Birgit Hogrefe. Litho Bagel Security-Print, Mönchengladbach)

2006 (8 June). Birth Centenary of Stefan Andres (writer). P 14.
3422 1541 55c. multicoloured .... 2·50 2·10

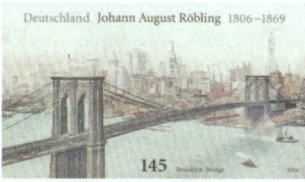

1542 Brooklyn Bridge, New York *(Illustration further reduced. Actual size 55×32 mm)*

(Des L. Menze. Litho)

2006 (8 June). Birth Bicentenary of Johan August Röbling (architect).

(a) Ordinary gum. P 14
3423 1542 145c. multicoloured .... 7·00 6·00

(b) Self-adhesive. Die-cut perf 11
3423a 1542 145c. multicoloured .... 8·00 7·25

1543 Car Number Plates    **1544** Berghauser Castle, Burganlage

(Des K. Erdmann. Litho German Bank Ptg Co, Leipzig)

2006 (13 July). Centenary of First Number Plates. P 14.
3424 1543 45c. multicoloured .... 2·30 1·70

(Des D. Dorfstecher. Litho)

2006 (13 July). P 14.
3425 1544 55c. multicoloured .... 2·50 2·10

1545 Flowering Rapeseed    **1546** Saskia van Uylenburgh

(Des J. Graf. Litho German Bank Ptg Co, Leipzig)

2006 (13 July). Summer. P 14.
3426 1545 55c. multicoloured .... 2·50 2·10
See also No. 3450.

(Des W. Nikkels. Litho Bagel Security-Print, Mönchengladbach)

2006 (13 July). 400th Birth Anniv of Rembrandt Harmenszoon van Rijn (Rembrandt) (artist). P 14.
3427 1546 70c. multicoloured .... 3·25 2·75

No. 3428 is vacant.

(Des J. Graf. Litho Bagel Security-Print, Mönchengladbach)

2006 (10 Aug). Lighthouses. Square designs as T **1505**. Multicoloured. P 14.
3429 45c. Neuland .... 2·10 1·70
3430 55c. Hohe Weg .... 2·50 2·10

No. 3431 is vacant.

1547 Valley    **1548** Valley and Skull

(Des J. Rieß. Litho Bagel Security-Print, Mönchengladbach)

2006 (10 Aug). Tourism. Schwarzwald. Sheet 145×70 mm. P 14.
MS3432 1547 55c. multicoloured .... 3·00 2·75

(Des Annegret Ehmke. Litho German Bank Ptg Co, Leipzig)

2006 (10 Aug). 150th Anniv of Discovery of Neanderthal Skull. P 14.
3433 1548 220c. multicoloured .... 10·50 9·50

1549 Cat and Envelopes    **1550** Hauptmann von Köpenick

(Des G. Fiedler. Litho German Bank Ptg Co, Leipzig)

2006 (7 Sept). For us Children. P 13½.
3434 1549 55c. multicoloured .... 2·50 2·10

163

GERMANY

(Des C. Wolff. Litho German Bank Ptg Co. Leipzig)

2006 (7 Sept). Centenary of Hauptmann von Köpenick (fraudulent identity of William Voigt) Affair. P 13½.
| 3435 | **1550** | 55c. multicoloured | 2·75 | 2·30 |

1551 Shipping and Trade

(Des J. Rieß. Eng L. Sjööblom. Recess and litho Austrian State Ptg Wks)

2006 (7 Sept). 650th Anniv of Hanseatic League (Städtehanse). P 13½.
| 3436 | **1551** | 70c. multicoloured | 3·50 | 3·25 |

1552 Fliegender Hamburger VT 877
(Illustration reduced. Actual size 55×32 mm)

(Des S. Klein and O. Neumann. Litho)

2006 (5 Oct). Welfare. Trains. T **1552** and similar horiz designs. Multicoloured.

(a) Ordinary gum. P 14
3437	45c. +20c. Type **1552**	3·25	3·00
3438	55c. +25c. Intercity Express ET 403	3·50	3·25
3439	55c. +25c. Trans Europe Express VT 11.5	3·50	3·25
3440	145c. +55c. Henschel-Wegmann-Zug 61 001	9·25	8·50

(b) Self-adhesive. Die-cut perf 11
| 3441 | 55c. +25c. As No. 3438 | 5·00 | 3·75 |
| 3437/3441 | Set of 5 | 22·00 | 20·00 |

No. 3441 was issued both in booklets with the surplus paper around the stamp retained and in coils with the surplus paper removed.

1553 Postcard, 1896

(Des Gerda and H. Neumann. Litho Bagel Security-Print, Mönchengladbach)

2006 (5 Oct). Stamp Day. P 14.
| 3442 | **1553** | 55c. multicoloured | 2·50 | 2·10 |

1554 Woodland

(Des J. Graf. Litho German Bank Ptg Co, Leipzig)

2006 (5 Oct). Autumn. P 14.
| 3443 | **1554** | 55c. multicoloured | 2·50 | 2·10 |

See also No. 3451.

1555 Hannah Arendt *(Illustration reduced. Actual size 55×32 mm)*

(Des Regina and P. Steiner. Litho)

2006 (5 Oct). Birth Centenary of Hannah Arendt (political theorist and philosopher). P 14.
| 3444 | **1555** | 145c. multicoloured | 8·50 | 6·75 |

1556 Eugen Bolz

(Des Susanne Österlee. Litho Bagel Security-Print, Mönchengladbach)

2006 (9 Nov). 125th Birth Anniv of Eugen Anton Bolz (Catholic politician). P 14.
| 3445 | **1556** | 45c. slate-blue and orange-yellow | 2·30 | 1·70 |

1557 The Nativity

(Des Annegret Ehmke. Litho German Bank Ptg Co, Leipzig)

2006 (9 Nov). Christmas. Paintings by Meister Franke. T **1557** and similar horiz design. Multicoloured. P 14.
| 3446 | 45c. +20c. Type **1557** | 2·75 | 2·50 |
| 3447 | 55c. +25c. Three Kings | 3·50 | 3·25 |

1558 Cardinal Höffner    **1559** Werner Forßmann

(Des C. Gassner. Litho German Bank Ptg Co, Leipzig)

2006 (9 Nov). Birth Centenary of Cardinal Joseph Höffner (Bishop of Münster and Archbishop of Cologne). P 14.
| 3448 | **1558** | 55c. multicoloured | 2·50 | 2·10 |

(Des J. Graf. Litho German Bank Ptg Co, Leipzig)

2006 (9 Nov). Seasons. Self-adhesive Booklet Stamps. Horiz designs as T **1524**. Multicoloured. Die-cut perf 11.
3449	55c. As Type **1535**	2·75	2·10
3450	55c. As Type **1545**	2·75	2·10
3451	55c. As Type **1554**	2·75	2·10
3452	55c. As Type **1524**	2·75	2·10
3449/3452	Set of 4	10·00	7·50

(Des F. Lüdtke. Litho)

2006 (9 Nov). 50th Anniv of Werner Forßmann's (surgeon and inventor of the heart catheter) Nobel Prize for Medicine. P 14.
| 3453 | **1559** | 90c. multicoloured | 4·50 | 4·25 |

1560 Street    **1561** Stars

164

(Des Susanne Öesterlee. Litho German Bank Ptg Co, Leipzig)

2007 (2 Jan). Furth Millenary.

(a) Ordinary gum. P 14
3454 1560 45c. multicoloured .... 2·30 1·90

(b) Self-adhesive booklet stamp. Die-cut perf 11
3455 1560 45c. multicoloured .... 2·30 1·90

(Des P. Effert. Litho and embossed Bagel Security-Print, Mönchengladbach)

2007 (2 Jan). Germany's Presidency of European Union. P 14.
3456 1561 55c. black, orange vermilion and chrome yellow .... 2·50 2·10

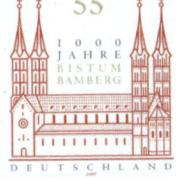

1562 Imperial Cathedral Façade **1563** Symbols of Saarland

(Des G. Fiedler. Litho German Bank Ptg Co, Leipzig)

2007 (2 Jan). Bamberg Diocese Millenary. P 14.
3457 1562 55c. rosine, bright blue and gold .... 2·50 2·10

(Des F. Lüdtke. Litho Bagel Security-Print, Mönchengladbach)

2007 (2 Jan–3 Mar). 50th Anniv of Federal Republic of Saarland.

(a) Ordinary gum. P 14
3458 1563 55c. multicoloured .... 2·50 2·10

(b) Self-adhesive booklet stamp. Die-cut perf 10½
3459 1563 55c. multicoloured (3.3) .... 2·50 2·10

1564 Ball and Hands

(Des S. Klein and O. Neuman. Litho Bagel Security-Print, Mönchengladbach)

2007 (2 Jan). Sport Promotion Fund (1st issue). World Handball Championship, Germany. P 13×13½.
3460 1564 55c. +25c. multicoloured .... 4·25 3·75
See also Nos. 3462/4 and **MS**3477.

1565 Engine Diagram and NSU Ro80

(Des Lorili and E. Jünger. Litho)

2007 (2 Jan). 50th Anniv of Rotary Engine designed by Felix Wankel. P 14.
3461 1565 145c. multicoloured .... 6·50 6·00

(Des S. Klein and O. Neuman. Litho Bagel Security-Print, Mönchengladbach)

2007 (8 Feb). Sport Promotion Fund (2nd issue). Horiz designs as T **1564**. Multicoloured. P 13×13½.
3462 45c. +20c. Canoeing (world championships, Wedau Park) .... 3·50 3·25
3463 55c. +25c. Gymnastics (world championships, Stuttgart) .... 4·00 3·50
3464 145c. +55c. Swimming (world pentathlon championships, Berlin) .... 9·25 8·50
3462/3464 Set of 3 .... 15·00 13·50

1566 Johann Senckenberg and Institute Building

(Des Angela Kühn. Litho)

2007 (8 Feb). 300th Birth Anniv of Johann Christian Senckenberg (physician and health reformer). P 14.
3465 1566 90c. multicoloured .... 4·25 3·75

1567 Claus Schenk Graf von Stauffenberg and Helmuth James Graf von Moltke

(Des Irmgard Hesse. Litho German Bank Ptg Co, Leipzig)

2007 (1 Mar). Birth Centenaries. P 14.
3466 1567 55c. vermilion and black .... 2·50 2·10

1568 Star of David **1569** Die Ausgrabung der Kreuze (Adam Elsheimer)

(Des Barbara Dimanski. Litho)

2007 (1 Mar). Jewish Centre, Munich. P 14.
3467 1568 55c. multicoloured .... 2·50 2·10

(Litho German Bank Ptg Co, Leipzig)

2007 (1 Mar). P 13½.
3468 1569 55c. multicoloured .... 2·75 2·10

1570 Signatories **1571** Paul Gerhardt and Music Score

(Des W. Schmidt. Litho German Bank Ptg Co, Leipzig)

2007 (1 Mar). 50th Anniv of Treaty of Rome. P 13½.
3469 1570 55c. multicoloured .... 2·50 2·10

2007 (1 Mar). 400th Birth Anniv of Paul Gerhardt. P 14.
3470 1571 55c. multicoloured .... 2·50 2·10

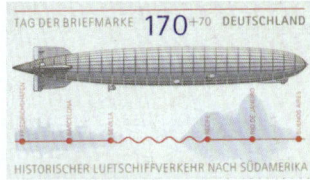

1572 LZ 127 Graf Zeppelin

GERMANY

(Des G. Gamroth. Litho)
2007 (1 Mar). Stamp Day. Sheet 105×70 mm. P 14.
MS3471 **1572** 170c.+70c. multicoloured........................... 12·50 11·50

1573 Writing a Letter

1574 Pope Benedict XVI

(Des Regina and Peter Steiner. Litho Bagel Security-Print, Mönchengladbach)
2007 (12 Apr). Post. T **1573** and similar square design. Each chrome yellow, black and scarlet vermilion. P 14.
3472 55c. Type **1573**................................. 2·30 2·10
3473 55c. Posting letter .... 2·30 2·10

(Des Antonia Graschberger. Litho German Bank Ptg Co, Leipzig)
2007 (12 Apr). 80th Birthday of Pope Benedict XVI. P 14.
3474 **1574** 55c. multicoloured........................... 2·50 2·10

1575 Universalis Cosmographia

(Des Werner Hans Schmidt. Recess and litho Enschedé)
2007 (12 Apr). 500th Anniv of World Map drawn by Martin Waldseemüller. P 14.
3475 **1575** 220c. multicoloured........................... 12·50 11·50

1576 Scouts

(Des Susanne Oesterlee. Litho German Bank Ptg Co, Leipzig)
2007 (3 May). Europa. Centenary of Scouting. P 14.
3476 **1576** 45c. multicoloured........................... 2·10 1·70

(Des Stefan Klein and Olaf. Neuman. Litho Bagel Security-Print, Mönchengladbach)
2007 (3 May). 40th Anniv of Sport Promotion Fund. Horiz designs as T **1564**. Multicoloured. P 13×13½.
MS3477 45c.+20c. As No. 3462; 55c.+25c. As No. 3460; 55c.+25c. As No. 3463; 145c.+55c. As No. 3464....................... 21·00 19·00

1577 Schloss

(Des Gerhard Lienemeyer. Litho)
2007 (3 May). Bellevue Schloss.
(a) Ordinary gum. P 14
3478 **1577** 55c. multicoloured........................... 2·75 2·30
(b) Self-adhesive gum. Die-cut 10×10½
3479 **1577** 55c. multicoloured........................... 3·00 2·30
No. 3479 was die-cut round to simulate perforations and had the surplus paper around the stamp removed.

1578 Schloss and Sculptures

(Des Lutz Menze. Litho German Bank Ptg Co, Leipzig)
2007 (3 May). 700th Anniv of Moyland Schloss. P 14.
3480 **1578** 85c. multicoloured........................... 4·25 3·25

1579 Early Festival Goers

(Des Johannes Graf. Litho Bagel Security-Print, Mönchengladbach)
2007 (3 May). 175th Anniv of Hambacher Fest (democratic festival).
(a) Ordinary gum. P 13×13½
3481 **1579** 145c. multicoloured........................... 6·50 5·50
(b) Self-adhesive booklet stamps. Die-cut 10×10½
3482 **1579** 145c. multicoloured........................... 7·00 5·50
No. 3482 was die-cut round to simulate perforations.

1580 Sawing legs from Chair

(Des Michael Kunter and Henning Wagenbreth. Litho)
2007 (14 June). 125th Birth Anniv of Valentin Ludwig Fey (Karl Valentin) (comedian and writer). P 14.
3483 **1580** 45c. multicoloured........................... 2·30 1·90

1581 'Nichts Schönres gab's für Tante Lotte Als Schwarze-Heidelbeer-Kompotte' (Behold Aunt Lotte's choicest snack: Blueberry compote, sweet and black)

1582 Paul Klinger and Nadia Grey (poster for film *Hengst Maestoso Austria*)

(Des Inigo Wulf. Litho German Bank Ptg Co, Leipzig)
2007 (14 June). For the Young. 175th Birth Anniv of Wilhelm Busch (poet and cartoonist). Sheet 165×75 mm containing T **1581** and similar square designs showing scenes from illustrated poem *Hans Huckebein–der Unglücksrabe* (the unlucky raven) by Wilhelm Busch. Multicoloured. P 14.
MS3484 45c.+20c. Type **1581**; 55c.+25c. 'Doch Huckebein verschleudert nur Die schöne Gabe der Natur' (But Huckebein, unused to thrift, Just squanders nature's precious gift); 55c.+25c. 'Die Tante naht voll Zorn und Schrecken; Hans Huckebein verläßt das Becken' (The aunt descends in shock and wrath. Hans Huckebein deserts his bath); 145c.+55c. 'Und schnell betritt er, angstbeflügelt, Die Wäsche, welche frisch gebügelt' (And tramples, on the wings of fright, The ironed laundry, clean and white)....................... 20·00 18·00

(Des Elisabeth Hau. Litho Litho Bagel Security-Print, Mönchengladbach)

2007 (14 June). Birth Centenary of Paul Karl Heinrich Klinksik (Paul Klinger) (actor). P 14.

| 3485 | **1582** | 55c. multicoloured | 4·50 | 3·75 |

(Des Johannes Graf. Litho Schwann-Bagel, Mönchengladbach)

2007 (12 July). Lighthouses. Square designs as T **1467**. Multicoloured. P 14.

| 3486 | 45c. Bremerhaven Oberfeuer | 2·30 | 1·70 |
| 3487 | 55c. Hörnum | 2·50 | 2·10 |

1583 House of Blackheads, Riga

(Des Sibylle Haase and Fritz Haase. Litho German Bank Ptg Co, Leipzig)

2007 (12 July). World Heritage Sites, Riga and Wismar. T **1583** and similar horiz design. Multicoloured. P 14.

| 3488 | 65c. Type **1583** | 2·75 | 2·50 |
| 3489 | 70c. City Hall and St George's Church, Wismar | 3·00 | 2·75 |

Stamps of a similar design were issued by Latvia.

1584 Banknotes and Coins from Various Currency Epochs

(Des Werner Hans Schmidt. Litho)

2007 (9 Aug). 50th Anniv of German Bundesbank (Federal bank). P 14.

| 3490 | **1584** | 55c. multicoloured | 2·75 | 2·10 |

1585 Saale River Plain

(Des Barbara Dimanski. Litho)

2007 (9 Aug). 75th Anniv of Saaletalsperre Bleiloch (dam across Saale valley). P 14.

| 3491 | **1585** | 55c. multicoloured | 2·50 | 2·10 |

1586 Kaiser Wilhelm Bridge

(Des Lutz Menze. Recess and litho Austrian State Ptg Wks, Vienna)

2007 (9 Aug). Centenary of Kaiser Wilhelm Bridge, Wilhelmshaven. P 14.

| 3492 | **1586** | 145c. multicoloured | 7·00 | 6·25 |

1587 Hedgehog and Hearts

(Des Regina and Olaf Jäger. Litho German Bank Ptg Co, Leipzig)

2007 (20 Sept). For us Children. P 14.

| 3493 | **1587** | 55c. multicoloured | 2·50 | 2·10 |

1588 Receiving a Letter    **1589** Symbols of Science

(Des Regina and Peter Steiner. Litho Bagel Security-Print, Mönchengladbach)

2007 (20 Sept). Post. T **1588** and similar square design. Multicoloured. P 14.

| 3494 | 55c. Type **1588** | 2·30 | 2·10 |
| 3495 | 55c. Reading letter | 2·30 | 2·10 |

(Des Nina Clausing. Litho)

2007 (20 Sept). 50th Anniv of Wissenschaftsrat (government scientific advisors). P 14.

| 3496 | **1589** | 90c. multicoloured | 4·50 | 4·25 |

1590 Stylised Building    **1591** Section of 'Limes' and Watch Towers

(Des Ingo Wulff. Litho German Bank Ptg Co, Leipzig)

2007 (11 Oct). Centenary of Deutscher Werkbund (artistic design group). P 13½.

| 3497 | **1590** | 55c. multicoloured | 2·50 | 2·10 |

(Des Annegret Ehmke. Litho Bagel Security-Print, Mönchengladbach)

2007 (11 Oct). World Heritage Site. 'The Roman Limes' (Roman camp, castle and walls). Sheet 105×70 mm. P 14.

| MS3498 | **1591** | multicoloured | 4·25 | 3·75 |

1592 Karl Freiherr Vom Stein

(Des Lutz Menze. Litho)

2007 (11 Oct). 250th Birth Anniv of Heinrich Friedrich Carl Freiherr Vom und Zum Stein (statesman and reformer). P 13½.

| 3499 | **1592** | 145c. multicoloured | 6·50 | 6·00 |

GERMANY

1593 Three Kings
1594 St. Elisabeth feeding Invalid 
1598 Liturgical Book and Gothic Wall Painting (detail), Reichenau Abbey
1599 Old Berlin Distillery

(Des Lorli and Ernst Jünger. Litho German Bank Ptg Co, Leipzig)

2007 (8 Nov). Christmas. T **1593** and similar square design. Multicoloured. P 13½.
3500	45c. +20c. Type **1593**	3·25	3·00
3501	55c. +25c. Virgin and Child	3·75	3·25

(Des Dieter Ziegenfeuter. Litho Bagel Security-Print, Mönchengladbach)

2007 (8 Nov). 800th Birth Anniv of St. Elisabeth von Thüringen. P 14.
3502	**1594**	55c. multicoloured	3·50	2·75

1595 Astrid Lindgren and Emil from *Lönneberga* (character from book)

(Des Lorli and Ernst Jünger. Recess and litho Austrian State Ptg Wks, Vienna)

2007 (8 Nov). Birth Centenary of Astrid Lindgren (children's author). P 14.
3503	**1595**	100c. multicoloured	4·50	4·25

A stamp of the same design was issued by Sweden.

1596 Brandenburg Gate, Berlin

(Des Andrea Voß Acker. Litho Enschedé)

2007 (27 Dec). 275th Birth Anniv of Carl Gotthard Langhans (architect). T **1596** and similar horiz design. Multicoloured.
(a) Ordinary gum. P 14
3504	55c. Type **1596**	2·75	2·10

(b) Self-adhesive booklet stamp. Die-cut perf 11
3505	55c. As No. 3504	3·25	2·10

1597 Guinea Pigs

(Des Andrea Voß Acker. Litho Enschedé)

2007 (27 Dec). Welfare. Pets. T **1597** and similar horiz designs showing animals and young. Multicoloured.
(a) Ordinary gum. P 14
3506	45c. +20c. Type **1597**	3·50	3·25
3507	55c. +25c. Dogs	3·75	3·25
3508	55c. +25c. Horses	3·75	3·25
3509	145c. +55c. Rabbits	9·75	9·00

(b) Self-adhesive. Die-cut perf 11
3510	55c. +25c. As No. 3508	4·50	3·75
3506/3510	Set of 5	23·00	20·00

No. 3510 was issued both in booklets with the surplus paper around the stamp retained and in coils with the surplus paper removed.

(Des Andrea Voß Acker. Litho Enschedé)

2008 (2 Jan). World Heritage Site. T **1598** and similar square design. Multicoloured.
(a) Ordinary gum. P 14
3511	45c. Type **1598**	2·10	1·70

(b) Self-adhesive booklet stamp. Die-cut perf 11
3512	45c. As No. 3511	2·30	1·90

(Des Antonia Graschberger. Litho Bagel Security-Print, Mönchengladbach)

2008 (2 Jan). 150th Birth Anniv of Heinrich Zille (artist). P 14.
3513	**1599**	55c. multicoloured	2·30	2·10

1600 '50 Jahre Bundeskartellamt'
1601 Cathedral Square 

(Des Werner Schmidt. Litho German Bank Ptg Co, Leipzig)

2008 (2 Jan). 50th Anniv of Bundeskartellamt (monopolies commission) (1st issue). P 14.
3514	**1600**	90c. multicoloured	4·25	4·00

See also No. 3528.

(Des Vera Braesecke-Kaul and Hilmar Kaul. Litho)

2008 (2 Jan). 1100th Anniv of Eichstätt. T **1601** and similar square design. Multicoloured.
(a) Ordinary gum. P 14
3515	145c. Type **1601**	7·00	6·50

(b) Self-adhesive. Die-cut perf 11
3516	145c. As No. 3515	7·50	7·00

No. 3516 was issued in coils with the surplus paper around the stamp removed.

1602 Decorative Pot with Shell Insert

(Des Lorli Jünger and Ernst Jünger. Litho German Bank Ptg Co, Leipzig)

2008 (2 Jan). 500th Birth Anniv of Wenzel Jamnitzer (goldsmith). P 14.
3517	**1602**	220c. multicoloured	11·50	10·50

1603 Der Arme Poet
1604 Fish and Heart ('Herzlichen Glückwunsch') (Congratulations) 

168

GERMANY

(Des Werner Hans Schmidt. Litho)

2008 (7 Feb). Birth Bicentenary of Carl Spitzweg (artist).

(a) Ordinary gum. P 14

| 3518 | **1603** | 55c. multicoloured | 2·75 | 2·30 |

(b) Self-adhesive gum. Die-cut perf 14

| 3518a | **1603** | 55c. multicoloured | 3·00 | 2·30 |

No. 3518a was issued in coils with the surplus paper around the stamp removed.

(Des James Rizzi. Litho German Bank Ptg Co, Leipzig)

2008 (7 Feb). Post. Greetings Stamps. T **1604** and similar horiz design. Multicoloured. P 14.

| 3519 | 55c. Type **1604** | 2·50 | 2·30 |
| 3520 | 55c. Cats ('Alles Gute') | 2·50 | 2·30 |

See also Nos. 3539/3540.

1605 Church Façade

(Des Heinz Schillinger. Litho Bagel Security-Print, Mönchengladbach)

2008 (7 Feb). Millenary of Bochum-Stiepel Village Church. P 14.

| 3521 | **1605** | 145c. multicoloured | 7·50 | 7·00 |

1606 Glider World Championships, Lüsse

(Des Andrea Voß-Acker. Litho Bagel Security-Print, Mönchengladbach)

2008 (13 Mar). Sports Promotion Fund. T **1606** and similar horiz designs. Multicoloured. P 13×13½.

3522	45c. +20c. Type **1606**	3·50	3·25
3523	55c. +25c. European Football Championships, Austria and Switzerland	3·75	3·50
3524	55c. +25c. Chess Olympiad, Dresden	3·75	3·50
3525	145c. +55c. Olympic Games, Beijing	9·00	8·25
3522/3525	*Set of 4*	18·00	17·00

1607 Helmut Käutner

(Des Kym Erdmann.)

2008 (13 Mar). Birth Centenary of Helmut Käutner (film director). P 14.

| 3526 | **1607** | 55c. multicoloured | 2·75 | 2·30 |

1608 Gnu Herd   **1609** Birds

(Des Detlef Glinski. Litho German Bank Ptg Co, Leipzig)

2008 (13 Mar). 150th Anniv of Frankfurt Zoological Society.

| 3527 | **1608** | 65c. multicoloured | 3·00 | 2·75 |

(Des Werner Schmidt. Litho German Bank Ptg Co, Leipzig)

2008 (13 Mar). 50th Anniv of Bundeskartellamt (monopolies commission) (2nd issue). Self adhesive booklet stamp. Die-cut perf 11½.

| 3528 | **1600** | 90c. multicoloured | 5·00 | 4·25 |

(Des Detlef Glinski. Litho German Bank Ptg Co, Leipzig)

2008 (10 Apr). Centenary State Bird Sanctuary, Seebach. P 14.

| 3529 | **1609** | 45c. multicoloured | 2·75 | 1·80 |

1610 Max Planck   **1611** Johann Wichern

(Des Grit Fiedler. Litho Bagel Security-Print, Mönchengladbach)

2008 (10 Apr). 150th Birth Anniv of Max Planck (physicist, Nobel Prize Winner-1918). P 14.

| 3530 | **1610** | 55c. multicoloured | 2·75 | 2·30 |

(Des Karen Scholz.)

2008 (10 Apr). Birth Bicentenary of Johann Hinrich Wichern (theologian). P 14.

| 3531 | **1611** | 55c. multicoloured | 2·75 | 2·30 |

1612 Knut (hand reared polar bear cub)

(Des Kym Erdmann)

2008 (10 Apr). Environmental Protection. P 14.

| 3532 | **1612** | 55c. +25c. multicoloured | 4·50 | 4·25 |

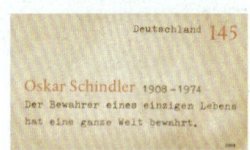

1613 'Der Bewahrer eines einzigen Lebens hat eine ganze Welt bewahrt' ((he who saves a single life saves the whole world) (translation of Hebrew engraving on Oskar Schindler's ring, gift of farewell from rescuee on 8 May 1945))

(Des Bianca Becker and Peter Kohl. Litho German Bank Ptg Co, Leipzig)

2008 (10 Apr). Birth Centenary of Oskar Schindler (industrialist who saved Jews during WWII). P 14.

| 3533 | **1613** | 145c. multicoloured | 6·50 | 6·00 |

1614 Photograph of German Players (5 April 1908) and Parts of Original Poster

(Des Thomas Serres. Litho Bagel Security-Print, Mönchengladbach)

2008 (10 Mar). Centenary of German Soccer Internationals. P 14.

| 3534 | **1614** | 170c. multicoloured | 9·50 | 8·75 |

169

GERMANY

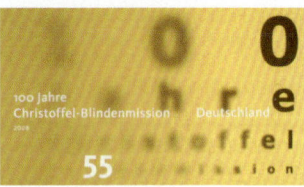

1615 Blurred Script

(Des Andrea Voß-Acker. Litho Bagel Security-Print, Mönchengladbach)

2008 (8 May). Centenary of Christian Blind Mission (Christoffel Blindoffmission) (charity founded by Pastor Ernst Jakob Christoffel for support of the blind worldwide). P 13×13½.
3535	**1615**	55c. multicoloured	2·75	2·30

1616 Sun and Moon ('Herzliche Grüße heartfelt greetings')

(Des James Rizzi. Litho German Bank Ptg Co, Leipzig)

2008 (8 May). Greetings Stamps. Europa. The Letter (3536/3538). T **1616** and similar horiz designs. Multicoloured.

(a) Ordinary gum. P 14
3536	55c. Type **1616**		2·75	2·30
3537	55c. Hands holding bird and flower ('Danke' (thank you))..........		2·75	2·30

(b) Self-adhesive booklet stamps. Die-cut perf 14
3538	55c. As Type **1616**	3·00	2·75
3539	55c. As No. 3520	3·00	2·75
3540	55c. As No. 3519	3·00	2·75
3541	55c. As No. 3537	3·00	2·75
3536/3541 Set of 6..		16·00	14·00

Nos. 3538/3541 were issued in booklets of 20 stamps (Nos. 3538/3539, each×5 and Nos. 3540/3541, each×5).

1617 Dornier Do J Wal

(Des Andrea Voß Acker. Litho)

2008 (12 June). Welfare. Aircraft. T **1617** and similar horiz designs. Multicoloured.

(a) Ordinary gum. P 14
3542	45c. +20c. Type **1617**		3·50	3·25
3543	55c. +25c. A380 Airbus		3·75	3·50
3544	55c. +25c. Junkers Ju 52		3·75	3·50
3545	145c. +55c. Messerschmitt-Bölkow-Blohm (MBB) BO 105		9·00	8·25

(b) Self-adhesive. Die-cut perf 14
3546	55c. +25c. As No. 3543.............................	5·00	4·25
3542/3546 Set of 5		23·00	20·00

No. 3546 was issued both in booklets with the surplus paper around the stamp retained and in coils with the surplus paper removed.

1618 Faces

(Des Corinna Rogger. Litho)

2008 (12 June). Community Service. P 14.
3547	**1618**	55c. multicoloured	2·75	2·30

1619 Steam Locomotive, Early Station and Passengers

1620 Warnemunde

(Des Lutz Menze. Litho German Bank Ptg Co, Leipzig)

2008 (3 July). 125th Anniv of Drachenfels Railway (Drachenfelsbahn) (rack railway line from Königswinter to summit of Drachenfels). P 14.
3548	**1619**	45c. multicoloured	2·30	1·80

(Des Johannes Graf. Litho Bagel Security-Print, Mönchengladbach)

2008 (3 July). Lighthouses. T **1620** and similar square designs. Multicoloured.

(a) Ordinary gum. P 14
3549	45c. Type **1620**	2·50	1·80
3550	55c. Amrum	2·50	2·30

(b) Self-adhesive booklet stamps. Die-cut perf 11
3551	55c. Hornum	2·75	2·30
3552	55c. As No. 3550	2·75	2·30
3549/3552 Set of 4		9·50	7·75

1621 Man at Table (drawing by Franz Kafka)

1622 Selbstporträt mit Rückenakt and Morgensonne

(Des Jens Müller and Karen Weiland. Litho)

2008 (3 July). 125th Birth Anniv of Franz Kafka (Czech writer).
3553	**1621**	55c. black	2·75	2·30

(Des Irmgard Hesse. Litho Bagel Security-Print, Mönchengladbach)

2008 (3 July). 150th Birth Anniv of Lovis Corinth (artist). P 14.
3554	**1622**	145c. multicoloured	7·50	7·00

1623 Gorch Fock

1624 Silhouette *Ringelnatz* (Ernst Moritz Engert)

(Des Heribert Birnbach. Litho Bagel Security-Print, Mönchengladbach)

2008 (7 Aug). 50th Anniv of *Gorch Fock* (sail training ship). P 14.
3555	**1623**	55c. multicoloured	2·75	2·30

(Des Victor Malsy. Litho Bagel Security-Print, Mönchengladbach)

2008 (7 Aug). 125th Birth Anniv of Joachim Ringelnatz (writer and artist). P 14.
3556	**1624**	85c. dull violet-blue and black	4·00	3·75

GERMANY

1625 Herman Schulze-Delitzsch

(Des Thomas Serres. Litho)

2008 (7 Aug). Birth Bicentenary of Herman Schulze-Delitzsch (politician and founder of German co-operative system). P 14.
3557 1625 90c. multicoloured .... 4·00 3·75

1626 Triceratops

(Des Werner Hans Schmidt. Litho Bagel Security-Print, Mönchengladbach)

2008 (4 Sept). Youth Stamp. Dinosaurs. Sheet 190×110 mm containing T **1626** and similar horiz designs. Multicoloured. P 14.
MS3558 45c.+20c. Type **1626**; 55c.+25c. Tyrannosaurus; 55c.+25c. Diplodocus; 145c.+55c. Plateosaurus .... 25·00 23·00

1627 Arrival of First Mail Coach in Ohrdruff

1628 Ronald, Günni and Jenny the Rat riding Blue Horse

(Des Carsten Wolff. Litho German Bank Ptg Co, Leipzig)

2008 (4 Sept). Stamp Day. Philatelic Treasures. P 14.
3559 1627 55c. multicoloured .... 3·00 2·50

(Des Christiane Hemmerich. Litho Bagel Security-Print, Mönchengladbach)

2008 (4 Sept). For us Children. P 14.
3560 1628 55c. multicoloured .... 3·00 2·50

1629 Old Bridge, Bad Säckingen-Stein/Aargau

(Des Bernadette Baltis. Litho)

2008 (4 Sept). Bridges. P 14.
3561 1629 70c. multicoloured .... 3·50 3·25
A stamp of a similar design was issued by Switzerland.

1630 Livestock Market

(Des Regina and Peter Steiner. Litho German Bank Ptg Co, Leipzig)

2008 (9 Oct). 500th Anniv of Gallimarkt (annual fair), Leer. P 14.
3562 1630 45c. multicoloured .... 3·00 2·00

1631 Disc and Two Bronze Swords

(Des Markus Weisbeck. Litho Bagel Security-Print, Mönchengladbach)

2008 (9 Oct). Archaeology. Sky Disc of Nebra (bronze plate with apparent astronomical phenomena and religious themes). P 14.
3563 1631 55c. multicoloured .... 3·00 2·50

1632 Lorenz Werthmann

1633 Aircraft in Flight

(Des Karen Scholz. Litho Bagel Security-Print, Mönchengladbach)

2008 (9 Oct). 150th Birth Anniv of Lorenz Werthmann (founder and first president of the German Caritas association). P 14.
3564 1632 55c. multicoloured .... 3·00 2·50

(Des Henning Wagenbreth. Litho)

2008 (9 Oct). Centenary of Hans Grade's First Powered Flight in Germany. P 14.
3565 1633 145c. multicoloured .... 7·00 6·50

Type **1634** is vacant.

(Des Henning Wagenbreth. Litho)

2008 (1 Nov). Winter. 450th Anniv (2005) of the 'Peace of Augsburg' (treaty marking the beginning of peaceful cohabitation of Catholics and Protestants) (3566). Self-adhesive booklet stamps. Vert designs as Types **1484** and **1511**. Multicoloured. Die-cut perf 11.
3566   55c. As Type **1484** .... 3·00 2·75
3567   55c. As Type **1511** .... 3·00 2·75
Nos. 3566/3567, each×5, were issued in booklets of ten stamps.

1635 *The Nativity* (Albrecht Dürer)

1636 Association Emblem

(Des Werner hans Schmidt. Litho)

2008 (13 Nov). Christmas. T **1635** and similar multicoloured design. P 14.
3568   45c. +20c. Type **1635** .... 3·25 3·00
3569   55c. +25c. *The Nativity* (Raffaello Santi) (horiz) .... 4·00 3·75
Stamps of a similar design were issued by the Vatican City.

(Des Dieter Ziegenfeuter. Litho Bagel Security-Print, Mönchengladbach)

2008 (13 Nov). 30th Anniv of Heart for Children Association (children's charity). P 14.
3570 1636 55c. scarlet-vermilion and black .... 3·00 2·50

171

GERMANY

1637 'Leben'

1638 *Nils Holgersson with Ganz* (book illustration by Wilhelm Schultz)

1642 Tangermünde Castle

1643 Theodor Heuss

(Des Barbara Dimanski. Litho German Bank Ptg Co, Leipzig)

2008 (13 Nov). 50th Anniv of Federal Association of Life (intellectual diasablities charity). P 14.
3571 1637 55c. multicoloured .... 3·00 2·50

(Des Gerhard Lienemeyer. Litho Bagel Security-Print, Mönchengladbach)

2008 (13 Nov). 150th Birth Anniv of Selma Ottilia Lovisz Lagerlöf (winner of Nobel Prize for Literature-1909). P 14.
3572 1638 100c. multicoloured .... 5·50 5·00

1639 Building Façade

1640 Plates with Cereal Grains

(Des Joachim Reiß. Litho Bagel Security-Print, Mönchengladbach)

2009 (2 Jan). 500th Anniv of Frankenberg Hall. T **1639** and similar square design. Multicoloured.

(a) Sheet stamp. PVA gum. P 14
3573 45c. Type **1639** .... 2·50 2·20

(b) Self-adhesive booklet stamp. Die-cut perf 11
3574 45c. As Type **1639** .... 2·50 2·20

No. 3574 was issued in booklets of ten stamps, with the surplus paper around the stamp retained.

(Des Corinna Rogger. Litho German Bank Ptg Co, Leipzig)

2009 (2 Jan). 50th Anniv of MISEREOR and Bread for the World (church charities). P 14.
3575 1640 55c. multicoloured .... 2·75 2·75

1641 Rainbow

(Des Dieter Ziegenfeuter. Litho)

2009 (2 Jan). Welfare Stamps. Celestial Phenomena. T **1641** and similar horiz designs. Multicoloured.

(a) Sheet stamps. PVA gum. P 14
3576 45c. +20c. Type **1641** .... 4·25 4·00
3577 55c. +25c. Aurora borealis .... 4·50 4·25
3578 55c. +25c. Sunset .... 4·50 4·25
3579 145c. +55c. Lightning .... 10·50 10·50

(b) Self-adhesive gum. Die-cut perf 11
3580 55c. +25c. As No. 3578 .... 4·50 4·00
3576/3580 Set of 5 .... 25·00 24·00

No. 3580 was issued both in booklets of ten stamps, with the surplus paper around the stamp retained, and in coils with the surplus paper removed.

(Des Jochen Berthold. Litho German Bank Ptg Co, Leipzig)

2009 (2 Jan). Tangermünde Castle Millenary. P 14.
3581 1642 90c. multicoloured .... 4·50 4·25

(Des Thomas Serres. Litho Bagel Security-Print, Mönchengladbach)

2009 (2 Jan). 125th Birth Anniv of Theodor Heuss (politician, writer and first FDR Head of State). P 14.
3582 1643 145c. multicoloured .... 7·25 7·00

1644 Heinz Erhardt

1645 Felix Mendelssohn

(Des Andreas Ahrens. Litho Bagel Security-Print, Mönchengladbach)

2009 (12 Feb). Birth Centenary of Heinz Erhardt (comedian). P 14.
3583 1644 55c. multicoloured .... 2·75 2·75

(Des Dieter Ziegenfeuter. Litho German Bank Ptg Co, Leipzig)

2009 (12 Feb). Birth Bicentenary of Jakob Ludwig Felix Mendelssohn Bartholdy (composer). P 14.
3584 1645 65c. multicoloured .... 3·25 3·25

1646 *The Propylaea in Munich*

1647 *The Firebird*

(Des Heribert Birnbach. Litho)

2009 (12 Feb). 225th Birth Anniv of Leo von Klenze (architect). P 14.
3585 1646 70c. multicoloured .... 3·75 3·50

(Des Thomas Serres. Litho German Bank Ptg Co, Leipzig)

2009 (12 Feb). Birth Centenary of Helmut Andreas Paul (HAP) Grieshaber (artist). P 14.
3586 1647 165c. multicoloured .... 8·50 8·00

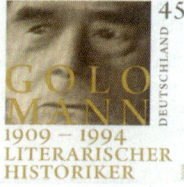

1648 Golo Mann

1649 Applying Stamp

(Des Gülsah Edis, Victor Malsy and Thomas Meyer. Litho Bagel Security-Print, Mönchengladbach)

2009 (12 Mar). Birth Centenary of Angelus Gottfried Thomas Mann, (Golo) Mann (historian and writer). P 14.
3587 1648 45c. multicoloured .... 2·50 2·20

GERMANY

(Des Nina Clausing. Litho German Bank
Ptg Co, Leipzig)

2009 (12 Mar). Post. T **1649** and similar vert design. Multicoloured.
P 14.
3588   55c. Type **1649**............................   3·00   3·00
3589   55c. Post Office..........................   3·00   3·00
See also Nos. 3597/8.

1650 Stahlradwagen    **1651** Hurdler

(Des Rudolf Grüttner. Litho)

2009 (12 Mar). 175th Birth Anniv of Gottlieb Wilhelm Daimler (engineer and motor vehicle pioneer). P 14.
3590   **1650**   170c. multicoloured............................   9·25   9·00

(Des Stephan Klein and Olaf Neuman. Litho Bagel
Security-Print, Mönchengladbach)

2009 (9 Apr). Sports Promotion Fund. International Association of Athletics Federations World Championship-Berlin 2009. T **1651** and similar horiz design. Multicoloured. P 14.
3591   45c. +20c. Type **1651**...................   4·75   4·50
    a. Booklet pane. Nos. 3591/3592, each×4.   40·00
3592   55c. +25c. Pole vaulter...............   5·00   4·75
3593   55c. +25c. Runners...................   5·00   4·75
3594   145c. +55c. Discus......................   12·00   11·50
3591/3594 Set of 4...............................   24·00   23·00
The booklet pane No. 3591a has lilac margins.

1652 Bernhard Grzimek    **1653** Planets

(Des Sybille Haase and Fritz Hasse)

2009 (9 Apr). Birth Centenary of Bernhard Grzimek (film maker). P 14.
3595   **1652**   55c. multicoloured............................   3·00   3·00

(Des Nina Clausing. Litho)

2009 (7 May). Europa. Astronomy. 400th Anniv of *Kepler's Laws*. P 14.
3596   **1653**   55c. multicoloured............................   3·00   3·00

(Des Nina Clausing. Litho German Bank Ptg Co, Leipzig)

2009 (7 May). Post. Vert designs as T **1649**. Multicoloured. P 14.
3597   55c. Transport ....   3·00   3·00
3598   55c. Delivery............................   3·00   3·00

1654 Eichstätt Letter
(showing first German
stamps, franked 1849)

(Des Ursula Lautenschläger. Litho Bagel
Security-Print, Mönchengladbach)

2009 (7 May). Stamp Day. P 14 (with irregular perf on either right or left vert side).
3599   **1654**   55c. +25c. multicoloured............   5·25   4·50
No. 3599 was printed in sheetlets of ten (2×5) stamps with irregular perfs along the centre. The irregular perforation gives an oak leaf shape when viewed across the sheet.

1655 Luther Memorials, Eisleben and Wittenberg

(Des Grit Fielder. Litho German Bank Ptg Co, Leipzig)

2009 (7 May). World Heritage Sites. P 14.
3600   **1655**   145c. multicoloured......................   8·00   7·75
A stamp of a similar design was issued by United Nations (Vienna).

1656 First Exhibition Poster,   **1657** *Mask* (Christian
Frankfurt 1909   Grovermann), *Emperor
    Agustus* (Jochen Hahnel),
    Hermann Monument,
    Teutoburg Forest and *Forest*
    (Thomas Serres)

(Des Andrea Voß-Acker. Litho)

2009 (4 June). Centenary of International Aerospace Exhibition. P 14.
3601   **1656**   55c. multicoloured......................   3·00   3·00
See also No. 3616a.

(Litho Leipzig Securities Printing)

2009 (4 June). Bimillenary of Varus (Teutoburg Forest) Battle. T **1657** and similar square design. Multicoloured.
    (a) Ordinary gum. P 14
3602   55c. Type **1657**.................................   3·00   3·00
    (b) Self-adhesive booklet stamp. Die-cut perf 11
3603   55c. As Type **1657** ....   3·50   3·00

1658 Illustration   **1659** Eifel National Park
from *Struwwelpeter*

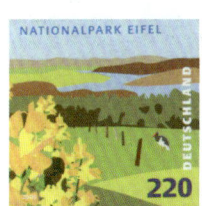

(Des Arne Sanger. Litho Bagel Security-Print,
Mönchengladbach)

2009 (4 June). Birth Bicentenary of Heinrich Hoffman (children's author and politician). P 14.
3604   **1658**   85c. multicoloured......................   5·00   4·75

(Des Greta Gröttrup. Litho Bagel Security-Print,
Mönchengladbach)

2009 (4 June). Sheet 105×70 mm. P 14.
MS3605   **1659**   220c. multicoloured..................   12·50   12·00

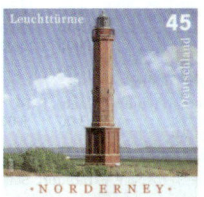

1660 Norderney    **1661** Early Campus

173

GERMANY

(Des Lutz Menze. Litho German Bank Ptg Co, Leipzig)

2010 (11 Feb). Sports Promotion Fund. Winter Paralympics (45c.+20c.) or Winter Olympic Games, Vancouver (55c.+25c.). T **1683** and similar horiz design. Multicoloured. P 14.

3642	45c. +20c. Type **1683**	4·25	3·50
3643	55c. +25c. Skier	5·00	4·50

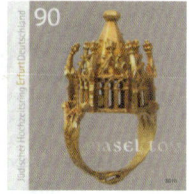

1684 Family playing **1685** Ring

(Des Henning Wagenbreth)

2010 (11 Feb). *Mensch ärgere dich nicht* (board game designed by Joseph Friedrich Schmidt). P 14.

3644	**1684**	55c. multicoloured	3·00	3·00

(Des Corinna Rogger. Litho German Bank Ptg Co, Leipzig)

2010 (11 Feb). 14th-century Jewish Wedding Ring found at Erfurt. P 14.

3645	**1685**	90c. multicoloured	5·25	5·00

1686 Ship **1687** Ariadne abandoned by Theseus

(Des Johannes Graf. Litho Bagel Security-Print, Mönchengladbach)

2010 (11 Mar). Post. Greeting Stamps (1st issue). T **1686** and similar horiz design. Multicoloured. P 14.

3646	55c. Type **1686**	3·50	3·00
3647	55c. Rainbow	3·50	3·00

See also Nos. 3649/3650, 3686*a/b* and 3701*a/b*.

(Des Werner Hans Schmidt. Litho Bagel Security-Print, Mönchengladbach)

2010 (11 Mar). Art. Painting by Maria Anna Catharina Angelica (Angelica) Kauffmann. P 14.

3648	**1687**	260c. multicoloured	16·00	14·00

(Des Johannes Graf. Litho Bagel Security-Print, Mönchengladbach)

2010 (8 Apr). Post. Greeting Stamps (2nd issue). Horiz designs as T **1686**. Multicoloured.

3649	55c. Dove	3·50	3·00
3650	55c. Angel carrying heart	3·50	3·00

1688 Footballers

(Des Lutz Menze. Litho German Bank Ptg Co, Leipzig)

2010 (8 Apr). Sports Promotion Fund. Football World Cup Championship, South Africa (55c.+25c.) or 2010 Ice Hockey World Cup, Germany (145c.+55c.). T **1688** and similar horiz design. Multicoloured. P 14.

3651	55c. +25c. Type **1688**	4·75	4·50
3652	145c. +55c. Ice hockey players	12·50	11·00

1689 Birds and Cliffs

(Des Elsenbach & Fienbork. Litho)

2010 (8 Apr). Centenary of Helgoland Ornithological Institute.

(a) Sheet 105×70 mm. Ordinary gum. P 14

MS3653	**1689**	145c. multicoloured	9·25	8·00

(b) Coil stamp. Self-adhesive. Die-cut perf 14

3654	**1689**	145c. multicoloured	9·25	8·00

1690 Robert Schumann **1691** Zampino the Magical Bear

(Des Karen Solz. Litho German Bank Ptg Co, Leipzig)

2010 (6 May). Birth Bicentenary of Robert Alexander Schumann (composer). P 14.

3655	**1690**	55c. multicoloured	3·00	3·00

(Des Grit Fielder. Litho German Bank Ptg Co, Leipzig)

2010 (6 May). Europa. Children's Books. P 14.

3656	**1691**	55c. multicoloured	3·00	3·00

1692 Bee **1693** Grey Seals

(Des Thomas Serres)

2010 (6 May). Bee Awareness Campaign.

(a) Ordinary gum. P 14

3657	**1692**	55c. multicoloured	3·00	3·00

(b) Self-adhesive gum. Die-cut perf 10½

3658	**1692**	55c. multicoloured	3·50	3·00

(Des Thomas Serres. Litho Bagel Security-Print, Mönchengladbach)

2010 (6 May). Environmental Protection. P 14.

3659	**1693**	55c. +25c. multicoloured	4·75	4·50

The premium was for marine conservation.

1694 Neuwerk **1695** Konrad Zuse

(Des Johannes Graf. Litho Bagel Security-Print, Mönchengladbach)

2010 (10 June). Lighthouses. T **1694** and similar square design. Multicoloured. P 14.

3660	45c. Type **1694**	2·50	2·40
3661	55c. Falshöft	3·00	3·00

(Des Klein und Neumann)

2010 (10 June). Birth Centenary of Konrad Zuse (engineer and computer pioneer). P 14.
3662 1695 55c. steel blue, pale blue and yellow-olive .... 3·00 3·00

1696 Ship and Figure holding Wine Glass (*Andrea Doria*)

(Des Udo Lindenburg. Litho German Bank Ptg Co, Leipzig)

2010 (1 July). Illustrations of Songs by Udo Lindenburg (rock musician and artist). T **1696** and similar horiz design. Multicoloured.

(a) Sheet stamps. Ordinary gum. P 14
3663 45c. Type **1696** .... 2·50 2·40
3664 55c. Train (*Sonderzug nach Pankow*) .... 3·00 3·00

(b) Size 38×22 mm. Self-adhesive booklet stamp. Die-cut perf 10
3665 45c. As Type **1696** .... 2·50 2·40
3666 55c. As No. 3664 .... 3·00 3·00

1697 Johann Friedrich Böttger (inventor of first process) demonstrates to August the Strong (painting by Paul Kießling)

1698 Four Seater Stagecoach

(Des Nadine Nill. Litho German Bank Ptg Co, Leipzig)

2010 (1 July). 300th Anniv of Porcelain Production in Europe. P 14.
3667 1697 55c. multicoloured .... 3·00 3·00
See also No. 3676.

(Des Nina Clausing)

2010 (1 July). Historic Mail Coaches. P 14.
3668 1698 145c. multicoloured .... 8·00 7·75

1699 *Deutschland*

(Des Werner Hans Schmidt. Litho Bagel Security-Print, Mönchengladbach)

2010 (12 Aug). Youth Stamps. Historic Steam Ships. T **1699** and similar horiz designs. Multicoloured. P 14.
3669 45c. +20c. Type **1699** .... 4·75 4·50
3670 55c. +25c. *Imperator* .... 5·00 4·75
3671 55c. +25c. *Aller* .... 5·00 4·75
3672 145c. +55c. *Columbus* .... 12·00 11·50
3669/3672 Set of 4 .... 24·00 23·00

1700 Bf 108 Taifun (D-EBEI) and Elly Beinhorn

(Des Klein & Neumann)

2010 (12 Aug). 75th Anniv of Elly Beinhorn's Long distance flight from Gliwice to Berlin, via Istanbul. P 14.
3673 1700 55c. black and carmine .... 3·00 3·00

1701 Mother Teresa

1702 Jorge Luis Borges

(Des Christof Gassner. Litho German Bank Ptg Co, Leipzig)

2010 (12 Aug). Birth Centenary of Agnes Gonxha Bojaxhiu (Mother Teresa) (founder of Missionaries of Charity). P 14.
3674 1701 70c. black and new blue .... 4·00 4·00

(Des Dario Canovas)

2010 (12 Aug). Frankfurt Bookfair. P 14.
3675 1702 170c. black, silver and scarlet-vermilion .... 9·25 9·00
A stamp of a similar design was issued by Argentina.

(Des Nadine Nill. Litho German Bank Ptg Co, Leipzig)

2010 (12 Aug). 300th Anniv of Porcelain Production in Europe. Booklet Stamp. Self-adhesive. Die-cut perf 10.
3676 1697 55c. multicoloured .... 3·00 3·00

1703 Bear cradling Child

1704 *Imperial German Post to Helgoland, Norderney, Sylt* (poster, 1880)

(Des Isabel Seliger. Litho Bagel Security-Print, Mönchengladbach)

2010 (9 Sept). For Us Children. P 14.
3677 1703 55c. multicoloured .... 3·00 3·00

(Des Johannes Graf. Litho German Bank Ptg Co, Leipzig)

2010 (9 Sept). Stamp Day. P 14.
3678 1704 55c. multicoloured .... 3·00 3·00

1705 Merry-go-Round

1706 Celebration of German Unity in Berlin

(Des Michael Kunter. Litho German Bank Ptg Co, Leipzig)

2010 (9 Sept). Bicentenary of Oktoberfest. P 14.
3679 1705 55c. multicoloured .... 3·00 3·00

2010 (9 Sept). 20th Anniv of Re-unification of Germany.
(a) Sheet stamp. Ordinary gum. P 14.
3680 1706 55c. multicoloured .... 3·00 3·00

(b) Coil stamp. Self-adhesive. Die-cut perf 10½.
3681 1706 55c. multicoloured .... 3·00 3·00

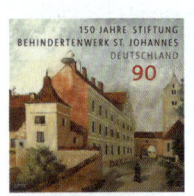

GERMANY

1707 Castle, Schweinspoint
1708 Baumann'sche House (Upper German), Eppingen (1582) 
1712 *Adler* Locomotive on First Journey from Nüremberg to Fürth on Bavarian Ludwig Railway
1713 Giant Slalom

(Des Annegret Ehmke. Litho Bagel Security-Print, Mönchengladbach)

2010 (9 Sept). 150th Anniv of St John Foundation for the Disabled. P 13½.
3682 **1707** 90c. multicoloured .... 5·25 5·00

(Des Dieter Ziegenfeuter)

2010 (7 Oct). Half-timbered Architecture (1st issue). T **1708** and similar square design. Multicoloured. P 14.
3683   45c. Type **1708** .... 2·50 2·40
3684   55c. Farmhouse (Low German), Trebel-Dunsche (1734)................................ 3·00 3·00
See also Nos. 3709/3710 and 3783.

1709 Ear of Corn

(Des Nicole Else Bach and Frank Fienborg. Litho Bagel Security-Print, Mönchengladbach)

2010 (7 Oct). Thanksgiving. P 14.
3685 **1709** 55c. multicoloured .... 3·00 3·00

1710 Friedrich Loeffler and Pathogen

(Des Kym Erdmann. Litho German Bank Ptg Co, Leipzig)

2010 (7 Oct). Centenary of Friedrich Loeffler Institute. P 13½.
3686 **1710** 85c. multicoloured .... 5·00 4·75

(Des Johannes Graf. Litho Bagel Security-Print, Mönchengladbach)

2010 (2 Nov). Post. Greeting Stamps (3rd issue). Self-adhesive. Horiz designs as T **1686**. Multicoloured. Die-cut perf 10.
3686*a*   55c. As No. 3649.................................... 3·00 3·00
3686*b*   55c. As No. 3650.................................... 3·00 3·00

1711 Madonna and Child

(Des Julia Warbanow. Litho Bagel Security-Print, Mönchengladbach)

2010 (11 Nov). Christmas. Crib by Sebastian Osterrieder, Church of Our Lady, Munich. T **1711** and similar horiz design. Multicoloured. P 13×13½.
3687   45c. +20c. Type **1711** .... 3·75 3·50
3688   55c. +25c. Adoration of the Magi .... 4·75 4·50
The premium was for the benefit of Federal Association of Voluntary Welfare Association.

(Des Iris Utikal and Michael Gais. Litho Enschedé)

2010 (11 Nov). 175th Anniv of German Railways. P 14.
3689 **1712** 55c. multicoloured .... 3·00 3·00

(Des Heribert Birnbach)

2010 (11 Nov). Alpine Ski World Championships 2011, Garmisch-Partenkirchen. P 14.
3690 **1713** 55c. multicoloured .... 3·00 3·00

1714 'WENN EINER DAUHN DEIHT.....' and Fritz Reuter
1715 Hands holding Coffeepot and Sandwich 

(Des Jens Müller and Karen Weiland. Litho German Bank Ptg Co, Leipzig)

2010 (11 Nov). Birth Bicentenary of Fritz Reuter (writer). P 13. P 14.
3691 **1714** 100c. multicoloured .... 5·50 5·50

(Des Gerhard Lienemeyer. German Bank Ptg Co, Leipzig)

2010 (11 Nov). 750th Anniv of Knappschaft (providing sickness, accident, and death benefits for miners). P 13½.
3692 **1715** 145c. black and carmine............................ 8·00 7·75

1716 Glider, 1920
1717 *Wanderer above the Sea of Fog* (Caspar David Friedrich) 

(Des Elisabeth Hau and Georg Brütting. Litho German Bank Ptg Co, Leipzig)

2011 (3 Jan). Rhön Gliding Competitions at Wasserkuppe. P 13½.
3693 **1716** 45c. multicoloured .... 2·50 2·40

(Des Werner Hans Schmidt)

2011 (11 Jan–5 May). German Painting.
(*a*) *Sheet stamp. Ordinary gum.* P 14.
3694 **1717** 55c. multicoloured .... 3·00 3·00
(*b*) *Self-adhesive. Die-cut perf 10½* (5 May).
3694*d* **1717** 55c. multicoloured .... 3·00 3·00
No. 3694*a* was printed with the surplus paper around the stamp removed.

1718 Dr. Sommer and Bello being Interviewed (*The Talking Dog*)

178

GERMANY

(Des Hans Günter Schmitz)

2011 (3 Jan). Welfare Stamps. Animated films by Loriot (Bernhard Victor Christoph Carl von Bülow). T **1718** and similar horiz designs. Multicoloured.

(a) Sheet stamp. Ordinary gum. P 14.

3695	45c. +20c. Type **1718**	4·75	4·50
3696	55c. +25c. Kloebner and Mueller-Luedenscheidt in the bath (*The Bathtub*)	5·00	4·75
3697	55c. +25c. Two racegoers (*At the Racecourse*)	5·00	4·75
3698	145c. +55c. Berta and her husband eating breakfast (*The Breakfast Egg*)	12·00	11·50

(b) Self-adhesive. Die-cut perf 11.

| 3699 | 55c. +25c. As No. 3697 | 4·75 | 4·50 |
| 3695/3699 | Set of 5 | 28·00 | 27·00 |

No. 3699 was issued both in coils and in booklets of ten stamps.

1719 National Park-Edersee Keller

(Des Julia Warbanow)

2011 (3 Jan). National Parks. P 13½.

| 3700 | **1719** | 145c. multicoloured | 8·00 | 7·75 |

See also No. 3715.

1720 Franz Liszt

(Des Jens Müller and Karen Weiland)

2011 (3 Feb). Birth Bicentenary of Franz Liszt (pianist and composer). P 13½×14.

| 3701 | **1720** | 55c. dull violet | 3·00 | 3·00 |

(Des Johannes Graf. Litho Bagel Security-Print, Mönchengladbach)

2011 (3 Feb). Post. Greeting Stamps (4th issue). Self-adhesive. Horiz designs as T **1686**. Multicoloured. Self-adhesive. Die-cut perf 10.

| 3701a | 55c. As No. 3646 | 3·00 | 3·00 |
| 3701b | 55c. As No. 3647 | 3·00 | 3·00 |

1721 Main Hall and Great Hall Pagodas, Old City, Nara Yakushi-ji

(Des Dieter Ziegenfeuter. Litho Bagel Security-Print, Mönchengladbach)

2011 (3 Feb). World Heritage Sites. T **1721** and similar horiz design. Multicoloured.

(a) Sheet stamp. Ordinary gum. P 13½×14.

| 3702 | 55c. Type **1721** | 3·00 | 3·00 |
| 3703 | 75c. Regensburg Cathedral | 4·25 | 4·25 |

(b) Self-adhesive booklet stamp. Die-cut perf 10½.

| 3703a | 75c. Regensburg Cathedral | 4·25 | 4·25 |
| 3702/3703a | Set of 3 | 10·50 | 10·50 |

Stamps of a similar design were issued by Japan.

1722 Countryside

(Des Joachim Rieß. Litho German Bank Ptg Co, Leipzig)

2011 (3 Feb–3 Mar). Werratal, View of Two Castles.

(a) Sheet stamp. Ordinary gum. P 14.

| 3704 | **1722** | 90c. multicoloured | 5·25 | 5·00 |

(b) Self-adhesive booklet stamp. Die-cut perf 10½ (3 March).

| 3704a | **1722** | 90c. multicoloured | 5·25 | 5·00 |

1722a Droplets on Leaf (water)   **1723** Alsfeld Town Hall

(Des John Graf. Litho Giesecke & Devrient GmbH, Security Printing, Leipzig)

2011 (3 Mar). Post. The Four Elements. T **1722a** and similar horiz designs. Multicoloured. P 13½×14.

3705	55c. Type **1722a**	3·00	3·00
3706	55c. Dunes (earth)	3·00	3·00
3707	55c. Erupting volcano (fire)	3·00	3·00
3708	55c. Clouds (air)	3·00	3·00
3705/3708	Set of 4	11·00	11·00

(Des Dieter Ziegenfeuter)

2011 (7 Apr). Half-timbered Architecture (2nd issue). T **1723** and similar square design. Multicoloured. P 14.

| 3709 | 45c. Type **1723** | 2·50 | 2·40 |
| 3710 | 55c. White Horse Inn, Hartenstein | 3·00 | 3·00 |

1724 Goalkeeper

(Des Wagenbreth Hennig. Litho Bagel Security-Print, Mönchengladbach)

2011 (7 Apr). Sports Promotion Fund, 2011. Women's Football World Cup (45c.+20c., 55c.+25c.), European Gymnastics Championships, Berlin (55c.+25c.) or Mönchengladbach Hockey Championship (145c.+55c.). T **1724** and similar horiz designs. Multicoloured. P 13½×14.

3711	45c. +20c. Type **1724**	4·75	4·50
3712	55c. +25c. Player kicking ball	5·00	4·75
3713	55c. +25c. Male gymnast using bars	5·00	4·75
3714	145c. +55c. Player with raised stick and ball	12·00	11·50
3711/3714	Set of 4	24·00	23·00

(Des Julia Warbanow)

2011 (7 Apr). National Parks. Booklet stamp. Self-adhesive. Die-cut perf 10.

| 3715 | **1719** | 145c. multicoloured | 8·00 | 7·75 |

1725 Light through Tree Trunks

(Des Hans Peter Hoch and Andreas Hoch)

2011 (5 May). Europa. Forests. P 13½×14.

| 3716 | **1725** | 55c. multicoloured | 3·00 | 3·00 |

1726 Benz Patent-Motorwagen and Patent Details

179

GERMANY

(Des Kym Erdmann. Litho Bagel Security-Print, Mönchengladbach)

2011 (5 May). 125th Anniv of First Automobile. P 13½.
3717   1726   55c. multicoloured .... 3·00   3·00

1727 External and Interior of Museum

1728 Chamber of Commerce Offices in Germany and DIHK Emblem

(Des Thomas Serres. Litho Bagel Security-Print, Mönchengladbach)

2011 (5 May). 150th Anniv of Wallraff-Richartz-Museum. P 14.
3718   1727   85c. multicoloured .... 5·00   4·75

(Des Nadine Nill. Litho Giesecke & Devrient GmbH, Security Printing, Leipzig)

2011 (5 May). 150th Anniv of Industry and Commerce Organisation (DIHK). P 13½×14.
3719   1728   145c. multicoloured .... 8·00   7·75

1729 Reich Insurance Code

(Des Andreas Ahrens)

2011 (5 May). Centenary of Insurance Code (Reich Insurance Code (RVO)). P 13½×14.
3720   1729   205c. scarlet-vermilion, silver and black .... 11·50   11·00

1730 Train

(Des Michael Kunter. Giesecke & Devrient GmbH, Security Ptg, Leipzig)

2011 (9 June). 125th Anniv of Mecklenburg Bäderbahn Steam-operated Narrow Gauge Railway ('Molli'). P 14.
3721   1730   45c. multicoloured .... 2·50   2·40

1731 Light at the end of the Tunnel

(Des Irmgard Hesse. Litho Bagel Security-Print, Mönchengladbach)

2011 (9 June). 50th Anniv of Amnesty International. P 14.
3722   1731   55c. multicoloured .... 3·00   3·00

1732 The First Gymnasium in Germany (lithograph)

(Des Annegret Ehmke)

2011 (9 June). Bicentenary of Friedrich Ludwig Jahn Turnplatz (first open air gymnasium). P 14.
3723   1732   165c. black and scarlet-vermilion .... 9·25   9·00

1733 Paddle-steamer

1734a Norderney

(Des Klein and Neumann. Litho Giesecke & Devrient GmbH, Security Ptg, Leipzig)

2011 (9 June). 175th Anniv of Saxon Steamship Company.
(a) Ordinary gum. Sheet 105×70 mm. P 14.
MS3724   1733   220c. multicoloured .... 13·00   13·00
(b) Self-adhesive booklet stamp. Die-cut perf 11.
3724a   220c. As Type **1733** .... 12·50   12·00

(Des Johannes Graf)

2011 (1 July). Lighthouses. Self-adhesive booklet stamps. T **1734a** and similar square design. Multicoloured. Die-cut perf 10.
3724b   45c. Type **1734a** .... 2·50   2·40
3724c   45c. Warnemünde .... 2·50   2·40

1734 Till Eulenspiegel

1735 Arngast Lighthouse

(Des Henning Wagenbreth. Giesecke & Devrient GmbH, Security Ptg, Leipzig)

2011 (7 July). 500th Anniv of Till Eulenspiegel (folklore trickster figure). P 14.
3725   1734   55c. multicoloured .... 3·00   3·00

(Des Johannes Graf. Litho Bagel Security-Print, Mönchengladbach)

2011 (7 July). Lighthouses. T **1735** and similar square design. Multicoloured. P 13½.
3726   55c. Type **1735** .... 3·00   3·00
3727   90c. Dahmeshöved .... 5·25   5·00

1736 Targets and 1861 Awards Ceremony

(Des John Graf)

2011 (7 July). 150th Anniv of German Shooting Federation. P 14.
3728   1736   145c. multicoloured .... 8·00   7·75

1737 Horse Head Nebula

GERMANY

(Des Werner H. Schmidt. Litho Giesecke & Devrient GmbH, Security Ptg, Leipzig)

2011 (11 Aug). For Us Children. Astronomy. T **1737** and similar horiz designs. Multicoloured. P 14.
3729	45c. +20c. Type **1737**	4·25	4·25
3730	55c. +25c. Solar System (left)	4·75	4·50
	a. Pair. Nos. 3730/31	9·75	9·25
3731	55c. +25c. Solar System (right)	4·75	4·50
3732	145c. +55c. Pleiades	11·00	11·00
3729/3732	Set of 4	22·00	22·00

1738 Archaeopteryx Fossil    **1739** Anniversary Emblem

(Des Julia Warbanow. Litho Bagel Security-Print, Mönchengladbach)

2011 (11 Aug). 150th Anniv of Discovery of Archaeopteryx. P 14.
3733	**1738** 55c. multicoloured	3·00	3·00

(Des Julia Warbanow)

2011 (11 Aug). 75th Anniv of Stamp Day in Germany. P 14.
3734	**1739** 55c. +25c. multicoloured	4·75	4·50

1740 Aquarium (Marie-Helen Geißelbrecht)    **1741** Stylised Tunnel and Shipping

(Litho Bagel Security-Print, Mönchengladbach)

2011 (15 Sept). For Us Children. P 14.
3735	**1740** 55c. multicoloured	3·00	3·00

(Des Bianca Becker and Peter Kohl)

2011 (15 Sept). Centenary of St Pauli Elbe Tunnel, Hamburg. P 13½×14.
3736	**1741** 55c. black, new blue and yellow	3·00	3·00

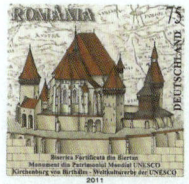

1742 Fortified Church, Birthälmer    **1743** Thermos Flask (Reinhold Burger, 1903), Currywurst and Teabag

(Des Popescu. Litho German Bank Ptg Co, Leipzig)

2011 (15 Sept). World Heritage Site. Birthälmer Fortified Church, Transylvania (Siebenbürgen). P 13½.
3737	**1742** 75c. multicoloured	4·25	4·25

Stamps of a similar design were issued by Romania.

(Des Thomas Serres)

2011 (13 Oct). At Home in Germany. German Designs for the Home. T **1743** and similar horiz design. Multicoloured. P 14.
3738	45c. Type **1743**	2·50	2·40
3739	55c. Gramophone (Emil Berliner, 1887), tape recorder (Fritz Pfleumer, 1928) and MP3 player (Fraunhofer Institute, 1987)	3·00	3·00

1744 White Calla Flower    **1745** Museum Building c. 1880

(Des Klein and Neumann)

2011 (13 Oct). Mourning Stamp. P 14.
3740	**1744** 55c. multicoloured	3·00	3·00

(Des Dieter Zeigenfeuter)

2011 (13 Oct). 175th Anniv of Alte Pinakothek Museum, Munich. P 14.
3741	**1745** 145c. multicoloured	8·00	7·75

1746 Kaiser Wilhelm Memorial Church    **1747** Embroidery (Guatemala)

(Des Ingo Wulff. Litho Giesecke & Devrient GmbH, Security Ptg, Leipzig)

2011 (10 Nov). 50th Anniv of New Kaiser Wilhelm Memorial Church. P 13.
3742	**1746** 55c. multicoloured	3·00	3·00

(Des Hau)

2011 (10 Nov). 50th Anniv of Adveniat (Christmas charitable campaign). P 13½×14.
3743	**1747** 55c. multicoloured	3·00	3·00

1748 St Martin (detail, stained glass window, St Martin's Church, Nettersheim)

(Des Karen Scholz. Litho Bagel Security-Print, Mönchengladbach)

2011 (10 Nov). Christmas. Welfare Stamps. T **1748** and similar horiz design. Multicoloured. P 13×13½.
3744	45c. +20c. Type **1748**	3·75	3·50
3745	55c. +25c. St Nicholas (detail) (stained glass window, St Nicholas's Church, Rheurdt)	4·75	4·50

1749 Emil Wiechert    **1750** Winter Landscape

(Des Carsten Wolff. Litho Bagel Security-Print, Mönchengladbach)

2011 (10 Nov). 150th Birth Anniv of Emil Weichert (geophysicist and seismologist). P 13½.
3746	**1749** 90c. multicoloured	5·25	5·00

(Des Andrea Voß-Acker. Litho Giesecke & Devrient GmbH, Security Ptg, Leipzig)

2012 (2 Jan). Post. Winter. P 13½×14.
3747	**1750** 45c. multicoloured	2·75	2·75

181

GERMANY

1751 Sea Cliffs
1752 *Frederick II (Anton Graff)* 

(Des Dieter Ziegenfeuter)

2012 (2 Jan). National Parks. Jasmund.

(a) Sheet stamp. Ordinary gum. P 13½.
3748	**1751**	55c. multicoloured	3·50	3·25

(b) Size 38×23 mm. Self-adhesive booklet stamp. Die-cut perf 10.
3749	**1751**	55c. multicoloured	3·50	3·25

(Des Gerhard Lienemeyer. Litho Giesecke & Devrient GmbH, Security Ptg, Leipzig)

2012 (2 Jan). 300th Birth Anniv of Frederick II of Prussia. P 13½.
3750	**1752**	55c. multicoloured	3·50	3·25

1753 Ruby

(Des Julia Warbanow. Litho Enschede)

2012 (2 Jan). Welfare Stamps. Jewels. T **1753** and similar designs. Multicoloured.

(a) Sheet stamps. Ordinary gum. P 14.
3751	55c. +25c. Type **1753**	5·00	4·75
3752	90c. +40c. Emerald	8·00	7·75
3753	145c. +55c. Sapphire	12·50	12·00

(b) Self-adhesive. Die-cut perf 11.
3754	55c. +25c. As Type **1753**	5·00	4·75
3751/3754 Set of 4		27·00	26·00

No. 3754 was printed both in coils, and booklets of ten stamps.

1754 Colour Spectrum 
1755 Zwinger Palace, Dresden (designed by Matthäus Daniel Pöppelmann in collaboration with sculptor Balthasar Permoser)

(Des Daniela Haufe and Detlef Fiedler. Litho Giesecke & Devrient GmbH, Security Ptg, Leipzig)

2012 (2 Jan). 225th Birth Anniv of Joseph von Fraunhofer (pioneer of scientific methodology in the field of optics and precision engineering and entrepreneur) (1st issue). P 13½.
3755	**1754**	90c. multicoloured	5·50	5·50

See also No. 3776.

(Des Lutz Menze. Litho Bagel Security-Print, Mönchengladbach)

2012 (2 Jan). 350th Birth Anniv of Matthäus Daniel Pöppelmann (master builder and architect) (1st issue). P 13½×14.
3756	**1755**	145c. multicoloured	9·00	8·75

See also No. 3765.

1756 Steam Locomotive
1757 Athletes skiing 

(Des Neumann. Litho Giesecke & Devrient GmbH, Security Ptg, Leipzig)

2012 (9 Feb). 125th Anniv of Harz Narrow-gauge Railways.

(a) Sheet stamp. Ordinary gum. P 14.
		45c. Type **1756**	2·75	2·75

(b) Size 38×24 mm. Self-adhesive booklet stamp. Die-cut perf 10.
3758		45c. As Type **1756**	2·75	2·75

(Des Jens Müller and Karin Weiland. Litho Bagel Security-Print, Mönchengladbach)

2012 (9 Feb). Biathlon Championship, Ruhpolding. P 14.
3759	**1757**	55c. multicoloured	3·50	3·25

1758 Lynx and Kitten
1759 *Blue Horse (Franz Marc)* 

(Des Thomas Serres. Litho German Bank Ptg Co, Leipzig)

2012 (9 Feb–1 Mar). Recolonisation of Native Fauna. T **1758** and similar horiz design.

(a) Ordinary gum. P 14.
3760	55c. Type **1758**	3·50	3·25
3761	55c. Moose	3·50	3·25

(b) Size 38×24 mm. Self-adhesive. Die-cut perf 10 (1 Mar).
3762	55c. As Type **1758**	3·50	3·25
3763	55c. As No. 3761	3·50	3·25
3760/3763 Set of 4		12·50	11·50

No. 3763 was printed in sheetlets of 20 stamps.

(Des Nina Clausing)

2012 (9 Feb). Centenary of Blue Rider Group (formed by artists Wassily Kandinsky and Franz Marc (German Expressionism)). P 14.
3764	**1759**	145c. multicoloured	9·00	8·75

(Des Lutz Menze. Litho Bagel Security-Print, Mönchengladbach)

2012 (9 Feb). 350th Birth Anniv of Matthäus Daniel Pöppelmann (master builder and architect) (2nd issue). Self-adhesive booklet stamp. Die-cut perf 10.
3765	145c. As Type **1755** (38×24 *mm*)	9·00	8·75

1760 Tree and Countryside in Spring
1761 *La Madonna di San Sisto* 

(Des Andrea Voß-Acker. Litho Giesecke & Devrient GmbH, Security Ptg, Leipzig)

2012 (1 Mar). Post. Spring.

(a) Sheet stamp. Ordinary gum. P 13½×14.
3766		55c. Type **1760**	3·50	3·25

(b) Size 38×24 mm. Self-adhesive booklet stamp. Die-cut perf 10.
3767		55c. As Type **1760**	3·50	3·25

(Des Werner H. Schmidt)

2012 (1 Mar). 500th Anniv of Sistine Madonna (*La Madonna di San Sisto*) (by Raphael) (1st issue). Sheet 98×134 mm. P 14.
MS3768	**1761**	55c. multicoloured	3·75	3·50

Stamps of a simlar design were issued by the Vatican City. See also No. 3811.

1762 Trees at Dusk

1763 Gerhard Mercator and Symbols of Cartography

(Des Silvia Runge)
2012 (1 Mar). Mourning Stamp. P 14.
3769   1762   55c. black .... 3·50   3·25

(Des Iris Utikal and Michael Gais. Litho Giesecke & Devrient GmbH, Security Ptg, Leipzig)
2012 (1 Mar). 500th Birth Anniv of Gerhard Mercator (Gerhard Kremer) (cartographer, surveyor and instrument maker). P 14.
3770   1763   220c. multicoloured .... 13·50   13·00

1764 Axel Springer

1765 Woman carrying Baskets on Yoke

(Des Nicole Elsenbach)
2012 (12 Apr). Birth Centenary of Axel Springer (journalist). P 14.
3771   1764   55c. black, scarlet-vermilion and pale yellow-ochre .... 3·50   3·25

(Des Ingo Wulff. Litho German Bank Ptg Co, Leipzig)
2012 (12 Apr). 50th Anniv of German Welthungerhilfe. P 14.
3772   1765   55c. multicoloured .... 3·50   3·25

1766 Football Match

(Des Jens Müller and Karen Weiland)
2012 (12 Apr). Sports Promotion Fund, 2012. Euro 2012, European Football Championships, Poland and Ukraine (3773), Olympic Games, London (3774) or World Team Table Tennis Championships, Dortmund (3775). T **1766** and similr horiz designs. Multicoloured. P 13½.
3773   55c. +55c. Type **1766** .... 5·00   4·75
3774   90c. +40c. Swimmers .... 8·00   7·75
3775   145c. +55c. Four players and table .... 12·50   12·00
3773/3775 Set of 3 .... 23·00   22·00

(Des Daniela Haufe and Detlef Fiedler. Litho Giesecke & Devrient GmbH, Security Ptg, Leipzig)
2012 (12 Apr). 225th Birth Anniv of Joseph von Fraunhofer (pioneer of scientific methodology in the field of optics and precision engineering and entrepreneur) (2nd issue). Size 38×24 mm. Self-adhesive booklet stamp. Die-cut perf 10.
3776   90c. As Type **1754** .... 5·50   5·50

1767 Crowd waving Flag

1768 Beach in Summer

(Des Stefan Klein and Olaf Neumann. Litho Bagel Security-Print, Mönchengladbach)
2012 (12 May). German Football Enthusiasm.
(a) Sheet stamp. Ordinary gum. P 14.
3777   1767   55c. multicoloured .... 3·50   3·25
(b) Self-adhesive booklet stamp. Die-cut perf 10.
3778   1767   55c. multicoloured .... 3·50   3·25

(Des Andrea Voß-Acker. Litho Giesecke & Devrient GmbH, Security Ptg, Leipzig)
2012 (2 May). Post. Summer. Europa. Visit Germany. P 13½×14.
3779   1768   55c. multicoloured .... 3·50   3·25

No. 3780 and T **1769** are left for Lighthouse, issued on 2 May 2012, not yet received.

1770 Scene from *Frog Prince* with Rubbish Bin as Frog Prince

1771 Johann Gottlieb Fichte

(Des Neumann)
2012 (2 May). Environmental Protection. P 14.
3781   1770   55c. +25c. multicoloured .... 5·00   4·75

(Des Dieter Ziegenfeuter)
2012 (2 May). 250th Birth Anniversary of Johann Gottlieb Fichte (philosopher). P 14.
3782   1771   70c. multicoloured .... 4·25   4·25

1772 Windeck House in Bad Münstereifel

1773 Silhouette Figures from Inside Cover of Original Edition of *Children's and Household Tales*

(Des Dieter Ziegenfeuter)
2012 (2 May). Half-timbered Architecture (3rd issue). P 14.
3783   1772   165c. multicoloured .... 10·00   10·00

(Des Barbara Dimanski)
2012 (14 June). Bicentenary of Grimm Brothers' Fairy Tales (*Children's and Household Tales*). P 14.
3784   1773   55c. multicoloured .... 3·50   3·25

1774 Pfälzerhütte and Buildings

(Des Corinna Rogger)
2012 (14 June). Pfälzerhütte (mountain hut and inn), Liechtenstein. P 14.
3785   1774   75c. multicoloured .... 4·75   4·50

GERMANY

1775 Mixed Choir

1776 Das Balkonzimmer (Adolph Menzel)

(Des Barbara Dimanski. Litho Giesecke & Devrient GmbH, Security Ptg, Leipzig)

2012 (14 June). 150th Anniv of German Choral Association. P 13½.
3786 **1775** 85c. multicoloured .... 5·25 5·00

Des Werner Hans Schmidt. Litho Bagel Security-Print, Mönchengladbach)

2012 (14 June). German Painting. P 14.
3787 **1776** 260c. multicoloured .... 16·00 16·00

1777 Borkum Lighthouse

1778 Apartment Name Plates

(Des Johannes Graf. Litho Bagel Security-Print, Mönchengladbach)

2012 (12 July). Lighthouses. T **1777** and similar square design. Multicoloured. P 13½.
3788   45c. Type **1777** .... 2·50 2·40
3789   55c. Arkona .... 3·00 3·00

(Des Jens Müller and Karen Weiland. Litho Bagel Security-Print, Mönchengladbach)

2012 (12 July). At Home in Germany. Diversity. P 14.
3790 **1778** 55c. multicoloured .... 3·50 3·25

1779 Parkland

(Des Marzanna Dabrowska)

2012 (12 July). World Heritage Site. Muskauer Park. P 14.
3791 **1779** 90c. multicoloured .... 5·50 5·50
A stamp of a similar design was issued by Poland.

1780 Dog, Cat and Fish

1781 Emperor Otto I

(Des Michael Okraj. Litho German Bank Ptg Co, Leipzig)

2012 (12 July). German Animal Protection Association Animal Shelters. P 14.
3792 **1780** 145c. multicoloured .... 9·00 8·75

(Des Ernst Kößlinger. Litho Bagel Security-Print, Mönchengladbach)

2012 (9 Aug). 1100th Birth Anniv of Emperor Otto I. P 14.
3793 **1781** 45c. multicoloured .... 2·75 2·75

1782 Symbols of Festival

(Des Peter Steiner and Regina Steiner. Litho Giesecke & Devrient GmbH, Security Ptg, Leipzig)

2012 (9 Aug). Bicentenary of Gäubodenfest, Straubing. P 13½×14.
3794 **1782** 55c. multicoloured .... 3·50 3·25

1783 Steam Locomotive S 3/6

(Des Stefan Klein and Olaf Neumann. Litho Giesecke & Devrient GmbH, Security Ptg, Leipzig)

2012 (9 Aug). Youth Stamps. Historic Steam Locomotives. T **1783** and similar horiz designs. Multicoloured. P 14.
3795   55c. +25c. Type **1783** .... 5·25 5·00
3796   90c. +40c. PTL 2/2 .... 8·50 8·00
3797   145c. +55c. Leopold Friedrich ..... 13·00 12·50
3795/3797 Set of 3 .... 24·00 23·00

1784 Four Car Set on Viaduct

(Des Olaf Neumann. Litho Giesecke & Devrient GmbH, Security Ptg, Leipzig)

2012 (9 Aug). Centenary of Mittenwald Railway. P 13½×14.
3798 **1784** 75c. multicoloured .... 5·00 4·75

1785 Children's Imagination

(Des Peter Steiner and Regina Steiner. Litho Bagel Security-Print, Mönchengladbach)

2012 (13 Sept). For Us Children. P 14.
3799 **1785** 55c. multicoloured .... 3·75 3·50

1786 Autumn Colour

(Des Andrea Voß-Acker. Litho Giesecke & Devrient GmbH, Security Ptg, Leipzig)

2012 (13 Sept). Post. Autumn in Germany. P 13½×14.
3800 **1786** 55c. multicoloured .... 3·75 3·50

1787 Airmail Envelope with 1902 5pf. Stamp

GERMANY

(Des Annegret Ehmke)
2012 (13 Sept). Stamp Day. Centenary of First Official Postal Flight in Germany. P 13½×14.
3801   **1787**   55c. multicoloured ....   3·75   3·50

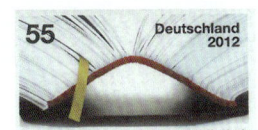

1788 Open Book

(Des Wilfried Korfmacher. Litho Giesecke & Devrient GmbH, Security Ptg, Leipzig)
2012 (13 Sept). Centenary of National Library. P 13½×14.
3802   **1788**   55c. multicoloured ....   3·75   3·50

1789 Page 76

(Des Annegret Ehmke. Litho Bagel Security-Print, Mönchengladbach)
2012 (13 Sept). Bicentenary of German Bible Society. P 13½×14.
3803   **1789**   85c. multicoloured ....   5·50   5·25

1790 Cross    **1791** Three Castles

(Des Andreas Ahrens. Litho Giesecke & Devrient GmbH, Security Ptg, Leipzig)
2012 (11 Oct). 50th Anniv of Second Vatican Ecumenical Council. P 14.
3804   **1790**   45c. gold and black ....   3·00   2·75

(Des Anna Berkenbusch. Litho Bagel Security-Print, Mönchengladbach)
2012 (11 Oct). Drei Gleichen (municipality), Thuringia. P 13½×14.
3805   **1791**   55c. pale brownish grey, grey and scarlet-vermilion ....   3·75   3·50

1792 Helmut Kohl    **1793** Anniversary Emblem

(Des Coordt von Mannstein. Litho Giesecke & Devrient GmbH, Security Ptg, Leipzig)
2012 (11 Oct). Helmut Kohl – Chancellor of Germany – Honorary Citizen of Europe. P 14.
3806   **1792**   55c. multicoloured ....   3·75   3·50

(Des Kitty Kahane. Litho Bagel Security-Print, Mönchengladbach)
2012 (11 Oct). Centenary of Domowina – Federation of Lusatian Sorbs. P 13½×14.
3807   **1793**   145c. multicoloured ....   9·50   9·00

1794 '3'

1795 Professors G. G. Gervinus, W. E. Albrecht, H. G. A. Ewald, F. C. Dahlmann, W. E. Weber, W. Grimm and J. Grimm

(Des Stefan Klein and Olaf Neumann. Litho Enschedé)
2012 (2 Nov). Supplementary Stamp.
(a) Sheet stamps. Ordinary gum. P 14
3808   **1794**   3c. multicoloured ....   1·00   95
(b) Size 38×22 mm. Booklet stamps. Self-adhesive. Die-cut perf 10
3808a **1794**   3c. multicoloured ....   1·00   95

(Des Stefan Klein and Olaf Neumann. Litho Giesecke & Devrient GmbH, Security Ptg, Leipzig)
2012 (2 Nov). 175th Anniv of Göttingen Seven (seven professors of University of Göttingen, who stood against King Ernst August of Hanover who decreed liberal state constitution suspended). P 14.
3809   **1795**   55c. multicoloured ....   3·75   3·50

1796 Gerhart Hauptmann and Book Titles    **1797** Madonna and Child (Raphael)

(Des Christof Gassner. Litho Bagel Security-Print, Mönchengladbach)
2012 (2 Nov). 150th Birth Anniv of Gerhart Hauptmann. P 13½.
3810   **1796**   55c. vermilion and black ....   3·75   3·50

(Des Werner Hans Schmidt. Litho Bagel Security-Print, Mönchengladbach)
2012 (2 Nov). 500th Anniv of Sistine Madonna (*La Madonna di San Sisto*) (by Raphael) (2nd issue). Self-adhesive. Die-cut perf 11.
3811   **1797**   55c. multicoloured ....   3·75   3·50

1798 Snow-covered Chapel

(Des Carsten Wolff. Litho)
2012 (2 Nov). Christmas. Welfare Stamps.
(a) Ordinary gum. P 13½
3812   **1798**   55c. +25c. multicoloured ....   5·25   5·00
(b) Self-adhesive gum. Die-cut perf 10½
3813   **1798**   55c. +25c. multicoloured ....   5·25   5·00

1799 Half-timbered Building, Dinkelsbühl, 1600 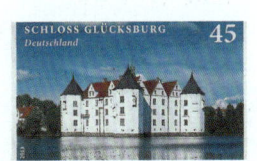   **1800** Glücksburg Schloss

185

GERMANY

(Des Dieter Ziegenfeuter)

2012 (6 Dec). Half-timbered Architecture. P 14.
3814   **1799**   58c. multicoloured .... 4·00   3·75

(Des Nicole Elsenbach and Franc Fienbork. Litho Bagel Security-Print, Mönchengladbach)

2013 (2 Jan). Prussian Schlosses. T **1800** and similar horiz design. Multicoloured.
(a) Sheet stamps. Ordinary gum. P 14
3815   45c. Type **1800** .... 3·00   2·75
3816   58c. Nüremberg Castle .... 4·00   3·75
(b) Self-adhesive. Die-cut perf 10
3816a   58c. Nüremberg Castle .... 4·00   3·75
No. 3816a was printed in single-sided booklets of ten stamps.

1801 Queen Nefertiti
1802 French and German Flags as Binoculars 

(Des Stefan Klein and Olaf Neumann)

2013 (2 Jan). Treasures from German Museums (1st issue). T **1801** and similar vert design. Multicoloured. P 14.
3817   58c. Type **1801** .... 4·00   3·75
3818   145c. Ishtar Gate .... 9·50   9·00
See also Nos. 3836, 3845, 3851, 3924, 3950, 3990, 4009, 4014, 4046, 40467, 4070 and 4094/4097.

(Des Thomas Serres. Litho Bagel Security-Print, Mönchengladbach)

2013 (2 Jan). 50th Anniv of Elysée Treaty. P 13½×14.
3819   **1802**   75c. multicoloured .... 5·00   4·75
Stamps of a similar design were issued by France.

1803 *Die Rasenbleiche* (The Bleaching) (Max Liebermann)
1804 German Cathedral and Konzerthaus, Gendarmenmarkt, Berlin (left) 

(Des Werner Hans Schmidt)

2013 (2 Jan). German Painting.
(a) Ordinary gum. P 14
3820   **1803**   240c. multicoloured .... 16·00   15·00
(b) Self-adhesive. Die-cut perf 10½
3821   **1803**   240c. multicoloured .... 16·00   15·00
No. 3821 was printed with the surplus paper around the stamp retained.

(Des Stefan Klein and Olaf Neumann. Litho Giesecke & Devrient GmbH, Security Ptg, Leipzig)

2013 (7 Feb). Panorama (1st issue). Multicoloured.
(a) Sheet stamps. Ordinary gum. P 14
3822   58c. Type **1804** .... 4·00   3·75
          a. Pair. Nos. 3822/3823 .... 8·25   7·75
3823   58c. Konzerthaus (right) and French
          Cathedral, Gendarmenmarkt .... 4·00   3·75
(b) Size 38×22 mm. Booklet stamps. Self-adhesive. Die-cut perf 10
3824   58c. As Type **1804** .... 4·00   3·75
3825   58c. As No. 3823 .... 4·00   3·75
Nos. 3824/3825 are separated by a die-cutting. Therefore No. 3824 has right vertical edge imperforate and No. 3825 has left edge imperforate.
See also Nos. 3869/3870, 3906/3909, 3921/3922, 3991/3994, 4048, 4049, 4144 and 4145.

1805 Lime Tree

(Des Andrea Voß-Acker)

2013 (7 Feb). Welfare Stamps. Flowering Trees. T **1805** and similar horiz designs. Multicoloured.
(a) Sheet stamps. Ordinary gum. P 14
3826   58c. +27c. Type **1805** .... 5·50   5·25
3827   90c. +40c. Bird Cherry .... 8·50   8·00
3828   145c. +55c. Horse Chestnut .... 13·00   12·50
(b) Self-adhesive. Die-cut perf 11
3829   58c. +27c. As Type **1805** .... 5·50   5·25
3826/3829 Set of 4 .... 29·00   28·00
No. 3826 was printed both in coils, and booklets of ten stamps.

1806 Castle Hubertusburg, Wermsdorf
1807 Tiger and Bear in Sailboat and Tiger Duck Swimming 

(Des Matthias Wittig. Litho Giesecke & Devrient GmbH, Security Ptg, Leipzig)

2013 (7 Feb). 250th Anniv of Hubertusburg Peace Treaty (ending Seven Years War). P 14.
3830   **1806**   90c. multicoloured .... 6·00   5·50

(Des Janosch and Grit Fiedler. Litho Giesecke & Devrient GmbH, Security Ptg, Leipzig)

2013 (1 Mar). 82nd Birth Anniv of Horst Eckert (Janosch) (children's author and illustrator). Multicoloured.
(a) Sheet stamps. Ordinary gum. P 13½
3831   45c. Type **1807** .... 3·00   2·75
3832   58c. Tiger, Tiger Duck, Bunny and Bear with
          presents celebrating Easter .... 4·00   3·75
(b) Size 38×22 mm. Booklet stamps. Self-adhesive. Die-cut perf 10
3833   45c. As Type **1807** .... 3·00   2·75
3834   58c. As No. 3832 .... 4·00   3·75
3831/3834 Set of 4 .... 12·50   11·50

1808 Cellist
1809 Friedrich Hebbel 

(Des Kitty Kahane)

2013 (1 Mar). 50th Anniv of Jugend musiziert (competition for young musicians). P 14.
3835   **1808**   58c. multicoloured .... 4·00   3·75

(Des Stefan Klein and Olaf Neumann)

2013 (1 Mar). Treasures from German Museums (2nd issue). Self-adhesive. Die-cut perf 12.
3836   58c. As No. 3817 .... 4·00   3·75

(Des Birgit Hogrefe. Litho Bagel Security-Print, Mönchengladbach)

2013 (1 Mar). Birth Bicentenary of Christian Friedrich (Friedrich) Hebbel (dramatist). P 14.
3837   **1809**   100c. greenish yellow and black .... 6·50   6·25

GERMANY

1810 A. H. Francke

1811 Symbols of Work of Red Cross

(Des Imme and Alessio Leonardi. Litho Bagel Security-Print, Mönchengladbach)

2013 (1 Mar). 350th Birth Anniv of August Hermann Francke (theologian and educator). P 13½×14.
3838   **1810**   205c. multicoloured .... 13·50   12·50

(Des Greta Göttrup)

2013 (4 Apr). 150th Anniv of Red Cross. P 14.
3839   **1811**   58c. black and scarlet-vermilion .... 4·00   3·75

1812 German Sports Badge

1813 Fehmarn Bridge

(Des Lorli Jünger and Ernst Jünger. Litho Bagel Security-Print, Mönchengladbach)

2013 (4 Apr). Centenary of German Sports Badge. P 14.
3840   **1812**   58c. multicoloured .... 4·00   3·75

(Des Heribert Birnbach)

2013 (4 Apr). 50th Anniv of Fehmarn Bridge.
    (a) Ordinary gum. P 13½
3841   **1813**   75c. multicoloured .... 5·00   4·75
    (b) Size 38×22 mm. Booklet Stamp. Self-adhesive. Die-cut perf 10
3842   **1813**   75c. multicoloured .... 5·00   4·75
No. 3842 was printed with the surplus paper around the stamp retained.

1814 Möhnetalsperre Dam

1815 Flag

(Des Gerda M. Neumann and Horst F. Neumann. Litho German Bank Ptg Co, Leipzig)

2013 (4 Apr). Centenary of Möhnetalsperre Dam (1st issue). P 14.
3843   **1814**   90c. multicoloured .... 6·00   5·50
See also No. 3851.

(Des Thomas Serres. Litho German Bank Ptg Co, Leipzig)

2013 (4 Apr). 150th Anniv of General German Workers' Association (ADAV). P 14.
3844   **1815**   145c. multicoloured .... 9·50   9·00

(Des Stefan Klein and Olaf Neumann)

2013 (4 Apr). Treasures from German Museums (3rd issue). Self-adhesive. Die-cut perf 12.
3845   145c. As No. 3818 .... 9·50   9·00

Type **1816** is vaccant.

1817 Richard Wagner

(Des Julia Warbanow. Litho Bagel Security Print GmbH & Co. KG, Mönchengladbach)

2013 (2 May). Birth Bicentenary of Richard Wagner (composer). P 13½×14.
3846   **1817**   58c. multicoloured .... 4·00   3·75

1818 Lloyd Paketzustellwagen, 1908

(Des Günter Gamroth. Litho Giesecke & Devrient GmbH, Security Ptg, Leipzig)

2013 (2 May). Europa. Postal Transport. P 13½×14.
3847   **1818**   58c. multicoloured .... 4·00   3·75

1819 Mouse preparing to Sprint

1819a Glücksburg

(Des Hans Werner Schmidt)

2013 (2 May). Sports Promotion Fund. *Sprint Mouse* (cartoon character by Uli Stein). T **1819** and similar horiz designs. Multicoloured. P 13½×14.
3848   58c. +27c. Type **1819** .... 6·50   6·25
3849   90c. +40c. Mouse wind surfing .... 8·50   8·00
3850   145c. +55c. Mouse using parallel bars .... 13·00   12·50
3848/3850 Set of 3 .... 25·00   24·00

(Des Gerda M. Neumann and Horst F. Neumann. Litho German Bank Ptg Co, Leipzig)

2013 (2 May). Centenary of Möhnetalsperre Dam (2nd issue). Booklet Stamp. Self-adhesive. Die-cut perf 10.
3851   90c. As Type **1814** .... 6·00   5·50

(Des Nicole Elsenbach and Franc Fienbork. Litho Giesecke & Devrient GmbH, Security Ptg, Leipzig)

2013 (6 June). Prussian Schlosses. Self-adhesive. P 10.
3852   **1819a**   45c. multicoloured .... 3·00   2·75

1820 East German Rose Garden

1821 Flügge Lighthouse

(Des Thomas Serres)

2013 (6 June). German Rose Show, Forst (Lausitz). Centenary of East German Rose Garden. P 13½×14.
3853   **1820**   45c. multicoloured .... 3·00   2·75

(Des Johannes Graf. Litho Bagel Security-Print, Mönchengladbach)

2013 (6 June). Lighthouses. T **1821** and similar square design. Multicoloured. P 13½.
3854   45c. Type **1821** .... 3·00   2·75
3855   58c. Büsum .... 4·00   3·75

1822 Camouflaged People and National Flag

(Des Stefan Klein and Olaf Neumann)

2013 (6 June). Bundeswehr – Working for Germany. P 13½.
3856   **1822**   58c. multicoloured .... 4·00   3·75

187

GERMANY

1823 Temple of the Sun, Bayreuth

(Des Matthias Wittig. Litho Giesecke & Devrient GmbH, Security Ptg, Leipzig)

2013 (6 June). Cultural History and Architecture. T **1823** and similar horiz design. Multicoloured. P 13½×14.
| 3857 | 75c. Type **1823**.. | 5·00 | 4·75 |
| 3858 | 150c. Hyangwonjong Pavilion, Gyeongbokgung Palace, Seoul................ | 10·00 | 9·25 |

Stamps of a similar design were issued by South Korea.

1824 'Dessau', Aircraft and Buildings

(Des Matthias Wittig and Jutta Ziemba)

2013 (1 July). 800th Anniv of Dessau. P 13½×14.
| 3859 | **1824** | 45c. bright orange and bright violet .. | 3·00 | 2·75 |

1825 Lower Saxony Wadden Sea

(Des Dieter Ziegenfeuter. Litho Giesecke & Devrient GmbH, Security Ptg, Leipzig)

2013 (1 July). Wild Germany. T **1825** and similar horiz design. Multicoloured. P 13½×14.
| 3860 | 58c. Type **1825**... | 4·00 | 3·75 |
| 3861 | 58c. Berchtesgaden National Park................ | 4·00 | 3·75 |

1826 Seascape

(Des Sybille Haase and Fritz Haase. Litho Bagel Security Print, Mönchengladbach)

2013 (1 July). Painting by Gerhard Richter.
(a) Ordinary gum. P 14
| 3862 | **1826** | 145c. multicoloured .... | 9·50 | 9·00 |

(b) Booklet Stamp. Self-adhesive gum. Die-cut perf 10
| 3863 | **1826** | 145c. multicoloured .... | 9·50 | 9·00 |

1827 Ocean and Coast

(Des Manfred Gottschall. Litho Bagel Security Print & Co. KG, Mönchengladbach)

2013 (18 July). Flood Relief. P 14.
| 3864 | **1827** | 58c. +42c. multicoloured............................ | 6·50 | 6·25 |

1828 Inscribed Ribbon

1829 *Carduelis carduelis* (Goldfinch)

(Des Iris Utikal and Michael Gais. Litho Giesecke & Devrient GmbH, Leipzig)

2013 (8 Aug). Birth Centenary of Julius Kardinal Döpfner (Cardinal and Archbishop of Munich and Freising). P 14.
| 3865 | **1828** | 58c. multicoloured .... | 4·00 | 3·75 |

(Des Julia Warbanow. Litho Bagel Security Print GmbH & Co. KG, Mönchengladbach)

2013 (8 Aug). Youth Stamps. Song Birds. T **1829** and similar square designs. Multicoloured. P 14.
3866	58c. +27c. Type **1829**................................	5·50	5·25
3867	90c. +40c. *Pyrrhula pyrrhula* (Bullfinch)..........	8·50	8·00
3868	145c. +55c. *Parus caeruleus* (Bluetit)................	13·00	12·50
3866/3868	Set of 3...	24·00	23·00

1830 Heidelberg (left)

1831 *Saxonia* (steam locomotive), 1843

(Des Stefan Klein and Olaf Neumann. Litho Giesecke & Devrient GmbH, Security Ptg, Leipzig)

2013 (5 Sept). Panorama (2nd issue). T **1830** and similar horiz design. Multicoloured.
3869	58c. Type **1830**...	4·00	3·75
	a. Horiz pair. Nos. 3869/3870......................	8·25	7·75
3870	58c. Heidelberg (right)	4·00	3·75

Nos. 3869/3870 were printed, *se-tenant*, in horizontal pairs within the sheet, each pair forming a composite design.

(Des Harry Scheuner. Litho Bagel Security Print GmbH & Co. KG, Mönchengladbach)

2013 (5 Sept). Stamp Day. Locomotives. P 13½.
| 3871 | **1831** | 58c. +27c. multicoloured........................ | 5·50 | 5·25 |

1832 Dame, King and Knave playing Skat

(Des Christoph Niemann. Litho Bundesdruckerei GmbH, Berlin)

2013 (13 Sept). Bicentenary of German Card Game Skatspiel. P 13½×14.
| 3872 | **1832** | 90c. multicoloured .... | 6·00 | 5·50 |

1833 Monument

(Des Astrid Grahl and Lutz Menze. Litho German Bank Ptg Co, Leipzig)

2013 (10 Oct). Centenary of Monument to the Battle of the Nations. P 14.
| 3873 | **1833** | 45c. multicoloured .... | 3·00 | 2·75 |

1834 Script
1835 Ludwig Leichhardt

(Des Katrin Stangl. Litho Bagel Security-Print, Mönchengladbach)

2013 (10 Oct). Birth Bicentenary of Georg Büchner. P 14.
3874   1834   58c. black, pale ochre and rose .... 4·00   3·75

(Des Gary Domoney and Karen Weiland. Litho)

2013 (10 Oct). Birth Bicentenary of Ludwig Leichhardt. P 14.
3875   1835   75c. multicoloured .... 5·00   4·75
A stamp of a similar design was issued by Australia.

1836 Willy Brandt
1837 Electromagnetic Rays

(Des Ingo Wulff. Litho Bundesdruckerei GmbH)

2013 (2 Nov). Birth Centenary of Willy Brandt (chancellor). P 13½×14.
3876   1836   58c. multicoloured .... 4·00   3·75

(Des Thomas and Martin Poschauko. Litho Bagel Security Print GmbH & Co. KG, Mönchengladbach)

2013 (2 Nov). 125th Anniv of Treatise *On Rays of Electric Force* by Heinrich Hertz. P 14.
3877   1837   58c. multicoloured .... 4·00   3·75

1838 Decorated Trees
1839 Three Kings

(Des Nicole Elsenbach & Franc Fienbork. Litho Giesecke & Devrient GmbH, Leipzig)

2013 (2 Nov). Christmas (1st issue).
         (a) Ordinary gum. P 13½
3878   1838   58c. multicoloured .... 4·00   3·75
         (b) Self-adhesive gum. Die-cut perf 10½
3879   1838   58c. multicoloured .... 4·00   3·75

(Des Kitty Kahane. Litho Bundesdruckerei GmbH)

2013 (2 Nov). Christmas (2nd issue). Welfare Stamps.
         (a) Ordinary gum. P 13½
3880   1839   58c. +27c. multicoloured .... 5·50   5·25
         (b) Self-adhesive gum. Die-cut perf 10½
3881   1839   58c. +27c. multicoloured .... 5·50   5·25

1840 Professor Hirsch in her Laboratory
1841 '2'

(Des Thomas Mayfried. Litho Bagel Security Print GmbH & Co. KG, Mönchengladbach)

2013 (2 Nov). Centenary of Award of Title of Professor to Rachel Hirsch (first woman in Prussia to be appointed professor of medicine). P 13½.
3882   1840   145c. multicoloured .... 9·50   9·00

(Des Stefan Klein and Olaf Neumann. Litho Enschedé (3383) or Giesecke & Devrient GmbH, Leipzig (3384))

2013 (5 Dec). Supplementary Stamp.
         (a) Sheet stamps. Ordinary gum. P 14
3883   1841   2c. multicoloured .... 1·00   95
         (b) Size 38×22 mm. Booklet stamps. Self-adhesive. Die-cut perf 10
3884   1841   2c. multicoloured .... 1·00   95

1842 Clouds

(Des Greta Gröttrup. Litho Bundesdruckerei GmbH)

2013 (5 Dec). Mourning Stamp. P 13½×14.
3885   1842   60c. multicoloured .... 4·00   3·75

1843 Salmon
1844 Lorsch Abbey

(Des Jens Müller. Litho Giesecke & Devrient GmbH, Leipzig)

2014 (2 Jan). Reintroduction of Fish Species. Atlantic Salmon. P 14.
3886   1843   45c. multicoloured .... 3·00   2·75
See also No. 3949.

(Des Harry Scheuner. Litho Bundesdruckerei GmbH)

2014 (2 Jan). World Heritage. 1250th Anniversary of Lorsch Abbey.
         (a) Ordinary gum. P 14
3887   1844   60c. multicoloured .... 4·00   3·75
         (b) Self-adhesive. Die-cut perf 10½
3888   1844   60c. multicoloured .... 4·00   3·75

1845 Fox Cubs

(Des Nicole Elsenbach and Franc Fienbork. Litho Giesecke & Devrient GmbH, Leipzig)

2014 (2 Jan). Young Animals. T **1845** and similar horiz design. Multicoloured.
         (a) Ordinary gum. P 14
3889   60c. Type **1845** .... 4·00   3·75
3890   60c. Hedgehogs .... 4·00   3·75
         (b) Self-adhesive. Die-cut perf 10
3891   60c. As Type **1845** .... 4·00   3·75
3892   60c. As No. 3890 .... 4·00   3·75

1846 Stolzenfels am Rhein Castle

(Des Nicole Eisenbach. Litho Bagel Security Print GmbH & Co. KG, Mönchengladbach)

2014 (2 Jan). Prussian Schlosses. P 14.
3893   1846   75c. multicoloured .... 5·00   4·75

GERMANY

1871 Nie Wieder Krieg (Never again war) (Kathe Kollwitz)
1872 Courier Coach 

(Des Astrid Grahl and Lutz Menze. Litho Bundesdruckerei GmbH)
2014 (7 Aug). Centenary of Start of World War I. P 14.
3935   1871   75c. black and grey .... 5·00   4·75

(Des Peter Steiner and Regina Steiner. Litho Bundesdruckerei GmbH)
2014 (1 Sept). Stamp Day. Lindau via Fussach to Milan Courier. P 14.
3936   1872   60c. multicoloured .... 4·00   3·75

1873 The Little Prince
1874 *Sonniger Weg* 

(Des Peter Steiner and Regina Steiner. Litho Bundesdruckerei GmbH)
2014 (1 Sept). 70th Death Anniv of Antoine de Saint-Exupéry.
  (a) Sheet stamps. Ordinary gum. P 14.
3937   1873   60c. multicoloured .... 4·00   3·75
  (b) Self-adhesive. Die-cut perf 10.
3938   60c. As Type 1873 .... 4·00   3·75
No. 3938 was printed in booklets of ten stamps.

(Des Irmgard Hesse. Litho Giesecke & Devrient GmbH, Security Ptg, Leipzig)
2014 (1 Sept). German Painting. Death Centenary of August Macke. P 14.
3939   1874   100c. multicoloured .... 6·50   6·25

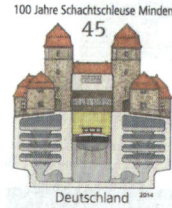

1875 Minden Lock
1876 Fagus Factory Buildings 

(Des Ursula Lautenschläger. Litho Giesecke & Devrient GmbH, Security Ptg, Leipzig)
2014 (2 Oct). Centenary of Minden Lock. P 14.
3940   1875   45c. multicoloured .... 3·00   2·75

(Des Christof Gassner. Litho Bundesdruckerei GmbH, Berlin)
2014 (2 Oct). World Heritage Site. Fagus Factory. P 14.
3941   1876   60c. multicoloured .... 4·00   3·75

1877 Anniversary Emblem
1878 Fahrenheit Scale 

(Des Matthias Beyrow. Litho Bagel Security-Print, Mönchengladbach)
2014 (2 Oct). 300th Anniv of External Financial Control. P 14.
3942   1877   145c. multicoloured .... 9·50   9·00

(Des Pschauko. Litho Bagel Security-Print, Mönchengladbach)
2014 (3 Nov). 300th Anniv of Fahrenheit Scale. P 14.
3943   1878   60c. vermilion and bright new blue ....   4·00   3·75

1879 Snowman in Snow Globe
1880 Shooting Star 

(Des Bianca Becker and Peter Kohl. Litho Giesecke & Devrient GmbH, Leipzig)
2014 (3 Nov). Christmas (1st issue). Snowman.
  (a) Ordinary gum. P 13½.
3944   1879   60c. multicoloured .... 4·00   3·75
  (b) Self-adhesive gum. Die-cut perf 10½.
3945   60c. As Type 1879 .... 4·00   3·75
No. 3944 is perforated around the globe enclosed in an outer perforated rectangle, No. 3945 has die-cut perforations around the globe only.
No. 3945 was printed in booklets of ten stamps.

(Des Nicole Elsenbach. Litho Bundesdruckerei GmbH)
2014 (3 Nov). Christmas (2nd issue). Welfare Stamps.
  (a) Ordinary gum. P 13½.
3946   1880   60c. +30c. multicoloured .... 6·00   5·50
  (b) Self-adhesive gum. Die-cut perf 10½.
3947   60c. +30c. As Type 1880 (36×22 mm).. 6·00   5·50
No. 3947 was printed in booklets of ten stamps.

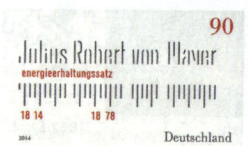

1881 'Julius Robert von Mayer' as Thermodynamic Scale

(Des Loebe. Litho Bagel Security-Print, Mönchengladbach)
2014 (3 Nov). Birth Bicentenary of Julius Robert von Mayer (physician and physicist). P 14.
3948   1881   90c. cream, black and vermilion .... 6·00   5·50

1882 Brown Trout

(Des Jens Müller. Litho Giesecke & Devrient GmbH, Security Ptg, Leipzig)
2014 (4 Dec). Reintroduction of Fish Species. Brown Trout (*Salmo trutta trutta*). P 13½×14.
3949   1882   45c. multicoloured .... 3·00   2·75

1883 *Heimsuchung* (Roger Van Der Weyden)
1884 Young Squirrels (*Sciurus vulgaris*)

GERMANY

(Des Stefan Klein and Olaf Neumann. Litho Bagel Security-Print, Mönchengladbach)

2014 (4 Dec). Treasures from German Museums (5th issue). P 14.
3950 **1883** 145c. multicoloured .... 9·50 9·00

(Des Nicole Elsenbach and Franc Fienbork. Litho Giesecke & Devrient GmbH, Security Ptg, Leipzig)

2015 (2 Jan). Young Animals. T **1884** and similar horiz design. Multicoloured.

(a) Ordinary gum. P 14.
3951 62c. Type **1884** .... 4·25 4·00
3952 62c. Wild Cat kittens (*Felis silvestris*) .... 4·25 4·00

(b) Self-adhesive. Die-cut perf 11.
3953 62c. As Type **1884** .... 4·25 4·00
3954 62c. As No. 3952 .... 4·25 4·00
3951/3954 Set of 4 .... 15·00 14·50

Nos. 3953/3954 were printed, each×5, in single-sided booklets of ten stamps.

1885 Marksburg Castle

(Des Nicole Elsenbach. Litho Bagel Security-Print, Mönchengladbach)

2015 (2 Jan). Prussian Schlosses. T **1885** and similar horiz design. Multicoloured.

(a) Sheet stamps. Ordinary gum. P 14.
3955 62c. Type **1885** .... 4·25 4·00
3956 80c. Ludwigslust Castle .... 5·25 5·00

(b) Self-adhesive. Die-cut perf 11.
3957 62c. As Type **1885** .... 4·25 4·00
3958 80c. As No. 3956 .... 5·25 5·00
3955/3958 Set of 4 .... 17·00 16·00

No. 3957/3958 were printed in coils.
No. 3958 was also printed in single-sided booklets of ten stamps.

1886 Western Pomerania Lagoon Area National Park

(Des Dieter Ziegenfeuter. Litho.)

2015 (2 Jan). Wild Germany. Multicoloured.

(a) Ordinary gum. Giesecke & Devrient GmbH, Security Ptg, Leipzig. P 14.
3959 **1886** 85c. multicoloured .... 5·50 5·25

(b) Self-adhesive. Bundesdruckerei GmbH, Berlin. Die-cut perf 11.
3960 85c. As Type **1886** .... 5·50 5·25

No. 3960 was printed both in booklets with the surplus paper around the stamp retained and in sheets with the surplus paper removed.

1887 Karl Leisner    **1888** The Spindle

(Des Daniela Haufe and Detlef Fiedler. Litho Bagel Security Print, Mönchengladbach)

2015 (5 Feb). Birth Centenary of Karl Leisner (Roman Catholic priest interned in Dachau concentration camp). P 14.
3961 **1887** 62c. multicoloured .... 4·25 4·00

(Des Astrid Grahl and Lutz Menze. Litho Enschedé)

2015 (5 Feb). Welfare Stamps. *Sleeping Beauty*. T **1888** and similar vert designs. Multicoloured.

(a) Sheet stamps. Ordinary gum. P 14.
3962 62c. +30c. Type **1888** .... 6·25 6·00
3963 85c. +40c. Sleep .... 8·50 8·00
3964 145c. +55c. The Kiss .... 13·00 12·50

(b) Self-adhesive. Die-cut perf 10½.
3965 62c. +30c. As Type **1888** .... 6·25 6·00
3962/3965 Set of 4 .... 31·00 29·00

No. 3965 was printed both in booklets of ten stamps with the surplus paper around the stamp retained and in sheets with the surplus paper removed.

1889 Felix travelling

(Des Grit Fielder (from illustrations by Constanza Droop). Litho Giesecke & Devrient GmbH, Security Printing, Leipzig)

2015 (2 Mar). Felix the Rabbit (character created by Annette Langen and Constanza Droop). T **1889** and similar horiz designs. Multicoloured.

(a) Sheet stamps. Ordinary gum. P 14.
3966 45c. Type **1889** .... 3·00 2·75
3967 62c. Felix writing letter .... 4·25 4·00

(b) Self-adhesive. Die-cut perf 11.
3968 62c. As No. 3967 .... 4·25 4·00
3966/3968 Set of 3 .... 10·50 9·75

No. 3968 was printed in single-sided booklets of ten stamps.

1890 University Library, West Façade    **1891** Large Disc Cross, Hildesheim Cathedral Treasure

(Des Anette Stahmer and André Heers. Litho Bagel Security-Print, Mönchengladbach)

2015 (2 Mar). 350th Anniv of Christian-Albrechts-Universität (University of Kiel) (1st issue). P 14.
3969 **1890** 62c. multicoloured .... 4·25 4·00

See also No. 3978.

(Des Sascha Lobe. Litho Bundesdruckerei GmbH, Berlin)

2015 (2 Mar). 1200th Anniv of Diocese of Hildesheim. P 14.
3970 **1891** 62c. black and gold .... 4·25 4·00

1892 Cityscape, 1650    **1893** Max and Moritz with Schneider Böck (The Bridge Breaks)

(Des Grit Fielder. Litho Bundesdruckerei GmbH, Berlin)

2015 (2 Mar). 900th Anniv of Köthen (Anhalt). P 14.
3971 **1892** 240c. black, rose-red and new blue .... 16·00 15·00

(Des Greta Gröttrup (after Wilhelm Busch). Litho Giesecke & Devrient GmbH, Security Ptg, Leipzig)

2015 (2 Apr). 150th Anniv of Max and Moritz (characters created by Wilhelm Busch). P 14.
3972 **1893** 62c. multicoloured .... 4·25 4·00

1894 Otto von Bismarck

(Des Dieter Ziegenfeuter. Litho Bundesdruckerei GmbH, Berlin)

2015 (2 Apr). Birth Bicentenary of Otto von Bismarck. P 14.
3973 **1894** 62c. black, scarlet-vermilion and grey .... 4·25 4·00

No. 3973 was printed both in sheets and in coils of 200 stamps.

193

GERMANY

1895 BMW 507

(Des Thomas Serres. Litho Bagel Security Print, Mönchengladbach)

2015 (2 Apr). Classic Cars. T **1895** and similar horiz design. Multicoloured.

(a) Ordinary gum. P 14.
3974	145c. Type **1895**................................	10·00	9·25
3975	145c. Mercedes Benz 220S...................	10·00	9·25

(b) Self-adhesive. Die-cut perf 10.
3976	145c. As Type **1895**...........................	10·00	9·25
3977	145c. As No. 3975...............................	10·00	9·25
3974/3977	*Set of 4*.............................	36·00	33·00

Nos. 3976/3977, were printed, each×5, in booklets of ten stamps with the surplus paper around the stamp retained and, individually, in sheets with the surplus paper removed.

(Des Anette Stahmer and André Heers. Litho Bagel Security-Print, Mönchengladbach)

2017 (7 May). 350th Anniv of Christian-Albrechts-Universität (University of Kiel) (2nd issue). Horiz design as T **1890**. Self-adhesive. Die-cut perf 11.
3978	62c. As Type **1890**............................	4·25	4·00

No. 3978 was printed in booklets of ten stamps with the surplus paper around the stamp retained, and both in sheets and coils with the surplus paper removed.

1896 Stormy Sea    **1897** Monkey riding Rocking Elephant

(Des Andreas Ahrens. Litho Bagel Security-Print, Mönchengladbach)

2015 (7 May). 150th Anniv of German Maritime Search and Rescue Service (DGZRS). P 14.
3979	**1896**	62c. multicoloured...................	4·25	4·00

(Des Kitty Kahane. Litho Giesecke & Devrient GmbH, Leipzig)

2015 (7 May). Europa. Old Toys. P 14.
3980	**1897**	62c. multicoloured...................	4·25	4·00

1898 Wheelchair Tennis    **1899** Bruno House

(Des Henning Wagenbreth. Litho Bagel Security-Print, Mönchengladbach)

2015 (7 May). Sports Promotion Fund. Disabled Sports. T **1898** and similar horiz designs. Multicoloured. P 14.
3981	62c. Type **1898**................................	6·50	6·25
3982	85c. Athletics.....................................	8·25	7·75
3983	145c. Skiing.......................................	13·00	12·50
3981/3983	*Set of 3*.............................	25·00	24·00

(Des Zvika Roitman. Litho Bundesdruckerei GmbH, Berlin)

2015 (7 May). 50th Anniv of Germany – Israel Diplomatic Relations. P 14.
3984	**1899**	80c. multicoloured...................	5·25	5·00

A stamp of a similar design was issued by Israel.

1900 Moritzburg    **1901** Miesbacher Costume

(Des Johannes Graf. Litho Bagel Security-Print, Mönchengladbach)

2015 (11 June). Lighthouses. T **1900** and similar square design. Multicoloured. P 14.
3985	45c. Type **1900**................................	3·00	2·75
3986	62c. Lindau.......................................	4·25	4·00

(Des Michael Kunter. Litho Giesecke & Devrient GmbH, Security Ptg, Leipzig)

2015 (11 June). 125th Anniv of First Bavarian Mountain Costume Association. P 14.
3987	**1901**	62c. multicoloured...................	4·25	4·00

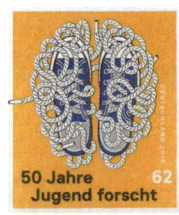

1902 Brain meets Sneaker    **1903** Children

(Des Matthias Beyrow. Litho Giesecke & Devrient GmbH, Security Ptg, Leipzig)

2015 (11 June). 50th Anniv of First Youth Science Competition. P 14.
3988	**1902**	62c. multicoloured...................	4·25	4·00

(Des Lisa Röper. Litho Giesecke & Devrient GmbH, Security Ptg, Leipzig)

2015 (11 June). 175th Anniv of First Kindergarten in Germany. P 14.
3989	**1903**	215c. multicoloured.................	14·00	13·50

(Des Stefan Klein and Olaf Neumann. Litho Giesecke & Devrient GmbH, Security Ptg, Leipzig)

2015 (11 June). Treasures from German Museums (6th issue). Vert design as T **1863**. Self-adhesive. Die-cut perf 10½.
3990	240c. As Type **1863**.........................	16·00	15·00

No. 3990 was printed in booklets of ten stamps.

1904 Chiemsee Lake, Bavaria (left)

(Des Stefan Klein and Olaf Neumann. Litho Giesecke & Devrient GmbH, Security Ptg, Leipzig)

2015 (1 July). Panorama (5th issue). T **1904** and similar horiz design. Multicoloured.

(a) Sheet stamps. Ordinary gum. P 14.
3991	45c. Type **1904**................................	3·00	2·75
	a. Horiz pair. Nos. 3991/3992..........	6·25	5·75
3992	45c. Lake (right)................................	3·00	2·75

(b) Self-adhesive. Die-cut perf 11.
3993	45c. As Type **1904** (38×22 mm)........	3·00	2·75
3994	45c. As No. 3992 (38×22 mm)..........	3·00	2·75
3991/3994	*Set of 4*.............................	11·00	10·00

Nos. 3991/3992 and 3993/3994, respectively, were printed, *se-tenant*, in horizontal pairs within the sheet, each pair forming a composite design.

Nos. 3993/3994 were printed, each×5, in single-sided booklets of ten stamps.

1905 'LEIPZIG'

(Des Anette Stahmer and André Heers. Litho Giesecke & Devrient GmbH, Security Ptg, Leipzig)
2015 (1 July). Millennary of Leipzig. P 14.
3995   **1905**   62c. orange .... 4·25   4·00

1906 Pina Bausch    **1907** Philipp Scheidemann

(Des Dieter Ziegenfeuter (from photograph by Wilfried Krüger). Litho Bundesdruckerei GmbH, Berlin)
2015 (1 July). 75th Birth Anniv of Pina Bausch (dancer, choreographer, dance teacher and theatre guide). P 14.
3996   **1906**   85c. black and salmon-pink .... 5·50   5·25

(Des Daniela Haufe and Detlef Fiedler. Litho Bagel Security-Print, Mönchengladbach)
1915 (1 July). 150th Birth Anniv of Philipp Heinrich Scheidemann (German politician, Social Democratic Party of Germany, proclaimed Germany a republic on 9 November 1918, during German Revolution, 1918–19). P 13½.
3997   **1907**   145c. black and bright vermilion .... 9·50   9·00

1908 Tall Ships    **1909** Grayling

(Des Johannes Graf. Litho Bagel Security-Print, Mönchengladbach)
2015 (6 Aug). International Tall Ships Festival, Bremerhaven. P 14.
3998   **1908**   62c. multicoloured .... 4·25   4·00

(Des Johannes Graf. Litho Bagel Security Print GmbH & Co. KG)
2015 (6 Aug). Youth Stamps. Freshwater Fish. T **1909** and similar horiz designs. Multicoloured. P 14.
3999   62c. +30c. Type **1909** .... 6·50   6·25
    a. Booklet pane. Nos. 3999×5 and 4001....
4000   85c. +40c. Barbel .... 8·25   7·75
4001   145c. +50c. Sturgeon .... 13·00   12·50
3999/4001 *Set of 3* .... 25·00   24·00
Nos. 3999×5 and 4001 were printed in booklets of six stamps, the booklet pane having enlarged illustrated margins.

1910 Asterix    **1911** Helmut Schön

(Des Thomas Steinacker (after Albert Uderz). Litho Bagel Security Print GmbH & Co. KG, Mönchengladbach)
2015 (1 Sept). Asterix (character created by René Goscinny and Albert Uderzo). T **1910** and similar multicoloured designs. Multicoloured.
(a) Booklet Stamps. Self-adhesive. Die-cut perf 11½×11.
4002   62c. Type **1910** .... 4·25   4·00

4003   62c. Obelix .... 4·25   4·00
(b) Miniature sheet. Ordinary gum. P 14.
MS4004 180×120 mm. 21c. Idefix (Dogmatix) (35×35 mm); 62c. Asterix (As Type **1910**); 62c. Obelix (As No. 4003) .... 11·50   11·00
Nos. 4002/4003 were printed, each×5, in booklets of ten stamps.

(Des Andreas Ahrens. Litho Giesecke & Devrient GmbH, Security Ptg, Leipzig)
2015 (1 Sept). Birth Centenary of Helmut Schön (footballer and manager). P 14.
4005   **1911**   62c. black and bright green .... 4·25   4·00

1912 Penny Black    **1913** The Last Supper

(Des Johannes Graf. Litho Bundesdruckerei GmbH)
2015 (1 Sept). Stamp Day. 175th Anniv of World's First Stamp. P 14.
4006   **1912**   62c. +30c. multicoloured .... 6·25   6·00

(Des Antonia Graschberger. Litho Bundesdruckerei GmbH, Berlin)
2015 (1 Oct). 500th Birth Anniv of Lucas Cronach the Younger (artist). P 14.
4007   **1913**   45c. multicoloured .... 3·00   2·75

1914 Anniversary Emblem    **1915** Mourning Women (Tilman Riemenschneider)

(Des Daniela Haufe and Detlef Fiedler. Litho Bagel Security-Print, Mönchengladbach)
2015 (1 Oct). 25th Anniv of German Re-unification. P 14.
4008   **1914**   62c. multicoloured .... 4·25   4·00

(Des Stefan Klein and Olaf Neumann. Litho Giesecke & Devrient GmbH, Leipzig)
2015 (1 Oct). Treasures from German Museums (7th issue). P 14.
4009   **1915**   62c. multicoloured .... 4·25   4·00

1916 Child unpacking Teddy Bear    **1917** 'Silent Night'

(Des Regina Kehn. Litho Giesecke & Devrient GmbH, Leipzig)
2015 (2 Nov). Christmas (1st issue). Give Pleasure. Multicoloured.
(a) Ordinary gum. P 13½.
4010   62c. Type **1916** .... 4·25   4·00
(b) Self-adhesive gum. Size 36×19 mm. Die-cut perf 10½.
4011   62c. As Type **1916** .... 4·25   4·00
No. 4011 was printed in single-sided booklets of ten stamps.

(Des Greta Gröttrup. Litho Giesecke & Devrient GmbH, Security Ptg, Leipzig)
2015 (2 Nov). Christmas (2nd issue). Welfare Stamps.
(a) Ordinary gum. P 13½.
4012   62c. +30c. Type **1917** .... 6·25   6·00

195

GERMANY

(b) Self-adhesive gum. Die-cut perf 10½.
4013   62c. +30c. As Type **1917** .... 6·25   6·00
No. 4013 was printed in booklets of ten stamps.

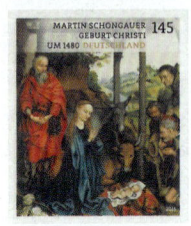

1918 Adoration of the Shepherds (Martin Schongauer)    **1919** '8'

(Des Stefan Klein and Olaf Neumann. Litho Bagel Security-Print, Mönchengladbach)

2015 (2 Nov). Treasures from German Museums (8th issue). P 14.
4014   **1918**   145c. multicoloured .... 9·50   9·00

(Des Stefan Klein and Olaf Neumann. Litho Enschedé)

2015 (2 Nov). Numeral.

(a) Ordinary gum. P 14.
4015   8c. Type **1919** .... 1·00   95

(b) Self-adhesive gum. Die-cut perf 10.
4015a   8c. As Type **1919** .... 1·00   95
No. 4015a was printed in single-sided booklets of 20 stamps.

1920 Microorganism    **1921** Flourite from Freiberg Area

(Des Andrea Voß-Acker. Litho Bundesdruckerei GmbH, Berlin)

2015 (3 Dec). Microworld (1st issye). T **1920** and similar horiz design. Multicoloured.

(a) Ordinary gum. P 14.
4016   70c. Type **1920** .... 4·50   4·25
4017   70c. Diatom .... 4·50   4·25

(b) Self-adhesive gum. Die-cut perf 10.
4018   70c. As Type **1920** .... 4·50   4·25
4019   70c. As No. 4017 .... 4·50   4·25
Nos. 4018/4019 were printed in coils of 100 stamps the designs alternating and the surplus paper around the stamp removed. See also No. 4066, 4131, 4132 and 4171.

(Des Elisabeth Hau. Litho Giesecke & Devrient GmbH, Security Ptg, Leipzig)

2015 (3 Dec). Bicentenary of Freiberg University of Mining and Technology.

(a) Ordinary gum. P 14.
4020   70c. Type **1921** .... 4·50   4·25

(b) Self-adhesive gum. Size 36×19 mm. Die-cut perf 10.
4021   70c. As Type **1921** .... 4·50   4·25
No. 4021 was printed in single-sided booklets of ten stamps.

1922 Heavenly Blossom above Yellow House    **1923** Ford Capri

(Des Sibylle Haase and Fritz Haase. Litho Giesecke & Devrient GmbH, Security Ptg, Leipzig)

2015 (3 Dec). 75th Death Anniv of Paul Klee (artist). P 14.
4022   **1922**   240c. multicoloured .... 16·00   15·00

(Des Thomas Serres. Litho Bagel Security Print Mönchengladbach)

2016 (2 Jan). Classic Cars. T **1895** and similar horiz design. Multicoloured.

(a) Ordinary gum. P 14.
4023   70c. Type **1923** .... 4·50   4·25
4024   70c. Porsche 911 Targa .... 4·50   4·25

(b) Self-adhesive. Size 36×19 mm. Die-cut perf 10.
4025   70c. As Type **1923** .... 4·50   4·25
4026   70c. As No. 4024 .... 4·50   4·25
Nos. 4025/4026, each×10, were printed, in single-sided booklets of 20 stamps.

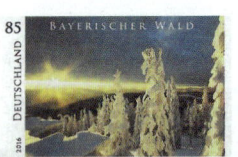

1924 Great Arber Mountain

(Des Dieter Ziegenfeuter. Litho Bundesdruckerei GmbH, Berlin)

2016 (2 Jan). Wild Germany. P 14.
4027   **1924**   85c. multicoloured .... 5·50   5·25

1925 Löwenburg Castle

(Des Nicole Elsenbach. Litho Bagel Security-Print, Mönchengladbach)

2016 (2 Jan). Prussian Schlosses. P 14.
4028   **1925**   90c. multicoloured .... 6·00   5·50

1926 Symbols of Schwetzingen    **1927** '112'

(Des Nicole Elsenbach. Litho Bagel Security-Print, Mönchengladbach)

2016 (2 Jan). 1250th Anniv of City of Schwetzingen.

(a) Ordinary gum. P 14.
4029   145c. Type **1926** .... 9·50   9·00

(b) Self-adhesive gum. Size 34×22 mm. Die-cut perf 10.
4029a   145c. As Type **1926** .... 9·50   9·00
No. 4029a was printed in single-sided booklets of ten stamps.

(Des Annette le Fort and André Heers. Litho Bagel Security-Print, Mönchengladbach)

2016 (11 Feb). 25th Anniv of 112 European Emergency Number. P 14.
4030   **1927**   45c. bright red and ultramarine .... 3·00   2·75

1928 Ernst Litfaß    **1929** In the Forest

(Des Gregor Schöner. Litho Giesecke & Devrient GmbH, Security Ptg, Leipzig)

2016 (11 Feb). Birth Bicentenary of Ernst Amandus Theodor (Ernst) Litfaß (printer and publisher). P 14.
4031   **1928**   70c. multicoloured .... 4·50   4·25

196

(Des Astrid Grahl and Lutz Menze. Litho Bundesdruckerei GmbH, Berlin)

2016 (11 Feb). Welfare Stamps. *Little Red Riding Hood.* T **1929** and similar vert designs. Multicoloured.

(a) Sheet stamps. Ordinary gum. P 14.

4032	70c. +30c. Type **1929**	6·50	6·25
4033	85c. +40c. 'What big teeth you have'	8·50	8·00
4034	145c. +55c. Huntsman kills wolf	13·00	12·50

(b) Self-adhesive. Die-cut perf 10½.

| 4035 | 70c. +30c. As Type **1929** | 6·50 | 6·25 |
| 4032/4035 | Set of 4 | 25·00 | 24·00 |

No. 4035 was printed both in coils, with the surplus paper around the stamp removed, and in booklets of ten stamps, with the surplus paper retained.

1930 Corvey Abbey

(Des Daniela Haufe and Detlef Fiedler. Litho Bundesdruckerei GmbH, Berlin)

2016 (1 Mar). World Heritage Site. Imperial Abbey of Corvey. P 14.

| 4036 | **1930** | 70c. black and gold | 4·50 | 4·25 |

1931 Greylag Goslings

(Des Nicole Elsenbach and Franc Fienbork. Litho Giesecke & Devrient GmbH, Security Ptg, Leipzig)

2016 (1 Mar). Young Animals. T **1931** and similar horiz design. Multicoloured.

(a) Ordinary gum. P 14.

| 4037 | 70c. Type **1931** | 4·50 | 4·25 |
| 4038 | 70c. Rabbits | 4·50 | 4·25 |

(b) Self-adhesive. Size 36×19 mm. Die-cut perf 10.

4039	70c. As Type **1931**	4·50	4·25
4040	70c. As No. 4038	4·50	4·25
4037/4040	Set of 4	16·00	15·00

Nos. 4039/4040 were printed, each×5, in single-sided booklets of ten stamps.

1932 Sanssouci Schloss    **1933** Dresden Frauenkirche

(Des Nicole Elsenbach. Litho Giesecke & Devrient GmbH, Security Ptg, Leipzig)

2016 (1 Mar). Prussian Schlosses (1st issue). P 13½×14.

| 4041 | **1932** | 85c. multicoloured | 5·50 | 5·25 |

See also No. 4150.

(Des Rudolf Grüttner and Sabine Matthes. Litho Bagel Security-Print, Mönchengladbach)

2016 (1 Mar). 350th Birth Anniv of George Bähr (architect).

(a) Ordinary gum. P 14.

| 4042 | 260c. Type **1933** | 17·00 | 16·00 |

(b) Self-adhesive gum. Die-cut perf 10½.

| 4043 | 260c. As Type **1933** | 17·00 | 16·00 |

No. 4043 was printed in single-sided booklets of ten stamps.

1934 Emblem    **1935** Nelly Sachs

(Des Thomas and Martin Poschauko. Litho Bundesdruckerei GmbH, Berlin)

2016 (7 Apr). 500th Anniv of Beer Purity Law. P 14.

| 4044 | **1934** | 45c. multicoloured | 3·00 | 2·75 |

(Des Daniela Haufe and Detlef Fiedler. Litho Giesecke & Devrient GmbH, Security Ptg, Leipzig)

2016 (7 Apr). 125th Birth Anniv of Nelly Sachs (writer). P 14.

| 4045 | **1935** | 70c. multicoloured | 4·50 | 4·25 |

(Des Stefan Klein and Olaf Neumann. Litho Bundesdruckerei GmbH, Berlin)

2016 (7 Apr). Treasures from German Museums (9th issue). Vert designs showing exhibits from museums. Multicoloured. P 14.

| 4046 | 70c. Emperor Charles V (Titian (Tiziano Vecellio)) | 4·50 | 4·25 |
| 4047 | 145c. Ivory Frigate (Jacob Zeller) | 9·50 | 9·00 |

Type **1936** is vacant.

1937 Mosel

(Des Stefan Klein and Olaf Neumann. Litho Bagel Security-Print, Mönchengladbach)

2016 (7 Apr). Panorama (6th issue). Mosel (1st issue). T **1937** and similar horiz design. Multicoloured. P 14.

4048	90c. Type **1937**	6·00	5·50
	a. Horiz pair. Nos. 4048/4049	12·50	11·50
4049	90c. Mosel (right)	6·00	5·50

Nos. 4048/4049 were printed, *se-tenant*, in horizontal pairs within the sheet, each pair forming a composite design.

(Des Nicole Elsenbach. Litho Giesecke & Devrient GmbH, Security Ptg, Leipzig)

2016 (7 Apr). Prussian Schlosses. Sanssouci Schloss (2nd issue). Size 39×22 mm. Self-adhesive. Die-cut perf 10.

| 4050 | 85c. As Type **1932** | 5·50 | 5·25 |

No. 4050 was printed in single-sided booklets of ten stamps.

1938 Cake

(Des Regina Kehn. Litho Bagel Security-Print, Mönchengladbach)

2016 (2 May). Greeting Stamps. T **1938** and similar horiz designs. Multicoloured.

(a) Ordinary gum. P 14.

4051	70c. Type **1938**	4·50	4·25
4052	70c. Flowers	4·50	4·25
4053	70c. Shoes	4·50	4·25

(b) Self-adhesive. Die-cut perf 10.

4054	70c. As Type **1938**	4·50	4·25
4055	70c. As No. 4052	4·50	4·25
4051/4055	Set of 5	12·00	11·50

Nos. 4054/4055, each×5, were printed, in single-sided booklets of ten stamps.

GERMANY

1939 Roller painting Contaminated Landscape Green
1940 Emblem

(Des Doxia Sergidou. Litho Bagel Security-Print, Mönchengladbach)

2016 (2 May). Europa. Think Green. P 14.
| 4056 | **1939** | 70c. multicoloured | 4·50 | 4·25 |

Post Europ decided that member countries should issue a joint stamp, 'Think Green', to that end a design-a-stamp competition was held which was won by Doxia Sergidou of Cyprus.

(Des Iris Utikal and Michael Gais. Litho Giesecke & Devrient GmbH, Security Ptg, Leipzig)

2016 (2 May). Centenary of Catholic Day in Leipzig. P 14.
| 4057 | **1940** | 70c. multicoloured | 4·50 | 4·25 |

1941 Black Madonna and Pilgrims' Chapel
1942 Football

(Eng Werner Hans Schmidt. Litho Bundesdruckerei GmbH, Berlin)

2016 (2 May). Shrines of Europe – Gnadenkapelle Shrine, Altötting. P 14.
| 4058 | **1941** | 85c. multicoloured | 5·50 | 5·25 |

(Des Stefan Klein and Olaf Neumann. Litho Bagel Security-Print, Mönchengladbach)

2016 (2 May). Panorama. Mosel (2nd issue). Horiz designs as T **1937**. Multicoloured. Self-adhesive. Die-cut perf 10.
| 4059 | | 90c. As Type **1937** | 6·00 | 5·50 |
| 4060 | | 90c. Mosel (right) | 6·00 | 5·50 |

Nos. 4059/60 were printed in horizontal pairs, each pair forming a composite design, in single-sided booklets of ten stamps.

(Des Thomas Serres. Litho Giesecke & Devrient GmbH, Security Ptg, Leipzig)

2016 (2 May). Sports Promotion Fund. Balls. T **1942** and similar square designs. Multicoloured. P 14.
4061		70c. +30c. Type **1942**	6·50	6·25
4062		85c. +40c. Rugby ball	8·25	7·75
4063		145c. +55c. Golf ball	13·00	12·50
4061/4063	Set of 3		25·00	24·00

1943 'Schrammsteine' Rock Formation
1944 Microorganism ('Nachtpfauenauge')

(Des Dieter Ziegenfeuter. Litho Giesecke & Devrient GmbH, Security Ptg, Leipzig)

2016 (2 June). Wild Germany.
(a) Sheet stamps. Ordinary gum. P 14.
| 4064 | | 45c. Type **1943** | 3·00 | 2·75 |

(b) Self-adhesive. Die-cut perf 9½.
| 4065 | | 45c. As Type **1943** | 3·00 | 2·75 |

No. 4065 was printed in single-sided booklets of ten stamps.

(Des Andrea Voß-Acker. Litho Bundesdruckerei GmbH, Berlin)

2016 (2 June). Microworld (2nd issue). T **1944** and similar horiz design. Multicoloured. P 14.
| 4066 | | 70c. Type **1944** | 4·50 | 4·25 |
| 4067 | | 250c. Microorganism ('Strahlentierchen') | 17·00 | 16·00 |

1945 Flags as Figures Embracing
1946 The Alps

(Des Maciej Jedrysik, Stefan Klein and Olaf Neumann. Litho Bagel Security-Print, Mönchengladbach)

2016 (2 June). 25th Anniv of Polish-German Youth Co-operation. P 14.
| 4068 | **1945** | 90c. multicoloured | 6·00 | 5·50 |

(Des Henning Wagenbreth. Litho Bagel Security-Print, Mönchengladbach)

2016 (2 June). Environmental Protection. P 14.
| 4069 | **1946** | 70c. +30c. multicoloured | 6·50 | 6·25 |

(Des Stefan Klein and Olaf Neumann. Litho Bundesdruckerei GmbH, Berlin)

2016 (2 June). Treasures from German Museums (10th issue). Vert design as No. 4047. Multicoloured. Self-adhesive. Die-cut perf 10½.
| 4070 | | 145c. Ivory Frigate (Jacob Zeller) | 9·50 | 9·00 |

No. 4070 was issued in coils of 100, with the surplus paper around the stamps removed.

1947 Staberhuk
1948 Glider in Flight

(Des Johannes Graf. Litho Bagel Security-Print, Mönchengladbach)

2016 (7 July). Lighthouses. T **1947** and similar square design. Multicoloured. P 14.
| 4071 | | 45c. Type **1947** | 3·00 | 2·75 |
| 4072 | | 70c. Kampen | 4·50 | 4·25 |

(Des Henning Wagenbreth. Litho Bundesdruckerei GmbH, Berlin)

2016 (7 July). 125th Anniv of First Glider Flight by Otto Lilienthal. P 14.
| 4073 | **1948** | 145c. multicoloured | 9·50 | 9·00 |

1949 Atlantic Herring

(Des Werner Hans Schmidt. Litho Bundesdruckerei GmbH)

2016 (4 Aug). Youth Stamps. Saltwater Fish. T **1949** and similar horiz designs. Multicoloured. P 14.
4074		70c. +30c. Type **1949**	6·50	6·25
4075		85c. +40c. Atlantic Cod	8·25	7·75
4076		145c. +55c. European Plaice	13·00	12·50
4074/4076	Set of 3		25·00	24·00

1950 Abbey Buildings

(Des Heribert Birnbach. Litho Giesecke & Devrient GmbH, Security Ptg, Leipzig)

2016 (4 Aug). 1200th Anniv of Münsterschwarzach Abbey, Schwarzach am Main, Bavaria. P 13½×14.
| 4077 | **1950** | 70c. multicoloured | 4·50 | 4·25 |

1951 Love Letters  **1952** Rhönschaf Sheep

(Des Christoph Niemann. Litho Giesecke & Devrient GmbH, Security Ptg, Leipzig)

2016 (1 Sept). Stamp Day. Love Letters. P 14.
4078 **1951** 70c. bistre and scarlet-vermilion............ 4·50 4·25

(Des Carsten Wolff. Bagel Security-Print GmbH, Mönchengladbach)

2016 (1 Sept). Old and Endangered Livestock Breeds – Rhönschaf and Deutsches Sattelschwein. Sheet 164×110 mm containing T **1952** and similar horiz design. Multicoloured.
MS4079 70c. Type **1952**; 85c. Deutsches Sattelschwein Pig............ 10·50 10·00

1953 Characters from the Series

(Des Thomas Steinacker. Litho Bundesdruckerei GmbH, Berlin)

2016 (1 Sept). German Television Legends. 50th Anniv of *Raumpatrouille Orion* (television programme). P 13½×14.
4080 **1953** 145c. multicoloured............ 9·50 9·00

1954 Cathedral Building and Schematic  **1955** Detail

(Des Markus Dreßen. Litho Giesecke & Devrient GmbH, Security Ptg, Leipzig)

2016 (6 Oct). St. Peter and Paul Cathedral, Naumburg. P 13½×14.
4081 **1954** 45c. multicoloured............ 3·00 2·75

(Des Daniela Haufe and Detlef Fiedler. Litho Bundesdruckerei GmbH, Berlin)

2016 (6 Oct). 175th Anniv of *Deutschlandlied* (A H Hoffmann von Fallersleben) – German National Anthem. P 14.
4082 **1955** 70c. orange-vermilion and gold............ 4·50 4·25

1956 Electric Transport  **1957** Archangel Gabriel appears to the Shepherds

(Des Bianca Becker and Peter Kohl. Litho Bagel Security-Print, Mönchengladbach)

2016 (6 Oct). Climate Protection. Electric Mobility. P 14.
4083 **1956** 190c. multicoloured............ 12·50 12·00

(Des Stefan Klein und Olaf Neumann. Litho Bundesdruckerei GmbH, Berlin)

2016 (2 Nov). Christmas (1st issue). Welfare Stamps.
(a) *Ordinary gum. P 13½.*
4084 70c. +30c. Type **1957**............ 6·50 6·25
(b) *Self-adhesive gum. Size 36×19 mm. Die-cut perf 10½.*
4085 70c. +30c. Type **1957**............ 6·50 6·25
No. 4085 was printed in single-sided booklets of ten stamps. See also Nos. 4087/4088.

1958 To Beauty

(Des Annette le Fort and André Heers. Litho Bagel Security-Print, Mönchengladbach)

2016 (2 Nov). 125th Anniv of Otto Dix (artist). P 14.
4086 **1958** 85c. multicoloured............ 5·50 5·25

(Des Stefan Klein und Olaf Neumann. Litho Giesecke & Devrient GmbH, Security Ptg, Leipzig)

2016 (30 Nov). Christmas (2nd issue). Horiz designs showing Christmas bauble. Multicoloured.
(a) *Ordinary gum. P 13½.*
4087 70c. Bauble and greetings............ 4·50 4·25
(b) *Self-adhesive gum. Size 36×19 mm. Die-cut perf 10½.*
4088 70c. As No. 4087............ 4·50 4·25
No. 4088 was printed in single-sided booklets of ten stamps. Type **1959** is vacant.

1960 Schlaufenstuhl (chair) (Luigi Colani)  **1961** Die Weser

(Des Sibylle Haase and Fritz Haase. Litho Giesecke & Devrient GmbH, Security Ptg, Leipzig)

2016 (8 Dec). German Design (1st issue). T **1960** and similar vert design. Multicoloured. P 14.
4089 70c. Type **1960**............ 4·50 4·25
4090 145c. Glasgefäße Gruppe (glass vases) (Hans Theo Baumann)............ 9·50 9·00
See also No. 4139.

(Des Lutz Menze and Astrid Grahl. Litho Bagel Security-Print, Mönchengladbach)

2016 (8 Dec)–**17**. Bicentenary of *Die Weser* (German steamship).
(a) *Sheet stamps. Ordinary gum. P 14.*
4091 **1961** 70c. multicoloured............ 4·50 4·25
(b) *Self-adhesive. Size 35×23 mm. Die-cut perf 10.*
4092 70c. As Type **1961** (2.1.17)............ 4·50 4·25
No. 4092 was printed in single-sided booklets of ten stamps.

1962 Topographie des Terrors  **1963** Pfefferfresser, Jungfern- und Haubenkranich

(Des Matthias Beyrow. Litho Giesecke & Devrient GmbH, Security Ptg, Leipzig)

2017 (2 Jan). 25th Anniv of Topography of Terror Foundation – Topographie des Terrors Documentation Centre (memorial and museum). P 14.
4093 **1962** 45c. black............ 3·00 2·75

GERMANY

(Des Stefan Klein and Olaf Neumann. Litho Bundesdruckerei GmbH, Berlin)

2017 (2 Jan). Treasures from German Museums (11th issue). T **1963** and similar multicoloured design. P 14.

(a) Ordinary gum.

4094	70c. Type **1963**..	4·50	4·25
4095	70c. Girl with a Wine Glass (Jan Vermeer van Delft) (vert)..	4·50	4·25

(b) Self-adhesive. Coil Stamps. Die-cut perf 11.

4096	70c. As Type **1963**...	4·50	4·25
4097	70c. As No. 4095 (vert)................................	4·50	4·25
4094/4097	Set of 4...	16·00	15·00

Nos. 4096/7 were issued in coils of 100, with the designs alternating and with the surplus paper around the stamps removed.

No. 4097 was laid at right-angles.

1964 Elbphilharmonie

1965 Detail from Luther's Handwritten Copy, Wittenberg, 1540

(Des Thomas Steinacker. Litho Bagel Security-Print, Mönchengladbach)

2017 (2 Jan–9 Feb). Opening of the Elbphilharmonie.

(a) Sheet stamps. Ordinary gum. P 14.

4098	145c. Type **1964**..	9·50	9·00

(b) Self-adhesive. Size 35×23 mm. Die-cut perf 10.

4099	145c. As Type **1964** (9.2.17)..........................	9·50	9·00

No. 4099 was printed in single-sided booklets of ten stamps.

(Des Peter Krüll. Litho Bundesdruckerei GmbH)

2017 (2 Jan). Martin Luther's Translation of the Bible . P 14.

4100	**1965** 260c. multicoloured..	17·00	16·00

1966 Schloss Ludwigsburg

1967 The Donkey, the Dog, the Cat and the Cock on the Road to Bremen

(Des Nicole Elsenbach. Litho Giesecke & Devrient GmbH, Security Ptg, Leipzig)

2017 (9 Feb). Prussian Schlosses. Schloss Ludwigsburg. P 13½×14.

4101	**1966** 70c. multicoloured..	4·50	4·25

See also no. 4123a.

(Des Astrid Grahl and Lutz Menze. Litho Bundesdruckerei GmbH)

2017 (9 Feb). Welfare Stamps. Die Bremer Stadtmusikanten (Bremen City Musicians). T **1967** and similar square designs. Multicoloured.

(a) Sheet stamps. Ordinary gum. P 14.

4102	70c. +30c. Type **1967**...................................	6·50	6·25
4103	85c. +40c. The animals standing on each other's backs to frighten the robbers.....	8·25	7·75
4104	145c. +55c. The animals in front of their new house...	13·00	12·50

(b) Self-adhesive. Die-cut perf 10½.

4105	70c. +30c. As Type **1967**...............................	6·50	6·25
4102/4105	Set of 4...	25·00	24·00

No. 4105 was printed both in booklets of ten stamps with the surplus paper around the stamp retained and in sheets with the surplus paper removed.

1968 Early City

1969 Knot

(Des Julia Warbanow. Litho Bundesdruckerei GmbH)

2017 (1 Mar). Millennary of Neunburg vorm Wald. P 14.

4106	**1968** 45c. claret and ultramarine......................	3·00	2·75

(Des Annette le Fort and André Heers. Litho Bundesdruckerei GmbH)

2017 (1 Mar). Germany, President of G20. P 14.

4107	**1969** 70c. multicoloured..	4·50	4·25

1970 Ottifant

(Des Thomas Steinacker. Litho Giesecke & Devrient GmbH, Security Ptg, Leipzig)

2017 (1 Mar). Greeting Stamps. The Ottifant (character created by Otto Waalkes).

(a) Ordinary gum. P 14.

4108	**1970** 70c. multicoloured..	4·50	4·25

(b) Self-adhesive. Size 35×23 mm. Die-cut perf 10.

4109	70c. As Type **1970**.......................................	4·50	4·25

No. 4109 was printed in single-sided booklets of ten stamps.

1971 Wild Boar Piglets

(Des Nicole Elsenbach and Franc Fienbork. Litho Giesecke & Devrient GmbH, Security Ptg, Leipzig)

2017 (1 Mar). Young Animals. T **1971** and similar horiz design. Multicoloured.

(a) Ordinary gum. P 14.

4110	85c. Type **1971**..	5·50	5·25
4111	85c. Polecats..	5·50	5·25

(b) Self-adhesive. Size 36×19 mm. Die-cut perf 10.

4112	85c. As Type **1971**.......................................	5·50	5·25
4113	85c. As No. 4111..	5·50	5·25
4110/4113	Set of 4...	20·00	19·00

Nos. 4112/4113 were printed, each×5, in single-sided booklets of ten stamps.

1972 Martin Luther

(Des Antonia Graschberger. Litho Bundesdruckerei GmbH Berlin)

2017 (13 Apr). 500th Anniv of the Reformation. P 14.

4114	**1972** 70c. multicoloured..	4·50	4·25

1973 VW Golf Series 1

(Des Thomas Serres. Litho Bagel Security-Print, Mönchengladbach)

2017 (13 Apr). Classic Cars. T **1973** and similar horiz design. Multicoloured.

(a) Ordinary gum. P 14.
| 4115 | 90c. Type **1973** | 6·00 | 5·50 |
| 4116 | 90c. Opel Manta A | 6·00 | 5·50 |

(b) Self-adhesive. Size 36×19 mm. Die-cut perf 10.
4117	90c. As Type **1973**	6·00	5·50
4118	90c. As No. 4116	6·00	5·50
4115/4118	Set of 4	22·00	20·00

Nos. 4117/4118, each×10, were printed, in single-sided booklets of 20 stamps.

1974 Rammelsberg Mine, Goslar Old Town and Upper Harz Water

(Des Nina Clausing. Litho Giesecke & Devrient GmbH, Security Ptg, Leipzig)

2017 (13 Apr). World Heritage Site. Bergwerk Rammelsberg, Old Town of Goslar, Oberharzer Wasserwirtschaft. P 14.
| 4119 | **1974** | 145c. multicoloured | 9·50 | 9·00 |

1975 Invitation

(Des Regina Kehn. Litho Giesecke & Devrient GmbH, Security Ptg, Leipzig)

2017 (11 May). Greeting Stamps. T **1975** and similar horiz design. Multicoloured.

(a) Ordinary gum. P 14.
| 4120 | 70c. Type **1975** | 4·50 | 4·25 |
| 4121 | 70c. Lily (Mourning Stamp) | 4·50 | 4·25 |

(b) Self-adhesive. Size 35×23 mm. Die-cut perf 10.
| 4122 | 70c. As No. 4121 | 4·50 | 4·25 |
| 4120/4122 | Set of 3 | 12·00 | 11·50 |

No. 4122 was printed in single-sided booklets of ten stamps.

1976 Schloss Wartburg

(Des Nicole Elsenbach. Litho Giesecke & Devrient GmbH, Security Ptg, Leipzig)

2017 (11 May). Europa Castles. Prussian Schlosses. Schloss Wartburg.

(a) Ordinary gum. P 13½×14.
| 4123 | **1976** | 70c. multicoloured | 4·50 | 4·25 |

(b) Self-adhesive. Booklet Stamps. Die-cut perf 11.
4123*a*	70c. As No. 4101	4·50	4·25
4123*b*	70c. As No. 4123	4·50	4·25
4123*a*/4123*b*	Set of 3	12·00	11·50

Nos. 4123*a*/*b*, each×10, were issued in booklets of 20 stamps.

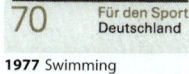

1977 Swimming

1978 Kiel-Holtenau

(Des Wilfried Korfmacher. Litho Bundesdruckerei GmbH)

2017 (11 May). Sports Promotion Fund. 50th Anniv of German Sports Assistance. T **1977** and similar square designs. Multicoloured. P 14.
4124	70c. +30c. Type **1977**	4·50	4·25
4125	85c. +40c. Fencing	5·50	5·25
4126	145c. +55c. Rowing	9·50	9·00
4124/4126	Set of 3	18·00	17·00

Nos. 4124/4126 were each printed in sheets of ten stamps and together, also in sheets of six stamps (Nos. 4124×4, 4125/6) and two stamp-size labels.

(Des Johannes Graf. Litho Bagel Security-Print, Mönchengladbach)

2017 (8 June). Lighthouses. T **1978** and similar square design. Multicoloured. P 14.
| 4127 | 45c. Type **1978** | 3·00 | 2·75 |
| 4128 | 70c. Bremerhaven Unterfeuer | 4·50 | 4·25 |

1979 Heinz Sielmann

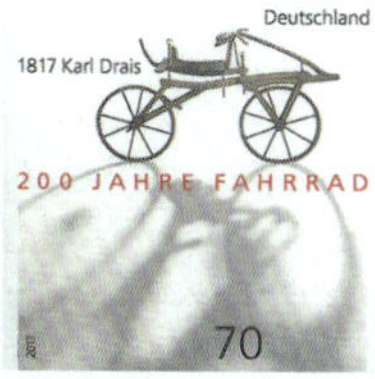

1980 First Bicycle

(Des Thomas Mayfried. Litho Giesecke & Devrient GmbH, Security Ptg, Leipzig)

2017 (8 June). Birth Centenary of Heinz Sielmann (wildlife photographer and conservationist).

(a) Sheet stamps. Ordinary gum. P 14.
| 4129 | **1979** | 45c. multicoloured | 3·00 | 2·75 |

(b) Self-adhesive. Size 36×19 mm. Die-cut perf 10.
| 4130 | 45c. As Type **1979** | 3·00 | 2·75 |

No. 4130 was printed in single-sided booklets of ten stamps.

(Des Rudolf Grüttner and Sabine Matthes. Litho Bagel Security-Print, Mönchengladbach)

2017 (13 July). Bicentenary of Invention of the Bicycle by Karl Drais. P 14.
| 4130*a* | **1980** | 70c. multicoloured | 4·50 | 4·25 |

1981 Human Hair

1982 Seal

(Des Andrea Voß-Acker. Litho Bundesdruckerei GmbH, Berlin)

2017 (13 July). Microworld (3rd issue). T **1981** and similar horiz design. Multicoloured. P 14.
| 4131 | 70c. Type **1981** | 4·50 | 4·25 |
| 4132 | 85c. Vitamin C | 5·50 | 5·25 |

(Des Stefan Klein and Olaf Neumann. Giesecke & Devrient GmbH, Security Ptg, Leipzig)

2017 (13 July). 150th Anniv of North German Confederation. P 14.
| 4133 | **1982** | 320c. multicoloured | 21·00 | 20·00 |

1983 Colour Television and Test Card

(Des Andreas Ahrens. Litho Bundesdruckerei GmbH)

2017 (10 Aug). 50th Anniv of Colour Television in Germany. P 14.
| 4134 | **1983** | 70c. multicoloured | 4·50 | 4·25 |

GERMANY

1984 Characters from *Urmel aus dem Eis*

(Des Anna Berkenbusch and Christian Gralingen. Litho Bagel Security-Print, Mönchengladbach)

2017 (10 Aug). Youth Stamps. Augsburger Puppenkiste Marionette Theatre, Augsburg. T **1984** and similar horiz designs. Multicoloured. P 14.

4135	70c. +30c. Type **1984**	6·50	6·25
4136	85c. +40c. Character from *Kleiner König Kalle Wirsch*	8·25	7·75
4137	145c. +55c. Character from *Kater Mikesch*	13·00	12·50
4135/4137	Set of 3	25·00	24·00

1985 Emblem

(Des Annette Le Fort and André Heers. Litho Bundesdruckerei GmbH, Berlin)

2017 (10 Aug). 400th Anniv of Fruchtbringende Gesellschaft Literary Society. P 14.

4138	**1985**	145c. emerald, gold and black	9·50	9·00

(Des Sibylle Haase and Fritz Haase. Litho Bundesdruckerei GmbH, Berlin)

2017 (10 Aug). German Design (2nd issue). Coil Stamp. Self-adhesive. Die-cut perf 13½.

4139	145c. As No. 4090	9·50	9·00

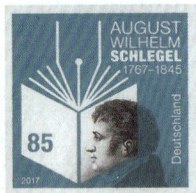

1986 Grapes   **1987** Schegel and Book

(Des Kym Erdmann. Litho Bagel Security Print, Mönchengladbach)

2017 (7 Sept). Wine Growing in Germany. P 14.

4140	**1986**	70c. multicoloured	4·50	4·25

(Des Birgit Hogrefe. Litho Bundesdruckerei GmbH, Berlin)

2017 (7 Sept). 250th Birth Anniv of August Wilhelm Schlegel (writer). P 14.

4141	**1987**	85c. azure and grey-black	5·50	5·25

1988 Fix and Foxi on Skateboards   **1989** Walter Rathenau

(Des Wilfried Korfmacher. Litho Bagel Security-Print, Mönchengladbach)

2017 (7 Sept). Stamp Day. *Fix and Foxi* (comic created by Rolf Kauka). P 14.

4142	**1988**	70c. +30c. multicoloured	6·50	6·25

(Des Jens Müller. Litho Giesecke & Devrient GmbH, Security Ptg, Leipzig)

2017 (7 Sept). 150th Birth Anniv of Walter Rathenau (statesman and Foreign Minister during the Weimar Republic). P 14.

4143	**1989**	250c. multicoloured	17·00	16·00

1990 Badische Weinstrasse

(Des Stefan Klein and Olaf Neumann. Litho Giesecke & Devrient GmbH, Wertpapierdruckerei Leipzig)

2017 (12 Oct). Panorama (7th issue). Badische Weinstrasse. T **1990** and similar horiz design. Multicoloured. P 14.

4144	45c. Type **1990**	3·00	2·75
	a. Horiz pair. Nos. 4143/4144	6·25	5·75
4145	45c. Badische Weinstrasse (right)	3·00	2·75

Nos. 4144/4145 were printed in horizontal pairs, each pair forming a composite design, in single-sided booklets of ten stamps.

1991 Scene from *Das Millionenspiel*   **1992** J. J. Winckelmann and Busts of Aphrodite and Adonis

(Des Thomas Steinacker. Litho Giesecke & Devrient GmbH, Security Ptg, Leipzig)

2017 (12 Oct). German Television Legends. 47th Anniv of *Das Millionenspiel* (television programme). P 14.

4146	**1991**	70c. multicoloured	4·50	4·25

(Des Susanne Stefanizen. Litho Bundesdruckerei GmbH, Berlin)

2017 (12 Oct). 300th Birth Anniv of Johann Joachim Winckelmann (German art historian and archaeologist). P 14.

4147	**1992**	70c. vermilion, turquoise-green and black	4·50	4·25

1993 Script   **1994** Maria Rast Chapel, Krün

(Des Peter Krull. Litho Bundesdruckerei GmbH, Berlin)

2017 (12 Oct). 50th Anniv of Justitia et Pax – German Commission for Justice and Peace. P 14.

4148	**1993**	145c. multicoloured	9·50	9·00

(Des Bettina Walter and Jennifer Dengler. Litho Giesecke & Devrient GmbH, Leipzig)

2017 (2 Nov). Christmas (1st issue). Welfare Stamps.

(a) Ordinary gum. P 14.

4149	**1994**	70c. multicoloured	4·50	4·25

(b) Self-adhesive gum. Size 36×19 mm. Die-cut perf 10.

4150		70c. As Type **1994**	4·50	4·25

No. 4150 was printed in single-sided booklets of ten stamps.

1995 Adoration of the Three Kings (Stefan Lochner)

(Des Heribert Birnbach. Litho Bundesdruckerei GmbH, Berlin)

2017 (2 Nov). Christmas (2nd issue).

(a) Ordinary gum. P 14.
4151	**1995**	70c. +30c. multicoloured............................	6·50	6·25

(b) Self-adhesive gum. Size 30×19 mm. Die-cut perf 10.
4152		70c. +30c. As Type **1995**............................	6·50	6·25

No. 4152 was printed in single-sided booklets of ten stamps.

1996 Mecklenburg Lake District
1997 Theodor Mommsen 

(Des Dieter Ziegenfeuter. Litho Bagel Security-Print, Mönchengladbach)

2017 (2 Nov). Wild Germany. T **1996** and similar horiz design. Multicoloured. P 14.
4153		70c. Type **1996**..............................	4·50	4·25
4154		90c. Reinhard Forest, Hessen..................	6·00	5·50

(Des Julia Warbanow. Litho Giesecke & Devrient GmbH, Leipzig)

2017 (2 Nov). Birth Bicentenary of Christian Matthias Theodor Mommsen (classical scholar, historian, jurist, journalist, politician and archaeologist). P 14.
4155	**1997**	190c. brown and black............................	12·50	12·00

1998 European Space Agency Satellite *Gaia*
1999 Heinrich Böll 

(Des Andrea Voß-Acker. Litho Bagel Security-Print, Mönchengladbach)

2017 (7 Dec). Astrophysics (1st issue). T **1998** and similar horiz design. Multicoloured. P 14.
4156		45c. Type **1998**..............................	3·00	2·75
4157		70c. Gravitational waves.......................	4·50	4·25

See also No. 4160.

(Des Dieter Ziegenfeuter. Litho Giesecke & Devrient GmbH, Security Ptg, Leipzig)

2017 (7 Dec). Birth Centenary of Heinrich Theodor Böll (writer). P 14.
4158	**1999**	70c. multicoloured...........................	4·50	4·25

2000 Stuttgart City Railway (designed by Herbert Lindinger)
2001 Falkenlust, Brühl 

(Des Sibylle Haase and Fritz Haase. Litho Giesecke & Devrient GmbH, Security Ptg, Leipzig)

2017 (7 Dec). German Design (1st issue). P 14.
4159	**2000**	145c. multicoloured...........................	9·50	9·00

See also No. 4172.

(Des Andrea Voß-Acker. Litho Bagel Security-Print, Mönchengladbach)

2018 (2 Jan). Astrophysics (2nd issue). Booklet Stamp. Multicoloured. Self-adhesive. Die-cut perf 10.
4160		70c. Gravitational waves (As No. 4157).........	4·50	4·25

(Des Nicole Elsenbach. Litho Giesecke & Devrient GmbH, Security Ptg, Leipzig)

2018 (2 Jan). Prussian Schlosses. Schloss Falkenlust. P 13½×14.
4161	**2001**	70c. multicoloured...........................	4·50	4·25

2002 Roe Deer
2003 Traditional German Breads 

(Des Nicole Elsenbach and Franc Fienbork. Litho Giesecke & Devrient GmbH, Security Ptg, Leipzig)

2018 (2 Jan). Young Animals. T **2002** and similar horiz design. Multicoloured. P 13½×14.
4162		85c. Type **2002**..............................	5·50	5·25
4163		85c. Harbour Seals............................	5·50	5·25

(Des Carsten Wolff. Litho Bagel Security-Print, Mönchengladbach)

2018 (2 Jan). German Bread Culture. P 14.
4164	**2003**	260c. multicoloured...........................	17·00	16·00

2004 Emblem
2005 Anniversary Emblem 

(Des Andreas Hoch. Litho Bagel Security-Print, Mönchengladbach)

2018 (1 Feb). Bicentenary of Friedrich-Wilhelms University, Bonn. P 14.
4165	**2004**	45c. multicoloured...........................	3·00	2·75

(Des Susann Stefanizen. Litho Giesecke & Devrient GmbH, Security Ptg, Leipzig)

2018 (1 Feb). 25th Anniv of Tafel – German Federation of Food Pantries (charity suppling surplus foods to the needy). P 13½×14.
4166	**2005**	70c. multicoloured...........................	4·50	4·25

2006 Frog Prince

(Des Johannes Graf. Litho Bundesdruckerei GmbH, Berlin)

2018 (1 Feb). Welfare Stamps. *The Frog Prince*. T **2006** and similar square designs. Multicoloured. P 14.

(a) Sheet stamps. Ordinary gum. P 14.
4167		70c. +30c. Type **2006**.........................	6·50	6·25
4168		85c. +40c. Ready to eat.......................	8·25	7·75
4169		145c. +55c. Drunken slumber..................	13·00	12·50
4167/4169	Set of 3...		25·00	24·00

203

GERMANY

(b) Self-adhesive. Die-cut perf 10½.

| 4170 | 70c. +30c. As Type **2006** | 4·50 | 4·25 |

No. 4170 was printed both in booklets of ten stamps with the surplus paper around the stamp retained and in sheets with the surplus paper removed.

(Des Andrea Voß-Acker. Litho Bundesdruckerei GmbH, Berlin)

2018 (1 Feb). Microworld (4th issue). Coil Stamp. Multicoloured. Self-adhesive. Die-cut perf 10.

| 4171 | 85c. Vitamin C (As No. 4132) | 5·50 | 5·25 |

(Des Sibylle Haase and Fritz Haase. Litho Giesecke & Devrient GmbH, Security Ptg, Leipzig)

2018 (1 Feb). German Design (2nd issue). Coil Stamp. Multicoloured. Self-adhesive. Die-cut perf 10.

| 4172 | 145c. Stuttgart City Railway (Herbert Lindinger) (As No. 4159) | 9·50 | 9·00 |

MACHINE LABELS

A

B Sanssouci Palace, Potsdam

1981 (2 Jan). Type **A** with value in black. Multicoloured design showing posthorn. Face values 5pf. to 99m.95 in 5pf. steps (10pf. steps on some machines from 14 April 1992).
Fixed values: 2.1.81 10, 40, 50, 60, 80, 90, 100, 120, 140, 150, 180, 210, 230, 280pf.
1.7.82 10, 20, 50, 60, 70, 80, 100, 110, 120, 130, 190, 250, 280, 300pf.
1.4.89 10, 20, 60, 80, 100, 140, 170, 180, 210, 240, 250, 320, 350pf.
18.2.91 10, 20, 60, 70, 80, 100, 140, 170, 320, 350pf.
15.3.91 10, 20, 40, 60, 80, 100, 140, 170, 180, 210, 240, 250, 320, 350pf.
20.3.91 10, 40, 60, 80, 100, 140, 170, 350pf.
1.4.93 10, 50, 80, 100, 130, 200, 250, 300, 350, 400, 700pf.

The use of various machines and printing methods can be identified by the different type styles of the face value inscription.

1993 (19 May). Type **B** with value in black. Multicoloured design showing Sanssouci Palace, Potsdam. Inscr 'DBP' at top left. Face values 5pf. or 10pf to 99m.95 or 99m.90 in 5 or 10pf. steps.
Fixed values: 19.5.93 10, 50, 80, 100, 130, 200, 250, 300, 350, 400, 700pf.
11.10.93 10, 50, 80, 100, 130, 200, 300, 400pf.
8.12.95 80, 100pf.
1.9.97 10, 40, 100, 110, 130, 220, 300, 440pf.
24.4.98 10, 50, 100, 200, 500pf.
24.4.98 100, 110, 220, 300, 440pf.

The use of various machines and printing methods can be identified by the different type styles of the face value inscription.

1999 (8 Mar). Type **B** with value in black. Multicoloured design showing Sanssouci Palace, Potsdam. With posthorn at top left. Face values 5pf. to 99m.95 in 5pf. steps.
Fixed values: 8.3.99 10, 40, 100, 110, 130, 220, 300, 440pf.

C

1999 (22 Oct). Type **C** with value in black. Multicoloured design showing three posthorns. With posthorn at top left. Face values 5pf. to 99m.95 in 5pf. steps.
Fixed values: 22.10.99 10, 40, 100, 110, 130, 220, 300, 440pf.

D Letter and Letterbox

2002 (4 Apr). Type **D** with value in black. Multicoloured design showing a letter and a letterbox. Face values 1c. to €36.81 in 35 fixed values (2002). Face values 1c. to €36 (from 2003).
Fixed values: 4.4.02 51c., 56c., €1.12, €1.53
1.1.03 45c., 55c., €1, €1.50
1.4.04 45c., 55c., €1, €1.55
1.1.06 45c., 55c., 65c., 70c.

E Brandenburg Gate, Berlin

2008 (24 Oct). Multicoloured designs as Type **E** but face values 1c. to €36.75.
Fixed values: 24.10.08 15c., 65c., 70c., €1.65, €1.70 (as Type **E**)
1.1.01 5c., 20c., 75c., €1.65, €2
1.1.13 3c., 5c., 15c., 20c., €1, €1.65
24.10.08 15c., 65c., 70c., €1.65, €1.70 (Post Tower, Bonn)
1.1.01 5c., 20c., 75c., €1.65, €2
1.1.13 3c., 5c., 15c., 20c., €1, €1.65

Also known with the face value imprint at top with the Euro symbol.

STAMP BOOKLETS

The following checklist covers, in simplified form, booklets issued by the Federal Republic. It is intended that it should be used in conjunction with the main listings and details of stamps and panes listed there are not repeated.

Many booklets exist in more than one version, differing, for example, in the postage rates listed or the advertisements on the cover. Such differences are not covered by this list, prices quoted being for the cheapest version.

Since 1979 booklets have been produced by various organisations containing issues for the Sport Promotion Fund, Humanitarian Relief Fund or Christmas. These were not official issues of the Post Office and are outside the scope of this catalogue.

Prices are for complete booklets

Booklet No.	Date	Contents and Cover Price	Price
SB50	30.10.51	Numeral and Posthorn (T **262**) 2 panes. Nos. 1046at and 1050a (2.50m.)	£1100
SB51	15.1.55	Heuss (T **286**) 3 panes. Nos. 1103a, 1105a and 1109a (2.50m.)	£275
SB52	3.56	Heuss (T **286**) 2 panes. Nos. 1103b and 1103c (1m.)	55·00
SB53	1958–60	Heuss (T **286**) and Numeral (T **306**) 1 pane (1m.)	
		(a) No. 1152bba (26.3.58)	42·00
		(b) No. 1152bca (2.60)	£160
SB54	19.1.60	Heuss (T **354a**) 1 pane. No. 1220×10 (1m.)	£5000
SB55	1.9.60	Heuss (T **286**) 1 pane. No. 1109b×10 (1m.)	15·00
SB56	10.61	Famous Germans. Dürer 1 pane. No. 1264a×10 (1m.)	33·00
SB57	23.7.63	Famous Germans. Albertus Magnus and Luther 2 panes. No. 1261a×10 and No. 1265a×10 (2m.)	42·00
SB58	23.7.63	Famous Germans. Bach 1 pane. No. 1266a×10 (2m.)	33·00
SB59	6.7.65	Albertus Magnus (T **372a**) and Tegel Castle 2 panes. No. 1261a×10 and No. 1360×10 (2m.)	24·00
SB60	2.66	German Architecture. Lorsch 1 pane. No. 1361×10 (2m.)	22·00
SB61	17.2.67	Brandenburg Gate (T **428**) 1 pane. No. 1412b (2m.)	8·50
SB62	8.3.68	Brandenburg Gate (T **428**) 1 pane. No. 1412c (2m.)	6·50
SB63	8.3.68	Brandenburg Gate (T **428**) 1 pane. No. 1413b (1m.)	7·00
SB64	11.71	Accident Prevention 1 pane. No. 1599×4 (1m.)	12·50
SB65	3.72	Accident Prevention 1 pane. No. 1597a (1m.)	
		(a) With posthorn on front cover	8·50
		(b) Without posthorn	5·25
SB66	18.8.72	Olympic Games, Munich 1 pane. No. 1629a (2m.)	12·50

GERMANY

SB67	11.72	Accident Prevention 1 pane. No. 1597b (2m.)	12·50
SB68	8.73	Accident Prevention 1 pane. No. 1596a (2m.)	16·00
SB69	1974	Accident Prevention 1 pane. No. 1597ca (2m.)	25·00
SB70	1.6.77	German Castles 1 pane. No. 1805ab (2m.)	7·75
SB71	1980–81	German Castles 1 pane. No. 1805ac (2m.)	
		(a) Without posthorn on front cover (4.80)	6·00
		(b) With posthorn (4.81)	5·75
SB72	10.80	German Castles 1 pane. No. 1805ad (3m.)	17·00
SB73	6.82	German Castles 1 pane. No. 1805ae (3m.)	10·50
SB74	6.89	Tourist Sights 1 pane. No. 2201ab (3m.)	10·00
SB75	1989–91	Tourist Sights 1 pane. No. 2201ac (5m.)	
		(a) Cover 58×51 mm (6.89)	18·00
		(b) 'City' cover, 110×70 mm (9.7.91)	18·00
SB76	4.90	German Castles. Litho 1 pane. No. 1805bb (2m.)	7·75
SB77	4.6.91	Tourist Sights. Self-adhesive Nos. 2377/2380, each×2 (5m.)	33·00
SB78	1993	Tourist Sights 1 pane. No. 2202ab (2m.)	
		(a) 'CeBIT'93' cover (24.3.93)	11·50
		(b) 'Abgabepreis 2 DM' cover (8.93)	11·50
SB79	1993–95	Tourist Sights 1 pane. No. 2201ad (3m.)	
		(a) Green cover inscr 'Postdienst' (11.93)	10·00
		(b) Pictorial cover inscr 'Deutsche Post AG' (1995)	10·00
SB80	5.5.94	Europa 1 pane. No. 2575×10 (10m.)	21·00
SB81	9.11.94	Tourist Sights 1 pane. No. 2202ac (5m.)	23·00
SB82	5.5.95	Tourist Sights 1 pane. No. 2213ab (10m.)	42·00
SB83	18.7.96	800th Anniv of Heidelberg (T **1149**) 1 pane. No. 2725a (10m.)	18·00
SB84	14.8.96	Tourist Sights 1 pane. No. 2201ae (5m.)	19·00
SB85	14.8.97	Tourist Sights 1 pane. No. 2657ab (11m.)	19·00
SB86	22.1.98	Tourist Sights 1 pane. No. 2656ab (10m.)	18·00
SB87	16.7.98	1100th Anniv of Nördlingen (T **1206**) 1 pane. No. 2828×10 (11m.)	20·00
SB88	14.1.99	1100th Anniv of Weimar (T **1244**) 1 pane. No. 2882×10 (10m.)	20·00
SB89	10.6.99	Tourist Sights 1 pane. No. 2658ab (11m.)	22·00
SB90	13.4.00	EXPO 2000 World's Hanover Fair, (T **1253**) No. 2959×10 (11m.)	£110
SB91	12.5.00	Europa (T **1299**) No. 2963×10 (11m.)	41·00
SB92	28.9.00	Tourist Sights 1 pane. No. 2994ab (11m.)	25·00
SB93	25.5.01	Tourist Sights Nos. 3001/3002, each×2 and No. 3003×8 (11m.)	60·00
SB94	12.7.01	Endangered Species Nos. 3055/6, each×5 (11m.)	29·00
SB95	13.9.01	Natural Heritage (T **1351**) No. 3069×20 (22m.)	90·00
SB95a	7.3.02	Millenary of Bautzen (T **1362**) No. 3086a×10 (€5.60)	75·00
SB96	8.8.02	UNESCO World Heritage (T **3182**) No. 3114×20 (€11.20.)	65·00
SB97	27.12.02	Tourist Sights No. 3165×4 and No. 3166×8 (€6.20)	41·00
SB98	13.2.03	Greetings Stamp (T **1412**) No. 3201×10 (€5.50)	26·00
SB99	12.6.03	Centenary of Oberndorf–Laufen Bridge (T **1428**) No. 3224×20 (€11)	70·00
SB100	7.8.03	German Cities No. 3233×10 (€4.50)	24·00
SB101	8.1.04	50th Anniv of Deutscher Musikrat (T **1431**) No. 3227a×10 (€14.40)	60·00
SB102	12.8.04	Greetings Stamps Nos. 3201 and 3286, each×5 (€5.40)	29·00
SB103	12.8.04	*Bremen*–1929 Winner of Blue Ribbon (T **1468**) No. 3283×20 (€11)	47·00
SB104	10.2.05	150th Anniv of Berlin Cathedral (T **1489**) 1 pane. No. 3343×10 (€9.50)	55·00
SB105	7.7.05	Lighthouses. Self-adhesive Nos. 3366a/3367, each×5 (€4.50)	24·00
SB106	3.11.05	Prussian Schlosses. New Palace, Sanssouci. (T **1507**) Self-adhesive No. 3386×10 (€22)	£120
SB107	1.12.05	Butterflies and Moths. Self-adhesive No. 3391×10 (€8)	44·00
SB108	2.1.06	Flowers. Self-adhesive No. Y3373×10 (€9)	41·00
SB109	2.1.06	650th Anniv of Charles IV's Golden Bull. (T **1526**) Self-adhesive No. 3397×10 (€9)	85·00
SB110	4.5.06	Upper Central Rhine Valley (Oberes Mittelrheintal). (T **1538**) Self-adhesive No. 3415×10 (€5.50)	29·00
SB111	5.10.06	Welfare. Trains. Self-adhesive No. 3441×10 (€8)	55·00
SB112	9.10.06	Seasons. Self-adhesive Nos. 3449/3452, each×5 (€11)	60·00
SB113	2.1.07	Furth Millenary. (T **1560**) Self-adhesive No. 3455×10 (€4.50)	24·00
SB114	3.3.07	50th Anniv of Federal Republic of Saarland. (T **1563**) Self-adhesive No. 3459×10 (€5.50)	26·00
SB115	3.5.07	175th Anniv of Hambacher Fest (T **1579**) Self-adhesive No. 3482×10 (€14.50)	75·00
SB116	27.12.07	275th Birth Anniv of Carl Gotthard Langhans. (T **1596**) Self-adhesive No. 3505×10 (€5.50)	34·00
SB117	27.12.07	Welfare. Horse. Self-adhesive No. 3510×10 (€8)	46·00
SB118	2.1.08	World Heritage Site. (T **1598**) Self-adhesive No. 3512×10 (€4.50)	24·00
SB119	13.3.08	50th Anniv of Bundeskartellamt. (T **1600**) Self-adhesive No. 3528×10 (€9)	55·00
SB120	8.5.08	Greetings Stamps. Self-adhesive Nos. 3538/3541 each×5 (€11)	65·00
SB122	12.6.08	Welfare. Aircraft. Self-adhesive No. 3546×10 (€8)	55·00
SB123	3.7.08	Lighthouses. Self-adhesive Nos. 3551/3552 each×5 (€5.50)	29·00
SB124	1.11.08	Winter. Self-adhesive Nos. 3566/3567 each×5 (€5.50)	31·00
SB124a	2.1.09	Frankenberg Hall. (T **1639**) Self-adhesive No. 3574×10 (€4.50)	26·00
SB125	2.1.09	Welfare. Celestial Phenomena. Self-adhesive No. 3580×10 (€8)	46·00
SB125a	2.1.09	Flowers. Self-adhesive No. Y3370×5 (€3.25)	29·00
SB125b	2.1.09	Flowers. Self-adhesive No. Y3371×5 (€3.50)	31·00
SB126	9.4.09	Sports Promotion Fund No. 3591a (€5.80)	41·00
SB127	4.6.09	Bimillennary of Varus Battle (T **1657**) Self-adhesive No. 3603×20 (€11)	75·00
SB128	2.7.09	600th Anniv of Leipzig University (T **1661**) Self-adhesive No. 3609×10 (€5.50)	39·00
SB128a	2.1.10	Bicentenary of Natural History Museum, Berlin (T **1678**) Self-adhesive No. 3631×10 (€4.50)	31·00
SB129	2.1.10	Welfare Fund. Self-adhesive Fruit No. 3636×10 (€8)	60·00
SB130	2.1.10	St Michael's Church Millennary (T **1682**) Self-adhesive No. 3641×10 (€22)	£150
SB131	1.7.10	Illustrations of Songs by Udo Lindenburg. (T **1696**) Self-adhesive No. 3665×10 (€4.50)	26·00
SB132	1.7.10	Illustrations of Songs by Udo Lindenburg. Self-adhesive No. 3666×10 (€5.50)	31·00
SB132a	12.8.10	Porcelain Production (T **1697**) Self-adhesive No. 3676×20 (€11)	65·00
SB133	12.11.10	Post. Greetings (3rd issue). Self-adhesive Nos. 3686a/3686b, each×5 (€5.50)	31·00
SB134	31.1.11	Welfare Stamps Self-adhesive No. 3699×10 (€8)	49·00
SB135	31.2.11	World Heritage Sites Self-adhesive No. 3703a×10 (€7.50)	44·00
SB136	31.2.11	Weratal (T **1722**) Self-adhesive No. 3704a×10 (€9)	60·00
SB137	1.3.11	Flowers. *Conuallaria majalis* Self-adhesive No. Y3364×10 (€4.50)	22·00

205

GERMANY

SB138	7.4.11	Sports Promotion Fund 1 pane Nos. 3711/12, each×4 (€5.80)..	40·00
SB139	7.4.11	National Parks (T **1719**) Self-adhesive No. 3715×10 (€14.50)...	85·00
SB140	9.6.11	175th Anniv of Saxon Steamship Company. (T **1733**) Self-adhesive No. 3724a×10 (€22)...	£140
SB141	1.7.11	Lighthouses Self-adhesive. Nos. 3724b/3724c, each×5 (€4.50)......	26·00
SB142	2.1.12	National Parks. (T **1751**) Self-adhesive No. 3749×10 (€5.50)...	36·00
SB143	2.1.12	Welfare Stamps. Jewels (T **1753**) Self-adhesive No. 3754×10 (€8)...	55·00
SB144	9.2.12	Harz Narrow-gauge Railways (T **1756**) Self-adhesive No. 3758×10 (€4.50)...	29·00
SB145	9.2.12	Recolonisation of Native Fauna. Lynx (T **1756**) Self-adhesive Nos. 3762/3, each×5 (€5.50)...	36·00
SB146	9.2.12	Matthäus Daniel Pöppelmann (T **1755**) Self-adhesive No. 3765×10 (€14.50)...	95·00
SB147	1.3.12	Post. Spring (T **1760**) Self-adhesive No. 3767×10 (€5.50)...	36·00
SB148	12.4.12	225th Birth Anniv of Joseph von Fraunhofer (T **1754**) Self-adhesive No. 3776×10 (€5.50)...	60·00
SB149	2.5.12	German Football Enthusiasm (T **1767**) Self-adhesive No. 3778×10 (€5.50)...	36·00
SB149a	2.11.12	Supplementary Stamp (T **1794**) Self-adhesive No. 3808a×20 (60c.)...	21·00
SB150	2.11.12	500th Anniv of Sistine Madonna (T **1797**) Self-adhesive No. 3811×10 (€5.50)...	39·00
SB151	2.11.12	Christmas. Welfare Stamp (T **1798**) Self-adhesive No. 3813×10 (€8)...	60·00
SB152	2.1.13	Prussian Schlosses Self-adhesive No. 3816a×10 (€5.80)...	41·00
SB153	2.1.13	German Painting (T **1803**) Self-adhesive No. 3821×10 (€24)...	£170
SB154	7.2.13	Panorama Self-adhesive. Nos. 3824/5, each×10 (€11.60)...	85·00
SB155	7.2.13	Welfare Stamps. Flowering Trees (T **1805**) Self-adhesive No. 3829×10 (€8.50)...	60·00
SB156	7.2.13	82nd Birth Anniv of Janosch (T **1807**) Self-adhesive No. 3833×10 (€4.50)...	31·00
SB157	7.12.13	82nd Birth Anniv of Janosch Self-adhesive. No. 3834×10 (€5.80)...	41·00
SB158	4.4.13	50th Anniv of Fehmarn Bridge (T **1813**) Self-adhesive No. 3842×10 (€7.50)...	55·00
SB159	2.5.13	Centenary of Möhnetalsperre Dam (T **1814**) Self-adhesive No. 3851×10 (€9)...	65·00
SB160	1.7.13	Paintings by Gerhard Richter (T **1826**) Self-adhesive No. 3863×10 (€14.50)...	£100
SB161	10.10.13	Flowers. *Dicentra spectabilis* Self-adhesive No. Y3374×10 (€10)...	46·00
SB162	2.11.13	Christmas (T **1838**) (1st issue) Self-adhesive No. 3879×10 (€5.80)...	41·00
SB163	2.11.13	Christmas (T **1839**) (2nd issue). Welfare Self-adhesive No. 3881×10 (€8.50)...	60·00
SB164	2.1.14	Young Animals Self-adhesive Nos. 3891/2, each×5 (€6)...	41·00
SB165	6.2.14	Welfare. *Hansel and Gretel* (T **1849**) Self-adhesive No. 3900×10 (€9, €11.60)...	65·00
SB166	1.3.14	Cartoons by Peter Gaymann Self-adhesive. No. 3903×10 (€6)...	41·00
SB167	3.4.14	Panorama Self-adhesive. Nos. 3908/9, each×5 (€4.50)...	41·00
SB168	8.5.14	Wild Germany Self-adhesive. Nos. 3916/17, each×5 (€6)...	41·00

No. SB169 is vacant.

SB170	1.9.14	70th Death Anniv of A. Saint-Exupery Self-adhesive No. 3938×10 (€6)...	41·00
SB171	3.11.14	Christmas (1st issue). (T **1879**) Self-adhesive Nos. 3945×10 (€6)...	41·00
SB172	3.11.14	Christmas (2nd issue). Self-adhesive Nos. 3947×10 (€9)...	65·00
SB173	4.12.14	Flowers. Peony. Self-adhesive No. Y3325×10 (€6.20)...	31·00
SB174	2.1.15	Young Animals. Self-adhesive Nos. 3953/3954, each×5 (€6.20)...	50·00
SB175	2.1.15	Prussian Schlosses. Self-adhesive No. 3958×10 (€8)...	60·00
SB176	2.1.15	Wild Germany. Self-adhesive No. 3960×10 (€8.50)...	60·00
SB177	5.2.15	Welfare Stamps. *Sleeping Beauty*. Self-adhesive No. 3965×10 (€9.20)...	70·00
SB178	2.3.15	Felix the Rabbit. Self-adhesive No. 3968×10 (€6.20)...	44·00
SB179	2.4.15	Classic Cars. Self-adhesive Nos. 3976/3977, each×5 (€14.50)...	£110
SB180	7.5.16	350th Anniv of Christian-Albrechts (University of Kiel) Self-adhesive No. 3978×10 (€6.20)...	44·00
SB181	11.6.15	Treasures for German Museums. Self-adhesive No. 3990×10 (€24)...	£170
SB182	1.7.15	Panorama. Self-adhesive No. 3993/3994, each×5 (€4.50)...	31·00
SB183	7.8.15	Youth Stamps. Freshwater Fish 1 pane. Nos. 3999×5, and 4001 (€4.55)...	47·00
SB184	1.9.15	Asterix, Self-adhesive Nos. 4002/4003, each×5 (€6.20)...	44·00
SB185	2.11.15	Christmas (1st issue). Self-adhesive No. 4011×10 (€6.20)...	44·00
SB186	2.11.15	Christmas (2nd issue). Self-adhesive No. 4013×10 (€9.20)...	70·00
SB187	3.12.15	Numeral. Self-adhesive No. 4015a×20 (€1.60)...	21·00
SB188	3.12.15	Bicentenary of University. Self-adhesive No. 4021×10 (€7)...	46·00
SB189	2.1.16	Classic Cars. Self-adhesive Nos. 4025/4026, each×10 (€29)...	95·00
SB190	2.1.16	125th Anniv of Schwetzingen. Self-adhesive No. 4029a×10 (€14.50)...	£100
SB191	11.2.16	Welfare Stamps. Little Red Riding Hood. Self-adhesive No. 4035×10 (€10)...	70·00
SB192	1.3.16	Young Animals. Self-adhesive Nos. 4039/4040, each×5 (€7)...	46·00
SB193	1.3.16	300th Birth Anniv of George Bähr No. 4043×10 (€26)...	£180
SB194	7.4.16	Prussian Schlosses. Self-adhesive No. 4050×10 (€8.50)...	60·00
SB195	2.5.16	Greetings. Self-adhesive Nos. 4054/4055, each×5 (€7)...	46·00
SB196	2.5.16	Panorama. Self-adhesive Nos. 4059/4060, each×5 (€9)...	65·00
SB197	2.6.16	Wild Germany. Self-adhesive No. 4065×10 (€4.50)...	31·00
SB198	2.11.16	Christmas (1st issue) No. 4085×10 (€11)...	70·00
SB199	30.11.16	Christmas (2nd issue) No. 4088×10 (€7)...	46·00
SB200	8.12.16	Bicentenary of Die Weser. Self-adhesive No. 4092×10 (€7)...	46·00
SB201	9.2.17	Opening of the Elbphilharmonie. Self-adhesive No. 4099×10 (€14.50)...	£100
SB202	9.2.17	Welfare Stamps. Die Bremer Stadtmusikanten Self-adhesive No. 4105×10 (€10)...	70·00
SB203	1.3.17	Greetings. Self-adhesive No. 4109×10 (€7)...	46·00
SB204	1.3.17	Young Animals. Self-adhesive Nos. 4112/4113, each×5 (€8.50)...	60·00
SB205	13.4.17	Classic Cars. Self-adhesive Nos. 4117/4118, each×10 (€36)...	£130
SB206	13.4.17	Greetings. Self-adhesive No. 4122×10 (€7)...	46·00
SB207	11.5.17	Europa Castles. Prussian Schlosses. Schloss Wartburg. Self-adhesive Nos. 4123a/b, each×10 (€14)...	95·00
SB208	8.6.17	Birth Centenary of Heinz Sielman No. 4130×10 (€4.50)...	31·00
SB209	10.8.17	500th Anniv of Reformation. Self-adhesive No. 4114 and 4123, each×4 (€5.60)...	37·00
SB210	2.11.17	Christmas (1st issue) No. 4150×10 (€7)...	46·00
SB211	2.11.17	Christmas (2nd issue) No. 4152×10 (€10)...	70·00
SB212	2.1.18	Astrophysics (2nd issue) No. 4160×10 (€7)...	46·00
SB213	1.2.18	Welfare Stamps. *The Frog Prince*. Self-adhesive No. 4170×10 (€10)...	46·00

DESIGN INDEX

I. Issues from 1945

This index covers all post-war issues for Allied Occupation areas (Nos. 899/956 and numbers prefixed A, F or R), West Berlin (numbers prefixed B) and German Federal Republic (No. 1033 onwards). It also includes those issues of East Germany (numbers prefixed E) inscribed 'DEUTSCHE POST'.

Where the same design, or subject, appears more than once in a set only the first number is given. Scenes and buildings are listed under the town or geographical area in which they are situated, except for the Berlin Building issues which are given separate entries. Portraits are listed under surnames only; those without surnames (e.g. rulers and some saints) are under forenames. Works of art and inventions are indexed under the artist's, or inventor's, name, where this appears on the stamp. In cases of difficulty part of the inscription has been used to identify the stamp.

This index should be used in conjunction with the Notes on Inscriptions on page 22.

112 ... 4030
2 ... 3883
20 ... 3622
3 ... 3808
50 JAHRE BUNDESWEHR ... 3384
8 ... 4015

A

Aachen ... 1681
Aachen Cathedral ... 2938
Abbe-Zeiss ... 1453
Able-bodied and Disabled Figures ... 3911
Accident ... 1088, 1596, B396
Accordion ... 3048
ADAC ... 3219
Adenauer ... **MS**1459, 1469, 1769, 2447, 3353
Adenauer and De Gaulle ... 2228
Adoration of the Magi ... 2260, 2748, 3625, B797, B836
Adoration of the Shepherd's (painting) ... 4014
Adoration of the Three King's (painting) ... 4151
Adorno ... 3236
Adveniat (Christmas charitable campaign) ... 1450, 2148, 3743
Advertisement pillars ... 3341
Aerobics ... 2757
Agriculture ... RB16, RC13, 1215
Ahrensburg ... 1812*c*, B524*c*
Aircraft ... 1482, 1771, 1857, 1886, 1918, 1959, 2241, 2357, 3347, 3542, 3565, B57, B225, B548, B567, B589
Airmail envelope ... 3801
Airport ... 1754*a*, B490*a*
Akademie der Künste ... 2720
Aktion Mensch ... 3911
Al-Kohol ... 1999
Albers, H. ... 2413
Albers, J. ... 2015, 2519
Albrechtsburg ... 3904
Allers ... B321
Alpen ... 2585
Alphabet ... 2025
Alpine Ski World Championship ... 3690
Alsfeld ... 1756
Altdorfer ... 1945
Alte Pinakothek Museum ... 3741
Altötting ... 2213, 2385, B787
AM Post ... A1
American Chamber of Commerce ... B546
Ammonite ... 2288
Amnesty International ... 1710, 3722
Andersen ... 3350
Andres ... 3422
Angel ... 1563, 2294, 2333, 2427, 3375, B378, B835
Angel and shepherds ... B608, B816
Animal Protection ... 3792
Animals ... 1206, 1416, 1434, 1454, 1613, 1984, 2303, **MS**2684, 3417, B285, B293, B310, **MS**B332, B414
Animated Films ... 3695
Anneke ... 2165, B744
Anniversary Emblem ... 3734, 3807
Annunciation ... 2934
Antarctic ... 1981
Apartment Names ... 3790
Apotheker ... 2340
Apple ... 3632, 4166
Aquaduct ... 3348
Aquarium ... 3735
Archaeology ... 1789, 1834, 1865, 3133, 3335, 3563
Archery ... 1626, 1992, B572, B574
Architecture ... **MS**2762, 3683, 3709, 3783, 3814
Archive Congress ... 2070
Arend ... 2162, 3444, B742
Armorial Lions ... 3103
Arms ... F1, FB42, FR42, FW40, RA1, RC1, RD27, R23, 1138, 1175, 1181, **MS**1703, 1832, 2277, 2372, B126, B147, B170, B573
Arms of Länder ... 2448, 2465, 2470, 2474, 2479, 2506, 2526, 2534, 2539, 2556, 2567, 2580, 2584, 2597
Arndt ... 1511
Arngast Lighthouse ... 3726
Arnim, A. von ... B609
Arnim, B. von ... B692
Arnold ... 3042
Arnstadt ... 3259
Arnweiler ... FR6, FR25, FR33
Arrows ... 1472, 2140, 3141
Art ... 3305, 3411, 3623, 3648
Artists ... 3202
Asam, C. D. ... 2274
Asam, E. G. ... 2471
Aschaffenburg ... 1181
Asterix (cartoon) ... 4002
Astronomy ... 3596, 3729
Astrophysics ... 4156, 4160
Athletes ... 3037
Athletes skiing ... 3759
Athletics ... 2056, 2120, B636, B678
Atlantic Cod ... 4075
Atlantic Herring ... 4074
'Aufbruch nach Europa' ... 2636
Augsburg ... 1588, 2077, 2082, 2690
Augustusburg Castle ... 2765
Aussätzigen-Hilfswerk ... 2000
Aussem ... 2152, B734
Ausstellungshallen ... B36*c*, B118
Automobilclub ... 2895
Automobiles ... *see* Motor cars
Autumn ... 3443, 3800
Aviators ... 3215
AVUS ... **MS**B395

B

Bach ... 1043, 1266, 2097, 2976, B199, B393
Bad Frankenhausen ... 2836
Bad Hersfeld ... 2117
Bad Meinberg ... 2219, B791
Bad Reichenhall ... 1502
Bad Tolz Leonhardifahrt (festival) ... 3379
Baden ... F4, FB42
Baden-Württemberg ... 1138, 1823, 2437, 2838, 3103
Badge ... 3840
Badger ... 3627
Badische Weinstrasse ... 4144
Baeck ... 1197
Bahr ... 4042
Baker ... 2125
Ballin ... 1185
Balloons ... 1856, 2486, B547
Balls ... 4061
Bamberg ... 1860, 2736
Bamberg Diocese ... 3457
Banknotes ... 3490
Barbarossa ... 1823
Barcelona ... 2186
Barlach ... B629, B811
Barrel-organ ... B849
Barth ... 2130
Basic Law ... **MS**2095
Basketball ... 1775, 2347, 3039, B694, B843
Bats ... 2933
Battle ... 2371
Bauernhaus ... 2678
Bauhaus ... 2014, 3264
Baumeister ... 2261
Bäumer ... 1686
Bausch ... 3996
Bautzen ... 3086
Bavaria ... 2448, 2839
Bavaria (statue) ... 2209, 2381, B783
Bavarian Forest ... 2806, 3349
Bavarian Mountain Costume Association ... 3987
Bavarian stamp ... 1501
Bayern *see* Bavaria
Bayreuth Opera House ... 2845
Bayreuther Festpiele ... 1788
Beach ... 3779
Bear (Berlin Emblem) ... RA1, R23, B68, B126, B147, B212, B226, B798
Bear and child ... 3677
Bebel ... R36, 2250
Bebenhausen ... FW6, FW19, FW29
Beck ... 1343*b*
Beckman ... 1692, 3202
Bee ... 3657
'Beendigung des Zweiten Weltkrieges' ... **MS**2634
Beer Purity Law ... 4044
Beethoven ... FR1, FR16, FR32, **MS**1233*a*, 1272, 1516, B87, B205
Beetles ... 2511
'Befreiung der Gefangenen...' ... **MS**2633
Begas ... B619
'Behinderte eingliedern' ... 1695
Behring ... 1123
Beinhorn ... 3673
Bell ... B75, B82, B101, B115, B151
Bellevue Castle ... B218, 3478
Belvedere ... B562
Benedict of Nursia ... 1933
Benediktinerabteien ... 2510
Bengel ... 2191
Benn ... B722
Benz ... 1278
Bergengruen ... 2477
Berghauser Castle ... 3425
Bergkristallreliquiar ... 2252
Bergwerk Rammelsberg ... 4119
Berlichingen ... 1916
Berlin ... RA1, R23, 2170, 2220d, 2465, 2472, 2501, 2651, 2657, 2840, 3226, B213, B760
Berlin (ship) ... B123
Berlin Cathedral ... 3342
Berlin Film Festival ... 2943
'Berlin Kulturstadt Europas' ... B798
Berlin subway ... 3098
Berliner Börse ... B701
Berliner Festwochen ... B373
Berliner Feuerwehr ... B507
Berliner Luftbrücke ... 2903
Berliner Zoo ... **MS**2577
Bernward, St., and St. Godehard ... 1250
Berries ... B585
Bessel ... 2067
Bethel ... 2415
Betzingen ... 2602
Beuth ... B627
Beuys ... 2518
Biathlon Championship ... 3759
'Bibelanstalt' ... 1296
Bible ... 3197, 4100
Bible text ... 4100
Bicycles ... *see* Cycles
Big Top ... 2270
Bingen ... 1899, 2842
Bird and flowers ... 2108, B706
Bird on hand ... 1966
Birds ... 1194, 1315, 1384, 2134, 2251, 2390, 2870, 3529, B261
Birds and Cliffs ... **MS**3653
Birth of Christ ... 3028
Bismarck ... 1388
Black Forest ... FB12, FB37
Black Forest Costume ... FB20, FB32
Blacksmiths ... B122
Blast furnace ... 1752, B489
Blaubeuren ... 2552
Blind School, Berlin ... 3405
Blood Donor ... 1687
Blücher ... 2490
Blue Horse (painting) ... 3764
Blue ribbon ... 3865
Blue Rider Group ... 3764
Blue Wonder Bridge ... 2956
Bluetit ... 3868
Blurred script ... 3535
Boats ... B467
Bobsleigh ... 2121, **MS**2344
Bochum-Stiepel Village Church ... 3521
Bockler ... 1722, B192
Bodelschwingh ... 1070, 1442, 1833, 2694
Boehm ... 2155*a*
Boll ... 4158
Bolz ... 3445
Bonhoeffer ... 1343*c*, 2628
Boniface, St. ... 1125
Bonn ... 1338, 1867, **MS**2136, 2262, 2419
Bonn–Copenhagen Declaration ... 2087
Book ... 2924
Book (open) ... 1634, 1932
Book Titles ... 3810
Bookbinder ... 2182
Bora ... 2884
Borchert ... 2716
Borges ... 3675
Borkum Lighthouse ... 3788
Born and Franck ... 2001
Borsig ... B122
Borussia Dortmund ... 2692
Böse Friederich ... 2570
Botanical Gardens ... B577
'Böttcher' ... B765
Böttger ... 1982
Bouquet ... B457
Bourse ... B144
Bowl ... 1790
Bowling ... 2088
Boxing ... 2620, 2944
Boy selling copperplate prints ... 1783
Bracelet ... 2195
Brahms ... 2027
Braille ... 3405
Brain ... 3988
Brandenburg ... 2470, 2841
Brandenburg Arms ... 2805

GERMANY / Design Index

Brandenburg Concertos ... B393
Brandenburg Gate ... A86, A106, 1412, 2331, 2341, B35, B111, B133, B184, B281, B300, E3042, 3504
Brandström ... 1071
Brandt ... 2549, 3876
Brauenlage ... 1749*a*, B487*a*
Braunkohlen-Förderbagger ... 1748, B486
Braunschweig ... 2624
Breaking Chains ... B110
Brecht ... 2834
Brehm ... B684
Breitscheid ... RB13
Bremen ... 1339, 1682, 2205, 2474, 2661, 2897
Bremen (ship) ... 1821, 3282
Bremen Bishopric ... 2193
Bremen City Musicians ... 4102
'Bremer Stadtmusikanten' ... 1984
Brentano ... 1869
Bricklayer ... 934, A42, R7, 2123, B7, B30
Bridge ... 2060, 2187, 3223, RF13, B219, 3561
Broadcasting ... 1679, 2406, **MS**B442
Broadcasting Exhibition ... B392, B621
Bronzekultwagen ... 1789
Brooch ... 2197
Brooklyn Bridge ... 3423
BROT für die Welt ... 1303, 1645
Brown Trout ... 3949
Bruckner ... 2739
Bruno House ... 3984
Brunsbüttel Lighthouse ... 3365
Brunswick ... 2200
Buber ... 1854
Bucer ... 3035
Bucerius ... 3416
Buchholz ... 2339
Buchner ... 3874
Bückeburg ... 2598
Buckle ... 2196
Büdingen ... 2416
Bugle ... B560
Building Exhibition ... B156
Building Façade ... 3573, 3969
Buildings ... 3259, 3497, 4077
Buk Lighthouse ... 3924
Bullfinch ... 3867
Bund Deutscher Amateurtheater ... 2473
Bund Deutscher Frauenvereine ... 2564
Bund Deutscher Philatelisten ... 2733
'Bund Länder Gemeinden' ... 2044
Bundesbank ... 3490
Bundesdruckerei ... B573
Bundesgartenschau ... 1817, B696
Bundesgerichtshof ... 2895
Bundesgrenzschutz ... 3044
Bundeshaus (Berlin) ... B841
Bundeskartellamt ... 3514, 3528
Bundesrat ... B147
Bundestag ... 1033, B126, B170
'Bundesverfassungs Gericht' ... 1772
Bundeswehr ... 2114
'Bürgerliches Gesetzbuch' ... 2734
Burning building ... 2257
Bürresheim ... 1812, B524
Busch ... 1200, 1993, **MS**3484
Buses ... B434
Butcher ... 2181
Butterflies and Moths ... 1290, 2052, 2361, 2449, 3387, B675
Butterfly, fish and plant ... 1951
Buxtehude (town) ... 1231
Buxtehude, D. ... 2190

C

Cake ... 4051
Calvin ... 1344, 3610
Camellia ... 3285
Camera ... 1748a, B486a, B704
Camouflaged People ... 3856
Cancellations ... 2045
Canoeing ... 1891, 2089, 2618, B680
Canzow Bell Tower ... 3065
Cap Polonio (ship) ... B529
Capital ... 2099
Car ... 3590, 4115
Car number plates ... 3424
Card game ... 3872
CARE ... 2688
'Caritas Verband' ... 2824
Carol singers ... 2046
Carpenter ... B719
Cars ... *see* Motor Cars
Carstens ... **MS**2010
'Cartellverband der Katholischen Deutschen Studentenverbindungen' ... 2131
Cartoons ... 3901
Castle ... 3682
Castle Hubertusburg ... 3830
Castles ... 1805, B519
Cathedral ... 3515, 3822, 4081
Catholic Congress ... 1244
Catholic Day ... 4057
Catholic Synod ... 1646
Catholic World Mission ... 1556
Catholics' Day ... 1165, 1295, 1349, 1420, 1470, 1557, 1868, B175
Cats ... 3272
Celebration ... 3620
Celebrations ... 3680
Celle ... 2203, B780
Cellist ... 3835
Centaur Head ... 1836
Ceramics ... 1982
Chamisso ... B610
Chaplin ... 3077
Chariot ... 1789
Charlemagne ... FR15, FR29, 2253
Charlottenburg ... 1810d, B42, B142, B522*c*, B646, B723, **MS**B761
Charta der Deutschen Chemical Fibre Research ... 1573
Chemical plant ... 1749, B487
Chemiefaserforschung ... 1573
Chickens ... 3373
Chicks ... 4037
Chiemsee Lake, Bavaria ... 3991
Child Protection ... 2869
Child with present ... 4010
Child's drawing ... 3571, 3799
Children ... 3989
Children building house ... 2287
Children of different races ... **MS**2321
Children on horse ... 3560
Children's books ... 3656
Children's cartoons ... 2851, 2907, 3057
Children's Church Services ... 3107
Children's villages ... 2913
Choir ... B807, **MS**3199
Christ (statues) ... 1420, B175, B302
Christmas ... 3139, 3245, 3299, 3380, 3446, 3500, 3568, 3625, 3687, 3743, 3812, 3878, 3880, 3944, 3946, 4010, 4012, 4149, 4151
Church ... 3287, 3737, 4012
Churchill ... **MS**1459
Circus ... 2267, 2446, 3111, B819
City Hall ... 3304
Civil code ... **MS**2634
Civil ruins ... 2734
Clarinet ... 3914
Claudius ... 1383, 2322
Clausewitz ... 1979
Clemenswerth Castle ... 2174
Cleopatra VII ... B670
Cliffs and Sea ... 3748
Climate Protection ... 3395
Climate zones ... 3293
Clocks ... 2101, 2480, 3142
Clouds ... 3252, 3395, 3885
Clown ... 2269, **MS**2538, 3111
Coach and horses ... B832
Coal mining ... 1189
Coastline ... 2850, 3132
Coburger Convent ... 2521
Cochem ... 1558
Cockerel ... B390
Cogwheel ... 1438, B149
Coin ... 1209, 2857
Coins ... 3490
Cologne ... A70, A76, 1165, 1180, 1937, 2243
Cologne Carnival ... 1643, 2755
Cologne Cathedral ... 3002, 3209
Colour spectrum ... 2176, 3755
Colour television ... 4134
Comenius ... 1565
Communications Museum ... 3131
Community Service ... 3547
Concord (ship) ... 2030
Cones ... 1908, B582
Conference ... 3927
'Confessio Augustana' ... 1929
Conservation ... 3912
Constance ... FB46
Contemporary design ... **MS**2780, **MS**2865, **MS**2922
Cooper ... B765
Copernicus ... 1652
Corinth ... 1877, 3554, B492
Corn (sheaf) ... R89
Costumes ... FB2, FB15, FB30, FR3, FR16, FR37, 2542, 2598
Cottbus ... 2220*b*
Coty ... 3353
Coubertin ... 1465
Council of Constance ... 3927
Council of Europe ... 2904
Countryside ... 2965, 3766
Court of Justice ... 2985
Court seal ... 3292
Courths-Mahler ... 2168*b*
'CRALOG und CARE' ... 1304
Cowboy and Indian ... 3619
Cranach ... 1620
Creation of the Animals (painting) ... 3924
Crocodile skeleton ... 2861
Cronach the Younger ... 4007
Cross ... 3804
Cross and shadow ... 2064
Cross country skier ... 3092
Cross of St. John ... 2902
Cross on orb ... 1898
Crosses ... 1174, 1243, 1311, 1450, 1470, 1488, 1556, 1557, 1706, 2051, 2114, B848
Crossing warden ... 2031
Crown ... 2254
Crowned head ... A70
Cultural Foundation ... 3100, 3198
Cultural History ... 3857
Cusanus ... 1218
Cut-out figures ... 3213
CVJM ... 1997
Cycles ... 2092, 4130*a*, B697
Cycling ... A112, 2346, 2886, B551, B679

D

Daimler ... 1277, 3590
Daisy ... 3306, B540
Dam ... 3843, 3851
Dancers ... 1960, B660
Dandelion ... 1840
Dante ... 1595
De Gaulle and Adenauer ... 2228
Decorated tree ... 3878
Decorative pots ... 3517
Deer ... 4162
Deggendorf ... 3099
Dehler ... 2821
Delp ... 1343*d*
'Denkmalschutz' ... 2137
Dentistry ... 2180
Dessau ... 3859
Dessau and Aircraft ... 3859
Dessau-Wörlitz Gardens ... 3113
Deutsche Einheit ... 2326
Deutsche Kultur u. Heimat ... B169
Deutsche Staatsoper ... 2472
Deutsche Welle ... 3214
'Deutsche Welthungerhilfe' ... 2223, 3124
Deutscher ... 2113
Deutscher Kinderschutzbund ... 3213
Deutscher Musikrat ... 3227
Deutscher Orden ... 2300
'Deutscher Verein für Öffentliche und Private Fürsorge' ... 1922
Deutscher Werkbund ... 3497
'Deutscher Zollverein' ... 2045
Deutsches Museum, Munich ... 3212
Deutsches Turnen ... 1210
Deutsches Turnfest ... B315
Deutschland (steam ship) ... 3669
Deutschmark ... 2857
DGB ... 2932
Diagram (mathematical) ... 1818
Diagram (scientific) ... 1345, 1426, 1453
'Diakonie' ... 1706
Diamonds ... 2766
Diatom ... 4017
'Die Ausgrabung der Kreuze' ... 3468
Die Brücke ... 3354
Die Weser (steamship) ... 4091
Diem ... 1467
Diesel ... 1203, 2809
Diesterweg ... B851
Dietrich ... 2786
Dinosaurs ... **MS**3558
Direktwahlen zum Europäischen Parliament ... 2565
Disabled athlete ... 3642, 3982
Disabled sports ... 3981
Disabled War Veterans Association ... 3031
Disc and swords ... 3563
Disc Cross ... 3970
Discus ... 2056
Dish Aerials ... B392
Distler ... 2485
Diving ... 2234
Dix ... 2423
DLRG ... 3244
'Documenta11' ... **MS**3108
'Documenta Kassel' ... **MS**2780
Dog, Cat and FIsh ... 3792
Dogs ... 2640, 2696
Dohnanyi ... 3087
Doll ... 1473, B316
Dominikus-Ringeisen-Werk ... 2915
Domowina ... 3807
'Donaueschinger Musiktage' ... 2741
Donhoff ... 3628
Dorsch ... 2337
Dortmund ... 2211, 2383, 2991, B786
Dove ... 945, R53, R54, 1470, 2880, 2899, B17, B33
'DPhG' ... B850
Drachenfels Railway ... 3548
Dragon ... **MS**2596, 3067
Drais ... 4130*a*
Dransfeld ... 2168, B747

GERMANY / Design Index

Drehstromübertragung 2411
Dresden RE34, 1359, 2220, 2659, B326, E3044, E3058, 3906
Dresden Catholic Church 3063
Dresden Opera House 3247
Dressage 1925, 2440
Droplets on leaf 3705
Droste-Hülshoff 1275, 3190, B207
Duden 1917
Duderstadt 2069
Duisburg 2414
Dumont 1802
Dunant 1085, 1090
Dürer 1264, 1586, 3411, B197, B391
Düsseldorf 1337, 2240
Düsseldorf Carnival 2949

E

E=mc^2 3368
Eagle (Arms) 380, 1357, 1488, 1567, **MS**1699, 2173, B147, B170, B573
Ear 1931
Ear of corn 3685
Early racing cars **MS**3617
East–West North Atlantic Flight 3215
Ebert 1568, 2950
Ebner-Eschenbach 1935
Eckert 3831
Ecksberg Pilgrimage Church 3101
Ecumenical Church Conference, Berlin 3220
Egk 3051
Ehrlich 1123
Eichendorff 1199, 2229
Eichstatt 3515
Eiermann 3291
Eifel 2678, 2709
Eifel National Park **MS**3605
Einkommende Zeitungen (newspaper) 2972
Einstein 1900, 3368
Eisenach 3001, E3046
Eisenbarth 1843
Eisenhower 3353
Elbe Mountains **MS**2860
Elbphilharmonie 4098
Electricity 3266
Electromagnetic Rays 3877
Electromagnetic waves 2026
Elephant and rainbow 4108
Elephants 2267
Elisabeth of Thüringia 1039, 1262, 1978, B195
Ellwagen 1363, B420
Elser 3195
Eltz 1807, B519
Elysee Treaty 3819
Emblem 3409, 3942, 4057, 4138, 4165
Emperor Otto I 3793
Endangered species 3116, 3263
'Ende des Krieges' 2635
'Energie sparen' 1983
'Energieforschung' 1965
Engels R37, 1566
Entdeckung Amerikas 2456
Entwicklungszusammenarbeit 1967
Environmental Protection 3252, 3532, 3781, 4069
Enztal Viaduct 3235
EPPE 2059
Erfurt 2455
Erhard 2172, 2756
Erhardt 3583
Ernst 2422
Ernst-Reuter Platz B270
Ernstroda 2546
ERP B71
Erste Haager Friedenskonferenz 2919
Erxleben 2155, B737
Erzberger 1723
Erzebirge 2586
Esslingen am Neckar 1862
Eucken 2342
Euregio Bodensee 2522
Euro (new currency) 3089
Europa 1167, 1187, 1212, 1234, 1251, 1281, 1297, 1320, 1350, 1404, 1424, 1438, 1460, 1484, 1520, 1583, 1618, 1661, 1696, 1733, 1782, 1824, 1860, 1892, 1927, 1960, 1994, 2025, 2060, 2096, 2128, 2186, 2241, 2275, 2313, 2456, 2518, 2574, 2635, 2713, 2768, 2847, **MS**2901, 2962, 3050, 3111, 3216, 3267, 3355, 3413, 3476, 3536, 3656, 3716, 3779, 3847, 3914, 3980, 4056
Europa Centre B271
Europäische Kunstausstellung B535
Europäischer Binnenmarkt 2493
Europäisches Patentamt 1952
Europarat 2278
European Central Bank 2859
European Emergency Number 4030
European Parliament 2059, 2272
European Plaice 4076
European Space Agency Satellite 4156
European Union 3268, 3456
European University Viadrina Frankfurt 3409
Evangelical Churches Day 1233, 1319, 1401, 1441, 1497, B210, B532
Evangelical Trombone Choirs 3905
Excavator 1748, B486
Exhibition 3601, 3616*a*
EXPO 2000 2658, 2898, 2936, 2959, 2966, 2979
External Financial Control 3942
Eyck B73
Eyes 2737
EZB 2859

F

Factory 1749, B487
Fagus Factory 3941
Fahrenheit scale 3943
Fairy Tales 1204, 1236, 1254, 1283, 1299, 1322, 1352, 1406, 1428, 1443, B231, B277, B289, B304
Falkenlust Castle 2765, 4161
Fallada 2528
Fallersleben 2409
'Familie schafft Zukunft' 2469
Family playing 3644
'Fastnacht' 2017
Faust 1910
Federahannes 2017
Federal Agency for Civic Education 3141
Federal Border Police 3044
Federal Constitutional Court 3073
Federal Employment Services 3105
Federal Republic **MS**1703, 2277, **MS**2906
Federal Social Court 3292
Federation of Trade Unions 2932
Fehmarn Bridge 3841
Feininger 3149
Felder 3128
Felix the Rabbit (cartoon) 3966
Fencing 2438, 4125, B552
'Ferienplätze für Berliner Kinder' B188
'Fernsehtechnik' B664
Festival 3794
Feuchtmayer B301
Feuerbach 1913, 3284
Fey 3483
Fichte 3782
FIFA 3257
Figurines 1506, B339
Film **MS**2677
Film Festival 2943, B349
Film reel 3079
Filmfestspiele 2943
FIP 1421, 1943
Fir trees RF1
Fire-service 3130, B507
Firebird 3586
First Automobile 3717
Fischer Bridge B219
Fish 1326, 3886, 3949, 3999, 4074, B388, B536
Fish and hearts 3519
'Five Crosses' 1161, 1233, 1319, 1401, 1441, 1962, B210, B532
Flag 3844
Flagon 2212
Flags 1914, 2272, 2318, 3073, 3268, 3278, 3346, B720
Flame (Human Rights) 1477
Flame (of Remembrance) B173
Flame (Olympic) 2561
Flatow, A. and G. 2724
Fleisser 3019
Flensburg 1370, B248
Fliedner 1084
'Fliege' B387
'Floh' 1570
Flood Plain 3895
Flood Relief 3864
Flowering trees 3826
Flowers 1306, 1396, 1712, 1762, 1796, 1839, 1873, 1907, 1938, 1972, 2004, 2013, 2024, 2038, 2073, 2107, 2350, 3211, 3306, 4052, B457, B494, B508, B540, B557, B577, B601, B622, B642, B665, B706
Flowers (jewelled) 2255
Flugge Lighthouse 3854
Flying Boat Do X 3298
Föhr 2542
Folk music 3048
Fontane 2612, B94, B344
Football 1707, 1924, 2232, 2560, 2692, 2735, 2820, 2830, 2866, 2923, 3109, 3204, 3253, 3256, 3398, **MS**3412, 3534, 3651, 3930
Football Association 2940
Football pitch 3773
For Us Children **MS**2538, **MS**2596, **MS**2684, **MS**2708, **MS**2781, **MS**2843, **MS**2921, **MS**2986, **MS**3071, **MS**3134, **MS**3228, **MS**3237, 3272, 3290, 3373, 3434, 3493, 3493, 3560, 3619, 3677, 3735, 3729, 3799
For You 3902
Forbmann 3453
Forchheim 3304
'Fördert die Forschung' 1140
Forell 2536
Forest 3894
Forests 3716
Fort 1721
Fossil 3733
Fossils 1865
Fox cubs 3889
'Fraiske Raid' 3404
Francis of Taxis 1440
Francis, St., of Assisi 2003
Franck and Born 2001
Francke 1099, 3838
Francke Charitable Institutions 2867
Franco-German Treaty 1647, 2228
Frank 1894
Frankenberg Hall 3573
Frankfurt Bookfair 3675
Frankfurt Fair 2301
Frankfurt-am-Main A74, 1098, 1206, 2106, 2201, 2286, 2313, 2377, 2411, 2558, B778
Fränkische Schweiz 2646
Französisches Gymnasium B829
Frauenkirche 3377
Fraunhofer 2176, 3776
Fraunhofer-Gesellschaft 2891
Frederick the Great 2138, B726
Frederik II of Prussia 3750
Freeclimbing 2760
Freemason's Museum 3102
Freiburg FB13, FB27, FB38, 1182, 1564, 1868, 2208, B782
Freiberg University of Mining and Technology 4020
Freie Volksbühne B840
'Freiheit der...' 2629
Freising 2715
French and German Flags 3819
Freshwater Fish 3999
'Frieden und Verständigung' 2080
Friedlandhilfe 1847
Friedrich II, Kaiser 2582
Friedrich, C. D. 1711
Friedrich Loeffler Institute 3686
Friedrich Wilhelm of Brandenburg 2622
Friedrich-Wilhelms University 4165
Froebel 1041
Frog 4167
'Fromme Helene' 1993
Fruchtbringgende Gesellschaft Library 4138
Fruit 3632
Fry 1082
Fuchs 3030
Fugger 1224
Fulda 2563
Funkturm B132
'Für Berliner...' B68
'Für den Umweltschutz' 2581
'Für Dich' 2982, 3081
'Für mehr Sicherheit...' 2407
Furrier B767
Furth 3454
Further Drachenstich 3067
Furtwängler B125, B712

G

G20 4107
Gabelsberger 2279
Gabin 3080
Gaertner B526
Gaia (satellite) 4156
Galen 1411, 2703
Gandersheim 1663
Gandhi 1504
Garbo 3078
Gardener 928, A36, R1, B1, B21
Garmisch-Partenkirchen 2499
Gartenbauausstellung 2024, 2516
Gasperi **MS**1459
Gaubodenfest 3794
Gauss 1818
Gauss (survey ship) **MS**3084
Gedenbibliothek B120
'Geheimnis der Erlösung...' 2257
Gelnhausen 1923
Gemen 1805*d*, B517*a*
Gendarmenmarkt 2732, B51
General German Workers' Association 3844
Genfer Flüchtlingskonvention 2405
George, H. 2533
George, St. 1260
Gera 2613
Gerhardt 1179, 1785, 3470
German–Denmark Relations 3346
German–French Co-operation Treaty 3196
German–Israel Relations 3984
German–Russian YouthForum 3278
German Air Traffic 3347
German Bible Society 3803
German bread 4164
German Catholic Women's Federation 3248
German Choral Association 3786
German design 3738, 4089, 4139, 4159, 4172
German Federal Armed Forces 3384

GERMANY / Design Index

German Football 3777
German Maritime Research 3979
German Museums 3817, 3836, 3845, 3924, 3950, 3990, 4009, 4014, 4046, 4070, 4094
German Paintings 3694, 3787, 3820
German Pavilion, Montreal **MS**2762
German Railways 3689
German Reunification 4008
German Rose Show 3853
German Shooting Federation 3728
German Soccer Internationals 3534
German Sports Badge 3840
German television 3142, 4146
German Unification 1567, B380
German Women 3190
'Gesundheit durch Vorsorge...Krebs' 1953
Giant Slalom 3690
Giehse 2157, B739
Giessen 1184
Gilly B413
Giotto (satellite) 2119
Girl selling trinkets 1782
Giza B671
Glassware 2143, B727
Glazier B716
'Gleichberechtigung' 2079
Glider 3693, 4073
Gliders 1959, B548
Gliding 3522
Glienicke Bridge 2829
Glienicke Palace B724
Globe 1140, 1450, 2317, 2343, 2475, B184, B809, B3059
Globe and rainbow 2626
Gluck 2221
Glücksburg 1805, 3852, B516
Glücksburg Schloss 3815
Gmelin 2248
Gnadenkapelle Shrine 4058
Gnu herd 3527
Goalkeeper 3711
Goblet 1792, 2143
Goerdeler 1343*e*
Goethe..A114, F11, FB47, FR46, FW44, RF7, **MS**RF11, R55, **MS**R59*a*, R61, 1270, 1985, 2920, B61, B203
Goethe Institute 3049
Goethe-Schiller (statue) E3041
Golden Bull 3396
Golden Hat 1834
Goldfinch 3866
Göltzsch Bridge 2931
Gontard B611
Gorch Fock (sail training ship) 3555
Gorilla 3053
Gosla 1606
Gottingen Seven 3809
Government **MS**3621
Graefe B553
Graffiti 3088
Gramophone and disc B772
Grapes 4140
Graph 2282
Gravitational waves 4157
Grayling 3999
Great Arber Mountain 4027
Greetings Stamps 3200, 3519, 3686*a*, 3701*a*, 4051, 4108, 4120
Gregorian calendar 2009
Greifswald 2958, 2997
Grey Seals 3659
Grien FB3, FB16, FB33, 2115, B710
Grieshaber 3586
Grimm 2084
Grimm Brothers Fairytales 3784
Grimma 3000
Grimmelshausen 1794
Gropius 2016
'Grosse Kurfürst' B808
'Grosse Neugierde' B606
Grosz 2507, B535
'Grundgedanken der Demokratie' 1969
Grundgesetz **MS**2905
'Grüne Woche' B500
Grunewald B119, B224, B607
Grzimek 3595
Guardini 2085
Guericke 3138
Guest workers 1950
Guinea Pigs 3506
Güschwitz RF15
Gutenberg FR9, FR23, 1124, 1263, 2948, B196
Gutenfels FR14, FR28, FR41
Gymnasium zum Grauen Kloster B456
Gymnastics 1777, 2022, 2057, 2266, 2619, 2945, B477, B617, B763
Gynaecology B703

H

Haass 1934
Haber B162
Hagenbeck **MS**2577
Hahn-Strassman 1346
Hahn 1901
Hahnemann 1150
Hainich National Park **MS**2954
Hairdressing 2124
Halberstadt 2702
Half-timbered Architecture 3683, 3709, 3783
Half-timbered Building 3814
Halle 3392
Halle an der Saale 2599
Halle Gate B220
Halley's comet 2119
Hambach 2218, B790
'Hambacher Fest' 1994, 3481
Hamburg 1227, 1331, 1655, 2036, 2072, 2187, 2206, 2273, 2293, 2479, 2666, 2893, B781
Hammer, Throwing the B803
Hand 1934, **MS**3066, 3197
Hand prints 2726
Handball 1890, 2304, B50
Handel **MS**1233*a*, 2096
Hands 2883, 3221, 3248
Hands and arms forming square 1967
Hands and Coffee Pot 3692
Handwerks 2973
Hanover 1330, 1812*d*, 2338, 2468, B524*d*
Hanover Trade Fair 955, A108
Hans Guck-in-die-Luft 2568
Hanseatic League 3436
Hansel and Gretal 3897
Happy Easter 3901
Harbig 1464
Hardenberg B429
Harp B72, B638
Harz 2529
Harz Narrow-gauge Railway 3757
Hauff 1844
Hauptmann R34, 1276, 1850, 2222, 3810, B208
Hausfrau 2311
Hausmann 2868
Havel B512
Havellandschaft 2647
Haydn **MS**1233*a*
Health awareness **MS**3066
Heart 2581, 3570
Heart for Children Association 3570
Hebbel 3837
Hebel FB1, FB14, FB28, 2091
Heck B163
Heckel 1691, 2591
Hedgehog 3493, 3890
Hedwig, St. 2547, B130
Hegel R38, 1517
Heidelberg 1642, 2141, 2725,3869
Heidelberg Catechism 1310
Heidi 3059
Heim B685
Heimatvertriebenen 2320
Heine F13, 1155, 1644, 2822
Heinemann 1535, **MS**2010, 2916, B350
Heinrich der Löwe 2650
Heisenberg 3085
Helena Sloman (ship) B528
'Helfer der Menschheit' 1169
'Helft Berlin!' A106
'Helft den Kindern' RB19
Heligoland 1078, 1641, 2210*a*, B785
Heligoland Ornithological Institute **MS**3653
Helicopter 1742, 3219, B481
Helmet 1835
Helmholtz 2594, B394
Helmsman 1903
Hensel 2167, B746
Herberger 2752
Herder 2589
Hermes 3230
Hertz 1178, 2557
Herzogsägmühle 2579
Hesse 1851, 2506, 2885
Hesse, H. 3126
Heuss 1103, 1219, **MS**2010, 3582, B178
Heuss-Knapp 1946, B174
High jumping 1780
Hildesheim 1250, 1379, 3004,
Hildesheim Cathedral 3970, B257
'Hilfswerk Ludwigshafen' FR30
Hindemith 2686
Hiorten (ship) 2876
Hips 1907
Hirsch 3882
Höch B834
Hochharz National Park **MS**3127
Hockey **MS**1781, B502, B505, B818
Hofer B556
Hoffman 3604, B421
Hoffman von Fallersleben 2409
Hoffner 3448
Hohe Rhön 2531
Hohenheim 1040
Holbein 1709
Hölderlin FW2, FW15, FW30, 1518, 2524
Höllental FB12, FB37
Holly 2235
Holsteinische Schweiz 2710
Holzel 3203
'Homöopathie' 2738
Honegger 2442
Hop cultivation 2858
Hoppegarten 2517
Horse-drawn carriage B837
Horse racing 2517, 2887
Horse riding 1925
Horses 1478, 2185, 2774, B328
Houses 1948
Hoyerswerda 2601
Hubertusburg Peace Treaty 3830
Hübler-Horn 2723
Huch 1719, 3929
Human hair 4131
Human rights 2880, 2889
Humboldt, A. von 1226, B167, B338
Humboldt, W. von B100, B693
Humperdinct 3288
'Hundert Jahre 1.Mai' 2310
Hurdling 3591, B678
Hutten 2239

I

IAF Congress E3058
IBRA München 1973 1658
iBRA'99, Nüremberg **MS**2900
ICC Berlin B566
ICE 2373
Ice hockey 1728, B661
Ice skater 3093
Idar-Oberstein 2766
IFRABA 1097
Ihrer 2150, B732
Imperial Abbey of Corvey 4036
Indian 2175
Industriegewerkschaft 2288
Industrie-undHandelskammer B144
Industry and Commerce Organisation Ingolstadt 3406
Inline skating 2758
Inscribed ribbon 3865
Insects 2052, 2397, 2511, B674
Installateur 2179
Insurance Code 3720
'Integration Ausländischer...' 1950
INTERBAU B156
International Aerospace Exhibition 3601, 3616*a*
International Congress Centre B566
International Horticultural Exhibition, Rostock 3211
International Peace Year 2134
International Space Station 3303
International Year of Disabled Persons 1947
Internationale Arbeitsorganisation 1486
Internationale Bauausstellung B770
Internationale Fernmeldeunion 2317
Internationale Funkausstellung 2406, 2535, B575, B826
Internationale Union für Geodasie 2037
Internationales Jahrder Familie 2555
Interparliamentary Union Conference 1867
Interpol 1653
Invitation 4120
Inzlingen 1808*b*, B520*b*
IOC 2561
Iphla '89 2271
IPPT B333
Iris B508
Isny FW38
Israel 3382
IVA '79 1895

J

Jahn B554
Jamnitzer 3517
Javelin B593
Jawlensky 1690
'Jederzeit Sicherheit' 1596, B396
Jena RF14
Jester 2225
Jewellery 1791, 2255, B773, B812
Jewels 3751
Jewish Museum, Berlin 3075
Jim Knopf 3060
Joachim B337
Jochum 3137
Johannes of Nepomuk 2504
Johannes XXIII 1505
Jonas 3221
Jousting 1737
Juchacz **MS**1499, 3192
Jüdisches Gemeindehaus B268
Judo B764
Jug B729
Jugend Forscht 2302
Jugendmarke (Youth Hostels) 1080, 1158
Jugendstil **MS**1815
Jugglers B822

GERMANY / Design Index

Juli 1944 **MS**2583
July Plot (20.7.1944) 1343*a*, **MS**2583, B116
Jünger 2846
Junkers W33 *Bremen* (aircraft) 3215

K

Kafka 2028, 3553
Kaisen 2192
Kaiser 2226
Kaiser Wilhelm Bridge 3492, 3492
Kaiser Wilhelm Church 3291, B106, B137, B265
Kaiser Wilhelm Memorial Church 3742
Kammergericht B314
Kampen Lighthouse 4072
Kandinsky 2463
Kant 1268, 1702, B201
Karl Freiherr Vom Stein 3499
Karlsbüste 2253
Kassel 2989
Kästner 2890
Katholikentage 2856
Kaub B245
Kautner 3526
Kayak *see* Canoeing
Kekule 1345
Kempis 1585
Kennedy 1358, B235
Kentenich 2100
Kepler 1594
Ketteler FR2, FR17, FR35, 1288, 1832
Kevelaer 2184
Kiel 1332, 2444, 2502
Kiel-Holtenau Lighthouse 4127
Kiel Regatta 1996
Kiesinger 3265
Kilian, Kolonat, Totnan 2281
Kinder gehören dazu 2287
'KINDERGOTTESDIENSTI' 3107
Kindermarke **MS**2538, **MS**2596, **MS**2684
King 1569
Kirchbach 3193
Kircheim Castle 2990
Kirchhoff B449
Kirchner 1693, 3135
Kisch 2090
Kites 2275
Kittens 3952
Klausener RB14, B681
Klee 1909, 4022
Kleist 1273, 3136, B206
Kleistpark B40
Klemperer B702
Klenze 3585
Klepper 2492
Klimarahmenkonvention 2626
Klinger 3485
Klopstock 1705
Klotz 2532
Knef 3191
Kneipp 1100, 2772
Knigge 3097
Knight 1512
Knights of St. John 2902
Knobelsdorff B448
Knot 4107
Koblenz 2434
Koch 1986, 3385, B186
Köenig 1451
Kohl 3806
Kokoschka 2118
Kolb 1718
Kolbe, G. B531, B628
Kolbe, M. 1664
Kolle 2706
Kollo B545
Kollwitz R33, 1126, 2152*a*, 2714
Köln *see* Cologne
Kölner Carnival 2755
Kolping 1149, 1398
Konferenz der Europäischen Kulturminister B683
Kongress der Internationalen Organisation der Obersten Rechnungskontrollbehörden B824
Kongresshall B146*a*
Königsberg 1377, B255
Konstanz FB46
Kopling 2984
Korczak 1864
Körner, H. 1803
Körner, T. **MS**2412
KOSOVO-HILFE 1999 2899
Köthen 3971
Krebshilfe 2896
Kreutzer FB53
Kreuzberg B493, B534, B612
'Kriegsgräberfürsorge' 1174, 1488
Kronach 3194
Krüger B323
Kulturstiftung 2917, 2960
'Kürschner' B767
Kyffhäuserdenkmal E3043

L

Labourer 932, A40, R5, B5, B28
Lagerlof 3572
Lampadius 2394
Lampel 3070
Landespostdirektion B134
'Landfrauenverband' 2848
Landscape 1930
Landshut 3250
Landwehr Canal B563
Lange 1684
Langen 1463
Langenfeld 2349
Langhans B646, 3504
Lantern 2395
Larkspur 3321
Lasker-Schüler 1720
Lassalle 1348
Laue 1902
Lauscha 2418
Leaves 3124
'Leben ohne Drogen' 2737
Lebenslanges Lernen 3070
Leber 2431
Lechfeld 1142
Lehmann 2163, B743
Lehmbruck 1700
Leibniz 1423, 1928, 2719
Leichhardt 3875
Leine Palace 2953
Leip 2537
Leipzig-Dresden Railway 3913
Leipzig RD27, 2467, 2593, 3995
Leipzig Fair 926, 951, 953, RD13, RD33, R31, R51, R60, 2761
Leipzig Gewandhaus Orchestra 2503
Leipzig University 3608
Leisner 3961
Leistikow B420
Lenné B827
Lennon 2238
Lessing 1269, B202
Lette-Verein 2370
Letter box 3243
Letter rack 2008
Leuschner 1343f, 2316
Lewandowski E3054
Lichtenberg Castle 1812*b*, B524*b*
Lichtenberg, G. C. 2464
Lichtenrade B564
Lichtenstein FW12, FW37, 1806*c*, B518*b*
Liebermann 1878, B419, B422
Liebig 1092, 1184, 3217
Liebknecht R50
Liegnitz 2371
Lifeboat 2312
Lifeguards 3244
Light and Tunnel 3722
Lightbulb 1911, 3266
Lighthouses 1741, 3279, 3365, 3429, 3486, 3549, 3606, 3660, 3724*b*, 3726, 3788, 3854, 3925, 3985, 4072, 4127, B480
Lilienthal **MS**2408, B92
Lilienthal Monument B140, B605
Lily 4121
Limburg 2098, 3638
Lime tree 3068, 3826
Lincke 2731, B152
Lindau Lighthouse 3986
Linde zu Himmelsberg 3068
Linden, Die B213
Lindgren 3503
Lion 2200, B777
Lion jug B813
List 2285
Liszt **MS**RF11, 2135, 3701
Litfab 4031
Little Red Riding Hood (fairy tale) 4032
Livestock Breeds **MS**4079
Löbe B499
Lock (canal) 2071
Locksmith B717
Locomotives *see* Railway engines
Löffelbagger 1751, B488*a*
Löhe 1612
Lorsch 1361, B238
Lorsch Abbey 3887
Lortzing 3033, B74
Love Letters 4078
Löwenberg 1381, B259
Löwenburg Castle 4028
Lower body **MS**3066
Lower Saxony 2953
Lower Saxony Wadden Sea 3860
Lübeck A98, 1065, 1229, 1672, 2299, 2663
Lübke 1342, 1447, **MS**2010, B228, B308
Lüders **MS**1499, 2790
Ludgerus, St. 2458
Ludwig II 2127
Ludwigshafen FR30
Lugwigslust Castle 3956
Ludwigstein 1806, B518
'Luftbrücke' B183, B451, B823
Luftbrückendenkmal B138
Lufthansa 1131, 1771
Luise Henriette von Oranien 2157*a*
Luise von Preussen 2166, B745
Lüneburg 1156
Lüneburger Heide 2808
Luther 1075, 1265, 1449, 1578, 2043, 2695, 4114, B198
Luther's Catechisms 1897
Luxemburg R50, 1685
Lynx and Kitten 3760

M

M A1
Maastricht Treaty 3249
Macke 1689, 2462, 3939
Macmillan 3353
Made in Germany 2249
Madonna (Nüremberg) 1077
Madonna and Child 2184, 3687, 3811
Magdeburg 2216*a*, 3374, E3047
Magnifying glass and stamp E4
Magnus 1261, 1927, B194
Mai 2310
Maidburg 2488
Maier 2292
Mail coaches 3668
Mail van B854
Main–Donau Canal 2478
Maintal 2587
Mainz FR10, FR22, 1289, 1336, 1738, 2978
Mainz Carnival 2225
Mainz Cathedral 3618
Mainz University 1828
Majolica B673
'Maler/Lackierer' B768
Maltese Cross 1500
Man holding head **MS**3066
Mann 1163, 1852, 3587
Map (Denmark–Germany) 1313, 2087
Map (S. America) 2148
Map (weather) 1654
Map (World) 1166, 2496, B588
Marburg University 1829
Marc 1688, 2461
Marcks 2264
Marconi 2638
Marggraf, Archard, Scheibler 2445
Maria Laach Abbey 1164
Maria Rast Chapel 4149
Marian Congress 2184
Marigolds 1797
Market 3562
Marksburg 1809, B521
Marksburg Castle 3955
Mars E3061
Marshall 1258
Marshall Plan 2773
Martin Luther University 3106
Martin, St. 2081
Marx FR5, FR20, FR34, R35, 1462
Mary, Virgin 2428
Match 2078
Materialprüfung B412
Mathematicians Congress 2862
Mauerstrasse B215
Maulbronn Monastery 2827
Max and Moritz 2306, 3972, B844
Max Planck Society 2835
May 2175
May Day 1396
Mayer, H. 1466
Mayer, R., and Stein 2227
Maze 2302
Mechanical calculator 3100
Mechanical shovel 1751, B488*a*
Mecklenburg-Vorpommern 2526
Mecklenburg 2623, 2682, 2894, 2992, 3007
Mecklenburg Lake District 4153
Mecklenburgische Seenplatte 2588
Medal B620
Medallion B597
Medical examination 2000
Meersburg 2247
'Mehr Sicherheit für Kinder!' 2752*a*
Meissen E3040
Meit B297
Meitner 2159, B740
Melanchthon 1242, 2754
Mellingen RF16
Memling 2607
Men and dog (cartoon) 3695
Mendel 2049
Mendelssohn, F. **MS**1233*a*, 2813, 3584
Mendelssohn, M. B576
'Menschenrechte' 1477, 1870
Menzei B95, B324
Mercator 3770
Mergenthaler B114

GERMANY / Design Index

Merian 2153, B735
Merry-go-Round 3679
Mespelbrunn 1810, B522
Meteorological Organisation 1654
Meyer, F. B463
Meyer, W. B464
Meyerheim B325
Michelangelo 2128
Michelstadt 2050
Micro-organism 4016
Microscope 3385, B412
Microworld 4016, 4066, 4131, 4171
Miegel 1882
Miesbacher costume 3987
Miller 1135, 3212
Mills 2814
Minden 2600
Minden Lock 3940
Minnesingers 1512, B345
MISEREOR (church charity) 1305, 2263, 3575
'Miteinander leben!' 2566
Mittelland Canal 3348
Mittenwald Railway 3798
Mixed choir 3786
Moby Dick (boat) B471
Modersohn-Becker 2151, 2713, B733
Mohnetalsperre Dam 3843, 3851
Moholy-Nagy 2014
Molecular chain 1573
Moltke 1343*g*, 3466
Mommsen 4155, B159
Monks (sculpture) B598
Monnet 1816, 2244
Monorail train 1754*c*, 1774, B490*c*
Monroe 3076
Monteverdi 2550
Monument 3873
Monument to the Battle of the Nations 3873
Moon E3060
Mophila 1985 2104
Mörike 1735, 3289
Moritzburg Lighthouse 3985
Morrison 2237
Mosel 4048, 4059
Moses receiving tablets 1897
Mother and Child 1725
Mother Teresa 3674
Moths *see* Butterflies
Motor cars 1987, 2032, 2116, 3144, 3238, 3974, 4023, B632
Motorcycles 1987, 2018, 2889, B656
Motor-racing 2888, **MS**3617, **MS**B395
Mountain Hut 3785
Mountains 3091, 4069
Mourning Stamp 3740, 3769, 3885
Mouse preparing to sprint 3848
Mouth 2128
Moyland Schloss 3480
Mozart 1154, **MS**2433, 3393
Muche 2705
Mueller, F. 2740
Mueller, O. B641
Müller B465
München *see* Munich
Münchhausen 1522
Mungsten bridge 2779
Munich A75, 1207, 1244, 1333, 1524, 1658, 1855, 2209, 2381, 2500, 2573, 3231, B783
Münster 2494
Münsterschwarzach Abbey 4077
Münter 2592
Museum building 3741
Museum exhibits 3102
Museum Façade 3718
Museum Island, Berlin 3129
Museums **MS**2136, B670
Music 1294, 2183
Music Competition 3835
Music notation 3227
Musical Instruments 3914
Musicians B804
Muskauer Park 3791
Mussel 3117

N

Nansen 1102
National Gallery **MS**2762, B47
National Library 3802
National Museum of German Art and Culture 3125
National Parks 3700, 3715, 3959
Native Flora and fauna 3760
Nativity 1912, 1944, 1977, 2011, 2115, 2149, 2224, 2295, 2430, 2690, 2749, 2826, 2879, 2935, 3029, 3245, B587, B669
NATO 1914, 2892
Natural History Museum, Berlin 3630
Nature Protection 1489, 2729, **MS**2771, 2850, **MS**2860, **MS**2954, 2965
NaturFreunde Deutschlands 3372
'Naturschutzgebiete' 1930
Naumburg B169
Nay 3123
Neanderthal skull 3433
Neckermann 2722
Necklet 1791
Nefertiti 2202, B779
Nepomuk, St. John of 2504
Neuber 1800
Neubrandenburg 1364, 2220*a*, B241
'Neue Postleitzahlen' 2505
Neue Synagoge E3055
Neukölln B136
Neumann 1267, 2171, B200
Neunburg vorm Wald 4106
Neuschwanstein 1808, B520
Neuss 1736, 2066
New Millennium 2937
Newspapers 2972
Newton 2495
Niederdeutschland 2680
Niedersachsen 2527
Niemöller 2435
Nietzsche 2981
Nikolai-Kirche B830
Nikolaus, St. B691
Nipkow B664
Nobel 2689
Nobel Peace Prize 3383
Nobel Prize 3262, 3385
Nocht 2987
Nofretete *see* Nefertiti
Norbert von Xanten 2062
Nord-Ostsee-Kanal 1528, 2637
Norddeutsche Moorlandschaft 2807
Norddeutsche Seewarte 2496
Norderney Lighthouse 3724*b*
Nördlingen 2828
Nordrhein-Westfalen 2534, 2957
Nordsee 2303
Nose 2129
'Notopfer Berlin' AT102, T1043, T1103
Numeral RB1, RD1, RD15, RE1, 899, 1152
Nüremberg 1279, 1587
Nussbaum 3302
Nuts 1905, B582

O

Oberammergau 1523
Oberammergau Passion Play 1243, 2051
Oberbayern 2681
Oberhof 2350
Oberlausitz 2648
Oberlin 1128
Oberndorf 2544
Oberndorf–Laufen Bridge 3223
Occupations RB22
Ocean and Coast 3864
Octant 1957
OECD 2140
'Öffnung der innerdeutschen Grenzen' 2611
'Ohmschen Gesetzes' 2574
Oil-rig 1754, B490
Oktoberfest 3679
Ollenhauer 3041
Olympia Stadium B42*b*
Olympic Games 1157, 1246, 1356, 1463, 1493, 1524, 1589, 1621, **MS**1625, 1629, 1768, 1779, 2721, B88
Open book 3802
Opera glasses 3928
Opera House (Berlin) B223, B266
'Opfern von Teilung…' 2689
Oppenheimer 1274
Optician 2122
Orchid 2073, B577, B686
Orff 2645
Organ pipes 2190, 2293
Ortenberg Altar 2149, B731
Osnabrück 1915
Ossietzky **MS**1767, B828
Otto-Langen 1347
Otto-Motor 1076
Otto-Peters 1683
Otto, St. B129
Ottobeuren 1341
Owl and cogwheel 1089

P

Paddle Steamer **MS**3724
Paderborn Diocese 2912
Page 76 3803
Paik **MS**2780
Paint sprayer B768
Painting 3811, 3924, 3950, 3990
Palais de l'Europe 1813
Palatinate F1
Palatinate house FR7, FR26, FR38
Palucca 2795
Pankok 2508
Panorama 3822, 3869, 3906, 3991, 4048, 4059, 4144
Pansies 1799
Paper aeroplanes 3258
Pappenheim 1129
Paracelsus 2551
Paralysed Games 1626
Paris 1312
Parkland 3791
Parliament **MS**2849
Parochialkirche B221
Passau 2952
Patentgesetz B534
Patrol vehicle 3219
Patrus, St. B131
Paulinchen 2569
Peace Conference, The Hague 2919
Peace of Augsburg Treaty 3566
Peaceful Revolution 3624
Pechstein B640, 2704
Pellworm Lighthouse 3926
Penny Black 4006
People's Congress R53, R54
Pesne B662
Pestalozzi 1072
Petrified forest, Chemnitz 3234
Pets 3506
Pfaueninsel Castle 1805c, 1811, B141, B517, B523
Pfitzner 2576
Pforzheim 2476
Pharmazeutische Gesellschaft B850
Philatelic treasures 3559
Philatelistenkongress 1658
Philharmonic Hall (Berlin) **MS**2762, B267, **MS**B761
Philharmonic Orchestra B72
Phlox 1796
Pied Piper 1863
Pigeons 1173, 1195
Piglets 4110
Pilgrimage Church, Neviges **MS**2762
Pillar 2099, B586
Pine cones 1908, B582
Pine martin 3417
Pinocchio 3057
Pippi Longstocking 3058
Pius XII 2068
Planck 3530, B99
Planetarium B274
Planets 3596
Plates of cereal grains 3575
Playing card 2139
Ploughman RB4, RB16, RC13
Poinsettia 1716
Polar Bear 3532
'Polarforschung' 1964
Polarstern (exploration ship) **MS**3084
Polecats 4111
Police 1166
Polish-German Youth Co-operation 4068
Pope Benedict XVI 3474
Pope John Paul II 3356
Pöppelmann 3756, 3765
Porcelain production 3667
Post! 2955, 3047, 3104, 3243, 3258, 3301, 3472, 3494, 3588, 3597, 3646, 3649, 3705, 3800, 3801
Post boxes 1717
Post bus 3357
Post office counter 1893
Post Office Headquarters B134
Post sorting office 2325
Post Wagon 3847
Postal codes 3222
Postal Conference 1312
Postal Museum 1627
Postal Service 3344, 3370
Postal transport B54, FR49, FW49, 1086, 1137, 1199, 1279, 3847, B333, E3052
Poster art 3216
Posthorn FB56, FR51, FW51, RF4, 2271
Posthorn with numeral 1045
Posthouse signs 1658, 1761, 1838, 1871, 1904, 1943
Postilion 2042, 2104, 2289, 2297, B117, B128, B154, B172, B839, E3050
Postman 3370
Postmen 2199, 2290, 2323, 2421, 2540, 2605, B831, B852, E2
'Postwesen' E3050
Postwoman 2676
Potato cultivation 2810
Potsdam 2523, E3045
Potsdam Edict B705
Potzdamer Platz B217
Pour le Mérite order 2460, B620
Power station 1750, B488
Presley 2236
Preussen (ship) 1820
Preysing B596
Primeval Beech Forest 3894
Primrose B559
Princess Charlotte (boat) B467
Princess kissing frog 3781
Printing press 1617
Prison window 1710
Prisoner of War 1091
Probst 2792
Professors 3809

GERMANY / Design Index

Protestant Conference	1665, 1962
Protestant Regional Church, Speyer	3287
Prussian Eagle	3032
Prussian Museums	B597
Prussian Schlosses	**MS**3369, 3386, 3815, 3852, 3893, 3904, 3955, 4028, 4041, 4050, 4101, 4123, 4161
Pumps	*see* Water pumps
Puning Temple, China	2864
Puppets	1559, 2276, B374
Purse reliquary	2198

Q

Quantentheorie	2575
Quantz	B441
Quedlinburg	2606
Queen Nefertiti	3817
Quidde	**MS**1767
Quill and sword	**MS**2412

R

R	2298
Raabe	1968
Rabbit and Chicken	3901
Rabbits	4038
Radar	1744, B483
Radio	1498, 3214, B212, B226, B303
Radio dial	1896
Radio tower	1402, B132, B212, B226, B303
Radio waves	3214
Radlader	1753, B498*a*
Radziwill	2615
Raiffeisen	1214, 2230
Railway carriages	E3053
Railway engines	1259, 1729, 1740, 1754*c*, 2112, 3871, B381, B472, B479
Railway signal	1145
Rainbow	3220, 3576
'Rainbow' in National Colours	2330
Raised hands	2947
Ramin	2877
Ranke	2685, B379, B721
Rastatt	FB6, FB19, FB29, FB50, 2207
Rathenau	4143, B93
Rau	3408
Rauch	B168, B525
Red Cross	FB42, FR42, FW40, 1090, 1314, 1399, 2256, 3839
Reformation	4114, B830
Refugees	1141, 1240, 1400, 1847
Regensburg	1861, 2627, 2993, 3008
Reger	2376
Regina Martyrum Church	1311, B269
Reichenau Abbey	3511
'Reichsgründung'	1567, B380
Reichstag	1335, **MS**2136, **MS**3621, B37, B230
Reinhardt	2548, B165
Reinheim	2212, B789
'Reinheitsgebot für Bier'	2029
Reis	1087, 1287, 2048
Reislinganbau	2298
Religious Freedom	3375
Rembrandt	3427
Rendsberg Viaduct	3046
Rentenversicherung	2282
Renz	2446
'Rettet den Tropischen Regenwald'	2465
Re-unification of Germany	3680
Reuter	3691
Reuter, E.	B112, B161, B825
Reuter, F.	2111
Reuter Power-station	B143
Rheinland-Pfalz	2539
Rheydt	1809*a*, B521*a*
Rhine	FR14, FR28, FR41
Rhineland	F2, FR42
Rhinoceros	3054
Ribbons	2131
Ribera	3083
Richter, L.	2063
Richter, W.	2595
Riemenschneider	1963, B299
Riese	1225, 2459
Riesen	B418
Rifles and target	2194
Rigging	1936
Rilke	3026
Ringelnatz	3556, B663
Rixdorf	B769
Road safety	1088, 1574, 1579, 2752*a*
Road sign	2975
Robin	1194
Robling	3423
Rock	3349
Rohe	2186, B713
Roland	2205
Roldán	3082
Rome	1727
Rome Treaty	1995
Röntgen	1073, 2625
Rooftops	3403

Rose and barbed wire	2013
Rose Garden	3853
Roses	2004, 3200, B459, B642
Rosette	2035
Rotary International	2188
Rothenburg	1503, 1757
Rowing	1776, **MS**1781, 1891,1958, 2439, 2832, 4126
Rubens	1826
Ruby	3751
Rudesheim	1656
Rudorff	B838
Rügen	2530, 2543
Ruhr 2010	3637
Ruhr Industrial Landscape	3229
Ruhrfestspiele, Recklinghausen	2717
Rummelsberg	2315
Runge	1831
Running	1991, 2120, 2946, 3036, 3255, B571, B618, B636

S

Saalburg	RF13
Saale River	3491
Saalelandschaft	2711
Saaletalsperre Bleiloch	3491
Saar-Lor-Lux	2819
Saar	F7, 1175
Saar River	2983
Saarbrücken	1340*a*, 1680
Saarland	2556, 3025, 3458
Sabria '70	1519
Sachs, H.	1770, 2604
Sachs, N.	2432, 3020, 4045
Sachsen	*see* Saxony
Sailing boat	3712
Sails	1936
Salmon	3886
Salomon	2169, B748
Saltwater Fish	4074
Salvaguardia	1795
Salzburg emigrants	B639
Samaritans	2258
Sanssouci Schloss	4041, 4050
Sapporo	1589
Sartorius	2693
Sauerbruch	B476
Sauerland	2649
Savigny	B166
Saxon State Orchestra	2881
Saxon Steamship Company	**MS**3724
Saxonia (steam locomotive)	3871
Saxony-Anhalt	2580, 3052
Saxony	RC1, 2567, 2679, 3043
Schad	2590
Schadow	3915, B413, B466
Schall	2454
Scheel	**MS**2010
Scheibe	B630
Schickard	1670
Scheidemann	3997
Schiller	F12, FW1, FW14, FW28, RF6, **MS**RF11, 1136, 1271, 3352, B185, B204
Schillergesellschaft	2631
Schiller Theatre	B145
Schindler	3533
Schinkel	3407, B98, B612
Schlaun	2630
Schlegel	4141
Schleiermacher	B164
Schlemmer	1733
Schleswig-Holstein	2584, 2746, 3064
Schleswig-Holstein Canal	2071
Schleswig	2204, 2214, 3251, B788
Schliemann	2328, E3056
Schloss (Berlin)	B216
Schloss Ludwigsburg	3271
Schlüter	B146, B298
Schmeling	3376
Schmid	2750
Schmidt-Rottluff	2617, B690
Schmidt	3261
Schneider, P.	2284
Schneider, R.	3218
Scholl	1343*a*, 2161
Schön	4005
Schöneberg	B36, B227
Schongauer	2427
Schoolchildren	1176
Schopenhauer	2231
Schreiber	B187
Schrimpf	2616
Schröder, R.	1846
Schröder, S.	1801
Schroeder	B193, B762
Schubert	2751
Schuhmann	2721
Schulpforta	2520
Schulze-Delitzsch	1211, 3557
Schumacher	1628, 2683
Schuman	**MS**1459

Schumann, C.	2156, B738
Schumann, R.	1160, 3655
Schurz	FB50, 1079, 1787
Schütz	1635
'Schutz der Menschenrechte'	1870
'Schutzt die Natur'	1489
Schwabisch Hall	3403
Schwalm	2545
Schwanenburg	1812*a*, B524*a*
Schwarzhaupt	2785
Schwarz-Rot-Gold	2318
Schwarz–Schilling	3269
Schwarzald	**MS**3432
Schwarzwälder	2744
Schweitzer	1724, 2939
Schwerin Castle	E3048
Schwetzingen	4029
Schwitters	2189
Scouting	2102
Script	3378, 3874, 4148
Sculpture	1696, 2917, 2960, 3072
Sea	1998, 3277
Sealions	B821
Seals	1828, 2300, 2301, 4163, B705
Seascape	3862
Seasons	3449
Second Vatican Ecumenical Council	3804
Selbert	2158
Semper	3247
Senckenberg	1101, 3465
Senefelder	1617
Sextant	B616
Sheep	**MS**4079
Shepherds	2878
Shepherds and Angel	B608
Ship-building	1746, B484
Ship in Envelope	3646
Ships	1183, 1395, 1399, 1819,2030, 273, B123, B467, B527
Shoes	4053
Shooting	B801
Shooting star	3946
Shot-putting	B521
Show jumping	1849, B715
Shrines of Europe	4058
'Sicherheit und Gesundheitsschutz…'	2497
Siebold	2701
Siegfried (boat)	B468
Sielmann	4129
Siemens	1433, 2491, B97
Sieveking	1148
Signatories	3469
Signature	3352
Silcher	2280
Sing-Akademie	2369
Sintenis	B800
Sistine Chapel	1726
Sistine Madonna	**MS**3768, 3811
Skating	2559, 3038, B802
Skatspiel (card game)	3872
Ski-jump	2499, 2831
Ski-runner	1768
Ski Championships	FW38
Skiing	1848, 1926, 2178, 2441, 2562, 2833, 3094, 3983
Slaby	B450
Sleeping Beauty (fairy tale)	3962
Slevogt	1879
Smoker	2335
Snail	3116
Snakes	1572
Snow-covered Chapel	3812
Snow globes	3944
Snowman	3944
Söderblom	1410
Soest	1365, B242
Song Birds	3866
Songs by Udo Lindenburg	3663
Sonnenschein	1083, 1784
Sorbische Sagen	2425
Sower	930, A38, R3, B3, B23
'Sozialversicherung'	1980
Space	2927
Space laboratory	1743, B482
Space satellites	1739, 2119, 2133, 2374, B478, B826
Spandau	2578, B155, B513, B631
Spener	2083
Sperber (boat)	B469
Speyer	1280, 2296, 2665
Spitzweg	2103, 3518
Spohr	**MS**1233*a*
Sports	2023, 2305, 2721, 2757, 2830, 2886, 2944, 3036, 3253, 3336, 3462, 3522
Sports Promotion Fund	**MS**3477, 3522, 3591, 3642, 3711, 3773, 3848, 3918, 3981, 4061, 4124
Spreewald	2712
Spreewälder	2742
Spring	3410, 3766
Springer	3771
Sprint Mouse	3848, 3918
Squirrels	3951

213

GERMANY / Design Index

St. Adalbert 2767
St. Boniface 3270
St. Catherine's Monastery 3062
St. Elisabeth von Thüringen 3502
St. John Foundation 3682
St. Marienstern Abbey 2844
St. Martin's Church 3250
St. Michael's Church, Hildesheim 3640
St. Peter and Paul Church B648
St. Peter's Cathedral 1727
Staatsbibliothek B561
Staberhuk Lighthouse 4071
'Stacheltier' B389
Stade 2554
Stadtautobahn B275
'Städtepartnerschaften' 2770
Stage coach 1976, 2105, 2142, 2291, 3936
Stage curtain 2718
Stained glass window **MS**1804, **MS**1845, 1868, **MS**1880, 2137, 3744, **MS**B515, **MS**B544, **MS**B565
Stamp centenaries B54, FR49, FW49, 1035, 1086, 1227, 1403, 1471
Stamp Day R49, 1761, 1795, 1838, 1871,1904, 1976, 2008, 2042, 2077, 2142, 2199, 2251, 2421, 2486, 2540, 2605, 2676, 2733, **MS**2811, 2876, 3016, 3298, 3357, 3442, **MS**3471, 3559, 3599, 3678, 3801, 3871, 3936, 4006, 4078, 4142, B80, B128, B154, B172, B423
Stamp exhibitions 1067, 1097, 1143, 1180, 1227, 1279, 1306, 1501, 1658, 2104, 2271, **MS**2321, B117
Stamps 1035, 1227, 1403, 1471, 1501, 1872, 2258, 2329, **MS**2900, E4
Stamps and stage coach 2142
Star of David 3467
Stars 2565, 3249, 3456
State Parliaments 2838, 2885,2893, 2897, 2953, 2957, 2978, 3025, 3043, 3052
Statue 4009
Staufer-Jahr 1823
Stauffenberg 1343*h*, 3466
Steam Locomotive 3548, 3757, 3795
Steam ships 3669
Steel girders 1773
Steglitz B276
Stein, Baron vom 1196
Stein, C. von 2168*a*
Stein, E. 2012
Stein, E. and Mayer 2227
'Steinmetz' B766
Stella **MS**2780
Stephan 949, 1038, 1153, **MS**2065, 2764, B54
Stephanie FB21
Stettin 1367, B244
Steuben 2609, B600
Stifter 1146, 3378
Stolz B599
Stonemason B766
Storm 2245
Stormy Sea 3979
Stoss 2294, B835
Stralsund 2417
Straubing 2763
Strauss 3923
Strauss, F. J. 2675
Strauss, J. 2914
Strauss, R. 2925, B121
Street lamps B578
Streetball 2759
Stresemann **MS**1767
Strobel 3018
'Strom für Berlin' B682
Struwwelpeter 2571
Students 3106
Sturgeon 4001
Sturmfels (ship) 1822
Stuttgart 1340, 1402, 1497, 1498, 1657, 1817
Stuttgart railway 4159, 4172
Suhl-Heinrichs 2220*c*
Suhr B177
Summer 3426, 3779
Sun 3252
Sun and moon 3536
Sunflower 3267, 3320
Supplementary Stamp 3883
Suspension bridge 3045
Suttner 2164, 3383
Swimming 1779, 4124, B504, B555, B714
Switchboard 1837
Sword and quill **MS**2412
Symbols of Music 3923
Symbols of Science 3496
Symbols of Work 3839

T

Table tennis 2265, B695
Tailor B718
Tall ships 3998
Tall Ships Festival 3998
Tangermünde Castle 3581
Target B574
Targets 3728
Tchaikovsky 2541
Technical High School B42
Technisches Hilfwerk 2975
Tegel Airport B462
Tegel Schloss 1360, B37, B258
Telecommunications 2242
Telecommunications Tower B275
'TelefonSeelsorge' 2875
Telegraph 1892, B655
Telemann 1949
Telephone 3034
Telephone exchange 2324
Telephone help lines 2875, 3034
Telephone lines B853
Telephones 1287, B533
Telescopes 1755, 1954, B491, B613
Television programs 4080
Television screen 1186, B303, B575
Tempelhof B41
Temple of the Sun, Bayreuth 3857
Tennis 2233
Terre des Hommes 2436
Tersteegen 2823
Test card 4134
Teusch 2154, B736
Thadden-Trieglaff 2410
Thaer 3115
Thälmann RB15, R41
Thanksgiving 3685
The Alps 4069
The Dream Eater (musical) 3932
The Four Elements 3705
The Frog Prince (book) 4167
The Last Supper (painting) 4007
The Little Prince (book) 3937
Theatre **MS**3260, **MS**RF11
Theatre association 2718
'Thesen-Anschlag' 1449
Think Green 4056
Thoma 2727
Thomas, St., of Aquinas 1694
Three Castles 3805
Three Kings A71, 2825, 3500, 3800, B626, B650, B731
Thüringer 2743
Thüringia 2597, 3072
Thurn & Taxis 1097, 1403
Tieck B440
Tiepolo 2707
Tiergarten B514
Tiger and Bear in sailboat 3831
Tiger tamer B819
Till Eulenspiegel 1814, 3725
'Tolerance' 3088
Tom Sawyer 3061
Topography of Terror (museum) 4093
Torso **MS**3066
Tourist sites 3150
Towers **MS**3498
Toys 1607, 3118, 3980, B407
Tractor 1747, B485
Trade Unions 1472
Trades 1458
Traffic 2407
Train 1729, 1743, 1774, 1895, 2112, 3437, 3721, B381, B472, B479, B810, B852
Train on Viaduct 3913
Tram-cars B382
Transport 1093, 1389, B375
'Transrapid' 1732
Trapeze artistes B820
Traunstein 1502
Treaty of Rome 3469
Treble clef B506
Tree (uprooted) 1240
Trees 1202, 2246, **MS**3127, 3229, 3252, 3716, B771
Trelleborg Ferry 3611
Tricycle .... *see* Cycles
Trier FR4, FR19, FR36, 1208, 1232, 1758, 2047
Trimm-aktion 2305
Trombonists 3905
Tropenmedizin 2987
Tschaikowski 2541
Tübingen University 1830
Tucholsky B711
Tunnel and Shipping 3736
Turbine Hall **MS**B761
Twisted pencils 4078
Two Women 3915
Type 2025
Typesetting 2370

U

Überherm 2654
Uhland FW21
UIT 1397
Ulm 1827
'Umweltschutz' 1666
UNESCO 2730, 2736, 2765, 2827, 2861, 2863, 3113, 3129, 3209, 3488
UNICEF 1432, 2525, 2726
United Nations 1147, 1673, 2035, 2639
University (Berlin) B139, B222, B272
University (Kiel) 3969, 3978
Unser Sandmännchen (children's TV programme) 3612
Unteres Odertal National Park **MS**3225
Upper Central Rhine Valley 3414
Uprising (East German) B110
UPU FB56, FR51, 1038, B35
Urania B799

V

Varnhagen von Ense 2156*a*
Varus Battle 3602
Vaterland (boat) B470
VdK 3031
VDU 2070
'Verband Deutscher Elektrotechniker' 2498
'Verband Deutscher Maschinen-und Anlagenbau...' 2487
Verden 2086
Vereinte Nationen .... *see* United Nations
'Verhütet...des Meeres' 1998
'Verhütet Verkehrs-Unfälle!' 1088
Viaduct 3235, 3798
Viermächte Konferenz B113
Villas B647
Vincent, St., de Paul 1069
Vinci 1074
Vinzenz-Konferenzen 2632
Virchow R39, B96
Vischering 1810*c*, B522*b*
Vitamin C 4132
'Vogelfluglinie' 1313
Vogt 2160, B741
Volkingen Blast Furnace 2730
Volksbund Deutsche Kriegsgräberfürsorge 2610
Volkskongress R53, R54
'Volkszählung' 2173
Volleyball 1778, 2621, B637, B817
Voluntary Fire Brigades 3130
Von Bismarck 3973
Von Gluck 3928
Von Mayer 3948
Von Schiller 3629
Voss 3040

W

Wagner 1468, 3846
Waisenbrücke B214
Waldsee FW20, FW32
Waldseemüller 3475
Wallot 2396
Walsrode 2126
'Wandern gibt Lebensfreude' 1704
Wangen FW3, FW16, FW33
Wankel 3461
Wappen von Hamburg (ship) 1819
Warburg 2033
Wartburg Schloss 4123
Water is Life 3912
Water lily 1193
Water polo B595, B842
Water pumps B651
Wattenmeer National Park 3277
Way of Human Rights (sculpture) 3125
Weber 3910
Weber, A. P. 2509
Weber, C. 1786, 2132
Weber, Die 2222
Weber, H. **MS**1499
Wedding ring 3645
Wedigh A104
Wegener B588
Wehner 2941
Weightlifting 2345, B594
Weilburg 2420
Weill 2951
Weimar **MS**RF11, 2656, 2882, E3041
Weiser 3017
Weissenburg 1366, B243
Welfare 3506, 3751
Welfare Stamps 3812, 3826, 3897, 3962, 4032, 4102, 4149, 4167
Wels 1671
Welt-Hauswirtschafts-Kongress 2468
Weltkongress der Internationalen Handelskammer Hamburg 2319
Weltpostkongress **MS**2065
Weltpostverein E1
Werfel 2652
Werner FW47
Wernigerode 2988, 3006
Werratal Castle 3704
Werth 2355
Werthmann 1127, 3564
Wesselmann **MS**2780
Western Pomerania Park **MS**2728
Westfälisches 2745

GERMANY / Design Index

Westphalia 2837
WESTROPA 1143
Wheat B500
Wheelchair sports 1626, 3254, B843
Wheelchair tennis 3981
White Calla Flower 3740
White Stork 3263
Wichern 1042, 3531
Widar (ship) B530
'Wie im Himmel…' B848
Wiechert 2980, 3746
'Wiederaufbau' RC17
Wieland **MS**RF11, 2034
Wiesbaden 1334, 2206*a*
Wigman 2147
Wild Germany 3860, 3895, 3916, 4163
Wilhelmsthal 1810*a*, B522*a*
William Voigt Affair 3435
Winckelmann 4147
Winding equipment 3229
Windsurfing 2058
Windthorst 2356
Wine glass and bottle 3355
Wine-making FR3, FR18, FR37, 1942, 4140
Winter **MS**2780, 3394
Winter Landscape 3747
Winter Olympic Games, Salt Lake City 3092
Wireless transmitter B153
Wissenschaftsrat 3496
Wittenberg 1378, B256
Wöhler 2002
Wolfgang, St. 2603
Wolfsburg 1807*a*, B519*a*
Woman 2942
Woman carrying baskets 3772
World Congress, Berlin 3074
World Cup Football Championship 3109, 3930
World Cup Football Championship,
  Germany 3204, 3398, **MS**3412
World Cup Football Championship,
  South Africa 3651
World Handball Championship 3460
World Heritage Sites **MS**3498, 3511, 3600, 3702,
  3737, 3791, 3887, 3894, 3941, 4036, 4119
World map 3475
World War I 3935
Worms FR8, FR21, FR39, 1578, 2614
Wormser Reichstag 2614
Worpswede 2283
Wrestling 2348
Wter 3912
Wuppertal 1067, 3045
Württemberg F3, FW40, 1198
Würzburg Palace 2863

X

X-ray apparatus 1745, B483*a*
Xanten (town) 1759
Xanten, N. von 2062

Y

Yachts 1996, 2177
Year of the Elderly 2883
Yellow Feather in Red (painting) 3123
Young animals 3889, 3951, 4037, 4110, 4162
Young firefighters 3931
Youth activities 1696, B452
Youth hostels 3616
Youth Science Competition 3988
Youth stamps 3612, 3795, 3866, 3932, 4135
Youth welfare 3118

Z

Zappel-Philipp 2572
'Zauberer' 1571
Zelter B91
Zeppelin 2443
Zeppelin (airship) 2977, **MS**3471
'Zerstörung von Städten' **MS**2634
Zille 1263, B160, 3513
Zimmermann 2099
Zinzendorf 2964
ZnS PbS 1452
Zoo 1206, **MS**B332, B536, B725
Zuckmayer 2747
Zugspitze Meteorological Station 2974
Zuse 3662
Zwiefalten FW13, FW27

215

GERMANY / Berlin (Western Sectors)

V. Berlin (Western Sectors)

The Soviet Government withdrew from the four-power control of Berlin on 1 July 1948 and the Western Sectors remained under American, British and French control. West Berlin was constituted a Land of the German Federal Republic on 1 September 1950. The first stamps to be used in the Western Sectors were Nos. A4/A5 and A7 of the British and American Zones, followed by Nos. A36/A52, which were on sale from 24 June to 31 August 1948 and remained valid until 19 September 1948. Stamps of the Russian Zone were also valid for postage in West Berlin as the East German mark was in use throughout Berlin at the time. However Russian Zone stamps were not on sale in West Berlin and their validity ceased there on 21 March 1949. Mixed franking of British and American Zones and Russian Zone stamps was also possible in the Western Sectors. Russian Zone stamps used in West Berlin comprise Nos. R1 to R50. They are worth more with West Berlin cancellations and very much more on cover.

1948. 100pfennig = 1 Deutsche Mark (East)
1949. 100pfennig = 1 Deutsche Mark (West)

The issues of 1948 to 1952 are inscribed 'DEUTSCHE POST', those of June 1952–55 'DEUTSCHE POST BERLIN' and thereafter 'DEUTSCHE BUNDESPOST BERLIN'.

(B **1**)

1948 (1 Sept). Allied Occupation issues optd with Type B **1**. On Pictorial issue of 1947–48. Nos. 928/48.

B1	2pf. brown-black	4·00	7·75
B2	6pf. violet	5·25	7·75
B3	8pf. vermilion	3·25	7·75
B4	10pf. yellow-green	4·00	2·30
B5	12pf. grey	3·25	2·30
B6	15pf. chocolate	18·00	£100
B7	16pf. blue-green	4·00	3·25
B8	20pf. light blue	9·75	11·50
B9	24pf. brown	2·75	80
B10	25pf. yellow-orange	26·00	80·00
B11	30pf. rose	7·75	13·00
B12	40pf. magenta	10·50	13·00
B13	50pf. ultramarine	13·00	39·00
B14	60pf. red-brown (No. 942)	5·25	80
B15	80pf. grey-blue	17·00	39·00
B16	84pf. emerald-green	23·00	£130
B17	1m. olive-green	65·00	£200
B18	2m. violet	70·00	£650
B19	3m. brown-lake	90·00	£900
B20	5m. indigo	£120	£1000
B1/B20 Set of 20		£450	£3000

1949 (20 Jan–21 Mar). West German currency. As Nos. B1/B20 but optd in red.

B21	2pf. brown-black (21.3)	4·50	4·00
B22	6pf. violet (21.3)	33·00	4·00
B23	8pf. vermilion (21.3)	60·00	7·75
B24	10pf. yellow-green	7·75	2·30
B25	15pf. chocolate	17·00	3·25
B26	20pf. light blue	5·75	2·00
B27	25pf. yellow-orange (21.3)	£130	70·00
B28	30pf. rose (21.3)	£120	8·50
B29	40pf. magenta (21.3)	£120	23·00
B30	50pf. ultramarine (21.3)	£120	13·00
B31	60pf. red-brown (No. 942)	17·00	1·00
B32	80pf. grey-blue (21.3)	£170	13·00
B33	1m. olive-green (21.3)	£700	£700
B34	2m. violet (21.3)	£400	£375
B21/B34 Set of 14		£1700	£1100

PRINTERS From No. B35 onwards all stamps were printed by the State Printing Works, Berlin, *unless otherwise stated*.

B **2** Schöneberg

B **3** Douglas C-54 Skymaster Transport over Tempelhof Airport

1949–54. Berlin Buildings as Types B **2**/**3**. W **230**. P 14.

(a) Size 22×18 mm. Typo

B35	1pf. olive-grey (20.3.49)	65	65
	a. Tête-bêche (vert pair)	1·80	2·10
	b. Booklet pane No B35×5 plus horizontal label (1.11.49)	46·00	
	ba. Do. but vert label (8.5.52)	£130	
B36	4pf. orange-brown (7.5.49)	1·30	65
	a. Tête-bêche (vert pair)	3·50	4·00
	b. Booklet pane. No. B36×5 plus horiz label (1.11.49)	46·00	
	ba. Do. but vert label (8.5.52)	£130	
B36c	4pf. orange-brown (22.1.54)	7·75	6·50
B37	5pf. blue-green (7.5.49)	1·60	65
B38	6pf. deep mauve (7.5.49)	2·50	2·00
B39	8pf. orange-red (7.5.49)	2·75	2·10
B40	10pf. bright green (7.5.49)	1·30	65
	a. Booklet pane. No. B40×5 plus horiz label (1.11.49)	£225	
	ab. Do. but with vert label (8.5.52)	£225	
B41	15pf. brown (30.5.49)	21·00	1·60
B42	20pf. bright scarlet (17.6.49)	7·75	65
	a. Booklet pane. No. B42×5 plus horiz label (1.11.49)	£225	
	ab. Do. but with vert label (8.5.52)	£225	
B42b	20pf. bright scarlet (29.8.53)	85·00	4·00
B43	25pf. yellow-orange (7.5.49)	39·00	1·60
B44	30pf. deep ultramarine (2.7.49)	18·00	1·30
B45	40pf. carmine-lake (7.5.49)	29·00	1·30
B46	50pf. brown-olive (2.7.49)	29·00	65
B47	60pf. brown-lake (7.5.49)	90·00	65
B48	80pf. grey-blue (7.5.49)	23·00	1·30
B49	90pf. emerald (7.5.49)	26·00	1·60

(b) Size 29½×24½ mm. Recess

B50	1Dm. olive-green (17.6.49)	39·00	2·00
B51	2Dm. dull purple (22.7.49)	£100	2·50
B52	3Dm. brown-red (25.10.49)	£400	26·00
B53	5Dm. dull ultramarine (25.10.49)	£200	26·00
B35/B53 Set of 21		£1000	75·00

Designs:—1pf., 3Dm. Brandenburg Gate; 4 (B36), 8, 40pf. Type B **2**; 4pf. (B36c), Exhibition building; 5, 25pf., 5Dm. Tegel Schloss; 6, 50pf. Reichstag Building; 10, 30pf. Kleistpark; 15pf., 1Dm. Type B **3**; 20 (B42), 80, 90pf. Technical High School; 20pf. (B42b), Olympia Stadium; 60pf. National Gallery; 2Dm. Gendarmenmarkt.

In the booklet panes with 'horiz label' the label reads the same way as the stamps; in those with 'vert label' the label is sideways to the stamps.

For 7pf. and 70pf. inscr 'DEUTSCHE POST BERLIN' see Nos. B118/B119.

B **4** Stephan Monument and Globe

B **5** Heinrich von Stephan Monument

1949 (11 Apr). 75th Anniv of Universal Postal Union. Litho. W **230**. P 14.

B54	B **4**	12pf. slate-blue	41·00	13·50
B55		16pf. blue-green	70·00	27·00
B56		24pf. red-orange	55·00	1·40
B57		50pf. brown-olive	£250	70·00
B58		60pf. lake-brown	£300	55·00
B59	B **5**	1Dm. yellow-olive	£200	£160
B60		2Dm. dull purple	£200	£120
B54/B60 Set of 7			£1000	£400

B **6** Goethe and scene from *Iphigene*

(B **7**)

(B **8**)

1949 (29 July). Birth Bicentenary of Goethe (poet). Type B **6** and similar designs showing Goethe and scenes from his works. W **230**. P 14.

B61	10pf. green	£190	95·00
B62	20pf. carmine	£200	95·00
B63	30pf. blue	55·00	70·00
B61/B63 Set of 3		£400	£225

Scenes from:—*Reineke Fuchs* (20pf.); *Faust* (30pf.).

Modern forgeries exist of Nos. B61/B63 imperforate on unwatermarked paper.

216

GERMANY / Berlin (Western Sectors)

1949 (1 Aug). Nos. 919, 936, 943 and 947 surch with Type B **7** (5pf.) or as Type B **8** (others), in green.

B64	**229**	5pf. on 45pf. scarlet	6·75	70
B65	**236**	10pf. on 24pf. brown	27·00	70
B66	**235**	20pf. on 80pf. grey-blue	95·00	23·00
B67	**237**	1m. on 3m. brown-lake	£225	30·00
B64/B67	Set of 4		£325	49·00

B **9** Alms Bowl and Bear

B **10**

(Des Goldammer. Litho)

1949 (1 Dec). Berlin Relief Fund. W 230. P 14.

B68	B **9**	10pf. +5pf. green	£140	£250
B69		20pf. +5pf. carmine	£160	£250
B70		30pf. +5pf. blue	£180	£300
B68/B70	Set of 3		£425	£700
MSB70a	111×65 mm. Nos. B68/B70 (sold at 1Dm.) (17.12.49)		£1300	£3000

VALIDITY. From 20 January 1950 the stamps of West Berlin were valid for use throughout West Germany.

(Des and eng Piwczyk. Recess)

1950 (1 Oct). European Recovery Programme. Wmk Type M **7** of Württemberg (Mult Crosses and Circles). P 14.

B71	B **10**	20pf. carmine-lake	£140	55·00

B **11** Harp

B **12** Singing Angels (after H. and J. van Eyck)

B **13** G. A. Lortzing

(Des A. Goldammer (10pf.), L. Schnell (30pf.). Eng L. Schnell. Recess)

1950 (29 Oct). Re-establishment of Berlin Philharmonic Orchestra. Wmk Type M **7** of Württemberg. P 14.

B72	B **11**	10pf. +5pf. yellow-green	70·00	55·00
B73	B **12**	30pf. +5pf. deep blue	£130	£120

(Des and eng L. Schnell. Recess)

1951 (22 Apr). Death Centenary of Lortzing (composer). Wmk Type M **7** of Württemberg. P 14.

B74	B **13**	20pf. brown-lake	80·00	75·00

B **14** Freedom Bell

B **15** Boy Stamp Collectors

B **16** Mask of Beethoven (taken from life, 1812)

(Des and eng L. Schnell. Recess)

1951 (1 May–6 Aug). Wmk Type M **7** of Württemberg. P 14.

B75	B **14**	5pf. brown (6.8)	3·50	11·00
B76		10pf. green (1.5)	24·00	34·00
B77		20pf. carmine (6.8)	13·50	34·00
B78		30pf. blue (1.5)	80·00	£120
B79		40pf. purple (5.8)	20·00	80·00
B75/B79	Set of 5		£130	£250

For stamps as T B **14** but with clapper of bell at right, see Nos. B82/B86, and with clapper in centre see Nos. B101/B105.

(Eng L. Schnell. Recess)

1951 (7 Oct). Stamp Day. Wmk Type M **7** of Württemberg. P 14.

B80	B **15**	10pf. +3pf. green	35·00	41·00
B81		20pf. +2pf. red	41·00	55·00

1951–52. As T B **14**, but re-engraved, with clapper of bell at right. Wmk Type M **7** of Württemberg. P 14.

B82	5pf. brown-olive (28.1.52)	3·50	3·50
B83	10pf. yellow-green (23.12.51)	10·00	6·75
B84	20pf. scarlet (23.12.51)	34·00	27·00
B85	30pf. deep blue (28.1.52)	90·00	70·00
B86	40pf. claret (28.1.52)	34·00	27·00
B82/B86	Set of 5	£150	£120

(Eng L. Schnell. Recess)

1952 (26 Mar). 125th Death Anniv of Beethoven (composer). No wmk. P 14.

B87	B **16**	30pf. blue	60·00	41·00

B **17** Olympic Torch

B **18** W. von Siemens (electrical engineer)

(Des A. Goldammer. Litho)

1952 (20 June). Olympic Games Festival, Berlin. Wmk Type M **7** of Württemberg. P 14.

B88	B **17**	4pf. yellow-brown	1·40	3·50
B89		10pf. green	16·00	23·00
B90		20pf. scarlet	24·00	35·00
B88/B90	Set of 3		37·00	55·00

(Des A. Goldammer. Eng J. Piwczyk (10pf), G. Schulz (15, 25pf.), L. Schnell (others). Recess)

1952–53. Famous Berliners. As T B **18** (portraits). W 230. P 14.

B91	4pf. brown (22.11.52)	95	95
B92	5pf. blue (24.1.53)	1·60	95
B93	6pf. brown-purple (24.6.53)	9·50	13·50
B94	8pf. brown-red (7.3.53)	3·50	4·00
B95	10pf. green (23.12.52)	4·75	95
B96	15pf. deep lilac (24.1.53)	24·00	24·00
B97	20pf. lake (12.10.52)	4·00	1·40
B98	25pf. olive green (27.5.53)	70·00	11·00
B99	30pf. purple (24.1.53)	27·00	13·50
B100	40pf. black-brown (2.5.53)	41·00	4·00
B91/B100	Set of 10	£170	65·00

Portraits:—4pf. C. F. Zelter (musician); 5pf. O. Lilienthal (aviator); 6pf. W. Rathenau (statesman); 8pf. T. Fontane (writer); 10pf. A. von Menzel (artist); 15pf. R. Virchow (pathologist); 20pf. T B **18**; 25pf. K. F. Schinkel (architect); 30pf.M. Planck (physicist); 40pf. W. von Humboldt (philologist).

1953. As T B **14**, but re-engraved, with clapper of bell in centre. W 230. P 14.

B101	5pf. bistre-brown (28.7.)	1·80	1·80
B102	10pf. green (9.10.)	3·50	2·75
B103	20pf. vermilion (26.9.)	9·50	5·50
B104	30pf. blue (26.9.)	16·00	16·00
B105	40pf. reddish violet (26.9.)	80·00	47·00
B101/B105	Set of 5	£100	65·00

B **19** Church before Bombing

B **20** Chainbreaker

(Des A. Goldammer. Eng G. Schulz (4, 10pf.), L. Schnell (others).Recess)

1953 (9 Aug). Kaiser Wilhelm Memorial Church Reconstruction Fund. T B **19** and similar vert design. W 230. P 14.

B106	B **19**	4pf. +1pf. deep brown	70	27·00
B107		10pf. +5pf. green	2·00	75·00
B108		20pf. +10pf. carmine-red	4·00	75·00
B109		30pf. +15pf. deep blue	27·00	£140
B106/B109	Set of 4		30·00	£275

Designs:—20pf., 30pf. Church after bombing.

217

GERMANY / Berlin (Western Sectors)

1953 (17 Aug). East German Uprising. T B **20** and another vert design inscr '17 JUNI 1953'. Typo. W **230**. P 14.
B110	20pf. black	13·50	2·75
B111	30pf. deep carmine-red	55·00	50·00

Designs:—20pf. T B **20**; 30pf. Brandenburg Gate.

B **21** Ernst Reuter
B **22** Conference Buildings 

(Des and eng L. Schnell. Recess)

1954 (18 Jan). Death of Ernst Reuter (Mayor of West Berlin). W **230**. P 14.
B112	B **21** 20pf. purple-brown	16·00	2·75

1954 (25 Jan). Four-Power Conference, Berlin. Typo. W **230**. P 14.
B113	B **22** 20pf. scarlet	13·50	7·50

B **23** O. Mergenthaler and Linotype Machine
(B **24**)

(Des H. Zapf. Eng G. Schulz. Recess)

1954 (11 May). Ottmar Mergenthaler Birth Centenary (Linotype machine inventor). W **230**. P 14.
B114	B **23** 10pf. myrtle-green	5·50	4·00

1954 (17 July). West German Presidential Election. No. B103 optd with T B **24**.
B115	20pf. vermilion	8·00	8·75

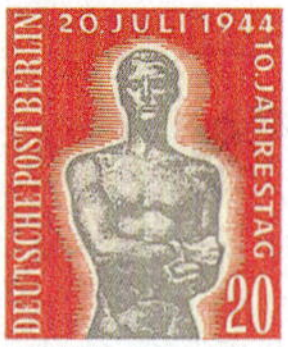

B **25** 'Germany in Bondage'
B **26** Prussian Postilion, 1827 

(Des R. Gerhardt. Typo)

1954 (20 July). Tenth Anniv of Attempt on Hitler's Life. W **230**. P 14.
B116	B **25** 20pf. grey and carmine	9·50	7·50

1954 (4 Aug). National Stamp Exhibition, Berlin. Litho. W **230**. P 14.
B117	B **26** 20pf. +10pf. blue, red, yellow and black	24·00	47·00

(Des A. Goldammer. Typo)

1954 (10 Aug–23 Oct). As Type B **2** but inscr 'DEUTSCHE POST BERLIN' at foot. W **230**. P 14.
B118	7pf. turquoise-green (10.8)	10·00	2·75
B119	70pf. yellow-olive (23.10)	£160	34·00

Designs:—7pf. Exhibition building; 70pf. Grunewald hunting lodge.

B **27** Memorial Library
B **28** Richard Strauss 

(Des H. Gorsch. Typo)

1954 (17 Sept). W **230**. P 14.
B120	B **27** 40pf. pale purple	18·00	5·50

(Des and eng L. Schnell. Recess)

1954 (18 Sept). Fifth Anniv of Death of Richard Strauss (composer). W **230**. P 14.
B121	B **28** 40pf. ultramarine	16·00	6·00

B **29** Blacksmiths at Work
B **30** Berlin (liner) 

(Des and eng L. Schnell. Recess)

1954 (25 Sept). Death Centenary of A. Borsig (industrialist). W **230**. P 14.
B122	B **29** 20pf. red-brown	12·00	3·00

(Des and eng G. Schulz. Recess)

1955 (12 Mar). W **230**. P 14.
B123	B **30** 10pf. deep bluish green	2·00	1·40
B124	25pf. deep ultramarine	12·00	6·00

B **31** Wilhelm Furtwängler (conductor)
B **32** 
B **33** Prussian Rural Postilion, 1760 

(Des and eng L. Schnell. Recess)

1955 (17 Sept). First Anniv of Death of Furtwängler. No wmk. P 14.
B125	B **31** 40pf. ultramarine	31·00	31·00

(Des R. Gerhardt. Litho)

1955 (17 Oct). Federal Parliament Session, Berlin. W **294**. P 14.
B126	B **32** 10pf. black, yellow and vermilion	1·20	1·40
B127	20pf. black, yellow and vermilion	8·00	15·00

(Des A. Goldammer. Litho)

1955 (27 Oct). Stamp Day and Philatelic Fund. W **294**. P 14.
B128	B **33** 25pf. +10pf. multicoloured	10·00	23·00

B **34** St. Otto
B **35** Radio Tower 
B **36** Radio Tower 

(Des R. Gerhardt. Eng P. Winkler (7pf.), E. Falz (10pf.), H.-J. Fuchs (20pf.). Recess)

1955 (26 Nov). 25th Anniv of Berlin Bishopric. T B **34** and similar vert designs inscr '25 JAHRE BISTUM BERLIN'. W **294**. P 14.
B129	7pf. +3pf. deep brown	1·40	4·00
B130	10pf. +5pf. deep myrtle-green	2·00	4·75
B131	20pf. +10pf. deep magenta	3·00	5·50
B129/B131	Set of 3	5·75	13·00

Designs:—7pf. T B **34**; 10pf. St. Hedwig; 20pf. St. Peter.

(Des A. Goldammer. Eng E. Falz (30, 40pf.), H.-J. Fuchs (50pf.,1, 3Dm.), G. Schulz (60pf.), H. Thorweger (70pf.))

1956–63. Berlin Buildings and Monuments. W **294**. P 14.

(a) T B **35**. Litho
B132	7pf. turquoise-green (1.3.56)	13·50	4·00

(b) As T B **36** with inscr at top. Litho (No. B133b), recess (No. B141/B146a) or typo (others)
B133	1pf. grey (23.2.57)	40	35
	a. Fluorescent paper (3.62)	40	35
B133b	3pf. reddish violet (fluorescent paper) (1.3.63)	55	45

GERMANY / Berlin (Western Sectors)

B134	5pf. mauve (23.2.57)	40	35
B135	7pf. turquoise-green (5.10.56)	40	35
B136	8pf. pale grey (22.6.56)	80	70
B136*a*	8pf. orange-red (14.2.59)	55	70
B137	10pf. green (10.7.56)	40	35
B138	15pf. chalky blue (10.7.56)	80	40
B139	20pf. carmine (10.7.56)	80	40
B140	25pf. purple-brown (9.8.56)	80	80
B141	30pf. grey-green (16.11.57)	1·60	1·60
B142	40pf. blue (30.7.57)	16·00	13·50
B143	50pf. deep yellow-olive (5.10.56)	1·60	1·60
B144	60pf. brown (16.11.57)	1·60	1·60
B145	70pf. violet (5.10.56)	36·00	22·00
B146	1Dm. yellow-olive (10.11.56)	3·50	4·50
B146*a*	3Dm. lake (26.4.58)	8·00	30·00
B132/B146*a* Set of 18		80·00	75·00

Designs: As T B **36**. Vert—8pf. (2), Town Hall, Neukölln; 10pf. Kaiser Wilhelm Memorial Church; 15pf. Airlift Monument; 25pf. Lilienthal Monument; 30pf. Pfaueninsel Castle; 50pf. Reuter Power-station. Horiz—1, 3pf. Brandenburg Gate; 5pf. PO Headquarters; 20pf. Free University; 40pf. Charlottenburg Castle; 60pf. Chamber of Commerce and Bourse; 70pf. Schiller Theatre. 24×30 mm—1Dm. *The Great Elector* (statue, Schlüter). 29½×25 mm—3Dm. Congress Hall, Berlin.

The 5, 7, 8 (both), 10, 15, 20, 25 and 70pf. were also issued in coils with every fifth stamp numbered on the back; the 7, 10 and 20pf. also exist in unnumbered coils.

B **37** Eagle and Arms of Berlin
B **38** 

(Des R. Gerhardt. Litho)
1956 (16 Mar). Federal Council Meeting. W **294**. P 14.
B147	B **37**	10pf. black, ochre and red	2·00	1·40
B148		25pf. black, ochre and red	6·75	6·75

(Des A. Goldammer. Eng E. Falz. Recess)
1956 (12 May). Centenary of German Engineers' Union. W **294**. P 14.
B149	B **38**	10pf. green	3·50	2·75
B150		20pf. deep rose-red	6·00	8·00

(B **39**)
B **40** P. Lincke 

1956 (9 Aug). Flood Relief Fund As No. B77 but colour changed, surch with T B **39**.
B151	B **14**	20pf. +10pf. bistre	6·75	7·50

(Des and eng L. Schnell. Recess)
1956 (3 Sept). Tenth Death Anniv of Lincke (composer). W **294**. P 14.
B152	B **40**	20pf. scarlet	4·00	4·75

B **41** Wireless Transmitter
B **42** Brandenburg Postilion, 1700 

(Des R. Gerhardt. Eng H.-J. Fuchs. Recess)
1956 (15 Sept). Industrial Exhibition. W **294**. P 14.
B153	B **41**	25pf. chocolate	11·00	16·00

(Des L. A. Helmcke. Litho)
1956 (26 Oct). Stamp Day and Philatelic Fund. W **294**. P 14.
B154	B **42**	25pf. +10pf. multicoloured	5·50	6·00

B **43** Spandau
B **44** Model of Hansa District 

(Des A. Goldammer. Eng G. Schulz. Recess)
1957 (7 Mar). 725th Anniv of Spandau. W **294**. P 14.
B155	B **43**	20pf. deep olive and red-brown	1·10	1·40

(Des R. Gerhardt. Eng H.-J. Fuchs (7pf.), E. Falz (20pf., 40pf.) Recess)
1957 (27 Apr–6 July). International Building Exhibition, Berlin. T B **44** and similar horiz designs inscr 'INTERBAU 6.7.—29.9.1957'. W **294**. P 14.
B156		7pf. chocolate	70	70
B157		20pf. carmine-red (6.7.57)	1·40	1·40
B158		40pf. deep ultramarine	3·50	4·00
B156/B158 Set of 3			5·00	5·50

Designs:—7pf. T B **44**; 20pf. Aerial view of Exhibition; 40pf. Exhibition Congress Hall.

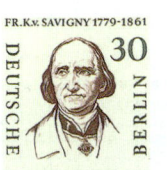

B **45** Friedrich K. von Savigny (jurist)
B **46** *Uta von Naumburg* (statue) 

(Des A. Degner. Eng E. Falz. Recess)
1957–59. T B **45** and similar vert portraits. W **294**. P 14.
B159		7pf. brown and blue-green (24.10.58)	40	40
B160		8pf. chocolate and grey (10.1.58)	40	40
B161		10pf. brown and green (29.9.58)	40	40
B162		15pf. sepia and chalky blue (30.9.57)	70	1·40
B163		20pf. +10pf. sepia and carmine-red (7.9.57)	1·40	1·60
B164		20pf. brown to carmine-red (5.12.58)	40	40
B165		25pf. sepia and lake (28.9.57)	1·60	1·90
B166		30pf. sepia and grey-green (22.6.57)	4·00	4·75
B167		40pf. sepia and grey-blue (6.5.59)	1·60	1·90
B168		50pf. sepia and yellow-olive (3.12.57)	8·00	12·00
B159/B168 Set of 10			17·00	23·00

Portraits:—7pf. T. Mommsen (historian); 8pf. H. Zille (painter); 10pf. E. Reuter (Mayor of Berlin); 15pf. F. Haber (chemist); 20pf.+10pf. L. Heck (zoologist); 20pf. F. Schleiermacher (theologian); 25pf. Max Reinhardt (theatrical producer); 30pf. T B **45**; 40pf. A. von Humboldt (naturalist); 50pf. C. D. Rauch (sculptor).

The premium on No. B163 was for the Berlin Zoo. No. B167 commemorates Humboldt's death centenary.

(Des H. Zimbal. Eng L. Schnell. Recess)
1957 (6 Aug). German Cultural Congress. W **294**. P 14.
B169	B **46**	25pf. lake-brown	1·60	2·00

B **47** 'Unity, Justice and Freedom'
B **48** Postilion, 1897–1925 

(Des R. Gerhardt. Litho)
1957 (15 Oct). Third Federal Parliament Assembly. W **294**. P 14.
B170	B **47**	10pf. black, ochre and vermilion	1·40	1·60
B171		20pf. black, ochre and vermilion	5·50	6·00

219

GERMANY / Berlin (Western Sectors)

(Des A. Goldammer. Litho)
1957 (23 Oct). Stamp Day. W **294**. P 14.
B172 B **48** 20pf. multicoloured .... 1·90 2·00

B **49** Torch of Remembrance
B **50** Elly Heuss-Knapp (social worker) 

(Des R. Gerhardt. Litho)
1957 (28 Oct). Seventh Congress of World War Veterans. W **294**. P 14.
B173 B **49** 20pf. blackish green, lemon and blue-green .... 2·00 1·40

(Des and eng L. Schnell. Recess)
1957 (30 Nov). Mothers' Convalescence Fund. W **294**. P 14.
B174 B **50** 20pf. +10pf. brown-red .... 2·75 4·50

B **51** Christ and Symbols of the Cosmos
B **52** Otto Suhr 

(Des E. Finke, after R. Ahrlé. Litho)
1958 (13 Aug). German Catholics' Day. W **294**. P 14.
B175 B **51** 10pf. black and blue-green .... 95 1·10
B176   20pf. black and magenta .... 1·80 2·75

(Des and eng L Schnell. Recess)
1958 (30 Aug). First Anniv of Death of Burgomaster Otto Suhr. W **294**. P 14.
B177 B **52** 20pf. scarlet .... 2·00 3·00
See also Nos. B187 and B193.

B **53** President Heuss
B **54** Symbolic Airlift 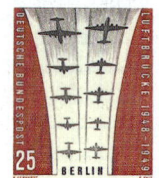

1959 (31 Jan–22 May). W **294**. P 14.
(a) Typo
B178 B **53** 7pf. blue-green (10.4) 55 70
B179   10pf. green (31.1) 55 70
B180   20pf. carmine (31.1) 95 70

(b) Recess
B181 B **53** 40pf. blue (22.5) .... 4·00 8·00
B182   70pf. violet (22.5) .... 15·00 19·00
B178/B182 Set of 5 .... 19·00 26·00
Nos. B178/B182 were also issued in coils with every fifth stamp numbered on the back.

(Des R. Gerhardt. Eng E. Falz. Recess)
1959 (12 May). Tenth Anniv of Berlin Airlift. W **294**. P 14.
B183 B **54** 25pf. black and brown-red .... 1·10 80

B **55** Brandenburg Gate, Berlin
B **56** Schiller 

(Des R. Gerhardt. Litho)
1959 (18 June). 14th World Communities Congress, Berlin. W **294**. P 14.
B184 B **55** 20pf. blue, red and pale blue .... 1·50 80

(Des R. Gerhardt. Eng H.-J. Fuchs. Recess)
1959 (10 Nov). Bicentenary of Birth of Schiller (poet). W **294**. P 14.
B185 B **56** 20pf. brown and scarlet 70 80

B **57** Robert Koch
B **58** Boy at Window 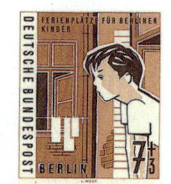

(Des R. Gerhardt. Eng H.-J. Braband. Recess)
1960 (27 May). 50th Anniv of Death of Koch (bacteriologist). W **294**. P 14.
B186 B **57** 20pf. brown-purple 70 80

(Des E. Fincke. Eng H.-J. Fuchs. Recess)
1960 (30 June). Fourth Anniv of Death of W. Schreiber (Mayor of Berlin, 1951–53). Portrait as T B **52**. W **294**. P 14.
B187   20pf. brown-red .... 95 1·20

(Des. L. Wüst. Litho)
1960 (15 Sept). Berlin Children's Holiday Fund. T B **58** and similar vert designs inscr. 'FERIENPLATZE FUR BERLINER KINDER'. W **294**. P 14.
B188   7pf. +3pf. deep brown, brown and yellow-brown 40 55
B189   10pf. +5pf. deep green, olive-green and yellow-green 40 55
B190   20pf. +10pf. deep brown, crimson and pink.. 95 95
B191   40pf. +20pf. deep blue, blue and pale blue ... 2·30 6·00
B188/B191 Set of 4 .... 3·75 7·25
Designs:—7pf. T B **58**; 10pf. Girl in street; 20pf. Girl blowing on Alpine flower; 40pf. Boy on beach.

B **59** H. Böckler
B **60** Dürer 

1961 (16 Feb). Tenth Anniv of Death of Böckler (politician). Litho. W **294**. P 14.
B192 B **59** 20pf. black and vermilion 55 70

> **FLUORESCENT PAPER** was used for all issues from No. B193 onwards unless otherwise stated.

(Des R. Gerhardt. Eng E. Falz. Recess)
1961 (3 June). Fourth Death Anniv of Louise Schroeder (Mayor of Berlin). Portrait as T B **52**. W **294**. P 14.
B193   20pf. chocolate and deep brown 70 70

(Des Michel and Kieser)
1961–62. Famous Germans. T B **60** and similar portraits. W **294**. P 14.
(a) Typo
B194   5pf. olive (18.9.61) 40 40
B195   7pf. yellow-brown (3.8.61) 40 70
B196   8pf. reddish violet (3.8.61) 40 70
B197   10pf. yellow-green (15.6.61) 40 40
   a. Tête-bêche (pair) (3.62) .... 1·60 4·00
B198   15pf. pale blue (18.9.61) 40 70
B199   20pf. carmine-red (28.6.61) 40 40
B200   25pf. orange-brown (7.10.61) 40 70

(b) Recess
B201   30pf. black-brown (7.10.61) 55 95
B202   40pf. blue (28.6.61) .... 95 1·80
B203   50pf. brown (1.12.61) .... 70 1·80
B204   60pf. claret (12.4.62) .... 70 2·00
B205   70pf. green (1.12.61) .... 95 2·00
B206   80pf. yellow-brown (1.12.61) .... 6·00 13·50
B207   1Dm. bluish violet (18.9.61) .... 3·50 6·00

B208	2Dm. green (12.4.62)		4·75	8·75
B194/B208	Set of 15		19·00	37·00

Portraits:—As Nos. 1261/1276 of German Federal Republic.
Nos. B194/B200, B202 and B205 were also issued in coils with every fifth stamp numbered on the back.

No. B209 is vacant.

B 61 'Five Crosses' Symbol and St. Mary's Church

B 62 Exhibition Emblem

(Des R. Gerhardt. Litho)

1961 (19 July). Tenth Evangelical Churches' Day. T B 61 and similar horiz design. W 294. P 14.

B210	10pf. violet and green		40	40
B211	20pf. violet and reddish purple		40	40

Designs:—10pf. T B 61; 20pf. 'Five Crosses' and Kaiser Wilhelm Memorial Church.

(Des R. Gerhardt. Eng E. Falz. Recess)

1961 (3 Aug). West Berlin Broadcasting Exhibition. W 294. P 14.

B212	B 62	20pf. deep brown and brown-red	55	70

B 63 'Die Linden' (1650)

B 64 Euler Gelberhund Biplane, 1912, and Boeing 707 Jetliner

(Des H. Hiller. Eng E. Falz (10,15, 40pf., 1Dm.); P. Nowraty (90pf.); H.-J. Fuchs (others). Recess)

1962–63. Old Berlin Series. T B 63 and similar horiz designs. W 294. P 14.

B213	7pf. sepia and brown (27.6.62)		40	40
B214	10pf. sepia and green (27.6.62)		40	40
B215	15pf. black and ultramarine (26.4.63)		40	40
B216	20pf. sepia and brown-red (17.9.62)		40	40
B217	25pf. sepia and yellow-olive (29.8.63)		40	40
B218	40pf. black and ultramarine (17.9.62)		40	70
B219	50pf. sepia and brown-purple (14.9.63)		70	70
B220	60pf. sepia and magenta (25.10.63)		80	80
B221	70pf. black and purple (27.7.62)		80	80
B222	80pf. sepia and carmine-red (24.5.63)		1·10	1·20
B223	90pf. sepia and orange-brown (6.12.63)		1·40	1·40
B224	1Dm. sepia and blue-green (7.12.62)		1·60	2·00
B213/B224	Set of 12		8·00	8·75

Designs:—7pf. T B **63**; 10pf. 'Waisenbrücke' (Orphans' Bridge), 1783; 15pf. Mauerstrasse, 1780; 20pf. Berlin Castle, 1703; 25pf. Potsdamer Platz, 1825; 40pf. Bellevue Castle, *circa* 1800, 50pf. Fischer Bridge, 1830; 60pf. Halle Gate, 1880; 70pf. Parochial Church, 1780; 80pf. University, 1825; 90pf. Opera House, 1780; 1Dm. Grunewald Lake, *circa* 1790.

(Des Michel and Kieser. Litho)

1962 (12 Sept). 50th Anniv of German Airmail Transport. W **294**. P 14.

B225	B **64**	60pf. black and blue	1·10	95

B **65** Exhibition Emblem

B **66** Town Hall, Schöneberg

B **67** Pres. Lübke

(Des after poster by W. Regel. Litho)

1963 (24 July). West Berlin Broadcasting Exhibition. W **294**. P 14.

B226	B **65**	20pf. ultramarine, green and light blue	55	55

(Des L. Wüst. Eng P. Nowraty. Recess)

1964 (30 May). 700th Anniv of Schöneberg. W **294**. P 14.

B227	B **66**	20pf. chocolate	55	55

(Des H. Schardt. Litho)

1964 (1 July). Re-election of President Lübke. No wmk. P 14.

B228	B **67**	20pf. carmine-red	40	40
B229		40pf. blue	70	70

See also Nos. B308/B309.

WEST GERMAN DESIGNS. Except where illustrated the following are stamps of West Germany additionally inscribed 'BERLIN'.

1964 (19 Sept). Capitals of the Federal Lands. As No. 1335.

B230	20pf. multicoloured	70	70

1964 (6 Oct). Humanitarian Relief and Welfare Funds. As Nos. 1352/5.

B231	10pf. +5pf. multicoloured	40	40
B232	15pf. +5pf. multicoloured	40	40
B233	20pf. +10pf. multicoloured	70	55
B234	40pf. +20pf. multicoloured	95	1·60
B231/B234	Set of 4	2·20	2·75

1964 (21 Nov). President Kennedy Commemoration. As No. 1358.

B235	40pf. ultramarine	80	95

1964 (15 Dec)–**69**. 12 Centuries of German Architecture.

(a) Size 18½×22½ mm. on slightly greyish paper. As Nos. 1359/1366.
Plain backgrounds

B236	10pf. brown (12.3.65)	40	40
	a. Tête-bêche (pair) (6.65)	1·10	2·00
B237	15pf. deep green (12.3.65)	40	40
B238	20pf. brown-red (12.3.65)	40	40
B239	40pf. ultramarine (12.3.65)	1·10	2·00
B240	50pf. bistre-brown	2·40	2·75
B241	60pf. scarlet	1·80	2·00
B242	70pf. bronze-green (29.5.65)	3·50	6·00
B243	80pf. chocolate	3·50	2·75
B236/B243	Set of 8	12·00	15·00

(b) Size 19½×24 mm. on creamy paper. As Nos. 1367/1381.
Coloured backgrounds

B244	5pf. bistre-brown (15.6.66)	40	40
B245	8pf. crimson (15.6.66)	40	40
B246	10pf. deep purple-brown (21.6.67)	40	40
B247	20pf. emerald-green (17.11.67)	40	40
B248	30pf. olive-green (7.1.66)	40	40
B249	30pf. rose-red (17.2.67)	40	40
B250	40pf. bistre (4.8.67)	95	1·40
B251	50pf. deep blue (4.8.67)	70	80
B252	60pf. orange-red (14.4.67)	2·75	3·50
B253	70pf. bronze-green (14.4.67)	1·40	1·40
B254	80pf. red-brown (21.6.67)	1·80	3·50
B255	90pf. black (15.6.66)	95	1·40
B256	1Dm. Prussian blue (7.11.66)	95	1·40
B257	1Dm.10 chestnut (13.12.66)	2·40	2·40
B258	1Dm.30 yellow-green (26.3.69)	4·00	4·00
B259	2Dm. purple (13.12.66)	4·00	3·50
B244/B259	Set of 16	20·00	23·00

Buildings:—8pf. Palatine Castle, Kaub; others, as Nos. 1359/1381 of West Germany.

Nos. B236/B239 and B242 were also issued in coils with every fifth stamp numbered on the back.

1965 (1 Apr). Child Welfare. As Nos. 1384/1387.

B261	10pf. +5pf. Woodcock	30	40
B262	15pf. +5pf. Ring-necked Pheasant	30	40
B263	20pf. +10pf. Black Grouse	30	40
B264	40pf. +20pf. Capercaillie	70	1·40
B261/B264	Set of 4	1·40	1·30

B **68** Kaiser Wilhelm Memorial Church

B **69** Bust of a Young Man (after C. Meit)

B **70** Broadcasting Tower and TV Screen

(Des H. Hiller. Eng P. Inowraty (10pf., 40pf., 80pf.), E. Falz (50pf., 1Dm.10), H.-J. Fuchs (others). Recess and litho)

1965–66. New Berlin. T B **68** and similar designs. Multicoloured. No wmk. P 14.

B265	10pf. Type B **68** (28.8.65)	40	40
B266	15pf. Opera House (23.10.65)	40	40
B267	20pf. Philharmonic Hall (23.10.65)	40	40

GERMANY / Berlin (Western Sectors)

B268	30pf. Jewish Community Centre (19.4.66)		40	40
B269	40pf. Regina Martyrum Memorial Church (28.8.65)		40	40
B270	50pf. Ernst Reuter Square (18.11.65)		40	55
B271	60pf. Europa Centre (19.4.66)		55	70
B272	70pf. Technical University, Charlottenburg (18.11.66)		80	80
B273	80pf. City Motorway (18.11.65)		80	80
B274	90pf. Planetarium (16.9.68)		95	1·40
B275	1Dm. Telecommunications Tower (16.9.66)		95	1·60
B276	1Dm.10 University Clinic, Steglitz (18.11.66)		95	1·80
B265/B276	Set of 12		6·75	8·75

Nos. B266/B270, B272, B274 and B276 are horiz designs.

1965 (6 Oct). Humanitarian Relief Funds. As Nos. 1406/1409.

B277	10pf. +5pf. Type **425**		30	40
B278	15pf. +5pf. Cinderella and birds with dress		30	40
B279	20pf. +10pf. Prince offering slipper to Cinderella		30	40
B280	40pf. +20pf. Cinderella and Prince on horse		60	1·30
B277/B280	Set of 4		1·40	2·30

1966–70. As Nos. 1412/1415a.

B281	**428**	10pf. chocolate (24.10.66)	40	40
		a. Tête-bêche (pair) (1966)	1·60	2·00
		b. Booklet pane. Nos. B281×4, B282×2 and B283×4 (13.12.66)	11·50	
		c. Booklet pane. Nos. B281×4 and B283×2 (7.70)	5·25	
B282		20pf. myrtle-green (24.10.66)	40	40
		a. Booklet pane. Nos. B282×2 and B283×2 (7.70)	4·00	
B283		30pf. carmine-red (1.4.66)	40	40
B284		50pf. deep blue (24.10.66)	90	65
B284a		100pf. Prussian blue (14.4.67)	7·25	7·75
B281/B284a	Set of 5		8·50	8·75

Nos. B281/B284a were also issued in coils with every fifth stamp numbered on the back.

1966 (22 Apr). Child Welfare. As Nos. 1416/1419.

B285	10pf. +5pf. Type **429**		40	40
B286	20pf. +10pf. Chamois		40	40
B287	30pf. +15pf. Fallow Deer		40	50
B288	50pf. +25pf. Red Deer		80	1·30
B285/B288	Set of 4		1·80	2·30

1966 (5 Oct). Humanitarian Relief Funds. As Nos. 1428/1431.

B289	10pf. +5pf. Type **435**		40	40
B290	20pf. +10pf. Frog dining with Princess		40	40
B291	30pf. +15pf. Frog Prince and Princess		65	40
B292	50pf. +25pf. In coach		65	1·30
B289/B292	Set of 4		1·90	2·30

Designs from Grimm's *The Frog Prince*.

1967 (4 Apr). Child Welfare. As Nos. 1434/1437.

B293	10pf. +5pf. Common Rabbit		40	40
B294	20pf. +pf. Stoat		40	40
B295	30pf. +15pf. Common Hamster		65	50
B296	50pf. +25pf. Red Fox		1·60	2·30
B293/B296	Set of 4		2·75	3·25

(Des E. Finke. Eng E. Falz (1Dm.10), H. Fuchs (others). Recess)

1967. Berlin Art Treasures. T B **69** and similar vert designs. P 14.

B297	10pf. sepia and bistre (21.6.67)		40	40
B298	20pf. blackish of and grey-blue (31.10.67)		40	40
B299	30pf. brown and olive (17.11.67)		40	40
B300	50pf. blackish brown and grey (14.10.67)		65	65
B301	1Dm. black and violet-blue (17.11.67)		1·30	1·30
B302	1Dm.10 deep brown and yellow-brown (21.6.67)		2·00	2·50
B297/B302	Set of 6		4·75	5·00

Designs:—10pf. T B **69**; 20pf. Head of *The Elector of Brandenburg* (statue by Schlüter); 30pf. *St. Mark* (statue by Riemenschneider); 50pf. Head from Quadriga, Brandenburg Gate; 1Dm. *Madonna* (carving by Feuchtmayer). Larger (221×39 *mm*), 1Dm.10 *Christ and St. John* (after carving from Upper Swabia, *circa* 1320).

(Des H. Kummer. Recess and litho)

1967 (19 July). West Berlin Broadcasting Exhibition. W **294**. P 14.

B303	B **70**	30pf. multicoloured	50	65

1967 (3 Oct). Humanitarian Relief Funds. As Nos. 1443/6.

B304	10pf. +5pf. multicoloured		40	40
B305	20pf. +10pf. multicoloured		40	40
B306	30pf. +15pf. multicoloured		40	65
B307	50pf. +25pf. multicoloured		90	1·30
B304/B307	Set of 4		1·90	2·50

1967 (14 Oct). Re-election of President Lübke. Design as T B **67**.

B308	B **67**	30pf. carmine-red	40	40
B309		50pf. blue	65	80

1968 (2 Feb). Child Welfare. As Nos. 1454/1457.

B310	10pf. +5pf. Wild Cat		40	80
B311	20pf. +10pf. European Otter		50	80
B312	30pf. +15pf. Eurasian Badger		90	1·60
B313	50pf. +25pf. Eurasian Beaver		2·75	3·50
B310/B313	Set of 4		4·00	6·00

B **71** Former Courthouse

B **72** Festival Emblems

(Des W. Welde. Eng E. Falz. Recess)

1968 (16 Mar). 500th Anniv of Berlin Magistrates' Court. P 14.

B314	B **71**	30pf. black	50	65

(Des R. Schmitt. Litho)

1968 (29 Apr). Athletics Festival, Berlin. P 14.

B315	B **72**	20pf. red, black and light grey	50	65

B **73** Doll of 1878

B **74** *The Newspaper Seller* (C. W. Allers, 1889)

(Des Heinz and Hella Schillinger. Litho)

1968 (3 Oct). Humanitarian Relief Funds. T B **73** and similar vert designs, showing reclining dolls. Multicoloured. P 14.

B316	10pf. +5pf. Type B **73**		40	40
B317	20pf. +10pf. Doll of 1850		40	40
B318	30pf. +15pf. Doll of 1870		40	40
B319	50pf. +25pf. Doll of 1885		75	1·30
B316/B319	Set of 4		1·80	2·30

(Des Finke. Eng H.-J. Fuchs (B320/2, B324/5), E. Falz (B323, B326/7). Recess)

1969. 19th-century Berliners. Contemporary Art. T B **74** and similar designs. P 14.

B320	5pf. black (26.3)		35	35
B321	10pf. deep maroon (6.2)		35	35
B322	10pf. brown (24.10)		35	35
B323	20pf. bronze-green (6.2)		40	40
B324	20pf. deep bluish green (24.10)		40	40
B325	30pf. red-brown (26.3)		90	65
B326	30pf. lake-brown (24.10)		90	65
B327	50pf. blue (26.3)		2·50	3·00
B320/B327	Set of 8		5·50	5·50

Designs: Horiz—No. B320, *The Cab-driver* (H. Zille, 1875). Vert—No. B321, T B **74**; No. B322, *The Bus-driver* (C. W. Allers, 1890); No. B323, *The Cobbler's Boy* (F. Kruger, 1839); No. B324, *The Cobbler* (A. von Menzel, 1833); No. B325, *The Borsig Forge* (P. Meyerheim, 1878); No. B326, *Three Berlin Ladies* (F. Kruger, 1839); No. B327, *At the Brandenburg Gate* (C. W. Allers, 1889).

1969 (6 Feb). Child Welfare. As Nos. 1478/1481.

B328	10pf. +5pf. brown, black and olive-yellow		40	50
B329	20pf. +10pf. chestnut, black and buff		50	90
B330	30pf. +15pf. blackish-brown, black and red		80	1·30
B331	50pf. +25pf. grey, yellow, black and blue		2·10	2·50
B328/B331	Set of 4		3·50	5·75

B **75** Orangutan Family

(Des Weber. Eng Fuchs (10pf., 20pf.), Falz (30pf., 50pf.). Recess and litho)

1969 (4 June). 125th Anniv of Berlin Zoo. Sheet 99×74 mm containing T B **75** and similar horiz designs. P 14×13½.

MSB332 10pf. black and yellow-brown; 20pf. black and yellow-green; 30pf. black and reddish purple; 50pf. black and light blue; (*sold for* 1Dm.30). 3·25 3·25

Designs:—10pf. T B **75**; 20pf. Dalmatian Pelican family; 30pf. Gaur and calf; 50pf. Common Zebra and foal.

The premium of 20pf. was for Zoo funds.

GERMANY / Berlin (Western Sectors)

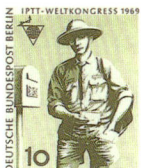

B 76 Postman

B 77 J. Joachim (violinist and Academy director: after A. von Menzel)

B 78 Railway Carriage (1835)

1969 (21 July). 20th Congress of Post Office Trade Union Federation (IPTT), Berlin. T B **76** and similar vert designs. P 14.

B333	10pf. deep olive and light yellow-olive	40	40
B334	20pf. blackish brown, yellow-brown and buff	40	40
B335	30pf. blackish violet and light ochre	90	1·00
B336	50pf. deep blue and light blue	1·80	2·10
B333/B336	Set of 4	3·25	3·50

Designs:—10pf. T B **76**; 20pf. Telephonist; 30pf. Technician; 50pf. Airmail Handlers.

(Des State Ptg Wks, Berlin. Photo)

1969 (12 Sept). Anniversaries. T B **77** and similar vert design. P 14.

B337	30pf. multicoloured	90	80
B338	50pf. multicoloured	1·60	2·10

Designs:—30pf. T B **77** (Centenary of Berlin Academy of Music); 50pf. *Alexander von Humboldt* (after J. Stieler: Birth Bicentenary). Stamps of a similar design were issued by Venezuela.

(Des Hella and Heinz Schillinger. Litho)

1969 (2 Oct–13 Nov). Humanitarian Relief Funds. Pewter Models. T B **78** and similar vert designs. Multicoloured. P 14.

(a) Inscr 'WOHLFAHRTSMARKE' (2 Oct)

B339	10pf. +5pf. Type B **78**	40	40
B340	20pf. +10pf. Woman feeding chicken (1850)	40	40
B341	30pf. +15pf. Market stall (1850)	65	65
B342	50pf. +25pf. Mounted postilion (1860)	1·70	1·70
B339/B342	Set of 4	2·75	2·75

(b) Christmas. Inscr 'WEIHNACHTSMARKE' (13 Nov)

B343	10pf. +5pf. The Three Kings	65	50

B 79 T. Fontane

B 80 Heinrich von Stretlingen

(Des State Ptg Wks, Berlin. Photo)

1970 (7 Jan). 150th Birth Anniv of Theodor Fontane (writer). P 14.

B344	B **79**	20pf. multicoloured	65	50

(Des P. Froitzheim. Photo)

1970 (5 Feb). Child Welfare. Miniatures of Minnesingers. T B **80** and similar vert designs. Multicoloured. P 14.

B345	10pf. +5pf. Type B **80**	40	40
B346	20pf. +10pf. Meinloh von Sevelingen	65	80
B347	30pf. +15pf. Burkhart von Hohenfels	90	1·00
B348	50pf. +25pf. Albrecht von Johannsdorf	2·10	2·50
B345/B348	Set of 4	3·75	4·25

B 81 Film 'Title'

B 82 Allegory of Folklore

(Des State Printing Works, Berlin. Photo)

1970 (18 June). 20th International Film Festival, Berlin. P 14.

B349	B **81**	30pf. multicoloured	80	90

1970–73.

B350	486	5pf. black (23.7.70)	40	40
B351		8pf. olive-brown (8.4.71)	1·20	1·70
B352		10pf. brown (23.10.70)	40	40
B353		15pf. bistre (20.6.72)	40	50
B354		20pf. deep green (23.10.70)	40	40
B355		25pf. deep yellow-green (27.8.71)	1·30	90
B356		30pf. lake-brown (6.1.71)	1·70	80
B357		40pf. brown-orange (8.4.71)	90	40
B358		50pf. steel-blue (8.4.71)	90	40
B359		60pf. deep ultramarine (25.6.71)	1·30	90
B360		70pf. agate (8.4.71)	1·20	1·00
B361		80pf. slate-green (8.4.71)	1·60	1·60
B362		90pf. deep claret (6.1.71)	3·00	4·00
B363		1Dm. yellow-olive (23.7.70)	1·60	1·20
B364		110pf. olive-grey (16.1.73)	2·00	2·00
B365		120pf. yellow-brown (8.3.72)	2·00	1·60
B366		130pf. ochre (20.6.72)	2·50	2·50
B367		140pf. deep bluish green (16.1.73)	2·50	2·50
B368		150pf. brown-lake (5.7.72)	2·50	2·00
B369		160pf. orange (8.3.72)	3·25	3·25
B370		170pf. orange (11.9.72)	2·50	2·75
B371		190pf. brown-purple (16.1.73)	3·25	3·00
B372		2Dm. bluish violet (6.1.71)	3·25	2·30
B350/B372	Set of 23		36·00	33·00

(Des H. Hiller. Litho)

1970 (4 Sept). 20th Berlin Folklore Week. P 14.

B373	B **82**	30pf. multicoloured	90	90

B 83 'Kasperl'

B 84 L. von Ranke (after painting by J. Schrader)

(Des E. de Vries. Litho)

1970 (6 Oct–12 Nov). Humanitarian Relief Funds. Puppets. Vert designs similar to T B **83**. Multicoloured. P 14.

(a) Relief Funds (6 Oct)

B374	10pf. +5pf. Type B **83**	40	40
B375	20pf. +10pf. 'Polichinelle'	40	40
B376	30pf. +15pf. 'Punch'	90	80
B377	50pf. +25pf. 'Pulcinella'	1·60	1·80
B374/B377	Set of 4	3·00	3·00

(b) Christmas (12 Nov)

B378	10pf. +5pf. Angel	50	50

(Des State Printing Works, Berlin. Photo)

1970 (23 Oct). 175th Birth Anniv of Leopold von Ranke (historian). P 14.

B379	B **84**	30pf. multicoloured	80	65

1971 (18 Jan). Centenary of German Unification.

B380	492	30pf. black, vermilion and orange	90	90

B 85 Class ET 165.8 Electric Train, 1933

B 86 Fly

(Des H. Hiller. Litho)

1971 (18 Jan–3 May). Berlin Rail Transport. T B **85** and similar horiz designs. Multicoloured. P 14.

B381	5pf. Class T.12 steam train, 1925 (3.5)	40	40
B382	10pf. Electric tram, 1890 (3.5)	40	40
B383	20pf. Horse tram, 1880 (3.5)	40	40
B384	30pf. Type B **85**	65	65
B385	50pf. Electric tram, 1950 (3.5)	2·50	2·30
B386	1Dm. Underground train No. 2431, 1971	3·25	3·25
B381/B386	Set of 6	6·75	6·75

(Des from Children's drawings. Litho)

1971 (5 Feb). Child Welfare. Drawings. T B **86** and similar horiz designs. Multicoloured. P 14.

B387	10pf. +5pf. Type B **86**	50	50
B388	20pf. +10pf. Fish	50	50

223

GERMANY / Berlin (Western Sectors)

B389	30pf. +15pf. Porcupine		80	90
B390	50pf. +25pf. Cockerel		2·10	2·20
B387/B390 Set of 4			3·50	3·75

B **87** *The Bagpiper* (copper engraving, Dürer, *c.* 1514)

B **88** Communications Tower, and Dish Aerials

(Des and eng H.-J. Fuchs. Recess)

1971 (21 May). 500th Birth Anniv of Albrecht Dürer. P 14.
B391	B **87**	10pf. black and brown	80	50

(Des H. Hiller. Photo)

1971 (14 July). International Broadcasting Exhibition, Berlin. P 14.
B392	B **88**	30pf. indigo, steel-blue and red	1·30	1·00

B **89** Bach and part of *2nd Brandenburg Concerto*

B **90** H. von Helmholtz (from painting by K. Morell-Kramer)

(Des E. Finke. Litho)

1971 (14 July). 250th Anniv of Bach's *Brandenburg Concertos*. P 14.
B393	B **89**	30pf. black, deep bronze-green, brown-red and pale flesh	1·30	1·00

(Des State Printing Works, Berlin. Photo)

1971 (27 Aug). 150th Birth Anniv of Hermann von Helmholtz (scientist). P 14.
B394	B **90**	25pf. multicoloured	90	65

B **91** Opel Racing-car (1921)

B **92** Dancing Men

(Des R. Gerhardt. Litho)

1971 (27 Aug). 50th Anniv of Avus Motor-racing Track. Sheet 100×75 mm, containing horiz designs as T B **91**. Multicoloured. P 14.
MSB395 10pf. Type B **91**; 25pf. Auto-Union (1936); 30pf. Mercedes-Benz SSKL (1931) 60pf. Mercedes racing with Auto-Union (1937) .... 2·50 2·30

1971–74. Accident Prevention. As Nos. 1596/1605.
B396	5pf. orange-red (29.10.71)	40	50
B397	10pf. reddish brown (8.3.72)	40	40
	a. Booklet pane. Nos. B397×2, B398×2, B400×2 and B401×2 (perf all edges) (11.72)	8·50	
	b. Perf 3 sides. Booklets (1974)	3·25	4·50
	ba. Booklet pane. Nos. B397b×2, B398a×2, B400a×2 and B401b×2 (imperf top and bottom) (1974)	29·00	
B398	20pf. violet (5.7.72)	40	40
	a. Perf 3 sides. Booklets (1974)	4·50	6·50
B399	25pf. myrtle green (10.9.71)	65	1·00
B400	30pf. carmine-red (8.3.72)	65	80
	a. Perf 3 sides. Booklets (1974)	3·25	4·50
B401	40pf. magenta (20.6.72)	65	90
	a. Tête-bêche (pair) (11.72)	5·00	7·75
	b. Perf 3 sides. Booklets (1974)	4·50	6·50
B402	50pf. turquoise-blue (16.1.73)	3·25	2·00
B403	60pf. ultramarine (10.9.71)	3·25	4·00
B404	70pf. ultramarine and emerald (5.6.73)	2·30	1·80
B405	100pf. olive (5.7.72)	3·25	2·00
B406	150pf. chestnut (11.9.72)	9·75	11·50
B396/B406 Set of 11 (cheapest)	22·00	23·00

Nos. B396/B406 were issued both in sheets and coils, the latter having every fifth stamp numbered on the back.

In booklet panes Nos. B397a and B397ba the stamps are arranged in different orders.

(Des H. and H. Schillinger. Litho)

1971 (5 Oct–11 Nov). Humanitarian Relief Funds. Wooden Toys. T B **92** and similar vert designs. Multicoloured. P 14.

(a) Inscr 'WOHLFAHRTSMARKE' (5 Oct)
B407	10pf. +5pf. Type B **92**	40	40
B408	25pf. +10pf. Horseman on wheels	40	55
B409	30pf. +15pf. Acrobat	95	95
B410	60pf. +30pf. Nurse and babies	1·80	2·00
B407/B410 Set of 4	3·25	3·50

(b) Christmas. Inscr 'WEIHNACHTSMARKE' (11 Nov)
| B411 | 10pf. +5pf. Angel with two candles | 70 | 55 |

B **93** Microscope

B **94** *F. Gilly* (after bust by Schadow)

(Des H. Hiller. Photo)

1971 (26 Oct). Centenary of Material-Testing Laboratory, Berlin. P 14.
| B412 | B **93** | 30pf. multicoloured | 80 | 70 |

(Des State Printing Wks, Berlin. Eng E. Falz. Recess)

1972 (4 Feb). Birth Bicentenary of Friedrich Gilly (architect). P 14.
| B413 | B **94** | 30pf. black and blue | 95 | 70 |

B **95** Boy raiding Bird's-nest

B **96** *Grunewaldsee* (A. von Riesen)

(Des H. Börnsen. Litho)

1972 (4 Feb). Youth Welfare. Protection of Animals. T B **95** and similar horiz designs. Multicoloured. P 14.
B414	10pf. +5pf. Type B **95**	40	40
B415	25pf. +10pf. Care of kittens	55	55
B416	30pf. +15pf. Man beating watch-dog	95	95
B417	60pf. +30pf. Animals crossing road at night	2·00	2·30
B414/B417 Set of 4	3·50	3·75

1972 (14 Apr). Paintings of Berlin Lakes. T B **96** and similar horiz designs. Multicoloured. Photo. P 14.
B418	10pf. Type B **96**	40	40
B419	25pf. *Wannsee* (Max Liebermann)	80	95
B420	30pf. *Schlachtensee* (W. Leistikow)	1·40	1·10
B418/B420 Set of 3	2·30	2·20

B **97** E. T. A. Hoffmann

B **98** *Max Liebermann* (self-portrait)

B **99** Stamp Printing-press

(Des J. H. Hiller. Eng H.-J. Fuchs. Recess)

1972 (18 May). 150th Death Anniv of E. T. A. Hoffman (poet and musician). P 14.
| B421 | B **97** | 60pf. black and bluish violet | 1·90 | 1·90 |

(Des State Printing Wks, Berlin. Photo)

1972 (18 July). 125th Birth Anniv of Max Liebermann (painter). P 14.
| B422 | B **98** | 40pf. multicoloured | 1·20 | 80 |

GERMANY / Berlin (Western Sectors)

(Des E. Finke. Eng E. Falz. Recess and litho)
1972 (20 Oct). Stamp Day. P 14.
B423   B **99**   20pf. blue, black and brown-red 95   55

1972 (5 Oct–10 Nov). Humanitarian Relief Funds. As Nos. 1636/1640.
(a) Relief Funds 19th-century Faience Chessman. Inscr 'WOHLFAHRTSMARKE' (5 Oct)
B424   20pf. +10pf. multicoloured 60   60
B425   30pf. +15pf. multicoloured 90   90
B426   40pf. +20pf. multicoloured .... 2·30   2·30
B427   70pf. +35pf. multicoloured .... 3·25   3·25
B424/B427 *Set of 4* .... 6·25   6·25

(b) Christmas. Inscr 'WEIHNACHTSMARKE'. Multicoloured (10 Nov)
B428   20pf. +10pf. The Holy Family 95   80

B **100** Prince von Hardenberg (after Tischbein)
B **101** Northern Goshawk 

(Des State Printing Wks, Berlin. Photo)
1972 (10 Nov). 150th Death Anniv of Karl August von Hardenberg (statesman). P 14.
B429   B **100**   40pf. multicoloured .... 1·10   80

(Des G. H. Magnus. Photo)
1973 (6 Feb). Youth Welfare. Birds of Prey. T B **101** and similar vert designs. Multicoloured. P 14.
B430   20pf. +10pf. Type B **101** 80   80
B431   30pf. +15pf. Peregrine Falcon .... 1·20   1·20
B432   40pf. +20pf. European Sparrow Hawk .... 1·60   1·80
B433   70pf. +35pf. Golden Eagle .... 2·75   3·00
B430/B433 *Set of 4* .... 5·75   6·00

B **102** Horse-bus, 1907
B **103** Ludwig Tieck 

(Des J. Hiller. Litho)
1973 (30 Apr–14 Sept). Berlin Buses. T B **102** and similar horiz designs. Multicoloured. P 14.
B434   20pf. Type B **102** 70   55
B435   20pf. Trolley-bus, 1933 (14.9) 70   55
B436   30pf. Motor-bus, 1919 .... 1·40   80
B437   30pf. Double-decker, 1970 (14.9) .... 1·90   80
B438   40pf. Double-decker, 1925 .... 2·00   1·20
B439   40pf. 'Standard' bus, 1973 (14.9) .... 2·00   1·20
B434/B439 *Set of 6* .... 7·75   4·50

(Des State Printing Wks, Berlin. Photo)
1973 (25 May). Birth Bicentenary of Ludwig Tieck (poet and writer). P 14.
B440   B **103**   40pf. multicoloured .... 1·20   80

B **104** Johann Quantz
B **105** Radio Set, 1926 

(Des E. Finke. Eng H-J. Fuchs. Recess and litho)
1973 (12 June). Death Bicentenary of Johann Quantz (composer). P 14.
B441   B **104**   40pf. black .... 1·40   1·10

(Des E. Finke. Litho)
1973 (23 Aug). 50 Years of German Broadcasting. Sheet 148×105 mm containing horiz designs as T B **105**. P 14.
MSB442   20pf. black and yellow; 30pf. black and bright green; 40pf. black and red; 70pf. black and new blue (*sold at 1.80Dm.*) .... 6·00   6·00
Designs:—20pf. T B **105**; 30pf. Hans Bredow and microphone of 1924; 40pf. Girl with TV and video tape-recorder; 70pf. TV camera.

B **106** 17th-century Hurdy-Gurdy
B **107** Georg W. von Knobelsdorff 

(Des I. Monson-Baumgart. Litho or recess and litho (B447))
1973 (5 Oct–9 Nov). Humanitarian Relief Funds. Musical Instruments. T B **106** and similar vert designs. Multicoloured. P 14.
(a) Inscr 'WOHLFAHRTSMARKE' (5 Oct)
B443   20pf. +10pf. Type B **106** 70   70
B444   30pf. +15pf. 16th-century drum .... 1·40   1·40
B445   40pf. +20pf. 18th-century lute .... 1·50   1·60
B446   70pf. +35pf. 16th-century organ .... 2·20   2·40
B443/B446 *Set of 4* .... 5·25   5·50

(b) Christmas. Inscr 'WEIHNACHTSMARKE' (9 Nov)
B447   20pf. +10pf. Christmas Star 95   95

(Des J. Hiller. Eng E. Falz. Recess)
1974 (15 Feb). 275th Birth Anniv of Georg W. von Knobelsdorff (architect). P 14.
B448   B **107**   20pf. chocolate 70   55

B **108** Gustav R. Kirchhoff
B **109** Adolf Slaby 

(Des J. Hiller. Eng H.-J. Fuchs. Recess and litho)
1974 (15 Feb). 150th Birth Anniv of Gustav R. Kirchhoff (physicist). P 14.
B449   B **108**   30pf. deep bluish green and grey 70   70

(Des E. Finke. Litho)
1974 (17 Apr). 125th Birth Anniv of Adolf Slaby (radio pioneer). P 14.
B450   B **109**   40pf. black and brown-red 95   80

B **110** Airlift Memorial
B **111** Photography 

(Des E. Finke. Photo)
1974 (17 Apr). 25th Anniv of Berlin Airlift. P 14.
B451   B **110**   90pf. multicoloured .... 3·75   2·75

(Des P. Lorenz. Photo)
1974 (17 Apr). Youth Welfare. Youth Activities. T B **111** and similar vert designs. Multicoloured. P 14.
B452   20pf. +10pf. Type B **111** 70   80
B453   30pf. +15pf. Athletics 70   80
B454   40pf. +20pf. Music .... 1·40   1·80
B455   70pf. +35pf. Voluntary service (Nurse) .... 2·20   2·40
B452/B455 *Set of 4* .... 4·50   5·25

GERMANY / Berlin (Western Sectors)

B **112** School Seal

B **113** Spring Bouquet

B **118** Steam Locomotive *Drache*, 1848

B **119** Ferdinand Sauerbruch

(Des J. Hiller. Photo)

1974 (16 July). 400th Anniv of Evangelical Grammar School, Berlin. P 14.
B456 B **112** 50pf. bluish grey, brown lake and gold .... 1·20 80

(Des Hella and Heinz Schillinger. Litho)

1974 (15 Oct–29 Oct). Humanitarian Relief Funds. Flowers. T B **113** and similar horiz designs. Multicoloured. P 14.

(a) Inscr '25 JAHRE WOHLFAHRTSMARKE' (15 Oct)
B457 30pf. +15pf. Type B **113** 70 70
B458 40pf. +20pf. Autumn bouquet .... 1·30 1·30
B459 50pf. +25pf. Bouquet of roses .... 1·40 1·40
B460 70pf. +35pf. Bouquet of winter flowers .... 2·00 2·40
B457/B460 Set of 4 .... 4·75 5·25

(b) Christmas. Inscribed 'WEIHNACHTSMARKE 1974' (29 Oct)
B461 30pf. +15pf. Christmas bouquet .... 1·40 1·60

(Des Hella and Heinz Schillinger. Litho)

1975 (15 Apr). Youth Welfare. Railway Locomotives. T B **118** and similar horiz designs. Multicoloured. P 14.
B472 30pf. +15pf. Type B **118** .... 1·40 1·10
B473 40pf. +20pf. Class 89 tank locomotive .... 1·40 1·40
B474 50pf. +25pf. Class 050 steam locomotive .... 2·75 2·30
B475 70pf. +35pf. Class 010 steam locomotive .... 3·50 4·00
B472/B475 Set of 4 .... 8·25 8·00

(Des E. Finke. Eng H.-J. Fuchs. Recess and litho)

1975 (15 May). Birth Centenary of Ferdinand Sauerbruch (surgeon). P 13½×14.
B476 B **119** 50pf. agate, red-brown and salmon-pink .... 1·40 95

B **114** Tegel Airport

B **115** *Venus* (F. E. Meyer)

B **120** Gymnastics Emblem

B **121** *Lovis Corinth* (self-portrait)

(Des E. Finke, Eng H.-J. Fuchs. Recess and litho)

1974 (15 Oct). Opening of Tegel Airport, Berlin. P 14.
B462 B **114** 50pf. deep violet-blue, light blue and bright yellow-green .... 1·90 1·10

(Des J. Hiller. Litho)

1974 (29 Oct). Berlin Porcelain Figures. T B **115** and similar vert designs. Multicoloured. P 14.
B463 30pf. Type B **115** 80 80
B464 40pf. *Astronomy* (W. C. Meyer) 95 95
B465 50pf. *Justice* (J. G. Müller) .... 1·20 1·20
B463/B465 Set of 3 .... 2·75 2·75

(Des E. Finke. Photo)

1975 (15 May). Gymnaestrada (Gymnastic games), Berlin. P 14.
B477 B **120** 40pf. black, gold and emerald 95 70

1975 (15 May)–**82**. Industry and Technology. As Nos. 1739/1755. P 14.
B478 5pf. bronze-green (14.11.75) 40 35
B479 10pf. deep magenta (14.8.75) 40 35
B480 20pf. orange-vermilion (17.2.76) 40 35
B481 30pf. slate-lilac (14.8.75) 55 40
B482 40pf. blue-green 80 40
B483 50pf. bright magenta 80 40
B483*a* 60pf. rose-red (16.11.78) .... 1·40 70
B484 70pf. blue (14.8.75) .... 1·50 80
B485 80pf. deep bluish green (15.10.75) .... 1·50 40
B486 100pf. deep brown .... 1·50 80
B486*a* 110pf. plum (16.6.82) .... 2·30 2·00
B487 120pf. deep blue (15.10.75) .... 2·00 1·60
B487*a* 130pf. deep claret (16.6.82) .... 3·75 2·40
B488 140pf. carmine-red (14.11.75) .... 2·00 2·30
B488*a* 150pf. brown-red (12.3.79) .... 4·50 2·00
B489 160pf. deep yellowish green (15.10.75) .... 4·00 2·30
B489*a* 180pf. sepia (12.7.79) .... 4·75 3·50
B489*b* 190pf. orange-brown (15.7.82) .... 4·75 4·00
B490 200pf. deep rose-lilac (14.11.75) .... 2·75 1·40
B490*a* 230pf. purple (17.5.79) .... 4·00 3·50
B490*b* 250pf. green (15.7.82) .... 6·75 4·00
B490*c* 300pf. brown-olive (15.7.82) .... 6·75 4·00
B491 500pf. blue-black (17.3.76) .... 9·50 6·75
B478/B491 Set of 23 .... 60·00 40·00

(Des State Ptg Wks, Berlin. Photo)

1975 (15 July). 50th Death Anniv of Lovis Corinth (painter). P 14.
B492 B **121** 50pf. multicoloured .... 1·40 95

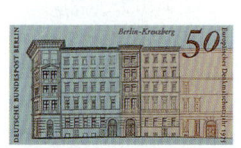

B **116** Gottfried Schadow

B **117** Princess Charlotte

(Des M. Pusch. Eng E. Falz. Recess)

1975 (15 Jan). 125th Death Anniv of Gottfried Schadow (sculptor). P 14.
B466 B **116** 50pf. purple-brown .... 1·40 95

(Des J. Hiller. Litho)

1975 (14 Feb). Berlin Pleasure Craft. T B **117** and similar horiz designs. Multicoloured. P 14.
B467 30pf. Type B **117** .... 1·10 55
B468 40pf. *Siegfried* .... 1·10 55
B469 50pf. *Sperber* .... 1·60 1·40
B470 60pf. *Vaterland* .... 1·80 1·40
B471 70pf. *Moby Dick* .... 2·40 2·40
B467/B471 Set of 5 .... 7·25 5·75

B **122** Buildings in Naunynstrasse, Berlin-Kreuzberg

B **123** Yellow Gentian

GERMANY / Berlin (Western Sectors)

(Des O. Rohse. Eng L. Lück. Recess and litho)
1975 (15 July). European Architectural Heritage Year. P 14.
B493   B **122**   50pf. multicoloured .... 1·40   1·10

(Des Hella and Heinz Schillinger. Litho)
1975 (15 Oct–14 Nov). Humanitarian Relief Funds. Alpine Flowers. T B **123** and similar vert designs. Multicoloured. P 14.

(a) Inscribed 'Wohlfahrtsmarke 1975' (15 Oct)
B494   30pf. +15pf. Type B **123** 95   95
B495   40pf. +20pf. Arnica 90   90
B496   50pf. +25pf. Cyclamen .... 1·10   1·10
B497   70pf. +35pf. Blue Gentian .... 1·90   1·90
B494/B497   Set of 4 .... 4·25   4·25

(b) Christmas. Inscribed 'Weihnachtsmarke 1975' (14 Nov)
B498   30pf. +15pf. Snow Heather .... 1·40   1·40
See also Nos. B508/B511, B540/B543 and B557/B560.

B **124** Paul Löbe

B **125** Ears of Wheat with inscription 'Grüne Woche'

(Des E. Finke. Eng E. Falz. Recess)
1975 (14 Nov). Birth Centenary of Paul Löbe (politician). P 14.
B499   B **124**   50pf. brown-red .... 1·40   95

(Des W. Hölter. Photo)
1976 (5 Jan). International Agriculture Week, Berlin. P 14.
B500   B **125**   70pf. lemon and emerald .... 1·40   1·30

B **126** Putting the Shot

B **127** Hockey

(Des Hella and Heinz Schillinger. Litho)
1976 (6 Apr). Youth Welfare. Training for Olympic Games. T B **126** and similar vert designs. Multicoloured. P 14.
B501   30pf. +15pf. Type B **126** .... 1·10   1·20
B502   40pf. +20pf. Hockey .... 1·10   1·20
B503   50pf. +25pf. Handball .... 1·20   1·40
B504   70pf. +35pf. Swimming .... 2·40   2·75
B501/B504   Set of 4 .... 5·25   6·00

(Des J. H. Hiller. Eng H.-J. Fuchs. Recess)
1976 (13 May). Women's International Hockey Championships. P 14.
B505   B **127**   30pf. deep green .... 1·40   70

B **128** Treble Clef

B **129** Fire Service Emblem

(Des D. von Horst-Voigt. Photo)
1976 (13 May). German Choristers' Festival. P 14.
B506   B **128**   40pf. multicoloured .... 1·40   95

(Des E. Finke. Litho)
1976 (13 May). 125th Anniv of Berlin Fire Service. P 14.
B507   B **129**   50pf. multicoloured .... 2·00   1·40

(Des Hella and Heinz Schillinger. Litho)
1976 (14 Oct). Humanitarian Relief Funds Garden Flowers. Vert designs similar to T B **123**. Multicoloured. P 14.
B508   30pf. +15pf. Iris 70   70
B509   40pf. +20pf. Wallflower 70   70
B510   50pf. +25pf. Dahlia .... 1·10   1·40
B511   70pf. +35pf. Larkspur .... 1·60   1·90
B508/B511   Set of 4 .... 3·75   4·25

B **130** Julius Tower, Spandau

B **131** *Annunciation to the Shepherds* (window, Frauenkirche, Esslingen)

(Des State Ptg Wks, Berlin. Eng E. Falz (30pf.), L. Lück (40pf.), H.-J. Fuchs (50pf.). Recess)
1976 (16 Nov). Berlin Views (1st series). T B **130** and similar horiz designs. P 14.
B512   30pf. blue-black and blue 95   70
B513   40pf. brown-black and deep brown .... 1·40   70
B514   50pf. greenish black and myrtle green .... 1·50   70
B512/B514   Set of 3 .... 3·50   1·90
Designs:—30pf. Yacht on River Havel; 40pf. T B **130**; 50pf. Lake and Victory Column, Tiergarten Park.
See also Nos. B562/B564, B605/B607 and B647/649.

(Des D. von Andrian. Eng State Ptg Wks. Berlin. Recess and litho)
1976 (16 Nov). Christmas. Sheet 71×101 mm. P 14.
MSB515   B **131** 30pf.+15pf. multicoloured .... 1·40   1·20

(Des Hella and Heinz Schillinger. Typo)
1977 (13 Jan)–**87**. German Castles. As Nos. 1805/1812d. P 14.
B516   10pf. deep blue (14.4.77) 40   35
       a. Perf 3 sides. Booklets (1.6.77) 45   55
      ab. Booklet pane. Nos. B516a×4, B518a×2
           and B520a×2 (1.6.77) .... 13·50
      ac. Booklet pane. Nos. B516a×2, B518a×2
           and B520bb a×2 (4.80) .... 7·00
      ad. Booklet pane. Nos. B516a×2, B518a×2,
           B520bb a×2 and B521ab×2 (10.80) .... 22·00
      ae. Booklet pane. Nos. B516a×4,
           B520bb a×2 and B522aab×2 (6.82) .... 21·00
       b. Litho* (1987) .... 2·40   5·50
B517   20pf. red-orange (14.4.77) 40   35
B517a   25pf. scarlet (11.1.79) .... 1·10   70
B518   30pf. bistre (14.4.77) 45   40
       a. Perf 3 sides. Booklets (1.6.77) .... 1·40   1·80
       b. Litho* (1987) .... 2·40   6·75
B518c   35pf. brown-red (16.6.82) 55   55
B519   40pf. blue-green (16.2.77) 55   40
B519a   40pf. deep brown (14.2.80) 95   55
B520   50pf. rose-carmine (17.5.77) 95   40
       a. Perf 3 sides. Booklets (1.6.77) .... 4·25   6·00
B520b   50pf. yellowish green (14.2.80) .... 1·10   55
       ba. Perf 3 sides. Booklets (4.80) .... 1·10   3·50
B521   60pf. bistre-brown .... 1·80   80
B521a   60pf. carmine (14.11.79) .... 1·60   80
       ab. Perf 3 sides. Booklets (10.80) .... 7·50   15·00
B522   70pf. new blue (17.5.77) .... 1·80   80
B522a   80pf. yellow-olive (16.6.82) .... 1·10   55
       ab. Perf 3 sides. Booklets (6.82) .... 8·00   12·00
B522b   90pf. ultramarine (11.1.79) .... 1·60   1·40
B522c   120pf. reddish violet (15.7.82) .... 1·80   1·60
B523   190pf. Venetian red (16.2.77) .... 2·40   2·40
B524   200pf. bronze green .... 2·50   2·40
B524a   210pf. red-brown (14.2.79) .... 3·50   2·75
B524b   230pf. deep bluish green (16.11.78) .... 3·50   2·75
B524c   280pf. greenish blue (15.7.82) .... 6·00   4·00
B524d   300pf. red-orange (16.6.82) .... 6·00   4·00
B516/B524d Set of 21 (*cheapest*) .... 36·00   26·00

Nos. B516/B524d were issued both in sheets and in coils, the latter having every fifth stamp numbered on the back.

The booklet panes are imperforate top and bottom, giving stamps imperf on one side.

*See note below No. 1812d of German Federal Republic.

227

GERMANY / Berlin (Western Sectors)

B **132** *Eugenia d'Alton* (Christian Rauch)

B **133** *Eduard Gaertner* (self portrait)

(Des J. H. Hiller. Photo)

1977 (13 Jan). 200th Birth Anniv of Christian Daniel Rauch (sculptor). P 14.
B525 B **132** 50pf. black .... 1·40   95

(Des D. von Horst-Voigt. Eng E. Falz. Recess and litho)

1977 (16 Feb). Death Centenary of Eduard Gaertner (artist). P 14.
B526 B **133** 40pf. black, apple-green and deep green .... 1·10   70

B **134** *Bremen Kogge*, 1380

B **135** *Female Figure*

(Des Hella and Heinz Schillinger. Litho)

1977 (14 Apr). Youth Welfare. Ships. T B **134** and similar horiz designs. Multicoloured. P 14.
B527   30pf. +15pf. Type B **134** 70   70
B528   40pf. +20pf. *Helena Sloman* (steam ship), 1850 80   95
B529   50pf. +25pf. *Cap Polonio* (liner), 1914 .... 1·40 1·60
B530   70pf. +35pf. *Widar* (bulk carrier), 1971 .... 1·90 2·00
B527/B530 Set of 4 .... 4·25 4·75

(Des E. Finke. Photo)

1977 (14 Apr). Birth Centenary of Georg Kolbe (sculptor). P 14.
B531 B **135** 30pf. olive-green and black 95   70

B **136** Crosses and Text

B **137** Telephones of 1905 and 1977

(Des State Ptg Wks, Berlin. Litho)

1977 (17 May). 17th Evangelical Churches Day. P 14.
B532 B **136** 40pf. yellow, black and dull blue-green 95   70

(Des J. H. Hiller. Litho)

1977 (13 July). International Broadcasting Exhibition, Berlin, and Centenary of Telephone in Germany. P 14.
B533 B **137** 50pf. buff, black and scarlet-vermilion .... 3·00 1·80

B **138** Imperial German Patent Office, Berlin-Kreuzberg

B **139** *Untitled Painting* (Georg Grosz)

(Des E. Finke. Eng H.-J. Fuchs. Recess and litho)

1977 (13 July). Centenary of German Patent Office. P 14.
B534 B **138** 60pf. black, red and grey .... 2·75 1·20

(Des State Ptg Wks, Berlin. Litho)

1977 (13 July). 15th European Art Exhibition. P 14.
B535 B **139** 70pf. multicoloured .... 1·60 1·80

B **140** Picasso Trigger Fish

B **141** *Madonna and Child* (stained glass window, Basilica of St. Gereon, Cologne)

(Des D. von Horst-Voigt. Photo)

1977 (16 Aug). 25th Anniv of Reopening of Berlin Aquarium. T B **140** and similar horiz designs. Multicoloured. P 14.
B536   20pf. Type B **140** 80   75
B537   30pf. Paddlefish .... 1·20 1·10
B538   40pf. Radiated Tortoise .... 1·60 1·40
B539   50pf. Rhinoceros Iguana .... 2·20 1·60
B536/B539 Set of 4 .... 5·25 4·25

(Des Hella and Heinz Schillinger. Litho)

1977 (13 Oct). Humanitarian Relief Funds Meadow Flowers. Vert designs similar to T B **123**. Multicoloured. P 14.
B540   30pf. +15pf. Daisy 55   55
B541   40pf. +20pf. Marsh Marigold 95   95
B542   50pf. +25pf. Sainfoin .... 1·10 1·40
B543   70pf. +35pf. Forget-me-not .... 1·70 2·00
B540/B543 Set of 4 .... 3·75 4·50

(Des C. Hansmann. Litho)

1977 (10 Nov). Christmas. Sheet 70×105 mm. P 14.
MSB544 B **141** 30pf.+15pf. multicoloured .... 1·40 1·40

B **142** Walter Kollo

B **143** Emblem of American Chamber of Commerce

(Des J. Hiller. Eng E. Falz. Recess)

1978 (12 Jan). Birth Centenary of Walter Kollo (composer). P 14.
B545 B **142** 50pf. deep brown and brown-red .... 1·60 1·30

(Des State Ptg Wks, Berlin. Eng H.-J. Fuchs. Recess)

1978 (13 Apr). 75th Anniv of American Chamber of Commerce in Germany. P 14.
B546 B **143** 90pf. deep blue and red .... 1·90 1·80

B **144** Montgolfier Balloon, 1783

(Des F. Haase. Litho)

1978 (13 Apr). Youth Welfare. Aviation History (1st series) T B **144** and similar horiz designs. Multicoloured. P 14.
B547   30pf. +15pf. Type B **144** 70   80
B548   40pf. +20pf. Lilienthal glider, 1891 95   1·10
B549   50pf. +25pf. Wright Type A biplane ..... 1·20 1·40
B550   70pf. +35pf. Etrich/Rumpler Taube,1910 .... 2·00 2·30
B547/B550 Set of 4 .... 4·25 5·00

See also Nos. B567/B570 and B589/B592.

GERMANY / Berlin (Western Sectors)

B 145 Cycling
B 146 Albrecht von Graefe 

(Des P. Lorenz. Litho)

1978 (13 Apr). Sport Promotion Fund. T B **145** and similar horiz design. Multicoloured. P 14.
B551	50pf. +25pf. Type B **145**	1·60	1·10
B552	70pf. +35pf. Fencing	2·20	1·90

(Des E. Finke. Eng H.-J. Fuchs. Recess)

1978 (22 May). 150th Birth Anniv of Albrecht von Graefe (pioneer of medical eye services). P 14.
B553	B **146**	30pf. black and red-brown	95	70

B 147 Friedrich L. Jahn
B 148 Swimming 

(Des E. Finke. Eng H.-J. Fuchs. Recess)

1978 (13 July). Birth Bicentenary of Friedrich Ludwig Jahn (pioneer of physical education). P 14.
B554	B **147**	50pf. deep carmine	1·40	95

(Des P. Lorenz. Litho)

1978 (17 Aug). Third World Swimming Championships. P 14.
B555	B **148**	40pf. multicoloured	1·90	1·40

B 149 The Boat

(Des State Ptg Wks, Berlin. Photo)

1978 (12 Oct). Birth Centenary of Karl Hofer (Impressionist painter). P 14.
B556	B **149**	50pf. multicoloured	1·40	1·10

(Des Hella and Heinz Schillinger. Litho)

1978 (12 Oct). Humanitarian Relief Funds Woodland Flowers. Vert designs similar to T B **123**. Multicoloured. P 14.
B557	30pf. +15pf. Solomon's Seal	80	80
B558	40pf. +20pf. Wood Primrose	95	95
B559	50pf. +25pf. Red Helleborine	1·40	1·50
B560	70pf. +35pf. Bugle	2·00	2·20
B557/B560	Set of 4	4·75	5·00

B 150 Prussian State Library
B 151 Madonna (stained glass window, Frauenkirche, Munich) 

(Des J. H. Hiller. Eng E. Falz. Recess)

1978 (16 Nov). Opening of New Prussian State Library Building. P 14.
B561	B **150**	90pf. deep olive and vermilion	2·40	1·90

(Des and eng E. Falz. Recess)

1978 (16 Nov). Berlin Views (2nd series). Horiz designs similar to T B **130**. P 14.
B562	40pf. black and blue-green	1·10	70
B563	50pf. black and bright purple	1·40	1·10
B564	60pf. black and light brown	1·60	1·20
B562/564	Set of 3	3·50	2·50

Designs:—40pf. Belvedere; 50pf Landwehr Canal; 60pf. Village Church, Lichtenrade.

(Des W. Fleckhaus. Litho)

1978 (16 Nov). Christmas. Sheet 65×92 mm. P 14.
MSB565	B **151**	30pf.+15pf. multicoloured	1·40	1·40

B 152 Congress Centre
B 153 Relay Runners 

(Des E. Finke. Eng E. Falz. Recess and litho)

1979 (14 Feb). Opening of International Congress Centre, Berlin. P 14.
B566	B **152**	60pf. black, blue and carmine	1·90	1·20

(Des F. Haase. Litho)

1979 (5 Apr). Youth Welfare Aviation History (2nd series). Horiz designs as T B **144**. Multicoloured. P 14.
B567	40pf. +20pf. Vampyr glider, 1921	1·10	1·10
B568	50pf. +25pf. Junkers Ju 52/3m D-2202 *Richthofen*, 1932	1·60	1·60
B569	60pf. +30pf. Messerschmitt Bf 108 D-1010, 1934	2·00	2·00
B570	90pf. +45pf. Douglas DC-3 NC-14988, 1935	2·75	2·75
B567/B570	Set of 4	6·75	6·75

(Des H. P. Hoch. Litho)

1979 (5 Apr). Sport Promotion Fund T B **153** and similar horiz design. Multicoloured. P 14.
B571	60pf. +30pf. Type B **153**	1·60	1·80
B572	90pf. +45pf. Archers	2·20	2·30

B 154 Old and New Arms
B 155 Arrows and Target 

(Des J. H. Hiller. Litho)

1979 (17 May). Centenary of State Printing Works. Berlin. P 14.
B573	B **154**	60pf. multicoloured	2·40	1·90

(Des E. Finke. Photo)

1979 (12 July). World Archery Championships. Berlin. P 14.
B574	B **155**	50pf. multicoloured	1·40	95

B 156 Television screen
B 157 Moses Mendelssohn 

(Des State Ptg Wks, Berlin. Photo)

1979 (12 July). International Broadcasting Exhibition, Berlin. P 14.
B575	B **156**	60pf. black, grey and orange-red	1·90	1·40

229

GERMANY / Berlin (Western Sectors)

B 183 Arms and View of Spandau, c. 1700

B 184 Daimler Steel-wheeled Car, 1889

(Des R. Gerstetter. Eng H.-J. Fuchs. Recess and litho.)

1982 (18 Feb). 750th Anniv of Spandau. P 14.
| B631 | B 183 | 60pf. multicoloured | 2·00 | 1·60 |

(Des Hella and Heinz Schillinger. Litho)

1982 (15 Apr). Youth Welfare Fund. Motor Cars. T B **184** and similar horiz designs. Multicoloured. P 14.
B632		40pf. +20pf. Type B **184**	1·10	1·20
B633		50pf. +25pf. Wanderer Puppchen, 1911	1·20	1·40
B634		60pf. +30pf. Adler limousine, 1913	1·40	1·60
B635		90pf. +45pf. DKW F1, 1913	2·40	2·75
B632/B635 Set of 4			5·50	5·25

B 185 Sprinting

B 186 Harp

(Des H. Buschfeld. Litho.)

1982 (15 Apr). Sport Promotion Fund. T B **185** and similar horiz design. Multicoloured. P 14.
| B636 | | 60pf. +30pf. Type B **185** | 1·60 | 1·40 |
| B637 | | 90pf. +45pf. Volleyball | 2·40 | 1·90 |

(Des R. Gerstetter. Embossed and litho.)

1982 (15 Apr). Centenary of Berlin Philharmonic Orchestra. P 14.
| B638 | B 186 | 60pf. brownish grey, brown-red and deep bluish green | 2·00 | 1·40 |

B 187 Emigrants reaching Prussian Frontier (woodcut after drawing by Adolph von Menzel)

B 188 Italian Stone Carriers (Max Pechstein)

(Des R. Gerstetter. Eng E. Falz. Recess and litho.)

1982 (5 May). 250th Anniv of Salzburg Emigrants' Arrival in Prussia. P 14.
| B639 | B 187 | 50pf. stone, blackish brown and yellow-brown | 1·40 | 95 |

(Des R. Schmidt. Photo.)

1982 (15 July). Paintings. T B **188** and similar horiz design. Multicoloured. P 14.
| B640 | | 50pf. Type B **188** | 1·60 | 1·20 |
| B641 | | 80pf. Two Girls Bathing (Otto Mueller) | 2·40 | 1·90 |

B 189 Floribunda-Grandiflora

B 190 Castle Theatre, Charlottenburg

(Des Hella and Heinz Schillinger. Litho.)

1982 (14 Oct). Humanitarian Relief Funds. Roses. T B **189** and similar vert designs. Multicoloured. P 14.
B642		50pf. +20pf. Type B **189**	1·60	1·60
B643		60pf. +30pf. Hybrid tea	1·60	1·60
B644		80pf. +40pf. Floribunda	2·75	2·75
B645		120pf. +60pf. Miniature rose	4·25	4·25
B642/B645 Set of 4			9·25	9·25

(Des R. Gerstetter. Eng E. Falz. Recess and litho.)

1982 (10 Nov). 250th Birth Anniv of Carl Gotthard Langhans (architect). P 14.
| B646 | B 190 | 80pf. brown-lake, brownish grey and black | 2·75 | 2·20 |

(Des R. Gerstetter. Eng H.-J. Fuchs (60pf.), E. Falz (others). Recess.)

1982 (10 Nov). Berlin Views (4th series). Vert designs as T B **130**. P 14.
B647		50pf. black and deep blue	1·60	1·20
B648		60pf. black and carmine-red	1·90	1·50
B649		80pf. black and chestnut	2·75	1·60
B647/B649 Set of 3			5·75	3·75
Designs:—50pf. Villa Borsig; 60pf. Sts. Peter and Paul Church; 80pf. Villa von der Heydt.

B 191 Adoration of the Kings (detail from St. Peter altar by Master Bertram)

B 192 Water Pump, Klausenerplatz

(Des B. K. Wiese. Litho.)

1982 (10 Nov). Christmas. P 14.
| B650 | B 191 | 50pf. +20pf. multicoloured | 1·60 | 1·40 |

(Des R. Gerstetter. Photo.)

1983 (13 Jan). Street Water Pumps. T B **192** and similar vert designs. Multicoloured. P 14.
B651		50pf. Type B **192**	2·00	1·40
B652		60pf. Chamissoplatz	2·30	1·40
B653		80pf. Schloss-strasse	2·75	2·20
B654		120pf. Kuerfirstendamm	4·00	3·50
B651/B654 Set of 4			10·00	7·75

B 193 Royal Prussian Telegraphy Inspectors at St. Anne's Church

B 194 Hildebrand & Wolfmüller, 1894

(Des and eng E. Falz. Recess.)

1983 (8 Feb). 150th Anniv of Berlin–Coblenz Optical-Mechanical Telegraph. P 14.
| B655 | B 193 | 80pf. blackish brown | 3·00 | 2·75 |

(Des H. Schillinger. Litho.)

1983 (12 Apr). Youth Welfare. Motorcycles. T B **194** and similar horiz designs. Multicoloured. P 14.
B656		50pf. +20pf. Type B **194**	1·40	95
B657		60pf. +30pf. Wanderer, 1908	2·00	1·80
B658		80pf. +40pf. DKW-Lomos, 1922	2·30	1·90
B659		120pf. +60pf. Mars, 1925	5·25	4·50
B656/B659 Set of 4			9·75	8·25

B 195 Latin American Dancing

B 196 La Barbarina (painting of Barbara Campanini)

GERMANY / Berlin (Western Sectors)

(Des F-D. Rothacker. Photo)
1983 (12 Apr). Sport Promotion Fund. T B **195** and similar horiz designs. Multicoloured. P 14.
B660   80pf. +40pf. Type B **195** .... 2·40   2·00
B661   120pf. +60pf. Ice hockey .... 3·75   3·50

(Des R. Schmidt. Photo)
1983 (5 May). 300th Birth Anniv of Antoine Pesne (artist). P 14.
B662   B **196**   50pf. multicoloured .... 1·60   1·40

B **197** Ringelnatz (silhouette by E.M. Engert)

B **198** Paul Nipkow's Picture Transmission System, 1884

(Des R. Schmidt. Litho)
1983 (14 July). Birth Centenary of Joachim Ringelnatz (poet and painter). P 14.
B663   B **197**   50pf. grey-olive, grey-brown and brown-lake .... 1·90   1·40

(Des R. Gerstetter. Litho)
1983 (14 July). International Broadcasting Exhibition, Berlin. P 14.
B664   B **198**   80pf. multicoloured .... 2·75   2·30

B **199** Mountain Windflower

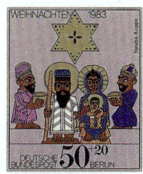

B **200** Nigerian Yoruba Crib

(Des Karin Blume. Litho)
1983 (13 Oct). Humanitarian Relief Funds. Endangered Alpine Flowers. T B **199** and similar vert designs. Multicoloured. P 14.
B665   50pf. +20pf. Type B **199** .... 1·10   1·10
B666   60pf. +30pf. Alpine Auricula .... 1·60   1·60
B667   80pf. +40pf. Little Primrose .... 3·00   3·00
B668   120pf. +60pf. Einsele's Aquilegia .... 4·25   4·50
B665/B668 *Set of 4* .... 9·00   9·25

(Des P. Steiner. Litho)
1983 (10 Nov). Christmas. P 14.
B669   B **200**   50pf. +20pf. multicoloured .... 1·60   1·60

B **201** Queen Cleopatra VII (Antikenmuseum)

B **202** *Trichius fasciatus*

(Des B. Görs. Litho)
1984 (12 Jan). Art Objects in Berlin Museums. T B **201** and similar square designs. Multicoloured. P 14.
B670   30pf. Type B **201** .... 1·60   1·40
B671   50pf. Statue of seated couple from Giza Necropolis (Egyptian Museum) .... 2·20   1·90
B672   60pf. Goddess with pearl turban (Ethnology Museum) .... 2·75   2·40
B673   80pf. Majolica dish (Applied Arts Museum) .... 3·75   3·50
B670/B673 *Set of 4* .... 9·25   8·25

(Des E. Nitsche. Litho)
1984 (12 Apr). Youth Welfare. Pollinating Insects. T B **202** and similar vert designs. Multicoloured. P 14.
B674   50pf. +20pf. Type B **202** .... 1·80   1·10
B675   60pf. +30pf. *Agrumenia carniolica* .... 1·80   1·40
B676   80pf. +40pf. *Bombus terrestris* .... 2·75   2·40
B677   120pf. +60pf. *Eristalis tenax* .... 4·00   4·00
B674/B677 *Set of 4* .... 9·25   8·00

B **203** Hurdling

B **204** Klausener

(Des F. Kefer and P. Munch. Litho)
1984 (12 Apr). Sport Promotion Fund. T B **203** and similar horiz designs. Multicoloured. P 14.
B678   60pf. +30pf. Type B **203** .... 2·75   1·90
B679   80pf. +40pf. Cycling .... 3·00   1·90
B680   120pf. +60pf. Four-seater kayaks .... 4·75   4·75
B678/B680 *Set of 3* .... 9·50   7·75

(Des and eng H.-J. Fuchs. Recess)
1984 (8 May). 50th Death Anniv of Dr. Erich Klausener (chairman of Catholic Action). P 14.
B681   B **204**   80pf. green and deep dull green .... 1·90   1·40

B **205** *Electric Power* (K. Sutterlin)

B **206** *Conference Emblem*

(Des R. Schmidt. Photo)
1984 (8 May). Centenary of Berlin Electricity Supply. P 14.
B682   B **205**   50pf. orange-yellow, red-orange and black .... 1·60   1·20

(Des R. Gerstetter. Litho)
1984 (8 May). Fourth European Ministers of Culture Conference, Berlin. P 14.
B683   B **206**   60pf. multicoloured .... 2·00   1·40

B **207** Alfred Brehm and White Stork

B **208** Heim (bust, Friedrich Tieck)

(Des R. Gerstetter. Recess and litho)
1984 (19 June). Death Centenary of Alfred Brehm (zoologist). P 14.
B684   B **207**   80pf. multicoloured .... 3·00   2·30

(Des and eng H.-J. Fuchs. Recess)
1984 (24 Aug). 150th Death Anniv of Ernst Ludwig Heim (medical pioneer). P 14.
B685   B **208**   50pf. black and brown-lake .... 1·90   1·40

B **209** *Listera cordata*

B **210** Sunflowers on Grey Background

(Des G. Jacki. Litho)
1984 (18 Oct). Humanitarian Relief Funds. Orchids. T B **209** and similar horiz designs. Multicoloured. P 14.
B686   50pf. +20pf. Type B **209** .... 2·50   1·60
B687   60pf. +30pf. *Ophrys insectifera* .... 2·50   1·60
B688   80pf. +40pf. *Epipactis palustris* .... 4·00   3·50
B689   120pf. +60pf. *Ophrys coriophora* .... 6·75   6·00
B686/B689 *Set of 4* .... 14·00   11·50

233

GERMANY / Berlin (Western Sectors)

(Des B. Görs. Litho)
1984 (8 Nov). Birth Centenary of Karl Schmidt-Rottluff (artist). P 14.
B690   B **210**   60pf. multicoloured .... 1·90   1·40

B **211** St. Nicholas

B **212** Bettina von Arnim

(Des P. Steiner. Litho)
1984 (8 Nov). Christmas. P 14.
B691   B **211**   50pf. +20pf. multicoloured .... 1·90   1·90

(Des B. Görs. Recess and litho)
1985 (21 Feb). Birth Bicentenary of Bettina von Arnim (writer). P 14.
B692   B **212**   50pf. blue-black, pale red-brown and brown lake .... 1·60   1·50

B **213** Humboldt (statue, Paul Otto)

B **214** Ball in Net

(Des B. Görs. Recess)
1985 (21 Feb). 150th Death Anniv of Wilhelm von Humboldt (philologist). P 14.
B693   B **213**   80pf. black, blue and brown-lake........... 3·00   2·50

(Des F.-D. Rothacker. Photo)
1985 (21 Feb). Sport Promotion Fund. T B **214** and similar horiz design. Multicoloured. P 14.
B694   80pf. +40pf. Type B **214** (50th anniv of basketball in Germany and European championships, Stuttgart)............................... 2·40   2·40
B695   120pf. +60pf. Table tennis (60th anniv of German Table Tennis Association)........... 4·00   4·00

B **215** Stylised Flower

B **216** Büssing Bicycle, 1868

(Des B. Görs. Litho)
1985 (16 Apr). Federal Horticultural Show, Berlin. P 14.
B696   B **215**   80pf. multicoloured .... 2·30   1·90

(Des H. Schillinger. Litho)
1985 (16 Apr). Youth Welfare. International Youth Year. Cycles. T B **216** and similar horiz designs. Multicoloured. P 14.
B697   50pf. +20pf. Type B **216**........................... 2·00   2·00
B698   60pf. +30pf. Child's tricycle, 1885.................. 2·00   2·00
B699   80pf. +40pf. Jaray bicycle, 1925 .... 2·75   3·00
B700   120pf. +60pf. Opel racing bicycle, 1925 .... 6·00   6·50
B697/B700 Set of 4 .... 11·50   12·00

B **217** Stock Exchange, 1863–1915

B **218** Otto Klemperer

(Des B. Görs. Eng E. Falz. Recess and litho)
1985 (7 May). 300th Anniv of Berlin Stock Exchange. P 14.
B701   B **217**   50pf. multicoloured .... 1·90   1·50

(Des B. Görs. Eng H.-J. Fuchs. Recess)
1985 (7 May). Birth Centenary of Otto Klemperer (orchestral conductor). P 14.
B702   B **218**   60pf. deep violet-blue................................ 2·30   1·90

B **219** Association Emblem

B **220** FE 3 Television Camera, 1935

(Des B. Görs. Litho)
1985 (16 July). 11th International Gynaecology and Obstetrics Association Congress, Berlin. Photo. P 14.
B703   B **219**   60pf. multicoloured .... 1·90   1·50

(Des B. Görs. Recess and litho)
1985 (16 July). International Broadcasting Exhibition, Berlin. P 14.
B704   B **220**   80pf. multicoloured .... 3·25   2·75

B **221** Seal of Brandenburg-Prussia and Preamble of Edict

B **222** Flowers, Strawberries and Ladybirds

(Des Antonia Graschberger. Eng H.-J. Fuchs. Recess and litho)
1985 (15 Oct). 300th Anniv of Edict of Potsdam (admitting Huguenots to Prussia). P 14.
B705   B **221**   50pf. slate-lilac and black .... 1·60   1·20

(Des H. Börnsen. Litho)
1985 (15 Oct). Humanitarian Relief Funds. T B **222** and similar horiz designs depicting motifs from borders of medieval prayer book. Multicoloured. P 14.
B706   50pf. +20pf. Type B **222**........................... 2·00   2·00
B707   60pf. +30pf. Flowers, Bird and Butterfly............ 2·75   2·75
B708   80pf. +40pf. Flowers, Bee and Butterfly............ 2·75   2·75
B709   120pf. +60pf. Flowers, Berries, Butterfly and Snail .... 3·50   4·00
B706/B709 Set of 4 .... 10·00   10·50

B **223** Adoration of the Kings (detail, Epiphany Altar)

B **224** Kurt Tucholsky

(Des F. Lüdtke. Litho)
1985 (12 Nov). Christmas. 500th Birth Anniv of Hans Baldung Grien (artist). P 14.
B710   B **223**   50pf. +20pf. multicoloured...................... 2·00   1·90

(Des R. Gerstetter. Litho)
1985 (12 Nov). 50th Death Anniv of Kurt Tucholsky (writer and journalist). P 14.
B711   B **224**   80pf. multicoloured .... 2·75   1·90

B **225** Furtwängler and Score

B **226** Rohe and National Gallery

(Des B. Görs. Eng E. Falz. Recess and litho)
1986 (16 Jan). Birth Centenary of Wilhelm Furtwängler (composer and conductor). P 14.
B712   B **225**   80pf. multicoloured .... 3·25   3·00

GERMANY / Berlin (Western Sectors)

(Des B. Görs. Eng E. Falz. Recess and litho)
1986 (13 Feb). Birth Centenary of Ludwig Mies van der Rohe (architect). P 14.
B713 B 226 50pf. multicoloured .... 1·90 2·00

B 227 Swimming

B 228 Glazier

(Des H. P. Hoch. Litho)
1986 (13 Feb). Sport Promotion Fund. T B **227** and similar horiz design. Multicoloured. P 14.
B714 80pf. +40pf. Type B 227 (European Youth Championships, Berlin)............... 3·00 3·50
B715 120pf. +55pf. Show Jumping (World Championships, Aachen)............ 3·75 4·00

(Des H. Schillinger. Litho)
1986 (10 Apr). Youth Welfare. Trades (1st series). T B **228** and similar horiz designs. Multicoloured. P 14.
B716 50pf. +25pf. Type B 228 .... 2·00 2·30
B717 60pf. +30pf. Locksmith................... 2·75 3·25
B718 70pf. +35pf. Tailor.......................... 2·75 3·25
B719 80pf. +40pf. Carpenter.................. 3·50 3·75
B716/B719 Set of 4 .... 10·00 11·50
See also Nos. B765/B768.

B 229 Flags

B 230 Ranke

(Des F. Lüdtke. Litho)
1986 (10 Apr). 16th European Communities Day. P 14.
B720 B 229 60pf. multicoloured .... 1·60 1·80

(Des R. Gerstetter. Litho)
1986 (5 May). Death Centenary of Leopold von Ranke (historian). P 14.
B721 B 230 80pf. agate and pale olive-grey.............. 2·75 2·30

B 231 Gottfried Benn

B 232 Charlottenburg Gate

(Des R. Schmidt. Eng H.-J. Fuchs. Recess)
1986 (5 May). Birth Centenary of Gottfried Benn (poet). P 14.
B722 B 231 80pf. royal blue .... 2·75 2·30

(Des and eng J. Kanior (50pf.), H.-J. Fuchs (60pf.) and W. Maurer (80pf.). Recess and litho)
1986 (20 June). Gateways. T B **232** and similar horiz designs. Multicoloured. P 14.
B723 50pf. Type B 232 .... 2·30 2·30
B724 60pf. Griffin Gate, Glienicke Palace................. 2·40 2·40
B725 80pf. Elephant Gate, Berlin Zoo .... 2·75 2·75
B723/B725 Set of 3 .... 6·75 6·75

B 233 *The Flute Concert* (detail, Adolph von Menzel)

B 234 Cantharus, 1st-century AD

(Des B. Görs. Photo)
1986 (14 Aug). Death Bicentenary of Frederick the Great. P 14.
B726 B 233 80pf. multicoloured .... 2·75 2·30

(Des P. Steiner. Litho A. Bagel, Düsseldorf)
1986 (16 Oct). Humanitarian Relief Funds. Glassware. B **234** and similar vert designs. Multicoloured. P 13.
B727 50pf. +25pf. Type B 234 .... 2·00 2·00
B728 60pf. +30pf. Beaker, 200 AD .... 2·75 2·75
B729 70pf. +35pf. Jug, 3rd-century AD .... 2·75 2·75
B730 80pf. +40pf. Diatreta, 4th-century AD........... 2·75 3·50
B727/B730 Set of 4 .... 9·25 10·00

B 235 *Adoration of the Three Kings* (Ortenberg altarpiece)

B 236 Berlin, 1650

(Des F. Lüdtke. Litho)
1986 (13 Nov). Christmas. P 14.
B731 B 235 50pf. +25pf. multicoloured.................. 1·60 1·80

1986 (13 Nov)–**89**. Famous German Women. As Nos. 2150/69. P 14.
B732 5pf. orange-brown and slate (9.2.89)............. 70 3·75
B733 10pf. yellow-brown and violet (14.4.88)......... 70 2·75
B734 20pf. deep turquoise-blue and carmine-lake (5.5.88) .... 2·75 6·75
B735 40pf. crimson and deep ultramarine (17.9.87) ... 2·20 6·75
B736 50pf. deep bluish green and olive-brown....... 3·50 4·75
B737 60pf. slate-lilac and bronze green (10.11.88) . 2·00 6·75
B738 80pf. red-brown and bottle green .... 2·30 4·75
B739 100pf. olive-grey and brown-red (10.11.88).... 3·50 2·75
B740 130pf. deep violet and Prussian blue (5.5.88)... 6·00 20·00
B741 140pf. brown-ochre and deep violet-blue (10.8.89) .... 8·00 20·00
B742 170pf. deep dull purple and deep olive (10.11.88) .... 4·00 16·00
B743 180pf. maroon and new blue (13.7.89) .... 6·00 23·00
B744 240pf. light brown and slate-green (10.11.88).. 5·75 23·00
B745 250pf. royal blue and bright magenta (13.7.89) .... 13·00 38·00
B746 300pf. deep green and plum (10.8.89) .... 13·50 34·00
B747 350pf. lake-brown and greenish black (10.11.88) .... 9·50 27·00
B748 500pf. brown-red and brown-olive (12.1.89) .. 15·00 60·00
B732/B748 Set of 17 .... 90·00 £275

Nos. B749/B759 are vacant.

(Des P. Steiner. Litho)
1987 (15 Jan). 750th Anniv of Berlin. P 14.
(*a*) As No. 2170
B760 833 80pf. multicoloured .... 3·25 2·75

(*b*) Sheet 130×100 mm containing T B **236** and similar horiz designs. Multicoloured
MSB761 40pf. Type B 236; 50pf. Charlottenburg Castle, 1830; 60pf. Turbine Hall; 80pf. Philharmonic and Chamber Music Concert Hall................ 8·00 8·00

B 237 Louise Schroeder

B 238 German Gymnastics Festival, Berlin

(Des R. Gerstetter. Eng H.-J. Fuchs. Recess)
1987 (12 Feb). Birth Centenary of Louise Schroeder (Mayor of West Berlin). P 14.
B762 B 237 50pf. sepia and carmine-vermilion/pale grey-brown........................... 1·90 1·90

1987 (12 Feb). Sport Promotion Fund. T B **238** and similar Multicoloured. P 14.
B763 80pf. +40pf. Type B 238 .... 2·75 2·75
B764 120pf. +55pf. World Judo Championships Essen .... 3·50 3·50

235

GERMANY / Berlin (Western Sectors)

(Des H. Schillinger. Litho)

1987 (9 Apr). Youth Welfare. Trades (2nd series). Horiz designs as T B **228**. Multicoloured. P 14.

B765	50pf. +25pf. Cooper	1·60	2·00
B766	60pf. +30pf. Stonemason	1·80	2·00
B767	70pf. +35pf. Furrier	2·75	3·00
B768	80pf. +40pf. Painter/lacquerer	2·75	2·75
B765/B768	Set of 4	8·00	8·75

B **239** *Bohemian Refugees* (detail of relief, King Friedrich Wilhelm I Monument, Berlin-Neukölln)

B **240** New Buildings

(Des B. Görs. Eng J. Kanior. Recess and litho)

1987 (5 May). 250th Anniv of Bohemian Settlement, Rixdorf. P 14.

B769	B **239**	50pf. sepia and sage green	1·40	1·60

(Des F. Lüdtke. Litho)

1987 (5 May). International Building Exhibition, Berlin. P 14.

B770	B **240**	80pf. silver, black and bright blue	2·30	2·00

B **241** Tree in Arrow Circle

B **242** Compact Disc and Gramophone

(Des R. Gerstetter. Litho)

1987 (16 July). 14th International Botanical Congress, Berlin. P 14.

B771	B **241**	60pf. multicoloured	1·50	1·80

(Des B. Görs. Litho)

1987 (16 July). International Broadcasting Exhibition, Berlin. Centenary of Gramophone Record. P 14.

B772	B **242**	80pf. multicoloured	2·20	2·00

B **243** 5th-century Bonnet Ornament

(Des F. Lüdtke. Litho)

1987 (15 Oct). Humanitarian Relief Funds. Precious Metal Work. T B **243** and similar horiz designs. Multicoloured. P 14.

B773	50pf. +25pf. Type B **243**	1·40	1·80
B774	60pf. +30pf. Athene plate, 1st-century BC	2·00	2·30
B775	70pf. +35pf. Armilla armlet, 1180	2·40	3·00
B776	80pf. +40pf. Snake bracelet, 300 BC	3·00	3·50
B773/B776	Set of 4	8·00	9·50

1987 (6 Nov)–**90**. Tourist Sights. As Nos. 2200/2219. P 14.

B777	5pf. turquoise-blue and grey (15.2.90)	55	80
B778	10pf. cobalt and indigo (14.1.88)	70	70
	a. Perf 3 sides. Booklets (6.89)	2·20	4·75
	ab. Booklet pane. Nos. B778a×4, B782a×2 and B786a×2	41·00	
	ac. Booklet pane. Nos. B778a×2, B783a×2, B786a×2 and B787a×2	80·00	
B779	20pf. flesh and Prussian blue (12.1.89)	70	1·40
B780	30pf. chestnut and turquoise-green	1·90	1·80
B781	40pf. chocolate, dull scarlet and ultramarine (11.8.88)	2·75	3·75
B782	50pf. ochre and ultramarine	2·75	2·00
	a. Perf 3 sides. Booklets (6.89)	8·75	15·00
B783	60pf. dull blue-green and greenish black	2·75	2·00
	a. Perf 3 sides. Booklets (6.89)	16·00	30·00
B784	70pf. flesh and Prussian blue (14.7.88)	2·75	4·75
B785	70pf. chestnut and dull violet-blue (21.6.90)	3·75	8·00
B786	80pf. brownish grey and deep bluish green	2·75	2·00
	a. Perf 3 sides. Booklets (6.89)	6·75	19·00
B787	100pf. blue-green and dull orange (9.2.89)	2·00	2·75
	a. Perf 3 sides. Booklets (6.89)	12·00	19·00
B788	120pf. turquoise-green and Venetian red (14.7.88)	4·00	6·00
B789	140pf. olive-bistre and bistre-yellow (12.1.89)	4·00	7·50
B790	300pf. flesh and red-brown (14.1.88)	8·00	8·00
B791	350pf. drab and deep ultramarine (9.2.89)	7·50	13·50
B777/B791	Set of 15	42·00	60·00

Nos. B777/B791 were each issued both in sheets and in coils, the latter having every fifth stamp numbered on the back.

Nos. B792/B796 are vacant.

B **244** *Adoration of the Magi* (13th-century Book of Psalms)

B **245** Heraldic Bear

(Des F. Lüdtke. Litho)

1987 (6 Nov). Christmas. P 14.

B797	B **244**	50pf. +25pf. multicoloured	1·60	1·60

(Des H. Schillinger. Litho)

1988 (14 Jan). Berlin, European City of Culture. P 14.

B798	B **245**	80pf. multicoloured	3·50	3·50

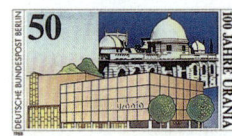

B **246** Old and New Buildings

B **247** *Large Pure-bred Foal* (bronze)

(Des Katharina Siegers. Litho)

1988 (18 Feb). Centenary of Urania Science Museum. P 14.

B799	B **246**	50pf. multicoloured	2·40	2·30

(Des B. Görs. Litho)

1988 (18 Feb). Birth Centenary of Renée Sintenis (sculptor). P 14.

B800	B **247**	60pf. multicoloured	1·60	1·60

B **248** Clay-pigeon Shooting

(Des H. G. Schmitz. Litho)

1988 (18 Feb). Sport Promotion Fund. Olympic Games. T B **248** and similar horiz designs. Multicoloured. P 14.

B801	60pf. +30pf. Type B **248**	2·40	2·40
B802	80pf. +40pf. Figure skating (pairs)	2·40	2·40
B803	120pf. +55pf. Throwing the hammer	3·50	3·50
B801/B803	Set of 3	7·50	7·50

B **249** Piano, Violin and Cello

(Des Antonia Graschberger. Litho)

1988 (14 Apr). Youth Welfare. Music. T B **249** and similar horiz designs. Multicoloured. P 14.

B804	50pf. +25pf. Type B **249**	2·00	2·00
B805	60pf. +30pf. Wind quintet	2·75	3·00
B806	70pf. +35pf. Guitar, recorder and mandolin	2·75	3·00
B807	80pf. +40pf. Children's choir	4·00	4·25
B804/B807	Set of 4	10·50	11·00

GERMANY / Berlin (Western Sectors)

B **250** The Great Elector and Family in Berlin Castle Gardens

B **251** Globe

(Des R. Gerstetter. Eng E. Falz. Recess and litho)

1988 (5 May). 300th Death Anniv of Friedrich Wilhelm, Elector of Brandenburg. P 14.
B808   B **250**   50pf. multicoloured .... 1·90   1·90

(Des B. Görs. Litho)

1988 (11 Aug). International Monetary Fund and World Bank Boards of Governors Annual Meetings, Berlin. P 14.
B809   B **251**   70pf. multicoloured .... 2·00   1·80

B **252** First Train leaving Potsdam Station

B **253** The Collector (bronze statue)

(Des B. Görs. Litho)

1988 (13 Oct). 150th Anniv of Berlin–Potsdam Railway. P 14.
B810   B **252**   10pf. multicoloured 95   80

(Des B. Görs. Litho)

1988 (13 Oct). 50th Death Anniv of Ernst Barlach (artist). P 14.
B811   B **253**   40pf. multicoloured .... 1·20   95

B **254** 18th-century Breast Ornament

B **255** Annunciation to the Shepherds (illus from *Henry the Lion's Gospel Book*)

(Des F. Lüdtke. Litho)

1988 (13 Oct). Humanitarian Relief Funds. Precious Metal Work. T B **254** and similar square designs. Multicoloured. P 14.
B812   50pf. +25pf. Type B **254**................................. 1·60   1·60
B813   60pf. +30pf. 16th-century lion-shaped jug ...... 1·90   1·90
B814   70pf. +35pf. 16th-century goblet .... 2·20   2·20
B815   80pf. +40pf. 15th-century cope clasp................. 2·75   2·75
B812/B815 Set of 4 .... 7·50   7·50

(Des Silvia Runge. Litho)

1988 (10 Nov). Christmas. P 14.
B816   B **255**   50pf. +25pf. multicoloured .... 2·20   2·20

B **256** Volleyball (European Championships)

B **257** Tigers and Tamer

(Des H. P. Hoch. Litho)

1989 (9 Feb). Sport Promotion Fund. T B **256** and similar horiz design. Multicoloured. P 14.
B817   100pf. +50pf. Type B **256**............................... 4·00   4·00
B818   140pf. +60pf. Hockey (Champions Trophy)........ 5·50   6·00

(Des E. Kößlinger. Litho)

1989 (20 Apr). Youth Welfare. Circus. T B **257** and similar horiz designs. Multicoloured. P 14.
B819   60pf. +30pf. Type B **257**............................... 2·75   2·75
B820   70pf. +30pf. Trapeze artistes............................ 3·50   3·50
B821   80pf. +35pf. Sealions....................................... 4·75   5·50
B822   100pf. +50pf. Jugglers..................................... 5·50   6·00
B819/B822 Set of 4 .... 15·00   16·00

B **258** US and UK Flags forming Aeroplanes

B **259** Emblem

(Des B. Görs. Photo)

1989 (5 May). 40th Anniv of Berlin Airlift. P 14.
B823   B **258**   60pf. multicoloured .... 1·90   2·20

(Des H. Schillinger. Litho)

1989 (5 May). 13th International Organisation of Chief Accountants Congress, Berlin. P 14.
B824   B **259**   80pf. multicoloured .... 3·00   2·75

B **260** Ernst Reuter

B **261** Satellite, Radio Waves and TV Screen

(Des G. Aretz. Recess and litho)

1989 (13 July). Birth Centenary of Ernst Reuter (politician and Mayor of West Berlin). P 14.
B825   B **260**   100pf. multicoloured .... 3·25   3·00

(Des B. Görs. Litho)

1989 (13 July). International Broadcasting Exhibition, Berlin. P 14.
B826   B **261**   100pf. multicoloured .... 2·75   2·75

B **262** Plan of Berlin Zoo and Lenné

B **263** Ossietzky and Masthead of *Die Weltbühne*

(Des B. Görs. Eng J. Kanior. Recess and litho)

1989 (10 Aug). Birth Bicentenary of Peter Joseph Lenné (landscape designer). P 14.
B827   B **262**   60pf. multicoloured .... 2·50   2·30

(Des B. Görs. Photo)

1989 (10 Aug). Birth Centenary of Carl von Ossietzky (journalist and peace activist). P 14.
B828   B **263**   100pf. multicoloured .... 3·00   3·00

B **264** Former School Building

B **265** St. Nicholas's Church, Berlin-Spandau

(Des B. Görs. Eng L. Lück. Recess and litho)

1989 (12 Oct). 300th Anniv of Berlin Lycée Français. P 14.
B829   B **264**   40pf. multicoloured .... 1·60   1·50

GERMANY / German Democratic Republic (East Germany)

E 8 Shepherd Playing Pipes
E 9 Dove, Globe and Stamp 
E 10 L. Euler 

(Des F. Jacob and E.P. Weis. Litho)

1950 (14 June). Death Bicentenary of J. S. Bach (composer). Type E **8** and similar types inscr 'BACH JAHR 1950'. Wmk R **2**. P 13×13½.

E15	12pf. +4pf. emerald-green	11·00	7·75
E16	24pf. +6pf. olive-bistre	11·00	7·75
E17	30pf. +8pf. red	13·50	13·00
E18	50pf. +16pf. light blue	27·00	23·00
E15/E18	Set of 4	55·00	46·00

Designs:—12pf. Type E **8**; 24pf. Girl playing hand-organ; 30pf. Bach; 50pf. Three singers.

(Des F. Gravenhorst. Litho)

1950 (1 July). Philatelic Exhibition (DEBRIA), Leipzig. Wmk R **2**. P 13.

E19	E **9**	84pf. +41pf. lake	65·00	17·00

See also No. **MSE29**a.

(Des G. Kreische. Litho)

1950 (10 July). 250th Anniv of Academy of Sciences, Berlin. Portraits as Type E **10** inscr '250 JAHRE DEUTSCHE AKADEMIE DER WISSENSCHAFTEN ZU BERLIN'. Wmk R **2**. P 13×12½.

E20	1pf. grey (Type E **10**)	6·75	2·50
E21	5pf. green (A. von Humboldt)	9·50	6·50
E22	6pf. violet (T. Mommsen)	19·00	6·50
E23	8pf. red-brown (W. von Humboldt)	23·00	13·00
E24	10pf. grey-green (H. von Helmholtz)	19·00	13·00
E25	12pf. blue (M. Planck)	16·00	5·25
E26	16pf. turquoise-blue (J. Grimm)	27·00	26·00
E27	20pf. reddish purple (W. Nernst)	24·00	21·00
E28	24pf. rose-red (G. W. Leibniz)	24·00	5·25
E29	50pf. ultramarine (A. von Harnack)	35·00	26·00
E20/E29	Set of 10	£180	£110

1950 (26 Aug). German Stamp Exhibition, DEBRIA. Sheet 92×52 mm. Imperf.

MSE29a Nos. E4 and E19 .... £200 £225

E 11 Miner
E 12 Ballot Box 

(Des F. Gravenhorst. Litho)

1950 (1 Sept). 750th Anniv of Opening of Mansfeld Copper Mines. T E **11** and similar horiz design. Wmk R **2**. P 13×13½.

E30	12pf. blue (Type E **11**)	9·50	10·50
	a. Deep ultramarine	£750	£950
	b. Light ultramarine	£275	£250
E31	24pf. scarlet (Copper smelting)	15·00	10·50

Prices for E30a/E30b are for properly used examples (not cancelled to order).

(Des F. Gravenhorst. Litho)

1950 (28 Sept). East German Elections. Wmk R **2**. P 13.

E32	E **12**	24pf. chestnut	22·00	6·50

E 13 Hand, Dove and Burning Building
E 14 Tobogganing 

(Des G. Martens. Litho)

1950 (15 Dec). Peace Propaganda. T E **13** and similar types inscr 'ERKAMPFT DEN FRIEDEN'. Wmk R **2**. P 13½×13.

E33	6pf. deep violet-blue	6·75	4·50
E34	8pf. brown	6·00	2·50
E35	12pf. turquoise-blue	7·50	5·75
E36	24pf. vermilion	8·00	4·00
E33/E36	Set of 4	25·00	15·00

Designs:—All include 'Hand and Dove'; 6pf. Tank, 8pf. T E **13**; 12pf. Atom-bomb explosion; 24pf. Rows of gravestones.

1951 (3 Feb). Second Winter Sports Meeting, Oberhof. T E **14** and similar type inscr '2. WINTER. SPORT-MEISTERSCHAFTEN OBERHOF 1951'. Litho. Wmk R **2**. P 13×13½.

E37	12pf. turquoise-blue (Type E **14**)	12·00	10·50
E38	24pf. carmine (Ski jumper)	16·00	13·00

E 15
E 16 Presidents Pieck and Bierut 

(Des Prof. Troggmayer. Litho)

1951 (4 Mar). Leipzig Spring Fair. Wmk R **2**. P 13×13½.

E39	E **15**	24pf. carmine	22·00	16·00
E40		50pf. ultramarine	23·00	16·00

(Des G. Martens. Litho)

1951 (22 Apr). Visit of Polish President to Berlin. Wmk R **2**. P 13×13½.

E41	E **16**	24pf. rose-red	27·00	23·00
E42		50pf. blue	27·00	23·00

E 17 Mao Tse-tung
E 18 Chinese Land Reform 

(Des G. Martens. Litho)

1951 (27 June). Friendship with China. Wmk R **2**. P 13×13½ (vert) or 13½×13 (horiz).

E43	E **17**	12pf. green	£120	33·00
E44	E **18**	24pf. carmine	£180	39·00
E45	E **17**	50pf. blue	£120	39·00
E43/E45	Set of 3		£375	£100

E 19 Youth Hoisting Flag
E 20 Symbols of Agriculture and Industry 

(Des K. Eigler and K. Bade. Litho)

1951 (3 Aug). Third World Youth and Students' Festival. T E **19** and similar vert design. Wmk R **2**. P 13×13.

E46	E **19**	12pf. chestnut and brown/grey-blue	18·00	9·00
E47	–	24pf. green and red/grey-blue	18·00	5·25
E48	E **19**	30pf. buff and blue-green/cream	20·00	9·75
E49	–	50pf. red and blue/grey-blue	20·00	9·75
E46/E49	Set of 4		70·00	30·00

Designs:—24pf, 50pf. Three girls dancing.

1951 (2 Sept). Five Year Plan. Typo. Wmk R **2**. P 13×12½.

E50	E **20**	24pf. yellow, red, black and lake	6·75	3·25

E 21 K. Liebknecht
E 22 Instructing Young Collectors

(Des P. Weiss. Litho)
1951 (7 Oct). 80th Birth Anniv of Liebknecht (revolutionary). Wmk R **2**. P 13½×13.
E51   E **21**   24pf. slate-violet and red.................... 8·00   3·25

(Des K. Bade and K. Eigler Litho)
1951 (28 Oct). Stamp Day. Wmk R **2**. P 13×13½.
E52   E **22**   12pf. blue.. 9·75   4·00

E **23** P. Bykov and E. Wirth   E **24** Skier

(Des E. Gruner and K. Wolf. Litho)
1951 (1–15 Dec). German Soviet Friendship. T E **23** and similar horiz portrait type. Wmk R **2**. P 13½×13.
E53   12pf. blue (15.12)................................. 7·50   5·25
E54   24pf. red (1.12)..................................... 8·75   6·50
Designs:—12pf. T E **23**; 24pf. Stalin and President Pieck.

(Des H. Liedtke and H. Weber. Litho)
1952 (12 Jan). Third Winter Sports Meeting, Oberhof. T E **24** and similar vert design inscr 'OBERHOF 1952'. Wmk R **2**. P 13½×13.
E55   12pf. blue-green (Type E **24**)............ 9·50   5·25
E56   24pf. blue (Ski jumper)......................... 9·75   6·50

E **25** Beethoven   E **26** President Gottwald

(Des K. Eigler and K. Wolf. Litho)
1952 (26 Mar). 125th Death Anniv of Beethoven (composer). T E **25** and similar vert portrait inscr '1827–1952'. Wmk R **2**. P 13½×13.
E57   12pf. blue and pale blue....................... 3·75   1·30
E58   24pf. chocolate and grey..................... 5·00   2·00
Designs:—12pf. Full face portrait; 24pf. T E **25**.

(Des K. Eigler. Photo Druckhaus Einheit)
1952 (1 May). Czechoslovak-German Friendship. Wmk R **2**. P 13½×13.
E59   E **26**   24pf. ultramarine............................ 5·50   2·75

E **27** Bricklayers   E **28** Cyclists

(Des K. Bade and K. Eigler. Eng K. Wolf. Litho)
1952 (1 May). National Reconstruction Fund. T E **27** and similar horiz designs inscr 'NATIONALES AUFBAUPROGRAMM'. Wmk R **2**. P 13×13½.
E60   12pf. +3pf. violet.................................. 3·75   1·20
E61   24pf. +6pf. brown-red........................... 2·75   1·30
E62   30pf. +10pf. green................................ 3·75   1·40
E63   50pf. +10pf. deep ultramarine.............. 4·50   2·50
E60/E63   Set of 4 .... 13·50   5·75
Designs:—12pf. Workers clearing debris; 24pf. T E **27**; 30pf. Carpenters; 50pf. Architect and workmen.

(Des H. Liedtke and H. Weber. Photo Druckhaus Einheit)
1952 (5 May). Fifth Warsaw-Berlin-Prague Peace Cycle Race. Wmk R **2**. P 13×13½.
E64   E **28**   12pf. blue.. 5·50   2·50

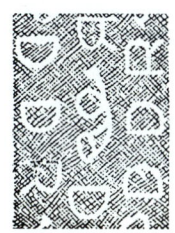

E **29** Handel   E **30** (Vertical)

(Des K. Eigler and K. Wolf. Litho)
1952 (5 July). Handel Festival, Halle. T E **29** and similar vert portraits. Wmk E **30** (vert). P 13½×13.
E65   6pf. brown and pale brown (Type E **29**)...... 4·75   2·00
E66   8pf. carmine and pink (Lortzing)............ 5·00   3·25
E67   50pf. deep and pale blue (Weber).......... 5·00   4·00
E65/E67   Set of 3 .... 13·50   8·25

(Ptd by G.B.N. and G.W.)
1952 (July)–**53**. As Nos. E 10/13 but Wmk E **30** (horiz). New value (5pf.).

(a) Typo. P 13×12½
E68   E **6**   5pf. emerald (22.9.52)..................... 13·50   5·25
             a. Wmk vert.................................... 47·00   26·00
E69   12pf. blue (9.52)............................... 55·00   2·50
             a. Wmk vert.................................... £425   £180
E70   24pf. brown-red (7.52)...................... 34·00   2·10
             a. Wmk vert.................................... 55·00   20·00

(b) 28×23 mm. P 13
E71   E **7**   1Dm. sage-green (*typo*) (1953)...... 47·00   26·00
E72   2Dm. brown-red (*litho*) (11.6.53)...... 46·00   5·25
E68/E72   Set of 5 .... £180   37·00

E **31** Victor Hugo (writer)   E **32** Machinery, Dove and Globe

(Des K. Eigler, Photo Druckhaus Einheit, Leipzig)
1952 (11 Aug). Cultural Anniversaries. T E **31** and similar horiz portraits. Wmk R **2**. P 13×13½.
E73   12pf. brown.. 5·50   6·50
E74   20pf. yellowish green........................... 5·50   6·50
E75   24pf. carmine-red................................ 5·50   6·50
E76   35pf. blue... 8·00   7·75
E73/E76   Set of 4 .... 22·00   25·00
Designs and anniversaries:—12pf. T E **31** (150th birth); 20pf. Leonardo da Vinci (artist) (500th birth); 24pf. Nikolai Gogol (writer) (death centenary); 35pf. Avicenna (physician) (born 980, design incorrectly inscr '952').

(Des K. Eigler, Photo Druckhaus Einheit, Leipzig)
1952 (7 Sept). Leipzig Autumn Fair. Wmk E **30** (horiz). P 13×13½.
E77   E **32**   24pf. carmine-red.......................... 4·00   2·00
E78   35pf. blue... 4·00   2·50

E **33** F. L. Jahn   E **34** University Building

(Des K. Eigler and K. Wolf. Litho)
1952 (15 Oct). Death Centenary of Jahn (patriot). Wmk E **30** (vert). P 13½×13.
E79   E **33**   12pf. deep violet-blue..................... 3·50   2·50
             a. Wmk horiz................................. 80·00   33·00

(Des E. Gruner. Photo Druckhaus Einheit, Leipzig)
1952 (18 Oct). 450th Anniv of Halle-Wittenberg University. Wmk E **30** (horiz). P 13×13½.
E80   E **34**   24pf. green...................................... 3·50   1·60

GERMANY / German Democratic Republic (East Germany)

E 35 Dove, Stamp and Flags
E 36 Dove, Globe and St. Stephen's Cathedral, Vienna 

(Des K. Eigler. Photo Druckhaus Einheit)

1952 (26 Oct). Stamp Day. Wmk E **30** (vert). P 13½×13.
| E81 | E **35** | 24pf. red-brown | 4·50 | 1·70 |

(Ptd by G.B.N. and G.W.)

1952–53. As Nos. R33/48 but Wmk E **30** (horiz).
E82	2pf. grey-black	5·25	7·75
	a. Wmk vert	£140	£200
E83	6pf. violet	4·75	3·50
	a. Wmk vert	55·00	20·00
E84	8pf. brown-red	3·25	3·25
	a. Wmk vert	34·00	20·00
E85	10pf. bluish green	9·50	5·25
	a. Wmk vert	£1900	£2000
E86	15pf. brown	22·00	21·00
E87	16pf. greenish blue	9·50	5·50
	a. Wmk vert		£16000
E88	20pf. brown-purple	13·50	4·75
	a. Wmk vert	£2750	£1800
E89	25pf. olive-green	£275	£375
E90	30pf. vermilion	30·00	13·00
	a. Wmk vert	£100	£100
E91	40pf. reddish purple	6·75	6·25
	a. Wmk vert	£6000	£8000
E92	50pf. ultramarine (3.53)	41·00	29·00
E93	60pf. deep green	8·00	5·25
	a. Wmk vert	24·00	34·00
E94	80pf. blackish blue	11·00	3·25
	a. Varnished surface (9.3.53)	13·50	£500
E95	80pf. bright carmine-red (16.4.53)	20·00	13·00
E96	84pf. purple-brown	£110	£140
E82/E96	Set of 15	£500	£550

(Des K. Eigler. Photo Druckhaus Einheit)

1952 (8 Dec). Peace Congress, Vienna. Wmk E **30** (vert). P 13½×13.
| E97 | E **36** | 24pf. bright carmine | 3·00 | 3·00 |
| E98 | | 35pf. deep blue | 3·00 | 5·25 |

E 37 President Pieck
E 38 Karl Marx 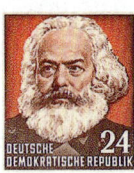

(Des K. Eigler. Photo Druckhaus Einheit or G.W. (E100))

1953–55. Wmk E **30** (horiz). P 13×13½.
E99	E **37**	1Dm. olive-green (2.2.53)	20·00	1·00
E100		1Dm. deep bronze-green (7.55)	£200	4·00
E101		2Dm. red-brown (3.1.53)	15·00	1·00

For similar design, Wmk E **100**, see Nos. E320/E321 and E539.

(Des K. Eigler, T. Thomas (20pf.), and Döbeln. Photo. 20pf., 35pf. Druckhaus Einheit, others G.W.)

1953 (14 Mar–10 Dec). 70th Death Anniv of Marx. T E **38** and similar designs. Wmk E **30** (horiz or vert). P 13×13½; 13½×13 (vert).
E102	6pf. orange-red and deep turquoise-green (5.5)	2·00	1·30
E103	10pf. brown and grey-green (5.5)	6·75	1·30
E104	12pf. carmine-lake and deep yellow-green (5.5)	2·00	1·30
E105	16pf. ultramarine and carmine-red (5.5)	5·50	3·25
E106	20pf. brown and ochre	2·00	1·30
E107	24pf. deep brown and orange-red	5·50	1·30
E108	35pf. maroon and ochre (5.5)	5·50	4·50
E109	48pf. red-brown and bronze-green (5.5)	2·75	1·30
E110	60pf. orange-red and lake-brown (5.5)	6·75	4·50
E111	84pf. sepia and blue	5·50	3·25
E102/E111	Set of 10	40·00	21·00

MSE111a Two sheets each 148×104 mm. (a) the six vert and (b) the four horiz designs. Perf (10.12) Set of 2 sheets | £250 | £400 |
| | c. Imperf (24.10) Set of 2 sheets | £250 | £400 |

Designs: Vert—6pf. Flag and foundry; 12pf. Flag and Spassky Tower, Kremlin; 20pf. Marx reading from *Das Kapital*; 24pf. T E **38**; 35pf. Marx addressing meeting; 48pf. Marx and Engels. Horiz—10pf. Marx, Engels and *Communist Manifesto*; 16pf. Marching crowd; 60pf. Flag and workers; 84pf. Marx in medallion and Stalin Avenue, Berlin.

E 39 Maksim Gorky
E 40 Cyclists 

(Des K. Eigler. Photo Druckhaus Einheit)

1953 (28 Mar). 85th Birth Anniv of Maksim Gorky (writer). Wmk E **30** (vert). P 13½×13.
| E112 | E **39** | 35pf. deep brown | 1·10 | 80 |

(Litho G.W.)

1953 (2 May). Sixth International Cycle Race. T E **40** and similar vert designs. Wmk E **30** (vert). P 13½×13.
E113	24pf. blue-green	3·75	3·25
E114	35pf. bright blue	2·00	2·00
E115	60pf. brown	2·75	2·50
	a. Wmk horiz		
E113/E115	Set of 3	7·75	7·00

Designs:—24pf. T E **40**; 35pf. Cyclists and countryside; 60pf. Cyclists in town.

E 41 Heinrich von Kleist (writer)
E 42 Miner 

(Des E. Gruner. Litho G.W.)

1953 (6 July). Seventh Centenary of Frankfurt-on-Oder. T E **41** and horiz views inscr '1253–1953'. Wmk E **30** (horiz). P 13×13½.
E116	16pf. brown	2·30	3·25
E117	20pf. deep bluish green	1·70	3·25
E118	24pf. scarlet	2·30	3·25
E119	35pf. bright blue	2·75	4·50
E116/E119	Set of 4	8·25	13·00

Designs:—16pf. T E **41**; 20pf. St. Mary's Church; 24pf. Frankfurt from R. Oder; 35pf. Frankfurt Town Hall and Coat of Arms.

> **REPRINTS**. Official reprints exist of Nos. E120/E137, E153/E176 and E189/E197, made for sale to collectors. These are always ungummed and may be detected by postmarks, which are machine-printed and glossy. Reprints of Nos. E120/E137 and E193 have 'E' of 'DEUTSCHE' over 'A'; originals have 'E' over 'T'. In the typographed issues both originals and reprints have the 'E' over the 'A'.

(Des E. Gruner. Litho G.W.)

1953 (10 Aug–Nov). Five Year Plan. T E **42** and similar vert designs. No imprint below designs. Wmk E **30** (horiz). P 13×12½.
E120	1pf. brownish black	2·75	90
E121	5pf. emerald	3·50	2·30
E122	6pf. violet	3·50	1·80
E123	8pf. orange-brown	4·75	2·50
E124	10pf. blue-green	3·50	2·00
E125	12pf. pale blue	4·75	2·10
	a. Wmk vert	£700	£275
E126	15pf. reddish violet	5·50	4·25
E127	16pf. blackish violet	11·00	5·75
E128	20pf. bronze-green	8·00	5·75
E129	24pf. carmine-red (21.11)	16·00	2·50
E130	25pf. deep green	11·00	7·75
E131	30pf. brown-red	23·00	8·50
E132	35pf. bright ultramarine	27·00	9·75
E133	40pf. rose-red	22·00	6·50
E134	48pf. bright mauve	22·00	6·50
E135	60pf. bright blue	22·00	11·50
E136	80pf. greenish blue	23·00	11·50
E137	84pf. brown	22·00	33·00
E120/E137	Set of 18	£200	£110

Designs:—1pf. T E **42**; 5pf. Woman turning wheel; 6pf. Workmen shaking hands; 8pf. Students; 10pf. Engineers; 12pf. Agricultural and industrial workers; 15pf. Teletypist; 16pf. Foundry worker; 20pf. Workers' health centre, Elster; 24pf. Stalin Avenue, Berlin; 25pf. Locomotive construction workers; 30pf. Folk dancers; 35pf. Stadium; 40pf. Scientist; 48pf. Zwinger, Dresden; 60pf. Launching ship; 80pf. Farm workers; 84pf. Workman and family.

For similar designs typographed, see Nos. E153/E176 and E310/E319.

GERMANY / German Democratic Republic (East Germany)

E 43 Mechanical Grab

E 44 G. W. von Knobelsdorff and Opera House, Berlin

(Des E. Gruner. Photo G.W.)

1953 (30 Aug). Leipzig Autumn Fair. T E **43** and similar horiz design. Wmk E **30** (horiz). P 13×13½.

E138	24pf. brown-red (Type E **43**)	4·50	4·25
E139	35pf. green (Potato-harvester)	4·75	4·50

(Des K. Eigler. Photo Druckhaus Einheit)

1953 (16 Sept). German Architects. T E **44** and similar horiz design. Wmk E **30** (horiz). P 13×12½.

E140	24pf. rose-magenta	3·75	1·60
	a. Wmk vert	70·00	39·00
E141	35pf. deep slate-blue	3·75	2·50

Designs:—24pf. T E **44**; 35pf. B. Neumann and Würzburg Palace.

E 45 Lucas Cranach

E 46 Nurse and Patient

(Des K. Eigler. Photo Druckhaus Einheit)

1953 (16 Oct). 400th Death Anniv of Cranach (painter). Wmk E **30** (horiz). P 13×13.

E142	E **45**	24pf. brown	4·75	2·00
		a. Wmk vert	60·00	90·00

(Des K. Eigler. Photo G.W.)

1953 (23 Oct). Red Cross. Wmk E **30** (vert). P 13½×13.

E143	E **46**	24pf. scarlet and brown	4·00	2·20
		a. Wmk horiz	£800	£250

E 47 Postman Delivering Letters

E 48 Lion

(Des E. Gruner. Photo G.W.)

1953 (25 Oct). Stamp Day. Wmk E **30** (vert). P 13½×13.

E144	E **47**	24pf. indigo	4·75	1·30
		a. Wmk horiz	£140	£200

(Des E. Gruner. Photo Druckhaus Einheit)

1953 (2 Nov). 75th Anniv of Leipzig Zoo. Wmk E **30** (horiz). P 13×13½.

| E145 | E **48** | 24pf. deep olive-brown | 3·50 | 1·30 |

E 49 Müntzer and Peasants

E 50 Franz Schubert

(Des K. Eigler and K. Bade. Photo G.W.)

1953 (9–30 Nov). German Patriots. T E **49** and similar horiz designs. Wmk E **30** (horiz). P 13×12½.

E146	12pf. red-brown	2·40	1·00
	a. Wmk vert	41·00	31·00
E147	16pf. brown (30.11)	2·40	1·00
	a. Wmk vert	95·00	£120
E148	20pf. carmine	2·40	65
	a. Wmk vert	50·00	80·00
E149	24pf. deep greenish blue	2·40	65
	a. Wmk vert		
E150	35pf. deep grey-green (30.11)	4·00	2·50
E151	48pf. sepia (30.11)	6·00	2·10
	a. Wmk vert		
E146/E151	Set of 6	18·00	7·00

Designs:—12pf. T E **49**; 16pf. Baron vom Stein and scroll; 20pf. Von Schill and cavalry; 24pf. Blücher and infantry; 35pf. Students marching; 48pf. Barricade, 1848 Revolution.

(Des K. Eigler. Photo Druckhaus Einheit)

1953 (13 Nov). 125th Death Anniv of Schubert. Wmk E **30** (vert). P 13½×13.

| E152 | E **50** | 48pf. orange-brown | 5·25 | 2·50 |

PRINTERS. Nos. E153 to E294 were printed by Graphische Werkstätten (=G.W.). Leipzig.

BOOKLET PANES. Specially printed booklet panes, in which the stamps are surrounded by perforated margins, are included in the listings under the lowest value in each pane. A checklist of booklets is given at the end of the section.

E 51 Miner

(Des E. Gruner. Die eng K. Wolf. Typo)

1953 (21 Nov)–**55**. As Nos. E120/E137 but designs redrawn in lines instead of dots, as in T E **51**. With designers' and engravers' names below design except Nos. E155, E158/E159, E161/E162 and E168. Wmk E **30** (horiz). P 13×12½.

E153	1pf. black	1·40	25
	a. Wmk vert	3·50	3·25
E154	5pf. emerald (28.12.53)	4·00	40
	a. Booklet pane. Nos. E154×3 and E158×3 (3.55)	47·00	
	b. Booklet pane. Nos. E154×3 and E164×3 (3.55)	47·00	
	c. Wmk vert	£550	£325
E155	6pf. violet	6·75	80
	a. Wmk vert	£450	£130
E156	8pf. orange-brown (28.12.53)	6·75	50
E157	10pf. blue-green	60·00	40
	a. Wmk vert	70·00	36·00
E158	10pf. light blue (22.1.55)	3·50	80
	a. Booklet pane. Nos. E158×4 and E164×2 (3.55)	43·00	
E159	12pf. greenish blue	8·00	50
	a. Wmk vert	34·00	16·00
E160	15pf. bright lilac (25.1.54)	30·00	90
	a. Wmk vert		£4000
E161	15pf. blackish violet (15.8.55)	6·00	90
E162	16pf. blackish violet	6·75	1·30
E163	20pf. bronze-green (6.2.54)	£120	1·30
	a. Wmk vert	£550	£200
E164	20pf. carmine-red (22.1.55)	3·50	80
E165	24pf. carmine-red (28.12.53)	11·00	50
	a. Wmk vert	£800	£800
E166	25pf. deep green	6·75	1·30
	a. Wmk vert	£700	£350
E167	30pf. brown-red	11·00	1·30
E168	35pf. ultramarine	8·00	1·60
E169	40pf. rose-red (15.2.54)	16·00	1·60
	a. Wmk vert	41·00	43·00
E170	40pf. bright mauve (22.1.55)	9·50	1·00
E171	48pf. bright mauve (28.12.53)	16·00	2·30
E172	50pf. bright blue (22.1.55)	15·00	1·20
	a. Wmk vert		
E173	60pf. bright blue	30·00	2·50
E174	70pf. brown (15.8.55)	18·00	1·60
E175	80pf. turquoise-blue	6·75	2·50
	a. Wmk vert	50·00	26·00
E176	84pf. brown (28.12.53)	27·00	2·50
E153/E176	Set of 24	£400	27·00

Designs:—10pf. blue, Agricultural and industrial workers; 15pf. violet, Foundry Worker; 20pf. red, Stalin Avenue, Berlin; 40pf. mauve, Zwinger, Dresden; 50pf. Launching ship; 70pf. Workman and family. Others as Nos. E120/E137.

Reprints exist; see note above No. E120.

The prices in the second column are postally used copies.

For similar designs, Wmk E **100** see Nos. E310/E319.

GERMANY / German Democratic Republic (East Germany)

E 52 G. E. Lessing
E 53 Conference Table and Crowd 
E 54 Stalin 

(Des K. Eigler. Photo)
1954 (20 Jan). 225th Birth Anniv of Lessing (writer). Wmk E **30** (vert). P 13½×13.
E177   E **52**   20pf. bronze-green ....   3·75   1·60

(Des E. Gruner. Photo)
1954 (25 Jan). Four-Power Conference, Berlin. Wmk E **30** (vert). P 13½×13.
E178   E **53**   12pf. blue ....   2·75   1·60

(Des K. Eigler. Photo)
1954 (5 Mar). First Anniv of Death of Stalin. Wmk E **30** (vert). P 13½×13.
E179   E **54**   20pf. sepia, red-orange and grey ....   4·75   1·70

E 55 Racing Cyclists
E 56 Folk Dancing 

(Des B. Petersen. Photo)
1954 (30 Apr). Seventh International Cycle Race. T E **55** and similar horiz design. Wmk E **30** (horiz). P 13×12½.
E180   12pf. sepia ....   2·75   1·30
E181   24pf. deep grey-green ....   3·50   2·00
Designs:—12pf. T E **55**; 24pf. Cyclists racing through countryside.

(Des K. Bade and K. Eigler (12pf.), K. Eigler (24pf.). Photo)
1954 (3 June). Second German Youth Assembly. T E **56** and similar vert design. Wmk E **30** (vert). P 13½×13.
E182   12pf. emerald (Type E **56**) ....   2·00   1·60
E183   24pf. brown-lake (Young people and flag) ....   2·00   1·60

E 57 F. Reuter 
EO 58

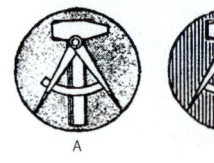

A   B   C
The three main types of centre

(Des K. Eigler. Photo)
1954 (12 July). 80th Death Anniv of Reuter (author). Wmk E **30** (vert). P 13½×13.
E184   E **57**   24pf. sepia ....   2·75   1·80

> **PRICES FOR ISSUED STAMPS.** During their period of use, stamps of T EO **58** were not issued in unused condition but later some were put on sale by the Philatelic Bureau for collectors. We quote prices only for postally used copies. The issued stamps also exist cancelled to order and are almost worthless.

> **REPRINTS.** Official reprints of Nos. EO185/EO201 were made for collectors. They are always ungummed and bear machine-printed cancellations. They can be distinguished by the diagonally dotted shading around the hammer. There is a faint line of dots surrounding the wide band around the hammer. In the originals this line is three dots wide but in the reprints there are five.

(Des K. Eigler)
1954–56. OFFICIAL. Wmk E **30** (horiz). P 13×12½.
(a) Litho. Centre Type A (15 Aug–1 Oct 1954)
EO185   EO **58**   5pf. bright emerald ....   —   65
                            a. Wmk vert ....   —   £250
EO186   6pf. bright violet ....   —   3·25
EO187   8pf. orange-brown ....   —   65
EO188   10pf. turquoise-green ....   —   65
EO189   12pf. greenish blue ....   —   65
EO190   15pf. deep lilac (1.10) ....   —   65
                            a. Wmk vert ....   —   39·00
EO191   16pf. deep lilac ....   —   1·30
EO192   20pf. olive-green ....   —   65
                            a. Wmk vert ....   —   £500
EO193   24pf. scarlet ....   —   80
EO194   25pf. dull blue-green (1.10) ....   —   6·50
                            a. Wmk vert ....   —   20·00
EO195   30pf. brown-red ....   —   65
EO196   40pf. rose-red ....   —   65
EO197   48pf. reddish lilac ....   —   16·00
EO198   50pf. reddish lilac (1.10) ....   —   90
                            a. Wmk vert ....   —   —
EO199   60pf. blue ....   —   1·00
EO200   70pf. brown. (1.10) ....   —   90
EO201   84pf. brown ....   —   46·00
EO185/EO201   Set of 17 ....   —   75·00

(b) Typo. Centre Type B (1954–1956)
EO202   EO **58**   5pf. bright emerald ....   —   80
                            a. Wmk vert ....   —   £160
EO203   10pf. turquoise-green ....   —   65
EO204   12pf. deep greenish blue ....   —   65
EO205   15pf. blackish lilac ....   —   65
EO206   20pf. olive-green (1956) ....   —   1·00
EO207   25pf. blue-green ....   —   4·00
EO208   30pf. brown-red ....   —   4·50
EO209   40pf. rose-red ....   —   90
EO210   50pf. reddish lilac ....   —   1·00
EO211   70pf. brown ....   —   2·50
                            a. Wmk vert ....   —   £550
EO202/EO211   Set of 10 ....   —   15·00
The 5, 10, 15, 20 and 40pf. also exist on granite paper, printed by both the Graphische Werkstätten and the German Bank Note Ptg Co.

(c) Typo. Centre Type C (1955)
EO212   EO **58**   20pf. olive-green ....   —   1·00
See Nos. EO295/EO302 for stamps of Type B with wmk E **100**.

E 58 Dam and Forest
E 59 Thälmann 

(Des K. Eigler. Litho)
1954 (16 Aug). Flood Relief Fund. No wmk. P 13×13½.
E185   E **58**   24pf. +6pf. green ....   1·40   1·30

(Des K. Eigler. Photo)
1954 (18 Aug). Tenth Death Anniv of Thälmann (politician). Wmk E **30** (vert). P 13½×13.
E186   E **59**   24pf. brown, indigo and red-orange ....   2·00   1·40
                        a. Wmk horiz ....   —   £500

E 60 Exhibition Buildings
(E 61)

(Des E. Gruner. Photo)
1954 (4 Sept). Leipzig Autumn Fair. Wmk E **30** (horiz). P 13×13½.
E187   E **60**   24pf. brown-red ....   1·50   1·30
E188   35pf. indigo ....   1·50   1·30

GERMANY / German Democratic Republic (East Germany)

1954 (1 Oct)–**55**. Surch as T E **61**. Wmk horiz.

E189	5pf. on 6pf. (E155)		2·00	80
	a. Wmk vert.		41·00	46·00
E190	5pf. on 8pf. (E156)		2·40	80
E191	10pf. on 12pf. (E159)		2·40	1·00
	a. Wmk vert.		41·00	50·00
E192	15pf. on 16pf. (E162)		2·00	80
	a. Wmk vert.		47·00	39·00
E193	20pf. on 24pf. (E129) (2.55)		£2750	£2500
	a. Brown-carmine (16.3.55)		2·00	1·00
E194	20pf. on 24pf. (E165)		3·50	1·00
	a. Wmk vert.		£550	£350
E195	40pf. on 48pf. (E171)		6·75	5·25
	a. Wmk vert.		£550	£325
E196	50pf. on 60pf. (E173)		6·75	3·50
E197	70pf. on 84pf. (E176)		18·00	4·00
	a. Wmk vert.		£400	£200
E189/E197 Set of 9 (cheapest)			39·00	15·00

The prices in the second column are for postally used copies. Cancelled-to-order stamps are almost worthless.

No. E193 (litho) was issued in error. To obviate speculation two million more were issued but in brown-carmine instead of the original carmine-red.

No. E193 was also reprinted in 1957 without gum and cancelled by machine as described in the note above No. E120.

E **62** President Pieck

E **63** Stamp of 1953

(Des E. Gruner. Photo)

1954 (6 Oct). Fifth Anniv of German Democratic Republic. Wmk E **30** (horiz). P 13×12½.

E198	E **62**	20pf. brown	4·75	2·10
E199		35pf. deep slate-blue	4·75	2·30

(Des K. Eigler. Photo)

1954 (23 Oct). Stamp Day. Wmk E **30** (vert). P 13×13½.

E200	E **63**	20pf. deep magenta	2·75	1·30
		a. Wmk vert.	70·00	20·00
MSE200b 60×80 mm. No. E200 imperf (sold at Dm. 30) (30.10.54)			65·00	65·00
		ba. Wmk vert.	£1400	£1600

E **64** Russian Pavilion

(E **65**)

(Des E. Gruner. Photo)

1955 (21 Feb). Leipzig Spring Fair. T E **64** and similar horiz design. Wmk E **30** (horiz). P 13×13½.

E201		20pf. purple (Type E **64**)	1·50	1·60
		a. Wmk vert.		65·00
E202		35pf. deep blue (Chinese Pavilion)	2·75	2·00
		a. Blue/yellowish	27·00	1·60

1955 (25 Feb). Flood Relief Fund. No. E185 surch with T E **65**.

E203	E **58**	20pf. +5pf. on 24pf.+6pf. green	1·60	90

E **66** Women of All Nations

E **67** Parade of Workers

(Des E. Gruner. Photo)

1955 (1 Mar). 45th Anniv of International Women's Day. Wmk E **30** (horiz). P 13×12½.

E204	E **66**	10pf. green	1·90	80
E205		20pf. scarlet	1·90	80

(Des E. Gruner. Photo)

1955 (15 Mar). International Conference of Municipal Workers, Vienna. Wmk E **30** (horiz). P 13×12½.

E206	E **67**	10pf. black and red	1·60	1·60

E **68** Monument to Fascist Victims, Brandenburg

E **69** Monument to Russian Soldiers, Treptow

(Des K. Eigler. Photo)

1955 (9 Apr). International Liberation Day. Wmk E **30** (vert). P 13½×13.

E207	E **68**	10pf. deep blue	1·40	1·30
E208		20pf. deep magenta	1·90	2·10
MSE208a 73×99 mm. Nos. E207/E208. Wmk horiz. Imperf			27·00	46·00

(Des K. Eigler. Photo)

1955 (15 Apr). Tenth Anniv of Liberation. Wmk E **30** (vert). P 12½×13.

E209	E **69**	20pf. deep magenta	2·75	2·00

> **BLOCKED VALUES.** From 1955 to 1983 most commemorative issues contained one 'blocked value'. Blocked values were not sold freely at post offices but were only available there at face value to registered permit-holding collectors. They were exported to the Philatelic Bureau at very much higher rates and are priced accordingly. Most used stamps of these blocked values were cancelled to order and our prices are for this condition. Postally used examples are worth more.

E **70** Schiller

E **71** Cyclists

(Des K. Eigler (5pf.), H. Götze (10pf.), E. Schoner (20pf.). Photo)

1955 (30 Apr). 150th Death Anniv of Schiller (poet). T E **70** and similar vert portraits. Wmk E **30** (vert). P 13½×13.

E210		5pf. deep grey-green (Type E **70**)	4·75	4·00
E211		10pf. blue (Full-face)	1·10	65
		a. Wmk horiz.		60·00
E212		20pf. deep red-brown (Facing left)	1·10	65
E210/E212 Set of 3			6·25	4·75
MSE212a 73×100 mm. Nos. E210/E212 (+15pf.) Wmk horiz. Imperf			32·00	39·00

(Des B. Petersen. Photo)

1955 (30 Apr). Eighth International Cycle Race. Wmk E **30** (vert). P 13½×13.

E213	E **71**	10pf. deep turquoise-green	1·30	1·00
E214		20pf. bright carmine	1·40	1·30

E **72** Karl Liebknecht

(Des K. Eigler (15pf.), B. Petersen and K. Eigler (others). Photo)

1955 (20 June). German Labour Leaders. T E **72** and similar horiz portraits. Wmk E **30** (horiz). P 13×12½.

E215		5pf. blue-green (Type E **72**)	55	50
E216		10pf. blue (A. Bebel)	80	65
E217		15pf. violet (F. Mehring)	11·00	7·75
E218		20pf. rose-red (E. Thälmann)	80	65
E219		25pf. deep blue (Clara Zetkin)	80	65
E220		40pf. carmine-red (Wilhelm Liebknecht)	4·00	80
E221		60pf. sepia (Rosa Luxemburg)	80	65
E215/E221 Set of 7			17·00	10·50

GERMANY / German Democratic Republic (East Germany)

E 73 Pottery
E 74 Workers and Charter 
E 79 Portrait of a Young Man (Dürer)
E 80 Mozart

(Des E. Gruner. Photo)

1955 (29 Aug). Leipzig Autumn Fair. T E **73** and similar horiz design inscr 'LEIPZIGER MESSE 4-9.9.1955'. Wmk E **30** (horiz). P 13×13½.
| E222 | 10pf. blue (Camera and microscope) | 1·40 | 90 |
| E223 | 20pf. bronze-green (Type E **73**) | 1·40 | 90 |

(Des B. Petersen. Litho)

1955 (3 Sept). Tenth Anniv of Land Reform. T E **74** and similar designs inscr '1945 BODENREFORM 1955'. Wmk E **30** (horiz, 20pf. or vert, others). P 13½×13 (vert) or 13×13½ (horiz).
E224	5pf. deep dull green	9·50	7·75
E225	10pf. deep ultramarine	1·40	65
E226	20pf. brown-red	1·40	65
E224/E226 Set of 3		11·00	8·25

Designs: Vert—5pf. T E **74**; 10pf. Bricklayers at work. Horiz—20pf. Combine-harvesters.

E 75 'Solidarity'
E 76 Engels Speaking 

1955 (10 Oct). Tenth Anniv of People's Solidarity Movement. Litho. Wmk E **30** (vert). P 13×13½.
| E227 | E **75** | 10pf. blue | 1·20 | 90 |

(Des T. Thomas. Photo)

1955 (7 Nov–10 Dec). 135th Birth Anniv of Engels. T E **76** and similar vert designs inscr '1820 1955'. Wmk E **30** (vert). P 13×13.
E228	5pf. greenish blue and yellow	55	35
	a. Wmk horiz	41·00	16·00
E229	10pf. deep violet-blue and yellow	1·10	35
E230	15pf. deep green and yellow	1·10	35
E231	20pf. purple-brown and orange	2·20	35
E232	30pf. orange-brown and slate	13·50	13·00
E233	70pf. grey-olive and rose-red	6·75	50
E228/E233 Set of 6		23·00	13·50
MSE233*a* 148×105 mm. Nos. E228/E233. Imperf (10.12.55)		£110	£200

Designs:—5pf. T E **76**; 10pf. Engels and Marx; 15pf. Engels and newspaper; 20pf. Portrait, facing right; 30pf. Portrait, facing left; 70pf. 1848 Revolution scene.

E 77 Magdeburg Cathedral
E 78 Georg Agricola 

(Des K. Eigler. Photo)

1955 (14 Nov). Historic Buildings. T E **77** and similar vert designs. Wmk E **30** (vert). P 13½×13.
E234	5pf. sepia	1·40	65
E235	10pf. bronze-green	1·40	65
E236	15pf. purple	1·40	65
E237	20pf. carmine	1·40	1·30
E238	30pf. red-brown	13·00	17·00
E239	40pf. indigo	2·75	1·30
E234/E239 Set of 6		19·00	19·00

Designs:—5pf. T E **77**; 10pf. State Opera House, Berlin; 15pf. Old Town Hall, Leipzig; 20pf. Town Hall, Berlin; 30pf. Erfurt Cathedral; 40pf. Zwinger, Dresden.

(Des K. Eigler. Litho)

1955 (21 Nov). Fourth Death Centenary of Agricola (scholar). Wmk E **30** (vert). P 13½×13.
| E240 | E **78** | 10pf. deep brown | 1·20 | 90 |

(Des E. Gruner. Photo)

1955 (15 Dec). Dresden Gallery Paintings (1st series). Vert designs as T E **79**. Wmk E **30** (vert). P 13½×13.
E241	5pf. red-brown	1·10	35
E242	10pf. brown	1·10	35
E243	15pf. reddish purple	38·00	36·00
E244	20pf. sepia	1·10	35
E245	40pf. bronze-green	1·10	65
E246	70pf. brown-red	2·75	1·30
E241/E246 Set of 6		41·00	35·00

Paintings:—5pf. T E **79**; 10pf. *The Chocolate Girl* (Liotard); 15pf. *Portrait of a Boy* (Pinturicchio); 20pf. *Self-portrait with Saskia* (Rembrandt); 40pf. *Maiden with Letter* (Vermeer); 70pf. *Sistine Madonna* (Raphael).

For other stamps as T E **79** see Nos. E325/E330 and E427/E431.

(Des K. Eigler. Photo)

1956 (27 Jan). Birth Bicentenary of Mozart (composer). T E **80** and similar vert portrait. Wmk E **30** (vert). P 13½×13.
| E247 | 10pf. grey-green (Type E **80**) | 20·00 | 16·00 |
| E248 | 20pf. chestnut (Portrait facing left) | 6·75 | 4·00 |

E 81 Ilyushin Il-14P DDR-ABA
E 82 Heinrich Heine 

(Des K. Eigler. Litho (5pf.), photo (others))

1956 (1 Feb). Establishment of Lufthansa (airline). T E **81** and similar horiz designs. Wmk E **30** (horiz). P 13½×12.
E249	5pf. yellow, red, blue and black	23·00	16·00
E250	10pf. myrtle-green	1·40	65
E251	15pf. blue	1·40	65
E252	20pf. brown-red	1·40	65
E249/E252 Set of 4		24·00	16·00

Designs:—5pf. Lufthansa flag; 10pf. T E **81**; 15pf. Ilyushin Il-14P DDR-ABF; 20pf. Ilyushin Il-14P DDR-ABA.

(Des K. Eigler. Photo)

1956 (17 Feb). Death Centenary of Heinrich Heine (poet). T E **82** and similar vert portrait. Wmk E **30** (vert). P 13½×13.
| E253 | 10pf. slate-green (Type E **82**) | 19·00 | 9·75 |
| E254 | 20pf. brown-red (Full-face) | 4·00 | 1·00 |

E 83 Mobile Cranes
EO 84 
E 84 E. Thälmann 

(Des E. Gruner. Photo)

1956 (25 Feb). Leipzig Spring Fair. Wmk E **30** (vert). P 13×13½.
| E255 | E **83** | 20pf. brown-red | 1·40 | 90 |
| E256 | 35pf. deep ultramarine | 2·00 | 1·40 |

1956 (1 Apr). OFFICIAL. For internal use. Litho. Wmk E **30** (horiz). P 13×12½.

			Postally Used	Can.to Order
EO257	EO **84**	5pf. black	4·75	40
EO258		10pf. black	1·60	40
EO259		20pf. black	95	40
EO260		40pf. black	6·75	45
EO261		70pf. black	£200	80

During their period of use the above were not issued in unused condition but later some were put on sale by the Philatelic Bureau for collectors. The original stamps exist postally used and cancelled to order with normal postmarks. They also exist overprinted with cancels in the sheet so that exactly a quarter segment appears on a corner of the stamp and these are worth less.

The issue was also officially reprinted ungummed and only with the machine-printed cancellations.

246

GERMANY / German Democratic Republic (East Germany)

(Des K. Eigler. Litho)

1956 (16 Apr–25 May). 70th Anniv of Birth of Thälmann (Communist leader). Wmk E **30** (horiz). P 13×13½.
E257 E **84** 20pf. black, drab and red .... 1·10   65
MSE257a 73×100 mm. No. E257 Imperf (25.5.56)........... 16·00 42·00

E **85** Hand, Laurels and Cycle Wheel
E **86** New Buildings, Old Market-place

(Des B. Petersen. Litho)

1956 (30 Apr). Ninth International Cycle Race. T E **85** and similar vert design. Wmk E **30** (vert). P 13½×13.
E258   10pf. green .... 1·40   50
E259   20pf. cerise .... 1·40   50
Designs:—10pf. T E **85**; 20pf. Arms of Warsaw, Berlin and Prague, and cycle wheel.

(Des H. Götze. Litho)

1956 (1 June). 750th Anniv of Dresden. T E **86** and similar vert designs. inscr '750 JAHRE DRESDEN'. Wmk E **30** (vert). P 13½×13.
E260   10pf. deep dull green 70   35
E261   20pf. carmine-red 70   35
E262   40pf. reddish violet .... 2·75 3·50
E260/E262 Set of 3 .... 3·75 3·75
Designs:—10pf. T E **86**; 20pf. Elbe Bridge; 40pf. Technical High School.

E **87** Workman
E **88** Robert Schumann
E **88a**

(Des B. Petersen. Litho)

1956 (30 June–8 Oct). Tenth Anniv of Industrial Reforms. Wmk E **30** (vert). P 13½×13.
E263   E **87** 20pf. red 80   40

(Des K. Eigler. Photo)

1956 (20 July). 100th Anniv of Death of Robert Schumann. Wmk E **30** P 13×13½.
(a) T E **88** (wrong music) (20 July)
E264   10pf. deep emerald .... 3·50 2·30
E265   20pf. scarlet .... 2·00   35
(b) T E **88a** (correct music) (8 Oct)
E266   10pf. deep emerald .... 8·00 2·75
E267   20pf. scarlet .... 4·75   65
T E **88** shows part of the music written by Franz Schubert for the poem *Wanderers Nachtlied* by Goethe. T E **88a** shows Schumann's music *Mondnacht*.

E **89** Footballers
E **90** Thomas Mann (author)

(Des B. Petersen. Litho)

1956 (25 July). Second Sports Festival, Leipzig. T E **89** and similar vert designs. Wmk E **30** (vert). P 13½×13.
E268   5pf. deep dull green (Type E **89**) 55   40
E269   10pf. deep blue (Javelin thrower) 55   40
E270   15pf. light purple (Hurdlers) .... 3·75 2·75
E271   20pf. bright carmine-red (Gymnast) 55   40
E268/E271 Set of 4 .... 4·75 3·50

(Des A. Bengs. Litho)

1956 (13 Aug). First Death Anniv of Thomas Mann. Wmk E **30** (vert). P 13½×13.
E272   E **90** 20pf. blue-black .... 1·80   90

E **91** J. B. Cinski
E **92** Lace

(Des K. Eigler. Photo)

1956 (20 Aug). Birth Centenary of Cinski (poet) Wmk E **30** (vert). P 13½×13.
E273   E **91** 50pf. chocolate .... 1·80   90

(Des W. Hoepfner. Photo)

1956 (1 Sept). Leipzig Autumn Fair. T E **92** and similar vert design. Wmk E **30** (vert). P 13½×13.
E274   10pf. green and black 70   65
E275   20pf. carmine-rose and black 70   65
Designs:—10pf. T E **92**; 20pf. Sailing dinghy.

E **93** Buchenwald Memorial

(Des P. Weiss. Litho)

1956 (8 Sept). Concentration Camp Memorials Fund. Wmk E **30** (vert). P 13½×13.
E276   E **93** 20pf. +80pf. rose-carmine .... 1·90 6·50
For similar stamp see No. E390.

E **94** Torch and Olympic Rings
EO **95**

(Des H. Zethmeyer. Litho)

1956 (28 Sept). Olympic Games. T E **94** and similar vert design inscr 'OLYMPISCHE SPIELE 1956'. Wmk E **30** (vert). P 13½×13.
E277   20pf. Venetian red (Type E **94**) .... 1·10   65
E278   35pf. slate-blue (Greek athlete) .... 1·40   90

CENTRAL COURIER SERVICE. This and later issues were for use on special postal services for confidential mail between Government officials and state-owned enterprises.

(Litho G.W.)

1956 (1 Oct). OFFICIAL. Central Courier Service. T EO **95**. Wmk E **30** (horiz). P 13½×12.

		Un	Postally Used	Can.to Order
EO279	10pf. black and bright purple	1·60	2·00	1·30
EO280	20pf. black and bright purple	£250	2·00	1·30
EO281	40pf. black and bright purple	2·75	3·25	1·30
EO282	70pf. black and bright purple	4·00	85·00	4·50

These were issued unused, postally used and cancelled to order with postmarks.
The 20pf. on yellowish paper with the watermark vertical is a reprint which was available unused but had no postal validity.
For these stamps bearing control figures see Nos. EO303/EO308.

E **95**

GERMANY / German Democratic Republic (East Germany)

(Des A. Bengs and R. Skribelka. Litho)
1956 (17 Oct). 500th Anniv of Greifswald University. Wmk E **30** (horiz). P 13×13½.
E279 E **95** 20pf. lake .... 1·10   65

E **96** Postal Carrier, 1450
E **97** E. Abbe 

(Des P. Hohler. Litho)
1956 (27 Oct). Stamp Day. Wmk E **30** (vert). P 13½×13.
E280   E **96**   20pf. brown-red .... 1·10   65

(Des R. Skribelka. Litho)
1956 (9 Nov). 110th Anniv of Zeiss Factory, Jena. T E **97** and similar designs inscr '1846 1956'. Wmk E **30** (horiz 20pf., vert others). P 12½×13 (vert) or 13×12½ (horiz).
E281   10pf. deep dull green 55   35
E282   20pf. red-brown 55   35
E283   25pf. indigo 80   50
E281/E283 Set of 3 .... 1·70   1·10
Designs: Horiz—20pf. Factory buildings. Vert—10pf. T E **97**; 25pf. Carl Zeiss.

E **98** 'African'
E **99** Indian Elephants 

(Des A. Bengs and R. Skribelka. Litho)
1956 (10 Dec). Human Rights Day. T E **98** and similar designs inscr 'TAG DER MENSCHENRECHTE'. Wmk E **30** (vert). P 13½×13.
E284   5pf. olive-green/*pale olive-green* ('Chinese') .   2·20   1·70
E285   10pf. chocolate/*pale pink* (Type E **98**)   40   40
E286   25pf. indigo/*pale lavender* ('European')   40   40
E284/E286 Set of 3 .... 2·75   2·30

(Des A. Bengs. Photo)
1956 (14 Dec). Berlin Zoological Gardens. T E **99** and similar designs inscr 'TIERPARK BERLIN'. Wmk E **30** (horiz). P 13½×12½.
E287   5pf. grey and black 40   25
E288   10pf. grey and deep green 40   25
E289   15pf. grey and deep purple .... 7·00   5·25
E290   20pf. grey and brown-red 40   25
E291   25pf. grey and deep olive-brown 40   25
E292   30pf. grey and deep blue 45   25
E287/E292 Set of 6 .... 8·25   5·75
Designs:—5pf. T E **99**; 10pf. Greater Flamingoes; 15pf. Black Rhinoceros; 20pf. Mouflon; 25pf. European Bison; 30pf. Polar Bear.

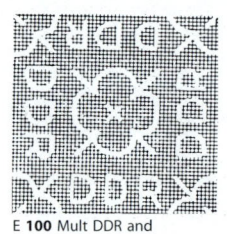

E **100** Mult DDR and Quatrefoils
(E **101**)

1956 (20 Dec). Egyptian Relief Fund. As No. E237 but litho, surch with T E **101**. Wmk E **100**.
E293   20pf. +10pf. carmine-red .... 1·20   65

HELFT DEM SOZIALISTISCHEN UNGARN
(E **102**) 
E **103** *Frieden* (freighter)

1956 (20 Dec). Hungarian Socialists' Relief Fund. As No. E237 but litho, surch with T E **102**. Wmk E **100**.
E294   20pf. +10pf. carmine-red .... 1·20   65

(Typo G.W. (Nos. EO295/EO302) or G.B.N. (Nos. EO295a/EO298a))
1957–60. OFFICIAL. T EO **58**. Centre Type B. Granite paper. Wmk E **100**. P 13×12½.

		Postally Used	Can.to Order
EO295	5pf. bright emerald	70	40
	a. Perf 14 (1958)	1·00	40
EO296	10pf. turquoise-green	70	40
	a. Perf 14 (1958)	1·00	40
EO297	15pf. blackish lilac	70	40
	a. Perf 14 (1958)	1·00	40
EO298	20pf. olive-green	70	40
	a. Perf 14 (1958)	90	40
EO299	30pf. brown-red (1958)	1·10	3·25
EO300	40pf. rose-red (1958)	1·00	40
EO301	50pf. red-lilac (2·60)	£3000	3·25
EO302	70pf. brown (1958)	£130	3·25

During their period of use the above were not issued in unused condition but were put on sale later by the Philatelic Bureau for collectors.
Prices quoted are for postally used and cancelled to order with postmarks.
The 5pf. to 40pf. perf 13×12½ were reprinted ungummed and with machine-printed cancellations.

PRINTERS. Nos. E295 onwards were printed by the German Bank Note Ptg Co., Leipzig, *unless otherwise stated.*

(Des A. Bengs and R. Skribelka. Litho)
1957 (1 Mar). Leipzig Spring Fair. T E **103** and similar horiz design inscr 'LEIPZIGER FRUHJAHRSMESSE 1957'. Wmk E **100**. P 13×12½.
E295   20pf. carmine (Type E **103**) 55   35
E296   25pf. blue (Class E251 electric locomotive)   55   35

1957 (1–15 Apr). OFFICIAL. Central Courier Service. T EO **95**. Optd with control figures in black or violet.
(a) Nos. EO279/EO282 (wmk) E **30** (1 April)

		Postally Un	Used	Can.to Order
EO303	10pf. black and bright purple	95	2·00	65
EO304	20pf. black and bright purple	2·75	2·00	65
EO305	40pf. black and bright purple	95	4·00	1·30
EO306	70pf. black and bright purple	4·75	85·00	6·25

(b) As Nos. EO279/EO280 but wmk E **100** and typo by G.B.N. (15 April)

| EO307 | 10pf. black and bright purple | 3·50 | 6·50 | 4·00 |
| EO308 | 20pf. black and bright purple | 2·75 | 5·25 | 3·25 |

These were issued unused, postally used and cancelled to order with postmarks.
The control figures designate the city and office in which each stamp was used. Some number sequences are scarce; our prices are for the most common.
Nos. EO307/EO308 without control figures come from remainder stock which had no postal validity.

E **104** Silver Thistle
E **105** Friedrich Fröebel and Children 

(Des E. Schoner. Photo G.W.)
1957 (12 Apr). Nature Protection Week. T E **104** and similar horiz designs inscr 'NATURSCHUTZWOCHE 14–20 APRIL 1957'. Wmk E **100**. P 13×12½.
E297   5pf. chocolate 40   25
E298   10pf. deep green .... 4·00   3·75
E299   20pf. light red-brown 40   25
E297/E299 Set of 3 .... 4·25   3·75
Designs:—5pf. T E **104**; 10pf. Green Lizard; 20pf. Lady's Slipper Orchid.

GERMANY / German Democratic Republic (East Germany)

(Des A. Bengs. Litho)

1957 (18 Apr). 175th Birth Anniv of Fröebel (educator). T E **105** and similar design inscr '1782–1852'. Wmk E **100**. P 13.

E300	10pf. black and olive-green	2·20	1·60
E301	20pf. black and light red-brown	40	25

Designs:—10pf. Children at play; 20pf. T E **105**.

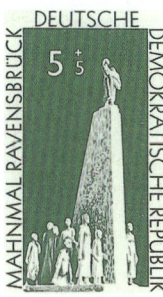

E **106** Ravensbrück Memorial

E **107** Cycle Race Route

1957 (25 Apr). Concentration Camp Memorials Fund. T E **106** and similar design inscr 'MAHNMAL RAVENSBRÜCK'. Wmk E **100**. P 13×13½ or 13½×13 (20pf.).

E302	5pf. +5pf. green	55	40
E303	20pf. +10pf. light carmine-red	70	65

Designs: Vert—5pf. T E **106**. Horiz—20pf. Memorial and environs. For stamp similar to No. E303, see No. E453.

(Des B. Petersen. Litho)

1957 (30 Apr). Tenth International Cycle Race. Wmk E **100**. P 13×13½.

E304	E **107**	5pf. orange	70	50

E **108** Coal Miner

E **109** Henri Dunant and Globe

(Des G. Heiss. Litho)

1957 (3 May). Coal Mining Industry. T E **108** and similar designs. Wmk E **100**. P 13½×13 (25pf.) or 13×12½ (others).

E305	10pf. deep myrtle-green and pale green	40	40
E306	20pf. deep brown and pale brown	40	40
E307	25pf. dull violet-blue and grey-blue	4·00	2·30
E305/E307	Set of 3	4·25	2·75

Designs: Vert—25pf. T E **108**. Horiz (39×21 *mm*)—10pf. Mechanical shovel and coal trucks; 20pf. Gantry.

(Des H. Rose and H. Priess. Photo G.W.)

1957 (7 May). International Red Cross Day. T E **109** and similar design. Wmk E **100**. P 13×12½.

E308	10pf. brown, red and green	40	40
E309	25pf. black, red and blue	40	40

Designs:—10pf. T E **109**; 25pf. Dunant wearing hat, and globe.

1957–60. As Nos. E154/E174 but Wmk E **100**.

A. P 13×12½. With designers' and engravers' names below design (except Nos. E311/E313 (1957–1959))

E310A	5pf. emerald (3.57)	95	65
	a. Booklet pane. Nos. E310A/E311A, each×3 (9.57)	45·00	
	b. Booklet pane. Nos. E310A and E314A, each×3 (9.57)	45·00	
	c. Booklet pane. Nos. E310A×6 (12.60)	6·00	
E311A	10pf. light blue (1.57)	9·50	90
	a. Booklet pane. Nos. E311A×4 and E314A×2 (9.57)	50·00	
E312A	10pf. blue-green (7.59)	95	1·30
	a. Booklet pane. No. E312A×6 (12.60)	6·00	
	b. Booklet pane. Nos. E312A and E314A×5 (12.60)	6·75	
E313A	15pf. blackish violet (1.57)	1·10	80
E314A	20pf. carmine-red (5.57)	55	80
E315A	25pf. deep green (1.57)	55	1·60
E316A	30pf. brown-red (1.57)	95	90
E317A	40pf. bright mauve (1.57)	1·60	90
E318A	50pf. bright blue (5.57)	2·00	90
E319A	70pf. brown (1.57)	4·00	90
E310A/E319A	Set of 10	20·00	8·75

B. P 14. Without imprints below design (1958–1959)

E310B	5pf. emerald (11.58)	1·10	50
E311B	10pf. light blue (8.58)	30	50
E312B	10pf. blue-green (7.59)	2·00	1·30
E313B	15pf. blackish violet (5.58)	1·10	50
E314B	20pf. carmine-red (1.59)	45	40
E316B	30pf. brown-red (5.59)	40	50
E317B	40pf. bright mauve (5.59)	40	50
E318B	50pf. bright blue (8.59)	45	1·00
E319B	70pf. brown (12.59)	45	1·70
E310B/E319B	Set of 9	6·00	6·25

Prices quoted apply to postally used, cancelled specimens being almost worthless.

No. E314B was re-issued on September 4th, 1959 in special sheets of 60 stamps and 40 labels inscr 'II. DEBRIA Berlin 1959' (German Stamp Exhibition). *Strip of 2 stamps with intervening label, unused,* £8·50.

(Photo G.W.)

1957–1958. As Nos. E100/E101 but Wmk E **100**.

			Postally	Can.to
		Un	Used	Order
E320	E **37** 1Dm. deep bronze-green	4·00	2·50	65
E321	2Dm. red-brown (1958)	8·00	2·50	65

E **110** Joachim Jungius (botanist)

E **111** Clara Zetkin and Flower

(Des K. H. Zethmeyer. Photo G.W.)

1957 (7 June). Scientists' Anniversaries. T E **110** and similar portraits. Wmk E **100**. P 13×13½.

E322	5pf. bistre-brown	2·75	2·00
E323	10pf. deep yellow-green	40	40
E324	20pf. light red-brown	40	40
E322/E324	Set of 3	3·25	2·50

Portraits:—5pf. T E **110**; 10pf. L. Euler (mathematician); 20pf. H. Hertz (physicist).

(Des E. Gruner. Photo G.W.)

1957 (26 June). Dresden Gallery Paintings (2nd series). Vert designs as T E **79**. Wmk E **100**. P 13½×13.

E325	5pf. sepia	55	40
E326	10pf. yellow-green	55	40
E327	15pf. olive-brown	55	40
E328	20pf. brown-red	55	40
E329	25pf. brown-purple	55	40
E330	40pf. blue-grey	8·00	3·50
E325/E330	Set of 6	9·75	5·00

Paintings:—5pf. *The Holy Family* (Mantegna); 10pf. *The Dancer, Barbarina Campani* (Carriera); 15pf. *Portrait of Morette* (Holbein the Younger); 20pf. *The Tribute Money* (Titian); 25pf. *Saskia with a Red Flower* (Rembrandt); 40pf. *A Young Standard-bearer* (Piazetta).

(Des R. Skribelka. Photo G.W.)

1957 (5 July). Birth Centenary of Clara Zetkin (patriot). Wmk E **100**. P 13×13½.

E331	E **111**	10pf. deep dull green and red	1·20	50

E **112** Bertolt Brecht

E **113** Congress Emblem

E **114** Fair Emblem

(Des I. Friebel. Photo G.W.)

1957 (14 Aug). First Death Anniv of Brecht (dramatist). Wmk E **100**. P 13½×13.

E332	E **112**	10pf. greyish green	55	40
E333		25pf. deep blue	80	40

(Des P. Weiss. Litho)

1957 (23 Aug). Fourth World Trade Unions Congress. Wmk E **100**. P 13½×13.

E334	E **113**	20pf. black and vermilion	1·10	50

(Des R. Skribelka. Litho)

1957 (30 Aug). Leipzig Autumn Fair. Wmk E **100**. P 13½×13.

E335	E **114**	20pf. carmine-red and orange-red	55	40
E336		25pf. blue and light blue	55	40

GERMANY / German Democratic Republic (East Germany)

E 115 Savings Bank Book
E 116 Postrider of 1563 
E 117 Revolutionary's Rifle, and Red Flag 

(Des H. Grohmann. Litho)
1957 (10 Oct). Savings Week. Wmk E **100**. P 13½×13.
| E337 | E **115** | 10pf. black and green/*grey* | 1·40 | 1·00 |
| E338 | | 20pf. black and magenta/*grey* | 55 | 50 |

(Des A. Bengs. Litho)
1957 (25 Oct). Stamp Day. Wmk E **100**. P 13½×13.
| E339 | E **116** | 5pf. blue-black/*beige* | 95 | 40 |

(Des J. Heartfield. Photo G.W.)
1957 (7 Nov). 40th Anniv of Russian Revolution. Wmk E **100**. P 12½×13.
| E340 | E **117** | 10pf. green and red | 40 | 40 |
| E341 | | 25pf. blue and red | 40 | 40 |

E 118 Artificial Satellite
E 119 Professor Ramin 

(Des E. R. Vogenauer. Litho)
1957 (7 Nov)–**58**. International Geophysical Year. T E **118** and similar vert designs. Wmk E **100**. P 12½×13.
E342		10pf. indigo	70	40
E343		20pf. carmine (5.2.58)	95	35
E344		25pf. light blue (5.2.58)	3·50	2·30
E342/E344	Set of 3		4·75	2·75

Designs:—10pf. T E **118**; 20pf. Stratosphere balloon; 25pf. Ship using echo-sounder.

(Des P. Weiss. Litho)
1957 (22 Nov). National Prize Composers. T E **119** and similar portrait. Wmk E **100**. P 13½×13.
| E345 | | 10pf. black and yellow-green | 1·80 | 1·60 |
| E346 | | 20pf. black and red-orange | 40 | 25 |

Portrait:—10pf. T E **119**; 20pf. Professor Abendroth.

E 120 Ernst Thälmann
E 121 
E 122 

(Des A. Bengs and R. Skribelka. Photo G.W.)
1957 (3 Dec)–**58**. National Memorials Fund. East German War Victims. T E **120** and similar portraits in grey; background colours below. Wmk E **100**. P 13½×13.
E347		20pf. +10pf. deep magenta (Type E **120**)	40	40
E348		25pf. +15pf. deep blue (R. Breitscheid)	40	40
E349		40pf. +20pf. violet (Father P. Schneider)	70	80
E347/E349	Set of 3		1·40	1·40
MSE349*a*	140×95 mm. Nos. E347/E349 (+20pf.)			
	Imperf (15.9.58)		80·00	£180

For similar portraits see Nos. E374/E378, E448/E452, E485/E487, E496/E500, E540/E544, E588/E592.

(Des E. R. Vogenauer. Litho)
1957 (13 Dec). AIR. Wmk E **100**. P 13×12½. (5pf. to 50pf.) or 13×13½ (others).
E350	E **121**	5pf. black and grey	6·00	35
E351		20pf. black and carmine	40	35
E352		35pf. black and bright bluish violet	40	35
E353		50pf. black and purple-brown	55	35
E354	E **122**	1Dm. olive and yellow	1·90	35
E355		3Dm. chocolate and yellow	3·00	80
E356		5Dm. deep grey-blue and yellow	6·75	1·20
E350/E356	Set of 7		17·00	3·50

In the following issue and later in Types EO **130**/EO **131** and EO **149**/EO **150**, one bar on either side of the control number signifies 10pf. and two bars, 20pf.

EO 123

EO 124

Thin Bars

1958 (2 Jan). OFFICIAL. Central Courier Service. Typo. From coils. Imperf×perf 10. Optd with control figures in red.
| EO357 | EO **123** | (10pf.) yellow | 95·00 | 8·50 |
| EO358 | EO **124** | (20pf.) yellow | £110 | 5·25 |

Reprints have the value bars 3·7 mm. long instead of 4·5 mm. and exist unused and cancelled 'UNGÜLTIG' (invalid).
See also Nos. EO371/EO378 and EO414/EO419.

E 123 Fair Emblem

(Des B. Rehm. Litho)
1958 (27 Feb). Leipzig Spring Fair. Wmk E **100**. P 13×13½.
| E357 | E **123** | 20pf. carmine-red | 55 | 25 |
| E358 | | 25pf. cobalt | 70 | 40 |

E 124 Transmitting Aerial and Posthorn
E 125 Zille at play 

(Des H. Priess. Litho)
1958 (6 Mar). Socialist Countries' Postal Ministers Conference, Moscow. T E **124** and similar horiz design. Wmk E **100**. P 13×12½.
| E359 | | 5pf. black and olive-grey | 1·40 | 1·00 |
| E360 | | 20pf. scarlet and deep salmon-pink | 70 | 35 |

Designs:—5pf. T E **124**; 20pf. As T E **124** but inscription in circle around transmitter and posthorn above figures of value.

(Des I. Friebel. Litho)
1958 (20 Mar). Birth Centenary of Heinrich Zille (painter). T E **125** and similar vert design. Wmk E **100**. P 13½×13.
| E361 | | 10pf. drab and deep green | 4·25 | 2·20 |
| E362 | | 20pf. drab and carmine (*Self-portrait*) | 1·10 | 40 |

E 126 Max Planck
E 127 Breeding Cow

GERMANY / German Democratic Republic (East Germany)

(Des R. Skribelka. Litho)

1958 (23 Apr). Birth Centenary of Planck (physicist). T E **126** and similar vert design. Wmk E **100**. P 13½×13.

E363	10pf. grey-olive	2·00	1·80
E364	20pf. deep magenta	70	40

Designs:–10pf. 'h' symbol of *Planck's Constant*; 20pf. T E **126**.

(Des H. Rose. Litho)

1958 (4 June). Sixth Markkleeberg Agricultural Exhibition. T E **127** and other horiz designs inscr '6. Landwirtschaftsausstellung der DDR in Markkleeberg'. Wmk E **100**. P 13×13½ (5pf.) or 13×12½ (others).

E365	5pf. black and grey	4·00	2·20
E366	10pf. green and pale emerald	70	40
E367	20pf. carmine-red and pink	70	40
E365/E367	Set of 3	4·75	2·75

Designs:—5pf. T E **127**. (39×22½ *mm*):—10pf. Chaff-cutter; 20pf. Beet-harvester.

E **128** Charles Darwin
E **129** Congress Emblem 

(Des R. Skribelka. Litho)

1958 (19 June). Centenary of Darwin's *Theory of Evolution*, and Bicentenary of Linnaeus's Plant Classification System. T E **128** and similar horiz portrait inscr '200 JAHRE SYSTEMA NATURAE'. Wmk E **100**. P 13×13½.

E368	10pf. black and blue-green	2·40	1·70
E369	20pf. black and brown-red	40	40

Portrait:—10pf. T E **128**; 20pf. Linnaeus (Carl von Linné).

(Des K. Sauer. Litho)

1958 (25 June). Fifth German Socialist Unity Party Congress. Wmk E **100**. P 13×13½.

E370	E **129** 10pf. scarlet	70	50

EO **130**

EO **131**

Thick Bars

1958–59. OFFICIAL. Central Courier Service. Typo. From coils. Imperf×perf 10. Optd with control figures in first colour given. Thick bars.

(a) On greenish granite paper (1.7.58)

EO371	EO **130** (10pf.) red on yellow	£100	10·50
EO372	EO **131** (20pf.) red on yellow	80·00	6·50

There are two types of letters: wide and condensed. Reprints of the first type have the value bars 27 mm. long instead of 36 mm. and in the 20pf. the bars are 15 mm. high instead of 08 mm. They exist unused and cancelled 'UNGÜLTIG' (invalid).

(b) Colours changed (1.10.58)

EO373	EO **130** (10pf.) chestnut on blue	41·00	10·50
EO374	EO **131** (20pf.) chestnut on blue	£100	6·50

There are two types of letters: wide 'A' and condensed 'M' or condensed 'A' and wide 'M'. Reprints of both types have the value bars 45 mm. long instead of 38 mm. and exist unused or cancelled 'UNGÜLTIG'.

(c) Colours changed again (12.58)

EO375	EO **130** (10pf.) violet on orange	38·00	13·00
EO376	EO **131** (20pf.) violet on orange	£140	10·50

Reprints have the distance between the value bars 315 mm. instead of 305 mm. and in the 20pf. the bars are 15 mm. high instead of 08 mm. They exist unused and cancelled 'UNGÜLTIG'. The original 10pf. also exists cancelled 'UNGÜLTIG'.

(d) Colours changed again (15.12.58)

EO377	EO **130** (10pf.) red on green	15·00	14·50
EO378	EO **131** (20pf.) red on green	19·00	7·25

There are three types: (*a*) value bars 37 mm. (*b*) value bars 45 mm. (*c*) as (*b*) but with condensed 'M'. Reprints of all three types exist only cancelled 'UNGÜLTIG'.

E **130** 'The Seven Towers of Rostock' and Ships
E **131** Mare and Foal 

(Des A. Bengs. Litho)

1958 (5 July–24 Nov). Rostock Port Reconstruction. T E **130** and similar vert designs. Wmk E **100**. P 13½×13.

E371	10pf. pale blue-green (24.11)	40	25
E372	20pf. orange-red	1·40	50
E373	25pf. light blue (24.11)	1·90	2·00
E371/E373	Set of 3	3·25	2·50

Designs:—10pf. *Freundschaft* (freighter) at quayside; 20pf. T E **130**; 25pf. *Frieden* (freighter) in Rostock harbour.
See also No. E494.

(Des A. Bengs and R. Skribelka. Photo G.W.)

1958 (11 July). Resistance Fighters. Vert portraits as T E **120**. Portraits grey-black; background colours below. Wmk E **100**. P 13½×13.

E374	5pf. +5pf. black-brown (A. Kuntz)	55	1·30
E375	10pf. +5pf. deep bronze-green (R. Arndt)	55	1·30
E376	15pf. +10pf. violet (Dr. K. Adams)	55	5·25
E377	20pf. +10pf. red-brown (R. Renner)	55	1·30
E378	25pf. +15pf. slate-black (W. Stoecker)	1·90	20·00
E374/E378	Set of 5	3·75	26·00

(Des E. Schoner. Photo G.W.)

1958 (22 July). 'Grand Prix of the DDR' Horse-show. Horiz designs as T E **131**. Wmk E **100**. P 13×12½.

E379	5pf. sepia (Type E **131**)	4·00	4·25
E380	10pf. bronze-green (Horse-trotting)	40	40
E381	20pf. red-brown (Racing horses)	40	40
E379/E381	Set of 3	4·25	4·50

E **132** J. A. Komenský (Comenius)
E **133** Camp Bugler 

(Des I. Friebel. Litho)

1958 (7 Aug). 300th Anniv of Publication of *Opera didactica omnia* by Comenius. T E **132** and similar horiz design. Wmk E **100**. P 13×13½.

E382	10pf. black and blue-green	2·75	1·80
E383	20pf. black and orange-brown	40	30

Designs:—10pf. T E **132**; 20pf. Komenský with pupils (from an old engraving).

(Des H. Klöpfel. Litho)

1958 (7 Aug). Tenth Anniv of East German Pioneer Organisation. T E **133** and similar horiz design. Wmk E **100**. P 12½×13.

E384	10pf. +5pf. bluish green	70	40
E385	20pf. +10pf. scarlet	70	40

Designs:—10pf. T E **133**; 20pf. Young Pioneers saluting.

E **134** University Seal

(Des E. Schoner. Litho)

1958 (19 Aug). 400th Anniv of Friedrich Schiller University, Jena. T E **134** and similar horiz design. Wmk E **100**. P 13×12½.

E386	5pf. black and grey	2·40	1·80
E387	20pf. grey and brown-red	55	40

Designs:—5pf. T E **134**; 20pf. University building.

GERMANY / German Democratic Republic (East Germany)

E 135 Model with hamster-lined Coat, and Leipzig Railway Station
E 136 Soldier climbing Wall 

(Des H. Priess. Litho)

1958 (29 Aug). Leipzig Autumn Fair. T E 135 and similar horiz design. Wmk E **100**. P 13×12½.
E388 10pf. chocolate and yellow-green...................... 55 40
E389 25pf. black and blue.................................... 55 40
Designs:—10pf. T E 135; 25pf. Model with Karakul fur coat and Leipzig Old Town Hall.

1958 (15 Sept). Concentration Camp Memorials Fund. Design as T E 93 but additionally inscribed '14. SEPTEMBER 1958' in black.
E390 E 93 20pf. +20pf. rose-carmine...................... 1·10 90

(Des O. Leisner. Litho)

1958 (19 Sept). First Summer Military Games, Leipzig. T E 136 and similar vert designs inscr 'I. SPARTAKIADE DER BEFREUNDETEN ARMEEN'. Wmk E **100**. P 13½×13.
E391 10pf. chocolate and light green...................... 2·75 1·60
E392 20pf. yellow and brown-red.......................... 55 40
E393 25pf. red and light blue................................ 55 40
E391/E393 Set of 3.. 3·50 2·20
Designs:—10pf. T E 136; 20pf. Games emblem; 25pf. Marching athletes with banner.

E 137 Warding-off the Atomic Bomb
E 138 17th-century Mail Cart 

(Des C. Sauer. Litho)

1958 (19 Sept). Campaign Against Atomic Warfare. Wmk E **100**. P 13.
E394 E 137 20pf. carmine-red............................... 55 25
E395 25pf. blue... 80 40

(Des A. Bengs. Litho)

1958 (23 Oct). Stamp Day. T E 138 and similar horiz design. Wmk E **100**. P 13×12½.
E396 10pf. deep green..................................... 3·50 2·00
E397 20pf. lake.. 70 35
Designs:—10pf. T E 138; 20pf. Modern postal sorting train and Baade-Bonin 152 jetliner.

E 139 Revolutionary and Soldier
E 140 Brandenburg Gate, Berlin 

(Des K. Zimmermann. Litho)

1958 (7 Nov). 40th Anniv of the November Revolution. Wmk E **100**. P 12½×13.
E398 E 139 20pf. deep dull purple and vermilion.. 15·00 25·00

(Des I. Friebel. Litho)

1958 (29 Nov). Brandenburg Gate Commemoration. Wmk E **100**. P 13×13½.
E399 E 140 20pf. carmine................................... 70 35
E400 25pf. deep blue................................... 4·75 2·50

E 141 Girl's Head (bas-relief)
E 142 African and European Youths 

(Des K. Wittkugel. Litho)

1958 (2 Dec). Antique Art Treasures (1st series). T E 141 and a similar vert design. Wmk E **100**. P 13½×13.
E401 10pf. black and blue-green......................... 2·40 1·70
E402 20pf. black and rose-red............................ 40 35
Designs:—10pf. T E 141; 20pf. Large Head (from Pergamon frieze). For similar designs see Nos. E475/E478.

(Des G. Stauf. Litho)

1958 (10 Dec). Tenth Anniv of Declaration of Human Rights. T E 142 and a similar horiz design. Wmk E **100**. P 13×12½.
E403 10pf. black and light blue-green................... 40 35
E404 25pf. black and light blue......................... 3·50 1·80
Designs:—10pf. T E 142; 25pf. Chinese and European girls.

E 143 Otto Nuschke
E 144 The Red Flag (Party Newspaper) 

(Des H. Klöpfel. Litho)

1958 (27 Dec). First Death Anniv of Vice-Premier Otto Nuschke. Wmk E **100**. P 13½×13.
E405 E 143 20pf. red.. 55 50

(Des H. Priess. Litho)

1958 (30 Dec). 40th Anniv of German Communist Party. Wmk E **100**. P 13×12½.
E406 E 144 20pf. red.. 70 50

E 145 President Pieck
E 146 Rosa Luxemburg (revolutionary) 

(Des A. Bengs. Photo G.W.)

1959 (3 Jan). President Pieck's 83rd Birthday. Wmk E **100**. P 13½×13.
E407 E 145 20pf. brown-red................................. 80 40
For 20pf. black, see No. E517/MSE517a.

(Des G. Stauf. Litho)

1959 (15 Jan). 40th Anniv of Deaths of Rosa Luxemburg and Karl Liebknecht. T E 146 and similar horiz design. Wmk E **100**. P 13×13½.
E408 10pf. black and deep turquoise-green........... 3·50 2·10
E409 20pf. black and brown-red...................... 40 25
Designs:—10pf. T E 146; 20pf. Karl Liebknecht (revolutionary).

E 147 Concert Hall, Leipzig
E 148 Schwarze Pumpe plant 

252

GERMANY / German Democratic Republic (East Germany)

(Eng K. Wolf, after R. Israel. Recess)

1959 (28 Feb). 150th Birth Anniv of Felix Mendelssohn-Bartholdy (composer). T E **147** and a similar horiz design. Wmk E **100**. P 14.
E410   10pf. myrtle-green/*pale green* 75   65
E411   25pf. deep blue/*pale blue* .... 2·75   4·50
Designs:—10pf. T E **147**; 25pf. Opening theme of Symphony in A major (*The Italian*).

(Des K-H. Bobbe. Litho)

1959 (28 Feb). Leipzig Spring Fair. T E **148** and a similar horiz design. Wmk E **100**. P 13×12½.
E412   20pf. cerise (Type E **148**) 55   35
E413   25pf. cobalt (Various cameras) 70   40

EO 149

EO 150

1959. OFFICIAL. Central Courier Service. New designs. Typo. From coils. Imperf×perf 10. Optd with control figures in one or two colours.

(a) 18 March
EO414   EO **149** (10pf.) red and violet on green .... 15·00   10·50
EO415   EO **150** (20pf.) blue and chestnut on yellow ...... 34·00   9·00
Reprints of the 20pf. have larger upright letters in the control overprint instead of smaller letters sloping to the right. They exist unused and cancelled 'UNGÜLTIG' (invalid).

(b) Colours changed (27 July)
EO416   EO **149** (10pf.) black on blue .... 19·00   £100
EO417   EO **150** (20pf.) green and blue on red .... 19·00   13·00
There are no reprints but these exist cancelled 'UNGÜLTIG'.

(c) Colours changed again (6 Nov)
EO418   EO **149** (10pf.) black and chestnut on blue ...... 65·00   £110
EO419   EO **150** (20pf.) violet and black on brown .... 44·00   9·00
Reprints of the 20pf. differ in the same way as No. EO415 and exist unused and cancelled 'UNGÜLTIG'.
In 1960 the colours were changed again four times but these were never postally used and so are not listed.

E **149** Boy holding Book for Girl    E **150** Handel's Statue, Oboe and Arms of Halle

(Des R. Skribelka. Litho)

1959 (2 Apr). Fifth Anniv of Youth Consecration. T E **149** and a similar vert design. Wmk E **100**. P 13½×13.
E414   10pf. black/*yellow-green* .... 2·75   1·70
E415   20pf. black/*salmon* 40   35
Designs:—10pf. T E **149**; 20pf. Girl holding book for boy.

(Des A. Bengs. Litho)

1959 (27 Apr). Death Bicentenary of Handel. T E **150** and a similar vert design inscr '1685–1759'. Wmk E **100**. P 13½×13.
E416   10pf. black and blue-green .... 3·00   1·80
E417   20pf. black and rose-red 40   40
Designs:—10pf. T E **150**; 20pf. Portrait of Handel (after oil painting by Thomas Hudson).

E **151** A. von Humboldt and Jungle Scene    E **152** Posthorn

(Des G. Thieme. Litho)

1959 (6 May). Death Centenary of Alexander von Humboldt (naturalist). T E **151** and similar vert design. Wmk E **100**. P 13½×13.
E418   10pf. bluish green .... 2·40   1·80
E419   20pf. brown-red 55   35
Designs:—10pf. T E **151**; 20pf. As T E **151** but with view of sleigh in forest.

(Des H. Klöpfel. Litho)

1959 (30 May). Socialist Countries' Postal Ministers Conference, Berlin. Wmk E **100**. P 13½×13.
E420   E **152**   20pf. black, yellow and red 55   35
E421   25pf. black, yellow and blue .... 1·40   1·30

E **153** Grey Heron    E **154** Common Cormorant

(Des W. Oehlke. Litho)

1959 (26 June). Nature Preservation. Horiz designs as T E **153**. Wmk E **100**. P 13×12½.
E422   5pf. lilac, black and light blue 40   35
E423   10pf. orange-brown, sepia and turquoise-blue 40   35
E424   20pf. blue, sepia, green and chestnut 40   35
E425   25pf. yellow, black, brown and reddish lilac .. 70   35
E426   40pf. yellow-orange, black and blue-grey ...... 10·00   5·75
E422/E426   Set of 5 .... 10·50   6·50
Designs:—5pf. T E **153**; 10pf. Eurasian Bittern; 20pf. Lily of the Valley and *Inachis io* (butterfly); 25pf. Eurasian Beaver; 40pf. *Apis mellifera* (bee) and Willow Catkin.

(Des E. Gruner. Photo G.W.)

1959 (29 June). Dresden Gallery Paintings (3rd series). Vert designs as T E **79**. Wmk E **100**. P 13½×13.
E427   5pf. olive-brown 40   35
E428   10pf. green 40   35
E429   20pf. deep orange-red 40   35
E430   25pf. brown 70   40
E431   40pf. lake .... 8·75   4·50
E427/E431   Set of 5 .... 9·50   5·25
Paintings:—5pf. *The Vestal Virgin* (Kauffman); 10pf. *The Needlewoman* (Metsu); 20pf. *Mlle. Lavergne reading a letter* (Liotard); 25pf. *Old woman with a brazier* (Rubens); 40pf. *Young man in black coat* (Hals).

(Des A. Brylka. Litho)

1959 (2 July). Birds of the Homeland. Bird designs as T E **154**. Wmk E **100**. P 13½×13.
E432   5pf. black and greenish yellow 40   35
E433   10pf. black and light green 40   35
E434   15pf. black and lavender .... 8·75   4·00
E435   20pf. black and rose-pink 40   35
E436   25pf. black and light blue 40   35
E437   40pf. black and light red 40   35
E432/E437   Set of 6 .... 9·75   5·25
Birds:—5pf. T E **154**; 10pf. Black Stork; 15pf. Eagle Owl; 20pf. Black Grouse; 25pf. Hoopoe; 40pf. Peregrine Falcon.

E **155**    E **156** Hoop Exercises

(Des H. Priess. Litho)

1959 (25 July). Seventh World Youth and Students' Festival, Vienna. T E **155** and similar design. Wmk E **100**. P 12½×13 (20pf.) or 13×12½ (25pf).
E438   20pf. deep rose-red 55   40
E439   25pf. blue .... 1·60   1·30
Designs: Vert—20pf. T E **155**; Horiz—25pf. White girl embracing African girl.

253

GERMANY / German Democratic Republic (East Germany)

(Des H. Priess. Litho)

1959 (10 Aug). Third German Gymnastic and Sports Festival Leipzig. Horiz designs as T E **156**. Wmk E **100**. P 13×13½.

E440	5pf. +5pf. orange-brown	40	35
E441	10pf. +5pf. deep bluish green	40	35
E442	20pf. +10pf. carmine	40	35
E443	25pf. +10pf. blue	40	35
E444	40pf. +20pf. bright purple	3·00	1·10
E440/E444	Set of 5	4·25	2·30

Designs:—5pf. T E **156**; 10pf. High jumping; 20pf. Vaulting; 25pf. Club exercises; 40pf. Fireworks over Leipzig Stadium.

E **157** Modern Leipzig Building
E **158** Glass Tea-set 

(Des F. Deutschendorf. Litho)

1959 (17 Aug). Leipzig Autumn Fair. Wmk E **100**. P 13×12½.

| E445 | E **157** 20pf. grey and rose-red | 70 | 50 |

(Des A. Bengs. Litho)

1959 (1 Sept). 75 Years of Jena Glassware. T E **158** and a similar design. Wmk E **100**. P 13×12½ (10pf.) or 12½×13 (25pf.).

| E446 | 10pf. turquoise-green | 40 | 35 |
| E447 | 25pf. blue | 3·25 | 2·00 |

Designs: Horiz—10pf. T E **158**. Vert—25pf. Laboratory retorts.

(Des R. Skribelka. Photo G.W.)

1959 (3 Sept). Ravensbrück Concentration Camp Victims. Portraits of women as T E **120**. Portraits in black; background colours below. Wmk E **100**. P 13½×13.

E448	5pf. +5pf. bistre-brown	40	40
E449	10pf. +5pf. blackish green	40	40
E450	15pf. +10pf. deep bluish violet	40	40
E451	20pf. +10pf. deep magenta	40	40
E452	25pf. +15pf. deep blue	70	1·60
E448/E452	Set of 5	2·10	3·00

Portraits:—5pf. T. Klose; 10pf. K. Niederkirchner; 15pf. C. Eisenblätter; 20pf. O. Benario-Prestes; 25pf. M. Grollmuss.

1959 (11 Sept). Concentration Camp Memorials Fund. Design as No. E303 but additionally inscr '12 SEPTEMBER 1959' in black.

| E453 | 20pf. +10pf. light carmine-red | 95 | 50 |

E **159** Russian Pennant on the Moon

(Des E. R. Vogenauer. Litho)

1959 (21 Sept). Landing of Russian Rocket on the Moon. Wmk E **100**. P 13½×13.

| E454 | E **159** 20pf. rose-red | 1·10 | 65 |

E **160** East German Flag and Combine-harvester
E **161** J. R. Becher 

(Des L. Grünewald. Litho)

1959 (6 Oct). Tenth Anniv of German Democratic Republic. Vert designs as T E **160**. East German Flag in black, red and yellow. Wmk E **100**. P 13½×13.

E455	5pf. red and black/buff	35	35
E456	10pf. red and black/grey	35	35
E457	15pf. red and black/pale yellow	35	35
E458	20pf. red and black/grey-lilac	35	35
E459	25pf. red and black/pale olive	35	35
E460	40pf. red and black/yellow	35	35
E461	50pf. red and black/salmon	35	35
E462	60pf. red and black/blue-green	35	35
E463	70pf. red and black/pale green	35	35
E464	1Dm. red and black/brown	70	80
E455/E464	Set of 10	3·50	3·50

Designs:—5pf. T E **160**. East German Flag and 10pf. Fritz Heckert convalescent home; 15pf. Zwinger Palace, Dresden; 20pf. Steel-worker; 25pf. Industrial chemist; 40pf. Leipzig Stadium; 50pf. Woman tractor-driver; 60pf. Ilyushin Il-14M aeroplane; 70pf. Shipbuilding; 1Dm. East Germany's first atomic reactor.

(Des H. Ilgenfritz. Litho)

1959 (27 Oct). First Death Anniv of Becher (poet). Wmk E **100**. P 13×13½.

| E465 | E **161** 20pf. deep slate and red | 2·20 | 40 |

This was issued in sheets with alternate horizontal rows of labels inscribed 'AUFERSTANDEN' etc. (part of the East German National Anthem), and with Becher's signature in deep slate on yellow background.

Price for E465 is with a label (*un* £ 3·25, *used* £1·30).

E **162** Schiller
E **163** 18th-century Courier and Milestone 

(Des H. Müller. Eng K. Wolf. Recess)

1959 (10 Nov). Birth Bicentenary of Schiller (poet). T E **162** and similar horiz design. Wmk E **100**. P 14.

| E466 | 10pf. deep grey-green/pale green | 2·50 | 1·80 |
| E467 | 20pf. lake/pink | 95 | 35 |

Designs:—10pf. Schiller's house, Weimar; 20pf T E **162**.

(Des A. Bengs. Litho)

1959 (17 Nov). Stamp Day. T E **163** and similar vert design. Wmk E **100**. P 13½×13.

| E468 | 10pf deep green | 2·30 | 1·70 |
| E469 | 20pf. carmine-lake | 40 | 35 |

Designs:—10pf. T E **163**; 20pf. Postwoman on motorcycle.

E **164** Eurasian Red Squirrels
E **165** Boxing 

(Des G. Stauf. Litho)

1959 (28 Nov). Forest Animals. Horiz designs as T E **164**. Wmk E **100**. P 13×12½.

E470	5pf. brown-red, deep brown, olive and grey (T E **164**)	70	35
E471	10pf. yellow-brown, brown and emerald (Brown Hares)	80	35
E472	20pf. yellow-bistre, olive, black and red (Roe Deer)	80	35
E473	25pf. orange-brown, deep brown, green and blue (Red Deer)	95	40
E474	40pf. yellow, deep brown and violet-blue (Lynx)	20·00	5·75
E470/E474	Set of 5	21·00	6·50

(Des K. Wittkugel. Litho)

1959 (29 Dec). Antique Art Treasures (2nd series). Designs as T E **141**. Wmk E **100**. P 13½×13.

E475	5pf. black and yellow	55	35
E476	10pf. black and blue-green	55	35
E477	20pf. black and rose-red	55	35
E478	25pf. black and light blue	1·80	1·30
E475/E478	Set of 4	3·00	2·10

Designs: Vert—5pf. Attic goddess (about 580 BC); 10pf. Princess of Tell el-Amarna (about 1360 BC); 20pf. Bronze horse of Toprak-Kale, Armenia (7th-century, BC). Horiz (49×28 *mm*)—25pf. Altar of Zeus, Pergamon (about 160 BC).

(Des O. Volkamer. Litho)

1960 (27 Jan). Olympic Games. T E **165** and similar horiz designs inscr 'OLYMPISCHE SOMMERSPIELE 1960' or 'WINTERSPIELE' etc. (20pf.). Wmk E **100**. P 13×13½.

| E479 | 5pf. yellow-brown and brown | 8·00 | 4·00 |
| E480 | 10pf. yellow-brown and green | 40 | 35 |

GERMANY / German Democratic Republic (East Germany)

E481	20pf. yellow-brown and carmine-red	40	35
E482	25pf. yellow-brown and blue	40	35
E479/E482	Set of 4	8·25	4·50

Designs:—5pf. T E **165**; 10pf. Running; 20pf. Ski jumping; 25pf. Sailing.

(Des F. Deutschendorf. Litho)

1960 (17 Feb). Leipzig Spring Fair. Designs similar to T E **157** but inscr 'LEIPZIGER FRUHJAHRSMESSE 1960'. Wmk E **100**. P 13×12½.

E483	20pf. grey and red	40	25
E484	25pf. grey and blue	40	25

Designs:—20pf. Northern Entrance, Technical Fair; 25pf. Ring Fair Building.

(Des R. Skribelka. Photo G.W.)

1960 (25 Feb). Sachsenhausen Concentration Camp Victims (1st series). Portraits in black as T E **120**. Wmk E **100**. P 13½×13.

E485	5pf. +5pf. drab (L. Erdmann)	40	40
E486	10pf. +5pf. black-green (E. Schneller)	40	40
E487	20pf. +10pf. reddish purple (L. Horn)	40	40
E485/E487	Set of 3	1·10	1·10

See also Nos. E496/E500.

E **166** Purple Foxglove

E **167** Lenin

(E **168**)

(Des I. Friebel. Litho)

1960 (7 Apr). Medicinal Flowers. Vert floral designs as T E **166**. Wmk E **100**. P 12½×12½.

E488	5pf. carmine, green and pale drab (T E **166**)	40	25
E489	10pf. olive-yellow, green and pale drab (Camomile)	40	25
E490	15pf. dull red, green and pale drab (Peppermint)	40	25
E491	20pf. violet, turquoise-blue and pale drab (Poppy)	40	25
E492	40pf. red, green, brown and pale drab (Wild Rose)	8·75	4·00
E488/E492	Set of 5	9·25	4·50

(Des L. Grünewald. Eng M. Sachs. Recess)

1960 (22 Apr). 90th Birth Anniv of Lenin. Wmk E **100**. P 14.

E493	E **167** 20pf. brown-red	70	40

1960 (28 Apr). Re-opening of Rostock Port. No. E371 optd with T E **168**.

E494	10pf. pale blue-green	1·10	65

E **169** Russian Soldier and Liberated Prisoner

E **170** Model and Plan of *Fritz Heckert* (liner)

(Des H. Böhnke. Litho)

1960 (5 May). 15th Anniv of Liberation. Wmk E **100**. P 13×13½.

E495	E **169** 20pf. rose-red	70	50

1960 (5 May–8 June). Sachsenhausen Concentration Camp Victims (2nd series). Portraits in black as T E **120**. Litho. Wmk E **100**. P 13½×13.

E496	10pf. +5pf. deep green (8.6)	40	25
E497	15pf. +5pf. deep violet (8.6)	1·40	90
E498	20pf. +10pf. lake (8.6)	40	25
E499	25pf. +10pf. deep slate-blue	40	40
E500	40pf. +20pf. red-brown	3·00	4·00
E496/E500	Set of 5	5·00	5·25

Portraits:—10pf. M. Lademann; 15pf. L. Breunig; 20pf. M. Thesen; 25pf. G. Sandtner; 40pf. H. Rothbarth.

(Des H. Priess. Litho)

1960 (23 June). Launching of Cruise Liner *Fritz Heckert*. T E **170** and similar horiz designs. Wmk E **100**. P 13½×13.

E501	5pf. slate, red and olive-yellow	40	25
E502	10pf. +5pf. black, red and yellow	40	25
E503	20pf. +10pf. black, red and blue	40	25
E504	25pf. black, yellow and cobalt	7·50	7·75
E501/E504	Set of 4	7·75	7·75

Designs:—5pf. T E **170**; 10pf. Liner under construction at Wismar; 20pf. Liner off Stubbenkammer; 25pf. Liner and Russian cruiser *Aurora* at Leningrad.

E **171** Lenin Statue, Eisleben

E **172** Masked Dancer (statuette)

(Des E. Schoner. Litho)

1960 (2 July). Lenin-Thälmann Statues. T E **171** and similar vert design. Wmk E **100**. P 13×13½.

E505	10pf. slate-green	40	40
E506	20pf. rose-red	40	40

Designs:—10pf. T E **171**; 20pf. Thälmann statue, Pushkin, USSR.

(Des J. Widmann. Litho)

1960 (28 July). 250th Anniv of Porcelain Industry, Meissen. T E **172** and similar vert designs. Wmk E **100**. P 12½×13.

E507	5pf. grey-blue and orange	40	35
E508	10pf. grey-blue and emerald	40	35
E509	15pf. grey-blue and purple	6·00	5·75
E510	20pf. grey-blue and red	40	35
E511	25pf. grey-blue and yellow-olive	40	35
E507/E511	Set of 5	6·75	6·50

Designs:—5pf. T E **172**; 10pf. Dish inscr with swords and '1710–1960'; 15pf. Otter; 20pf. Potter; 25pf. Coffee-pot.

E **173** Racing Cyclist

E **174** Opera House, Leipzig

(Des E. Schoner. Litho)

1960 (3 Aug). World Cycling Championships. T E **173** and horiz design. Wmk E **100**. P 13×13½ (20pf.) or 13×12½ (25pf.).

E512	20pf. +10pf. carmine-red, blue, black, yellow and green	40	40
E513	25pf. +10pf. deep brown, drab and grey-blue	2·40	4·50

Designs:—20pf. T E **173**. (38½×21 *mm*) 25pf. Racing cyclists on track.

(Des F. Deutschendorf. Litho)

1960 (29 Aug). Leipzig Autumn Fair. T E **174** and similar horiz design. Wmk E **100**. P 13×13½.

E514	20pf. grey and carmine-red (Type E **174**)	55	35
E515	25pf. light brown and light blue (Export goods)	55	50

E **175** Sachsenhausen Memorial

E **176** 18th-century Rook

GERMANY / German Democratic Republic (East Germany)

(Des R. Skribelka. Litho)

1960 (8 Sept)–**61**. Concentration Camp Memorial Fund. Wmk E **100**. P 13×13½.

E516	E **175**	20pf. +10pf. rosine	70	50
		a. *Carmine-red* plus label (20.4.61) ..	1·90	80

No. E516a includes a *se-tenant* label bearing a 12 line inscription referring to 100,000 inmates of the camp.

(Litho G.W.)

1960 (10 Sept). President Pieck Mourning Issue. P 13½×13.

E517	E **145**	20pf. black	80	50
MSE517a	88×108 mm. No. E517. Imperf		2·40	3·75

(Des H. Ilgenfritz. Recess)

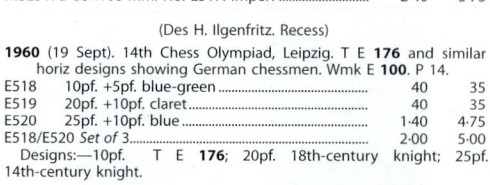

1960 (19 Sept). 14th Chess Olympiad, Leipzig. T E **176** and similar horiz designs showing German chessmen. Wmk E **100**. P 14.

E518	10pf. +5pf. blue-green	40	35
E519	20pf. +10pf. claret	40	35
E520	25pf. +10pf. blue	1·40	4·75
E518/E520	Set of 3	2·00	5·00

Designs:—10pf. T E **176**; 20pf. 18th-century knight; 25pf. 14th-century knight.

E **177** Mail Vans

E **178** Medal of 1518 showing Hans Burgkmair (painter)

(Des A. Bengs. Litho)

1960 (6 Oct). Stamp Day. T E **177** and similar horiz design. Wmk E **100**. P 13×12½.

E521	20pf. yellow, black and magenta	40	35
E522	25pf. mauve, black and blue	5·25	2·50

Designs:—20pf. T E **177**; 25pf. 19th-century railway mail-coach.

(Des O. Volkamer. Litho)

1960 (20 Oct). 400th Anniv of Dresden Art Collections. T E **178** and similar vert design. Wmk E **100**. P 12½×13.

E523	20pf. ochre, green and buff	40	25
E524	25pf. black and cobalt	2·75	3·00

Designs:—20pf. T E **178**; 25pf. *Dancing Peasants* (after Dürer).

E **179** Count N. von Gneisenau

E **180** R. Virchow

(Des P. Weiss. Litho)

1960 (27 Oct). Birth Bicentenary of Von Gneisenau. T E **179** and similar vert portrait. Wmk E **100**. P 13×12½ (20pf.) or 12½×13 (25pf.).

E525	E **179**	20pf. black and brown-red	40	30
E526	–	25pf. blue	2·30	2·20

(Des E. Schoner. Litho)

1960 (4 Nov). 250th Anniv of Berlin Charity and 150th Anniv of Humboldt University, Berlin. Horiz designs as T E **180**. Wmk E **100**. P 13×12½.

E527	5pf. black and yellow-ochre	40	25
E528	10pf. black and dull green	40	25
E529	20pf. black, grey and chestnut	40	25
E530	25pf. black and blue	40	25
E531	40pf. black and carmine	4·00	2·30
E527/E531	Set of 5	5·00	3·00

Designs:—5pf. T E **180**. (Berlin Charity: As T E **180**)—10pf. Robert Koch; 40pf. W. Griesinger. (Humboldt University)—20pf. University building and statues; 25pf. Plaque with profiles of Von Humboldt brothers.

Nos. E527/E531 were each issued in separate sheets of 50. Nos. E527 and E530 and Nos. E528/E529 respectively were also issued together in vertical *se-tenant* pairs within sheets of 50 stamps.

E **181** Scientist with notebook

E **182** Young Socialists' Express (double-decker train)

(Des G. Stauf. Litho)

1960 (10 Nov). Chemical Workers' Day. T E **181** and similar horiz designs. Wmk E **100**. P 13×13½.

E532	5pf. blue-grey and red	35	35
E533	10pf. emerald and yellow-orange	35	35
E534	20pf. red and light blue	35	35
E535	25pf. ultramarine and yellow	3·00	3·75
E532/E535	Set of 4	3·75	4·25

Designs:—5pf. T E **181**; 10pf. Chemical worker with fertiliser: 20pf. Girl with jar, and Trabant car; 25pf. Laboratory assistant and synthetic dress.

(Des D. Dorfstecher. Litho)

1960 (5 Dec). 125th Anniv of German Railways. T E **182** and similar horiz designs. Wmk E **100**. P 13×12½ (20pf.) or 12½×13 (others).

E536	10pf. black and green	40	40
E537	20pf. black and vermilion	40	40
	a. Imperf (vert pair)	15·00	7·25
E538	25pf. black and blue	8·00	7·75
E536/E538	Set of 3	8·00	7·75

Designs:—10pf. T E **182**. 43×25 mm—20pf. Sassnitz Harbour station and train ferry *Sassnitz*. As T E **182**—25pf. Stephenson locomotive *Adler* (1835) and Class V180 diesel locomotive.

E **183** President Pieck

E **184** High-voltage Switchgear

1961 (3 Jan). 85th Birth Anniv of President Pieck. Litho. Wmk E **100**. P 13×13½.

E539	E **183**	20pf. brown-red and black	70	50

1961 (6 Feb). Concentration Camp Victims. Portraits as T E **120** in black; background colours below. Wmk E **100**. P 13½×13.

E540	5pf. +5pf. emerald	35	35
E541	10pf. +5pf. bluish green	35	35
E542	15pf. +5pf. reddish violet	1·90	3·75
E543	20pf. +10pf. carmine-red	35	35
E544	25pf. +10pf. blue	35	35
E540/E544	Set of 5	3·00	4·75

Portraits:—5pf. W. Kube; 10pf. H. Günther; 15pf. Elvira Eisenschneider; 20pf. Hertha Lindner; 25pf. H. Tschäpe.

(Des D. Dorfstecher. Litho)

1961 (3 Mar). Leipzig Spring Fair. T E **184** and similar vert design. Wmk E **100**. P 13½×13.

E545	10pf. deep slate and emerald	55	40
E546	25pf. deep slate and bright blue	55	40

Designs:—10pf. T E **184**; 25pf. Fair Press Centre.

E **185** Lilienstein, Saxony

E **186** *Ros* (trawler)

(Des E. Gruner. Die-eng O. Volkamer (E549, E551), M. Sachs (others). Typo)

1961 (14 Mar–22 June). Landscapes and Historical Buildings. T E **185** and similar designs. Wmk E **100**. P 14.

E547	5pf. grey (22.6)	35	35
E548	10pf. blue-green (22.6)	35	35
E549	20pf. red-brown	40	40
E550	20pf. brown-red (22.6)	35	35
E551	25pf. deep blue	40	40
E547/E551	Set of 5	1·70	1·70

Designs: Vert—5pf. Ruins of Rudelsburg; 10pf. Wartburg; 20pf. (E549) T E **185**; 20pf. (E550) Town Hall, Wernigerode. Horiz—25pf. Brocken, Oberharz.

(Des D. Dorfstecher (10pf., 25pf.), G. Stauf (20pf., 40pf.). Eng M. Sachs (10pf., 40pf.), G. Stauf (20pf.), O. Volkamer (25pf.). Recess)

1961 (10 Apr). Deep Sea Fishing Industry. T E **186** and similar horiz designs. Wmk E **100**. P 14.

E552	10pf. deep grey-green		35	35
E553	20pf. brown-purple		35	35
E554	25pf. slate-blue		35	35
E555	40pf. slate-violet		3·75	2·75
E552/E555	Set of 4		4·25	3·50

Designs:—10pf. T E **186**; 20pf. Hauling nets; 25pf. *Robert Koch* (trawler); 40pf. Processing Atlantic Cod.

E **187** Cosmonaut in Capsule

(Des H. Urbschat. Litho)

1961 (18–20 Apr). First Manned Space Flight. T E **187** and similar horiz designs. Wmk E **100**. P 13½×12½.

E556	10pf. rosine and turquoise-green		2·00	1·30
E557	20pf. rosine (20.4)		2·00	1·30
E558	25pf. greenish blue (20.4)		7·50	7·75
E556/E558	Set of 3		10·50	9·25

Designs:—10pf. Space rocket leaving globe; 20pf. T E **187**; 25pf. Capsule's parachute descent.

E **188** Marx, Engels, Lenin and Demonstrators

(Des K. Sauer and O. Volkamer. Litho)

1961 (20 Apr). 15th Anniv of Socialist Unity Party. Wmk E **100**. P 13½×13.

E559	E **188**	20pf. bright scarlet	80	50

E **189** Common Zebra

(Des H. Naumann. Litho)

1961 (9 May). Centenary of Dresden Zoo. T E **189** and similar horiz design inscr '1861—1961'. Wmk E **100**. P 13½×12½.

E560	10pf. black and green		8·00	7·75
E561	20pf. black and deep magenta		1·40	65

Designs:—10pf. T E **189**; 20pf. Eastern Black-and-white Colobus.

E **190** Pioneers playing Volleyball

E **191** Floor Exercises

(Des I. Friebel. Litho)

1961 (25 May). Pioneers Meeting, Erfurt. T E **190** and similar horiz designs. Wmk E **100**. P 13½×12½.

E562	10pf. +5pf. green, yellow, black and magenta		35	25
E563	20pf. +10pf. magenta, yellow, black and blue		35	25
E564	25pf. +10pf. violet, yellow, black and magenta		5·25	4·00
E562/E564	Set of 3		5·25	4·00

Designs:—10pf. T E **190**; 20pf. Folk dancing; 25pf. Model aeroplane construction.

(Des W. Bley. Litho)

1961 (3 June). Third European Women's Gymnastics Championships, Leipzig. T E **191** and similar designs. Wmk E **100**. P 13×13½ (25pf.) or 13½×13 (others).

E565	10pf. green		35	25
E566	20pf. magenta		35	25
E567	25pf. blue		9·00	7·25
E565/E567	Set of 3		8·75	7·00

Designs:—Vert—10pf. T E **191**; 20pf. Gymnast. Horiz—25pf. Exercise on parallel bars.

E **192** Salt Miners and Castle

E **193** Folding Canoe

(Des G. Voigt. Litho)

1961 (22 June). 1,000th Anniv of Halle (Saale). T E **192** and similar horiz design. Wmk E **100**. P 13×12½.

E568	10pf. black, yellow and green		2·30	1·30
E569	20pf. black, yellow and carmine		2·30	1·30

Designs:—10pf. T E **192**; 20pf. Scientist and Five Towers of Halle.

(Des O. Volkamer. Litho)

1961 (6 July). World Canoeing Championships. T E **193** and similar horiz design. Wmk E **100**. P 13½×12½.

E570	5pf. slate-blue and grey		5·25	4·25
E571	10pf. bronze-green and grey		35	25
E572	20pf. brown-purple and grey		35	25
E570/E572	Set of 3		5·25	4·25

Designs:—5pf. T E **193**; 10pf. Canadian canoe: 20pf. Canadian two-seater canoe.

E **194** Line-casting

E **195** Old Weighhouse, Leipzig

(Des A. Bengs. Litho)

1961 (21 July). World Angling Championships. T E **194** and similar horiz design. Wmk E **100**. P 13½×12½.

E573	10pf. blue-green and cobalt (Type E **194**)		3·50	2·50
E574	20pf. brown and light blue (River-fishing)		1·40	1·30

(Des D. Dorfstecher (10pf.), M. Bruckels (25pf.). Litho)

1961 (23 Aug). Leipzig Autumn Fair. T E **195** and similar vert design. Wmk E **100**. P 13½×13.

E575	10pf. yellow-olive and blue-green		35	25
E576	25pf. light blue and ultramarine		1·80	50

Designs:—10pf. T E **195**; 25pf. Old Stock Exchange, Leipzig.

E **196** Walter Ulbricht

E **197** Dahlia

E **198** Liszt and Berlioz (after von Kaulbach and Prinzhofer)

(Des K. Wolf (E586/E587). Recess E586/E587) or typo (others))

1961 (29 Aug)–71. T E **196** or larger 24×29 mm. (Dm. values). Wmk E **100**. P 14.

E577	5pf. grey-blue	40	40
	a. Booklet pane. No. E577×8 (16.11.62)	19·00	
E578	10pf. bluish green	45	50
	a. Booklet pane. No. E578×8 (16.11.62)	18·00	
E579	15pf. purple	75	25
E580	20pf. carmine-red	70	50
E581	25pf. deep turquoise-blue (2.1.63)	55	25
E582	30pf. carmine (2.1.63)	35	25
E582a	35pf. deep blue-green (8.7.71)	90	80
E583	40pf. bluish violet (2.1.63)	35	25
E584	50pf. blue (11.2.63)	40	25

257

GERMANY / German Democratic Republic (East Germany)

E584a	60pf. olive-green (9.12.64)	55	40
E585	70pf. brown (11.2.63)	55	25
E585a	80pf. greenish blue (6.12.67)	80	65
E586	1DM. bronze-green (25.6.63)	1·40	1·20
E587	2DM. brown (25.6.63)	2·75	1·30
E577/E587	Set of 14	9·75	6·50

The 5, 10, 20 and 50pf. were also issued in coils. From 1967 these coils had every fifth stamp numbered on the back.

Nos. E578/E579 and E584/E585 exist on paper watermarked Type R **2**, but their status is uncertain.

For Nos. E586/E587 but with value expressed as 'MDN', see Nos. E805/E806 and expressed as 'M', Nos. E1197/E1198 and E1255.

1961 (7 Sept). Concentration Camps Memorials Fund. Portraits as T E **120** in grey and black; background colours below. Litho. Wmk E **100**. P 13½×13 (5pf, 10pf, 20pf) or 13½ (others).

E588	5pf. +5pf. emerald	35	40
E589	10pf. +5pf. blue-green	35	40
E590	20pf. +10pf. mauve	35	40
E591	25pf. +10pf. blue	35	40
E592	40pf. +20pf. lake	3·25	8·50
E588/E592	Set of 5	4·25	9·00

Portraits:—5pf. C. Schönhaar; 10pf. H. Baum; 20pf. Liselotte Herrmann. (41×32½ *mm*)—25pf. Sophie and Hans Scholl; 40pf. Hilde and Hans Coppi.

1961 (13 Sept). International Horticultural Exhibition. T E **197** and similar vert designs. Photo. Wmk E **100**. P 14.

E593	10pf. red, yellow and green (Tulips)	70	40
E594	20pf. red, yellow and red-brown (Type E **197**)	70	40
E595	40pf. red, yellow and greenish blue (Rose)	15·00	14·50
E593/E595	Set of 3	15·00	14·00

(Des F. Deutschendorf. Eng G. Stauf (5pf.), O. Volkamer (10pf.), M. Sachs (20pf., 25pf.). Recess)

1961 (19 Oct–23 Nov). 150th Anniv of Liszt. T E **198** and similar vert designs inscr '1811–1886'. Wmk E **100**. P 14.

E596	5pf. black (23.11)	40	25
E597	10pf. bluish green	3·50	3·75
E598	20pf. carmine-red	40	25
E599	25pf. ultramarine (23.11)	4·00	4·50
E596/E599	Set of 4	7·50	8·00

Designs:—5pf. T E **198**; 10pf. Young hand of Liszt (from French sculpture, Liszt Museum, Budapest); 20pf. Liszt (after Rietschel); 25pf. Liszt and Chopin (after Bartolini and Bovy).

E **199** TV Camera and Screen

E **200** G. S. Titov with Young Pioneers

(Des D. Dorfstecher and M. Brückels. Litho)

1961 (25 Oct). Stamp Day. T E **199** and similar horiz design. Wmk E **100**. P 13×13½.

E600	10pf. black and blue-green	2·75	4·25
E601	20pf. black and red	35	40

Designs:—10pf. T E **199**; 20pf. Studio microphone and radio tuning-scale.

(Des K. Sauer. Litho)

1961 (11 Dec). Second Russian Manned Space Flight. T E **200** and similar designs. Wmk E **100**. P 13½.

E602	5pf. bluish violet and carmine	40	25
E603	10pf. deep green and carmine	40	25
E604	15pf. reddish violet and blue	13·50	14·50
E605	20pf. carmine and blue	40	25
E606	25pf. blue and carmine	40	25
E607	40pf. deep blue and carmine	2·40	80
E602/E607	Set of 6	16·00	15·00

Designs: Vert—10pf. Titov in Leipzig. Horiz—5pf. T E **200**; 15pf. Titov in space suit; 20pf. Titov receiving Karl Marx Order from Ulbricht; 25pf. *Vostok 2* rocket in flight; 40 pf. Titov and Ulbricht in Berlin.

E **201** *Formica rufa* (Ant)

E **202** Zum Kaffeebaum

(Des H. Naumann. Photo)

1962 (16 Feb). Fauna Protection Campaign (1st series). T E **201** and similar horiz designs. Wmk E **100**. P 14.

E608	5pf. olive-yellow, brown and black	6·75	9·75
E609	10pf. red-brown and light green	35	35
E610	20pf. brown and carmine	35	35
E611	40pf. yellow, black and violet	95	65
E608/E611	Set of 4	7·50	10·00

Designs:—5pf. T E **201**; 10pf. Weasels (*Mustela nivalis*); 20pf. Eurasian Common Shrews (*Soricidae*); 40pf. Common Long-eared Bat (*Chiroptera*).

See also Nos. E699/E703.

(Des D. Dorfstecher and M. Brückels. Litho)

1962 (22 Feb). Leipzig Spring Fair. Designs as T E **202**. Wmk E **100**. P 13½×13.

E612	10pf. sepia and olive green	35	25
E613	20pf. black and light red	55	25
E614	25pf. maroon and blue	1·40	1·30
E612/E614	Set of 3	2·10	1·60

Designs:—10pf. T E **202**; 20pf. Gohliser Schlösschen; 25pf. Romanus-Haus.

E **203** Pilot and Mikoyan Gurevich MiG-17 Jet Fighters

E **204** Danielle Casanova

(Des G. Stauf. Litho)

1962 (1 Mar). Sixth Anniv of East German People's Army. T E **203** and similar horiz designs. Wmk E **100**. P 13×12½.

E615	5pf. light blue	40	25
E616	10pf. bluish green	40	25
E617	20pf. red	40	25
E618	25pf. ultramarine	40	50
E619	40pf. brown	2·75	2·30
E615/E619	Set of 5	4·00	3·25

Designs:—5pf. T E **203**; 10pf. Soldiers and armoured car; 20pf. Factory guard; 25pf. Sailor and Habich 1 class minesweeper; 40pf. Tank and driver.

(Des and eng O. Volkamer (5pf., 25pf.), M. Sachs (10pf., 40pf.), G. Stauf (20pf.). Recess)

1962 (22 Mar). Concentration Camps Memorial Fund. Camp Victims. T E **204** and similar vert portrait designs. Wmk E **100**. P 14.

E620	5pf. +5pf. black	35	25
E621	10pf. +5pf. deep bluish green	35	25
E622	20pf. +10pf. brown-purple	35	25
E623	25pf. +10pf. blue	40	25
E624	40pf. +20pf. deep maroon	2·75	3·50
E620/E624	Set of 5	3·75	4·00

Portraits:—5pf. T E **204**; 10pf. Julius Fucik; 20pf. Johanna J. Schaft; 25pf. Pawel Finder; 40pf. Soja A. Kosmodemjanskaja.

E **205** Racing Cyclists and Prague Castle

E **206** Johann Fichte

(Des L. Grünewald. Litho)

1962 (26 Apr). 15th International Peace Cycle Race. T E **205** and similar horiz designs. Wmk E **100**. P 13×12½.

E625	10pf. red, black, blue and green	35	35
E626	20pf. +10pf. red, black, blue and yellow	35	35
E627	25pf. yellow, black, red and light blue	2·30	2·20
E625/E627	Set of 3	2·75	2·50

Designs:—10pf. T E **205**; 20pf. Cyclists and Palace of Culture and Science, Warsaw; 25pf. Cyclist and Town Hall, East Berlin.

(Des D. Dorfstecher (10pf.), K. Hennig (20pf.). Litho)

1962 (17 May). Birth Bicentenary of Johann Fichte (philosopher). T E **206** and similar horiz design. Wmk E **100**. P 13×13½.

E628	10pf. green and black	2·75	3·00
E629	20pf. red and black	40	40

Designs:—10pf. Fichte's birthplace, Ramenau; 20pf. T E **206**.

E 215 Dove   E 216 National Theatre, Helsinki

E 207 Cross of Lidice    E 208 Dimitrov at Leipzig

(Des D. Dorfstecher and K. Hennig (E 213/E 214); R. Skribelka (others). Litho.)

1962 (17 July). World Youth Festival Games, Helsinki. Wmk E **100**. P 14 (Nos. E642/E643) or 13½×13 (others).

E640	E **211**	5pf. multicoloured	3·50	5·00
		a. Block of 4. Nos. E640/E641 and E644/E645	15·00	
E641	E **212**	5pf. multicoloured	3·50	5·00
E642	E **213**	10pf. +5pf. multicoloured	55	30
		a. Horiz pair. Nos. E642/3	2·00	1·80
E643	E **214**	15pf. +5pf. multicoloured	55	30
E644	E **215**	20pf. multicoloured	3·50	5·00
E645	E **216**	20pf. multicoloured	3·50	5·00
E640/E645	Set of 6		13·50	19·00

The 5 and 20pf. values were issued together in *se-tenant* blocks of four and the 10 and 15pf. values in *se-tenant* pairs within their sheets. Each block and pair form the composite designs illustrated.

(Des P. Weiss. Litho.)

1962 (7 June). 20th Anniv of Destruction of Lidice. Wmk E **100**. P 12½×13.

E630	E **207**	20pf. red and black	40	25
E631		25pf. blue and black	1·60	2·10

(Des A. Bengs. Photo)

1962 (18 June). 80th Birth Anniv of G. Dimitrov (Bulgarian statesman). T E **208** and similar vert design. Wmk E **100**. P 14.

E632		5pf. black and bluish green	95	65
		a. Pair. Nos. E632/E633, plus 1 central label	9·50	65·00
E633		20pf. black and bright carmine	40	25

Designs:—5pf. T E **208**; 20pf. Portrait of Dimitrov as Premier of Bulgaria.

Nos. E632/E633 were issued both in separate sheets of 50 stamps and also together in sheets of 30 stamps and 15 inscribed labels, arranged in *se-tenant* pairs with an intervening label.

E 217 Free-style Swimming   E 218 Municipal Store, Leipzig

(Des H. Priess. Litho.)

1962 (7 Aug). Tenth European Swimming Championships, Leipzig. T E **217** and similar horiz designs. Wmk E **100**. P 13×13½.

E646		5pf. turquoise-blue and orange	35	35
E647		10pf. turquoise-blue	35	35
E648		20pf. +10pf. turquoise blue and magenta	35	35
E649		25pf. turquoise-blue and ultramarine	35	35
E650		40pf. turquoise-blue and violet	2·00	2·00
E651		70pf. turquoise-blue and red-brown	35	35
E646/E651	Set of 6		3·50	3·50

Designs:—5pf. T E **217**; 10pf. Back stroke; 20pf. High diving; 25pf. Butterfly stroke; 40pf. Breast stroke; 70pf. Water-polo.

Nos. E646/E651 were issued both in separate sheets of 50 stamps and together in *se-tenant* blocks of six within sheets of 60 stamps (*Price per block*: £4·00 *un*).

E 209 Maize-planting Machine    E 210 *Frieden* (freighter)

(Des H.-J. Walch. Litho.)

1962 (26 June). Tenth DDR Agricultural Exhibition, Markkleeberg. T E **209** and similar horiz designs. Multicoloured. Wmk E **100**. P 13×12½.

E634		10pf. T E **209**	35	25
E635		20pf. Milking shed	35	25
E636		40pf. Combine-harvester	2·75	2·30
E634/E636	Set of 3		3·00	2·50

(Des H. Priess (10pf.), C. Schneider (others). Litho.)

1962 (2 July). Fifth Baltic Sea Week, Rostock. T E **210** and similar designs inscr '715 JULI 1962'. Wmk E **100**. P 13½×13 (20pf.) or 13×13½ (others).

E637		10pf. turquoise and blue	35	25
E638		20pf. brown-red and light yellow	35	25
E639		25pf. bistre and blue	3·50	3·25
E637/E639	Set of 3		3·75	3·50

Designs: Horiz—10pf. Map of the Baltic Sea inscr 'Meer des Friedens' ('Sea of Peace'); 25pf. T E **210**. Vert—20pf. Railway-station hotel, Rostock.

(Des D. Dorfstecher. Eng G. Stauf. Recess and photo)

1962 (28 Aug). Leipzig Autumn Fair. T E **218** and similar vert designs. Wmk E **100**. P 14.

E652		10pf. black and green	35	25
E653		20pf. black and red	55	35
E654		25pf. black and blue	1·40	1·30
E652/E654	Set of 3		2·10	1·70

Designs:—10pf. T E **218**; 20pf. Mädler Arcade, Leipzig; 25pf. Leipzig Airport and nose of Ilyushin Il-14M aeroplane.

E 211 Brandenburg Gate. Berlin   E 212 Youth of Three Races

E 213 Folk Dancers   E 214 Youth of Three Nations

E 219 Transport and Communications    E 219a P. Popovich and A. Nikolaev

259

GERMANY / German Democratic Republic (East Germany)

(Des A. Bengs. Litho)

1962 (3 Sept). Tenth Anniv of Friedrich List Transport High School, Dresden. Wmk E **100**. P 13½×13.
E655   E **219**   5pf. black and blue 55   30

(Des H. Urbschat. Litho)

1962 (13 Sept). *Vostok 3* and *Vostok 4* Space Flights. Sheet 89×108 mm. Wmk E **100**. Facsimile perfs.
MSE655a   E **219a**   70pf. yellow-green, indigo and yellow .... 5·50   9·00

E **220** René Blieck
E **221** Television Screen and Call-sign 

(Eng M. Sachs (20pf.), O. Volkamer (others). Recess)

1962 (4 Oct). Concentration Camp Victims. Memorials Fund. T E **220** and similar portraits. Wmk E **100**. P 14.
E656   5pf. +5pf. grey-blue 35   35
E657   10pf. +5pf. bluish green 35   35
E658   15pf. +5pf. violet 35   35
E659   20pf. +10pf. brown-purple 35   35
E660   70pf. +30pf. chocolate .... 3·00   4·25
E656/E660 Set of 5 .... 4·00   5·00
Portraits: Vert—5pf. T E **220**; 10pf. Dr. A Klahr; 15pf. J. Diaz; 20pf. J. Alpari. Horiz (39×21 mm)—70pf. Seven Cervi brothers.

(Des A. Bengs. Litho)

1962 (25 Oct). Tenth Anniv of German Television and Stamp Day. T E **221** and similar horiz design inscr 'TAG DER BRIEFMARKE 1962'. Wmk E **100**. P 13½×13.
E661   20pf. deep dull purple and emerald 35   35
E662   40pf. deep dull purple and magenta .... 2·75   3·00
Designs:—20pf. T E **221**; 40pf. Children with stamp album.

E **222** Gerhart Hauptmann
E **222a** Gagarin and *Vostok 1* 

(Des D. Dorfstecher. Litho)

1962 (15 Nov). Birth Centenary of Gerhart Hauptmann (author). Wmk E **100**. P 13½×13½.
E663   E **222**   20pf. black and red 70   30

(Des H. Urbschat. Litho)

1962 (28 Dec). Five Years of Russian Space Flights. Sheet 127×108 mm. Multicoloured. Wmk E **100**. P 12½×13.
MSE663a 5pf. Dogs Bielka and Strelka; 10pf. Type E **222a**; 15pf. *Sputniks 1, 2* and *3*; 20pf. Titov and *Vostok 2*; 25pf. *Luniks 1* and *2*; 30pf. Nikolaev and Popovich; 40pf. Interplanetary station and spacecraft; 50pf. *Lunik 3*.. 55·00   80·00

E **223** Pierre de Coubertin
E **224** Party Flag 

(Des A. Bengs and R. Skribelka. Litho)

1963 (2 Jan). Birth Centenary of Pierre de Coubertin (reviver of Olympic Games). T E **223** and similar vert design. Wmk E **100**. P 13½×13.
E664   20pf. carmine and grey (Type E **223**) 35   35
E665   25pf. blue and ochre (Stadium) .... 2·75   4·00

(Des K. Sauer. Litho)

1963 (15 Jan). Sixth Socialist Unity Party Day. Wmk E **100**. P 13×13½.
E666   E **224**   10pf. red, black and yellow 55   30

E **225** Insecticide Sprayer

(Des D. Dorfstecher and K. Hennig. Litho)

1963 (6 Feb). Malaria Eradication. T E **225** and similar horiz designs. Wmk E **100**. P 13×12½.
E667   20pf. black, brown-red and red-orange 35   35
E668   25pf. black, red, violet and light blue 35   35
E669   50pf. black, yellow, yellow-olive and light green .... 2·00   2·10
E667/E669 Set of 3 .... 2·40   2·50
Designs:—20pf. T E **225**. As T E **225** but central design depicting. 25pf. Rod of Aesculapius; 50pf. Mosquito.

E **226** Red Fox (Silver Fox race)
E **227** Barthels Hof, Leipzig (1748–1872) 

(Des D. Dorfstecher, K. Hennig and G. Stauf. Photo)

1963 (14 Feb). International Fur Auctions, Leipzig. T E **226** and similar horiz design. Wmk E **100**. P 14.
E670   20pf. indigo and rose-red 35   35
E671   25pf. indigo and light blue .... 2·40   3·75
Designs:—20pf. T E **226**; 25pf. Karakul Lamb.

(Des D. Dorfstecher. Recess and photo)

1963 (26 Feb). Leipzig Spring Fair. T E **227** and similar vert designs. Wmk E **100**. P 14.
E672   10pf. black and olive-yellow 35   25
E673   20pf. black and orange-brown 55   40
E674   25pf. black and light blue .... 2·00   2·10
E672/E674 Set of 3 .... 2·50   2·50
Designs:—10pf. T E **227**; 20pf. New Town Hall Leipzg; 25pf. Clocktower, Karl Marx Square, Leipzig.

E **227a** Laboratory Worker and Apparatus
E **228** J. G. Seume (writer) and Scene from *Syracuse Walk* (birth bicentenary) 

1963 (12 Mar). Chemistry for Freedom and Socialism. Sheet 105×74 mm with T E **227a** and similar horiz design. Litho. Imperf. No gum.
MSE674a 50pf. blue and black (E **227a**); 70pf. blue and grey (Oil refinery) .... 6·75   39·00

(Des I. Friebel. Litho)

1963 (9 Apr). Cultural Anniversaries. T E **228** and similar horiz designs. Wmk E **100**. P 13×12½.
E675   5pf. black and greenish yellow 35   35
E676   10pf. black and blue-green 35   35
E677   20pf. black and red-orange 35   35
E678   25pf. black and light blue .... 2·75   3·25
E675/E678 Set of 4 .... 3·50   3·75
Designs:—5pf. T E **228**; 10pf. F. Hebbel (dramatist) and scene from *Mary Magdalene* (150th birth anniv); 20pf. G. Büchner (writer) and scene from *Woyzeck* (150th birth anniv); 25pf. R. Wagner (composer) and scene from *The Flying Dutchman* (150th birth anniv).

GERMANY / German Democratic Republic (East Germany)

E 229 Nurse bandaging Patient

E 230 W. Bohne (runner)

(Des H. Rose. Litho)

1963 (14 May). Red Cross Centenary. T E **229** and similar horiz design. Wmk E **100**. P 13×12½.
E679	10pf. black, blue-green, grey and red		1·90	1·80
E680	20pf. black, grey and red		35	35

Designs:—10pf. T E **229**; 20pf. Barkas type B 1000 ambulance.

(Des G. Stauf. Eng M. Sachs (5pf., 15pf.), O. Volkamer (10pf., 20pf.), Sachs and Volkamer (25pf.). Recess and photo)

1963 (27 May). Concentration Camps Memorial Fund. Sportsmen Victims (1st series). T E **230** and similar vert portraits. Designs black. Wmk E **100**. P 14.
E681	5pf. +5pf. pale greenish yellow	40	45
E682	10pf. +5pf. pale yellow-green	40	45
E683	15pf. +5pf. pale mauve	40	45
E684	20pf. +10pf. pale pink	40	45
E685	25pf. +10pf. pale blue	3·25	8·50
E681/E685	Set of 5	4·25	9·25

Sportsmen:—5pf. T E **230**; 10pf. W. Seelenbinder (wrestler); 15pf. A. Richter (cyclist); 20pf. H. Steyer (footballer); 25pf. K. Schlosser (mountaineer).

Nos. E681/E685 were issued in sheets with *se-tenant* stamp-size labels depicting the various sports associated with the sportsmen.

See also Nos. E704/E708.

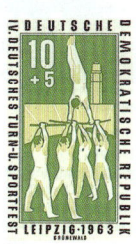

E 231 Gymnastics

E 232 E. Pottier (lyricist) and Opening Bars of *The Internationale*

(Des L. Grünewald. Litho)

1963 (13 June). Fourth East German Gymnastic and Sports Festival, Leipzig. T E **231** and similar vert designs. Wmk E **100**. P 12½×13.
E686	10pf. +5pf. olive-yellow, green and black	35	25
E687	20pf. +10pf. violet, red and black	40	25
E688	25pf. +10pf. light green, greenish blue and black	5·50	4·50
E686/E688	Set of 3	5·75	4·50

Designs:—10pf. T E **231**; 20pf. Dederon kerchief exercises; 25pf. Relay-racing.

(Des W. Kosak. Litho)

1963 (18 June). 75th Anniv of *The Internationale* (song). T E **232** and similar horiz design. Wmk E **100**. P 13×13½.
E689	20pf. black and red	35	35
E690	25pf. black and blue	1·90	2·10

Designs:—20pf. T E **232**. 25pf. As 20pf. but portrait of P.-C. Degeyter.

E 233 V. Tereshkova and *Vostok 6*

E 234 V. Bykovsky and *Vostock 5*

(Des R. Skribelka and A. Bengs. Photo)

1963 (18 July). Second Team Manned Space Flights. Wmk E **100**. P 13½×14.
E691	E **233**	20pf. black, new blue and slate-blue	1·40	40
		a. Horiz pair. Nos. E691/E692	3·00	85
E692	E **234**	20pf. black, slate-blue and new blue	1·40	40

Nos. E691/E692 were issued together in horizontal *se-tenant* pairs within the sheet, each pair forming a composite design.

E 235 Motorcyclist (Motocross Championships, Apolda)

E 236 Treblinka Memorial

(Des F. Deutschendorf. Eng Margot Sachs (10pf., 25pf.), O. Volkamer (20pf.). Recess and photo)

1963 (30 July). World Motorcycle Racing Championships. T E **235** and similar designs. Wmk E **100**. P 14.
E693	10pf. myrtle green and emerald	5·50	5·75
E694	20pf. brown-red and carmine-red	40	40
E695	25pf. deep dull blue and greenish blue	40	40
E693/E695	Set of 3	5·75	6·00

Designs:—10pf. T E **235**. 39×22 mm—20pf. Motorcyclist; 25pf. Two motorcyclists cornering.

(Des P. Weiss. Litho)

1963 (20 Aug). Erection of Treblinka Memorial, Poland. Wmk E **100**. P 13×13½.
E696	E **236**	20pf. deep blue and orange-red	55	40

E 237 Transport

E 238 Transport

(Des D. Dorfstecher. Litho)

1963 (27 Aug). Leipzig Autumn Fair. Wmk E **100**. P 13½×13.
E697	E **237**	10pf. multicoloured	1·20	25
		a. Horiz pair. Nos. E697/E698	2·50	55
E698	E **238**	10pf. multicoloured	1·20	25

Nos. E697/E698 were issued together in horizontal *se-tenant* pairs within the sheet, each pair forming a composite design.

(Des H. Naumann. Photo)

1963 (10 Sept). Fauna Protection Campaign (2nd series). Horiz designs as T E **201**. Fauna in natural colours. Wmk E **100**. P 14.
E699	10pf. yellow-green	35	35
E700	20pf. red	35	35
E701	30pf. carmine-lake	35	35
E702	50pf. deep blue	5·50	5·25
E703	70pf. red-brown	95	90
E699/E703	Set of 5	6·75	6·50

Designs:—10pf. Stag Beetle (*Lucanus cervus*); 20pf. Salamander (*Salamandra salamandra*); 30pf. European Pond Tortoise (*Emys orbicularis*); 50pf. Green Toad (*Bufo viridis*); 70pf. West European Hedgehogs (*Erinaceus europaeus*).

(Des G. Stauf. Eng M. Sachs (5pf., 15pf.), O. Volkamer (20pf., 40pf.), Sachs and Volkamer (10pf.). Recess and photo)

1963 (24 Sept). Concentration Camps Memorial Fund. Sportsmen Victims (2nd series). Vert portraits as T E **230**. Designs black. Wmk E **100**. P 14.
E704	5pf. +5pf. pale yellow	40	40
E705	10pf. +5pf. pale green	40	40
E706	15pf. +5pf. pale violet	40	40
E707	20pf. +10pf. pale red	40	40
E708	40pf. +20pf. pale blue	3·75	5·50
E704/E708	Set of 5	4·75	6·50

Sportsmen:—5pf. H. Tops (gymnast); 10pf. Kate Tucholla (hockey-player); 15pf. R. Seiffert (swimmer); 20pf. E. Grube (athlete); 40pf. K. Biedermann (canoeist).

Nos. E704/E708 were issued in sheets with *se-tenant* stamp-size labels depicting the various sports.

GERMANY / German Democratic Republic (East Germany)

(Des P. Weiss. Photo)

1964 (16 Sept). Centenary of 'First International'. Wmk E **100**. P 14.
E775	E **258**	20pf. black and red	35	25
E776		25pf. black and blue	1·10	1·00

(Des A. Bengs and H. J. Gadegast. Litho)

1964 (23 Sept). National Stamp Exhibition, East Berlin. T E **259** and similar vert designs. Wmk E **100**. P 13×13½.
E777	10pf. +5pf. blue-green and orange	40	25
E778	20pf. +10pf. blue and bright purple	55	40
E779	50pf. red-brown and grey	3·00	2·30
E777/E779	Set of 3	3·50	2·75

Designs:—10pf. T E **259**; 20pf., 12pf. 'Peace' stamp of 1950; 50pf., 5pf. 'Dresden Paintings' stamp of 1955.

E **260** Modern Buildings and Flag (Reconstruction)

E **261** Mönchgut (Rügen) Costume

(Des D. Dorfstecher and K. Hennig. Litho)

1964 (6 Oct). 15th Anniv of German Democratic Republic. T E **260** and similar horiz designs. Multicoloured. Wmk E **100**. P 13½×13.
E780	10pf. T E **260**	55	50
E781	10pf. Surveyor and conveyor (Coal)	55	50
E782	10pf. Scientist and chemical works (Chemical Industry)	55	50
E783	10pf. Guard and chemical works (Chemical Industry)	55	50
E784	10pf. Milkmaid and dairy pen (Agriculture)	55	50
E785	10pf. Furnaceman and mills (Steel)	55	50
E786	10pf. Student with microscope and lecture hall (Education)	55	50
E787	10pf. Operator and lathe (Engineering)	55	50
E788	10pf. Scientist and planetarium (Optics)	55	50
E789	10pf. Girl with cloth, and loom (Textiles)	55	50
E790	10pf. Docker and ship at quayside (Shipping)	55	50
E791	10pf. Leipzig buildings and 'businessmen' formed of Fairemblem (Exports)	55	50
E792	10pf. Building worker and flats (New Construction)	55	50
E793	10pf. Sculptor modelling and Dresden gateway (Culture)	55	50
E794	10pf. Girl skier and holiday resort (Recreation)	55	50
E780/E794	Set of 15	7·50	6·75
MSE794a	210×285 mm. Nos. E780/E794. No gum. Imperf	90·00	£130

(Des I. Friebel Photo)

1964 (25 Nov). Provincial Costumes (1st series). T E **261** and similar vert designs. Multicoloured. Wmk E **100**. P 14.
E795	5pf. Type E **261**	12·50	8·25
	a. Pair. Nos. E795/E796	26·00	18·00
E796	5pf. Mönchgut (male)	12·50	8·25
E797	10pf. Spreewald (female)	3·00	1·60
	a. Pair. Nos. E797/E798	6·25	3·50
E798	10pf. Spreewald (male)	3·00	1·60
E799	20pf. Thüringen (female)	3·00	1·60
	a. Pair. Nos. E799/E800	6·25	3·50
E800	20pf. Thüringen (male)	3·00	1·60
E795/E800	Set of 6	33·00	21·00

The stamps of the same face value were issued together in se-tenant pairs within the sheet.
See also Nos. E932/E937 and E1073/E1076.

E **261a** Observation of Sun's Activity

(Des H. Urbschat. Litho)

1964 (29 Dec). Quiet Sun Year. Three sheets, each 108×90 mm, incorporating stamp as T E **261a**. Multicoloured. Wmk E **100**. P 13½×13.
MSE801 (a) 25pf. Rocket over part of Earth; (b) 40pf. Type E **261a**; (c) 70pf. Earth and rocket routes Price for 3 sheets .... 17·00   31·00

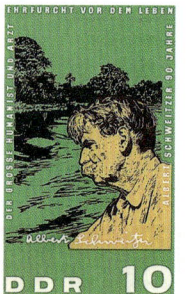

E **262** Dr. Schweitzer and Lambarene River

E **263** August Bebel

(Des P. Weiss. Photo)

1965 (14 Jan). 90th Birthday of Dr. Albert Schweitzer. T E **262** and similar vert designs. Wmk E **100**. P 14.
E802	10pf. yellow, black and green	1·10	25
E803	20pf. yellow, black and red	1·10	25
E804	25pf. yellow, black and blue	6·00	3·50
E802/E804	Set of 3	7·50	3·50

Designs:—10pf. T E **262**; 20pf. Schweitzer and nuclear disarmament marchers; 25pf. Schweitzer and part of a Bach organ prelude.

1965 (10 Feb). As Nos. E586/E587 (Ulbricht), but values expressed in MDN instead of DM.
E805	1 MDN. bronze-green	80	2·00
E806	2 MDN. brown	95	3·25

MDN signifies Mark der Deutschen Notenbank.
For stamps with value expressed as M see Nos. E1197/E1198 and E1255.

(Des P. Weiss. Photo)

1965 (22 Feb). 125th Birth Anniv of August Bebel (founder of Social Democratic Party). Wmk E **100**. P 14.
E807	E **263**	20pf. pale yellow, olive-brown and red	70	25

For similar types, see Nos. E814, E815, E839, E842 and E871.

E **264** Fair Medal (obverse)

E **265** Giraffe

(Des D. Dorfstecher. Photo)

1965 (25 Feb). Leipzig Spring Fair and 800th Anniv of Leipzig Fair. T E **264** and similar vert designs. Wmk E **100**. P 14.
E808	10pf. gold and magenta	40	25
E809	15pf. gold and magenta	40	25
E810	25pf. multicoloured	95	40
E808/E810	Set of 3	1·60	80

Designs:—10pf. T E **264**; 15pf. Fair medal (reverse); 25pf. Chemical works.

(Des A. Bengs. Photo)

1965 (24 Mar). Tenth Anniv of East Berlin Zoo. T E **265** and similar but horiz designs. Wmk E **100**. P 14.
E811	10pf. grey and emerald-green (Type E **265**)	35	25
E812	25pf. grey and deep ultramarine (Iguana)	40	25
E813	30pf. grey and sepia (Black Wildebeest)	3·50	2·30
E811/E813	Set of 3	3·75	2·50

(Des P. Weiss. Photo)

1965 (24 Mar). 120th Anniv of W. C. Röntgen (physicist). Vert design as T E **263**. Wmk E **100**. P 14.
E814	10pf. pale yellow, bistre-brown and emerald	80	25

GERMANY / German Democratic Republic (East Germany)

(Des P. Weiss. Photo)

1965 (15 Apr). 700th Anniv of Dante's Birth. Vert design as T E **263**. Wmk E **100**. P 14.

| F815 | 50pf. pale yellow, bistre-brown and yellow | 3·00 | 40 |

E **266** Belyaev and Leonov
E **267** Boxing Gloves 

(Des A. Bengs. Litho)

1965 (15 Apr). Space Flight of *Voskhod 2*. T E **266** and similar horiz design. Wmk E **100**. P 13½×13.

| E816 | 10pf. carmine-red (Type E **266**) | 55 | 25 |
| E817 | 25pf. bright blue (Leonov in space) | 3·50 | 2·50 |

(Des K. Hennig. Photo)

1965 (27 Apr). European Boxing Championships, Berlin. T E **267** and similar vert design. Wmk E **100**. P 13½×13.

| E818 | 10pf. +5pf. red, blue, black and gold (Type E **267**) | 35 | 25 |
| E819 | 20pf. gold, black and red (Boxing glove) | 1·40 | 1·30 |

E **268** Dimitrov denouncing Fascism
E **269** Transmitter Aerial and Globe 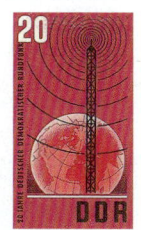

(Des K. Sauer. Photo)

1965 (5 May). 20th Anniv of Liberation. T E **268** and similar horiz designs. Multicoloured. Wmk E **100**. P 14.

E820	5pf. +5pf. Type E **268**	40	40
E821	10pf. +5pf. Distributing Communist Manifesto	40	40
E822	15pf. +5pf. Soldiers of International Brigade fighting in Spain	40	40
E823	20pf. +10pf. 'Freedom for Ernst Thälmann' demonstration	40	40
E824	25pf. +10pf. Founding of 'Free Germany' National Committee (Moscow)	40	40
E825	40pf. Ulbricht and Weinert distributing Manifesto on Eastern Front	40	40
E826	50pf. Liberation of concentration camps	40	40
E827	60pf. Hoisting Red Flag on Reichstag	4·75	4·50
E828	70pf. Bilateral demonstration of Communist and Socialist parties	40	40
E820/E828	Set of 9	7·25	7·00

(Des L. Grünewald. Litho)

1965 (12 May). 20th Anniv of East German Broadcasting Service. T E **269** and similar vert design. Wmk E **100**. P 12½×13.

| E829 | 20pf. black, light red and cerise | 55 | 25 |
| E830 | 40pf. black and violet-blue | 2·40 | 1·40 |

Designs:—20pf. T E **269**; 40pf. Radio workers.

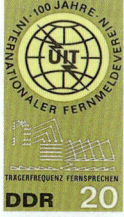

E **270** ITU Emblem and Radio Circuit Diagram
E **271** FDGB Emblem 

(Des K.-H. Bobbe. Litho)

1965 (17 May). Centenary of International Telecommunications Union. T E **270** and similar vert design. Wmk E **100**. P 12½×13.

| E831 | 20pf. black, greenish yellow and yellow-olive | 70 | 25 |
| E832 | 25pf. black, pale mauve and light violet | 3·50 | 80 |

Designs:—20pf. T E **270**; 25pf. ITU emblem and switch diagram.

(Des P. Weiss. Photo)

1965 (10 June). 20th Anniv of the Free German (FDGB) and World Trade Unions. T E **271** and similar design inscr '20 JAHRE WELTGEWERKSCHAFTSBUND'. Wmk E **100**. P 13½×14 (20pf.) or 14 (25pf.).

| E833 | 20pf. gold and red | 70 | 40 |
| E834 | 25pf. black, new blue and gold | 2·75 | 90 |

Designs: Vert:—20pf. T E **271**. Horiz (39×21½ *mm*):—25pf. Workers of two hemispheres.

E **272** Industrial Machine
E **273** Marx and Lenin 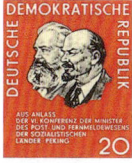
E **274** Congress Emblem

(Des M. Gottschall. Photo)

1965 (16 June). 800th Anniv of Karl-Marx-Stadt (formerly Chemnitz). T E **272** and similar vert designs. Wmk E **100**. P 13½×14.

E835	10pf. light emerald and gold	40	25
E836	20pf. carmine-red and gold	40	25
E837	25pf. new blue and gold	1·90	1·00
E835/E837	Set of 3	2·40	1·40

Designs:—10pf. T E **272**; 20pf. Red Tower, Chemnitz; 25pf. Town Hall, Chemnitz.

(Des G. Stauf. Photo)

1965 (21 June). Socialist Countries' Postal Ministers Conference, Peking. Wmk E **100**. P 13½×13.

| E838 | E **273** | 20pf. black, pale yellow and orange-red | 95 | 30 |

(Des P. Weiss. Photo)

1965 (5 July). 90th Birth Anniv of Dr. Wilhelm Külz (politician). Vert design as T E **263**. Wmk E **100**. P 14.

| E839 | 25pf. pale yellow, bistre-brown and greenish blue | 1·50 | 30 |

(Des A. Bengs. Litho)

1965 (5 July). World Peace Congress, Helsinki. Wmk E **100**. P 13.

| E840 | E **274** | 10pf. +5pf. emerald and ultramarine | 40 | 25 |
| E841 | 20pf. +5pf. ultramarine and red | 80 | 50 |

(Des P. Weiss. Photo)

1965 (28 July). 75th Birth Anniv of Erich Weinert (poet). Vert design as T E **263**. Wmk E **100**. P 14.

| E842 | 40pf. pale yellow, bistre-brown and cerise | 80 | 30 |

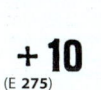

(E **275**)
E **276** Rebuilt Weigh-house and Modern Buildings, Katharinenstrasse 

1965 (23 Aug). 'Help for Vietnam' No. E780 surch. with T E **275**.

| E843 | E **260** | 10pf. +10pf. multicoloured | 70 | 30 |

(Des K.-H. Bobbe and D. Dorfstecher. Photo)

1965 (25 Aug). 800th Anniv of Leipzig. T E **276** and similar horiz designs. No Wmk. P 14.

E844	10pf. brown-purple, ultramarine and gold	35	25
E845	25pf. yellow-orange, sepia and gold	35	25
E846	40pf. yell-orange, sepia, olive-green and gold	40	25
E847	70pf. ultramarine and gold	3·25	1·40
E844/E847	Set of 4	4·00	1·90

Designs:—10pf. T E **276**; 25pf. Old Town Hall; 40pf. Opera House and new GPO; 70pf. Stadt Leipzig Hotel.

For stamps in miniature sheets, see No. MSE851.

265

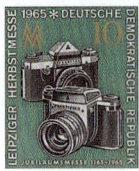

GERMANY / German Democratic Republic (East Germany)

E 277 Praktica and Praktisix Cameras

E 278 Show Jumping

(Des D. Dorfstecher. Photo)

1965 (2 Sept). Leipzig Autumn Fair. T E **277** and similar vert designs. No Wmk. P 14.

E848	10pf. black, gold and green	55	25
E849	15pf. black, yellow, gold and magenta	55	25
E850	25pf. black. pale blue, gold and blue	1·20	40
E848/E850	Set of 3	2·10	80

Designs:—10pf. T E **277**; 15pf. Clavichord and electric guitar; 25pf. Zeiss microscope.

1965 (4 Sept). Leipzig Philatelic Exhibition, INTERMESS III. Nos. E844/E847 in two miniature sheets each 137×99 mm.

MSE851 (a) Nos. E844 and E847; (b) Nos, E845/E846 (sold for 1 MDN.75) Set of 2 sheets .... 8·75 10·50

(Des K. Hennig. Litho)

1965 (15 Sept). World Modern Pentathlon Championships. Leipzig. T E **278** and similar vert designs. Multicoloured. No wmk. P 13½×13.

E852	10pf. T E **278**	40	25
E853	10pf. Swimming	40	25
E854	10pf. Running	3·75	4·00
E855	10pf. +5pf. Fencing	40	25
E856	10pf. +5pf. Pistol-shooting	40	25
E852/E856	Set of 5	4·75	4·50

E 279 Aleksei Leonov

E 280 Memorial at Putten, Netherlands

(Des J. Riess. Photo)

1965 (1 Oct). Visit of Soviet Cosmonauts to East Germany. T E **279** and similar designs. Wmk E **100**. P 13½×14.

E857	20pf. dull blue, silver and vermilion	90	90
	a. Horiz strip of 3. Nos. E857/E859	4·00	
E858	20pf. dull blue, silver and vermilion	90	90
E859	25pf. multicoloured	90	90
E857/E859	Set of 3	2·40	2·40

Designs:—E857, T E **279**. As T E **279**—No. E858, Pavel Belyaev. 48×29 mm—No. E859, *Voskhod 2* and Leonov in space.

Nos. E857/E859 were issued together in horizontal *se-tenant* strips of three stamps within the sheet.

(Des P. Weiss. Litho)

1965 (19 Oct). Putten War Victims Commemoration. Wmk E **100**. P 13×13½.

E860	E **280** 25pf. black, pale yellow and new blue	1·40	30

E 281 Stoking Furnace (from old engraving)

E 282 Red Kite

(Des W. Klemke. Litho)

1965 (13 Nov). Bicentenary of Mining School, Freiberg. T E **281** and similar horiz designs. Multicoloured. No wmk. P 13×12½.

E861	10pf. Type E **281**	40	25
E862	15pf. Mining ore (old engraving)	95	1·30
E863	20pf. Ore	40	25
E864	25pf. Sulphur	40	25
E861/E864	Set of 4	1·90	1·80

(Des A. Bengs. Photo)

1965 (8 Dec). Birds of Prey. T E **282** and similar vert designs. Multicoloured. No wmk. P 14.

E865	5pf. Type E **282**	35	25
E866	10pf. Lammergeier	35	25
E867	20pf. Common Buzzard	40	25
E868	25pf. Common Kestrel	40	25
E869	40pf. Northern Goshawk	70	25
E870	70pf. Golden Eagle	6·00	3·75
E865/E870	Set of 6	7·50	4·50

(Des P. Weiss. Photo)

1965 (8 Dec). 150th Birth Anniv of A. von Menzel (painter). Vert design as T E **263**. Wmk E **100**. P 14.

E871	10pf. pale yellow, bistre-brown and orange-red	1·40	30

E 283 Otto Grotewohl

E 284 Extract from Newsletter

(Des A. Bengs. Photo)

1965 (14 Dec). Grotewohl Commemoration. Wmk E **100**. P 14.

E872	E **283** 20pf. black	1·20	30

(Des P. Weiss. Photo)

1966 (3 Jan). 50th Anniv of Spartacus Group Conference. Miniature sheet 138×98 mm. T E **284** and similar horiz design. No wmk. P 14.

MSE873 20pf. black and rosine (Type E **284**); 50pf. black and rosine (Karl Liebknecht and Rosa Luxemburg) .... 3·50 9·00

E 285 Ladies' Single-seater

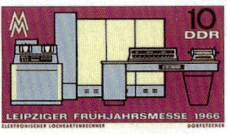

E 286 Electronic Punch card Computer

(Des D. Dorfstecher and K. Hennig. Litho)

1966 (25 Jan). World Tobogganing Championships, Friedrichroda. T E **285** and similar horiz designs. No wmk. P 13½×13.

E874	10pf. green, deep green and light yellow-olive	35	25
E875	20pf. blue, deep blue and bright carmine	35	25
E876	25pf. blue, blue-black and light greenish blue	2·00	1·30
E874/E876	Set of 3	2·40	1·60

Designs:—10pf. T E **285**; 20pf. Men's double-seater; 25pf Men's single-seater.

(Des D. Dorfstecher. Photo)

1966 (24 Feb). Leipzig Spring Fair. T E **286** and similar horiz design. No wmk. P 13×12½.

E877	10pf. black, pale yellow, light blue and magenta	40	25
E878	15pf. black, salmon, light green and blue	1·80	40

Designs:—10pf. T E **286**; 15pf. Drilling and milling plant.

E 287 Soldier and National Gallery, Berlin

E 288 J. A. Smoler

266

GERMANY / German Democratic Republic (East Germany)

(Des P. Weiss. Photo)

1966 (1 Mar). Tenth Anniv of National People's Army. T E **287** and similar horiz designs. Each printed in blackish olive, black, greyish olive and greenish yellow. Wmk E **100**. P 14.

E879	5pf. Type E **287**	40	25
E880	10pf. Brandenburg Gate	40	25
E881	20pf. Industrial plant	40	25
E882	25pf. Combine-harvester	1·80	1·30
E879/E882	Set of 4	2·75	1·80

Each value shows the profile of the soldier.

(Des J. Hansky and G. Stauf. Litho)

1966 (1 Mar). 150th Birth Anniv of Jan Smoler (Sorb patriot and savant). T E **288** and similar vert design. No wmk. P 13×13½.

E883	20pf. black, red and blue	40	25
E884	25pf. black, red and blue	95	80

Designs:—20pf. T E **288**; 25pf. House of the Sorbs, Bautzen.

E **289** Good Knowledge Badge

E **290** Luna 9 on Moon

(Des D. Dorfstecher. Litho)

1966 (7 Mar). 20th Anniv of Freie Deutsche Jugend (Socialist Youth Movement). No wmk. P 13½×13.

E885	E **289**	20pf. bright blue, black, yellow and red	95	30

(Des W. Pochanke and G. Stauf. Photo)

1966 (7 Mar). Moon Landing of *Luna 9*. No wmk. P 14.

E886	E **290**	20pf. multicoloured	3·50	65

E **291** Road Signs

E **292** Marx and Lenin Banner

(Des H. Detlefsen (15pf.), M. Gottschall (others). Litho)

1966 (28 Mar). Road Safety. T E **291** and similar horiz designs. P 13×13½.

E887	10pf. red, light greenish blue and blue	35	25
E888	15pf. black, olive-yellow and blue-green	35	25
E889	25pf. black, new blue and bistre	35	25
E890	50pf. black, yellow and red	1·60	1·00
E887/E890	Set of 4	2·40	1·60

Designs:—10pf. T E **291**; 15pf. Child on scooter crossing in front of car; 25pf. Cyclist and hand-signal; 50pf. Motorcyclist, glass of beer and ambulance.

(Des K. Sauer (10pf.), P. Weiss (25pf.), K. Hennig (others). Photo.)

1966 (31 Mar). 20th Anniv of Socialist Unity Party (SED). T E **292** and similar designs. No wmk. P 14.

E891	5pf. yellow, black, blue and carmine	40	25
E892	10pf. yellow, black and carmine	40	25
E893	15pf. black and green	40	25
E894	20pf. black and carmine	40	25
E895	25pf. black, yellow and carmine	2·75	2·00
E891/E895	Set of 5	4·00	2·75

Designs: Vert—5pf. Party badge and demonstrators; 15pf. Marx, Engels and manifesto; 20pf. Pieck and Grotewohl. Horiz—10pf. T E **292**; 25pf. Workers greeting Ulbricht.

E **293** WHO Building

(Des D. Dorfstecher. Litho)

1966 (26 Apr). Inauguration of World Health Organisation Headquarters, Geneva. No wmk. P 13×12½.

E896	E **293**	20pf. multicoloured	70	50

E **294** Spreewald

E **295** Lace Flower

(Des G. Stauf. Litho)

1966 (17 May). National Parks. T E **294** and similar horiz designs. Multicoloured. No wmk. P 13×12½.

E897	10pf. Type E **294**	35	25
E898	15pf. Königsstuhl (Isle of Rügen)	35	25
E899	20pf. Sächsische Schweiz	35	25
E900	25pf. Westdarss	40	25
E901	30pf. Teufelsmauer	3·25	1·70
E902	50pf. Feldberg Lakes	40	25
E897/E902	Set of 6	4·50	2·75

(Des W. Rahm. Litho)

1966 (26 May). Plauen Lace. Floral patterns as T E **295**. No Wmk. P 13.

E903	10pf. myrtle-green and light green	35	25
E904	20pf. indigo and light blue	35	25
E905	25pf. deep brown-red and light red	40	25
E906	50pf. deep bluish violet and lilac	3·75	2·00
E903/E906	Set of 4	4·25	2·50

E **296** Lily of the Valley

E **297** Parachutist on Target

(Des L. Grünewald. Photo and recess)

1966 (28 June–16 Aug). International Horticultural Show, Erfurt. T E **296** and similar vert designs. Multicoloured. No wmk. P 14×13½.

E907	20pf. Type E **296** (16.8)	35	25
E908	25pf. Rhododendrons	40	25
E909	40pf. Dahlias	55	40
E910	50pf. Cyclamen	6·50	5·75
E907/E910	Set of 4	7·00	6·00

(Des K. Hennig. Litho)

1966 (12 July). Eighth World Parachute Jumping Championships, Leipzig. T E **297** and similar vert designs. No wmk. P 12½×13.

E911	10pf. new blue, black and bistre	35	35
E912	15pf. magenta, black, bright blue and pale blue	95	90
E913	20pf. black, bistre and light blue	35	35
E911/E913	Set of 3	1·50	1·40

Designs:—10pf. T E **297**; 15pf. Group descent; 20pf. Free fall.

E **298** Hans Kahle and Music of *The Thälmann Column*

(Des G. Stauf, after K. Sauer. Photo)

1966 (15 July). 30th Anniv of International Brigade in Spain. T E **298** and similar horiz designs. Multicoloured. No wmk. P 14.

E914	5pf. Type E **298**	40	25
E915	10pf. +5pf. W. Bredel and open-air class	40	25
E916	15pf. H. Beimler and Madrid streetfighting	40	25

GERMANY / German Democratic Republic (East Germany)

E917	20pf. +10pf. H. Rau and march-past after Battle of Brunete	40	25
E918	25pf. +10pf. H. Marchwitza and soldiers	40	25
E919	40pf. +10pf. A. Becker and Ebro battle	2·75	2·00
E914/E919	Set of 6	4·25	3·00

E **299** Canoeing

(Des K. Hennig. Litho)

1966 (16 Aug). World Canoeing Championships, Berlin. T E **299** and similar horiz design. Multicoloured. No wmk. P 13×12½.

E920	10pf. +5pf. Type E **299**	40	25
E921	15pf. Kayak doubles	1·90	1·60

E **300** Television set

(Des D. Dorfstecher. Litho)

1966 (29 Aug). Leipzig Autumn Fair. T E **300** and similar horiz design. No wmk. P 13×12½.

E922	10pf. black, grey, pale stone and blue-green	1·10	25
E923	15pf. black, grey, pale stone and carmine	2·40	40

Designs:—10pf. T E **300**; 15pf. Electric typewriter.

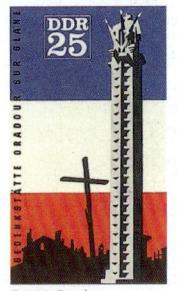

E **301** Oradour Memorial

E **302** Blood Donors

(Des P. Weiss. Litho)

1966 (9 Sept). Oradour-sur-Glane War Victims Commemoration. Wmk E **100**. P 13×13½.

E924	E **301**	25pf. black, blue and red	70	40

(Des H. Priess. Photo)

1966 (13 Sept). International Health Co-operation. T E **302** and similar designs. Wmk E **100**. P 14.

E925	5pf. red and emerald	40	25
E926	20pf. +10pf. red and violet	70	25
E927	40pf. red and greenish blue	3·00	90
E925/E927	Set of 3	3·75	1·30

Designs: Horiz—5pf. T E **302**; 20pf. International Co-operation Year emblem. Vert—40pf. Health symbol.

E **303** Weightlifting ('snatch')

E **304** Congress Hall

(Des G. Bläser and K.-H. Bobbe. Litho)

1966 (22 Sept). World and European Weightlifting Championships, Berlin. T E **303** and similar horiz design. No wmk. P 13½×13.

E928	15pf. black and light brown	2·40	2·30
E929	20pf. +5pf. black and violet-blue	70	25

Designs:—15pf. T E **303**; 20pf. Weightlifting ('jerk').

(Des D. Dorfstecher. Litho)

1966 (10 Oct). Sixth International Journalists' Congress, Berlin. T E **304** and similar design. No wmk. P 13.

E930	10pf. new blue, black, yellow and lake	80	65
E931	20pf. yellow and deep blue	35	35

Design: Horiz—10pf. T E **304**. Vert—20pf. Emblem of International Organisation of Journalists.

(Des I. Friebel. Photo)

1966 (25 Oct). Provincial Costumes (2nd series). Vert designs as T E **261**. Multicoloured. No wmk. P 14.

E932	5pf. Altenburg (female)	70	30
	a. Horiz pair. Nos. E932/E933	1·50	1·00
E933	10pf. Altenburg (male)	70	30
E934	10pf. Mecklenburg (female)	70	30
	a. Horiz pair. Nos. E934/E935	1·50	1·00
E935	15pf. Mecklenburg (male)	70	30
E936	20pf. Magdeburger Börde (female)	3·50	2·50
	a. Horiz pair. Nos. E936/E937	7·25	5·25
E937	30pf. Magdeburger Börde (male)	3·50	2·50
E932/E937	Set of 6	9·00	5·50

Nos. E932/E933, E934/E935 and E936/E937 were respectively issued together in horizontal se-tenant pairs within their sheets.

E **305** 'Vietnam is Invincible'

E **306** Oil Rigs and Pipeline Map

(Des G. Schütz. Litho)

1966 (25 Oct). Aid for Vietnam. No wmk. P 13½×13.

E938	E **305**	20pf. +5pf. black and light pink	1·10	40

(Des P. Weiss. Litho)

1966 (8 Nov). Inauguration of International Friendship Oil Pipeline. T E **306** and similar horiz design. No wmk. P 13½×13.

E939	20pf. black and red	30	25
E940	25pf. black and greenish blue	1·40	65

Designs:—20pf. T E **300**; 25pf. Walter Ulbricht Oil Works, Leuna, and pipeline map.

E **307** Black Phantom Tetra
(*Megalamphodus megalopterus*)

(Des H. Priess. Litho)

1966 (8 Nov). Aquarium Fish. T E **307** and similar horiz designs. Multicoloured. No wmk. P 13½×13.

E941	5pf. Type E **307**	35	25
E942	10pf. Cardinal Tetra (inscr *Cheirodon axelrodi*)	35	25
E943	15pf. Rio Grande Cichlid (inscr *Cichlasoma cynoguttatum*)	4·00	3·25
E944	20pf. Blue Gularis (inscr *Aphyosemion coeruleum*)	35	25
E945	25pf. Ramirez's Dwarf Cichlid (inscr *Microgeophagus ramirezi*)	40	25
E946	40pf. Honey Gourami (inscr *Colisa chuna*)	55	30
E941/E946	Set of 6	5·50	4·00

E **308** Horse (detail from Ishtar Gate)

(Des K. Hennig. Photo)

1966 (23 Nov). Babylonian Art Treasures, Vorderasiatisches Museum, Berlin. T E **308** and similar designs. Multicoloured. No wmk. P 13½×14 (horiz) or 14×13½ (vert).

E947	10pf. Type E **308**	35	35
E948	20pf. Mythological animal, Ishtar Gate	35	35
E949	25pf. Lion facing right (*vert*)	35	35
E950	50pf. Lion facing left (*vert*)	95	1·80
E947/E950	Set of 4	1·80	2·50

GERMANY / German Democratic Republic (East Germany)

E 309 The Wartburg from the East

E 310 *Gentiana pneumonanthe*

(Des J. Riess. Litho)

1966 (23 Nov). 900th Anniv of the Wartburg (Castle). T E **309** and similar vert designs. No wmk. P 13×13½.
E951	10pf. +5pf. deep grey-blue (Type E **309**)	70	25
E952	20pf. olive-green (Castle bailiwick)	70	25
E953	25pf. maroon (Residence)	1·40	55
E951/E953	Set of 3	2·50	95

(Des W. Klemke. Litho)

1966 (8 Dec). Protected Plants (1st series). T E **310** and similar vert designs. Multicoloured. No wmk. P 12½×13.
E954	10pf. Type E **310**	35	25
E955	20pf. *Cephalanthera rubra*	40	25
E956	25pf. *Arnica montana*	2·30	1·30
E954/E956	Set of 3	2·75	1·60

See also Nos. E1177/E1182 and E1284/E1289.

E 311 Son leaves Home

E 312 Worlitz Castle

1966 (8 Dec). Fairy Tales. *The Wishing Table*. T E **311** and similar horiz designs. Multicoloured. No wmk. P 13½×13.
E957	5pf. Type E **311**	40	50
	a. Sheetlet of 6. Nos. E957/E962	4·00	
E958	10pf. Feasting at the table	40	50
E959	20pf. The thieving inn-keeper	1·10	1·20
E960	25pf. The magic donkey	1·10	1·20
E961	30pf. The cudgel in the sack	40	50
E962	50pf. Return of the son	40	50
E957/E962	Set of 6	3·50	4·00

Nos. E957/E962 were issued together in *se-tenant* sheetlets of six stamps.
See also Nos. E1045/E1050, E1147/E1152, E1171/E1176, E1266/E1271, E1437/E1442, E1525/E1530, E1623/E1628, E1711/E1716, E1811/E1813, E1902/E1907, E1996/E2001 and E2092/E2097.

(Des D. Dorfstecher. Photo)

1967 (24 Jan). Principal East German Buildings. (1st series). T E **312** and similar designs. Multicoloured. P 14.
E964	5pf. Type E **312**	35	25
E965	10pf. Stralsund Town Hall	35	25
E966	15pf. Chorin Monastery	40	25
E967	20pf. Ribbeck Houses, Berlin	40	25
E968	25pf. Moritzburg, Zeitz	40	25
E969	40pf. Old Town Hall, Potsdam	2·40	1·30
E964/E969	Set of 6	3·75	2·30

See also Nos. E1100/E1103 and E1155/E1160.

E 313 Rifle-shooting

E 314 Multilock Loom

(Des J. Riess. Litho)

1967 (15 Feb). World Biathlon Championships, Altenberg. T E **313** and similar horiz designs. No wmk. P 13×12½.
E970	10pf. greenish blue, olive-drab and magenta	35	20
E971	20pf. blackish olive, light greenish blue and emerald	35	20
E972	25pf. bronze-green, turquoise-blue and yellow-olive	1·20	80
E970/E972	Set of 3	1·70	1·10

Designs:—10pf. T E **313**; 20pf. Shooting on skis; 25pf. Riflemen racing on skis.

(Des D. Dorfstecher. Litho)

1967 (2 Mar). Leipzig Spring Fair. T E **314** and similar vert design. Wmk E **100**. P 13½×13.
E973	10pf. light blue-green, grey and purple	40	25
E974	15pf. bistre and blue	1·60	40

Designs:—10pf. T E **314**; 15pf. Zeiss tracking telescope.

WATERMARK. From No. E975 all issues are *without* watermark, *unless otherwise stated*.

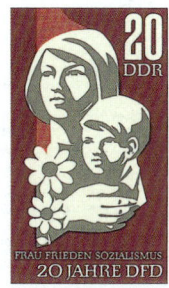

E 315 Mother and Child

(Des H. Detlefsen. Litho)

1967 (7 Mar). 20th Anniv of German Democratic Women's Federation. T E **315** and similar vert design. P 13½×13.
E975	20pf. olive-grey, red and brown-purple	40	25
E976	25pf. brown, greenish blue and blue	1·40	1·20

Designs:—20pf. T E **315**; 25pf. Professional woman.

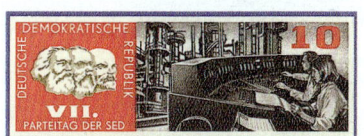

E 316 Industrial Control Desk

(Des K. Sauer. Photo (Nos. E977/E980). Des H. Detlefsen. Litho (Nos. E981/E984).

1967 (22 Mar–6 Apr). Socialist Party Rally. Multicoloured. P 14.
(a) First Series. T E **316** and similar horiz designs (22 March)
E977	10pf. Type E **316**	40	40
E978	20pf. Ulbricht meeting workers	40	40
E979	25pf. Servicemen guarding industrial plants	40	40
E980	40pf. Agricultural workers and harvesters	80	1·30
E977/E980	Set of 4	1·80	2·30

Each with inset portraits of Marx, Engels and Lenin.

(b) Second Series. Designs as T E **316** but vert (6 April)
E981	5pf. Agricultural worker	35	35
E982	10pf. Teacher and pupil	35	35
E983	15pf. Socialist family	70	80
E984	20pf. Servicemen	35	35
E981/E984	Set of 4	1·60	1·70

Each with inset portraits as above.

E 317 *Portrait of a Girl* (after F. Hodler)

269

GERMANY / German Democratic Republic (East Germany)

(Des A. Bengs. Photo)

1967 (29 Mar). Dresden Gallery Paintings (1st series). T E **317** and similar designs. Multicoloured. P 14.

E985	20pf. Type E **317**	35	25
E986	25pf. *Peter at the Zoo* (H. Hakenbeck)	35	25
E987	30pf. *Venetian Episode* (R. Bergander)	35	25
E988	40pf. *Tahitian Women* (Gauguin) (*horiz*)	35	25
E989	50pf. *The Grandchild* (J. Scholtz)	2·75	2·10
E990	70pf. *Cairn in the Snow* (C. D. Friedrich) (*horiz*)	55	40
E985/E990	*Set of* 6	4·25	3·25

See also Nos. E1114/E1119 and E1249/E1254.

REGISTRATION STAMPS. 'SELF-SERVICE POST OFFICE'. These registration labels embody a face value to cover the registration fee and have franking value to this extent. They are issued in pairs from automatic machines together with a certificate of posting against a 50pf. coin. The stamps are serially numbered in pairs and inscribed with the name of the town of issue.

The procedure is to affix one label to the letter (already franked with stamps for carriage of the letter) and complete page 1 of the certificate of posting which is then placed in the box provided, together with the letter. The duplicate label is affixed to the second page of the certificate and retained for production as evidence in the event of a claim.

They are not obtainable over the post office counter.

ER **318**

ER **319**

1967–83. REGISTRATION. Typo.

(a) Thin transparent paper. Imperf×perf 12

ER991	ER **318** 50pf. carmine and black (13.4.67)	43·00	

(b) Thick white paper. Imperf×perf 9½ or imperf×perf 12

ER992	ER **318** 50pf. black and carmine	9·50	

(c) Thin transparent paper. Imperf×perf 12½

ER993	ER **319** 50pf. carmine (3.68)	2·75	

*(d) As T ER **319**, but with a solid frame. Thin transparent paper Imperf×perf 10*

ER994	50pf. carmine (7.83)	2·75	

The right-hand label of Nos. ER993/ER994 are inscr 'Auf Einlieferungsschein Kleben!' (=stick onto the delivery coupon).

Unused prices are for pairs.

See No. ER1089.

E **318** Barn Owl (*Tyto alba*)

E **319** Cycle Wheels

(Des E. Mailick. Photo)

1967 (27 Apr). Protected Birds. T E **318** and similar vert designs. Multicoloured. P 14.

E991	5pf. Type E **318**	35	25
E992	10pf. Common Crane (*Grus grus*)	35	25
E993	20pf. Peregrine Falcon (*Falco peregrinus*)	35	25
E994	25pf. Bullfinches (*Pyrrhula pyrrhula*)	35	25
E995	30pf. Common Kingfisher (*Alcedo atthis*)	6·75	3·50
E996	40pf. Common Roller (*Coracias garrulus*)	55	25
E991/E996	*Set of* 6	7·75	4·25

(Des A. Wagner and M. Baumann. Litho)

1967 (10 May). 20th Warsaw-Berlin-Prague Cycle Race. T E **319** and similar horiz design. Wmk E **100**. P 13×12½.

E997	10pf. violet-black and orange-yellow	35	25
E998	25pf. carmine and light greenish blue	80	65

Designs:—10pf. T E **319**; 25pf. Racing cyclists.

E **320** Tom Cat

E **321** Girl with Grapes (Gerard Dou)

(Des G. Schütz, from children's drawings. Litho)

1967 (1 June). International Children's Day. T E **320** and similar horiz designs. Multicoloured. P 13×12½.

E999	5pf. Type E **320**	35	25
E1000	10pf. Snow White	35	25
E1001	15pf. Fire Brigade	35	25
E1002	20pf. Cockerel	35	25
E1003	25pf. Vase of Flowers	35	25
E1004	30pf. Children Playing with Ball	1·80	1·30
E999/E1004	*Set of* 6	3·25	2·30

(Des F. Deutschendorf. Photo)

1967 (7 June). Paintings Missing from German National Galleries (after World War II). T E **321** and similar designs. P 14.

E1005	5pf. blue and pale blue	35	25
E1006	10pf. deep orange-brown and pale orange-brown	35	25
E1007	20pf. bright green and pale yellow-green	35	25
E1008	25pf. reddish purple and pale purple	35	25
E1009	40pf. olive-green and pale green	35	25
E1010	50pf. sepia and pale brown	2·50	1·70
E1005/E1010	*Set of* 6	3·75	2·75

Designs: Horiz—5pf. *Three Horsemen* (after Rubens); 20pf. *Spring Idyll* (after H. Thoma). Vert—10pf. T E **321**; 25pf. *Portrait of W. Schroeder-Devrient* (after K. Begas); 40pf. *Young Girl in Straw Hat* (after S. Bray); 50pf. *The Four Evangelists* (after Jordaens).

E **322** Exhibition Emblem

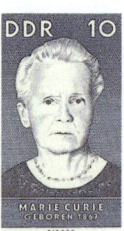

E **323** Marie Curie (Birth Centenary)

E **324** Jack of Diamonds

(Des A. Bengs. Litho)

1967 (14 June). 15th Agricultural Exhibition, Markkleeberg. P 12½×13.

E1011	E **322** 20pf. red, deep bluish green and yellow	55	40

(Des M. Bitzer. Recess)

1967 (6 July–27 Sept). Birth Anniversaries. T E **323** and similar vert portraits. P 14.

E1012	5pf. red-brown (27.9)	40	25
E1013	10pf. deep blue	40	25
E1014	20pf. claret	40	25
E1015	25pf. sepia (27.9)	40	25
E1016	40pf. blackish green (27.9)	1·40	90
E1012/E1016	*Set of* 5	2·75	1·70

Designs:—5pf. G. Herwegh (poet–150th); 10pf. T E **323**; 20pf. Käthe Kollwitz (artist–centenary); 25pf. J. J. Winckelmann (archaeologist–250th); 40pf. T. Storm (poet–150th).

(Des K.-H. Bobbe. Photo)

1967 (18 July). German Playing-Cards. T E **324** and similar vert designs. Multicoloured. P 14×13½.

E1017	5pf. Type E **324**	35	25
E1018	10pf. Jack of Hearts	35	25
E1019	20pf. Jack of Spades	35	25
E1020	25pf. Jack of Clubs	8·75	5·00
E1017/E1020	*Set of* 4	8·75	5·25

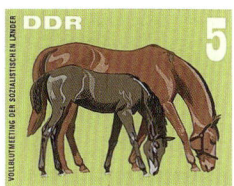

GERMANY / German Democratic Republic (East Germany)

E 325 Mare and Filly

E 326 Kitchen Equipment

(Des K. Hennig and G. Bläser. Litho)

1967 (15 Aug). Thoroughbred-Horses Meeting, Berlin. T E **325** and similar designs. Multicoloured. P 13½.
E1021	5pf. Type E **325**	40	25
E1022	10pf. Stallion	40	25
E1023	20pf. Horse-racing	40	25
E1024	50pf. Two fillies (*vert*)	5·50	3·25
E1021/E1024	Set of 4	6·00	3·50

(Des A. Bengs. Photo)

1967 (30 Aug). Leipzig Autumn Fair. T E **326** and similar horiz design. Multicoloured. P 14.
E1025	10pf. Type E **326**	70	25
E1026	15pf. Fur coat and Interpelz brandmark	1·50	65

E 327 Max Reichpietsch and *Friedrich der Grosse* (battleship), 1914–18

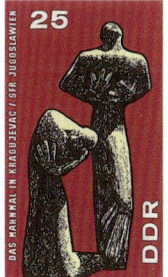

E 328 Kragujevac Memorial

(Des H. Schneider. Litho)

1967 (5 Sept). 50th Anniv of Revolutionary Sailors' Movement T E **327** and similar horiz designs. P 13½×13.
E1027	10pf. multicoloured	35	25
E1028	15pf. multicoloured	2·00	90
E1029	20pf. multicoloured	70	25
E1027/E1029	Set of 3	2·75	1·30

Designs:—10pf. T E **327**; 15pf. Albin Köbis and *Prinzregent Luitpold* (battleship), 1914–18; 20pf. Sailors' demonstration and *Seydlitz* (battle cruiser), 1914–18.

(Des P. Weiss. Litho)

1967 (20 Sept). Victims of Kragujevac (Yugoslavia) Massacre. P 13×13½.
E1030	E **328**	25pf. black, greenish yellow and brown-lake	1·20	50

E 329 Worker and Dam (Electrification)

E 330 Martin Luther (from engraving by Lucas Cranach the Elder)

(Des M. Gottschall, J. Riess and H. Detlefesen. Photo)

1967 (6 Oct). 50th Anniv of October Revolution. T E **329** and similar horiz designs. P 14.
E1031	5pf. black, red-orange and carmine	35	25
E1032	10pf. black, carmine and bistre	35	25
E1033	15pf. black, carmine and light olive-grey	35	25
E1034	20pf. black, carmine and red-orange	55	25
E1035	40pf. black, carmine and red-orange	4·00	3·25
E1031/E1035	Set of 5	5·00	3·75
MSE1036	127×83 mm. Nos. E1034/E1035. Imperf (sold for 85pf.)	2·20	5·75

Designs:—5pf. Worker and newspaper headline 'Hands off Soviet Russia!'; 10pf. T E **329**; 15pf. Treptow Memorial (Victory over Fascism); 20pf. German and Soviet soldiers (Friendship); 40pf. Lenin and *Aurora* (Russian cruiser). Each with hammer and sickle.

(Des and eng G. Stauf. Recess and photo)

1967 (17 Oct). 450th Anniv of Reformation. T E **330** and similar designs. P 14.
E1037	20pf. black and mauve	40	25
E1038	25pf. black and light blue	40	25
E1039	40pf. black and light bistre	4·75	1·30
E1037/E1039	Set of 3	5·00	1·60

Designs: Horiz—25pf. Luther's house, Wittenberg. Vert—20pf. T E **330**; 40pf. Castle church, Wittenberg.

> **IMPERFORATES AND MISSING COLOURS.** Many issues between Nos. E1040/E1042 and Nos. E1760/E1764 exist imperforate or additionally with one or more colours omitted. These come from progressive proofs which were never available for postal purposes.

E 331 Young Workers

E 332 Goethe's House, Weimar

(Des J. Riess. Recess and litho)

1967 (15 Nov). Tenth Masters of Tomorrow Fair, Leipzig. T E **331** and similar designs. P 14.
E1040	20pf. black, gold and turquoise-blue	80	65
	a. Horiz strip of 3. Nos. E1040/E1042	5·00	
E1041	20pf. black, gold and turquoise-blue	80	65
E1042	25pf. multicoloured	80	65
E1040/E1042	Set of 3	2·20	1·80

Designs:—E1040, T E **331**. As T E **331**—No. E1041, Young man and woman. 51×29 mm—E1042, Presentation of awards.

Nos. E1040/E1042 were issued together in horizontal *se-tenant* strips of three within the sheet.

(Des D. Dorfstecher and K.-H. Bobbe. Recess and litho)

1967 (27 Nov). Cultural Places. T E **332** and similar horiz design. P 13×12½.
E1043	20pf. black, brown and light olive-grey	40	25
E1044	25pf. olive, brown and light yellow-olive	2·50	85

Designs:—20pf. T E **332**; 25pf. Schiller's House, Weimar.

E 333 Queen and Courtiers

(Des G. Bläser. Litho)

1967 (27 Nov). Fairy Tales. *King Thrushbeard*. T E **333** and similar horiz designs showing different scenes. P 13½×13.
E1045	5pf. multicoloured	40	40
	a. Sheetlet of 6. Nos. E1045/E1050	7·00	
E1046	10pf. multicoloured	40	40
E1047	15pf. multicoloured	1·40	1·60
E1048	20pf. multicoloured	1·40	1·60
E1049	25pf. multicoloured	40	40
E1050	30pf. multicoloured	40	40
E1045/E1050	Set of 6	4·00	4·25

Nos. E1045/E1050 were issued together in *se-tenant* sheetlets of six stamps.

E 334 Peasants and Modern Farm Buildings

(Des J. Riess. Litho)

1967 (6 Dec). 15th Anniv of Agricultural Co-operatives. P 13×12½.
E1052	E **334**	10pf. sepia, blue-green and yellow-olive	55	25

271

GERMANY / German Democratic Republic (East Germany)

E 335 Nutcrackers

E 336 Ice Skating

(Des D. Dorfstecher. Photo)

1967 (6 Dec). Popular Art of the Erzgebirge. T E **335** and similar vert design. P 13½×14.
| E1053 | 10pf. multicoloured | 1·10 | 65 |
| E1054 | 20pf. multicoloured | 35 | 25 |

Designs:—10pf. T E **335**; 20pf. Angel and miner with candles (carved figures).

(Des D. Dortstecher and R. Platzer. Litho)

1968 (17 Jan). Winter Olympic Games, Grenoble. T E **336** and similar vert designs. P 13½×13.
E1055	5pf. blue, red and light blue	35	25
E1056	10pf. +5pf. ultramarine, red and light turquoise-blue	35	25
E1057	15pf. ultramarine, red, yellow and light ultramarine	35	25
E1058	20pf. ultramarine, red and light greenish blue	35	25
E1059	25pf. greenish blue, black, red and light blue	35	25
E1060	30pf. ultramarine, red and light greenish blue	5·50	1·80
E1055/E1060	Set of 6	6·50	2·75

Designs:—5pf. T E **336**; 10pf. Luge; 15pf. Slalom; 20pf. Ice hockey; 25pf. Figure skating (pairs); 30pf. Cross-country skiing.

E 337 Actinometer

E 338 Venus 4

(Des J. Riess and M. Gottschall. Litho)

1968 (24 Jan). 75th Anniv of Potsdam Meteorological Observatory, and World Meteorological Day (23rd March) T E **337** and similar designs. P 13½×13.
E1061	10pf. black, orange-red and bright purple	70	50
	a. Horiz strip of 3. Nos. E1061/E1063	4·75	
E1062	20pf. black, deep blue, light blue and red	70	50
E1063	25pf. black, greenish yellow and yellow-olive	70	50
E1061/E1063	Set of 3	1·90	1·40

Designs:—10pf. T E **337**. 50×28 mm—20pf. Satellite picture of clouds. As T E **337**—25pf. Cornfield by day and night.

Nos. E1061/E1063 were issued together in horizontal se-tenant strips of three within the sheet.

(Des M. Gottschall. Photo)

1968 (24 Jan). Soviet Space Achievements. T E **338** and similar horiz design. Multicoloured. P 14.
| E1064 | 20pf. Type E **338** | 35 | 25 |
| E1065 | 25pf. Cosmos 186 and 188 coupled | 1·80 | 90 |

E 339 Illegal Struggle
(man, wife and child)

(Des A. Bengs, after W. Womacka. Photo)

1968 (21 Feb). Stained Glass Windows, Sachsenhausen National Memorial Museum. T E **339** and similar vert designs. Multicoloured. P 14×13½.
E1066	10pf. Type E **339**	35	25
E1067	20pf. Liberation	35	25
E1068	25pf. Partisans' Struggle	70	40
E1066/E1068	Set of 3	1·30	80

E 340 Type DE 1 Diesel-Electric Locomotive
(built for Brazil)

(Des D. Dorfstecher. Photo)

1968 (29 Feb). Leipzig Spring Fair. T E **340** and similar horiz design. Multicoloured. P 14.
| E1069 | 10pf. Type E **340** | 55 | 30 |
| E1070 | 15pf. Deep sea trawler | 1·50 | 65 |

E 341 Maksim Gorky

E 342 Ring-necked Pheasants
(*Phasianus colchicus*)

(Des G. Preuss. Eng G. Faulwasser (20pf.), M. Bitzer (25pf.). Recess)

1968 (14 Mar). Birth Centenary of Maksim Gorky (writer). T E **341** and similar vert design. P 14.
| E1071 | 20pf. dull purple and claret | 55 | 30 |
| E1072 | 25pf. dull purple and claret | 1·10 | 55 |

Designs:—20pf. T E **341**; 25pf. Fulmar (from Song of the Stormy Petrel—poem).

(Des I. Friebel. Photo)

1968 (14 Mar). Provincial Costumes (3rd series). Vert designs as T E **261**. Multicoloured. P 14.
E1073	10pf. Hoyerswerda (female)	35	25
E1074	20pf. Schleife (female)	35	25
E1075	40pf. Crostwitz (female)	40	25
E1076	50pf. Spreewald (female)	4·50	1·60
E1073/E1076	Set of 4	5·00	2·10

(Des H. Naumann. Litho)

1968 (26 Mar). Small Game. T E **342** and similar horiz designs. Multicoloured. P 13½×13.
E1077	10pf. Type E **342**	35	35
E1078	15pf. Grey Partridges (*Perdix perdix*)	35	35
E1079	20pf. Mallards (*Anas platyrhynchos*)	35	35
E1080	25pf. Greylag Geese (*Anser anser*)	35	35
E1081	30pf. Wood Pigeons (*Columba palumbus*)	35	35
E1082	40pf. Brown Hares (*Lepus europaeus*)	5·00	8·75
E1077/E1082	Set of 6	6·00	9·50

E 343 Karl Marx

E 344 Fritz Heckert
(after E. Hering)

(Des P. Weiss Photo)

1968 (25 Apr). 150th Birth Anniv of Karl Marx. T E **343** and similar vert designs. P 14.
E1083	10pf. black and yellow-green	40	40
	a. Horiz strip of 3. Nos. E1083/E1085	2·00	
E1084	20pf. black, olive-yellow and crimson	40	40
E1085	25pf. black, olive-yellow and crimson	40	40
E1083/E1085	Set of 3	1·10	1·10

MS E1086 126×86 mm. Nos. E1083/E1085. Imperf........... 2·30 6·75
 Designs:—10pf. Title-page of *Communist Manifesto*; 20pf. T E **343**;
 25pf. Title-page of *Das Kapital*.
 Nos. E1083/E1085 were issued together in horizontal *se-tenant*
strips of three within the sheet.

(Des J. Riess. Photo)

1968 (25 Apr). Seventh Confederation of Free German Trade Unions
 Congress. T E **344** and similar vert design. Multicoloured. P 14.
E1087   10pf. Type E **344** 35   35
E1088   20pf. Young workers and new tenements 40   40

ER **345**

1968 (16 May). REGISTRATION. For Parcel Post. Typo. Thin transparent
 paper. Imperf×perf 12½.
ER1089 ER **345**   50pf. black................................ 11·00
 See notes after No. E990.

E **345** Hammer and Anvil (The right to work)
E **346** Vietnamese Mother and Child  

(Des H. Detlefsen. Litho)

1968 (8 May). Human Rights Year. T E **345** and similar vert designs.
 P 13½×13.
E1089   5pf. light magenta and brown-purple........... 35   25
E1090   10pf. light bistre and olive-brown 35   25
E1091   25pf. light blue and deep turquoise-blue ...... 1·40 70
E1089/E1091 Set of 3 .... 1·90 1·10
 Designs:—5pf. T E **345**; 10pf. Tree and Globe (The right to live);
25pf. Dove and Sun (The right to peace).

(Des G. Schütz. Litho)

1968 (8 May). Aid for Vietnam. P 13½×13.
E1092 E **346**   10pf. +5pf. multicoloured 40   25

E **347** Angling (World Championships, Güstrow)
E **348** Brandenburg Gate and Torch 

(Des J. Riess. Photo)

1968 (6 June). Sporting Events. T E **347** and similar horiz designs.
 P 14.
E1093   20pf. slate-blue, olive-green and carmine....... 55   40
E1094   20pf. deep blue, turquoise-blue and olive
            green... 55   45
E1095   20pf. maroon, brown-red and greenish blue . 1·00   90
E1093/E1095 Set of 3 .... 1·90 1·60
 Designs:—No. E1093, T E **347**; No. E1094, Sculling (European
Women's Rowing Championships, Berlin); No. E1095, High jumping
(Second European Youth Athletic Competitions).

(Des R. Patzer. Litho)

1968 (20 June). German Youth Sports Days. T E **348** and similar vert
 design. Multicoloured. P 13½×13.
E1096   10pf. Type E **348** 35   25
E1097   25pf. Stadium plan and torch....................... 1·50 95

E **349** Festival Emblem
E **350** Walter Ulbricht 

(Des K. Hennig. Litho)

1968 (20 June). Peace Festival, Sofia. P 13½×13.
E1098 E **349**   20pf. +5pf. multicoloured..................... 55   25
E1099   25pf. multicoloured............................. 1·30   70

(Des D. Dorfstecher. Photo)

1968 (25 June). Principal East German Buildings (2nd series). Designs
 as T E **312**. Multicoloured. P 14.
E1100   10pf. Town Hall, Wernigerode....................... 35   35
E1101   20pf. Moritzburg Castle, Dresden 35   35
E1102   25pf. Town Hall, Greifswald.......................... 35   35
E1103   30pf. New Palace, Potsdam......................... 1·40 1·40
E1100/E1103 Set of 4 .... 2·20 2·20
 Design sizes: Vert (24×29 *mm*)—10pf., 25pf. Horiz (51½×29½ *mm*)—
20pf., 30pf.

(Des J. Riess. Recess and photo)

1968 (27 June). 75th Birthday of Walter Ulbricht (Chairman of Council
 of State). P 14.
E1104 E **350**   20pf. black, deep carmine and orange   1·00   25

E **351** Ancient Rostock
E **352** Dr. K. Landsteiner (physician and pathologist; birth centenary) 

(Des D. Dorfstecher. Photo)

1968 (4 July). 750th Anniv of Rostock. T E **351** and similar horiz
 design. Multicoloured. P 14.
E1105   20pf. Type E **351** 35   25
E1106   25pf. Rostock, 1968 85   70

(Des G. Stauf. Eng G. Faulwasser (10pf., 20pf., 25pf.),
M. Bitzer(others). Recess)

1968 (17 July). Celebrities' Anniversaries (1st series). T E **352** and
 similar horiz designs. P 14.
E1107   10pf. olive-grey 35   25
E1108   15pf. black.. 35   25
E1109   20pf. brown... 35   25
E1110   25pf. slate-blue.. 35   25
E1111   40pf. deep claret.. 1·30   80
E1107/E1111 Set of 5 .... 2·40 1·60
 Designs:—10pf. T E **352**; 15pf. Dr. E. Lasker (chess master, birth
centenary); 20pf. Hans Eisler (composer, 70th birth anniv); 25pf. Ignaz
Semmelweis (physician, 150th birth anniv); 40pf. Max von Pettenkofer
(hygienist, 150th birth anniv).
 See also Nos. E1161/E1164, E1256/E1261 and MS E1352.

E **353** Zlin Z-226 Trener 6 DM-WKM looping
E **354** At the Seaside (Womacka) 

(Des L. Grünewald. Litho)

1968 (13 Aug). Aerobatics World Championships, Magdeburg. T E **353**
 and similar vert design. Multicoloured. P 12½×13.
E1112   10pf. Type E **353** 35   25
E1113   25pf. Stunt flying.. 1·10   70

273

GERMANY / German Democratic Republic (East Germany)

(Des F. Deutschendorf. Photo)

1968 (20 Aug). Dresden Gallery Paintings (2nd series). T E **354** and similar multicoloured designs. P 14.

E1114	10pf. Type E **354**		35	25
E1115	15pf. *Peasants Mowing Mountain Meadow* (Egger-Lenz)		35	25
E1116	20pf. *Portrait of a Farmer's Wife* (Leibl)		35	25
E1117	40pf. *Portrait of my Daughter* (Venturelli)		70	25
E1118	50pf. *High-school Girl* (Michaelis)		70	25
E1119	70pf. *Girl with Guitar* (Castelli)		4·25	1·80
E1114/E1119	Set of 6		6·00	2·75

The 20pf. to 70pf. values are vert designs.

E **355** Model Trains
E **356** Spremberg Dam

(Des D. Dorfstecher. Photo)

1968 (29 Aug). Leipzig Autumn Fair. P 14.

E1120	E **355**	10pf. multicoloured	55	40

(Des P. Weiss. Litho)

1968 (11 Sept). East German Post-War Dams. T E **356** and similar multicoloured designs. P 13×12½ (horiz) or 12½×13 (vert).

E1121	5pf. Type E **356**	35	35
E1122	10pf. Pöhl Dam (*vert*)	35	35
E1123	15pf. Ohra Valley Dam (*vert*)	70	70
E1124	20pf. Rappbode Dam	40	40
E1121/E1124	Set of 4	1·60	1·60

E **357** Sprinting

(Des K. Hennig. Photo)

1968 (18 Sept). Olympic Games, Mexico. T E **357** and similar multicoloured designs. P 14.

E1125	5pf. Type E **357**	35	30
E1126	10pf. +5pf. Pole vaulting (*vert*)	35	30
E1127	20pf. +10pf. Football (*vert*)	35	30
E1128	25pf. Gymnastics (*vert*)	35	30
E1129	40pf. Water-polo (*vert*)	45	30
E1130	70pf. Sculling	3·00	2·20
E1125/E1130	Set of 6	4·25	3·25

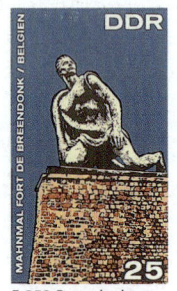

E **358** Breendonk Memorial, Belgium
E **359** *Cicindela campestris*

(Des P. Weiss. Litho)

1968 (10 Oct). Breendonk War Victims Commemoration. P 13×13½.

E1131	E **358**	25pf. multicoloured	75	30

(Des H. Priess. Litho)

1968 (16 Oct). Beetles. T E **359** and similar vert designs. Multicoloured. P 13½×13.

E1132	10pf. Type E **359**	35	30
E1133	15pf. *Cychrus caraboides*	35	30
E1134	20pf. *Adalia bipunctata*	35	30
E1135	25pf. *Carabus arvensis* (*Carabus arcensis*)	3·75	3·00
E1136	30pf. *Hister bipustulatus*	45	30
E1137	40pf. *Clerus mutillarius* (*Pseudoclerops mutillarius*)	45	30
E1132/E1137	Set of 6	5·25	4·00

E **360** Lenin and Letter to Spartacus Group

(Des M. Gottschall. Litho)

1968 (29 Oct). 50th Anniv of German November Revolution. T E **360** and similar horiz designs. P 13×12½.

E1138	10pf. black, vermilion and olive-yellow	35	35
E1139	20pf. black, vermilion and olive-yellow	35	35
E1140	25pf. black, vermilion and olive-yellow	85	85
E1138/E1140	Set of 3	1·40	1·40

Designs:—10pf. T E **360**; 20pf. Revolutionaries and title of Spartacus newspaper *Die Rote Fahne*; 25pf. Karl Liebknecht and Rosa Luxemburg.

E **361** *Lailio-cattleya alba. rubra* ('Maggie Raphaela')

(Des M. Gottschall. Photo)

1968 (12 Nov). Orchids. Designs as T E **361**. Multicoloured. P 13.

E1141	5pf. Type E **361**	35	30
E1142	10pf. *Paphiopedilum albertianum*	35	30
E1143	15pf. *Cattleya fabia*	35	30
E1144	20pf. *Cattleya aclandiae*	35	30
E1145	40pf. *Sobralia macrantha*	45	30
E1146	50pf. *Dendrobium alpha*	3·25	2·20
E1141/E1146	Set of 6	4·50	3·25

E **362** Trying on the Boots
E **363** Young Pioneers

(Des G. Bläser. Litho)

1968 (27 Nov). Fairy Tales. *Puss in Boots*. Horiz designs as T E **362**, showing different scenes. P 13½×13.

E1147	5pf. multicoloured	35	35
	a. Sheetlet of 6. Nos. E1147/E1152	5·75	
E1148	10pf. multicoloured	35	35
E1149	15pf. multicoloured	1·70	1·70
E1150	20pf. multicoloured	1·70	1·70
E1151	25pf. multicoloured	35	35
E1152	30pf. multicoloured	35	35
E1147/E1152	Set of 6	4·25	4·25

Nos. E1147/E1152 were issued together in *se-tenant* sheetlets of six stamps.

(Des I. Uhlich. Litho)

1968 (3 Dec). 20th Anniv of Ernst Thälmann's *Young Pioneers*. T E **363** and similar horiz design. Multicoloured. P 13×13½.

E1153	10pf. Type E **363**	35	30
E1154	15pf. Young pioneers (*different*)	1·20	55

(Des D. Dorfstecher. Photo)

1969 (15 Jan). Principal East German Buildings (3rd series). Multicoloured designs as T E **312**. P 14.

E1155	5pf. Town Hall, Tangermünde	35	30
E1156	10pf. State Opera House, Berlin	35	30
E1157	20pf. Rampart Pavilion, Dresden Castle	35	30
E1158	25pf. Patrician's House, Luckau	1·50	1·00
E1159	30pf. Dornburg Castle	35	30
E1160	40pf. Zum Stockfisch Inn, Erfurt	45	30
E1155/E1160	Set of 6	3·00	2·30

The 5, 20, 25 and 40pf. are vert designs.

GERMANY / German Democratic Republic (East Germany)

(Des G. Stauf. Eng G. Faulwasser (10pf., 20pf.). M. Bitzer (others). Recess)

1969 (5 Feb). Celebrities' Anniversaries (2nd series). Horiz designs as T E **352**. P 14.

E1161	10pf. olive	35	30
E1162	20pf. chocolate	35	30
E1163	25pf. deep blue	1·50	70
E1164	40pf. brown	35	30
E1161/E1164	Set of 4	2·30	1·40

Designs:—10pf. M. A. Nexö (Danish poet—birth centenary); 20pf. O. Nagel (painter—75th birth anniv); 25pf. A. von Humboldt (naturalist–bicentenary of birth); 40pf. T. Fontane (writer–150th birth anniv).

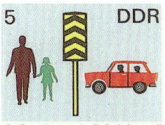

E **364** Pedestrian Crossing

E **365** E-512 Combine-harvester

(Des W. Heinrich. Litho)

1969 (18 Feb). Road Safety. T E **364** and similar horiz designs. Multicoloured. P 13×13½.

E1165	5pf. Type E **364**	35	30
E1166	10pf. Traffic lights	35	30
E1167	20pf. Class 103 electric locomotive and railway crossing sign	35	30
E1168	25pf. Motor-vehicle overtaking	85	70
E1165/E1168	Set of 4	1·70	1·40

(Des D. Dorfstecher. Photo)

1969 (26 Feb). Leipzig Spring Fair. T E **365** and similar horiz design. Multicoloured. P 14.

E1169	10pf. Type E **365**	35	30
E1170	15pf. Planeta-Variant lithograph printing-press	45	30

E **366** Jorinde and Joringel

E **367** Spring Snowflake (*Leucojum vernum*)

(Des G Bläser. Litho)

1969 (18 Mar). Fairy Tales. *Jorinde and Joringel*. Horiz designs as T E **366**, showing different scenes. P 13½×13.

E1171	5pf. multicoloured	35	40
	a. Sheetlet of 6. Nos. E1171/E1176	3·25	
E1172	10pf. multicoloured	35	40
E1173	15pf. multicoloured	85	1·00
E1174	20pf. multicoloured	85	1·00
E1175	25pf. multicoloured	35	40
E1176	30pf. multicoloured	35	40
E1171/E1176	Set of 6	2·75	3·25

Nos. E1171/E1176 were issued together in *se-tenant* sheetlets of six stamps.

(Des F. Deutschendorf. Photo)

1969 (15 Apr). Protected Plants (2nd series). T E **367** and similar vert designs. Multicoloured. P 14.

E1177	5pf. Type E **367**	35	30
E1178	10pf. Yellow Pheasant's-eye (*Adonis vernalis*)	35	30
E1179	15pf. Globe Flower (*Trollius europaeus*)	35	30
E1180	20pf. Martagon Lily (*Lilium martagon*)	35	30
E1181	25pf. Sea Holly (*Eryngium maritimum*)	4·75	2·75
E1182	30pf. *Dactylorchis latifolia*	60	30
E1177/E1182	Set of 6	6·00	3·75

E **368** Plantation of Young Conifers

E **369** Symbols of the Societies

(Des H. Naumann. Litho)

1969 (23 Apr). Forest Fire Prevention. T E **368** and similar vert designs. Multicoloured. P 12½×13.

E1183	5pf. Type **368**	45	30
E1184	10pf. Lumber, and resin extraction	45	30
E1185	20pf. Forest stream	45	30
E1186	25pf. Woodland camp	3·25	1·70
E1183/E1186	Set of 4	4·25	2·30

(Des C. Wolfgramm (10pf.), A. Bengs (15pf.). Litho)

1969 (23 Apr). 50th Anniv of League of Red Cross Societies. T E **369** and similar vert design. Multicoloured. P 12½×13.

E1187	10pf. Type E **369**	45	30
E1188	15pf. Similar design with symbols in oblong	2·50	85

E **370** Erythrite (Schneeberg)

E **371** Women and Symbols

(Des L. Grünewald. Photo)

1969 (21 May). East German minerals. T E **370** and similar vert designs. Multicoloured. P 14.

E1189	5pf. Type **370**	35	30
E1190	10pf. Florite (Halsbrücke)	35	30
E1191	15pf. Galena (Neudorf)	35	30
E1192	20pf. Smoky Quartz (Lichtenburg)	35	30
E1193	25pf. Calcite (Niederrabenstein)	1·50	1·00
E1194	50pf. Silver (Freiberg)	45	30
E1189/E1194	Set of 6	3·00	2·30

(Des J. Riess. Recess)

1969 (28 May). Second DDR Women's Congress. T E **371** and similar horiz design. P 14.

E1195	20pf. claret and blue	35	30
E1196	25pf. blue and brown-red	1·60	55

Designs:—20pf. T E **371**; 25pf. Women and symbols.
The symbols on both designs represent agriculture, industry and science.

1969 (4 June). As Nos. E586/E587, but with face values expressed in M (Mark).

E1197	1m. bronze-green	75	2·10
E1198	2m. brown	85	2·40

E **372** Badge of DDR Philatelists' Association

E **373** Armed Volunteers

(Des K. Hennig. Photo)

1969 (4 June). DDR 20th Anniversary Stamp Exhibition, Magdeburg (First issue). P 14.

E1199	E **372**	10pf. gold, bright blue and red	60	30

See also Nos. E1233/E1234.

275

GERMANY / German Democratic Republic (East Germany)

(Des G. Schütz. Litho)
1969 (4 June). Aid for Vietnam. P 13.
E1200 E **373** 10pf. +5pf. multicoloured 60 30

E **374** Development of Youth
E **375** Inaugural Ceremony 

(Des J. Riess. Litho)
1969 (4 June). International Peace Meeting, East Berlin. T E **374** and similar multicoloured designs. P 13.
E1201	10pf. Type E **374**	1·00	1·40
	a. Horiz strip of 3. Nos. E1201/E1203	4·50	
E1202	20pf. +5pf. Berlin landmarks (50×28 *mm*)	1·00	1·40
E1203	25pf. Workers of the World	1·00	1·40
E1201/E1203	Set of 3	2·75	3·75

Nos. E1201/E1203 were issued together in horizontal *se-tenant* strips of three within the sheet.

(Des J. Riess. Recess and photo)
1969 (18 June). Fifth Gymnastics and Athletic Meeting, Leipzig. T E **375** and similar horiz designs. Multicoloured. P 14.
E1204	5pf. Type E **375**	35	30
E1205	10pf. +5pf. Gymnastics	35	30
E1206	15pf. Athletes' parade	35	30
E1207	20pf. +5pf. Sport Art Exhibition	35	30
E1208	25pf. Athletic events	3·00	85
E1209	30pf. Presentation of colours	35	30
E1204/E1209	Set of 6	4·25	2·10

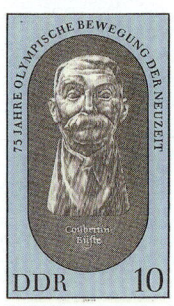

E **376** Pierre de Coubertin (from bust by W. Förster)
E **377** Knight 

(Des G. Stauf. Recess and photo)
1969 (20 June). 75th Anniversary of Coubertin's Revival of Olympic Games Movement. T E **376** and similar vert design. P 14×13½.
E1210	10pf. sepia, black and light blue	45	30
E1211	25pf. sepia, black and light red	1·30	1·30

Designs:—10pf. T E **376**; 25pf. Coubertin monument, Olympia.

(Des G. Stauf. Photo)
1969 (29 July). World Sports Championships. T E **377** and similar vert designs. P 14.
E1212	20pf. gold, vermilion and maroon	45	30
E1213	20pf. gold, pale ochre, vermilion and green	45	30
E1214	20pf. gold, red-brown, black, pale yellow-olive and ultramarine	45	30
E1212/E1214	Set of 3	1·20	80

Designs and events:—No. E1212, T E **377** (16th World Students' Team Chess Championship, Dresden); No. E1213, Cycle wheel (World Covered Court Championships, Erfurt); No. E1214, Ball and net (Second World Volleyball Cup).

E **378** Fair Display Samples
E **379** Rostock 

(Des D. Dorfstecher. Litho)
1969 (27 Aug). Leipzig Autumn Fair. P 12½×13.
E1215 E **378** 10pf. multicoloured 45 40

(Des G. Voigt and A. Lipsch. Photo)
1969 (23 Sept). 20th Anniversary of German Democratic Republic (1st issue). East German Towns. T E **379** and similar multicoloured designs, all horiz except for **MS**E1228. P 14.
E1216	10pf. Type E **379**	35	30
E1217	10pf. Neubrandenburg	35	30
E1218	10pf. Potsdam	35	30
E1219	10pf. Eisenhüttenstadt	35	30
E1220	10pf. Hoyerswerda	35	30
E1221	10pf. Magdeburg	35	30
E1222	10pf. Halle-Neustadt	35	30
E1223	10pf. Suhl	35	30
E1224	10pf. Dresden	35	30
E1225	10pf. Leipzig	35	30
E1226	10pf. Karl-Marx-Stadt	35	30
E1227	10pf. East Berlin	35	30
E1216/E1227	Set of 12	3·75	3·25
MSE1228	88×110 mm. 1m. East Berlin and DDR emblem (30×52 *mm*)	3·25	8·00

E **380** Flags and Rejoicing Crowd (½–size illustration)
E **381** TV Tower, East Berlin 

(Des G. Stauf, Litho)
1969 (6 Oct). 20th Anniversary of German Democratic Republic. (2nd issue). Sheet 110×154 mm. P 13×12½.
MSE1229 E **380** 1m. multicoloured .... 3·75 7·00

(Des H. Detlefsen. Photo)
1969 (6 Oct). 20th Anniversary of German Democratic Republic (3rd issue). Completion of East Berlin TV Tower. T E **381** and similar vert designs. Multicoloured. P 13½×14 or 14 (**MS**E1232).
E1230	10pf. Type E **381**	35	30
E1231	20pf. Globe of Tower on TV screen	45	30
MSE1232	96×115 mm. 1m. TV Tower and receiver	2·50	7·00

The design of No. **MS**E1232 is larger, 21½×60½ mm.

E **382** Von Guericke Memorial, Cathedral and Hotel International, Magdeburg

(Des K. Hennig. Litho)
1969 (28 Oct). DDR 20th Anniversary Stamp Exhibition Magdeburg (2nd issue). T E **382** and similar horiz design. Multicoloured. P 13×12½.
E1233	10pf. Type E **382**	35	30
E1234	40pf. +10pf. Von Guericke's vacuum experiment	1·90	1·10

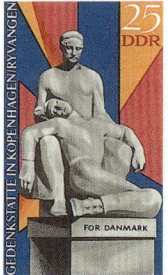

E **383** Ryvangen Memorial
E **384** UFI Emblem

GERMANY / German Democratic Republic (East Germany)

(Des M. Gottschall and J. Riess. Litho)

1969 (28 Oct). War Victims' Memorial, Ryvangen (Copenhagen). P 13.
E1235 E **383**   25pf. multicoloured .... 1·20   30

(Des J. Bertholdt. Litho)

1969 (28 Oct). 36th International Fairs Union (UFI) Congress. Leipzig. P 13.
E1236 E **384**   10pf. multicoloured 35   30
E1237   15pf. multicoloured .... 3·00   55

E **385** ILO Emblem

E **386** University Seal and Building

(Des D. Dorfstecher. Photo)

1969 (12 Nov). 50th Anniversary of International Labour Organisation. P 14.
E1238 E **385**   20pf. silver and blue-green 35   30
E1239   25pf. silver and magenta .... 3·00   55

(Des J. Bertholdt. Litho)

1969 (12 Nov). 550th Anniversary of Rostock University. T E **386** and similar vert design. Multicoloured. P 12½×13.
E1240 E **386**   10pf. Type E **386** 45   30
E1241   15pf. Steam-turbine rotor and curve
                         (University emblem) .... 2·20 40

E **387** Horseman Pastry-mould

E **388** Antonov An-24B

(Des D. Dorfstecher. Litho)

1969 (25 Nov). Lausitz Folk Art. Vert designs as T E **387**. P 13.
E1242   10pf. red-brown, black and cinnamon ...... 1·70 1·70
               a. Horiz pair. Nos. E1242 and E1244 ...... 6·75
E1243   20pf. +5pf. multicoloured 60   55
E1244   50pf. multicoloured .... 3·00 2·75
E1242/E1244 Set of 3 .... 4·75 4·50
Designs:—10pf. T E **387**; 20pf. Plate; 50pf. Pastry in form of African couple.
Nos. E1242 and E1244 were issued together in horizontal *se-tenant* pairs within the sheet.

(Des E. and G. Bormann. Litho)

1969 (2 Dec). Interflug Aircraft. T E **388** and similar horiz designs. Multicoloured. P 13×12½.
E1245   20pf. Type E **388** 35   30
E1246   25pf. Ilyushin Il-18 .... 2·00 1·70
E1247   30pf. Tupolev Tu-134 35   30
E1248   50pf. Mil Mi-8 helicopter DM-SPA 45   30
E1245/E1248 Set of 4 .... 2·75 2·30
See also Nos. E1467/E1470.

E **389** Siberian Teacher (Svechnikov)

(Des H. Naumann and F. Deutschendorfer. Photo)

1969 (10 Dec). Dresden Gallery Paintings (3rd series). T E **389** and similar square designs. Multicoloured. P 13.
E1249   5pf. Type E **389** 35   30
E1250   10pf. *Steel-worker* (Serov) 35   30
E1251   20pf. *Still Life* (Aslamasjan) 35   30
E1252   25pf. *A Warm Day* (Romas) .... 1·70 1·70
E1253   40pf. *Springtime Again* (Kabatchek) ... 45   30
E1254   50pf. *Man by the River* (Makovsky) 45   30
E1249/E1254 Set of 6 .... 3·25 3·00

1970 (20 Jan). Coil stamp. Value expressed in M. Type. Wmk E **100**. P 14.
E1255 E **196**   1m. yellow-olive .... 1·50 7·75
No. E1255 only comes from coil rolls of 1,000 with black control numbers on every fifth stamp.

(Des G. Stauf. Eng G. Faulwasser (5, 10, 40pf.), M. Bitzer (others). Recess)

1970 (20 Jan). Celebrities' Anniversaries (3rd series). Horiz designs similar to T E **352**. P 14.
E1256   5pf. deep violet-blue 45   30
E1257   10pf. sepia 45   30
E1258   15pf. ultramarine 45   30
E1259   20pf. purple 60   30
E1260   25pf. greenish blue .... 3·75 1·10
E1261   40pf. crimson 75   30
E1256/E1261 Set of 6 .... 5·75 2·30
Designs:—5pf. E. Barlach (sculptor and playwright–birth centenary); 10pf. J. Gutenberg (printer–500th death anniv (1968)); 15pf. K. Tucholsky (author–80th birth anniv); 20pf. Beethoven (birth bicentenary); 25pf. F. Hölderlin (poet–birth bicentenary); 40pf. G. W. F. Hegel (philosopher–birth bicentenary).
See also No. MSE1352.

E **390** Red Fox

(Des A. Bengs. Photo)

1970 (5 Feb). 525th International Fur Auction, Leipzig. T E **390** and similar horiz designs. Multicoloured. P 13½×14.
E1262   10pf. Rabbit 35   30
E1263   20pf. Type E **390** 35   30
E1264   25pf. European Mink .... 4·75 4·25
E1265   40pf. Common Hamster 60   30
E1262/E1265 Set of 4 .... 5·50 4·75

E **391** Little Brother and Little Sister

E **392** Telephone and Electrical Switchgear

(Des G. Bläser. Litho)

1970 (17 Feb). Fairy Tales. *Little Brother and Little Sister*. Horiz designs as T E **391** showing different scenes. P 13½×13.
E1266   5pf. multicoloured 45   55
               a. Sheetlet of 6. Nos. E1266/E1271 ... 4·75
E1267   10pf. multicoloured 45   55
E1268   15pf. multicoloured .... 1·00 1·10
E1269   20pf. multicoloured .... 1·00 1·10
E1270   25pf. multicoloured 45   55
E1271   30pf. multicoloured 45   55
E1266/E1271 Set of 6 .... 3·50 4·00
Nos. E1266/E1271 were issued together in *se-tenant* sheetlets of six stamps.

(Des M. Gottschall. Litho)

1970 (24 Feb). Leipzig Spring Fair. T E **392** and similar multicoloured design. P 13×12½ (10pf.) or 12½×13 (15pf.).
E1272   10pf. Type E **392** 35   30
E1273   15pf. High-voltage transformer (*vert*) .. 85   40

277

GERMANY / German Democratic Republic (East Germany)

E **393** Horseman's Gravestone (AD 700)

(Des G. Voigt. Photo)

1970 (10 March). Archaeological Discoveries. T E **393** and similar square designs. P 13.

E1274	10pf. pale olive, black and olive-green	45	30
E1275	20pf. black, yellow and scarlet	45	30
E1276	25pf. blue-green, black and yellow	1·20	2·00
E1277	40pf. chestnut, black and chocolate	45	30
E1274/E1277	Set of 4	2·30	2·50

Designs:—10pf. T E **393**; 20pf. Helmet (AD 500); 25pf. Bronze basin (1000 BC); 40pf. Clay drum (2500 BC).

E **394** Lenin and *Iskra* (=the Spark) press

(Des G. Stauf. Eng M. Bitzer (10, 25, 70pf.), G. Faulwasser (20, 40pf.), G. Stauf (1m.). Recess and photo)

1970 (16 Apr). Birth Centenary of Lenin. T E **394** and similar multicoloured designs. P 13½×14 or 14×13½ (1m.).

E1278	10pf. Type E **394**	35	30
E1279	20pf. Lenin and Clara Zetkin	35	30
E1280	25pf. Lenin and book, *State and Revolution*	3·25	2·75
E1281	40pf. Lenin monument, Eisleben	35	30
E1282	70pf. Lenin Square, East Berlin	60	30
E1278/E1282	Set of 5	4·50	3·50
MSE1283	118×84 mm. 1m. Lenin (*vert*)	3·25	10·50

(Des M. Gottschall. Photo)

1970 (28 Apr). Protected Plants (3rd series). Vert designs similar to T E **367**. Multicoloured. P 14.

E1284	10pf. Sea Kale (*Crambe maritima*)	35	30
E1285	20pf. Pasqueflower (*Pulsatilla vulgaris*)	35	30
E1286	25pf. Fringed Gentian (*Gentiana ciliata*)	3·00	3·00
E1287	30pf. Military Orchid (*Orchis militaris*)	35	30
E1288	40pf. Labrador Tea (*Ledum palustre*)	45	30
E1289	70pf. Round-leaved Wintergreen (*Pyrola rotundifolia*)	60	35
E1284/E1289	Set of 6	4·50	4·00

E **395** Capture of the Reichstag, 1945

E **396** Shortwave Aerial

(Des G. Stauf (10pf.), M. Gottschall (20, 25pf.), C. Sauer and G. Stauf (70pf.). Litho)

1970 (5 May). 25th Anniversary of Liberation from Fascism. T E **395** and similar multicoloured designs. P 13.

E1290	10pf. Type E **395**	45	30
E1291	20pf. Newspaper headline, Kremlin and State Building, East Berlin	45	30
E1292	25pf. CMEA Building, Moscow and flags	2·20	1·10
E1290/E1292	Set of 3	2·75	1·50
MSE1293	135×105 mm. 70pf. Buchenwald Monument (*horiz*)	3·00	8·50

(Des M. Gottschall. Litho)

1970 (13 May). 25th Anniversary of German Democratic Republic Broadcasting Service. T E **396** and similar multicoloured design. P 13.

E1294	10pf. Type E **396**	1·00	1·00
	a. Horiz pair. Nos. E1294/E1295	3·75	3·25
E1295	15pf. Radio Station, East Berlin (50×28 *mm*)	1·50	1·40

Nos. E1294/E1295 were issued together in horizontal *se-tenant* pairs within the sheet.

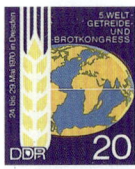

E **397** Globe and Ear of Corn

E **398** Fritz Heckert Medal

(Des J. Bertholdt. Litho)

1970 (19 May). Fifth World Corn and Bread Congress, Dresden. T E **397** and similar vert design Multicoloured. P 13.

E1296	20pf. Type E **397**	1·30	1·30
	a. Horiz strip. Nos. E1296/E1297 plus label	5·00	5·00
E1297	25pf. Palace of Culture and ear of corn	1·30	1·30

Nos. E1296/E1297 were issued as a triptych with an intervening stamp-sized label inscribed in four languages.

(Des A. Bengs. Litho)

1970 (9 June). 25th Anniversaries of German Confederation of Trade Unions and World Trade Union Federation (Federation Syndicale Mondiale). T E **398** and similar horiz design. Multicoloured. P 13×12½.

E1298	20pf. Type E **398**	35	30
E1299	25pf. FSM emblem	1·00	85

E **399** Gods Amon, Shu and Tefnut

(Des J. Bertholdt. Photo)

1970 (23 June). Sudanese Archaeological Excavations by Humboldt University Expedition. T E **399** and similar multicoloured designs showing carvings from Lions' Temple, Musawwarat. P 13½.

E1300	10pf. Type E **399**	35	30
E1301	15pf. King Arnekhamani	35	30
E1302	20pf. Cattle frieze	35	30
E1303	25pf. Prince Arka	1·40	1·10
E1304	30pf. God Arensnuphis (*vert*)	35	30
E1305	40pf. War elephants and prisoners	35	30
E1306	50pf. God Apedemak	35	30
E1300/E1306	Set of 7	3·25	2·50

E **400** Road Patrol

E **401** DKB Emblem

(Des H. Zill. Litho)

1970 (23 June). 25th Anniv of German Peoples' Police. T E **400** and similar horiz designs. P 13×12½.

E1307	5pf. Type E **400**	45	30
E1308	10pf. Policewoman with children	45	30
E1309	15pf. Radio patrol car	45	30
E1310	20pf. Railway policeman and Class SVT18.16 diesel-hydraulic locomotive	45	30
E1311	25pf. River police in patrol boat	4·25	60
E1307/E1311	Set of 5	5·50	1·60

GERMANY / German Democratic Republic (East Germany)

(Des G. Voigt. Photo)

1970 (1 July). 25th Anniv of Deutscher Kulturbund (cultural association). T E **401** and similar vert design. P 14.
E1312	10pf. chocolate, silver and blue	3·25	3·75
	a. Horiz strip. Nos. E1312/E1313 plus label	10·00	12·00
E1313	25pf. chocolate, gold and blue	3·25	3·75

Designs:—10pf. T E **401**; 25pf. Johannes Becher medal.
Nos. E1312/E1313 were issued together *se-tenant* with an intervening inscribed label.

E **402** Arms of DDR and Poland

(Des M. Gottschall. Litho)

1970 (1 July). 20th Anniversary of Görlitz Agreement on the Oder-Neisse Border. P 13×12½.
E1314	E **402**	20pf. multicoloured	60	30

E **403** Pommel-horse

(Des A. Bengs. Photo)

1970 (14 July). Third Children and Young People's Sports Days. T E **403** and similar horiz design. Multicoloured. P 14.
E1315	10pf. Type E **403**	35	30
E1316	20pf. +5pf. Hurdling	75	30

E **404** Boy Pioneer with Neckerchief

(Des H. Detlefsen. Photo)

1970 (28 July). Sixth Pioneers Meeting, Cottbus. T E **404** and similar horiz design. Multicoloured. P 13×12½.
E1317	10pf. +5pf. Type E **404**	45	55
	a. Horiz pair. Nos. E1317/E1318	1·50	2·75
E1318	25pf. +5pf. Girl pioneer with neckerchief	45	55

No. E1317/E1318 were issued together in horizontal *se-tenant* pairs within the sheet, each pair forming a composite design.

E **405** Cecilienhof Castle

E **406** Pocketwatch and Wristwatch

(Des B. Steinwendner. Litho)

1970 (28 July). 25th Anniv of Potsdam Agreement. T E **405** and similar designs. P 13.
E1319	10pf. olive-yellow, carmine-vermilion and black	45	40
	a. Horiz strip of 3. Nos. E1319/E1321	2·00	
E1320	20pf. black, carmine-vermilion and olive-yellow	45	40
E1321	25pf. black and carmine-vermilion	45	40
E1319/E1321	Set of 3	1·20	1·10

Designs:—10pf. T E **405**. As T E **405**—20pf. 'Potsdam Agreement' in four languages. 77×28 mm—25pf. Conference delegates around the table.
Nos. E1319/E1321 were issued together in horizontal *se-tenant* strips of three within the sheet.

(Des D. Dorfstecher. Photo)

1970 (25 Aug). Leipzig Autumn Fair. P 13½×14.
E1322	E **406**	10pf. multicoloured	60	30

E **407** T. Neubauer and M. Poser

E **408** Pres. Ho-Chi-Minh

(Des M. Gottschall. Photo)

1970 (2 Sept). Anti-Fascist Resistance. T E **407** and similar design. P 13×12½ (20pf.) or 12½×13 (25pf.).
E1323	20pf. maroon, red and indigo	35	35
E1324	25pf. yellow-olive and magenta	45	40

Designs: Horiz—20pf. T E **407**. Vert—25pf. *Motherland* (detail, Soviet War Memorial, Treptow, Berlin).

(Des K.–H. Bobbe. Litho)

1970 (2 Sept). Aid for Vietnam and Ho-Chi-Minh Commemoration. P 13.
E1325	E **408**	20pf. +5pf. black, red and rose	75	30

E **409** Compass and Map

(Des K.–H. Bobbe. Litho)

1970 (15 Sept). World Orienteering Championships. T E **409** and similar horiz design. Multicoloured. P 13×12½.
E1326	10pf. Type E **409**	35	30
E1327	25pf. Runner and three map sections	2·00	55

E **410** *Forester Scharf's Birthday* (Nagel)

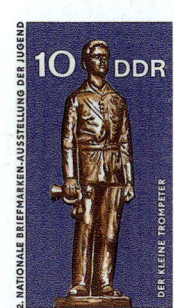

E **411** *The Little Trumpeter* (Weineck Memorial, Halle)

(Des K. Wittkugel (25, 40, 50pf.), K. Wittkugel and H. Naumann (others). Litho (25, 30pf.) or photo (others))

1970 (22 Sept). The Art of Otto Nagel, Käthe Kollwitz and Ernst Barlach. T E **410** and similar vert designs. P 14×13½.
E1328	10pf. multicoloured	35	30
E1329	20pf. multicoloured	35	30
E1330	25pf. blackish brown and plum reddish mauve	1·50	1·70
E1331	30pf. black and salmon-pink	35	30
E1332	40pf. black and chrome-yellow	35	30
E1333	50pf. black and yellow	40	30
E1328/E1333	Set of 6	3·00	3·00

Designs:—10pf. T E **410**; 20pf. *Portrait of a Young Girl* (Nagel); 25pf. *No More War* (Kollwitz); 30pf. *Mother and Child* (Kollwitz); 40pf. Sculptured head from Gustrow Cenotaph (Barlach); 50pf. *The Fluteplayer* (Barlach).

(Des G. Voigt. Photo)

1970 (1 Oct). Second National Youth Stamp Exhibition, Karl-Marx-Stadt. T E **411** and similar vert design. Multicoloured. P 14×13½.
E1334	10pf. Type E **411**	35	55
E1335	15pf. +5pf. East German 25pf. stamp of 1959	35	55

279

GERMANY / German Democratic Republic (East Germany)

E **412** Flags Emblem

(Des K. Bernsdorf and H. Wendt. Litho)

1970 (1 Oct). 'Comrades-in-Arms' Warsaw Pact Military Manoeuvres. P 13×12½.
| E1336 | E **412** | 10pf. multicoloured | 35 | 35 |
| E1337 | | 20pf. multicoloured | 45 | 40 |

E **413** Musk Ox (*Ovibos moschatus*)

E **414** UN Emblem and Headquarters, New York

(Des H. Naumann. Photo)

1970 (6 Oct). Animals in East Berlin Tierpark (Zoo). T E **413** and similar vert designs. Multicoloured. P 14.
E1338	10pf. Type E **413**	60	30
E1339	15pf. Whale-headed Stork	60	30
E1340	20pf. Addax (*Addax nasomaculatus*)	1·00	55
E1341	25pf. Sun Bear (*Helarctos malayanus*)	9·00	8·75
E1338/E1341	Set of 4	10·00	9·00

(Des M. Gottschall. Photo)

1970 (20 Oct). 25th Anniversary of United Nations. P 13.
| E1342 | E **414** | 20pf. multicoloured | 1·20 | 40 |

E **415** Engels

E **416** *Epiphyllum hybr.*

(Des and eng G. Stauf (10pf.). Des G. Stauf. Eng M. Bitzer (others). Recess and photo)

1970 (24 Nov). 150th Birth Anniv of Friedrich Engels. T E **415** and similar vert designs. P 14×13½.
E1343	10pf. black, light drab and red-orange	45	30
E1344	20pf. black, myrtle-green and red-orange	45	30
E1345	25pf. black, crimson and red-orange	2·20	1·10
E1343/E1345	Set of 3	2·75	1·50

Designs:—10pf. T E **415**; 20pf. Marx, Engels and *Communist Manifesto*; 25pf. Engels and *Anti-Dühring*.

(Des M. Gottschall. Photo)

1970 (2 Dec). Cacti Cultivation in the DDR. T E **416** and similar vert designs. Multicoloured. P 14.
E1346	5pf. Type E **416**	35	30
E1347	10pf. *Astrophytum myriostigma*	35	30
E1348	15pf. *Echinocereus salm-dyckianus*	35	30
E1349	20pf. *Selenicereus grandiflorus*	35	30
E1350	25pf. *Hamatoc setispinus*	3·00	2·50
E1351	30pf. *Mamillaria boolii*	35	30
E1346/E1351	Set of 6	4·25	3·50

(Des G. Stauf. Eng M. Bitzer. Recess)

1970 (10 Dec). Birth Bicentenary of Beethoven. As No. E1259, but colour and face value changed, in sheet 81×55 mm. P 14×13½.
| MSE1352 | 1m. slate-green | 3·00 | 5·00 |

E **417** Dancer's Mask, Bismarck Archipelago

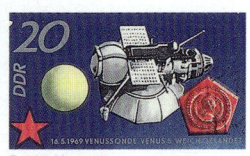

E **418** Venus 5

(Des G. Voigt. Photo)

1971 (12 Jan). Exhibits from the Ethnological Museum, Leipzig. T E **417** and similar square designs. P 13.
E1353	10pf. multicoloured	35	30
E1354	20pf. brown and red-orange	35	30
E1355	25pf. multicoloured	1·20	85
E1356	40pf. blackish brown and brown-red	40	30
E1353/E1356	Set of 4	2·10	1·60

Designs:—10pf. T E **417**; 20pf. Bronze head, Benin; 25pf. Tea-pot, Thailand; 40pf. Zapotec earthenware Jaguar-god, Mexico.

(Des H. Zill. Litho)

1971 (11 Feb). Soviet Space Research. T E **418** and similar horiz designs. Multicoloured. P 13×12½.
E1357	20pf. Type E **418**	45	65
	a. Sheetlet of 8. Nos. E1357/E1364	5·50	
E1358	20pf. Orbital space station	45	65
E1359	20pf. *Luna 10* and *Luna 16*	85	1·10
E1360	20pf. Various Soyuz spacecraft	85	1·10
E1361	20pf. *Proton 1* satellite and Vostok rocket	85	1·10
E1362	20pf. *Molniya 1* communications satellite	85	1·10
E1363	20pf. Yuri Gagarin and *Vostok 1*	45	65
E1364	20pf. Aleksei Leonov in space	45	65
E1357/E1364	Set of 8	4·75	6·25

Nos. E1357/E1364 were issued together in *se-tenant* sheetlets of eight stamps.

E **419** K. Liebknecht

E **420** J. R. Becher (poet) (80th Birth Anniv)

(Des G. Voigt. Photo)

1971 (23 Feb). Birth Centenaries of Karl Liebknecht and Rosa Luxemburg (revolutionaries). T E **419** and similar vert portrait. P 14.
E1365	20pf. brown-lilac, gold and black	75	70
	a. Horiz pair. Nos. E1365/E1366	1·60	1·50
E1366	20pf. brown-lilac, gold and black	75	70

Designs:—20pf. T E **419**; 25pf. Rosa Luxemburg.

Nos. E1365/E1366 were issued together in horizontal *se-tenant* pairs within the sheet.

(Des G. Stauf. Eng M. Bitzer (5, 15pf.), G. Stauf (10, 20pf.), I. Volkamer (25, 50pf.). Recess)

1971 (23 Feb). Celebrities' Birth Anniversaries. T E **420** and similar vert portraits. P 14.
E1367	5pf. light brown	35	30
E1368	10pf. ultramarine	35	30
E1369	15pf. black	35	30
E1370	20pf. brown-purple	35	30
E1371	25pf. blue-green	95	80
E1372	50pf. indigo	40	30
E1367/E1372	Set of 6	2·50	2·10

Designs:—5pf. T E **420**; 10pf. H. Mann (writer–centenary); 15pf. J. Heartfield (artist–80th birth anniv); 20pf. W. Bredel (70th anniv); 25pf. F. Mehring (politician–125th anniv); 50pf. J. Kepler (astronomer–400th anniv).

See also Nos. E1427 and E1451/E1455.

280

GERMANY / German Democratic Republic (East Germany)

E 421 Soldier and Army Badge

(Des K. Bernsdorf. Photo)
1971 (1 Mar). 15th Anniversary of People's Army. P 13½×14.
E1373 E 421 20pf. multicoloured 60 30

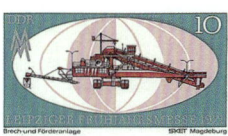

E 422 Sket Mobile Ore-crusher    E 423 Proclamation of the Commune

(Des H. Detlefsen. Litho)
1971 (9 Mar). Leipzig Spring Fair. T E 422 and similar horiz design. Multicoloured. P 13×12½.
E1374 10pf. Type E 422 .... 35 30
E1375 15pf. Dredger *Takraf* 35 30

(Des F. Deutschendorf. Photo)
1971 (9 Mar). Centenary of the Paris Commune. T E 423 and similar square designs. P 13.
E1376 10pf. black, stone and carmine 60 30
E1377 20pf. black, stone and carmine 60 30
E1378 25pf. black, pale buff and carmine 85 75
E1379 30pf. black, pale brownish grey and carmine 60 30
E1376/E1379 Set of 4 .... 2·40 1·50
Designs:—10pf. T E 423; 20pf. Women at the Place Blanche barricade; 25pf. Cover of *L'Internationale*; 30pf. Title page of Karl Marx's *The Civil War in France*.

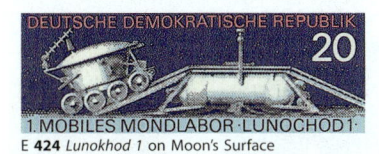

E 424 *Lunokhod 1* on Moon's Surface

(Des H. Detlefsen. Photo)
1971 (30 Mar). Moon Mission of *Lunokhod 1*. P 14.
E1380 E 424 20pf. pale turquoise-blue, chalky blue and carmine-red .... 1·00 55

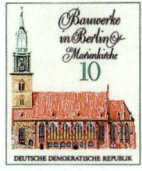

E 425 St. Mary's Church 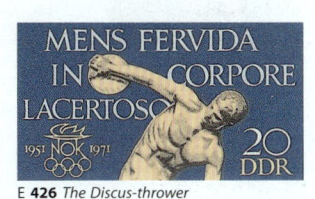   E 426 The Discus-thrower

(Des D. Dorfstecher. Photo)
1971 (6 Apr). Berlin Buildings. T E 425 and similar multicoloured designs. P 13½.
E1381 10pf. Type E 425 .... 35 30
E1382 15pf. Köpenick Castle (*horiz*) 35 30
E1383 20pf. Old Library (*horiz*) 35 30
E1384 25pf. Ermeler House .... 4·75 4·00
E1385 50pf. New Guardhouse (*horiz*) 40 30
E1386 70pf. National Gallery (*horiz*) 60 30
E1381/E1386 Set of 6 .... 6·00 5·00

(Des D. Dorfstecher. Litho)
1971 (6 Apr). 20th Anniversary of DDR National Olympic Committee. P 13.
E1387 E 426 20pf. multicoloured .... 1·30 40

E 427 Handclasp and XXV Symbol    E 428 Schleife Costume

(Des H. Detlefsen. Litho and embossed)
1971 (20 Apr). 25th Anniv of Socialist Unity Party. P 13.
E1388 E 427 20pf. black, bright scarlet and gold ... 60 30

(Des H. Leitner and F. Deutschendorf. Litho)
1971 (4 May). Sorbian Dance Costumes. Vert designs as T E 428. Multicoloured. P 13.
E1389 10pf. Type E 428 .... 35 30
E1390 20pf. Hoyerswerda 35 30
E1391 25pf. Cottbus .... 1·00 1·40
E1392 40pf. Kamenz 40 40
E1389/E1392 Set of 4 .... 1·90 2·20
For 10pf. and 20pf. in smaller format, see Nos. E1443/E1444.

E 429 *Self-portrait c.1500*    E 430 Construction Worker

1971 (18 May). 500th Birth Anniversary of Albrecht Dürer (artist). T E 429 and similar vert designs showing Dürer's works. Multicoloured. P 12½×13.
E1393 10pf. Type E 429 .... 45 30
E1394 40pf. *Three Peasants* 45 30
E1395 70pf. *Philipp Melanchthon* .... 3·00 1·40
E1393/E1395 Set of 3 .... 3·50 1·80

(Des L. Grünewald. Photo)
1971 (9 June). Eighth Socialist Unity Party Conference (1st issue). T E 430 and similar vert designs. Multicoloured. P 14.
E1396 5pf. Type E 430 .... 35 30
E1397 10pf. Technician 35 30
E1398 20pf. Farm girl 35 30
E1399 25pf. Soldier 60 45
E1396/E1399 Set of 4 .... 1·50 1·20

E 431 Conference Emblem    E 432 Internees

281

GERMANY / German Democratic Republic (East Germany)

(Des M. Gottschall. Photo)
1971 (9 June). Eighth SED Party Conference (2nd issue). P 13½.
E1400 E **431** 20pf. gold, orange-red and magenta 60 30

(Des D. Dorfstecher Litho)
1971 (22 June). 20th Anniv of International Resistance Federation (FIR). T E **432** and similar vert design showing details from F. Cremer's lithograph *Buchenwaldzyklus*. P 13.
E1401 20pf. black and deep yellow-ochre .... 85 1·00
  a. Horiz strip. Nos. E1401/E1402 plus label 2·00 2·50
E1402 25pf. black and light blue .... 85 1·00
Designs:—20pf. T E **432**; 25pf. *Attack on Guard*.
Nos. E1401/E1402 were issued together *se-tenant* with intervening inscribed label.

E **433** Cherry Stone with 180 Carved Heads

E **434** Mongolian Arms

(Des G. Voigt. Photo)
1971 (22 June). Art Treasures of Dresden's Green Vaults. T E **433** and similar square designs. Multicoloured. P 13.
E1403 5pf. Type E **433** 35 35
E1404 10pf. Insignia of the Golden Fleece *c.* 1730 ... 35 35
E1405 15pf. Nüremberg jug, *c.* 1530 .... 35 35
E1406 20pf. Mounted Moorish drummer figurine, *c.* 1720 .... 35 35
E1407 25pf. Writing-case. 1562 .... 1·00 1·00
E1408 30pf. St. George medallion, *c.* 1570 .... 35 35
E1403/E1408 *Set of 6* .... 2·50 2·50

(Des M. Gottschall. Litho)
1971 (6 July). 50th Anniversary of Mongolian People's Republic. P 13.
E1409 E **434** 20pf. multicoloured 60 40

E **435** Child's Face

E **436** Servicemen

(Des M. Gottschall. Photo)
1971 (13 July). 25th Anniv of United Nations Children's Fund. P 13.
E1410 E **435** 20pf. multicoloured 75 35

(Des K. Bernsdorf. Photo)
1971 (12 Aug). Tenth Anniversary of Berlin Wall T E **436** and similar vert design. Multicoloured. P 13½.
E1411 20pf. Type E **436** .... 1·20 40
E1412 35pf. Brandenburg Gate .... 3·00 1·70

E **437** *Ivan Franko* (liner)

(Des J. Bertholdt. Eng M. Bitzer (10, 15, 40, 50pf.), G. Faulwasser (20, 25pf.). Recess)
1971 (24 Aug). East German Shipbuilding Industry. T E **437** and similar horiz designs. P 14.
E1413 10pf. purple-brown 35 30
E1414 15pf. deep blue and light yellow-brown 35 30
E1415 20pf. deep green 35 30
E1416 25pf. slate-blue .... 1·90 1·70
E1417 40pf. more-lake 35 30
E1418 50pf. ultramarine 35 30
E1413/E1418 *Set of 6* .... 3·25 3·00

Designs:—10pf. T E **437**; 15pf. *Irkutsk* (freighter); 20pf. *Rostock* (freighter), 1966; 25pf. *Junge Welt* (fish-factory ship); 40pf. *Hansel* (container ship); 50pf. *Akademik Kurchatov* (research ship).

E **438** Vietnamese Woman and Child

E **439** MAG-Butadien Plant

(Des J. Riess. Recess and photo)
1971 (2 Sept). Aid for Vietnam. P 13½.
E1419 E **438** 10pf. +5pf. multicoloured 60 30

(Des J. Riess. Litho)
1971 (2 Sept). Leipzig Autumn Fair. T E **439** and similar vert design showing chemical plants. P 13.
E1420 10pf. violet, magenta and light olive-green ... 35 35
E1421 25pf. violet, pale olive-green and new blue ... 45 40
Designs:—10pf. T E **439**; 25pf. SKL reactor plant.

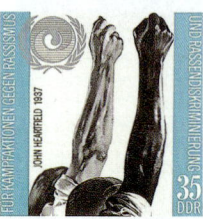

E **440** Upraised Arms (after motif by J. Heartfield)

E **441** Tupolev Tu-134 Mail Plane at Airport

(Des J. Reiss. Recess and photo)
1971 (23 Sept). Racial Equality Year. P 13.
E1422 E **440** 35pf. black, silver and turquoise-blue .. 60 30

(Des J. Reiss. Eng G. Faulwasser (10pf.), M. Bitzer (25pf.). Recess and photo)
1971 (5 Oct). Philatelists' Day. T E **441** and similar horiz design. P 14.
E1423 10pf. +5pf. steel-blue, lake and yellow-green 45 30
E1424 25pf. lake, yellow-green and greenish blue 75 70
Designs:—10pf. T E **441**; 25pf. Milestones and Zürner's measuring cart.

E **442** Wiltz Memorial, Luxembourg

E **443** German Violin

(Des H. Detlefsen (25pf.), M. Gottschall (35pf.). Photo)
1971 (5 Oct). Monuments. T E **442** and similar vert design. Multicoloured. P 13½.
E1425 25pf. Type E **442** 45 35
E1426 35pf. Karl Marx monument, Karl-Marx-Stadt.. 75 35

(Des G. Stauf. Eng H. Nebel. Recess)
1971 (13 Oct). 150th Birth Anniv of Rudolf Virchow (physician). Vert design as T E **420**, but with portrait of Virchow. P 14.
E1427 40pf. plum 75 35

(Des D. Dorfstecher. Photo)
1971 (26 Oct). Musical Instruments in Markneukirchen Museum. T E **443** and similar vert designs. Multicoloured. P 14.
E1428 10pf. North African darbuka 35 30
E1429 15pf. Mongolian morin chuur 35 30
E1430 20pf. Type E **443** 35 30

282

GERMANY / German Democratic Republic (East Germany)

E1431	25pf. Italian mandolin		35	30
E1432	40pf. Bohemian bagpipes		35	30
E1433	50pf. Sudanese kasso		1·60	1·40
E1428/E1433	Set of 6		3·00	2·50

E **444** Dahlta O 10 A Theodolite

E **445** Donkey and Windmill

(Des D. Uttikal. Photo)

1971 (9 Nov). 125th Anniversary of Carl Zeiss Optical Works, Jena. T E **444** and similar designs. P 13½×14.

E1434	10pf. black, new blue and red	75	75
	a. Horiz strip of 3. Nos. E1434/E1436	3·75	
E1435	20pf. black, new blue and red	75	75
E1436	25pf. new blue, bright lemon and deep ultramarine	75	75
E1434/E1436	Set of 3	2·00	2·00

Designs:—10pf. T E **444**. As T E **444**—20pf. Ergaval microscope. 52×29 mm—25pf. Planetarium.

Nos. E1434/E1436 were issued together in horizontal *se-tenant* strips of three within the sheet.

(Des E. and G. Bläser. Litho)

1971 (23 Nov). Fairy Tales. *The Town Musicians of Bremen*. T E **445** and similar horiz designs, showing different scenes. P 13½×13.

E1437	5pf. multicoloured	45	30
	a. Sheetlet of 6. Nos. E1437/E1442	4·25	
E1438	10pf. multicoloured	45	30
E1439	15pf. multicoloured	1·00	1·40
E1440	20pf. multicoloured	1·00	1·40
E1441	25pf. multicoloured	45	30
E1442	30pf. multicoloured	45	30
E1437/E1442	Set of 6	3·50	3·50

Nos. E1437/E1442 were issued together in *se-tenant* sheetlets of six stamps.

1971 (23 Nov). Booklet Stamps. Sorbian Dance Costumes. As Nos. E1389/E1390 but smaller, size 23×28 mm. P 13.

E1443 E **428**	10pf. multicoloured		45	35
	a. Booklet pane. No. E1443×4		1·90	
	b. Booklet pane. Nos. E1443×2 and E1444×2		4·00	
E1444	20pf. multicoloured		1·00	70

Nos. E1443/E1444 were only issued in booklets.

E **446** Tobogganing

(Des M. Gottschall. Photo)

1971 (7 Dec). Winter Olympic Games, Sapporo, Japan (1972). T E **446** and similar horiz designs. P 13½×14.

E1445	5pf. black, bluish green and magenta	35	30
E1446	10pf. +5pf. black, new blue and magenta	35	30
E1447	15pf. +5pf. black, blue-green and blue	35	30
E1448	20pf. black, magenta and violet	35	30
E1449	25pf. black, bluish violet and magenta	2·50	2·00
E1450	70pf. black, ultramarine and violet	40	30
E1445/E1450	Set of 6	3·75	3·25

Designs:—5pf. T E **446**; 10pf. Figure skating; 15pf. Speed skating; 20pf. Cross-country skiing; 25pf. Biathlon; 70pf. Ski jumping.

(Des G. Stauf. Eng G. Faulwasser (10, 35pf.), M. Bitzer (20, 50pf.), H. Nebel (25 pf.). Recess)

1972 (25 Jan). Celebrities' Anniversaries. Vert designs similar to T E **420**. P 14.

E1451	10pf. light grey-green	35	35
E1452	20pf. reddish mauve	35	35
E1453	25pf. royal blue	35	35
E1454	35pf. light brown	35	35
E1455	50pf. reddish lilac	1·60	2·10
E1451/E1455	Set of 5	2·75	3·25

Designs:—10pf. J. Tralow (writer—90th birth anniv); 20pf. L. Frank (writer—90th birth anniv); 25pf. K. A. Kocor (composer—150th birth anniv); 35pf. H. Schliemann (archaeologist—150th birth anniv); 50pf. F. Caroline Neuber (actress—275th birth anniv).

E **447** Gypsum from Eisleben

E **448** Vietnamese Woman

(Des L. Grünewald. Photo)

1972 (22 Feb). Minerals. T E **447** and similar square designs. Multicoloured. P 13.

E1456	5pf. Type E **447**	45	30
E1457	10pf. Zinnwaldite, Zinnwald	45	30
E1458	20pf. Malachite, Ullersreuth	45	30
E1459	25pf. Amethyst, Wiesenbad	45	30
E1460	35pf. Halite, Merkers	45	30
E1461	50pf. Proustite, Schneeberg	1·70	1·80
E1456/E1461	Set of 6	3·50	3·00

(Des J. Riess. Litho)

1972 (22 Feb). Aid for Vietnam. P 13.

E1462 E **448**	10pf. +5pf. multicoloured	60	30

E **449** Soviet Exhibition Hall

E **450** Anemometer of 1896 and Koppen's Chart of 1876

(Des L. Grünewald. Photo)

1972 (7 Mar). Leipzig Spring Fair. T E **449** and similar horiz design. Multicoloured. P 14.

E1463	10pf. Type E **449**	35	30
E1464	25pf. East German and Soviet flags	45	40

(Des M. Gottschall. Litho)

1972 (23 Mar). International Meteorologists Meeting, Leipzig. Three sheets each 85×57 mm. Multicoloured. P 13×12½.

MSE1465	20pf. Type E **450**; 35pf. Weather station and clouds; 70pf. Satellite and weather map	4·00	4·75

E **451** WHO Emblem

E **452** Kamov Ka-26 Helicopter

(Des D. Dorfstecher. Photo)

1972 (4 Apr). World Health Day. P 13.

E1466 E **451**	35pf. deep ultramarine, silver and light blue	60	30

(Des G. Bormann. Photo)

1972 (25 Apr). East German Aircraft. T E **452** and similar horiz designs. Multicoloured. P 14.

E1467	5pf. Type E **452**	35	35
E1468	10pf. Letov Z-37 Cmelak crop sprayer DM-SMC	35	35
E1469	35pf. Ilyushin Il-62M jetliner	40	35
E1470	1m. Tailfin of Ilyushin Il-62M	2·50	2·75
E1467/E1470	Set of 4	3·25	3·50

E **453** Wrestling

GERMANY / German Democratic Republic (East Germany)

(Des M. Gottschall. Photo)

1972 (16 May). Olympic Games, Munich. T E **453** and similar horiz designs. Multicoloured. P 14.

E1471	5pf. Type **453**	35	30
E1472	10pf. +5pf. High diving	35	30
E1473	20pf. Pole vaulting	35	30
E1474	25pf. +10pf. Rowing	35	30
E1475	35pf. Volleyball	40	30
E1476	70pf. Gymnastics	5·00	3·00
E1471/E1476	Set of 6	6·00	4·00

E **454** Soviet and East German Flags

(Des J. Riess. Recess and photo)

1972 (24 May). 25th Anniv of German–Soviet Friendship Society. T E **454** and similar horiz design. Multicoloured. P 14.

E1477	10pf. Type E **454**	1·90	1·40
E1478	20pf. Brezhnev (USSR) and Honecker (DDR)	1·90	1·40

E **455** Steel Workers

E **456** Karneol Rose

(Des H. Heise. Litho)

1972 (24 May). Trade Unions Federation Congress. T E **455** and similar vert design. P 13.

E1479	10pf. deep magenta, red-orange and ochre	60	30
	a. Horiz strip. Nos. E1479/E1480 plus label	1·60	1·30
E1480	35pf. bright blue and ochre	60	30

Designs:—10pf. T E **455**; 35pf. Students. Nos. E1479/E1480 were issued together *se-tenant* with an intervening inscribed label.

(Des M. Gottschall. Photo)

1972 (13 June). International Rose Exhibition. German Species. T E **456** and similar square designs. Multicoloured. P 13.

E1481	5pf. Type E **456**	35	30
E1482	10pf. Berger's Rose	35	30
E1483	15pf. Charme	2·50	2·40
E1484	20pf. Izetka Spreeathen	35	30
E1485	25pf. Köpernicker Sommer	35	30
E1486	35pf. Professor Knöll	40	30
E1481/E1486	Set of 6	3·75	3·50

For 10pf., 25pf. and 35pf. in smaller format, see Nos E1497/E1499.

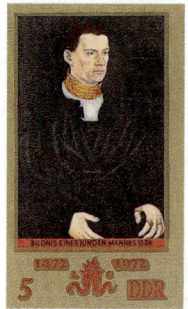

E **457** Portrait of Young Man

E **458** Compass and Motorcyclist

(Des H. Naumann. Photo)

1972 (4 July). 500th Birth Anniv of Lucas Cranach the Elder (painter). T E **457** and similar multicoloured designs. P 14.

E1487	5pf. Type E **457**	35	35
E1488	20pf. Mother and Child	35	35
E1489	35pf. Margarete Luther	40	40
E1490	70pf. Nymph (horiz)	3·50	5·00
E1487/E1490	Set of 4	4·25	5·50

(Des M. Gottschall. Photo)

1972 (8 Aug). Sports and Technical Sciences Association. T E **458** and similar horiz designs. Multicoloured. P 13.

E1491	5pf. Type E **458**	35	30
E1492	10pf. Light aeroplane and parachute	35	30
E1493	20pf. Target and obstacle race	35	30
E1494	25pf. Radio set and Morse key	1·00	1·00
E1495	35pf. Wilhelm Pieck (brigantine) and propeller	35	30
E1491/E1495	Set of 5	2·20	2·00

E **459** Young Worker Reading (J. Damme)

(Des H. Naumann. Photo)

1972 (22 Aug). International Book Year. P 14.

E1496	E **459** 50pf. multicoloured	1·00	55

1972 (22 Aug). Booklet Stamps. German Roses. As Nos. E1482 and E1485/E1486 but smaller, size 24×28 mm. P 13.

E1497	10pf. multicoloured	35	30
	a. Booklet pane. No. E1497×4	1·50	
E1498	25pf. multicoloured	2·00	75
	a. Booklet pane. Nos. E1498×2 and E1499×2	8·25	
E1499	35pf. multicoloured	2·00	75
E1497/E1499	Set of 3	4·00	1·60

Nos. E1497/E1499 were only issued in booklets.

E **460** Overhead Projector

E **461** G. Dimitrov

(Des F. Deutschendorf. Litho)

1972 (29 Aug). Leipzig Autumn Fair. T E **460** and similar design. P 12½×13 (10pf.) or 13×12½ (25pf.).

E1500	10pf. black and carmine	35	30
E1501	25pf. black and blue-green	45	40

Designs: Horiz—10pf. T E **460**. Vert—25pf. Slide projector.

(Des M. Gottschall. Litho)

1972 (19 Sept). 90th Birth Anniv of Georgi Dimitrov (Bulgarian statesman). P 13.

E1502	E **461** 20pf. black and carmine-red	75	40

E **462** Catching Birds (Egyptian Relief Painting, c. 2400 BC)

E **463** Red Cross Team and Patient

GERMANY / German Democratic Republic (East Germany)

(Des M. Gottschall. Photo)

1972 (19 Sept). Interartes Stamp Exhibition, East Berlin. T E **462** and similar multicoloured designs. P 14.

E1503	10pf. Type E **462**	35	30
E1504	15pf. +5pf. Persian Spearman (glazed tile, c. 500 BC)	1·50	1·10
E1505	20pf. Anatolian Tapestry, c. 1400 BC	35	30
E1506	35pf. +5pf. The Grapesellers (Max Lingner, 1949) (horiz)	35	30
E1503/E1506	Set of 4	2·30	1·80

(Des H. Detlefsen. Litho)

1972 (3 Oct). East German Red Cross. T E **463** and similar designs. P 13.

E1507	10pf. deep ultramarine, greenish blue and red	60	40
	a. Horiz strip of 3. Nos. E1507/E1509	2·10	
E1508	15pf. deep ultramarine, greenish blue and red	60	40
E1509	35pf. red, greenish blue and deep ultramarine	60	40
E1507/E1509	Set of 3	1·60	1·10

Designs:—10pf. T E **463**. As T E **463**—15pf. Sea rescue launch. 50×28 mm—35pf. World map on cross, and transport.

Nos. E1507/E1509 were issued together in horizontal, *se-tenant* strips of three within the sheet.

E **464** Terrestrial Globe (J. Praetorius, 1568)

E **465** Monument

(Des D. Dorfstecher. Photo)

1972 (17 Oct). Terrestrial and Celestial Globes. T E **464** and similar vert designs. Multicoloured. P 14.

E1510	5pf. Arab celestial globe, 1279	35	30
E1511	10pf. Type E **464**	35	30
E1512	15pf. Globe clock (J. Reinhold and G. Roll, 1586)	3·75	4·50
E1513	20pf. Globe clock (J. Bürgi, 1590)	35	30
E1514	25pf. Armillary sphere (J. Moeller, 1687)	35	30
E1515	35pf. Heraldic celestial globe, 1690	40	35
E1510/E1515	Set of 6	5·00	5·50

(Des R. Platzer. Litho)

1972 (24 Oct). Inauguration of German–Polish Resistance Memorial. Berlin. P 12½×13.

E1516	E **465** 25pf. multicoloured	75	30

E **466** Educating Juveniles

(Des J. Riess. Photo)

1972 (2 Nov). Juvenile Inventions Exhibition. T E **466** and similar horiz design. Multicoloured. P 13½×14.

E1517	10pf. Type E **466**	45	40
	a. Horiz strip. Nos. E1517/E1518 plus label	1·30	1·50
E1518	25pf. Youths with welding machine	45	40

Nos. E1517/E1518 were issued together *se-tenant* with an intervening half stamp-size label bearing inscription and emblems of exhibition.

E **467** Mauz and Hoppel (Cat and Hare)

E **468** The Snow Queen

(Des E. and G. Bläser. Litho)

1972 (28 Nov). Children's TV Characters. T E **467** and similar horiz designs. Multicoloured. P 13½×13.

E1519	5pf. Type E **467**	45	40
	a. Sheetlet of 6. Nos. E1519/E1524	4·75	
E1520	10pf. Fuchs and Elster (Fox and Magpie)	45	40
E1521	15pf. Herr Uhu (Eagle Owl)	1·30	1·40
E1522	20pf. Frau Igel and Borstel (Hedgehogs)	1·30	1·40
E1523	25pf. Schnuffel and Pieps (Dog and Mouse)	45	40
E1524	35pf. Paulchen (Paul from the Children's Library)	45	40
E1519/E1524	Set of 6	4·00	4·00

Nos. E1519/E1524 were issued together in *se-tenant* sheetlets of six stamps.

(Des E. and G. Bläser. Litho)

1972 (28 Nov). Fairy Tales. *The Snow Queen* by Hans Christian Andersen. T E **468** and similar vert designs showing different scenes. P 13×13½.

E1525	5pf. multicoloured	45	40
	a. Sheetlet of 6. Nos. E1525/E1530	5·00	
E1526	10pf. multicoloured	1·00	1·40
E1527	15pf. multicoloured	45	40
E1528	20pf. multicoloured	45	40
E1529	25pf. multicoloured	1·00	1·40
E1530	35pf. multicoloured	45	40
E1525/E1530	Set of 6	3·50	4·00

Nos. E1525/E1530 were issued together in *se-tenant* sheetlets of six stamps.

E **469** Heinrich Heine

E **470** Arms of USSR

(Des D. Dorfstecher. Litho)

1972 (5 Dec). 175th Birth Anniv of Heinrich Heine (poet). Sheet 60×86 mm. P 12½×13.

MSE1531	E **469** 1m. black, brown-red and olive	3·00	2·75

(Des L. Grünewald. Photo)

1972 (5 Dec). 50th Anniv of USSR. P 14.

E1532	E **470** 20pf. multicoloured	75	35

E **471** Leninplatz, East Berlin

E **472** M. da Caravaggio

(Des M. Gottschall)

1973 (23 Jan)–**75**.

(a) Size 29×24 mm. Recess. P 14×13½

E1533	5pf. blue-green (10.4.73)	45	40
E1534	10pf. emerald (10.4.73)	70	40
E1535	15pf. deep magenta (13.6.73)	75	40
E1536	20pf. bright magenta	1·50	40
E1537	25pf. deep turquoise-green (13.6.73)	1·60	40

GERMANY / German Democratic Republic (East Germany)

E1538	30pf. red-orange (20.11.73)	75	55
E1539	35pf. greenish blue	1·50	55
E1540	40pf. slate-violet (18.9.73)	85	55
E1541	50pf. deep blue (18.9.73)	1·00	55
E1542	60pf. purple (22.1.74)	1·40	70
E1543	70pf. brown-purple (18.9.73)	1·30	70
E1544	80pf. deep ultramarine (22.1.74)	1·70	85
E1545	1m. deep olive (18.9.73)	2·00	85
E1546	2m. carmine-red (20.11.73)	2·50	1·10
E1546a	3m. bright magenta (11.6.74)	7·00	2·00
E1533/E1546a	Set of 15	22·50	9·30

(b) Coil Stamps. Size 22×18 mm. Photo. P 14

E1547	5pf. blue-green (16.4.74)	45	30
E1548	10pf. emerald (26.7.73)	1·10	1·00
E1549	20pf. bright magenta (26.7.73)	1·10	1·00
E1549a	25pf. deep turquoise-green (4.3.75)	80	55
E1550	50pf. blue (16.4.74)	1·30	1·00
E1550a	1m. grey-olive (9.7.74)	3·00	3·25
E1547/E1550a	Set of 6	7·00	6·25

Designs:—5pf. Eastern White Pelican and Alfred Brehm House, Tierpark, Berlin; 10pf. Neptune Fountain and Rathausstrasse, Berlin; 15pf. Apartment Blocks, Fishers' Island, Berlin; 20pf. T E **471**; 25pf. TV Tower, Alexander Square, Berlin; 30pf. Workers' Memorial, Halle; 35pf. Karl-Marx-Stadt; 40pf. Brandenburg Gate, Berlin; 50pf. New Guardhouse, Berlin; 60pf. Crown Gate and Zwinger, Dresden; 70pf. Old Town Hall, Leipzig; 80pf. Rostock-Warnemunde; 1m. Soviet War Memorial, Treptow; 2m. and 3m. Arms of East Germany.

The coil stamps have every fifth stamp numbered on the back. Nos. E1548/E1549 were also issued in sheets.

No. E1549 was issued both with matt gum and on thinner paper with shiny gum.

For designs 22×18 mm but recess, see Nos. E2197/E2211.

(Des G. Stauf. Litho)

1973 (23 Jan). Cultural Anniversaries. T E **472** and similar vert designs. P 13.

E1551	5pf. brown	1·20	1·10
E1552	10pf. grey-green	35	30
E1553	20pf. reddish purple	35	30
E1554	25pf. cobalt	35	30
E1555	35pf. claret	35	30
E1551/E1555	Set of 5	2·30	2·10

Designs:—5pf. T E **472** (painter, 400th birth anniversary); 10pf. Friedrich Wolf (dramatist, 85th birth anniversary); 20pf. Max Reger (composer, birth centenary); 25pf. Max Reinhardt (impresario, birth centenary); 35pf. Johannes Dieckmann (politician, 80th birth anniversary).

E **473** *Lebachia speciosa*

(Des G. Voigt. Photo)

1973 (6 Feb). Fossils in Palaeontological Collection, Berlin Natural History Museum. T E **473** and similar square designs. Multicoloured. P 13.

E1556	10pf. Type E **473**	35	30
E1557	15pf. *Sphenopteris hollandica*	35	30
E1558	20pf. *Pterodactylus kochi*	35	30
E1559	25pf. *Botryopteris*	35	30
E1560	35pf. Archaeopteryx (*Archaeopteryx lithographica*)	35	30
E1561	70pf. *Odontopleura ovata*	2·50	2·50
E1556/E1561	Set of 6	3·75	3·50

E **474** Copernicus

(Des G. Stauf. Litho)

1973 (13 Feb). 500th Birth Anniv of Copernicus. P 13½×13.

E1562	E **474** 70pf. multicoloured	1·50	70

E **475** National Flags

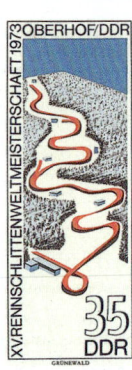

E **476** Bobsleigh Course

(Des M. Gottschall. Litho)

1973 (13 Feb). Tenth World Youth and Students' Festival, Berlin (1st issue). T E **475** and similar vert design. Multicoloured. P 12½×13.

E1563	10pf. +5pf. Type E **475**	35	35
E1564	25pf. +5pf. Youths and Peace Dove	45	40

See also Nos. E1592/**MSE**1597.

(Des L. Grünewald. Litho)

1973 (13 Feb). 15th World Bobsleigh Championships, Oberhof. P 12½×13.

E1565	E **476** 35pf. multicoloured	75	55

E **477** Combine-harvester

E **478** Firecrest

(Des H. Detlefsen. Litho)

1973 (6 Mar). Leipzig Spring Fair. T E **477** and similar horiz design. Multicoloured. P 13×12½.

E1566	10pf. Type E **477**	35	35
E1567	25pf. Automatic lathe	60	55

(Des G. Voigt. Photo)

1973 (20 Mar). Songbirds. T E **478** and similar horiz designs. Multicoloured. P 14.

E1568	5pf. Type E **478**	35	35
E1569	10pf. White-winged Crossbill	35	35
E1570	15pf. Bohemian Waxwing	35	35
E1571	20pf. Bluethroats	35	35
E1572	25pf. Goldfinch	35	35
E1573	35pf. Golden Oriole	35	35
E1574	40pf. Grey Wagtail	40	30
E1575	50pf. Wallcreeper	4·25	4·25
E1568/E1575	Set of 8	6·00	6·00

E **479** Class 211 Electric Locomotive No. 200-3

(Des D. Glinski. Litho)

1973 (22 May). Railway Rolling Stock. T E **479** and similar horiz designs. Multicoloured. P 13×12½.

E1576	5pf. Type E **479**	45	30
E1577	10pf. Refrigerator wagon	45	30
E1578	20pf. Long-distance passenger carriage	45	30
E1579	25pf. Tank wagon	45	30
E1580	35pf. Double-deck carriage	45	30
E1581	85pf. Passenger carriage	3·75	3·25
E1576/E1581	Set of 6	5·50	4·25

GERMANY / German Democratic Republic (East Germany)

E 480 *King Lear* (Shakespeare) (directed by Wolfgang Langhoff)

E 481 H. Matern

(Des L. Grünewald Photo)
1973 (29 May). Famous Theatrical Productions. T E 480 and similar square designs. Multicoloured. P 13.
E1582	10pf. Type E 480	35	30
E1583	25pf. *A Midsummer Night's Dream* (opera by Benjamin Britten) (directed by Walter Felsenstein)	35	30
E1584	35pf. *Mother Courage* (Bertholt Brecht) (directed by author)	1·30	1·10
E1582/E1584	Set of 3	1·80	1·50

(Des G. Stauf. Litho)
1973 (13 June). 80th Birth Anniv of Hermann Matern (politician). P 13½×13.
E1585	E 481	40pf. claret	75	40

E 482 Goethe and House

E 483 Firework Display

(Des D. Dorfstecher. Litho)
1973 (26 June). Cultural Celebrities and Houses in Weimar. T E 482 and similar vert designs. Multicoloured. P 12½×13.
E1586	10pf. Type E 482	35	30
E1587	15pf. C. M. Wieland (writer)	35	30
E1588	20pf. F. Schiller (writer)	35	30
E1589	25pf. J. G. Herder (writer)	35	30
E1590	35pf. Lucas Cranach the Elder (painter)	35	30
E1591	50pf. Franz Liszt (composer)	3·75	2·00
E1586/E1591	Set of 6	5·00	3·25

(Des M. Gottschall and H. Detlefsen (**MS**E1597). Litho)
1973 (3–26 July). World Festival of Youth and Students, East Berlin (2nd issue). T E 483 and similar vert designs. Multicoloured. P 12½×13.
E1592	5pf. Type E 483	35	30
	a. Booklet pane. No. E1592×4	2·00	
E1593	15pf. Students (International Solidarity)	30	25
E1594	20pf. Young workers (Economic Integration)	35	30
	a. Booklet pane. No. E1594×4 (26.7)	2·00	
E1595	30pf. Students (Aid for Young Nations)	1·50	70
E1596	35pf. Youth and Students' Emblems	30	25
E1592/E1596	Set of 5	2·75	1·70
MSE1597	86×107 mm. 50pf. Emblem and Brandenburg Gate (26.7)	2·00	1·40

E 484 Walter Ulbricht

E 485 Power Network

(Des and eng K. Wolf. Recess)
1973 (8 Aug). Death of Walter Ulbricht. P 14.
E1598	E 484	20pf. black	1·00	55

(Des H. Detlefsen. Photo)
1973 (14 Aug). Tenth Anniv of 'Peace' United Energy Supply System. P 14.
E1599	E 485	35pf. bright orange, claret and pale blue	75	55

E 486 Leisure Activities

(Des M. Gottschall. Photo)
1973 (28 Aug). Leipzig Autumn Fair. T E 486 and similar horiz design depicting pastimes. Multicoloured. P 14.
E1600	10pf. Type E 486	35	30
E1601	25pf. Yacht, guitar and power drill	60	40

Nos. E1600/E1601 publicised the Expovita exhibition within the Fair.

E 487 Militiaman and Emblem

E 488 Red Flag encircling Globe

(Des J. Riess. Litho)
1973 (11 Sept). 20th Anniv of Workers' Militia. T E 487 and similar multicoloured designs. P 13×12½ or 12½×13 (50pf.).
E1602	10pf. Type E 487	35	30
E1603	20pf. Militia guard	60	30
MSE1604	61×87 mm. 50pf. Militiamen (*vert*)	1·90	1·70

(Des J. Riess. Photo)
1973 (11 Sept). 15th Anniv of Review 'Problems of Peace and Socialism'. P 14.
E1605	E 488	20pf. red and gold	85	40

E 489 Langenstein-Zwieberge Memorial

E 490 UN HQ and Emblems

(Des H. Detlefsen. Photo)
1973 (18 Sept). Langenstein-Zwieberge Monument. P 14.
E1606	E 489	25pf. multicoloured	85	40

(Des M. Gottschall. Photo)
1973 (19 Sept). Admission of German Democratic Republic to United Nations Organisation. P 13.
E1607	E 490	35pf. multicoloured	85	40

E 491 *Young Couple* (G. Glombitza)

E 492 Congress Emblem

(Des M. Gottschall. Photo)
1973 (4 Oct). Philatelists' Day and Third Young Philatelists' Exhibition, Halle. P 14.
E1608	E 491	20pf. +5pf. multicoloured	60	30

287

GERMANY / German Democratic Republic (East Germany)

(Des H. Detlefsen. Photo)
1973 (11 Oct). Eighth World Trade Union Congress, Varna, Bulgaria. P 14.
E1609　E **492**　35pf. multicoloured .... 75　55

E **493** Vietnamese Child
E **494** Launching Rocket 

(Des M. Gottschall. Photo)
1973 (11 Oct). Solidarity with Vietnam. P 14.
E1610　E **493**　10pf. +5pf. multicoloured .... 60　30

(Des M. Gottschall and G. Probock. Photo)
1973 (23 Oct). Soviet Science and Technology Days. T E **494** and similar multicoloured designs. P 14.
E1611　　　10pf. Type E **494** .... 35　30
E1612　　　20pf. Soviet map and emblem (*horiz*) .... 35　30
E1613　　　25pf. Oil refinery .... 1·50　1·10
E1611/E1613 Set of 3 .... 2·00　1·50

E **495** L. Corvalan
E **496** Child with Doll (C. L. Vogel) 

(Des J. Riess. Photo)
1973 (5 Nov). Solidarity with the Chilean People. T E **495** and similar vert design. Multicoloured. P 14.
E1614　　　10pf. +5pf. Type E **495** .... 35　35
E1615　　　25pf. +5pf. President Allende .... 75　70

(Des H. Naumann. Photo)
1973 (13 Nov). Paintings by Old Masters. T E **496** and similar vert designs. Multicoloured. P 14.
E1616　　　10pf. Type E **496** .... 35　30
E1617　　　15pf. *Madonna with Rose* (Parmigianino) .... 35　30
E1618　　　20pf. *Woman with Fair Hair* (Rubens) .... 35　30
E1619　　　25pf. *Lady in White* (Titian) .... 35　30
E1620　　　35pf. *Archimedes* (D. Fetti) .... 35　30
E1621　　　70pf. *Flower Arrangement* (Jan D. de Heem) .... 4·00　2·75
E1616/E1621 Set of 6 .... 5·25　3·75

E **497** Flame Emblem
E **498** Catching the Pike 

(Des D. Dorfstecher. Photo)
1973 (20 Nov). 25th Anniv of Declaration of Human Rights. P 13.
E1622　E **497**　35pf. multicoloured .... 85　55

(Des G. Bläser. Litho)
1973 (4 Dec). Fairy Tales. *At the Bidding of the Pike*. T E **498** and similar vert designs, showing different scenes. P 13½×13.
E1623　　　5pf. multicoloured .... 45　40
　　　　　a. Sheetlet of 6. Nos. E1623/E1628 .... 5·00
E1624　　　10pf. multicoloured .... 1·50　2·10
E1625　　　15pf. multicoloured .... 45　40
E1626　　　20pf. multicoloured .... 45　40
E1627　　　25pf. multicoloured .... 1·50　2·10
E1628　　　35pf. multicoloured .... 45　40
E1623/E1628 Set of 6 .... 4·25　5·25
　Nos. E1623/E1628 were issued together in *se-tenant* sheetlets of six stamps.

E **499** E. Hoernle

(Des G. Stauf. Photo)
1974 (8 Jan). Socialist Personalities. T E **499** and similar vert portraits. P 13.
E1629　　　10pf. olive-grey .... 45　30
E1630　　　10pf. slate-lilac .... 45　30
E1631　　　10pf. deep blue .... 45　30
E1632　　　10pf. brown-purple .... 45　30
E1633　　　10pf. grey-green .... 45　30
E1634　　　10pf. chestnut .... 45　30
E1635　　　10pf. chalky blue .... 45　30
E1636　　　10pf. olive-drab .... 45　30
E1629/E1636 Set of 8 .... 3·25　2·20
　Personalities:—No. E1629, T E **499**; No. E1630, Etkar Andre; E1631, Paul Merker; E1632, Hermann Duncker; E1633, Fritz Heckert; E1634, Otto Grotewohl; E1635, Wilhelm Florin; E1636, Georg Handke.
　See also Nos. E1682/E1684.

E **500** Pablo Neruda (Chilean Poet)

(Des H. Detlefsen. Photo)
1974 (22 Jan). Pablo Neruda Commemoration. P 14.
E1637　E **500**　20pf. multicoloured .... 80　45

E **501** Comecon Emblem
E **502** *Echinopsis multiplex* 

(Des J. Riess. Photo)
1974 (22 Jan). 25th Anniv of Council for Mutual Economic Aid. P 13.
E1638　E **501**　20pf. multicoloured .... 80　30

(Des M. Gottschall. Photo)
1974 (12 Feb). Cacti. T E **502** and similar vert designs. Multicoloured. P 14.
E1639　　　5pf. Type E **502** .... 40　30
E1640　　　10pf. *Lobivia haageana* .... 40　30
E1641　　　15pf. *Parodia sanguiniflora* .... 4·00　3·75
E1642　　　20pf. *Gymnocal monvillei* .... 40　30
E1643　　　25pf. *Neoporteria rapifera* .... 40　30
E1644　　　35pf. *Notocactus concinnus* .... 45　35
E1639/E1644 Set of 6 .... 5·50　4·75

288

GERMANY / German Democratic Republic (East Germany)

E 503 Handball Players

E 504 High-tension Testing Plant

(Des J. Riess. Litho)

1974 (26 Feb). Eighth Men's World Indoor Handball Championships. T E **503** and similar vert designs. P 13×13½.
E1645	5pf. multicoloured	60	60
	a. Horiz strip of 3. Nos. E1645/E1647	1·90	
E1646	10pf. multicoloured	60	60
E1647	35pf. multicoloured	60	60
E1645/E1647 Set of 3..		1·60	1·60

Nos. E1645/E1647 were issued together in horizontal *se-tenant* strips of three within the sheet, each strip depicting an indoor handball match in progress.

(Des H. Nebel. Photo)

1974 (5 Mar). Leipzig Spring Fair. T E **504** and similar multicoloured design. P 13.
E1648	10pf. Type E **504**	40	30
E1649	25pf. Robotron computer (*horiz*)	60	45

E 505 *Rhodophyllus sinuatus*

E 506 Gustav Kirchhoff (physicist: 150th Birth Anniv)

(Des F. Deutschendorf. Litho)

1974 (19 Mar). Poisonous Fungi. T E **505** and similar vert designs. Multicoloured. P 13.
E1650	5pf. Type E **505**	40	30
E1651	10pf. *Boletus satanas*	40	30
E1652	15pf. *Amanita pantherina*	40	30
E1653	20pf. *Amanita muscaria*	40	30
E1654	25pf. *Gyromitra esculenta*	40	30
E1655	30pf. *Inocybe patouillardii*	45	30
E1656	35pf. *Amanita phalloides*	45	30
E1657	40pf. *Clitocybe dealbata*	3·00	2·10
E1650/E1657 Set of 8..		5·25	3·75

(Des G. Stauf. Litho)

1974 (26 Mar). Celebrities' Birth Anniversaries. T E **506** and similar vert portraits. P 13.
E1658	5pf. black and grey	40	30
E1659	10pf. deep ultramarine and cobalt................	40	30
E1660	20pf. crimson and rose	40	30
E1661	25pf. slate-green and turquoise-green	40	30
E1662	35pf. chocolate and light brown	1·20	1·00
E1658/E1662 Set of 5..		2·50	2·00

Portraits:—5pf. T E **506**; 10pf. Immanuel Kant (philosopher, 250th); 20pf. Ehm Welk (writer, 90th); 25pf. Johann Herder (author, 230th); 35pf. Lion Feuchtwanger (novelist, 90th).

E 507 Globe and 'PEACE'

E 508 Tractor Driver

(Des H. Detlefsen. Photo)

1974 (16 Apr). 25th Anniv of First World Peace Congress. P 13.
E1663	E **507** 35pf. multicoloured	80	60

(Des H. Detlefsen. Photo)

1974 (30 Apr). 25th Anniv of German Democratic Republic. T E **508** and similar square designs. Multicoloured. P 13.
E1664	10pf. Type E **508**	40	35
E1665	20pf. Students	40	35
E1666	25pf. Woman worker	40	35
E1667	35pf. East German family.............................	1·70	1·50
E1664/E1667 Set of 4..		2·50	2·30

E 509 Buk Lighthouse, 1878

(Des J. Bertholdt. Litho)

1974 (7 May). Lighthouses (1st series). T E **509** and similar vert designs. Multicoloured. P 14.
E1668	10pf. Type E **509**	40	30
E1669	15pf. Warnemünde lighthouse, 1898............	40	30
E1670	20pf. Darsser Ort lighthouse, 1848...............	40	30
E1671	35pf. Arkona lighthouse in 1827 and 1902 ...	40	30
E1672	40pf. Greifswalder Oie lighthouse, 1855	2·20	1·70
E1668/E1672 Set of 5..		3·50	2·50

See also Nos. E1760/E1764.

E 510 *Man and Woman looking at the Moon*

E 511 Self-portrait

E 512 Lace Pattern

(Des J. Riess. Recess (No. **MS**E1677). Des H. Naumann. Photo (others))

1974 (21 May). Birth Bicentenary of Caspar Friedrich (painter). Horiz designs showing paintings as T E **510**, and T E **511**. Multicoloured (except No. **MS**E1677). P 14 (**MS**E1677) or 13½×14 (others).
E1673	10pf. Type E **510**	40	30
E1674	20pf. *The Stages of Life* (seaside scene)	40	30
E1675	25pf. *Heath near Dresden*	3·00	3·00
E1676	35pf. *Trees in the Elbe Valley*	45	30
E1673/E1676 Set of 4..		3·75	3·50
MSE1677 80×55 mm. E **511** 70pf. sepia..........................		2·50	3·25

(Des M. Gottschall. Litho)

1974 (11 June). Plauen Lace. T E **512** and similar vert designs showing lace patterns. P 13½×13.
E1678	10pf. black and violet	40	30
E1679	20pf. black, red-brown and bistre.................	40	30
E1680	25pf. black, blue and turquoise-blue............	2·30	1·90
E1681	35pf. black, magenta and bright rose...........	40	30
E1678/E1681 Set of 4..		3·25	2·50

(Des G. Stauf. Litho)

1974 (9 July). Socialist Personalities. Vert designs similar to T E **499**. P 13½×13.
E1682	10pf. deep turquoise-blue.............................	45	30
E1683	10pf. deep violet	45	30
E1684	10pf. light brown	45	30
E1682/E1684 Set of 3..		1·20	80

Designs:—No. E1682, R. Breitscheid; E1683, K. Bürger; E1684, C. Moltmann.

289

GERMANY / German Democratic Republic (East Germany)

E 513 Show Jumping

E 514 Crane lifting Diesel Locomotive

E 517 Arms of East Germany and Family

E 518 James Watt (paddle-steamer) and Modern Freighter

(Des H. Naumann. Photo)

1974 (13 Aug). International Horse-breeders' Congress, Berlin. T E **513** and similar multicoloured designs. P 14.

E1685	10pf. Type E 513	40	35
E1686	20pf. Horse and trap (*horiz*)	40	35
E1687	25pf. Haflinger draught horses (*horiz*)	2·75	3·25
E1688	35pf. Horse-racing (*horiz*)	45	35
E1685/E1688	Set of 4	3·50	3·75

(Des P. Reissmüller. Litho)

1974 (27 Aug). Autumn Fair, Leipzig. T E **514** and similar horiz design. Multicoloured. P 13×12½.

E1689	10pf. Type E 514	45	30
E1690	25pf. Agricultural machine	60	45

E 515 The Porcelain Shop

(Des M. Gottschall. Photo)

1974 (10 Sept). 'Mon Plaisir' Exhibits in Dolls' Village, Castle Museum, Arnstadt. T E **515** and similar vert designs. Multicoloured. P 14.

E1691	5pf. Type E 515	40	35
E1692	10pf. Fairground Crier	40	35
E1693	15pf. Wine-tasting in Cellar	40	35
E1694	20pf. Cooper and Apprentice	40	35
E1695	25pf. Bagpiper playing for Dancing Bear	2·30	2·20
E1696	35pf. Butcher's Wife and Crone	40	35
E1691/E1696	Set of 6	3·75	3·50

E 516 Ardeatine Caves Memorial, Rome

(Des H. Detlefsen. Photo)

1974 (24 Sept). International War Memorials. T E **516** and similar horiz design. P 13½×14.

E1697	35pf. black, light green and rose-carmine	60	60
E1698	35pf. black, new blue and rose-carmine	60	60

Designs:—No. E1697, T E **516**; No. E1698, Resistance memorial, Châteaubriant, France.

(Des H. Detlefsen. Photo)

1974 (3 Oct). 25th Anniv of German Democratic Republic. Sheet 90×108 mm. P 13.

MSE1699 E 517	1m. multicoloured	3·00	2·75

(Des M. Gottschall. Photo)

1974 (9 Oct). Centenary of Universal Postal Union. Mail Transport. T E **518** and similar vert designs. Multicoloured. P 14.

E1700	10pf. Type E 518	40	30
E1701	20pf. Steam and diesel locomotives	40	30
E1702	25pf. Early airliner and Tupolev Tu-134	40	30
E1703	35pf. Early mail coach and modern truck	1·90	1·50
E1700/E1703	Set of 4	2·75	2·20

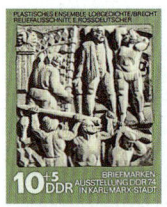

E 519 The Revolutionaries (E. Rossdeutscher)

E 520 The Sun shines for All (G. Mlosch)

(Des M. Gottschall. Litho)

1974 (24 Oct). DDR 1974 Stamp Exhibition. Sculptures in Karl-Marx-Stadt. T E **519** and similar vert designs in black, stone and dull yellowish green. P 13.

E1704	10pf. +5pf. Type E 519	45	35
	a. Horiz strip of 3. Nos. E1704/E1706	1·50	
E1705	20pf. The Dialetics (J. Jastram)	45	35
E1706	25pf. The Party (M. Wetzel)	45	35
E1704/E1706	Set of 3	1·20	95

Nos. E1704/E1706 were issued together in horizontal *se-tenant* strips of three within the sheet.

(Des H. Detlefsen. Litho)

1974 (26 Nov). Children's Paintings. T E **520** and similar vert designs. Multicoloured. P 13½×14.

E1707	20pf. Type E 520	60	60
	a. Sheetlet of 4. Nos. E1707/E1710 plus label	2·50	
E1708	20pf. My Friend Sascha (Birk Ozminski)	60	60
E1709	20pf. Carsten, best Swimmer in the Class (Michael Kluge)	60	60
E1710	20pf. Me and the Blackboard (Petra Westphal)	60	60
E1707/E1710	Set of 4	2·20	2·20

Nos. E1707/E1710 were issued together in sheetlets of four stamps and one large label depicting a Pioneer orchestra.

E 521 The Woodchopper

E 522 Still Life (R. Paris)

GERMANY / German Democratic Republic (East Germany)

(Des E. and G. Bläser. Litho)

1974 (3 Dec). Fairy Tales. *Twittering To and Fro* by A. Tolstoi. T E **521** and similar vert designs showing scenes from the story. P 13×13½.

E1711	10pf. multicoloured	40	35
	a. Sheetlet of 6. Nos. E1711/E1716	5·25	
E1712	15pf. multicoloured	1·70	1·60
E1713	20pf. multicoloured	40	35
E1714	30pf. multicoloured	40	35
E1715	35pf. multicoloured	1·70	1·60
E1716	40pf. multicoloured	40	35
E1711/E1716	Set of 6	4·50	4·25

Nos. E1711/E1716 were issued together in *se-tenant* sheetlets of six stamps.

(Des H. Naumann. Photo)

1974 (17 Dec). Paintings from Berlin Museums. T E **522** and similar multicoloured designs. P 13½×14 (horiz) or 14½×13 (vert).

E1717	10pf. Type E **522**	40	30
E1718	15pf. *Girl in Meditation* (W. Lachnit) (*vert*)	40	30
E1719	20pf. *Fisherman's House* (H. Hakenbeck) (*vert*)	40	30
E1720	35pf. *Girl in Red* (R. Bergander)	45	30
E1721	70pf. *Parents* (W. Sitte) (*vert*)	3·00	2·30
E1717/E1721	Set of 5	4·25	3·25

E **523** Banded Jasper

E **524** Martha Arendsee

(Des L. Grünewald. Photo)

1974 (17 Dec). Gemstones in Mining Academy Collection, Freiberg. T E **523** and similar horiz designs. Multicoloured. P 14×13½.

E1722	10pf. Type E **523**	40	30
E1723	15pf. Smoky quartz	40	30
E1724	20pf. Topaz	40	30
E1725	25pf. Amethyst	40	30
E1726	35pf. Aquamarine	45	30
E1727	70pf. Agate	3·00	2·30
E1722/E1727	Set of 6	4·50	3·50

(Des G. Stauf. Litho)

1975 (14 Jan). 90th Birth Anniv of Martha Arendsee (socialist). P 13½×13.

| E1728 | E **524** | 10pf. rose-carmine | 60 | 30 |

E **525** Peasants doing Forced Labour

E **526** Women and Emblem

(Des K. Müller. Photo)

1975 (11 Feb). 450th Anniv of Peasants' War. T E **525** and similar vert designs, showing contemporary woodcuts. P 12½×13.

E1729	5pf. black, pale sage-green and bluish grey	60	60
	a. Sheetlet of 6. Nos. E1729/E1734 plus label	4·75	
E1730	10pf. black, pale olive-sepia and bluish grey	60	60
E1731	20pf. black, pale azure and bluish grey	60	60
E1732	25pf. black, pale yellow-stone and bluish grey	1·10	1·00
E1733	35pf. black, pale claret and bluish grey	1·10	1·00
E1734	50pf. black, pale brownish grey and bluish grey	60	60
E1729/E1734	Set of 6	4·25	4·00

Designs:—5pf. T E **525**; 10pf. Paying tithes; 20pf. Thomas Mentzer; 25pf. Armed peasants; 35pf. Flag of Liberty; 50pf. Peasants on trial.

Nos. E1729/E1734 were issued together in sheets of six stamps and one double stamp-size inscribed label.

(Des J. Riess. Litho)

1975 (25 Feb). International Women's Year. T E **526** and similar vert designs showing women of different nations. P 13.

E1735	10pf. multicoloured	45	45
	a. Horiz strip of 3. Nos. E1735/E1737	1·50	
E1736	20pf. multicoloured	45	45
E1737	25pf. multicoloured	45	45
E1735/E1737	Set of 3	1·20	1·20

Nos. E1735/E1737 were issued together in horizontal *se-tenant* strips of three within the sheet.

E **527** Pentakta A 100 (microfilm camera)

E **528** Hans Otto (actor) (1900–1933)

(Des J. Bertholdt. Photo)

1975 (4 Mar). Spring Fair, Leipzig. T E **527** and similar horiz design. Multicoloured. P 14.

E1738	10pf. Type E **527**	45	30
E1739	25pf. SKET (cement works)	45	45

(Des G. Stauf. Litho)

1975 (18 Mar). Celebrities' Birth Annivs. T E **528** and similar vert designs. P 13.

E1740	5pf. deep grey blue	40	30
E1741	10pf. deep claret	40	30
E1742	20pf. dull blue-green	40	30
E1743	25pf. sepia	40	30
E1744	35pf. chalky blue	1·60	95
E1740/E1744	Set of 5	3·00	1·90

Designs:—5pf. T E **528**; 10pf. Thomas Mann (author) (1875–1955); 20pf. Dr. Albert Schweitzer (medical missionary) (1875–1965); 25pf. Michelangelo (artist) (1475–1564); 35pf. André Marie Ampère (physicist) (1775–1836).

E **529** Blue and Yellow Macaws

E **530** Soldiers, Industry and Agriculture

(Des R. Zieger. Litho)

1975 (25 Mar). Zoo Animals. T E **529** and similar multicoloured designs. P 13½×13 (vert) or 13×13½ (horiz).

E1745	5pf. Type E **529**	45	30
E1746	10pf. Orangutan	45	30
E1747	15pf. Ibex	45	30
E1748	20pf. Indian Rhinoceros (*horiz*)	45	30
E1749	25pf. Pygmy Hippopotamus (*horiz*)	45	30
E1750	30pf. Grey Seals (*horiz*)	45	30
E1751	35pf. Tiger (*horiz*)	45	30
E1752	50pf. Common Zebra	2·75	3·00
E1745/E1752	Set of 8	5·25	4·50

(Des M. Gottschall and J. Riess. Photo)

1975 (6 May). 20th Anniv of Warsaw Treaty. P 13½×14.

| E1753 | E **530** | 20pf. multicoloured | 2·00 | 60 |

E **531** Soviet Memorial, Berlin-Treptow

E **532** Ribbons with 'Komsomol' and 'FDJ' Badges

291

GERMANY / German Democratic Republic (East Germany)

(Des H. Detlefsen. Photo)
1975 (6 May). 30th Anniv of Liberation. T E **531** and similar vert designs. Multicoloured. P 14.
E1754	10pf. Type E **531**	40	35
E1755	20pf. Detail of Buchenwald memorial	40	35
E1756	25pf. Woman voluntary worker	40	35
E1757	35pf. Socialist economic integration	1·20	1·00
E1754/E1757	*Set of 4*	2·20	1·80
MSE1758	109×90 mm. 50pf. Soldier planting Red flag on Reichstag. Imperf	1·90	2·30

(Des H. Detlefsen. Photo)
1975 (13 May). Third Youth Festival of Friendship, Halle. P 14.
E1759	E **532**	10pf. multicoloured	80	30

(Des J. Bertholdt. Litho)
1975 (13 May). Lighthouses (2nd series). Vert designs similar to T E **509**. Multicoloured. P 13½×14.
E1760	5pf. Timmendorf lighthouse	45	30
E1761	10pf. Gellen lighthouse	45	30
E1762	20pf. Sassnitz lighthouse	45	30
E1763	25pf. Dornbusch lighthouse	45	30
E1764	35pf. Peenemünde lighthouse	1·60	1·20
E1760/E1764	*Set of 5*	3·00	2·20

E **533** Wilhelm Liebknecht and August Bebel

E **534** Dove and 'Scientific Co-operation between Socialist Countries'

(Des J. Riess. Photo)
1975 (21 May). Centenary of Marx's *Programmkritik* and Gotha Unity Congress. T E **533** and similar vert designs. P 13½×14.
E1765	10pf. deep brown, cinnamon and scarlet	45	35
	a. Horiz strip of 3. Nos. E1765/E1767	1·50	
E1766	20pf. multicoloured	45	35
E1767	25pf. deep brown, cinnamon and scarlet	45	35
E1765/E1767	*Set of 3*	1·20	95

Designs:—10pf. T E **533**; 20pf. Tivoli (meeting place at Gotha) and title-page of the Minutes of the *Unity Congress*; 25pf. Karl Marx and Friedrich Engels.
Nos. E1765/E1767 were issued together in horizontal *se-tenant* strips of three within the sheet.

(Des G. Voigt and Prof. Womacka. Litho)
1975 (10 June). 25th Anniv of Eisenhüttenstadt. P 13×13½.
E1768	E **534**	20pf. multicoloured	60	30

E **535** Construction Workers

E **536** Automatic Clock, 1585

(Des H. Detlefsen. Photo)
1975 (10 June). 30th Anniv of Free German Trade Unions Association. P 14×13½.
E1769	E **535**	20pf. multicoloured	60	30

(Des D. Dorfstecher and L. Ziratzki. Photo)
1975 (24 June). Ancient Clocks. T E **536** and similar vert designs. Multicoloured. P 14.
E1770	5pf. Type E **536**	40	30
E1771	10pf. Astronomical Mantlepiece clock, 1560	40	30
E1772	15pf. Automatic clock, 1600	2·30	2·20
E1773	20pf. Mantlepiece clock, 1720	40	30
E1774	25pf. Mantlepiece clock, 1700	40	30
E1775	35pf. Astronomical clock, 1738	40	30
E1770/E1775	*Set of 6*	3·75	3·25

E **537** Jacob and Wilhelm Grimm's German Dictionary

(Des A. Bengs. Litho)
1975 (2 July). 275th Anniv of Academy of Sciences. T E **537** and similar horiz designs. P 13.
E1776	10pf. black, sage-green and deep claret	40	30
E1777	20pf. black and ultramarine	40	30
E1778	25pf. black, greenish yellow and emerald	40	30
E1779	35pf. multicoloured	1·60	1·30
E1776/E1779	*Set of 4*	2·50	2·00

Designs:—10pf. T E **537**; 20pf. Karl Schwarzschildt's Observatory, Tautenburg; 25pf. Electro-microscope and chemical plant; 35pf. Intercosmic satellite.

E **538** Runner with Torch

E **539** Map of Europe

(Des W. Bremer. Litho)
1975 (15 July). Fifth National Youth Sports Day. T E **538** and similar vert designs. P 13½×13.
E1780	10pf. black and pink	40	30
E1781	20pf. black and lemon	40	30
E1782	25pf. black and cobalt	40	30
E1783	35pf. black and bright yellow-green	1·60	1·30
E1780/E1783	*Set of 4*	2·50	2·00

Designs:—10pf. T E **538**; 20pf. Hurdling; 25pf. Swimming; 35pf. Gymnastics.

(Des J. Bertholdt. Photo)
1975 (30 July). European Security and Co-operation Conference, Helsinki. P 13.
E1784	E **539**	20pf. multicoloured	80	45

E **540** Asters

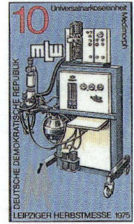

E **541** Medimorph (Anaesthetising machine)

(Des H. Naumann. Photo)
1975 (19 Aug). Flowers. T E **540** and similar vert designs. Multicoloured. P 14.
E1785	5pf. Type E **540**	40	30
E1786	10pf. Pelargoniums	40	30
E1787	20pf. Gerberas	40	30
E1788	25pf. Carnation	40	30
E1789	35pf. Chrysanthemum	45	30
E1790	70pf. Pansies	4·25	3·50
E1785/E1790	*Set of 6*	5·75	4·50

GERMANY / German Democratic Republic (East Germany)

(Des J. Bertholdt. Photo)
1975 (28 Aug). Autumn Fair, Leipzig. T E **541** and similar multicoloured design. P 14.
E1791	10pf. Type E **541**	40	30
E1792	25pf. Zschopau (MZ) TS 250 motorcycle (horiz)	80	45

E **542** School Crossing

(Des J. Riess. Litho)
1975 (9 Sept). Road Safety. T E **542** and similar horiz designs. Multicoloured. P 13×12½.
E1793	10pf. Type E **542**	40	30
E1794	15pf. Policewoman controlling traffic	2·50	1·30
E1795	20pf. Policeman assisting motorist	40	30
E1796	25pf. Car having check-up	40	30
E1797	35pf. Road safety instruction	40	30
E1793/E1797	Set of 5	3·75	2·30

E **543** Launch of Soyuz

E **544** Clenched Fist and Red Star

(Des J. Bertholdt. Photo)
1975 (15 Sept). Apollo–Soyuz Space Link. T E **543** and similar multicoloured designs. P 14×13½ (vert) or 13½×14 (horiz).
E1798	10pf. Type E **543**	40	30
E1799	20pf. Spaceships in linking manoeuvre	40	30
E1800	70pf. The completed link (83×33 *mm*)	3·00	2·50
E1798/E1800	Set of 3	3·50	2·75

(Des M. Gottschall. Litho)
1975 (23 Sept). 'International Solidarity'. P 13.
E1801	E **544**	10pf. +5pf. black, orange-red and brown-olive	60	30

E **545** Weimar in 1650 (Merian)

E **546** Vienna Memorial (F. Cremer)

(Des D. Dorfstecher. Litho)
1975 (23 Sept). Millenary of Weimar. T E **545** and similar designs. P 13½×13 (horiz) or 13×13½ (vert).
E1802	10pf. sepia, pale green and green	40	30
E1803	20pf. multicoloured	40	30
E1804	35pf. multicoloured	95	75
E1802/E1804	Set of 3	1·60	1·20

Designs: Horiz—10pf. T E **545**. Vert—20pf. Buchenwald memorial. Horiz—35pf. Weimar buildings (975–1975).

(Des L. Grünewald. Photo)
1975 (14 Oct). Austrian Patriots Monument, Vienna. P 14×13½.
E1805	E **546**	35pf. multicoloured	80	30

E **547** Louis Braille

E **548** Post Office Gate, Wurzen

(Des M. Gottschall. Photo)
1975 (14 Oct). International Braille Year. T E **547** and similar horiz designs. Multicoloured. P 14.
E1806	20pf. Type E **547**	40	30
E1807	35pf. Hands reading braille	40	30
E1808	50pf. An eye-ball, eye-shade and safety goggles	2·50	2·20
E1806/E1808	Set of 3	3·00	2·50

(Des J. Riess. Photo)
1975 (21 Oct). National Philatelists' Day. T E **548** and similar horiz design. Multicoloured. P 14×13½.
E1809	10pf. +5pf. Type E **548**	80	75
E1810	20pf. Post Office, Bärenfels	40	30

E **549** The Emperor's New Clothes

(Des G. Bläser. Litho)
1975 (18 Nov). Fairy Tales. *The Emperor's New Clothes* by Hans Christian Andersen. T E **549** and similar horiz designs showing scenes from the story. P 14×13½.
E1811	20pf. multicoloured	80	75
	a. Sheetlet of 3. Nos. E1811/E1813	3·00	
E1812	35pf. multicoloured	1·20	1·20
E1813	50pf. multicoloured	80	75
E1811/E1813	Set of 3	2·50	2·40

Nos. E1811/E1813 were issued together in *se-tenant* sheetlets of three stamps.

E **550** Tobogganing

E **551** Wilhelm Pieck

(Des J. Riess. Photo)
1975 (2 Dec). Winter Olympic Games, Innsbruck (1976). T E **550** and similar horiz designs. Multicoloured. P 13½×14.
E1814	5pf. Type E **550**	40	30
E1815	10pf. +5pf. Bobsleigh track	40	30
E1816	20pf. Speed-skating rink	40	30
E1817	25pf. +5pf. Ski-jump	45	30
E1818	35pf. Skating rink	45	30
E1819	70pf. Skiing	3·50	2·50
E1814/E1819	Set of 6	5·00	3·50
MSE1820	80×55 mm. 1m. Innsbruck (33×28 *mm*). P 14×13½	4·00	3·00

(Des G. Stauf. Litho)
1975 (30 Dec). Birth Centenary of Wilhelm Pieck (statesman). P 13½×13.
E1821	E **551**	10pf. blackish brown and new blue	45	30

(Des G. Stauf. Litho)
1976 (13 Jan). Members of German Workers' Movement. Vert designs similar to T E **551**. P 13½×13.
E1822	10pf. blackish brown and dull rose	40	30
E1823	10pf. blackish brown and bright green	40	30
E1824	10pf. blackish brown and dull orange	40	30
E1825	10pf. blackish brown and bright reddish violet	40	30
E1822/E1825	Set of 4	1·40	1·10

GERMANY / German Democratic Republic (East Germany)

Designs:—No. E1822 Ernst Thälmann; E1823, Georg Schumann; E1824. Wilhelm Koenen; E1825, John Schehr.
No. E1822 in black and violet is a colour changeling.

E 552 Organ, Rötha
E 553 Richard Sorge 
E 558 Telecommunications Satellite Tracking Radar
E 559 Marx, Engels, Lenin and Socialist Party Emblem

(Des G. Voigt. Photo)

1976 (27 Jan). Gottfried Silbermann (organ builder) Commemoration. T E **552** and similar vert designs. Multicoloured. P 14.

E1826	10pf. Type E **552**	40	30
E1827	20pf. Organ, Freiberg	40	30
E1828	35pf. Organ, Fraureuth	40	30
E1829	50pf. Organ, Dresden	2·30	1·50
E1826/E1829	Set of 4	3·25	2·20

(Dies G. Stauf. Litho)

1976 (3 Feb). Dr. Richard Sorge (Soviet agent) Commemoration. Sheet 82×65 mm. Imperf.
MSE1830 E **553** 1m. black and pale olive-grey .... 3·50 3·25

1976 (27 Apr). Intersputnik. P 13½×14.
E1837   E **558**   20pf. multicoloured 60   30

(Des M. Köenig (10pf.), J. Bertholdt (20pf.), M. Gottschall (1m.). Photo)

1976 (11 May). Ninth Socialist Unity Party Congress, Berlin. T E **559** and similar designs. P 14×13½ (10pf.) or 13½×14 (others).
| E1838 | 10pf. vermilion, gold and carmine-lake | 45 | 30 |
| E1839 | 20pf. multicoloured | 45 | 30 |
MSE1840 110×91 mm. E **557** 1m. multicoloured........... 2·75   2·30
Designs: Horiz—10pf. T E **559**; 20pf. Industrial site, housing complex and emblem.

E 554 Servicemen and Emblem
E 560 Cycling

(Des K. Müller. Litho)

1976 (24 Feb). 20th Anniv of National Forces (NVA). T E **554** and similar horiz design. Multicoloured. P 14.
| E1831 | 10pf. Type E **554** | 40 | 30 |
| E1832 | 20pf. NVA equipment | 60 | 45 |

(Des J. Riess. Photo)

1976 (18 May). Olympic Games, Montreal. T E **560** and similar horiz designs. Multicoloured. P 13½×14.
E1841	5pf. Type E **560**	40	30
E1842	10pf. +5pf. Modern swimming-pool	40	30
E1843	20pf. Modern sports-hall	40	30
E1844	25pf. Regatta course	40	30
E1845	35pf. +10pf. Rifle-range	45	30
E1846	70pf. Athletics	4·00	3·25
E1841/E1846	Set of 6	5·50	4·25
MSE1847 81×55 mm 1m. Modern sports stadium (33×28 mm) .... 3·00   2·75

E 555 Telephone and Inscription
E 556 Block of Flats, Leipzig

(Des D. Glinski. Litho)

1976 (2 Mar). Telephone Centenary. P 13½×13.
E1833   E **555**   20pf. greenish blue 60   30

(Des P. Reissmüller Photo)

1976 (9 Mar). Spring Fair, Leipzig. T E **556** and similar multicoloured design. P 14.
| E1834 | 10pf. Type E **556** | 40 | 35 |
| E1835 | 25pf. *Prometey* (deep sea trawler) (*horiz*) | 80 | 45 |

E 561 Intertwined Ribbon and Emblem
E 562 *Himantoglossum bircinum* 

(Des J. Riess. Photo)

1976 (25 May). Tenth Youth Parliament Conference, Berlin. T E **561** and similar horiz design. Multicoloured. P 14.
| E1848 | 10pf. Type E **561** | 40 | 30 |
| E1849 | 20pf. Members of Youth Parliament and stylised industrial plant | 45 | 45 |

E 557 Palace of Republic, Berlin

(Des J. Bertholdt. Photo) (Des M. Gottschall. Photo)

1976 (22 Apr). Opening of Palace of Republic, Berlin. P 13½×14.
E1836   E **557**   10pf. multicoloured .... 1·40   30
See also No. MSE1840.

(Des L. Grünewald. Litho)

1976 (15 June). Flowers. T E **562** and similar vert designs. Multicoloured. P 12½×13.
E1850	10pf. Type E **562**	40	30
E1851	20pf. *Dactylorhiza incarnata*	40	30
E1852	25pf. *Anacamptis pyramidalis*	40	30
E1853	35pf. *Dactylorhiza sambucina*	45	30
E1854	40pf. *Orchis coriophora*	45	30
E1855	50pf. *Cypripedium calceolus*	4·25	3·00
E1850/E1855	Set of 6	5·75	4·00

294

GERMANY / German Democratic Republic (East Germany)

E 563 Shetland Pony (H. Drake)

E 564 Marx, Engels, Lenin and Red Flag

(Des K. Wittkugel. Photo)

1976 (22 June). Statuettes from Berlin Museums. T E **563** and similar designs. P 13½×14 (horiz) or 14×13½ (vert).

E1856	10pf. blackish brown and turquoise-green	40	30
E1857	20pf. blackish brown and brown-ochre	40	30
E1858	25pf. blackish brown and pale orange	40	30
E1859	35pf. blackish brown and apple-green	40	30
E1860	50pf. blackish brown and salmon-pink	3·00	2·50
E1856/E1860 Set of 5		4·25	3·25

Designs: Horiz—10pf. T E **563**. Vert—20pf. *Tanzpause* (W. Arnold); 25pf. *Am Strand* (L. Engelhardt); 35pf. *Herman Duncker* (W. Howard); 50pf. *Das Gespräch* (G. Weidanz).

(Des M. Gottschall. Photo)

1976 (29 June). European Communist Parties' Conference. P 14.

| E1861 | E **564** | 20pf. blue, deep carmine and dull scarlet | 80 | 30 |

E 565 State Carriage, 1790

E 566 Gera in 1652

(Des K.-H. Bobbe. Photo)

1976 (27 July). 19th-century Horse-drawn Vehicles. T E **565** and similar horiz designs. Multicoloured. P 14.

E1862	10pf. Type E **565**	40	30
E1863	20pf. Russian trap, 1800	40	30
E1864	25pf. Carriage, 1840	40	30
E1865	35pf. State carriage, 1860	40	30
E1866	40pf. Stage-coach, 1850	45	30
E1867	50pf. Carriage, 1889	4·75	4·00
E1862/E1867 Set of 6		6·00	5·00

(Des J. Riess. Litho)

1976 (5 Aug). National Philatelists' Day. Gera. T E **566** and similar horiz design. Multicoloured. P 13½×12½.

E1868	10pf. +5pf. Type E **566**	40	30
	a. Horiz strip of 2. Nos. E1868/E1869 plus label	1·30	1·00
E1869	20pf. Gera buildings	40	30

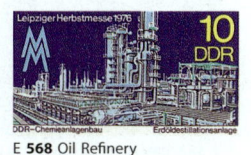

Nos. E1868/E1869 were issued together *se-tenant* with an intervening half stamp-size label showing town Arms.

E 567 Boxer

E 568 Oil Refinery

(Des J. Riess. Litho)

1976 (17 Aug). Domestic Dogs. T E **567** and similar horiz designs. Multicoloured. P 14.

E1870	5pf. Type E **567**	40	35
E1871	10pf. Airedale Terrier	40	35
E1872	20pf. Alsatian	40	35
E1873	25pf. Collie	40	35
E1874	35pf. Schnauzer	40	35
E1875	70pf. Great Dane	4·00	3·75
E1870/E1875 Set of 6		5·50	5·00

(Des G. Stauf. Litho)

1976 (1 Sept). Autumn Fair, Leipzig. T E **568** and similar horiz design. Multicoloured. P 13×12½.

| E1876 | 10pf. Type E **568** | 40 | 30 |
| E1877 | 25pf. Library, Leipzig | 60 | 30 |

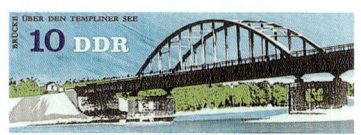

E 569 Railway Bridge, Templin Lake

(Des P. Reissmüller. Photo)

1976 (21 Sept). East German Bridges. T E **569** and similar horiz designs. Multicoloured. P 14.

E1878	10pf. Type E **569**	40	30
E1879	15pf. Adlergestell Railway Bridge, Berlin	40	30
E1880	20pf. River Elbe railway bridge, Rosslau	40	30
E1881	25pf. Göltzschtal Railway Viaduct	40	30
E1882	35pf. Elbe River Bridge, Magdeburg	40	30
E1883	50pf. Grosser Dreesch Bridge, Schwerin	3·00	3·00
E1878/E1883 Set of 6		4·50	4·00

E 570 Memorial Figures

E 571 Brass Jug, *c*. 1500

(Des L. Grünewald. Photo)

1976 (5 Oct). Patriots' Memorial, Budapest. P 13½×14.

| E1884 | E **570** | 35pf. multicoloured | 80 | 60 |

(Des G. Voight. Photo)

1976 (19 Oct). Exhibits from the Applied Arts Museum, Köpenick Castle, Berlin. T E **571** and similar vert designs. Multicoloured. P 14.

E1885	10pf. Type E **571**	40	30
E1886	20pf. Faience covered vase, *c*. 1710	40	30
E1887	25pf. Porcelain 'fruit-seller' table centre, *c*. 1768	40	30
E1888	35pf. Silver 'basket-carrier' statuette, *c*. 1700	40	30
E1889	70pf. Coloured glass vase, *c*. 1900	3·50	3·25
E1885/E1889 Set of 5		4·50	4·00

E 572 Berlin TV Tower

E 573 Spadetail Guppy

(Des H. Detlefsen. Litho)

1976 (19 Oct). Sozphilex 77 Stamp Exhibition, East Berlin (1st issue). P 13.

| E1890 | E **572** | 10pf. +5pf. blue, black and light red | 60 | 30 |

See also Nos. E1962/**MS**E1965.

(Des R. Zieger. Litho)

1976 (9 Nov). Aquarium Fish. Guppies. T E **573** and similar horiz designs. Multicoloured. P 13.

E1891	10pf. Type E **573**	40	30
E1892	15pf. Lyretail	40	30
E1893	20pf. Flagtail	40	30
E1894	25pf. Swordtail	40	30
E1895	35pf. Triangle	40	30
E1896	70pf. Roundtail	3·75	3·00
E1891/E1896 Set of 6		5·25	4·00

GERMANY / German Democratic Republic (East Germany)

E 574 Clay Pots, *c.* 3000 BC

E 575 The Miller and the King

E 578 Spring near Plaue, Thuringia

E 579 Book Fair Building

(Des D. Dorfstecher. Photo)

1976 (23 Nov). Archaeological Discoveries in the German Democratic Republic. T E **574** and similar diamond-shaped designs. Multicoloured. P 13.

E1897	10pf. Type E **574**	40	30
E1898	20pf. Bronze cult vessel on wheels, *c.* 1300 BC	40	30
E1899	25pf. Roman gold aureus of Tetricus I, AD 270–273	40	30
E1900	35pf. Viking cross-shaped pendant, 10th-century AD	40	30
E1901	70pf. Roman glass beaker, 3rd-century AD	3·50	3·25
E1897/E1901	Set of 5	4·50	4·00

(Des P. Rosié. Litho)

1976 (14 Dec). Fairy Tales. *Rumpelstiltskin*. T E **575** and similar vert designs showing scenes from the story. P 13.

E1902	5pf. multicoloured	45	30
	a. Sheetlet of 6. Nos. E1902/E1907	4·25	
E1903	10pf. multicoloured	1·10	1·00
E1904	15pf. multicoloured	45	30
E1905	20pf. multicoloured	45	30
E1906	25pf. multicoloured	1·10	1·00
E1907	30pf. multicoloured	45	30
E1902/E1907	Set of 6	3·50	3·00

Nos. E1902/E1907 were issued together in *se-tenant* sheetlets of six stamps.

E 576 *The Air* (Rosalba Carriera)

E 577 Arnold Zweig (author)

(Des H. Naumann. Photo)

1976 (14 Dec). Paintings by Old Masters from the National Art Collection, Dresden. T E **576** and similar vert designs. Multicoloured. P 13½×14.

E1908	10pf. Type E **576**	40	30
E1909	15pf. *Madonna and Child* (Murillo)	40	30
E1910	20pf. *Viola Player* (Bernardo Strozzi)	40	30
E1911	25pf. *Ariadne Forsaken* (Angelica Kauffmann)	40	30
E1912	35pf. *Old Man in Black Cap* (Bartolomeo Nazzari)	40	30
E1913	70pf. *Officer reading a Letter* (Gerard Teborch)	4·00	2·50
E1908/E1913	Set of 6	5·50	3·50

(Des G. Stauf. Litho)

1977 (8 Feb). German Celebrities. T E **577** and similar horiz designs. P 13½×12½.

E1914	10pf. brownish black and brown-rose	40	30
E1915	20pf. brownish black and grey	40	30
E1916	35pf. brownish black and green	40	30
E1917	40pf. brownish black and bright turquoise-blue	1·60	1·50
E1914/E1917	Set of 4	2·50	2·20

Designs:—10pf. T E **577**; 20pf. Otto von Guericke (scientist); 35pf. Albrect D. Thaer (agriculturalist); 40pf. Gustav Hertz (physicist).

(Des J. Riess. Litho)

1977 (24 Feb). Natural Phenomena. T E **578** and similar vert designs. Multicoloured. P 12½×13.

E1918	10pf. Type E **578**	40	30
E1919	20pf. Rock face near Jonsdorf	40	30
E1920	25pf. Oaks near Reuterstadt Stavenhagen	40	30
E1921	35pf. Rocky ledge near Saalburg	40	30
E1922	50pf. Erratic boulder near Furstenwalde/Spree	2·50	2·20
E1918/E1922	Set of 5	3·75	3·00

(Des J. Bertholdt. Photo)

1977 (8 Mar). Leipzig Spring Fair. T E **579** and similar horiz design. Multicoloured. P 14.

E1923	10pf. Type E **579**	40	30
E1924	25pf. Aluminium casting machine	45	30

E 580 Senftenberg Costume, Zly Komorow

E 581 Carl Friedrich Gauss

(Des H. Detlefsen. Photo)

1977 (22 Mar). Sorbian Historical Costumes. T E **580** and similar vert designs. Multicoloured. P 14.

E1925	10pf. Type E **580**	40	30
E1926	20pf. Bautzen, Budyšin	40	30
E1927	25pf. Klitten, Kletno	40	30
E1928	35pf. Nochten, Wochozy	40	30
E1929	70pf. Muskau, Mužakow	4·00	3·00
E1925/E1929	Set of 5	5·00	3·75

(Des G. Stauf. Litho)

1977 (19 Apr). Birth Bicentenary of Carl Friedrich Gauss (mathematician). P 13×12½.

E1930	E **581**	20pf. black and cobalt	1·10	45

E 582 Start of Race

E 583 Three Flags

(Des B. Lindner and R. Diedrichs. Photo)

1977 (19 Apr). 30th International Peace Cycle Race. T E **582** and similar vert designs. Multicoloured. P 13½×14.

E1931	10pf. Type E **582**	45	45
	a. Horiz strip of 3. Nos. E1931/E1933	1·60	
E1932	20pf. Spurt	45	45
E1933	35pf. Race finish	45	45
E1931/E1933	Set of 3	1·20	1·20

Nos. E1931/E1933 were issued together in horizontal *se-tenant* strips of three within the sheet.

GERMANY / German Democratic Republic (East Germany)

(Des L. Grünewald. Photo)
1977 (3 May). Ninth Congress of Free German Trade Unions Association. P 13.
E1934 E **583** 20pf. multicoloured 60 30

E **584** VKM Channel Converter and Filters

E **585** Shooting

(Des J. Bertholdt. Litho)
1977 (17 May). World Telecommunications Day. P 13½.
E1935 E **584** 20pf. black, new blue and red.............. 95 30

(Des E. Haller. Photo)
1977 (17 May). 25th Anniv of Sports and Technical Sciences Association. T E **585** and similar horiz designs. P 14.
E1936 10pf. black, pale blue and deep mauve........... 40 30
E1937 20pf. black, pale flesh and deep bluish green.. 40 30
E1938 35pf. black, pale green and red...................... 1·40 1·30
E1936/E1938 Set of 3.. 2·00 1·70
Designs:—10pf. T E **585**; 20pf. Diving; 35pf. Model boats.

E **586** Accordion, 1900

E **587** Bathsheba at the Fountain

(Des D. Dorfstecher. Photo)
1977 (14 June). Old Musical instruments from Vogtland. T E **586** and similar vert designs. Multicoloured. P 14.
E1939 10pf. Type E **586** 40 30
E1940 20pf. Treble viola da gamba, 1747 .... 40 30
E1941 25pf. Oboe, 1785; Clarinet, 1830, Flute, 1817 40 30
E1942 35pf. Concert zither, 1891 .... 40 30
E1943 70pf. Trumpet, 1860.. 4·00 3·50
E1939/E1943 Set of 5.. 5·00 4·25

(Des H. Naumann. Photo)
1977 (28 June). 400th Birth Anniv of Peter Paul Rubens. Dresden Gallery Paintings. T E **587** and similar designs. Multicoloured. P 14.
E1944 10pf. Type E **587** 40 30
E1945 15pf. *Mercury and Argus* (horiz) 40 30
E1946 20pf. *The Drunk Hercules* 40 30
E1947 25pf. *Diana's Return from Hunting* (horiz) 40 30
E1948 35pf. *The Old Woman with the Brazier* 45 30
E1949 50pf. *Leda with the Swan* (horiz).................... 5·75 3·75
E1944/E1949 Set of 6.. 7·00 4·75

E **588** Soviet and East German Flags

(Des K. Müller. Photo)
1977 (28 June). 30th Anniv of German-Soviet Friendship Society. Sheet 80×55 mm. P 14.
MSE1950 E **588** 50pf. multicoloured........................... 2·50 2·30

E **589** Tractor and Plough

(Des D. Glinski. Litho)
1977 (12 July). Modern Agricultural Techniques. T E **589** and similar horiz designs. Multicoloured. P 13×12½.
E1951 10pf. Type E **589** 40 30
E1952 20pf. Fertiliser spreader on truck 40 30
E1953 25pf. Potato digger and loader....................... 40 30
E1954 35pf. High-pressure collecting press............... 40 30
E1955 50pf. Milking machine .... 3·50 3·00
E1951/E1955 Set of 5.. 4·50 3·75

E **590** High Jump

(Des R.-J. Lehmann. Litho)
1977 (19 July). Sixth Gymnastics and Athletic Meeting. Sixth Children and Young Peoples Sports Days, Leipzig. T E **590** and similar horiz designs. Multicoloured. P 13×12½.
E1956 5pf. Type E **590** 40 30
E1957 10pf. +5pf. Running.. 40 30
E1958 20pf. Hurdling... 40 30
E1959 25pf. +5pf. Gymnastics.................................... 40 30
E1960 35pf. Dancing.. 40 30
E1961 40pf. Torch bearer and flags........................... 3·00 3·00
E1956/E1961 Set of 6.. 4·50 4·00

E **591** *Bread for Everybody* (Wolfram Schubert)

E **592** 'Konsument' Department Store, Leipzig

E **593** Bust of Dzerzhinsky and Young Pioneers

(Des H. Naumann. Photo)
1977 (16 Aug). Sozphilex 77 Stamp Exhibition, East Berlin (2nd issue). T E **591** and similar designs. Multicoloured. P 13×12½ (**MS**E1965) or 14 (others).
E1962 10pf. Type E **591** 45 30
E1963 25pf. *... when Communists are Dreaming* (Walter Womacka) 95 75
MSE1964 Two sheets each 77×110 mm. (a) No. E1962×4; (b) No. E1963×4 *Set of two sheets*............ 6·25 5·25
MSE1965 85×54 mm. 50pf.+20pf. *World Youth Song* (Lothar Zitzmann) (horiz)................................... 2·75 2·20

(Des P. Reismüller. Photo)
1977 (30 Aug). Leipzig Autumn Fair. T E **592** and similar vert design. Multicoloured. P 14.
E1966 10pf. Type E **592** 60 30
E1967 25pf. Carved bowl and Thuringian blown-glass vases 60 45

(Des G. Stauf. Litho)
1977 (6 Sept). Birth Centenary of Feliks E. Dzerzhinsky (founder of Soviet Cheka). Sheet 127×69 mm containing T E **593** and similar vert design. Multicoloured. P 12½×13.
MSE1968 20pf. Type E **593**; 35pf. Portrait..................... 2·50 3·00

E **594** Steam Locomotive *Muldenthal*, 1861

E **595** *Aurora* (Russian cruiser)

297

GERMANY / German Democratic Republic (East Germany)

(Des H. Detlefsen. Photo)

1977 (13 Sept). Transport Museum, Dresden. T E **594** and similar horiz designs. Multicoloured. P 14.

E1969	5pf. Type E **594**	45	30
E1970	10pf. Dresden tram, 1896	45	30
E1971	20pf. Hans Grade's monoplane, 1909	45	30
E1972	25pf. Phanomobil tricar, 1924	45	30
E1973	35pf. River Elbe passenger steamer, 1837	4·75	3·50
E1969/E1973	Set of 5	6·00	4·25

(Des M. Gottschall. Photo)

1977 (20 Sept). 60th Anniv of October Revolution. T E **595** and similar designs. Multicoloured. P 12½×13 (**MS**E1976) or 14 (others).

E1974	10pf. Type E **595**	60	30
E1975	25pf. Assault on Winter Palace	95	75
MSE1976	55×86 mm. 1m. Lenin (vert)	3·75	3·00

E **596** Soviet Memorial

E **597** Flaming Torch

(Des J. Riess. Litho)

1977 (20 Sept). Soviet Memorial, Berlin-Schönholz. P 14.
E1977 E **596** 35pf. multicoloured 80 30

(Des R. Platzer. Litho)

1977 (18 Oct). 'Solidarity'. P 13½×14.
E1978 E **597** 10pf. +5pf. multicoloured 60 30

E **598** Ernst Meyer

E **599** Heinrich von Kleist

(Des G. Stauf. Litho)

1977 (18 Oct). Socialist Personalities. T E **598** and similar vert designs. Portaits in sepia, background colours below. P 14.

E1979	10pf. light bistre	40	35
E1980	10pf. light Venetian red	40	35
E1981	10pf. light greenish blue	40	35
E1979/E1981	Set of 3	1·10	95

Designs:—No. E1979, T E **598**; No. E1980, August Frolich; No. E1981, Gerhart Eisler.

(Des P. Rosié. Litho)

1977 (18 Oct). Birth Bicentenary of Heinrich von Kleist (poet). Sheet 82×54 mm. P 14.
MSE1982 E **599** 1m. black and deep red .... 5·00 3·75

E **600** Rocket pointing Right

E **601** Mouflons

(Des G. Schutz. Photo)

1977 (8 Nov). 20th Masters of Tomorrow Fair, Leipzig. T E **600** and similar horiz design. P 14.

E1983	10pf. rose-red, silver and black	45	30
	a. Horiz strip of 2. Nos. E1983/E1984 plus label	1·10	1·00
E1984	20pf. blue, gold and black	45	30

Designs:—10pf. T E **600**; 20pf. Rocket pointing left.
Nos. E1983/E1984 were issued together se-tenant with an intervening half stamp-size label bearing inscription and emblems of exhibition.

(Des H. Naumann. Photo)

1977 (15 Nov). Hunting. T E **601** and similar vert designs. Multicoloured. P 14.

E1985	10pf. Type E **601**	40	30
E1986	15pf. Red Deer	4·00	3·75
E1987	20pf. Shooting Ring-necked Pheasant	40	30
E1988	25pf. Red Fox and Mallard	45	30
E1989	35pf. Tractor driver with Roe Deer Fawn	45	30
E1990	70pf. Wild Boars	60	30
E1985/E1990	Set of 6	5·75	4·75

E **602** Firemen with Scaling Ladders

E **603** Traveller and King

(Des J. Bertholdt. Litho)

1977 (22 Nov). Fire Brigade. T E **602** and similar designs. Multicoloured. P 14.

E1991	10pf. Type E **602**	40	30
E1992	20pf. Children visiting fire brigade (vert)	40	30
E1993	25pf. Fire engines in countryside	40	30
E1994	35pf. Artificial respiration (vert)	40	30
E1995	50pf. Fire-fighting tug	3·75	3·25
E1991/E1995	Set of 5	4·75	4·00

(Des P. Rosié. Litho)

1977 (22 Nov). Fairy Tales. Six World Travellers (Brothers Grimm). T E **603** and similar vert designs showing scenes from the story. P 13×13½.

E1996	5pf. multicoloured	40	30
	a. Sheetlet of 6. Nos. E1996/E2001	4·75	
E1997	10pf. multicoloured	1·40	1·30
E1998	20pf. multicoloured	40	30
E1999	25pf. multicoloured	40	30
E2000	35pf. multicoloured	1·40	1·30
E2001	60pf. multicoloured	40	30
E1996/E2001	Set of 6	4·00	3·50

Nos. E1996/E2001 were issued together in se-tenant sheetlets of six stamps.

E **604** Rosehips

E **605** Amilcar Cabral

(Des Hannelore Heise. Photo)

1978 (10 Jan). Medicinal Plants. T E **604** and similar horiz designs. Multicoloured. P 14.

E2002	10pf. Type E **604**	40	30
E2003	15pf. Birch leaves	40	30
E2004	20pf. Camomile flowers	40	30
E2005	25pf. Coltsfoot	40	30
E2006	35pf. Lime flowers	40	30
E2007	50pf. Elder flowers	4·00	3·75
E2002/E2007	Set of 6	5·50	4·75

(Des L. Grünewald. Litho)

1978 (17 Jan). Amilcar Cabral Commemoration (nationalist leader of Guinea-Bissau). P 13½×14.
E2008 E **605** 20pf. multicoloured 80 60

GERMANY / German Democratic Republic (East Germany)

E **606** Town Hall, Suhl-Heinrichs

E **607** Post Office Van, 1921

(Des L. Grünewald. Photo)
1978 (24 Jan). Half-timbered Buildings. T E **606** and similar vert designs. Multicoloured. P 13½×14.

E2009	10pf. Type E **606**	40	30
E2010	20pf. Farmhouse, Niederoderwitz	40	30
E2011	25pf. Farmhouse, Strassen	40	30
E2012	35pf. House, Quedlinburg	40	30
E2013	40pf. House, Eisenach	3·75	3·25
E2009/E2013 Set of 5		4·75	4·00

(Des H. Detlefsen. Litho)
1978 (9 Feb). Postal Transport. T E **607** and similar horiz designs. Multicoloured. P 13×12½.

E2014	10pf. Type E **607**	40	35
	a. Block of 4. Nos. E2014/E2017	3·50	
E2015	20pf. Postal truck, 1978	80	75
E2016	25pf. Railway mail coach, 1896	95	85
E2017	35pf. Railway mail coach, 1978	1·20	1·20
E2014/E2017 Set of 4		3·00	2·75

Nos. E2014/E2017 were issued together in *se-tenant* blocks of four within the sheet.

E **608** Ear-pendant, 11th-century

E **609** Royal House, Market Square, Leipzig

(Des K.-H. Bobbe. Photo)
1978 (21 Feb). Slavonic Treasures. T E **608** and similar vert designs. Multicoloured. P 13½×14.

E2018	10pf. Type E **608**	40	30
E2019	20pf. Ear-ring, 10th-century	40	30
E2020	25pf. Bronze tag, 10th-century	40	30
E2021	35pf. Bronze horse, 12th-century	45	30
E2022	70pf. Arabian coin, 8th-century	3·00	3·00
E2018/E2022 Set of 5		4·25	3·75

(Des P. Reissmüller. Photo)
1978 (7 Mar). Leipzig Spring Fair. T E **609** and similar vert design. P 13½×14.

E2023	10pf. orange-yellow, black and red	40	30
E2024	25pf. bright green, black and red	80	60

Designs:—10pf. T E **609**; 25pf. Universal measuring instrument, U MK10/1318.

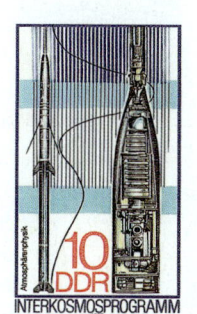

E **610** M-100 Meteorological Rocket

E **611** Samuel Heinicke (founder)

(Des J. Bertholdt. Photo)
1978 (21 Mar). Interkosmos Space Programme. T E **610** and similar vert designs. Multicoloured. P 14×13½.

E2025	10pf. Type E **610**	40	35
E2026	20pf. *Interkosmos 1* satellite	40	35
E2027	35pf. *Meteor* satellite with Fourier spectrometer	1·90	1·70
E2025/E2027 Set of 3		2·40	2·20
MSE2028 90×109 mm. 1m. MKF-6 multispectral camera		4·75	3·50

(Des J. Riess. Litho)
1978 (4 Apr). Bicentenary of First National Deaf and Dumb Educational Institution. T E **611** and similar horiz design. Multicoloured. P 13×12½.

E2029	20pf. Type E **611**	40	35
E2030	25pf. Child learning alphabet	1·20	1·20

E **612** Radio-range Tower, Dequede, and Television Transmission Van

E **613** Saxon Miner in Gala Uniform

(Des J. Bertholdt. Photo)
1978 (25 Apr). World Telecommunications Day. T E **612** and similar vert design. Multicoloured. P 14×13½ (10pf.) or 13½×14 (20pf.).

E2031	10pf. Type E **612**	45	30
E2032	20pf. Equipment in Berlin television tower, and Dresden television tower	45	45

(Des E. Haller. Litho)
1978 (9 May). 19th-Century Gala Uniforms of Mining and Metallurgical Industries. T E **613** and similar vert designs. Multicoloured. P 12½×13.

E2033	10pf. Type E **613**	40	30
E2034	20pf. Freiburg foundry worker	40	30
E2035	25pf. School of Mining academician	40	30
E2036	35pf. Chief Inspector of Mines	2·30	1·50
E2033/E2036 Set of 4		3·25	2·20

E **614** Lion Cub (*Panthera leo*)

E **615** Loading Container

(Des Hannelore Heise and M. Lissmann. Photo)
1978 (23 May). Centenary of Leipzig Zoo. T E **614** and similar horiz designs. Multicoloured. P 14.

E2037	10pf. Type E **614**	45	30
E2038	20pf. Leopard cub (*Panthera pardus*)	45	30
E2039	35pf. Tiger cub (*Panthera tigris*)	45	30
E2040	50pf. Snow Leopard cub (*Uncia uncia*)	2·50	2·20
E2037/E2040 Set of 4		3·50	2·75

(Des D. Glinski. Litho)
1978 (13 June). Container Goods Traffic. T E **615** and similar vert designs. Multicoloured. P 12½×13.

E2041	10pf. Type E **615**	40	30
E2042	20pf. Placing container on truck	40	30
E2043	35pf. Diesel locomotive and container wagons	40	30
E2044	70pf. Placing containers on *Boltenhagen* (container ship)	3·50	2·50
E2041/E2044 Set of 4		4·25	3·00

GERMANY / German Democratic Republic (East Germany)

E **616** Clay Ox (Egyptian Museum, Leipzig)

E **617** Justus von Liebig

E **620** Trooper with Halberd (Hans Schäufelein)

E **621** Multicar 25 Truck

(Des M. Gottschall. Photo)

1978 (20 June). Ancient African Works of Art in Egyptian Museums at Leipzig and Berlin. T E **616** and similar designs. Multicoloured. P 14.

E2045	5pf. Type E **616**	40	30
E2046	10pf. Clay head of woman (Leipzig)	40	30
E2047	20pf. Gold bangle (Berlin) (horiz)	40	30
E2048	25pf. Gold ring plate (Berlin)	40	30
E2049	35pf. Gold signet-ring plate (Berlin)	40	30
E2050	40pf. Necklace (Berlin) (horiz)	2·30	1·90
E2045/E2050	Set of 6	3·75	3·00

(Des G. Stauf. Litho)

1978 (18 July). Celebrities' Birth Anniversaries. T E **617** and similar vert designs. P 13½×12½.

E2051	5pf. black and yellow-ochre	40	30
E2052	10pf. black and grey-blue	40	30
E2053	15pf. black and apple green	40	30
E2054	20pf. black and cobalt	40	30
E2055	25pf. black and red	40	30
E2056	35pf. black and bright green	40	30
E2057	70pf. black and drab	2·75	2·20
E2051/E2057	Set of 7	4·75	3·50

Designs:—5pf. T E **617** (agricultural chemist–175th birth anniv); 10pf. Joseph Dietzgen (writer–150th); 15pf. Alfred Döblin (novelist–100th); 20pf. Hans Loch (politician–80th); 25pf. Theodor Brugsch (scientist–100th); 35pf. Friedrich Ludwig Jahn (gymnast–200th); 70pf. Albrecht von Graefe (ophthalmatician–150th).

E **618** Cottbus, 1730

(Des J. Riess. Litho)

1978 (18 July). Fifth National Youth Stamp Exhibition, Cottbus. T E **618** and similar horiz design. Multicoloured. P 13½×12.

E2058	10pf. +5pf. Type E **618**	45	45
	a. Horiz strip of 2. Nos. E2058/E2059 plus label	95	95
E2059	20pf. Modern Cottbus	45	45

Nos. E2058/E2059 were issued together *se-tenant* with an intervening half stamp-size label bearing inscription and Cottbus Arms.

E **619** Havana Buildings and Festival Emblem

(Des M Gottschall. Litho)

1978 (25 July). 11th World Youth and Students' Festival, Havana. T E **619** and similar horiz design. Multicoloured. P 13½×12½.

E2060	20pf. Type E **619**	60	60
	a. Horiz strip of 2. Nos. E2060/E2061 plus label	1·40	1·40
E2061	35pf. East Berlin buildings and Festival emblem	60	60

Nos. E2060/E2061 were issued together *se-tenant* with an intervening half stamp-size inscribed label.

(Des H. Naumann. Litho)

1978 (25 July). Drawings in Berlin State Museum. Sheet 110×98 mm containg T E **620** and similar vert designs, each brownish black and stone. P 13½×14.

MSE2062 10pf. Type E **620**; 20pf. *Woman reading a Letter* (Jean Antoine Watteau); 25pf. *Seated Boy* (Gabriel Metsu); 30pf. *Young Man cutting a Loaf* (Cornelis Saftleven); 35pf. *St. Anthony in a Landscape* (Matthias Grünewald); 50pf. *Man seated in an Armchair* (Abraham van Diepenbeeck) .... 5·50 5·25

(Des J. Bertholdt. Photo)

1978 (29 Aug). Leipzig Autumn Fair. T E **621** and similar vert design. Multicoloured. P 14.

E2063	10pf. Type E **621**	40	30
E2064	25pf. 'Three Kings' Fair building, Petersstrasse	80	60

E **622** Soyuz Spaceship and Emblems

(Des J. Bertholdt. Photo)

1978 (4 Sept). Soviet-East German Space Flight (1st issue). P 13½×14.

E2065	E **622**	20pf. multicoloured	80	45

See also Nos. E2069/**MS**E2073.

E **623** Mauthausen Memorial

(Des L. Grünewald. Photo)

1978 (5 Sept). War Victims' Memorial, Mauthausen, Austria. P 14.

E2066	E **623**	35pf. multicoloured	80	45

E **624** WMS Unit on the March

E **625** Soyuz, MKF 6M Camera and Space Station

(Des M. König and R. Diedrichs. Photo)

1978 (19 Sept). 25th Anniv of Workers' Militia Squads. T E **624** and similar horiz design. Multicoloured. P 14.

E2067	20pf. Type E **624**	80	60
	a. Horiz strip of 2. Nos. E2067/E2068 plus label	1·70	1·60
E2068	35pf. Members of Red Army, National People's Army and WMS	80	60

Nos. E2067/E2068 were issued together *se-tenant* with an intervening half stamp-size label bearing the WMS emblem.

GERMANY / German Democratic Republic (East Germany)

(Des D. Glinski (20pf.), J. Bertholdt (others). Litho)
1978 (21 Sept). Soviet-East German Space Flight (2nd issue). T E **625** and similar designs. Multicoloured. P 14 (1m.), 13×13½ (20pf.) or 13½×13 (others).

E2069	5pf. Type E **625**	40	30
E2070	10pf. Albert Einstein and Soyuz	40	30
E2071	20pf. Sigmund Jahn (first East German cosmonaut) (*vert*)	40	30
E2072	35pf. Salyut, Soyuz and Otto Lilienthal monoplane glider	1·60	1·50
E2069/E2072	Set of 4	2·50	2·20
MSE2073	110×90 mm. 1m. Space station and cosmonauts Valeri Bykovski and Jähn (54×32 *mm*)	3·75	3·50

E **626** Human Pyramid

E **627** African behind Barbed Wire

(Des L. Grünewald. Photo)
1978 (26 Sept). The Circus. T E **626** and similar vert designs. Multicoloured. P 14.

E2074	5pf. Type E **626**	60	1·00
	a. Block of 4. Nos. E2074/E2077	8·00	
E2075	10pf. Elephant on tricycle	1·10	1·50
E2076	20pf. Performing horse	1·90	2·50
E2077	35pf. Polar Bear kissing girl	3·00	5·00
E2074/E2077	Set of 4	6·00	9·00

Nos. E2074/E2077 were issued together in *se-tenant* blocks of four within the sheet.

(Des H. Detlefsen after sketch by Lola Gruner. Litho)
1978 (3 Oct). International Anti-Apartheid Year. P 12½×13.

E2078	E **627** 20pf. multicoloured	80	30

E **628** Construction of Natural Gas Pipe Line

E **629** *Parides hahneli* (*Papilio hahneli*)

(Des P. Reissmüller. Litho)
1978 (3 Oct). Construction of 'Friendship Line' (Drushba-Trasse) by East German Youth. P 13×12½.

E2079	E **628** 20pf. multicoloured	80	30

(Des H. Zill. Photo)
1978 (24 Oct). 250th Anniv of Dresden Scientific Museums. T E **629** and similar vert designs. Multicoloured. P 13½×14.

E2080	10pf. Type E **629**	40	30
E2081	20pf. *Agama lehmanni*	40	30
E2082	25pf. Agate	40	30
E2083	35pf. *Palaeobatrachus diluvianus*	40	30
E2084	40pf. Mantlepiece clock, *c*. 1720	45	30
E2085	50pf. Table telescope, *c*. 1750	4·00	3·25
E2080/E2085	Set of 6	5·50	4·25

E **630** Wheel-lock Gun, 1630

(Des L. Grünewald. Photo)
1978 (21 Nov). Sporting Guns from Suhl. T E **630** and similar horiz designs. Multicoloured. P 14.

E2086	5pf. Type E **630**	45	30
	a. Vert strip of 3. Nos. E2086, E2088 and E2090	2·30	
E2087	10pf. Double-barrelled gun, 1978	45	30
	a. Vert strip of 3. Nos. E2087, E2089 and E2091	3·25	
E2088	20pf. Spring-cock gun, 1780	45	45
E2089	25pf. Superimposed double-barrelled gun, 1978	60	60
E2090	35pf. Percussion gun, 1850	95	85
E2091	70pf. Three-barrelled gun, 1978	1·90	1·70
E2086/E2091	Set of 6	4·25	3·75

Nos. E2086/E2091 were issued together in vertical *se-tenant* strips of three in sheets containing either 5, 20 and 35pf. or 10, 25 and 70pf.

E **631** Old Woman and Youth

E **632** Chaffinches

(Des P. Rosié. Litho)
1978 (21 Nov). Fairy Tales. *Rapunzel*. (Brothers Grimm). T E **631** and similar vert designs showing scenes from the story. P 13×13½.

E2092	10pf. multicoloured	45	30
	a. Sheetlet of 6. Nos. E2092/E2097	5·50	
E2093	15pf. multicoloured	1·70	1·60
E2094	20pf. multicoloured	45	30
E2095	25pf. multicoloured	45	30
E2096	35pf. multicoloured	1·70	1·60
E2097	50pf. multicoloured	45	30
E2092/E2097	Set of 6	4·75	4·00

Nos. E2092/E2097 were issued together in *se-tenant* sheetlets of six stamps.

(Des M. Gottschall. Photo)
1979 (9 Jan). Songbirds. T E **632** and similar vert designs. Multicoloured. P 13½×14.

E2098	5pf. Type E **632**	45	30
E2099	10pf. European Nuthatch	45	30
E2100	20pf. European Robin	45	30
E2101	25pf. Common Rosefinches	45	30
E2102	35pf. Blue Tit	45	30
E2103	50pf. Linnets	4·25	2·40
E2098/E2103	Set of 6	5·75	3·50

E **633** Chabo (Siro)

E **634** Telephone Exchanges of 1900 and 1979

(Des A. Bertram. Litho)
1979 (23 Jan). Poultry. T E **633** and similar horiz designs. Multicoloured. P 14.

E2104	10pf. Type E **633**	40	30
E2105	15pf. Crows head	40	30
E2106	20pf. Porcelain-colour Feather-footed Dwarf	40	30
E2107	25pf. Saxonian	40	30
E2108	35pf. Phoenix	40	30
E2109	50pf. Striped Italian	4·00	3·00
E2104/E2109	Set of 6	5·50	4·00

(Des R.-J. Lehmann. Photo)
1979 (6 Feb). Telephone and Telegraph Communication. T E **634** and similar horiz design. Multicoloured. P 13½×14.

E2110	20pf. Type E **634**	40	30
E2111	35pf. Transmitting telegrams in 1880 and 1979	1·40	1·20

301

GERMANY / German Democratic Republic (East Germany)

E 635 Albert Einstein

E 636 Max Klinger House, Leipzig

(Des J. Riess. Litho)

1979 (20 Feb). Birth Centenary of Albert Einstein (physicist). Sheet 55×86 mm. P 13½×14.

| MSE2112 | E 635 | 1m. pinkish brown, deep brown and yellow-brown | 4·00 | 3·50 |

(Des H. Scheuner. Litho)

1979 (6 Mar). Leipzig Spring Fair. T E **636** and similar horiz design. Multicoloured. P 14.

| E2113 | 10pf. Type E **636** | 40 | 30 |
| E2114 | 25pf. Horizontal drill and milling machine | 60 | 45 |

E 637 Otto Hahn

(Des G. Stauf. Litho)

1979 (20 Mar). Celebrities' Birth Anniversaries. T E **637** and similar horiz designs. P 13×12½.

E2115	5pf. agate and flesh	40	30
E2116	10pf. agate and azure	40	30
E2117	20pf. agate and pale olive-bistre	40	30
E2118	25pf. agate and pale green	40	30
E2119	35pf. agate and turquoise-blue	40	30
E2120	70pf. agate and carmine-rose	4·00	2·20
E2115/E2120	Set of 6	5·50	3·25

Designs:—5pf. T E **637** (physicist, birth centenary); 10pf. Max von Laue (physicist, centenary); 20pf. Arthur Scheunert (physiologist, centenary); 25pf. Friedrich August Kekule (chemist, 150th); 35pf. Georg Forster (explorer and writer, 225th); 70pf. Gotthold Ephraim Lessing (playwright and essayist, 250th).

E 638 *Radebeul* (container ship), *Sturmvogel* (tug) and Shipping Route Map

(Des J. Bertholdt. Photo)

1979 (20 Mar). World Navigation Day. P 13½×14.

| E2121 | E 638 | 20pf. multicoloured | 1·20 | 45 |

E 639 Horch 8, 1911

E 640 MXA Electric Locomotive

(Des J. Riess. Litho)

1979 (3 Apr). Zwickau Motor Industry. T E **639** and similar horiz design. Multicoloured. P 14×13½.

E2122	20pf. Type E **639**	60	60
	a. Sheetlet of 3. Nos. E2122/E2123 plus label	3·50	
E2123	35pf. Trabant 601 S de luxe, 1978	1·10	1·00

Nos. E2122/E2123 were issued together in *se-tenant* sheetlets containing the two stamps and an intervening label depicting the motorcar factory, Zwickau.

(Des D. Glinski. Photo)

1979 (17 Apr). East German Locomotives and Wagons. T E **640** and similar square designs. Multicoloured. P 13.

E2124	5pf. Type E **640**	45	30
E2125	10pf. Self-discharging wagon	45	30
E2126	20pf. Diesel locomotive No. 110836.4	45	30
E2127	35pf. Railway car transporter	1·60	1·20
E2124/E2127	Set of 4	2·75	1·90

E 641 Durga (18th-century)

E 642 Children Playing

(Des M. Gottschall. Photo)

1979 (8 May). Indian Miniatures. T E **641** and similar vert designs. Multicoloured. P 14×13½.

E2128	20pf. Type E **641**	40	30
E2129	35pf. Mahavira (15th/16th-century)	40	30
E2130	50pf. Todi Ragini (17th-century)	45	30
E2131	70pf. Asavari Ragini (17th-century)	4·25	4·00
E2128/E2131	Set of 4	5·00	4·50

(Des L. Luders. Photo)

1979 (22 May). International Year of the Child. T E **642** and similar vert design. Multicoloured. P 14.

| E2132 | 10pf. Type E **642** | 40 | 40 |
| E2133 | 20pf. Overseas aid for children | 80 | 75 |

E 643 Construction Work on Leipziger Strasse Complex

E 644 Torchlight Procession of Free German Youth, 1949

(Des R.-J. Lehmann. Litho)

1979 (22 May). Berlin Project of Free German Youth Organisation. T E **643** and similar horiz design. Multicoloured. P 13×12½.

| E2134 | 10pf. Type E **643** | 40 | 40 |
| E2135 | 20pf. Berlin-Marzahn building site | 60 | 60 |

(Des L Grünewald Photo)

1979 (22 May). National Youth Festival T E **644** and similar horiz design. Multicoloured. P 14.

E2136	10pf. +5pf. Type E **644**	45	45
	a. Horiz strip of 2. Nos. E2136/E2137 plus label	95	95
E2137	20pf. Youth rally	45	45

Nos. E2136/E2137 were issued together *se-tenant* with an intervening half stamp-size label bearing the Festival emblem and an inscription.

E 645 Exhibition Emblem

E 646 *Rostock* (train ferry), 1977

(Des M. König. Photo)

1979 (5 June). agra 79 Agricultural Exhibition, Markkleeberg. P 14.

| E2138 | E **645** | 10pf. multicoloured | 80 | 30 |

GERMANY / German Democratic Republic (East Germany)

(Des H. Zill Photo)

1979 (26 June). 70th Anniv of Sassnitz–Trelleborg Railway Ferry. T E **646** and similar horiz design. Multicoloured. P 14.

E2139	20pf. Type E **646**	60	60
	a. Horiz strip of 2. Nos. E2139/E2140 plus label	1·50	1·50
E2140	35pf. *Rugen* (train ferry)	60	60

Nos. E2139/E2140 were issued together *se-tenant* with an intervening half stamp-size label showing a map of the ferry route.

E **647** Hospital Classroom    E **648** Cycling

(Des J. Riess. Litho)

1979 (26 June). Rehabilitation. T E **647** and similar horiz design. Multicoloured. P 13×12½.

E2141	10pf. Type E **647**	40	30
E2142	35pf. Wheelchair-bound factory worker	95	75

(Des L. Luders. Litho)

1979 (3 July). Seventh Children and Young People's Sports Day, Berlin. T E **648** and similar horiz design. Multicoloured. P 13×12½.

E2143	10pf. Type E **648**	40	30
E2144	20pf. Roller-skating	95	75

E **649** Dahlia 'Rubens'    E **650** Goose-thief Fountain, Dresden

(Des Evelyne and K.-H. Bobbe. Photo)

1979 (17 July). iga International Garden Exhibition, Erfurt. Dahlias. T E **649** and similar square designs. Multicoloured. P 13.

E2145	10pf. Type E **649**	40	30
E2146	20pf. 'Rosalie'	40	30
E2147	25pf. 'Corinna'	40	30
E2148	35pf. 'Enzett-Dolli'	40	30
E2149	50pf. 'Enzett-Carola'	45	30
E2150	70pf. 'Don Lorenzo'	4·75	4·25
E2145/E2150	Set of 6	6·00	5·25

(Des J. Riess. Litho (**MS**E2153) or photo (others))

1979 (7 Aug). National Stamp Exhibition, Dresden. T E **650** and similar multicoloured designs. P 13×12½ (**MS**E2153) or 14 (others).

E2151	10pf. +5pf. Type E **650**	95	75
E2152	20pf. Dandelion fountain, Dresden	40	30
MSE2153	86×55 mm. 1m. Dresden buildings (*horiz*)	3·75	3·25

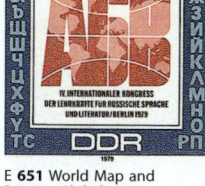

E **651** World Map and Russian Alphabet    E **652** Italian Lira da Gamba, 1592

(Des H. Detlefsen. Photo)

1979 (7 Aug). Fourth International Congress of Russian Language and Literature Teachers, Berlin. P 13.

E2154	E **651**	20pf. multicoloured	60	50

(Des H. Detlefsen. Photo)

1979 (21 Aug). Musical Instruments in Leipzig Museum. T E **652** and similar vert designs. Multicoloured. P 14×13½.

E2155	20pf. Type E **652**	40	30
E2156	25pf. French serpent, 17th/18th-century	40	30
E2157	40pf. French barrel-lyre, 1750	45	30
E2158	85pf. German tenor flugelhorn, 1850	4·25	3·25
E2155/E2158	Set of 4	4·75	3·75

E **653** Horseracing

(Des H. Naumann. Litho)

1979 (21 Aug). 30th International Congress on Horse-breeding in Socialist Countries, Berlin. T E **653** and similar horiz design. Multicoloured. P 14.

E2159	10pf. Type E **653**	40	30
E2160	25pf. Dressage (*pas de deux*)	1·60	1·40

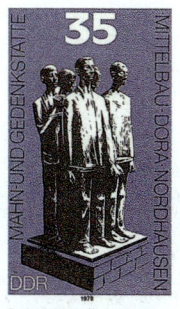

E **654** Mittelbau-Dora Memorial    E **655** Teddy Bear

(Des H. Detlefsen. Photo)

1979 (28 Aug). Mittelbau-Dora Memorial, Nordhausen. P 14.

E2161	E **654**	35pf. black and blue-violet	95	60

(Des J. Bertholdt Photo)

1979 (28 Aug). Leipzig Autumn Fair. T E **655** and similar horiz design. Multicoloured. P 14.

E2162	10pf. Type E **655**	40	30
E2163	25pf. Grosser Blumenberg building, Richard Wagner Square	45	30

E **656** Philipp Dengel    E **657** Building Worker and Flats

(Des G. Stauf. Litho)

1979 (11 Sept). Socialist Personalities. T E **656** and similar vert designs. P 13½×14.

E2164	10pf. blackish brown, pale green and deep green	40	30
E2165	10pf. blackish brown, slate-blue and indigo	40	30
E2166	10pf. blackish brown, stone and bistre	40	30
E2167	10pf. blackish brown, pale Venetian red and bistre-brown	40	30
E2164/E2167	Set of 4	1·40	1·10

Designs:—No. E2164, T E **656**; No. E2165, Otto Buchwitz; E2166, Bernard Koenen; E2167, Heinrich Rau.

303

GERMANY / German Democratic Republic (East Germany)

(Des L. Grünewald. Photo)

1979 (2 Oct). 30th Anniv of German Democratic Republic. T E **657** and similar multicoloured designs. P 14×13½ (**MS**E2172) or 13 (others).

E2168	5pf. Type E **657**		40	30
E2169	10pf. Boy and girl		40	30
E2170	15pf. Soldiers		80	50
E2171	20pf. Miner and Soviet soldier		40	30
E2168/E2171 Set of 4			1·80	1·30
MSE2172 90×110 mm. 1m. Family and flats (29×51 mm)			3·00	2·75

E **658** Girl applying Lipstick (1966/7)

E **659** Vietnamese Soldier, Mother and Child

(Des E. Haller and G. Stauf. Photo)

1979 (6 Nov). Meissen Porcelain. T E **658** and similar vert designs. Multicoloured. P 14×13½.

E2173	5pf. Type E **658**		40	30
	a. Block of 4. Nos. E2173/E2176		3·75	
E2174	10pf. 'Altozier' coffee-pot (18th-century)		40	30
E2175	15pf. 'Grosser Ausschnitt' coffee-pot (1973/4)		45	45
E2176	20pf. Vase with lid (18th-century)		60	60
E2177	25pf. Parrot with cherry (18th-century)		80	75
	a. Block of 4. Nos. E2177/E2180		7·25	
E2178	35pf. Harlequin with tankard (18th-century)		1·20	1·20
E2179	50pf. Flower girl (18th-century)		1·70	1·70
E2180	70pf. Sake bottle (18th-century)		2·30	2·30
E2173/E2180 Set of 8			7·00	6·75

Nos. E2173/E2176 were issued together in *se-tenant* blocks of four within sheets of 16 stamps, and Nos. E2177/E2180 were likewise arranged.

(Des G. Preuss. Litho)

1979 (6 Nov). Invincible Vietnam. P 14.

E2181	E **659** 10pf. +15pf. black orange-red		80	45

E **660** Rag-doll, 1800

E **661** Balance on Ice (Johanna Starke)

(Des A. Bertram. Litho)

1979 (20 Nov). Dolls. T E **660** and similar vert designs. Multicoloured. P 13½×14.

E2182	10pf. Type E **660**		40	40
	a. Sheetlet of 6. Nos. E2182/E2187		5·75	
E2183	15pf. Ceramic doll, 1960		1·90	1·80
E2184	20pf. Wooden doll, 1780		40	40
E2185	35pf. Straw puppet, 1900		40	40
E2186	50pf. Jointed doll, 1800		1·90	1·80
E2187	70pf. Tumbler-doll, 1820		40	40
E2182/E2187 Set of 6			4·75	4·75

Nos. E2182/E2187 were issued together in *se-tenant* sheetlets of six stamps.

(Des M. Gottschall. Photo)

1980 (15 Jan). Olympic Winter Games, Lake Placid. T E **661** and similar multicoloured designs showing artworks. P 13½×14 (10pf.) or 14×13½ (others).

E2188	10pf. *Bobsleigh Start* (Gunter Rechn) (*horiz*)		40	30
E2189	20pf. Type E **661**		40	30
E2190	25pf. +10pf. *Ski Jumpers* (plastic sculpture, Günter Schütz)		40	30
E2191	35pf. *Speed Skaters at the Start* (Axel Wunsch)		2·75	2·00
E2188/E2191 Set of 4			3·50	2·50
MSE2192 79×55 mm. 1m. *Skiing Girls* (Lothar Zitmann) (29×24 mm)			4·00	3·25

E **662** Stille Musik Rock Garden, Grossedlitz

(Des C. Gabriel. Photo)

1980 (29 Jan). Baroque Gardens. T E **662** and similar horiz designs. Multicoloured. P 13½×14.

E2193	10pf. Type E **662**		40	30
E2194	20pf. Belvedere Orangery, Weimar		40	30
E2195	50pf. Flower garden, Dornburg Castle		45	30
E2196	70pf. Park, Rheinsberg Castle		2·75	2·75
E2193/E2196 Set of 4			3·50	3·25

1980 (29 Jan)–81. Designs as Nos. E1533/E1546a, and new design (10pf.), but smaller, 22×18 mm. Recess. P 14.

E2197	5pf. blue-green		40	30
E2198	10pf. emerald		45	30
E2199	15pf. deep magenta (18.3.80)		80	75
E2200	20pf. magenta		95	40
E2201	25pf. deep turquoise-green (10.6.80)		80	60
E2202	30pf. red-orange (10.2.81)		95	75
E2203	35pf. new blue (13.5.80)		95	60
E2204	40pf. slate-violet (26.8.80)		1·70	1·10
E2205	50pf. royal blue (14.10.80)		1·10	60
E2206	60pf. purple (6.10.81)		1·40	1·00
E2207	70pf. purple-brown (21.4.81)		1·40	1·10
E2208	80pf. deep ultramarine (6.10.81)		1·70	1·40
E2209	1m. deep olive (11.11.80)		1·90	1·40
E2210	2m. carmine-red (14.10.80)		3·50	1·50
E2211	3m. bright magenta (21.7.81)		5·50	2·40
E2197/E2211 Set of 15			21·00	13·00

New design:—10pf. Palace of the Republic, Berlin.

The 5, 10, 15, 35, 50, 70pf. and 2m. were issued both with matt gum and on thinner paper with shiny gum.

E **663** Cable-laying Machine and Dish Aerial

(Des M. Gottschall. Photo)

1980 (5 Feb). Post Office Activities. T E **663** and similar horiz design. Multicoloured. P 13½×14.

E2212	10pf. Type E **663**		40	30
E2213	20pf. TV Tower, Berlin, and television		45	30

E **664** Johann Wolfgang Döbereiner

E **665** Karl Marx University, Leipzig

304

GERMANY / German Democratic Republic (East Germany)

(Des G. Stauf. Litho)

1980 (26 Feb). Celebrities' Birth Anniversaries. T E **664** and similar horiz designs. P 13×12½.

E2214	5pf. brownish black and olive-bistre	40	30
E2215	10pf. black and cerise	40	30
E2216	20pf. brownish black and bright green	40	30
E2217	25pf. black and blue	40	30
E2218	35pf. black and bright blue	40	30
E2219	70pf. brownish black and Venetian red	2·50	2·00
E2214/E2219	Set of 6	4·00	3·25

Designs:—5pf. T E **664** (chemist, birth bicentenary); 10pf. Frédéric Joliot-Curie (chemist, 80th); 20pf. Johann Friedrich Naumann (zoologist, bicentenary); 25pf. Alfred Wegener (explorer and geophysicist, centenary); 35pf. Carl von Clausewitz (Prussian general, bicentenary); 70pf. Helene Weigel (actress, 80th).

(Des P. Reismüller. Photo)

1980 (4 Mar). Leipzig Spring Fair. T E **665** and similar horiz design. Multicoloured. P 14.

E2220	10pf. Type E **665**	40	30
E2221	25pf. ZT 303 tractor	60	45

E **666** Werner Eggerath

E **667** Cosmonauts and Interkosmos Emblem

(Des G. Stauf. Litho)

1980 (18 Mar). 80th Birth Anniv of Werner Eggerath (socialist). P 13½× 14.

E2222	E **666**	10pf. blackish brown and brown-red	95	60

(Des Yu. K. Lewanowsky and D. Glinski. Litho)

1980 (11 Apr). Interkosmos Programme. Sheet 109×89 mm. P 13½×14.

MSE2223	E **667**	1m. multicoloured	3·75	3·25

E **668** On the Horizontal Beam (sculpture, Erich Wurzer)

E **669** Flags of Member States

(Des M. Gottschall. Photo)

1980 (22 Apr). Olympic Games, Moscow (1st issue). T E **668** and similar horiz designs showing artworks Multicoloured. P 13½×14.

E2224	10pf. Type E **668**	45	30
E2225	20pf. +5pf. Runners before the Winning Post (Lothar Zitzmann)	45	30
E2226	50pf. Coxless Four (Wilfried Falkenthal)	2·50	2·10
E2224/E2226	Set of 3	3·00	2·40

See also Nos. E2247/**MS**E2250.

(Des R.-J. Lehmann. Photo)

1980 (13 May). 25th Anniv of Warsaw Pact. P 14.

E2227	E **669**	20pf. multicoloured	95	30

E **670** Co-operative Society Building (W. Gropius)

E **671** Rostock Buildings

(Des L. Grünewald. Photo)

1980 (27 May). Bauhaus Architecture. T E **670** and similar multicoloured designs. P 13½×14 (vert) or 14×13½ (horiz).

E2228	5pf. Type E **670**	45	30
E2229	10pf. Socialist Memorial Place (M. van der Rohe) (horiz)	45	30
E2230	15pf. Monument to the Fallen of March 1922 (W. Gropius)	45	30
E2231	20pf. Steel building, 1926 (G. Muche and R. Paulick) (horiz)	45	30
E2232	50pf. Trade Union school (H. Meyer)	60	30
E2233	70pf. Bauhaus building (W. Gropius) (horiz)	3·75	3·25
E2228/E2233	Set of 6	5·50	4·25

(Des J. Bertholdt. Photo)

1980 (10 June). 18th Workers' Festival, Rostock. T E **671** and similar horiz design. Multicoloured. P 14.

E2234	10pf. Type E **671**	40	30
E2235	20pf. Costumed dancers	60	45

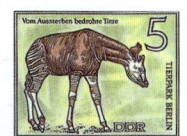

E **672** Radar Complex, Berlin-Schönefeld Airport

E **673** Okapi

(Des Eva and G. Bormann. Litho)

1980 (10 June). Aeroaozphilex 1980 International Airmail Exhibition, Berlin. T E **672** and similar horiz designs. Multicoloured. P 13×12½.

E2236	20pf. Type E **672**	60	60
	a. Block of 4. Nos. E2236/E2239	4·25	
E2237	25pf. Ilyushin Il-62M at Schönefeld Airport	60	60
E2238	35pf. PZL-106A Kruk crop-spraying aeroplane	95	90
E2239	70pf. Antonov An-2 aerial photography biplane and multispectrum camera	1·90	1·80
E2236/2239	Set of 4	3·50	3·50
MSE2240	64×95 mm. 1m.+10pf. Ilyushin Il-62 M jetliner and globe	4·25	3·75

Nos. E2236/E2239 were issued together in *se-tenant* blocks of four within the sheet.

(Des A. Bengs. Litho)

1980 (24 June). Endangered Animals. T E **673** and similar horiz designs. Multicoloured. P 14×13½.

E2241	5pf. Type E **673**	40	30
E2242	10pf. Lesser Pandas	40	30
E2243	15pf. Maned Wolf	40	30
E2244	20pf. Arabian Oryx	40	30
E2245	25pf. White-eared Pheasant	40	30
E2246	35pf. Musk Oxen	3·50	2·40
E2241/E2246	Set of 6	5·00	3·50

(Des M. Gottschall. Photo)

1980 (8 July). Olympic Games. Moscow (2nd issue). Multicoloured designs as T E **668**. P 14.

E2247	10pf. *Judo* (Erhard Schmidt)	40	30
E2248	20pf. +10pf. *Swimmer* (Willi Sitte) (vert)	40	30
E2249	50pf. *Spurt* (sculpture, Siegfried Schreiber)	2·75	2·00
E2247/E2249	Set of 3	3·25	2·30
MSE2250	79×55 mm. 1m. *Spinnakers* (Karl Raetsch) (29×24 *mm*)	4·25	3·50

E **674** Suhl, 1700

E **675** Huntley Microscope

305

GERMANY / German Democratic Republic (East Germany)

(Des J. Riess. Litho)

1980 (22 July). Sixth National Youth Stamp Exhibition, Suhl. T E **674** and similar horiz design. Multicoloured. P 13×12½.
E2251	10pf. +5pf. Type E **674**	60	60
	a. Horiz strip of 2. Nos. E2251/E2252 plus label	1·30	1·30
E2252	20pf. Modern Suhl	60	60

Nos. E2251/E2252 were issued together se-tenant with an intervening half stamp-size label bearing the Suhl Arms.

(Des G. Voigt. Photo)

1980 (12 Aug). Carl Zeiss Optical Museum, Jena. T E **675** and similar vert designs. Multicoloured. P 14.
E2253	20pf. Type E **675**	60	60
	a. Block of 4. Nos. E2253/E2256	4·25	
E2254	25pf. Magny microscope, 1751	60	60
E2255	35pf. Amici microscope, 1845	1·10	1·10
E2256	70pf. Zeiss microscope, 1873	1·60	1·50
E2253/E2256	Set of 4	3·50	3·50

Nos. E2253/E2256 were issued together in se-tenant blocks of four within the sheet.

E **676** Majdanek Memorial

(Des J. Riess. Photo)

1980 (26 Aug). War Victims' Memorial, Majdanek, Poland. P 13½×14.
| E2257 | E **676** | 35pf. multicoloured | 95 | 60 |

E **677** Information Centre, Leipzig

(Des J. Riess. Photo)

1980 (26 Aug). Leipzig Autumn Fair. T E **677** and similar horiz design. Multicoloured. P 14.
E2258	10pf. Type E **677**	40	30
E2259	25pf. Carpet-knitting machine	95	45

E **678** Palace of Republic, Berlin

E **679** Laughing Boy with Flute

(Des K.-H. Bobbe. Photo)

1980 (9 Sept). 67th Interparliamentary Conference, Berlin. P 14.
| E2260 | E **678** | 20pf. multicoloured | 1·40 | 45 |

(Des H. Naumann. Photo)

1980 (23 Sept). 400th Birth Anniv of Frans Hats (artist). T E **679** and similar multicoloured designs. P 14×13½.
E2261	10pf. Type E **679**	40	30
E2262	20pf. *Portrait of Young Man in Drab Coat*	40	30
E2263	25pf. *The Mulatto*	40	30
E2264	35pf. *Portrait of Young Man in Black Coat*	1·90	1·50
E2261/E2264	Set of 4	2·75	2·20
MSE2265	80×55 mm. 1m. red-brown (*Self-portrait*) (29×23 mm)	4·00	3·00

E **680** Clenched Fist and Star

E **681** Leccinum versipelle (*Leccinum testaceo scabrum*)

(Des G. Voigt. Photo)

1980 (14 Oct). 'Solidarity'. P 13×13½.
| E2266 | E **680** | 10pf. +5pf. greenish blue and vermilion | 1·10 | 30 |

1980 (28 Oct). Edible Mushrooms. T E **681** pnd similar vert designs. Multcoloured. P 13×13½.
E2267	5pf. Type E **681**	40	30
E2268	10pf. *Boletus* (*Boletus miniatoporus erythropus*)	40	30
E2269	15pf. *Agaricus campestris* (*Agaricus campester*)	40	30
E2270	20pf. *Xerocomus badius*	40	30
E2271	35pf. *Boletus edulis*	45	30
E2272	70pf. *Cantharellus cibarius*	3·50	3·00
E2267/E2272	Set of 6	5·00	4·00

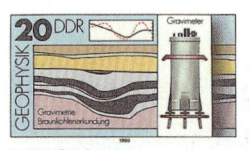

E **682** Gravimetry

(Des L. Grünewald. Litho)

1980 (11 Nov). Geophysics. T E **682** and similar horiz designs. Multicoloured. P 13×12½.
E2273	20pf. Type E **682**	60	30
	a. Block of 4. Nos. E2273/E2276	4·25	
E2274	25pf. Bore-hole measuring	80	60
E2275	35pf. Seismic prospecting	95	90
E2276	50pf. Seismology	1·60	1·50
E2273/E2276	Set of 4	3·50	3·00

Nos. E2273/E2276 were issued together in se-tenant blocks of four within the sheet.

E **683** Radebeul–Radeburg Steam Locomotive

E **684** Toy Steam Locomotive, 1850

(Des D. Glinski. Litho)

1980 (25 Nov). Narrow-gauge Railways (1st series). T E **683** and similar horiz designs. Multicoloured. P 13×12½.
E2277	20pf. Type E **683**	60	60
	a. Horiz strip of 2. Nos. E2277 and E2279 plus label	1·70	1·70
E2278	20pf. Bad Doberan–Ostseebad Kühlungsborn steam locomotive	60	60
	a. Horiz strip of 2. Nos. E2278 and E2280 plus label	1·70	1·70
E2279	25pf. Radebeul–Radeburg passenger carriage	60	60
E2280	35pf. Bad Doberan-Ostseebad Kühlungsborn passenger carriage	60	60
E2277/E2280	Set of 4	2·20	2·20

Nos E2277 and E2279 were issued together se-tenant with an intervening half stamp-size label bearing a map of the railway route; Nos. E2278 and E2280 were similarly issued together.

See also Nos. E2342/E2345, E2509/E2512 and E2576/E2579.

GERMANY / German Democratic Republic (East Germany)

(Des A.Bertram. Litho)

1980 (Dec). Historical Toys. T E **684** and similar vert designs. Multicoloured. P 13½×14.

E2281	10pf. Type E **684**	45	45
	a. Sheetlet of 6. Nos. E2281/E2286	5·75	
E2282	20pf. Aeroplane, 1914	1·90	1·80
E2283	25pf. Steam roller, 1920	45	45
E2284	35pf. Sailing ship, 1825	45	45
E2285	40pf. Car, 1900	1·90	1·80
E2286	50pf. Balloon, 1920	45	45
E2281/E2286 Set of 6		5·00	4·75

Nos. E2281/E2286 were issued together in *se-tenant* aheetlets of six stamps.

E **685** Mozart    E **686** *Malus pumila*

(Des M. Gottschall. Litho)

1981 (13 Jan). 225th Birth Anniv of Wolfgang Amadeus Mozart (composer). Sheet 55×80 mm. P 13½×14.

MSE2287 E **685** 1m. black, carmine-rose and stone..... 4·75 3·50

(Des Evelyne and K.-H. Bobbe. Photo)

1981 (13 Jan). Rare Plants in Berlin Arboretum. T E **686** and similar multicoloured designs. P 14.

E2288	5pf. Type E **686**	40	30
E2289	10pf. *Halesia carolina* (horiz)	40	30
E2290	20pf. *Colutea arborescens*	40	30
E2291	25pf. *Paulownia tomentosa*	40	30
E2292	35pf. *Lonicera periclymenum* (horiz)	45	30
E2293	50pf. *Calycanthus floridus*	4·00	3·25
E2288/E2293 Set of 6		5·50	4·25

E **687** Heinrich von Stephan    E **688** Soldiers on Parade

(Des G. Stauf. Litho)

1981 (20 Jan). 150th Birth Anniv of Heinrich von Stephan (founder of Universal Postal Union). P 13×13½.

E2294 E **687** 10pf. black and bistre-yellow .... 1·10 45

(Des H. Zill. Photo)

1981 (27 Jan). 25th Anniv of National People's Army. T E **688** and similar horiz design. Multicoloured. P 14.

E2295	10pf. Type E **688**	45	30
E2296	20pf. Marching soldiers	60	30

E **689** Marx and Lenin

(Des J. Riess. Photo)

1981 (10 Feb). Tenth Socialist Unity Party Congress, Berlin (1st issue). P 13½×14.

E2297 E **689** 10pf. multicoloured .... 1·10 30

See also Nos. E2309/MSE2313.

E **690** Counter Clerks

(Des R.-J. Lehmann. Litho)

1981 (10 Feb). Post Office Training. T E **690** and similar horiz designs. Multicoloured. P 13½×14.

E2298	5pf. Type E **690**	40	30
E2299	10pf. Telephone engineers	40	30
E2300	15pf. Radio communications	40	30
E2301	20pf. Rosa Luxemburg Engineering School, Leipzig	45	30
E2302	25pf. Friedrich List Communications School, Dresden	2·20	1·50
E2298/E2302 Set of 5		3·50	2·40

E **691** Erich Baron 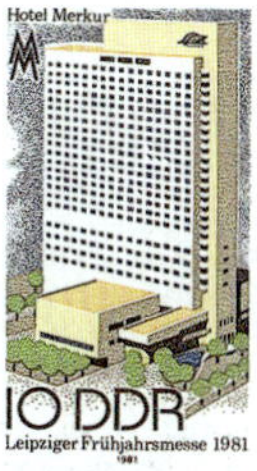   E **692** Hotel Merkur, Leipzig

(Des G. Stauf. Litho)

1981 (24 Feb). Socialist Personalities. T E **691** and similar vert designs. P 13½×14.

E2303	10pf. brownish black and dull green	45	30
E2304	10pf. brownish black and olive-bistre	45	30
E2305	10pf. brownish black and grey-blue	45	30
E2306	10pf. brownish black and pale reddish brown	45	30
E2303/E2306 Set of 4		1·60	1·10

Designs:—No. E2303, T E **691**; No. E2304, Conrad Blenkle; E2305, Arthur Ewert; E2306, Walter Stoecker.

(Des P. Reissmüller. Photo)

1981 (10 Mar). Leipzig Spring Fair. T E **692** and similar horiz design. Multicoloured. P 14.

E2307	10pf. Type E **692**	40	30
E2308	25pf. Open-cast mining machine	80	45

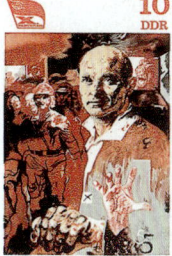

E **693** *Ernst Thälmann* (Willi Sitte) 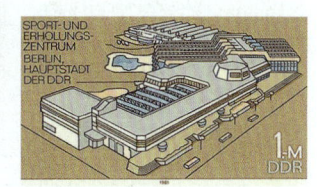   E **694** Sports Centre

(Des D. Glinski. Photo)

1981 (24 Mar). Tenth Socialist Unity Party Congress, Berlin (2nd issue). T E **693** and similar vert designs depicting paintings. Multicoloured. P 14×13½.

E2309	10pf. Type E **693**	40	30
E2310	20pf. *Brigadier* (Bernhard Heisig)	40	30
E2311	25pf. *Festival Day* (Rudolf Bergander)	1·60	1·20
E2312	35pf. *Comrades in Arms* (Paul Michaelis)	40	30
E2309/E2312 Set of 4		2·50	1·90

MSE2313 108×82 mm. 1m. *When Communists are Dreaming* (Walter Womacka) .... 3·00 2·50

GERMANY / German Democratic Republic (East Germany)

(Des J. Riess. Litho)

1981 (24 Mar). Sports Centre, Berlin. Sheet 110×90 mm. P 13½×14.
MSE2314 E **694** 1m. multicoloured .... 4·25 3·75

E **695** Plugs and Socket

E **696** Heinrich Barkhausen

(Des K.-H. Bobbe. Litho)

1981 (21 Apr). Conservation of Energy. P 12½×13.
E2315 E **695** 10pf. black and red-orange 45 30
No. E2315 was issued both in sheets of 50 and in sheets of ten.

(Des G. Stauf. Litho)

1981 (5 May). Celebrities' Birth Anniversaries. T E **696** and similar horiz designs. P 13×12½.
E2316   10pf. black and blue 40 30
E2317   20pf. brownish black and Venetian red 40 30
E2318   25pf. brownish black and grey-brown .... 4·25 3·00
E2319   35pf. black and bright violet 45 30
E2320   50pf. brownish black and apple green 60 30
E2321   70pf. brownish black and light olive-sepia 95 30
E2316/E2321 Set of 6 .... 6·25 4·00
Designs:—10pf. T E **696** (physicist, birth centenary); 20pf. Johannes R. Becher (writer, 90th); 25pf. Richard Dedekind (mathematician, 150th); 35pf. Georg Philipp Telemann (composer, 300th); 50pf. Adelbert von Chamisso (poet and naturalist, bicentenary); 70pf. Wilhelm Raabe (novelist, 150th).

E **697** Free German Youth Members and Banner

E **698** Wörlitz Park

(Des H. Detlefsen. Litho)

1981 (19 May). 11th Free German Youth Parliament, Berlin. T E **697** and similar horiz design. Multicoloured. P 13×12½.
E2322   10pf. Type E **697** 45 45
         a. Horiz strip of 2. Nos. E2322/E2323 plus label .... 1·10 1·10
E2323   20pf. Free German Youth members instructing foreign students 45 45
Nos. E2322/E2323 were issued together se-tenant with an intervening half stamp-size label bearing the Parliament emblem.

(Des D. Dorfstecher. Litho)

1981 (9 June). Landscaped Parks. T E **698** and similar vert designs. Multicoloured. P 12½×13.
E2324   5pf. Type E **698** 40 30
E2325   10pf. Tiefurt Park, Weimar 40 30
E2326   15pf. Maxwalde 40 30
E2327   20pf. Branitz Park 40 30
E2328   25pf. Treptow Park, Berlin .... 3·00 2·30
E2329   35pf. Wiesenburg Park 45 30
E2324/E2329 Set of 6 .... 4·50 3·50

E **699** Children at Play and Sport

E **700** Berlin Theatre

(Des J. Riess. Photo)

1981 (23 June). Eighth Children and Young People's Sports Days. Berlin. T E **699** and similar horiz design. Multicoloured. P 14.
E2330   10pf. +5pf. Type E **699** .... 1·10 75
E2331   20pf. Artistic gymnastics 45 30

(Des A. Bengs. Eng G. Stauf. Recess and photo)

1981 (23 June). Birth Bicentenary of Karl Friedrich Schinkel (architect). T E **700** and similar horiz design, each black and stone. P 14.
E2332   10pf. Type E **700** .... 1·70 30
E2333   25pf. Old Museum, Berlin .... 4·00 1·70

E **701** Throwing the Javelin from a Wheelchair

E **702** House, Zaulsdorf

(Des J. Riess. Litho)

1981 (23 June). International Year of Disabled Persons. T E **701** and similar horiz design. Multicoloured. P 13×12½.
E2334   5pf. Type E **701** 45 30
         a. Horiz strip of 2. Nos. E2334/E2335 plus label 95 70
E2335   15pf. Disabled people in art gallery 45 30
Nos. E2334/E2335 were issued together se-tenant with an intervening half stamp-size label depicting the IYDP emblem.

(Des L. Grünewald. Photo)

1981 (7 July). Half-timbered Buildings. T E **702** and similar multicoloured designs. P 14.
E2336   10pf. Type E **702** 40 30
E2337   20pf. 'Sugar-loaf' cottage. Gross Zicker (horiz) 40 30
E2338   25pf. Farmhouse, Weckersdorf 40 30
E2339   35pf. House, Pillgram (horiz) 45 30
E2340   50pf. House, Eschenbach 60 30
E2341   70pf. House, Ludersdorf (horiz) .... 5·25 4·00
E2336/E2341 Set of 6 .... 6·75 5·00

(Des D. Glinski. Litho)

1981 (21 July). Narrow-gauge Railways (2nd series). Horiz designs as T E **683**. P 13×12½.
E2342   5pf. black and orange-vermilion 45 30
         a. Horiz strip of 2. Nos. E2342 and E2344 plus label .... 1·00 80
E2343   5pf. black and orange-vermilion 45 30
         a. Horiz strip of 2. Nos. E2343 and E2345 plus label .... 1·00 80
E2344   15pf. multicoloured 45 30
E2345   20pf. multicoloured 45 30
E2342/E2345 Set of 4 .... 1·60 1·10
Designs:—No. E2342, Freital–Kurort Kipsdorf steam locomotive; E2343, Putbus–Göhren steam locomotive; E2344, Freital–Kurort Kipsdorf luggage van; E2345, Putbus–Göhren passenger carriage.
Nos. E2342 and E2344 were issued together se-tenant with an intervening half-stamp size label bearing a map of the railway route; Nos. E2343 and E2345 were similarly arranged.

E **703** Chemical Works

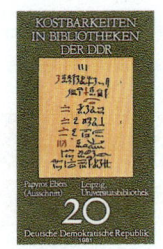

E **704** Ebers Papyrus (Leipzig University Library)

(Des E. Haller. Photo)

1981 (18 Aug). Leipzig Autumn Fair. T E **703** and similar horiz design. Multicoloured. P 14.
E2346   10pf. Type E **703** 40 30
E2347   25pf. New Draper's Hall 80 60

308

GERMANY / German Democratic Republic (East Germany)

(Des K. Müller. Photo)
1981 (18 Aug). Precious Books in East German Libraries. T E **704** and similar vert designs. Multicoloured. P 14.
E2348	20pf. Type E **704**	40	30
E2349	35pf. Maya manuscript (Dresden Library)	40	30
E2350	50pf. Miniature from *Les six visions Messire Francoys Petrarque* (Berlin State Library)	2·75	2·75
E2348/E2350	Set of 3	3·25	3·00

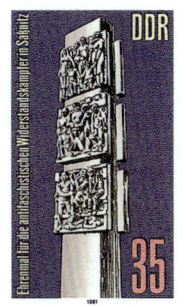

E **705** Sassnitz Memorial

E **706** Henbane and Incense Burner

(Des H. Detlefsen. Photo)
1981 (8 Sept). Resistance Fighters' Memorial, Sassnitz. P 14.
E2351	E **705**	35pf. multicoloured	95	60

(Des K. Hennig. Photo)
1981 (22 Sept). Early Medical Equipment in Karl Sudhoff Institute, Leipzig. T E **706** and similar multicoloured designs. P 14.
E2352	10pf. Type E **706**	40	30
E2353	20pf. Dental instruments	40	30
E2354	25pf. Forceps	40	30
E2355	35pf. Bladder knife and hernia shears	45	30
E2356	50pf. Speculum and gynaecological forceps (*vert*)	4·75	4·50
E2357	85pf. Triploid elevators (*vert*)	95	60
E2352/E2357	Set of 6	6·50	5·75

E **707** Letter from Friedrich Engels, 1840

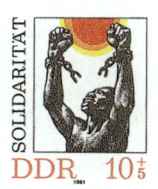

E **708** African breaking Chains

(Des J. Riess. Photo)
1981 (6 Oct). Stamp Day. T E **707** and similar horiz design. Multicoloured. P 14.
E2358	10pf. +5pf. Type E **707**	1·60	1·10
E2359	20pf. Postcard from Karl Marx, 1878	45	30

(Des R.-J. Lehmann. Photo)
1981 (6 Oct). 'Solidarity'. P 14.
E2360	E **708**	10pf. +5pf. multicoloured	95	30

E **709** Tug

E **710** Windmill, Dabel

(Des P. Reissmüller. Photo)
1981 (20 Oct). Inland Shipping. T E **709** and similar horiz designs. Multicoloured. P 14.
E2361	10pf. Type E **709**	45	30
E2362	20pf. Tug and barges	45	30
E2363	25pf. Diesel-electric paddle-ferry, River Elbe	45	30
E2364	35pf. Ice-breaker in Oder estuary	45	30
E2365	50pf. *Schonewalde* (motor barge)	60	30
E2366	85pf. Dredger	5·00	4·50
E2361/E2366	Set of 6	6·75	5·50

(Des J. Bertholdt. Photo)
1981 (10 Nov). Windmills. T E **710** and similar vert designs. Multicoloured. P 14.
E2367	10pf. Type E **710**	40	30
E2368	20pf. Pahrenz	40	30
E2369	25pf. Dresden-Gohlis	40	30
E2370	70pf. Ballstädt	3·00	2·75
E2367/E2370	Set of 4	3·75	3·25

E **711** Snake, 1850

E **712** Coffee Pot, 1715

(Des A. Bertram. Litho)
1981 (24 Nov). Historical Toys. T E **711** and similar horiz designs. Multicoloured. P 13½×13.
E2371	10pf. Type E **711**	45	45
	a. Sheetlet of 6. Nos. E2371/E2376	5·75	
E2372	20pf. Teddy bear, 1910	45	45
E2373	25pf. Goldfish, 1935	1·90	1·80
E2374	35pf. Hobby-horse, 1850	1·90	1·80
E2375	40pf. Pull-along duck, 1800	45	45
E2376	70pf. Clockwork frog, 1930	45	45
E2371/E2376	Set of 6	5·00	4·75

Nos. E2371/E2376 were issued together in *se-tenant* sheetlets of six stamps.

(Des M. Gottschall (**MS**E2381), L. Luders (others). Litho (**MS**E2381), photo (others))
1982 (26 Jan). 300th Birth Anniv of Johann Friedrich Böttger (founder of Meissen China Works). T E **712** and similar vert designs. Multicoloured. P 14.
E2377	10pf. Type E **712**	40	40
	a. Block of 4. Nos. E2377/E2380	3·50	
E2378	20pf. Vase decorated with flowers, 1715	60	60
E2379	25pf. *Oberon* (figurine), 1969	95	90
E2380	35pf. Vase *Day and Night*, 1979	1·20	1·20
E2377/E2380	Set of 4	2·75	2·75
MSE2381	89×110 mm. 50pf. Portrait medal; 50pf. Banger's Seal	5·00	3·75

Nos. E2377/E2380 were issued together in *se-tenant* blocks of four within the sheet.

E **713** Post Office, Bad Liebenstein

E **714** Alpine Marmot

(Des R.-J. Lehmann. Photo)
1982 (9 Feb). Post Office Buildings. T E **713** and similar horiz designs. Multicoloured. P 14.
E2382	20pf. Type E **713**	40	30
E2383	25pf. Telecommunications Centre, Berlin	40	30
E2384	35pf. Head Post Office, Erfurt	45	30
E2385	50pf. Head Post Office, Dresden	3·50	2·50
E2382/E2385	Set of 4	4·25	3·00

(Des Hannelore Heise. Photo)
1982 (23 Feb). International Fur Auction, Leipzig. T E **714** and similar horiz designs. Multicoloured. P 14.
E2386	10pf. Type E **714**	40	30
E2387	20pf. Polecat	40	30
E2388	25pf. European Mink	45	30
E2389	35pf. Beech Marten	2·30	2·00
E2386/E2389	Set of 4	3·25	2·50

309

GERMANY / German Democratic Republic (East Germany)

E 715 Silhouette of Goethe

E 716 West Entrance to Fairground

(Des J. Riess. Litho)

1982 (9 Mar). Johann Wolfgang von Goethe and Friedrich von Schiller (writers) Commemoration. Sheet 110×90 mm containing T E **715** and similar vert design. Multicoloured. P 14.
MSE2390 50pf. Type E **715** (150th death anniv); 50pf. Silhouette of Schiller (175th death (1980) and 225th birth (1984) annivs) .... 5·50 4·25

(Des J. Riess. Litho)

1982 (9 Mar). Leipzig Spring Fair. T E **716** and similar horiz design. Multicoloured. P 13×12½.
E2391 10pf. Type E **716** 40 30
E2392 25pf. Seamless steel tube plant, Riesa Zeithain 60 45

E 717 Dr. Robert Koch

E 718 Max Fechner

(Des L. Grünewald. Litho)

1982 (23 Mar). Centenary of Discovery of Tubercle Bacillus. Sheet 80×55 mm. P 14.
MSE2393 E **717** 1m. multicoloured .... 4·00 3·25

(Des G. Stauf. Recess)

1982 (23 Mar). Socialist Personalities. T E **718** and similar vert designs. P 14.
E2394 10pf. chocolate 40 30
E2395 10pf. deep grey-green 40 30
E2396 10pf. blackish lilac 40 30
E2397 10pf. deep turquoise-blue 40 30
E2398 10pf. grey-olive 40 30
E2394/E2398 Set of 5 .... 1·80 1·40
Designs:—No. E2394, T E **718**; No. E2395, Ottomar Geschke; E2396, Helmut Lehmann; E2397, Herbert Warnke; E2398, Otto Winzer.

E 719 Meadow Saffron (*Colchicum autumnale*)

E 720 Decorative Initial 'I'

(Des Evelyne and K.-H. Bobbe. Litho)

1982 (6 Apr). Poisonous Plants. T E **719** and similar vert designs. Multicoloured. P 14.
E2399 10pf. Type E **719** 40 30
E2400 15pf. Bog Arum (*Calla palustris*) 40 30
E2401 20pf. Labrador Tea (*Ledum palustre*) 40 30
E2402 25pf. Bryony (*Bryonia dioica*) 40 30
E2403 35pf. Monkshood (*Aconitum napellus*) 45 30
E2404 50pf. Henbane (*Hyoscyamus niger*) .... 3·00 2·50
E2399/E2404 Set of 6 .... 4·50 3·50

(Des K.-H. Bobbe. Photo)

1982 (20 Apr). International Art of the Book Exhibition, Leipzig. T E **720** and similar vert design. P 14.
E2405 15pf. multicoloured 80 75
        a. Horiz strip of 2. Nos. E2405/E2406 plus label .... 1·70 1·60

E2406 35pf. grey-brown, Indian red and black 80 75
Designs:—15pf. T E **720**; 35pf. Exhibition emblem.
Nos. E2405/E2406 were issued together *se-tenant* with an intervening label bearing a quotation by Johannes Becher.

E 721 Mother with Child (Walter Womacka)

E 722 Osprey

(Des D. Glinski. Photo)

1982 (20 Apr). Tenth Free German Trade Unions Association Congress, Berlin. T E **721** and similar multicoloured designs. P 14.
E2407 10pf. black, bright scarlet and bright lemon . 45 30
E2408 20pf. multicoloured 45 30
E2409 25pf. multicoloured .... 1·10 90
E2407/E2409 Set of 3 .... 1·80 1·40
Designs: Horiz—20pf. *Discussion by Collective of Innovators* (Willi Neubert). Vert—10pf. T E **721**; 25pf. *Young Couple* (Karl-Heinz Jakob).

(Des H. Zill. Photo)

1982 (18 May). Protected Birds. T E **722** and similar multicoloured designs. P 14.
E2410 10pf. Type E **722** 45 30
E2411 20pf. White-tailed Sea Eagle (*horiz*) 45 30
E2412 25pf. Little Owl 45 30
E2413 35pf. Eagle Owl .... 2·75 2·30
E2410/E2413 Set of 4 .... 3·75 3·00

E 723 Old and Modern Buildings

E 724 Memorial Medal

(Des J. Bertholdt. Photo)

1982 (8 June). 19th Workers' Festival, Neubrandenburg. T E **723** and similar horiz design. Multicoloured. P 14.
E2414 10pf. Type E **723** 40 30
E2415 20pf. Couple in traditional costume 80 60

(Des L. Grünewald. Photo)

1982 (8 June). Birth Centenary of Georgi Dimitrov (Bulgarian statesman). Sheet 80×55 mm. P 14.
MSE2416 E **724** 1m. multicoloured .... 5·50 5·25

E 725 Frieden (freighter)

(Des J. Bertholdt. Photo)

1982 (22 June). Ocean-going Ships. T E **725** and similar horiz designs. Multicoloured. P 14.
E2417 5pf. Type E **725** 40 30
E2418 10pf. *Fichtelberg* (roll-on roll-off freighter) 40 30
E2419 15pf. *Brocken* (heavy cargo carrier) 40 30
E2420 20pf. *Weimar* (container ship) 40 30
E2421 25pf. *Vorwärts* (freighter) 40 30
E2422 35pf. *Berlin* (container ship) .... 2·50 2·20
E2417/E2422 Set of 6 .... 4·00 3·25

310

GERMANY / German Democratic Republic (East Germany)

E 726 Members' Activities

E 727 Bird Wedding

(Des M. Gottschall. Litho)

1982 (22 June). 30th Anniv of Sports and Science Association. P 13×12½.
E2423 E 726 20pf. multicoloured 80   30

(Des H. Scheuner. Litho)

1982 (6 July). Sorbian Folk Customs. T E **727** and similar horiz designs. Multicoloured. P 13×12½.
E2424 10pf. Type E **727** 40   30
       a. Block of 6. Nos. E2424/E2429 .... 5·75
E2425 20pf. Shrove Tuesday procession 50   30
E2426 25pf. Egg rolling 65   60
E2427 35pf. Painted Easter eggs .... 1·10 1·10
E2428 40pf. St. John's Day riders .... 1·30 1·20
E2429 50pf. Distribution of Christmas gifts to hard-
             working children .... 1·60 1·60
E2424/E2429 Set of 6 .... 5·00 4·50
Nos. E2424/E2429 were issued together in *se-tenant* blocks of six within the sheet.

E 728 Schwerin, 1640

E 729 Flag and Pioneers

(Des J. Riess. Litho)

1982 (6 July). Seventh National Youth Stamp Exhibition, Schwerin. T E **728** and similar horiz design. Multicoloured. P 13×12½.
E2430 10pf. +5pf. Type E **728** 65   60
       a. Horiz strip of 2. Nos. E2430/E2431 plus
             label .... 1·70 1·40
E2431 20pf. Modern Schwerin 65   60
Nos. E2430/E2431 were issued together *se-tenant* with an intervening half stamp-size label depicting Schwerin arms.

(Des R.–J. Lehmann. Photo)

1982 (20 July). Seventh Pioneers Meeting, Dresden. T E **729** and similar horiz design. Multicoloured. P 14.
E2432 10pf. +5pf. Type E **729** 95   80
E2433 20pf. Trumpet and drum 40   30

E 730 Stormy Sea (Ludolf Backhuysen)

(Des H. Naumann. Photo)

1982 (10 Aug). Paintings in Schwerin State Museum. T E **730** and similar multicoloured designs. P 14.
E2434 5pf. Type E **730** 40   30
E2435 10pf. *Music making at Home* (Frans van
             Mieris) (vert) 40   30
E2436 20pf. *The Watchman* (Care) (Fabritius) (vert) ... 40   30
E2437 25pf. *Company of Peasants* (Adriaen
             Brouwer) 50   30
E2438 35pf. *Breakfast Table with Ham* (Willem
             Claesz Heda) 50   30
E2439 70pf. *River Landscape* (Jan van Goyen) .... 3·75 2·75
E2434/E2439 Set of 6 .... 5·25 3·75

E 731 Karl-Marx-Stadt

(Des J. Riess. Photo)

1982 (24 Aug). 13th Socialist Countries' Postal Ministers Conference, Karl-Marx-Stadt. P 14.
E2440 E **731** 10pf. multicoloured 95   60
Nos. E2440 was issued with *se-tenant* half stamp-size label depicting communications equipment.

E 732 Stentzlers Hof

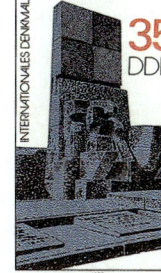

E 733 Auschwitz-Birkenau Memorial

(Des L. Grünewald. Litho)

1982 (24 Aug). Leipzig Autumn Fair. T E **732** and similar horiz design. Multicoloured. P 13×12½.
E2441 10pf. Type E **732** 40   30
E2442 25pf. Amber box, ring and pendant 50   45

(Des H. Detlefsen. Photo)

1982 (7 Sept). War Victims' Memorial, Auschwitz-Birkenau. P 14.
E2443 E **733** 35pf. dull blue, black and brown-red ... 80   60

E 734 Federation Badge

E 735 *Anemone hupehensis*

(Des K.-H. Bobbe. Litho)

1982 (7 Sept). Ninth International Federation of Resistance Fighters Congress, Berlin. P 14.
E2444 E **734** 10pf. multicoloured 80   45

(Des K. Müller. Photo)

1982 (21 Sept). Autumn Flowers. T E **735** and similar horiz designs. Multicoloured. P 14.
E2445 5pf. Type E **735** 40   30
E2446 10pf. French Marigolds (*Tagetes patula*) 40   30
E2447 15pf. Gazania 40   30
E2448 20pf. Sunflower (*Helianthus annuus*) 40   30
E2449 25pf. Annual Chrysanthemum
             (*Chrysanthemum carinatum*) 50   30
E2450 35pf. Cosmea (*Cosmos bipinnatus*) .... 3·75 2·75
E2445/E2450 Set of 6 .... 5·25 3·75

E 736 Palestinian Family

E 737 B 1000 Ambulance

(Des P. Korn. Litho)

1982 (21 Sept). Solidarity with Palestinian People. P 14.
E2451 E **736** 10pf. +5pf. multicoloured 80   45

(Des M. Gottschall. Litho)

1982 (5 Oct). IFA Vehicles. T E **737** and similar horiz designs. Multicoloured. P 13×12½.
E2452 5pf. Type E **737** 50   30
E2453 10pf. Road cleaner 50   30

311

GERMANY / German Democratic Republic (East Germany)

E2454	20pf. LD 3000 omnibus	50	30
E2455	25pf. LD 3000 lorry	50	30
E2456	35pf. W 50 lorry	50	30
E2457	85pf. W 50 milk tanker	4·50	3·50
E2452/E2457 Set of 6		6·25	4·50

E 738 Fair Emblem

E 739 Aircraft and Envelope

(Des E. Haller. Litho)

1982 (19 Oct). 25th Masters of Tomorrow Fair, Leipzig. P 14.

E2458	E **738**	20pf. multicoloured	65	30

(Des D. Glinski. Photo)

1982 (26 Oct)–87. AIR. P 14.

E2459	E **739**	5pf. black and greenish blue (4.10.83)	40	30
E2460		15pf. black and bright mauve (6.10.87)	40	60
E2461		20pf. black and dull orange (4.10.83)	50	30
E2462		25pf. black and olive-bistre (6.10.87)	75	55
E2463		30pf. black and blue-green	50	30
E2464		40pf. black and deep dull green	65	30
E2465		1m. black and blue	1·90	95
E2466		3m. black and deep yellow-brown (10.4.84)	5·50	3·00
E2467		5m. black and scarlet-vermilion (10.9.85)	8·00	2·75
E2459/E2467 Set of 9			17·00	8·25

The 20 and 25pf. were issued both with matt gum and on thinner paper with shiny gum.

Nos. E2468/E2470 are vacant.

E **740** Seal of Eisleben, 1500

E **741** Carpenter

(Des G. Schmidt. Photo)

1982 (9 Nov). 500th Birth Anniv of Martin Luther (Protestant reformer) (1st issue). T E **740** and similar vert designs. Multicoloured. P 14.

E2471	10pf. Type E **740**	50	30
E2472	20pf. Luther as Junker Jög, 1521	50	30
E2473	35pf. Seal of Wittenberg, 1500	80	30
E2474	85pf. Luther (after Cranach)	6·50	4·00
E2471/E2474 Set of 4		7·50	4·50

The 20pf. was issued both in sheets of 25 and sheets of ten stamps. See also No. MSE2548.

(Des A. Bertram. Litho)

1982 (23 Nov). Mechanical Toys. T E **741** and similar vert designs. Multicoloured. P 14.

E2475	10pf. Type E **741**	40	40
	a. Sheetlet of 6. Nos. E2475/E2480	6·25	
E2476	20pf. Shoemaker	2·20	2·20
E2477	25pf. Baker	40	40
E2478	35pf. Cooper	40	40
E2479	40pf. Tanner	2·20	2·20
E2480	70pf. Wheelwright	40	40
E2475/E2480 Set of 6		5·50	5·50

Nos. E2475/E2480 were issued together in *se-tenant* sheetlets of six stamps.

E **742** Johannes Brahms

E **743** Franz Dahlem

(Des J. Riess. Litho)

1983 (11 Jan). 150th Birth Anniv of Johannes Brahms (composer). Sheet 55×80 mm. P 14.

MSE2481 E **742** 1m.15 pale sage green, grey-brown and sepia		5·50	4·25

(Des G. Stauf. Recess)

1983 (25 Jan). Socialist Personalities. T E **743** and similar vert designs. P 14.

E2482	10pf. chocolate	40	30
E2483	10pf. deep grey-green	40	30
E2484	10pf. blackish olive	40	30
E2485	10pf. blackish lilac	40	30
E2486	10pf. deep blue	40	30
E2482/E2486 Set of 5		1·80	1·40

Designs:—No. E2482, T E **743**; No. E2483, Karl Maron; E2484, Josef Miller; E2485, Fred Oelssner; E2486, Siegfried Rädel.

E **744** Telephone Handset and Push-buttons

E **745** Otto Nuschke

(Des D. Glinski. Photo)

1983 (8 Feb). World Communications Year. T E **744** and similar horiz designs. P 14.

E2487	5pf. light brown, black and deep brown	50	30
E2488	10pf. new blue, deep turquoise-blue and deep greenish blue	50	30
E2489	20pf. dull blue-green, myrtle green and greenish black	50	30
E2490	35pf. multicoloured	2·75	1·60
E2487/E2490 Set of 4		3·75	2·30

Designs:—5pf. T E **744**; 10pf. Aerials and tankers (Rügen Radio); 20pf. Aircraft, container ship, letter and parcel; 35pf. Optical fibre cables.

(Des K. Müller. Photo)

1983 (8 Feb). Birth Centenary of Otto Nuschke (politician). P 14.

E2491	E **745**	20pf. stone, black and chestnut	95	35

E **746** Stolberg Town Hall

E **747** Petershof

(Des H. Zill. Photo)

1983 (22 Feb). Historic Town Halls. T E **746** and similar designs. Multicoloured. P 14.

E2492	10pf. Type E **746**	50	30
E2493	20pf. Gera (*vert*)	50	30
E2494	25pf. Pössneck (*vert*)	50	30
E2495	35pf. Berlin	2·75	2·00
E2492/E2495 Set of 4		3·75	2·50

(Des D. Glinski. Photo)

1983 (8 Mar). Leipzig Spring Fair. T E **747** and similar horiz design. Multicoloured. P 14.

E2496	10pf. Type E **747**	50	30
E2497	25pf. Robotron micro-electronic calculator	80	45

GERMANY / German Democratic Republic (East Germany)

E **748** Paul Robeson

E **749** Harnack, Schulze-Boysen and Sieg

(Des D. Lindner. Litho)

1983 (22 Mar). 85th Birth Anniv of Paul Robeson (singer). P 13×12½.
| E2498 | E **748** | 20pf. mutlicoloured | 65 | 45 |

(Des G. Stauf. Litho)

1983 (22 Mar). 40th Death Anniv of Arvid Harnack, Harro Schulze-Boysen and John Sieg (Resistance workers). Sheet 80×55 mm. P 13×12½.
| MSE2499 | E **749** | 85pf. black and pale yellow-olive | 3·00 | 2·75 |

E **750** Karl Marx and Newspaper Mastheads

(Des J. Riess (**MS**E2506), M. Gottschall (others). Litho)

1983 (11 Apr). Death Centenary of Karl Marx. T E **750** and similar horiz designs. Multicoloured. P 13×12½.
E2500	10pf. Type E **750**	30	30
E2501	20pf. Marx, Lyons silk weavers and title page of *Deutsche Französische Jahrbücher*	30	30
E2502	35pf. Marx, Engels and *Communist Manifesto*	50	30
E2503	50pf. Marx and German, Russian and French versions of *Das Kapital*	50	35
E2504	70pf. Marx and part of letter to Wilhelm Bracke containing commentary on German Workers' Party Programme	80	45
E2505	85pf. Globe and banner portraying Marx, Engels and Lenin	4·75	4·75
E2500/E2505	Set of 6	6·50	5·75
MSE2506	81×56 mm. 1m.15, Karl Marx (26×32 *mm*). P 14.	4·75	3·75

E **751** Athene

E **752** Chancery Hourglass with Wallmount, 1674

(Des K.-H. Bobbe. Photo)

1983 (19 Apr). Sculptures in Berlin State Museum. T E **751** and similar vert design. P 14.
| E2507 | 10pf. deep brown, ochre and deep violet-blue | 50 | 30 |
| E2508 | 20pf. deep brown, ochre and deep olive | 80 | 45 |
Designs:—10pf. T E **751**; 20pf. *Amazon*.

(Des D. Glinski. Litho)

1983 (17 May). Narrow-gauge Railways (3rd series). Horiz designs as T E **683**. P 13×12½.
E2509	15pf. grey, black and orange-vermilion	80	80
	a. Horiz strip of 2. Nos. E2509/E2510 plus label	1·90	1·90
E2510	20pf. multicoloured	80	80
E2511	20pf. grey, black and orange-vermilion	80	80
	a. Horiz strip of 2. Nos. E2511/E2512 plus label	1·90	1·90
E2512	50pf. orange-brown, black and grey	80	80
E2509/E2512	Set of 4	3·00	3·00
Designs:—No. E2509, Wernigerode–Nordhausen steam locomotive; E2510, Wernigerode–Nordhausen passenger carriage; E2511, Zittau–Kurort Oybin/Kurort Jonsdorf steam locomotive; E2512, Zittau–Kurort Oybin/Kurort Jonsdorf luggage van.

Nos. E2509/E2510 were issued together *se-tenant* with intervening half stamp-size label bearing a map of the railway route; Nos. E2511/E2512 were similarly arranged.

(Des J. Riess. Photo)

1983 (7 June). Hourglasses and Sundials. T E **752** and similar vert designs. Multicoloured. P 14.
E2513	5pf. Type E **752**	40	30
E2514	10pf. Chancery hourglass, 1700	40	30
E2515	20pf. Horizontal table sundial, 1611	40	30
E2516	30pf. Equatorial sundial, 1750	45	30
E2517	50pf. Equatorial sundial, 1760	80	45
E2518	85pf. 'Noon Gun' table sundial, 1800	5·00	4·75
E2513/E2518	Set of 6	6·75	5·75
The 20pf. was issued both in sheets of 50 and in sheets of eight stamps.

E **753** *Coryphantha elephantidens*

(Des M. Gottschall. Photo)

1983 (21 June). Cultivated Cacti. T E **753** and similar vert designs. Multicoloured. P 14.
E2519	5pf. Type E **753**	40	30
E2520	10pf. *Thelocactus schwarzii*	40	30
E2521	20pf. *Leuchtenbergia principis*	40	30
E2522	25pf. *Submatucana madrsoniorum*	45	30
E2523	35pf. *Oroya peruviana*	45	30
E2524	50pf. *Copiapoa cinerea*	3·25	2·75
E2519/E2524	Set of 6	4·75	3·75

E **754** Thimo and Wilhelm

E **755** Glasewaldt and Zinna defending the Barricade, Berlin, 1848 (Theodor Hosemann)

(Des L. Grünewald. Photo)

1983 (5 July). Founders of Naumberg Cathedral. T E **754** and similar square designs showing statues in the West Choir. Multicoloured. P 13.
E2525	20pf. Type E **754**	80	80
	a. Block of 4. Nos. E2525/E2528	5·75	
E2526	25pf. Gepa and Gerburg	95	95
E2527	35pf. Hermann and Reglindis	1·10	1·10
E2528	85pf. Eckehard and Uta	2·75	2·75
E2525/E2528	Set of 4	5·00	5·00
Nos. E2525/E2528 were issued together in *se-tenant* blocks of four within the sheet.

(Des H. Detlefsen. Litho)

1983 (5 July). Junior Sozphilex 1983 Stamp Exhibition, Berlin. T E **755** and similar horiz design. P 12½×13 (10pf.) or 13×12½ (20pf.).
| E2529 | 10pf. +5pf. pale cinnamon, black and carmine-red | 1·30 | 1·10 |
| E2530 | 20pf. multicoloured | 50 | 30 |
Designs:—10pf. T E **755**; 20pf. *Instruction at the Polytechnic*, (Harald Metzkes).

E **756** Simón Bolivar and Alexander von Humboldt

E **757** Exercise with Balls

313

GERMANY / German Democratic Republic (East Germany)

(Des H. Detlefsen. Photo)
1983 (19 July). Birth Bicentenary of Simón Bolivar. P 14.
E2531 E **756** 35pf. black, olive-sepia and deep yellow-brown .... 1·10 60

(Des R.-J. Lehmann. Photo)
1983 (19 July). Seventh Gymnastics and Sports Festival and Ninth Children and Young People's Sports Days, Leipzig. T E **757** and similar horiz designs. Multicoloured. P 14.
E2532 10pf. +5pf. Type E **757** .... 1·10 80
E2533 20pf. Volleyball 40 30

E **758** Arms of Cottbus

E **759** Central Fair Palace

(Des H. Stier. Photo)
1983 (9 Aug). Town Arms (1st series). T E **758** and similar vert designs. P 14.
E2534 50pf. multicoloured .... 1·60 1·20
E2535 50pf. multicoloured .... 1·60 1·20
E2536 50pf. scarlet-vermilion, black and silver .... 1·60 1·20
E2537 50pf. multicoloured .... 1·60 1·20
E2538 50pf. black, bright scarlet and silver .... 1·60 1·20
E2534/E2538 Set of 5 .... 7·25 5·50
Designs:—No. E2534, T E **758**. As T E **758** No. E2535, Dresden; E2536, Erfurt; E2537, Frankfurt-on-Oder. 21×39 mm—No. E2538, Berlin. See also Nos. E2569/E2573 and E2644/E2648.

(Des O. Volkamer. Photo)
1983 (30 Aug). Leipzig Autumn Fair. T E **759** and similar horiz design. Multicoloured. P 14.
E2539 10pf. Type E **759** 40 30
E2540 25pf. Microchip 95 45

E **760** Militiaman

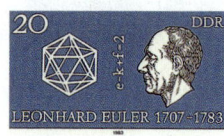

E **761** Euler, Formula and Model

(Des H. Naumann. Photo)
1983 (6 Sept). 30th Anniv of Workers' Militia. Sheet 63×86 mm. P 12½×13.
MSE2541 E **760** 1m. multicoloured .... 4·50 3·00

(Des A. Bengs. Litho)
1983 (6 Sept). Death Bicentenary of Leonhard Euler (mathematician). P 13×12½.
E2542 E **761** 20pf. blue and black 95 45

(Des P. Korn. Litho)
1983 (20 Sept). Public Palaces and Gardens of Potsdam-Sanssouci. T E **762** and similar horiz designs. Multicoloured. P 13×12½.
E2543 10pf. Type E **762** 40 20
E2544 20pf. Chinese tea house 50 30
E2545 40pf. Charlottenhof Palace 80 45
E2546 50pf. Film museum (former stables) .... 4·75 4·75
E2543/E2546 Set of 4 .... 5·75 5·25

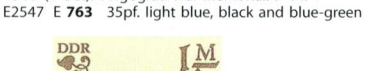

(Des M. Gottschall. Photo)
1983 (4 Oct). Volgograd War Memorial. P 14.
E2547 E **763** 35pf. light blue, black and blue-green 95 45

E **764** D.M.L. (Dr. Martin Luther)

E **765** Learning to Read and Write

(Des G. Schmidt. Litho)
1983 (18 Oct). 500th Birth Anniv of Martin Luther (Protestant reformer) (2nd issue). Sheet 108×83 mm. P 14.
MSE2548 E **764** 1m. multicoloured .... 5·50 4·75

(Des K. Hennig. Litho)
1983 (8 Nov). 'Solidarity with Nicaragua'. P 14.
E2549 E **765** 10pf. +5pf. multicoloured 65 30

E **766** Cockerel

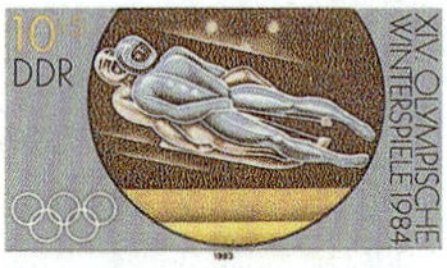

E **767** Luge

(Des J. Bertholdt. Photo)
1983 (8 Nov). Thuringian Glass. T E **766** and similar vert designs. Multicoloured. P 14.
E2550 10pf. Type E **766** 50 30
E2551 20pf. Beaker 50 30
E2552 25pf. Vase 50 30
E2553 70pf. Goblet .... 4·25 3·00
E2550/E2553 Set of 4 .... 5·25 3·50

(Des J. Riess. Photo)
1983 (22 Nov). Winter Olympic Games, Sarajevo (1984). T E **767** and similar horiz designs. P 14.
E2554 10pf. +5pf. multicoloured 50 30
E2555 20pf. +10pf. multicoloured 50 30
E2556 25pf. multicoloured 50 30
E2557 35pf. multicoloured .... 3·25 2·00
E2554/E2557 Set of 4 .... 4·25 2·50
MSE2558 83×57 mm. 85pf. new blue and silver. P 13×12½ .... 3·50 3·00
Designs:—10pf. T E **767**; 20pf. Cross-country skiing and ski jumping; 25pf. Cross-country skiing; 35pf. Biathlon; 85pf. Olympic Centre, Sarajevo.

E **762** Sanssouci Castle

E **763** Mother Homeland (Yevgeni Vuzhetich)

E **768** Dove and Greeting in German and English

E **769** Dr. Otto Schott (chemist)

GERMANY / German Democratic Republic (East Germany)

(Des K. Hennig. Photo)

1983 (22 Nov). New Year. Sheet 93×83 mm containing T E **768** and similar horiz designs, each showing dove and greeting in named languages. Multicoloured. P 14.
MSE2559 10pf. Type E **768**; 20pf. German and Russian; 25pf. French and German; 35pf. Spanish and German .... 3·50 3·50

(Des J. Bertholdt. Litho)

1984 (10 Jan). Centenary of Jena Glass. P 12½×13.
E2560 E **769** 20pf. multicoloured 80 45

E **770** Friedrich Ebert

E **771** Felix Mendelssohn

(Des G. Stauf. Recess)

1984 (24 Jan). Socialist Personalities. T E **770** and similar vert designs. P 14.
E2561 10pf. black 40 30
E2562 10pf. bottle green 40 30
E2563 10pf. blue-black 40 30
E2561/E2563 Set of 3 .... 1·10 80

Designs:—No. E2561, T E **767**; No. E2562, Fritz Grosse; E2563, Albert Norden.

(Des M. Gottschall. Litho)

1984 (24 Jan). 175th Birth Anniv of Felix Mendelssohn Bartholdy (composer). Sheet 82×57 mm. P 14.
MSE2564 E **771** 85pf. multicoloured .... 2·20 2·20

E **772** Milestones, Mühlau and Oederan

E **773** Old Town Hall, Leipzig

(Des M. Gottschall. Photo)

1984 (7 Feb). Postal Milestones. T E **772** and similar vert designs. Multicoloured. P 14.
E2565 10pf. Type E **772** 40 30
E2566 20pf. Milestones, Johanngeorgenstadt and Schönbrunn 65 45
E2567 35pf. Distance column, Freiberg 80 60
E2568 85pf. Distance column, Pegau .... 1·60 1·60
E2565/E2568 Set of 4 .... 3·00 2·75

(Des H. Stier. Photo)

1984 (21 Feb). Town Arms (2nd series). Vert designs as T E **758**. P 14.
E2569 50pf. multicoloured 95 80
E2570 50pf. bright scarlet, black and silver 95 80
E2571 50pf. multicoloured 95 80
E2572 50pf. multicoloured 95 80
E2573 50pf. multicoloured .... 1·60 1·60
E2569/E2573 Set of 5 .... 4·75 4·25

Designs:—No. E2569, Gera; E2570, Halle; E2571, Karl-Marx-Stadt; E2572, Leipzig; E2573, Magdeburg.

(Des O. Volkamer. Photo)

1984 (6 Mar). Leipzig Spring Fair. T E **773** and similar horiz design. Multicoloured. P 14.
E2574 10pf. Type E **773** 40 30
E2575 25pf. Body stamping press 65 45

(Des D. Glinski. Litho)

1984 (20 Mar). Narrow-gauge Railways (4th series). Designs as T E **683**. P 13×12½.
E2576 30pf. grey, black and orange-red 50 45
  a. Horiz strip of 2. Nos. E2576 and E2577 plus label .... 2·10 1·80

E2577 40pf. grey, black and orange-red 65 60
  a. Horiz strip of 2. Nos. E2577/E2578 plus label .... 1·60 1·50
E2578 60pf. multicoloured 80 80
E2579 80pf. multicoloured .... 1·30 1·20
E2576/E2579 Set of 4 .... 3·00 2·75

Designs:—30pf. Cranzahl–Kurort Oberwiesenthal steam locomotive; 40pf. Selketalbahn steam locomotive; 60pf. Selketalbahn passenger carriage; 80pf. Cranzahl–Kurort Oberwiesenthal passenger carriage. Nos. E2576 and 52579 were issued together se-tenant with an intervening half stamp-size label bearing a map of the railway route; Nos. E2577/E2578 were similarly arranged.

E **774** Town Hall, Rostock

E **775** Telephone, Letter, Pencil and Headquarters

(Des H. Zill. Photo)

1984 (24 Apr). Seventh International Society for Preservation of Monuments General Assembly, Rostock and Dresden. T E **774** and similar multicoloured designs. P 14.
E2580 10pf. Type E **774** 40 30
E2581 15pf. Albrecht Castle, Meissen 40 30
E2582 40pf. Gateway, Rostock (vert) 95 60
E2583 85pf. Stables, Dresden .... 2·40 2·00
E2580/E2583 Set of 4 .... 3·75 3·00

(Des P. Korn. Photo)

1984 (8 May). 25th Meeting of Posts and Telecommunciations Commission of Council of Mutual Economic Aid, Cracow. P 14.
E2584 E **775** 70pf. multicoloured .... 1·40 60

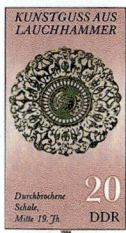

E **776** Cast Iron Bowl

E **777** String Puppet

(Des P. Korn. Photo)

1984 (22 May). Cast Iron from Lauchhammer. T E **776** and similar vert design. Multicoloured. P 14.
E2585 20pf. Type E **776** 50 30
E2586 85pf. Climber (Fritz Cremer) .... 1·80 1·70

(Des B. Lindner. Photo)

1984 (5 June). Puppets. T E **777** and similar vert design. Multicoloured. P 14.
E2587 50pf. Type E **777** .... 1·10 1·10
E2588 80pf. Hand puppet .... 1·90 1·90

E **778** Marchers with Flags

E **779** Gera Buildings

(Des R.-J. Lehmann. Litho)

1984 (5 June). National Youth Festival, Berlin. T E **778** and similar horiz design. Multicoloured. P 13×12½.
E2589 10pf. +5pf. Type E **778** 50 30
  a. Horiz strip of 2. Nos. E2589/E2590 plus label .... 1·10 80
E2590 20pf. Young construction workers 50 45

Nos. E2589/E2590 were issued together se-tenant with intervening half stamp-size label bearing festival emblem and inscription.

315

GERMANY / German Democratic Republic (East Germany)

(Des J. Bertholdt. Litho)

1984 (19 June). 20th Workers' Festival, Gera. T E **779** and similar horiz design. Multicoloured. P 13×12½.

E2591	10pf. Type E **779**	50	30
	a. Horiz strip of 2. Nos. E2591/E2592 plus label	1·10	80
E2592	20pf. Couple in traditional costume	50	45

Nos. E2591/E2592 were issued together *se-tenant* with intervening half stamp-size label bearing festival emblem.

E 780 Salt Carrier  E 781 Bakers' Seal, Berlin

(Des G. Voigt. Litho)

1984 (3 July). National Stamp Exhibition, Halle. T E **780** and similar vert design. Multicoloured. P 14.

E2593	10pf. +5pf. Type E **780**	40	30
E2594	20pf. Citizen of Halle with his bride	65	45

(Des E. Haller. Litho)

1984 (7 Aug). Historical Seals of 1442. T E **781** and similar vert designs. Multicoloured. P 14.

E2595	5pf. Type E **781**	65	30
	a. Block of 4. Nos. E2595/E2598	7·50	
E2596	10pf. Wool weavers, Berlin	1·10	60
E2597	20pf. Wool weavers, Cölln on Spree	2·10	80
E2598	35pf. Shoemakers, Cölln on Spree	3·50	3·00
E2595/E2598	Set of 4	6·50	4·25

Nos. E2595/E2598 were issued together in *se-tenant* blocks of four within the sheet.

E 782 New Flats and Restored Terrace  E 783 Frege House, Katharine Street

(Des J. Riess. Litho)

1984 (21 Aug). 35th Anniv of German Democratic Republic (1st issue). T E **782** and similar horiz designs. Multicoloured. P 14.

E2599	10pf. Type E **782**	40	30
E2600	20pf. Surface mining	65	60
MSE2601	80×55 mm. 1m. Privy Council building	2·40	2·20

See also Nos. E2604/MSE2607 and E2609/MSE2613.

(Des M. Gottschall. Photo)

1984 (28 Aug). Leipzig Autumn Fair. T E **783** and similar vert design. Multicoloured. P 14.

E2602	10pf. Type E **783**	40	30
E2603	25pf. Crystal jar from Olbernhau	65	45

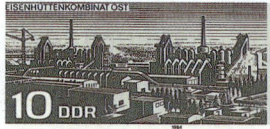

E 784 East Ironworks

(Des D. Glinski. Litho (MSE2064), photo (others))

1984 (11 Sept). 35th Anniv of German Democratic Republic (2nd issue) and similar horiz designs. Multicoloured. P 14.

E2604	10pf. Type E **784**	40	30
E2605	20pf. Soldiers, Mil Mi-8 helicopter, tank and warship	50	45
E2606	25pf. Petro-chemical complex, Schwedt	65	45
E2604/E2606	Set of 3	1·40	1·10
MSE2607	110×90 mm. 1m. bright carmine (Family and new flats) (51×29 *mm*)	3·00	2·75

E 785 Members of the Resistance (Arno Wittig)

(Des H. Detlefsen. Photo)

1984 (18 Sept). Resistance Memorial, Georg-Schumann Building, Dresden Technical University. P 14.

E2608	E **785**	35pf. multicoloured	1·40	60

E 786 Construction Workers

(Des J. Riess. Photo)

1984 (4 Oct). 35th Anniv of German Democratic Republic (3rd issue). T E **786** and similar multicoloured designs. P 14.

E2609	10pf. Type E **786**	40	30
E2610	20pf. Soldiers	50	30
E2611	25pf. Industrial workers	65	45
E2612	35pf. Agricultural workers	80	80
E2609/E2612	Set of 4	2·10	1·70
MSE2613	108×88 mm. 1m. Dove and National Arms (*vert*)	2·20	2·20

E 787 Magdeburg, 1551  E 788 Spring

(Des J. Riess. Litho)

1984 (4 Oct). Eighth National Youth Stamp Exhibition, Magdeburg. T E **787** and similar horiz design. Multicoloured. P 13×12½.

E2614	10pf. +5pf. Type E **787**	40	30
	a. Horiz strip of 2. Nos. E2614/E2615 plus label	1·00	85
E2615	20pf. Modern Magdeburg	40	30

Nos. E2614/E2615 were issued together *se-tenant* with intervening half stamp-size label bearing the Arms of Magdeburg.

(Des H. Detlefsen. Litho (MSE2620) or photo (others))

1984 (23 Oct). Statuettes by Balthasar Permoser in Green Vault, Dresden. T E **788** and similar vert designs. Multicoloured. P 14.

E2616	10pf. Type E **788**	40	30
E2617	20pf. *Summer*	50	30
E2618	35pf. *Autumn*	80	80
E2619	70pf. *Winter*	1·60	1·60
E2616/E2619	Set of 4	3·00	2·75
MSE2620	144×115 mm. No. E2617×8. P 12½×13	5·00	5·00

E 789 Entwined Cable and Red Star  E 790 Falkenstein Castle

(Des H. Detlefsen. Photo)

1984 (23 Oct). 'Solidarity'. P 14.

| E2621 | E **789** | 10pf. +5pf. multicoloured | 80 | 45 |

GERMANY / German Democratic Republic (East Germany)

(Des Snechana Russewa-Hoyer. Litho)

1984 (6 Nov). Castles (1st series). T E **790** and similar horiz designs. Multicoloured. P 14.

E2622	10pf. Type E **790**	50	30
E2623	20pf. Kriebstein Castle	50	30
E2624	35pf. Ranis Castle	1·30	95
E2625	80pf. Neuenburg	1·90	1·60
E2622/E2625	Set of 4	3·75	2·75

See also Nos. E2686/E2689 and E2742/E2745.

E **791** Queen and Princess

E **792** Anton Ackermann

(Des W. Klemke. Litho)

1984 (27 Nov). Fairy Tales. *Dead Tsar's Daughter and the Seven Warriors* by Pushkin. T E **791** and similar horiz designs. Multicoloured. P 13½×13.

E2626	5pf. Type E **791**	80	45
	a. Sheetlet of 6. Nos. E2626/E2631	14·50	
E2627	10pf. Princess and dog outside cottage	80	45
E2628	15pf. Princess and seven warriors	5·50	3·00
E2629	20pf. Princess holding poisoned apple	5·50	3·00
E2630	35pf. Princess awakened by Prince	80	45
E2631	50pf. Prince and Princess on horse	80	45
E2626/E2631	Set of 6	13·00	7·00

Nos. E2626/E26231 were issued together in *se-tenant* sheetlets of six stamps.

(Des G. Stauf. Recess)

1985 (8 Jan). Socialist Personalities. T E **792** and similar vert designs. P 14.

E2632	10pf. brownish black	40	30
E2633	10pf. chocolate	40	30
E2634	10pf. slate-purple	40	30
E2632/E2634	Set of 3	1·10	80

Designs:—No. E2632, T E **792**; No. E2633, Alfred Kurella; E2634, Otto Schön.

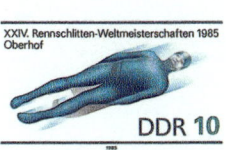

E **793** Luge

E **794** Letterbox, 1850

(Des G. Lenz. Photo)

1985 (22 Jan). 24th World Luge Championships, Oberhof. P 14.

E2635	E **793**	10pf. multicoloured	65	35

(Des B. Lindner. Litho)

1985 (5 Feb). Letterboxes. T E **794** and similar vert designs. P 14.

E2636	10pf. bistre and black	40	40
	a. Block of 4. Nos. E2636/E2639	2·50	
E2637	20pf. black, yellow-ochre and vermilion	40	40
E2638	35pf. multicoloured	65	60
E2639	50pf. olive-bistre, black and greenish grey	95	95
E2636/E2639	Set of 4	2·20	2·10

Designs:—10pf. T E **794**; 20pf. Letterbox, 1860; 35pf. Letterbox, 1900; 50pf. Letterbox, 1920.

Nos. E2636/E2639 were issued both in separate sheets of 50 stamps and in sheets of 40 containing the four values printed together in *se-tenant* blocks (*Price for se-tenant block*: £1·90 un).

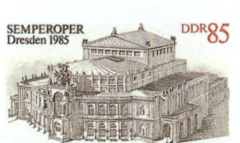

E **795** Semper Opera House, 1985

E **796** Bach Statue, Leipzig

(Des P. Kraus. Recess and litho)

1985 (12 Feb). Re-opening of Semper Opera House, Dresden. Sheet 57×80 mm. P 13×12½.

MSE2640	E **795** 85pf. reddish brown, brownish grey and carmine-lake	2·10	2·50

(Des O. Volkamer. Photo)

1985 (5 Mar). Leipzig Spring Fair. T E **796** and similar vert design. Multicoloured. P 14.

E2641	10pf. Type E **796**	40	30
E2642	25pf. Meissen porcelain pot	65	45

E **797** Johann Sebastian Bach

E **798** Liberation Monument

(Des M. Gottschall and J. Riess. Litho)

1985 (19 Mar). 300th Birth Anniv of Bach and Handel and 400th Birth Anniv of Schutz (composers). Sheet 90×114 mm containing T E **797** and similar vert designs, together with *se-tenant* horiz labels. P 14.

MSE2643	10pf. blue and bistre; 20pf brown-purple and bistre; 85pf. grey-olive and bistre	4·50	4·75

Designs:—10pf. T E **797**; 20pf. Georg Friedrich Handel; 85pf. Heinrich Schütz.

(Des H. Stier. Photo)

1985 (9 Apr). Town Arms (3rd series). Vert designs as T E **758**. Multicoloured. P 14.

E2644	50pf. Neubrandenberg	95	80
E2645	50pf. Potsdam	95	80
E2646	50pf. Rostock	95	80
E2647	50pf. Schwerin	95	80
E2648	50pf. Suhl	1·60	1·60
E2644/E2648	Set of 5	4·75	4·25

(Des H. Zill. Photo)

1985 (16 Apr). Liberation Monument, Seelow Heights. P 14.

E2649	E **798**	35pf. multicoloured	95	60

E **799** Egon Erwin Kisch

E **800** Sigmund Jähn and Valeri Bykovski

(Des L. Grünewald. Photo)

1985 (23 Apr). Birth Centenary of Egon Erwin Kisch (journalist). P 14.

E2650	E **799**	35pf. multicoloured	95	80

No. E2650 was issued with *se-tenant* half stamp-size label showing Kisch's birthplace.

(Des H. Detlefsen (**MS**E2655), M. Gottschall (others). Litho (**MS**E2655), photo (others))

1985 (7 May). 40th Anniv of Defeat of Fascism. T E **800** and similar vert designs. Multicoloured. P 14.

E2651	10pf. Type E **800**	40	40
E2652	20pf. Adolf Hennecke as miner	50	45
E2653	25pf. Agricultural workers reading paper	50	45
E2654	50pf. Laboratory technicians	95	1·10
E2651/E2654	Set of 4	2·10	2·20
MSE2655	55×81 mm. 1m. Soviet war memorial, Berlin Treptow (22×40 *mm*). P 12½×13	2·40	2·30

317

GERMANY / German Democratic Republic (East Germany)

E **801** Flags forming 'Frieden' (Peace)

(Des H. Detlefsen. Litho)

1985 (14 May). 30th Anniv of Warsaw Pact. P 13×12½.
E2656 E **801** 20pf. multicoloured 80 45

E **807** Support Steam-engine, Gera, 1833

E **808** Students reading

(Des D. Glinski. Photo)

1985 (9 July). Steam Engines. T E **807** and similar horiz design. Multicoloured. P 14.
E2667 10pf. Type E **807** 40 30
E2668 85pf. Balance steam-engine, Freiberg, 1848... 1·80 1·60

(Des R.-J. Lehmann. Litho)

1985 (23 July). 12th World Youth and Students' Festival, Moscow. T E **808** and similar horiz design. Multicoloured. P 13×12½.
E2669 20pf. +5pf. Type E **808**................................. 50 45
a. Horiz strip of 2. Nos. E2669/E2670 plus label... 1·40 1·40
E2670 50pf. Students with raised arms.................... 80 80
Nos. E2669/E2670 were printed together *se-tenant* with intervening half stamp-size label bearing festival emblem.

E **802** Emblem and Berlin Buildings

(Des P. Reissmüller. Litho)

1985 (21 May). 12th Free German Youth Parliament, Berlin. T E **802** and similar horiz design. Multicoloured. P 13×12½.
E2657 10pf. +5pf. Type E **802**................................. 50 30
a. Horiz strip of 2. Nos. E2657/E2658 plus label... 1·10 75
E2658 20pf. Flags, Ernst Thälmann and emblem 50 30
Nos. E2657/E2658 were printed together *se-tenant* with intervening half stamp-size label showing Parliament emblem.

E **803** 'Solidarity' and Dove on Globe

E **804** Olympic Flag

(Des J. Riess. Photo)

1985 (28 May). 'Solidarity'. P 14.
E2659 E **803** 10pf. +5pf. multicoloured 65 30

(Des P. Korn. Litho)

1985 (28 May). 90th International Olympic Committee Meeting, Berlin. P 14.
E2660 E **804** 35pf. multicoloured................................ 2·10 1·60
No. E2660 was issued with *se-tenant* stamp-size label depicting Olympic flame and running track.

E **809** Diver at Turning Post

(Des H. Zill. Photo)

1985 (13 Aug). Second World Orienteering Diving Championship, Neuglobsow. T E **809** and similar horiz design. Multicoloured. P 14.
E2671 10pf. Type E **809** 40 30
E2672 70pf. Divers... 1·60 1·60

E **810** Bose House, St. Thomas Churchyard

E **811** Passenger Mail Coach (relief, Hermann Steinemann)

(Des O. Volkamer. Photo)

1985 (27 Aug). Leipzig Autumn Fair. T E **810** and similar vert design. Multicoloured. P 14.
E2673 10pf. Type E **810** 40 30
E2674 25pf. J. Scherzer Bach-trumpet..................... 80 45

(Des D. Glinski. Litho)

1985 (10 Sept). Sozphilex '85 Stamp Exhibition, Berlin. T E **811** and similar vert design. Multicoloured. P 13×12½.
E2675 5pf. Type E **811** 40 40
a. Horiz pair. No. E2675/E2676 .... 95 90
b. Booklet pane. Nos.E2675a×4 .... 4·00
E2676 20pf. +5pf. Team of horses........................... 50 45
Nos. E2675/E2676 were printed together in horizontal *se-tenant* pairs within the sheet, each pair forming a composite design.
The booklet pane has a perforated margin decorated with the exhibition emblem.

E **805** '40' and Emblem

E **806** Harpy Eagle

(Des D. Glinski. Photo)

1985 (11 June). 40th Anniv of Free German Trade Unions Federation. P 14.
E2661 E **805** 20pf. multicoloured................................ 65 35

(Des Andrea Soest. Photo)

1985 (25 June). Protected Animals. T E **806** and similar horiz designs. Multicoloured. P 14.
E2662 5pf. Type E **806** 40 30
E2663 10pf. Red-breasted Geese............................ 40 30
E2664 20pf. Spectacled Bear.................................. 45 35
E2665 50pf. Bantengs.. 95 80
E2666 85pf. Sunda Gavial....................................... 1·90 1·90
E2662/E2666 Set of 5... 3·75 3·25

318

GERMANY / German Democratic Republic (East Germany)

E 812 Electrification of Railway

E 813 Gertrauden Bridge

(Des H. Detlefsen. Litho)

1985 (24 Sept). Railways. T E **812** and similar vert designs. Multicoloured. P 12½×13.

E2677	20pf. Signal box	50	30
E2678	25pf. Andreas Schubert (engineer),steam locomotive *Saxonia*, 1838, and electric locomotive Type BR250	65	45
E2679	50pf. Type E **812**	1·30	1·10
E2680	85pf. Leipzig Central Station	1·90	1·90
E2677/E2680 *Set of 4*		4·00	3·50

(Des P. Korn. Litho (**MSE**2685), photo (others))

1985 (8 Oct). Berlin Bridges. T E **813** and similar horiz designs. Multicoloured. P 14.

E2681	10pf. Type E **813**	40	40
E2682	20pf. Jungfern Bridge	50	45
E2683	35pf. Weidendammer Bridge	80	80
E2684	70pf. Marx-Engels Bridge	1·30	1·20
E2681/E2684 *Set of 4*		2·75	2·50
MSE2685 107×128 mm. No. E2682×8. Litho. P 13 ×12½		6·50	6·25

(Des Snechana Russewa-Hoyer. Litho)

1985 (15 Oct). Castles (2nd series). Horiz designs as T E **790**. Multicoloured. P 14.

E2686	10pf. Hohnstein Castle	40	40
E2687	20pf. Rochsburg	40	40
E2688	35pf. Schwarzenberg Castle	65	60
E2689	80pf. Stein Castle	1·90	1·90
E2686/E2689 *Set of 4*		3·00	3·00

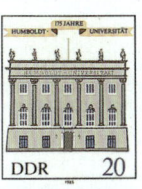

E 814 Humboldt University

E 815 Cecilienhof Castle and UN Emblem

(Des K.-H. Bobbe. Litho)

1985 (22 Oct). 175th Anniv of Humboldt University, Berlin (E2690) and 275th Anniv of Berlin Charité (training clinic)) (E2691). T E **814** and similar vert design. Multicoloured. P 14.

E2690	20pf. Type E **814**	50	35
E2691	85pf. New and old Charité buildings	1·90	1·90

(Des H. Detlefsen. Photo)

1985 (22 Oct). 40th Anniv of United Nations Organisation. P 13.

E2692 E **815**	85pf. multicoloured	1·90	95

E 816 Elephants on Balls

E 817 Grimm Brothers

(Des R.-J. Lehmann. Photo)

1985 (12 Nov). Circus. T E **816** and similar vert designs. Multicoloured. P 14.

E2693	10pf. Type E **816**	65	60
	a. Block of 4. Nos. E2693/E2696	6·75	
E2694	20pf. Trapeze artiste	95	95
E2695	35pf. Acrobats on monocycles	1·90	1·90
E2696	50pf. Tigers and trainer	3·00	2·75
E2693/E2696 *Set of 4*		5·75	5·50

Nos. E2693/E2696 were printed together in *se-tenant* blocks of four within the sheet.

(Des W. Klemke. Litho)

1985 (26 Nov). Birth Bicentenaries of Jacob and Wilhelm Grimm (folklorists). T E **817** and similar horiz designs. Multicoloured. P 13½×13.

E2697	5pf. Type E **817**	50	30
	a. Sheetlet of 6. Nos. E2697/E2702	4·50	
E2698	10pf. *The Valiant Tailor*	50	30
E2699	20pf. *Lucky John*	1·10	2·30
E2700	25pf. *Puss in Boots*	1·10	2·30
E2701	35pf. *The Seven Ravens*	50	30
E2702	85pf. *The Sweet Pap*	50	30
E2697/E2702 *Set of 6*		3·75	5·25

Nos. E2697/E2702 were issued together in *se-tenant* sheetlets of six stamps.

E 818 Water Pump, Berlin, 1900

E 819 Saxon Postilion

(Des D. Glinski. Recess and litho (35pf.), recess (others))

1986 (21 Jan). Water Supply. T E **818** and similar vert designs. P 14.

E2703	10pf. myrtle green and crimson	40	30
E2704	35pf. agate, orange-brown and bronze green	65	45
E2705	50pf. brown-purple and deep olive	1·10	1·10
E2706	70pf. deep blue and brown	1·40	1·40
E2703/E2706 *Set of 4*		3·25	3·00

Designs:—10pf. T E **818**; 35pf. Water tower, Berlin-Altglienicke, 1906; 50pf. Waterworks, Berlin-Friedrichshagen, 1893; 70pf. Rappbode dam, 1959.

(Des M. Gottschall)

1986 (4 Feb). Postal Uniforms of 1850. T E **819** and similar vert designs. Multicoloured.

A. Photo. P 14

E2707A	10pf. Type E **819**	50	30
E2708A	20pf. Prussian postman	80	45
E2709A	85pf. Prussian postal official	2·20	2·00
E2710A	1m. Postal official from Mecklenburg region	3·00	2·75
E2707A/E2710A *Set of 4*		5·75	5·00

B. Litho. P 12½×13

E2707B	10pf. Type E **819**	50	30
	a. Block of 4. Nos. E2707B/E2710B	6·75	
E2708B	20pf. Prussian postman	65	45
E2709B	85pf. Prussian postal official	2·20	2·00
E2710B	1m. Postal official from Mecklenburg region	3·00	2·75
E2707B/E2710B *Set of 4*		5·75	5·00

Nos. E2707B/E2710B were printed together in *se-tenant* blocks of four within the sheet.

E 820 Flag

E 821 Flag

(Des Ursula Abramowski-Lautenschläger. Photo)

1986 (18 Feb). 40th Anniv of Free German Youth. P 14.

E2711 E **820**	20pf. lemon, deep new blue and black	80	60

319

GERMANY / German Democratic Republic (East Germany)

(Des H. Zill. Photo)
1986 (18 Feb). 30th Anniv of National People's Army. P 14.
E2712   E **821**   20pf. multicoloured .... 1·60   95
    No. E2712 was issued with *se-tenant* half stamp-size inscribed label.

E **822** Exhibition Hall

(Des J. Bertholdt. Litho)
1986 (11 Mar). Leipzig Spring Fair. T E **822** and similar horiz design. Multicoloured. P 13×12½.
E2713   35pf. Type E **822** 65   45
E2714   50pf. *Atlantik 488* (factory trawler)............. 95   80

E **823** Yuri Gagarin and Vostok

(Des D. Glinski. Litho)
1986 (25 Mar). 25th Anniv of Manned Space Flight. T E **823** and similar horiz designs. Multicoloured. P 14.
E2715   40pf. Type E **823** (first man in space)............ 65   85
    a. Block of 4. Nos. E2715/E2718 .... 4·25
E2716   50pf. Cosmonauts Valeri Bykovski and Sigmund Jahn, space station and Interkosmos emblem 80   95
E2717   70pf. Space probe *Venera*, orbit around Venus and spectrometer .... 1·10   1·20
E2718   85pf. Reconnaissance camera MKF-6, photo, *Soyuz 22* spaceship, aeroplane and research ship .... 1·40   1·60
E2715/E2718 Set of 4 .... 3·50   4·25
    Nos. 2715/E2718 were printed together in *se-tenant* blocks of four within the sheet.

E **824** Marx, Engels and Lenin

E **825** Memorial

(Des P. Kraus. Litho)
1986 (8 Apr). 11th Socialist Unity Party of Germany Day. T E **824** and similar horiz designs. P 13½×13.
E2719   10pf. black, scarlet-vermilion and silver 40   40
E2720   20pf. scarlet-vermilion, black and silver 50   45
E2721   50pf. multicoloured 95   95
E2722   85pf. black, scarlet-vermilion and silver .... 1·90   1·90
E2719/E2722 Set of 4 .... 3·50   3·25
MSE2723 80×55 mm. 1m. multicoloured. P 13×14 ...... 2·20   2·50
    Designs:—10pf. T E **824**; 20pf. Ernst Thälmann (birth centenary); 50pf. Wilhelm Pieck and Otto Grotewohl, April 1946; 85pf. Family; 1m. Construction worker holding symbolic key.

(Des P. Kraus. Photo)
1986 (15 Apr). Opening of Ernst Thälmann Park, Berlin. P 14.
E2724   E **825**   20pf. multicoloured 80   60

E **826** Horse-drawn Tram, Dresden, 1886

E **827** Orangutan

(Des J. Bertholdt. Photo)
1986 (20 May). Trams. T E **826** and similar horiz designs. Multicoloured. P 14.
E2725   10pf. Type E **826** 40   40
E2726   20pf. Leipzig, 1896 50   45
E2727   40pf. Berlin, 1919 .... 1·10   1·20
E2728   70pf. Halle, 1928 .... 1·90   1·60
E2725/E2728 Set of 4 .... 3·50   3·25

(Des R. Zieger. Litho)
1986 (27 May). 125th Anniv of Dresden Zoo. T E **827** and similar vert designs. Multicoloured. P 14.
E2729   10pf. Type E **827** 50   30
E2730   20pf. Eastern Black-and-white Colobus............. 80   60
E2731   50pf. Mandrill .... 1·60   1·60
E2732   70pf. Ring-tailed Lemurs .... 1·90   1·90
E2729/E2732 Set of 4 .... 4·25   4·00

E **828** City Seal, 1253

E **829** Couple, Tractor and House

(Des D. Glinski. Recess (70pf., 1m.), (recess and litho (others))
1986 (3 June). 750th Anniv of Berlin. T E **828** and similar designs. P 12½×13 (vert) or 13×12½ (horiz).
E2733   10pf. sepia, pale bistre and lake-brown 50   30
E2734   20pf. blackish olive, pale sage green and reddish brown 95   45
E2735   50pf. black, brown and brown-red .... 1·90   1·20
E2736   70pf. deep yellow-green and deep brown....... 3·25   2·00
E2733/E2736 Set of 4 .... 6·00   3·50
MSE2737 54×80 mm. 1m. blackish green .... 2·50   2·75
    Designs: Horiz—20pf. City map, 1648; 50pf. Oldest City Arms. Vert—10pf. T E **828**; 70pf. St. Nicholas's Church, 1832; 1m. Cabinet building tower.
    See also Nos, E2780/**MS**E2784 and **MS**E2828.

(Des H. Zill. Litho)
1986 (17 June). 21st Workers' Festival, Magdeburg. T E **829** and similar horiz design. Multicoloured. P 13×12½.
E2738   20pf. Type E **829** 65   60
    a. Horiz strip of 2. Nos. E2738/E2739 plus label .... 1·40   1·30
E2739   50pf. Port and town of Magdeburg 65   60
    Nos. E2738/E2739 were issued together *se-tenant* with intervening half stamp-size label bearing festival emblem.

E **830** Berlin, 1652

E **831** Schwerin Castle

(Des J. Riess. Litho)
1986 (22 July). Ninth Youth Stamp Exhibition, Berlin. T E **830** and similar horiz design. Multicoloured. P 13×12½.
E2740   10pf. +5pf. Type E **830** 50   45
    a. Horiz strip of 2. Nos. E2740/E2741 plus label .... 1·10   95
E2741   20pf. Historic and modern Berlin 50   45
    Nos. E2740/E2741 were issued together *se-tenant* with intervening half stamp-size label showing 1338 city Seal.

(Des Snechana Russewa-Hoyer. Litho)
1986 (29 July). Castles (3rd series). T E **831** and similar horiz designs. Multicoloured. P 13×12½.
E2742   10pf. Type E **831** 40   30
E2743   20pf. Güstrow castle 50   30
E2744   85pf. Rheinsberg castle .... 1·80   1·70
E2745   1m. Ludwigslust castle .... 2·40   2·30
E2742/E2745 Set of 4 .... 4·50   4·25
    Nos. E2742/E2743 were each issued both in sheets of 50 and in sheetlets of four stamps.

320

GERMANY / German Democratic Republic (East Germany)

E 832 Soldiers and Girl before Brandenburg Gate

(Des L. Grünewald. Litho)
1986 (5 Aug). 25th Anniv of Berlin Wall. P 14.
E2746 E 832 20pf. multicoloured .... 1·80 95

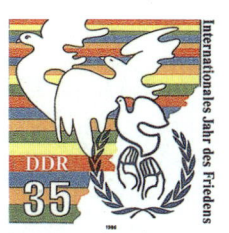

E 833 Doves flying from Emblem

E 834 Ring-Messehaus

(Des Steffi Kaiser. Photo)
1986 (5 Aug). International Peace Year. P 13.
E2747 E 833 35pf. multicoloured .... 1·10 80

(Des O. Volkamer. Litho)
1986 (19 Aug). Leipzig Autumn Fair. Sheet 82×57 mm containing T E 834 and similar vert design. Multicoloured. P 14.
MSE2748 25pf. Type E 834; 85pf. Merchants displaying cloth .... 2·50 2·50

E 835 Rostock, 1637

E 836 Man with Rifle

(Des P. Reissmüller. Photo)
1986 (2 Sept). Coins. T E 835 and similar square designs. P 13.
E2749 10pf. black, silver and vermilion 40 30
E2750 35pf. black, silver and greenish blue 65 45
E2751 50pf. multicoloured 95 80
E2752 85pf. black, silver and light royal blue .... 1·60 1·60
E2753 1m. black, silver and deep bluish green .... 2·20 2·20
E2749/E2753 Set of 5 .... 5·25 4·75
 Designs:—10pf. T E 835; 35pf. Nordhausen, 1660; 50pf. Erfurt, 1633; 85pf. Magdeburg, 1638; 1m. Stralsund, 1622.

(Des E. Haller. Photo)
1986 (2 Sept). 44th World Sports Shooting Championships, Suhl. T E 836 and similar vert designs. P 14.
E2754 20pf. black, myrtle green and brownish grey 50 30
E2755 70pf. black, bright scarlet and brownish grey .... 1·60 1·40
E2756 85pf. black, new blue and brownish grey .... 1·90 1·70
E2754/E2756 Set of 3 .... 3·50 3·00
 Designs:—20pf. T E 836; 70pf. Woman with pistol; 85pf. Man with double-barrelled shotgun.

E 837 Guard and Boundary Post

E 838 Hemispheres and Red Banner

(Des K. Bernsdorf. Photo)
1986 (9 Sept). 40th Anniv of Border Guards. P 14.
E2757 E 837 20pf. multicoloured .... 1·30 85

(Des H. Detlefsen. Photo)
1986 (9 Sept). 11th World Trade Unions Congress, Berlin. P 14.
E2758 E 838 70pf. multicoloured .... 1·90 1·60
 No. E2758 was issued with *se-tenant* inscribed label.

E 839 German Members Memorial, Friedrichshain

E 840 Memorial

(Des M. Gottschall. Photo)
1986 (11 Sept). 50th Anniv of Formation of International Brigades in Spain. P 14.
E2759 E 839 20pf. dull brown, black and bright crimson 80 45

(Des H. Detlefsen. Photo)
1986 (23 Sept). 25th Anniv of Sachsenhausen Memorial. P 14.
E2760 E 840 35pf. black, turquoise-green and blue. ... 95 60

E 841 Double-deck Train Ferry Loading Ramps

(Des J. Bertholdt. Photo)
1986 (23 Sept). Opening of Mukran–Klaipeda Railway Ferry Service. T E 841 and similar horiz design. Multicoloured. P 14.
E2761 50pf. Type E 841 .... 80 80
  a. Horiz pair. Nos. E2761/E2762 .... 1·70 1·70
E2762 50pf. *Mukran* (train ferry) 80 80
 Nos. E2761/E2762 were printed together in horizontal *se-tenant* pairs, each pair forming a composite design.

E 842 Help for Developing Countries

E 843 Weber (after F. Jügel)

(Des J. Riess. Photo)
1986 (4 Nov). 'Solidarity'. P 14.
E2763 E 842 10pf. +5pf. multicoloured 65 45

(Des J. Riess. Litho)
1986 (4 Nov). Birth Bicentary of Carl Maria von Weber (composer). Sheet 82×57 mm. P 14.
MSE2764 E 843 85pf. multicoloured .... 2·40 2·20

E 844 Indira Gandhi

E 845 Candle Holder, 1778

321

GERMANY / German Democratic Republic (East Germany)

(Des H. Detlefsen. Photo)

1986 (18 Nov). Second Death Anniv of Indira Gandhi (Indian Prime Minister). P 14.

| E2765 | E **844** | 10pf. stone and agate | 65 | 35 |

(Des H. Scheuner. Litho)

1986 (18 Nov). Candle Holders from the Erzgebirge. T E **846** and similar horiz designs. Multicoloured. P 14.

E2766		10pf. Type E **846**	50	30
		a. Sheetlet of 6. Nos. E2766/E2771	4·50	
E2767		20pf. Candle holder, 1796	50	30
E2768		25pf. Candle holder, 1810	1·10	1·10
E2769		35pf. Candle holder, 1821	1·10	1·10
E2770		40pf. Candle holder, 1830	50	30
E2771		85pf. Candle holder, 1925	50	30
E2766/E2771 Set of 6			3·75	3·00

Nos. E2766/E2771 were issued together in *se-tenant* sheetlets of six stamps.

E **846** Roland Statue, Stendal

E **847** Post Office, Freiberg

(Des Andrea Soest. Photo)

1987 (20 Jan). Statues of Roland (1st series). T E **846** and similar vert designs. P 14.

E2772		10pf. light brown, deep brown and yellow	40	30
E2773		20pf. light brown, deep brown and new blue	50	30
E2774		35pf. light brown, deep brown and reddish orange	65	60
E2775		50pf. light brown, deep brown and deep yellow-green	1·10	1·10
E2772/E2775 Set of 4			2·50	2·10

Designs:—10pf. T E **846**; Statues at—20pf. Halle; 35pf. Brandenburg; 50pf. Quedlinburg.

See also Nos. E2984/E2987.

(Des H. Detlefsen. Photo)

1987 (3 Feb). Post Offices. T E **847** and similar horiz designs. P 14.

E2776		10pf. black, brown-red and dull blue	40	40
		a. Block of 4. Nos. E2776/E2779	4·50	
E2777		20pf. multicoloured	50	45
E2778		70pf. multicoloured	1·10	1·10
E2779		1m.20 multicoloured	2·20	2·20
E2776/E2779 Set of 4			3·75	3·75

Designs:—10pf. T E **847**; 20pf. Perleberg; 70pf. Weimar; 1m.20, Kirschau.

Nos. E2776/E2779 were issued both in separate sheets and together in sheets containing ten *se-tenant* blocks.

(Des D. Glinski. Recess)

1987 (17 Feb). 750th Anniv of Berlin (2nd issue). Designs as T E **828**. P 12½×13 (20pf.) or 13×12½ (others).

E2780		20pf. chocolate and blue-green	50	30
E2781		35pf. bottle green and carmine-lake	80	55
E2782		70pf. deep blue and dull vermilion	1·60	1·40
E2783		85pf. brown-olive and emerald	2·40	2·00
E2780/E2783 Set of 4			4·75	3·75

MSE2784 4 sheets, 75×108 mm 107×75 mm (others).
(a) 10pf.×4, As No. E2780; (b) 10pf.×4, As No. E2781; (c) 20pf.×4, As No. E2782; (d) 20pf.×4, As No. E2783 ..... 8·00 10·00

Designs: Vert—20pf. Ephraim Palace. Horiz—35pf. New buildings, Alt Marzahn; 70pf. Marx-Engels Forum; 85pf. Friedrichstadtpalast.

E **848** Woman with Flower in Hair

E **849** Fair Hall 20

(Des P. Reissmüller and J. Schumann. Litho)

1987 (3 Mar). 40th Anniv and 12th Congress (Berlin) of German Democratic Women's Federation. P 13½.

| E2785 | E **848** | 10pf. deep violet-blue, vermilion and silver | 65 | 60 |

(Des J. Riess. Litho)

1987 (10 Mar). Leipzig Spring Fair. T E **849** and similar horiz design. Multicoloured. P 13×12½.

| E2786 | | 35pf. Type E **849** | 65 | 50 |
| E2787 | | 50pf. Traders at Weighbridge, 1804 (Christian Geissler) | 1·30 | 1·20 |

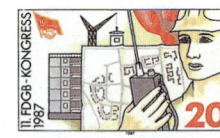

E **850** Clara Zetkin

E **851** Construction Industry

(Des G. Stauf. Recess)

1987 (24 Mar). Socialist Personalities. T E **850** and similar vert designs. Multicoloured. P 14.

E2788		10pf. deep slate-purple	50	30
E2789		10pf. brownish black	50	30
E2790		10pf. black	50	30
E2791		10pf. bottle green	50	30
E2788/E2791 Set of 4			1·80	1·10

Designs:—No. E2788, T E **850**; No. E2789, Fritz Gäbler; E2790, Walter Vesper; E2791, Robert Siewert.

(Des P. Korn. Litho)

1987 (7 Apr). 11th Federation of Free German Trade Unions Congress, Berlin. T E **851** and similar horiz design. Multicoloured. P 13×12½.

E2792		20pf. Type E **851**	40	40
		a. Horiz strip of 2. Nos. E2792/E2793 plus label	1·50	1·50
E2793		50pf. Communications industry	95	95

Nos. E2792/E2793 were issued together *se-tenant* with intervening half stamp-size inscribed label.

E **852** Flag, World Map and Doves

E **853** Museum and Karl August Lingner (founder) (after Robert Sterl)

(Des R. Link. Photo)

1987 (7 Apr). Tenth Congress of German Red Cross, Dresden. P 14.

| E2794 | E **852** | 35pf. multicoloured | 95 | 60 |

(Des B. Lindner. Photo)

1987 (7 Apr). 75th Anniv of German Hygiene Museum, Dresden. P 14.

| E2795 | E **853** | 85pf. multicoloured | 1·80 | 1·60 |

E **854** Old and New Farming Methods

E **855** Ludwig Uhland (poet)

(Des J. Bertholdt. Litho)

1987 (21 Apr). 35th Anniv of Agricultural Co-operatives. P 13×12½.

| E2796 | E **854** | 20pf. multicoloured | 80 | 60 |

(Des M. Gottschall. Litho)

1987 (5 May). Birth Anniversaries. T E **855** and similar horiz designs. Multicoloured. P 13×12½.

E2797		10pf. Type E **855** (bicentenary)	40	40
E2798		20pf. Arnold Zweig (writer, centenary)	50	45
E2799		35pf. Gerhart Hauptmann (writer, 125th anniv)	80	80
E2800		50pf. Gustav Hertz (physicist, centenary)	1·30	1·20
E2797/E2800 Set of 4			2·75	2·50

322

GERMANY / German Democratic Republic (East Germany)

E 856 Bream (*Abramis brama*)

E 857 Woman holding Baby

1987 (19 May)–**88**. Freshwater Fish. T E **856** and similar horiz designs. Multicoloured. P 13×12½.

E2801	5pf. Type E **856**	50	30
E2802	10pf. Brown Trout (*Salmo trutta fario*)	50	45
	a. No imprint date. Booklets (29.11.88)	50	45
	ab. Booklet pane. No. E2802a×4 (29.11.88)	2·10	
E2803	20pf. Wels (*Silures glanis*)	50	30
E2804	35pf. European Grayling (*Thymallus thymallus*)	80	80
E2805	50pf. Barbel (*Barbus barbus*)	1·10	80
E2806	70pf. Northern Pike (*Esox lucius*)	1·60	1·60
E2801/E2806	Set of 6	4·50	3·75

The 10 and 20pf. were each issued both in sheets of 50 and in sheetlets of four stamps.
The booklet pane was issued with matt or shiny gum.

(Des J. Bertholdt. Litho.)

1987 (16 June). 'Solidarity'. Anti-apartheid Campaign. P 14.

E2807	E **857**	10pf. +5pf. multicoloured	65	45

E 858 Horse-drawn Hand-pumped Fire Engine, 1756

E 859 Ludwig Lazarus Zamenhof (inventor)

1987 (16 June). Fire Engines. T E **858** and similar horiz designs. Multicoloured. P 13×12½.

E2808	10pf. Type E **858**	40	40
	a. Block of 4. Nos. E2808/E2811	3·75	
E2809	25pf. Steam engine, 1903	50	45
E2810	40pf. Model LF 15, 1919	95	95
E2811	70pf. Model LF 16-TS 8, 1971	1·60	1·60
E2808/E2811	Set of 4	3·00	3·00

Nos. E2808/E2811 were issued both in separate sheets and together in *se-tenant* blocks of four stamps.

(Des E. Haller. Litho.)

1987 (7 July). Centenary of Esperanto (invented language). Sheet 55×80 mm. P 14.

MSE2812 E **859**	85pf. multicoloured	1·90	2·50

E 860 Otters

E 861 Tug-of-War

(Des Ursula Abramowski-Lautenschläger. Photo)

1987 (7 July). Endangered Animals. European Otter (*Lutra lutra*). T E **860** and similar horiz designs Multicoloured. P 14.

E2813	10pf. Type E **860**	40	30
E2814	25pf. Otter swimming	50	35
E2815	35pf. Otter	80	60
E2816	60pf. Otter's head	1·90	1·90
E2813/E2816	Set of 4	3·25	2·75

(Des R.-J. Lehmann. Photo)

1987 (21 July). Eighth Gymnastics and Sports Festival and 11th Children and Young People's Sports Days, Leipzig. T E **861** and similar horiz designs. Multicoloured. P 14.

E2817	5pf. Type E **861**	40	30
E2818	10pf. Handball	40	30
E2819	20pf. +5pf. Long jumping	50	30
E2820	35pf. Table tennis	65	45
E2821	40pf. Bowling	95	80
E2822	70pf. Running	1·40	1·40
E2817/E2822	Set of 6	3·75	3·25

E 862 Association Activities

E 863 Head Post Office, Berlin, 1760

(Des J. Riess. Litho.)

1987 (4 Aug). 35th Anniv of Association of Sports and Technical Sciences. P 13×12½.

E2823	E **862**	10pf. multicoloured	65	30

(Des J. Bertholdt. Photo)

1987 (11 Aug). Stamp Day. T E **863** and similar horiz design. Multicoloured. P 14.

E2824	10pf. +5pf. Type E **863**	40	40
	a. Horiz strip of 2. Nos. E2824/E2825 plus label	85	90
E2825	20pf. Wartenberg Palace	40	45

Nos. E2824/E2825 were issued together *se-tenant* with intervening half stamp-size label showing a postal wagon.

E 864 Market Scene (left)

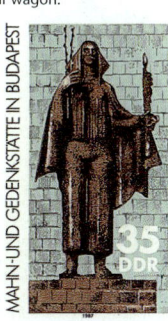

E 865 Memorial Statue (József Somogyi)

(Des G. Scheuner. Litho.)

1987 (25 Aug). Leipzig Autumn Fair. Sheet 80×58 mm containing T E **864** and similar vert design showing *Market Scene* by Christian Geissler. Multicoloured. P 13½×13.

MSE2826	40pf. T E **864**; 50pf. *Market Scene* (right)	2·40	2·30

(Des M. Gottschall. Photo)

1987 (8 Sept). War Victims' Memorial, Budapest. P 14.

E2827	E **865**	35pf. multicoloured	80	45

E 866 Memorial, Ernst Thälmann Park

E 867 Weidendamm Bridge (Arno Mohr)

(Des D. Glinski. Recess and litho)

1987 (8 Sept). 750th Anniv of Berlin (3rd issue). Sheet 80×55 mm. P 14.

MSE2828 E **866**	1m.35 black, stone and vermilion	3·25	3·00

(Des M. Gottschall. Litho.)

1987 (22 Sept). Tenth Art Exhibition, Dresden. T E **867** and similar multicoloured designs. P 14.

E2829	10pf. Type E **867**	40	45
E2830	50pf. *They only wanted to learn Reading and Writing* (Nicaragua) (Willi Sitte)	95	1·10

323

GERMANY / German Democratic Republic (East Germany)

E2831	70pf. *Big Mourning Man* (Wieland Förster)	1·30	1·40
E2832	1m. *Vase* (Gerd Lucke) (*horiz*)	1·90	2·20
E2829/E2832	Set of 4	4·00	4·75

E **868** Red Flag, Smolny Building (Leningrad), *Aurora* and Lenin

E **869** Youth using Personal Computer

E **874** *Tillandsia macrochlamys*

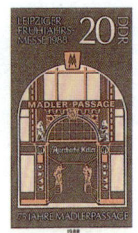

E **875** Mädler-passage Entrance

(Des J. Riess. Photo)

1987 (27 Oct). 70th Anniv of Russian Revolution. T E **868** and similar horiz design. Multicoloured. P 14.

E2833	10pf. Type E **868**	50	30
E2834	20pf. Moscow Kremlin towers	50	30

(Des P. Reissmüller. Litho)

1987 (3 Nov). 30th Masters of Tomorrow Fair, Leipzig. T E **869** and similar horiz design. Multicoloured. P 13×12½.

E2835	10pf. Type E **869**	50	30
E2836	20pf. ZIM 10-S robot-welder........................	50	30

(Des D. Glinksi. Litho)

1988 (16 Feb). Bromeliads. T E **874** and similar vert designs. Multicoloured. P 14.

E2852	10pf. Type E **874**	30	30
E2853	25pf. *Tillandsia bulbosa*	50	35
E2854	40pf. *Tillandsia kalmbacheri*	80	80
E2855	70pf. *Guzmania blassii*	1·30	1·20
E2852/E2855	Set of 4	2·50	2·40

(Des H. Scheuner. Litho)

1988 (8 Mar). Leipzig Spring Fair. 75th Anniv of Mädler-passage (fair building). T E **875** and similar vert design, each sepia, salmon and salmon-pink. P 12½×13.

E2856	20pf. Type E **875**	50	30
E2857	70pf. *Faust and Mephistopheles* (bronze statue, Matthieu Molitor)	1·90	1·20

E **870** Annaberg, 1810

E **871** Ski Jumping

E **876** Joseph von Eichendorff

E **877** Saddler, Mühlhausen, 1565

(Des H. Scheuner. Litho)

1987 (24 Nov). Christmas Pyramids from the Erzgebirge. T E **870** and similar vert designs. Multicoloured. P 12½×13.

E2837	10pf. Type E **870**	50	60
	a. Sheetlet of 6. Nos. E2837/E2842	4·50	
E2838	20pf. Freiberg, 1830	1·10	1·20
E2839	25pf. Neustädtel, 1870	50	60
E2840	35pf. Schneeberg, 1870	50	60
E2841	40pf. Lößnitz, 1880	1·10	1·20
E2842	85pf. Seiffen, 1910	50	60
E2837/E2842	Set of 6	3·75	4·25

Nos. E2837/E2842 were issued together in *se-tenant* sheetlets of six stamps.

(Des J. Riess. Litho)

1988 (8 Mar). Birth Bicentenary of Joseph von Eichendorff (writer). Sheet 82×55 mm. P 14.

MSE2858 E **876** 70pf. brown-olive, drab and pale slate-blue... 2·50 2·20

(Des K.-H. Bobbe. Photo)

1988 (22 Mar). Historic Seals. T E **877** and similar vert designs Multicoloured. P 14.

E2859	10pf. Type E **877**	40	40
	a. Block of 4. Nos. E2859/E2862	2·50	
E2860	25pf. Butcher, Dresden, 1564	50	45
E2861	35pf. Smith, Nauen, 16th-century	65	60
E2862	50pf. Clothier, Frankfurt-on-Oder, 16th-century	80	80
E2859/E2862	Set of 4	2·10	2·00

Nos. E2859/E2862 were issued both in separate sheets of 50 and together in *se-tenant* blocks of four within sheets of 40 stamps.

(Des M. Gottschall. Photo)

1988 (19 Jan). Winter Olympic Games, Calgary. T E **871** and similar multicoloured designs. P 14.

E2843	5pf. Type E **871**	50	30
E2844	10pf. Speed skating...................................	50	30
E2845	20pf. +10pf. Four-man bobsleigh	80	60
E2846	35pf. Biathlon	95	80
E2843/E2848	Set of 4	2·50	1·80

MSE2847 80×55 mm. 1m.20 Two-man and single luge (*horiz*) .... 3·25 2·75

E **872** Berlin-Buch Post Office

E **873** Brecht Bertolt

E **878** Georg Forster Antarctic Research Station

E **879** Wismar

(Des J. Riess. Photo)

1988 (2 Feb). Postal Buildings. T E **872** and similar horiz designs. Multicoloured. P 14.

E2848	15pf. Type E **872**	50	30
E2849	20pf. Postal museum	80	30
E2850	50pf. Berlin-Marzahn general post office.........	1·90	1·20
E2848/E2850	Set of 3	3·00	1·60

(Des P. Reissmüller. Litho)

1988 (22 Mar). 12th Anniv of Georg Forster Antarctic Research Station. P 13×12½.

E2863 E **878** 35pf. multicoloured 95 60

(Des R.-J. Lehmann. Litho)

1988 (2 Feb). 90th Birth Anniv of Bertolt Brecht (writer). Sheet 58×82 mm. P 13×12½.

MSE2851 E **873** 70pf. olive-grey, black and brown-red .... 2·10 2·75

(Des J. Bertholdt. Photo)

1988 (5 Apr). Northern Towns of the Democratic Republic. T E **879** and similar horiz designs. P 14.

E2864	5pf. black, turquoise-green and turquoise-blue	40	30
E2865	10pf. black, yellow-ochre and deep brown	40	30
E2866	25pf. black, azure and dull ultramarine...........	50	30
E2867	60pf. black, salmon-pink and carmine-red......	1·10	95

324

GERMANY / German Democratic Republic (East Germany)

E2868	90pf. black, apple green and yellowish green	1·60	1·60
E2869	1m.20 black, yellow-brown and carmine-vermilion	2·10	2·00
E2864/E2869	Set of 6	5·50	5·00

Designs:—5pf. T E **879**; 10pf. Anklam; 25pf. Ribnitz-Damgarten; 60pf. Stralsund; 90pf. Bergen; 1m.20 Greifswald.

E **880** Ulrich von Hutten

E **881** Chorin and Neuzelle Monasteries, Industrial and Agricultural Symbols

(Des Ursula Abramowski-Lautenschläger. Litho)

1988 (5 Apr). 500th Birth Anniv of Ulrich von Hutten (humanist). Sheet 54×80 mm. P 12½×13.

MSE2870 E **880**	70pf. black, yellow-brown and ochre	1·70	1·60

(Des P. Kraus. Litho)

1988 (7 June). 22nd Workers' Arts Festival, Frankfurt-on-Oder. T E **881** and similar horiz design. Multicoloured. P 13×12½.

E2871	20pf. Type E **881**	50	45
	a. Horiz strip. Nos. E2871/E2872 plus label	1·60	1·70
E2872	50pf. Buildings of Frankfurt	95	1·10

Nos. E2871/E2872 were issued together *se-tenant* with intervening half stamp-size label showing festival emblem and dancers.

E **882** Cosmonauts Sigmund Jähn and Valery Bykovski

(Des P. Kraus. Litho)

1988 (21 June). Tenth Anniv of USSR–East German Manned Space Flight (1st issue). T E **882** and similar horiz designs. Multicoloured. P 14.

E2873	5pf. Type E **882**	50	30
E2874	10pf. MKS-M multi-channel spectro-meter	50	30
E2875	20pf. Mir–Soyuz space complex	50	45
E2873/E2875	Set of 3	1·40	95

See also Nos. E2894/E2896.

E **883** Erfurt, 1520

E **884** Swearing-in Ceremony

(Des J. Riess. Photo)

1988 (21 June). Tenth Youth Stamp Exhibition, Erfurt and Karl-Marx-Stadt. T E **883** and similar horiz designs. Multicoloured. P 14.

E2876	10pf. +5pf. Type E **883**	40	45
	a. Horiz strip of 2. Nos. E2876 and E2878 plus label	95	1·20
E2877	20pf. +5pf. Chemnitz, 1620	50	60
	a. Horiz strip of 2. Nos. E2877 and E2879 plus label	1·70	2·10
E2878	25pf. Modern view of Erfurt	50	60
E2879	50pf. Modern view of Karl-Marx-Stadt (formerly Chemnitz)	1·10	1·40
E2876/E2879	Set of 4	2·30	2·75

Nos. E2876 and E2878 were issued together *se-tenant* with intervening half stamp-size label depicting Erfurt city Arms; Nos. E2877 and E2879 were similarly arranged with label showing Karl-Marx-Stadt city Arms.

(Des J. Riess. Photo)

1988 (5 July). 35th Anniv of Workers' Militia Squads. T E **884** and similar horiz designs. Multicoloured. P 14.

E2880	5pf. Type E **884**	50	30
E2881	10pf. Tribute to Ernst Thälmann	50	30
E2882	15pf. Parade	50	30
E2883	20pf. Arms distribution	50	30
E2880/E2883	Set of 4	1·80	1·10

E **885** Balloons and Doves over Karl-Marx-Stadt

E **886** Swimming

(Des Andrea Soest. Litho)

1988 (19 July). Eighth Pioneers Meeting, Karl-Marx-Stadt. T E **885** and similar horiz designs. Multicoloured. P 13×12½.

E2884	10pf. Type E **885**	50	45
	a. Horiz strip of 2. Nos. E2884/E2885 plus label	1·10	95
E2885	10pf. +5pf. Doves, balloons and Pioneers	50	45

Nos. E2884/E2885 were issued together *se-tenant* with intervening half stamp-size label showing Pioneers emblem.

(Des H. Detlefsen. Photo)

1988 (9 Aug). Olympic Games, Seoul. T E **886** and similar horiz designs. Multicoloured. P 14.

E2886	5pf. Type E **886**	40	40
E2887	10pf. Handball	40	40
E2888	20pf. +10pf. Hurdling	65	60
E2889	25pf. Rowing	65	60
E2890	35pf. Boxing	75	75
E2891	50pf. +20pf. Cycling	1·40	1·40
E2886/E2891	Set of 6	3·75	3·75
MSE2892	55×80 mm. 85pf. Relay race	3·75	4·00

Designs as Nos. E2886, E2888/E2889 and **MS**E2892, but with inscr 'SPIELE DER XX111. OLYMPIADE 1984' were prepared for those games but not issued.

E **887** Examining Fair Goods, 1810

E **888** Buchenwald Memorial (Fritz Cremer)

(Des Simone Arnold. Litho)

1988 (30 Aug). Leipzig Autumn Fair and 175th Anniv of Battle of Leipzig. Sheet 110×90 mm containing T E **887** and similar vert designs. Multicoloured. P 14.

MSE2893	5pf. Type E **887**; 15pf. Battle of Leipzig Monument; 100pf. Fair, 1820	4·00	3·50

(Des P. Kraus. Litho)

1988 (30 Aug). Tenth Anniv of USSR–East German Manned Space Flight (2nd issue). As Nos. E2873/E2875 but values changed. Multicoloured. P 14.

E2894	10pf. As No. E2873	50	45
E2895	20pf. As No. E2874	65	60
E2896	35pf. As No. E2875	1·30	1·20
E2894/E2896	Set of 3	2·20	2·00

Nos. E2894/E2896 were each issued in sheetlets of four stamps.

(Des H. Detlefsen. Photo)

1988 (13 Sept). War Memorials. T E **888** and similar horiz design. P 14.

E2897	10pf. myrtle green, black and light brown	50	30
E2898	35pf. multicoloured	80	60

Designs:—10pf. T E **888**; 35pf. Resistance Monument, Lake Como, Italy (Gianni Colombo).

325

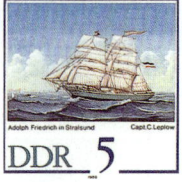

GERMANY / German Democratic Republic (East Germany)

E **889** Adolph Friedrich at Stralsund: Captain C. Leplow (E. Laschke)

E **890** Medical Scene and African Child

(Des J. Bertholdt Litho)

1988 (20 Sept). 500th Anniv of Stralsund Shipping Company. Captains' Paintings. T E **889** and similar square designs. Multicoloured. P 13.

E2899	5pf. Type E **889**	65	45
E2900	10pf. *Gartenlaube* of Stralsund; Captain J. F. Krüger (A. Laschky)	65	45
E2901	70pf. Brigantine *Auguste Mathilde* of Stralsund: Captain I. C. Grünwaldt (Johnsen-Seby Bergen)	1·60	1·60
E2902	1m.20 Brig *Hoffnung* of Cologneon-Rhine: Captain G. A. Luther (anon)	2·40	2·30
E2899/E2902 Set of 4		4·75	4·25

(Des M. Gottschall. Photo)

1988 (4 Oct). 'Solidarity'. P 14.
E2903 E **890** 10pf. +5pf. multicoloured .... 1·60 1·60
No. E2903 was issued with *se-tenant* half stamp-size label bearing a quotation by Wilhelm Pieck.

E **891** Magdeburg Drawbridge

E **892** Menorah

(Des J. Bertholdt. Photo)

1988 (18 Oct). Drawbridges and Ship Lifts. T E **891** and similar horiz designs. Multicoloured. P 14.

E2904	5pf. Type E **891**	40	30
E2905	10pf. Lift, Magdeburg-Rothensee Canal	40	30
E2906	35pf. Lift, Niederfinow	65	55
E2907	70pf. Bridge and lock, Altfriesack	1·30	1·20
E2908	90pf. Drawbridge, Rugendamm	1·60	1·60
E2904/E2908 Set of 5		4·00	3·50

(Des D. Glinski. Photo)

1988 (8 Nov). 50th Anniv of 'Kristallnacht' (Nazi pogrom). P 14.
E2909 E **892** 35pf. reddish purple, bright lemon and black 95 60

E **893** In the Boat

E **894** Lace (Regine Wengler)

(Des H. Detlefsen. Litho)

1988 (8 Nov). Birth Centenary of Max Lingner (artist). T E **893** and similar vert designs. Multicoloured. P 14.

E2910	5pf. Type E **893**	65	45
E2911	10pf. *Mademoiselle Yvonne*	65	45
E2912	20pf. *Free, Strong and Happy*	65	45
E2913	85pf. *New Harvest*	2·10	1·70
E2910/E2913 Set of 4		3·75	2·75

(Des H. Scheuner. Litho)

1988 (22 Nov). Bobbin Lace from the Erzgebirge. T E **894** and similar vert designs showing pieces of lace made by person named. Each black, light brown and yellow. P 12½×13.

E2914	20pf. Type E **894**	50	45
	a. Sheetlet of 6. Nos. E2914/E2919	4·50	
E2915	25pf. Wally Tilp	1·10	1·10
E2916	35pf. Elisabeth Mehnert-Pfabe	50	45
E2917	40pf. Ute Siewert	50	45
E2918	50pf. Regine Siebdraht	1·10	1·10
E2919	85pf. Elise Schubert	50	45
E2914/E2919 Set of 6		3·75	3·50

Nos. E2914/E2919 were issued together in *se-tenant* sheetlets of six stamps.

E **895** WHO Emblem

E **896** Dr. Wolf

(Des Gudrun Lenz. Photo)

1988 (22 Nov). 40th Anniv of World Health Organisation. P 14.
E2920 E **895** 85pf. silver, ultramarine and grey .... 1·90 95

(Des Andrea Soest. Litho)

1988 (22 Nov). Birth Centenary of Dr. Friedrich Wolf (writer). Sheet 87×59 mm. P 14.
MSE2921 E **896** 110pf. grey, black and vermilion .... 2·40 3·50

E **897** Members' Flags

E **898** Edith Baumann

(Des M. Gottschall. Photo)

1989 (10 Jan). 40th Anniv of Council of Mutual Economic Aid. P 13.
E2922 E **897** 20pf. multicoloured 95 45

(Des G. Stauf. Recess)

1989 (24 Jan). Socialist Personalities. T E **898** and similar vert designs. P 14.

E2923	10pf. purple-brown	40	30
E2924	10pf. bottle green	40	30
E2925	10pf. sepia	40	30
E2926	10pf. deep blue	40	30
E2923/E2926 Set of 4		1·40	1·10

Designs:—No. E2923, T E **898**; No. E2924, Otto Meier; E2925, Alfred Oelssner; E2926, Fritz Selbmann.

E **899** Philipp Reis Telephone, 1861

E **900** Johann Beckmann (technologist, 250th anniv)

(Des P. Korn. Litho)

1989 (7 Feb). Telephones. T E **899** and similar horiz designs. Multicoloured. P 14.

E2927	10pf. Type E **899**	40	40
	a. Block of 4. Nos. E2927/E2930	3·75	
E2928	20pf. Siemens & Halske wall telephone, 1882	50	45
E2929	50pf. OB 03 wall telephone, 1903	95	95

GERMANY / German Democratic Republic (East Germany)

E2930	85pf. OB 05 desk telephone, 1905	1·60	1·60
E2927/E2930	Set of 4	3·00	3·00

Nos. E2927/E2930 were issued both in separate sheets of 50 and together in *se-tenant* blocks of four within sheets of 40 stamps.

(Des M. Gottschall. Photo)

1989 (28 Feb). Birth Anniversaries. T E **900** and similar horiz designs. Multicoloured. P 14.

E2931	10pf. Type E **900**	40	30
E2932	10pf. Rudolf Mauersberger and church choir (musician, centenary)	40	30
E2933	10pf. Carl von Ossietzky and masthead of *Die Weltbühne* (journalist and peace activist, centenary)	40	30
E2934	10pf. Ludwig Renn and International Brigades flag (writer, centenary)	40	30
E2935	10pf. Adam Scharrer and cover of *Stateless People* (novelist, centenary)	40	30
E2931/E2935	Set of 5	1·80	1·40

E **901** Handelshof Fair Building (80th anniv)

E **902** Müntzer (after Christoph van Stichen and Romeyn de Hooghe)

(Des O. Volkamer. Litho)

1989 (7 Mar). Leipzig Spring Fair. T E **901** and similar horiz design. Multicoloured. P 14.

E2936	70pf. Type E **901**	1·40	1·20
E2937	85pf. Naschmarkt bake-house and bread shop, 1690	1·80	1·70

(Des G. Schmidt. Litho)

1989 (21 Mar). 500th Birth Anniv of Thomas Müntzer (religious reformer) (1st issue). Sheet 86×66 mm. P 13×12½.

MSE2938 E **902**	110pf. black and buff	2·50	3·50

See also Nos. E2967/**MS**E2972.

E **903** Friedrich List (economist and promoter of railway system)

E **904** Tea Caddy

(Des D. Glinski. Litho)

1989 (4 Apr). 150th Anniv of Leipzig–Dresden Railway (first German long-distance service). T E **903** and similar horiz designs. P 14.

E2939	15pf. sepia, pale brown and bronze green	65	45
E2940	20pf. black, dull green and brown-red	65	30
E2941	50pf. black, bistre and deep carmine	1·10	1·10
E2939/E2941	Set of 3	2·20	1·70

Designs:—15pf. T E **903**; 20pf. Dresdner Station, Leipzig, 1839; 50pf. Leipziger Station, Dresden, 1839.

(Des J. Riess. Litho)

1989 (18 Apr). Meissen Porcelain, 250th Anniv of Onion Design. T E **904** and similar vert designs. Each grey-brown, deep blue and dull ultramarine.

A. Size 24×42 mm. P 12½×13

E2942A	10pf. Type E **904**	50	45
E2943A	20pf. Vase	50	60
E2944A	35pf. Bread board	80	1·10
E2945A	70pf. Coffee pot	1·60	1·90
E2942A/E2945A	Set of 4	3·00	3·75

B. Size 31×54 mm. P 14

E2942B	10pf. Type E **904**	65	30
	a. Block of 4. Nos. E2942B/E2945B	4·50	
E2943B	20pf. Vase	65	45
E2944B	35pf. Bread board	95	80
E2945B	70pf. Coffee pot	1·90	1·90

E2942B/E2945B	Set of 4	3·75	3·00

Nos. E2942A/E2945A were issued in separate sheets and Nos. E2942B/E2945B were issued together in *se-tenant* blocks of four stamps within the sheet.

E **905** Renaissance Initial 'I'

E **906** Chollima Statue, Pyongyang

(Des Evelyne and K.-H. Bobbe. Photo)

1989 (2 May). Seventh International Typography Exhibition, Leipzig. T E **905** and similar vert designs. P 14.

E2946	20pf. multicoloured	50	30
E2947	50pf. black, yellow and sage green	95	80
E2948	1m.35 carmine, black and bluish grey	2·75	2·75
E2946/E2948	Set of 3	3·75	3·50

Designs:—20pf. T E **905**; 50pf. Art Nouveau initial 'B'; 1m.35 Modern initial 'A's.

(Des R.-J. Lehmann. Litho)

1989 (9 May). 13th World Youth and Students' Festival, Pyongyang, North Korea (E2949) and Free German Youth Whitsun Festival, Berlin (E2950). T E **906** and similar horiz design. Multicoloured. P 13×12½.

E2949	20pf. Type E **906**	65	80
	a. Horiz strip of 2. Nos. E2949/E2950 plus label	1·40	1·70
E2950	20pf. +5pf. Berlin buildings	65	80

Nos. E2949/E2950 were issued together *se-tenant* with intervening half stamp-size label showing Free German Youth emblem.

E **907** Princess Louise

E **908** JENEVAL Interference Microscope

E **909** Front Page of Address.

(Des J. Riess. Photo)

1989 (16 May). 225th Birth Anniv of Johann Gottfried Schadow (sculptor). T E **907** and similar vert design showing details of Princesses. P 14.

E2951	50pf. Type E **907**	1·30	95
E2952	85pf. *Princess Friederike*	2·20	1·90

(Des E. Haller. Photo)

1989 (16 May). Centenary of Carl Zeiss Foundation, Jena. T E **908** and similar vert design. Multicoloured. P 14.

E2953	50pf. Type E **908**	80	80
	a. Horiz strip of 2. Nos. E2953/E2954 plus label	2·50	2·50
E2954	85pf. ZKM 01-250 C bi-coordinate measuring instrument	1·60	1·60

Nos. E2953/E2954 were issued together *se-tenant* with intervening label bearing portrait of Ernst Abbe (physicist and Zeiss's partner).

(Des P. Kraus. Photo)

1989 (23 May). Bicentenary of Inaugural Address to Jena University by Friedrich Schiller (writer and philosopher). T E **909** and similar vert design. Each yellow-ochre, black and grey. P 14.

E2955	25pf. Type E **909**	50	60
	a. Horiz strip of 2. Nos. E2955/E2956 plus label	2·00	2·30
E2956	85pf. Part of address	1·40	1·60

Nos. E2955/E2956 were issued together *se-tenant* with intervening label showing bust and signature of Schiller.

327

GERMANY / German Democratic Republic (East Germany)

E **910** A. E. Brehm

E **911** Storming the Bastille

(Des Andrea Soest. Litho)

1989 (13 June). 160th Birth Anniv of Alfred Edmund Brehm and 125th Death Anniv of Christian Ludwig Brehm (naturalists). Sheet 110×80 mm containing T E **910** and similar vert design. Multicoloured. P 14.
MSE2957 50pf. Type E **910**; 85pf. C. L. Brehm .... 4·00   19·00

(Des J. Riess. Photo)

1989 (4 July). Bicentenary of French Revolution. T E **911** and similar square designs. Multicoloured. P 13.
E2958   5pf. Type E **911** 40   60
E2959   20pf. Sans-culottes 50   60
E2960   90pf. Invading the Tuileries .... 1·60   2·50
E2958/E2960 Set of 3 .... 2·30   3·25

E **912** Haflingers

E **913** Till Eulenspiegel Fountain

(Des Ursula Abramowski-Lautenschläger. Litho)

1989 (18 July). 40th International Horse Breeding in Socialist States Congress, Berlin. T E **912** and similar horiz designs. Multicoloured. P 13½.
E2961   10pf. Type E **912** 40   40
E2962   20pf. English thoroughbreds (racehorses) 40   40
E2963   70pf. Heavy horses (plough team) .... 1·30   1·20
E2964   110pf. Thoroughbreds (dressage) .... 2·10   2·00
E2961/E2964 Set of 4 .... 3·75   3·50

(Des J. Riess. Litho)

1989 (8 Aug). National Stamp Exhibition, Magdeburg. Magdeburg Fountains by Heinrich Apel. T E **913** and similar horiz design. Multicoloured. P 13×12½.
E2965   20pf. Type E **913** 40   30
E2966   70pf. +5pf. Devil's fountain .... 1·60   1·40

Nos. E2965/E2966 were each issued both in sheets of 50 stamps and in sheets of 20 stamps, five labels showing the German Bank Note Ptg Co emblem and four horizontal inscribed gutters.

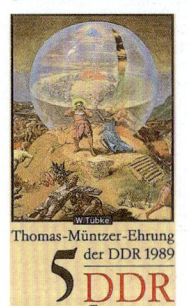

E **914** Annunciation to the Peasants

E **915** New Fair Building

(Des G. Schmidt. Litho)

1989 (22 Aug). 500th Birth Anniv of Thomas Müntzer (2nd issue). T E **914** and similar vert designs showing details of *Early Bourgeois Revolution in Germany* by Werner Tubke. Multicoloured. P 14.
E2967   5pf. Type E **914** 40   45
E2968   10pf. Fountain of Life 40   45
E2969   20pf. *Müntzer in the Battle* 50   45
E2970   50pf. *Lutheran Cat Battle* 95   1·20
E2971   85pf. *Justice, Jester* .... 2·10   2·30
E2967/E2971 Set of 5 .... 4·00   4·25
MSE2972 99×142 mm. No. E2969×4 .... 3·50   3·50

(Des H. Zill. Litho)

1989 (22 Aug). Leipzig Autumn Fair. Sheet 105×75 mm containing T E **915** and similar horiz design. Multicoloured. P 14.
MSE2973 50pf. Type E **915**; 85pf. New fair building (different) .... 3·00   4·25

E **916** African Children

E **917** Mother Group (Fritz Cremer)

(Des R.-J. Lehmann. Photo)

1989 (5 Sept). 'Solidarity'. P 14.
E2974 E **916** 10pf. +5pf. multicoloured 50   45

(Des J. Riess. Photo)

1989 (5 Sept). 30th Anniv of Ravensbruck War Victims' Memorial. P 14.
E2975 E **917** 35pf. multicoloured 80   80

E **918** 'Adriana'

(Des M. Gottschall. Litho)

1989 (19 Sept). *Epiphyllums*. T E **918** and similar square designs. Multicoloured. P 13.
E2976   10pf. Type E **918** 40   40
E2977   35pf. 'Fire Magic' 80   60
E2978   50pf. 'Franzisko' .... 1·30   1·20
E2976/E2978 Set of 3 .... 2·30   2·00

E **919** Dove, Flag and Schoolchildren

(Des J. Riess. Litho)

1989 (3 Oct). 40th Anniv of German Democratic Republic. T E **919** and similar horiz designs. Multicoloured. P 14.
E2979   5pf. Type E **919** 50   45
E2980   10pf. Combine-harvester and agricultural workers 50   45
E2981   20pf. Political activists working together 65   80
E2982   25pf. Industrial workers 80   80
E2979/E2982 Set of 4 .... 2·20   2·30
MSE2983 113×93 mm. 135pf. Construction workers (54×32 mm) .... 9·50   7·00

(Des Andrea Soest. Photo)

1989 (7 Nov). Statues of Roland (2nd series). Vert designs as T E **846**. Multicoloured. P 14.
E2984   5pf. Zerbst 40   30
E2985   10pf. Halberstadt 40   30
E2986   20pf. Buch-Altmark 45   30
E2987   50pf. Perleberg 95   95
E2984/E2987 Set of 4 .... 2·00   1·70

GERMANY / German Democratic Republic (East Germany)

E 920 Jawaharlal Nehru

E 921 Schneeberg, 1860

(Des H. Detlefsen. Photo)

1989 (7 Nov). Birth Centenary of Jawaharlal Nehru (Indian statesman). P 14.
| E2988 | E 920 | 35pf. red-brown and black | 80 | 80 |

(Des H. Scheuner. Recess and litho)

1989 (28 Nov). Chandeliers from the Erzgebirge. T E 921 and similar vert designs. Multicoloured. P 14.
E2989	10pf. Type E 921	50	45
	a. Sheetlet of 6. Nos. E2989/E2994	4·50	
E2990	20pf. Schwarzenberg, 1850	1·10	1·10
E2991	25pf. Annaberg, 1880	50	45
E2992	35pf. Seiffen, 1900	50	45
E2993	50pf. Seiffen, 1930	1·10	1·10
E2994	70pf. Annaberg, 1925	50	45
E2989/E2994	Set of 6	3·75	3·50

Nos. E2989/E2994 were issued together in *se-tenant* sheetlets of six stamps.

E 922 Bee on Apple Blossom

E 923 *Courier* (Albrecht Dürer)

(Des Ursula Abramowski-Lautenschläager. Litho)

1990 (9 Jan). The Honey Bee (*Apis mellifera*). T E 922 and similar horiz designs. Multicoloured. P 14.
E2995	5pf. Type E 922	40	40
E2996	10pf. Bee on Heather	40	40
E2997	20pf. Bee on Rape	45	40
E2998	50pf. Bee on Clover	1·30	1·20
E2995/E2998	Set of 4	2·30	2·20

(Des E. Kößlinger. Litho)

1990 (12 Jan). 500th Anniv of Regular European Postal Services (1st issue). P 13½×13½.
| E2999 | E 923 | 35pf. chocolate, cinnamon and grey-brown | 95 | 1·20 |

See also Nos. E3050/E3053.

E 924 Erich Weinert

E 925 19th-century Sign, Blankenburg

(Des G. Stauf. Litho)

1990 (16 Jan). Socialist Personalities. T E 924 and similar vert design. P 14.
| E3000 | 10pf. deep blue | 50 | 45 |
| E3001 | 10pf. bistre-brown | 50 | 45 |

Designs:—No. E3000, T E 924; No. E3001, Bruno Leuschner.

(Des J. Bertholdt)

1990 (6 Feb). Posthouse Signs. T E 925 and similar vert designs. Multicoloured.

A. Size 24×30 mm. Photo. P 14
E3002A	10pf. Type E 925	50	30
E3003A	20pf. Royal Saxony sign (19th-century)	50	30
E3004A	50pf. German Empire sign (1870s)	1·60	1·20
E3005A	110pf. German Empire auxiliary station sign (1900s)	3·25	2·75
E3002A/E3005A	Set of 4	5·25	4·00

B. Size 32×42 mm. Litho. P 13½
E3002B	10pf. Type E 925	80	30
	a. Block of 4. Nos. E3002B/E3005B	6·75	
E3003B	20pf. Royal Saxony sign (19th-century)	80	45
E3004B	50pf. German Empire sign (1870s)	1·60	1·20
E3005B	110pf. German Empire auxiliary station sign (1900s)	3·25	2·75
E3002B/E3005B	Set of 4	5·75	4·25

Nos. E3002A/E3005A were issued in separate sheets of 50 stamps and Nos. E3002B/E3005B were issued together in *se-tenant* blocks of four stamps within sheets of 16.

E 926 August Bebel

E 927 Drawings by Leonardo da Vinci

(Des P. Kraus. Photo)

1990 (20 Feb). 150th Birth Anniv of August Bebel (politician). P 14.
| E3006 | E 296 | 20pf. black, olive-grey and bright scarlet | 95 | 95 |

(Des J. Riess. Litho)

1990 (20 Feb). Lilienthal '91 European Airmail Exhibition. Historic Flying Machine Designs. T E 927 and similar square designs. Multicoloured. P 13.
E3007	20pf. Type E 927	50	30
E3008	35pf. +5pf. Melchior Bauer's man-powered aeroplane design, 1764	95	95
E3009	50pf. Albrecht-Ludwig Berblinger's man-powered flying machine, 1811	1·30	1·10
E3010	90pf. Otto Lilienthal's design for mono plane glider	2·20	2·20
E3007/E3010	Set of 4	4·50	4·00

E 928 St. Nicholas's Church, Leipzig, and Demonstrators

E 929 Warrior's Head

(Des J. Kohler and J. Fiedler. Photo)

1990 (28 Feb). 'We Are The People'. P 13.
| E3011 | E 928 | 35pf. +15pf. multicoloured | 1·90 | 1·40 |

(Des W. Ebert. Photo)

1990 (6 Mar). Museum of German History, Berlin. Stone Reliefs by Andreas Schlüter. T E 929 and similar vert design. P 14.
| E3012 | 40pf. yellow-ochre, olive-green and black | 1·10 | 1·60 |
| E3013 | 70pf. multicoloured | 1·60 | 1·90 |

Designs:—40pf. T E 929; 70pf. Warrior's head (*different*).

E 930 Fair Seal, 1268

E 931 Kurt Tucholsky (writer, centenary)

(Des O. Volkamer. Litho)

1990 (6 Mar). Leipzig Spring Fair and 825th Anniv of Leipzig. T E 930 and similar vert design. Multicoloured. P 12½×13.
| E3014 | 70pf. Type E 930 | 2·75 | 1·40 |
| E3015 | 85pf. Fair Seal, 1497 | 3·00 | 1·70 |

A 1m. stamp showing the two parts of Germany and inscribed 'EUROPA' with text commemorating 18 March parliamentary elections is bogus.

329

GERMANY / German Democratic Republic (East Germany)

(Des D. Glinski. Photo)
1990 (20 Mar). Birth Anniversaries. T E **931** and similar horiz design. P 14.
E3016	10pf. black, dull green and deep green	65	60
E3017	10pf. black, drab and brown-red	65	60

Designs:—No. E3016, T E **931**; No. E3017, Friedrich Adolph Wilhelm Diesterweg (educationist, bicentenary).

E **932** *Solidarity of Labour* (Walter Crane)

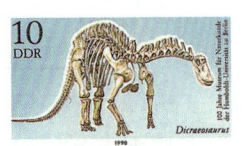

E **933** Dicraeosaurus

(Des E. Haller. Photo)
1990 (3 Apr). Centenary of Labour Day. T E **932** and similar vert design. P 14.
E3018	10pf. grey, black and vermilion	95	95
E3019	20pf. vermilion, grey and black	1·40	1·60

Designs:—10pf. T E **932**; 20pf. Red carnation.

(Des U. Lange. Litho)
1990 (17 Apr). Centenary of Natural Science Museum, Berlin. Dinosaur Skeletons. T E **933** and similar multicoloured designs. P 13×12½ (horiz) or 12½×13 (vert).
E3020	10pf. Type E **933**	50	30
E3021	25pf. Kentrurosaurus	50	35
E3022	35pf. Dysalotosaurus	65	60
E3023	50pf. Brachiosaurus (vert)	95	95
E3024	85pf. Skull of brachiosaurus (vert)	2·10	2·00
E3020/E3024	Set of 5	4·25	3·75

No. E3021 was issued both in sheets of 50 and in sheetlets of four stamps.

E **934** Penny Black

E **935** Edward Hughes and 1855 Printing Telegraph

(Des M. Gottschall. Litho)
1990 (8 May). 150th Anniv of the Penny Black. T E **934** and similar vert designs. P 14.
E3025	20pf. black, bright mauve and deep magenta	80	80
E3026	35pf. +15pf. brown-red, grey-lilac and black..	1·40	1·40
E3027	110pf. multicoloured	3·75	3·75
E3025/E3027	Set of 3	5·25	5·25

Designs:—20pf. T E **934**; 35pf. Saxony 1850 3pf. stamp; 110pf. First East Germany stamp, 1949.

(Des J. Riess. Litho)
1990 (15 May). 125th Anniv of International Telecommunications Union. T E **935** and similar vert designs. Multicoloured. P 14.
E3028	10pf. Type E **935**	65	60
E3029	20pf. Distribution rods from Berlin-Köpenick post office	65	60
E3030	25pf. Transmitting tower and radio control desk	65	60
E3031	50pf. *Molniya* communications satellite and globe	2·10	2·00
E3028/E3031	Set of 4	3·75	3·50
MSE3032	82×56 mm. 70pf. Philipp Reis (telephone pioneer)	4·25	4·00

E **936** Pope John Paul II

E **937** Halle (18th-century)

(Des J. Riess. Litho)
1990 (15 May). Pope's 70th Birthday. P 14.
E3033	E **936**	35pf. multicoloured	1·90	2·30

(Des J. Riess. Litho)
1990 (5 June). 11th Youth Stamp Exhibition, Halle. T E **937** and similar horiz design. Multicoloured. P 13×12½.
E3034	10pf. +5pf. Type E **937**	65	95
	a. Horiz strip of 2. Nos. E3034/E3035 plus label	1·40	2·00
E3035	20pf. Modern Halle	65	95

Nos. E3034/E3035 were issued together *se-tenant* with intervening half stamp-size label showing city Arms.

E **938** Rules of Order of Teutonic Knights, 1264

(Des R.-J. Lehmann. Litho)
1990 (19 June). Exhibits in German State Library, Berlin. T E **938** and similar horiz designs. Multicoloured. P 13×12½.
E3036	20pf. Type E **938**	95	45
E3037	25pf. World map from *Rudimentum Novitiorum*, 1475	95	45
E3038	50pf. *Chosrou and Schirin* by Nizami (18th-century Persian manuscript)	2·50	1·40
E3039	110pf. Book cover from Amalia musical	4·50	3·50
E3036/E3039	Set of 4	8·00	5·25

West German Currency

On 1 July 1990 the Ostmark was abolished and replaced by the West German Deutsche Mark.

E **939** Albrechts Castle and Cathedral, Meissen

E **940** Different Alphabets

(Des H. Detlefsen. Photo)
1990 (2 July–Oct). Tourist Sights. T E **939** and similar horiz designs. P 14.
E3040	10pf. dull ultramarine	80	60
E3041	30pf. deep olive	1·60	80
	a. Booklet pane. No. E3041×8 (2.10.90)	13·50	
E3042	50pf. blue-green	1·60	1·20
	a. Booklet pane. No. E3042×6 (2.10.90)	13·50	
E3043	60pf. lake-brown	1·60	1·60
E3044	70pf. deep brown	1·60	1·60
E3045	80pf. brown-red	1·60	1·90
E3046	100pf. deep carmine	2·40	2·00
E3047	200pf. violet	4·75	4·25
E3048	500pf. emerald	9·50	9·25
E3040/E3048	Set of 9	13·00	21·00

Designs:—10pf. T E **939**; 30pf. Goethe-Schiller Monument, Weimar; 50pf. Brandenburg Gate, Berlin; 60pf. Kyffhäuser Monument; 70pf. Semper Opera House, Dresden; 80pf. Sanssouci Palace, Potsdam; 100pf. Wartburg Castle, Eisenach; 200pf. Magdeburg Cathedral; 500pf. Schwerin Castle.

The booklet panes each have a margin around the outer edges.
The 50pf. was issued both in sheets and in coils, the latter having every fifth stamp numbered on the back.

(Des M. Gottschall. Photo)
1990 (24 July). International Literacy Year. P 14.
E3049	E **940**	30pf. +5pf. on 10pf.+5pf. multicoloured	1·90	2·00

No. E3049 was not issued without surcharge.

E **941** Letter-carrier (from playing card) and Messenger, 1486

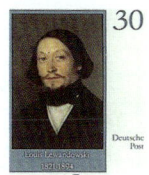

E **942** Louis Lewandowski (choir conductor)

(Des J. Riess. Litho)

1990 (28 Aug). 500th Anniv of Regular European Postal Services (2nd issue). T E **941** and similar horiz designs. P 13×12½.

E3050	30pf. black, olive-sepia and grey-olive............	80	80
E3051	50pf. black, carmine-rose and dull violet-blue..	1·10	1·10
E3052	70pf. black, yellow-brown and brown-lake.....	1·40	1·90
E3053	100pf. black, sage green and slate-blue...........	2·40	2·30
E3050/E3053	Set of 4..	5·25	5·50

Designs:—30pf. T E **941**; 50pf. *Courier* (Albrecht Dürer) and post rider, 1590; 70pf. Open wagon, 1595, and mail carriage, 1750; 100pf. Travelling post office vans, 1842 and 1900.

(Des Gudrun Lenz. Litho)

1990 (18 Sept). Reconstruction of New Synagogue, Berlin. T E **942** and similar vert design. Multicoloured. P 14.

E3054	30pf. Type E **942**	65	60
E3055	50pf. +15pf. New Synagogue.................................	1·30	1·20

E **943** Heinrich Schliemann and Two-handled Vessel

E **944** Dresden

(Des G. Fiedler. Photo)

1990 (2 Oct). Death Centenary of Heinrich Schliemann (archaeologist). T E **943** and similar multicoloured design. P 14.

E3056	30pf. Type E **943**	80	80
E3057	50pf. Schliemann and double pot (*horiz*)........	1·60	1·60

(Des D. Glinski. Photo)

1990 (2 Oct). 41st International Astronautics Federation Congress, Dresden. T E **944** and similar horiz designs. P 14.

E3058	30pf. black and bluish grey	50	45
E3059	50pf. multicoloured	95	95
E3060	70pf. indigo, sage green and blue..................	1·60	2·00
E3061	100pf. multicoloured	2·20	2·20
E3058/E3061	Set of 4..	4·75	5·00

Designs:—30pf. T E **944**; 50pf. Earth; 70pf. Moon; 100pf. Mars.

On 3 October 1990 the territory of the Democratic Republic was absorbed into the Federal Republic of Germany. Stamps inscribed 'DDR' ceased to be valid from that date. East German stamps inscribed 'Deutsche Post' remained on sale until 31 December 1990 and were valid until 31 Dec 1991.

STAMP BOOKLETS

The following check list covers, in simplified form, booklets issued in East Germany. It is intended that it should be used in conjunction with the main listings and details of stamps and panes listed there are not repeated.

Prices are for complete booklets

Booklet No.	Date	Contents and Cover Price	Price
ESB1	3.55	Five Year Plan. Wmk E **30** 3 panes. Nos. E154a, E154b and E158a (2m.)..	£200
ESB2	9.57	Five Year Plan. Wmk E **100** 3 panes. Nos. E310Aa, E310Ab and E311Aa (2m.)..	£250
ESB3	12.60	Five Year Plan. Wmk E **100** 3 panes. Nos. E310Ac, E312Aa and E312Ab (2m.)..	26·00
ESB4	16.11.62	Ulbricht (T E **196**) 3 panes. Nos. E577a and E578a×2 (2m.)..	£100
ESB5	23.11.71	Sorbian Dance Costumes 4 panes. Nos. E1443a×2 and E1443b×2 (2m.)..	35·00
ESB6	22.8.72	German Roses 3 panes. Nos. E1497a×2 and E1498a (2m.)..	11·50
ESB7	26.7.73	World Festival of Youth and Students 2 panes. Nos. E1592a and E1594a (1m.)..	4·50
ESB8	10.9.85	Sozphilex '85 2 panes. No. E2675b (2m.40)................	8·25
ESB9	29.11.88	Freshwater Fish 5 panes. No. E2802ab (2m.)................	11·00
ESB10	2.10.90	Tourist Sights 2 panes. Nos. E3041a and E3042a (6m.40)	28·00

The above listing covers booklets issued by the central administration containing specially printed panes. Between 1971 and 1990 other booklets, to the value of 1 or 2 marks, with various cover designs were sold in post offices. These booklets were filled locally with various stamps taken from normal sheets, and the same cover design can therefore be found with different contents. These booklets are outside the scope of this catalogue.

Belgian Occupation, 1919-1921

I. FOR BELGIAN FORCES IN THE RHINELAND

100 Centimes = 1 Belgian Franc

Stamps of Belgium overprinted or surcharged

51 King Albert 
52 Cloth Hall, Ypres 
53 Dinant 
54 Louvain 
55 Freeing of the Scheldt 
56 Annexation of the Congo 
57 King Albert at Furnes 
58 Three Kings of Belgium 
63 Perron at Liège 
73 Hotel de Ville, Termonde

D 66

ALLEMAGNE / DUITSCHLAND (1)
ALLEMAGNE / DUITSCHLAND (2)

1919 (20 Sept)–**21**. Optd at Marines with Type **1** (Nos. 1/8) or **2** (others).

1	51	1c. orange	50	1·00
2		2c. brown	50	1·00
3		3c. grey (II) (1.6.21)	50	4·00
4		5c. green	1·00	2·00
5		10c. carmine	2·00	4·00
6		15c. dull violet (II)	1·00	2·00
7		20c. purple	1·60	2·00
8		25c. blue	2·00	3·25
9	63	25c. blue (1.6.21)	6·50	20·00
10	52	35c. black and chestnut	2·00	2·00
11	53	40c. black and green	2·00	4·00
12	54	50c. black and carmine	9·75	18·00
13	73	65c. black and claret (1.6.21)	5·25	20·00
14	55	1f. violet	36·00	33·00
		a. opt as Type **1**	46·00	39·00
15	56	2f. slate	65·00	80·00
		a. opt as Type **1**	65·00	80·00
16	57	5f. deep blue ('FRANK')	14·50	20·00
		a. opt as Type **1**	20·00	26·00
17	58	10f. sepia	80·00	£100
		a. opt as Type **1**	90·00	£130
1/17	Set of 17 (cheapest)		£200	£275

These stamps were valid for use until 30 April 1931.

II. FOR THE DISTRICTS OF EUPEN AND MALMEDY

Stamps of Belgium overprinted or surcharged

100 Pfennig = 1 Mark

EUPEN & MALMÉDY 10 PF. (3)
EUPEN & MALMÉDY 1 Mk 25 (4)

1920 (15 Jan). Surch as Type **3** or **4** (Nos. 23/4).

18	51	5pf. on 5c. green	50	1·60
19		10pf. on 10c. carmine	50	1·80
20		15pf. on 15c. dull violet (II)	90	2·30
21		20pf. on 20c. purple	90	3·00
22		30pf. on 25c. blue	1·30	3·25
23	54	75pf. on 50c. black and carmine (R.)	26·00	33·00
24	55	1m. 25pf. on 1f. violet (R.)	36·00	34·00
18/24	Set of 7		60·00	70·00

Eupen (5)
Eupen (6)

1920 (20 Mar)–**21**. Optd as Type **5** or **6** (65c. to 10f.).

25	51	1c. orange	65	1·60
26		2c. brown (I or II)	65	1·60
27		3c. grey (II) (3.21)	1·00	5·50
28		5c. green	1·00	1·60
29		10c. carmine	1·70	2·20
30		15c. dull violet (II)	2·30	2·20
31		20c. purple	2·50	2·50
32		25c. blue	2·30	3·25
33	63	25c. blue (3.21)	7·75	25·00
34	52	35c. black and chestnut	3·25	3·25
35	53	40c. black and green	4·00	4·00
36	54	50c. black and carmine	10·50	13·00
37	73	65c. black and claret (3.21)	5·75	30·00
38	55	1f. violet	42·00	33·00
39	56	2f. slate	70·00	55·00
40	57	5f. deep blue ('FRANK')	23·00	20·00
41	58	10f. sepia	£100	85·00
25/41	Set of 17		£250	£250

Malmédy (7) **Malmédy** (8) **Malmédy** (9)

1920 (5 Mar)–**21.** Optd Type **7** (1c. to 25c.), **8** (35c. to 50c.), **9** (65c. to 10f.).

42	**51**	1c. orange	80	1·60
43		2c. brown	80	1·60
44		3c. grey (II) (3.21)	80	5·50
45		5c. green (I or II)	1·20	1·60
46		10c. carmine	1·70	2·20
47		15c. violet (II)	2·50	2·50
48		20c. purple	3·25	3·25
49		25c. blue	2·50	3·25
50	**63**	25c. blue (3.21)	7·75	25·00
51	**52**	35c. black and chestnut	3·25	3·25
52	**53**	40c. black and green	3·25	4·00
53	**54**	50c. black and carmine	13·00	13·00
54	**73**	65c. black and claret (3.21)	5·75	31·00
55	**55**	1f. violet	42·00	33·00
56	**56**	2f. slate	70·00	55·00
57	**57**	5f. deep blue ('FRANK')	23·00	29·00
58	**58**	10f. sepia	£100	£100
42/58 Set of 17			£250	£275

1920 (5 Mar–20 Mar). POSTAGE DUE (numeral stamps inscr 'A PAYER TE BETALEN').

*(a) Optd with Type **5** (20 Mar)*

D1	**D 66**	5c. green	1·70	2·00
D2		10c. carmine	3·25	3·25
D3		20c. olive-green	6·50	7·75
D4		30c. blue	6·50	7·75
D5		50c. grey	33·00	26·00
D1/D5 Set of 5			46·00	42·00

*(b) Optd with Type **7** (5 Mar)*

D6	**D 66**	5c. green	3·25	2·00
D7		10c. carmine	6·50	3·25
D8		20c. olive-green	23·00	23·00
D9		30c. blue	13·00	14·50
D10		50c. grey	26·00	21·00
D6/D10 Set of 5			65·00	55·00

No plebiscite was held but voters who desired the territory to remain in Germany were required to sign a public register. Few did this and on 20 September 1920 the Council of the League of Nations placed the territory under Belgian sovereignty.

German Occupation Issues, 1914-1918

A. BELGIUM

100 Centimes = 1 Franc

German troops invaded Belgium on 4 August 1914 and, until they were held by the British Army in front of Ypres in October-November, they overran the country. They occupied all the country except the area round Ypres and to the west of the R. Yser until the final Allied offensive of 28 September 1918 regained much territory. Under the terms of the Armistice of 11 November, all German forces left Belgium.

Belgien
3 Centimes
(1)

Belgien
1 Franc
(2)

✻ 1 Fr. 25 C. ✻

Belgien
(3)

1914 (1 Oct). Stamps of Germany, surch as Type **1** or with Type **2/3**.

1	**17**	3c. on 3pf. brown	50	80
2		5c. on 5pf. green	50	80
3		10c. on 10pf. carmine	50	80
4		25c. on 20pf. ultramarine	4·00	4·00
5		50c. on 40pf. black and carmine	6·50	11·50
6		75c. on 60pf. magenta	3·25	3·25
7		1f. on 80pf. black and carmine/*rose*	4·50	4·50
8	**18**	1f.25c. on 1m. red	46·00	38·00
9	**20**	2f.50c. on 2m. blue	46·00	38·00
1/9 Set of 9			£100	90·00

✻ 1 F. 25 Cent. ✻

Belgien
2 Cent.
(4)

Belgien
(5)

1916–18. Stamps of Germany, surch as Type **4** or **5** ('Cent' for 'Centimes' and 'F' for 'Franc' (or 'Fr.')).

10	**24**	2c. on 2pf. grey (1.10.18)	40	1·80
11	**17**	3c. on 3pf. brown	1·20	2·50
12		5c. on 5pf. green	1·30	4·00
13	**24**	8c. on 7½pf. orange	1·20	3·50
14	**17**	10c. on 10pf. carmine	1·40	2·50
15	**24**	15c. on 15pf. yellow-brown	3·25	3·25
16		15c. on 15pf. slate-violet (1917)	1·60	3·25
17	**17**	20c. on 25pf. black and red/*yellow* (1918)	50	2·30
18		25c. on 20pf. ultramarine	1·40	2·75
19		40c. on 30pf. black and orange/*buff*	50	1·60
20		50c. on 40pf. black and carmine	1·60	3·25
21		75c. on 60pf. magenta	2·20	65·00
22		1f. on 80pf. black and carmine/*rose*	3·25	25·00
23	**18**	1f.25c. on 1m. red (26×17 holes) (1918)	£500	£160
		a. 25×17 holes	11·00	11·00
24	**20**	2f.50c. on 2m. blue (26×17 holes)	49·00	48·00
		a. 25×17 holes	80·00	£120
		ba. Error On 1m. red		£38000
25	**22**	6f.25c. on 5m. lake and black (2.17)	85·00	90·00
10/25 Set of 16 (*cheapest*)			£150	£250

13 examples, all used in Charleroi, of No. 24ba are known.

333

GERMAN OCCUPATION ISSUES, 1914-1918

B. EASTERN MILITARY COMMAND AREA

(Russian Baltic Provinces)

After their conquest of Russian Poland in the summer of 1915, the German armies broke through into the Russian Baltic Provinces and took Vilna on 18 September. In further advances they occupied Courland and most of Livonia by the end of 1915. In a renewed offensive in 1917 Riga was taken on 2 September. Under the terms of the Treaty of Brest-Litovsk, 3 March 1918, the Germans occupied the rest of the Baltic Provinces of Russia, later to be known as Estonia. Latvia and Lithuania. For postal purposes all this area was known as the Postal Territory of the Commander-in-Chief, East (*Postgebiet Oberbefehishaber Ost*).

100 Pfennig = 1 Mark

Postgebiet Ob. Ost
(1)

1916 (15 Jan)–**18**. Contemporary stamps of Germany optd with Type **1**.

1	24	2½pf. grey (1.8.16)	80	2·50
2	17	3pf. brown	40	1·00
3		5pf. green	1·20	2·75
4	24	7½pf. orange (1.8.16)	80	3·25
5	17	10pf. carmine	7·50	2·75
6	24	15pf. yellow-brown (1.8.16)	6·25	6·50
7		15pf. slate-violet (1917)	1·70	3·25
8	17	20pf. ultramarine	5·00	3·25
9		25pf. black and red/*yellow* (1.8.16)	50	1·60
10		40pf. black and carmine	5·00	10·50
11		50pf. black and purple/*buff* (1.8.16)	4·00	5·25
12	18	1m. red (26×17 holes) (1.8.16)	£225	£300
		a. 25×17 holes	16·00	10·50
1/12a *Set of* 12 (*cheapest*)			44·00	48·00

C. ESTONIA

100 Pfennig = 1 Mark

The German postal service in the Baltic area was closed on 28 December 1918. Most offices in Estonia had closed by the end of November 1918, Walk staying open until 19 December 1918.

40 Pfg.
(1)

1918 (4 Mar). Issue for Dorpat (Tartu). Stamps of Russia, Arms, surch as Type **1**, by C. Mattiesen, Tartu.

1	20pf. on 10k. blue	44·00	£140
	a. Light blue	£350	
2	40pf. on 20k. carmine and blue	44·00	£140

Nos. 1/2 were officially valid for postage until 16 March but later cancellations are known.

D. POLAND

A German offensive in Galicia on 1 May 1915 broke through the Russian lines and all Poland was in German hands by the end of August. In 1916 Poland was named the 'General-Government, Warsaw' and on 5 November 1916, Germany and Austria proclaimed a 'Polish Kingdom'; Pilsudski sat on the Council of State of this till he resigned in protest against German control. On 15 October 1917, the Germans set up a Regency Council, which exercised control under German supervision, and took charge of affairs on 12 October 1918 when the Central Powers were on the verge of collapse.

100 Pfennig = 1 Mark

Russisch-Polen   **Gen.-Gouv. Warschau**
(1)   (2)

Contemporary stamps of Germany overprinted.

1915 (12 May). With Type **1**.

1	17	3pf. brown	1·30	65
2		5pf. green	1·40	65
3		10pf. carmine	1·40	1·00
4		20pf. ultramarine	7·75	1·00
5		40pf. black and carmine	8·75	4·50
1/5 *Set of* 5			19·00	7·00

Nos. 1/5 were for use in the Lodz region.

1916 (1 Aug)–**17**. With Type **2**.

6	24	2½pf. grey	1·20	2·50
7	17	3pf. brown	1·20	3·75
8		5pf. green	1·30	4·50
9	24	7½pf. orange	1·60	2·75
10	17	10pf. carmine	5·25	2·75
11	24	15pf. yellow-brown	4·50	4·00
12		15pf. slate-violet (1917)	1·30	2·75
13	17	20pf. deep blue	6·50	3·25
		a. Violet-blue	85·00	£140
		b. Ultramarine	5·25	7·75
14		30pf. black and orange/*buff*	10·50	18·00
15		40pf. black and carmine	4·00	2·75
16		60pf. magenta	4·00	3·75
6/16 *Set of* 11			37·00	46·00

The area north-east of Warsaw was part of the Eastern Military Command Area, which also included the Baltic Provinces of Russia.

During the period of German occupation several municipal councils organised local postal delivery services. Most used handstamps to indicate payment but the following towns issued stamps, some of which were quickly suppressed by the military authorities: Sosnowiec, Warsaw, Zawiercie. Bialystok (in the Eastern Command Area). Przedborz and Zarki in the Austrian occupied area also issued stamps.

E. ROMANIA

Romania entered the war against the Central Powers on 27 August 1916; after early successes her troops were defeated and by January 1917 all Romania S.E. of the River Sereth was in German, Austro-Hungarian or Bulgarian occupation.

100 Bani = 1 Leu
100 Pfennig = 1 Mark

M.V.i.R.   **M.V.i.R.**
25 Bani   **10 Bani**
(1)   (2)

('M. V.i.R.' = Militärverwaltung in Rumänien) (Military Administration in Romania)

Contemporary stamps of Germany surcharged.

1917 (1 June). Surch as Tyoe **1** (value in black).

1	24	15b. on 15pf. slate-violet (R.)	1·30	1·70
		a. Black surcharge		
		b. Surch double		
2	17	25b. on 20pf. ultramarine	1·30	1·70
3		40b. on 30pf. black and orange/*buff* (R.)	26·00	46·00
		a. Black surcharge		
		b. Surch double		

1917 (2 July)–**18**. Surch as Type **2**.

4	17	10b. on 10pf. rose carmine	2·10	2·50
5	24	15b. on 15pf. slate-violet (1918)	9·00	10·50
6	17	25b. on 20pf. blue	5·25	7·75
7		40b. on 30pf. black and orange/*buff*	2·30	2·75
		a. '40' omitted (pos. 21)	£225	

Rumänien   **Gultig**
25 Bani   **9. Armee**
(3)   (4)

1918 (1 Mar). Surch as T **3**.

8	17	5b. on 5pf. green	1·30	3·00
9		10b. on 10pf. carmine	1·30	2·75
10	24	15b. on 15pf. slate-violet	40	80
11	17	25b. on 20pf. ultramarine	1·30	2·75
12		40b. on 30pf. black and orange/*buff*	40	65

1918 (10 Mar). Ninth Army Post. Optd with Type **4**.

13	17	10pf. carmine	65·00	£130
14	24	15pf. dark violet	23·00	65·00
15	17	20pf. blue	3·25	5·25
16		30pf. black and orange/*buff*	23·00	46·00

POSTAL TAX STAMPS

Stamps of Romania overprinted

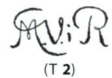

(T 1)   (T 2)   (T 3)

1917 (1 June). Large fiscal stamp of Romania (King's portrait, inscr 'TIMBRU FISCAL'), optd with Type T **1**, reading upwards.

T1	10b. brown (R.)	£180	70·00

1917 (25 June). T T **41** optd with Type T **2**. P 13½, 11½ or 13½×11½.

T2	5b. black (R.)	1·60	6·50
T3	10b. brown	1·60	5·75

1917 (10 Aug)–**18**. T T **41** optd with Type T **3**. P 13½, 11½ or 13½×11½.

T4	5b. black (R.) (1.10.18)	3·25	9·00
	a. Black overprint	£130	£1300
T5	10b. brown	36·00	39·00
T6	10b. purple (1917)	3·25	10·50

1917 (15 Sept). Fiscal type as in Type T **1** in new colour, optd with Type T **3**.

T7	10b. yellow (R.)	16·00	£110

POSTAGE DUE STAMPS

1918 (1 July). Type D **38** of Romania optd as Type T **3**, in red.

A. Wmkd

D1A	5b. blue/*greenish yellow*	31·00	£160
D2A	10b. blue/*greenish yellow*	31·00	£160

B. No wmk

D1B	5b. blue/*greenish yellow*	20·00	23·00
D2B	10b. blue/*greenish yellow*	20·00	36·00
D3B	20b. blue/*greenish yellow*	5·25	5·25
D4B	30b. blue/*greenish yellow*	5·25	5·25
D5B	50b. blue/*greenish yellow*	5·25	5·25

The 20, 30 and 50b. with watermark show forged overprints.

1918 (Sept). POSTAL TAX. T TD **42** of Romania optd as Type T **3**.

D6	10b. red/*greenish*	5·25	33·00

F. WESTERN MILITARY COMMAND AREA

(Military Zone in Belgium and Northern France)

Until the issue of the stamps listed below, with values in French currency, the stamps issued for the German Occupation of Belgium were in use in the Lines of Communication Area West (Etappengebiet West). This comprised the areas occupied by the German army from 1914 to 1918 in the French departments of the Nord, Pas de Calais, Somme, Oise, Aisne, Marne, Ardennes, Meuse and Meurthe et Moselle, as well as West Flanders in Belgium.

100 Centimes = 1 Franc

(1)   (2)

1916 (1 Dec). Contemporary stamps of Germany surch as T **1** or **2** ('Cent.' for 'Centimes' and 'F' or 'Fr.' for 'Franc').

1	**17**	3c. on 3pf. brown	65	1·80
2		5c. on 5pf. green	2·00	3·25
3	**24**	8c. on 7½pf. orange	1·30	3·75
4	**17**	10c. on 10pf. carmine	4·00	5·25
5	**24**	15c. on 15pf. yellow-brown	65	1·80
6	**17**	25c. on 20pf. ultramarine	1·60	5·25
7		40c. on 30pf. black and orange/*buff*	1·60	3·25
8		50c. on 40pf. black and carmine	1·60	4·50
9		75c. on 60pf. rose-purple	13·00	26·00
10		1f. on 80pf. black and lake/*carmine*	5·25	33·00
11	**18**	1f.25c. on 1m. red (26×17 holes)	£140	
		a. 25×17 holes	50·00	50·00
		b. Opt as double	£200	
12	**20**	2f.50c. on 2m. deep blue (26×17 holes)	90·00	50·00
		a. Opt double	£800	
		b. 25×17 holes	£450	£1800
		c. Dark cobalt (25×17 holes)	65·00	£130
1/12	*Set of 12 (cheapest)*		£130	£170

Allenstein

100 Pfennig = 1 Mark

On 11 July 1920 a plebiscite was held under the Treaty of Versailles in this district of East Prussia. There was a vote of 98% in favour of remaining in Germany. The district was occupied by Soviet troops in 1945 and has since been administered by Poland under the name of Olsztyn.

PLÉBISCITE

OLSZTYN
ALLENSTEIN
(1)   (2)

1920 (3 Apr–3 Aug). Types of Germany (wmk Lozenges) optd with Type **1** at State Printing Office, Berlin. Mark values (*a*) Engraved, (*b*) Surface-printed.

1	**17**	5pf. green	65	2·00
2		10pf. carmine	65	2·00
3	**24**	15pf. slate-violet	65	2·00
4		15pf. dull purple-brown (3.8)	9·00	20·00
5	**17**	20pf. violet-blue	65	2·50
6		30pf. black and orange/*buff*	65	2·50
7		40pf. black and carmine	65	2·00
8		50pf. black and purple/*buff*	65	2·00
9		75pf. black and dark green-black	65	2·00
10	**18**	1m. red (*a*)	2·50	9·00
		a. Opt double	£450	£1800
11		1m.25 yellow-green (*b*)	2·50	8·50
		a. Opt double		
12		1m.50 brown (*b*)	1·60	6·75
13	**20**	2m.50 lilac-rose (*b*)	65·00	£225
		a. Claret	4·00	18·00
		b. Purple	4·00	26·00
14	**21**	3m. violet-black (*a*)	4·00	9·75
		a. Opt double	£450	£1800
1/14	*Set of 14 (cheapest)*		26·00	80·00

1920 (May–June). Stamps as last, but optd with Type **2**.

15	**17**	5pf. green	65	1·60
16		10pf. carmine	65	1·60
17	**24**	15pf. slate-violet	65	1·60
18		15pf. dull purple brown (25.6)	33·00	65·00
19	**17**	20pf. violet-blue	1·00	2·50
20		30pf. black and orange/*buff*	65	1·60
21		40pf. black and carmine	65	1·60
22		50pf. black and purple/*buff*	65	1·60
23		75pf. black and dark green-black	1·00	2·50
24	**18**	1m. red (*a*)	2·30	6·25
		a. Opt inverted		
25		1m.25 yellow-green (*b*)	2·30	6·25
26		1m.50 brown (*b*)	1·60	6·25
27	**20**	2m.50 claret (*b*)	4·00	10·50
		a. Purple (*b*)	5·25	21·00
28	**21**	3m. violet-black (*a*)	2·75	5·25
		a. Opt inverted		
		b. Opt double		
15/28	*Set of 14*		47·00	£100

The 40pf. carmine, No. 144a, was also overprinted and placed on sale after the plebiscite but was only used on internal parcels and also exists cancelled by favour.

The international use of these stamps was discontinued on 20 August but they could be used internally until the end of October.

335

Danzig

1920. 100 Pfennig = 1 Mark
1923. 100 Pfennig = 1 Danzig Gulden

FREE CITY

By the Treaty of Versailles, 28 June 1919, Danzig, with surrounding territory, was created a Free City as from 10 January 1920. Unoverprinted stamps of Germany were in use from 10 January to 13 June 1920.

USED PRICES. Used prices for Nos. 1/177 are for cancelled-to-order examples.

(1) Danzig (2) 10

(Optd by State Ptg Wks, Berlin)

1920 (14 June–21 Dec). Stamps of Germany, 1905–1920, optd with Type **1**.

1	17	5pf. green	50	80
		a. Pair, one with opt omitted	£530	
2	30	10pf. carmine	50	50
3	24	15pf. dull purple-brown	50	50
4	17	20pf. violet-blue	50	1·70
5		30pf. black and orange/*buff*	50	50
6		40pf. carmine (No. 144a) (13.9)	50	50
7		50pf. black and purple/*buff*	65	50
		a. Pair, one with opt omitted	£225	
8	18	1m. carmine (No. 113)	65	90
		a. Pair, one with opt omitted	£130	
9		1m.25 blackish green-blue	65	90
10		1m. brown (20.7)	1·30	2·50
11	20	2m. blue (No. 94B)	4·50	10·50
		a. Surch double	£600	
12		2m.50 claret	4·50	7·25
		a. Pair, one with opt omitted		
13	21	3m. violet-black (No. 95B) (20.7)	13·00	18·00
		a. Pair, one with opt omitted	£2500	
14	17	4m. carmine and black (21.12)	6·25	9·00
15	22	5m. carmine and black (No. 96A)	£4000	
15a		5m. carmine and black (No. 96B)	4·00	5·75
		ab. Frame inverted	£24000	
		ac. Surch double	£1400	
1/15a (ex. 15) *Set of* 15			35·00	55·00

Nos. 89 and 140/141 of Germany also exist with this overprint, but were not sold to the public.

(Surch by J. Sauer, Danzig)

1920. Nos. 4 and 5 with additional surch as Type **2**.

16		5 on 30pf. (V.) (1.11)	40	40
17		10 on 20pf. (R.) (17.8)	40	40
		a. Surch double	£170	
18		25 on 30pf. (G.) (10.8)	40	40
		a. Surch inverted	£130	£400
19		60 on 30pf. (Br.) (20.11)	1·00	1·70
		a. Surch double	£130	£450
20		80 on 30pf. (V.) (20.11)	1·00	1·70
16/20 *Set of* 5			3·00	4·25

(3) Danzig (3a) DANZIG

(Optd by J. Sauer, Danzig)

1920 (20–30 Aug). Stamps of Germany optd.

(a) With Type **3** *or larger (1m.)*

21	24	2pf. grey (B.) (30.8)	£160	£300
22		2½pf. grey (B.)	£225	£450
23	17	3pf. brown (B.) (30.8)	16·00	26·00
		a. Opt double	£120	
24		5pf. green (B.)	80	1·20
		a. Opt double	£130	
25	24	7½pf. orange (B.) (30.8)	60·00	85·00
26	17	10pf. carmine (B.) (30.8)	5·25	10·50
27	24	15pf. slate-violet (B.)	1·00	1·20
		a. Opt double	£130	
28	17	20pf. dark violet blue (B.)	1·00	1·20
29		25pf. black and red/*yellow* (R.)	1·00	1·20
30		30pf. black and orange/*buff* (R.) (30.8)	80·00	£140
31		40pf. black and carmine (R.) (30.8)	3·25	4·00
		a. Opt double		
		b. Opt inverted	£325	
32		50pf. black and purple/*buff* (R.)	£250	£450
32a		60pf. magenta (B.) (30.8)	£1800	£3250
33		75pf. black and blue-green (30.8) (R.)	1·00	1·20
34		80pf. black and carmine/*rose* (R.) (30.8)	3·75	6·50
34a	18	1m. carmine (R.) (30.8)	£1800	£3250
		ab. Opt double	£6500	

(b) With Type **3a**

34b	20	2m. blue (94B) (R.) (30.8)	£1800	£3250
		a. Opt double		

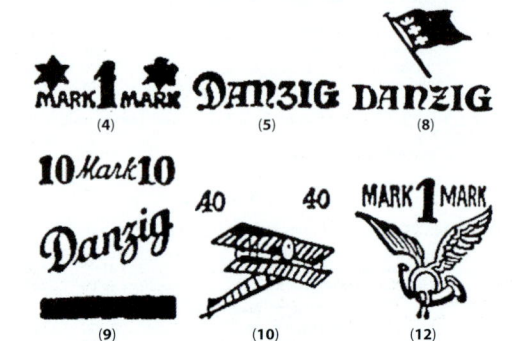

(4) 1 MARK (5) 1 MARK (8) DANZIG DANZIG

(9) 10 Mark 10 Danzig (10) 40 40 (12) MARK 1 MARK

(Surch by J. Sauer, Danzig)

1920. No. 5 of Danzig and T **17** and **24** of Germany, but with burelé background added, surch as Type **4** to **9**.

(a) Background in grey (20 Aug)

A. Burelé background with points upward toward the right

35A	17	1m. on 30pf. black and orange/*buff*	1·30	2·30
36A		1¼m. on 3pf. brown (R.)	1·60	2·30
37A	24	2m. on 35pf. red-brown (B.)	2·30	2·30
38A		3m. on 7½pf. orange (G.)	1·60	2·30
39A		5m. on 2pf. grey (R.)	1·60	3·25
40A		10m. on 7½pf. orange	4·00	11·50

B. Burelé background with points downward toward the left

36B	17	1¼m. on 3pf. brown (R.)	50·00	65·00
37B	24	2m. on 35pf. red-brown (B.)	£650	£450
38B		3m. on 7½pf. orange (G.)	39·00	26·00
39B		5m. on 2pf. grey (R.)	39·00	46·00
40B		10m. on 7½pf. orange	8·50	20·00

(b) Background in lilac (1 Nov)

A. Burelé background with points upward toward the right

40Aa	17	1m. on 30pf.	£130	48·00
40Ab		1¼m. on 3pf. (R.)	7·75	9·75
40Ac	24	2m. on 35pf. (B.)	20·00	60·00
40Ad		3m. on 7½pf. (G.)	3·25	4·00
40Ae		5m. on 2pf. (R.)	2·00	4·00
40Af		10m. on 7½pf.	2·00	3·25

B. Burelé background with points downward toward the left

40Ba	17	1m. on 30pf.	2·00	4·00
40Bb		1¼m. on 3pf. (R.)	10·50	17·00
40Bc	24	2m. on 35pf. (B.)	46·00	80·00
40Bd		3m. on 7½pf. (G.)	65·00	£130
40Be		5m. on 2pf. (R.)	13·00	13·00
40Bf		10m. on 7½pf.	21·00	46·00

The bar in T **9** is of network pattern, not solid as shown in our illustration.

All values exist without burelé background, and all except Nos. 39A and 37B/40B with background double.

1920 (29 Sept). AIR. No. 6 of Danzig surch as Type **10** and **12**.

41	17	40 on 40pf. carmine (B.)	2·00	4·50
		a. Surch double	£250	£400
42		60 on 40pf. carmine (R.)	2·00	4·50
		a. Surch double	£200	£400
43		1m. on 40pf. carmine (B.)	2·00	4·50
		a. Surch double	£200	£400

On the 60pf. the aeroplane is reversed.

DANZIG

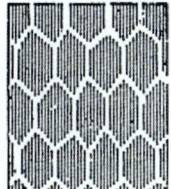

13 Hanse Kogge **14** **14a** Large Honeycomb

(Typo J. Sauer, Danzig)

1921 (31 Jan–11 Mar). Constitution of 1920. W **14a**.

(a) Zigzag roulette (31 Jan)

44	13	5pf. purple and brown	35	35
		a. Centre inverted	£140	
45		10pf. slate-violet and orange	35	35
		a. Centre inverted	£140	
46		25pf. carmine and green	80	1·00
		a. Centre inverted	£140	
47		40pf. carmine	5·75	5·25
48		80pf. ultramarine	65	80
49	14	1m. slate and red	2·50	3·25
		a. Centre inverted	£160	
50		2m. deep green and blue	7·75	7·75
		a. Centre inverted	£160	
51		3m. emerald and black	3·25	4·50
		a. Centre inverted	£160	
52		5m. red and slate	3·25	4·50
		a. Centre inverted	£160	
53		10m. chestnut and deep green	4·00	7·25
		a. Centre inverted	£160	

(b) P 14 (11 Mar)

54	13	25pf. carmine and green	80	1·30
		a. Centre inverted	65·00	
55		40pf. carmine	80	1·30
56		80pf. ultramarine	9·00	16·00

Nos. 44 and 45 but with centres in red are believed to be proofs.
All values exist imperforate *(Price for set of 10: £650 un)*.

15 Sabaltnig P111 over Danzig **16** **(17)**

(Des M. Buchholz. Typo J. Sauer, Danzig)

1921 (3 May)–**22**. AIR. P 14 (T **15**) or zigzag roulette (T **16**). W **14a**.

57	15	40pf. emerald	40	65
		b. Wmk sideways	90·00	£130
58		60pf. dull purple	40	65
		b. Wmk sideways	£140	£200
59		1m. carmine	40	65
60		2m. bistre-brown	40	65
		b. Wmk sideways	£130	£275
61	16	5m. blue-violet	2·00	3·25
		b. Wmk sideways	£2250	£4000
		ba. Imperf pair	£4500	£8000
62		10m. olive-green (15.5.22)	3·25	7·25
		b. Wmk sideways	39·00	£200

Nos. 57/62 are also known imperforate *(Price per set of 6 £325)*.
See also Nos. 112/119.

1921 (6 May). No. 33 surch with T **17**, in blue-black.

63		60 on 75pf. black and blue-green	1·60	1·30
		a. Surch double	£160	£170
		b. Surch double, one inverted	£130	£120

18 **19** **D M** (O **20**)

(Des Prof. Petersen. Typo J. Sauer)

1921 (3 June)–**22**. W **14a**. P 14.

64	18	5pf. orange	25	25
65		10pf. grey-brown	25	25
66		15pf. green	25	25
67		20pf. slate	25	25
68		25pf. deep green	25	25
69		30pf. red and blue	25	25
		a. Centre inverted	£130	£225
70		40pf. red and green	25	25
		a. Centre inverted	£130	£225
71		50pf. red and deep green	25	25
72		60pf. carmine	65	65
73		75pf. purple (1.2.22)	40	40
74		80pf. red and slate-black	50	65
75		80pf. bright green (1.2.22)	40	40
76		1m. red and orange	80	65
		a. Centre inverted	£130	£225
77		1.20m. blue	2·00	2·00
78		1.25m. red and purple (1.2.22)	40	40
79		1.50m. slate (29.7.22)	25	65
80		2m. red and grey	4·50	8·50
81		2m. carmine (1.2.22)	40	40
82		2.40m. carmine and sepia (1.2.22)	2·00	3·25
83		3m. red and purple (*wmk sideways*)	13·00	16·00
		a. Wmk upright	£130	£250
84		3m. carmine (29.7.22)	25	65
85		4m. indigo (1.2.22)	2·00	3·25
86		5m. deep green (9.11.22)	25	50
		a. Wmk sideways	46·00	90·00
87		6m. carmine (30.10.22)	25	50
88		8m. pale blue (29.7.22)	80	2·50
89		10m. orange (9.11.22)	25	50
90		20m. yellow-brown (30.10.22)	25	50

See also Nos. 106/111.

(Des M. Buchholz. Typo J. Sauer)

1921 (1 Aug)–**22**. W **14a**. Zigzag roulette.

91	19	5m. green, black and red	2·00	4·50
		a. Wmk sideways	2·00	5·00
91b		9m. orange and red (1.2.22)	4·50	13·00
		ba. Wmk sideways	4·50	13·00
92		10m. blue, black and red (1922)	2·00	4·50
		a. Wmk sideways	2·00	5·00
93		20m. black and red	2·00	4·50
		a. Wmk sideways	2·00	5·00

Nos. 76 to 93 have a background of faint grey network. Some stamps in this and the following issues are known without network.

1921 (25 Aug)–**22**. OFFICIAL. Optd with T O **20**. W **14a**.

O94	18	5pf. orange	40	40
		a. Opt double	50·00	
O95		10pf. grey-brown	40	40
		a. Opt double	50·00	
		b. Opt inverted	90·00	
O96		15pf. green	40	40
O97		20pf. slate	40	40
		a. Opt inverted		
O98		25pf. deep green	40	40
		a. Opt double	50·00	
		b. Wmk sideways	£450	£650
O99		30pf. red and blue	90	90
		a. Opt double	50·00	
O100		40pf. red and green	40	40
		a. Opt double	50·00	
O101		50pf. red and deep green	40	40
O102		60pf. carmine	40	40
O103		75pf. purple (15.2.22)	25	65
		a. Opt double	85·00	
O104		80pf. red and slate-black	1·30	2·00
O105		80pf. bright green (15.2.22)	25	4·25
		a. Wmk sideways	13·00	50·00
O106		1m. red and orange	40	40
O107		1.20m. blue	2·00	2·00
O108		1.25m. red and purple (15.2.22)	25	65
O109		1.50m. slate (29.7.22)	50	80
O110		2m. red and grey	26·00	21·00
		a. Opt inverted	£170	
O111		2m. carmine (15.2.22)	25	65
O112		2.40m. carmine and sepia (15.2.22)	2·00	4·25
O113		3m. red and purple (*wmk sideways*)	16·00	18·00
O114		3m. carmine (29.7.22)	50	80
O115		4m. indigo (15.2.22)	2·00	1·60
		a. Opt inverted		
O116		5m. deep green (21.11.22)	50	80
		a. Wmk sideways	13·00	20·00
O117		6m. carmine (30.10.22)	50	80
O118		10m. orange (21.11.22)	50	80
O119		20m. yellow-brown (16.12.22)	50	80

DANZIG

D 20    **20**

1921 (1 Oct)–**22**. POSTAGE DUE. Typo. W **14a** (sideways). P 14.

(a) Value in 'pfennig' (figures only)

D94	D **20**	10pf. purple	50	80
D95		20pf. purple	50	80
		a. Wmk upright	£200	
D96		40pf. purple	50	80
D97		60pf. purple	50	80
D98		75pf. purple (10.6.22)	50	80
		a. Wmk upright	£130	
D99		80pf. purple	50	80
		a. Wmk upright	£130	
D100		120pf. purple	50	80
D101		200pf. purple (10.6.22)	1·30	1·70
D102		240pf. purple	50	1·70
		a. Wmk upright	£200	
D103		300pf. purple (10.6.22)	1·30	1·70
D104		400pf. purple	1·30	1·70
D105		500pf. purple	1·30	1·70
D106		800pf. purple (1.2.22)	1·30	1·70

(b) Value in 'marks' (numeral followed by 'M')

D107	D **20**	20m. purple (30.10.22)	1·30	1·70

See also Nos. D112/D122.

(Des E. Hellingrath. Typo J. Sauer)

1921 (16 Oct). Tuberculosis Week. W **14a**. Zigzag roulette (1.20m.) or P 14 (others).

93b	**20**	30pf. (+30pf.) green and orange	65	1·60
93c		60pf. (+60pf.) carmine and yellow	2·00	2·50
93d		1.20m. (+1.20m.) indigo and orange (25×29 mm)	3·25	3·75

21

(Des M. Buchholz. Typo J. Sauer)

1922. W **14a**. Zigzag roulette.

94	**21**	50m. red and gold	90·00	£180
		a. Wmk sideways	13·00	21·00
		b. Crimson and gold	3·25	10·50
		ba. Wmk sideways	3·25	8·50
95		100m. red and bronze-green	11·50	20·00
		a. Wmk sideways	5·25	9·00

The 50m. has a grey overprinted network. On the 100m. it is brown. The designs of the stamps differ in detail.

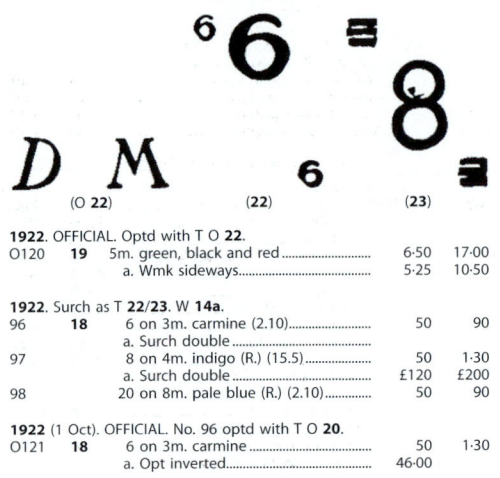

(O 22)   **(22)**   **(23)**

1922. OFFICIAL. Optd with T O **22**.

O120	**19**	5m. green, black and red	6·50	17·00
		a. Wmk sideways	5·25	10·50

1922. Surch as T **22/23**. W **14a**.

96	**18**	6 on 3m. carmine (2.10)	50	90
		a. Surch double		
97		8 on 4m. indigo (R.) (15.5)	50	1·30
		a. Surch double	£120	£200
98		20 on 8m. pale blue (R.) (2.10)	50	90

1922 (1 Oct). OFFICIAL. No. 96 optd with T O **20**.

O121	**18**	6 on 3m. carmine	50	1·30
		a. Opt inverted	46·00	

24 Small Honeycomb    **25**

25a    **26**

(Des M. Buchholz. Typo J. Sauer)

1922 (Nov)–**23** (Feb). W **24** (sideways). P 14.

99	**25**	50m. red and pale blue (21.11.22)	25	65
		a. Wmk upright	80	1·30
100	**25a**	100m. red and deep olive (14.12.22)	25	65
		a. Wmk upright	1·60	1·30
101		150m. red and purple (23.1.23)	25	65
102	**26**	250m. red and purple (24.1.23)	65	65
103		500m. red and slate (24.1.23)	65	65
104		1000m. pink and black-brown (24.1.23)	65	65
105		5000m. red and silver (27.2.23)	2·50	9·75

Nos. 99/105 have background of faint grey network.
See also Nos. 136/141.

1922 (Dec)–**23** (Sept). W **24** (sideways on 4, 6m.). P 14.

106	**18**	4m. indigo (16.12.22)	25	65
107		5m. deep green (1.23)	80	1·30
		a. Wmk sideways	25	65
107b		6m. carmine (9.23)	£3250	
108		10m. orange (1.23)	80	1·30
		a. Wmk sideways	25	65
109		20m. yellow-brown (1.23)	80	1·30
		a. Wmk sideways	25	65
110		40m. pale blue (15.5.23)	40	90
111		80m. scarlet (15.5.23)	40	90

Nos. 106/111 have background of faint grey network.

1922 (Dec)–**23** (Feb). OFFICIAL. Optd as T O **20**. W **24** (sideways on 4m.).

O122	**18**	4m. indigo (16.12.22)	40	1·00
O123		5m. deep green (1.23)	1·30	4·00
		a. Wmk sideways	40	1·30
O124		10m. orange (1.23)	1·30	4·00
		a. Wmk sideways	40	1·00
O125		20m. yellow-brown (1.23)		
		a. Wmk sideways	40	1·00
O126	**25**	50m. red and pale blue (10.1.23)	1·30	4·00
		a. Wmk sideways	40	1·00
O127	**25a**	100m. red and olive-green (21.2.23)	1·30	4·00
		a. Wmk sideways	40	1·00

See also Nos. O142/O147.

1923 (Jan–Apr). POSTAGE DUE. W **24** (sideways on 100 to 400pf.). P 14.

(a) Value in 'pfennig' (figures only)

D112	D **20**	100pf. purple	1·30	1·30
D113		200pf. purple	4·50	6·50
D114		300pf. purple	1·30	1·30
D115		400pf. purple	1·30	1·30
D116		500pf. purple	1·30	1·70
		a. Wmk sideways	1·30	1·30
D117		800pf. purple	2·20	6·50

(b) Value in 'marks'

D118	D **20**	10m. purple	1·30	1·70
		a. Wmk sideways	1·30	1·30
D119		20m. purple	£160	
		a. Wmk sideways	1·30	1·30
D120		50m. purple	£100	
		a. Wmk sideways	1·30	1·30
D121		100m. purple	1·30	1·70
D122		200m. purple	1·30	1·70

Nos. D121/D122 have background of faint grey network.
Nos. D119 and D120 were prepared for the surcharges.
Remainders of these two stamps with upright watermark were placed on sale, but were not used by the post office.

DANZIG

27

1923 (Jan–Apr). AIR. Typo. W **24** (sideways). Zigzag roulette (5, 10, 20m.) or P 14 (others).

112	**15**	40pf. emerald (3.1)	90	3·25
113		60pf. dull purple (3.1)	90	3·25
114		1m. carmine (3.1)	90	3·25
115		2m. bistre-brown (3.1)	90	3·25
116	**16**	5m. blue-violet (3.1)	90	1·60
117		10m. olive-green (3.1)	90	1·60
118		20m. yellow-brown (10.1)	90	1·60
		a. Background omitted	26·00	20·00
119	**15**	25m. pale blue (5.2)	65	1·20
120	**27**	50m. orange (27.4)	65	1·20
		a. Background omitted	33·00	26·00
		b. Wmk upright	£100	
121		100m. scarlet (27.4)	65	1·20
		a. Background omitted	26·00	39·00
		b. Wmk upright	£100	
122		250m. black-brown (27.4)	1·00	1·20
		a. Background omitted	26·00	39·00
123		500m. carmine (27.4)	1·00	1·20
		a. Background omitted	26·00	39·00
		b. Wmk upright	£100	

Nos. 118 and 120/123 have background of faint grey network.

28

(Des Max Buchholz. Typo J. Sauer)

1923 (15 Mar). Poor People's Fund. W **24**. P 14.

123c	**28**	50 +20m. lake	40	1·00
123d		100 +30m. dull purple	40	1·00

Nos. 123c/123d have background of faint grey network.

1923 (Mar–Sept). Typo. W **24** (sideways except 3000m.). P 14.

124	**29**	250m. scarlet and purple (15.5)	40	90
125		300m. scarlet and emerald (22.3)	40	65
126		500m. scarlet and slate (29.6)	40	90
		a. Wmk upright	£250	£400
127		1000m. brown (24.7)	25	90
128		1000m. scarlet and black-brown (30.7)	40	90
		a. Wmk upright	£350	£400
129		3000m. scarlet and violet (13.8)	40	90
130		5000m. pink (15.8)	25	65
131		20000m. pale blue (25.8)	25	65
132		50000m. green (1.9)	25	65
133		100000m. deep blue (6.9)	25	65
134		250000m. purple (11.9)	25	65
135		500000m. slate (16.9)	25	65

Nos. 124/135 have background of faint grey network.

1923 (July–Aug). W **24** (sideways on 200m. to 20000m.). P 14.

136	**25**	50m. pale blue (20.7)	40	90
137	**25a**	100m. olive-green (29.7)	40	90
138	**25**	200m. orange (20.7)	40	90
139	**26**	10000m. scarlet and orange (8.8)	1·00	1·00
140		20000m. scarlet and pale blue (13.8)	1·00	1·70
141		50000m. scarlet and green (20.8)	1·00	1·70

Nos. 136/141 have background of faint grey network.

29

1923 (July). OFFICIAL. Optd as T O **20**. W **24** (sideways on Nos. O144/O147).

O142	**25**	50m. pale blue (21.7)	40	1·30
		a. Opt inverted	39·00	
O143	**25a**	100m. olive-green (29.7)	40	1·30
O144	**25**	200m. orange (29.7)	40	1·30
		a. Opt inverted	39·00	
O145	**29**	300m. scarlet and emerald (2.7)	40	1·00
O146		500m. scarlet and slate (21.7)	40	1·30
O147		1000m. scarlet and black-brown (29.7)	40	1·30

(30) T = Tausend (thousand)
(31) 
(32) 
(33) 
(34) M = Million or Millionen 

1923 (Aug–Oct). W **24**.

(a) Surch as T **30**. Wmk sideways (except No. 145)

142	**25**	40T. on 200m. orange (1.9)	1·30	3·25
		a. Surch double	£130	
143		100T. on 200m. orange (1.9)	1·30	3·25
144		250T. on 200m. orange (1.9)	9·75	22·00
145	**25a**	400T. on 100m. olive-green (24.9)	90	1·00
146	**29**	500T. on 50000m. green (8.9)	65	1·00

No. 145 has 'Tausend' in different type and a fleuron instead of bars. No. 146 has only one bar.

(b) Surch as T **31**. Wmk sideways

147	**29**	1M. on 10000m. orange (13.9)	5·75	10·50
148		1M. on 10000m. carmine (19.9)	40	1·00
149		2M. on 10000m. carmine (19.9)	40	1·00
150		3M. on 10000m. carmine (23.9)	40	1·00
151		5M. on 10000m. carmine (23.9)	50	1·00
		a. Surch double	£130	
152		10M. on 10000m. lavender (15.10)	65	1·20
		a. Wmk upright	£120	
153		20M. on 10000m. lavender (15.10)	65	1·20
		a. Wmk upright	£120	
154		25M. on 10000m. lavender (15.10)	25	1·20
155		40M. on 10000m. lavender (22.10)	25	1·20
		a. Surch double	80·00	
156		50M. on 10000m. lavender (15.10)	25	1·20

(c) Surch with T **32** and 33. Wmk sideways

157	**26**	100000 on 20000m. scarlet and pale blue (R.) (14.8)	1·30	9·75
158		10M. on 1000000m. orange (1.10)	65	2·00

No. 158 was not issued without the surcharge and has a background of faint grey network.

(d) Surch as T **34**, in red. Wmk sideways

159	**29**	100M. on 10000m. lavender (22.10)	25	1·20
160		300M. on 10000m. lavender (23.10)	25	1·20
161		500M. on 10000m. lavender (23.10)	25	1·20

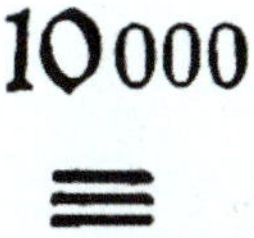

(D **35**)  **35** Etrich/Rumpler Taube
(36) 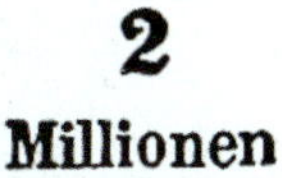

1923 (1 Oct). POSTAGE DUE. Surch as T D **35**.

D162	D **20**	1000 on 10m. purple	£200	
D163		5000 on 50m. purple	65	1·30
D164		10000 on 20m. purple	65	1·30
D165		50000 on 500m. purple	65	1·30
D166		100000 on 20m. purple	1·30	2·50

(Des M. Buchholz. Typo J. Sauer)

1923 (18 Oct). AIR. W **24**. P 14.

162	**35**	250000m. scarlet (wmk sideways)	50	2·00
		a. Wmk upright	80·00	£325
		ab. Imperf	80·00	
163		500000m. scarlet (wmk sideways)	50	2·00
		a. Wmk upright	80·00	£325
		ab. Imperf	80·00	
164	**35**	2M. on 10000m. scarlet. Surch as T **36**. scarlet (wmk sideways)	50	2·00
		a. Wmk upright	£160	£325
		ab. Error. Surch omitted	20·00	85·00
165		5M. on 50000m. scarlet (wmk sideways)	50	2·00
		a. Wmk upright	£180	£325
		ab. Error. Surch omitted	65·00	
		ac. Error. Stamp inscribed 10000m.	65·00	£250

No. 165ac exists on position 73 in the sheet of 100.

339

DANZIG

10 Pfennige (37) **1 Gulden** (38) **38a** Octagonal Mesh

1923 (31 Oct–5 Nov). Surch as T **37** or **38**. W **38a**.

166	**25**	5pf. on 50m. carmine	80	65
167		10pf. on 50m. carmine	80	65
168	**25a**	20pf. on 100m. carmine	80	65
169	**25**	25pf. on 50m. carmine	5·75	13·00
170		30pf. on 50m. carmine	5·75	3·25
171	**25a**	40pf. on 100m. carmine	3·75	3·25
172		50pf. on 100m. carmine	3·75	4·50
173		75pf. on 100m. carmine	13·00	26·00
174	**26**	1g. on 1000000m. carmine (5.11)	7·25	9·75
175		2g. on 1000000m. carmine (5.11)	20·00	26·00
176		3g. on 1000000m. carmine (5.11)	36·00	£100
177		5g. on 1000000m. carmine (5.11)	42·00	£100
166/177 *Set of 12*			£130	£250

D **39**    **39**   (O **40**)

1923 (24 Nov)–**27**. POSTAGE DUE. Typo. W **38a**. P 14.

D178	D **39**	5pf. blue and black	1·30	1·30
D179		10pf. blue and black	65	1·30
D180		15pf. blue and black (13.12.27)	2·00	2·50
D181		20pf. blue and black	2·10	3·25
D182		30pf. blue and black	13·00	3·25
D183		40pf. blue and black	3·75	5·25
D184		50pf. blue and black	3·75	4·00
D185		60pf. blue and black	20·00	31·00
D186		100pf. blue and black	29·00	17·00
D187		3g. blue and carmine (13.12.27)	14·50	80·00
D178/D187 *Set of 10*			80·00	£130

See also Nos. D263/D267.

(Des M. Buchholz. Typo)

1924 (19 Jan)–**38**. W **24** (sideways). P 14.

177a	**39**	3pf. brown (24.2.27)	4·00	3·25
		b. On pale yellow paper (10.35)	1·90	2·30
178		5pf. orange	26·00	3·50
		a. Interrupted perf (1932)	39·00	16·00
		b. On pale yellow paper (2.35)	4·50	90
		c. Wmk upright	£170	
		d. Pale yellow paper. Interrupted perf (10.35)	18·00	14·50
178e		7pf. yellow-green (27.4.33)	2·50	4·50
178f		8pf. yellow-green (14.8.37)	2·50	9·75
179		10pf. green	20·00	4·25
		a. Interrupted perf (1932)	46·00	20·00
		b. On pale yellow paper (3.35)	9·00	80
		c. Do. Interrupted perf (11.35)	26·00	17·00
179d		10pf. bright blue-green (24.6.37)	7·75	2·50
		e. Interrupted perf (24.8.37)	17·00	23·00
180		15pf. grey	6·50	1·00
180a		15pf. vermilion (20.8.25)	7·75	1·70
		b. On pale yellow paper (2.35)	3·25	1·70
181		20pf. red and carmine-red (26.1.24)	26·00	1·00
182		20pf. slate (20.6.35)	4·00	4·00
183		25pf. red and slate (12.3.24)	39·00	5·75
184		25pf. carmine-red (5.6.35)	26·00	2·50
185		30pf. red and deep green (12.3.24)	23·00	1·30
		a. Red and yellow-green	65·00	4·25
186		30pf. purple (21.8.35)	4·00	6·50
186a		35pf. blue (2110.25)	7·75	2·30
187		40pf. light blue and deep blue (14.2.24)	20·00	1·60
188		40pf. vermilion and brown (15.4.35)	10·50	20·00
189		40pf. deep blue (26.6.35)	4·00	5·75
190		50pf. red and deep blue (12.3.24)	26·00	13·00
		a. On pale yellow paper (3.38)	29·00	50·00
190b		55pf. vermilion and deep claret (4.37)	13·00	23·00
191		60pf. scarlet and bottle green (15.4.35)	10·50	29·00
192		70pf. vermilion and yellow-green (5.9.35)	4·00	11·50
193		75pf. red and purple (12.3.24)	16·00	13·00
		a. On pale yellow paper (1938)	13·00	46·00
194		80pf. vermilion and reddish brown (5.9.35)	4·00	11·50

1924 (1 Mar)–**25**. OFFICIAL. Optd with T O **40**.

O195	**39**	5pf. orange	3·25	5·25
O196		10pf. green	3·25	5·25
O197		15pf. grey	3·25	5·25
O198		15pf. vermilion (1925)	29·00	16·00
O199		20pf. red and carmine-red	3·25	3·25
O200		25pf. red and slate (12.3.24)	29·00	42·00
O201		30pf. red and yellow-green (12.3.24)	4·50	5·75
O202		35pf. blue (1925)	90·00	80·00
O203		40pf. light blue and deep blue	10·50	13·00
O204		50pf. red and deep blue (12.3.24)	33·00	65·00
O205		75pf. red and purple (12.3.24)	65·00	£180

Double overprints are fakes.

40 Etrich/Rumpler Taube    **41** Aeroplane    **42** Oliva

(Des M. Buchholz. Typo J. Sauer)

1924 (5 June). AIR. No. 199 has network background. W **24** (upright). P 14.

195	**40**	10pf. vermilion	35·00	5·75
196		20pf. cerise	3·50	2·50
197		40pf. brown	5·00	3·25
198		1g. deep green	5·00	7·25
199	**41**	2½g. plum	29·00	55·00
		a. Without network background	£100	£325

All values exist imperforate.

(Des and eng E. Hellingrath. Recess Berlin State Ptg Works)

1924 (22 Sept–28 Nov). T **42** and similar designs. Wmk Lozenges (T **23** of Germany). P 14.

200		1g. black and yellow-green	33·00	70·00
201		2g. black and purple	70·00	£170
202		3g. black and blue (28.11)	7·75	7·75
203		5g. black and lake (28.11)	7·75	13·00
204		10g. black and brown (28.11)	33·00	£170
200/204 *Set of 5*			£140	£400

Designs: Horiz—1g. T **42**; 2g. Krantor and River Mottlau; 3g. Zoppot. Vert—5g. St. Mary's Church; 10g. Town Hall and Langemarkt.

44 Fountain of Neptune   (**45**)

1925 (1 Jan)–**32**. As last, colours changed.

205		1g. black and orange	26·00	6·50
		a. Black and bright red-orange (5.32)	26·00	20·00
206		2g. black and carmine	5·75	13·00

See also No. 275.

(Recess Berlin State Ptg Works)

1929 (7 July). International Philatelic Exhibition. Various frames. P 14.

207	**44**	10pf. (+10pf.) black and green	4·00	7·25
208		15pf. (+15pf.) black and carmine	4·00	7·25
209		25pf. (+25pf.) black and blue	13·00	46·00
		a. Black and ultramarine	80·00	£425
207/209 *Set of 3*			19·00	55·00

DANZIG

1930 (15 Nov). Tenth Anniv of Constitution of Free City of Danzig. Optd with T **45**.

210	**39**	5pf. orange	4·00	5·75
211		10pf. green (V.)	5·25	7·25
212		15pf. vermilion	9·00	17·00
213		20pf. red and carmine-red	4·50	9·00
214		25pf. red and slate	6·50	17·00
215		30pf. red and yellow-green	13·00	39·00
216		35pf. blue (R.)	50·00	£160
217		40pf. light blue and deep blue (R.)	17·00	60·00
218		50pf. red and deep blue	50·00	£130
219		75pf. vermilion and purple	50·00	£140
220	**42**	1g. black and orange (R.)	50·00	£130
210/220 *Set of 11*			£225	£650

(46) (D 47) (47) ('Winterhilfswerk')

1932 (23 July). Danzig International Air Post Exhibition ('Luposta'). Nos. 200/204 surch as T **46**.

221		10pf. +10pf. on 1g. (G.)	14·50	36·00
222		15pf. +15pf. on 2g. (P.)	14·50	36·00
223		20pf. +20pf. on 3g. (B.)	14·50	36·00
224		25pf. +25pf. on 5g. (R.)	14·50	36·00
225		30pf. +30pf. on 10g. (Br.)	14·50	36·00
221/225 *Set of 5*			65·00	£160

On Nos. 222 and 224/225 the surcharge is in four lines; on Nos. 224/225 '1932' is the second line.

1932 (20 Dec). POSTAGE DUE. Surch as T D **47**. W **38a**. P 14.

D226	D **39**	5 on 40pf. blue and black (R.)	6·50	13·00
D227		10 on 60pf. blue and black (R.)	50·00	16·00
D228		20 on 100pf. blue and black (R.)	4·25	13·00
D226/D228 *Set of 3*			55·00	38·00

1934 (15 Jan). Winter Relief Work Charity stamps. Surch with T **47**.

226	**39**	5pf. +5pf. orange	14·50	33·00
227		10pf. +5pf. green	36·00	80·00
228		15pf. +5pf. vermilion	21·00	60·00
226/228 *Set of 3*			65·00	£160

(48) (49)

1934 (28 Dec)–**36**. Nos. 178*e* and 186*a* surch.

229	**48**	6 on 7pf. yellow-green (R.)	1·30	2·50
230		8 on 7pf. yellow-green (B.) (5.6.35)	3·25	3·75
		a. Red surch (14.7.36)	2·00	4·00
		b. Green surch (23.12.36)	1·30	4·00
231	**49**	30 on 35pf. bright blue (B.)	16·00	39·00
229/231 *Set of 3 (cheapest)*			17·00	41·00

No. 232 is vacant.

50 Junkers F-13   **51**   **52** Stockturm, 1346

(Des M. Buchholz. Typo Post Office Ptg Wks, Danzig)

1935 (25 Oct). AIR. W **24** (upright, except on 1g.). P 14.

233	**50**	10pf. salmon	2·50	1·30
		a. Error. 'DANZIO' instead of 'DANZIG' (pos. 3)	50·00	£180
		b. Error. 'STADL' instead of 'STADT' (pos. 4)	50·00	£180
234		15pf. orange-yellow	2·50	2·00
235		25pf. bottle green	2·50	2·50
236		50pf. blue	13·00	16·00
237	**51**	1g. bright purple	5·25	22·00
233/237 *Set of 5*			23·00	39·00

See also Nos. 263/266.

(Des M. Buchholz. Typo)

1935 (23 Dec). Winter Relief Fund. Designs inscr 'Für das Winterhilfswerk', as T **52**. W **24** (sideways on No. 239). P 14.

238		5pf. +5pf. orange	1·00	2·50
239		10pf. +5pf. green	1·80	4·00
240		15pf. +10pf. scarlet	4·25	5·75
238/240 *Set of 3*			6·25	11·00

Designs: Horiz—5pf. T **52**; 10pf. The Lege Tor. Vert—15pf. Georgshalle, 1487.

54 Brösen War Memorial   **55** Frauentor and Observatory   **56** 'D(anziger) L(uftschutz) B(und)'

(Des M. Buchholz. Typo Post Office Ptg Wks, Danzig)

1936 (23 June). 125th Anniv of Brösen. As T **54** (inscr '125 JAHRE OSTSEEBAD BRÖSEN'). W **24** (sideways on horiz stamps). P 14.

241		10pf. deep green	1·60	2·00
242		25pf. carmine	2·10	3·75
243		40pf. light blue	3·75	7·25
241/243 *Set of 3*			6·75	11·50

Designs: Horiz—10pf. Brösen Beach; 25pf. Zoppot end of Brösen Beach. Vert—40pf. T **54**.

1936 (25 Nov). Winter Relief Fund. As T **55** (inscr 'WINTERHILFE'). W **24** (sideways on horiz stamps). P 14.

244		10pf. +5pf. green	2·50	7·75
245		15pf. +5pf. blue-green	2·50	10·50
246		25pf. +10pf. maroon	4·00	16·00
247		40pf. +20pf. brown and maroon	5·25	18·00
248		50pf. +20pf. pale blue and deep blue	9·00	26·00
244/248 *Set of 5*			21·00	70·00

Designs: Vert—10pf. Milchkannenturm; 15pf. T **55**; 25pf. Krantor. Horiz—40pf. Langgartertor; 50pf. Hohestor.

1937 (27 Mar). Air Defence League. Typo. W **24** (sideways). P 14.

249	**56**	10pf. deep blue	90	2·00
250		15pf. dull purple	2·50	4·00

57 Marienkirche, Danzig   **57a** Danziger Dorf, Magdeburg

(Des W. Lüdtcke. Typo)

1937 (6 June). First National Philatelic Exhibition, Danzig ('DAPOSTA'). Sheets 147×104 mm. W **24** (sideways). P 14.

(a) POSTAGE

| MS251 | **57** | 50pf. blue-green/*toned* | 6·50 | £180 |

(b) AIR

| MS252 | | 50pf. blue/*toned* | 6·50 | £180 |

Design:—No. **MS**252 Marienkirche and Junkers F-13.

(Des W. Brandt. Typo)

1937 (30 Oct). Foundation of Danzig Community, Magdeburg. T **57a** and similar type, inscr 'Danziger Dorf in Magdeburg'. W **24** (sideways on 25pf.). P 14.

253		25pf. (+25pf.) carmine	4·50	9·00
		a. Wmk upright	17·00	65·00
254		40pf. (+40pf.) vermilion and blue	4·50	9·00

Designs: Vert—25pf. T **57a**. Horiz—40pf. Village and Arms of Danzig and Magdeburg.

1937 (28 Nov). Danzig Productivity Show. Sheet 146×105 mm.

| MS254*a* | Nos. 253/254 (*sold for* 1g.50) | 80·00 | £600 |

DANZIG / POLISH POST IN DANZIG

58 Madonna and Child
59 Schopenhauer 
61 Teutonic Knights
62 Gregor Mendel

(Des M. Buchholz. Typo)

1937 (13 Dec). Winter Relief Fund. As T **58** (statues inscr 'WINTERHILFSZUSCHLAG' or 'WINTERHILFE' (Nos. 258/259)). W **24**. P 14.

255	5pf. +5pf. violet		4·00	13·00
256	10pf. +5pf. brown		4·00	9·75
257	15pf. +5pf. orange and light blue		4·00	14·50
258	25pf. +10pf. green and blue-green		5·25	20·00
259	40pf. +25pf. blue and carmine		9·00	26·00
255/259 Set of 5			24·00	75·00

Designs:—5pf. T **58**; 10pf. Mercury; 15pf. The 'Golden Knight'; 25pf. Fountain of Neptune; 40pf. St. George and the Dragon.

(Des M. Buchholz, after J. Hamel (15pf.), L. S. Ruhl (25pf.) and Daguerre (40pf.). Photo State Ptg Wks, Berlin)

1938 (22 Feb). 150th Birth Anniv of Schopenhauer (philosopher). As T **59** (portraits inscr 'Schopenhauer 1788–1860'). P 14.

260	15pf. blue		2·30	4·00
261	25pf. sepia		5·50	13·00
262	40pf. red		2·30	5·25
260/262 Set of 3			9·00	20·00

Designs:—Portraits of Schopenhauer as an old man (15pf.) and as a young man (25pf.).

1938 (5 May)–**39**. POSTAGE DUE. W **97** of Germany (Swastikas). P 14.

D263	D **39**	10pf. blue and black (21.5.39)	2·00	£120
D264		30pf. blue and black	3·25	£100
D265		40pf. blue and black (21.5.39)	9·75	£200
D266		60pf. blue and black (21.5.39)	9·75	£200
D267		100pf. blue and black	16·00	£130
D263/D267 Set of 5			37·00	£650

1938–39. AIR. W **97** of Germany (Swastikas). P 14.

263	**50**	10pf. salmon (7.38)	2·00	6·50
264		15pf. orange-yellow (8.7.38)	3·25	21·00
265		25pf. bottle green (7.38)	2·50	11·00
266		50pf. blue (13.2.39)	6·50	£100
263/266 Set of 4			13·00	£120

1938–39. W **97** of Germany (Swastikas). P 14.

267	**39**	3pf. brown (28.9.38)	1·30	11·50
268		5pf. orange (23.7.38)	1·30	13·00
		a. Interrupted perf (24.8.38)	2·00	11·50
269		8pf. yellow-green (9.38)	6·50	50·00
270		10pf. green (10.38)	1·30	3·25
		a. Interrupted perf (18.7.38)	4·00	16·00
271		15pf. scarlet (23.7.38)	2·50	20·00
272		25pf. carmine (23.7.38)	2·00	10·50
273		40pf. indigo (19.7.38)	3·25	46·00
274		50pf. scarlet and blue (14.7.39)	3·25	£200
275	**42**	1g. black and orange (10.38)	10·50	£180
267/275 Set of 9			29·00	£475

60 Yacht *Peter von Danzig* (1936)

(Des H. Gruber (Nos. 276/279), O. Lienau (No. 280). Photo State Ptg Wks, Berlin)

1938 (28 Nov). Winter Relief Fund. As T **60** (ship types inscr 'W H W'). No wmk. P 14.

276	5pf. +5pf. bottle green		2·20	2·75
277	10pf. +5pf. deep orange-brown		2·20	5·25
278	15pf. +10pf. olive-green		2·50	5·25
279	25pf. +10pf. deep blue		3·75	7·75
280	40pf. +15pf. purple-brown		5·25	11·50
276/280 Set of 5			14·50	29·00

Designs:—5pf. T **60**; 10pf. Dredger *Fu Shing*; 15pf. Liner *Columbus*; 25pf. Liner *Hansestadt Danzig*; 40pf. Sailing vessel *Peter von Danzig* (1472).

(Photo State Ptg Wks, Berlin)

1939 (7 Jan). 125th Anniv of Prussian Annexation. As T **61** (historical designs). No wmk. P 14.

281	5pf. deep green		·90	3·25
282	10pf. deep orange-brown		1·30	4·00
283	15pf. indigo		2·00	4·50
284	25pf. chocolate		2·50	6·50
281/284 Set of 4			6·00	16·00

Designs:—5pf. T **61**; 10pf. Danzig–Swedish treaty of neutrality, 1630; 15pf. Danzig united to Prussia, 2.1.1814; 25pf. Stephen Baton's defeat at Weichselmunde, 1577.

(Photo State Ptg Wks, Berlin)

1939 (29 Apr). Anti-Cancer Campaign. As T **62** (medical-scientists' portraits). No wmk. P 13×14½.

285	10pf. red-brown		1·00	1·30
286	15pf. black		1·00	3·25
287	25pf. olive-green		2·00	4·50
285/287 Set of 3			3·50	8·25

Portraits:—10pf. T **62**; 15pf. Robert Koch; 25pf. Wilhelm Konrad Röntgen.

On 1 September, 1939, Danzig was reabsorbed into Germany. Since 1945 it has been part of Poland.

STAMP BOOKLETS

The following checklist covers, in simplified form, booklets issued by Danzig. It is intended that it should be used in conjunction with the main listings and details of stamps and panes listed there are not repeated.

Booklets differing in the colour of cover or in the text on the front cover are separately priced. Booklets also occur with other differences, for example in the text on the inside covers; these are not covered by this list, but prices are generally the same for each version.

Prices are for complete booklets

Booklet No.	Date	Contents and Cover Price	Price
SB1	9.25-26	Arms (T **39**) 1 pane, No. 178×6; 1 pane, No. 179×6; 1 pane, No. 180a×6 (1g.80)	
		(a) Grey cover	£1000
		(b) Pink cover (1.26)	£12000
SB2	4.28-34	Arms (T **39**) 1 pane, No. 178×10 1 pane No. 179×10; 1 pane, No. 180a×10 (3g.)	
		(a) Front cover inscr 'Post- und Telegraphenverwaltung...'. Brown cover.	£8500
		(b) As a. but pink cover (4.30)	£10000
		(c) As a. but green cover (1.33)	£5000
		(d) Cover inscr 'Landespostdirektion...'. Pink cover. (1.34)	
SB3	1.36	Arms (T **39**) 1 pane, No. 178b×10; 1 pane, No. 179b×10; 1 pane, No. 180b×10 (3g.)	£17000
SB4	5.37	Arms (T **39**) 1 pane, No. 178b×10; 1 pane, No. 179d×10; 1 pane, No. 180b×10 (3g.)	£11000
SB5	9.38	Arms (T **39**) 1 pane, No. 268×10; 1 pane, No. 270×10; 1 pane No. 271×10 (3g.)	£19000

POLISH POST IN DANZIG

The Poles operated a postal service in Danzig with a post office by the harbour.

100 Groszy = 1 Zloty

Stamps of Poland overprinted

PORT GDAŃSK (R **1**)   PORT GDAŃSK (R **2**)   PORT GDAŃSK (R **3**)

1925 (5 Jan). Nos. 218/228 (Arms) optd with Type R **1**.

R1	40	1g. yellow-brown	70	4·00
R2		2g. grey-brown	70	9·50
R3		3g. orange	70	5·50
R4		5g. sage-green	20·00	13·50
R5		10g. blue-green	6·75	5·50
R6		15g. scarlet	38·00	13·50
R7		20g. light blue	2·00	2·75
R8		25g. claret	2·00	2·75
R9		30g. bright violet	2·00	2·75
R10		40g. slate	2·00	2·75
R11		50g. magenta	6·75	4·00
R1/R11 Set of 11			75·00	55·00

1926 (12 Apr). Nos. 244/245 optd with Type R **1**.

R12	44	5g. green (Town Hall, Poznán)	60·00	70·00
R13		10g. violet (King Sigismund Monument. Warsaw)	16·00	27·00

1926–29. Optd with Type R **2**.

R14	44	5g. green (No. 244a)	2·00	3·50
R15	45	10g. violet (No. 245a) (1927)	2·00	3·50
R16	46	15g. carmine (No. 246a) (Wawel Castle)	34·00	6·75
		a. Optd on No. 246	80·00	95·00
R17	48	20g. carmine (Ship) (15.2.28)	4·00	3·50
R18	51	25g. yellow-brown (Marshal Pilsudski)	6·75	8·00
R19	57	1z. slate-black/cream (Pres. Mościcki) (30.11.29)	38·00	60·00
R14/R19 Set of 6			80·00	75·00

Inverted overprints of Nos. R14/R15, R17 and R24 are now believed to be private productions made from the original clichés.

1929 (28 May)–**30**. Optd with Type R **3**.

R21	61	5g. violet (Arms)	2·00	3·50
R22		10g. green (1930)	2·00	3·50
R23	59	15g. deep blue (Sienkiewicz) (5.1.30)	5·50	10·00
R24	61	25g. red-brown	4·00	3·50
R21/R24 Set of 4			12·00	18·00

See note below No. R19.

(R **4**)   (R **5**)   R **6** Port of Danzig

1933 (1 July). No. 273a (Mościcki) optd with Type R **4**. P 11½.

R25	57	1z. slate-black/cream (V.)	£100	£225

1934 (22 Sept)–**35**. Nos. 284a/285a (Arms) optd with Type R **3**.

R26	65	5g. violet	4·75	11·00
R27		10g. green (30.10.35)	50·00	£180
R28		15g. claret	4·75	11·00
R26/R28 Set of 3			55·00	£180

1936–37. Nos. 313, 315, 317, 319 and 321 optd as Type R **5** in one or (Nos. R30 and R31) in two lines.

(a) Typo (Aug–Sept 1936)

R29	79	5g. violet-blue (Dog's Rock) (15.8.36)	4·00	41·00
R30		15g. greenish blue (MS *Pilsudski*) (10.9.36)	4·00	41·00
R31		5g. violet (Czestochowa) (25.10.37)	1·50	20·00

(b) Recess (Sept 1936–June 1937)

R32		15g. brown-lake (Lwów University) (5.6.37)	1·50	20·00
R33		25g. deep blue green (Belvedere Palace) (10.9.36)	4·00	13·50

(Des W. Boratynski. Eng M. Dutczynskr Recess Govt Ptg Wks, Warsaw)

1938 (11 Nov). 20th Anniv of Polish Independence. P 12½×13.

R34	R **6**	5g. red-orange	70	34·00
R35		15g. red-brown	70	34·00
R36		25g. purple	70	34·00
R37		55g. bright blue	2·00	55·00
R34/R37 Set of 4			3·75	£140

Stamps inscribed 'GDANSK' showing a Crown surmounting two Maltese Crosses were issued by a Polish Defence organisation but they were not put on sale at the post office.

The Polish Post Office was closed on 1 September 1939 when Danzig was incorporated into Germany.

Marienwerder

100 Pfennig = 1 Mark

By the treaty of Versailles, 1919, a plebiscite was to be held to determine whether this district of West Prussia should belong to Germany or Poland and an Interallied Commission was appointed to supervise this.

1 (2)

(Recess Officine Grafiche Coen, Milan)

1920 (13 Mar–13 Apr). Inscr 'COMMISSION INTERALLIÉE' at top. Papermaker's wmk, O.B.M. and two Stars or P. & C.M. in sheet. P 11½.

1	**1**	5pf. green	1·00	4·00
2		10pf. red (13.4)	1·00	3·25
3		15pf. slate	1·00	4·50
4		20pf. orange-brown	1·00	3·25
5		25pf. blue	1·00	4·50
6		30pf. orange (13.4)	1·40	4·50
7		40pf. brown (13.4)	1·00	5·25
8		50pf. violet	1·00	4·00
9		60pf. red-brown (13.4)	6·50	6·50
10		75pf. chocolate (13.4)	1·40	4·00
11		1m. brown and green (13.4)	1·00	3·25
12		2m. purple (13.4)	3·25	7·50
13		3m. vermilion (13.4)	7·75	11·50
14		5m. blue and carmine (13.4)	46·00	33·00
1/14 Set of 14			65·00	90·00

Printings were made on thick bluish and greyish paper and on thin yellowish paper.

All values exist imperforate (*Price:* £60 *each un*).

1920 (27 Mar–11 May). Stamps of Germany (W **23**), optd as in Type **2**.

15	**17**	5pf. green (8.5)	23·00	46·00
		a. Opt inverted	£200	£325
16		20pf. ultramarine (8.5)	11·50	46·00
		a. Opt inverted	£100	£225
		b. Opt double	£130	
17		50pf. black and purple/buff (9.4)	£600	£1300
		a. On cream (90a) (11.5)	£1300	£4500
18		75pf. black and blue-green	7·75	15·00
		a. Opt inverted	£100	£225
19		80pf. black and carmine/rose	£120	£200
20	**18**	1m. carmine-red (No. 93B)	£130	£250
			£650	
15/20 Set of 6			£800	£1700

An official proof sheet was made of the 1m. with the overprint in sans-serif capitals in black. This also exists with the overprint more widely spaced between the lines in seriffed capitals, both in black and in red, whilst the 75pf. and 80pf. exist with the normal overprint in red but they were all private productions None of these was issued although copies have passed through the post.

1920 (21 Apr–11 May). Stamps of Germany (W **23**), surch as Type **2**.

21	**24**	1m. on 2pf. grey	46·00	80·00
22		2m. on 2½pf. grey (11.5)	23·00	33·00
23	**17**	3m. on 3pf. brown (10.5)	23·00	33·00
24	**24**	5m. on 7½pf. orange (11.5)	23·00	33·00
21/24 Set of 4			£100	£160

There are minor varieties of lettering in T **2**, consisting of accented 'e' of different type in 'Interalliee', 'M' of 'Mark' or 'Marienwerder' with straight or slanting strokes, with or without serifs and two types of figures '2' and '5'.

(3)   4

MARIENWERDER / MEMEL

1920 (9–16 July). Stamps of Germany (offset ptg, W **23**) optd with Type **3**.

25	**18**	1m. carmine-red (16.7)	4·00	11·50
26		1m.25 green	5·25	13·50
27		1m.50 brown	6·50	16·00
28	**20**	2m.50 claret (16.7)	4·00	13·50
25/28 Set of 4			18·00	49·00

1920 (11 July–3 Aug). Inscr 'PLEBISCITE' at top. P 11½.

29	**4**	5pf. green (3.8)	5·75	3·25
30		10pf. red(3.8)	5·75	3·25
31		15pf. slate (3.8)	21·00	22·00
32		20pf. orange-brown (3.8)	4·00	3·25
33		25pf. blue (3.8)	22·00	29·00
34		30pf. orange (3.8)	4·00	2·50
35		40pf. brown (3.8)	4·00	2·50
36		50pf. violet (3.8)	3·25	3·25
37		60pf. red-brown (3.8)	10·50	9·00
38		75pf. chocolate (3.8)	10·50	9·00
39		1m. brown and green (16.7)	4·00	2·50
40		2m. purple	4·00	2·50
41		3m. vermilion	4·00	3·25
42		5m. blue and carmine	6·50	4·50
29/42 Set of 14			£100	90·00

The plebiscite was held on 11 July 1920 and resulted in a vote of 92% in favour of remaining in Germany. Marienwerder was restored to Germany on 16 August 1920 and German stamps were used there until 1945, since when it has been administered by Poland under the name of Kwidzyn.

Memel

100 Pfennig = 1 Mark

Following the First World War Germany surrendered the city of Memel, situated on the Baltic coast of Lithuania, to the Allies. Under the terms of the Treaty of Versailles in 1919 France was granted the administration of Memel under the auspices of the League of Nations.

Types of France Surcharged

13 'Olivier Merson' type **15** Sower **18** Sower without ground

(1) MEMEL 30 pfennig (2) MEMEL 3 mark (A) 4 (B) 4

1920 (7 July)–**22**. Stamps of France surch as Type **1** (5pf to 50pf.) or **2** (others).

(a) On ordinary white paper

1	**18**	5pf. on 5c. green (21.10.20)	1·30	5·75
2		10pf. on 10c. red	1·00	4·50
3		20pf. on 25c. blue	2·00	6·50
		a. Wider space between surch figures	13·00	46·00
4		30pf. on 30c. orange	1·30	5·75
5		50pf. on 35c. violet	50	5·75
6	**13**	60pf. on 40c. red and pale blue	65	6·50
7		80pf. on 45c. deep green and blue (8.20)	2·00	7·75
8		1m. on 50c. cinnamon and lavender (8.20)	90	6·50
9		1m.25 on 60c. violet and blue (5.9.20)	2·10	16·00
10		2m. on 1f. lake and yellow-green (9.20)	1·00	5·75
11		3m. on 2f. orange and blue-green (R.) (27.1.21)	39·00	£120
12		3m. on 5f. deep blue and buff	36·00	£120
13		4m. on 2f. orange and blue-green ('4' as A) (6.12.20)	80	6·50
		a. Figure 4 as B	46·00	£130
14		10m. on 5f. deep blue and buff (R.) (16.12.20)	5·25	26·00
15		20m. on 5f. deep blue and buff (R.) (27.1.21)	70·00	£250
1/15 Set of 15			£150	£550

(b) On greyish granite ('G.C.') paper

16	**18**	5pf. on 5c. blue-green	4·50	33·00
17		10pf. on 10c. red (9.20)	33·00	£160
18		30pf. on 30c. orange	11·50	26·00
19		40pf. on 20c. chocolate	11·50	26·00
20		50pf. on 35c. violet	£160	£650
21	**13**	60pf. on 40c. red and pale blue	5·50	26·00
		a. Wider space between surch figures	46·00	£160
22		80pf. on 45c. deep green and blue	11·50	50·00
23		1m. on 50c. cinnamon and lavender	23·00	13·00
24		2m. on 1f. lake and yellow-green	4·50	26·00
24a		4m. on 2f. orange and blue-green	8·50	60·00
16/24a Set of 10			£250	£950

Memelgebiet (3) Memelgebiet (4)

MEMEL

1920 (1 Aug). Stamps of Germany (W **23**), optd with Type **3** or **4** (mark values).

25	**17**	5pf. deep green	6·25	17·00
26		10pf. bright carmine	3·25	16·00
27		10pf. orange	50	5·75
28	**24**	15pf. purple-brown	4·50	21·00
29	**17**	20pf. ultramarine	2·00	9·00
30		30pf. black and orange/*buff*	2·20	13·50
		a. On cream (No. 88*a*)	£650	£1300
31		30pf. dull blue (Plate II)	65	5·75
32		40pf. black and carmine	45	5·75
33		50pf. black and purple/*buff*	50	5·75
		a. On cream (No. 90*a*)	£275	£1000
34		60pf. olive-green	2·50	10·50
35		75pf. black and blue-green	4·50	36·00
36		80pf. ultramarine (Plate II)	2·30	16·00
37	**18**	1m. carmine-red (25×17 perforation holes)	50	5·75
38		1m.25 green	22·00	85·00
39		1m.50 brown	7·75	48·00
40	**20**	2m. deep blue (25×17 perforation holes)	9·00	21·00
		a. 26×17 perforation holes	£1200	£3250
41		2m.50 claret (*shades*) 26×17 perforation holes	20·00	£100
25/41 Set of 17			80·00	£375

(5) (6)

1921 (Apr)–**22**. Nos. 2/3, 5, 8, 10, 19 and 49 further surch as Type **5** in red (No. 44) or blue (others).

42	**18**	15 on 10pf. on 10c. red	65	3·25
		a. Surch inverted	£100	£400
43		15 on 20pf. on 25c. blue (15.11.21)	65	5·25
		a. Surch inverted	£100	
		b. Wider space between surch figures	13·00	39·00
44		15 on 50pf. on 35c. violet (2.12.21)	65	5·25
		a. Surch inverted	£100	
45		60 on 40pf. on 20c. chocolate	65	3·25
		a. Surch inverted	£100	£350
		b. Opt '60' double	£170	£350
46	**13**	75 on 60pf. on 40c. red and pale blue (27.1.22)	1·30	6·50
47		1,25 on 1m. on 50c. cinnamon and lavender (6.1.22)	1·00	3·25
48		5,00 on 2m. on 1f. lake and yellow green (7.1.22)	1·60	7·75
		a. Surch inverted	£250	£900
		b. Opt '5,00' double	£500	£1800
42/48 Set of 7			5·75	31·00

1921 (14 May). Stamps of France surch as Type **2** but with initial of 'Pfennig' or 'Mark' a capital letter.

49	**13**	60pf. on 40c. red and pale blue	7·75	33·00
50		3m. on 60c. violet and blue (R.)	4·00	13·00
51		10m. on 5f. deep blue and buff (R.)	4·00	14·50
		a. Figures '10' widely spaced	23·00	70·00
52		20m. on 45c. deep green and blue (R.)	10·50	46·00
49/52 Set of 4			21·00	95·00

The value in the surcharge on No. 50 is in italic type. In No. 51 the figures '10' are spaced 1.5 mm apart and in No. 51a 1.9 mm.

1921 (6–31 July). AIR. Nos. 6/8, 10, 13 and 49/50 further optd with Type **6** in blue.

53	**13**	60pf. on 40c. red and pale blue (No. 6)	50·00	£250
		a. Type **6** with coloured dot in centre of top bar of 'T' (31.7)	70·00	£450
54		60pf. on 40c. red and pale blue (No. 49) (Type **6** with coloured dot in centre of top bar of 'T') (31.7)	6·50	33·00
		a. Opt Type **6** inverted	£250	
		b. Type **6** without dot in 'T'		
55		80pf. on 45c. deep green and blue	6·50	33·00
56		1m. on 50c. cinnamon and lavender	7·75	23·00
		a. Type **6** with coloured dot in centre of top bar of 'T' (31.7)	7·75	65·00
57		2m. on 1f. lake and yellow-green	5·75	26·00
		a. Opt Type **6** inverted	£250	
58		3m. on 60c. violet and blue	5·25	26·00
		a. Opt Type **6** inverted	£400	
59		4m. on 2f. orange and blue-green ('4' as A)	6·50	33·00
		a. Figure 4 as B	£130	£500
53/59 Set of 7			80·00	£375

No. 54b occurs on one position in sheets of 25 (pos. 42, 43 and 67).

(7) (8)

1922 (2 Jan–Dec). Stamps of France surch.

(a) As Type **7**

60	**18**	5pf. on 5c. orange	40	2·30
61		10pf. on 10c. scarlet (24.1)	1·30	9·00
62		10pf. on 10c. green (18.1)	40	2·30
63		15pf. on 10c. green (18.1)	40	2·30
64		20pf. on 20c. chocolate (24.1)	13·00	65·00
65		20pf. on 25c. blue (24.1)	13·00	65·00
66		25pf. on 5c. orange (22.3)	40	2·30
67		30pf. on 35c. scarlet (18.1)	2·00	9·00
68		35pf. on 35c. violet (12.9)	25	1·30
69	**15**	50pf. on 50c. deep blue (24.1)	40	2·30
70	**18**	75pf. on 35c. violet (22.3)	50	2·30
71	**15**	75pf. on 15c. slate-green (12.9)	25	1·30
72	**18**	1m. on 35c. violet (12.9)	25	1·30
73		1¼m. on 30c. scarlet (12.9)	25	1·30
74		3m. on 5c. orange (12.22)	65	7·75
75	**15**	6m. on 15c. slate-green (C.) (12.22)	1·30	8·50
76	**18**	8m. on 30c. scarlet (12.22)	1·30	22·00
60/76 Set of 17			32·00	£180

(b) As Type **8**

77	**13**	40pf. on 40c. red and pale blue (3.1)	40	2·30
78		80pf. on 45c. deep green and blue (24.1)	50	2·30
79		1m. on 40c. red and pale blue (15.4)	50	4·00
		a. Opt double	£225	£700
80		1m.25 on 60c. violet and blue (C.) (19.4)	60	3·25
81		1m.50 on 45c. deep green and blue (C.) (9.4)	50	4·00
82		2m. on 45c. deep green and blue (12.9)	1·30	4·50
83		2m. on 1f. lake and yellow-green (15.4)	50	4·00
84		2¼m. on 40c. red and pale blue (12.9)	35	1·30
85		2½m. on 60c. violet and blue (12.9)	1·30	4·50
86		3m. on 60c. violet and blue (C.) (19.4)	2·00	8·50
87		4m. on 45c. deep green and blue (12.9)	25	1·30
88		5m. on 1f. lake and yellow-green (22.4)	50	4·50
89		6m. on 60c. violet and blue (12.9)	25	1·30
90		6m. on 2f. orange and blue-green (15.4)	50	4·25
91		9m. on 1f. lake and yellow-green (12.9)	25	1·30
92		9m. on 5f. deep blue and buff (C.) (22.4)	65	5·25
93		10m. on 45c. deep green and blue (C.) (12.22)	1·30	8·50
94		12m. on 40c. red and pale blue (12.9)	65	4·00
95		20m. on 40c. red and pale blue (12.22)	1·30	8·50
96		20m. on 2f. orange and blue-green (12.9)	65	4·00
97		30m. on 60c. violet and blue (12.22)	1·30	8·50
98		30m. on 5f. deep blue and buff (12.9)	4·50	33·00
99		40m. on 1f. lake and yellow-green (12.22)	1·30	11·00
100		50m. on 2f. orange and blue-green (12.9)	13·00	80·00
101		80m. on 2f. orange and blue-green (C.) (12.22)	1·30	11·00
102		100m. on 5f. deep blue and buff (12.22)	2·00	23·00
77/102 Set of 26			33·00	£200

On Type **7** five stamps in each sheet (positions 121-125) the word 'MEMEL' is 31 mm from the figure of value instead of 21 mm (*Price about 3 times normal*).

Nos. 82, 87, 89, 91, 94, 96, 98 and 100 exist with space 3½ mm (instead of 2 mm) between the figure of value and 'MARK' (*Prices from £4·00 to £65·00*). Nos. 82, 87 and 93 are also found with 6 mm spacing between 'MEMEL' and 'MARK' (*Price £7·75 each*).

(9) (10)

345

MEMEL / LITHUANIAN OCCUPATION

57	10c. on 400m. olive-brown ('10' as N) (12.5)	16·00	33·00
	a. '10' as O	47·00	90·00
	b. '10' as P	23·00	46·00
	c. '10' as Q	£160	£325
	d. '1' as O, '0' as N	20·00	39·00
	e. '1' as Q, '0' as O	31·00	65·00
58	30c. on 500m. purple ('30' as R) (28.5)	10·50	26·00
	a. '30' as S	16·00	39·00
	b. '3' as E, '0' as O	31·00	80·00
	c. '3' as G, '0' as N	31·00	80·00
59	1l. on 1000m. pale blue ('1' as T) (18.5)	33·00	90·00
	a. 'MARKW'	£160	£400
	b. '1' as U	50·00	£160
	c. '1' as V	60·00	£170
	d. '1' as W	65·00	£180
	e. '1' as X	80·00	£225
	f. '1' as Y	48·00	£140
	g. '1' as Z	£225	£450
	h. '1' as ZA	£225	£450

Nos. 51/9 were each surcharged in sheets of 100 comprising the following number of each variety in the sheet.
2c.— Nos. 51/52 38, Nos. 51a/52a 31, Nos. 51b/52b 17, Nos. 51c/52c 14
3c.— Nos. 53/54 38, Nos. 53a/54a 37, Nos. 53b/54b 16, Nos. 53c/54c 7, Nos. 53d/54d 2
5c.— No. 55 35, No. 55a 31, No. 55b 20, No. 55c 14 No. 56 72, No. 56a 28
10c.— No. 57 40, No. 57a 28, No. 57b 9, No. 57c 18, No. 57d 4, No. 57e 1
30c.— No. 58 72, No. 58a 4, No. 58b 4, No. 58c 20
1l.— No. 59 41, No. 59a 13, No. 59b 15, No. 59c 11, No. 59d 8, No. 59e 19, No. 59f. 6, No. 59g 1, No. 59h 1

The surcharges on Nos. 56 and 58 have the word 'CENT.' smaller.

1923 (May). Type **5** and **6** surch as T **13** ('CENT.'), but figures of surch bold, as in T **14** and **15**.

60	**5**	2c. on 10m.	9·75	£120
61		2c. on 20m.	33·00	£225
62		2c. on 50m.	11·50	£140
63		3c. on 10m.	26·00	£160
		a. Surch double	£250	£1000
64		3c. on 40m.	39·00	£350
65	**6**	5c. on 100m.	18·00	60·00
		a. Surch double	£180	£550
66		10c. on 400m.	£250	£1100
67	**5**	15c. on 25m.	£250	£1100
68	**6**	50c. on 1000m.	10·50	20·00
		a. 'MARKW'	£130	£450
		b. Surch double	£180	£550
69		1l. on 1000m.	13·00	39·00
		a. 'MARKW'	£225	£700
		b. Surch double	£180	£600

50   1
CENT.   LITAS
(14)   (15)

1923 (June). Type **7/9** Surch as T **14** or **15**.

70	**7**	15c. on 40m. olive-green	8·50	49·00
71		30c. on 50m. brown	8·50	38·00
		a. Surch double	£100	£425
72		30c. on 80m. green	8·50	60·00
73		30c. on 100m. scarlet	8·50	26·00
74	**8**	50c. on 200m. blue	8·50	49·00
75		50c. on 300m. brown	8·50	26·00
		a. Surch double	£100	£450
		b. Surch inverted	£100	£450
76		50c. on 400m. purple	8·50	46·00
		a. Surch inverted	£120	£500
77		50c. on 500m. orange	8·50	26·00
		a. Surch double	£100	£425
78		1l. on 600m. olive-green	8·50	55·00
79	**9**	1l. on 800m. blue	9·75	60·00
80		1l. on 1000m. purple	9·75	60·00
81		1l. on 2000m. scarlet	9·75	60·00
82		1l. on 3000m. green	9·75	60·00

Numerous forgeries of this set are known.

1923 (Nov). Nos. 2,4,5 and 8 further surch as T **16**. Narrow figures as illustration.

83	10c. on 25m. on 5c. (C.)	50·00	£200
	b. Thick broad figures	£600	£2000
84	15c. on 100m. on 25c. (G.)	65·00	£600
	a. Surch inverted	£650	£3750
	b. Thick broad figures	£1000	£3000
85	30c. on 400m. on 1l. (C.)	13·00	80·00
	b. Thick broad figures	£325	£1600
86	60c. on 50m. on 25c. (G.)	65·00	£500
	b. Thick broad figures	£400	£4250

Thick broad figures occur once in the sheet.

1923 (Dec). Type **7/8** surch as T **17**, in deep green. Narrow figures as illustration.

87	**7**	15c. on 50m. brown	£350	£3250
		b. Thick broad figures	£2000	£8000
88		25c. on 100m. scarlet	£140	£2000
		b. Thick broad figures	£1800	£5000
89	**8**	30c. on 300m. brown	£275	£2000
		b. Thick broad figures	£1600	£6000
90		60c. on 500m. orange	£170	£2000
		b. Thick broad figures	£1000	£4000

30   15
Centu   Centu
(18)   (19)

1923 (Dec). Type **5** and **6** surch as T **18** or **19** in 'Centu' or 'Centai'.

91	**18**	15c. on 10m. (G.)	46·00	£300
92		15c. on 20m. (G.)	5·25	50·00
93		15c. on 25m. (G.)	8·50	£100
94		15c. on 40m. (G.)	4·00	50·00
95		15c. on 50m. (R.)	4·50	39·00
		a. Surch inverted	£100	
96	**19**	15c. on 100m. (G.)	4·50	39·00
		a. Surch inverted	£100	
97		15c. on 400m. (G.)	4·00	33·00
98		15c. on 1000m. (R.)	£100	£800
		a. 'MARKW'	£650	£2750
		b. Surch inverted	£325	£1300
99	**18**	25c. on 10m. (G.)	18·00	£170
100		25c. on 20m. (G.)	4·50	50·00
101		25c. on 25m. (G.)	9·00	80·00
102		25c. on 25m. (G.)	7·75	80·00
		a. Surch inverted	£100	
103		25c. on 50m. (R.)	4·50	39·00
		a. Surch inverted	£100	
104	**19**	25c. on 100m. (G.)	4·00	39·00
105		25c. on 400m. (G.)	4·00	39·00
106		25c. on 1000m. (R.)	£100	£800
		a. 'MARKW'	£650	£3000
		b. Surch inverted	£325	£1300
107	**18**	30c. on 10m. (G.)	49·00	£325
108		30c. on 20m. (G.)	7·75	65·00
109		30c. on 25m. (G.)	9·00	£100
110		30c. on 40m. (G.)	6·50	39·00
		a. Surch in red		
111		30c. on 50m. (R.)	5·25	39·00
		a. Surch inverted	£100	
112	**19**	30c. on 100m. (G.)	5·25	39·00
		a. Surch inverted	£100	
113		30c. on 400m. (G.)	5·25	39·00
114		30c. on 1000m. (R.)	£100	£800
		a. 'MARKW'	£650	£3250
		b. Surch inverted	£325	£1300

A variety with tall '5' with straight top in the 15c. and 25c. surcharges is scarce.

By the Memel Statute of 8 May 1924, the Memel district became an autonomous region in Lithuania. It was returned to Germany on 22 March 1939; since 1945 it has been known as Klaipeda and is now part of Lithuania.

15   60
Centu   CENT.
(16)   (17)

Saar

1920–May 1921. 100 Pfennig = 1 Mark
May 1921–March 1935. 100 Centimes = 1 Franc
1935–1947. 100 Pfennig = 1 Reichsmark
1947. 100 Pfennig = 1 Saarmark
November 1947–July 1959. 100 Centimes = 1 Franc
From 1959. West German currency

I. LEAGUE OF NATIONS COMMISSION (1920–1935)

By the Treaty of Versailles, 28 June 1919, the Saar district of Germany was to be placed under the administration of a League of Nations Commission for 15 years, at the end of which its future was to be decided by plebiscite; during this period France was to have ownership of the coal mines in the Saar.

Sarre (1)   **Sarre** (1a)   **Sarre** (1b)

Sarre (2)

Three types of overprint Type 1:
T **1**. Large letters, without short control line beneath bar, 10.7 mm. long.
T **1a**. As T **1** but with short control line beneath bar.
T **1b**. Smaller letters, narrower spacing and with short control line beneath bar, 10.5 mm. long.

1920 (29 Jan–3 Mar). Stamps of Germany, 1905–1919, overprinted with Type **1** or Type **2** (No. 17) by Hofer Brothers, Saarbrücken.

1	24	2pf. yellowish-grey (31.1)	2·50	7·75
		a. Opt inverted	£500	£900
		b. Opt Type **1a** (28.2)	£250	£700
		c. Opt Type **1b** (3.3)	7·75	33·00
		ca. Opt double	£3250	£4250
2		2½pf. grey (5.2)	16·00	46·00
		a. Opt inverted	£600	£1000
		b. Opt Type **1a** (28.2)	£850	£1600
		c. Opt Type **1b** (1.3)	2·50	9·00
3	17	3pf. brown (7.2)	1·70	4·50
		a. Opt inverted	£500	£900
		b. Opt Type **1a** (28.2)	£275	£600
		c. Opt Type **1b** (1.3)	2·10	7·25
4		5pf. green	80	1·70
		b. Opt Type **1a** (28.2)	20·00	£100
		c. Opt Type **1b** (1.3)	80	1·60
		ca. Opt double	£1300	£2250
5	24	7½pf. orange	1·00	2·75
		b. Opt Type **1a** (28.2)	80·00	£275
		c. Opt Type **1b** (1.3)	7·75	39·00
6	17	10pf. rose-carmine	90	2·10
		a. Opt double	£1200	£2000
		c. Opt Type **1b** (1.3)	90	1·70
7	24	15pf. slate-violet	80	1·70
		a. Opt double	£1300	£2250
		c. Opt Type **1b** (1.3)	80	1·70
8	17	20pf. violet-blue	80	1·70
		a. Opt double	£1000	£1600
		c. Opt Type **1b** (1.3)	80	2·00
9		25pf. black and red/*yellow* (6.2)	16·00	33·00
		a. Opt inverted	£1300	£4000
		c. Opt Type **1b** (1.3)	£180	£550
10		30pf. black and orange/*buff* (5.2)	29·00	60·00
		c. Opt Type **1b** (1.3)	70·00	£170
11	24	35pf. red-brown (5.2)	90	2·10
		a. Opt inverted	£800	£1700
		c. Opt Type **1b** (1.3)	23·00	90·00
12	17	40pf. black and carmine (4.2)	90	2·10
		a. Opt inverted	£800	£1700
		b. Opt Type **1a** (28.2)	2·75	9·75
		c. Opt Type **1b** (1.3)	4·00	13·00
		ca. Opt inverted	£900	£1600
13		50pf. black and purple/*cream* (5.2)	90	1·70
		a. Opt inverted	£650	£1200
		b. Opt Type **1a** (28.2)	2·50	8·50
		c. Opt Type **1b** (1.3)	90	1·70
14		60pf. deep purple (9.2)	90	2·10
		a. On rose-purple	£475	£1300
		c. Opt Type **1b** (1.3)	80	1·70
15		75pf. black and blue-green (4.2)	80	2·00
		a. Opt inverted	£400	£650
		c. Opt Type **1b** (1.3)	1·00	2·00
16		80pf. black and bright carmine/*carmine* (9.2)	£300	£475
		c. Opt Type **1b** (1.3)	£325	£500
17	18	1m. carmine-red (26×17 perforation holes) (3.2)	£1700	£2500
		a. Opt double	£13000	
		b. 25×17 perforation holes	46·00	65·00
		ba. Opt double	£1700	£3000
		bb. Opt inverted	£1200	£2250
1/17		Set of 17 (*cheapest*)	£375	£600

A 3m. value was prepared but never issued.

SARRE (3)   **Sarre** (4)

1920 (1 Mar). Stamps of Bavaria optd with Type **3** (5pf. to 60pf.) as Type **3**, but larger (1m. to 3m.) or Type **4** (5, 10m.) by Hofer Brothers, Saarbrücken.

18	15	5pf. yellow-green	1·20	2·50
19		10pf. scarlet	1·20	2·50
19a		15pf. carmine	1·60	3·00
20		15pf. scarlet	11·50	31·00
21		20pf. blue	1·00	2·50
22		25pf. grey	18·00	26·00
23		30pf. orange	10·50	18·00
24		40pf. olive	17·00	26·00
25		50pf. chocolate	3·25	7·25
26		60pf. blue-green	5·25	13·00
27	16	1m. grey-brown	39·00	60·00
28		2m. deep violet	£100	£225
29		3m. scarlet	£200	£250
30	17	5m. Prussian blue	£1300	£1400
31		10m. green	£225	£425
18/31		Set of 15	£1700	£2250

The 2, 3, 7½pf. and 20m. values in this set also exist overprinted, but were not regularly issued (*Price* 2pf. £1400 *un*, £8000 *used*. 3pf. £130 *un*, £100 *used*. 7½pf. £50·00 *un*, £450 *used*. 20m. £195000 *un*.).

SAARGEBIET (5)   **SAARGEBIET** (6)

1920 (10 Apr–21 Oct). Stamps of Germany, 1905–1920, optd with Type **5** (18 *mm* long on 1.25 and 1.50m.) or **6** (2.50m.).

32	17	5pf. green	40	80
		a. Opt inverted	26·00	£250
33		5pf. red-brown (21.10)	80	1·30
34		10pf. bright carmine	40	80
		a. Opt inverted	80·00	£550
35		10pf. orange (21.10)	80	80
36	24	15pf. slate-violet	40	80
		a. Opt inverted	46·00	£400
37	17	20pf. violet-blue	40	80
		a. Opt inverted	60·00	
38		20pf. green (21.10)	1·60	80
39		30pf. black and orange/*buff*	65	80
40		30pf. dull blue (Pl II) (21.10)	90	1·20
41		40pf. black and carmine	50	80
42		40pf. carmine (Pl II) (21.10)	1·70	1·20
43		50pf. black and purple/*buff*	90	80
44		60pf. deep purple	1·00	80
		a. Opt inverted	£130	£500
45		75pf. black and blue-green	1·20	80
		a. Opt inverted	£180	
46	18	1m.25 green	4·50	2·00
		a. Opt inverted	£160	
47		1m.50 brown	3·25	2·00
		a. Opt inverted	£160	£1300
48	20	2m.50 claret	7·75	22·00
49	17	4m. carmine and black (21.10)	14·50	36·00
32/49		Set of 18	37·00	65·00

349

SAAR

Mark 10 Mark

(7)   (8)

1921 (4–5 Feb). No. 45 of Saar and No. 102 of Germany surch with Type **7** or as Type **8** respectively.

50	**17**	20 on 75pf. black and blue-green	65	2·00
		a. Opt inverted	39·00	£120
		b. Opt double	90·00	£225
51	**24**	5m. on 15pf. brown-purple (5.2)	9·00	26·00
52		10m. on 15pf. brown-purple (5.2)	9·75	31·00
50/52 Set of 3			17·00	55·00

9 Miner
10 Gothic Chapel, Mottlach
11 Colliery Shafthead
12 Burbach Steelworks
(13)

(Des A. Montader. Typo Vaugirard, Paris)

1921 (19 Feb–21 Apr). T **11** and similar horiz designs, **9**, **10** and **12**. P 12½.

53		5pf. violet and olive (19.3)	50	80
		a. Tête-bêche (vert pair)	5·75	33·00
		b. Tête-bêche (horiz pair)	£140	£500
		c. Centre inverted	£140	£500
54		10pf. orange and blue (23.3)	50	80
55		20pf. slate and green (22.3)	50	1·70
		a. Tête-bêche (vert pair)	10·50	65·00
		b. Tête-bêche (horiz pair)	21·00	£120
		c. Perf 10½	36·00	£375
		ca. Tête-bêche (vert pair)	£170	£1000
		cb. Tête-bêche (horiz pair)	£325	£1300
56		25pf. blue and brown (1.3)	65	1·30
		a. Tête-bêche (vert pair)	11·50	65·00
		b. Tête-bêche (horiz pair)	31·00	£160
57		30pf. brown and blue-green (21.2)	65	1·20
		a. Tête-bêche (vert pair)	20·00	£100
		b. Tête-bêche (horiz pair)	31·00	£160
		c. Error of colour. Brown and olive (20.2)	4·00	36·00
		ca. Tête-bêche (vert pair)	21·00	£120
		cb. Tête-bêche (horiz pair)	46·00	£225
58		40pf. scarlet	65	80
		a. Tête-bêche (vert pair)	31·00	£130
		b. Tête-bêche (horiz pair)	65·00	£250
59		50pf. black and grey (11.4)	1·60	6·50
60		60pf. brown and red (18.4)	2·50	5·75
61		80pf. blue (22 Mar)	1·20	1·70
		a. Tête-bêche (vert pair)	34·00	£180
		b. Tête-bêche (horiz pair)	85·00	£400
62		1m. black and red (5.4)	1·30	2·50
63		1m.25 green and brown (11.4)	1·60	3·25
64		2m. black and orange (18.4)	4·00	6·50
65		3m. sepia and brown (5.4)	5·25	16·00
		a. Centre inverted	£200	
66		5m. violet and yellow (18.4)	16·00	36·00
67		10m. brown and yellow-green (9.4)	20·00	39·00
68		25m. blue, black and red (21.4)	50·00	£130
53/68 Set of 16			95·00	£225

Designs:—5pf. Mill above Mettlach; 20pf. Pit-head, Reden; 25pf. River traffic, Saarbrücken; 30pf. R. Saar at Mettlach; 40pf. Slag-heap, Volklingen; 50pf. Signal-gantry, Saarbrücken; 80pf. 'Old Bridge', Saarbrücken; 1m. Wire-rope Railway; 2m. Town Hall, Saarbrücken; 3m. Pottery, Mettlach; 5m. St. Ludwigs Church; 10m. Chief Magistrate's and Saar Commissioner's Offices.

There were two inverted stamps in the sheets of 5, 20, 25, 30, 40 and 80pf.

For similar designs in French currency see Nos. 84/97.

1921 (30 Apr–May). French currency. 1921 Pictorials surch as T **13** (No. 83 surch '5 FRANKEN' and three bars). P 12½.

70		3c. on 20pf. slate and green (R.)	65	80
		a. Stamps and surch tête-bêche (vert pair)	7·75	50·00
		b. Stamps and surch tête-bêche (horiz pair)	10·50	65·00
		c. Perf 10½	7·75	£250
		ca. Stamps and surch tête-bêche (vert pair)	34·00	
		cb. Stamps and surch tête-bêche (horiz pair)	65·00	
71		5c. on 25pf. blue and brown (R.)	65	80
		a. Stamps and surch tête-bêche (vert pair)	£160	£650
		b. Stamps and surch tête-bêche (horiz pair)	£325	£1300
72		10c. on 30pf. brown and green (B.)	65	80
		a. Stamps and surch tête-bêche (vert pair)	7·75	42·00
		b. Stamps and surch tête-bêche (horiz pair)	10·50	65·00
73		15c. on 40pf. scarlet (Bk.)	80	80
		a. Stamps and surch tête-bêche (vert pair)	£160	£650
		b. Stamps and surch tête-bêche (horiz pair)	£225	£1100
		c. Surch inverted	£160	£800
74		20c. on 50pf. black and grey (R.)	65	80
		a. Perf 10½		
75		25c. on 60pf. brown and red (B.)	80	80
76		30c. on 80pf. blue (Bk.)	2·50	1·70
		a. Stamps and surch tête-bêche (vert pair)	21·00	£100
		b. Stamps and surch tête-bêche (horiz pair)	42·00	£200
		c. Surch inverted (5.21)	£225	£1000
77		40c. on 1m. black and red (B.)	3·25	80
78		50c. on 1m.25 green and brown (Bk.) (5.21)	5·25	1·70
		a. Perf 10½	£120	£225
79		75c. on 2m. black and orange (B.)	7·75	3·25
80		1f. on 3m. black and brown (B.)	7·75	4·00
81		2f. on 5m. violet and yellow (B.)	20·00	10·50
82		3f. on 10m. brown and yellow-green (Bk.)	29·00	42·00
83		5f. on 25m. blue, black and red (B.) (5.21)	29·00	60·00
70/83 Set of 14			£100	£120

No. 73b occurs in the same sheet as normal surcharges.

1922 (1 Mar–Dec). Type **9**, etc. (typo), redrawn, larger size (except T **12** (5f.), slightly smaller). Values in French currency. Designs similar to 1921 issue as noted below. P 12½×13½, 13½×12½ (Nos. 85 and 96) or 12 (No. 97).

84		3c. olive-green (as 1m.) (4.22)	65	1·00
85		5c. black and orange (as 10pf.)	65	65
86		10c. green (as 80pf.)	65	65
87		15c. brown (as 1m.)	2·00	65
88		20c. blue and yellow (as 2m.) (12.22)	22·00	65
89		25c. red and yellow (as 2m.) (4.22)	9·50	3·75
90		30c. carmine and yellow (as 40pf.) (5.22)	3·25	3·50
91		40c. brown and yellow (as 3m.) (5.22)	2·30	65
92		50c. deep blue and yellow (as 25pf.) (5.22)	1·60	65
93		75c. green and yellow (as 3m.) (5.22)	22·00	39·00
94		1f. red-brown (as 5m.) (5.22)	4·00	1·30
95		2f. violet (as 1m.25) (5.22)	9·00	5·25
96		3f. myrtle and orange (as 60pf.) (5.22)	39·00	10·50
97		5f. red-brown and chocolate (as 25m.) (7.22)	39·00	70·00
84/97 Set of 14			£140	£120

Nos. 84/97 are also known imperforate.

See also Nos. 98/101.

14 Madonna of Blieskastel

Two types of opt for 25c. and 1f.

I. Small opening to 'A'. Middle bar of first 'E' nearer to top.
II. Wide opening to 'A'. Bar of 'E' central.

1922 (1 June)–**24**. OFFICIAL. Nos. 84/94 optd with T O **14**.

O98		3c. olive-green (R.)	1·60	60·00
O99		5c. black and orange (R.)	65	65
O100		10c. green (R.)	65	50
O101		15c. brown (B.)	65	50
O102		20c. blue and yellow (R.)	65	50
O103		25c. red and yellow (I) (B.)	6·50	2·00
O104		30c. carmine and yellow (B.)	65	50
O105		40c. brown and yellow (B.)	90	50
O106		50c. deep blue and yellow (R.)	90	50
O107		75c. green and yellow (R.)	39·00	46·00
O108		1f. red-brown (I) (B.)	80·00	26·00
		a. Type II (1924)	20·00	4·00
O98/O108a Set of 11 (cheapest)			65·00	£100

1923 (Sept–Oct). As Nos. 87/89 and 93 but colours changed.

98	15c. orange	4·00	65
99	20c. turquoise-blue and yellow (10.23)	6·50	65
100	25c. carmine and yellow (10.23)	4·00	65
101	75c. blackish green and yellow (10.23)	50·00	5·25
98/101	Set of 4	60·00	6·50

1923 (Nov)–**24**. OFFICIAL. Nos. 98/101 optd with T O **14**.

O109	15c. orange (B.)	4·00	80
O110	20c. turquoise-blue and yellow (R.)	4·00	80
O111	25c. carmine and yellow (I) (B.)	4·00	80
	a. Type II (1924)	26·00	4·00
O112	75c. blackish green and yellow (R.)	7·75	4·00
O109/O112	Set of 4	18·00	5·75

(Des H. Wagner. Photo Vaugirard)

1925 (9 Apr). P 13½×12½ (45c.) or 12 (10f.).

102	**14**	45c. plum (23×27 *mm*)	4·50	8·50
103		10f. brown (31×36 *mm*)	26·00	39·00

> **PRINTERS.** All the following issues until 1934 were printed in photogravure by Vaugirard, Paris.

15 Army Medical Service

16 Maternity Nursing Service

1926 (25 Oct). Welfare Fund. P 13½.

104	**15**	20c. +20c. blackish olive	13·00	33·00
105		40c. +40c. sepia	13·00	33·00
106		50c. +50c. red-orange	13·00	33·00
107	**16**	1f.50 +1f.50 blue	31·00	80·00
104/107		Set of 4	65·00	£160

Designs: As T **15**—40c. Hospital Work (Nurse and patient); 50c. Child Welfare (Children at a spring).

17 Fountain, St. Johann, Saarbrücken

18 Tholey Abbey

1926 (26 Dec)–**32**. T **17**, **18** and similar types. P 13½.

108	10c. brown (15.1.27)	1·20	80
109	15c. deep myrtle (15.1.27)	65	1·70
110	20c. orange-brown	65	80
111	25c. greenish blue (15.1.27)	1·20	80
112	30c. green (15.1.27)	1·60	80
113	40c. sepia (15.1.27)	1·20	80
114	50c. deep lake (15.1.27)	1·60	80
114*a*	60c. orange (15.4.30)	6·50	90
115	75c. maroon (15.1.27)	1·20	80
116	80c. orange (15.1.27)	4·00	14·50
116*a*	90c. carmine-red (20.4.32)	20·00	29·00
117	1f. violet (15.1.27)	4·00	80
118	1f.50 blue (15.1.27)	9·75	80
119	2f. brown-lake (15.1.27)	10·50	80
120	3f. deep olive (15.1.27)	22·00	2·10
121	5f. deep brown (15.1.27)	23·00	11·50
108/121	Set of 16	£100	60·00

Designs: Vert—10c., 30c. T **17**. Horiz—15c., 75c. Saar Valley near Güdingen; 20c., 40c., 90c. View from Saarlouis fortifications; 25c., 50c. T **18**; 60c., 80c., 1f. Colliery shafthead; 1f.50, 2f., 3f., 5f. Burbach Steelworks.

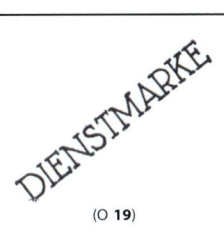

(O **19**)

19 Breguet 14 Biplane over Saarbrücken

1927 (Jan)–**34**. OFFICIAL. Stamps of 1926–1932 optd with T O **19**.

(a) Angle of 32° and extending to frame of stamp (inverted on 30c)

O122	30c. green (C.)	9·00	1·30
O123	40c. sepia (Verm.)	9·00	1·30
O124	50c. deep lake (B.)	33·00	1·30
O125	75c. maroon (C.)	10·50	1·30
O126	1f. violet (R.)	9·00	1·30
O127	2f. brown-lake (B.)	23·00	2·50
O122/O127	Set of 6	85·00	8·00

(b) Angle of 23° to 25° not touching frame (inverted on 10c. and 30c.) (1929–1934)

O128	10c. brown (B.) (1934)	3·25	4·00
O129	15c. deep myrtle (B.) (1934)	3·25	10·50
O130	20c. orange-brown (B.) (1931)	3·25	2·50
O131	25c. deep. blue (B.) (1934)	4·00	10·50
O132	30c. green (R.)	3·25	80
O133	40c. sepia (R.)	3·25	50
O134	50c. deep lake (B.)	6·50	65
O135	60c. orange (Blk.) (1930)	2·00	50
O136	75c. maroon (Verm.)	4·00	1·30
O137	1f. violet (Verm.)	4·00	65
O138	2f. brown-lake (B.)	4·00	65
O128/O138	Set of 11	37·00	29·00

1927 (1 Oct). Welfare Fund. Nos. 104/107 optd '1927–1928'.

122	20c. +20c. blackish olive	21·00	55·00
123	40c. +40c. sepia	21·00	55·00
124	50c. +50c. red-orange	18·00	49·00
125	1f.50 +1f.50 blue	29·00	£120
122/125	Set of 4	80·00	£250

1928 (20 Sept). AIR. P 13½.

126	**19**	50c. brown-lake	6·50	6·50
127		1f. violet	10·50	7·75

20 The blind beggar, by Dyckmanns

21 Charity, by Raphael

(24)

1928 (23 Dec). Christmas Charity. P 13½.

128	**20**	40c. (+40c.) sepia	20·00	£120
129		50c. (1+50c.) claret	20·00	£120
130		1f. (+1f.) violet	20·00	£120
131	–	1f.50 (+1f.50) greenish blue	20·00	£120
132	–	2f. (+2f.) brown-lake	23·00	£170
133	–	3f. (+3f.) olive-green	23·00	£225
134	**21**	10f. (+10f.) chocolate	£600	£6500
128/134		Set of 7	£650	£6500

Design: As T **20**—1f.50 to 3f. *Almsgiving* by Schiestl. See also Nos. 135/141, 143/149 and 150/156.

1929 (23 Dec). Christmas Charity. Paintings as T **20**. P 13½.

135	40c. (+15c.) green	3·25	9·00
	a. 'SAARGEBIFT'	31·00	£100
136	50c. (+20c.) brown-vermilion	6·50	16·00
137	1f. (+50c.) plum	6·50	18·00
138	1f.50 (+75c.) greenish blue	6·50	18·00
139	2f. (+1f.) lake	6·50	18·00
140	3f. (+2f.) deep green	13·00	42·00
141	10f. (+8f.) sepia	80·00	£225
135/141	Set of 7	£110	£300

Paintings:—40c. to 1f. *Orphaned* by H. Kaulbach; 1f.50 to 3f. *St. Ottilia* by M. Feuerstein; 10f. *The Little Madonna* by Ferruzzio.

1930 (28 Mar)–**34**. Nos. 114 and 116 surch as T **24**.

141*a*	40c. on 50c. deep lake (1.11.34)	2·50	2·50
142	60c. on 80c. orange	3·25	4·00

SAAR

1931 (20 Jan). Christmas Charity. Paintings as T **20**. P 13½.

143	40c. (+15c.) chestnut	13·00	39·00
144	60c. (+20c.) vermilion	13·00	39·00
145	1f. (+50c.) lake	13·00	80·00
146	1f.50 (+75c.) greenish blue	20·00	80·00
147	2f. (+1f.) chocolate	20·00	80·00
148	3f. (+2f.) green	33·00	80·00
149	10f. (+10f.) red-brown	£160	£475
143/149	Set of 7	£250	£750

Paintings:—40c. 60c. 1f.50. *The Safetyman* (miner and lamp) by F. Zolnhofer; 1f., 2f., 3f. *The Good Samaritan* by J. Heinemann; 10f. *At the Window* by F. G. Waldmüller.

1931 (23 Dec). Christmas Charity. Paintings as T **20**. P 13½.

150	40c. (+15c.) sepia	21·00	60·00
151	60c. (+20c.) vermilion	21·00	60·00
152	1f. (+50c.) claret	26·00	90·00
153	1f.50 (+75c.) blue	31·00	90·00
154	2f. (+1f.) lake	36·00	90·00
155	3f. (+2f.) blackish green	46·00	£160
156	5f. (+5f.) red-brown	£160	£500
150/156	Set of 7	£300	£950

Paintings:—40c. to 1f. *St. Martin* by F. Boehle: 1f.50 to 3f. *Charity* by Ridgway-Knight; 5f. *The Widow's Mite* by Dubufe.

29 Focke Wulf A-17 Möwe over Saarbrücken Airport

30 Kirkel Castle Ruins

1932 (20 Apr). AIR. P 13½.

157	**29** 60c. orange-vermilion	10·50	7·75
158	5f. brown	70·00	£160

1932 (20 Dec). Christmas Charity. Views as T **30**. P 13½.

159	40c. (+15c.) sepia	16·00	36·00
160	60c. (+20c.) vermilion	16·00	36·00
161	1f. (+50c.) purple	23·00	65·00
162	1f.50 (+75c.) blue	33·00	80·00
163	2f. (+1f.) lake	33·00	90·00
164	3f. (+2f.) blackish green	90·00	£275
165	5f. (+5f.) red-brown	£200	£475
159/165	Set of 7	£375	£950

Designs: Vert—40c. T **30**; 60c. Blieskastel Church; 1f. Ottweiier Church; 1f.50, St. Michael's Church, Saarbrücken; 2f. Cathedral and fountain, St. Wendel; 3f. St. John's Church, Saarbrücken. Horiz—5f. Kerpen Castle, Illingen.

32 Scene of the Disaster

33 'Love'

(Des J. Lempereur)

1933 (1 June). Neunkirchen Explosion Disaster. P 13½.

166	**32** 60c. (+60c.) vermilion	26·00	33·00
167	3f. (+3f.) blackish green	60·00	£120
168	5f. (+5f.) red-brown	60·00	£120
166/168	Set of 3	£130	£250

1934 (15 Mar). Christmas Charity. Designs as T **33**. P 13½.

169	40c. (+15c.) sepia	9·00	26·00
170	60c. (+20c.) vermilion	9·00	26·00
171	1f. (+50c.) mauve	11·50	36·00
172	1f.50 (+75c.) blue	23·00	60·00
173	2f. (+1f.) lake	21·00	60·00
174	3f. (+2f.) blackish green	23·00	60·00
175	5f. (+5f.) red-brown	50·00	£140
169/175	Set of 7	£130	£375

Designs:—(Nos. 169/174 from statues by C. L. Pozzi in the church of St. Louis and St. Arnual Abbey, Saarbrücken): 60c. *Solicitude*; 1f. *Peace*; 1f.50 *Consolation*; 2f. *Welfare*; 3f. *Truth* 5f. *Countess Elisabeth von Nassau-Suarbrücken*.

VOLKSABSTIMMUNG 1935

(**35**)

1934 (1 Nov). Saar Plebiscite. Optd as T **35**, in same colours as stamps. Opt reads vertically upwards on 10c. and 30c.

(a) POSTAGE. Nos. 108/115, 116a/121 and 103

176	10c. brown	65	90
177	15c. deep myrtle	65	90
178	20c. orange-brown	1·00	2·20
179	25c. deep blue	1·00	2·20
180	30c. green	65	90
181	40c. sepia	65	1·20
182	50c. deep lake	1·20	2·20
183	60c. orange	65	90
184	75c. maroon	1·20	2·20
185	90c. carmine-red	1·20	2·30
186	1f. violet	1·20	2·50
187	1f.50 blue	2·10	5·25
188	2f. brown-lake	3·25	7·75
189	3f. deep olive	7·75	16·00
190	5f. deep brown	33·00	50·00
191	10f. brown	39·00	£100
176/191	Set of 16	85·00	£180

(b) AIR. Nos. 126/127 and 157/158

192	50c. brown-lake	6·50	11·50
193	60c. orange-vermilion	5·25	4·50
194	1f. violet	11·50	16·00
195	5f. brown	16·00	23·00
192/195	Set of 4	35·00	50·00

1934 (1 Dec). Christmas Charity. Saar Plebiscite. Nos. 169/175 optd vertically upwards as T **35** in same colours as stamps.

196	40c. (+15c.) sepia	5·75	23·00
197	60c. (+20c.) vermilion	5·75	23·00
198	1f. (+50c.) mauve	18·00	42·00
199	1f.50 (+75c.) blue	11·50	42·00
200	2f. (+1f.) lake	18·00	60·00
201	3f. (+2f.) blackish green	17·00	50·00
202	5f. (+5f.) red-brown	25·00	65·00
196/202	Set of 7	90·00	£275

II. RETURN TO GERMANY

After the plebiscite the Saar returned to Germany on 1 March 1935 and German stamps were used from then until 1945. The Saar was then placed under French occupation, and the general issue for the French Zone (Germany Nos. F1/F13) was used until the following special issues were made.

III. FRENCH OCCUPATION

36 Coal-miner

37 Loop of the Saar

(Des V. K. Jonynas. Photo F. Burda, Offenburg)

1947 (Jan–Mar). T **36/37** and similar designs. Yellowish paper. Brownish gum. Wmk Wavy Lines (12, 45, 75pf.) or no wmk (others). P 14.

203	2pf. grey	45	65
204	3pf. yellow-orange	45	80
205	6pf. blue-green	45	65
206	8pf. carmine	45	50
207	10pf. mauve	45	65
208	12pf. olive-green	45	65
209	15pf. brown	45	10·50
210	16pf. ultramarine	45	65
211	20pf. lake (20.1)	45	65
212	24pf. red-brown	45	65
213	25pf. magenta	90	36·00
214	30pf. yellow-green	45	1·30
215	40pf. violet	45	2·00
216	45pf. carmine	1·00	26·00
217	50pf. slate-violet	1·00	36·00
218	60pf. violet	90	36·00
219	75pf. greenish blue (20.1)	45	65
220	80pf. brown-orange	45	65
221	84pf. brown	45	65
222	1m. green	45	80
203/222	Set of 20	10·00	£140

Designs: As T **36**—2pf. to 12pf. Coal-miner; 15pf. to 24pf. Steelworkers; 25pf. to 50pf. Sugar Beet Harvesters; 60pf. to 80pf. Mettlach Abbey, 1m. T **37**. As T **37**: Vert—84pf. Marshal Ney.

For the short-lived introduction of the Saarmark, a second printing was prepared in November 1947 with slight differences in the designs and the 1m. value expressed as '1 SM'. Of these only the 12, 15 and 24pf. were issued to a few post offices but they were not valid for use after 27 November when the French currency was restored. They were used for the provisional surcharges, Nos. 223/235B and a few unsurcharged copies exist as a result of sheets sticking together and failing to receive the surcharge, and these usually have an albino surcharge. They differ from the original printing also through being on white paper with white gum.

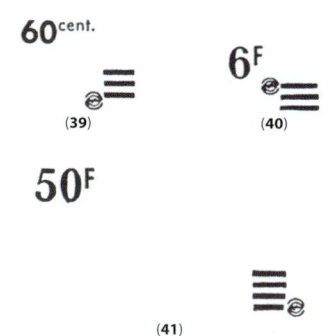

60^{cent.} **6**^F

(39)   (40)

50^F

(41)

(Surch by Malstatt-Burbacher Printing Works)

1947 (17 Nov). Change to French currency. Surch as T **39/41**.

A. Nos. 203, etc. on yellowish paper with brownish gum

223A	10c. on 2pf. grey		£140	£600
	a. Surch inverted		£850	£3250
224A	60c. on 3pf. yellow-orange		£130	£1400
	a. Surch inverted		£700	£2250
225A	1f. on 10pf. mauve		13·00	29·00
	a. Surch inverted		£450	£2500
226A	2f. on 12pf. olive-green		2·50	3·25
	a. Surch inverted		£850	£3250
227A	3f. on 15pf. brown		£1200	£4000
228A	4f. on 16pf. ultramarine		26·00	£200
	a. Surch inverted		£850	£2250
229A	5f. on 20pf. lake		£500	£7500
	a. Surch inverted		£1000	£10000
230A	6f. on 24pf. red-brown		1·30	7·75
	a. Surch inverted		£1800	£6000
231A	9f. on 30pf. yellow-green		£140	£1400
	a. Surch inverted		£325	£1400
232A	10f. on 50pf. slate-violet		£2000	£8000
233A	14f. on 60pf. violet		£275	£1600
234A	20f. on 84pf. brown		8·50	13·00
235A	50f. on 1m. on 1Sm. green		£225	£550
	a. Surch inverted		£700	£2250
223A/235A	Set of 13		£4250	£23000

B. November printing. White paper with white gum (see note below No. 222)

223B	10c. on 2pf. grey		40	90
	a. Surch inverted		65·00	£1000
224B	60c. on 3pf. yellow-orange		40	1·80
	a. Surch inverted		39·00	£1000
225B	1f. on 10pf. mauve		40	90
226B	2f. on 12pf. olive-green		1·00	2·50
	a. Surch inverted		90·00	£1000
227B	3f. on 15pf. brown		50	2·30
	a. Surch inverted		£325	£1400
228B	4f. on 16pf. ultramarine		50	13·00
	a. Surch inverted		£120	£1200
229B	5f. on 20pf. lake		50	1·70
	a. Surch inverted		50·00	£1000
230B	6f. on 24pf. red-brown		50	1·00
	a. Surch inverted		£1700	£5000
231B	9f. on 30pf. yellow-green		65	1·80
	a. Surch inverted		£225	£2500
232B	10f. on 50pf. slate-violet		65	34·00
	a. Surch inverted		£650	£3750
233B	14f. on 60pf. violet		1·00	22·00
234B	20f. on 84pf. brown		2·30	35·00
	a. Surch inverted		£130	£1300
235B	50f. on 1m. on 1Sm. green		2·30	35·00
	a. Surch inverted		£140	£650
223B/235B	Set of 13		10·00	£150

Double surcharges and many other errors and varieties exist on this issue.

> **PRINTERS.** From 1948 to 1956 recess-printed stamps were printed at the Mint, Paris, and those in photogravure by Vaugirard, Paris, *unless otherwise stated.*

42 Clasped Hands

43 Builders

44 Saar Valley

46 Floods in St. Johann, Saarbrücken

(Des Decaris. Eng Dufresne (10c. to 1f.), Piel (2f., 3f.), Mazèlin (4f., 5f.), Cottet (6f., 9f., 25f. to 200f.), Decaris (10f. to 50f.). Recess.)

1948 (1 Apr). Various designs.

*(a) POSTAGE. As T **42**. P 14×13*

236	42	10c. brown-red	1·20	3·25
237		60c. greenish blue	1·20	3·25
238		1f. black	50	50
239	–	2f. carmine	65	50
240	–	3f. sepia	65	50
241		4f. scarlet	65	50
242	–	5f. violet	65	50
243		6f. brown-red	1·20	50
244		9f. brown-red	7·75	80

Designs:—2f., 3f. Man's head; 4f., 5f. Woman's head; 6f., 9f. Miner's head.

*(b) POSTAGE. As T **43**. P 13*

245	–	10f. blue	4·50	1·30
246	–	14f. purple	6·50	1·80
247	43	20f. brown-red	13·00	1·80
248	–	50f. grey-blue	22·00	4·50

Designs:—10f. Blast-furnace chimney; 14f. Foundry; 50f. Façade of Mettlach Abbey.

(c) AIR. P 13

249	44	25f. scarlet	7·75	5·25
250		50f. greenish blue	4·50	4·00
251		200f. carmine	46·00	60·00
236/251	Set of 16		£110	80·00

1948 (12 Oct). Flood Disaster Relief Fund. Flood scenes as T **46**, inscr 'HOCHWASSER HILFE 1947–48'. Photo. P 13½.

(a) POSTAGE

252	5f. +5f. yellow-green	7·50	60·00
253	6f. +4f. purple	7·50	50·00
254	12f. +8f. scarlet	11·00	80·00
255	18f. +12f. blue	14·50	80·00
252/255	Set of 4	36·00	£250
MS255a	147×104 mm. Nos. 252/255 imperf	£1300	£4500

(b) AIR. Inscr 'LUFTPOST'

256	25f. +25f. sepia	39·00	£400
MS256a	90×60 mm. No. 256	£800	£3000

Designs: Horiz—5f. Flooded industrial area; 12f. Landtag building, Saarbrücken; 25f. Floods at Ensdorf, Saarlouis. Vert—6f. T**46**; 18f. Flooded street, Saarbrücken.

47 Map of Saarland

48 Hikers and Ludweiler Hostel

1948 (15 Dec). First Anniv of Constitution. Photo. P 13½.

257	47	10f. brown-red	3·50	6·50
258		25f. deep blue	5·00	13·00

1949 (11 Jan). Youth Hostels Fund. T **48** and similar type. Photo. P 13½.

259	8f. +7f. brown	5·75	£170
260	10f. +7f. green	7·25	£170

Designs:—8ft. T**48**; 10f. Hikers and Weisskirchen hostel.

SAAR

49 Chemical Research
50 Mare and Foal 
O **51** Arms 

(Des Mees. Photo)

1949 (2 Apr). Saar University. P 13.
| 261 | **49** | 15f. carmine | 11·50 | 80 |

(Des Beutin. Photo)

1949 (25 Sept). Horse Day, 1949. T **50** and similar type inscr 'TAG DES PFERDES 1949'. P 13½.
| 262 | | 5f. +5f. brown-red | 20·00 | 50·00 |
| 263 | | 25f. +15f. blue | 26·00 | 60·00 |

Designs:—15f. T **50**; 25f. Two horses in steeple-chase.

(Des Mees. Eng Cortot. Recess)

1949 (1 Oct). OFFICAL. P 14×13.
O264	O **51**	10c. deep carmine	80	31·00
O265		30c. greenish black	80	36·00
O266		1f. blue-green	80	1·70
O267		2f. vermilion	3·25	2·00
O268		5f. blue	4·00	1·70
O269		10f. black	1·70	1·70
O270		12f. magenta	14·50	18·00
O271		15f. deep blue	1·70	1·70
O272		20f. green	5·25	2·00
O273		30f. mauve	15·00	7·75
O274		50f. purple	4·50	6·50
O275		100f. red-brown	£150	£500
O264/O275	Set of 12		£180	£550

51 Symbolic of Typography
52 Labourer and Foundry 
53 Detail from *Moses Striking the Rock* after Murillo 

(Des Winter (10c., 5f., 30f., 60f., 100f.); F. Tschersovsky (60c., 1f., 3f.); Schmidt (10f.); Mees (6f., 8f., 12f., 15f., 18f., 45f.); Schnei (20f., 25f.). Photo)

1949–51. Various designs. P 13×13½.

*(a) As T **51***
264		10c. brown-purple (30.11.49)	50	3·25
265		60c. black (27.4.51)	50	3·25
266		1f. brown-red (30.11.49)	2·00	50
267		3f. deep brown (16.6.51)	13·00	65
268		5f. violet (3.4.50)	3·25	50
269		6f. green (16.6.51)	17·00	65
270		8f. olive (15.2.51)	2·00	1·00
271		10f. brown-orange (3.4.50)	7·75	50
272		12f. deep green (30.11.49)	23·00	50
273		15f. scarlet (3.4.50)	11·50	50
274		18f. magenta (16.6.51)	4·50	8·50

*(b) As T **52***
275		20f. greenish grey (28.4.50)	3·25	50
276		25f. blue (30.11.49)	33·00	50
277		30f. brown-lake (15.2.51)	29·00	80
278		45f. purple (15.2.51)	7·75	90
279		60f. olive-green (16.6.51)	13·00	3·25
280		100f. sepia (30.11.49)	17·00	4·00
264/280	Set of 17		£170	27·00

Designs: As T **51**—10c. Building trade; 60c. Beethoven; 1 and 3f. Heavy Industries; 5f. Slag heap; 6f. and 15f. Colliery; 8f. Posthorn and Telephone; 10f. T **51**; 12f. and 18f. Pottery. As T **52**; 25f. Blast furnace worker; 60f. Landsweiler; 100f. Wiebelskirchen. (Horiz)—30f. St. Arnual; 45f. 'Giant's Boot', Rentrisch.

1949 (20 Dec). National Relief Fund. T **53** and similar paintings. Recess. P 13.
281		8f. +2f. slate-blue	13·00	65·00
282		12f. +3f. yellowish green	16·00	80·00
283		15f. +5f. claret	23·00	£130
284		25f. +10f. blue	39·00	£200
285		50f. +20f. brown-purple	60·00	£375
281/285	Set of 5		£140	£750

Paintings:—8f. T **53**; 12f. *Our Lord healing the Paralytic* (Murillo); 15f. *The Sick Child* (Metsu); 25f. *St. Thomas of Villanueva* (Murillo); 50f. *Madonna of Blieskastel*.

54 Adolf Kolping
55 Peter Wust 

1950 (3 Apr). Honouring Adolf Kolping (miners' padre). Photo. P 12×12½.
| 286 | **54** | 15f. +5f. lake | 42·00 | £130 |
| | | a. Error. 'GFSELLEN' | | |

1950 (3 Apr). Death Centenary of Peter Wust (philosopher). Photo. P 13×13½.
| 287 | **55** | 15f. carmine-lake | 21·00 | 12·50 |

56 Mail Coach

(Des H. Cheffér. Eng F. Tschersovsky. Recess)

1950 (22 Apr). Stamp Day. P 13.
| 288 | **56** | 15f. +5f. purple-brown and brown-red | £120 | £180 |

57 'Food for the Hungry'
58 St. Peter 
59 Town Hall, Ottweiler 

(Des. L. Schmidt. Recess)

1950 (28 Apr). Red Cross Fund. Cross in red. P 13.
| 289 | **57** | 25f. +10f. brown-lake | 44·00 | £100 |

(Des and eng R. Serres. Recess)

1950 (29 June). Holy Year. P 13.
290	**58**	12f. yellow-green	5·25	17·00
291		15f. brown-red	7·75	16·00
292		25f. blue	13·00	34·00
290/292	Set of 3		23·00	60·00

1950 (10 July). 400th Anniv of Ottweiler. Photo. P 13×13½.
| 293 | **59** | 10f. yellow-brown | 10·50 | 13·00 |

61
62 St. Lutwinus enters Monastery 

(Des F. Tschersovsky. Photo)

1950 (8 Aug). Admission to the Council of Europe T **61** and similar design. P 13½×13.

(a) POSTAGE
| 294 | **61** | 25f. blue | 60·00 | 20·00 |

SAAR

(b) AIR. Inscr 'LUFTPOST'

| 295 | 200f. brown lake | £225 | £400 |

Design: Horiz—200f. as T **61** but with a dove in flight over book.

(Eng R. Serres (8f., 50f.), Dufresne (12f.) and P. Munier (15f., 25f.). Recess)

1950 (10 Nov). National Relief Fund. T **62** and similar designs. P 13.
296	8f. +2f. brown	16·00	50·00
297	12f. +3f. green	14·50	50·00
298	15f. +5f. red-brown	20·00	85·00
299	25f. +10f. blue	21·00	£120
300	50f. +20f. claret	31·00	£200
296/300	Set of 5	90·00	£450

Designs:—12f. Lutwinus builds Mettlach Abbey; 15f. Lutwinus as Abbot of Monastery; 25f. Bishop Lutwinus confirming children at Rheims; 50f. Lutwinus succours the sick and needy.

63 Orphans **64** Mail-carriers, 1760

(Des F. L. Schmidt. Eng J. Piel. Recess)

1951 (28 Apr). Red Cross Fund. Cross in red. P 13.
| 301 | **63** | 25f. +10f. deep green | 31·00 | £100 |

(Des Mees. Eng Cheffér. Recess)

1951 (29 Apr). Stamp Day. P 13.
| 302 | **64** | 15f. brown-purple | 15·00 | 31·00 |

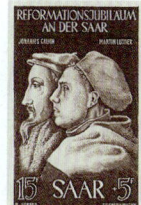

65 Allegory **66** Flowers and Building **67** Calvin and Luther

(Des F. Tschersovsky Photo)

1951 (12 May). Saar Fair. P 13½.
| 303 | **65** | 15f. blue-green | 5·00 | 11·00 |

(Des Mazèlin. Eng Blum. Recess)

1951 (16 June). Horticultural Show, Bexbach. P 13.
| 304 | **66** | 15f. | 5·00 | 2·75 |

(Des R. Serres. Eng F. Tschersovsky. Recess)

1951 (31 Oct). 375th Anniv of Reformation in Saar. P 13.
| 305 | **67** | 15f. +5f. purple-brown | 6·25 | 12·50 |

68 *The Good Mother* (Lepicié) **69** Mounted Postman

(Des Mees. Eng Sander (15f., 30f.), H. Cheffér (others). Recess)

1951 (3 Nov). National Relief Fund. Vert designs showing paintings as T **68**. P 13.
306	12f. +3f. green	10·50	31·00
307	15f. +5f. violet	13·00	31·00
308	18f. +7f. brown-lake	11·50	31·00
309	30f. +10f. blue	20·00	60·00
310	50f. +20f. purple-brown	33·00	£120
306/310	Set of 5	80·00	£250

Paintings:—15f. *Outside the Theatre* (Kampf); 18f. *Sisters of Charity* (Browne); 30f. *The Good Samaritan* (Bassano); 50f. *St. Martin and the Poor* (Van Dyck).

(Des F. Tschersovsky Eng H. Cheffér. Recess)

1952 (29 Mar). Stamp Day. P 13.
| 311 | **69** | 30f. +10f. deep blue | 20·00 | 46·00 |

70 Athlete bearing Olympic Flame **71** Globe and Emblem **72** Red Cross and Refugees

(Des F. Tschersovsky (15f.), Gandon (30f.). Eng J Piel (15f.), H. Blum (30f.). Recess)

1952 (29 Mar). 15th Olympic Games, Helsinki. T **70** and similar vert design. P 13.
| 312 | 15f. +5f. deep green | 9·75 | 20·00 |
| 313 | 30f. +5f. deep blue | 9·75 | 22·00 |

Designs:—15f. T **70**; 30f. Hand, laurels and globe.

(Des Bur. Eng J. Piel. Recess)

1952 (26 Apr). Saar Fair. P 13.
| 314 | **71** | 15f. brown-lake | 4·00 | 2·20 |

(Des Hossfeld. Eng P. Munier. Recess)

1952 (2 May). Red Cross Week. P 13.
| 315 | **72** | 15f. scarlet | 5·75 | 2·20 |

73 GPO Saarbrücken **74** *Count Stroganov as a Boy* (Greuze)

(Des Kratz (1f., 15f.), Mees (2f., 30f.), Frantzen (3f., 18f., 500f.), Geiss (5f., 12f.), Grittmann (6f.). Eng Mazèlin (1f., 3f., 15f., 18f.), Dufresne (2f., 500f.), Barlangue (5f., 12f., 30f.), Munier (6f.). Recess)

1952–55. T **73** and similar views. (I) Without inscr in or below design. (II) With inscr. P 13.
316	1f. deep bluish green (II) (23.3.53)	40	40
317	2f. reddish violet (23.3.53)	40	40
318	3f. carmine-lake (3.5.53)	40	40
319	5f. deep turquoise-green (I) (1.10.52)	7·75	40
320	5f. deep turquoise-green (II) (3.54)	40	40
321	6f. maroon (1.8.53)	65	40
322	10f. deep olive-brown (19.12.53)	65	40
323	12f. emerald (II) (12.3.53)	1·20	40
324	15f. black-brown (I) (1.10.52)	13·00	40
325	15f. black-brown (II) 11.53)	5·75	40
326	15f. carmine-red (II) (10.1.55)	50	40
327	18f. brown-purple (18.3.55)	4·50	7·75
329	30f. deep bright blue (3.5.53)	1·60	1·60
334	500f. brown-lake (1.8.53)	26·00	£100
316/334	Set of 14	55·00	£100

Designs: Horiz—1f., 15f. (×3), Colliery shafthead; 2f., 10f. Ludwigs High School, Saarbrücken; 3f., 18f. Gersweiler Bridge; 5f. (×2), 12f. as T **73**; 6f. Mettlach Bridge; 30f. Saarbrücken University Library. Vert—500f. St. Ludwigs Church, Saarbrücken.

(Des and eng J. Piel (15f.), Cheffér (18f.); Gandon (30f.). Recess)

1952 (3 Nov). National Relief Fund. Vert designs as T **74**. P 13.
335	15f. +5f. purple-brown	5·25	18·00
336	18f. +7f. lake	7·75	23·00
337	30f. +10f. blue	10·50	26·00

SAAR

335/337 Set of 3.. 21·00 60·00
Paintings:—18f. *The Holy Shepherd* (Murillo); 30f. *Portrait of a Boy* (Kraus).

75 Fair Symbol    **76** Postilions

(Des Ring. Eng Gandon. Recess)

1953 (23 Apr). Saar Fair. P 13.
338   75   15f. deep bright blue.......................   4·00   2·50

(Des Mees. Eng H. Cheffér. Recess)

1953 (3 May). Stamp Day. P 13.
339   76   15f. blue..   11·00   21·00

77 Henri Dunant    **78** Boy with Bird (Rubens)    **79** St. Benedict Blessing St. Maurus

(Eng Gandon. Recess)

1953 (3 May). Red Cross Week and 125th Anniv of Birth of Henri Dunant (founder of Red Cross). P 13.
340   77   15f. +5f. deep purple-brown and red...   4·50   12·50

(Des and eng Dufresne (15f.), Gandon (18f.), Mazèlin (30f.). Recess)

1953 (16 Nov). National Relief Fund Paintings as T **78**. P 13.
341   15f. +5f. reddish violet.......................   5·25   9·00
342   18f. +7f. lake.....................................   5·25   9·75
343   30f. +10f. blackish olive ....   7·75   16·00
341/343 Set of 3...   16·00   31·00
Designs:—Vert—15f. *Clarice Strozzi* (Titian) Horiz—18f. *Caritas (detail)* (Rubens).

(Eng J. Piel. Recess)

1953 (18 Dec). Tholey Abbey Fund. P 13.
344   79   30f. +10f. black ....   4·25   13·00

80 Saar Fair    **81** Postal Motor Coach

(Des Ring. Eng Dufresne. Recess)

1954 (10 Apr). Saar Fair. P 13.
345   80   15f. green...   4·00   1·60

(Des Mees. Eng H. Cheffér. Recess)

1954 (9 May). Stamp Day. P 13.
346   81   15f. scarlet ....   16·00   22·00

82 Red Cross and Child    **83** Madonna and Child (Holbein)

(Des F. L. Schmidt. Eng J. Piel. Recess)

1954 (10 May). Red Cross Week. P 13.
347   82   15f. +5f. chocolate............................   5·25   11·50

(Eng Pheulpin (5f.), Munier (10f.), Mazèlin (15f.). Recess)

1954 (14 Aug). Marian Year. T **83** and similar vert portraits. P 13.
348   5f. carmine-red..................................   4·00   5·25
349   10f. deep green..................................   4·00   5·25
350   15f. ultramarine.................................   5·25   9·00
348/350 Set of 3...   12·00   18·00
Designs:—5f. T **83**; 10f. *Sistine Madonna* (Raphael); 15f. *Madonna and Child with Pear* (Dürer).

84 Street Urchin with a Melon (Murillo)    **85** Cyclist and Flag    **86** Rotary Emblem and Industrial Plant

(Eng Munier (5f.) Pheulpin (10f.), Cheffér (15f.). Recess)

1954 (15 Nov). National Relief Fund. Paintings as T **84**. P 13.
351   5f. +3f. scarlet...................................   1·60   2·30
352   10f. +5f. deep green...........................   1·60   2·30
353   15f. +7f. bright violet.........................   1·60   3·25
351/353 Set of 3...   4·25   7·00
Designs:—5f. T **84**; 10f. *Maria de Medici* (A. Bronzino), 15f. *Baron Emil von Maucler* (J.F. Dietrich).

(Des Bartz. Photo)

1955 (28 Feb). World Cross-Country Cycle Race. P 13×13½.
354   85   15f. bright blue, red and olive-black.....   65   1·20

(Des F. L. Schmidt. Photo)

1955 (28 Feb). 50th Anniv of Rotary International. P 13×13½.
355   86   15f. deep chestnut............................   65   1·60

87 Exhibitors' Flags    **88** Nurse and Baby

(Des Ring. Photo)

1955 (18 Apr). Saar Fair. P 13×13½.
356   87   15f. yellow, red, blue and deep grey-green.........   65   1·20

(Des F. L. Schmidt. Photo)

1955 (5 May). Red Cross Week. P 13½.
357   88   15f. +5f. black and red   90   1·70

89 Postman  **(90)**

(Des F. L. Schmidt. Eng H. Cheffér)

1955 (8 May). Stamp Day. P 13.
358   **89**   15f. brown-purple .... 3·50   4·25

1955 (22 Oct). Referendum. Nos. 326/327 and 329 optd with T **90**.
359   15f. carmine-red 80   1·30
360   18f. brown-purple 80   1·00
361   30f. deep bright blue .... 1·00   1·30
359/361 Set of 3 .... 2·30   3·25

91 Mother (Dürer)    **92**    **93** Radio Tower

(Eng Serres (5f.), Mazèlin (10f.), Pheulpin (15f.). Recess)

1955 (10 Dec). National Relief Fund. T **91** and similar vert designs inscr '1955'. P 13.
362   5f. +3f. deep green .... 1·00   2·20
363   10f. +5f. olive-green .... 1·40   2·75
364   15f. +7f. bistre .... 2·00   3·50
362/364 Set of 3 .... 4·00   7·50
  Designs:—5f. T **91**; 10f. *The Praying Hands* (Dürer); 15f. *The Old Man from Antwerp* (Dürer).

(Des Ring. Photo Courvoisier)

1956 (14 Apr). Saar Fair. P 11½.
365   **92**   15f. bright yellow-green and brown-lake 65   1·60

(Des Mees. Photo Courvoisier)

1956 (6 May). Stamp Day. P 11½.
366   **93**   15f. deep green and turquoise-green .. 65   1·60

94 Casualty Station    **95**

(Des Mees. Recess)

1956 (7 May). Red Cross Week. P 13.
367   **94**   15f. +5f. sepia 65   1·60

(Des Serres. Recess)

1956 (25 July). Olympic Games. P 13.
368   **95**   12f. +3f. deep bluish green and deep dull green 90   1·20
369   15f. +5f. sepia and brown-purple 90   1·20

96 Winterberg Memorial    **97** *Portrait of Lucrezia Grivelli* (da Vinci)

(Eng Fenneteaux. Recess)

1956 (29 Oct). Winterberg Memorial Reconstruction Fund. P 13.
370   **96**   5f. +2f. green 50   80
371   12f. +3f. bright purple 50   80
372   15f. +5f. deep olive-brown 50   1·00
370/372 Set of 3 .... 1·40   2·30

(Eng Mazèlin (5f.), Piel (10f.), Gandon (15f.). Recess)

1956 (10 Dec). National Relief Fund. T **97** and similar vert paintings inscr '1956'. P 13.
373   5f. +3f. deep blue 50   50
374   10f. +5f. lake 50   80
375   15f. +7f. deep green 50   1·30
373/375 Set of 3 .... 1·40   2·30
  Designs:—5f. T **97**; 10f. *Saskia* (Rembrandt); 15f. *Lady Playing Spinet* (Floris).

IV. RETURN TO GERMANY

The Saar again returned to Germany on 1 January 1957, as a result of the referendum held in 1955. The issues inscribed 'SAARLAND' which follow were authorised by the German Federal Republic for postal use prior to the reintroduction of German currency in the Saar Territory.

PRINTERS. All the succeeding issues were printed at the State Printing Works, Berlin, *unless otherwise stated*.

98 Arms of the Saar    **99** President Heuss

(Des H. Kern. Litho A. Bagel, Düsseldorf)

1957 (1 Jan). Return of the Saar to Germany. W **294** of West Germany. P 13×13½.
376   **98**   15f. Prussian blue and orange-red 60   65

1957 (1 Jan–25 May). W **294** of West Germany. P 14.
(a) Typo
377   **99**   1f. emerald 40   35
378   2f. bright reddish violet (5.4) 40   35
379   3f. pale bistre-brown 40   35
380   4f. mauve (5.4) 50   1·30
381   5f. yellow-olive 40   35
382   6f. rose-red (5.4) 40   80
383   10f. grey (5.4) 40   50
384   12f. orange 40   35
385   15f. turquoise-green 40   35
386   18f. carmine .... 1·00   4·00
387   25f. bright reddish lilac (5.4) 80   1·30
(b) Recess
388   **99**   30f. purple 80   1·30
389   45f. bronze-green (5.4) .... 1·80   4·50
390   50f. chocolate .... 1·80   2·10
391   60f. brown-red (5.4) .... 2·50   5·25
392   70f. red-orange (5.4) .... 4·75   7·75
393   80f. olive .... 1·60   6·00
394   90f. deep grey (5.4) .... 4·50   10·50
(c) Larger size (24×29½ mm). Recess
395   **99**   100f. carmine-red .... 4·00   13·00
396   200f. deep lilac (25.5) .... 10·50   42·00
377/396 Set of 20 .... 34·00   90·00

SAAR

100 Iron Foundry

(Des F. L. Schmidt. Litho A. Bagel, Düsseldorf)

1957 (20 Apr). Saar Fair. W **294** of West Germany. P 13×13½.
397　**100**　15f. carmine-lake and brownish black..　60　65

101 Arms of Merzig and St. Pierre Church

(Des E. Grittmann. Eng E. Falz. Recess)

1957 (25 May). Centenary of Merzig. W **294** of West Germany. P 14.
398　**101**　15f. deep bright blue.............................　40　65

1957 (16 Sept). Europa. As Nos. 1187/1188 of West Germany but inscr 'SAAR/LAND'.
399　　20f. brown-orange and yellow..................　1·00　1·70
400　　35f. violet and pink....................................　1·60　2·30

1957 (1 Oct). Humanitarian Relief Fund. As Nos. 1189/1192 of West Germany but inscr 'SAARLAND'.
401　　6f. +4f. black and yellow-brown...............　40　40
402　　12f. +6f. black and yellow-green................　40　50
403　　15f. +7f. black and blue.............................　50　65
404　　30f. +10f. black and blue...........................　65　1·20
401/404 Set of 4..　1·80　2·50

1957 (5 Oct). International Correspondence Week. As No. 1195 of West Germany but inscr 'SAARLAND'.
405　　15f. black and carmine...............................　50　65

1957. As T **99** but redrawn with letter 'F' after figure of value and colours changed.

(a) Litho
406　　1f. greenish slate (5.12.57)........................　50　40
407　　3f. blue (5.12.57)......................................　50　40
408　　5f. yellow-olive (2.11.57)...........................　50　40
409　　6f. brown (5.12.57)...................................　50　80
410　　10f. violet (2.11.57)...................................　50　40
411　　12f. brown-orange (2.11.57).....................　50　40
412　　15f. grey-green (2.11.57)..........................　65　40
413　　18f. slate-grey (5.12.57)............................　3·25　7·75
414　　20f. light yellow-olive (20.12.57)...............　2·00　5·25
415　　25f. orange-brown (20.12.57)...................　65　65
416　　30f. mauve (5.12.57).................................　1·60　65
417　　35f. brown (20.12.57)................................　4·00　5·25
418　　45f. turquoise-green (5.12.57)...................　3·25　6·50
419　　50f. purple-brown (5.12.57)......................　1·60　3·25
420　　70f. green (20.12.57).................................　7·75　9·00
421　　80f. chalky blue (20.12.57)........................　4·00　8·50
422　　90f. carmine (20.12.57).............................　9·00　10·50

(b) Recess (24×29½ mm)
423　　100f. yellow-orange (20.12.57)..................　9·00　11·50
424　　200f. green (20.12.57)...............................　14·50　42·00
425　　300f. blue (20.12.57).................................　16·00　47·00
406/425 Set of 20..　70·00　£140

1958 (9 Jan). 50th Death Anniv of Busch. As Nos. 1200/1201 of West Germany, but inscr 'SAARLAND'.
426　　12f. yellow-olive and black........................　40　40
427　　15f. light red and black.............................　40　65

1958 (5 Mar). Forest Fires Prevention Campaign. As No. 1202 of West Germany, but inscr 'SAARLAND'.
428　　15f. black and orange-red.........................　60　80

1958 (18 Mar). Birth Centenary of Rudolf Diesel (engineer). As No. 1203 of West Germany but inscr 'SAARLAND'.
429　　12f. deep bluish green...............................　60　80

1958 (1 Apr). Berlin Students' Fund. As Nos. 1204/1205 of West Germany, but inscr 'SAARLAND'.
430　　12f. +6f. brown-red, black and green........　40　50
431　　15f. +7f. olive-brown, green and red.........　50　65

102 Saarbrücken Town Hall and Fair Emblem　　**103** Homburg

1958 (10 Apr). Saar Fair. Litho. W **294** of West Germany. P 14.
432　　**102**　15f. claret.................................　50　65

(Des H. Lau. Eng E. Falz. Recess)

1958 (14 June). 400th Anniv of Homburg. W **294** of West Germany. P 14.
433　　**103**　15f. olive-green........................　50　65

1958 (21 July). 150th Anniv of German Gymnastics. As No. 1210 of West Germany but inscr 'SAARLAND'.
434　　12f. black, green and pale grey.................　50　65

1958 (29 Aug). 150th Anniv of Birth of Schulze-Delitzsch. As No. 1211 of West Germany, but inscr 'SAARLAND'.
435　　12f. light green..　50　65

1958 (13 Sept). Europa. As Nos. 1212/1213 of West Germany, but inscr 'SAARLAND'.
436　　12f. blue and green...................................　90　1·60
437　　30f. red and blue......................................　1·20　2·30

1958 (1 Oct). Humanitarian Relief and Welfare Funds. As Nos. 1214/1217 of West Germany but inscr 'SAARLAND'.
438　　6f. +4f. brown, yellow-brown and chestnut...　40　45
439　　12f. +6f. red, yellow and green..................　40　45
440　　15f. +7f. blue, green and red....................　80　90
441　　30f. +10f. yellow, green and blue..............　80　1·20
438/441 Set of 4..　2·20　2·75

1959 (6 Mar). 500th Birth Anniv of Fugger. As No. 1224 of West Germany but inscr 'SAARLAND'.
442　　15f. black and brown-red..........................　50　65

104 Hands holding Crates　　**105** Saarbrücken

1959 (1 Apr). Saar Fair. Litho. W **294** of West Germany. P 14.
443　　**104**　15f. lake....................................　50　65

1959 (1 Apr). 50th Anniv of Greater Saarbrücken. Recess. W **294** of West Germany. P 14.
444　　**105**　15f. blue....................................　50　65

1959 (6 May). Death Centenary of Von Humboldt. As No 1226 of West Germany but inscr 'SAARLAND'.
445　　15f. Prussian blue.....................................　65　80

The Saar Territory ceased issuing stamps on 6 July 1959, when German currency and the stamps of West Germany came into use.

STAMP BOOKLET

The price is for complete booklet

Booklet No.	Date	Contents and Cover Price	Price
SB1	6.12.24	Miner (Type **9**) and Town Hall 1 pane, No. 85×8; 1 pane, No. 99×8; 1 pane, No. 100×8 (4f.)................	£2500

Schleswig (Slesvig)

100 Pfennig = 1 German Mark
100 Öre = 1 Danish Krone

By the Treaty of Versailles, 1919, Schleswig was divided into two zones, in each of which a plebiscite was to be held. In the northern Zone 1, on 10 February 1920, 75% of the voters were in favour of inclusion in Denmark. In Zone 2, on 14 March 1920, 80% of the voters were in favour of remaining in Germany. Zone 1 was incorporated in Denmark on 9 July 1920.

Earlier issues for Schleswig are listed under German States.

1 Arms
2 Arms
3 Rural View
3a

(Des August Carstens. Typo H. H. Thiele, Copenhagen)

1920 (25 Jan). W **3a**. P 14×14½.

1	**1**	2½pf. grey	25	1·60
2		5pf. green	25	1·60
3		7½pf. brown	25	1·60
4		10pf. bright carmine	25	1·60
5		15pf. claret	25	1·60
6		20pf. bright blue	25	1·60
7	**2**	25pf. orange	50	1·60
8		35pf. grey-brown	65	2·00
9		40pf. violet	50	1·60
10		75pf. turquoise-green	65	1·60
11	**3**	1m. grey-brown	65	1·60
12		2m. bright blue	90	2·50
13		5m. green	2·00	3·25
14		10m. red	5·75	6·50
1/14 Set of 14			12·00	27·00

1920 (26 Jan). OFFICIAL. Nos. 1/14 optd 'C.L.S.' (='Comission Interalliée Slesvig'), in blue-black.

O15	**1**	2½pf. grey	£100	£140
O16		5pf. green	£100	£170
O17		7½pf. brown	£100	£140
O18		10pf. bright carmine	£100	£200
O19		15pf. claret	65·00	£100
O20		20pf. bright blue	£100	£100
O21	**2**	25pf. orange	£200	£275
O22		35pf. grey-brown	£200	£275
O23		40pf. violet	£170	£275
O24		75pf. turquoise-green	£200	£425
O25	**3**	1m. grey-brown	£200	£400
O26		2m. bright blue	£275	£425
O27		5m. green	£425	£650
O28		10m. red	£800	£1000
O15/O28 Set of 14			£2750	£4000

1. ZONE
(4)

1920 (21 May). As Nos. 1/14, but values in Danish currency, optd with Type **4**, in blue.

29	**1**	1ö. grey	25	4·00
30		5ö. green	25	3·25
31		7ö. brown	25	2·50
32		10ö. bright carmine	25	2·50
33		15ö. claret	25	4·50
34		20ö. deep blue	25	4·50
35	**2**	25ö. orange	25	13·00
36		35ö. grey-brown	1·30	23·00
37		40ö. violet	40	7·75
38		75ö. turquoise-green	65	13·00
39	**3**	1k. grey-brown	90	21·00
40		2k. bright blue	10·50	80·00
41		5k. red	5·25	80·00
42		10k. red	11·50	£140
29/42 Set of 14			29·00	£350

Upper Silesia

100 Pfennig = 1 Mark

By the Treaty of Versailles, 1919, a plebiscite was to be held in Upper Silesia, in Germany, to determine whether the inhabitants of part of the area wished to be included in Poland.

1

(Typo Govt Ptg Wks, Paris)

1920 (20 Feb). P 14×13½.

1	**1**	2½pf. slate	65	1·30
2		3pf. chocolate	65	2·00
3		5pf. green	40	1·30
4		10pf. chestnut	65	2·10
5		15pf. violet	40	1·30
6		20pf. blue	40	1·30
7		50pf. maroon	7·75	13·00
8		1m. pink	7·75	18·00
9		5m. orange	7·75	18·00
1/9 Set of 9			24·00	50·00

No. 10 is vacant.

(2) (3) (4) (5) (6) (7) (8)

(Surch by Erdm. Raabe, Oppeln)

1920 (Mar). Type **1** Surch.

11	**3**	5pf. on 15pf. violet	£250	£900
12	**2**	5pf. on 20pf. blue	1·80	5·25
13	**3**	5pf. on 20pf. blue	2·50	6·50
14	**4**	10pf. on 20pf. blue (R.)	1·80	5·25
15	**5**	10pf. on 20pf. blue (R.)	3·25	8·50
16	**6**	50pf. on 5m. orange	47·00	£100
17	**7**	50pf. on 5m. orange	60·00	90·00
18	**8**	50pf. on 5m. orange	65·00	£140

No. 11 in violet was printed in error.
Other minor differences exist in the figures of Type **2** to **8**, but we only list the most prominent.

9
10 Coal-mine in Silesia

(Typo Govt Ptg Wks, Paris)

1920 (26 Mar). P 13½×14 (Type **9**) or 14×13½ (Type **10**).

19	**9**	2½pf. slate	50	1·30
20		3pf. dull maroon	90	1·30
21		5pf. green	50	1·30
22		10pf. red	90	1·30
23		15pf. violet	90	1·30
24		20pf. blue	1·30	3·25
25		25pf. grey-brown	1·70	3·25
26		30pf. orange-yellow	1·30	1·30
27		40pf. olive-green	1·30	1·70
28	**10**	50pf. slate	1·70	1·30
29		60pf. blue	90	2·50
30		75pf. green	2·50	3·25
31		80pf. maroon	2·50	1·70
32		1m. magenta	2·50	1·30
33		2m. grey-brown	2·50	1·30
34		3m. violet	2·10	1·30

UPPER SILESIA

35		5m. orange	6·50	9·00
19/35	Set of 17		27·00	34·00

Plébiscite 20 mars 1921. (11)   **Plébiscite 20. mars 1921.** (12)   **4 M** (13)

1921 (20 Mar). Types **9** and **10** optd.

36	11	10pf. red	6·50	16·00
37		15pf. violet	6·50	16·00
38		20pf. blue	9·00	22·00
39		25pf. grey-brown (R.)	20·00	50·00
		a. Opt inverted		
40		30pf. orange-yellow	17·00	33·00
41		40pf. olive-green (R.)	17·00	33·00
42	12	50pf. slate (R.)	17·00	46·00
43		60pf. blue	20·00	39·00
44		75pf. green	20·00	46·00
		a. Opt inverted		£1300
45		80pf. maroon	33·00	60·00
46		1m. magenta	39·00	£100
36/46	Set of 11		£180	£425

Double and inverted overprints exist, also numerous errors, including '1921' omitted.

1922 (Mar). Surch as T **13**.

47	10	4m. on 60pf. olive-green	1·30	3·25
48		10m. on 75pf. red	2·00	4·50
49		20m. on 80pf. orange	10·50	26·00
47/49	Set of 3		12·50	30·00

INTER-ALLIED COMMISSION

C.I.H.S. (O **14**)   **C. G. H. S.** (O **15**)

1920 (14 Feb). Stamps of Germany handstamped with T O **14**, in blue.

(a) Postage stamps

O1	24	2pf. yellowish grey		£5000
O2		2½pf. grey	£2750	£1200
O3	17	3pf. brown		£1100
O4		5pf. green	£1600	£800
O5	24	7½pf. orange	£2750	£1300
O6	17	10pf. carmine	£1000	£500
O7	24	15pf. slate-violet	£1000	£400
O8	17	20pf. violet-blue	£1000	£500
O9		25pf. black and red/*yellow*		£5000
O10		30pf. black and orange/*rose*	£1800	£425
O11	24	35pf. red-brown	£1800	£400
O12	17	40pf. black and carmine	£1200	£400
O13		50pf. black and purple/*rose*	£1200	£400
O14		60pf. rose-purple	£1800	£400
O15		75pf. black and blue-green	£1000	£400
O16		80pf. black and lake/*carmine*		£5000
O17	18	1m. carmine-red	£2750	£1200
O18	20	2m. deep blue		£5000

(b) War Charity. Nos. 105/106

O19	17	10 +5pf. carmine	
O20	24	15 +5pf. slate-violet	

(c) National Assembly at Weimar. Nos. 107/110

O21	26	10pf. carmine	£2000	£1600
O22	27	15pf. blue and chocolate		£1600
O23	28	25pf. scarlet and green		£6500
O24		30pf. scarlet and purple	£2000	£2000

Nos. O4, O7, O8, O10/O17 and O22 exist with red overprint. The above were in use between 14 and 19 February pending the arrival of Nos. 1/9.

1920–22. Official stamps of Germany optd with T O **15**, in black.

(a) Types O **31** *and O* **32**, *etc. (with figures '21') (April 1920)*

O25		5pf. green	50	4·50
O26		10pf. carmine	50	4·50
O27		15pf. chocolate	50	4·50
O28		20pf. deep blue	50	4·50
O29		30pf. orange/*buff*	50	4·50
O30		50pf. violet/*buff*	1·30	5·25
O31		1m. red/*buff*	10·50	21·00
O25/O31	Set of 7		13·00	44·00

(b) Types O **31**, *O* **32**, *etc but without figures (July 1920–1922)*

O32		5pf. green	1·30	13·00
O33		10pf. carmine	40	4·50
O34		15pf. brown-purple	40	4·50
O35		20pf. deep blue	40	4·50
O36		30pf. orange/*buff*	40	4·50
O37		40pf. carmine (10.20)	40	4·50
O38		50pf. violet/*buff*	40	4·50
O39		60pf. purple-brown (5.21)	40	4·50
O40		1m. red/*buff*	40	4·50
O41		1m.25 indigo/*yellow* (9.21)	40	5·25
O42		2m. blue (wmk Lozenges) (9.20)	13·00	20·00
O43		2m. blue (wmk Mesh) (2.22)	40	5·25
O44		5m. red/*yellow*	40	5·25
O32/O44	Set of 13		17·00	75·00

Many stamps may be found with this overprint inverted, sideways, double, etc., but some of these are from printer's waste.

After the plebiscite of 20 March 1921, Upper Silesia was divided between Germany and Poland.

German Occupation Issues, 1939–1945

A. ALBANIA

September 1943–1929 November 1944

100 Qint = 1 Franc

Stamps of Albania

63 King Victor Emmanuel
64 Broken Columns, Botrint 

(70) 
71 War Refugees

1943.

(a) Nos. 352/363 surch (or optd only as T 70, in purple-brown (15q.) or red (others)).

389	–	1q. on 3q. red-brown	1·90	13·00
		a. '1944' for '1943'	£350	£800
390	–	2q. olive-brown	1·90	13·00
		a. '1643' for '1943'	£350	£800
		b. '1948' for '1943'	£350	£800
391	–	3q. red-brown	1·90	13·00
		a. '1643' for '1943'	£350	£800
		b. '1948' for '1943'	£350	£800
		c. '1944' for '1943'	£350	£800
392	–	5q. green	1·90	13·00
		a. Opt inverted	£550	
		b. '1948' for '1943'	£350	£800
393	63	10q. brown	1·90	13·00
		a. Opt inverted	£550	
		b. '1948' for '1943'	£350	£800
394	–	15q. scarlet	1·90	13·00
		a. '1643' for '1943'	£325	£550
395	–	25q. bright blue	1·90	13·00
		a. '1643' for '1943'	£350	£800
		b. '1948' for '1943'	£350	£800
396	–	30q. bright violet	1·90	13·00
397	–	50q. on 65q. brown-lake	2·50	20·00
		a. '1944' for '1943'	£350	£800
398	–	65q. brown-lake	2·50	20·00
		a. '1944' for '1943'	60·00	£130
399	–	1f. blue-green	17·00	39·00
		a. '1944' for '1943'	£350	£850
400	–	2f. lake	21·00	£130
401	64	3f. olive-black	£140	£325

(b) EXPRESS LETTER. No. E373 optd as in T 70, in lake-brown

E402	E 67	25q. bright violet	55·00	50·00
389/E402	Set of 14		£225	£600

Desings:—Nos. 389/391 Gheg Women; No. 390 Tosk Man; No. 392 Tosk Woman; Nos. 397/398 Profile portait of King Victo Emmanuel; No. 399 Krujë Fortress; No. 400 Bridge over River Kivi at Mes.
There were several settings of the overprint. One setting contained two errors, '1643' and '1948' on positions 29 and 51; the '1944' error on the qind values is on position 18 of a different setting.
The '1' in '14' and '1943', and also in the surcharge on No. 389, is found in two different fonts: with a horizontal serif at the top or with a shorter oblique serif. Different combinations are found throughout the settings, with the conjunction of two oblique-serifed figures being the least common.

(Photo State Ptg Wks, Vienna)

1944 (22 Sept). War Refugees Relief Fund. P 14.

402	71	5q. +5q. green	7·75	26·00
403		10q. +5q. brown	7·75	26·00
404		15q. +5q. lake	7·75	26·00
405		25q. +10q. blue	7·75	26·00
406		1f. +50q. olive	7·75	26·00
407		2f. +1f. violet	7·75	26·00
408		3f. +1f.50 orange	7·75	26·00
402/408	Set of 7		49·00	£160

B. BOHEMIA AND MORAVIA

German Protectorate

16 March 1939–8 May 1945

100 Haleru = 1 Koruna

After Slovakia declared its independence on 14 March 1939, the President of Czechoslovakia was induced to agree to a German protectorate over Bohemia and Moravia, the Czech areas of Czechoslovakia.

> **PRINTERS**. All stamps and overprints were produced by the Czech Graphic Union, Prague.

Stamps of Czechoslovakia

34 National Arms 
59 J. A. Komenský (Comenius) 
60a Gen. M. R. Stefánik

61 Pres. Masaryk 
64 Banská Bystrica

65 Podébrady

(1)

1939 (15 July). Stamps of Czechoslovakia variously optd as Type **1**.

1	34	5h. deep ultramarine	65	7·50
2		10h. brown	65	7·50
3		20h. vermilion	75	7·50
4		25h. blue-green	40	12·50
5		30h. purple	65	7·50
6	59	40h. blue	5·00	30·00
7	77	50h. blue-green	40	7·50
8	60a	60h. violet	5·00	35·00
9	61	1k. claret	90	12·50
10		1k. claret (No. 395)	75	7·50
11	–	1k.20 purple (No. 354)	4·00	30·00
12	64	1k.50 carmine	4·00	40·00
13	–	1k.60 olive-green (No. 355a)	5·75	45·00
		a. Error: 'MAHNEN'	80·00	£900
14	–	2k. green (No. 356)	1·80	40·00
15	–	2k.50 blue (No. 357)	4·00	30·00
16	–	3k. chocolate (No. 358)	4·00	40·00
17	65	4k. violet	7·00	45·00
18	–	5k. grey-green (No. 361)	7·00	55·00
19	–	10k. blue (No. 362)	7·50	90·00
1/19	Set of 19		55·00	£500

Designs:—No. 11 Palanok Castle; No. 13 St. Barbara's Church, Kutná Hora; No. 14 Zvíov Castle; No. 15 Streino Castle; No. 16 Hrubá Skála Castle; No. 18 Town Hall, Olomouc; No. 19 Bratislava and Danube.
Overprint sizes:—Nos. 1/6, 17½×16 mm; No. 7, 23×13½ mm; Nos. 8/10, 18×15½ mm; Nos. 11/16, 19½×18 mm; Nos. 17 and 19, 28½×18 mm; No. 18, 23½×23½ mm.

GERMAN OCCUPATION ISSUES, 1939–1945

2 Linden Leaves and Buds
3 Karluv Tyn Castle 
4 Brno Cathedral 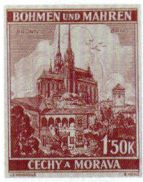
5 Zlin 

(Des K. Vik. Eng K. Seizinger (40, 60h., 2k., 2k.50) Des and eng B. Heinz (50h.). Des J. C. Voudrouš. Eng B. Heinz (1k., 1k.20, 1k.50, 3, 5, 10, 20k.). Des V. Silovsky. Eng B. Heinz (4k.) T **2** photo, others recess.)

1939–40. Type **2** and views as Type **3** to **5**. P 14 (Type **2**) or 12½ (others).

20	**2**	5h. blue (30.8.39)	20	50
21	–	10h. sepia (30.8.39)	20	65
22	–	20h. scarlet (30.8.39)	20	50
23	–	25h. blue-green (30.8.39)	20	50
24	–	30h. purple (30.8.39)	20	50
25	–	40h. blue (29.7.39)	20	50
26	**3**	50h. green (29.7.39)	20	50
27	–	60h. violet (29.7.39)	20	50
28	–	1k. claret (29.7.39)	20	50
29	**4**	1k.20 purple (29.7.39)	40	90
30	–	1k.50 carmine (29.7.39)	20	50
31	–	2k. green (29.7.39)	20	75
32	–	2k.50 green (29.7.39)	20	50
33	**5**	3k. mauve (4.11.40)	20	50
34	–	4k. slate (4.11.40)	20	65
35	–	5k. green (30.8.39)	65	1·30
36	–	10k. ultramarine (30.8.39)	55	1·50
37	–	20k. brown (30.8.39)	1·60	3·25
20/37 Set of 18			5·50	13·00

Designs: As T **3**—40h. Svikov Castle; 60h. St. Barbara's Church, Kutná Hora; 1k. St. Vitus's Cathedral, Prague. As T **4**—2k. and 2k.50, Olomouc. As T **5**—4k. Iron works, Morayska-Ostrava; 5k., 10k. and 20k. Karlsburg, Prague.

Nos. 29/37 were each issued in sheets of 100 stamps and 12 blank labels.

N **6** Dove
D **6** 

(Des J. Benda. Typo)

1939 (25 Aug). NEWSPAPER. Imperf.

N38	N **6**	2h. yellow-brown	40	50
N39	–	5h. pale blue	40	50
N40	–	7h. orange-vermilion	40	50
N41	–	9h. emerald-green	40	50
N42	–	10h. brown-lake	40	50
N43	–	12h. bright ultramarine	40	50
N44	–	20h. deep green	40	50
N45	–	50h. red-brown	40	65
N46	–	1k. grey-olive	65	1·30
N38/N46 Set of 9			3·50	5·00

These stamps exist perforated privately.

(Des A. Erhardt. Typo)

1939 (1 Dec)–40. POSTAGE DUE. P 14.

D38	D **6**	5h. lake	35	50
D39	–	10h. lake	35	50
D40	–	20h. lake	35	50
D41	–	30h. lake	35	50
D42	–	40h. lake	35	50
D43	–	50h. lake	35	50
D44	–	60h. lake	35	50
D45	–	80h. lake (10.6.40)	35	50
D46	–	1k. ultramarine	35	65
D47	–	1k.20 ultramarine (10.6.40)	45	65
D48	–	2k. ultramarine	1·40	1·90
D49	–	5k. ultramarine	1·60	2·50
D50	–	10k. ultramarine	2·30	3·25
D51	–	20k. ultramarine	4·00	5·00
D38/D51 Set of 14			11·50	16·00

P **6**

(Des A. Erhardt. Photo)

1939–40. PERSONAL DELIVERY. P 13½.

P38	P **6**	50h. blue (1940)	3·25	4·50
		a. Tête-bêche (pair)	12·50	25·00
P39	–	50h. carmine	2·10	5·00
		a. Tête-bêche (pair)	7·50	15·00

No. P38 was for the prepayment of the Personal Delivery charge and No. P39 was used when the charge was collected on receipt of the letter.

(Des A. Schaumann. Eng I. Goldschmied (Nos 41/43))

1940–41. Colour changed and new values.

(a) Type **2**. Photo. P 14

38	30h. yellow-brown (1.6.41)	20	40
39	40h. orange (3.40)	20	40
40	50h. slate-green (20.12.40)	20	40
38/40 Set of 3		55	1·10

(b) As Type **2** but redrawn (Leaves and Flowers). Recess. P 12½ (28.7.41)

41	60h. violet	20	40
42	80h. red-orange	30	40
43	1k. brown	30	40
41/43 Set of 3		70	1·11

(Des K. Vik (50h., 1k. 50), V. Silovsky (80h., 3, 6, 10k.), J. C. Vondrouš (others). Eng I. Goldschmied (2, 6, 8k.), K. Seizinger (1k.50), L. B. Heinz (others). Recess)

1940–41. Various views, as 1939–40. P 12½.

(a) 19×23 mm

44	50h. blue-green (31.3.40)	30	40
45	80h. blue (29.6.40)	25	50
46	1k.20 violet-brown (Brno) (10.6.40)	50	40
47	1k.20 carmine (Prague) (1941)	30	40
48	1k.50 lilac-rose (1941)	30	45
49	2k. grey-green (20.12.40)	40	40
50	2k. light blue (1941)	30	50
51	2k.50 ultramarine (1941)	65	90
52	3k. olive (1941)	80	1·30

(b) 30×24 mm

53	5k. blue-green (20.1.40)	40	40
54	6k. lilac-brown (20.11.40)	40	90
55	8k. slate-green (31.12.40)	40	50
56	10k. blue (20.11.40)	75	50
57	20k. chocolate-brown (1.10.40)	1·50	3·75
44/57 Set of 14		6·50	10·00

Designs:—50h. Neuhaus Castle; 80h., 3k. Pernstyn Castle; 1k.20 (violet-brown) and 2k.50 Brno Cathedral (as T **4**, but reduced); 1k.20 (carmine) St. Vitus's Cathedral, Prague; 1k.50 St. Barbara's Church, Kutná Hora; 2k. (×2) Pardubitz Castle; 5k. Bridge at Beching; 6k. Samson Fountain, Budweis; 8k. Kremsier; 10k. Wallenstein Palace, Prague; 20k. Karlsburg, Prague.

Nos. 53/57 were each issued in sheets of 100 stamps and 12 blank labels.

6 Red Cross Nurse and Wounded Soldier
(N **7**)
O **7** Numeral and Laurel Wreath 

(Des Max Geyer. Photo)

1940 (29 June). Red Cross Relief Fund. P 13½.

58	**6**	60h. +40h. indigo	1·00	1·90
59	–	1k.20 +80h. plum	1·00	1·90

Nos. 58/59 were issued in sheets of 50, *se-tenant* with 50 stamp-size labels, showing emblem, prices given are for stamps with labels.

1940. NEWSPAPER. For Bulk Postings. No. N42 optd with Type N **7**.

| N60 | N **6** | 10h. brown-lake | 40 | 1·30 |

(Des A. Erhardt. Typo)

1941 (1 Jan). OFFICIAL. P 14.

O60	O **7**	30h. yellow-brown	25	40
O61	–	40h. slate-blue	25	40

O62	50h. emerald-green		25	40
O63	60h. deep green		25	40
O64	80h. vermilion		50	40
O65	1k. brown		25	40
O66	1k.20 carmine		25	40
O67	1k.50 maroon		40	40
O68	2k. light blue		40	40
O69	3k. olive-green		40	40
O70	4k. bright purple		50	75
O71	5k. yellow		1·30	1·50
O60/O71 Set of 12			4·50	5·75

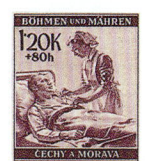

7 Patient in Hospital

8 Antonín Dvořák

1941 (20 Apr). Red Cross Relief Fund. Photo. P 13½.

60	**7**	60h. +40h. indigo	1·10	2·50
61		1k.20 +80h. plum	1·10	2·50

Issued with *se-tenant* labels as Nos. 58/59, prices given are for stamps with labels.

(Des J. Sejpka. Eng J Goldschmied. Recess.)

1941 (25 Aug). Birth Centenary of Antonín Dvořák (composer). P 12½.

62	**8**	60h. grey-violet	50	1·30
63		1k.20 sepia	50	1·30

Issued with *se-tenant* labels as Nos. 58/59, prices given are for stamps with labels.

9 Harvesting

10 Blast furnace, Pilsen

(Des J. Sejpka (Type **9**), V. Silovsky (Type **10**). Photo)

1941 (7 Sept). Prague Fair. P 13½.

64	**9**	30h. red-brown	25	65
65		60h. green	25	65
66	**10**	1k.20 plum	25	65
67		2k.50 blue	25	2·50
64/67 Set of 4			90	4·00

11 Ständetheater, Prague

12 Mozart

(Des M. Geyer (T **11**), A. Langenberger (T **12**). Photo)

1941 (26 Oct). 150th Death Anniv of Mozart. P 13½.

68	**11**	30h. +30h. brown	50	1·00
69		60h. +60h. green	50	1·00
70	**12**	1k.20 +1k.20 scarlet	50	1·00
71		2k.50 +2k.50 blue	1·00	2·00
68/71 Set of 4			2·30	4·50

Each issued with *se-tenant* labels, depicting bars of music (Nos. 68/69) or a piano (70/71), prices given are for stamps with labels.

(13)

14 Adolf Hitler

1942 (15 Mar). Third Anniv of German Occupation. Nos. 47 and 51 optd with T **13**.

72		1k.20 carmine (B.)	65	1·90
73		2k.50 ultramarine (R.)	65	1·90

(Des J. Sejpka. Eng J. Goldschmied. Recess)

1942 (20 Apr). Hitler's 53rd Birthday. P 12½.

74	**14**	30h. +20h. brown	20	50
75		60h. +40h. green	20	50
76		1k.20 +80h. maroon	20	50
77		2k.50 +1k.50 blue	40	1·60
74/77 Set of 4			1·00	2·75

Each issued in sheets of 100 stamps and 12 blank labels, prices given are for stamps with labels.

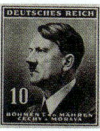

15 Adolf Hitler

16 Nurse and Patient

(Des J. Sejpka. Eng J. Goldschmied (Nos. 84/99)).

1942. As T **15** (various sizes).

(a) Photo. 17½×21½ mm. P 14 (1 July)

78		10h. black	20	40
79		30h. green	20	40
80		40h. indigo	20	40
81		50h. blackish green	20	40
82		60h. violet	20	40
83		80h. orange-red	20	40

(b) Recess. 18½×21 mm. P 12½ (1 July)

84		1k. chocolate	20	40
85		1k.20 carmine	25	50
86		1k.50 claret	25	50
87		1k.60 blue-green	25	50
88		2k. light blue	25	50
89		2k.40 chestnut	25	50

(c) Recess. 19×24 mm. P 12½ (22 July)

90		2k.50 ultramarine	25	50
91		3k. olive-green	25	50
92		4k. purple	25	50
93		5k. green	25	50
94		6k. purple-brown	25	65
95		8k. indigo	25	65

(d) Recess. 24×30 mm. P 12½ (22 July)

96		10k. grey-green	25	1·30
97		20k. slate-violet	40	1·30
98		30k. scarlet	55	3·00
99		50k. blue	1·10	3·75
78/99 Set of 22			5·75	16·00

Nos. 96/99 were each issued in sheets of 100 stamps and 12 blank labels.

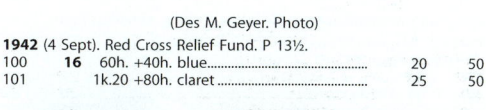

(Des M. Geyer. Photo)

1942 (4 Sept). Red Cross Relief Fund. P 13½.

100	**16**	60h. +40h. blue	20	50
101		1k.20 +80h. claret	25	50

17 Mounted Postman

18 Peter Parler

N **19** Dove

(Des A. Erhardt. Photo)

1943 (10 Jan). Stamp Day. P 13½.

102	**17**	60h. purple	25	90

(Des A. Langenberger. Photo)

1943 (29 Jan). Winter Relief Fund. As T **18** (busts). P 13½.

103		60h. +40h. violet	20	40
104		1k.20 +80h. carmine	20	40
105		2k.50 +1k.50 blue	20	40
103/105 Set of 3			55	1·10

Designs:—60h. Charles IV; 1k.20, T **18**; 2k.50, King John of Luxembourg.

GERMAN OCCUPATION ISSUES, 1939–1945

(Des J. Benda. Typo)
1943 (15 Feb). NEWSPAPER. Imperf.
N106	N **19**	2h. yellow-brown	15	25
N107		5h. pale blue	15	25
N108		7h. orange-vermilion	15	25
N109		9h. emerald-green	15	25
N110		10h. brown-lake	15	25
N111		12h. bright ultramarine	15	25
N112		20h. deep green	15	25
N113		50h. red-brown	15	25
N114		1k. grey-olive	15	25
N106/N114 Set of 9			1·20	2·00

O **19** Eagle and Numeral

19 Adolf Hitler

(Des A. Erhardt. Typo)
1943 (15 Feb). OFFICIAL. P 14.
O106	O **19**	30h. yellow-brown	20	65
O107		40h. slate-blue	20	65
O108		50h. grey-green	20	65
O109		60h. violet	20	65
O110		80h. vermilion	20	65
O111		1k. purple-brown	20	65
O112		1k.20 carmine	20	65
O113		1k.50 red-brown	20	65
O114		2k. light blue	20	65
O115		3k. olive-green	20	65
O116		4k. bright purple	20	65
O117		5k. blue-green	20	65
O106/O117 Set of 12			2·20	7·00

(Des and eng J. Schmidt.)
1943 (20 Apr). Hitler's 54th Birthday. (Recess). P 12½.
106	**19**	60h. +1k.40 violet	25	1·00
107		1k.20 +3k.80 carmine	25	1·00

Each issued in sheets of 100 stamps and 12 blank labels.

20 Scene from *The Mastersingers of Nüremberg*

21 Richard Wagner

(Des A. Langenberger (1k. 20), A. Erhardt (others). Photo)
1943 (22 May). 130th Birth Anniv of Richard Wagner. T **20**, **21**, and similar type. P 13½.
108	**20**	60h. violet	20	65
109	**21**	1k.20 carmine	20	65
110	–	2k.50 ultramarine	20	75
108/110 Set of 3			55	1·80

Design:—2k.50, Blacksmith scene from *Siegfried*.

22 Reinhard Heydrich

23 Arms of Bohemia and Moravia and Red Cross

(Des F. Rotter. Photo)
1943 (28 May). First Death Anniv of Reinhard Heydrich (German Governor). P 13½.
111	**22**	60h. +4k.40 black	50	2·50

(Des A. Erhardt. Photo)
1943 (16 Sept). Red Cross Relief Fund. P 13½.
112	**23**	1k.20 +8k.80 black and carmine	40	75

24 National Costumes

25 Arms of Bohemia and Moravia

(Des A. Erhardt. Photo)
1944 (15 Mar). Fifth Anniv of German Occupation. P 13½.
113	**24**	1k.20 +3k.80 carmine	25	50
114	**25**	4k.20 +10k.80 brown	25	50
115	**24**	10k. +20k. blue	25	50
113/115 Set of 3			70	1·40

26 Adolf Hitler

27 Smetana

(Des A. Erhardt. Photo)
1944 (20 Apr). Hitler's 55th Birthday. P 13½.
116	**26**	60h. +1k.40 brown	25	50
117		1k.20 +3k.80 green	25	50

(Des J. Sejpka. Eng J. Goldschmied. Recess)
1944 (12 May). 60th Death Anniv of Bedřich Smetana (composer). P 12½.
118	**27**	60h. +1k.40 grey-green	25	50
119		1k.20 +3k.80 claret	25	50

Each issued in sheets of 100 stamps and 12 blank labels.

28 St. Vitus's Cathedral, Prague

29 Adolf Hitler

(Des and eng J. Schmidt. Recess)
1944 (21 Nov). P 12½.
120	**28**	1k.50 brown-purple	25	50
121		2k.50 slate-violet	25	65

Each issued in sheets of 100 stamps and 12 blank labels.

(Des J. Schmidt after photograph by H. Hoffmann. Eng J. Goldschmied. Recess)
1944. P 12½.
122	**29**	4k.20 blue-green	40	90

Bohemia and Moravia were freed from German rule during April and early May, 1945, and the Sudeten German inhabitants were then deported to Germany. Issues of stamps for Czechoslovakia were resumed.

C. ESTONIA

1941–1944

100 Kopeks = 1 Rouble

2

3 Long Hermann Tower Reval (Tallinn)

(Des V. Krass. Typo Ilutrukk, Tartu)
1941 (7–12 Aug). Tartu issue. P 11½.

A. Thick chalky paper with brownish gum
3A	**2**	15 (k.) brown	16·00	25·00
4A		20 (k.) green	13·50	20·00
5A		30 (k.) blue	13·50	19·00

B. Ordinary paper with white gum
3B	**2**	15 (k.) brown (12.8)	16·00	22·00
4B		20 (k.) green (12.8)	12·50	19·00
5B		30 (k.) blue (12.8)	12·50	19·00

Used prices are for cancelled-to-order examples.
Nos. 3B/5B exist imperforate from a limited printing, only a few of which were placed on sale at Tartu.
Originally issued for local use, the above were made available for use throughout Estonia until 31 March 1942. However, not many were used since the German Eastern Command stamps came into use on 1 December 1941. Shades differ in the two printings.

(Des H. Sarap. Photo Ilutrukk, Tartu)
1941 (29 Sept). Reconstruction Fund. Type **3** and similar designs. Thick paper with lilac-grey network background. P 11½.
6	15 +15 (k.) sepia	60	6·50
7	20 +20 (k.) bright purple	60	6·50
8	30 +30 (k.) indigo	60	6·50
9	50 +50 (k.) blue-green	60	13·00
10	60 +60 (k.) rose-carmine	90	11·00
11	100 +100 (k.) slate	1·30	13·00
6/11	*Set of 6*	4·25	50·00

Designs: Horiz—20k. Stone bridge, Tartu; 30k. Narva Castle; 50k. View of Tallinn. Vert—15k. Type **3**; 60k. Tartu University; 100k. Narva Castle.
Nos. 6/11 exist imperf from a limited printing which was sold at post offices. Nos. 6/8 also exist imperf in larger quantities from a second printing, but these imperforates were sold in Germany only. Miniature sheets were not valid for postage.

Stamps inscribed or overprinted 'EESTI POST' are local issues which are outside the scope of this catalogue.
German stamps overprinted 'OSTLAND' (listed under Russia in this section) were used from 1 December 1941 until the Russian re-occupation of Estonia in 1944.

D. FRANCE

1940–1944
100 Pfennig = 1 Mark

The provinces of Alsace and Lorraine were occupied by the Germans in 1940. On 29 July 1940 the French departments of Haut Rhin and Bas Rhin, in Alsace, were combined with Baden to form the Gau of Elsass-Baden, and on 30 November the department of Moselle, in Lorraine, was combined with Saarpfalz to form the new Gau of Westland.

ALSACE
Elsaß
(1)

1940 (15 Aug). Stamps of Germany optd with Type **1**. W **97**. P 14.
1	**94**	3pf. bistre-brown	45	90
2		4pf. slate-blue	90	1·80
3		5pf. emerald-green	45	90
4		6pf. deep green	45	90
		a. Opt inverted	£1800	£4000
5		8pf. orange-red	45	90
		a. Opt inverted	£2250	
6		10pf. chocolate	45	1·30
7		12pf. carmine	45	90
8		15pf. claret	1·00	1·80
9		20pf. light blue	1·00	1·80
10		25pf. ultramarine	1·30	2·75
11		30pf. bronze-green	2·00	2·75
12		40pf. magenta	2·00	2·75
13		50pf. black and green	2·75	4·50
14		60pf. black and claret	3·00	5·25
15		80pf. black and blue	4·25	7·75
16		100pf. black and yellow	9·75	8·50
1/16	*Set of 16*		28·00	41·00

LORRAINE
Lothringen
(1)

1940 (21 Aug). Stamps of Germany optd with Type **1**. W **97**. P 14.
1	**94**	3pf. bistre-brown	1·00	1·60
2		4pf. slate-blue	1·00	1·60
3		5pf. emerald-green	1·00	1·60
4		6pf. deep green	1·00	1·00
5		8pf. orange-red	1·00	1·60
6		10pf. chocolate	1·00	1·00
7		12pf. carmine	1·00	1·00
8		15pf. claret	1·00	1·60
9		20pf. light blue	1·30	2·00
10		25pf. ultramarine	1·30	2·00
11		30pf. bronze-green	1·30	2·30
12		40pf. magenta	1·30	2·30
13		50pf. black and green	2·50	4·50
14		60pf. black and claret	2·50	5·25
15		80pf. black and blue	4·25	5·75
16		100pf. black and yellow	6·50	10·50
1/16	*Set of 16*		26·00	41·00

Both issues were in use until 31 December 1941, after which German stamps were used. Alsace and Lorraine were re-conquered for France late in 1944.

E. IONIAN ISLANDS

1943–1944

In September 1943, after the armistice between the Kingdom of Italy and the Allies, German troops took over control of the Ionian Islands from Italian forces.

ZANTE

Greek Civil Administration

100 Centesimi = 1 Lira = 8 Drachma

ΕΛΛΑΣ
2·X·43

(1)

1943 (22 Oct). Stamps of Italian Occupation of Ionian Islands (optd 'ISOLE JONIE') further handstamped with Type **1** in black.

(a) POSTAGE. T **102** *and* **103**
1	25c. green	50·00	80·00
	a. Optd with Type **1** in red	80·00	£120
2	50c. bright violet	50·00	80·00
	a. Optd with Type **1** in red	80·00	£120

(b) AIR. T **110**
3	50c. sepia	65·00	£120
	a. Optd with Type **1** in red	£325	£500

The 10c. value exists with handstamp in black and in red but was not issued.
Inverted handstamps exist.

In 1941 whilst under Italian military occupation contemporary Greek stamps were handstamped 'OCCUPAZIONE/MILITARE DI/ZANTE/1–5–XIX'. These are rare and outside the scope of this catalogue.

F. LATVIA

1941–1945

Stamps of Russia

141 Farm Girl **146** Factory Girl  **147** Farm Girl

242a Miner  **242c** Infantryman  **242d** Airman

365

GENERAL ISSUES

100 Kopeks = 1 Rouble

LATVIJA
1941.
1. VII
(1)

1941 (July). Russian stamps of 1936–1939 optd with Type **1**.
1	**242a**	5k. scarlet (847a) (18.7)	85	5·75
2	**146**	10k. deep blue (727f) (18.7)	85	5·75
3	**242c**	15k. blue-green (847c) (19.7)	46·00	£100
4	**141**	20k. green (727h) (17.7)	85	5·75
5	**242d**	30k. blue (847d) (17.7)	85	5·75
6	**147**	50k. grey-brown (buff) (727m) (23.7)	3·50	14·00
1/6 Set of 6			48·00	£120

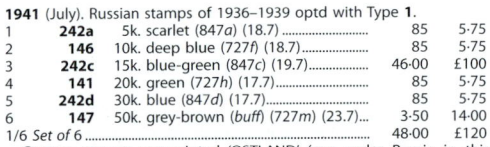

German stamps overprinted 'OSTLAND' (see under Russia in this section) were used from 4 November 1941 until the Russian re-occupation of Latvia in 1944–1945.

COURLAND

The German troops in this part of Latvia, N.W. of Riga, were cut off by the Russians when the latter reached the Baltic north of Memel (Klaipeda) in October 1944.

100 Pfenninge = 1 Reichsmark

KURLAND (1)   Kurland (2)

1945 (20 Apr). Hitler stamps of Germany surch with Type **1**. by the *Kurzemes vārds* Press.
1	**173**	6 on 5pf. olive-green (772)	55·00	95·00
		a. Surch inverted		
2		6 on 10pf. brown (775)	20·00	38·00
		a. Surch inverted	£140	£250
		b. Surch double	£120	£225
3		6 on 20pf. blue (781)	12·00	22·00
		a. Surch inverted	£140	£250
		b. Surch double	£120	£225

There are three types of '6' in this surcharge.

1945 (20 Apr). No. M805 of Germany surch with Type **2** for ordinary postal use.

A. P 13½
4A	M **185**	12 on (–) chestnut	60·00	£110
		a. Surch inverted	£225	£375
		b. Surch double	£225	£375

B. Roul
4B	M **185**	12 on (–) chestnut	9·50	24·00
		a. Surch inverted	£110	£190
		b. Surch double	95·00	£170

Nos. 4A/4B exist bisected and used on airmail letters from the troops.

G. LITHUANIA

1941–1944

100 Kopeks = 1 Rouble

Stamps of Russia
(For other images see section F. Latvia)

139 Factory Girl 
226 Soviet Flag at North Pole 
242f Arms of USSR

---

228 Machine Gunners

NEPRIKLAUSOMA
LIETUVA
1941-VI-23
(1)

1941 (23 June). Russian stamps of 1936–1940 optd with Type **1** or larger (80k.), by Spindulys Ptg Works, Kaunas.
1	**139**	2k. apple-green (727d)	55·00	£225
2	**242a**	5k. scarlet (847a)	2·75	18·00
3	**146**	10k. deep blue (727h)	2·75	18·00
4	**242c**	15k. blue-green (847c)	2·75	18·00
5	**141**	20k. green (727i)	2·75	18·00
6	**242d**	30k. blue (847d)	2·75	18·00
7	**147**	50k. grey-brown (buff) (727n)	10·00	36·00
8	**242f**	60k. carmine (847f)	18·00	70·00
9	–	80k. bright ultramarine (905)	18·00	70·00
1/9 Set of 9			£100	£450

VILNIUS
(2)

1941 (16 July). Issue for Vilnius and South Lithuania. Russian stamps of 1936–1939 optd with Type **2** or larger (80k, 1r), by Spindulys Ptg Works, Kaunas.
10	**242a**	5k. scarlet (847a)	1·80	6·00
11	**146**	10k. deep blue (727h)	1·80	6·00
12	**242c**	15k. blue-green (847c)	1·80	6·00
13	**141**	20k. green (727i)	4·75	18·00
14	**242d**	30k. blue (847d)	4·75	12·00
15	**147**	50k. grey-brown (buff) (727n)	4·75	12·00
16	**242f**	60k. carmine (847f)	4·75	14·50
17	**226**	80k. red and carmine (772)	£425	£350
18	**228**	1r. black and scarlet (779) (G.)	£1200	£1100
10/18 Set of 9			£1500	£1400

Lithuania was incorporated in the German administrative area 'Ostland' on 17 July 1941.
German stamps overprinted 'OSTLAND' (see under Russia in this section) were used from 4 November 1941 until the Russian re-occupation of Lithuania in 1944.

H. LUXEMBOURG

1940–1944

100 Pfennig = 1 Reichsmark

Luxemburg (67)   5 Rpf (68)   −60 Rpf (69)

1940 (1 Oct). T **94** of Germany (Hindenburg. W **97**), optd with T **67**.
397	3pf. bistre-brown	45	80
398	4pf. slate-blue	45	80
399	5pf. emerald-green	45	80
400	6pf. deep green	45	80
401	8pf. orange-red	45	80
402	10pf. chocolate	45	80
403	12pf. carmine	45	80
404	15pf. claret	1·00	1·60
405	20pf. light blue	1·00	1·80
406	25pf. ultramarine	1·00	2·50
407	30pf. bronze-green	1·00	2·50
408	40pf. magenta	1·30	2·50
409	50pf. black and green	2·30	5·25
410	60pf. black and claret	2·50	5·25
411	80pf. black and blue	5·00	10·50

366

GERMAN OCCUPATION ISSUES, 1939–1945

412		100pf. black and yellow	8·50	10·50
397/412		*Set of 16*	24·00	43·00

Stamps of Luxembourg

32 Grand Duchess Charlotte

47 Gateway of the Three Towers

52 Vianden

65 Allegory of Medicinal Spring

1940 (5 Dec). Various types of Luxembourg surch as T **68** or **69**.

413	32	3Rpf. on 15c. black	25	50
414		4Rpf. on 20c. orange	25	50
415		5Rpf. on 35c. green	25	50
416		6Rpf. on 10c. olive-green	25	50
417		8Rpf. on 25c. chocolate	25	50
418		10Rpf. on 40c. olive-brown	25	50
419		12Rpf. on 60c. blue-green	25	50
420		15Rpf. on 1f. carmine	25	50
421		20Rpf. on 50c. red-brown	25	1·00
422		25Rpf. on 5c. mauve	25	2·00
423		30Rpf. on 70c. violet	25	1·00
424		40Rpf. on 75c. bistre-brown	65	2·00
425		50Rpf. on 1¼f. blue-green	30	1·00
426	65	60Rpf. on 2f. rose-red	2·75	16·00
427	47	80Rpf. on 5f. blue-green	95	3·25
428	52	100Rpf. on 10f. deep green	1·30	4·50
413/428		*Set of 16*	7·75	31·00

1941 (12 Jan). Nos. 739/747 of Germany (1940 Winter Relief Fund) optd as T **67**, but larger (21½ *mm* long instead of 17 *mm*).

429		3pf. +2pf. brown	30	1·00
430		4pf. +3pf. indigo	30	1·00
431		5pf. +3pf. yellow-green	30	1·00
432		6pf. +4pf. grey-green	30	1·00
433		8pf. +4pf. red-orange	30	1·00
434		12pf. +6pf. carmine	30	1·00
435		15pf. +10pf. brown-purple	45	2·50
436		25pf. +15pf. blue	65	5·75
437		40pf. +35pf. purple	2·10	9·75
429/437		*Set of 9*	4·50	22·00

From 1 January 1942 to 1944 German stamps were used in Luxembourg, which was incorporated in the Moselland Gau of Germany on 9 May 1941.

I. POLAND

General Government, 1939–1945

100 Groszy = 1 Zloty

German armies invaded Poland on 1 September 1939 and on 17 September Russian troops invaded from the east. On 28 September Poland was divided between Russia and Germany; Germany annexed the territory she had lost in 1919–1921 and also parts of the provinces of Lodz, Warsaw, Cracow and Bialystok; on 12 October the rest of the area seized by Germany became a protectorate called the General-Government. Russian stamps were used in the area to the east of River Bug, annexed by the Soviet Union.

Stamps of Poland

82 Marshal Smigly-Rydz

83 President Moscicki

85 Boleslaw the Brave

88 'Warmth'

89a (No. 357)

D 88

(**91**) Deutsche Post OSTEN

(**92**) 2 GR. General-Gouvernement

1939 (1–4 Dec). T **94** of Germany (Hindenburg) surch as T **91**. Wmk Swastikas. P 14×14½.

359		6g. on 3pf. bistre-brown	40	65
360		8g. on 4pf. slate-blue	40	65
361		12g. on 6pf. deep green	40	65
362		16g. on 8pf. orange-red (4.12)	90	2·00
363		20g. on 10pf. chocolate (4.12)	40	65
364		24g. on 12pf. carmine	40	65
365		30g. on 15pf. claret (4.12)	90	2·00
366		40g. on 20pf. light blue (4.12)	90	65
367		50g. on 25pf. ultramarine	90	1·30
368		60g. on 30pf. bronze-green	90	65
369		80g. on 40pf. magenta (4.12)	90	1·30
370		1z. on 50pf. black and green	2·00	2·50
371		2z. on 100pf. black and yellow	4·00	4·25
359/371		*Set of 13*	12·00	16·00

1940 (Feb–Mar). Stamps of Poland. 1937–1939, optd as T **92**, at State Ptg Wks, Vienna.

(a) Stamps overprinted

372	85	2g. on 5g. red-orange	35	50
373		4g. on 5g. red-orange	35	50
374	–	6g. on 10g. green (337)	35	50
375	–	8g. on 10g. green (337)	35	50
376	–	10g. on 10g. green (337)	35	50
377	89a	12g. on 15g. red-brown (I)	35	50
		a. Type II	1·60	4·00
378		16g. on 15g. red-brown (357)	35	50
379	82	24g. on 25g. slate-blue	2·00	4·00
380	–	24g. on 25g. purple (340)	35	50
381	–	30g. on 30g. rose-red (341)	35	50
382	88	30g. on 5g.+5g. red-orange	40	90
383	83	40g. on 25g. purple	65	1·30
384	88	40g. on 25g.+10g. purple	40	90
385		50g. on 50g. magenta (I) (343)	35	90
		a. Type II	5·00	11·50
386	82	50g. on 55g. blue	50	1·30
387	–	60g. on 55g. bright blue (344)	10·50	23·00
388	–	80g. on 75g. blue-green (345)	10·50	23·00

367

GERMAN OCCUPATION ISSUES, 1939–1945

388a	88	1z. on 55g.+15g. blue	5·75	14·50
389	–	1z. on 1z. orange (346)	11·00	23·00
390	–	2z. on 2z. carmine (347)	4·00	9·00
391	–	3z. on 3z. slate-blue (348)	5·25	13·00
372/391		Set of 21	49·00	£110

(b) Postage Dues overprinted

391a	50g. on 20g. blue-green (D353)	1·80	5·25
391b	50g. on 25g. blue-green (D354)	7·75	21·00
391c	50g. on 30g. blue-green (D355)	23·00	46·00
391d	50g. on 50g. blue-green (D356)	1·30	4·00
391e	50g. on 1z. blue-green (D357)	2·50	5·25
391a/391e	Set of 5	33·00	75·00

Two types of 12g. and 50g. Type I is as in T **92**. In Type II the figures of value are very close to the 'G' and 'I' of 'General'.

PRINTER. All stamps from Nos. O392 to 477 were printed at the State Printing Works, Vienna.

O **93** Copernicus Memorial, Cracow (**94**)

(Des W. Kreb. Design photo; figures of value typo)

1940 (5 Apr–5 Aug). OFFICIAL. As Type O **93**.

(a) 31×23 mm. P 12½ (5 Apr)

O392	6g. pale brown	95	3·50
O393	8g. grey	95	3·50
O394	10g. pale green	95	3·50
O395	12g. deep green	95	2·50
O396	20g. deep brown	95	4·00
O397	24g. brown-red	15·00	2·50
O398	30g. crimson-lake	1·30	4·00
O399	40g. deep violet	1·30	7·50
O400	48g. pale olive	4·50	7·50
O401	50g. blue	1·30	4·00
O402	60g. deep olive	95	2·75
O403	80g. purple	95	3·50

(b) 35×26 mm. P 13½×14 (5 Apr)

O404	1z. purple and grey	2·50	7·50
O405	3z. red-brown and grey	2·50	7·50
O406	5z. orange and grey	3·75	9·00
O392/O406	Set of 15	35·00	65·00

(c) Size 21×16 mm

O407	6g. brown (5.8)	95	2·00
O408	8g. grey (5.8)	95	2·30
O409	10g. blue-green (5.8)	1·30	2·50
O410	12g. deep green (5.8)	95	2·30
O411	20g. deep brown (22.7)	95	2·00
O412	24g. brown-red (5.8)	95	2·00
O413	30g. crimson-lake (22.7)	1·30	2·50
O414	40g. deep violet (22.7)	1·30	2·50
O415	50g. blue (22.7)	1·30	2·50
O407/O415	Set of 9	9·00	19·00

(Des Prof. Puchinger. Photo)

1940 (5 Aug)–**41**. Views as T **93**. P 14.

392	6g. brown	40	1·00
393	8g. chestnut	40	1·00
394	8g. blue-black (8.9.41)	85	90
395	10g. emerald	25	40
396	12g. deep green	3·25	1·00
397	12g. violet (8.9.41)	45	50
398	20g. deep brown	25	40
399	24g. lake	25	40
400	30g. reddish violet	25	40
401	30g. purple (8.9.41)	45	90
402	40g. blue-black	25	40
403	48g. red-brown (8.9.41)	90	1·60
404	50g. blue	25	40
405	60g. deep olive	25	40
406	80g. deep violet	65	65
407	1z. reddish purple (9.9.40)	3·25	1·70
408	1z. blue-green (8.9.41)	80	1·60
392/408	Set of 17	12·00	12·50

Designs:—6g. Florian Gate, Cracow; 8g. Castle Keep, Cracow; 10g. Cracow Gate, Lublin; 12g. T **93**; 20g. Church of the Dominicans, Cracow; 24g. Wawel Castle, Cracow; 30g. Old Church in Lublin; 40g. Arcade, Cloth Hall, Cracow; 48g. Town Hall, Sandomir; 50g. Town Hall, Cracow; 60g. Courtyard of Wawel Castle, Cracow; 80g. St. Mary's Church, Cracow; 1z. Bruhl Palace, Warsaw.

1940 (17 Aug). Red Cross Fund. Pictorial types of 1940–1941 (colours changed), surch as T **94**, in red.

409	12g. +8g. greyish olive	2·30	5·00
410	24g. +16g. greyish olive	2·30	5·00
411	50g. +50g. greyish olive	3·00	7·25
412	80g. +80g. greyish olive	3·00	9·75
409/412	Set of 4	9·50	24·00

95   **96**

(Nos. 413/419. Des O. Engelhardt-Kyffhäuser. Eng F. Lorber. Recess)

1940 (26 Oct). First Anniv of German Occupation. T **95** and similar types. Thick straw-coloured paper. P 14½.

413	12g. +38g. deep green	1·80	4·50
414	24g. +26g. red	1·80	4·50
415	30g. +20g. deep violet	2·75	7·75
413/415	Set of 3	5·75	15·00

Designs:—12g. T **95**; 24g. Woman with scarf; 30g. Fur-capped peasant (as T **96**).

1940 (1 Dec). Winter Relief Fund. P 12½.

416	**96**	12g. +8g. deep green	80	2·50
417		24g. +16g. red	80	3·00
418		30g. +30g. purple-brown	1·90	4·00
419		50g. +50g. blue	1·90	4·25
416/419		Set of 4	4·75	12·50

D **97**   **97** Cracow

1940 (1 Dec). DELIVERY. Photo. P 14.

D420	D **97**	10g. red-orange	65	2·00
D421		20g. red-orange	65	2·00
D422		30g. red-orange	65	2·20
D423		50g. red-orange	1·70	3·50
D420/D423		Set of 4	3·25	8·75

Ordinary postage stamps only paid for delivery to the nearest sub-office and the above were applied in addition to pay for delivery to the addressee.

(Des Gessner and W. Kreb. Eng F. Lorber. Recess)

1941 (20 Apr). P 14½.

420	**97**	10z. grey and red	1·60	4·00

Issued in sheets of eight.

98 The Barbican, Cracow   **99** Adolf Hitler

(Des Fahringer and Gessner. Eng F. Lorber. Recess)

1941 (22 May–10 July). T **98** and similar horiz design. P 13½×14.

421	2z. blue (22.5)	1·00	1·30
422	4z. green (10.7)	1·00	2·50

Designs:—2z. T **98**; 4z. Tyniec Monastery. See also Nos. 465/468.

(Des W. Dachauer. Eng F. Lorber)

1941 (26 Oct)–**44**.

(a) Photo. P 14

423	**99**	2g. grey	20	50
424		6g. yellow-brown	20	50
425		8g. deep grey-blue	20	50
426		10g. yellow-green	20	50
427		12g. deep violet	20	50
428		16g. red-orange	1·90	3·25
429		20g. deep brown	20	50
430		24g. lake	20	50

431		30g. purple		20	50
432		32g. deep blue-green		35	65
433		40g. blue		20	50
434		48g. chocolate		1·60	1·30
435		50g. deep blue (7.43)		30	1·00
436		60g. olive (7.43)		30	1·00
437		80g. deep purple (7.43)		30	1·00
423/437		Set of 15		6·00	11·50

(b) Recess. P 12½ (7.4.42–44)

438	99	50g. deep blue		65	1·40
439		60g. olive		65	1·40
440		80g. reddish purple		65	1·40
441		1z. deep green		65	1·40
		a. Perf 14 (1944)		1·30	20·00
442		1z.20 purple-brown		80	2·10
		a. Perf 14 (1944)		2·75	26·00
443		1z.60 violet-indigo		80	2·10
		a. Perf 14 (1944)		2·75	33·00
438/443		Set of 6		3·75	8·75

1942 (20 Apr). Hitler's 53rd Birthday. As T **99**, but premium inserted in design. Recess. Thick straw-coloured paper. P 11.

444		30g. +1z. reddish purple		45	2·50
445		50g. +1z. blue		45	2·50
446		1z.20 +1z. brown		45	2·50
444/446		Set of 3		1·20	6·75

100 Modern Lublin  **101** Nicolas Copernicus

1942 (15 Aug). 600th Anniv of Lublin. T **100** and similar design. Photo. P 12½.

447	–	12g. +8g. purple		25	1·00
448	**100**	24g. +6g. red-brown		25	1·00
449	–	50g. +50g. dull blue		25	2·00
450	**100**	1z. +1z. green		55	2·40
447/450		Set of 4		1·20	5·75

Designs:—12g, 50g. Lublin, after an ancient engraving.

(Des W. Dachauer. Eng F. Lorber. Recess)

1942 (20 Nov). Third Anniv of German Occupation. T **101** and similar portraits. P 13½×14.

451	–	12g. +18g. violet (Veit Stoss (Vit Stvosz))		20	65
452	–	24g. +26g. lake (Hans Dürer)		20	65
453	–	30g. +30g. purple (J. Schuch)		20	65
454	–	50g. +50g. blue (J. Elsner)		20	1·00
455	**101**	1z. +1z. green		25	1·30
451/455		Set of 5		95	3·75

O 102  **102** Adolf Hitler

(Des W. Kreb. Design photo; value typo)

1943 (16 Feb). OFFICIAL. P 14.

O456	O **102**	6g. yellow-brown		25	90
O457		8g. grey-blue		25	90
O458		10g. light green		25	90
O459		12g. violet		25	90
O460		16g. brown-orange		25	90
O461		20g. brown-olive		25	90
O462		24g. brown-lake		25	1·00
O463		30g. reddish purple		25	1·00
O464		40g. blue		25	1·00
O465		60g. olive		25	1·00
O466		80g. dull purple		25	1·00
O467		100g. slate		35	1·80
O456/O467		Set of 12		2·75	11·00

(Des W. Dachauer. Eng F. Lorber. Recess)

1943 (20 Apr). Hitler's 54th Birthday. P 14.

456	**102**	12g. +1z. violet		40	2·20
457		24g. +1z. carmine		40	2·20
458		84g. +1z. green		40	2·20
456/458		Set of 3		1·10	6·00

102a  **103** Cracow Gate, Lublin

1943 (24 May). 400th Death Anniv of Nicolas Copernicus (astronomer). T **101** (colour changed) optd with T **102a**.

459	**101**	1z. +1z. reddish purple		50	2·50

Issued in sheets of ten.
Examples of the 1z. reddish purple without overprint exist; their status is unclear.

(Des W. Kreb. Frame photo. Centre embossed)

1943 (13 Aug–Sept). Fourth Anniv of Nazi Party in German-occupied Poland. T **103** and similar designs. P 14.

460		12g. +38g. green		25	1·00
461		24g. +76g. red		25	1·00
462		30g. +70g. purple		25	1·00
463		50g. +1z. blue		25	1·00
464		1z. +2z. grey		25	1·00
460/464		Set of 5			4·50

Designs:—12g. T **103**; 24g. Cloth Hall, Cracow; 30g. Administrative Building, Radom; 50g. Bruhl Palace, Warsaw; 1z. Town Hall, Lwow.

103a Lwow  **104** Adolf Hitler

(Des Fahringer (2z., 4z.), F. Prufimeyer (6z.), Gessner (10z.). Eng F. Lorber. Recess)

1943–44. T **103a** and similar horiz designs. P 13½×14 or 14×13½ (10z.).

465		2z. deep green (10.4.44)		20	40
466		4z. slate-violet (10.4.44)		90	2·00
467		6z. agate (11.2.44)		45	1·30
468		10z. grey and chestnut (26.10.43)		50	2·00
465/468		Set of 4		1·80	5·25

Designs:—2z. The Barbican, Cracow; 4z. Tyniec Monastery; 6z. T **103a**; 10z. Cracow.

(Des W. Kreb. Photo)

1944 (20 Apr). Hitler's 55th Birthday. P 14.

469	**104**	12g. +1z. green		25	1·60
470		24g. +1z. red-brown		25	1·60
471		84g. +1z. violet		25	1·60
469/471		Set of 3		70	4·25

105 Konrad Celtis  **105a** Cracow Castle

(Des W. Dachauer. Eng F. Lorber. Recess)

1944 (15 July). Culture Funds. T **105** and similar portraits. P 14.

472		12g. +18g. green		20	2·00
473		24g. +26g. red		20	2·00
474		30g. +30g. purple		20	2·50
475		50g. +50g. blue		20	3·25
476		1z. +1z. brown		20	3·25
472/476		Set of 5		90	11·50

Designs:—12g. T **105**; 24g. Andreas Schluter; 30g. Hans Boner; 50g. Augustus the Strong; 1z. Gottlieb Pusch.

(Des P. Stubinger. Eng R. Zenziger. Recess)

1944 (26 Oct). Fifth Anniv of German Occupation. P 13½.

477	**105a**	10z. +10z. greenish black and carmine		10·50	65·00
		a. Grey-black and red		10·50	65·00

Issued in sheets of eight.

J. RUSSIA

1941–1945

100 Pfennig = 1 Reichsmark

The areas under German occupation in 1941–1945 were divided for administration into (i) OSTLAND, comprising the former Baltic States and White Russia; and (ii) UKRAINE.

OSTLAND (1)	UKRAINE (2)

1941 (4 Nov)–43. Issue for Ostland. Stamps of Germany (Adolf Hitler) optd with Type **1**.

1	**173**	1pf. grey	20	40
2		3pf. yellow-brown	20	40
3		4pf. slate	20	40
		a. Coil pair. Nos. 3 and 5 (1942)	3·25	
4		5pf. yellow-green	20	40
5		6pf. violet	20	40
6		8pf. scarlet	20	40
7		10pf. brown (*recess*)	1·00	2·30
8		10pf. brown (*typo*) (1943)	50	5·25
9		12pf. carmine (*recess*)	1·00	2·30
10		12pf. scarlet (*typo*) (1943)	50	4·50
11		15pf. brown-lake	20	40
12		16pf. turquoise-green	20	40
13		20pf. blue	20	40
14		24pf. orange-brown	20	40
15		25pf. ultramarine	20	40
16		30pf. olive-green	20	40
17		40pf. magenta	20	40
18		50pf. myrtle green	20	40
19		60pf. red-brown	20	40
20		80pf. indigo	20	1·00
1/20 *Set of 20*			5·50	19·00

1941 (14 Nov)–43. Issue for Ukraine. Stamps of Germany optd with Type **2**.

21	**173**	1pf. grey	20	40
22		3pf. yellow-brown	20	40
23		4pf. slate	20	40
24		5pf. yellow-green	20	40
25		6pf. violet	20	40
26		8pf. scarlet	20	40
27		10pf. brown (*recess*)	85	2·50
28		10pf. brown (*typo*) (1943)	45	5·50
29		12pf. carmine (*recess*)	85	2·50
30		12pf. scarlet (*typo*) (1943)	45	5·00
31		15pf. brown-lake	20	40
32		16pf. turquoise-green	20	40
33		20pf. blue	20	40
34		24pf. orange-brown	20	40
35		25pf. ultramarine	20	40
36		30pf. olive-green	20	40
37		40pf. magenta	20	40
38		50pf. myrtle green	20	40
39		60pf. red-brown	20	40
40		80pf. indigo	20	40
21/40 *Set of 20*			5·25	20·00

K. SERBIA

From 30 August 1941 Serbia was in theory an independent state, ruled by a Serbian government under General Nedic; in fact it was under German military rule.

The territory comprised most of the pre-1913 Serbia (except for areas around Pirot and Uranje) and a wedge, the Banat, between the Tisza and the old Romanian frontier, extending to just south of Szeged.

Stamps of Yugoslavia

80 St. Naum Convent, Lake Ohrid

99 King Petar II

104 Zagred Cathedral and Junkers Ju 86

D 56

PRINTER. All the following issues were printed at the Government Printing Works, Belgrade.

(G **1**)

1941 (5 June). Nos. 414/426 of Yugoslavia (1939 King Peter II issue), optd with Type G **1** on paper with coloured network.

G1	**99**	25p. black	80	13·00
G2		50p. orange	80	6·50
G3		1d. green	80	6·50
G4		1d.50 scarlet	80	6·50
G5		2d. carmine-rose	80	6·50
G6		3d. red-brown	2·30	50·00
G7		4d. bright blue	1·70	10·50
G8		5d. blue	2·30	26·00
G9		5d.50 dull violet	2·30	26·00
G10		6d. deep blue	2·30	26·00
G11		8d. chocolate	4·25	39·00
G12		12d. violet	4·25	39·00
G13		16d. purple	5·00	£130
G14		20d. light blue	20·00	£450
G15		30d. pink	43·00	£1800
G1/G15 *Set of 15*			80·00	£2250

GD 2   GD 3

(Des S. Grujić. Typo.)

1941 (24 June). POSTAGE DUE. Unissued Postage Due stamps optd 'SERBIEN' as Types GD **2** and GD **3**. P 12½.

GD16	GD **2**	0d.50 violet	1·70	65·00
GD17		1d. claret	1·70	65·00
GD18		2d. deep blue	1·70	65·00
GD19		3d. scarlet	1·70	£100
GD20	GD **3**	4d. blue	2·50	£225
GD21		5d. orange	2·50	£225
GD22		10d. violet	5·25	£600
GD23		20d. green	16·00	£1600
GD16/GD23 *Set of 8*			30·00	£2750

1941 (19 July). AIR. Nos. 360/367 and 443/444 of Yugoslavia (pictorial air stamps), optd as Type G **1** on paper with coloured network. P 12½, 12½×11½ or 11½×12½.

G16	**80**	50p. brown (R.)	13·00	£275
G17	–	1d. bright green (R.)	13·00	£275
G18	–	2d. slate-blue (R.)	13·00	£275
G19	–	2d.50 carmine (Br.)	13·00	£275
G20	**80**	5d. violet (R.)	13·00	£275
G21	–	10d. lake (Br.)	13·00	£275
G22	–	20d. bluish green (R.)	21·00	£275
G23	–	30d. bright blue (R.)	21·00	£275
G24	**104**	40d. blue-green (R.)	22·00	£1000
		a. Perf 11		
G25	–	50d. slate-blue (R.)	34·00	£1800
		a. Perf 11½		
G16/G25 *Set of 10*			£160	£4500

Designs:—1d., 10d. Rab Harbour; 2d., 20d. Sarajero; 2d.50, 30d. Ljubljana; 50d. Suspension Bridge, Belgrade.

The overprint 'SERBIEN' on the above Air Mail set is larger than in Type G **1** and reads diagonally up on Nos. G19, G23 and G25, and down on the remainder: The angle of the letters varies according to the shape of the stamp.

6 A/D

SERBIEN
(G **2**)   (G **3**)

1941 (28 July). AIR. As last, without network opt, surch as Type G **2**.

G26	1d. on 10d. lake (Br.)	8·75	£325
G27	3d. on 20d. bluish green (R.)	8·75	£325
G28	6d. on 30d. bright blue (R.)	8·75	£325
G29	8d. on 40d. blue-green (R.)	16·00	£650
G30	12d. on 50d. slate-blue (R.)	22·00	£1400
G26/G30	Set of 5	60·00	£2750

1941 (1 Sept). Nos. G1/G15 optd with Type G **3** in black on paper with coloured network.

G31	**99**	25p. black	90	39·00
G32		50p. orange	90	9·00
G33		1d. green	90	9·00
G34		1d.50 scarlet	90	9·00
G35		2d. carmine-rose	1·00	9·00
G36		3d. red-brown	1·40	34·00
G37		4d. bright blue	1·40	9·00
G38		5d. blue	1·40	17·00
G39		5d.50 dull violet	2·75	34·00
G40		6d. deep blue	2·75	34·00
G41		8d. chocolate	3·00	50·00
G42		12d. violet	3·50	50·00
G43		16d. purple	4·25	£170
G44		20d. light blue	4·25	£500
G45		30d. pink	30·00	£1700
G31/G45	Set of 15		55·00	£2500

G **4** Smederevo Fortress    G **5** Refugees

(Des S. Grujić. Litho)

1941 (22 Sept). Smederevo Explosion Relief Fund. P 11½×12½.

G46	G **4**	0.50d. +1d. brown	1·40	3·25
G47	G **5**	1d. +2d. green	1·40	4·00
G48		1.50d. +3d. purple	2·75	5·75
		a. Perf 12½	7·25	26·00
G49	G **4**	2d. +4d. blue	2·75	9·00
G46/G49	Set of 4		7·50	20·00

Miniature sheets (149×109 mm) comprising Nos. G47 and G49, colours changed and with high premiums.

MSG49a	1d.+49d. red, 2d.+48d. green P 11½	£200	£1200
MSG49b	1d.+49d. green, 2d.+48d. red Imperf	£200	£1200

G **6** Christ and the Virgin Mary

(Des Lj. Cucaković. Litho)

1941 (5 Dec). Prisoners of War Fund. P 12×11½.

A. With pink burelage

G50A	G **6**	0.50d. +1.50d. brown-red	90	10·50
G51A		1d. +3d. grey-green	90	10·50
G52A		2d. +6d. rosine	90	10·50
G53A		4d. +12d. blue	90	10·50
G50A/G53A	Set of 4		3·25	38·00

B. Without burelage

G50B	G **6**	0.50d. +1.50d. brown-red	3·00	33·00
G51B		1d. +3d. grey-green	3·00	33·00
G52B		2d. +6d. rosine	3·00	33·00
G53B		4d. +12d. blue	3·00	33·00
G50B/G53B	Set of 4		11·00	£120

The above were each printed in two panes of 25 (5×5) of which 20 have the burelage and the five in the centre (in the form of a cross) are without burelage. In addition four of the stamps with the burelage (positions 7, 9, 17 and 19) bear a large double-lined 'C' (resembling an 'E'), two normal and two reversed (*Price each value, either state, £29.00 un, £120 used*).

G **7**    G **8**

(Des S. Grujić. Litho)

1942 (1 Jan). Anti-Masonic Exhibition. Types G **7** and G **8** and similar designs dated '22.X.1941'. P 11½×12 (horiz) or 12×11½ (vert).

G54	0.50d. +0.50d. brown	1·70	5·75
G55	1d. +1d. green	1·70	5·75
G56	2d. +2d. carmine-lake	1·70	10·50
G57	4d. +4d. indigo	1·70	10·50
G54/G57	Set of 4	6·00	29·00

Designs: Horiz—0.50d. Type G **7**; 1d. Hand grasping snake. Vert—2d. Type G **8**; 4d. Peasant demolishing masonic symbols.

G **9** Kalenic    GD **10**    GD **11**

(Des N. K. Džange. Typo)

1942 (10 Jan)–**43**. Type G **9** and similar designs showing monasteries. P 12×11½ (vert) or 11½×12 (horiz).

G58	0d.50 violet	35	80
G59	1d. scarlet (3.9.42)	35	80
G60	1d.50 brown (3.9.42)	2·00	10·50
G61	1d.50 green (1943)	35	80
G62	2d. purple (12.1.42)	35	80
G63	3d. blue (3.9.42)	2·00	10·50
G64	3d. pink (1943)	35	80
G65	4d. ultramarine	35	80
G66	7d. grey-green	35	80
G67	12d. claret	35	5·25
G68	16d. grey-black (3.9.42)	2·75	5·75
G58/G68	Set of 11	8·50	34·00

Designs: Vert—0d.50, Lazarica; 1d. Type G **9**; 1d.50, Ravanica; 12d. Gornjak; 16d. Studenica. Horiz—2d. Manasija; 3d. Ljubostinja; 4d. Sopocani; 7d. Zica.

1942 (10 Jan). POSTAGE DUE. Typo. P 12½.

GD69	GD **10**	1d. claret and green	1·80	13·00
GD70		2d. deep blue and red	1·80	13·00
GD71		3d. scarlet and blue	1·80	20·00
GD72	GD **11**	4d. blue and red	1·80	20·00
GD73		5d. orange and blue	2·75	50·00
GD74		10d. violet and red	2·75	50·00
GD75		20d. green and red	20·00	£225
GD69/GD75	Set of 7		29·00	£350

1942 (24 Mar). As Nos. G50/G53, colours changed and without burelage. Thick paper. P 11½.

G68a	0.50d. +1.50d. brown	2·30	6·50
G68b	1d. +3d. blue-green	2·30	6·50
G68c	2d. +6d. carmine	2·30	6·50
G68d	4d. +12d. ultramarine	2·30	6·50
G68a/G68d	Set of 4	8·25	23·00

The above were printed in the same sheet formation as Nos. 650/653 except that in place of the five central stamps in the form of a cross there were four blank labels and a centre label which bears the Serbian Arms.

371

GERMAN OCCUPATION ISSUES, 1939–1945

(G 10)  — G **11** Mother and Children

1942 (5 July). AIR. T **99** of Yugoslavia optd with burelage in green and surch as Type G **10**.

G69	2 on 2d. carmine-rose	60	3·25
G70	4 on 4d. bright blue	60	3·25
G71	10 on 12d. violet	60	6·50
G72	14 on 20d. light blue	60	6·50
G73	20 on 30d. pink	1·00	26·00
G69/G73	Set of 5	3·00	41·00

(Des S. Grujić. Litho)

1942 (13 Sept). War Orphans' Fund. P 11½.

G74	G **11**	2d. +6d. violet	11·50	25·00
G75		4d. +8d. blue	11·50	25·00
G76		7d. +13d. green	11·50	25·00
G77		20d. +40d. lake	11·50	25·00
G74/G77	Set of 4		41·00	90·00

GO **12**  — G **12** Broken Sword  — GD **13**

(Des S. Grujic. Typo)

1943 (1 Jan). OFFICIAL. P 12½.
GO78 GO **12** 3d. claret .... 1·30 4·00

(Des S. Grujić. Litho)

1943 (16 May). War Invalids' Relief Fund. T G **12** and similar designs. P 12×11½ (vert) or 11½×12 (horiz).

G78	1.50d. +1.50d. chocolate	3·50	6·50
G79	2d. +3d. blue-green	3·50	6·50
G80	3d. +5d. magenta	5·75	9·00
G81	4d. +10d. blue	5·75	10·50
G78/G81	Set of 4	17·00	29·00

MSG81*a* Two sheets, each 149×110 mm. Thick paper. P 11½. (a) 1d.50+48d.50, 4d.+46d. (b) 2d.+48d., 3d.+47d. £375 £1700
Designs: Horiz—2d. Fallen standard bearer, 3d. Wounded soldier (seated). Vert—1.50d. and 3d. Nurse tending soldier.

(Des V. Guljević. Typo)

1943 (1 July). POSTAGE DUE. P 12½.

GD82	GD **13**	0d.50 black	2·30	13·00
GD83		3d. violet	2·30	13·00
GD84		4d. blue	2·30	13·00
GD85		5d. green	2·30	13·00
GD86		6d. orange	2·30	50·00
GD87		10d. scarlet	4·00	50·00
GD88		20d. ultramarine	17·00	£100
GD82/GD88	Set of 7		29·00	£225

За пострадале од англо-американског терор. бомбардовања Ниша — 20-X-1943

G **13** Post Rider — +3 (G **14**)

(Des S. Grujić. Litho)

1943 (15 Oct). Postal Centenary. As T G **13** (dated '15.X.1843—15.X.1943'). P 12½.

G82	3d. red and lilac	1·80	9·00
G83	8d. claret and grey-green	1·80	9·00
G84	9d. green and brown	1·80	9·00
G85	30d. brown and green	1·80	9·00
G86	50d. blue and red-brown	1·80	9·00
G82/G86	Set of 5	8·00	41·00

Designs: Vert—3d. T G **13**. Horiz—8d. Horse wagon; 9d. Railway van; 30d. Postal motor van; 50d. Junkers Ju 52/3m mail plane.
The above were issued in special sheets containing each value in a block of four, the 3d. and 8d. at top left and right; the 30d. and 50d. at bottom left and right; and the 9d. in the centre with labels containing a shield on either side with the date '15-X-1843' at left and '15-X-1943' at right (*Price for sheet* £60.00 *un*, £160 *used*).

1943 (11 Dec). Bombing of Nish Relief Fund. 'Monasteries' issue of 1942–1943 optd with green network and surch with additional value as Type G **14**.

G87	0d.50 +2d. violet	90	80·00
G88	1d. +3d. scarlet	90	80·00
G89	1d.50 +4d. green	90	80·00
G90	2d. +5d. purple	90	80·00
G91	3d. +7d. pink	90	80·00
G92	4d. +9d. ultramarine	90	80·00
G93	7d. +15d. grey-green	1·60	80·00
G94	12d. +25d. claret	1·60	£375
G95	16d. +33d. grey-black	2·30	£600
G87/G95	Set of 9	9·75	£1400

L. YUGOSLAVIA

1941–1945

DALMATIA

Stamps of Italy

98 Romulus, Remus and Wolf  — **99** Julius Caesar  — **100** Augustus the Great

101 Italia  — **102** King Victor Emmanuel III  — **103** King Victor Emmanuel III

110 Pegasus  — **111** Wings  — **112** Angel

113

D **141**  — D **142**

GERMAN OCCUPATION ISSUES, 1939–1945

E 132    **E 133**

The areas in Dalmatia under Italian control were occupied by the Germans after the armistice of 8 September 1943 between the Kingdom of Italy and the Allies.

ZARA (Zadar)

Italian Currency

Deutsche Besetzung Zara (1)   **ZARA** (2)

1943 (9 Oct). Imperial series of Italy, 1929–1942, optd with Type **1**.

1	98	5c. brown	£120	£225
2	100	10c. sepia	7·25	20·00
3	101	15c. blue-green	10·00	33·00
4	99	20c. carmine	7·25	22·00
5	102	25c. green	7·25	22·00
6	103	30c. brown	7·25	22·00
7	101	35c. blue	£325	£700
		a. Wmk inverted	£4000	£13000
8	102	75c. carmine	21·00	50·00
9	99	1l. violet	7·50	22·00
10	102	1l.25 blue	8·50	33·00
11	100	1l.75 orange-vermilion	25·00	85·00
12	101	2l. brown-lake	£120	£180
13	98	2l.55 grey-green	£325	£850
14		3l.70 bright violet	£1800	£3750
15		5l. carmine	£120	£200
16	101	10l. violet	£1400	£2500
17	99	20l. yellow-green	£13000	£26000
18	100	25l. blue-black	£43000	£80000
19	103	50l. deep violet	£33000	£55000

1943 (9 Oct). War Propaganda stamps of Italy (Nos. 571/574) optd with Type **1**, on stamp and attached label.

20	103	50c. bright violet (Navy)	42·00	£100
21		50c. bright violet (Army)	42·00	£100
22		50c. bright violet (Air Force)	42·00	£100
23		50c. bright violet (Militia)	42·00	£100
20/23 *Set of 4*			£150	£350

1943 (9 Oct). EXPRESS LETTER Nos. E350/E351 of Italy optd as Type **1**, but larger.

E24	E 132	1l.25 green	18·00	46·00
E25		2l.50 red-orange	£180	£300

1943 (9 Oct). AIR. Nos. 270/277 of Italy optd with Type **1**, larger on **2**.

26	111	25c. grey-green	14·50	33·00
27	110	50c. sepia	14·50	33·00
28	112	75c. chestnut	£450	£850
29	111	80c. orange-vermilion	39·00	£110
30	112	1l. bright violet	18·00	39·00
31	113	2l. blue	46·00	£110
32	110	5l. green	£7000	£15000
33		10l. carmine-red	£26000	£46000

1943 (9 Oct). AIR EXPRESS No. E370 of Italy optd with Type **1**, but larger.

E34	E 133	2l. blue-black	38·00	80·00

1943 (9 Oct). POSTAGE DUE. Italian Postage Due stamps of 1934 optd as Type **1**, sideways.

D35	D 141	5c. chocolate	43·00	£160
D36		10c. blue	43·00	£160
D37		20c. bright carmine	43·00	£160
D38		25c. green	£700	£1600
D39		30c. orange-vermilion	43·00	£160
D40		40c. sepia	43·00	£160
D41		50c. bright violet	43·00	£160
D42		60c. slate-blue	£700	£1600
D43	D 142	1l. orange	£700	£1600
D44		2l. green	£1100	£2250
D45		5l. bright violet	£700	£1600
D35/D45 *Set of 11*			£3750	£8500

1943 (4 Nov). Imperial series of Italy, 1929–1942, optd with Type **2**.

46	103	50c. bright violet	13·00	33·00
47	102	75c. carmine	13·00	33·00
48		1l.25 blue	80·00	£200
46/48 *Set of 3*			95·00	£250

1943 (4 Nov). War Propaganda stamps of Italy (Nos. 563/570), optd with Type **2**, on stamp and attached label.

49	102	25c. green (Navy)	29·00	55·00
50		25c. green (Army)	29·00	55·00
51		25c. green (Air Force)	29·00	55·00
52		25c. green (Militia)	29·00	55·00
53	103	30c. brown (Navy)	29·00	55·00
54		30c. brown (Army)	29·00	55·00
55		30c. brown (Air Force)	29·00	55·00
56		30c. brown (Militia)	29·00	55·00
49/56 *Set of 8*			£200	£400

1943 (4 Nov). EXPRESS LETTER Nos. E350/E351 of Italy, optd with Type **2**, twice.

E57	E 132	1l.25 green	17·00	65·00
E58		2l.50 red-orange	£225	£450

BRAĆ

The following issue for the island of Brać, south of Split, was authorised by the Head of the Army Fieldpost, with the approval of the Commander of the Panzer Army.

Croatian Currency

1944 (May). Island Welfare Fund. King Peter II stamps of Yugoslavia, 1939, and a Postage Due stamp, optd 'BRA' and value in kuna, No. 6 also optd 'FRANCO', by Jadran Printing Works, Dubrovnik.

1	99	2 +2k. on 25p. black (R.)	£275	£800
2		4 +4k. on 50p. orange	£250	£850
3		8 +8k. on 2d. carmine-rose	£275	£800
4		16 +16k. on 25p. black (R.)	£250	£850
5		32 +32k. on 2d. carmine-rose	£250	£800
6	D 56	50 +50k. on 1d. magenta (D260 II)	£250	£800
1/6 *Set of 6*			£1400	£4500

Similar charity issues were prepared for the islands of Hvar and Korula, but these were not issued.

GULF OF KOTOR

Italian and German Currency

This part of Dalmatia, annexed by Italy in 1941, was occupied by the Germans after the armistice of 8 September 1943 between the Kingdom of Italy and the Allies.

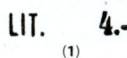

Deutsche Militär-verwaltung Kotor   **0,10 R.M. Boka Kotorska**

LIT. 4.- (1) 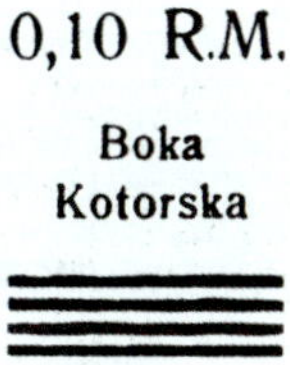   (2)

1944 (10 Feb). Imperial series of Italy, 1929, surch as Type **1**, by State Printing Works, Cetinje.

1	100	0.50 LIT. on 10c. sepia (R.)	80·00	£140
2	102	1 LIT. on 25c. green (R.)	£170	£300
		a. Wmk inverted		
3	103	1.50 LIT. on 50c. bright violet (R.)	80·00	£140
		a. Wmk inverted		
4		3 LIT. on 30c. brown (R.)	80·00	£140
5	99	4 LIT. on 20c. carmine	80·00	£140
6		10 LIT. on 20c. carmine	80·00	£140
1/6 *Set of 6*			£500	£900

1944 (16 Sept). Nos. 419/420 of Yugoslavia (1939 King Peter II issue), surch as Type **2**, by State Printing Works, Cetinje.

7	99	0,10 R.M. on 3d. red-brown	20·00	8·50
		a. Wmk inverted		
8		0,15 R.M. on 3d. red-brown	20·00	8·50
9		0,25 R.M. on 4d. bright blue	20·00	14·50
10		0,50 R.M. on 4d. bright blue	20·00	24·00
7/10 *Set of 4*			70·00	

Pictorial designs inscribed 'BOKA KOTORSKA' were printed in Vienna but were not issued.

Stamps similar to Nos. 1/6 were prepared for use in Podgorica but were not issued.

MACEDONIA

Bulgarian Currency

On 8 September 1944 Bulgaria, which had occupied Macedonia, signed an armistice and Macedonia was occupied by German troops and declared its independence, which lasted until German troops left on 13 November.

GERMAN OCCUPATION ISSUES, 1939–1945

Stamps of Bulgaria

140 Grapes

156 Bugler at Camp

157 Folk Dancers

МАКЕДОНИЯ
8. IX. 1944

1 лв.
(1)

30 лв.
(2)

1944 (28 Oct). Stamps of Bulgaria, 1940–1944, surch.

(a) As Type **1**

1	140	1l. on 10st. orange (B.)	5·75	26·00
2	–	3l. on 15st. blue (450) (R.)	5·75	26·00

(b) As Type **2**

3	–	6l. on 10st. blue (469) (R.)	7·25	39·00
4	–	9l. on 15st. deep blue-green (470) (R.)	7·25	39·00
5	–	9l. on 15st. blackish olive (471) (R.)	11·00	46·00
6	–	15l. on 4l. olive-black (504) (R.)	38·00	90·00
7	156	20l. on 7l. blue (R.)	55·00	£100
8	157	30l. on 14l. brown (B.)	65·00	£170
1/8		Set of 8	£180	£475

Designs:—No. 2 Beehive; No. 3 Threshing; No. 4, No. 5 Ploughing with Oxen; No. 6 Hoisting the Flag.
Numerous errors occur in these surcharges.

MONTENEGRO

Italian and German Currency

German forces took over Montenegro from Italy after the armistice of September 1943.

Stamp of Montenegro

Deutsche Militaer-Verwaltung Montenegro
0.50 LIRE
(1)

УСТАВ
Constitution Николајев
1905
(5)

1943 (22 Nov). Nos. 419/420 of Yugoslavia (1939 King Peter II issue), surch as Type **1**.

76	99	50c. on 3d. red-brown	9·75	46·00
77	–	1l. on 3d. red-brown	9·75	46·00
78	–	11.50 on 3d. red-brown	9·75	46·00
79	–	2l. on 3d. red-brown	17·00	90·00
80	–	4l. on 3d. red-brown	17·00	90·00
81	–	5l. bright blue	17·00	90·00
82	–	8l. on 4d. bright blue	43·00	£180
83	–	10l. on 4d. bright blue	50·00	£275
84	–	20l. on 4d. bright blue	£110	£650
76/84		Set of 9	£250	£1400

1943. Appointment of National Administrative Committee. Optd 'Nationaler/Verwaltungsausschuss/10. xi.1943'.

(a) POSTAGE. On Nos. 64/68 of Italian Occupation of Montenegro (National Poem Commemoratives)

85	–	25c. green	33·00	£300
86	–	50c. rose-magenta	33·00	£300
87	–	1l.25 blue	33·00	£300
88	–	2l. blue-green	33·00	£300
89	–	5l. carmine/*buff*	£400	£4000

(b) AIR. On Nos. 70/74 of Italian Occupation (of Montenegro)

90	5	50c. brown	33·00	£300
91	–	1l. ultramarine	33·00	£300
92	–	2l. rose-magenta	33·00	£300
93	–	5l. green	33·00	£300
94	–	10l. purple/*buff*	£4750	£34000

Designs:—1l. Coastline; 2l. Budva; 5l. Mt. Lovcen; 10l. Lake of Scutari.

Flücht-lingshilfe Montenegro
0,15 + 0,85 RM.
(2)

Flüchtlingshilfe Montenegro
0,15 + 1,35 RM.
(3)

1944 (22 May). Refugees' Fund. Surch as Type **2** or **3** in German Currency.

(a) With Type **2** *on Nos. 419/420 of Yugoslavia*

95	99	0.15 +0.85Rm. on 3d. red-brown	33·00	£300
96	–	0.15 +0.85Rm. on 4d. bright blue	33·00	£300

(b) As Type **2** *on Nos. 64/67 of Italian Occupation (of Montenegro)*

97	–	0.15 +0.85Rm. on 25c. green	33·00	£300
98	–	0.15 +1.35Rm. on 50c. rose-magenta	33·00	£300
99	–	0.25 +1.75Rm. on 1l.25 blue	33·00	£300
100	–	0.25 +1.75Rm. on 2l. blue-green	33·00	£300

(c) AIR. As Type **3** *on Nos. 70/72 of Italian Occupation (of Montenegro)*

101	–	0.15 +0.85Rm. on 50c. brown	33·00	£300
102	–	0.25 +1.25Rm. on 1l. ultramarine	33·00	£300
103	–	0.50 +1.50Rm. on 2l. rose-magenta	33·00	£300
95/103		Set of 9	£275	£2500

+ Crveni krst Montenegro
0.50 + 2.50 RM.
(4)

+ Crveni krst Montenegro
0.25 + 2.75 RM.
(5)

1944 (Aug). Red Cross. Surch as Type **4** or **5** in German currency in red.

(a) With Type **4** *on Nos. 419/420 of Yugoslavia*

104	99	0.50 +2.50Rm. on 3d. red-brown	29·00	£275
105	–	0.50 +2.50Rm. on 4d. bright blue	29·00	£275

(b) As Type **5** *on Nos. 64/65 of Italian Occupation (of Montenegro)*

106	–	0.15 +0.85Rm. on 25c. green	29·00	£275
107	–	0.15 +1.35Rm. on 50c. rose-magenta	29·00	£275

(c) AIR. As Type **5** *on Nos. 70/72 of Italian Occupation (of Montenegro)*

108	–	0.25 +1.75Rm. on 50c. brown	29·00	£275
109	–	0.25 +2.75Rm. on 1l. ultramarine	29·00	£275
110	–	0.50 +2Rm. on 2l. rose-magenta	29·00	£275
104/110		Set of 7	£180	£1700

SLOVENIA

Italian Currency

Following the armistice of September 1943, German forces took over Italian Slovenia.

PRINTERS. Types **3**/**8** were overprinted at the Ljudska Printing Works, Ljubljana.

GERMAN OCCUPATION ISSUES, 1939–1945

IMAGES. See section L. Yugoslavia (Dalmatia) for images of Italian stamps.

(3) (4)

1944 (5 Jan–Mar). Stamps of Italy optd with Type **3** or **4**.

(a) On Postage stamps Nos. 238, etc. (5 Jan)

65	4	5c. brown (B.) (T **98**)	60	8·50
66	3	10c. sepia (B.) (T **100**)	60	8·50
67	4	15c. blue-green (C.) (T **101**)	60	8·50
68	3	20c. carmine (B.) (T **99**)	60	8·50
69	4	25c. green (C.) (T **102**)	60	8·50
70	3	30c. brown (B.) (T **103**)	60	8·50
71	4	35c. blue (Br.) (T **101**)	60	8·50
72	3	50c. bright violet (C.) (T **103**)	60	12·00
73	4	75c. carmine (B.) (T **102**)	60	18·00
74	3	1l. violet (B.) (T **99**)	60	18·00
75	4	1l.25 blue (C.) (T **102**)	60	6·00
76	3	1l.75 orange-vermilion (G.) (T **100**)	12·00	42·00
77	4	2l. brown-lake (B.) (T **101**)	60	12·00
78	3	10l. violet (B.) (T **101**)	22·00	95·00

Surcharged with new value

79	–	2l.55 on 5c. brown (Bk.) (T **98**)	4·75	22·00
80	4	5l. on 25c. green (B.) (T **102**)	4·75	36·00
81	–	20l. on 20c. carmine (G.) (T **99**)	26·00	£110
82	3	25l. on 2l. brown-lake (G.) (T **101**)	22·00	£225
83	4	50l. on 1l.75 orange-vermilion (O.) (T **100**)	95·00	£350
65/83	Set of 19		£170	£900

In No. 79 the overprint inscriptions are at each side of the eagle.

(b) On Air stamps Nos. 270, etc (18 Mar)

84	4	25c. grey-green (C.) (T **111**)	20·00	70·00
85	3	50c. sepia (B.) (T **110**)	20·00	£225
86	4	75c. chestnut (G.) (T **112**)	20·00	70·00
87	3	1l. bright violet (C.) (T **112**)	20·00	£225
88	4	2l. blue (B.) (T **113**)	20·00	£160
89	3	5l. green (C.) (T **110**)	20·00	£225
90	4	10l. carmine-red (G.) (T **110**)	20·00	£160
84/90	Set of 7		£130	£1000

(c) On Air Express stamp No. E370 (18 Mar)

E91	3	2l. blue-black (B.) (T E **133**)	23·00	£160

(d) On Express Letter stamp No. E350 (11 Feb)

E92	3	1l.25 green (G.) (T E **132**)	20·00	43·00

(D 5) (D 6)

1944 (26 Feb). POSTAGE DUE. Nos. D395, etc of Italy optd as Type D **5**.

D93	D 5	5c. chocolate (Br.) (T D **141**)	4·75	£120
D94	–	10c. blue (␣) (T D **141**)	4·75	£120
D95	D 5	20c. bright carmine (C.) (T D **141**)	1·80	12·00
D96	–	25c. green (G.) (T D **141**)	1·80	12·00
D97	D 5	50c. bright violet (V.) (T D **141**)	1·80	12·00
D98	–	1l. orange (C.) (T D **142**)	1·80	12·00
D99	D 5	2l. green (B.) (T D **142**)	1·80	12·00

*Surcharged as Type D **6***

D100	D 6	30c. on 50c. bright violet (Bk.) (T D **141**)	4·75	£120
D101	–	40c. on 50c. chocolate (B.) (T D **141**)	4·75	£120
D93/D101	Set of 9		25·00	£475

In Nos. D93/D101 values with a hyphen in the type column have the overprint with the alternative language predominating.

(5)

1944 (18 Mar). Red Cross. Express Letter stamps, T E **132** of Italy surch as Type **5**.

102	5	1l.25 +50l. green (O.)	70·00	£900
103	–	2l.50 +50l. red-orange (O.)	70·00	£900

(6)

1944 (18 Mar). Homeless Relief Fund. Express Letter stamps, T E **132** of Italy surch as Type **6**.

104	–	1l.25 +50l. green (B.)	70·00	£900
105	5	2l.50 +50l. red-orange (G.)	70·00	£900

(7) (8)

1944 (18 Mar). AIR. Orphans' Fund. Nos. 270 etc. of Italy, surch as Type **7**.

106	7	25c. +10l. grey-green (B.) (T **111**)	26·00	£600
107	–	50c. +10l. sepia (B.) (T **110**)	26·00	£600
108	7	75c. +10l. chestnut (B.) (T **112**)	26·00	£600
109	–	1l. +20l. bright violet (B.) (T **112**)	26·00	£600
110	7	2l. +20l. blue (C.) (T **113**)	26·00	£600
111	–	5l. +20l. green (B.) (T **110**)	26·00	£600
106/111	Set of 6		£140	£3250

1944 (18 Mar). AIR. Winter Relief Fund. Nos. 270 etc., of Italy, surch as Type **8**.

112	8	25c. +10l. grey-green (B.) (T **111**)	26·00	£600
113	–	50c. +10l. sepia (B.) (T **110**)	26·00	£600
114	8	75c. +10l. chestnut (B.) (T **112**)	26·00	£600
115	–	1l. +20l. bright violet (B.) (T **112**)	26·00	£600
116	8	2l. +20l. blue (Br.) (T **113**)	26·00	£600
117	–	5l. +20l. green (B.) (T **110**)	26·00	£600
112/117	Set of 6		£140	£3250

In Nos. 102/117 the values with a hyphen in the type column have the overprint with the alternative language predominating.

9 Railway Viaduct, Borovnice   **10** Church in Novo Mesto

1945. Various landscape designs inscr 'PROVINZ LAIBACH' at top as Type **9/10**. P 11½×10½ (vert) or 10½×11½ (horiz).

118	5c. black-brown	55	6·00
119	10c. orange	55	6·00
120	20c. lake-brown	55	6·00
121	25c. deep green	55	6·00
122	50c. violet	55	6·00
123	75c. scarlet	55	6·00
124	1l. olive-green	55	6·00
125	1l.25 blue	55	12·00
126	1l.50 grey-green	55	12·00
127	2l. bright blue	85	14·50
128	2l.50 brown	85	14·50
129	3l. bright magenta	1·80	24·00
130	5l. red-brown	2·75	24·00
131	10l. blue-green	6·00	£110
132	20l. blue	36·00	£375
133	30l. carmine	£180	£1400
118/133	Set of 16	£200	£1800

Designs: Vert—5c. Stalagmites, Križna Jama; 50c. Type **10**; 1l.25, Kocevje; 1l.50, Borovnice Falls; 3l. Castle, Zuzemberg; 30l. View and Tabor Church. Horiz—10c. Zirknitz Lake; 20c. Type **9**; 25c. Farm near Ljubljana; 75c. View from Ribnica; 1l. Old Castle, Ljubljana; 2l. Castle, Kostanjevica; 2l.50, Castle, Turjak; 5l. View on River Krka; 10l. Castle, Otoec; 20l. Farm at Dolenjskom.

375

M. GERMAN OCCUPATION OF CHANNEL ISLANDS

GUERNSEY

WAR OCCUPATION ISSUES

Stamps issued under the authority of the Guernsey States during the German Occupation.

BISECTS. On 24 December 1940 authority was given, by Post Office notice, that prepayment of penny postage could be effected by using half a British 2d. stamp, diagonally bisected. Such stamps were first used on 27 December 1940.

The 2d. stamps generally available were those of the Postal Centenary issue, 1940 (S.G. 482) and the first colour of the King George VI issue (S.G. 465). These are listed under Nos. 482a and 465b. A number of the 2d. King George V, 1912–1922, and of the King George V photogravure stamp (S.G. 442) which were in the hands of philatelists, were also bisected and used.

Stamps of Great Britain

106
120
128
134 Queen Victoria and King George VI

Example of bisected 2d. Postal Centenary stamp

The Bisects

1940 (27 Dec).

(a) Stamps of King George V

Cat. No.			Price on Cover
BS1	**106**	1912–1922 2d. orange	£300
BS2		1924–1926 2d. orange	£300
BS3	**120**	1934–1936 2d. orange	£325

(b) Stamps of King George VI

BS4	**128**	1937 1d. scarlet	£700
BS5		1938 2d. orange	50·00
BS6	**134**	1940 Stamp Centenary 1d. scarlet	£700
BS7		1940 Stamp Centenary 2d. orange	40·00
BS8		1940 Stamp Centenary 2½d. ultramarine	£1500
BS9		1940 Stamp Centenary 3d. violet	

Forged postmarks on fake bisects are known from Guernsey Head Post Office ('2 JA 41'), Market Place ('19 FE 41' or '7 AP 41'), St. Sampson ('27 DE 40') and The Vale ('18 FE 41').

The bisects are priced on philatelic cover. Those which were used commercially are worth more, particularly Nos. BS5 and BS7.

Invalidated: 22.2.41 (last postings were postmarked 24.2.41.)

1a Loops (½-size illustration)

(Des E. W. Vaudin. Typo Guernsey Press Co Ltd)

1941–44. Rouletted.

(a) White paper. No wmk

1	1	½d. light green (7.4.41)	6·00	3·50
		a. Emerald-green (6.41)	6·00	2·00
		b. Bluish green (11.41)	35·00	13·00
		c. Bright green (2.42)	22·00	10·00
		d. Dull green (9.42)	4·00	2·00
		e. Olive-green (2.43)	45·00	25·00
		f. Pale yellowish green (7.43 and later) (shades)	4·00	3·00
		g. Imperf (pair)	£250	
		h. Imperf between (horiz pair)	£800	
		i. Imperf between (vert pair)	£950	
2		1d. scarlet (18.2.41)	3·25	2·00
		a. Pale vermilion (7.43) (etc.)	5·00	2·00
		b. Carmine (1943)	3·50	2·00
		c. Imperf (pair)	£200	90·00
		d. Imperf between (horiz pair)	£800	
		da. Imperf vert (centre stamp of horiz strip of 3)		
		e. Imperf between (vert pair)	£950	
		f. Printed double (scarlet shade)	£150	
3		2½d. ultramarine (12.4.44)	18·00	15·00
		a. Pale ultramarine (7.44)	15·00	12·00
		b. Imperf (pair)	£550	
		c. Imperf between (horiz pair)	£1250	

*(b) Bluish French bank-note paper. W **1a** (sideways)*

4	1	½d. bright green (11.3.42)	32·00	25·00
5		1d. scarlet (9.4.42)	18·00	25·00

The dates given for the shades of Nos. 1/3 are the months in which they were printed as indicated on the printer's imprints. Others are issue dates.

JERSEY

WAR OCCUPATION ISSUES

Stamps issued under the authority of the Jersey States during the German Occupation.

THE GERMAN OCCUPATION

1940–1945

Soon after the commencement of the occupation of Jersey by German forces on 1 July 1940 orders were given by the German Commandant to the Islands Postmaster for stocks of the currently available stamps to be forwarded to the Jersey printers, J. T. Bigwood, for overprinting with a swastika and 'JERSEY 1940'. All values of the 1937–1938 definitives from ½d. to 10s., excluding the 1d., were so overprinted as were the 1940 Postal Centenary stamps, excluding the 1d., but whilst this was in progress the Bailiff of Jersey protested to the German Commandant who referred the matter to Berlin and was ordered to destroy the stocks. Four complete sets to 1s., and a few singles, however, are known to exist. At the same time Bigwoods prepared a local 1d. stamp incorporating the Arms of Jersey and the words 'ETATS DE JERSEY'. These were printed in imperforate sheets of 30 (10×3) and are known with and without a swastika and '1940' overprint. These also were destroyed with the exception of two sheets of each which have been cut up for collectors and a damaged sheet with the overprint which is complete. There is also a complete sheet of the unoverprinted stamp in the National Postal Museum.

Jersey eventually issued locally printed ½d. and 1d. stamps, the 1d. on 1 April 1941 and the ½d. on 29 January 1942. No distinct shades exist though both values come on newsprint paper and, in addition, the 1d. is known on chalk-surfaced paper.

In June 1943 a pictorial set of six stamps from ½d. to 3d. was issued, the designer being the well-known Jersey artist Edmund Blampied. Two values, the 1d. and 2½d., are known on newsprint paper.

Both these and the earlier issues remained on sale until 13 April 1946 after which date they could no longer be used.

376

GERMAN OCCUPATION ISSUES, 1939–1945

The Swastika Overprints

1940. Prepared for use but not issued. Stamps of Great Britain overprinted by J. T. Bigwood, States Printers.

(a) On 1937–1939 definitive issue.

Cat. No	Type No.		Unused
SW1	1	½d. green	£3250
SW2		1½d. red-brown	£3250
SW3		2d. orange	£3250
SW4		2½d. ultramarine	£3250
SW5		3d. violet	£3250
SW6		4d. grey-green	£3250
SW7		5d. brown	£3250
SW8		6d. purple	£3250
SW9		7d. emerald-green	£3250
SW10		8d. bright carmine	£3250
SW11		9d. deep olive-green	£3250
SW12		10d. turquoise-blue	£3250
SW13		1s. bistre-brown	£3250

(b) On 1940 Stamp Centenary issue

SW14	2	½d. green	£3250
SW15		1½d. red-brown	£3250
SW16		2d. orange	£3250
SW17		2½d. ultramarine	£3250
SW18		3d. violet	£3250

3  **4**

(Des R. W. Cutland. Typo J. T. Bigwood)

1940. Prepared for use but not issued. No wmk. Imperforate.

SW19	3	1d. scarlet	£3000
SW20	4	1d. scarlet	£3000

5

(Des Major N. V. L. Rybot. Typo *Jersey Evening Post*, St. Helier)

1941–43. White paper (thin to thick). No wmk. P 11.

1	5	½d. bright green (29.1.42)	8·00	6·00
		a. Imperf between (vert pair)	£900	
		b. Imperf between (horiz pair)	£800	
		c. Imperf (pair)	£300	
		d. On greyish paper (1.43)	12·00	12·00
2		1d. scarlet (1.4.41)	8·00	5·00
		a. Imperf between (vert pair)	£900	
		b. Imperf between (horiz pair)	£800	
		c. Imperf (pair)	£325	
		d. On chalk-surfaced paper	55·00	48·00
		e. On greyish paper (1.43)	14·00	14·00

6 Old Jersey Farm  **7** Portelet Bay

8 Corbière Lighthouse  **9** Elizabeth Castle

10 Mont Orgueil Castle  **11** Gathering Vraic (seaweed)

(Des E. Blampied. Eng H. Cortot. Typo French Govt Works, Paris)

1943–44. No wmk. P 13½.

3	6	½d. green (1.6.43)	12·00	12·00
		a. Rough, grey paper (6.10.43)	15·00	14·00
4	7	1d. scarlet (1.6.43)	3·00	50
		a. On newsprint (28.2.44)	3·50	75
5	8	1½d. brown (8.6.43)	8·00	5·75
6	9	2d. orange-yellow (8.6.43)	7·50	2·00
7	10	2½d. blue (29.6.43)	3·00	1·00
		a. On newsprint (25.2.44)	1·00	1·75
		ba. Thin paper*	£225	
8	11	3d. violet (29.6.43)	3·00	2·75
3/8	*Set of 6*		30·00	21·00

*On No. 7ba the design shows clearly through the back of the stamp.

Cameroun

100 Pfennig = 1 Mark

FORERUNNERS. Forerunners, i.e. unoverprinted stamps of Germany used in colonies and post offices abroad before introduction of their own stamps, are listed with Z numbers. Prices quoted are for the cheapest version of each stamp used as a true forerunner, prices varying according to postmark. In many cases such stamps used after the introduction of overprinted stamps are worth less than those with the equivalent postmark used before. Prices are for loose stamps with full cancellation; poor cancels are worth less. Stamps on piece with exceptionally clear postmarks and stamps on covers or postcards are worth more.

ERRORS. Errors such as double and inverted surcharges were never issued but come from waste sheets which later leaked out of the printers.

A   B

'YACHT' KEY TYPES. Types A and B, representing the ex-Kaiser's yacht *Hohenzollern*, were in use throughout the German colonies, inscribed with the name of the particular colony for which they were issued.

Type A was printed by typography and Type B was recess-printed, both by Imperial Printing Office, Berlin.

Frame Type I

Centre Type I

Frame Type II

Centre Type II

Plates. There are two types of design according to the length of the name of the colony. Type I with plain scroll and Type II with folded scroll at the top.

The top value of each Colony (5m., 3r. or 2½d.) is printed in two colours and therefore has two plates; there are two types of the centre plates to fit the two types of frame plates and it sometimes happened that centre plates were used with frame plates for which they were not intended.

Where this occurred either the lines of shading from the sky run across the protruding folds (Centre Type I) or there are two clear spaces in the sky below the top scroll (Centre Type II).

In the lists which follow '(I)' means that both plates are Type I and '(II)' means that both are Type II. Combinations of plates are listed separately.

Perforations. Type A (low values) is perforated 14. In Type B (high values) there are three types of perforation, all measuring about 14½. They are distinguishable by the number of holes along the horizontal and down the vertical sides of the stamps thus:—
(a) 26×17 holes
(b) 25×17 holes
(c) 25×16 holes

Wmk Lozenges

Watermark. Some values listed on paper watermarked Lozenges were prepared for use and sold in Berlin, but owing to the war of 1914–1918 were not issued in the colonies.

On 14 July 1884, by agreement between Dr. Gustav Nachtigal and local rulers, the coastal area round Douala became the German Protectorate of Kamerun. The protectorate was extended inland to Lake Chad in 1894 and in 1911 territory giving access to the Congo and Ubangi Rivers was acquired from France in return for German recognition of a French protectorate in Morocco.

The first postal agency in Kamerun was opened on 1 February 1887; this became a post office on 6 January 1897. Until 1 June 1901 it used the 'KAMERUN' cancellation but on that date its name was changed to Duala. Other agencies were opened at Viktoria on 12 December 1888 (in December 1900 the spelling was changed to Victoria); Bibundi on 5 July 1891 (closed 8 January 1897, re-opened 22 May 1906; Gross-Batanga on 1 March 1893 (closed 31 December 1893); Kribi on 10 August 1894; Rio del Rey officially on 9 January 1897, but cancellations are known as a dispatching office from 20 October 1896; and Buea on 15 February 1900. Unoverprinted German stamps were used from these dates.

PRICES. Prices quoted below are for 'KAMERUN' cancellations dated between 1.2.87 and 31.12.88 and from 14.8.89 to May 1897 (except for No. Z1). Other date cancellations and postmarks of the other postal agencies are worth more, except for stamps used after May 1897 which are worth about 25% less than those used before.

1887–1900. Stamps of Germany cancelled with circular postmarks of Cameroun offices.

(a) Nos. 38b/38e (Numeral inscr 'DEUTSCHE REICHS-POST')

Z1	7	2m. dull rose (1.2.87)	£2000
		a. Mauve (6.6.89)	£1300
		b. Deep claret (23.1.91)	£450
		c. Red-lilac (1.2.00)	£1600

(b) Nos. 39/44 (Numeral or Eagle inscr 'DEUTSCHE REICHS-POST')

Z2	5	3pf. green (9.10.87)	£2500
Z3		5pf. mauve (8.3.87)	£400
Z4	6	10pf. rose (8.2.87)	£2000
		a. Carmine (14.2.87)	£250
Z5		20pf. pale blue (14.2.87)	£100
		a. Bright blue	£100

CAMEROUN

Z6	25pf. deep chestnut (8.4.88)		£3500
Z7	50pf. pale grey-olive (8.4.87)		£275
	a. Dull olive-green		£225
	b. Blackish olive		£2000
	c. Bronze-green		£400

(c) Nos. 46/51 (Numeral or Eagle inscr 'REICHSPOST')

Z8	8	3pf. brown (11.3.90)		£160
		a. Grey-brown (1892)		85·00
Z9		5pf. green (2.6.90)		£110
		a. Yellow-green (1891)		85·00
Z10	9	10pf. rose-carmine (6.1.90)		£1800
		a. Carmine (1895)		39·00
Z11		20pf. ultramarine (10.1.90)		£160
		a. Dull blue (1891)		£100
Z12		25pf. orange-yellow (22.4.90)		£300
		a. Orange (1894)		£250
Z13		50pf. lake-mauve (14.4.90)		£6000
		a. Chocolate (6.4.91)		85·00

Dates are those of earliest known use.

Examples of other shades of the 3pf. brown (Nos. 46c/46d) are known used from 1897, after the introduction of the overprinted stamps (*Price* £65).

Nos. Z2/Z7 were valid until 31 January 1891 and Nos. Z1 and Z8/Z13 until 30 September 1901.

Kamerun

(K **1**)

1897 (Apr)–**98**. Stamps of Germany, 1889, optd with Type K **1**.

K1	8	3pf. grey-brown (8.97)	30·00	65·00
		a. Yellow-brown (1898)	17·00	26·00
		b. Reddish brown (1898)	£100	£375
K2		5pf. green	10·50	13·00
K3	9	10pf. carmine	7·25	7·75
K4		20pf. ultramarine	7·25	11·50
		a. Bisected (*on cover*) (3.10.98)		†£26000
K5		25pf. orange	30·00	65·00
K6		50pf. red-brown (10.97)	23·00	42·00
		a. Chocolate	23·00	42·00
K1/K6		Set of 6 (*cheapest*)	85·00	£150

1900 (10 Nov)–**11**. No wmk.

K7	A	3pf. brown	2·20	2·50
K8		5pf. green	18·00	2·10
K9		10pf. carmine	60·00	19·00
K10		20pf. ultramarine	39·00	3·75
		a. Bisected (*on cover*) (19.5.11)		†£12000
K11		25pf. black and red/*yellow*	2·50	8·50
K12		30pf. black and orange/*buff*	3·00	7·25
K13		40pf. black and carmine	3·00	6·50
K14		50pf. black and purple/*buff*	3·00	9·75
K15		80pf. black and carmine/*rose*	4·00	17·00
K16	B	1m. carmine (*a*)	£100	£120
K17		2m. blue (*a*)	8·50	£120
K18		3m. violet-black (*a*)	8·50	£180
K19		5m. carmine and black (II) (*a*)	£275	£800
K7/K19		Set of 13	£475	£1200
K7s/K19s		Optd 'Specimen' Set of 13	£600	

2pf. grey is a proof.

No. K10a was used at Longji and covers show an impression of the postal agency's negative seal next to the bisect.

1905 (Oct)–**19**. Wmk Lozenges.

K20	A	3pf. brown (3.10.18*)	1·30	
K21		5pf. green	1·30	2·50
		a. Booklet pane. No. K21×5 plus label (1.10.11)	£1000	
		b. Booklet pane. Nos. K21×2 and K22×4 (1913)	£110	
K22		10pf. carmine (12.06)	4·00	2·50
		a. Booklet pane. No. K22×5 plus label (1.10.11)	£1000	
K23		20pf. ultramarine (*shades*) (1.14)	6·25	£200
K24	B	1m. carmine (*a*) (1.15*)	18·00	
		a. 25×17 holes (1919*)	20·00	
K25		5m. carmine and black (II) (*a*) (8.13)	80·00	£6000
		a. 25×17 holes (1919*)	48·00	

*These stamps were only on sale in Berlin.

STAMP BOOKLETS

Prices are for complete booklets.

Booklet No.	Date	Contents and Cover Price	Price
SB1	1.10.11	Yacht	
		4 panes, No. K21a; 2 panes, No. K22a (2m.)	£8000
SB2	1913	Yacht	
		3 panes, No. K21×6; 1 pane, No. K21b; 1 pane, No. K22×6 (2m.)	£250

No. SB2 was on sale in Berlin only.

In 1914–1916 Kamerun was occupied by British and French forces and on 4 March 1916 was provisionally divided between France and Britain, the latter receiving a strip of territory along the Nigerian border. This arrangement was recognised by the peace settlement of 1919, with the proviso that what had been the German protectorate before 1911 was to be administered by the two powers under League of Nations mandates. In 1946 the mandates were changed to trusteeships under the United Nations.

BRITISH OCCUPATION

Allied operations against the German protectorate of Kamerun commenced in September 1914 and were completed in 18 February 1916. The territory was divided, under an Anglo-French agreement, on 31 March 1916, with the British administering the area in the west along the Nigerian border. League of Nations mandates were issued for the two sections of Cameroon on 20 July 1922, which were converted into United Nations trusteeships in 1946.

Supplies of Kamerun stamps were found on the German steamer *Professor Woermann*, captured at Freetown, and these were surcharged, probably in Sierra Leone, and issued by the Cameroons Expeditionary Force at Duala in July 1915.

> **PRICES FOR STAMPS ON COVER**
>
> The stamps of British Occupation of Cameroons are rare used on cover.

A   B

C.E.F.   C.E.F.

1d.   **1**s.

(1)   (2)

SETTINGS. Nos. B1/B3 were surcharged from a setting of 100 (10×10) with the face value changed for the 1d.

Nos. B4 and B6/B9 were surcharged from a common setting of 50 (5×10) with the face value amended.

No. B5 was surcharged from a setting of ten in a vertical strip repeated across the sheet. The figures of the surcharge on this are in a different style from the remainder of the pence stamps.

Nos. B10/B13 were surcharged from a common setting of 20 (4×5) with the face value amended.

d.   *d.*

Normal   Different fount 'd' (R. 2/10, 6/9, 10/10)

1*d.*   1*d.*

'1' with thin serifs (R. 5/1)   Short '4' (R. 10/2, 10/7)

5ˢ   5ˢ.

's' broken at top (R. 3/1)   's' inverted (R. 3/4)

CAMEROUN / CAROLINE ISLANDS

1915 (12 July). Stamps of German Kamerun. Types A and B, surch as T **1** (Nos. B1/B9) or **2** (Nos. B10/B13) in black or blue.

B1	A	½d. on 3pf. brown (No. K7) (B.)	13·00	55·00
		a. Different fount 'd'	£180	£425
B2		½d. on 5pf. green (No. K21 wmk lozenges) (B.)	7·00	10·00
		a. Different fount 'd'	85·00	£140
		b. Surch double	†	£1000
		ba. Surch double, one albino	£400	
B3		1d. on 10pf. carmine (No. K22 wmk lozenges) (B.)	1·25	9·50
		a. '1' with thin serifs	13·00	70·00
		b. Surch double	£425	
		ba. Surch double, one albino	£160	
		c. '1d.' only double	£2000	
		d. Surch triple, two albino	£400	
		e. Surch in black	12·00	55·00
		ea. '1' with thin serifs	£275	
B4		2d. on 20pf. ultramarine (No. K23 wmk lozenges)	3·50	22·00
		a. Surch double, one albino	£400	
B5		2½d. on 25pf. black and red/*yellow* (No. K11)	20·00	55·00
		a. Surch double	£13000	
		ab. Surch double, one albino	£1500	
B6		3d. on 30pf. black and orange/*buff* (No. K12)	13·00	60·00
		a. Large '3' (R. 3/5, 3/10)	£1500	
		b. Surch triple, two albino	£475	
B7		4d. on 40pf. black and carmine (No. K13)	14·00	60·00
		a. Short '4'	£1000	£1800
		b. Surch triple, two albino	£375	
		c. Surch quadruple, three albino	£1500	
B8		6d. on 50pf. black and purple/*buff* (No. K14)	13·00	60·00
		a. Surch double, one albino	£375	
B9		8d. on 80pf. black and carmine/*rose* (No. K15)	13·00	60·00
		a. Surch triple, two albino	£1600	
B10	B	1s. on 1m. carmine (No. K16)	£200	£900
		a. 's' inverted	£1000	£3750
B11		2s. on 2m. blue (No. K17)	£225	£1000
		a. 's' inverted	£1000	£3750
		b. Surch double, one albino	£2750	
B12		3s. on 3m. violet-black (No. K18)	£225	£1000
		a. 's' inverted	£1000	£4000
		b. 's' broken at top	£900	
		c. Surch double	£15000	
		ca. Surch triple, two albino	£2750	
B13		5s. on 5m. carmine and black (No. K25a wmk lozenges)	£275	£1100
		a. 's' inverted	£1300	£4500
		b. 's' broken at top	£1200	
B1/B13 Set of 13			£900	£4000

The 1d. on 10pf. was previously listed with 'C.E.F.' omitted. This was due to misplacement, so that all stamps (except for a pair in the Royal Collection) from the bottom row show traces of the overprint on the top perforations.

Examples of all values exist showing a forged Duala, Kamerun postmark dated '11 10 15'. Another forged cancel dated '16 11 15' is also known. This can be identified by the lack of a serif on the index letter 'b'.

Caroline Islands

100 Pfennig = 1 Mark

GENERAL NOTES. See beginning of Cameroun.

The Caroline Islands in the Western Pacific Ocean were discovered in 1526 and claimed by Spain in 1875. The claim was contested by Germany, but arbitration by the Pope awarded the islands to Spain. Germany purchased rights to a protectorate from Spain in 1899.

(1)   (2)

1899–1900. Stamps of Germany, 1889, optd.

*(a) Overprint sloping as Type **1** (48 degrees) (12.10.99)*

1	8	3pf. grey-brown	£900	£1000
2		5pf. green	£900	£900
3	9	10pf. carmine	90·00	£190
4		20pf. ultramarine	90·00	£190
5		25pf. orange	£2250	£4000
6		50pf. chocolate	£950	£2250

*(b) Overprint sloping as Type **2** (56 degrees). (5.00)*

7	8	3pf. grey-brown	17·00	19·00
8		5pf. green	24·00	24·00
9	9	10pf. carmine	24·00	26·00
10		20pf. ultramarine	31·00	38·00
11		25pf. orange	70·00	85·00
12		50pf. chocolate	70·00	85·00
7/12 Set of 6			£200	£250

'YACHT' KEY TYPES and PERFORATIONS. For details of types A and B representing the ex-Kaiser's yacht *Hohenzollern*, and for perforation types (a), (b) and (c) see beginning of Cameroun.

1901 (7 Jan)–**10**. No wmk.

13	A	3pf. brown (7.1.01)	1·40	2·40
14		5pf. green (7.1.01)	1·40	3·00
15		10pf. carmine (7.1.01)	1·40	6·50
		a. Bisected (*on card*) (25.4.05)	†	£600
16		20pf. ultramarine (7.1.01)	1·70	12·00
		a. Bisected (*on cover*) (12.7.10)	†	£12000
17		25pf. black and red/*yellow* (7.1.01)	2·00	19·00
18		30pf. black and orange/*buff* (7.1.01)	2·00	19·00
19		40pf. black and carmine (7.1.01)	2·00	22·00
20		50pf. black and purple/*buff* (7.1.01)	2·75	30·00
21		80pf. black and carmine/*rose* (7.1.01)	4·00	34·00
22	B	1m. carmine (a)	6·00	85·00
23		2m. blue (a)	9·50	£120
24		3m. violet-black (a)	14·50	£200
25		5m. carmine and black (Frame II, Centre I) (a)	£225	£700
13/25 Set of 13			£250	£1100
13s/25s Optd 'Specimen' Set of 13			£600	

2pf. grey is a proof.

A typhoon at Ponape on 20 April 1906 destroyed the post office, the normal cancellation and much of the stamp stock. When the office re-opened on 25 April surviving stocks of the 10pf. were bisected and used as 5pf. stamps (No. 15a) (*Price of piece* £85). Such use continued until 9 July with the bisects cancelled with the negative post office seal as shown above.

5 pf
(3)

1910 (12 July). No. 13 handstamped with T **3**.
26   A   5pf. on 3pf. brown... † £7500

    No. 26 exists with handstamp inverted or double.

The unexpected arrival of a German naval squadron at Ponape in July 1910 led to the exhaustion of available supplies of both the 5pf. and 10pf. values. They were initially replaced by the 5pf. on 3pf. surcharge (No. 26) and by a bisect of the 20pf. (No. 16a) with a normal postmark and impression of the negative post office seal (as above but 'KAROLINEN' the same size as 'PONAPE') struck alongside (*Price on piece* £3500). Subsequent sendings had the postage paid in cash or were forwarded to the Marshall Islands for franking.

1915–19. Wmk Lozenges.
27	A	3pf. brown (5.19)..	1·20
28		5pf. green..	17·00
29		5m. carmine and black (II) (*a*) (1.15)......	60·00
		b. 25×17 holes (1919)	50·00

Nos. 27 and 29/29b were never issued in the Caroline Islands, but were on sale in Berlin. Stocks of No. 28 only exist from remainders auctioned in 1923.

The islands were occupied by Japan from 7 October 1914 and on 17 December 1920 became a Japanese mandated territory. In the Second World War the Japanese stronghold of Peleliu was captured by US forces on 25 November 1944; the main Japanese naval base of Truk was destroyed by air bombing on 17–18 February 1944. On 18 July 1947 the Caroline Islands became a United States trust territory.

German East Africa

1893. 64 Pesa = 1 Rupee
1905. 100 Heller = 1 Rupee

GENERAL NOTES. See beginning of Cameroun.

In November 1884 Karl Peters, a leader of the German colonial movement, made a treaty with a chief near Usambara, who was declared to be independent of the Sultan of Zanzibar who claimed to rule the mainland of what is now Tanzania. Similar treaties followed, and on 27 February 1885 Germany established a protectorate over the coast of East Africa from the Umba River in the north to the Rovuma River in the south.

LAMU

A postal agency was opened on the island of Lamu, which belonged to the Sultan of Zanzibar, on 22 November 1888 and used unoverprinted stamps of Germany. It closed on 31 March 1891 when the area was transferred to Great Britain.

1888–91. Stamps of Germany cancelled with circular postmark 'LAMU/OSTAFRIKA'.

(a) No. 38b (Numeral inscr 'DEUTSCHE REICHS-POST')
Z1	7	2m. dull rose (26.10.89)....................	£8000

(b) Nos. 39/44 (Numeral or Eagle inscr 'DEUTSCHE REICHSPOST')
Z2	5	3pf. green (3.2.91)............................	£6000
Z3		5pf. mauve (13.6.89)........................	£700
Z4	6	10pf. carmine (8.6.89)......................	£600
Z5		20pf. bright blue (2.12.88)................	£550
Z6		25pf. deep chestnut (9.90)................	—
Z7		50pf. dull olive-green (19.1.89)........	£1400

(c) Nos. 46/51 (Numeral or Eagle inscr 'REICHSPOST')
Z8	8	3pf. brown (6.1.91)	£900
Z9		5pf. green (3.2.91)	£700
		a. Yellow-green (1891)	£700
Z10	9	10pf. rose (6.1.91)	£900
Z11		20pf. ultramarine (3.2.91)................	£950
		a. Dull blue (1891).........................	
Z12		25pf. orange-yellow (27.2.91)..........	£1200
Z13		50pf. chocolate (27.2.91)..................	£1800

Dates are those of earliest known use.

Remainders of Nos. Z3/Z4 were sold with backdated cancellations; prices quoted are for genuinely used copies, remainders being almost worthless. These remainders, which when *on piece* are usually on buff-coloured paper, were cancelled as follows: various dates in 1888, 12.3.89, 12.8.89, 21.9.89, 17.12.89, 20.7.90 and 12.8.90.

ZANZIBAR

A postal agency opened in Zanzibar on 27 August 1890 and used unoverprinted stamps of Germany. It closed on 31 July 1891.

1890–91. Stamps of Germany cancelled with circular postmark 'ZANZIBAR/KAISERL DEUTSCHE/POSTAGENTUR'.

(a) Nos. 38b/38d (Numeral inscr 'DEUTSCHE REICHS-POST')
Z14	7	2m. mauve (1.9.90)............................	£6000
		a. Deep claret (9.11.90)	£2000
		b. Dull rose (25.4.91).......................	£1400

(b) Nos. 46/51 (Numeral or Eagle inscr 'REICHSPOST')
Z15	8	3pf. brown (24.3.91)..........................	£475
Z16		5pf. green (4.10.90)	£300
		a. Yellow-green...............................	£250
Z17	9	10pf. rose (31.8.90)	£250
Z18		20pf. ultramarine (31.8.90)	£225
		a. Dull blue......................................	£170
Z19		25pf. orange-yellow (24.3.91)..........	£950
Z20		50pf. lake-brown (1.9.90)	£900
		a. Chocolate.....................................	£475

Dates are those of earliest known use.

Prices quoted are for cancellations in black; most cancellations in blue are worth more.

Examples of Nos. 40/42 of Germany exist with Zanzibar postmarks. These are backdated philatelic cancellations, genuinely used examples being unknown.

381

German New Guinea

100 Pfennig = 1 Mark

GENERAL NOTES. See beginning of Cameroun.

On 16 November 1884, ten days after the south-eastern part of New Guinea became a British protectorate, the north-eastern part of the island was declared to be a German protectorate and was named Kaiser-Wilhelms-Land. At the same time a German protectorate was declared over the Bismarck archipelago, consisting of New Pomerania (now New Britain), New Mecklenburg (now New Ireland) and New Hanover; and also over the Admiralty Islands and the northern Solomon Islands. On 14 November 1899 these Solomon Islands, except Bougainville and Buka, were ceded to the United Kingdom in return for the renunciation of British claims in Samoa.

Postal agencies were opened at Finschhafen on 15 February 1888 (closed 19 March 1891 but re-opened 15 July 1904); Hatzfeldthafen on 1 April 1888 (closed 30 September 1891); Kerawara on 4 April 1888 (used 'Matupi' cancellation until May 1888, closed June 1890); Konstantinhafen on 15 May 1888 (closed 30 September 1891); Stephansort on 14 December 1889 (closed between 30 July 1892 and 14 February 1893); Herbertshöhe in June 1890 (used 'Kerawara' cancellation until December 1890); Friedrich-Wilhelmshafen on 1 March 1892; Matupi on 1 November 1894 (closed 31 January 1906); and Berlinhafen on 22 May 1898. Unoverprinted stamps of Germany were used from these dates.

PRICES. Prices for Nos. Z1 and Z2/Z7 are for Finschhafen postmarks, those of most other postal agencies being worth more. Prices for Nos. Z1*a* and Z8/Z13 are for the cheapest cancel found on each stamp, prices varying according to post office and type of postmark. Prices for No. Z8 are however for cancellations before 1899; cancellations after this date are worth about 50% less.

1888–98. Stamps of Germany cancelled with circular postmarks of German New Guinea postal agencies.

(a) Nos. 38c/38d (Numeral inscr 'DEUTSCHE REICHS-POST')

Z1	7	2m. mauve (1890)	£3500
		a. Deep claret (1891)	£600

(b) Nos. 39/44 (Numeral or Eagle inscr 'DEUTSCHE REICHS-POST')

Z2	5	3pf. green (24.1.90)	£5500
Z3		5pf. mauve (29.4.88)	£700
Z4	6	10pf. carmine (16.4.88)	£600
Z5		20pf. bright blue (16.2.88)	£300
Z6		25pf. deep chestnut (1890)	£6500
Z7		50pf. dull olive-green (21.2.88)	£475

(c) Nos. 46/51 (Numeral or Eagle inscr 'REICHSPOST')

Z8	8	3pf. brown (23.6.91)	£180
		a. Grey-brown (1892)	£110
		b. Orange-brown (1898)	£140
Z9		5pf. green (30.1.91)	£250
		a. Yellow-green (1891)	£120
Z10	9	10pf. rose (2.5.90)	£120
		a. Carmine (1894)	70·00
Z11		20pf. ultramarine (2.9.90)	£250
		a. Dull blue (1892)	70·00
Z12		25pf. orange-yellow (23.6.91)	£475
		a. Orange (1894)	£350
Z13		50pf. lake-brown (24.1.90)	£1300
		a. Chocolate (1891)	95·00

Dates are those of earliest known use.

Nos. Z2/Z7 were valid until 31 January 1891 and Nos. Z1 and Z8/Z13 until 30 September 1901.

(Deutsch-Neu-Guinea) (1)

1897 (22 Sept)–**99**. Stamps of Germany, 1889, optd with T **1**.

1	8	3pf. bistre-brown (7.98)	48·00	85·00
		a. Grey-brown (1899)	12·00	14·50
		b. Reddish brown (1899)	£200	£350
2		5pf. green	6·50	7·50
3	9	10pf. carmine	9·50	12·50
4		20pf. ultramarine	14·00	18·00
5		25pf. orange (7.98)	40·00	80·00
6		50pf. chocolate	48·00	70·00
1/6 Set of 6 (*cheapest*)			£120	£180

'YACHT' KEY TYPES and PERFORATIONS. For details of Types A and B representing the ex-Kaiser's yacht Hohenzollern, and for perforation types (*a*), (*b*) and (*c*), see beginning of Cameroun.

1901 (Jan–15 Mar). No wmk.

7	A	3pf. brown	1·80	1·80
8		5pf. green	9·50	1·80
9		10pf. carmine	32·00	4·75
10		20pf. ultramarine	2·40	4·75
11		25pf. black and red/*yellow*	2·40	24·00
12		30pf. black and orange/*buff*	2·40	30·00
13		40pf. black and carmine	2·40	34·00
14		50pf. black and purple/*buff*	3·00	29·00
15		80pf. black and carmine/*rose*	5·50	41·00
16	B	1m. carmine (*a*) (15.3)	13·00	80·00
17		2m. blue (*a*) (15.3)	13·00	£110
18		3m. violet-black (*a*) (15.3)	18·00	£225
19		5m. carmine and black (I) (*a*) (15.3)	£250	£700
7/19 *Set of* 13			£325	£1200
7s/19s Optd '*Specimen*' *Set of* 13			£600	

2pf. grey is a proof.

1914–19. Wmk Lozenges.

20	A	3pf. brown (1919)	1·60
21		5pf. green	2·40
22		10pf. carmine	2·40
23	B	5m. carmine and black (I) (*a*)	70·00
		a. 25×17 holes	£1200
		b. Frame I, Centre II (*a*)	55·00
		c. Frame I, Centre II (*b*)	48·00

No. 20 is inscribed 'DEUTSCH-NEU-GUINEA' (as Nos. 7/19). Nos. 21/23 'DEUTSCH-NEUGUINEA'.

Nos. 20/23 were only on sale in Berlin.

On 11 September 1914, Australian forces landed in New Pomerania and the German forces in New Guinea surrendered ten days later. On 17 December 1920 Australia received a Mandate of the League of Nations to administer the territories of the former German protectorate.

NEW GUINEA

PRICES FOR STAMPS ON COVER	
Nos. 1/30	from × 3
Nos. 31/32	
Nos. 33/49	from × 3
Nos. 50/59	from × 2
Nos. 60/62	
Nos. 63/64	from × 2
Nos. 64c/64q	
Nos. O1/O2	from × 8

AUSTRALIAN OCCUPATION

Stamps of German New Guinea surcharged

G.R.I. **G.R.I.**
2d.   **1s.**   **1**
(1)   (2)   (3)

SETTINGS. The 'G.R.I' issues of New Guinea were surcharged on a small hand press which could only accommodate one horizontal row of stamps at a time. In addition to complete sheets the surcharges were also applied to multiples and individual stamps which were first lightly affixed to plain paper backing sheets. Such backing sheets could contain a mixture of denominations, some of which required different surcharges.

Specialists recognise 12 settings of the low value surcharges (1d. to 8d.):

Setting 1   (Nos. 1/4, 7/11) shows the bottom of the 'R' 6 mm from the top of the 'd'
Setting 2   (Nos. 16/19, 22/26) shows the bottom of the 'R' 5 mm from the top of the 'd'
Setting 3   was used for the Official stamps (Nos. O1/O2)
Setting 4,   which included the 2½d. value for the first time, and
Setting 5   showed individual stamps with either 6 mm or 5 mm spacing.

These five settings were for rows of ten stamps, but the remaining seven, used on odd stamps handed in for surcharging, were applied as strips of five only. One has, so far, not been reconstructed, but of the remainder three show the 6 mm spacing, two the 5 mm and one both.

On the shilling values the surcharges were applied as horizontal rows of four and the various settings divide into two groups, one with 3½ to 4½ mm between the bottom of the 'R' and the top of numeral, and the second with 5½ mm between the 'R' and numeral. The first group includes the very rare initial setting on which the space is 4 to 4½ mm.

GERMAN NEW GUINEA

G.R.I. **G.R.I.** **G.R.I.**
2d. **1d.** **1s.**
'1' for 'I'   Short '1'   Large 'S'
(Setting 1)   (Setting 1)   (Setting 1)

1914 (17 Oct)–**15**. Stamps of 1901 surch.

(a) As Type 1. 'G.R.I.' and value 6 mm apart

1	1d. on 3pf. brown	£750	£850
	a. '1' for 'I'	£2000	£2250
	b. Short '1'	£2000	£2250
	c. '1' with straight top serif (Setting 6)	£2000	
	d. 'I' for '1' (Setting 12)	£3500	
2	1d. on 5pf. green	85·00	£110
	a. '1' for 'I'	£350	£425
	b. Short '1'	£350	£425
	c. '1' with straight top serif (Settings 6 and 9)	£475	£550
3	2d. on 10pf. carmine	90·00	£120
	a. '1' for 'I'	£400	£500
4	2d. on 20pf. ultramarine	90·00	£110
	a. '1' for 'I'	£375	£425
	e. Surch double, one 'G.R.I.' albino	£5500	
	f. Surch inverted	£16000	
5	2½d. on 10pf. carmine (27.2.15)	95·00	£200
	a. Fraction bar omitted (Setting 9)	£3500	£3500
6	2½d. on 20pf. ultramarine (27.2.15)	£110	£225
	a. Fraction bar omitted (Setting 9)	†	£9500
7	3d. on 25pf. black and red/*yellow*	£375	£450
	a. '1' for 'I'	£1100	£1300
8	3d. on 30pf. black and orange/*buff*	£475	£500
	a. '1' for 'I'	£1300	£1500
	e. Surch double	£15000	£15000
9	4d. on 40pf. black and carmine	£475	£500
	a. '1' for 'I'	£1500	
	e. Surch double	£4000	£4750
	f. Surch inverted	£16000	
10	5d. on 50pf. black and purple/*buff*	£850	£1000
	a. '1' for 'I'	£2250	£3000
	e. Surch double	£16000	
	f. Surch inverted	£16000	
11	8d. on 80pf. black and carmine/*rose*	£1000	£1500
	a. '1' for 'I'	£3250	£4250
	d. No stop after 'd'	£4250	
	e. Error. Surch 'G.R.I. 4d.'	£15000	

(b) As Type 2. 'G.R.I.' and value 3½ to 4 mm apart

12	1s. on 1m. carmine	£3500	£4250
	a. Large 's'	£13000	£13000
13	2s. on 2m. blue	£3250	£4000
	a. Large 's'	£12000	£14000
	c. Error. Surch 'G.R.I. 5s.'	£45000	
	d. Error. Surch 'G.R.I. 2d.' corrected by handstamped 'S'	£50000	
14	3s. on 3m. violet-black	£5500	£7000
	a. Large 's'	£16000	
	b. No stop after 'I' (Setting 3)	£13000	£13000
15	5s. on 5m. carmine and black	£14000	£16000
	a. Large 's'	£29000	
	b. No stop after 'I' (Setting 3)	£18000	£20000
	c. Error. Surch 'G.R.I. 1s.'	£85000	

G.R.I. **G.R.I.**
3d. **5d.**
Thick '3'   Thin '5'
(Setting 2)   (Setting 2)

1914 (16 Dec)–**15**. Stamps of 1901 surch.

(a) As Type 1. 'G.R.I.' and value 5 mm apart

16	1d. on 3pf. brown	£100	£110
	a. 'I' for '1' (Setting 11)	£750	
	b. Short '1' (Setting 2)	£325	
	c. '1' with straight top serif (Settings 2 and 6)	£150	£180
	e. Surch double	£1500	£1800
	f. Surch double, one inverted	£8000	
	g. Surch inverted	£6000	
	h. Error. Surch 'G.R.I. 4d.'	£17000	
17	1d. on 5pf. green	35·00	50·00
	b. Short '1' (Setting 2)	£130	£190
	c. '1' with straight top serif (Setting 2)	50·00	80·00
	e. 'd' inverted	†	£3750
	f. '1d' inverted	†	£11000
	g. 'G.R.I.' without stops or spaces	£11000	
	ga. 'G.R.I.' without stops, but with normal spaces	—	£11000
	h. 'G.I.R.' instead of 'G.R.I.'	£13000	£14000
	i. Surch double	£5000	£6000
18	2d. on 10pf. carmine	50·00	60·00
	e. No stop after 'd' (Setting 2)	£180	£250
	f. Stop before, instead of after, 'G' (Settings 4 and 5)	£11000	
	g. Surch double	£16000	£16000
	h. Surch double, one inverted	—	£13000
	i. Vert pair with No. 20	£20000	
	j. In horiz pair with No. 20	£28000	
	k. Error. Surch 'G.R.I. 1d.'	£12000	£12000
	l. Error. Surch 'G.I.R. 3d.'	£13000	
19	2d. on 20pf. ultramarine	50·00	70·00
	e. No stop after 'd' (Setting 2)	£130	£190
	f. No stop after 'I' (Setting 11)	£1500	
	g. 'R' inverted (Settings 4 and 5)	—	£9000
	h. Surch double	£3500	£5000
	i. Surch double, one inverted	£4750	£7000
	j. Surch inverted	£10000	
	k. Albino surch (in horiz pair with normal)	£23000	
	l. In vert pair with No. 21	£18000	£21000
	m. Error. Surch 'G.R.I. 1d.'	£13000	£15000
20	2½d. on 10pf. carmine (27.2.15)	£225	£350
21	2½d. on 20pf. ultramarine (27.2.15)	£2000	£2500
	a. Error. Surch 'G.R.I. 3d.' (in vert pair with normal)	£40000	
22	3d. on 25pf. black and red/*yellow*	£190	£250
	e. Thick '3'	£600	£750
	f. Surch double	£11000	£13000
	g. Surch inverted	£11000	£13000
	h. Surch omitted (in horiz pair with normal)	£13000	
	i. Error. Surch 'G.R.I. 1d.'	£20000	
23	3d. on 30pf. black and orange/*buff*	£170	£225
	e. No stop after 'd' (Setting 2)	£800	
	f. Thick '3'	£550	
	g. Surch double	£4000	£4500
	h. Surch double, one inverted	£4500	£5500
	i. Surch double, both inverted	£13000	£14000
	j. Surch inverted	£10000	
	k. Albino surch	£12000	
	l. Surch omitted (in vert pair with normal)	£13000	
	m. Error. Surch 'G.R.I. 1d.'	£12000	£15000
24	4d. on 40pf. black and carmine	£180	£275
	e. Surch double	£3500	
	f. Surch double, one inverted	£5000	
	g. Surch double, both inverted	£13000	
	h. Surch inverted	£9500	
	i. Error. Surch 'G.R.I. 3d.'	£9000	
	ia. Surch 'G.R.I. 1d.' inverted	£19000	
	j. Error. Surch 'G.R.I. 3d.' double	£27000	
	k. No stop after 'I' (Setting 11)	£3250	
25	5d. on 50pf. black and purple/*buff*	£325	£400
	e. Thin '5'	£1400	£3250
	f. Surch double	£4500	£5500
	g. Surch double, one inverted	£10000	£10000
	h. Surch double, both inverted	£13000	£14000
	i. Surch inverted	£10000	
	j. Error. Surch 'G.I.R. 3d.'	£22000	
26	8d. on 80pf. black and carmine/*rose*	£425	£600
	e. Surch double	£7000	£8000
	f. Surch double, one inverted	£7000	£8000
	g. Surch triple	£9500	£10000
	h. Surch inverted	£14000	
	i. Error. Surch 'G.R.I. 3d.'	£18000	

(b) As Type 2. 'G.R.I.' and value 5½ mm apart

27	1s. on 1m. carmine	£5000	£8000
	a. No stop after 'I' (Setting 7)	£12000	
28	2s. on 2m. blue	£5000	£8000
	a. No stop after 'I' (Setting 7)	£12000	
29	3s. on 3m. violet-black	£10000	£15000
	a. 'G.R.I.' double	£45000	
30	5s. on 5m. carmine and black	£40000	£45000

1915 (1 Jan). Nos. 18 and 19 further surch with Type **3**.

31	1d. on 2d. on 10pf.	£28000	£28000
32	1d. on 2d. on 20pf.	£28000	£17000

German New Guinea Registration Labels surcharged

4

4a

385

G.R.I.
3d.
Sans serif 'G'
and different '3'

1915 (Jan). Registration Labels surch 'G.R.I. 3d.' in settings of five or ten and used for postage. Each black and red on buff. Inscr '(Deutsch Neuguinea)' spelt in various ways as indicated. P 14 (No. 43) or 11½ (others).

I. With name of town in sans-serif letters as Type 4

33	**Rabaul** '(Deutsch Neuguinea)'	£275	£325
	a. 'G.R.I. 3d.' double	£5000	£6500
	b. No bracket before 'Deutsch'	£900	£1300
	ba. No bracket and surch double	£16000	
	d. '(Deutsch-Neuguinea)'	£425	£550
	da. 'G.R.I. 3d.' double	£16000	£16000
	db. No stop after 'I'	£900	
	dc. 'G.R.I. 3d' inverted	£16000	
	dd. No bracket before 'Deutsch'	£1500	£2000
	de. No bracket after 'Neuguinea'	£1500	£2000
34	**Deulon** '(Deutsch Neuguinea)'	£26000	£28000
35	**Friedrich-Wilhelmshafen** '(Deutsch Neuguinea)'	£250	£800
	a. No stop after 'd'	£450	
	b. 'G' omitted	£7500	
	c. Sans-serif 'G'	£16000	
	d. Sans-serif 'G' and different '3'	£14000	
	e. Surch inverted	†	£16000
	f. '(Deutsch-Neuguinea)'	£275	£800
	fa. No stop after 'd'	£475	
36	**Herbertshohe** '(Deutsch Neuguinea)'	£300	£850
	a. No stop after 'd'	£500	
	b. No stop after 'I'	£900	£1800
	c. 'G' omitted	£8500	
	d. Surch omitted (in horiz pair with normal)	£18000	
	e. '(Deutsch Neu-Guinea)'	£500	£1000
	f. '(Deutsch-Neuguinea)'		
37	**Kawieng** '(Deutsch-Neuguinea)'	£1000	
	a. No bracket after 'Neuguinea'	£3750	
	b. 'Deutsch Neu-Guinea'	£325	£650
	ba. No stop after 'd'	£550	
	bb. 'G.R.I.' double	£8000	
	bc. '3d.' double	£8000	
	bd. 'G' omitted	£8500	
38	**Kieta** '(Deutsch-Neuguinea)'	£450	£800
	a. No bracket before 'Deutsch'	£1600	£2750
	b. No stop after 'd'	£850	
	c. Surch omitted (right hand stamp of horiz pair)	£16000	
	e. No stop after 'I'	£1300	
	f. 'G' omitted	£8000	
39	**Manus** '(Deutsch Neuguinea)'	£325	£900
	a. 'G.R.I. 3d.' double	£9000	
	b. No bracket before 'Deutsch'	£1500	£2500
40	**Stephansort** '(Deutsch Neu-Guinea)'	—	£4500
	a. No stop after 'd'	†	£8500

II. With name of town in letters with serifs as T 4a

41	**Friedrich Wilhelmshafen** '(Deutsch-Neuguinea)'	£275	£750
	b. No stop after 'd'	£450	£1100
	c. No stop after 'I'	£850	£1600
	d. No bracket before 'Deutsch'	£1600	£2250
	e. No bracket after 'Neuguinea'	£1600	£2250
42	**Kawieng** '(Deutsch Neuguinea)'	£250	£650
	a. No stop after 'd'	£475	
	b. No stop after 'I'		
43	**Manus** '(Deutsch-Neuguinea)'	£4250	£5000
	a. No stop after 'I'	£8500	£8000

Examples of Nos. 33db, 36b, 38e, 41c and 43a also show the stop after 'R' either very faint or missing completely.

Stamps of Marshall Islands surcharged

SETTINGS. The initial supply of Marshall Islands stamps, obtained from Nauru, was surcharged with Setting 2 (5 *mm* between 'R' and 'd') on the penny values and with the 3½ to 4 setting on the shilling stamps.
Small quantities subsequently handed in were surcharged, often on the same backing sheet as German New Guinea values, with Settings 6, 7 or 12 (all 6 mm between 'R' and 'd') for the penny values and with a 5½ mm setting for the shilling stamps.

1914 (16 Dec). Stamps of 1901 surch.

*(a) As T **1**. 'G.R.I.' and value 5 mm apart*

50	1d. on 3pf. brown	£110	£170
	c. '1' with straight top serif (Setting 2)	£180	£300
	d. '.G.R.I.' and '1' with straight top serif (Settings 4 and 5)	†	£14000
	e. Surch inverted		£9000
51	1d. on 5pf. green	80·00	85·00
	c. '1' with straight top serif (Settings 2 and 11)	£140	£160
	d. 'I' for '1' (Setting 11)	£1200	
	e. '1' and 'd' spaced	£300	£325
	f. Surch double	£3750	
	g. Surch inverted	£5000	
52	2d. on 10pf. carmine	27·00	50·00
	e. No stop after 'G' (Setting 2)	£850	
	f. Surch double	£3750	
	g. Surch double, one inverted	£5500	
	h. Surch inverted	£7000	
	i. Surch sideways	£10000	
53	2d. on 20pf. ultramarine	27·00	50·00
	e. No stop after 'd' (Setting 2)	70·00	£110
	g. Surch double	£4000	£6500
	h. Surch double, one inverted	£10000	£10000
	i. Surch inverted	£11000	£11000
54	3d. on 25pf. black and red/*yellow*	£450	£550
	e. No stop after 'd' (Settings 2 and 11)	£850	£1100
	f. Thick '3'	£1000	£1400
	g. Surch double	£4250	£4750
	h. Surch double, one inverted	£4750	
	i. Surch inverted	£13000	
55	3d. on 30pf. black and orange/*buff*	£475	£600
	e. No stop after 'd' (Setting 2)	£900	£1200
	f. Thick '3'	£1100	
	g. Surch inverted	£9000	
	h. Surch double	£7000	
56	4d. on 40pf. black and carmine	£170	£250
	e. No stop after 'd' (Setting 2)	£425	£650
	f. 'd' omitted (Setting 2)	†	£7000
	g. Surch double	£7000	£8000
	h. Surch triple	£14000	
	i. Surch inverted	£10000	
	j. Error. Surch 'G.R.I. 1d.'	£17000	
	k. Error. Surch 'G.R.I. 3d.'	£17000	
57	5d. on 50pf. black and purple/*buff*	£300	£375
	e. Thin '5'	£3750	
	f. 'd' omitted (Setting 2)	£2000	
	g. Surch double	£10000	
	h. Surch inverted	£16000	
58	8d. on 80pf. black and carmine/*rose*	£475	£700
	e. Surch double	£10000	
	f. Surch double, both inverted	£13000	£14000
	g. Surch triple	£16000	
	h. Surch inverted	£11000	

*(b) As Type **2**. 'G.R.I.' and value 3½–4 mm apart*

59	1s. on 1m. carmine	£4000	£5000
	b. No stop after 'I'	£6000	£9000
	e. Surch double	£45000	
	f. Error. Additional surch '1d.'	£45000	
60	2s. on 2m. blue	£1900	£4000
	b. No stop after 'I'	£3500	£6000
	e. Surch double	£45000	
	f. Surch double, one inverted	£42000	£42000
61	3s. on 3m. violet-black	£6500	£9500
	b. No stop after 'I'	£8500	
	e. Surch double	£40000	£45000
62	5s. on 5m. carmine and black	£14000	£15000
	e. Surch double, one inverted	†	£65000

1915 (Jan). Nos. 52 and 53 further surch with Type **3**.

63	1d. on 2d. on 10pf. carmine	£200	£275
	a. '1' double	£16000	
	b. '1' inverted	£19000	£19000
	c. Small '1'	£650	
64	1d. on 2d. on 20pf. ultramarine	£4000	£2500
	a. On No. 53e	£9000	£4000
	b. '1' inverted	£19000	£19000

The surcharged '1' on No. 63c is just over 4 mm tall. Type **3** is 6 mm tall.

1915. Stamps of 1901 surch.

*(a) As Type **1**. 'G.R.I.' and value 6 mm apart*

64c	1d. on 3pf. brown	£3500	
	cc. '1' with straight top serif (Setting 6)	£4250	
	cd. 'I' for '1' (Setting 12)	£16000	
64d	1d. on 5pf. green	£3500	
	dc. '1' with straight top serif (Setting 6)	£4250	
	dd. 'I' for '1' (Setting 12)	£4250	
	de. Surch inverted	£16000	
	df. Surch double	£16000	
64e	2d. on 10pf carmine	£4500	
	ea. Surch sideways	£16000	
64f	2d. on 20pf. ultramarine	£4000	
	fe. Surch inverted	£16000	
64g	2½d. on 10pf. carmine	£27000	
64h	2½d. on 20pf. ultramarine	£40000	
64i	3d. on 25pf. black and red/*yellow*	£6500	
64j	3d. on 30pf. black and orange/*buff*	£6500	
	je. Error. Surch G.R.I. 1d.'	£18000	
64k	4d. on 40pf. black and carmine	£6500	
	ke. Surch double	£18000	

	kf. Surch inverted	£18000	
64l	5d. on 50pf. black and purple/*buff*	£6000	
	le. Surch double	£18000	
64m	8d. on 80pf. black and carmine/*rose*	£7500	
	me. Surch inverted	£18000	

(b) As Type **2**. *'G.R.I.' and value 5½ mm apart*

64n	1s. on 1m. carmine	£17000
	na. Large 's' (Setting 5)	£21000
	nb. No stop after 'I' (Setting 7)	£21000
64o	2s. on 2m. blue	£14000
	a. Large 's' (Setting 5)	£19000
	b. Surch double, one inverted	£55000
64p	3s. on 3m. violet-black	£27000
	pa. Large 's' (Setting 5)	£38000
	pb. No stop after 'I' (Setting 7)	£38000
	pe. Surch inverted	£65000
64q	5s. on 5m. carmine and black	£38000
	qa. Large 's' (Setting 5)	£50000

OFFICIAL STAMPS

O. S.
G.R.I.
1d.
(O **1**)

1915 (27 Feb). Stamps of 1901 surch as Type O **1**. 'G.R.I.' and value 3½ mm apart.

O1	1d. on 3pf. brown	35·00	75·00
	a. '1' and 'd' spaced	85·00	£170
	b. Surch double	£5500	
O2	1d. on 5pf. green	£100	£140
	a. '1' and 'd' spaced	£200	£300

German Post Offices in China

1898. 100 Pfennig = 1 Mark
1905. 100 Cents = 1 Dollar

An Imperial German Postal Agency was opened in the consulate at Shanghai on 16 August 1886. Branch offices were added at Chefoo ('Tschifu') (8 June 1892) and Tientsin (October 1889). Tientsin became a postal agency (with its own cancellation) on 1 April 1893 and, with Chefoo, became a full post office on 1 January 1900.

Further German post offices were later opened at Amoy (12 June 1902), Canton (2 June 1902), Chefoo ('Tschifu') (1 January 1900) Foochow ('Futschau') (18 June 1900), Hankow ('Hankau') (1 April 1900); Ichang ('Itschang') (11 February 1903), Nanking (1 January 1903), Peking (11 September 1900), Shanhaikwan (1 September 1901), Swatow ('Swatau') (17 May 1904), Tongku (September 1900), Tschinkiang (28 October 1901), Tsinanfu (16 March 1904) and Weihsien (1 June 1902).

> **PRICES.** Nos. Z1/Z1*a* and Z2/Z7 are found only with the circular postmark 'KAISERLICH / DEUTSCHE / POSTAGENTUR / SHANGHAI'. Prices for Nos. Z8/Z13 are for stamps with full cancellations dated before 1 September 1900, and are for the most common type of Shanghai postmark found on each stamp. Poor cancels are worth less. Stamps on piece with exceptionally clear postmarks and stamps on cover or postcards are worth more. Less common Shanghai postmarks and postmarks of other offices are worth more. Prices for Nos. Z1*b*/Z1*c* are similarly for the most common type of postmark.

1886–**1901**. Stamps of Germany cancelled with postmarks of German post offices in China.

(a) Nos. 38b/38e (Numeral inscr 'DEUTSCHE REICHS-POST')

Z1	**7**	2m. dull rose (5.9.86)	£900
		a. Mauve (23.8.89)	£900
		b. Deep claret (27.9.91)	39·00
		c. Red-lilac (18.1.01)	£140

(b) Nos. 39/44 (Numeral or Eagle inscr 'DEUTSCHE REICHS-POST')

Z2	**5**	3pf. green	—
Z3		5pf. mauve (28.8.86)	£130
Z4	**6**	10pf. carmine (28.8.86)	£130
Z5		20pf. pale blue (28.8.86)	
		a. Bright blue	46·00
Z6		25pf. deep chestnut	—
Z7		50pf. pale grey-olive (28.8.86)	£100
		a. Dull olive-green	80·00
		b. Bronze-green	£170

(c) Nos. 46/51 (Numeral or Eagle inscr 'REICHSPOST')

Z8	**8**	3pf. brown (2.5.90)	£350
		a. Grey-brown (1891)	£100
Z9		5pf. green (28.1.90)	£140
		a. Yellow-green (1891)	£100
Z10	**9**	10pf. rose (7.6.90)	49·00
		a. Carmine (1895)	26·00
Z11		20pf. ultramarine (7.3.90)	70·00
		a. Dull blue (1891)	43·00
Z12		25pf. orange-yellow (1.5.91)	£225
		a. Orange (1894)	£160
Z13		50pf. lake-brown (26.9.90)	£250
		a. Chocolate (1891)	65·00

Dates are those of earliest known use.
Examples of other shades of the 3pf. brown (Nos. 46*c*/46*d*) are known used from 1898, after the introduction of overprinted stamps.
For Nos. 46/51 of Germany cancelled from September 1900 see Nos. Z14/Z19.

> **ERRORS.** Errors such as double and inverted overprints or surcharges were never issued but come from waste sheets which later leaked out of the printers.

GERMAN POST OFFICES IN CHINA

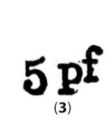

(1) (2) (3) **5 pf**

1898. Stamps of Germany, 1889–1990, optd 'China'.

(a) Overprint sloping as Type 1 (48°) (1 Mar–June)

1	8	3pf. grey-brown (6.98)	£3000	
		a. Bistre-brown	£225	£39000
2		5pf. green	25·00	28·00
3	9	10pf. carmine	50·00	17·00
4		20pf. ultramarine	23·00	17·00
5		25pf. orange (4.98)	80·00	£100
6		50pf. chocolate	34·00	29·00

(b) Overprint sloping as Type 2 (56°) (Dec)

7	8	3pf. grey-brown	9·00	8·75
		a. Bistre-brown	21·00	23·00
		b. Red-brown	65·00	£200
8		5pf. green	5·00	4·50
9	9	10pf. carmine	9·00	9·75
10		20pf. ultramarine	26·00	29·00
11		25pf. orange	46·00	50·00
12		50pf. chocolate	23·00	22·00
7/12	Set of 6		£100	£110

1900 (7 July). Foochow provisional. Handstamped with Type **3**.

13	9	5pf. on 10pf. carmine (No. 3)	£1000	£1800
14		5pf. on 10pf. carmine (No. 9)	£900	£1700

The first printing of 8 July comprised 100 of No. 13 and 1400 of No. 14 and there was a second printing on 7 November consisting of 2500 of No. 13. It follows therefore that copies of No. 13 showing dated postmarks prior to November 1900 are very rare (*Price* £10,000).

From September 1900 to 31 August 1901, during the Boxer uprisings, unoverprinted stamps of Germany were used by the Tientsin expedition. Postmarks used were 'KAISERLICH DEUTSCHEFELDPOST / CHINA', 'KAIS. DEUTSCHE / FELDPOST- / EXPEDITION', 'K. D. FELDPOST EXPED. / DES / OSTASIATISCHEN / EXPEDITIONSCORPS' and 'K. D. FELDPOSTSTATION No 2' to '10' (Field station No. 1 was in Kiaochow). These German stamps are also found cancelled up to the end of 1902 by various German post offices in China, while unoverprinted stamps of Kiaochow were used by Peking and Field station No. 2 (which was at Peking) from April to November 1901.

Prices for Nos. Z14/Z32 are for the cheapest version of each stamp, prices varying according to postmark.

1900 (1 Sept)–**01**.

(a) Stamps of Germany cancelled with postmarks of Field stations or offices in China, dated from September 1900

(i) Nos. 46/51 (Numeral or Eagle inscr 'REICHSPOST')

Z14	8	3pf. orange-brown	£1000
		a. Bistre-brown	£1000
Z15		5pf. green	£2500
Z16	9	10pf. carmine	£1200
Z17		20pf. ultramarine	£2000
Z18		25pf. orange	£4250
Z19		50pf. chocolate	£4750

(ii) Nos. 52/65 (Germania or various pictorial designs)

Z20	10	3pf. brown	£400
Z21		5pf. green	£120
Z22		10pf. carmine	70·00
Z23		20pf. blue	£180
Z24	11	25pf. black and red/yellow	£4500
Z25		30pf. black and orange/rose	£425
Z26		40pf. black and carmine	£500
Z27		50pf. black and purple/rose	£500
Z28		80pf. black and carmine/carmine	£500
Z29	12	1m. carmine-red	£900
Z30	13	2m. blue	£1100
Z31	14	3m. violet-black	£1000
Z32	15	5m. crimson and black	—

The 25pf. and 5m. were not supplied to the post offices, but are known used.

(b) Nos. 11/23 of Kiaochow cancelled with circular postmarks of Peking or Field station No. 2 (April 1901)

Z33	A	3pf. brown	£450
Z34		5pf. green	£450
Z35		10pf. carmine	£500
Z36		20pf. ultramarine	£700
Z37		25pf. black and red/yellow	£1400
Z38		30pf. black and orange/buff	£1600
Z39		40pf. black and carmine	£1200
Z40		50pf. black and purple/buff	£1400
Z41		80pf. black and carmine/rose	£2000
Z42	B	1m. carmine	£2250
Z43		2m. blue	£2750
Z44		3m. violet-blue	£5000
Z45		5m. carmine and black	£10000

(4) **China** (5) **China**

1900 (24 Nov)–**01** (Jan). Tientsin provisionals. Stamps of Germany (inscr 'REICHSPOST') handstamped with Type **4**.

15	10	3pf. brown (1.01)	£1000	£1300
16		5pf. green (1.01)	£650	£600
17		10pf. carmine (1.01)	£1600	£1400
18		20pf. blue (1.01)	£1300	£1600
19	11	30pf. black and orange/rose (1.01)	£8000	£8000
20		50pf. black and purple/rose	£33000	£23000
21		80pf. black and carmine/rose (1.01)	£8000	£7500

The 25 and 40pf. and 2 and 3 marks are known with this overprint but were not issued.

1901 (Feb)–**04**. Stamps of Germany (inscr 'REICHSPOST') optd with Type **5**, horizontally, (on 3m. vertically at sides).

22	10	3pf. brown	2·30	3·25
23		5pf. green	2·30	2·50
24		10pf. carmine	4·00	2·00
25		20pf. ultramarine	5·25	2·50
26	11	25pf. black and red/yellow	16·00	26·00
27		30pf. black and orange/rose	16·00	21·00
28		40pf. black and carmine	16·00	16·00
29		50pf. black and purple/rose	16·00	16·00
30		80pf. black and carmine/rose	18·00	18·00
31	12	1m. carmine	44·00	55·00
32	13	2m. blue	44·00	47·00
33	14	3m. violet-black (I) (R.)	80·00	£100
		a. Type II	£100	£130
35	15	5m. lake and black (I)	£2250	£4000
		a. Type II (4.04)	£350	£500
		b. Hand-painted borders (I)	£350	£500
22/35b	Set of 13 (cheapest)		£500	£700
22s/35s	Optd 'Specimen' Set of 11		£1200	

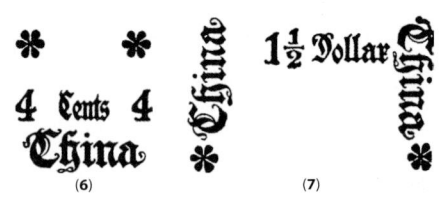

(6) **4 Cents 4 China** (7) **1½ Dollar China**

In Type 7 the word 'China' can be vertical or horizontal.

1905 (1 Oct). Chinese currency. Stamps of Germany (inscr 'DEUTSCHES REICH') surch as Type **6** (cent values) and **7** (dollar values). No wmk.

36	17	1c. on 3pf. brown	4·75	5·75
37		2c. on 5pf. green	4·75	2·50
38		4c. on 10pf. carmine	9·00	2·50
39		10c. on 20pf. ultramarine	4·75	2·75
40		20c. on 40pf. black and carmine	31·00	11·50
41		40c. on 80pf. black and carmine/rose	49·00	22·00
42	18	½d. on 1m. carmine (26×17)	26·00	33·00
		a. 25×16 perforation holes	£120	£110
43	20	1d. on 2m. blue	26·00	36·00
44	21	1½d. on 3m. violet-black (26×17) (R.)	£450	£200
		a. 25×16 perforation holes	26·00	80·00
45	22	2½d. on 5m. lake and black	£170	£500
36/45	Set of 10 (cheapest)		£325	£650

1905–19. As last, but wmk Lozenges.

46	17	1c. on 3pf. brown	80	2·10
47		2c. on 5pf. green (1911)	60	2·10
48		4c. on 10pf. carmine (1911)	80	2·50
49		10c. on 20pf. ultramarine (1913)	1·30	11·00
50		20c. on 40pf. black and carmine (1908)	1·80	5·75
51		40c. on 80pf. black and carmine/rose	2·10	85·00
52	18	½d. on 1m. carmine-red (26×17) (1906)	26·00	£100
		a. Bright rose-red (25×17) (1918)	10·00	
53	20	1d. on 2m. deep blue (26×17) (1907)	17·00	65·00
		a. Bright blue (25×17) (1918)	17·00	
54	21	1½d. on 3m. slate-purple (26×17) (R.) (1912)	46·00	£200
		a. Violet-black (1913)	33·00	£2500
		b. Do. (25×17) (1918)	13·00	
55	22	2½d. on 5m. +/*-carmine and black (I) (26×17) (1906)	£180	£225
		a. Type II (1918)	50·00	
		b. Do. (25×17) (1919)	50·00	
46/55b	Set of 10 (cheapest)		90·00	£650

Nos. 52a, 53a, 54b, 55a/55b were only on sale in Berlin.

German Post Offices in China were closed down on 17 March 1917.

German Post Offices in Morocco

100 Centimos = 1 Peseta

German post offices were established on 20 December 1899 at Tangier; in Casablanca, Larache, Mazagan, Mogador, Rabat and Saffi. Further offices followed at Alkassar (27 May 1901), Arsila (1 May 1911), Asimmur (1 October 1908), Fes (27 May 1901), Fes-Mellah (27 October 1902), Marrakesch (11 July 1900), Meknes (27 May 1901) and Tetuan (19 December 1906).

ERRORS. Errors such as double and inverted surcharges were never issued but come from waste sheets which later leaked out of the printers.

(1) Marocco 10 Centimos

1899 (20 Dec). Stamps of Germany, 1889, surch as T **1**.

1	**8**	3c. on 3pf. grey-brown	5·50	3·50
2		5c. on 5pf. green	5·50	3·50
3	**9**	10c. on 10pf. carmine	14·50	14·50
4		25c. on 20pf. ultramarine	29·00	23·00
5		30c. on 25pf. orange	42·00	50·00
6		60c. on 50pf. red-brown	36·00	60·00
1/6 Set of 6			£120	£140

(2) Marocco 3 Centimos (3) 1 Pes. 25 cts. Marocco

1900 (20 Oct–Dec). Stamps of Germany, (inscr 'REICHSPOST') surch as Type **2** (3c. to 1p.) and **3**.

7	**10**	3c. on 3pf. brown	1·90	3·50
8		5c. on 5pf. green	2·40	2·40
9		10c. on 10pf. carmine	3·50	2·40
10		25c. on 20pf. ultramarine	4·75	4·25
11	**11**	30c. on 25pf. black and red/*yellow*	14·50	23·00
12		35c. on 30pf. black and orange/*rose*	11·00	9·50
13		50c. on 40pf. black and carmine	11·00	9·50
14		60c. on 50pf. black and purple/*rose*	22·00	46·00
15		1p. on 80pf. black and carmine/*rose*	20·00	30·00
16	**12**	1p.25c. on 1m. carmine	48·00	70·00
17	**13**	2p.50c. on 2m. blue	55·00	85·00
		a. Type II	£140	£225
18	**14**	3p.75c. on 3m. violet-black (I) (R.)	70·00	£100
		a. Type II	95·00	£130
19	**15**	6p.25c. on 5m. lake and black (I) (12.00)	£475	£850
		a. Type II (thinner surch)	£2500	
		b. Hand-painted borders (I)	£275	£475
7/19b Set of 13 (cheapest)			£475	£750
7s/19s Optd 'Specimen' Set of 13			£900	

M t 1900 Straight serifs   **M t** 1903 Sloping serifs

1903 (Apr–25 Nov). As last but surch in different type, 'M' and 't' with sloping serifs.

20	**10**	5c. on 5pf. green (25.11)	£110	18·00
21	**12**	1p.25c. on 1m. carmine	£550	£300
22	**13**	2p.50c. on 2m. blue	£800	£170
		a. Type II	£1700	£350
23	**14**	3p.75c. on 3m. violet-black (I) (R.)	£2000	£375
		a. Type II	£2500	£475
24	**15**	6p.25c. on 5m. lake and black (II)	£300	£400

(4) Marocco 5 Centimos (5) 6 Pef. 25 Cts. Marocco

1905 (30 Sept). Stamp of Germany (inscr 'REICHSPOST') surch with Type **4**.

25	**10**	5c. on 5pf. green	12·00	34·00

1905 (1 Oct). Stamps of Germany (inscr 'DEUTSCHES REICH') surch as Type **4** (3c. to 1p.) and **5**. No wmk.

26	**17**	3c. on 3pf. brown	4·00	5·00
27		5c. on 5pf. green	7·25	1·70
28		10c. on 10pf. carmine	13·00	1·70
29		25c. on 20pf. ultramarine	29·00	5·50
30		30c. on 25pf. black and red/*yellow*	9·50	9·25
31		35c. on 30pf. black and orange/*buff*	14·50	9·00
32		50c. on 40pf. black and carmine	14·50	12·00
33		60c. on 50pf. black and purple/*buff*	31·00	36·00
34		1p. on 80pf. black and carmine/*rose*	31·00	29·00
35	**18**	1p.25c. on 1m. carmine (26×17)	£140	£225
		a. 25×16 perforation holes	80·00	55·00
36	**20**	2p.50c. on 2m. blue	£160	£225
37	**21**	3p.75c. on 3m. violet-black (26×17) (R.)	£225	£275
		a. 25×16 perforation holes	65·00	85·00
38	**22**	6p.25c. on 5m. lake and black	£250	£300
26/38 Set of 13 (cheapest)			£650	£700

1906 (Mar)–11. As last but wmk Lozenges.

39	**17**	3c. on 3pf. brown	13·00	3·00
40		5c. on 5pf. green (5.06)	10·00	1·80
41		10c. on 10pf. carmine (10.06)	10·00	1·80
42		25c. on 20pf. ultramarine (1.07)	30·00	12·00
43		30c. on 25pf. black and red/*yellow* (3.11)	30·00	24·00
44		35c. on 30pf. black and orange/*buff* (4.08)	24·00	16·00
45		50c. on 40pf. black and carmine (12.08)	48·00	£225
46		60c. on 50pf. black and purple/*buff* (3.11)	42·00	26·00
47		1p. on 80pf. black and carmine/*rose* (4.11)	£180	£425
48	**18**	1p.25c. on 1m. carmine	95·00	£275
49	**20**	2p.50c. on 2m. blue (6.06)	95·00	£275
50	**22**	6p.25c. on 5m. lake and black	£180	£475
39/50 Set of 12			£700	£1600

1911 (23 Jan)–**18**. As last, but name spelt 'Marokko'.

51	**17**	3c. on 3pf. brown	85	1·20
52		5c. on 5pf. green (2.8.11)	85	1·60
53		10c. on 10pf. carmine (2.8.11)	85	1·70
54		25c. on 20pf. ultramarine (2.8.11)	95	2·00
55		30c. on 25pf. black and red/*yellow* (5.11)	2·40	24·00
56		35c. on 30pf. black and orange/*buff* (2.8.11)	2·40	13·00
57		50c. on 40pf. black and carmine (5.11)	1·90	7·75
58		60c. on 50pf. black and purple/*buff* (5.11)	3·75	55·00
59		1p. on 80pf. black and carmine/*rose* (5.11)	2·40	36·00
60	**18**	1p.25c. on 1m. carmine-red (26×17) (5.11)	7·25	95·00
		a. Bright rose-red (25×17) (1918)	4·25	
61	**20**	2p.50c. on 2m. deep blue (26×17) (5.11)	12·00	70·00
		a. Greenish blue (25×17) (1918)	36·00	
62	**21**	3p.75c. on 3m. slate-purple (26×17) (R.) (16.3.11)	17·00	£300
		a. Violet-black (1918)	12·00	
		b. Slate-purple (25×17) (1918)	24·00	
63	**22**	6p.25c. on 5m. carmine and black (26×17) (15.11)	30·00	£500
51/63 Set of 13 (cheapest)			65·00	£1000

Nos. 60a, 61a and 62a/62b were only on sale in Berlin.

German post offices in French Morocco (Asimmur, Casablanca, Fes, Fes-Mellah, Marrakesch, Mazagan, Meknes, Mogador, Rabat and Saffi) were closed down on 4 August 1914 with Tangier in the International Zone following on 19 August 1914. Those offices in Spanish Morocco (Arsila, Alkassar, Larache and Tetuan) continued to function until 16 June 1919.

German Post Offices in Turkish Empire

1884. 40 Para = 1 Piaster
1908. 100 Centimes = 1 Franc

The first German postal agency was opened in Constantinople on 1 March 1870, and this became a post office in 1871. A second office in Constantinople (Stambul) was opened on 1 January 1876 and a third (Pera) on 1 March 1900. Other offices were opened at Jaffa on 1 October 1896 and at Beirut, Jerusalem and Smyrna on 1 March 1900. Unoverprinted stamps of North German Confederation and of German Empire were used at first.

PRICES. Prices for Nos. Z1/Z44 are for the most common types of 'CONSTANTINOPEL' postmark found on each stamp, less common types and postmarks of other offices are worth more. Stamps on piece with exceptionally clear postmarks and stamps on cover or postcards are worth more.

1870–71. Nos. 19/29 and 38/39 of North German Confederation cancelled with circular postmark for Constantinople (Nos. Z1/Z6) or pen-cancelled (Nos. Z7/Z8).

Z1	1	¼g. purple (15.6.70)	
		a. Pale mauve (13.10.71)	£3000
Z2		1⁄3g. green (3.5.70)	£1600
Z3		½g. orange (3.5.70)	£475
Z4		1g. rose-carmine (4.3.70)	£425
Z5		2g. ultramarine (3.3.70)	£425
Z6		5g. bistre (10.3.70)	£950
Z7	3	10g. grey (20.5.70)	£3500
Z8	4	30g. pale blue	£9000

1872–99. Stamps of Germany pen-cancelled (Nos. Z16/Z17 and Z32/Z32*a*) or with circular postmarks of German offices in Turkish Empire.

(a) Nos. 1/7 (Eagle with small shield) and 14/15 (numerals)

Z9	1	¼g. violet (3.1.72)	£800
Z10		1⁄3g. yellow-green (10.1.72)	£600
Z11		½g. orange-vermilion (10.1.72)	£550
Z12		½g. orange-yellow (10.5.72)	£850
Z13		1g. rose-carmine (3.1.72)	£120
Z14		2g. blue (2.1.72)	£120
Z15		5g. bistre (2.1.72)	£475
Z16	2	10g. grey (23.2.72)	£2500
Z17	3	30g. blue (14.5.72)	£4750

(b) Nos. 16/22 (Eagle with large shield) and 29 (numerals)

Z18		¼g. purple (10.4.73)	£850
Z19		1⁄3g. yellow-green (27.12.73)	£850
		a. Pale blue-green	£4250
Z20		½g. orange (13.9.72)	£120
Z21		1g. rose-carmine (26.2.73)	95·00
Z22		2g. blue (8.10.72)	95·00
Z23		2½g. chestnut (21.11.72)	£170
Z24	4	2½g. chestnut (24.4.74)	£120
		a. '1' in fraction to left of '2'	£1700
Z25	1	5g. bistre	£250

(c) Nos. 31/35 and 38 (Numeral or Arms incr 'DEUTSCHE REICH-POST' AND 'PFENNIGE'.)

Z26	5	3pf. green (4.1.75)	£950
Z27		5pf. mauve (28.1.75)	£120
Z28	6	10pf. carmine (20.3.75)	60·00
Z29		20pf. blue (3.3.75)	48·00
Z30		25pf. red-brown (16.2.75)	£225
		a. Yellow-brown	£300
		b. Deep brown	£450
Z31		50pf. grey-black (1.3.75)	£325
		a. Grey	
Z32		50pf. grey-green (19.10.77)	£425
		a. Deep olive-green	
Z33	7	2m. dull violet (3.3.75)	£850
		a. Purple (29.2.81)	£900
		b. Dull rose (12.2.84)	£600
		c. Mauve (9.4.89)	£600
		d. Deep claret (14.7.91)	£120
		e. Red-lilac (23.1.99)	£250

(d) Nos. 39/44 (inscr 'DEUTSCHE REICHS-POST' and 'PFENNIG')

Z34	5	3pf. green (5.1.84)	£850
Z35		5pf. mauve (30.3.80)	£110
Z36	6	10pf. rose (27.1.80)	60·00
		a. Carmine	
Z37		20pf. ultramarine (30.7.80)	36·00
		a. Dull blue (1882)	36·00
Z38		25pf. yellow-brown (7.10.80)	£425
		a. Red-brown (1883)	
Z39		50pf. pale grey-olive (1.6.80)	£375

Dates are those of earliest known use.

Nos. 46/51 of Germany (inscr 'REICHSPOST') were not issued in the Turkish Empire. They were however valid for postage until 30 September 1901 and copies brought in privately were used. Minimum prices are 3pf. £42; 5pf. £65; 10pf. £34; 20pf. £38; 25pf. £200; 50pf. £350.

Stamps of Germany surcharged

10 PARA 10
(1)

1 PIASTER 1
(2)

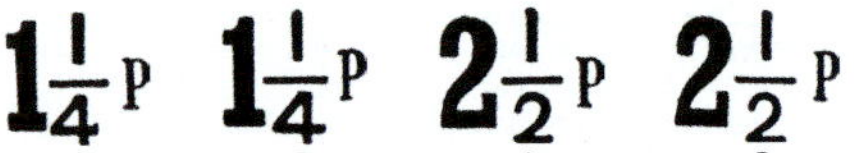

$1\frac{1}{4}$P
A.

$1\frac{1}{4}$P
B.

$2\frac{1}{2}$P
A.

$2\frac{1}{2}$P
B.

A. Middle of 'P' of 'PIASTER' below fraction bar.
B. Middle of 'P' above fraction bar.

1884 (25 Jan–Apr). Type **5** and **6** (inscr 'DEUTSCHE REICHS-POST' and 'PFENNIG') surch.

1	1	10pa. on 5pf. mauve	85·00	48·00
2		20pa. on 10pf. rose	£120	£120
3	2	1pi. on 20pf. ultramarine	95·00	12·00
		a. Blue surcharge (4.84)	£3500	£110
4		1¼pi. on 25pf. red-brown (A.)	£190	£400
5		1¼pi. on 25pf. red-brown (B.)	£190	£400
6		2½pi. on 50pf. grey-green (A.)	£160	£120
7		2½pi. on 50pf. myrtle-green (A.)	£425	£300
8		2½pi. on 50pf. grey green (B.)	£190	£225
1/8 *Set of* 5 (*cheapest*)			£600	£650

Reprints of all values exist.

10 PARA 10
(3)

1 PIASTER 1
(4)

$1\frac{1}{4}$ PIASTER $1\frac{1}{4}$
(5)

1889 (1 Oct). Type **8** and **9** (Numeral or Arms inscr 'REICHSPOST') surch.

9	3	10pa. on 5pf. yellow-green	70·00	55·00
10		10pa. on 5pf. blue-green	5·50	6·00
11	1	20pa. on 10pf. rose	14·50	5·50
12	4	1pi. on 20pf. ultramarine	9·50	3·50
13		1pi. on 20pf. dull blue	60·00	17·00
14	5	1¼pi. on 25pf. orange-yellow	36·00	31·00
15		2½pi. on 50pf. lake-brown	£300	£180
16		2½pi. on 50pf. chocolate	55·00	36·00
9/16 *Set of* 5 (*cheapest*)			£110	75·00

20 PARA 20
(6)

1 PIASTER 1
(7)

$1\frac{1}{2}$ Piaster $1\frac{1}{2}$
(8)

5 PIASTER 5
(9)

15 PIASTER 15   15 PIASTER 15
(10)

1900 (10 Oct). T **10** to **15** ('Germania', GPO or scenes) inscr 'REICHSPOST' surch.

17	6	10pa. on 5pf. green	2·75	3·00
18		20pa. on 10pf. carmine	4·25	3·50
19	7	1pi. on 20pf. ultramarine	7·25	3·00
20	8	1¼pi. on 25pf. black and red/*yellow*	9·50	7·25
21		1½pi. on 30pf. black and orange/*buff*	9·50	7·25
22	7	2pi. on 40pf. black and carmine	9·50	7·25
23	8	2½pi. on 50pf. black and lilac/*buff*	19·00	20·00
24	7	4pi. on 80pf. black and carmine/*rose*	22·00	20·00
25	9	5pi. on 1m. carmine	55·00	60·00
26		10pi. on 2m. blue	48·00	65·00
27	10	15pi. on 3m. violet-black (R.)	70·00	£170
28	9	25pi. on 5m. lake and black (I)	£1000	£2000
		a. Hand-painted borders (I)	£350	£700
		b. Surch double		£15000
		c. Type II	£300	£650
17/28c *Set of* 12 (*cheapest*)			£500	£900
17s/28s Optd 'Specimen' *Set of* 12			£900	

20 PARA 20   5 PIASTER 5
(11)   (12)

1902 (25 Oct)–**04.** Same stamps but surch with altered letter 'A' with serif at top, as T **11/12**.

29	**11**	10pa. on 5pf. green (11.04)	14·50	20·00
30		20pa. on 10pf. carmine (11.04)	46·00	29·00
31		1pi. on 20pf. ultramarine	13·00	11·00
32	**12**	5pi. on 1m. dull lake (3.03)	£225	£160
33		10pi. on 2m. blue (9.11.04)	£250	£400
34		25pi. on 5m. lake and black (II) (4.03)	£300	£850

20 Para 20   1 Piaster 1
(13)   (14)

5 Piaster 5
(15)

15 Piaster 15
(16)

1905 (1 Oct). T **17, 18, 20, 21** and **22** ('Germania', GPO or scenes) inscr 'DEUTSCHES REICH' surch. No wmk.

35	**13**	10pa. on 5pf. green	5·50	3·75
36		20pa. on 10pf. carmine	14·50	4·75
37	**14**	1pi. on 20pf. ultramarine	29·00	3·00
38		1¼pi. on 25pf. black and red/*yellow*	14·50	12·00
39		1½pi. on 30pf. black and orange/*buff*	22·00	24·00
40		2pi. on 40pf. black and carmine	36·00	36·00
41		2½pi. on 50pf. black and purple/*buff*	14·50	36·00
42		4pi. on 80pf. black and carmine/*rose*	42·00	26·00
43	**15**	5pi. on 1m. carmine (26×17)	£120	65·00
		a. 25×16 perforation holes	70·00	70·00
44		10pi. on 2m. blue	60·00	70·00
45	**16**	15pi. on 3m. violet-black (R.)	70·00	85·00
46	**15**	25pi. on 5m. lake and black	£350	£850
35/46	Set of 12 (cheapest)		£650	£1100

1905 (Nov)–**12.** As last, but wmk Lozenges.

47	**13**	10pa. on 5pf. green (5.06)	3·50	1·40
48		20pa. on 10pf. carmine (9.06)	7·25	1·40
49	**14**	1pi. on 20pf. ultramarine (6.06)	9·50	1·40
50		1¼pi. on 25pf. black and red/*yellow* (3.07)	19·00	19·00
51		1½pi. on 30pf. black and orange/*buff* (12.05)	19·00	16·00
52		2pi. on 40pf. black and carmine (12.05)	9·50	2·75
53		2½pi. on 50pf. black and purple/*buff* (6.06)	14·50	26·00
54		4pi. on 80pf. black and carmine/*rose* (1.06)	24·00	34·00
55	**15**	5pi. on 1m. carmine (3.07)	55·00	48·00
56		10pi. on 2m. blue (5.06)	55·00	70·00
57	**16**	15pi. on 3m. violet-black (R) (1912)	95·00	£700
58	**15**	25pi. on 5m. lake and black	48·00	£120
47/58	Set of 12		£325	£950

10 Centimes
(17)

1908 (5 Aug). T **17**, inscr 'DEUTSCHES REICH'. Wmk Lozenges, surch as T **17**.

60		5c. on 5pf. green	3·00	4·25
61		10c. on 10pf. carmine	4·25	7·25
62		25c. on 20pf. ultramarine	9·50	36·00
63		50c. on 40pf. black and carmine	48·00	90·00
64		100c. on 80pf. black and carmine/*rose*	85·00	95·00
60/64	Set of 5		£130	£200
60s/64s	Optd 'Specimen' Set of 5		£400	

All German post offices in the Turkish Empire were closed down on 30 September 1914.

German South-West Africa

100 Pfennig = 1 Mark

GENERAL NOTES. See beginning of Cameroun.

In 1883 Adolf Lüderitz, a Bremen merchant, bought from the natives a tract of territory north of the lower Orange River and set up a trading station at Angra Pequena. A German protectorate over the area was proclaimed on 24 April 1884, and this was extended over Namaqualand and Damaraland on 28 October. Boundaries with Angola were agreed in 1886 and with Cape Colony in 1890, when also the acquisition of the 'Capriv strip' gave the protectorate access to the Zambesi.

OTYIMBINGUE

A postal agency was opened at Otyimbingue on 7 July 1888. Because of rebellions from 1888 this agency was forced to change location frequently. The 'OTYIMBINGUE' (spelt with 'y') postmark was used at the following places: July–8 November 1888 Otyimbingue, November–December 1888 Usab, December 1888–8 July 1889 Walvis Bay (in British territory), July–September 1889 Otyimbingue, September–October 1889 Garinuab, October 1889–13 March 1890 Tsaobis, 13 March 1890–November 1891 Otyimbingue, 7 December 1891–March 1892 Windhoek. This cancellation was discontinued after March 1892, Windhoek receiving its own canceller.

Unoverprinted stamps of Germany were used during this period; prices quoted below are for the cheapest version of each stamp, prices varying according to date of cancellation.

1888–91. Stamps of Germany cancelled with circular postmark 'OTYIMBINGUE / DEUTSCH / SUDWEST-AFRIKA'.

(a) Nos. 38b and 38d (Numeral inscr 'DEUTSCHE REICHS-POST')

Z1	**7**	2m. dull rose (1888)	£3750
		a. Deep claret (29.6.91)	£3250

(b) Nos. 39/44 (Numeral or Eagle inscr 'DEUTSCHE REICHS-POST')

Z2	**5**	3pf. green	—
Z3		5pf. mauve (10.10.88)	£950
Z4	**6**	10pf. carmine (10.8.88)	£950
Z5		20pf. bright blue (10.10.88)	£850
Z6		25pf. deep chestnut	—
Z7		50pf. dull olive-green (10.8.88)	£1100
		a. Blackish olive	£1100

(c) Nos. 46/51 (Numeral or Eagle inscr 'REICHSPOST')

Z8	**8**	3pf. brown (6.9.91)	£550
Z9		5pf. green (18.4.91)	£475
		a. Yellow-green	£475
Z10	**9**	10pf. rose (12.2.91)	£425
Z11		20pf. ultramarine (14.3.91)	£225
		a. Dull blue (14.3.91)	£225
Z12		25pf. orange-yellow (28.7.91)	£850
Z13		50pf. lake-brown	—
		a. Chocolate (18.4.91)	£850

Dates are those of earliest known use.

OTHER POST OFFICES IN GERMAN SOUTH-WEST AFRICA

From March 1892 Windhoek had its own canceller. The Otyimbingue office was re-opened on 1 July 1895 but from this date used the canceller 'OTJIMBINGUE', spelt with 'j'. Other offices were opened in 1895 at Swakopmund (30 May), Omaruru (1 August), Okahandja (12 August), Gibeon (1 October), Cap Cross (10 October), Keetmanshoop (15 October) and Lüderitzbucht (12 November), and at Warmbad on 2 January 1896, Uhabis on 30 January 1896 and Rehoboth on 14 December 1896. These offices all used unoverprinted German stamps from these dates.

391

GERMAN SOUTH-WEST AFRICA

Many other offices and agencies were opened from 1897 when the first overprinted stamps appeared. Unoverprinted stamps are however known with the following cancellations: Bethanien (opened 15.7.89), Gobabis (1.8.98), Grootfontein (17.10.99), Gross-Barmen (12.3.98), Haris (18.2.00), Hasis (6.4.00), Hatzamas (1.3.00), Hohewarte (22.4.98), Jakalswater (1.5.99), Kapenousseu (1.10.01), Karibib (1.7.00), Khanrivier (10.8.98), Kubas (17.12.00), Kubub (16.1.00), Kuis (1.2.00), Maltahöhe (12.99), Marienthal (1.2.00), Okombahe (20.11.99), Otavi (18.10.99), Outjo (20.2.98), Ramansdrift (21.6.99), Rössing (16.6.98), Seeis (1.5.98), Ukamas (11.6.99) and Waterberg (21.10.99).

PRICES. Prices for Nos. Z14/Z20 are for the most common type of postmark found on each stamp; in most cases this is the 'WINDHOEK' cancellation. Most other postmarks are worth more. Prices for Nos. Z15/Z20 are for stamps used before May 1897 (Nos. Z15/Z18), November 1898 (No. Z20) or June 1900 (No. Z19); stamps used from these dates are worth about half those used before.

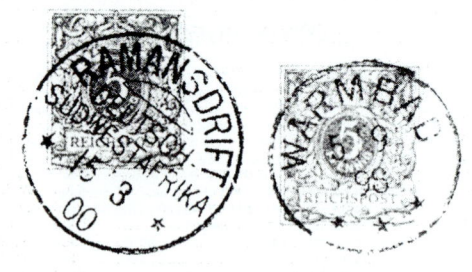

1892–99. Stamps of Germany cancelled with circular postmarks of German South-West Africa offices.

(a) Nos. 38d/38e (Numeral inscr 'DEUTSCHE REICHS-POST')

Z14	7	2m. deep claret...	60·00
		a. Red-lilac (10.11.99).................................	£120

(b) Nos. 46/51 (Numeral or Eagle inscr 'REICHSPOST')

Z15	8	3pf. grey-brown..	95·00
Z16		5pf. green...	48·00
Z17	9	10pf. rose...	£425
		a. Carmine (22.5.95)......................................	36·00
Z18		20pf. ultramarine..	£225
		a. Dull blue...	£100
Z19		25pf. orange-yellow.......................................	£600
		a. Orange (1895)..	£475
Z20		50pf. lake-brown..	£120
		a. Chocolate..	90·00

Examples of other shades of the 3pf. (Nos. 46c/46d) are known used from 1899, after the introduction of the overprinted stamps (*Price* £42).

Nos. Z14/Z20 were valid for postage until 31 October 1901.

(1)   (2)

1897–1900. Stamps of Germany, 1889, optd.

(a) With Type 1 (with hyphen) (May–June 1897)

1	8	3pf. grey-brown...................................	12·00	18·00
		a. Bistre-brown..................................	70·00	£3750
		b. Reddish brown...............................	£275	
2		5pf. green..	6·50	7·25
3	9	10pf. carmine.......................................	34·00	24·00
4		20pf. ultramarine..................................	9·50	8·50
1/4	Set of 4	....	55·00	50·00

The 25 and 50pf. were prepared for issue, but not sent to the colony. *Price* £325 *each, unused.*

(b) Optd with Type 2 (without hyphen) (Oct 1898–June 1900)

5	8	3pf. grey-brown (1899)........................	6·00	31·00
		a. Bistre-brown..................................	12·00	18·00
6		5pf. green (1899).................................	5·50	4·75
7	9	10pf. carmine......................................	5·50	6·00
		a. Bisected (*on cover*) (6.00).................	†	£1400
8		20pf. ultramarine (12.98).....................	19·00	22·00
9		25pf. orange (6.00)...............................	£500	£600
10		50pf. chocolate....................................	22·00	18·00
5/10	Set of 6	....	£500	£600

The above are local release dates.

No. 7a was used as 5pf. values on postcards at Keetmanshoop in June and July 1900.

No. 9 was not placed on general sale at post offices until June 1900. A quantity of these stamps was sent to the Windhoek office in October 1899 but these were all sold to a single person. A few of these were sold back to the Director of Posts who used them to frank letters but none were available to the general public.

'YACHT' KEY TYPES and PERFORATIONS. For details of Types A and B representing the ex-Kaiser's yacht *Hohenzollern*, and for perforation types (a), (b) and (c) see beginning of Cameroun.

1901 (Jan). No wmk.

11	A	3pf. brown..	6·00	2·40
12		5pf. green...	29·00	2·40
13		10pf. carmine.......................................	20·00	1·20
14		20pf. ultramarine..................................	43·00	2·20
15		25pf. black and red/*yellow*................	2·40	8·50
16		30pf. black and orange/*buff*..............	£120	4·00
17		40pf. black and carmine.....................	2·75	4·75
18		50pf. black and purple/*buff*...............	3·00	4·75
19		80pf. black and carmine/*rose*............	3·00	13·00
20	B	1m. carmine (*a*).................................	£180	46·00
21		2m. blue (*a*).......................................	46·00	55·00
22		3m. violet-black (*a*).............................	48·00	70·00
23		5m. carmine and black (I) (*a*)............	£300	£250
11/23	*Set of 13*	....	£700	£425
11s/23s	Optd 'Specimen' *Set of 13*..................	£800	

2pf. grey is a proof.

1906–19. Wmk Lozenges.

24	A	3pf. brown (9.2.07)...............................	1·20	5·50
25		5pf. green (5.06)..................................	1·20	2·00
		a. Booklet pane. No. 25×5 plus label (1.10.11)...	£700	
		b. Booklet pane. Nos. 25×2 and 26×4 (1.6.14)...................................	80·00	
26		10pf. carmine (9.06)............................	1·40	2·20
		a. Booklet pane. No. 26×5 plus label (1.10.11)...	£700	
27		20pf. ultramarine (1911).....................	1·40	5·50
28		30pf. black and orange/*buff* (8.13)....	9·00	
29	B	1m. carmine (*a*) (5.12).......................	18·00	£110
		a. 25×17 holes (1919).......................	60·00	
30		2m. blue (*a*) (11.11)............................	18·00	£110
		a. 25×17 holes (1919).......................	60·00	
31		3m. violet-black (*b*) (1919)..................	20·00	
32		5m. carmine and black (I) (*a*) (13.1.06).	55·00	£550
		a. Frame I, Centre II (*b*) (1919)..........	80·00	

Nos. 29a, 30a, 31 and 32a were only on sale in Berlin.

After a rebellion in South Africa, aided by arms supplied from German South-West Africa, had been crushed in December 1914, South African troops invaded the protectorate. The German forces capitulated on 9 July 1915.

On 17 December 1920 the League of Nations conferred a mandate of administration of the territory on His Britannic Majesty, to be exercised by the Government of South Africa.

STAMP BOOKLETS

Prices are for complete booklets

Booklet No.	Date	Contents and Cover Price	Price
SB1	1.10.11	Yacht	
		1 pane, No. 25a; 2 panes, No. 26a (2m.)...	£7000
SB2	1914	Yacht	
		3 panes, No. 25×6; 1 pane, No. 25b; 1 pane, No. 26×6 (2m.)	
		(a) Front cover lettered 'C', back cover with advert...........................	£250
		(b) Front cover unlettered, back cover with postal tariff....................	£7000

Kiaochow

1900. 100 Pfennig = 1 Mark
1905. 100 Cents = 1 Dollar

GENERAL NOTES. See beginning of Cameroun. Colonial types are inscribed with the German name 'Kiautschou'.

On 14 November 1897 the port of Tsingtao was occupied by German naval forces after the murder of two German missionaries in Shantung. By a treaty of 6 March 1898 the Kiaochow (now Kiaohsien) territory of 117 square miles, including Tsingtao, was leased by China to Germany for 99 years.

The first civilian postal agency in Kiaochow was opened at Tsingtao on 6 March 1898; this became a post office in June 1900. At first it used the cancellers 'TSINTANFORT MARINEFELDPOST' or 'TSINTANFORT', but from May 1898 several types of 'TSINTAU' or 'TSINGTAU' cancellers were used. Other offices were opened at Tapatur on 23 July 1900 and at Tsangkou on 1 April 1901. In addition to the postmarks of these offices cancellations of field stations are found as follows: 'KIAUTSCHOU', 'KIAUTSCHOU DEUTSCHE POST', 'K. D. FELD-POSTSTATION No 1' and 'KAUMI DEUTSCHE POST', and also railway postmarks. The 'KIAUTSCHOU' postmarks were later used at all offices. Unoverprinted German stamps and stamps of German Post Offices in China were used up to 1902.

PRICES. Prices for Nos. Z1/Z19 are for the most common types of 'TSINTAU' or 'TSINGTAU' postmark found on each stamp; less common types and other Kiaochow postmarks are worth more.

1898–1900. Stamps of Germany cancelled with circular or oval postmarks of Kiaochow offices.

(a) Nos. 38d/38e (Numeral inscr 'DEUTSCHES REICHS-POST')

Z1	**7**	2m. deep claret (26.1.98)	£750
		a. Red-lilac (20.2.00)	£1000

(b) Nos. 46/51 (Numeral or Arms inscr 'REICHPOST')

Z2	**8**	3pf. grey-brown	80·00
		a. Orange-brown	75·00
		b. Bistre-brown	£225
Z3		5pf. green	95·00
Z4	**9**	10pf. carmine	47·00
Z5		20pf. ultramarine	£170
Z6		25pf. orange	£350
Z7		50pf. chocolate	£400

1898 (26 Jan). Stamps of German Post Offices in China cancelled with postmarks of Kiaochow offices.

(a) Nos. 1/6

Z8		3pf. bistre-brown	£17000
Z9		5pf. green	28·00
Z10		10pf. carmine	22·00
Z11		20pf. ultramarine	22·00
Z12		25pf. orange	£120
Z13		50pf. chocolate	£100

(b) Nos. 7/12

Z14		3pf. grey-brown	28·00
		a. Bistre-brown	22·00
		b. Red-brown	£200
Z15		5pf. green	22·00
Z16		10pf. carmine	22·00
Z17		20pf. ultramarine	£375
Z18		25pf. orange	£170
Z19		50pf. chocolate	£120

ERRORS. Errors surch as double and inverted overprints or surcharges were never issued but come from waste sheets which later leaked out of the printers.

5 Pfg. (1) **5 Pfg.** (2) **5 Pfg.** (3)
5 Pfg. (4) **5 Pfg.** (5) **5 Pfg.** (6)

1900 (9 May). Issued at Tsingtao. Stamps of German POs in China, surch with Type **1** to **6**.

(a) On No. 3 ('China' sloping 48°)

1	**1**	5Pfg. on 10pf. carmine	£225	£180
2	**2**	5Pfg. on 10pf. carmine	£130	£150

(b) On No. 9 ('China' sloping 56°)

3	**1**	5Pfg. on 10pf. carmine	65·00	75·00
4	**2**	5Pfg. on 10pf. carmine	65·00	75·00
5	**3**	5Pfg. on 10pf. carmine	65·00	75·00
6	**4**	5Pfg. on 10pf. carmine	65·00	75·00
7	**5**	5Pfg. on 10pf. carmine	65·00	75·00
8	**6**	5Pfg. on 10pf. carmine		

Most examples of Nos. 1/8 show a manuscript horizontal line either across the entire design or through the original value only.

1900 (19 July). Issued at Tsingtao. No. 3 of German POs in China, surch as Type **1**, but '5Pf.' instead of '5Pfg'.

8a		5Pf. on 10pf. carmine	£4500	£5500

With additional handstamp '5'

9		5 on 5Pf. on 10pf. carmine	£55000	£66000

With additional handstamp '5Pf.'

10		5Pf. on 5Pf. on 10pf. carmine	£11000	£17000

The surcharge on No. 8a was difficult to see on the horizontal rows 5 and 10 of the setting of 50. Examples from these rows had an additional handstamp, either '5' or '5Pf.', applied to them.

'YACHT' KEY TYPES and PERFORATIONS. For details of types A and B representing the ex-Kaiser's yacht *Hohenzollern*, and for perforation types (a), (b) and (c) see beginning of Cameroun.

1901 (Jan). German currency. No wmk.

11	A	3pf. brown	2·75	2·75
12		5pf. green	2·75	2·20
13		10pf. carmine	3·25	2·75
14		20pf. ultramarine	10·00	11·00
15		25pf. black and red/*yellow*	18·00	22·00
16		30pf. black and orange/*buff*	18·00	22·00
17		40pf. black and carmine	21·00	26·00
18		50pf. black and purple/*buff*	21·00	31·00
19		80pf. black and carmine/*rose*	39·00	70·00
20	B	1m. carmine (*a*)	65·00	£120
21		2m. blue (*a*)	£110	£140
22		3m. violet-black (*a*)	£110	£275
23		5m. carmine and black (Frame II, centre I) (*a*)	£300	£900
11/23 Set of 13			£650	£1500

For Nos. 11/23 cancelled with Peking or Field station No. 2 postmarks, see Nos. Z33/Z45 of German Post Offices in China.

1905 (1 Oct). Chinese currency. No wmk.

24	A	1c. brown	1·70	2·20
25		2c. green	2·40	2·20
26		4c. carmine	6·00	2·20
27		10c. ultramarine	11·00	7·25
28		20c. black and carmine	44·00	26·00
29		40c. black and carmine/*rose*	£130	£130
30	B	½d. carmine (*c*)	95·00	£110
31		1d. blue (*a*)	£275	£170
		a. 25×16 holes	£200	£180
32		1½d. violet-black (*a*)	£1500	£2250
33		2½d. carmine and black (II) (*a*)	£2000	£6500
		a. 25×16 holes	£2750	£4500
24s/33s Optd 'Specimen' Set of 10			£800	

1905–18. Wmk Lozenges.

34		1c. brown (6.06)	1·70	2·20
		a. Yellow-brown	85	
35		2c. green (3.09)	1·50	1·80
		a. Dark green	85	2·75
36		4c. carmine (11.09)	1·30	1·70
37		10c. ultramarine (1.09)	1·40	5·00
38		20c. black and carmine (12.08)	3·75	22·00
		a. Black and red	2·20	
39		40c. black and carmine/*rose* (12.05)	4·25	70·00
40	B	½d. carmine (*a*) (10.07)	13·00	90·00
		a. 25×17 holes (1918)	10·50	
41		1d. blue (*a*) (2.06)	17·00	£110
		a. 25×17 holes (1918)	12·50	
42	B	1½d. violet-black (*a*) (18.10.05)	28·00	£275
		a. 25×17 holes (1918)	28·00	
43		2½d. carmine and black (II) (*a*) (10.05)	65·00	£650
		a. 25×17 holes (1918)	39·00	

In the First World War, Tsingtao surrendered to Japanese forces after a three months siege on 7 November 1914. The Japanese later occupied much of Shantung province, which was not returned to China until 4 February 1922, after the Washington Disarmament Conference of 1921–1922.

Mariana Islands

100 Pfennig = 1 Mark

GENERAL NOTES. See beginning of Cameroun.

The Mariana Islands in the Western Pacific Ocean were under Spanish rule until 1899, when Germany purchased rights to a protectorate over them. German administration commenced on 17 November 1899.

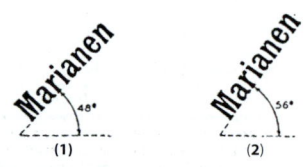

(1) *Marianen* 48°   (2) *Marianen* 56°

1899–1900. Stamps of Germany, 1889, optd.

(a) With Type 1 (18.11.99)

1	8	3pf. grey-brown	£3000	£3000
2		5pf. green	£3500	£2500
3	9	10pf. carmine	£275	£300
4		20pf. ultramarine	£275	£300
5		25pf. orange	£3750	£3750
6		50pf. chocolate	£3750	£3500

(b) With Type 2 (5.00)

7	8	3pf. grey-brown	18·00	43·00
8		5pf. green	24·00	46·00
9	9	10pf. carmine	30·00	65·00
10		20pf. ultramarine	36·00	£180
11		25pf. orange	90·00	£225
12		50pf. chocolate	90·00	£300
7/12		Set of 6	£250	£750

'YACHT' KEY TYPES and PERFORATIONS. For details of Types A and B representing the ex-Kaiser's yacht *Hohenzollern*, and for perforation types (a), (b) and (c) see beginning of Cameroun.

1901 (Jan). No wmk.

13	A	3pf. brown	1·60	2·40
14		5pf. green	1·60	2·75
15		10pf. carmine	1·60	6·00
16		20pf. ultramarine	1·80	10·00
17		25pf. black and red/*yellow*	2·40	18·00
18		30pf. black and orange/*buff*	2·40	19·00
19		40pf. black and carmine	2·40	19·00
20		50pf. black and purple/*buff*	3·00	22·00
21		80pf. black and carmine/*rose*	3·50	36·00
22	B	1m. carmine (*a*)	6·50	£100
23		2m. blue (*a*)	9·00	£130
24		3m. violet-black (*a*)	12·00	£190
25		5m. carmine and black (II) (*a*)	£225	£700
13/25		Set of 13	£250	£1100
13s/25s		Optd 'Specimen' Set of 13	£600	

1916–19. Wmk Lozenges.

26	A	3pf. brown (5.19)	1·40	
27	B	5m. carmine and black (II) (*a*) (6.16)	60·00	
		a. 25×17 holes	48·00	

Nos. 26/27a were only on sale in Berlin.

The islands were occupied by Japan on 14 October 1914 and from 17 December 1920 were a Japanese mandated territory. From 18 July 1947 they have been a United States trust territory. In a referendum held on 17 June 1975 the inhabitants voted for the establishment of a US Commonwealth with internal self-government.

Marshall Islands

100 Pfennig = 1 Mark

GENERAL NOTES. See beginning of Cameroun.

The Marshall Islands consist of the islands of Jaluit and Majuro and 865 other small islands and atolls in the north central Pacific Ocean. They were discovered by Spanish sailors in 1529 and explored by Captains Marshall and Thomas Gilbert in 1788. After a treaty had been made with the chiefs of Jaluit in 1878, they were made a German protectorate, to include Nauru, on 15 October 1885.

A postal agency opened at Jaluit on 29 March 1889. Unoverprinted German stamps were used from this date; prices quoted below are for the most common type of postmark found on each stamp, variations such as no year date or coloured cancellations being worth more.

1889–1900. Stamps of Germany cancelled with circular postmark 'JALUIT/MARSCHALL-INSELN' (to 23.5.1900) or 'JALUIT MARSHALL INSELN' (from 21.5.1900).

(a) Nos. 38b/38e (Numeral inscr 'DEUTSCHE REICHS-POST')

ZG1	7	2m. dull rose (8.4.89)	£3500
		a. Mauve (1891)	£4250
		b. Deep claret (28.1.92)	£1200
		c. Red-lilac (11.9.00)	£6500

(b) Nos. 39/44 (Numeral or Eagle inscr 'DEUTSCHE REICHS-POST')

ZG2	5	3pf. green (16.2.91)	£1300
ZG3		5pf. mauve (10.4.89)	£550
ZG4	6	10pf. carmine (1.6.89)	£425
ZG5		20pf. bright blue (18.4.89)	£250
ZG6		25pf. deep chestnut (14.3.90)	—
ZG7		50pf. dull olive-green (7.5.89)	£850
		a. Bronze-green (1890)	£850

(c) Nos. 46/51 (Numeral or Eagle inscr 'REICHSPOST')

ZG8	8	3pf. brown (16.2.91)	£425
		a. Grey-brown (1892)	£350
ZG9		5pf. green (16.2.91)	£425
		a. Yellow-green (1892)	£425
ZG10	9	10pf. rose (14.3.90)	£350
		a. Carmine (1895)	£300
ZG11		20pf. ultramarine (14.3.90)	£250
		a. Dull blue (1891)	£180
ZG12		25pf. orange-yellow (28.10.91)	£800
		a. Orange (1895)	£550
ZG13		50pf. lake-brown (14.3.90)	
		a. Chocolate (1891)	£450

Dates are those of earliest known use.
Examples of other shades of the 3pf. brown (Nos. 46c/46d) are known used from 1899, after the introduction of the overprinted stamps (*Price* £300).
The 2m. and Nos. ZG8/ZG13 were valid for postage until 30 September 1901.

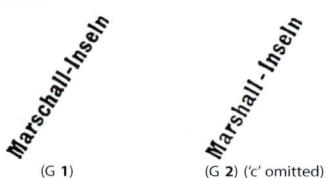

(G 1) *Marschall-Inseln*   (G 2) *Marshall-Inseln* ('c' omitted)

1897–1900. Stamps of Germany, 1889, optd.

(a) With Type G 1 (1897–1899)

G1	8	3pf. grey-brown (21.7.99)	£5500	£3000
		a. Pale brown	£5500	£3000
G2		5pf. green (21.7.99)	£800	£650
G3	9	10pf. carmine (8.97)	90·00	£130
		a. Bisected (*on card*) (2.00)	†	£36000
G4		20pf. ultramarine (4.97)	90·00	£140

394

No. G3a was used as a 5pf. at Jaluit between February and April 1900 to frank postcards.

The 25 and 50pf. were prepared for use but were not issued in the colony, although examples are known used. *Price £190 each unused.*

(b) With Type G 2 (22 November 1899–1900)

G5	8	3pf. grey-brown (4.00)	6·50	7·75
		a. Yellow-brown	£425	£1600
G6		5pf. green	13·00	18·00
G7	9	10pf. carmine (1900)	18·00	23·00
		a. Bisected (on card) (2.12.00)	†	£9000
G8		20pf. ultramarine (1900)	23·00	36·00
G9		25pf. orange	26·00	60·00
G10		50pf. red-brown	42·00	65·00
		a. Bisected (on card) (2.10.00)	†	£54000
G5/G10 *Set of 6*			£120	£190

Nos. G7a and G10a were used at Jaluit between 2 and 10 December 1900 to provide 5pf. and 25pf. frankings for postcards and registered postcards.

'YACHT' KEY TYPES and PERFORATIONS. For details of Types A and B representing the ex-Kaiser's yacht *Hohenzollern*, and for perforation types (a), (b) and (c) see beginning of Cameroun.

1901 (Jan–Mar). No wmk.

G11	A	3pf. brown	95	2·40
G12		5pf. green	95	2·40
G13		10pf. carmine	95	6·50
G14		20pf. ultramarine	1·30	13·00
G15		25pf. black and red/*yellow*	1·40	23·00
G16		30pf. black and orange/*buff*	1·40	23·00
G17		40pf. black and carmine	1·40	23·00
G18		50pf. black and purple/*buff*	2·20	34·00
G19		80pf. black and carmine/*rose*	4·25	50·00
G20	B	1m. carmine (*a*) (3.01)	6·00	£120
G21		2m. blue (*a*) (3.01)	8·50	£170
G22		3m. violet-black (*a*) (3.01)	12·50	£300
G23		5m. carmine and black (I) (*a*) (3.01)	£225	£700
G11/G23 *Set of 13*			£250	£1300
G11s/G23s Optd 'Specimen' *Set of 13*			£600	

1916–19. Wmk Lozenges.

G24	A	3pf. brown (1919)	1·20	
G25	B	5m. carmine and black (II) (*b*)	55·00	
		a. Frame I, Centre II (a) (1919)	55·00	
		b. Frame I, Centre II (b) (1919)		

Nos. G24/G25b were only on sale in Berlin.

The Marshall Islands were occupied by Japanese forces on 29 September 1914, except for Nauru which fell to the Australians on 6 November 1914.

Samoa

100 Pfennig = 1 Mark

GENERAL NOTES. See beginning of Cameroun.

The Samoa islands, in the Central Pacific Ocean, were discovered by the Dutch explorer Jakob Roggeveen in 1722. Missionary activities began there in 1830. In 1839 Captain Wilkes, an American, made a trading agreement with Samoan chiefs and from 1850 Hamburg merchants set up trading establishments. Treaties of 1878 with the USA and of 1879 with Germany secured Pago Pago and Apia as naval stations for those countries respectively. A complex history ensued of rivalries between candidates for the kingship and between American, British and German traders during the period 1880 to 1899. This led to no lasting settlement, in spite of two three-power conferences, till in 1899 the Samoan monarchy was abolished and the United Kingdom withdrew her claims on Samoa in return for acquisitions elsewhere. On 2 December 1899 the Samoa islands were divided between the United States and Germany, the latter obtaining those to the east of Longitude 170°W. The islands of Savaii, Upolu (with Apia, the chief town), Manono and Apolima became a German protectorate.

A German postal agency opened at Apia on 21 September 1886. Unoverprinted German stamps were used from this date; prices given below are for the most common type of quoted postmark found on each stamp with a cancellation before May 1900. Less common types and other Apia cancellations are worth more; cancellations from May 1900 are worth about 25% less than those before this date.

1886–99. Stamps of Germany cancelled with circular postmark 'APIA / KAISERL DEUTSCHE / POSTAGENTUR' or other Apia postmarks.

(a) Nos. 38b/38e (Numeral inscr 'DEUTSCHE REICHS-POST')

ZG1	7	2m. dull rose (4.1.89)	£12000
		a. Mauve (25.2.90)	£1800
		b. Deep claret (9.11.92)	£350
		c. Red-lilac (10.8.99)	£1900

(b) Nos. 39/44 (Numeral or Eagle inscr 'DEUTSCHE REICHS-POST')

ZG2	5	3pf. green (1890)	£1400
ZG3		5pf. mauve (19.12.87)	£550
ZG4	6	10pf. carmine (14.12.86)	£275
ZG5		20pf. pale blue (17.10.86)	£250
		a. Bright blue (1889)	£275
ZG6		25pf. deep chestnut (1890)	—
ZG7		50pf. pale grey-olive (1886)	£170
		a. Dull olive-green (1888)	£120
		b. Bronze green (1889)	£250

(c) Nos. 46/51 (Numeral or Eagle inscr 'REICHSPOST')

ZG8	8	3pf. brown (28.4.92)	£225
		a. Grey-brown (1892)	90·00
		b. Orange-brown (1899)	95·00
		c. Bistre-brown (1899)	95·00
ZG9		5pf. green (26.3.90)	£140
		a. Yellow-green (1891)	£140
ZG10	9	10pf. rose (29.3.90)	70·00
		a. Carmine (1894)	40·00
ZG11		20pf. ultramarine (24.6.90)	95·00
		a. Dull blue (1891)	70·00
ZG12		25pf. orange-yellow (14.9.92)	£650
		a. Orange (1894)	£475
ZG13		50pf. lake-brown (28.1.90)	£700
		a. Chocolate (1891)	80·00

Dates are those of earliest known use.

Nos. ZG5 and ZG7 with postmark 'APIA / DEUTSCHE / POSTDAMPFSCHIFFS- / AGENTUR' are priced the same as above; this postmark on other stamps is worth more than quoted prices.

The 2m. and Nos. ZG8/ZG13 were valid for postage until 30 September 1901.

(G **1**)

1900 (Apr). Stamps of Germany, 1889, optd with Type G **1**.

G1	8	3pf. grey-brown	13·00	18·00
G2		5pf. green	17·00	24·00
G3	9	10pf. carmine	13·00	24·00
G4		20pf. ultramarine	26·00	41·00
G5		25pf. orange	55·00	£110
G6		50pf. chocolate	55·00	£100
G1/G6 *Set of 6*			£160	£275

395

SAMOA

'YACHT' KEY TYPES and PERFORATIONS. For details of Types A and B representing the ex-Kaiser's yacht *Hohenzollern*, and for perforation types (a), (b) and (c) see beginning of Cameroun.

1900 (10 Dec)–**01**. No wmk.

G7	A	3pf. brown	1·40	1·60
G8		5pf. green	1·40	1·60
G9		10pf. carmine	1·40	1·60
G10		20pf. ultramarine	1·40	3·00
G11		25pf. black and red/*yellow*	1·60	17·00
G12		30pf. black and orange/*buff*	1·90	14·50
G13		40pf. black and carmine	1·90	17·00
G14		50pf. black and purple/*buff*	1·90	18·00
G15		80pf. black and carmine/*rose*	3·75	42·00
G16	B	1m. carmine (*a*) (1.01)	4·75	85·00
G17		2m. blue (*a*) (1.01)	6·50	£140
G18		3m. violet-black (*a*) (1.01)	11·00	£200
G19		5m. carmine and black (II) (*a*) (1.01)	£250	£700
G7/G19 Set of 13			£250	£1100
G7s/G19s Optd 'Specimen' Set of 13			£600	

The 2pf. grey in Type A is a proof.

1915–19. Wmk Lozenges.

G20	A	3pf. brown (1919)	1·40
G21		5pf. green (1919)	1·80
G22		10pf. carmine (1919)	1·80
G23	B	5m. carmine and black (II) (*a*)	65·00
		a. 25×17 holes (1919)	48·00

Nos. G20/G23a were only on sale in Berlin.

On 29 August 1914 German Samoa was occupied by New Zealand forces. In 1920 New Zealand received a mandate from the League of Nations to administer the islands, which became a New Zealand Trust Territory in 1946. On 1 January 1962 the islands became independent as Western Samoa (Samoa i Sisifo).

NEW ZEALAND OCCUPATION

The German Islands of Samoa surrendered to the New Zealand Expeditionary Force on 30 August 1914 and were administered by New Zealand until 1962.

G.R.I.   **G.R.I.**

1 d.   **1 Shillings.**

(13)   (14)

SETTINGS. Nos. 101/109 were surcharged by a vertical setting of ten, repeated ten times across the sheet. Nos. 110/114 were from a horizontal setting of four repeated five times in the sheet.

Nos. 101b, 102a and 104a occurred on position 6. The error was corrected during the printing of No. 102.
Nos. 101c, 102c, 104d and 105b are from position 10.
Nos. 101d, 102e and 104b are from position 1.
No. 108b is from position 9.

(Surch by *Samoanische Zeitung*, Apia)

1914 (3 Sept). German Colonial issue (ship) (no wmk) inscr 'SAMOA' surch as T **13** or **14** (mark values).

101	½d. on 3pf. brown	60·00	16·00
	a. Surch double	£750	£600
	b. No fraction bar	90·00	42·00
	c. Comma after 'I'	£700	£425
	d. '1' to left of '2' in '½'	85·00	40·00
102	½d. on 5pf. green	65·00	21·00
	a. No fraction bar	£140	60·00
	c. Comma after 'I'	£425	£180
	d. Surch double	£750	£600
	e. '1' to left of '2' in '½'	£110	45·00
103	1d. on 10pf. carmine	£100	40·00
	a. Surch double	£800	£650
104	2½d. on 20pf. ultramarine	60·00	14·00
	a. No fraction bar	95·00	42·00
	b. '1' to left of '2' in '½'	90·00	42·00
	c. Surch inverted	£1100	£1000
	d. Comma after 'I'	£550	£350
	e. Surch double	£750	£650
105	3d. on 25pf. black and red/*yellow*	80·00	40·00
	a. Surch double	£1100	£800
	b. Comma after 'I'	£5000	£1100
106	4d. on 30pf. black and orange/*buff*	£130	60·00
107	5d. on 40pf. black and carmine	£130	70·00
108	6d. on 50pf. black and purple/*buff*	65·00	35·00
	a. Surch double	£1100	£1000
	b. Inverted '9' for '6'	£180	£100
109	9d. on 80pf. black and carmine/*rose*	£200	£100
110	'1 shillings' on 1m. carmine	£3250	£3500
111	'1 shilling' on 1m. carmine	£11000	£7000
112	2s. on 2m. blue	£3500	£3000
113	3s. on 3m. violet-black	£1400	£1200
	a. Surch double	£10000	£11000
114	5s. on 5m. carmine and black	£1200	£1000
	a. Surch double	£13000	£14000

No. 108b is distinguishable from 108, as the 'd' and the '9' are not in a line, and the upper loop of the '9' turns downwards to the left.

UNAUTHORISED SURCHARGES. Examples of the 2d. on 20pf., 3d. on 30pf., 3d. on 40pf., 4d. on 40pf., 6d. on 80pf., 2s. on 3m. and 2s. on Marshall Islands 2m., together with a number of errors not listed above, were produced by the printer on stamps supplied by local collectors. These were not authorised by the New Zealand Military Administration.

Togo

1897. 100 Pfennig = 1 Mark

GENERAL NOTES. See beginning of Cameroun.

The lagoons along the coast of Togo were for long the resort of slavers. In the 18th and early 19th-centuries British, Dutch, French and Portuguese slave-traders all had stations there. Later in the 19th-century merchants from Bremen engaged in more normal trade with the small kingdoms of Togo and Klein-Popo, and on 5 July 1884 Dr. Gustav Nachtigal, German Imperial Commissioner, persuaded the King of Togo to place his country under German protection. German claims to large areas in the interior led to long negotiations with France and the United Kingdom, but by 1899 all the boundaries were agreed.

Postal agencies were opened in Klein-Popo on 1 March 1888 and in Lome on 1 March 1890. Unoverprinted German stamps were used from these dates; prices quoted below are for the cheapest version of each stamp, prices varying according to post office, type of postmark and date of cancellation. Prices for Nos. ZG8/ZG13 are however for stamps used before June 1897 (5, 10, 20pf.) or middle of 1898 (others); stamps used after these dates are worth about 25% less than those used before.

1888–1900. Stamps of Germany cancelled with circular postmark 'KLEIN-POPO' or 'LOME/TOGOGEBIET'.

(a) Nos. 38b/38e (Numeral inscr 'DEUTSCHE REICHS-POST')

ZG1	7	2m. dull rose (17.5.89)	£2500
		a. Mauve (2.9.91)	£11000
		b. Deep claret (3.1.92)	£120
		c. Red-lilac (14.2.00)	£1200

(b) Nos. 39/44 (Numeral or Eagle inscr 'DEUTSCHE REICHS-POST')

ZG2	5	3pf. green (7.7.88)	£2500
ZG3		5pf. mauve (19.7.88)	£350
ZG4	6	10pf. carmine (29.4.88)	£300
ZG5		20pf. bright blue (14.5.88)	£225
ZG6		25pf. deep chestnut (1890)	—
ZG7		50pf. dull olive-green (29.4.88)	£450
		a. Blackish olive	£950
		b. Bronze green (1889)	£650

(c) Nos. 46/51 (Numeral or Eagle inscr 'REICHSPOST')

ZG8	8	3pf. brown (24.4.91)	£180
		a. Grey-brown (1892)	85·00
ZG9		5pf. green (19.5.90)	£100
		a. Yellow-green (1890)	90·00
ZG10	9	10pf. rose (26.12.89)	55·00
		a. Carmine (1895)	29·00
ZG11		20pf. ultramarine (14.12.89)	65·00
		a. Dull blue (1891)	42·00
ZG12		25pf. orange-yellow (9.4.91)	£600
		a. Orange (1894)	£475
ZG13		50pf. lake-brown (11.12.89)	£650
		a. Chocolate (1891)	90·00

Prices quoted for Nos. ZG1/ZG1a and ZG2/ZG7 are for 'KLEIN-POPO' cancellation.
Dates are those of earliest known use.
Examples of other shades of the 3pf. brown (Nos. 46c/46d) are known used from 1898, after the introduction of the overprinted stamps (*Price* £60).
The 2m. and Nos. ZG8/ZG13 were valid for postage until 30 September 1901.

(G 1)

1897 (June)**–98.** Stamps of Germany, 1889, optd with Type **1**.

G1	8	3pf. grey-brown (1898)	7·75	10·00
		a. Bistre-brown	13·00	36·00
		b. Deep brown	70·00	£190
G2		5pf. green (8.97)	7·25	4·00
G3	9	10pf. carmine	8·50	4·50
G4		20pf. ultramarine	8·50	19·00
G5		25pf. orange (1898)	55·00	85·00
G6		50pf. chocolate (1.98)	55·00	85·00
G1/G6	Set of 6 (*cheapest*)		£130	£190

'YACHT' KEY TYPES and PERFORATIONS. For details of types A and B representing the ex-Kaiser's yacht *Hohenzollern*, and for perforation types (a), (b) and (c) see beginning of Cameroun.

1900 (Nov). No wmk.

G7	A	3pf. brown	1·40	1·80
G8		5pf. green	17·00	3·00
G9		10pf. carmine	31·00	2·40
G10		20pf. ultramarine	1·40	2·20
G11		25pf. black and red/*yellow*	1·40	14·50
G12		30pf. black and orange/*buff*	1·90	14·50
G13		40pf. black and carmine	1·40	14·50
G14		50pf. black and purple/*buff*	1·90	11·00
G15		80pf. black and carmine/*rose*	3·50	24·00
G16	B	1m. carmine (*a*)	4·75	80·00
G17		2m. blue (*a*)	7·75	£120
G18		3m. violet-black (*a*)	10·00	£225
G19		5m. carmine and black (II) (*a*)	£200	£700
G7/G19	Set of 13		£250	£1100
G7s/G19s Optd 'Specimen' Set of 13			£600	

1909–19. Wmk Lozenges.

G20	A	3pf. brown (1919)	1·20	
G21		5pf. green (8.09)	1·80	3·00
G22		10pf. carmine (1912)	2·40	£170
G23	B	5m. carmine and black (II) (*a*) (1.15)	46·00	
		a. 25×17 holes (1919)	26·00	

Nos. G20 and G23/G23a were only on sale in Berlin.
In the First World War French troops from Dahomey and British troops from the Gold Coast invaded Togo early in August 1914 and the German forces surrendered on 27 August. Until 1919 Togo was under Anglo-French military occupation.

ANGLO-FRENCH OCCUPATION

FRENCH ISSUES

100 Centimes = 1 Franc

26 August 1914–7 May 1919

TOGO
Occupation
franco-anglaise

(1)

1914 (8 Oct). Yacht Stamps of German Togo optd at Porto Novo, Dahomey, with Type **1**, the 3pf. and 5pf. surch in addition. Wmk Lozenges (No. 2) or no wmk (others).

1	A	05 on 3pf. brown (I)	£110	£100
		a. Type II	£100	95·00
		b. Type III	£120	£110
		c. Type IV	£150	£150
		d. Type V	£275	£250
		e. Type VI	£275	£250
2		10 on 5pf. green (I)	55·00	29·00
		a. Type II	31·00	31·00
		b. Type III	65·00	70·00
		c. Surch double (Type I)	£1500	£1500
3		20pf. ultramarine	80·00	70·00
		a. 'TOGO' and 'Occupation' spaced 3½ mm apart	£1100	£1100
4		25pf. black and red/*yellow*	£100	£100
5		30pf. black and orange/*salmon*	£140	£140
6		40pf. black and carmine	£700	£800
7		80pf. black and carmine/*rose*	£700	£800

The overprint was set up in groups of 50 (10×5) repeated twice on each sheet. For the two surcharges the settings were made up as follows:
05 on 3pf. Type I—18, Type II—17, Type III—11, Type IV—2, Type V—1, Type VI—1
10 on 5pf. Type I—3, Type II—22, Type III—25
All values have a narrow 'O' in 'Occupation' on positions 1, 4, 38 and 43 of the setting. The 10 on 5pf. surcharge shows a broken serif on the figure '1' from positions 10, 16 and 23.
No. 2 is known bisected and used at Anecho.

TOGO

TOGO
Occupation
franco-anglaise
(2)

**Occupation
franco-
anglaise**
(3)

1915 (Jan). Yacht Stamps of German Togo optd with Type **2** (No. 8 additionally handstamped with new value) at the Catholic Mission, Lomé. Wmk Lozenges (Nos. 9 and 10) or no wmk (others).

8	A	05 on 3pf. brown	£27000	£6500
9		5pf. green	£1300	£650
10		10pf. carmine	£1500	£650
		a. Opt inverted	£40000	£23000
11		20pf. ultramarine	£1800	£1500
12		25pf. black and red/*yellow*	£21000	£10000
13		30pf. black and orange/*salmon*	£21000	£10000
14		40pf. black and carmine	£21000	£10000
15		50pf. black and purple/*buff*	£30000	£18000
16	B	1m. carmine	—	£83000
17		2m. blue	£36000	£32000
18		3m. violet-black		£55000
19		5m. carmine and black	£55000	£66000

Stamp of Dahomey

6 Climbing Palm-tree

1916. Type **6** of Dahomey optd with Type **3**. Chalk-surfaced paper.

20	6	1c. black and violet	35	1·80
21		2c. rose and chocolate	45	1·60
22		4c. brown and black	55	2·00
		a. Opt double	£600	£600
23		5c. green and yellow-green	90	2·50
24		10c. rose and orange-red	85	1·60
25		15c. purple and red	2·20	2·50
26		20c. chocolate and grey	1·00	3·00
27		25c. blue and ultramarine	1·50	2·75
28		30c. violet and chocolate	1·70	4·50
29		35c. black and brown	2·20	5·75
30		40c. orange and black	1·80	2·40
31		45c. ultramarine and grey	2·10	3·50
32		50c. brown and chocolate	2·10	3·00
33		75c. violet and blue	8·00	13·50
34		1f. black and green	10·50	24·00
35		2f. chocolate and orange-yellow	15·00	19·00
36		5f. Prussian blue and violet	18·00	40·00
20/36		*Set of 17*	60·00	£120

All values except the 15c., 25c. and 35c. also exist on ordinary paper.

The 2c. is known bisected and used at Noepe on 19 April 1921.

On 7 May 1919 the Supreme Council of the Allies gave a mandate to France and the United Kingdom to administer Togo, and on 10 July the two powers agreed on a divison of the country. The administration of the British area was amalgamated with that of the Gold Coast but French Togo became a separate entitiy. The town of Lomé was at first in the British area but by a convention of 30 September 1920 went to France in exchange for another area further north.

BRITISH ISSUES

PRICES FOR STAMPS ON COVER	
Nos. H1/H7	from × 6
No. H8	—
No. H9	from × 6
No. H10	from × 2
No. H11	—
Nos. H12/H13	from × 6
Nos. H14/H16	—
Nos. H17/H19	from × 12
Nos. H20/H26	—
Nos. H27/H28	from × 20
No. H29	—
Nos. H30/H31	from × 6
Nos. H32/H33	—

French forces invaded southern Togo on 8 August 1914 and the British had entered Lomé by the same date, examples of Gold Coast stamps being known cancelled there on the 8th. The German administration surrendered on 26 August 1914.

The territory was jointly administered under martial law, but was formally divided between Great Britain and France, effective 1 October 1920. League of Nations mandates were issued for both areas from 20 July 1922.

100 pfennig = 1 mark

Stamps of German Colonial issue Yacht Types 1900 and 1909–1914 (5pf. and 10pf.)

**TOGO
Anglo-French
Occupation**
(1)

Half penny
(2)

SETTINGS. Nos. H1/H33 were all overprinted or surcharged by the Catholic Mission, Lomé.

The initial setting for the 3pf. to 80pf. was of 50 (10×5), repeated twice on each sheet of 100. Overprints from this setting, used for Nos. H1/H9, had the lines of type 3 mm apart.

Nos. H1/H2 were subsequently surcharged, also from a setting of 50, to form Nos. H12/H13. The surcharge setting showed a thin dropped 'y' with small serifs on R. 1/1–2, 2/1, 3/1, 4/1 and 5/1–2.

The type from the overprint and surcharge was then amalgamated in a new setting of 50 on which the lines of the overprint were only 2 mm apart. On this amalgamated setting, used for Nos. H27/H28, the thin 'y' varieties were still present and R. 4/7 showed the second 'O' of 'TOGO' omitted.

The surcharge was subsequently removed from this '2 mm' setting which was then used to produce Nos. H17/H19. The missing 'O' was spotted and corrected before any of the 30pf. stamps were overprinted.

The remaining low values of the second issue, Nos. H14/H16 and H20/H22, were overprinted from settings of 25 (5×5), either taken from the last setting of 50 or from an amended version on which there was no space either side of the hyphen. This slightly narrower overprint was subsequently used for Nos. H29/H33. It shows the top of the second 'O' broken so that it resembles a 'U' on R. 1/5.

The mark values were overprinted from settings of 20 (5×4), showing the same differences in the spacing of the lines as on the low values.

It is believed that odd examples of some German colonial values were overprinted from individual settings in either spacing.

1914 (17 Sept*). Optd with Type **1** by Catholic Mission, Lomé. Wide setting. Lines 3 mm apart.

H1	3pf. brown	£130	£100
H2	5pf. green	£130	£100
H3	10pf. carmine (Wmk Lozenges)	£130	£100
	a. Opt inverted	£10000	£3000
	b. Opt *tête-bêche* in vert pair	†	£8500
	c. No wmk	†	£5500
H4	20pf. ultramarine	42·00	50·00
H5	25pf. black and red/*yellow*	40·00	50·00
H6	30pf. black and orange/*buff*	50·00	60·00
H7	40pf. black and carmine	£225	£250
H8	50pf. black and purple/*buff*	£13000	£11000
H9	80pf. black and carmine/*rose*	£275	£275
H10	1m. carmine	£5000	£2750
H11	2m. blue	£13000	£15000
	a. 'Occupation' double	£24000	£16000
	b. Opt inverted	£16000	

*The post office at Lomé was open for four hours on 17 September, before closing again on instructions from Accra. It finally reopened on 24 September.

The *tête-bêche* overprint on the 10pf. is due to the sheet being turned round after the upper 50 stamps had been overprinted so that vertical pairs from the two middle rows have the overprint *tête-bêche*.

1914 (1 Oct). Nos. H1 and H2 surch as Type **2**.

H12	½d. on 3pf. brown	£160	£140
	a. Thin 'y' in 'penny'	£400	£350
H13	1d. on 5pf. green	£160	£140
	a. Thin 'y' in 'penny'	£400	£350

**TOGO
Anglo-French
Occupation**
(3)

**TOGO
Anglo-French
Occupation
Half penny**
(4)

1914 (Oct).

(a) Optd with Type **3**. *Narrow Setting. Lines 2 mm apart.*
'Anglo-French' measures 16 mm

H14	3pf. brown	£6500	£1100
H15	5pf. green	£1500	£750
H16	10pf. carmine	†	£3000
	a. No wmk	†	£7000
H17	20pf. ultramarine	32·00	12·00
	a. 'TOG'	£3500	£2500
	b. Nos. H4 and H17 *se-tenant* (vert pair)	£9000	
H18	25pf. black and red/*yellow*	42·00	35·00
	a. 'TOG'	£12000	
H19	30pf. black and orange/*buff*	20·00	29·00
H20	40pf. black and carmine	£6000	£1600
H21	50pf. black and purple/*buff*	†	£9000
H22	80pf. black and carmine/*rose*	£3250	£2250
H23	1m. carmine	£8000	£4250
H24	2m. blue	†	£14000
H25	3m. violet-black	†	£100000
H26	5m. lake and black	†	£100000

(b) Narrow setting, but including value, as Type **4**

H27	½d. on 3pf. brown	48·00	26·00
	a. 'TOG'	£425	£300
	b. Thin 'y' in 'penny'	75·00	60·00
H28	1d. on 5pf. green	7·00	4·25
	a. 'TOG'	£130	£110
	b. Thin 'y' in 'penny'	12·00	15·00

In the 20pf. one half of a sheet was overprinted with the wide setting (3 *mm*), and the other half with the narrow setting (2 *mm*), so that vertical pairs from the middle of the sheet show the two varieties of the overprint.

TOGO
Anglo-French
Occupation
(**6**)

1915 (7 Jan). Optd as Type **6**. The words 'Anglo-French' measure 15 mm instead of 16 mm as in Type **3**.

H29	3pf. brown	£9000	£2500
H30	5pf. green	£225	£130
	a. 'Occupation' omitted	£12000	
H31	10pf. carmine	£200	£130
	a. No wmk	†	£7000
H32	20pf. ultramarine	£1400	£400
H32*a*	40pf. black and carmine	†	£9000
H33	50pf. black and purple/*buff*	£16000	£11000

This printing was made on another batch of German Togo stamps, found at Sansane-Mangu.

INDEX

Albania (German Occupation) 362
Allenstein 336
Allied Military Post
 (British and American Zones) 53
Allied Occupation 53
Alsace (German Occupation) 366
Alsace and Lorraine
 (German Occupation, 1870-1871) 22
American, British and Soviet Russian
 Zones (1946-1948) 53
Anglo-French Occupation (Togo) 398

Baden (French Zone, 1947-1949) 57
Baden (German State) 1
Bavaria 1
Belgian Forces in the Rhineland
 (Belgian Occupation, 1919-1921) 333
Belgian Occupation (1919-1921) 333
Belgium (German Occupation 1914-1918) 334
Bergedorf 7
Berlin (Machine Labels) 240
Berlin (Western Sectors) 217
Berlin-Brandenburg (Russian Zone) 60
Bohemia and Moravia
 (German Occupation) 362
Brač (German Occupation) 374
Bremen 7
British and American Zones (1948-1949) 55
British and American Zones
 (Allied Military Zones) 53
Brunswick 8
British Issues (Togo) 399

Cameroun 379
Caroline Islands 381
Channel Islands 377
Courland (German Occupation) 367

Dalmatia (German Occupation) 373
Danzig 337
Danzig (Polish Post in Danzig) 343
Design Index (1871 to 1945) 51
Design Index (from 1945) 208
Districts of Eupen and Malmedy 333

East Germany
 (German Democratic Republic) 240
East Saxony (Russian Zone) 62
Eastern Military Command Area
 (German Occupation) 335
Empire (Germany) 23
Estonia (German Occupation, 1914-1918) 335
Estonia (German Occupation, 1941-1944) 365
Eupen 333

France (German Occupation) 366
Free City (Danzig) 337
French Occupation (Saar) 353
French Zone (Baden, 1947-1949) 57
French Zone (General Issues, 1945-1946) 57
French Zone
 (Rhineland-Palatinate, 1947-1949) 58
French Zone (Saar, 1945-1947) 59
French Zone (Württemberg, 1947-1949) 59

German Democratic Republic
 (East Germany) 240
German East Africa 382
German East Africa (Mafia Island) 384
German East Africa (other Post Offices) 383
German Federal Republic 64
German New Guinea 385
German New Guinea (New Guinea) 385
German Occupation (Albania) 362
German Occupation
 (Alsace and Lorraine, 1870-1871) 22

German Occupation
 (Bohemia and Moravia) 362
German Occupation (Eastern Military
 Command Area (Russian Baltic
 Provinces)) 335
German Occupation (Estonia, 1914-1918) 335
German Occupation (Estonia, 1941-1944) 365
German Occupation (France) 366
German Occupation (Ionian Islands) 366
German Occupation (Latvia) 366
German Occupation (Lithuania) 367
German Occupation (Luxembourg) 367
German Occupation (Poland, 1914-1918) 335
German Occupation (Poland, 1939-1945) 368
German Occupation (Romania) 335
German Occupation (Russia) 371
German Occupation (Serbia) 371
German Occupation
 (Western Military Command Area) 336
German Occupation (Yugoslavia) 373
German Occupation Issues (1914-18) 334
German Occupation Issues (1939-45) 362
German Occupation of Belgium 334
German Post Offices in China 388
German Post Offices in Morocco 390
German Post Offices in Turkish Empire 391
German South-West Africa 392
German South-West Africa
 (other Post Offices) 392
German States 1
Germany (Empire) 23
Germany (Machine Labels) 205
Germany Reunified 115
Guernsey (German Occupation) 377
Gulf of Kotor (German Occupation) 374

Hamburg 8
Hanover 9
Heligoland 19

Inscriptions on Stamp Designs 22
Ionian Islands (German Occupation) 366

Jersey (German Occupation) 377

Kiaochow (Kiautschou) 394
Kiautschou (Kiaochow) 394

Lamu (German East Africa) 382
Latvia (German Occupation) 366
League of Nations Commission (Saar) 350
Lithuania (German Occupation) 367
Lithuanian Occupation of Memel 347
Lorraine (German Occupation) 366
Lübeck 10
Luxembourg (German Occupation) 367

Macedonia (German Occupation) 374
Machine Labels (Berlin) 240
Machine Labels (Germany) 205
Malmedy 333
Mafia Island (German East Africa) 384
Mariana Islands 395
Marienwerder 344
Marshall Islands 395
Mecklenburg-Schwerin 10
Mecklenburg-Strelitz 11
Mecklenburg-Vorpommern (Russian Zone) 60
Memel 345
Memel (Lithuanian Occupation) 347
Montenegro (German Occupation) 375

New Guinea (German New Guinea) 385
New Zealand Occupation (Samoa) 397
North German Confederation 21
Northern District (Thurn and Taxis) 14

Oldenburg 11
Otyimbingue (German South-West Africa) 392

Poland (German Occupation) 335
Poland (German Occupation, 1939-1945) 368
Polish Post in Danzig 343
Post Offices in East Africa 383
Post Offices in German South-West Africa 392
Provincial Administrations (Russian Zone) 60
Provisional Government
 (Schleswig-Holstein) 13
Prussia 12

Rhineland-Palatinate (French Zone) 58
Romania (German Occupation) 335
Russia (German Occupation) 371
Russian Zone 60
Russian Zone (Berlin-Brandenburg
 (OPD Berlin)) 60
Russian Zone (East Saxony (OPD Dresden)) 62
Russian Zone (General Issues) 63
Russian Zone (Mecklenburg-Vorpommern
 (OPD Schwerin)) 60
Russian Zone (Provincial Administrations) 60
Russian Zone (Saxony (OPD Halle)) 61
Russian Zone (Thuringia (OPD Erfurt)) 62
Russian Zone (West Saxony (OPD Leipzig)) 61

Saar (French Occupation) 353
Saar (French Zone) 59
Saar (League of Nations Commission,
 1920-1935) 350
Saar (Return to Germany) 353, 358
Samoa 396
Samoa (New Zealand Occupation) 397
Saxony 12
Saxony (Russian Zone) 61
Schleswig 13
Schleswig (Slesvig) 360
Schleswig-Holstein 13
Schleswig-Holstein (Joint Administration
 by Austria and Prussia) 13
Schleswig-Holstein
 (Provisional Government) 13
Serbia (German Occupation) 371
Slesvig (Schleswig) 360
Slovenia (German Occupation) 375
Southern District (Thurn and Taxis) 15

The Weimar Republic 27
Third Reich 36
Thuringia (Russian Zone) 62
Thurn and Taxis 14
Togo 398
Togo (Anglo-French Occupation) 398
Togo (British Issues) 399
Togo (French Issues) 398

Upper Silesia 360
Upper Silesia (Inter-Allied Commission) 361

Weimar Republic 27
West Germany 64
West Saxony (Russian Zone) 61
Western Military Command Area
 (German Occupation) 336
Württemberg 15
Württemberg (French Zone) 59

Yugoslavia (German Occupation) 373

Zante (German Occupation) 366
Zanzibar (German East Africa) 382

STANLEY GIBBONS
Est 1856

Dear Catalogue User,

As a collector and Stanley Gibbons catalogue user for many years myself, I am only too aware of the need to provide you with the information you seek in an accurate, timely and easily accessible manner. Naturally, I have my own views on where changes could be made, but one thing I learned long ago is that we all have different opinions and requirements.

I would therefore be most grateful if you would complete the form overleaf and return it to me. Please contact Lorraine Holcombe (lholcombe@stanleygibbons.com) if you would like to be emailed the questionnaire.

Very many thanks for your help.

Yours sincerely,

Hugh Jefferies,
Editor.

Hugh Jefferies (Catalogue Editor)
Catalogue Questionnaire Responses
Stanley Gibbons Limited
7 Parkside, Ringwood
Hampshire BH24 3SH
United Kingdom

Questionnaire
2018 Germany

1. **Level of detail**
   Do you feel that the level of detail in this catalogue is:
   a. too specialised ○
   b. about right ○
   c. inadequate ○

2. **Frequency of issue**
   How often would you purchase a new edition of this catalogue?
   a. Annually ○
   b. Every two years ○
   c. Every three to five years ○
   d. Less frequently ○

3. **Design and Quality**
   How would you describe the layout and appearance of this catalogue?
   a. Excellent ○
   b. Good ○
   c. Adequate ○
   d. Poor ○

4. How important to you are the prices given in the catalogue:
   a. Important ○
   b. Quite important ○
   c. Of little interest ○
   d. Of no interest ○

5. Would you be interested in an online version of this catalogue?
   a. Yes ○
   b. No ○

6. Do you like the new format?
   a. Yes ○
   b. No ○

7. What changes would you suggest to improve the catalogue? E.g. Which other indices would you like to see included?
   ....
   ....
   ....
   ....

8. Which other Stanley Gibbons Catalogues do you buy?
   ....
   ....
   ....
   ....

9. Would you like us to let you know when the next edition of this catalogue is due to be published?
   a. Yes ○
   b. No ○
   If so please give your contact details below.
   Name: ....
   Address:..
   ....
   ....
   ....
   Email: ....
   Telephone:...

10. Which other Stanley Gibbons Catalogues are you interested in?
    a. ....
    b. ....
    c. ....

Many thanks for your comments.

Please complete and return it to: Hugh Jefferies (Catalogue Editor)
Stanley Gibbons Limited, 7 Parkside, Ringwood, Hampshire BH24 3SH, United Kingdom
or, email: lholcombe@stanleygibbons.com to request a soft copy

Stanley Gibbons

Stamp Catalogues

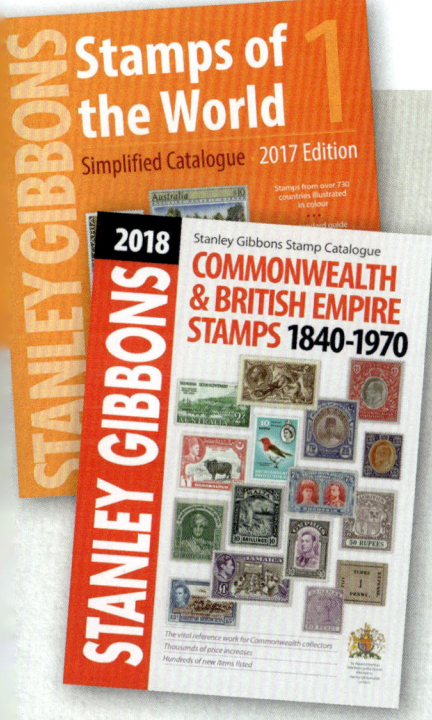

Commonwealth & British Empire Stamps 1840–1970 (120th edition, 2018)

King George VI (9th edition, 2018)

Commonwealth Country Catalogues

Australia & Dependencies (10th Edition, 2016)
Bangladesh, Pakistan & Sri Lanka (3rd edition, 2015)
Belize, Guyana, Trinidad & Tobago (2nd edition, 2013)
Brunei, Malaysia & Singapore (5th edition, 2017)
Canada (6th edition, 2016)
Cyprus, Gibraltar & Malta (4th edition, 2014)
East Africa with Egypt & Sudan (4th edition, 2018)
Eastern Pacific (3rd edition, 2015)
Falkland Islands (7th edition, 2016)
Hong Kong (5th edition, 2015)
India (including Convention & Feudatory States) (5th edition, 2018)
Indian Ocean (3rd edition, 2016)
Ireland (6th edition, 2015)
Leeward Islands (3rd edition, 2017)
New Zealand (6th edition, 2016)
Northern Caribbean, Bahamas & Bermuda (4th edition, 2016)
St. Helena & Dependencies (6th edition, 2017)
Southern & Central Africa (2nd edition, 2014)
West Africa (2nd edition, 2012)
Western Pacific (4th edition, 2017)
Windward Islands & Barbados (3rd edition, 2015)

Stamps of the World 2018

Volume 1	Abu Dhabi – Charkhari
Volume 2	Chile – Georgia
Volume 3	German Commands – Jasdan
Volume 4	Jersey – New Republic
Volume 5	New South Wales – Singapore
Volume 6	Sirmoor – Zululand

Great Britain Catalogues

2018 Collect British Stamps (69th edition, 2018)
Collect Channel Islands & Isle of Man (30th edition, 2016)
Great Britain Concise Stamp Catalogue (33rd edition, 2018)

Great Britain Specialised

Volume 1	Queen Victoria (16th edition, 2012)
Volume 2	King Edward VII to King George VI (14th edition, 2015)
Volume 3*	Queen Elizabeth II Pre-decimal issues (12th edition, 2011)
Volume 4	Queen Elizabeth II Decimal Definitive Issues – Part 1 (10th edition, 2008)
	Queen Elizabeth II Decimal Definitive Issues – Part 2 (10th edition, 2010)

Foreign Countries

Antarctica (2nd edition, 2012)
Arabia (1st edition, 2016)
Austria and Hungary (8th Edition 2014)
Belgium & Luxembourg (1st edition, 2015)
Central America (3rd edition, 2007)
China (11th edition, 2015)
Czech Republic and Slovakia (1st edition, 2017)
Denmark and Norway (1st edition, 2018)
Finland and Sweden (1st edition, 2017)
France, Andorra and Monaco (1st edition, 2015)
French Colonies (1st edition, 2016)
Germany (12th edition, 2018)
Japan & Korea (5th edition, 2008)
Netherlands & Colonies (1st edition, 2017)
North East Africa (2nd edition 2017)
Poland (1st edition, 2015)
Russia (7th edition, 2014)
South-East Asia (5th edition, 2012)
United States of America (8th edition, 2015)

*Currently out of stock.

We have catalogues to suit every aspect of stamp collecting

Our catalogues cover stamps issued from across the globe - from the Penny Black to the latest issues. Whether you're a specialist in a certain reign or a thematic collector, we should have something to suit your needs. All catalogues include our famous SG numbering system, making it as easy as possible to find the stamp you're looking for.

STANLEY GIBBONS
LONDON 1856

399 Strand, WC2R 0LX, London
Phone: +44 1425 472 363 | Email: support@stanleygibbons.com
www.stanleygibbons.com

Germany Order Form

STANLEY GIBBONS Est 1856

YOUR ORDER

Stanley Gibbons account number

Condition (mint/UM/ used)	Country	SG No.	Description	Price	Office use only
			POSTAGE & PACKING	£3.60	
			TOTAL		

The lowest price charged for individual stamps or sets purchased from Stanley Gibbons Ltd, is £1.

Payment & address details

Name
Address (We cannot deliver to PO Boxes)
Postcode
Tel No.
Email

PLEASE NOTE Overseas customers MUST quote a telephone number or the order cannot be dispatched. Please complete ALL sections of this form to allow us to process the order.

- Cheque (made payable to Stanley Gibbons Ltd)
- I authorise you to charge my
  - Mastercard Visa Diners Amex Maestro

Card No.
Valid from
Expiry date
Issue No. (Maestro only)
CVC No. (4 if Amex)
(Maestro only)

CVC No. is the last three digits on the back of your card (4 if Amex)

Signature
Date

4 EASY WAYS TO ORDER

Post to
Mark Pegg,
Stamp Mail Order Department, Stanley Gibbons Ltd, 399 Strand, London, WC2R 0LX, England

Call
020 7836 8444
+44 (0)20 7836 8444

Fax
020 7557 4499
+44 (0)20 7557 4499

Click
mpegg@stanleygibbons.com

Come and Visit us at 399 Strand

1856   1896   1936   1976   2017

- Get advice from our experienced and knowledgeable staff
- See first hand our superb range of top quality stamps, albums and accessories
- Get insider tips on how to enhance and expand your collection
- Ask for guidance on techniques for care and storage of your stamps and covers
- View our specialist material
- All Stanley Gibbons stamps come with a lifetime guarantee of authenticity from our stamp specialists.

Everything for the stamp collector.

399 Strand opening hours
Mon-Fri 9am-5.30pm • Sat 9:30am-5.30pm • Sun Closed

For more information visit
stanleygibbons.com

STANLEY GIBBONS
LONDON 1856

399 Strand, WC2R 0LX, London
Phone: +44 1425 472 363 | Email: support@stanleygibbons.com
www.stanleygibbons.com

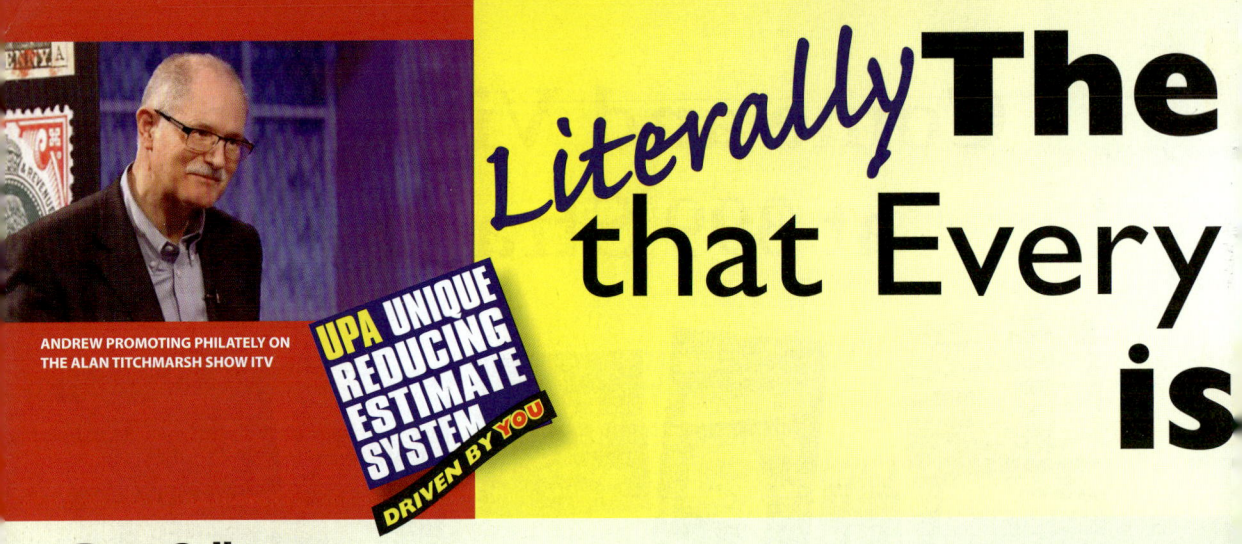

ANDREW PROMOTING PHILATELY ON
THE ALAN TITCHMARSH SHOW ITV

UPA UNIQUE REDUCING ESTIMATE SYSTEM — DRIVEN BY YOU

Literally **The** that Every is

Dear Colleague,

For the first time, in this open letter, I'm going to give you the thinking, the 'mindset' if you will, of how and why my stamp auction thrives where others do not...

As many of you will attest. At certain 'peak' times in our auction 'cycle,' I personally answer the telephone to callers. It's a wonderfully enjoyable and rewarding thing for me to do, because, you kindly inform me of your likes and dislikes, about us, and other auctions that you may have dealt with before discovering U P A...

One of the most common 'threads' that I have learnt from You, and from other Dealers and Auctioneers, is simply 'how does U P A do it?' How is it that we have become the largest Stamp Auction in the UK and almost the largest globally? How can we afford to expend more upon advertising worldwide than most dealers sell in a year? Simply put: How can we afford to offer more and charge less – indeed – how can we afford to offer more and charge you no extra w-h-a-t-s-o-e-v-e-r ??

The fundamental reason why is because, unlike others, everything we do is Driven by You.. Over the course of the past 18 years I have discovered that combining this 'bottom-up' thinking with offering **simply MASSIVE Philatelic Choice** – permits us to offer you a Unique Collector-Driven Stamp Auction Experience. Think about it: whilst the rest of our philatelic industry works 'top-down' – issuing diktats, regulation, charges and fees, and few guarantees – ever increasingly we throw these off encouraged by more and more collectors joining us, who crucially continue to participate in auction after auction... rewarding us by their loyalty, enriching their collections... enabling us, in turn, to reward them.

...So that, when you inform us that You don't like 'X' (extra shipping and insurance charges), and You dislike 'Y' (paying credit card charges) and you positively abhor paying 'Z' – up to 25% buyer's premiums... (particularly when you may realise that you are possibly or probably paying a buyer's premium upon that dealer's own stamps that they are selling to You)... we take that valuable knowledge you've imparted and 'dial' it back into our auction system, not purely for your benefit BUT for our mutual benefit because over the 18 years that U P A has been auctioning I have discovered that if we have enough participating bidders in our auctions we can offer you a **radically superior service and a radically different deal than others**...

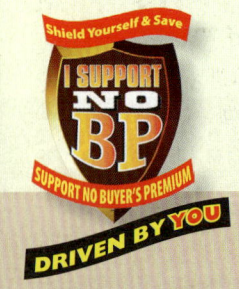

1st £55 FREE WINNINGS

Shield Yourself & Save
I SUPPORT NO BP — SUPPORT NO BUYER'S PREMIUM
DRIVEN BY YOU

NO SURCHARGE — VISA MasterCard
DRIVEN BY YOU

NEW POST-FREE UPA Loyalty Bonus ✓
DRIVEN BY YOU

Discover the Difference
UNIVERSAL PHILATELIC AUCTIONS
SINCE 1958
Philately Understood

Difference is thing we Do Driven by You...

To me it is logical that when you configure your auction to really give collectors what they seek, mixing in a unique reducing-estimate-auction system, blended with hundreds and thousands of simply massive philatelic choice – these are the reasons why more Collectors bid in my U P A auctions than any other auction in the UK and almost all others globally. Consider that each U P A auction adds up to 250 different new bidders when most stamp auctions only have a few hundred bidders TOTAL – the SCALE of Your SUPPORT permits us to 'square' the circle so that, hopefully, we can offer collectors like you **True Philatelic VAL-YOU for Money**...

How can you help? Simply by participating regularly in our auctions permits us to give back, producing the most expensive and the best post-free auction catalogues you may ever receive whilst staying in business. Your continued support is powering our new Loyalty Post-Free System. So, all that I would respectfully ask and encourage you to do – is join the 2,184 different Collectors and Dealers from 58 different countries worldwide, who participated in my last auction U P A #69, creating new philatelic world records of participation and in some cases of realisations – whilst an astonishing 90% of bidders were successful... and those lots that remained unsold carried forward at **ever decreasing estimate and reserve** thereby creating the nucleus of this auction with a 'sprinkling' of more than 8,000 new lots of absolutely extraordinary NEW material... whereby, ultimately collectors like You determine values, not catalogues…

My wife and I, and members of our super Team, wish you Happy Hunting and great Philatelic Fun. With thanks for Your continued support. Please do tell your Philatelic Friends. They'll receive the best Philatelic Thank You for joining us and you'll be rewarded too!

It's So Easy – START Now

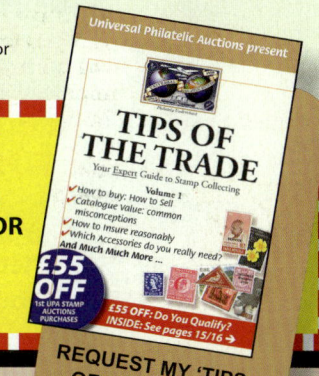

Andrew McGavin, Managing Director
Universal Philatelic Auctions UPA,

To Collect Your NEXT £20 20,000± lot Auction Catalogue FREE Request Yours **NOW**

Simply – telephone one of my Team on **01451 861111** to request Your **NEXT FREE January, April, July or October U P A Catalogue** NOW… OR turn to one of my 1st £55 Auction Winnings FREE coupon pages in this catalogue, visit www.upastampauctions.co.uk to view/bid on-line OR request your 362 page, 1 kg catalogue on-line, mailed quickly so you can test my auction without spending a penny, … Join 2,184 bidders, 90% successful, in my last auction. **Start Bidding and winning now…**

REQUEST MY 'TIPS OF THE TRADE' FREE BOOKLET

UNIVERSAL PHILATELIC AUCTIONS (SG-GERMANY) 4
The Old Coalyard, West End Northleach, Glos. GL54 3HE UK Tel:
01451 861111 • Fax: 01451 861297

"This is My Promise to YOU"

1st £55 FREE WINNINGS

"Massive Philatelic Choice in a Unique Reducing Estimate System Delivering VAL-YOU with Absolutely NO Buyer's Premium PLUS ALL Lots Guaranteed"

Andrew McGavin, Managing Director Universal Philatelic Auctions

I SUPPORT NO BP — Shield Yourself & Save — SUPPORT NO BUYER'S PREMIUM

UPA UNIQUE REDUCING ESTIMATE SYSTEM — DRIVEN BY YOU

THE COLLECTORS' SECRET WEAPON

Discover the Difference — UNIVERSAL PHILATELIC AUCTIONS — Philately Understood

CLOSING DATE: 5PM TUESDAY 10TH APRIL 2018

CATALOGUE £20

ALL LOTS - 100% NO-QUIBBLE - GUARANTEED

REQUEST YOUR FREE CATALOGUE

– send the coupon / simply request your next *FREE* catalogue in any way today!

info@upastampauctions.co.uk • www.upastampauctions.co.uk

OR VIEW / BID ON-LINE NOW – we'll take your £55 off
ONE OFFER PER COLLECTOR'S HOUSEHOLD

Do it today
1st £55 FREE

REQUEST FREE CATALOGUE TODAY

NEW CLIENTS

1st £55 FREE

Name..
Address..
....
....
Postcode.................... Tel....................
Country...
email...

SG-GERMANY

TIPS OF THE TRADE — Your Expert Guide to Stamp Collecting — Volume 1
- How to buy; How to sell
- Catalogue Value: common misconceptions
- How to house stamps economically
- Which accessories do you really need
- And Much Much More

£55 OFF: Do You Qualify? INSIDE: See pages 15/16

REQUEST MY 'TIPS OF THE TRADE' FREE BOOKLET

REQUEST YOUR FREE CATALOGUE

Returning UPA client? Not purchased for 12 months: £26 deducted if you spend more than £52, mention offer when requesting catalogue

UNIVERSAL PHILATELIC AUCTIONS SG-GERMANY
4 The Old Coalyard, West End Northleach, Glos. GL54 3HE UK
Tel: 01451 861111 • Fax: 01451 861297

UPA UNIQUE REDUCING ESTIMATE SYSTEM — DRIVEN BY YOU